OUTBOARD MOTOR

service manual

volume I · 11th edition

INTERTEC PUBLISHING CORP.

P.O. Box 12901, Overland Park, KS 66282-2901

1573

Cover photo courtesy of: American Suzuki Motor Corporation

OUTBOARD MOTOR

service manual
volume 1 · 11th edition

Chief	Federal	Mercury	Sears
Chrysler	Force	Pathfinder	Sportfisher
Clinton	Golden Jet	Seaco	Suzuki
Cruise 'N Carry	Hanimex	Seacruiser-Grant	Tanaka
Eska	Hiawatha	Seagull	Tohatsu
Evinrude	Johnson	Sea Hawk	Wizard
Explorer	Mariner	Sea King	Yamaha

Covers Motors Below 30 Horsepower

INTERTEC PUBLISHING CORP.

President	*Group Vice President*
Jack Hancock	Bill Wiesner

EDITORIAL

Editorial Director /Editor	*Associate Editor*	*Editorial Assistants*
Randy Stephens	Mark Jacobs	Irma Allread
		Shirley Renicker

Inventory/Production Manager
Terry Distin

MARKETING

Marketing Director	*Advertising Manager*	*Advertising Assistant*	*Graphic Designer*
Chris Charlton	Diane Wilmot	Katherine Nelms	Anita Blattner

SALES & ADMINISTRATION

Sales & Marketing Manager	*Customer Service & Administration Manager*
Roger Cobb	Joan Jackson
Dutch Sadler	

Marketing Coordinator
Lynn Reynolds

The following books and guides are published by **INTERTEC PUBLISHING CORP.**

ABOS/INTERTEC BLUE BOOKS AND TRADE-IN GUIDES

Recreational Vehicles	Outdoor Power Equipment	Agricultural Tractors	Lawn and Garden Tractors
Motorcycles and ATVs	Snowmobiles	Boats and Motors	Personal Watercraft

INTERTEC SERVICE MANUALS

Lawn and Garden Tractors	Outdoor Power Equipment	Personal Watercraft	Motorcycles
Snowmobiles	Recreational Vehicles	Boat Motors and Drives	
Gasoline and Diesel Engines			

CLYMER SHOP MANUALS

Boat Motors and Drives	Motorcycles and ATVs	Snowmobiles	Personal Watercraft

AIRCRAFT BLUEBOOK-PRICE DIGEST

Airplanes	Helicopters

I&T SHOP MANUALS

Tractors

CONTENTS

CONTENTS CONT.

DUAL DIMENSIONS

This service manual provides specifications in both the Metric (SI) and U.S. Customary systems of measurement on some models. The first specification is given in the measuring system used during manufacture, while the second specification (given in parenthesis) is the converted measurement. For instance, a specification of "0.28 mm (0.011 inch)" would indicate that the equipment was manufactured using the metric system of measurement and the U.S. equivalent of 0.28 mm is 0.011 inch.

DESIGN FUNDAMENTALS
OPERATING PRINCIPLES

ENGINE TYPES

The power source for the outboard motor does not differ basically from that used to power automobiles, farm or garden tractors, lawn mowers, or many other items of power equipment in use today. All are technically known as "Internal Combustion, Reciprocating Engines".

The source of power is heat formed by the burning of a combustible mixture of petroleum products and air. In a reciprocating engine, this burning takes place in a closed cylinder containing a piston. Expansion resulting from the heat of combustion applies pressure on the piston to turn a shaft by means of a crank and connecting rod.

The fuel mixture may be ignited by means of an electric spark (Otto Cycle Engine) or by the heat of compression (Diesel Cycle). The complete series of events which must take place in order for the engine to run may occur in one revolution of the crankshaft (referred to as Two-Stroke Cycle), or in two revolutions of the crankshaft (Four-Stroke Cycle).

OTTO CYCLE, In a spark ignited engine, a series of five events are required in order to provide power. This series of events are called the **Cycle** (or Work Cycle) and is repeated in each cylinder as long as work is done. The series of events which comprise the work cycle are as follows:

1. The mixture of fuel and air is pushed or drawn into the cylinder, by reducing cylinder pressure to less than the outside pressure, or by applying an initial, higher pressure to the fuel charge.

2. The mixture is compressed, or reduced in volume.

3. The mixture is ignited by a timed electric spark.

4. The burning fuel:air mixture expands, forcing the piston down, thus converting the generated chemical energy into mechanical power.

5. The burned gases are exhausted from the cylinder so that a new cycle can begin.

The series of events comprising the work cycle are commonly referred to as INTAKE, COMPRESSION, IGNITION, EXPANSION (POWER) and EXHAUST.

DIESEL CYCLE. The Diesel Cycle differs from the Otto Cycle in that air alone is drawn into the cylinder during the intake period, then compressed to a much greater degree. The air is heated by compression. Instead of an electric spark, a finely atomized charge of fuel is injected into the combustion chamber where it combines with the heated air and ignites spontaneously. The power and exhaust strokes are almost identical to those of the Otto Cycle.

FOUR-STROKE CYCLE. In a reciprocating engine, each movement of the piston (in or out) in the cylinder is referred to as a Stroke. Thus, one complete revolution of the engine crankshaft accompanies two strokes of the piston.

The most simple and efficient engine design from the standpoint of fuel and exhaust gas mixture movement is the Four-Stroke Cycle shown schematically in fig. 1-1. The first event of the work cycle coincides with the first stroke of the piston as shown at "A". Downward movement of the piston draws a fresh charge of the fuel:air mixture into the cylinder. View "B" shows the compression of the fuel mixture which occurs during the second stroke of the cycle. Ignition occurs at about the time the piston reaches the top of the cylinder on the compression stroke, resulting in the expansion of the burning fuel:air mixture, and in the power stroke as shown at "C". The fourth stroke of the cycle empties the cylinder of the burned gases as shown at "D", and the cylinder is ready for the beginning of another work cycle.

The fact that a full stroke of the piston is available for each major mechanical event of the cycle is ideal, from the standpoint of efficiency, and four-stroke engines are generally most economical where fuel costs alone are considered.

Individual cylinders are often combined and connected in series to the shaft to increase power output. Engine operation is also smoothed by increasing the number of power impulses per crankshaft revolution. A single cylinder, four-stroke cycle engine (with only one power impulse for two shaft revolutions) must have a heavy flywheel to store and deliver the developed energy between power strokes. Increasing the number of cylinders to two, three or four enables the design engineer to increase engine power without a corresponding increase

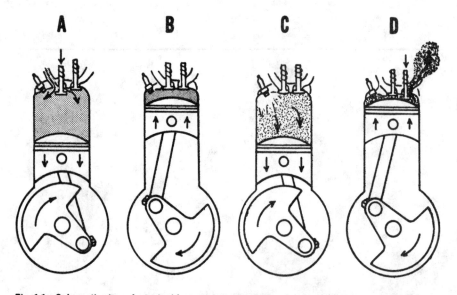

Fig. 1-1—Schematic view of a typical four-stroke cycle engine showing basic principles of operation. Two revolutions of the crankshaft are required to complete the cycle. The first, or INTAKE stroke is shown at "A". As the piston moves downward in cylinder the intake valve is opened allowing a combustible mixture of fuel and air to enter cylinder. The intake valve closes as the piston moves upward in the second, or COMPRESSION stroke as shown in "B." The compressed charge is ignited, and expansion of the burning mixture forces the piston down in the POWER stroke "C". The exhaust valve opens as the piston moves upward in the fourth, or EXHAUST stroke "D", and the cylinder is cleared of burned gases for the beginning of another cycle.

in engine weight.

The four-stroke cycle requires a more complicated system of valving, which adds materially to the weight and original cost of the engine. This fact, coupled with the fact that two revolutions of the crankshaft are required for each power stroke, causes the two-stroke engine to compare more favorably when horsepower to weight ratio is considered; and because of the weight advantage, the two-stroke engine has probably reached its highest degree of development for outboard motor use.

TWO-STROKE CYCLE. In a two-stroke cycle engine, the five events of intake, compression, ignition, power and exhaust must take place in two strokes of the piston; or one revolution of the crankshaft. Thus, a compressed fuel charge is fired each time the piston reaches the top of the cylinder, and each downward stroke is a power stroke. In order to accomplish this, the initial pressure of the incoming fuel-air mixture must be raised to a point somewhat higher than the lowest pressure existing in the cylinder, or a fresh charge of fuel could not be admitted and the engine would not run. This elevation of pressure requires the use of an air pump, or compressor, of approximately the same volume as the cylinder itself. Coincidentally, such an air pump is available with a minimum of additional parts, cost, or friction losses by utilizing the opposite side of the piston and cylinder as the pump. Such engines are called "Crankcase Scavenged," and are almost universally used in the outboard motor industry.

Figure 1-2 shows a schematic view of the crankcase scavenged, reed valve type, two-stroke cycle engine commonly used. The general sequence of events required for operation is as follows: As the piston moves outward from the crankshaft as shown in view "B", the volume of the closed crankcase is enlarged and the pressure lowered, causing air to be drawn through the carburetor (C), where it is mixed with fuel. This mixture is then drawn through the reed valve (R) and into the crankcase. At the same time, a previous charge of fuel is being compressed between head of piston and closed end of cylinder as shown by the darkened area. As the piston approaches top center, a timed spark ignites the compressed fuel charge and the resultant expansion moves the piston downward on the power stroke. The reed valve (R) closes, and downward movement of piston compresses the next fuel charge in the crankcase as shown in view "A". When the piston nears the bottom of its stroke, the crown of piston uncovers the exhaust port (EX)

in cylinder wall, allowing the combustion products and remaining pressure to escape as shown by the wavy arrow. Further downward movement of piston opens the transfer port (TP) leading from the crankcase to cylinder; and the then higher crankcase pressure forces the compressed fuel:air mixture through

transfer port into the cylinder. The baffle which is built into crown of piston deflects the incoming charge upward, and most of the remaining exhaust gases are driven from the combustion chamber by this fresh charge. Two-stroke cycle, crankcase scavenged engines are sometimes produced with a

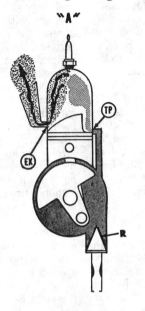

Fig. 1-2—Schematic view of two-stroke cycle, crankcase scavenged engine used in most outboard motors. The same series of events shown in Fig. 1-1 takes place in one revolution of the crankshaft by using the crankcase as a scavenging pump.

　C. Carburetor
　R. Reed valve
　TP. Transfer port
　EX. Exhaust port

Fig. 1-3—Two-stroke cycle, three port engine. Principles are similar to reed valve or rotary valve types except that a third, intake port is located in cylinder wall and opened and closed by the piston skirt.

　C. Carburetor
　EX. Exhaust port
　IP. Intake port
　TP. Transfer port

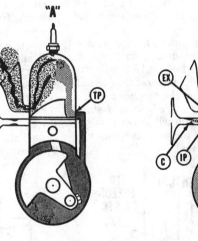

Fig. 1-4—Two-stroke cycle rotary valve engine. The incoming fuel charge is controlled by a rotary valve attached to the crankshaft. The opening in valve (RO) and crankcase (SO) align at the proper time to admit a fresh charge, then close to allow intial crankcase compression.

　C. Carburetor
　RO. Opening in rotating member
　SO. Opening in crankcase wall

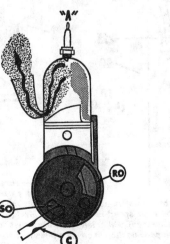

fuel induction system other than the inlet reed valve. Although they are not extensively used in outboard motor manufacture, they are mentioned in passing and illustrated schematically in Fig. 1-3 and Fig. 1-4.

In the crankcase scavenged engine, most of the friction parts requiring lubrication are located in the fuel intake system. Lubrication is accomplished by mixing the required amount of oil with the fuel, so that a small amount of oil in the form of a fine mist is drawn into the crankcase with each fuel charge. It should be pointed out that the new oil brought into the crankcase can little more than supplement the losses, therefore it is necessary that the friction parts be well lubricated at the time the engine is started. The use of too much oil in the fuel mixture results in plug fouling, excessive carbon, and poor performance, as well as being wasteful.

FUEL SYSTEM

CARBURETOR. The function of the carburetor is to atomize the fuel and mix it with the air flowing into the engine. The carburetor must also meter the fuel to provide the proper fuel:air ratio for the different engine operating conditions, and the proper density of total charge to satisfy the power and speed requirements.

A gasoline-air mixture is normally combustible between the limits of 25 parts air to 1 part fuel, and 8 parts air to 1 part fuel. Because much of the fuel will not vaporize when the engine is cold, a rich mixture is required for cold starting. The exact ratio will depend on the temperature and the volatility (ability to vaporize) of the fuel.

Carburetor operation is based on the venturi principle, in which a gas or liquid flowing through a restriction (venturi) will increase in speed and decrease in pressure, acting in much the same way as water passing through the nozzle of a garden hose. Refer to Fig. 1-5.

An extension tube (nozzle) from the fuel reservoir is inserted into the air passage with the opening at approximately the narrowest part of the venturi, and the fuel level in the reservoir is maintained at just below the opening of the nozzle. When air passes through the venturi, fuel spills over into the air stream in amounts relative to the pressure drop. If the level in fuel bowl is too high, fuel will spill over into carburetor when engine is not operating. If fuel level is too low, a sufficient amount may not be pulled into the the air stream during certain periods of operation, and a lean mixture could result. The fuel level is usually maintained by means of a float as shown in Fig. 1-6.

A simple carburetor which relies only on the venturi principle will supply a progressively richer mixture as engine speed is increased, and will not run at all at idle speeds. The carburetor must therefore be modified if the engine is to perform at varying speeds. The first step in modification is usually the addition of a separate fuel mixing and metering system designed to operate only at slow engine speeds. A fairly representative idle system is shown schematically in Fig. 1-7. An idle passage is drilled in the carburetor body as shown, leading from the fuel chamber to the air horn at the approximate location of the throttle valve (1). When the throttle valve is closed, the air flow is almost shut off. This reduces the pressure in the inlet

manifold, and therefore the density of the charge in the combustion chamber. The pressure drop at the venturi which is shown in Fig. 1-5 ceases to exist, and fuel cannot be drawn from the main fuel nozzle. The high manifold vacuum above the throttle valve (1 – Fig. 1-7) draws fuel up the idle passage through idle jet (5) then through primary idle orifice (2) into the intake manifold. At the same time, air is being drawn through the secondary idle orifice (3) and air metering orifice (4) to mix with the fuel in the idle passage. The sizes of the two orifices (2 and 3) and the idle jet (5) are carefully calculated and controlled. The amount of air passing through metering orifice (4) can be adjusted by the idle mixture adjusting needle (6) to obtain the desired fuel:air mixture for smooth idle.

When throttle valve (1) is opened slightly to a fast idle position (as indicated by the broken lines) both the primary and secondary idle orifices (2 and 3) are subjected to high manifold vacuum. The incoming flow of air through secondary orifice (3) is cut off, which increases the speed of fuel flow through idle jet (5). This supplies the additional fuel needed to properly mix with the greater volume of air passing around the throttle butterfly valve. As the throttle valve is further opened and edge of valve moves away from the idle orifices, the idle fuel system ceases to operate and fuel mixture is again controlled by the venturi of the main fuel system.

In many applications, the main fuel system and idle system will supply the fuel requirements for all operating conditions. In other cases, an additional economizer system is incorporated,

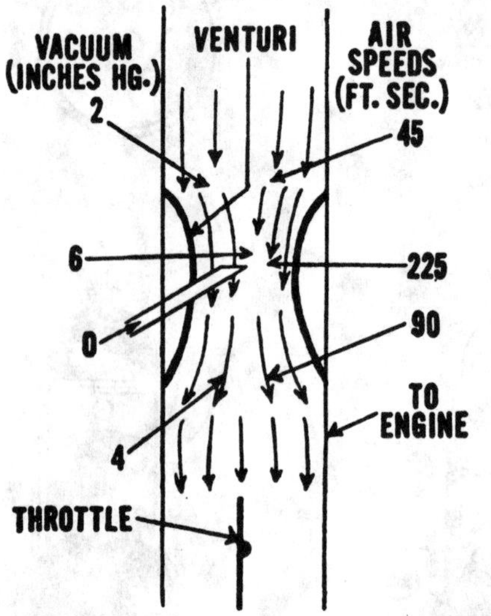

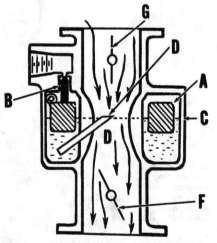

Fig. 1-5—Schematic view of venturi principle. Right hand figures show how air speed is increased by the restriction (venturi) while left hand figures show the accompanying drop in air pressure.

VACUUM (INCHES HG.) VENTURI AIR SPEEDS (FT. SEC.)

TO ENGINE

THROTTLE

Fig. 1-6—Schematic view of a simple float-type carburetor. The buoyancy of float (A) closes the fuel inlet valve (B) to maintain the fuel at a constant level (C). The pressure drop in the venturi causes fuel to flow out nozzle (D) which protrudes just above the fuel level. Throttle valve is at (F) and choke valve at (G).

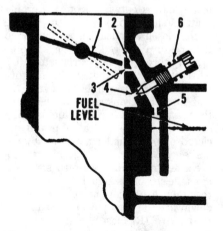

FUEL LEVEL

Fig. 1-7—The addition of a separate idle fuel system permits delivery of a correct fuel mixture over a wider range of engine speeds.

1. Throttle valve	4. Air metering orifice
2. Upper idle orifice	5. Idle fuel jet
3. Lower idle orifice	6. Idle mixture level

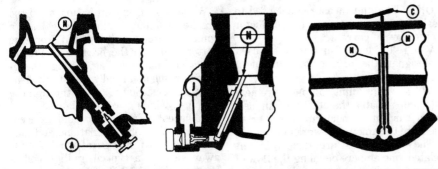

Fig. 1-8—The main fuel metering system may be of many types. Three typical systems are shown. In the left-hand view, the maximum fuel flow through nozzle (N) may be adjusted by the mixture needle (A). In the center view, maximum fuel flow is controlled by the carefully calibrated fixed jet (J). In the right-hand view, the stepped metering needle (M) is moved vertically by a cam (C) on throttle shaft, thus limiting maximum flow to predetermined amounts which vary with throttle setting.

the crankcase, but completely seals off any flow back through the carburetor during the downward stroke of the piston.

FUEL PUMP. All but the smallest motors normally use a remote fuel tank from which fuel is pumped to the carburetor. Most two-stroke motors use the pulsating, pressure and vacuum impulses in one crankcase to operate the fuel pump. Refer to Fig. 1-10. Operation is as follows:

When the piston moves upward in the cylinder as shown in view "A", a vacuum is created on the back side of diaphragm "D". As the diaphragm moves away from the fuel chamber, inlet check valve (5) opens against the pressure of spring (6) to admit fuel from tank as shown by arrow. When the piston moves downward as shown in view "B", the diaphragm moves into the fuel chamber, causing the inlet check valve to close. The outlet check valve (4) opens and fuel flows to the carburetor. When the carburetor float chamber becomes full and carburetor inlet valve closes, the fuel pump diaphragm will remain in approximately the position shown in "A", but will maintain pressure on carburetor fuel line until additional fuel is required.

On some of the larger motors, a two stage fuel pump of similar construction is connected to two separate crankcases of the motor.

On four-stroke cycle engines, the pump diaphragm is spring loaded in one direction and lever operated in the other. The lever may be actuated by any means, the most common being an eccentric cam on the engine camshaft. As the cam turns, the diaphragm pulsates in much the same way as that described for the pressure-vacuum unit. The strength of the diaphragm return spring determines the standby fuel pressure which will be maintained at the carburetor.

which provides a leaner fuel-air mixture for part throttle operation. Accelerator pumps or an accelerating well which are usually needed for automotive operation are not normally used on outboard motors.

An accelerator pump can be used, however. The accelerator pump can be lever operated or spring operated and vacuum controlled. The purpose of an accelerator pump is to provide an additional charge of fuel at the moment of throttle opening, before balance is restored to the high speed fuel system.

High speed mixture adjustment is controlled by a fixed jet, a fuel adjustment needle, or by a stepped metering rod which is synchronized with the throttle valve. Refer to Fig. 1-8 for a schematic view of the systems.

The basic design of diaphragm type carburetors is shown in Fig. 1-9. Fuel is delivered to inlet (1) by gravity with fuel tank above carburetor, or under pressure from a fuel pump. Atmospheric pressure is maintained on lower side of diaphragm (D) through vent hole (V). When choke plate (C) is closed and engine is cranked, or when engine is running, pressure at orifice (O) is less than atmospheric pressure; this low pressure, or vacuum, is transmitted to fuel chamber (F) above diaphragm through nozzle channel (N). The higher (atmospheric) pressure at lower side of diaphragm will then push the diaphragm upward compressing spring (S) and allowing inlet valve (IV) to open and fuel will flow into the fuel chamber. Some diaphragm type carburetors are equipped with an internal fuel pump.

REED VALVES. The inlet reed (or leaf) valve is essentially a check valve which permits the air-fuel mixture to move in only one direction through the engine. It traps the fuel charge in the crankcase, permitting the inlet pressure to be raised high enough to allow a full charge to enter the cylinder against the remaining exhaust pressure during the short period of time the transfer ports are open. The ideal design for the valve is one which offers the least possible resistance to the flow of gases entering

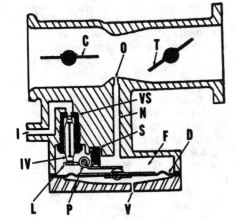

Fig. 1-9—Cross-section drawing of basic design diaphragm type carburetor. Atmospheric pressure actuates diaphragm (D).

C. Choke
D. Diaphragm
F. Fuel chamber
I. Fuel inlet
IV. Inlet valve needle
L. Lever
N. Nozzle
O. Orifice
P. Pivot pin
S. Spring
T. Throttle
V. Vent
VS. Valve seat

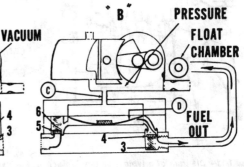

Fig. 1-10—Schematic view of a typical, crankcase operated, diaphragm type fuel pump. Pressure and vacuum pulsations from crankcase pass through connection (C) to rear of diaphragm (D) which induces a pumping action on fuel line as shown.

3. Valve spring
4. Outlet check valve
5. Inlet check valve
6. Valve spring

IGNITION SYSTEM

The timed spark which ignites the fuel charge in the cylinder may be supplied by either a magneto or battery ignition system. To better understand the operation of the components and the differences and similarities of the two systems, they will be combined in this section and the functions of the various units explained and compared.

IGNITION SYSTEM THEORY. In the modern ignition system, a relatively weak electric current of 6 to 12 volts and 2 to 5 amperes is transformed into a momentary charge of minute amperage and extremely high (10,000-25,000) voltage, capable of jumping the spark plug gap in the cylinder and igniting the fuel charge.

To understand the ignition system theory, electricity can be thought of as a stream of electrons flowing through a conductor. The pressure of the stream can be increased by restricting volume, or the volume increased by reducing the resistance to movement, but the total amount of power cannot be increased except by employing additional outside force. The current has an inertia of motion and resists being stopped once it has started flowing. If the circuit is broken suddenly, the force will tend to pile up temporarily, attempting to convert the speed of flow into energy.

A short list of useful electrical terms and a brief explanation of their meanings is as follows:

AMPERE. The unit of measurement used to designate the amount, or quantity of flow of an electrical current.

OHM. The unit measurement used to designate the resistance of a conductor to the flow of current.

VOLT. The unit of measurement used to designate the force, or pressure of an electrical current

WATT. The unit of measurement which designates the abililty of an electrical current to perform work; or to measure the amount of work performed.

The four terms are directly interrelated, one ampere equaling the flow of current produced by one volt against a resistance of one ohm. One watt designates the work potential of one ampere at one volt in one second.

BATTERY IGNITION

Fig. 1–11 shows a very simple battery ignition circuit for a single cylinder engine. The system uses breaker points to control the time of ignition. The system may be called a "total loss ignition" if there is no provision for recharging the battery while the engine is running and the intensity of the spark will diminish as the battery's electromotive Force (emF) is reduced.

When the timer cam is turned so the breaker (contact) points are closed, a complete circuit is completed from the battery through the breaker points, to the coil primary winding, through the ignition switch and finally back to the battery. The electricity flowing through the primary winding of the ignition coil establishes a magnetic field concentrated in the core laminations and surrounding the windings of wire. A cutaway view of a typical ignition coil is shown in Fig. 1-12. The cam is mechanically connected to rotate a specific amount in relation to the crankshaft. At the proper time, the cam will push the breaker points apart, opening the circuit and preventing current from flowing through the primary windings. The interruption stops the flow of current quickly which causes the magnetic field surrounding the primary windings to collapse. Stopping the magnetic field does not cause the field to fade away, but results in a very fast movement from around the coil windings and through the metal lamination, back to the center of the coil primary windings. As the magnetic field collapses, it quickly passes (cuts) through the primary and secondary windings creating an emf as high as 250 volts in the primary and up to 25,000 volts in the secondary windings. The condenser, which is wired parallel with the breaker points absorbs the self-induced current in the primary circuit, then discharges this current when the breaker points close.

Due to resistance of the primary winding, a certain period of time is required for maximum primary current flow after the breaker contact points are closed. At high engine speeds, the points remain closed for a smaller interval of time, hence the primary current does not build up to the maximum and secondary voltage is somewhat less than at low engine speed. However, coil design is such that the minimum voltage available at high engine speed exceeds the normal maximum voltage required for the ignition spark.

Notice that the ignition switch opens to stop current flow to the primary winding which also stops the high voltage necessary for ignition.

Other variations for this battery ignition are possible. Many use solid state electrical components to open and close the primary circuit in place of the mechanical breaker points.

MAGNETO IGNITION

Two of the principal reasons for utilizing a magneto ignition in place of a battery ignition are: Reduced weight and minimum dependence on other systems for ignition.

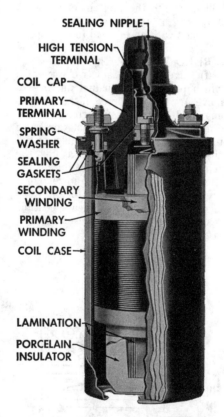

SEALING NIPPLE

HIGH TENSION TERMINAL

COIL CAP

PRIMARY TERMINAL

SPRING WASHER

SEALING GASKETS

SECONDARY WINDING

PRIMARY WINDING

COIL CASE

LAMINATION

PORCELAIN INSULATOR

Fig. 1-12—Cut-away view of typical battery ignition system coil. Primary winding consists of approximately 200-250 turns (loops) of heavier wire; secondary winding consists of several thousand turns of fine wire. Laminations concentrate the magnetic lines of force and increase efficiency of the coil.

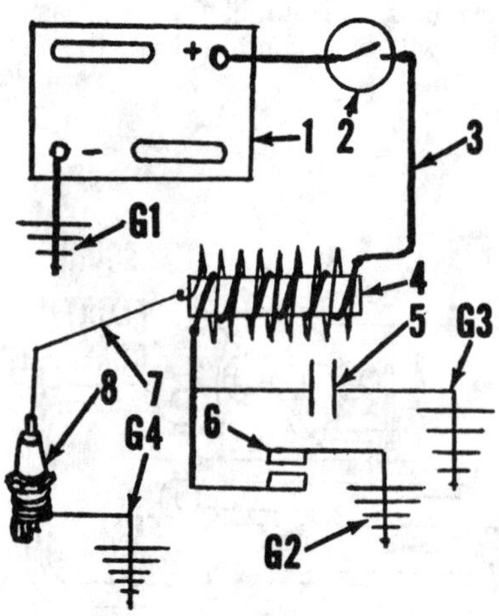

Fig. 1-11—Diagram of a typical battery ignition system. Refer to text for principles of operation.

1. Battery
2. Ignition switch
3. Primary circuit
4. Ignition coil
5. Condenser
6. Contact points
7. Secondary circuit
8. Spark plug

G1 through G4. Ground connections

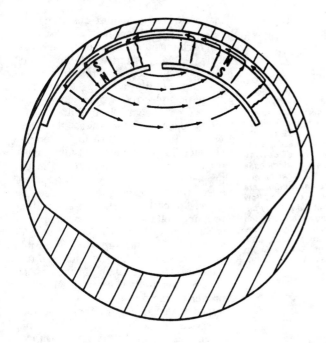

Fig. 1-13—Cut-away view of typical engine flywheel used with flywheel magneto type ignition system. The permanent magnets are usually cast into the flywheel. For flywheel type magnetos having the ignition coil and core mounted to outside of flywheel, magnets would be flush with outer diameter of flywheel.

coil windings and the breaker points which have now been closed by action of the cam.

At the instant the movement of the lines of force cutting through the coil winding sections is at the maximum rate, the maximum flow of current is obtained in the primary circuit. At this time, the cam opens the breaker points interrupting the primary circuit and, for an instant, the flow of current is absorbed by the condenser as illustrated in Fig. 1-16. An emf is also induced in the secondary coil windings, but the voltage is not sufficient to cause current to flow across the spark plug gap.

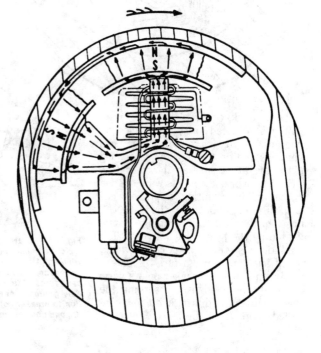

Fig. 1-14—View showing flywheel turned to a position so lines of force of the permanent magnets are concentrated in the left and center core legs and are interlocking the coil windings.

Flywheel Magneto With Breaker Points

Refer to Fig. 1-13 for a cut-away view of a typical flywheel. The arrows indicate lines of force (flux) of the permanent magnets which are carried by the flywheel. As indicated by the arrows, direction of force of the magnetic field is from the north pole (N) of the left magnet to the south pole (S) of the right magnet.

Figs. 1-14, 1-15, 1-16 and 1-17 illustrate the operational cycle of the flywheel type magneto. In Fig. 1-14 the flywheel magnets are located over the left and center legs of the armature (ignition coil) core. As the magnets moved into this position, their magnetic field was attracted by the armature core and a potential voltage (emf) was induced in the coil windings. However, this emf was not sufficient to cause current to flow across the spark plug electrode gap in the high tension circuit and the points were open in the primary circuit.

In Fig. 1-15, the flywheel magnets have moved to a new position to where there magnetic field is being attracted by the center and right legs of the armature core, and is being withdrawn from the left and center legs. As indicated by the heavy black arrows, the lines of force are cutting up through the section of coil windings between the left and center legs of the armature and are cutting down through the coil windings section between the center and right legs. If the left hand rule is applied to the lines of force cutting through the coil sections, it is seen that the resulting emf induced in the primary circuit will cause a current to flow through the primary

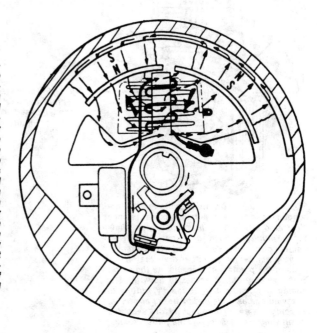

Fig. 1-15—View showing flywheel turned to a position so that lines of force of the permanent magnets are being withdrawn from the left and center core legs and are being attracted by the center and right core legs. While this event is happening, the lines of force are cutting up through the coil windings section between the left and center legs and are cutting down through the section between the right and center legs as indicated by the heavy black arrows. As the breaker points are now closed by the cam, a current is induced in the primary ignition circuit as the lines of force cut through the coil windings.

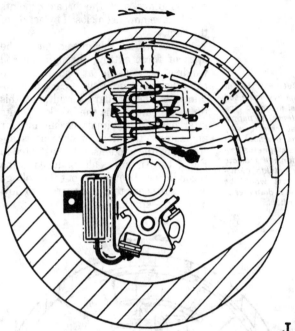

Fig. 1-16—The flywheel magnets have now turned slightly past the position shown in Fig. 1-15 and the rate of movement of lines of magnetic force cutting through the coil windings is at the maximum. At this instant, the breaker points are opened by the cam and flow of current in the primary circuit is being absorbed by the condenser, bringing the flow of current to a quick, controlled stop. Refer now to Fig. 1-17.

magnetic field to collapse at such a rapid rate to induce a very high voltage in the coil high tension or secondary windings. This voltage, often 10,000 to 25,000 volts, is sufficient to break down the resistance of the air gap between the spark plug electrodes and a current will flow across the gap. This creates the ignition spark which ignites the compressed fuel-air mixture in the engine cylinder. Point opening (or timing) must occur when the engine piston is in the proper position for the best performance. Point opening must also be timed to occur when the alternating primary voltage is at its peak or the secondary voltage will be weak and spark plug may not fire. It is impossible or impractical in the average shop to measure the alternating primary current relative to flywheel position, so the proper timing for peak voltage is determined by design engineers and becomes a service specification variously referrmd to as **Edge Gap**, **Break Away Gap** or **Pole Shoe Break**.

The flow of current in the primary windings created a strong electromagnetic field surrounding the coil windings and up through the center leg of the armature core as shown in Fig. 1-17. As the breaker points were opened by the cam, interrupting the primary circuit, this magnetic field starts to collapse cutting the coil windings as indicated by the heavy black arrows. The emf induced in the primary circuit would be sufficient to cause a flow of current across the opening breaker points were it not for the condenser absorbing the flow of current and bringing it to a controlled stop. This allows the electro-

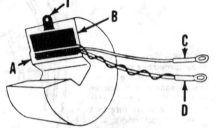

Fig. 1-18—Drawing showing construction of a typical flywheel magneto ignition coil. Primary winding (A) consists of about 200 turns of wire. Secondary winding (B) consists of several thousand turns of fine wire. Coil primary and secondary ground connection is (D); primary connection to breaker point and condenser terminal is (C); and coil secondary (high tension) terminal is (T).

Flywheel Magnetos Without Breaker Points

BREAKERLESS SYSTEM. The solid state (breakerless) magneto ignition system may operate on the same basic principles as the conventional type flywheel magneto previously described. The main difference is that the breaker contact points are replaced by a solid state electronic Gate Controlled Switch (GCS) which has no moving parts. Since, in a conventional system breaker points are closed for a longer period of crank-

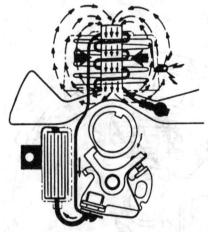

Fig. 1-17—View showing magneto ignition coil, condenser and breaker points at same instant as illustrated in Fig. 1-16, however, arrows shown above illustrate lines of force of the electromagnetic field established by current in primary coil windings rather than the lines of force of the permanent magnets. As the current in the primary circuit ceases to flow, the electromagnetic field collapses rapidly, cutting the coil windings as indicated by heavy arrows and inducing a very high voltage in the secondary coil winding resulting in the ignition spark.

Fig. 1-19—Exploded view of a typical flywheel magneto of the type used on outboard motors.

1. Condenser
2. Contact points
3. Magneto coil
4. Stator plate
5. Coil laminations
6. Washers
7. Mounting adapter
8. Friction washer
9. Throttle control cam
10. Spacer

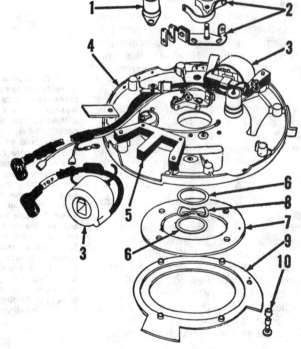

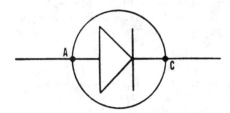

Fig. 1-20—In a diagram of an electrical circuit, the diode is represented by the symbol shown above. The diode will allow current to flow in one direction only, from cathode (C) to anode (A).

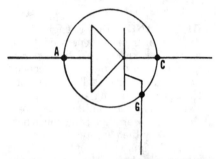

Fig. 1-21—The symbol used for a Gate controlled Switch (GCS) in an electrical diagram is shown above. The GCS will permit current to flow from cathode (C) to anode (A) when "turned on" by a positive electrical charge at gate (G) terminal.

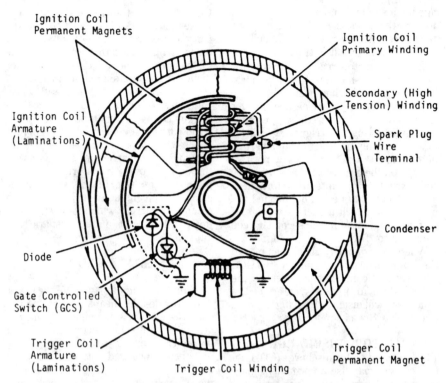

Fig. 1-22—Schematic diagram of typical breakerless magneto igniton system. Refer to Figs. 1-23, 1-24 and 1-25 for schemtic views of operating cycle.

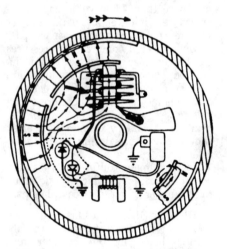

Fig. 1-23—View showing flywheel of breakerless magneto system at instant of rotation where lines of force of ignition coil magnets are being drawn into left and center legs of magneto armature. The diode (see Fig. 1-20) acts as a closed set of breaker points in completing the primary ignition circuit at this time.

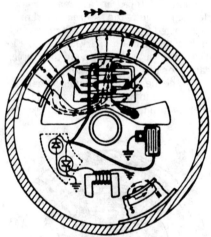

Fig. 1-24—Flywheel is turning to point where magnetic flux lines through armature center leg will reverse direction and current through primary coil circuit will reverse. As current reverses, diode which was previously conducting will shut off and there will be no current. When magnetic flux lines have reversed in armature center leg, voltage potential will again build up, but since GCS is in "OFF" state, no current will flow. To prevent excessive voltage build up, the condenser acts as a buffer.

shaft rotation than is the "GCS", a diode has been added to the circuit to provide the same characteristics as closed breaker points.

The same basic principles for electromagnetic induction of electricity and formation of magnetic fields by electrical current as outlined for the coventional flywheel type magneto also apply to the solid state magneto. Therefore the principles of the different components (diode and GCS) will complete the operating principles of the solid state magneto.

The diode is represented in wiring diagrams by the symbol shown in Fig. 1-20. The diode is an electronic device that will permit passage of electrical current (electrons) in one direction only. In electrical schematic diagrams, electron flow is sometimes opposite to direction arrow part of symbol is pointing.

The symbol shown in Fig. 1-21 is used to represent the gate controlled switch (GCS) in wiring diagrams. The GCS acts as a switch to permit passage of current from cathode (C) terminal to anode (A) terminal when in "ON" state and will not permit electric current to flow when in "OFF" state. The GCS can be turned "ON" by a positive surge of electricity at the gate (G) terminal and will remain "ON" as long as current remains positive at the gate terminal or as long as current is flowing through the GCS from cathode (C) terminal to anode (A) terminal.

The basic components and wiring diagram for the solid state breakerless magneto are shown schematically in Fig. 1-22. In Fig. 1-23, the magneto rotor (flywheel) is turning and the ignition coil magnets have just moved into position so that their lines of force are cutting the ignition coil windings and producing a negative surge of current in the primary windings. The diode allows current to flow and action is same as conventional magneto with breaker

points closed. As rotor (flywheel) continues to turn as shown in Fig. 1-24, direction of magnetic flux lines will reverse in the armature center leg. Direction of current will change in the primary coil circuit and the previously conducting diode will be shut off. At this point, neither diode is conducting. Voltage begins to build up as rotor continues to turn the condenser and acts as a buffer to prevent excessive voltage build up at the GCS before it is triggered.

When the rotor reaches the approximate position shown in Fig. 1-25, maximum flux density has been achieved in the center leg of the armature. At this time the GCS is triggered. Triggering is accomplished by the triggering coil armature moving into the field of a permanent magnet which induces a positive voltage on the gate of the GCS. Primary coil current flow results in the formation of an electro-magnetic field around the primary coil which inducts a voltage of sufficient potential in the secondary coil windings to "fire" the spark plug.

When the rotor (flywheel) has moved the magnets past the armature, the GCS will cease to conduct and revert to the "OFF" state until it is triggered. The condenser will discharge during the time that the GCS was conducting.

CAPACITOR DISCHARGE SYSTEM. The capacitor discharge (CD) ignition system may use a permanent magnet rotor (flywheel) to induce a current in a coil, but unlike the conventional flywheel magneto and solid state breakerless magneto described previously, the current is stored in a capacitor (condenser). Then the stored current is discharged through a transformer coil to create the ignition spark. Refer to Fig. 1-26 for a schematic of a typical capacitor discharge ignition system.

As the permanent flywheel magnets pass by the input generating coil (1), the current produced charges capacitor (6).

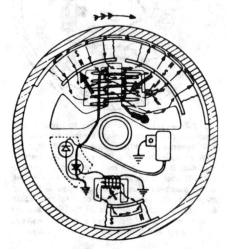

Fig. 1-25—With flywheel in the approximate position shown, maximum voltage potential is present in windings of primary coil. At this time the triggering coil armature has moved into the field of a permanent magnet and a positive voltage is induced on the gate of the GCS. The GCS is triggered and primary coil current flows resulting in the formation of an electromagnetic field around the primary coil which inducts a voltage of sufficient potential in the secondary windings to "fire" the spark plug.

Only half of the generated current passes through diode (3) to charge the capacitor. Reverse current is blocked by diode (3) but passes through Zener diode (2) to complete the reverse circuit. Zener diode (2) also limits maximum voltage of the forward current. As the flywheel continues to turn and magnets pass the trigger coil (4), a small amount of electrical current is generated. This current opens the gate controlled switch (5) allowing the capacitor to discharge through the pulse transformer (7). The rapid voltage rise in the transformer primary coil induces a high voltage secondary current which forms the ignition spark when it jumps the spark plug gap.

SPARK PLUG

In any spark ignition engine, the spark plug provides the means for igniting the compressed fuel-air mixture in the cylinder. Before an electric charge can move across an air gap, the intervening air must be charged with electricity, or ionized. The spark plug gap becomes more easily ionized if the spark plug ground (G4 – Fig. 1-11) is of negative polarity. If the spark plug is properly gapped and the system is not shorted, not more than 7,000 volts may be required to initiate a spark. Higher voltage is required as the spark plug warms up, or if compression pressures or the distance of the air gap is increased. Compression pressures are highest at full throttle and relatively slow engine speeds, therefore, high voltage requirements or a lack of available secondary voltage most often shows up as a miss during maximum acceleration from a slow engine speed. There are many different types and sizes of spark plugs which are designed for a number of specific requirements.

THREAD SIZE. The threaded, shell portion of the spark plug and the attaching holes in the cylinder are manufactured to meet certain industry established standards. The diameter is referred to as "Thread Size." Those com-

Fig. 1-26—Schematic diagram of a typical capacitor discharge ignition system.
1. Generating coil
2. Zener diode
3. Diode
4. Trigger coil
5. Gate controlled switch
6. Capacitor
7. Pulse transformer (coil)
8. Spark plug

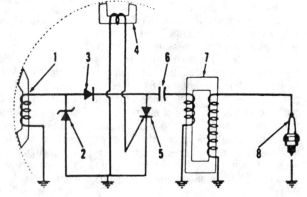

monly used are: 10 mm, 14 mm, 18 mm, 7/8 inch and 1/2 inch pipe. The 14 mm plug is almost universal for outboard motor use.

REACH. The length of the thread, and the thread depth in cylinder head or wall are also standardized throughout the industry. This dimension is measured from gasket seat of head to cylinder end of thread. Four different reach plugs commonly used are: 3/8 inch, 7/16 inch, 1/2 inch and 3/4 inch. The first two mentioned are the only ones commonly used in outboard motors.

HEAT RANGE. During engine operation, part of the heat generated during combustion is transferred to the spark plug, and from the plug to the coolant water through the shell threads and gasket. The operating temperature of the spark plug plays an important part in the engine operation. If too much heat is retained by the plug, the fuel-air mixture may be ignited by contact with the heated surface before the ignition spark occurs. If not enough heat is retained, partially burned combustion products (soot, carbon and oil) may build up on the plug tip resulting in "fouling" or shorting out of the plug. If this happens, the secondary current is dissipated uselessly as it is generated instead of bridging the plug gap as a useful spark, and the engine will misfire.

The operating temperature of the plug tip can be controlled, within limits, by altering the length of the path the heat must follow to reach the threads and gasket of the plug. Thus, a plug with a short, stubby insulator around the center electrode will run cooler than one with a long, slim insulator. Most plugs in the more popular sizes are available in a number of heat ranges which are interchangeable within the group. The proper heat range is determined by engine design and the type of service. Like most other elements of design, the plug type installed as original equipment is usually a compromise and is either the most suitable plug for average condi-

Fig. 1-27—Spark plug tip temperature is controlled by the length of the path heat must travel to reach the coolant medium.

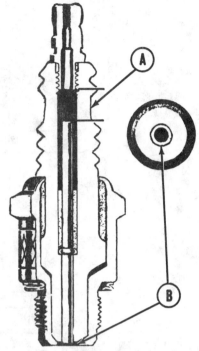

Fig. 1-29—A specially designed surface gap plug offers exceptional freedom from carbon fouling. Features include an air gap (A) in the center element and a circular gap (B) which burns clean. Special voltages are required, and the plug is not interchangeable with other types.

tions; or the best plug to meet the two extremes of service expected. No one spark plug, however, can be ideally suited for long periods of slow-speed operation such as trolling, and still be the best possible type for high-speed operation. Refer to SPARK PLUG SERVICING, in SERVICE FUNDAMENTALS section, for additional information on spark plug selection.

SPECIAL TYPES. Sometimes, engine design features or operating conditions call for special plug types designed for a particular purpose. Special types include SHIELDED PLUGS which are extensively used for inboard marine applications and RESISTOR PLUGS, with built-in resitance. Of special interest when dealing with outboard motors is the two-stroke spark plug shown in the left hand view, Fig. 1-28. In the design of this plug, the ground electrode is shortened so its end aligns with center of insulated electrode rather than completely overlapping as with the conventional plug. This feature reduces the possibility of the gap bridging over by carbon formations. A second special type designed for outboard motor use is the SURFACE GAP plug shown in Fig. 1-29. This spark plug was engineered by Champion Spark Plug Company for use in high-output motors. This plug is capable of efficient operation over a wide range of conditions. It cannot however, be interchanged with a conventional spark plug.

COOLING SYSTEM

The cooling system on most motors consists of a water intake located on the lower motor leg, a coolant pump, and in many cases, a thermostat to control the coolant temperature. As with all internal combustion engines, the cooling system must be designed to maintain a satisfactory operating temperature, rather than the coolest possible temperature. This is made additionally

difficult in the case of the outboard motor because the coolant liquid is not contained in a separate reservoir where coolant temperature can be controlled. Because the temperature of the incoming liquid cannot be controlled, the only possible means of regulating the operating temperature is by the control of the amount of coolant flowing in the system.

On most outboard motors, the flow is held at a relatively constant level regardless of engine speed, by the design of the coolant pump. Refer to Fig. 1-30. At slow engine speeds the rubber impeller blades follow the contour of the offset housing as shown by the solid line. The pump functions as a positive displacement pump, drawing water in (IN) as area between impeller blades increases. Water is forced into outlet passage (OUT) and up into power head as area decreases. As engine speed increases, pump rotative speed and water pressure forces impeller blade away from outside of housing as shown by the

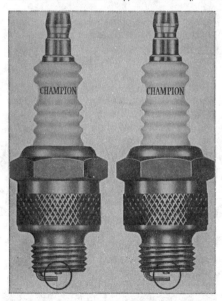

Fig. 1-28—The two stroke plug shown at left, is one of the more important special types in the outboard motor industry.

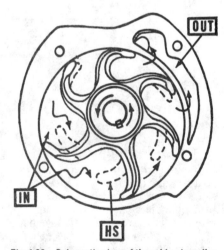

Fig. 1-30—Schematic view of the rubber impeller type water pump which maintains an approximately equal volume of coolant flow at most operating speeds. Water is drawn into pump (IN) as area between vanes increases and is forced into power head (OUT) as area decreases. At high speeds (HS) the blades remain curved and pump operates mostly by centrifugal action.

broken lines (HS). At full speed, the pump operates almost entirely as a centrifugal pump.

Later production motors often use a thermostat to assist in maintaining an efficient operating fumperature. The thermostat may recirculate the coolant

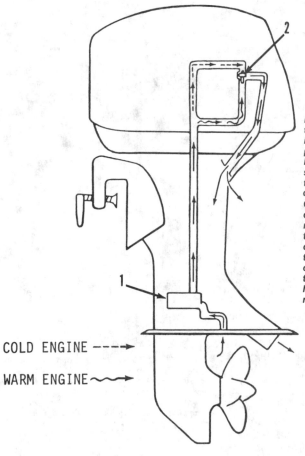

COLD ENGINE ---->

WARM ENGINE ~~~>

Fig. 1-31—Bypass type of thermostat operation used in some motors. When power head temperature is below normal the thermostat (2) closes coolant outlet through power head and opens the bypass outlet. Coolant flow then follows course shown by broken arrows. As operating temperature is reached, thermostat opens coolant passages through power head and closes bypass. The coolant then flows through power head as shown by wavy arrow. The coolant pump is in lower unit as shown by (1).

water in the power head until operating temperature is reached, then open to allow the heated liquid to be exhausted; or, may bypass the power head with the circulated liquid until operating temperature is reached, then circulate coolant through block. Refer to Fig. 1-31.

In almost all liquid-cooled motors, the coolant liquid passes from the power head into the engine exhaust system. The entrance of the water cools the exhaust stream and the exhaust housing which is usually part of the lower motor leg.

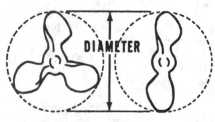

Fig. 1-32—The proper method of measuring the diameter of a two-blade and three-blade propeller is as shown.

DRIVE UNIT FUNDAMENTALS

PROPELLER

An outboard motor propeller moves a boat through the water in somewhat the same manner that a wood screw passes through a piece of wood. Propellers are rated by diameter, pitch and the number of blades; diameter being the distance across a circle described by blade tips as shown in Fig. 1-32, and pitch the forward thrust imparted in one revolution of the propeller as shown by Fig. 1-33. The correct propeller diameter is determined by motor design, especially the items of horsepower and propeller shaft gear ratio, and should usually not be changed from that recommended by the manufacturer. Propeller pitch is more nearly comparable to the transmission gear ratio of an automobile and should be individually selected to suit the conditions of boat design and usage.

Efficiency is greatest when the propeller operates with only moderate slippage, the actual amount depending to a

certain degree upon the application. Normal slippage on a racing hull may be as low as 10 percent, while a slow speed hull may normally be allowed 50-60 percent.

NOTE: Slippage is the difference between the distance a boat actually moves forward with each turn of the propeller, and the theoretical distance indicated by the pitch. For example, a boat equipped with a 12-inch (30.5 cm) pitch propeller which moves forward 9 inches (22.9 cm) with each revolution of the propeller shaft has 25 percent slippage.

The potential speed of a boat depends as much on the design of the boat as upon the power of the motor. Although there are many individual types, most boats will fall into one of two broad categories: (A) the displacement hull; and (B) the planing hull. Refer to Fig. 1-34. When not moving, any boat will displace its own weight in water. A displacement

hull will run at nearly the standing depth when under way. A planing hull will ride up on the water as shown at (2) as it approaches cruising speed, offering much less resistance to the forward movement.

A displacement hull is the only logical design for slow moving boats which cannot attain planing speed. They are also more stable in rough water and ride somewhat easier than a planing hull. A displacement hull requires a minimum pitch propeller as shown at (A – Fig. 1-33). A three-blade propeller offering maximum thrust area is usually used.

Speed is as important as power in the efficient operation of a planing hull. Maximum resistance is encountered as the boat moves into planing position, and peak slippage occurs at that time. Once planing position has been attained, forward speed will increase to the limits imposed by propeller speed and pitch. A two-blade propeller is capable of attaining a somewhat faster forward speed

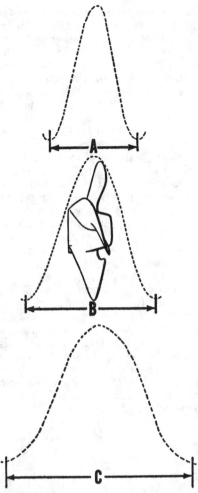

Fig. 1-33—Propeller pitch indicates the theoretical forward movement in one revolution of propeller if there were no slippage. Flat pitch propellers (A) can be likened to low gear in an automobile; while extreme pitch (C) is similar to high gear or overdrive.

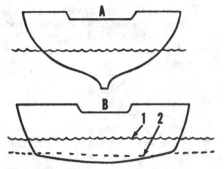

Fig. 1-34—Outboard hulls fall into two general classes; the displacement hull shown at (A) and the planing hull shown at (B). In the displacement hull, the waterline is about the same height on hull when boat is at anchor or under way. The planing hull (B) rises in the water as speed increases, and in extreme conditions barely touches the water surface.

A. Displacement hull
B. Planing hull
1. Standing waterline
2. Planing waterline

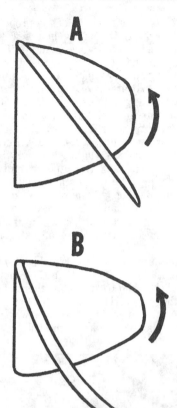

Fig. 1-35—The propeller pitch may be at a constant angle as shown at (A); or of a varying angle (cupped) as shown at (B).

than a three-blade propeller of the same pitch. Planing hulls require a longer pitch propeller, falling somewhere between that shown at (B) and (C), Fig. 1-33.

A propeller is not ideally suited to the same boat and motor under all operating conditions. If a light runabout with a small motor is used to pull a water skier, a lower pitch propeller may be required. The same holds true of a moderate horsepower motor when pulling two or more skiers. A three-blade propeller is usually preferable for water skiing. Top speed may be somewhat reduced over that of a comparable two-blade unit, but performance will usually be improved.

There is no set rule for matching a propeller, boat and motor. The general practice is to select a propeller which will allow the properly tuned and adjusted motor to run in the recommended operating speed range at wide-open throttle. Too little propeller pitch will

cause motor to over-speed, while too much pitch will not allow the motor to reach the proper speed.

Outboard motor propellers are usually made of aluminum or bronze, although some plastic propellers have been made. Stainless steel is sometimes used for racing propellers.

Propellers may be designed with a constant, flat pitch throughout the entire length of the blade as shown at "A"–Fig. 1-35, or with a cupped blade which increases in pitch toward the trailing edge as shown at "B". The flat blade propellers operate efficiently only at relatively slow rotative speeds. Above a certain critical speed, water is moved from the blade area faster than additional water can flow into the area behind the blades, causing "cavitation" and erratic behavior. The extreme turbulence and shock waves caused by cavitation rapidly reduces operating efficiency. The critical speed varies with propeller diameter, the traveling speed of the blade tips being the determining factor. Propeller shape also affects the critical speed, as does any obstruction ahead of the propeller which diverts the water flow. A propeller with curved blades is usually designed for higher speed operation than one with flat blades.

GEARCASE AND LOWER HOUSING

The power head delivers power to a drive shaft which is geared to turn a propeller shaft, thus delivering thrust to propel the boat. The gears, shafts and supporting bearings are contained in a lightweight housing or gearcase. In early motors and in some of today's trolling motors, the power transmitted was small. In today's larger motors, how-

ever, speed and pressure is considerable, requiring precision construction and close attention to bearing and gear clearances.

In spite of the necessity for strength and rigidity, the gearcase must interfere as little as possible with the smooth flow of water to the propeller. This is especially important at the higher speeds where propeller cavitation is a problem. To perform efficiently, the gearcase must be kept as small as possible and well streamlined, as shown in Fig. 1-36 and Fig. 1-37.

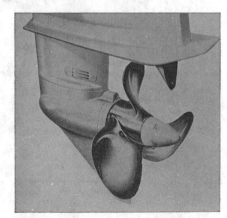

Fig. 1-36—High power, high performance lower unit showing streamlined configuration to eliminate drag and improve the performance.

The operating height of the propeller is important. If too low in the water, speed and efficiency are reduced; if too near the surface, cavitation results, also affecting performance. The manufacturers of boats have standardized the transom height to nominally 15 inches (38.1 cm) for small fishing boats and light utility boats; and 20 inches (50.8 cm) for the larger, faster boats. Actual height is usually slightly greater than the nominal height. Outboard motors are designed for installation on either of the standard height transoms. Most outboard motors can be converted to either a long or short shaft motor by the installation (or removal) of an extension kit.

An outboard motor should operate with the plate (5 – Fig. 1-37) running parallel to and barely below the surface of the water. This is usually (but not necessarily) parallel to and even with the lower planing surface of the hull.

The lower unit also serves as the rudder to steer the boat. Because the direction of thrust turns with the rudder, the system is unusually efficient, especially at slow speeds and in reverse. This makes the outboard unit extremely easy to maneuver in and around docks or other places where maneuverablity at slow speed is important.

The lower portion of the outboard motor propeller continuously operates in slightly less disturbed water than the upper portion. Because of this, the lower portion of the propeller has a tendency to walk the stern of the boat in a direction opposite to its movement. Thus, if a motor is equipped with a propeller which rotates counterclockwise (A – Fig. 1-38), the stern of the boat will move to port as shown by arrow "C"; and boat will pull to starboard when set on a dead ahead course. The opposite will occur if motor is equipped with a propeller rotating clockwise as shown at (B). To compen-

sate for this tendency, some motors are equipped with an adjustable trim tab. Other motors have the lower unit slightly offset with relation to the true centerline for the same reason. When two motors are used, the two propellers are often designed to rotate in opposite directions, and the effect is self-cancelling.

On most outboards, the engine exhaust is vented to the outside underneath the water level to silence engine noise (See 6 – Fig. 1-27). The exhaust usually enters in the disturbed water area immediately behind the propeller to minimize back pressure in the exhaust system. The coolant water as it leaves the power head enters the hot exhaust gases, thus cooling the exhaust and the lower motor housing that serves as the exhaust housing.

Because of variation in the planing angle and built-in transom angle in different types of boats, provision must be made for adjustment of the thrust, or tilt angle (3 – Fig. 1-37). Force of thrust should be parallel to the direction of travel when in planing position. A minor adjustment in the tilt angle can make considerable difference in the speed and performance of the unit.

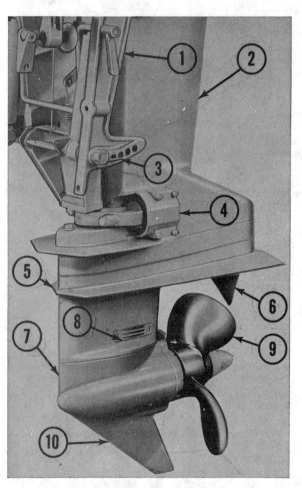

Fig. 1-37 — Lower unit, attaching brackets and associated parts showing nomenclature.

1. Stern brackets
2. Lower motor leg
3. Tilt pin
4. Shock mount
5. Antiventilation plate
6. Exhaust outlet
7. Gearcase
8. Water inlet
9. Propeller
10. Skeg

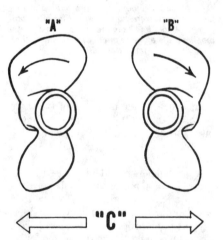

Fig. 1-38 — Propellers may be of counterclockwise rotation as shown at "A" or clockwise rotation as shown at "B". The rotation of the propeller has a tendency to pull the stern of the boat off-course in the direction shown by arrow "C".

SERVICE FUNDAMENTALS
PERIODIC SERVICING

Many of the troubles related to outboard motors will be much easier to repair if noticed before they result in extensive damage and sometimes the lack of proper servicing is the primary cause of failure. The following service and inspection schedule can be used as a guide. If the motor is operated under severe conditions, the intervals should be shortened.

NOTE: This schedule of mid-season service, off-season storage and pre-season preparations is taken from the Marine Service Manual of Recommended Practices which is copyrighted by the Boating Industry Association.

MID-SEASON (OR EVERY 50 HOURS)

1. Drain and flush gearcase. Refill to correct level using manufacturer's recommended lubricant.
2. Remove and clean fuel filter bowl. Replace fuel bowl element. Always use new filter bowl gasket.
3. Clean and regap spark plugs to recommended gap. Replace worn or burnt spark plugs. (Use new gaskets and torque plugs to manufacturer's recommendations).
4. Check propeller for correct pitch. Replace if propeller is worn, chipped or badly bent.
5. Lubricate all grease fittings, using manufacturer's recommended lubricant.
6. Check remote control box, cables and wiring harness.
7. Check steering controls; lubricate mechanical steering.
8. Lubricate all carburetor and magneto linkages with manufacturer's recommended lubricant.
9. Adjust tension on magneto and/or generator drive belts.
10. Clean and coat battery terminals with grease.
11. Check water pump and thermostat operation.
12. Check breaker points' condition and timing.
13. Check carburetor and ignition synchronization.
14. Check carburetor adjustment.

OFF-SEASON STORAGE

Operate motor in test tank, or on boat, at part throttle with shift lever in neutral. Rapidly inject rust preventative oil (with pump type oil can) into carburetor air intake, or intakes, until motor is smoking profusely. Stop motor immediately to prevent burning oil out of cylinders. This will lubricate and protect internal parts of powerhead while motor is in storage. If motor was last operated in salt water, run it in fresh water before preparing it for storage.

1. Place motor on a stand in normal upright position. Remove motor cover.
2. Retard throttle all the way and disconnect spark plug leads. Manually rotate motor flywheel several times to draing the water from water pump.
3. Drain carburetor float chamber. Remove fuel filter bowl – drain, clean and replace filter element and gasket.
4. Clean and lubricate electric starter drive mechanism.
5. Completely drain and clean fuel tank.
6. Remove propeller and check for condition and pitch. Clean and liberally lubricate propeller shaft. Replace propeller drive pin if bent or worn. Replace propeller using new cotter pin or tab lockwasher.
7. Drain and refill gearcase, using the manufacturers recommended lubricant.

8. Wipe over entire external motor surface with a clean cloth soaked in light oil.
9. Store in an upright position in a dry, well-ventilated room. To prevent accidental starting, leave spark plug leads disconnected.
10. Remove battery from boat and keep it charged while in storage.

PRE-SEASON PREPARATION

1. Remove, clean, inspect and properly gap spark plugs. Replace defective plugs. (Use new gaskets and torque plugs to manufacturer's recommendations.)
2. Remove oil level plug from gearcase and check for proper oil level.
3. Thoroughly clean and refinish surfaces as required.
4. Check battery for full charge and clean terminals. Clean and inspect battery cable connections. Check polarity before installing battery cables. Cover cable connections with grease to prevent corrosion.
5. If possible, run motor in test tank prior to installing on boat. Check water pump and thermostat operation.

Proper maintenance is important.

SALT WATER CARE

Motors that are operated in salt water require some special care to combat the possibility of corrosion resulting from such use. If possible, tilt motor out of water and flush cooling system and outside of lower unit with fresh water immediately after each use.

Special care is needed if motor is used in salt water.

The aluminum-silicon alloys used for outboard motor castings are relatively resistant to corrosion from oxidation but are very susceptible to galvanic action and the resultant corrosion if unprotected.

Oxidation is the destruction of a useful form of metal resulting from a chemical combination of the element with oxygen. Although oxidation can occur under water, the most favorable environment is the atmosphere under extreme conditions of warmth and humidity. Rust is an iron oxide and the best known example of oxidation. The oxidation of aluminum leaves a white, powdery coating on the surface of the metal which protects it from further oxidation, and aluminum can withstand years of exposure to the atmosphere without harmful effect.

Briefly described, galvanic action is an electrical process where atoms of one metal are carried in a solution and deposited on the surface of a dissimilar metal. Chrome or nickel plating are controlled forms of galvanic action. Each metallic element has a particular degree of susceptibility to galvanic corrosion, and pure aluminum is second only to magnesium in this scale. The aluminum alloys are somewhat less susceptible than pure metal, and galvanic action can be effectively stopped by painting or other surface protection. Aluminum parts are protected by a process known as anodizing, which deposits a hard, protective coating of aluminum oxide over the surface. The anodized surface is impervious to corrosion from any source, but is only effective if unbroken. Scratches or abrasion can expose the unprotected metal.

Galvanic action is more prevalent in salt water because of the presence of minerals in the water which makes it more effective as a conductor. The action can be hastened by the presence of stray electric currents, and batteries or other sources of electricity should be disconnected when not in use. Some protection is offered by attaching a small block of more susceptible metal in the water near the part to be protected. This small block then becomes the target of galvanic action and is consumed, but the valuable part is spared.

All motors, but especially those used in salt water, should have an adequate coverage of approved paint. Paint bonds well to an anodized aluminum surface, but is difficult to apply to uncoated aluminum. Use only an approved paint, applied according to instructions.

WARNING: Most manufacturers do not recommend the use of antifouling paint on any part of the motor. Antifouling paints contain mercury or copper which can cause galvanic corrosion in the presence of aluminum.

TROUBLE-SHOOTING

Intelligent service is normally divided into two basic functions; that of determining the cause of trouble, and correcting the trouble after cause has been determined. The cause may be obvious in many cases, where broken, worn or damaged parts are apparent. Repair in these cases becomes merely a matter of renewal and adjustment. Many of the performance problems, however, are not so apparent and the first task of the experienced service technician is that of determining the cause.

The experienced serviceman generally develops and follows a logical sequence in trouble-shooting which will most likely lead him quickly to the source of trouble. Some of the points to check may not be applicable to certain outboard motors.

NOTE: This sequence (items 1 through 27) is taken from the Marine Service Manual or Recommended Practices which is copyrighted by the Boating Industry Association.

1. Manual starter rope pulls out, but pawls do not engage.
   A. Friction spring bent or burred.
   B. Excess grease on pawls or spring.
   C. Pawls bent or burred.

Develop an orderly procedure when trouble-shooting.

2. Starter rope does not return.
   A. Recoil spring broken or binding.
   B. Starter housing bent.
   C. Loose or missing parts.

3. Clattering manual starter.
   A. Friction spring bent or burred.
   B. Starter housing bent.
   C. Excess grease on pawls or spring.
   D. Dry starter spindle.

4. Electric starter inoperative.
   A. Loose or corroded connections or ground.
   B. Starting circuit safety switch open, or out of adjustment.
   C. Under capacity or weak battery or corroded battery terminals.
   D. Faulty starter solenoid.
   E. Moisture in electric starter motor.
   F. Broken or worn brushes in starter motor.
   G. Faulty fields.
   H. Faulty armature.
   I. Broken wire in harness or connector.
   J. Faulty starter key or push button switch.
   K. Worn or frayed insulation.

5. Electric starter does not engage but solenoid clicks.
   A. Loose or corroded connections or ground.
   B. Weak battery.
   C. Faulty starter solenoid.
   D. Broken wire in electric harness.
   E. Loose or stripped post on starter motor.
   F. See steps in number 4.

6. Hard to start or won't start.
   A. Empty gas tank.
   B. Gas tank air vent not open.
   C. Fuel lines kinked or severely pinched.
   D. Water or dirt in fuel system.
   E. Clogged fuel filter or screens.
   F. Motor not being choked to start.
   G. Engine not primed – pump primer system.
   H. Carburetor adjustments too lean (not allowing enough fuel to start engine).
   I. Timing and sychronizing out of adjustment.
   J. Manual choke linkage bent – auto choke out of adjustment.
   K. Spark plugs improperly gapped, dirty or broken.
   L. Fuel tank primer inoperative (pressurized system).
   M. Ignition points improperly gapped, burned or dirty.

   N. Loose, broken wire or frayed insulation in electrical system.
   O. Reed valves not seating or stuck shut.
   P. Weak coil or condenser.
   Q. Faulty gaskets.
   R. Cracked distributor cap or rotor.
   S. Loose fuel connector.
   T. Electronic ignition component malfunction.

7. Low speed miss or motor won't idle smoothly and slowly enough.
   A. Too much oil – too little oil.
   B. Timing and sychronizing out of adjustment.
   C. Carburetor idle adjustment (mixture lean or rich).
   D. Ignition points improper (gap, worn or fouled).
   E. Weak coil or condenser.
   F. Loose or broken ignition wires.
   G. Loose or worn magneto plate.
   H. Spark plugs (improper gap or dirty).
   I. Head gasket, reed plate gasket (blown or leaking).
   J. Reed valve standing open or stuck shut.
   K. Plugged crankcase bleeder, check valves, or lines.
   L. Leaking crankcase halves.
   M. Leaking crankcase seals (top or bottom.)
   N. Exhaust gases returning through intake manifold.
   O. Electronic ignition component malfunction.

8. High speed miss or intermittent spark.
   A. Spark plugs improperly gapped or dirty.
   B. Loose, leaking or broken ignition wires.
   C. Breaker points (improper gap or dirty; worn cam or cam follower).
   D. Weak coil or condenser.
   E. Water in fuel.
   F. Leaking head gasket or exhaust cover gasket.
   G. Spark plug heat range incorrect.
   H. Engine improperly timed.
   I. Carbon or fouled combustion chambers.
   J. Magneto or distributor poorly grounded.
   K. Distributor oiler wick bad.
   L. Electronic ignition component malfunction.

9. Coughs, spits, slows.
   A. Idle or high speed needles set too lean.
   B. Carburetor not synchronized.

   C. Leaking gaskets in induction system.
   D. Obstructed fuel passages.
   E. Float level set too low.
   F. Improperly seated or broken reeds.
   G. Fuel pump pressure line ruptured.
   H. Fuel pump (punctured diaphragm), check valves stuck open or closed, fuel lines leak.
   I. Poor fuel tank pressure (pressurized system).
   J. Worn or leaking fuel connector.

10. Vibrates excessively or runs rough and smokes.
   A. Idle or high speed needles set too rich.
   B. Too much oil mixed with gas.
   C. Carburetor not synchronized with ignition properly.
   D. Choke not opening properly.
   E. Float level too high.
   F. Air passage to carburetor obstructed.
   G. Bleeder valves or passages plugged.
   H. Transom bracket clamps loose on transom.
   I. Prop out of balance.
   J. Broken motor mount.
   K. Exhaust gases getting inside motor cover.
   L. Poor ignition – see number 8.

11. Runs well, idles well for a short period, then slows down and stops.
   A. Weeds or other debris on lower unit or propeller.
   B. Insufficient cooling water.
   C. Carburetor, fuel pump, filter or screens dirty.
   D. Bleeder valves or passages plugged.
   E. Lower unit bind (lack of lubrication or bent.)
   F. Gas tank air vent not open.
   G. Not enough oil in gas.
   H. Combustion chambers and spark plugs fouled, causing preignition.
   I. Spark plug heat range too high or too low.
   J. Wrong propeller (preignition).
   K. Slow speed adjustment too rich or too lean.

12. Won't start, kicks back, backfires into lower unit.
   A. Spark plug wires reversed.
   B. Flywheel key sheared.
   C. Distributor belt timing off (magneto or battery ignition.)
   D. Timing and sychronizing out of adjustment.
   E. Reed valves not seating or broken.

13. No acceleration, low top Rpm.
    A. Improper carburetor adjustments.
    B. Improper timing and synchronization.
    C. Spark plugs (improper gap or dirty).
    D. Ignition system malfunction.
    E. Faulty coil or condenser.
    F. Loose, leaking or broken ignition wires.
    G. Reed valves not properly seated or broken.
    H. Blown head or exhaust cover gasket.
    I. Weeds on lower unit or propeller.
    J. Incorrect propeller.
    K. Insufficient oil in gas.
    L. Insufficient oil in lower unit.
    M. Fuel restrictions.
    N. Scored cylinder – stuck rings.
    O. Marine growth, hooks, rockers or change in load of boat.
    P. Sticky magneto plate.
    Q. Carbon build-up on piston head at deflector.

14. No acceleration, idles well but when put to full power dies down.
    A. High or low speed needle set too lean.
    B. Dirt or packing behind needles and seats.
    C. High speed nozzle obstructed.
    D. Float level too low.
    E. Choke partly closed.
    F. Improper timing and synchronization.
    G. Fuel lines or passages obstructed.
    H. Fuel filter obstructed. Fuel pump not supplying enough fuel.
    I. Not enough oil in gas.
    J. Breaker points improperly gapped or dirty.
    K. Bent gearcase or exhaust tube.

15. Engine runs at high speed only by using hand primer.
    A. Carburetor adjustments.
    B. Dirt or packing behind needles and seat.
    C. Fuel lines or passages obstructed.
    D. Fuel line leaks.
    E. Fuel pump not supplying enough fuel.
    F. Float level too low.
    G. Fuel filter obstructed.
    H. Fuel tank or connector at fault.

16. No power under heavy load.
    A. Wrong propeller.
    B. Weeds or other debris on lower unit or propeller.
    C. Breaker points improperly gapped or dirty.
    D. Stator plate loose.

    E. Ignition timing over advanced or late.
    F. Faulty carburetion and/or faulty ignition.
    G. Prop hub slips.
    H. Scored cylinders or rings stuck.
    I. Carbon build up on piston head at deflector.

17. Cranks over extremely easy on one or more cylinders.
    A. Low compression.
       1. Worn or broken rings.
       2. Scored cylinder or pistons.
       3. Blown head gasket.
       4. Loose spark plugs.
       5. Loose head bolts.
       6. Crankcase halves improperly sealed.
       7. Burned piston.

18. Engine won't crank over.
    A. Manual start lock improperly adjusted.
    B. Pistons rusted to cylinder wall.
    C. Lower unit gears, prop shaft rusted or broken.
    D. Broken connecting rod, crankshaft or driveshaft.
    E. Coil heels binding on flywheel.
    F. Engine improperly assembled.

19. Motor overheats.
    A. Motor not deep enough in water.
    B. Not enough oil in gas or improperly mixed.
    C. Bad thermostat.
    D. Seals or gaskets (burned, cracked or broken).
    E. Impeller key not in place or broken.
    F. Plugged water inlet, outlet or cavity.
    G. Obstruction in water passages.
    H. Broken, pinched or leaking water lines.
    I. Improper ignition timing.
    J. Motor not assembled properly.
    K. Shorted heat light wiring.
    L. Bad water pump impeller, plate, housing or seal.

20. Motor stops suddenly, freezes up.
    A. No oil in gas, or no gas.
    B. Insufficient cooling water.
    C. No lubricant in gearcase.
    D. Rusted cylinder or crankshaft.
    E. Bent or broken rod, crankshaft, drive shaft, prop shaft, stuck piston.
    F. Bad water pump or plugged water passages.

21. Motor knocks excessively.
    A. Too much or not enough oil in gas.
    B. Worn or loose bearings, pistons, rods or wrists pins.
    C. Over advanced ignition timing.
    D. Carbon in combustion chambers and exhaust ports.

    E. Manual starter not centered.
    F. Flywheel nut loose.
    G. Flywheel hitting coil heels.
    H. Bent shift rod (vibrating against exhaust tube).
    I. Loose assemblies, bolts or screws.

22. Generator will not charge.
    A. Battery condition.
    B. Connections loose or dirty.
    C. Drive belt loose or broken.
    D. Faulty regulator or cutout relay.
    E. Field fuse or fusible wire in regulator blown.
    F. Generator not polarized (dc generators).
    G. Open generator windings.
    H. Worn or sticking brushes and/or slip rings.
    I. Faulty rectifier diodes (ac generators).
    J. Faulty ammeter.

23. Low generator output and a low battery.
    A. High resistance at battery terminals.
    B. High resistance in charging circuit.
    C. Faulty ammeter.
    D. Low regulator setting.
    E. Faulty rectifier diodes (ac generators).
    F. Faulty generator.

24. Excessive battery charging.
    A. Regulator set too high.
    B. Regulator contacts stuck.
    C. Regulator voltage winding open.
    D. Regulator improperly grounded.
    E. High resistance in field coil.
    F. Regulator improperly mounted.

25. Excessive fuel consumption.
    A. Hole in fuel pump diaphragm.
    B. Deteriorated carburetor gaskets.
    C. Altered or wrong fixed jets.
    D. Jets improperly adjusted.
    E. Carburetor casting porous.
    F. Float level too high.
    G. Loose distributor pulley.

26. Shifter dog jumps.
    A. Worn shifter dog or worn gear dogs.
    B. Worn linkage.
    C. Remote control adjustment.
    D. Gearcase loose or sprung.
    E. Exhaust housing bent.
    F. Linkage out of adjustment.

27. Electric shift inoperative or slips.
    A. Improper remote control installation.
    B. Faulty coils.
    C. Faulty springs.
    D. Faulty clutch and gear.
    E. Faulty bearings.
    F. Wrong lubricant.
    G. Loose or sprung gearcase.
    H. Shorted wiring.

SPECIAL NOTES ON TROUBLE-SHOOTING

AIR-COOLED MOTORS. Overheating, low power and several other problems on air-cooled motors can sometimes be traced to improper cooling. Make certain that all shrouds are in place before starting motor. Check for dirt or debris accumulated on or between cooling fins. Broken cooling fins can sometimes cause a localized "hot spot."

SPARK PLUG APPEARANCE DIAGNOSIS. The appearance of a spark plug will be altered by use, and an examination of the plug tip can contribute useful information which may assist in obtaining better spark plug life. It must be remembered that the contributing factors differ in two-stroke and four-stroke engine operation and, although the appearance of two spark plugs may be similar, the corrective measures may depend on whether the engine is of two-stroke or four-stroke design. Fig. 2-1 through Fig. 2-6 are provided by Champion Spark Plug Company to illustrate typical observed conditions in two-stroke engines. Listed also are the probable causes and suggested corrective measures.

GENERAL MAINTENANCE

LUBRICATION

Refer to each motor's individual section for recommended type and amount of lubricant used for power head (engine) and gearcase.

FUEL: OIL RATIO. Most two-stroke cycle engines are lubricated by oil that is mixed with the fuel. It is important that the manufacturer's recommended type of oil and fuel:oil ratio be closely followed. Excessive oil or improper fuel type oil will cause low power, plug fouling and excessive carbon build-up. Insufficient amount of oil will result in inadequate lubrication and rapid internal damage. The recommended ratios and type of oil are listed in LUBRICATION paragraph for each motor. Oil should be mixed with gasoline in a separate container before it is poured into the fuel tank. Unleaded gasoline such as marine white should be used when possible. The following table may be useful in mixing the correct ratio.

RATIO	Gasoline	Oil
10:1	.63 Gallon	½ Pint
14:1	.88 Gallon	½ Pint
15:1	.94 Gallon	½ Pint
16:1	1.00 Gallon	½ Pint
20:1	1.25 Gallons	½ Pint
22:1	1.38 Gallons	½ Pint
24:1	1.50 Gallons	½ Pint
25:1	1.56 Gallons	½ Pint
50:1	3.13 Gallons	½ Pint
100:1	6.25 Gallons	½ Pint
10:1	5 U.S. Gallons	4 Pints 64 Fl. Oz.
14:1	5 U.S. Gallons	3 Pints 45¾ Fl. Oz.
15:1	5 U.S. Gallons	2¾ Pints 42½ Fl. Oz.
16:1	5 U.S. Gallons	2½ Pints 40 Fl. Oz.
20:1	5 U.S. Gallons	2 Pints 32 Fl. Oz.
22:1	5 U.S. Gallons	1¾ Pints 29 Fl. Oz.
24:1	3 U.S. Gallons	1 Pint 16 Fl. Oz.
25:1	4 U.S. Gallons	1¼ Pints 20½ Fl. Oz.
50:1	3 U.S. Gallons	½ Pint 7¾ Fl. Oz.
100:1	3 U.S. Gallons	¼ Pint 4 Fl. Oz.

SPARK PLUGS

The recommended type of spark plug, heat range and electrode gap is listed in the CONDENSER SERVICE DATA table for the individual motor. Under light loads or low speed (trolling), a spark plug of the same size with a higher (hotter) heat range may be installed. If subjected to heavy loads or high speed, a colder plug may be necessary.

The spark plug electrode gap should be adjusted on most plugs by bending the ground electrode. Refer to Fig. 2-7. Some spark plugs have an electrode gap which is not adjustable.

Before a plug is cleaned with abrasive, it should be thoroughly degreased with a nonoily solvent and air-dried to prevent a build up of abrasive in recess of plug.

After plug is cleaned by abrasive, and before gap is set, the electrode surfaces between the grounded and insulated electrodes should be cleaned and returned as nearly as possible to original shape by filing with a point file. Failure to properly dress the points can result in high secondary voltage requirements, and misfire of the plugs.

Spark plugs are usually cleaned by abrasive action commonly referred to as "sand blasting." Actually, ordinary sand is not used, but a special abrasive which is nonconductive to electricity even when melted, thus the abrasive cannot short out the plug current. Extreme care should be used in cleaning the plugs after sand blasting, because any particles of abrasive left on the plug may cause damage to piston rings, piston or cylinder walls.

Fig. 2-1—Two-stroke cycle engine plug of correct heat range. Insulators light tan to gray with few deposits. Electrodes not burned.

Fig. 2-2—Damp or wet black carbon coating over entire firing end of plug. Could be caused by prolonged trolling, rich carburetor mixture, too much oil in fuel, crankcase bleed passage plugged, or low ignition voltage. Could also be caused by incorrect heat range (too cold) for operating conditions. Correct the defects or install a hotter plug.

Fig. 2-3—Electrodes badly eroded, deposits white or light gray and gritty, insulator has "blistered" appearance. Could be caused by lean carburetor mixture, fast timing, overloading, or improperly operating cooling system. Could also be caused by incorrect heat range (too hot) for operating conditions. Check timing, carburetor adjustment and cooling system. If recommended operating speed cannot be obtained after tune-up, install flatter pitch propeller. If timing, carburetor adjustment, cooling system and engine speed are correct, install a colder plug.

CARBURETOR

The bulk of carburetor service consists of cleaning, inspection and adjustment. After considerable service it may become necessary to overhaul the carburetor and renew worn parts to restore original operating efficiency. Although carburetor condition affects engine operating economy and power, the ignition system and engine compression must also be considered to determine and correct causes. Also, make certain that the fuel:oil ratio is correct and that fuel is fresh (not last year's).

CLEANING AND INSPECTION. Before dismantling carburetor for cleaning and inspection, clean all external surfaces and remove accumulated dirt and grease. If fuel starvation is suspected, all filters in carburetor, fuel pump and/or tank should be inspected. Because of inadequate fuel handling methods, rust and other foreign matter may sometimes block or partially block these filters. Under no circumstances

should these filters be removed from the fuel system. If filters are removed, the blockage will most likely occur within the carburetor and cleaning will be frequent and more difficult.

Refer to appropriate motor repair section for carburetor exploded or cross sectional views. Disassemble the carburetor and note any discrepancies which may cause a malfunction.

Wear of the fuel inlet needle, needle seat, or the float linkage can cause a change in carburetor fuel level and possible flooding. Fuel inlet needle and seat are usually furnished as a matched set, and should be renewed if a groove is noticeable in the valve; or if neoprene seat is damaged on models so equipped. On models with brass seat and tapered steel valve needle, install seat, drop needle into position; then tap outer end of needle with a small hammer to even the seat.

Carburetor flooding can sometimes be caused by a loose fuel valve seat, loose nozzle, cracked carburetor body or binding float. Consider all of these possibilities when service is indicated.

When reassembling, be sure float level (or fuel level) is properly adjusted as listed in the CARBURETOR paragraph of the appropriate motor repair section.

Except for improper fuel, the most common cause of carburetor malfunction is the formation of gum and varnish which plugs or partially plugs the small drillings or calibrated orifices within the

Fig. 2-4—Gray, metallic aluminum deposits on plug. This condition is caused by internal engine damage. Engine should be overhauled and cause of damage corrected.

Fig. 2-6—Gap bridging. Usually results from the same causes outlined in Fig. 2-5.

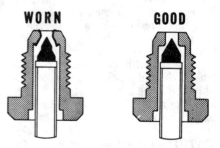

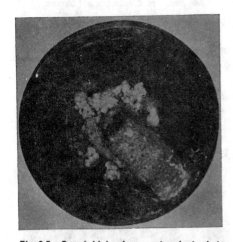

Fig. 2-5—Core bridging from center electrode to shell. Fused deposits sometimes have the appearance of tiny beads or glasslike bubbles. Caused by excessive combustion chamber deposits which in turn could be the result of; excessive carbon from prolonged usage; use of improper oil or incorrect fuel:oil ratio; high speed operation immediately following prolonged trolling.

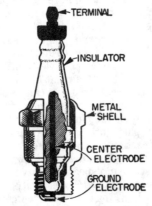

Fig. 2-7—Cross-sectional view of spark plug showing construction and nomenclature.

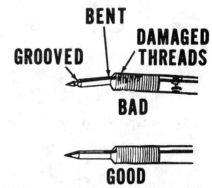

Fig. 2-9—Mixture adjustment needles should be renewed if damaged as shown at top. Never attempt to straighten a bent needle.

carburetor which control fuel flow. This build-up can be of two types, the most common being the gradual accumulation of hard varnish, sometimes mixed with dirt, which slowly builds up on all fuel system surfaces after long use. Over a period of time these deposits change the balance (calibration) of the carburetor or assist in completely blocking some small passsages making carburetor removal necessary. To do a thorough job of cleaning, the carburetor must be completely disassembled, the parts cleaned as recommended by the manufacturer, then the passages blown out with compressed air. It is impractical in most instances to attempt to clean the small passages with needles or wires, although this method is recommended by some. Exercise extreme caution to prevent enlarging passages and be sure that no hidden cross passages are plugged.

A second type of gum is formed by the decomposition of gasoline which is allowed to stand for long periods of time without being used. This form of gum can completely plug the carburetor passages, often causing the fuel inlet valve to stick. Preservative additives have been developed for gasoline which lessens the danger from this type of damage, but the fuel system including the carburetor should be drained when not is use to prevent such damage. This gum can only be loosened by prolonged soaking in a carbon dissolving solvent. Sometimes gum or varnish builds up around the throttle shaft causing the throttle to stick.

Wear damage is slight on the outboard motor carburetor. The throttle valve is not subject to frequent movement or dust abrasion, so wear of throttle valve, shaft and seals is usually negligible. If the throttle shaft does not move freely, check for gum or varnish buildup around shaft. The orifice of metering jets is subject to wear from prolonged use, but such wear cannot be detected by ordinary means. Because the jets are relatively inexpensive, it is common practice to renew them whenever carburetor is disassembled rather than to take a chance on the amount of wear.

Allied to wear damage, but usually from a different cause, is the groove around the tapered point of the mixture adjustment needle valves on carburetors so equipped. Refer to Fig. 2-9. This groove is usuallly caused by carelessness or ignorance, and is the result of bottoming the needle too tightly in the adjustment orifice. A groove on needle prevents the fine gradation of adjustment usually required of a metering needle, making it impossible to make and hold the correct mixture adjustment. When a damaged needle is found, it

should be discarded and a new part installed. It should be noted, however, the seat for the needle valve may also be damaged and accurate adjustment may not be possible even with a new needle. When adjusting the valve, always screw the needle down only lightly with the fingers until it bottoms, then back the needle out the number of turns suggested in the individual motor service sections.

ADJUSTMENT. Before attempting to adjust the carburetor, make certain that fuel used is fresh and contains the proper amount and recommended type of oil. Also, make certain that engine compression or ignition system is not the real problem. Check fuel system for air or fuel leaks and clean all of the fuel system filters. When adjusting the carburetor, make certain that exhaust fumes are properly vented and not allowed to be drawn into engine. Also, use the correct test wheel (or propeller) and do not allow motor to overheat.

Carburetor should be adjusted at the altitude that motor is to be operated. At high elevations, because the air is less dense, the main fuel adjustment on some carburetors should be set leaner than at sea level. Some carburetors have a high speed (main) adjustment needle and have a fixed main jet. On models with adjustment needle, the initial setting is listed in the individual motor section. On carburetors with fixed jets available in various sizes, the standard size is listed. At higher altitudes it may be necessary to install a main jet with smaller metering hole (orifice). In some cases, a propeller with less pitch should be installed to permit the recommended high rpm.

To adjust, first obtain the initial setting recommended in the individual motor section.

NOTE: Be careful when turning needles in and do not force, or damage to needle and/or seat may result.

Generally the initial setting for adjusting needles is too rich but should

allow motor to start. Run the motor until it reaches normal operating temperature, then adjust needles until fuel mixture is correct throughout entire range of rpm. It is preferable to set mixtures slightly rich. If mixture is too lean, motor may overheat and result in serious damage. If a "flat spot" or "4-cycling" condition cannot be corrected by adjusting carburetor, check synchronization between ignition timing advance and carburetor throttle opening as outlined in SPEED CONTROL LINKAGE section for individual motors.

SPEED CONTROL LINKAGE

The speed control on most outboard motors advances the ignition timing and opens the carburetor throttle valve as the handle is moved to the fast position. To provide correct operation, the throttle valve must be opened exactly the right amount as the ignition timing is changed. Refer to the motor repair section for models which have adjustments to synchronize "throttle" opening with the ignition timing.

A "flat spot" or "4-cycling" condition that cannot be corrected by adjusting carburetor (fuel mixture) is usually caused by incorrect throttle to ignition synchronization and/or ignition system malfunction.

REED VALVES

On two-stroke cycle motors, the incoming fuel-air mixture must be compressed in order for the mixture to properly reach the engine cylinder. On engines utilizing reed type carburetor to crankcase intake valve, a bent or broken reed may not allow compression build up in the crankcase. This condition is usually most noticeable at low speed. Thus, if such an engine seems otherwise OK, remove and inspect the reed valve unit. Refer to appropriate repair section in this manual for information on individual models.

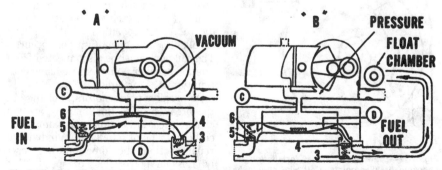

Fig. 2-10—Schematic view of a typical, crankcase operated, diaphragm type fuel pump. Pressure and vacuum pulsations from crankcase pass through connection (C) to rear of diaphragm (D) which induces a pumping action on fuel line as shown.

FUEL PUMP

Diaphragm type fuel pumps can be operated mechanically, electrically or by the vacuum and pressure pulsations in the two-stroke cycle engine crankcase. Refer to Fig. 2-10. Vacuum in the crankcase draws the diaphragm (D) in, pulling fuel past the inlet check valve (5) as shown in view "A". As the piston moves down in the cylinder, pressure is created in the crankcase. The pressure is directed to the back of diaphragm via passage (C) and diaphragm is forced out and trapped fuel is directed to the carburetor past the outlet check valve (4) as shown in view "B".

Passage (C) must be properly sealed. On some motors, the fuel pump is attached directly to the crankcase and passage (C) is sealed with a gasket. Other motors use a hose between the crankcase and fuel pump. Fuel lines (hoses) must not leak air or fuel and fuel filters should be clean. The check valves (4 & 5) should be correctly installed and not leak.

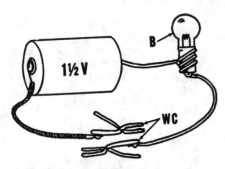

Fig. 2-11—A light can be easily constructed as shown for checking continuity. Bulb (B) should light when wire clamps (WC) are touching.

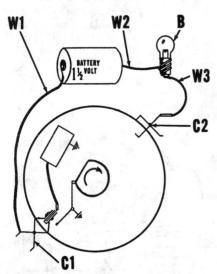

Fig. 2-12—Drawing of typical installation for checking breaker points. Coil wire should be disconnected from terminal before clamp (C1) is connected.

IGNITION SYSTEM

For a quick test of the ignition system, remove the spark plug and hold the spark plug wire with an insulated tool about 1/8-1/4 inch (3.17-6.35 mm) away from cylinder head. Have someone spin the motor and note the condition of spark. Although spark may not be visible in bright daylight, a distinct snap will be noted as the spark jumps gap. On breaker point models, if spark is weak or erratic, adjust breaker point gap and be sure to note point condition. If spark is weak although points are in good condition and properly adjusted, examine the condition of point, condenser and coil wiring, and the insulation on the magneto coils. On all models, look for broken or worn insulation or broken wires. Also check for loose or corroded connections. On models with electronic ignition control, if no external damage is noted, then refer to appropriate model section for electronic ignition control component testing. On motors equipped with a stop switch, check condition of switch and associated wiring. Renew any parts which are damaged or in poor condition.

IGNITION TIMING. On most motors, the ignition timing is advanced as the speed control handle is moved to the fast position. Refer to the SPEED CONTROL LINKAGE section for synchronizing throttle opening to the ignition timing.

Some motors have fixed ignition timing and engine speed is changed only by changing the carburetor throttle valve opening. Fixed ignition timing is usually adjustable but does not change with engine running. Refer to the appropriate motor section for method of adjusting the fixed ignition timing.

On two cylinder motors, ignition timing should be synchronized to fire the cylinders evenly. Refer to the individual motor section for method of checking and adjusting. A timing light constructed as shown in Fig. 2-11 or a continuity (ohm) meter can be used to indicate exact position that ignition breaker points open (ignition occurs). The coil wire must be disconnected from ignition breaker points before using continuity meter (or light).

On breaker point motors, a change in the breaker point (maximum) gap will change the ignition timing. Recommended breaker point gap listed in individual repair sections should be followed closely. Loss of power, loss of speed, "flat spot" and/or overheating may be caused by incorrect breaker point gap.

BREAKER POINTS. Breaker points are usually located under the flywheel. Holes are sometimes provided in the flywheel for checking and adjusting however, flywheel usually must be removed for renewal of ignition points.

Using a small screwdriver, separate and inspect condition of contacts. If burned or deeply pitted, points should be renewed. If contacts are clean to grayish in color, disconnect coil lead wire from breaker point terminal. Connect one lead (C1–Fig. 2-12) to the insulated breaker point terminal and the other (C2) to engine (ground). Light should burn with points closed and go out with points open. If light does not burn, little or no contact is indicated and points should be cleaned or renewed and contact maximum gap should be reset.

NOTE: IN some cases, new breaker point contact surfaces may be coated with oil or wax.

If light does not go out when points are opened, timing light is not connected properly or breaker point insulation is defective.

Adjust breaker point gap as follows unless manufacturer specifies adjusting breaker gap to obtain correct ignition timing. First, turn engine so that points are closed to be sure that the contact surfaces are in alignment and seat squarely. Then turn engine so that breaker point opening is maximum and adjust breaker gap to manufacturer's specification. Be sure to recheck gap after tightening breaker point base retaining screws.

CONDENSER. To check condition of the condenser without special test equipment, proceed as follows: The condenser case and wire should be visually checked for any obvious damage. Remove condenser, then connect one end of test lamp (Fig. 2-11) to terminal at end of condenser wire and other end to condenser case. If light goes on, condenser is shorted and should be renewed. It is usually a good practice to renew condenser when new breaker points are installed. If breaker points become pitted rapidly, condenser is usually faulty.

IGNITION COIL. If a coil tester is available, condition of coil can be checked. Sometimes, an ignition coil may perform satisfactorily when cold but fail after engine has run for some time and coil is hot. Check coil when hot if this condition is indicated.

MAGNETO AIR GAP. To fully concentrate the magnetic field of the flywheel, magnets pass as closely to the armature core as possible without danger of metal-to-metal contact. The clearance between the flywheel magnets and the legs of the armature core is called the armature air gap.

On magnetos where the armature and high tension coil are located outside of the flywheel rim, adjustment of the armature air gap is made as follows: Turn the engine so the flywheel magnets are located directly under the legs of the armature core and check the clearance between the armature core and flywheel magnets. If the measured clearance is not within manufacturer's specifications, loosen the armature mounting screws and place shims at thickness equal to minumum air gap specification between the magnets and armature core. The magnets will pull the armature core against the shim stock. Tighten the armature core mounting screws, remove the shim stock and turn the engine through several revolutions to be sure the flywheel does not contact the armature core.

Where the armature core is located under or behind the flywheel, the following methods may be used to check and adjust armature air gap: On some engines, slots or openings are provided in the flywheel through which the armature air gap can be checked. Some engine manufacturers provide a cutaway flywheel or a positioning ring that can be used to correctly set the armature air gap.

Another method of checking the armature air gap is to remove the flywheel and place a layer of plastic tape equal to the minimum specified air gap over the legs of the armature core. Reinstall flywheel and turn engine through several revolutions and remove flywheel; no evidence of contact between the flywheel magnets and plastic tape should be noticed. Then cover the legs of the armature core with a layer of tape of thickness equal to the maximum specified air gap, then reinstall flywheel and turn engine through several revolutions. Indication of the flywheel magnets contacting the plastic tape should be noticed after the flywheel is again removed. If the magnets contact the first thin layer of tape applied to the armature core legs, or if they do not contact the second thicker layer of tape, armature air gap is not within specifications and should be adjusted.

NOTE: Before loosening armature core mounting screws, inscribe a mark on mounting plate against edge of armature core so adjustment of air gap can be gauged.

MAGNETO EDGE GAP. The point of maximum acceleration of the movement of the flywheel magnetic field through the high tension coil (and therefore, the point of maximum current induced in the primary coil windings) occurs when the trailing edge of the flywheel magnet is slightly past the left hand leg of the armature core. The exact point of maximum primary current is determined by using electrical measuring devices, the distance between the trailing edge of flywheel magnet and the leg of the armature core at this point is measured and becomes a service specification. This distance, which is stated either in thousandths of an inch or in degrees of flywheel rotation, is called the Edge Gap or "E" Gap.

For maximum strength of the ignition spark, the breaker points should just start to open when the flywheel magnets are at the specified edge gap position. Usually, edge gap is nonadjustable and will be maintained at the proper dimension if the contact breaker points are adjusted to the recommended gap and the correct breaker cam is installed. However, magneto edge gap can change (and spark intensity thereby reduced) due to the following:

a. Flywheel drive key sheared.
b. Flywheel drive key worn (loose).
c. Keyway in flywheel or crankshaft worn (oversized).
d. Loose flywheel retaining nut which can also cause any above listed difficulty.
e. Excessive wear on breaker cam.
f. Breaker cam loose or improperly installed on crankshaft.
g. Excessive wear on breaker point rubbing block so points cannot be properly adjusted.

COOLING SYSTEM

When cooling system problems are suspected, first check the water inlet for partial or complete stoppage. If water inlet is clear, refer to the appropriate section and check condition of pump, water passages, gaskets, sealing surfaces and thermostat (if so equipped).

The following conditions can cause motor to overheat with cooling system operating properly.

1. Incorrect type of oil or incorrect fuel-oil ratio.
2. Fuel mixture too lean.
3. Clogged exhaust or exhaust leaking into cooling system.
4. Incorrect ignition timing.
5. Throttle not correctly synchronized to ignition advance.

6. Motor overloaded.
7. Incorrect propeller.
8. Missing or bent shields, fins or blower housing. (On air cooled models, never attempt to run engine without all shields in place).

Various types of temperature indicating devices (including heat sensitive sticks or crayons) are available for checking the operating temperature.

WATER PUMP. Most motors use a rubber impeller type water pump. Refer to Fig. 2-13. At slow engine speed, the impeller blades follow the contour of the offset housing as shown by the solid lines. With this type pump, the impeller blades may be damaged (or completely broken off) if turned in opposite direction of normal rotation. If impeller is damaged, all water passages should be cleaned. Some water passages may be blocked and result in overheating of the blocked area.

GENERATING SYSTEMS

Refer to the individual motor section for explanation of generating system used. Some motors use a combined starter-generator unit, others use combined flywheel alternator – flywheel magneto and others use a belt driven, automotive type generator.

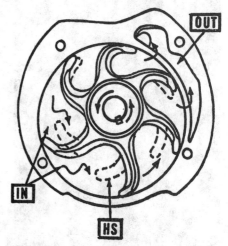

Fig. 2-13—Drawing of impeller type pump. Water is drawn into pump (IN) as area between vanes increases and is forced into power head (OUT) as area decreases. At high speeds the blades remain curved as shown by the broken lines (HS) and pump operates mostly by centrifugal action. Blades may be broken or damaged if turned in reverse of normal direction of rotation.

GENERAL REPAIRS

Because of the close tolerance of the interior parts, cleanliness is of utmost importance. It is suggested that the exterior of the motor and all nearby areas be absolutely clean before any repair is started. Manufacturer's recommended torque values for tightening screw fasteners should be followed closely. The soft threads in aluminum castings are often damaged by carelessness in overtightening fasteners or in attempting to loosen or remove seized fasteners.

Commonly recommended tightening torques, for common screw sizes, are listed below. These recommendations should be followed if specific recommendations are not given in the individual service sections.

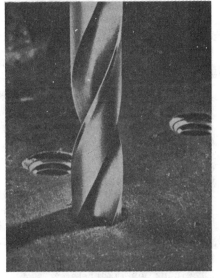

Fig. 2-14—First step in repairing damaged threads is to drill out old threads using exact size drill recommended in instructions provided with thread repair kit. Drill all the way through an open hole or all the way to bottom of blind hole, making sure hole is straight and that centerline of hole is not moved in drilling process. (Series of photos provided by Heli-Coil Corp., Danbury, Conn.)

SCREW SIZE	TORQUE
#4	4-6 in.-lbs.
	(0.5-0.7 N·m)
#6	8-11 in.-lbs.
	(0.9-1.2 N·m)
#8	15-20 in.-lbs.
	(1.7-2.3 N·m)
#10	25-35 in.-lbs.
	(2.8-3.9 N·m)
#12	35-40 in.-lbs.
	(3.9-4.5 N·m)
¼ inch	60-80 in.-lbs.
	(6.8-9 N·m)
5/16 inch	120-140 in.-lbs.
	(13.5-15.8 N·m)
3/8 inch	220-240 in.-lbs.
	(24.8-27.1 N·m)
7/16, ½ inch	340-360 in.-lbs.
	(38.4-40.7 N·m)

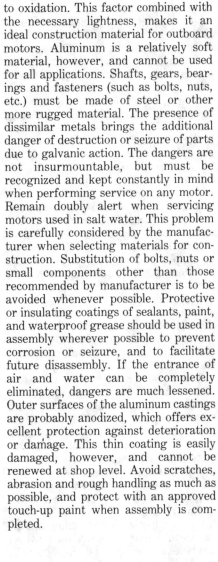

Aluminum offers unusual resistance to oxidation. This factor combined with the necessary lightness, makes it an ideal construction material for outboard motors. Aluminum is a relatively soft material, however, and cannot be used for all applications. Shafts, gears, bearings and fasteners (such as bolts, nuts, etc.) must be made of steel or other more rugged material. The presence of dissimilar metals brings the additional danger of destruction or seizure of parts due to galvanic action. The dangers are not insurmountable, but must be recognized and kept constantly in mind when performing service on any motor. Remain doubly alert when servicing motors used in salt water. This problem is carefully considered by the manufacturer when selecting materials for construction. Substitution of bolts, nuts or small components other than those recommended by manufacturer is to be avoided whenever possible. Protective or insulating coatings of sealants, paint, and waterproof grease should be used in assembly wherever possible to prevent corrosion or seizure, and to facilitate future disassembly. If the entrance of air and water can be completely eliminated, dangers are much lessened. Outer surfaces of the aluminum castings are probably anodized, which offers excellent protection against deterioration or damage. This thin coating is easily damaged, however, and cannot be renewed at shop level. Avoid scratches, abrasion and rough handling as much as possible, and protect with an approved touch-up paint when assembly is completed.

REPAIRING DAMAGED THREADS

Damaged threads in castings can be repaired by use of thread repair kits which are recommended by a number of manufacturers. Use of thread repair kits is not difficult, but instructions must be carefully followed. Refer to Figs. 2-14 through 2-16 which illustrate the use of thread repair kits manufactured by the Heli-Coil Corporation, Danbury, Connecticut.

Heli-Coil thread repair kits are available through the parts departments of most engine and equipment manufacturers. The thread inserts are available in all National Coarse (USS) sizes from number 4 to 1½ inch. National Fine (SAE) sizes from number 6 to 1½ inch and metric sizes 5 MM X 0.9 MM, 6 MM X 1.0 MM, 8 MM X 1.25 MM, 10 MM X 1.50 MM and 12 MM X 1.25 MM. Also, sizes for repairing 14MM and 18MM spark plug ports are available.

Fig. 2-15—Special drill taps are provided which are the correct size for OUTSIDE of the insert. A standard size tap cannot be substituted.

Fig. 2-16—Shown is the insert and a completed repair. Special tools are provided in kit for installation, together with the necessary instructions.

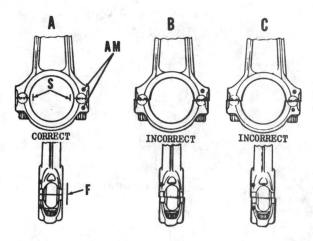

Fig. 2-17—Most connecting rods are provided with marks (AM) which should be aligned as shown in view "A". Bearing surface (S) and sides (F) should be smooth and all machine marks on rod and cap should be perfectly aligned. If cap is reversed as shown in view "B", bearing surface will not be smooth and marks will not be aligned. If incorrect rod cap is installed, machined surfaces will not be smooth even if marks on rod and cap are aligned as shown in view "C".

DISASSEMBLY AND ASSEMBLY

Outboard motors, especially the smaller types, are relatively simple in construction. The larger, more powerful units remain simple in design for the most part, but sometimes offer additional problems in disassembly and assembly.

Two or more identical pistons, rings, connectings rods and bearings may be used in a motor, but parts should never be interchanged when reassembling. As parts are removed, they should all be marked to identify the correct position. All wearing parts seat to the mating parts during operation. If parts are mixed during reassembly, a new wear pattern is established and early failure may result. Connecting rods are made with the cap and only this one cap will fit the rod perfectly. Refer to Fig. 2-17. If the original cap is incorrectly installed (as shown in view "B" – Fig. 2-17) or if another rod cap is installed (View "C" – Fig. 2-17), the bearing surface will not be smooth and true. Most connecting rods have raised marks (AM) on rod and cap to facilitate reassembly. Some manufacturers machine the rod as one piece and fracture (break) the cap away. The broken joint will fit together perfectly only when correctly installed.

A given amount of heat applied to aluminum will cause it to expand a greater amount than will steel under similar conditions. Because of the different expansion characteristics, heat is usually recommended for easy installation of bearings, pins, etc., in aluminum or magnesium castings. Sometimes, heat can be used to free parts that are seized or where an interference fit is used. Heat, therefore, becomes a service tool and the application of heat, one of the required service techniques. An open flame is not usually advised because it destroys the paint and other protective coatings and because a uniform and controlled temperature with open flame is difficult to obtain. Methods commonly

used for heating are: 1. In oil or water, 2. With a heat lamp, 3. Electric hot plate, 4. In an oven or kiln. See Fig. 2-18. The use of hot water or oil gives a fairly accurate temperature control but is somewhat limited as to the size and type of part that can be handled. Thermal crayons are available which can be used to determine the temperature of a heated part. These crayons melt when the part reaches specified temperature, and a number of crayons for different temperatures are available Temperature indicating crayons are usually available at welding equipment supply houses.

The crankcase and inlet manifold must be completely sealed against both vacuum and pressure. Exhaust manifold and cylinder head must be sealed against water leakage and pressure. Mating surfaces of water inlet, and exhaust areas between power head and lower unit must form a tight seal.

When disassembled, it is recommended that all gasket surfaces, and mating surfaces without gaskets, be carefully checked for nicks, burrs and warped surfaces which might interfere with a tight seal. The cylinder head, cylinder head cover, head end of

cylinder block, and some mating surfaces of manifolds and crankcase may be checked, and lapped if necessary, to provide a smooth surface. Flat surfaces can be lapped by using a surface plate or a smooth piece of plate glass, and a sheet of fine sandpaper or lapping compound. Use a figure-eight motion with minimum pressure, and remove only enough metal to eliminate the imperfection. Finish lap using lapping compound or worn emery cloth. Thoroughly clean the parts with new oil on a clean, soft rag, then wash with soapsuds and clean rags.

Mating surfaces of crankcase halves may be checked on the lapping block, and high spots or nicks removed, but surface must not be lowered. Bearing clearances must not be lessened by removing metal from the joint. If extreme care is used, a slightly damaged crankcase may be salvaged in this manner.

Gaskets and sealing surfaces should be lighly and carefully coated with an approved gasket cement or sealing compound unless the contrary is stated.

Make sure entire surface is coated, but avoid letting excesss cement squeeze out into crankcase, bearings or other passages.

PISTON, RINGS, PIN AND CYLINDER

When servicing pistons, rings and cylinders, it is important that all recommended tolerances be closely observed. Parts that are damaged should be carefully examined to determine the cause. A scored piston as shown in Fig. 2-19 is obviously not a result of normal wear and if the cause is not corrected, new parts may be similarly damaged in a short time. Piston scoring can be caused by overheating, improper fuel:oil mixture, carburetor out of adjustment, in-

Fig. 2-18—Heat can be used efficiently as a disassembly and assembly tool. Heating crankcase halves on electric hot plate (above) will allow bearings to be easily removed.

Fig. 2-19—If parts are excessively damaged, cause should be determined and corrected before returning motor to service.

Fig. 2-20—Gap between ends of ring should be within recommended limits.

Fig. 2-22—Ring side clearance in groove should be measured with gage as shown. Clearance should be within recommended limits and the same all the way around piston.

Fig. 2-23—A cross-hatch pattern as shown should be obtained by moving hone up and down cylinder bore as it is being turned by slow speed electric drill.

correct ignition timing and/or speed control linkage not correctly adjusted.

Before installing new piston rings, check ring end gap as follows: Position the ring near the top of cylinder bore. The bottom of piston (skirt) should be used to slide the ring in cylinder to locate ring squarely in bore. Measure the gap between end of ring using a feeler gage as shown in Fig. 2-20. Slide the ring down in the cylinder to the area of transfer and exhaust ports and again measure gap. Rings may break if end gap is too tight at any point; but, will not seal properly if gap is too wide. Variation in gap indicates cylinder wear (usually near the ports).

Ring grooves in the piston should be carefully cleaned and examined. Use caution when cleaning to prevent damage to piston. Carelessness can result in poor motor performance and possibly extensive internal engine damage. Refer to Fig. 2-21. When installing rings on piston, expand only far enough to slip over the piston and **do not twist rings.** After installing rings on piston, use feeler gage to measure ring side clearance in groove as shown in Fig. 2-22. Excessive side clearance will prevent an effective seal and may cause rings to break.

Cylinder bore should be honed to remove glaze from cylinder walls before installing new piston rings. Ridge at top and bottom of ring travel should be removed by honing. If ridge is not removed, new rings may catch enough to bend the ring lands as shown at (G–Fig. 2-21). The finished cylinder should have light cross-hatched pattern as shown in Fig. 2-23. After honing, wash cylinder assembly with soap and water to remove all traces of abrasive. After cylinder is dry, swab cylinder bore with oil making sure that it is absolutely clean.

Some manufacturers have oversize piston and ring sets available for use in repairing engines in which the cylinder bore is excessively worn and standard size piston and rings cannnot be used. If care and approved procedures are used in oversizing the cylinder bore, installation of an oversize piston and ring set should result in a highly satisfactory overhaul.

The cylinder bore may be oversized by using either a boring bar or a hone; however, if a boring bar is used it is usually recommended the cylinder bore be finished with a hone. Refer to Fig. 2-23. Before attempting to rebore or

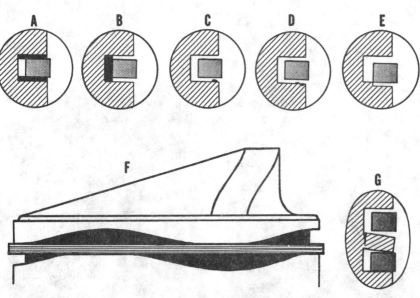

Fig. 2-21—Piston ring grooves must be clean and not damaged to provide a good seal.

A. Carbon on sides of groove may cause ring to stick in groove.
B. Carbon on bottom (back) of groove may prevent rings from compressing.
C. Small pieces of carbon
& (C) or nicks (D) in
D. groove will prevent a good seal.
E. If groove is worn as shown, renew the piston.
F. If groove is not straight, renew piston.
G. Renew piston if ring land is bent.

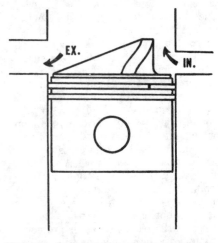

Fig. 2-24—Deflector type piston must be installed with long sloping side toward exhaust port and inlet deflector on transfer port side.

hone the cylinder to oversize, carefully measure the cylinder bore to be sure that new, standard size piston and rings will not fit within tolerance. Also, it may be possible that the cylinder is excessively worn or damaged and that reboring or honing to largest oversize will not clean up the worn or scored surface.

When assembling piston to connecting rod, observe special precautions outlined in the individual motor sections. Deflector type pistons must be installed with long sloping side toward exhaust port and the inlet deflector toward the transfer ports as shown in Fig. 2-24. If connecting rod has an oil hole at piston pin or crankpin end, hole should be toward top of motor. If piston pin has one closed end, it is normally installed toward exhaust port side of piston.

CONNECTING ROD, CRANKSHAFT AND BEARINGS

Before detaching connecting rods from crankshaft, mark rods and caps for correct assembly to each other and to proper cylinder. Most damage to ball and roller bearings is evident after visual inspection and turning the assembled bearing by hand. If bearing shows evidence of overheating, renew the complete assembly. On models with plain (bushing) bearings, check the crankpin and main bearing journals for wear with a micrometer. Crankshaft journals will usually wear out-of-round with most wear on side that takes the force of power stroke (strokes). If main bearing clearances are excessive, new crankcase seals may not be able to prevent pressure from blowing fuel and oil around crankshaft. All crankcase seals should be renewed when crankshaft, connecting rods and bearings are serviced.

SUBMERGED MOTOR

Almost all motors except small fishing motors are equipped for bolting to the transom. If motor is securely fastened by bolting, water damage cannot occur unless boat is swamped, overturned, or sunk. A safety chain will assist in the recovery of a small motor which vibrates loose and falls overboard. The same arrangement on a large motor could be dangerous, as the transom could be knocked out of boat by a wild motor.

There is a danger from two types of damage when a motor has been submerged. If motor was running when dropped, mechanical damage can result from the inability of water to compress. If mechanical damage is avoided, corrosive action can start almost immediately, especially in salt water.

Problems may develop if motor is dropped overboard.

Corrosion damage is most apt to occur after the motor has been removed from the water as corrosive action is greatest in the presence of heat and oxygen. In case of mechanical damage or for salt water submersion even where no actual damage exists, complete disassembly of the power head is indicated. In addition to the necesssary hand tools, fresh water under pressure, and alcohol and oil should be available. Proper care of a submerged motor, therefore, usually indicates that the motor be brought in to a suitable shop for service. If considerable time must elapse before service can be performed, it is best to keep motor submerged in fresh water, adding ice, if available, to keep the water cool. If fresh water is not available, motor is better off submerged in salt water than brought out to air dry.

If an attempt is to be made to run the motor without disassembly, remove the cowling and rinse off any silt or sand. Remove the spark plugs, carburetor and reed valve, if possible; then turn motor over slowly with starter to pump any water out of power head. Blow water from the magneto, spark plugs and wiring. Pour or spray alcohol into the crankcase and cylinders, trying to cover

as many of the metal surfaces as possible. the alcohol will combine with the water remaining in the engine, allowing it to be removed by flushing out, and later by evaporation. Disassemble and clean the carburetor, fuel pump, fuel lines and tank and refill with a fresh fuel:oil mixture. If a spray gun is available, spray a new coating of oil in the crankcases and spark plug holes. After motor is reassembled, it should start if magneto coils are not shorted out by moisture. Do not dry magneto parts in an oven. Excess heat will damage insulation. Check for silt in cooling system inlet before attempting to start the motor. If motor is started, it should be run for at least thirty minutes after it is warm, to give the remaining drops of water an opportunity to evaporate and disappear. The most likely points of corrosion damage are the main bearings and crankshaft journals, especially the lower one, as water drains into these parts and cannot be drained out or thrown out by centrifugal force. Even one drop of water can cause etching of the crankshaft or needle roller which will cause noise and early failure if bearings are of this type.

If silt or sand is present, in cases of salt water submersion, or where mechanical damage exists, the motor should be disassembled and cleaned. The corrosion factors of salt water or the presence of silt will cause early failure and are almost impossible to remove by flushing.

If the motor is to be disassembled, speed is essential, and the motor should be protected as much as possible from corrosion until disassembly is begun. Submersion in some type of liquid will inhibit corrosion temporarily. If several hours must elapse before disassembly can be started, keeping the parts submerged may limit the damage. In the case of large motors where complete submersion would be difficult, remove power head from lower unit and submerge the power head only. Remove the electrical units if tools are available. Alcohol offers the best protection if available. There is no special advantage of oil over fresh water if disassembly is to take place within 24 hours, and it most certainly should.

When motor is disassembled, scrub the parts thoroughly in hot, soapy water and air dry, then immerse in oil or spray with an oil mist until parts are completely coated. Ball or roller bearings which cannot be disassembled for cleaning should be renewed if their condition is at all questionable. It is very difficult to be sure that all traces of silt are removed from such bearings, and renewal at this time is usually cheaper than risking early failure.

CHRYSLER

US MARINE CORP.
105 Marine Drive
Hartford, Wisconsin 53027

3.5 AND 3.6 MODELS
(PRIOR TO 1978)

3.5 HP MODELS

Year Produced	Model
1969	3039, 3049, 3139

3.6 HP MODELS

Year Produced	Model
1970	32HA, 32BA, 33HA, 33BA
1971 & 1972	32HB, 32BB, 33HB, 33BB
1973, 1974, 1976 & 1977	32HC, 32BC, 33HC, 33BC

CONDENSED SERVICE DATA

TUNE-UP	3.5 HP	3.6 HP
Hp/rpm	3.5/4500	3.6/4500
Bore – Inches	2-1/16	2-1/16
Stroke – Inches	1-9/16	1-9/16
Number of Cylinders	1	1
Displacement – Cu. In.	5.18	5.18
Compression at Cranking Speed (Average)	65-75 psi	65-75 psi
Spark Plug – Champion	H8J	H8J
Electrode gap	0.030 in.	0.030 in.
Magneto – Point gap	0.020 in.	0.020 in.
Carburetor:		
Make	Tillotson	Tillotson
Model	MD124A	CO-1A
Adjustment	See text	See text
Fuel:Oil Ratio	16:1	25:1*

SIZES – CLEARANCES	3.5 HP	3.6 HP
Piston Rings:		
End gap	**	**
Side clearance	**	**
Piston to Cylinder Clearance	**	**
Piston Pin:		
Diameter	**	**
Clearance (Rod)	**	**
Clearance (Piston)	**	**
Crankshaft Bearing Type:		
Main Bearing	Bushing	Bushing
Crankpin	Bushing	Bushing
Crankshaft Bearing Clearance:		
Main Bearing	**	**
Crankpin	**	**
Crankshaft end play	**	**
Rod side clearance	**	**
Lower Unit:		
Bushing diametral clearance		
Pinion shaft	**	**
Propeller shaft	**	**

*Fuel to oil ratio should be increased to 16:1 for the first three hours of running (break-in and for severe service.
**Publication Not Authorized by Manufacturer.

TIGHTENING TORQUES (All Values in Inch-Pounds)	3.5 HP	3.6 HP
Connecting Rod	75-80	75-80
Flywheel Bolt	300	300
Spark Plug	120-180	120-180
Standard Screws:		
No. 10-24	30	30
No. 10-32	35	35
No. 12-24	45	45
¼-20	70	70
5/16-18	160	160
3/8-16	270	270

LUBRICATION

The power head is lubricated by oil mixed with the fuel. Mix ½ pint of oil with each gallon of gasoline to obtain 16:1 fuel to oil ratio. The fuel to oil ratio may be reduced to 25:1 for 3.6 hp motors after the first 3 hours of running (break-in). Mix ⅓ pint of oil with each gallon of gasoline for 25:1 ratio. Gasoline and oil should be thoroughly mixed, using a separate container, before filling fuel tank. Manufacturer recommends use of no-lead automotive gasoline although regular and premium grades may be used if octane rating is 85 or higher.

The lower unit gears and bearings are lubricated by oil contained in the gearcase. Only a noncorrosive, out-board gear oil, EP90 such as "Chrysler Outboard Gear Lube" or equivalent should be used. The gearcase should be drained and refilled every 100 hours or every six months, and fluid maintained at the level of the upper (vent) plug hole.

To fill the gearcase, have the motor in upright position and fill through the lower plug hole in port side of gearcase until fluid reaches level of upper gear vent plug. Have both plugs removed while refilling. Reinstall and tighten both plugs securely, using new gaskets if necessary, to assure a water tight seal.

FUEL SYSTEM

CARBURETOR. A Tillotson MD124A float type carburetor (Fig. C1-1) is used on 3.5 hp models. A Tillotson CO-1A carburetor (Fig. C1-2) is used on 3.6 hp models. Refer to the appropriate following paragraphs for adjustment and service.

Tillotson MD124A carburetors are provided with two mixture adjustment needles. Normal initial setting for both the high speed needle (12 – Fig. C1-1) and the idle mixture needle (23) is one turn open from closed position. Carburetor must be readjusted after motor is warm for best performance under normal load. To adjust the float, remove and invert the fuel bowl assembly (6). With the bowl held upside down, the lowest point of float, at free end, should project approximately 1/64 inch below gasket surface of bowl. Adjust by bending the vertical valve fork on float. Float must be removed to renew the inlet needle assembly (7). When installing float, make sure that slot in float lever engages the groove in needle.

Tillotson CO-1A carburetors are equipped with an adjustable idle mixture needle (11 – Fig. C1-2) and a fixed main jet (9). Initial setting for the idle mixture needle (11) is one turn out from lightly seated. The main jet standard size (0.037) will normally be correct from sea level to 3000 ft. altitude. Jet size 0.035 is recommended from 3000 to 6000 ft. altitude and size 0.033 is recommended above 6000 ft. Remove carburetor from engine to adjust float height. Remove bowl (3) and invert carburetor body (14). Bottom of float (top when inverted) should be 13/32 inch from gasket surface

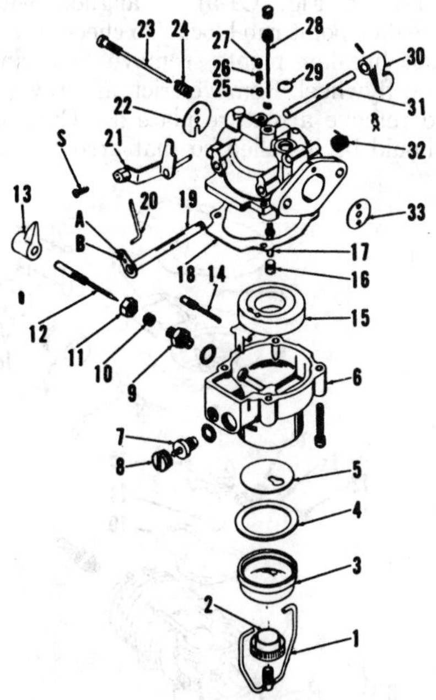

Fig. C1-1 – Exploded view of carburetor used on 3½ hp motors.

A. Outer hole	
B. Inner hole	16. Plug
S. Screw	17. Main nozzle
1. Bail	18. Gasket
2. Nut	19. Throttle shaft
3. Sediment bowl	20. Link
4. Gasket	21. Follower
5. Screen	22. Choke plate
6. Float chamber	23. Idle mixture needle
7. Inlet needle & seat	24. Spring
8. Plug	25. Friction pin
9. Gland nut	26. Spring
10. Packing	27. Plug
11. Nut	28. Idle tube
12. Main adjustment	29. Expansion ring
needle	30. Lever
13. Knob	31. Shaft
14. Float shaft	32. Spring
15. Float	33. Throttle plate

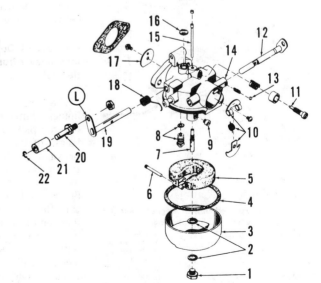

Fig. C1-2 – Exploded view of carburetor used on 3.6 hp models.

1. Retaining screw
2. Gasket
3. Float bowl
4. Gasket
5. Float
6. Float pin
7. Main nozzle
8. Inlet valve
9. Main jet
10. Choke
11. Idle mixture needle
12. Choke shaft
13. Choke detent ball
14. Carburetor body
15. Bypass tube
16. Welch plug
17. Throttle pin
18. Return spring
19. Throttle shaft
20. Follower
21. Roller
22. Clip

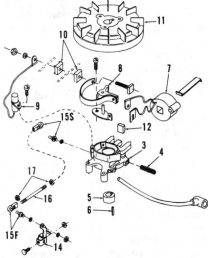

Fig. C1-3—The operating linkage should be adjusted to synchronize carburetor throttle opening to the magneto timing. Refer to text for method of checking.

of carburetor body. Adjust by bending tang on float arm. Pin (6) and float (5) must be removed before fuel inlet valve (8) can be removed.

SPEED CONTROL LINKAGE. The speed control lever is connected to the magneto stator plate to advance or retard the ignition timing. Throttle linkage is synchronized to open the throttle as magneto timing is advanced. It is very important that the throttle linkage be properly synchronized for best performance.

3.5 HP Adjustment. Make certain that throttle link (20 – Fig. C1-1) is in the inner hole (B) of throttle shaft (19). Move the speed control lever until lever is centered over the idle mixture needle (23) on control panel. With speed control lever in this position, follower arm (21) should just contact the control cam and begin to open throttle plate. Adjust by loosening clamp screw (S) and shortening or lengthening link (20).

3.6 HP Adjustment. To check and adjust the speed control linkage, the fuel tank should be removed. Move the speed control from low toward high speed and

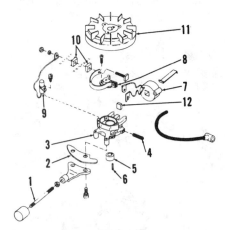

Fig. C1-4 — Exploded view of magneto assembly used on 3.5 hp models.

1. Speed control lever	7. Coil
2. Throttle cam	8. Breaker points
3. Armature plate	9. Condenser
4. Friction screw	10. Insulators
5. Cam	11. Flywheel
6. Key	12. Oil wick

Fig. C1-5 — Exploded view of magneto assembly and throttle control used on 3.6 hp models.

3. Armature plate	10. Insulators
4. Friction screw	11. Flywheel
5. Breaker cam	12. Felt wick
6. Key	14. Throttle cam
7. Coil	15. Rod ends
8. Breaker points	16. Control rod
9. Condenser	17. Locknuts

notice when the throttle cam (14 – Fig. C1-5) just contacts the roller (21 – Fig. C1-2). A mark (T – Fig. C1-3) is located on the throttle cam and should be at the center of the roller when they just touch. Bend the lever (L – Fig. C1-2) as necessary to correct the point of contact between cam and roller.

CAUTION: Do not bend lever enough to loosen lever from end of carburetor throttle shaft.

The length of the magneto control linkage can be adjusted after the carburetor pick-up point is correct. Initial length of the control link should be approximately 3½ inches measured between rod ends (15F & 15S – Fig. C1-5). Move the speed control until mark (T – Fig. C1-3) on cam is centered at the throttle roller as shown and check the location of the rod end (15S – Fig. C1-5). The center of rod end should be aligned with mark as shown at (M – Fig. C1-3). The rod ends can be pulled from the ball studs for easy adjustment of control rod

length. Tighten locknuts (17 – Fig. C1-5) after adjustment is complete.

REED VALVE. The reed valve unit (5, 6 & 7 – Fig. C1-6) is located on inlet manifold between carburetor and the crankcase. The reed valve assembly can be checked when the carburetor is removed for service. Reed petals should seat very lightly against the reed plate throughout their entire length. Check seating visually. Reed stop setting should be 11/64 inch when measured from end of reed stop (7) to seating surface on inlet manifold (5). Renew reeds if petals are broken, cracked, warped, rusted or bent. Never attempt to bend a reed petal or to straighten a damaged reed. Broken reed petals are sometimes caused by a bent or damage reed stop. Seating surface of reed plate should be smooth and flat.

IGNITION SYSTEM

Champion H8J, Autolite AL5XM or AC type M43L spark plug should be used. Electrode gap should be 0.030 inch. Breaker point gap should be 0.020 inch when mark on ignition cam (5 – Fig. C1-4 or Fig. C1-5) is aligned with breaker point rub block. To check or adjust breaker points, remove fuel tank and flywheel. Remove friction screw (4) to remove armature plate (3). Cam (5) should be installed so that arrow is up

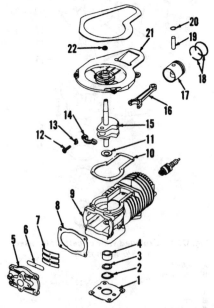

Fig. C1-6 — Exploded view of typical power head assembly.

1. Gasket	12. Screw
2. Snap ring	13. Lock
3. Washer	14. Cap
4. Collar	15. Crankshaft
5. Intake manifold	16. Connecting rod
6. Valve reed	17. Piston
7. Reed stop	18. Piston rings
8. Gasket	19. Piston pin
9. Crankcase	20. Retainer
10. Gasket	21. Upper support plate
11. Thrust washer	22. Seal

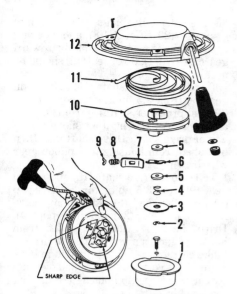

Fig. C1-7 — Exploded and assembled views of starter common to 3.5 hp motors. Spring (4) is assembled between top washer (5) and pulley (10) for starters used on 3.6 hp models.

1. Cup	7. Shoe plate
2. "E" ring	8. Spring
3. Washer	9. Retainer
4. Spring	10. Pulley
5. Fiber washer	11. Recoil spring
6. Lever	12. Housing

and pointing in direction of rotation. Friction screw (4) should be tightened enough to maintain speed control setting. Tapered bore in flywheel and end of crankshaft should be clean and dry before installing flywheel. Tighten flywheel retaining screw to 300 inch-pounds torque.

COOLING SYSTEM

The power head is air cooled by a fan integral with the flywheel, which forces air through cooling fins on the cylinder.

On 3.5 hp motors, a cooling tube is located in the lower unit. This tube picks up water from behind the propeller, below the antiventilation plate and directs it into the exhaust portion of the lower housing. Later (3.6 hp) motors are equipped with a rubber impeller type water pump which pumps water into the exhaust housing.

The water pump used on late models is located between the gearcase and drive shaft housings. Install impeller (22 – Fig. C1-8) in housing (23) while turning impeller in counterclockwise direction. Slots in impeller must be down.

POWER HEAD

R&R AND DISASSEMBLE. Remove fuel tank, flywheel (11 – Fig. C1-4 or Fig. C1-5), carburetor and inlet manifold (reed assembly). Remove friction screw (4) and lift off the magneto armature plate assembly (3). Remove the six screws attaching power head to

lower unit and lift off power head assembly.

The fuel tank support plate (21 – Fig. C1-6) also serves as crankshaft main bushing and seal. Remove the support plate (21), snap ring (2) and thrust washer (3). Remove connecting rod cap (14) and push piston and rod to top of cylinder, then lift the crankshaft (15) and thrust washer (11) from crankcase. Connecting rod and piston can be withdrawn after crankshaft is out.

Engine components are now accessible for overhaul as outlined in appropriate following paragraphs. Assemble as outlined in ASSEMBLY paragraph.

ASSEMBLY. When reassembling, make sure all joint and gasket surfaces are clean, free from nicks and burrs and hardened cement or carbon. The crankcase and inlet manifold must be completely sealed against both vacuum and pressure. The cooling fins must be straight, clean and undamaged. Collar (4 – Fig. C1-6) should be pressed into crankcase until edge extends 0.020 inch beyond crankcase gasket surface on 3.5 hp models. Collar is not used on 3.6 hp models.

Use new gaskets for assembly and coat gasket surfaces lightly and evenly with a good, nonhardening type gasket sealer.

PISTON, PIN, RINGS AND CYLINDER. Piston is fitted with three rings which should be installed with the beveled inner edge toward closed end of piston.

When installing piston in cylinder, the long tapering side of piston head should be installed down, toward the exhaust port. All friction surfaces should be lubricated with new engine oil when assembling.

CONNECTING ROD, BEARINGS AND CRANKSHAFT. The aluminum connecting rod is fitted with a cast-in bronze bearing surface which rides directly on the crankshaft. Crankshaft main bearing bushings are cast into crankcase (9 – Fig. C1-6) and support plate (21). Crankshaft end play is controlled by thrust washer (11) and should be 0.002-0.012 inch. Renew thrust washer if end play exceeds 0.015 inch.

Check the crankshaft and bearings for wear, scoring or out-of-round condition. Oversize and undersize parts are not available.

Make certain that marks on connecting rod and rod cap are aligned when assembling. Tighten connecting rod screws to 75-80 inch-pounds torque, then lock in place with lock plates (13). All friction surfaces should be coated with oil during assembly.

MANUAL STARTER

The complete starter assembly except for cup (1 – Fig. C1-7) can be lifted off after removing the attaching hardware.

To disassemble, unseat and remove "E" ring (2), then withdraw parts (3 through 9). Note order of assembly for

Fig. C1-8 — Exploded view of lower unit. Lip of seal (5) should be toward gearcase and lip of seal (12) should be up toward motor. Water pump (22) is not used on 3.5 hp units.

1. Nut	
2. Propeller	
3. Shear pin	
4. Seal retainer	
5. Seal	
6. Cap	
7. Gasket	
8. Propeller shaft & gear	
9. Drive pinion	
10. Filler plug	
11. Vent plug	
12. Seal	
13. Seal retainer	
14. Drive pin	
15. Drive shaft	
16. Cover	
17. Steering friction nut	
18. Tilt friction nut	
19. Water tube	
20. Gearcase housing	
21. Drive shaft housing	
22. Water pump impeller	
23. Pump housing	
24. Water tube seal	
25. Back plate	

washers and spring used. Starter parts used on 3.6 hp models are arranged differently than shown. Refer to Fig. C1-7. Withdraw pulley (10) from housing (12), leaving spring (11) coiled in housing unless renewal is indicated. The starter rope is secured to pulley (10) by a clip which is part of the rope unit. Starter rope should be 48 inches long. When reassembling the unit, wind the spring (11) three full turns on pulley (10) to establish correct spring tension, before installing handle.

The two shoe plates (7) should be installed with sharp edge positioned as shown in the assembled view (Fig. C1-7).

LOWER UNIT

PROPELLER AND DRIVE PIN. Shear pin protection is carefully engineered for each unit. Protection depends on shear pin material as well as size. Although, in an emergency, the shear pin may be replaced by one of any available material, the correct shear pin should be installed as soon as possible to ensure maximum performance and protection.

Stainless steel, 5/32 x 1-3/16 inch shear pins are available in a pack of 6 (manufacturer's part number K-238). To renew the shear pin it is necessary to first remove the propeller. Left hand rotation, 7½ inch diameter, 4½ inch pitch, 2 blade, aluminum propeller is used.

R&R AND OVERHAUL. Most service on the lower unit can be performed by detaching the gearcase housing from drive shaft and exhaust housing.

Always renew all seals and gaskets when gearcase has been removed or disassembled. Bushings are cast into gearcase (20 – Fig. C1-8) and housing cap (6). Lip of seal (5) should be toward gearcase (front); lip of seal (12) should be up toward motor.

To remove drive shaft (15) and pinion gear (9) from 3.5 hp motor, remove cap (6), pull propeller shaft (8) from housing and remove snap ring (not shown) from end of drive shaft. Drive shaft may then be pulled from housing and pinion gear withdrawn.

To remove drive shaft (15) and pinion gear (9) from 3.6 hp motor, remove cap (6), propeller shaft (8), water pump housing (23), impeller (22) and drive pin (14). Drive shaft may then be pulled from housing and pinion gear withdrawn. Make certain that hole provided in back plate (25) is correctly positioned over detent in water pump housing (23) during reassembly.

CHRYSLER
3.5 (1980 to 1984) AND
4.0 HP (1977 to 1984) MODELS

3.5 HP MODELS

Year Produced	Model
1980	32 H0D
1981	32 H1D
1982	32 H2E
1983	32H3
1984	32H4

4.0 HP MODELS

Year Produced	Model
1977	42HB, 42BB, 43HB, 47HB, 47BB
1978	42H8C, 42B8C, 42H8D, 42B8D, 42H8E, 42B8E, 47H8C, 47B8C, 47H8D, 47B8D, 47H8E, 47B8E
1979	42H9F, 42B9F, 47H9F, 47B9F
1980	42H0G, 42B0G, 43H0A, 47H0G, 47B0G
1981	42H1H, 42B1H, 43H1B, 43B1B
1982	42H2J, 42B2J
1983	42H3
1984	42H4

CONDENSED SERVICE DATA

TUNE-UP

HP/rpm	3.5/4500
	4.0/5250
Bore – Inches	2
Stroke – Inches	1-19/32
Number of Cylinders	1
Displacement – Cu. In.	5.0
Compression at Cranking Speed (Average, with recoil starter)	110-125 psi
Spark Plug:	
Champion	L86 (Canada RL86)
Electrode gap	0.030 in.
Magneto:	
Breaker point gap	0.020 in.
Fuel:Oil Ratio	50:1

SIZES – CLEARANCES

Piston Ring End Gap	0.006-0.011 in.
Piston to Cylinder Clearance	0.0035-0.005 in.
Piston Pin:	
Diameter	0.43750-0.43765 in.
Clearance (Rod)	Needle Bearing
Clearance (Piston)	0.00035 in. tight to 0.0001 in. loose

SIZES – CLEARANCES (CONT.)

Crankshaft Journal Diameters:	
Lower Main	0.7874-0.7878 in.
Upper Main	0.8125-0.8130 in.
Crankpin	0.7493-0.7496 in.

TIGHTENING TORQUES
(All Values in Inch-Pounds)

Connecting Rod	75-85
Cylinder Head	130
Flywheel Nut	204
Main Bearing Bolts	70
Spark Plug	120-180
Standard Screws:	
6-32	9
10-24	30
10-32	35
12-24	45
¼-20	70
5/16-18	160
⅜-16	270

LUBRICATION

The power head is lubricated by oil mixed with the fuel. One-sixth (1/6) pint of two-stroke engine oil should be mixed with each gallon of gasoline. Manufacturer recommends use of no-lead automotive gasoline although regular or premium grade gasoline may be used if octane rating is 85 or higher. Gasoline and oil should be thoroughly mixed.

The lower unit gears and bearings are lubricated by oil contained in the gearcase. Manufacturer recommends Chrysler Outboard Gear Lube for use in gearcase. The gearcase should be drained and refilled every 100 hours or once each year, and fluid maintained at the level of the upper (vent) plug hole.

FUEL SYSTEM

CARBURETOR. All 4 hp models produced in 1977 are equipped with the single barrel float type carburetor shown in Fig. C2-1. All 3.5 and 4 hp models produced after 1977 are equipped with the single barrel float type carburetor shown in Fig. C2-2. Initial setting of idle mixture screw (7 – Fig. C2-1 or Fig. C2-2) is one turn open. High speed mixture on 4 hp models produced in 1977 is adjusted by turning lever (20 – Fig. C2-1) located under support plate. Lever (20) is attached to high speed mixture screw (19). Turning screw (19) clockwise will lean high speed mixture. High speed mixture on all 1978 and later models is controlled by a high speed jet (17 – Fig. C2-2) and is nonadjustable. Idle speed on all 3.5 hp models and 4 hp models produced in 1977 is nonadjustable. Idle speed on 4 hp models after 1977 is adjusted by a throttle stop and should be 800-1200 rpm.

Adjust float level so float is parallel to float bowl gasket surface. Be sure float support spring (11–Fig. C2-1 or Fig. C2-2) is installed so spring pressure helps float close fuel inlet valve. Install throttle plate so stamped letter is towards engine and holes in throttle plate are on carburetor idle mixture screw side. Install choke plate so stamped number is towards carburetor front and oblong slot is on fuel inlet side.

SPEED CONTROL LINKAGE. The speed control lever is connected to the magneto stator plate to advance or retard ignition timing. Throttle linkage is synchronized to open the throttle as magneto timing is advanced.

To check speed control linkage, turn speed control lever until throttle cam shown in Fig. C2-3 contacts cam follower (F). Mark (M) on throttle cam should be in center of cam follower when cam contacts follower. If mark is not aligned with cam follower centerline, loosen throttle cam retaining screw and relocate cam. Recheck synchronization after relocating cam.

REED VALVES. On 4 hp models produced in 1977, reed stop (22–Fig. C2-1) and reed petals (23) are attached

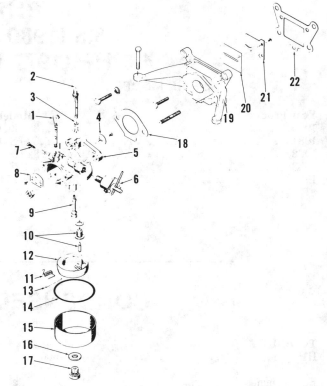

Fig. C2-2 – Exploded view of carburetor used on 3.5 hp models and 4 hp models after 1977.

1. Choke shaft
2. Throttle shaft
3. Spring
4. Throttle plate
5. Carburetor body
6. Fuel valve
7. Idle mixture screw
8. Choke plate
9. Nozzle
10. Fuel inlet valve
11. Float spring
12. Float
13. Float pin
14. Gasket
15. Float bowl
16. Washer
17. High speed jet
18. Gasket
19. Intake manifold
20. Reed petals
21. Reed stop
22. Gasket

to a vee type reed block (24) located between the carburetor and intake manifold. On all other models, reed stop (21–Fig. C2-2) and reed petals (20) are attached directly to engine side of intake manifold (19). Inspect reed petals and renew petals if they are broken, cracked or bent. Never attempt to straighten a bent reed. Tip of reed petal must not stand open more than 0.006 inch from contact surface. Reed stop opening should be 0.24-0.26 inch.

IGNITION

Breaker points are accessible after flywheel is removed. Breaker point gap should be 0.020 inch when index mark on breaker cam is aligned with breaker point rubbing block.

Tapered bore of flywheel and crankshaft end must be clean, dry and smooth before installing flywheel. Renew chipped or cracked flywheels. Flywheel and crankshaft tapers may be cleaned by using fine valve grinding compound. Apply grinding compound to tapers and

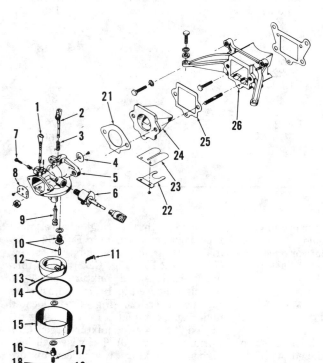

Fig. C2-1 – Exploded view of carburetor used on 1977 4 hp models.

1. Choke shaft
2. Throttle shaft
3. Spring
4. Throttle plate
5. Carburetor body
6. Fuel valve
7. Idle mixture screw
8. Choke plate
9. Nozzle
10. Fuel inlet valve
11. Float spring
12. Float
13. Float pin
14. Gasket
15. Float bowl
16. Needle seat
17. Spring
18. "O" ring
19. High speed mixture screw
20. Lever
21. Gasket
22. Reed stop
23. Reed petals
24. Reed block
25. Gasket
26. Intake manifold

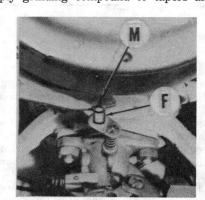

Fig. C2-3 – Cam follower (F) should be centered on cam mark (M) when cam contacts follower.

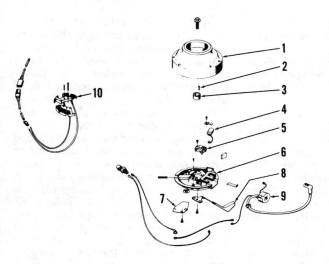

Fig. C2-4 — Exploded view of ignition components.

1. Flywheel
2. Key
3. Breaker cam
4. Condenser
5. Breaker points
6. Stator plate
7. Cam
8. Speed control lever
9. Ignition coil
10. Alternator stator

Fig. C2-7 — Install piston assembly so open end of piston pin (P) is towards flywheel and connecting rod match mark (M) is towards port side of engine.

rotate flywheel back and forth approximately one quarter turn. Do not spin flywheel on crankshaft. Clean flywheel and crankshaft tapers thoroughly.

COOLING SYSTEM

All models are equipped with a rubber impeller water pump. When cooling system problems are encountered, first check the water inlet for plugging or partial stoppage, then if not corrected, remove the lower unit gearcase and check the condition of water pump, water passages and sealing surfaces.

To detach gearcase from motor leg, remove shift coupling cover and loosen shift coupling screw shown in Fig. C2-5. Remove the two screws securing gearcase to motor leg and remove gearcase. Remove impeller cover (4 – Fig. C2-9), impeller (5) and water pump body (8).

Be sure impeller correctly engages drive pin (26) during assembly. Apply a suitable sealant to gearcase. Pull lower shift rod up as far as possible and move gear shift lever to neutral position (horizontal). Align shift rod with coup-

ling and water line with seal and mate gearcase with motor leg. Tighten shift coupling screw and install cover.

POWER HEAD

R&R AND OVERHAUL. To remove power head, remove upper and lower engine covers, starter, fuel tank, flywheel, stator and carburetor. Disconnect stop switch leads. Unscrew two screws securing handle support plate to power head and remove plate. Unscrew six screws and separate power head from motor leg.

Remove cylinder head. Drive out crankcase locating pins, unscrew crankcase screws and separate crankcase from cylinder. Crankshaft and piston assemblies are now accessible. Refer to appropriate paragraph for overhaul of power head components.

Inspect crankcase and cylinder mating surfaces for nicks, burrs or warpage. Use a suitable sealant on crankcase and cylinder mating surfaces before

assembly. Install crankshaft seals with lips towards crankcase. Be sure locating ring around crankshaft lower main bearing is seated in grooves in cylinder and crankcase. Tighten crankcase screws to 70 in.-lbs. Assembly is reverse of disassembly. Drive shaft splines should be coated with a suitable anticorrosion substance.

PISTON, PIN, RINGS AND CYLINDER. When properly assembled, connecting rod match marks will be towards port side of engine, piston pin open end will be towards flywheel and piston ring locating pins will be on same side of piston as piston pin open end. See Fig. C2-7. The piston is equipped with two piston rings which must be installed so beveled inner edge is towards piston crown.

CONNECTING ROD, CRANKSHAFT AND BEARINGS. Assemble connecting rod, piston and pin as outlined in previous section. Install rod and piston assembly in cylinder so alignment

Fig. C2-6 — Exploded view of engine used on all models.

1. Cylinder
2. Gasket
3. Cylinder head
4. Crankcase
5. Dowel pin
6. Rod cap
7. Bearing cage
8. Bearing rollers (16)
9. Seal
10. Seal
11. Crankshaft
12. Seal
13. Bearing
14. Bearing
15. Connecting rod
16. Piston
17. Piston pin
18. Snap ring
19. Piston rings

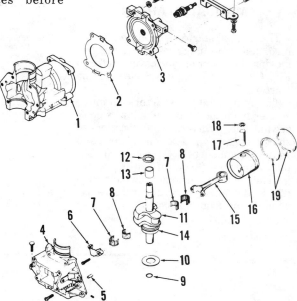

Fig. C2-5 — View showing location of shift rod coupling (C).

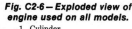

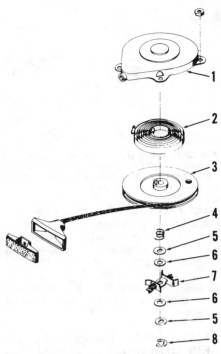

Fig. C2-8 — Exploded view of manual starter.

1. Starter housing
2. Rewind spring
3. Rope pulley
4. Spring
5. Washer
6. Fiber washer
7. Friction shoe assy.
8. "E" ring

mark on rod is towards port side of engine. Connecting rod rides on a caged roller bearing with sixteen rollers. Be sure marks on rod and cap are correctly aligned. Tighten rod screws to 75-85 in.-lbs.

Crankshaft upper main bearing is a needle roller bearing while a ball bearing is used on lower end of crankshaft. Lower bearing and crankshaft are available as a unit assembly only.

MANUAL STARTER

The manual starter is mounted on the fuel tank and is accessible after removing the upper engine cover. Refer to Fig. C2-8 for an exploded view of the starter.

To disassemble starter, remove starter from fuel tank and allow rope to rewind into starter. Note location of sharp edges on friction shoes and remove components (4 through 8). Lift pulley and rope (3) out of housing (1) being careful not to dislodge rewind spring (2). If damaged, carefully remove rewind spring from housing.

Install lightly lubricated rewind spring in housing in counterclockwise direction from outer spring end. Wind a 48 inch long rope on pulley in clockwise direction as viewed from rewind spring side of pulley. Lightly lubricate pulley bore and install pulley in housing making certain that inner and outer ends of spring are hooked in pulley and housing. Turn pulley three turns clockwise to preload rewind spring, pass rope end through housing and tie a knot in the rope. Pull rope out as far as possible and then try to turn pulley counterclockwise. Pulley should turn an additional 1/8-1/3 turn before bottoming out rewind spring. Check sharp end of friction shoes (7) and sharpen or renew as necessary. Install components (4 through 8). Make certain that friction shoe assembly is installed properly. If properly installed, sharp ends of friction shoes will extend when rope is pulled.

LOWER UNIT

R&R AND OVERHAUL. Refer to Fig. C2-9 for exploded view of lower unit. All 3.5 hp models are constant drive and do not use components (1, 2, 3, 9 and 13). On 1981 through 1984 3.5 hp models, propeller and propeller shaft (19) are splined and bevel gear (14) is secured to propeller shaft with a thrust pin (28) in place of components (16, 17 and 18).

Remove water pump as previously outlined. Remove propeller nut (27), then drive out propeller thrust pin and remove propeller. Remove any burrs or rust from exposed end of propeller shaft. Remove four screws holding retainer (24) to bearing housing (21). Install two screws in threaded holes of retainer and using a suitable puller, remove retainer. Propeller shaft assembly may be withdrawn after removal of retainer. Remove pinion gear (15) and bevel gear (14).

Assemble by reversing disassembly procedure. Shift rod seal (7) should have raised bead up. Shift pin (13) is installed in propeller shaft with round end forward, towards cam (9). Install bevel gear (14) and pinion gear (15). Pinion gear is secured with drive shaft (25). Install propeller shaft seal (22) with lip towards propeller.

Fig. C2-9 — Exploded view of gearcase.

1. Shift coupling
2. Pin
3. Shift rod
4. Cover
5. Impeller
6. Water tube seal
7. Shift rod seal
8. Water pump body
9. Shift cam clutch
10. Seal
11. "O" ring
12. Gearcase
13. Clutch shift pin
14. Bevel gear
15. Pinion gear
16. Clutch
17. Clutch guide pin
18. Spring
19. Propeller shaft
20. Spacer
21. Bearing housing
22. Seal
23. "O" ring
24. Retainer
25. Drive shaft
26. Impeller pin
27. Propeller nut
28. Thrust pin

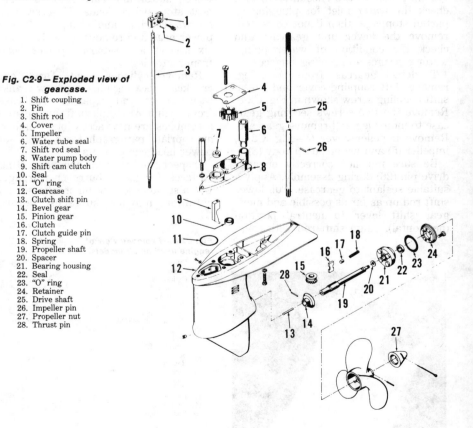

CHRYSLER 4.9 AND 5 HP
(1974, 1975 and 1976)

CONDENSED SERVICE DATA

TUNE-UP

Hp/rpm	4.9/4500
	5/4750
Bore—Inches	1¾
Stroke—Inches	1-9/16
Number of Cylinders	2
Displacement—Cu.	
Inches	7.52

Compression at
Cranking Speed
(Average):

HA, BA	60-70 psi
HB, BB	70-80 psi
HC, HD, BC, BD	90-100 psi

Spark Plug:

Champion	L10
Electrode Gap—Inch	0.030

Magneto:

Point Gap—Inch	0.020
Timing	See text

Carburetor:

Make	Amal

Fuel: Oil Ratio:

Normal	48:1
Break-In & Severe	
Service	24:1

SIZES—CLEARANCES

Piston Rings:

End Gap	*
Side Clearance	*

Piston to Cylinder

Clearance	*

Piston Pin:

Diameter	*
Clearance (rod)	*
Clearance (piston)	*

Crankshaft bearings:

Upper Main	Caged Needles
Lower main	Bushing
Crankpin	Loose Needles
Center Main	Loose Needles

Rod Side Clearance	*
Crankshaft end play	*

*Publication Not Authorized by Manufacturer.

TIGHTENING TORQUES
[All Values in Inch-Pounds]

Flywheel Nut	480
Cylinder Head	80
Spark Plug	120-180
Connecting Rod	
Screws	80

Standard Screws:

No. 10-24	30
No. 10-32	35
No. 12-24	45
¼-20	70
5-16-18	160
3/8-16	270

LUBRICATION

Power head is lubricated by oil mixed with the fuel. For normal service after break-in, mix 1/6 pint of two-stroke engine oil with each gallon of gasoline. For severe service and during break-in, the recommended ratio is one third (⅓) pint of oil per gallon of gasoline. Manufacturer recommends use of no-lead automotive gasoline although regular or premium gasoline may be used if octane rating is 85 or higher. Gasoline and oil should be thoroughly mixed.

The lower unit gears and bearings are lubricated by oil contained in the gear case. Only a non-corrosive, leaded, EP90, outboard gear oil such as "Chrysler Outboard Gear Lube" should be used. The gear case should be drained and refilled every 30 hours and fluid maintained at the level of the upper (vent) plug hole.

To fill the gearcase, have the motor in upright position and fill through the lower plug hole in the side of gearcase until fluid reaches level of upper plug hole. Reinstall and tighten both plugs securely, using new gaskets if necessary, to assure a water tight seal.

FUEL SYSTEM

CARBURETOR. All models are equipped with an Amal float type carburetor. Refer to Fig. C3-1 for an

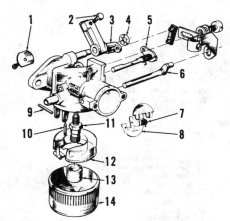

Fig. C3-1—Exploded view of Amal carburetor. Refer to Fig. C3-2 for installation of throttle plate (1).

1. Throttle plate	8. Choke plate
2. Speed control screw	9. Float pin
3. Throttle lever	10. Inlet fuel valve
4. Lockwasher	11. Main jet
5. Throttle shaft	12. Float
6. Choke shaft	13. Fuel filter
7. Spring	14. Float bowl

exploded view of carburetor.

Idle mixture and float level are non-adjustable. Refer to SPEED CONTROL LINKAGE for adjustment of throttle linkage. Standard main jet (11—Fig. C3-1) size is 52CC. Throttle plate (1) must be installed so that punch mark (P—Fig. C3-2) on throttle plate is to the top and facing the flange end of the carburetor.

SPEED CONTROL LINKAGE. The speed control lever is connected to the magneto stator plate to advance or retard the ignition timing. Throttle linkage is synchronized to open the throttle as magneto timing is advanced.

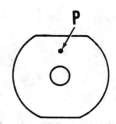

Fig. C3-2—Install throttle plate (1—Fig. C3-1) with punch mark (P) to top and facing flange end of carburetor.

It is very important that the throttle linkage be properly synchronized for best performance.

To synchronize linkage, remove upper engine cover. Position speed control lever so that mark (Fig. C3-3) on stator plate is aligned with crankcase parting line. Turn adjusting screw (S—Fig. C3-3) until throttle lever just contacts cam plate on underside of stator plate.

REED VALVES. The inlet reed valves are attached to the reed valve plate located between the intake manifold and the crankcase. Remove carburetor and intake manifold for access to the reed valves. Reed petals should seat very lightly against reed plate and should not be bowed more than 1/64 inch. Seating surface of reed plate should be smooth and flat. Reed petal ends should not stand open more than 0.005 inch. Never attempt to bend a reed petal or straighten a damaged

petal. Ends of reed stops (2—Fig. C3-4) should be 0.24-0.26 inch from reed plate. Broken petals are sometimes caused by a bent or damaged reed stop.

IGNITION

Breaker point gap must be the same for both sets of points and should be set at 0.020 inch. Remove flywheel for access to breaker points and note mark on breaker point cam which indicates highest point of cam. Align rub block on breaker points with mark on cam when setting breaker point gap.

The tapered bore in flywheel and end of crankshaft must be clean, dry and smooth. Tighten flywheel nut to 35-40 ft.-lbs.

POWER HEAD

R&R AND DISASSEMBLY. Use the following procedure for engine disassembly: Remove fuel cap and wire retainer, unscrew upper engine cover screws and move upper engine cover sufficiently to tie a knot in the starter rope. Tie a knot in the starter rope, detach starter handle from end of starter rope and remove upper engine cover from engine. Detach steering handle and choke knob and unscrew four screws securing lower engine cover to engine. Remove "O" ring (15—Fig. C3-13) from tabs at rear of cover and screw in outboard mounting screws. Remove lower engine cover by lowering cover and passing split end of cover past the motor leg. Unscrew four retaining screws and remove fuel tank. Remove carburetor. Disconnect spark plug wire and remove flywheel. Unscrew friction screw (12—Fig. C3-5) in stator plate. Unscrew stator plate retaining screws and remove stator plate.

To remove engine from motor leg, remove pivot bolt (8—Fig. C3-6) and

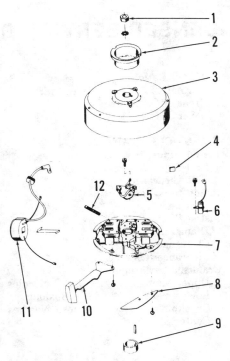

Fig. C3-5—Exploded view of ignition. Friction screw adjusts movement of speed control lever (10).

1. Nut	7. Stator plate
2. Starter cup	8. Cam plate
3. Flywheel	9. Point cam
4. Cam felt	10. Speed control lever
5. Breaker points	11. Coil
6. Condenser	12. Friction screw

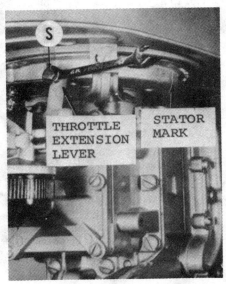

Fig. C3-3—Refer to text for speed control adjustment.

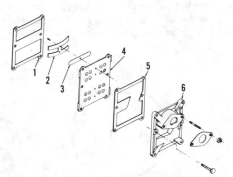

Fig. C3-4—View of reed valve assembly.

1. Gasket	4. Reed plate
2. Reed stop	5. Gasket
3. Reed petal	6. Intake manifold

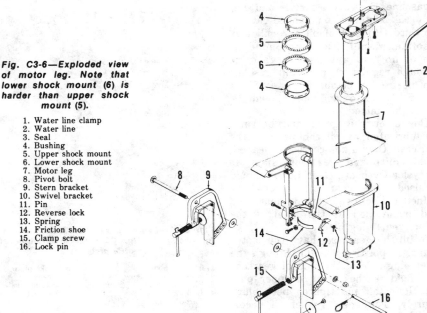

Fig. C3-6—Exploded view of motor leg. Note that lower shock mount (6) is harder than upper shock mount (5).

1. Water line clamp
2. Water line
3. Seal
4. Bushing
5. Upper shock mount
6. Lower shock mount
7. Motor leg
8. Pivot bolt
9. Stern bracket
10. Swivel bracket
11. Pin
12. Reverse lock
13. Spring
14. Friction shoe
15. Clamp screw
16. Lock pin

lock pin (16). Unscrew four retaining screws and separate swivel bracket halves (10) from motor leg. Unscrew powerhead mounting screws and separate powerhead from motor leg.

Refer to appropriate paragraphs for overhaul of engine components.

ASSEMBLY. Make sure all joint and gasket surfaces are clean, free from nicks and burrs and hardened cement or carbon. The crankcase and inlet manifold must be completely sealed against vacuum and pressure. Exhaust manifold and cylinder head must be sealed against water leakage and pressure. Mating surfaces of exhaust areas between powerhead and motor leg must form a tight seal.

Whenever powerhead is disassembled, it is recommended that all gasket surfaces, and mating surfaces without gaskets, be carefully checked for nicks and burrs and warped surfaces which might interfere with a tight seal. The cylinder head, head end of cylinder block, and some mating sufaces of manifolds and crankcase may be lapped if necessary to obtain a flat surface. Do not remove any more metal than is necessary.

Mating surfaces of crankcase may be checked on the lapping block, and high spots or nicks removed, but the surface must not be lowered. If extreme care is used, a slightly damaged crankcase may be salvaged in this manner. In case of doubt, renew the crankcase assembly.

A heavy, non-fibrous grease should be used to hold loose needle bearings in position during assembly. All friction surfaces should be lubricated with new engine oil. Check frequently as power head is being assembled, for binding or locking. If encountered, remove the cause before proceeding with the assembly.

Gasket and sealing surfaces should be lightly and carefully coated with a non-hardening gasket cement. Make sure entire surface is coated, including bore around top main bearing and bore around lower main seal. Avoid letting excess cement squeeze out into crankcase, bearings, or other passages. When installing crankcase screws, tighten those next to the main bearings and dowels first. Crankshaft seals (4, 20 and 24—Fig. C3-7) should be renewed each time crankshaft is removed. Refer to CONDENSED SERVICE DATA table for tightening torques.

Before reinstalling power head on motor leg, make certain that gasket surface is clean and a new gasket is positioned so that passage (Fig. C3-8) is covered. Ridge of bottom of crankcase must fit between water seal (Fig. C3-8) and end of water line.

PISTONS, PINS, RINGS AND CONNECTING RODS. Pistons and rod assemblies can be removed after cylinder head and reed plate are removed from engine. Unscrew rod screws being careful not to lose bearing rollers as rod and cap are separated. Push rod and piston out cylinder head end of engine.

NOTE: Do not interchange piston or rod components from one cylinder to the other.

Connecting rod rides on 14 caged roller bearings. Inspect connecting rod, crankshaft journal and bearings for excessive wear or damage. Piston rings are installed with beveled edge towards top of piston (Fig. C3-9). Piston must be heated to approximately 200°F. with a hot air gun, in an oven or in hot oil before the piston pin can be removed or installed. Piston must be installed on connecting rod so that

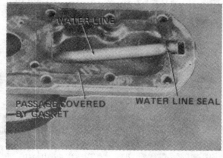

Fig. C3-8—Gasket (25—Fig. C3-7) must cover passage in motor leg. Ridge on bottom of crankcase must fit between water line seal and end of water line.

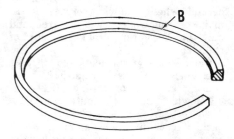

Fig. C3-9—Install piston rings with bevel (B) towards piston dome.

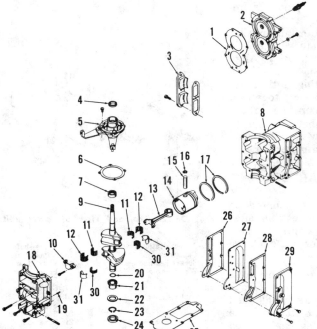

Fig. C3-7—Exploded view of powerhead

1. Head gasket
2. Cylinder head
3. Transfer port cover
4. Seal
5. Bearing housing
6. Gasket
7. Bearing
8. Cylinder block
9. Crankshaft
10. Rod cap
11. Bearing rollers (14)
12. Bearing cage
13. Connecting rod
14. Piston
15. Piston pin
16. Snap ring
17. Piston rings
18. Crankcase
19. Dowel pin
20. "O" ring
21. Bushing
22. Thrust washer
23. Snap ring
24. Seal
25. Gasket
26. Gasket
27. Exhaust port plate
28. Gasket
29. Exhaust cover
30. Bearing rollers
31. Bearing liners

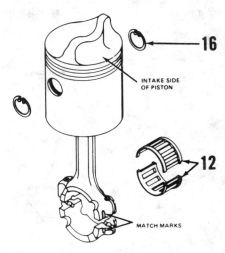

Fig. C3-10—Intake side of piston and match marks on connecting rod must be on same side. Notched ends of bearing cages (12) must be towards flywheel. Sharp edges of snap rings (16) must be out.

intake side of piston (steep side of piston dome) and match marks on rod are on same side. Refer to Fig. C3-10. Install piston pin snap rings (16—Fig. C3-10). Install sharp edge out and end gap of snap ring at 6 or 12 o'clock position. Notched end of bearing cages (12) must be installed toward flywheel end of engine. Coat bearing cages with a suitable grease to hold bearing rollers and install rod and piston assembly. Be sure ring end gaps are around locating pins in ring grooves when sliding piston into bore. Tighten connecting rod screws to 10 in.-lbs., check rod alignment and then tighten rod screws to a final torque of 80 in.-lbs. Install cylinder head gasket with side marked "TOP" towards cylinder head. Tighten cylinder head cap screws in steps of 40, 65 and 80 in.-lbs. in sequence shown in Fig. C3-11.

CRANKSHAFT, CRANKCASE AND SEALS. Upper crankshaft bearing and seal are contained in housing (5—Fig. C3-7). Bearing (7) and seal (4) may be pressed from housing after housing screws are removed and housing is separated from crankcase. Access to crankshaft and main bearings is obtained after connecting rod assemblies and crankcase are removed. Be careful when removing crankcase as main bearing rollers will be free and may be lost. Lift crankcase out of cylinder block.

Clean mating surfaces and inspect components. Center crankshaft main bearing consists of a liner (31—Fig. C3-7) which forms the outer race and 26 loose bearing rollers (30). Note that back of each liner has a bump which must align with hole in bearing bore of crankcase or cylinder block. To install crankshaft, place components (20, 21, 22 and 23) on crankshaft. Sharp edge of

snap ring (23) must be out. Place one bearing liner half in cylinder block with a light coating of grease and install 13 bearing rollers. Install crankshaft, remaining 13 bearing rollers and other half of bearing liner so that liners mesh together. Apply sealant to mating surfaces and install crankcase on cylinder block. Tighten crankcase screws to 80 in.-lbs. Apply grease to lips of crankcase seal (24) and drive seal into bore until fully seated. Complete reassembly of powerhead by reversing disassembly procedure.

COOLING SYSTEM

WATER PUMP. The engine is cooled by water circulated by an impeller type water pump located in the anti-cavitation plate. When cooling problems are encountered, first check the water inlet for plugging or partial stoppage. If water inlet is clear, proceed to inspection of water passages and water pump.

To gain access to water pump, unscrew anti-cavitation plate screws (3 and 4—Fig. C3-12) and separate lower unit from motor leg. Remove screws securing anti-cavitation plate to gear housing and separate the plate and housing assemblies. Remove water pump impeller (5) from anti-cavitation plate and inspect for damage or excessive wear. Inspect water seal (1) and renew if damaged. Apply a suitable sealant to bore of tube before installing water seal (1). Pump impeller pin (13) must be removed before pump plate (6) can be removed from gear housing.

Reassembly of water pump is reverse of disassembly, but the following points should be noted. Install impeller (5) in anti-cavitation plate with slot in impeller hub facing gear housing. Align impeller drive pin (13) with slot in impeller (5) when mating anti-cavitation plate and gear housing together. Apply an anti-seize compound to the upper splines of drive shaft (12) and to threads of rear screw (4) between anti-cavitation plate and motor leg.

MANUAL STARTER

The manual starter is mounted on the fuel tank and is accessible after removing the upper engine cover. Refer to Fig. C3-13 for an exploded view of the starter.

To disassemble starter, remove starter from fuel tank. Remove rope and insert (4) from rope handle and allow rope to rewind into starter. Note location of sharp edges on friction

shoes and remove components (6 thru 11). Lift pulley and rope (3) out of housing (1) being careful not to dislodge rewind spring (2). If damaged, carefully remove rewind spring from housing.

Install lightly lubricated rewind spring in housing in counter-clockwise direction from outer spring end. Wind a 48-inch long rope on pulley in clockwise direction as viewed from rewind spring side of pulley. Lightly lubricate pulley bore and install pulley in housing making certain that inner and outer ends of spring are hooked in pulley and housing. Turn pulley three turns clockwise to pre-load rewind spring, pass rope end through housing and tie a knot in the rope. Pull rope out as far as possible and then try to turn pulley counterclockwise. Pulley should turn an additional 1/8-1/3 turn before bottoming out rewind spring. Check sharp end of friction shoes (8) and sharpen or renew as necessary. Install spring (6), washer (7), friction shoe assembly (8), washers (9 & 10) and "E" ring (11). Make certain that friction shoe assembly is installed properly. If properly installed, sharp ends of friction shoes will extend when rope is pulled.

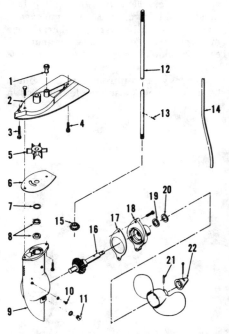

Fig. C3-12—Exploded view of lower unit.

1. Seal	12. Drive shaft
2. Anti-cavitation plate	13. Impeller pin
3. Cap screw	14. Water line
4. Socket head screw	15. Pinion gear
5. Water pump impeller	16. Propeller shaft
6. Pump plate	17. Gasket
7. Seal retainer	18. Cap
8. Seals	19. Seal
9. Gear housing	20. Seal retainer
10. Oil level screw	21. Shear pin
11. Drain plug	22. Nut

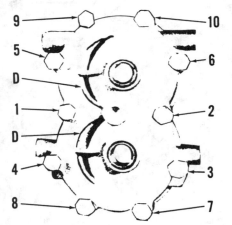

Fig. C3-11—Install cylinder head with depressions (D) on exhaust side. Tighten cylinder head screws in sequence shown above.

LOWER UNIT

PROPELLER AND DRIVE PIN. Lower unit protection is provided by a shear pin (21—Fig. C3-12). Protection is determined by shear pin material and size. In an emergency, the shear pin can be replaced by one of any material, but the correct shear pin should be installed as soon as possible to insure maximum protection.

Standard propeller size is 7½ inch diameter with 6 inch pitch and left hand rotation.

R&R AND OVERHAUL. To disassemble gear housing, separate gear housing from anti-cavitation plate as outlined in WATER PUMP section. Unscrew drain plug and drain gear lubricant. Remove impeller drive pin (13—Fig. C3-12) and pump plate (6). Withdraw drive shaft (12). Remove propeller, unscrew cap screws (18) and remove cap and propeller shaft (16). Remove pinion gear (15) and separate propeller shaft and cap.

Install drive shaft seals (8) with lips towards anti-cavitation plate. Lip of seal (19) must be towards gear housing. Drive seal retainer (20) in behind seal (19) until retainer is bottomed against seal. Tighten cap screws (18) to 65-75 in.-lbs.

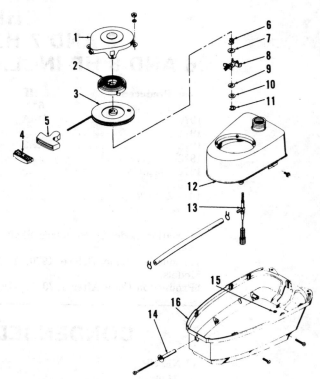

Fig. C3-13—Exploded view of manual starter, fuel tank and lower engine cover.

1. Starter housing
2. Rewind spring
3. Rope pulley
4. Insert
5. Rope handle
6. Spring
7. Fiber washer
8. Friction shoe assy.
9. Fiber washer
10. Washer
11. "E" ring
12. Fue tank
13. Fuel valve
14. Choke knob
15. "O" ring
16. Lower engine cover

CHRYSLER
5 AND 7 HP (1969 to 1971)
6 AND 8 HP INCL. SAILOR (1971 to 1977)

Year Produced	5 HP	6 HP	7 HP	8 HP
1969	5*‡	.....	7*‡	.....
1970	5*§A	.....	7*§A	.....
1971	.....	6*§A	.....	8*§A
1972	.....	6*§C	.....	8*§C
1973	.....	6*§D	.....	8*§C, D
1974	.....	6*§E, F	.....	8*§E, F
1975	.....	6*§G	.....	8*§G
1976 & 1977	.....	6*§G, H 60HA, B (Sailor)	.....	8*§G, H

*Variation Code: 0—Standard Shaft, 1—Long Shaft, 2—Standard Shaft, 3—Long Shaft.
†Production Code Before 1970, 1, 3 & 5—U.S.A. Models, 2, 4 & 6—Canada Models.
§Production Code After 1970, H—U.S.A. Models, B—Canada Models.

CONDENSED SERVICE DATA

TUNE-UP	5 & 6 HP	7 & 8 HP
Hp/rpm	5/4750 6/5000	7/4750 8/5000
Bore—Inches	1-7/8	2
Stroke—Inches	1-5/8	1-5/8
Number of Cylinders	2	2
Displacement—Cu. Inches	8.99	10.2
Compression at Cranking Speed (Average)	5 Hp, 75-85 psi 6 Hp, 85-95 psi	7 Hp, 90-100 psi 8 Hp, 100-110 psi
Spark Plug:		
Champion	L4J	L4J
Electrode Gap—Inch	0.030	0.030
Magneto:		
Point Gap—Inch	0.020	0.020
Timing	See Text	See Text
Carburetor:		
Make	Tillotson	Tillotson
Model	MD**	MD**
Fuel—Oil Ratio	††48:1	††48:1

SIZES—CLEARANCES	5 & 6 HP	7 & 8 HP
Piston Rings:		
End Gap	*	*
Side Clearance	*	*
Piston to Cylinder Clearance	*	*
Piston Pin:		
Diameter	*	*
Clearance (Rod)	*	*
Clearance (Piston)	*	*
Crankshaft Bearings:		
Upper Main	Ball	Ball
Lower Main	Bushing or Caged Needle	Bushing or Caged Needle
Crankpin	Loose Needles	Loose Needles
Center Main	Loose Needles	Loose Needles
Rod Side Clearance	*	*
Crankshaft End Play	*	*

*Publication Not Authorized by Manufacturer.
**1972 and later 6 hp models and all 8 hp models are equipped with CO type carburetors.
††Use a 24:1 fuel to oil ratio to break in a freshly overhauled engine.

TIGHTENING TORQUES (All Values in Inch-Pounds)	5 & 6 HP	7 & 8 HP
Flywheel Nut	480	480
Cylinder head	125	125
Spark Plug	120-180	120-180
Connecting Rod Screws	90	90
Standard Screws:		
No. 10-24	30	30
No. 10-32	35	35
No. 12-24	45	45
¼-20	70	70
5/16-18	160	160
3/8-16	270	270

LUBRICATION

Power head is lubricated by oil mixed with the fuel. For normal service after break-in, mix 1/6 pint of two-stroke engine oil with each gallon of gasoline. For severe service and during break-in the recommended ratio is one third (⅓) pint of oil per gallon of gasoline. Manufacturer recommends use of automotive no-lead gasoline although regular or premium gasoline may be used if octane rating is 85 or higher. Gasoline and oil should be thoroughly mixed.

The lower unit gears and bearings are lubricated by oil contained in the gear case. Only a non-corrosive, leaded EP90, outboard gear oil such as "Chrysler Outboard Gear Lube" should be used. The gear case should be drained and refilled every 30 hours and fluid maintained at the level of the upper (vent) plug hole.

To fill the gearcase, have the motor in upright position and fill through the lower plug hole in the side of gearcase until fluid reaches level of upper plug hole. Reinstall and tighten both plugs securely, using new gaskets if necessary, to assure a water tight seal.

FUEL SYSTEM

CARBURETOR. Tillotson type CO carburetors are used on 1972 and later 6 hp models and all 8 hp models. Refer to Fig. C4-1. All other models are equipped with Tillotson type MD carburetors. Refer to Fig. C4-2. Initial setting of idle mixture screw (A—Fig. C4-3) is one turn out from a lightly seated position. Final adjustment of carburetor must be made with engine at normal operating temperature and motor running with normal load. Standard main jet sizes should be correct for operation below 5000 ft. altitude. Standard main jet for all models equipped with MD type carburetors is 0.039 inch. Standard size main jet is 0.037 inch with CO6A, 0.032 inch with CO6B and 0.033 inch with CO6C carburetor. Standard size main jet for 8 hp models is 0.049 inch with CO4A, 0.047 inch with CO4B and 0.045 inch with CO4C, CO4D or CO6C.

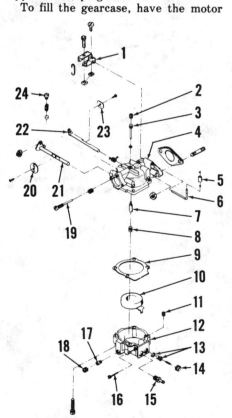

Fig. C4-1—Exploded view of CO type carburetor.

1. Adjusting arm
2. By-pass tube
3. Throttle cam roller
4. Throttle cam follower
5. Idle screw
6. Throttle body
7. Main nozzle
8. Float
9. Gasket
10. Float bowl
11. Retaining screw
12. Main jet
13. Inlet valve
14. Choke friction ball
15. Choke assembly
16. Choke shaft
17. Throttle shaft
18. Throttle plate
19. Throttle return spring
20. Welch plug

Fig. C4-2—Exploded view of MD type carburetor.

1. Adjusting arm
2. Idle plug screw
3. Idle tube
4. Throttle body
5. Throttle cam roller
6. Throttle cam follower
7. Nozzle
8. Main nozzle plug
9. Gasket
10. Float
11. Set screw
12. Float bowl
13. Inlet valve
14. Plug
15. Fuel connector
16. Float pin
17. Main jet
18. Plug screw
19. Idle screw
20. Choke plate
21. Choke shaft
22. Throttle shaft
23. Throttle plate
24. Choke detent plug

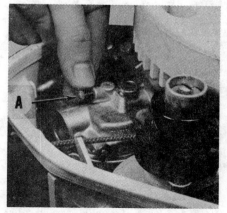

Fig. C4-3—Final adjustment of idle mixture should be done with engine under load and at operating temperature.

End of float (10—Fig. C4-2) opposite pivot in MD type carburetors should be 1/64 inch below surface of float bowl (12) with float bowl inverted. Correct float height of CO type carburetor is 13/32 inch. Height is checked by inverting carburetor body and measuring distance from bottom of float to gasket surface of carburetor body. Refer to Fig. C4-4. Adjustment is accomplished by bending tang on float.

SPEED CONTROL LINKAGE. The speed control lever or grip is connected to the magneto stator plate to advance or retard the ignition timing. Throttle linkage is synchronized to open the throttle as magneto timing is advanced. It is very important that the throttle linkage be properly synchronized for best performance.

Throttle pick-up point is adjusted in the following manner: with engine turned off, turn idle speed stop screw (14—Fig. C4-6) until pick-up mark on throttle cam plate (Fig. C4-5) is in approximate position shown. Turn speed control grip slowly until throttle cam touches roller on throttle cam

follower. Continue to turn speed control grip until carburetor throttle shaft (17—Fig. C4-1 or 22—Fig. C4-2) begins to move. Pick-up mark on throttle cam should be even with or no more than 1/32 inch from roller at this time. Turn screw (A—Fig. C4-5) to adjust throttle pick-up point. Make final adjustment of idle speed stop screw (14—Fig. C4-6) with engine running to obtain idle speed of 700 rpm in forward gear.

REED VALVES. The inlet reed valves are located on reed plate between inlet manifold and crankcase. The reed petals should seat very

lightly against the reed plate throughout their entire length, with the least possible tension. Check seating visually. End of reed stops (2—Fig. C4-7) should be 17/64 inch from reed plate (4) when installed.

Renew reeds if petals are broken, cracked, warped, rusted or bent. Never attempt to bend a reed petal or to straighten a damaged reed. Never install a bent or damaged reed. Seating surface of reed plate should be smooth and flat. When installing reeds or reed stop, make sure that petals are centered over the inlet holes in reed plate, and that the reed stops are centered over reed petals.

FUEL PUMP. A diaphragm type fuel pump is mounted on the side of power head cylinder block and ported to the upper crankcase. Pressure and vacuum pulsations from the crankcase are directed through the port (1—Fig. C4-8) to the rear of the diaphragm (2). When the powerhead piston moves upward in its cylinder, vacuum in the crankcase draws the diaphragm inward and fuel enters the pump through filter

Fig. C4-4—Float level of CO type carburetor should be 13/32 inch measured at (A).

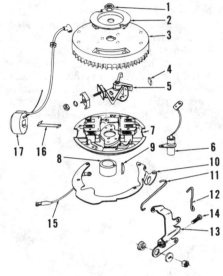

Fig. C4-6—Exploded view of flywheel and breaker assembly base plate used.

1. Nut
2. Starter collar
3. Flywheel
4. Felt wiper
5. Breaker points
6. Condenser
7. Base plate
8. Point cam
9. Woodruff key
10. Throttle cam
11. Throttle link
12. Speed control link
13. Control lever
14. Idle stop screw
15. Ground wire
16. Wedge spring
17. Coil/plug lead

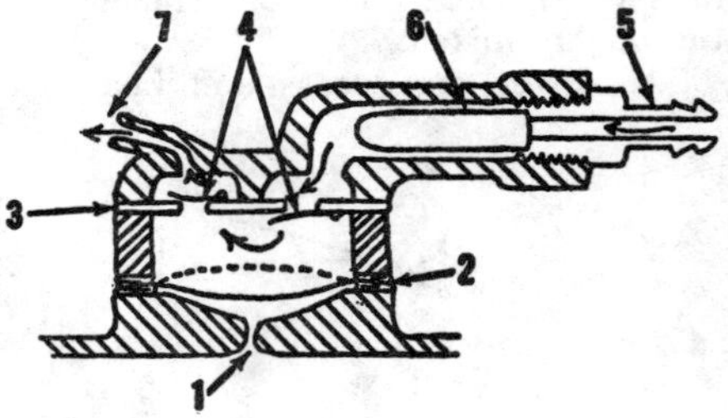

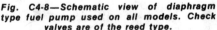

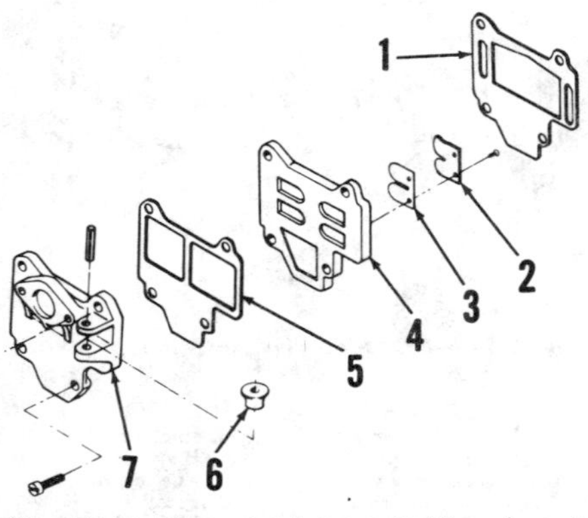

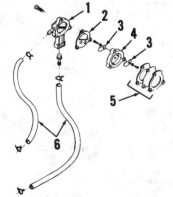

Fig. C4-8—Schematic view of diaphragm type fuel pump used on all models. Check valves are of the reed type.

1. Pressure port
2. Diaphragm
3. Reed plate
4. Check valve
5. Inlet fitting
6. Filter
7. Outlet

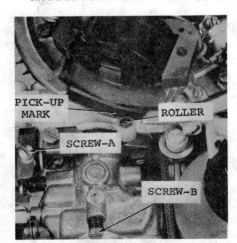

Fig. C4-5—View of throttle pick-up point timing. Adjust pick-up point by turning screw (A). Refer to text for procedure.

Fig. C4-7—View of inlet manifold and reed plate assembly.

1. Gasket
2. Reed stop
3. Reed petal
4. Reed plate
5. Gasket
6. Start rope pulley
7. Manifold

Fig. C4-9—Exploded view of fuel pump assembly common to all models.

1. Pump cover
2. Gasket
3. Pump valve (2 used)
4. Plate
5. Diaphragm & gaskets
6. Fuel lines

(6) and the inlet reed valve (4) in reed plate (3). As power head forces the diaphragm outward into fuel chamber, and fuel passes through the outlet reed valve into carburetor line (7).

Defective or questionable parts should be renewed. Pump valves (3—Fig. C4-9) should seat lightly and squarely on reed plate (4). Diaphragm should be renewed if air leaks or cracks are found, or if deterioration is evident.

IGNITION

Breaker point gap should be 0.020 inch for each set of points, and can be adjusted after the flywheel is removed. Both sets of points must be adjusted exactly alike.

NOTE: High point of breaker cam coincides with location of flywheel key.

Align key with the contact point rub block when adjusting points.

The tapered bore in flywheel and end of crankshaft must be clean, dry and smooth before installing flywheel. The flywheel nut should be torqued to 480 inch-pounds torque. Spark plug electrode gap should be set at 0.030 inch.

COOLING SYSTEM

WATER PUMP. All motors are equipped with a rubber impeller type water pump. When cooling system problems are encountered check the water inlet for plugging or partial stoppage. Remove lower unit gearcase and inspect water passages, water pump and sealing surfaces if previous check revealed nothing.

Water pump is removed in the following manner: Remove four screws that secure lower unit. Pull lower unit away from motor leg and remove shift rod screw (A—Fig. C4-10). Pull lower unit free of motor. Remove screws holding water pump to lower unit and slide pump off drive shaft.

NOTE: Pumps on some motors are secured with three screws. The longest of these three screws must be installed next to the seal (8—Fig. C4-15).

When reassembling water pump, make certain that slot in impeller is down toward back plate. A top plate (34—Fig. C4-15) is used only in pumps secured by three screws. Top plate is installed between impeller and pump body. A drive shaft seal is used only on pump bodies secured with four screws. Make certain tabs on water tube seal

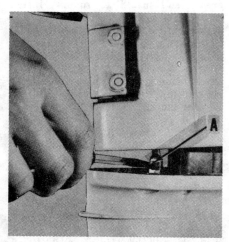

Fig. C4-10—Remove shift rod screw (A) to free lower unit. Socket head screws are used on late models.

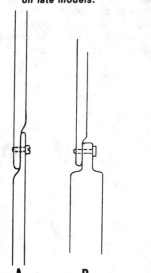

Fig. C4-11—Upper and lower shift rods must be aligned as shown in view "A" for all models except Sailor or view "B" for Sailor models.

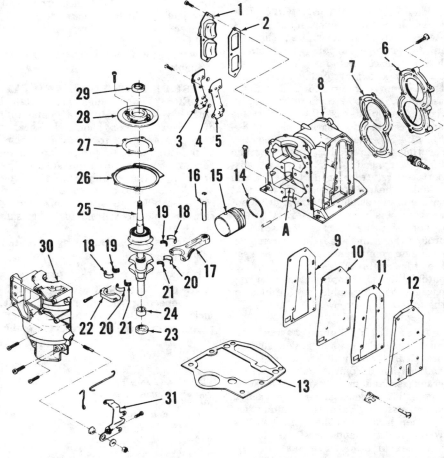

Fig. C4-12—Exploded view of power head. Construction is similar to all models.

1. Transfer port cover	12. Exhaust cover	21. Rod bearing rollers (24 per set)
2. Gasket	13. Gasket	22. Rod cap
3. Drain cover & check valves	14. Piston rings	23. Crankshaft seal
4. Drain screens	15. Piston	24. Lower main bearing
5. Gasket	16. Piston pin	25. Crankshaft
6. Cylinder head	17. Connecting rod	26. Stator ring
7. Head gasket	18. Main bearing liner	27. Bearing cage gasket
8. Cylinder block	19. Main bearing rollers (26 per set)	28. Bearing cage
9. Exhaust cover gasket	20. Rod bearing liner	29. Crankshaft seal
10. Exhaust plate		30. Crankcase half
11. Exhaust cover gasket		31. Speed control lever

are fully seated in pump on reassembly. Make certain that all seals are in good condition and lubricated with a light grease on reassembly. Screws that secure pump body should be coated with an anti-seize compound before installation.

Center line of screw hole in lower shift rod (4—Fig. C4-15 or 5—Fig. C4-16) must be 3/16 inch (plus or minus 3/64 inch) below top of lower unit gear case with unit in neutral. Same tolerance applies to top of motor leg extension (32—Fig. C4-15), if used. A longer lower shift rod is used on these models.

Shift rods should be aligned as shown in Fig. C4-11. If rods are assembled incorrectly, shift rod seal may be damaged. Be sure that water tube is seated in seal when assembling.

POWER HEAD

R&R AND DISASSEMBLY. Disassemble motor for overhaul as follows: Remove engine top cowl, tie a slip knot in starter rope at pulley and remove handle. Disconnect fuel line (at carburetor) and magneto control link, then remove magneto and starter assembly. Remove carburetor adapter flange/reed plate assembly, starter and upper crankshaft bearing cage (28—Fig. C4-12). Remove the six screws securing power head to motor leg and lift power head off. Remove exhaust port covers, transfer port covers and cylinder head. Remove screws that secure crankcase half (30) and drive out locating pins between cases. A screwdriver may be used at pry points around the crankcase to aid in removal.

Engine components are now accessible for removal and overhaul as outlined in the appropriate following paragraphs. Assemble as outlined in the following section.

ASSEMBLY. When reassembling, make sure all joint and gasket surfaces are clean, free from nicks and burrs and hardened cement or carbon. The crankcase and inlet manifold must be completely sealed against both vacuum and pressure. Exhaust manifold and cylinder head must be sealed against water leakage and pressure. Mating surfaces of exhaust areas between power head and motor leg must form a tight seal.

Whenever power head is disassembled, it is recommended that all gasket surfaces, and mating surfaces without gaskets, be carefully checked for nicks and burrs and warped surfaces which might interfere with a tight seal. The cylinder head, head end of cylinder block, and some mating surfaces of

manifolds and crankcase may be checked, and lapped if necessary, to provide a smooth surface. Do not remove any more metal than is necessary.

Make certain that all mating surfaces are clean and then coated with a non-hardening type sealer, such as Loctite "Fit-All", before installing crankcase cover. Coat all screws with a non-hardening type sealer and install in case cover. Screws around main bearings (5/16 inch) should be tightened to 155-165 inch-pounds torque. Apply a coating of light grease between the lips of a new lower main seal (23) and install seal on crankshaft with spring loaded tip toward outside of crankcase. Drive seal into bore until fully seated then stake engine case in two places with a center punch. Punch marks should be 180° apart and about 1/8 inch from mating surfaces of cylinder block and crankcase cover. Marks should be placed 1/16 inch from seal bore and should force material a minimum of 0.005 inch out over seal backing.

Oversize or undersize parts are not available.

PISTON, PINS, RINGS AND CYLINDERS. Piston rings are installed with beveled edge toward dome (top) of piston. Pistons should be heated before attempting to remove or reinstall piston pins. If pistons are to be reused, they must be reinstalled in the original position. Apply a light coating of SAE 30 motor oil to pistons and rings. Install pistons with long sloping side of dome toward exhaust port side of cylinder.

Oversize pistons and rings are not available.

CONNECTING RODS, BEARINGS AND CRANKSHAFT. Before detaching connecting rods from crankshaft, make certain that rod and rod cap are properly marked for correct assembly

to each other and in the cylinder. The loose needle bearings at crankpin end of connecting rod should be kept with each assembly and not intermixed if they are to be reused.

The cast aluminum connecting rods have 2 steel bearing liners and 24 loose rollers each. Use light grease to hold rollers in position on reassembly. Make certain the correlation marks on the rod and the rod cap are aligned and torque rod cap bolts to 85-95 inch-pounds torque.

Upper crankshaft main bearing is not available as a spare part. Crankshaft and bearing may be returned to manufacturer in exchange for a rebuilt assembly. Center crankshaft main bearing consists of liner (18—Fig. C4-12) which forms outer race and 26 loose needle rollers (19). To assemble center main bearing, place one half of liner in cylinder block with a light coating of grease and install 12 rollers. Install crankshaft, remaining 14 rollers and other half of bearing liner. Position lower main bearing on crankshaft 1/16-3/16 inch from top of bearing bore in cylinder block (A—Fig. C4-12). Lower main seal (23) is installed after assembling crankcase cover (30) to cylinder block.

MANUAL STARTER

Refer to Fig. C4-14 for exploded view of recoil starter assembly common to all models.

To disassemble, remove motor top cowl and flywheel. Remove screw (12—Fig. C4-14) and install rewind key (Chrysler Special Tool #2985) in top of spring arbor (7) where screw (12) was installed. Tighten rewind key and then apply a slight amount of counter-clockwise force so that pinion pin (8) may be removed. Use caution as rewind spring (6) is now free to unwind and will spin the arbor (7) and the rewind key. Slowly allow rewind key to turn and

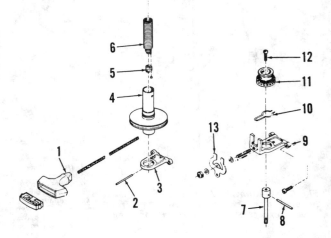

Fig. C4-14—View of recoil starter components used on later 6 and 8 hp models. Early models do not use starter interlock (13).

1. Pull handle
2. Spring pin
3. Lower bracket
4. Start spool and shaft
5. Spring retainer
6. Rewind spring
7. Spring arbor
8. Pinion pin
9. Upper bracket
10. Pinion spring
11. Starter pinion gear
12. Screw
13. Starter interlock

unwind the recoil spring. Pinion, arbor and spring may be lifted free of starter at this time.

Starter rope may be removed after removing upper bracket (9) and starter spool (4). Wind rope in spool counter-clockwise as viewed from top of spool.

Rewind spring should be greased before reinstallation. Assemble arbor (7), spring (6) and spring retainer (5) and install in spool. Grease inside of pinion gear (11) and install on top of arbor. Use rewind key to turn arbor and rewind spring 3½-4 turns counter-clockwise as viewed from the top. Align holes in spool, arbor and slot in pinion gear and partially install pin (8). Remove rewind key while holding end of pin and then complete installation of pin. Install screw (12) in top of starter.

LOWER UNIT

All Models Except Sailor

PROPELLER AND THRUST PIN. A 5/32 x 1-3/16 inch thrust pin is used in all motors. Standard propeller on 5 and 6 hp motors is a 7 inch diameter, 4¾ inch pitch aluminum unit. Standard propeller on 7 and 8 hp motors is a 7½ inch diameter, 6¼ inch pitch aluminum unit. Propellers on all models are two bladed and have right-hand (clockwise) rotation.

R&R AND OVERHAUL. Refer to Fig. C4-15. Remove fill and vent plugs from lower unit and drain all lubricant. Remove four screws that secure lower unit motor leg. Remove gear shift rod screw (A—Fig. C4-10) and separate lower unit from motor leg. Remove screws securing water pump body (9—Fig. C4-15). Remove pump body and drive shaft. Remove thrust pin and propeller. Remove any burrs or rust from exposed end of propeller shaft. Remove two screws holding bearing cage (29) to gear housing. Install two 10-24 x 1½ screws in threaded holes on inside of bearing cage and attach a suitable puller to remove bearing cage.

Shaft seal (30) is not renewable on 1971 and later models. Propeller shaft (21) may be pulled from unit after removal of bearing cage (29). Thrust washer (26) is not used in 1970 and earlier models but, must be reinstalled if fitted. Remove pinion gear (16) and then forward bevel gear (20) after removing propeller shaft. Shift pin (19) is installed in propeller shaft with round end out (forward). Shift cam (6) may be removed by pulling lower shift rod (4) up and removing seal (5) with shift cam.

Assemble by reversing disassembly procedure. Lower shift rod seal (5) should have outside coated with a non-

hardening sealer, such as "Loctite" Fit All, before installation. Install bevel gear (20) and pinion gear (16). Pinion gear is secured with drive shaft (14). Install propeller shaft, thrust washer (if used) and rear bevel gear (27). Propeller shaft seal (30) is installed with spring loaded lip toward propeller. Backlash and mesh position are not adjustable.

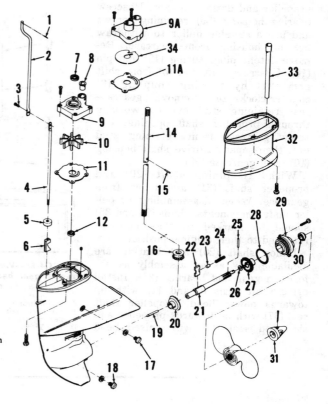

Fig. C4-15—Exploded view of lower drive unit except on Sailor models.

1. Spring pin
2. Upper shift rod
3. Shift rod screw
4. Lower shift rod
5. Shift rod oil seal
6. Shift cam clutch
7. Drive shaft seal
8. Water tube seal
9. Pump body
9A. Pump body
10. Pump impeller
11. Pump back plate
11A. Back plate
12. Drive shaft seal
14. Drive shaft
15. Impeller drive pin
16. Bevel pinion gear
17. Housing plug
18. Housing plug
19. Clutch shift pin
20. Bevel gear
21. Propeller shaft
22. Clutch
23. Clutch guide pin
24. Clutch spring
25. Propeller pin
26. Washer
27. Bevel gear & bearing
28. Shaft seal
29. Shaft bearing cage
30. Drive shaft seal
31. Propeller nut
32. Motor leg extension
33. Inlet water tube extension
34. Top plate

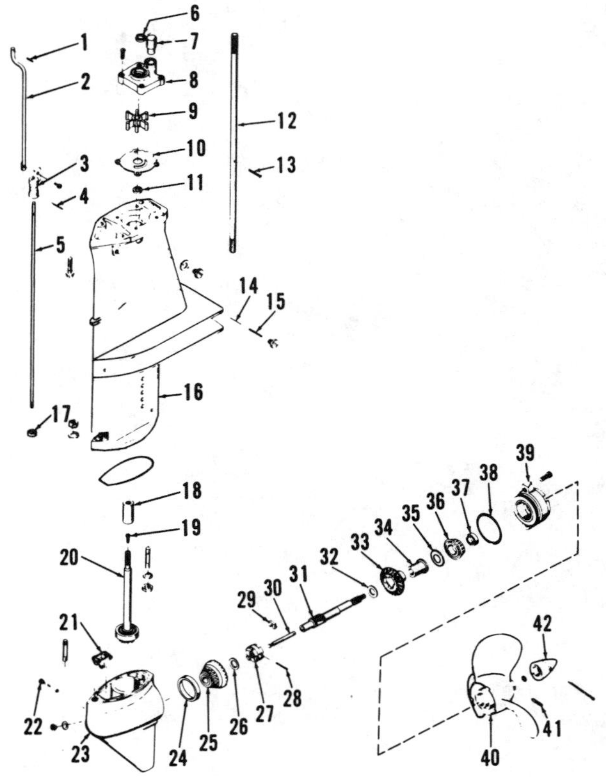

Fig. C4-16—Exploded view of lower drive unit used on 6 hp Sailor models.

1. Spring pin
2. Upper shift rod
3. Connector
4. Spring pin
5. Lower shift rod
6. Seal
7. Water seal
8. Water pump housing
9. Impeller
10. Back plate
11. Seal
12. Drive shaft
13. Impeller drive pin
14. Detent pin
15. Detent spring
16. Drive shaft housing
17. Shift seal
18. Drive shaft coupling
19. Screw
20. Pinion shaft & bearing
21. Pivot coupling
22. Pivot pin
23. Gearcase
24. Bearing cup
25. Forward gear & bearing
26. Shim
27. Shift coupling
28. Shift pin
29. Shift yoke
30. Shift shaft
31. Propeller shaft
32. Thrust washer
33. Reverse gear
34. Bushing
35. Shim
36. Bearing cone
37. Seal
38. Seal
39. Bearing cage
40. Propeller
41. Thrust pin
42. Nut

Sailor Models

R&R AND OVERHAUL. Refer to Fig. C4-16 for an exploded view of lower drive unit used on Sailor models. To disassemble lower drive, remove water pump as previously outlined. Withdraw drive shaft (12), remove propeller and drain lubricant. Unscrew bearing housing (39) retaining screws and use a suitable puller to withdraw bearing housing from gearcase. Remove detent plug, spring (15) and pin (14). Unscrew shift rod (5) from shift arm (21) by turning coupling (3) counter-clockwise. Remove gearcase rear retaining stud nut by working through propeller shaft opening. Unscrew gearcase front retaining stud nut, then separate drive shaft housing (16) from gearcase (23).

Withdraw pinion shaft (20) and propeller shaft (31) assemblies from gearcase. When disassembling propeller shaft components, shims (26 and 35) should be marked so they may be returned to their original position.

Pinion shaft (20) and bearing are available only as an assembly as are forward gear and bearing (25). Install drive shaft seals (6 and 11) with lip towards power head, propeller shaft seal (37) with lip towards propeller and shift rod seal (17) with raised bead

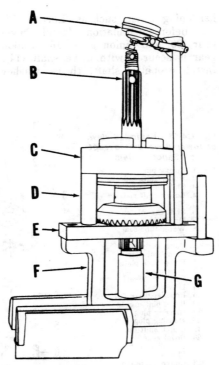

Fig. C4-17—View of set-up for checking reverse gear backlash using Chrysler tools noted below.

A. Dial indicator
B. Propeller shaft
C. Bearing housing
D. Tool T8995

E. Tool T8982
F. Tool T8924-1
G. Tool T8982A

towards power head. Short splined end of drive shaft (12) is inserted into coupling (18).

Screw (19) must be adjusted to obtain desired engagement between crankshaft and drive shaft (12). With pinion shaft assembly (20) in gearcase (23), distance from top of screw (19) to gearcase mating surface should be 7-3/8 inches.

To adjust reverse gear backlash, proceed as follows: Install thrust washer (32), reverse gear (33), bushing (34) and bearing (36) on propeller shaft (31). Bearing (36) must bottom against other components. Install bearing housing (39), without "O" ring (38), on propeller shaft and place assembly in Chrysler special tools shown in Fig. C4-17. Be sure all screws are tight. Propeller shaft end play should be 0.004-0.006 inch to obtain desired reverse gear backlash. Note end play, disassemble propeller shaft assembly and install shims (35) necessary to obtain desired end play.

Check propeller shaft end play after reverse gear backlash has been adjusted. Install components (24 through 39) except "O" ring (38) in gearcase and measure propeller shaft end play. Install shims (26) necessary to obtain 0.004-0.006 inch end play.

CHRYSLER 6, 7.5 AND 8 HP (1978-1984)
(Incl. Sailor)

6 HP MODELS

Year Produced	Model
1978	62H8J, 62B8J, 67H8A, 67B8A
1979	60H9C, 60B9C, 61H9B, 61B9B, 62H9K, 62H9L, 64H9E, 67H9B, 67H9C
1980	60H0D, 60B0D, 61H0C, 61B0C, 64H0F, 65H0A, 65B0A
1981	64H1G, 64B1G
1982	64H2H, 64B2H

7.5 HP MODELS

Year Produced	Model
1979	70H9A, 70B9A, 71H9A, 71B9A, 72H9B, 72B9B, 75H9A, 75B9A, 77H9A, 77B9A
1980	72H0C, 72B0C, 77H0B, 77B0B
1981	71H1B, 71B1B, 72H1D, 72B1D, 77H1C, 77B1C
1982	71H2C, 71B2C, 72H2E, 72B2E
1983	71H3D, 71B3D, 72H3F, 72B3F
1984	71H4, 71B4, 72H4, 72B4

8 HP MODELS

Year Produced	Model
1978	82H8J, 82B8J, 87H8A, 87B8A

CONDENSED SERVICE DATA

TUNE-UP

Hp/rpm	6/4750 7.5/4750	8/5250
Bore – Inches	2.0	2.0
Stroke – Inches	1.584	1.584
Number of Cylinders	2	2
Displacement – Cu. In.	10.0	10.0
Compression at Cranking Speed (Average, with recoil starter)	115-130 psi	115-130 psi
Spark Plug:		
Champion	L86	L86
Electrode gap	0.030 in.	0.030 in.
Ignition:		
Type –		
Models 64H9E, 64H0F		
64H1G, 64B1G, 64H2H, 64B2H	Breaker Point	.....
All Other Models	Breakerless	Breakerless
Breaker Point Gap –		
(Models so equipped)	0.020 in.	.....
Fuel:Oil Ratio	50:1	50:1

TIGHTENING TORQUES
(All Values in Inch-Pounds)

Connecting Rod	75-85
Cylinder Head	130
Flywheel Nut	40 ft.-lbs.
Main Bearing Bolts	70
Spark Plug	120-180
Standard Screws:	
6-32	9
10-24	30
10-32	35
12-24	45
¼-20	70
5/16-18	160
⅜-16	270

LUBRICATION

The power head is lubricated by oil mixed with the fuel. One-sixth (1/6) pint of two-stroke engine oil should be mixed with each gallon of gasoline. Manufacturer recommends use of no-lead automotive gasoline although regular or premium grade gasoline may be used if octane rating is 85 or higher. Gasoline and oil should be thoroughly mixed.

The lower unit gears and bearings are lubricated by oil contained in the gearcase. Manufacturer recommends Chrysler Outboard Gear Lube for use in gearcase. The gearcase should be drained and refilled every 100 hours or once each year, and fluid maintained at the level of the upper (vent) plug hole.

FUEL SYSTEM

CARBURETOR. All models are equipped with the single barrel float type carburetor shown in Fig. C8-1. Initial idle mixture screw (5) setting is one turn open. Refer to following table for recommended main jet sizes:

6 HP

Altitude	Jet Size	Part Number
Sea Level-3000 ft.	0.039	10096
3000-5000 ft.	0.038	10093
5000-7000 ft.	0.037	10086
Above 7000 ft.	0.036	10094

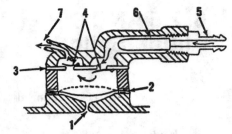

Fig. C8-2—Schematic view of diaphragm type fuel pump. Check valves are of the reed type.

1. Pressure port	
2. Diaphragm	5. Inlet fitting
3. Reed plate	6. Filter
4. Check valves	7. Outlet

7.5 AND 8 HP

Altitude	Jet Size	Part Number
Sea Level-3000 ft.	0.041	10089
3000-5000 ft.	0.040	10097
5000-7000 ft.	0.039	10096
Above 7000 ft.	0.038	10093

Adjust float level so float is parallel to float bowl gasket surface. Be sure float support spring (14) is installed so spring pressure helps float close fuel inlet valve. Install throttle plate with stamped letter towards carburetor rear and with throttle plate hole on idle mixture screw side of carburetor. Install choke plate so stamped number is towards carburetor front and oblong slot is on fuel inlet side.

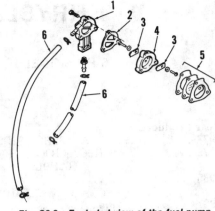

Fig. C8-3—Exploded view of the fuel pump.

1. Pump housing	4. Plate
2. Gasket	5. Diaphragm & gaskets
3. Pump valve (2 used)	6. Fuel lines

SPEED CONTROL LINKAGE. The speed control lever is connected to the ignition stator plate to advance or retard ignition timing. Throttle linkage is synchronized to open throttle as ignition timing is advanced.

Refer to IGNITION TIMING section and check full advance adjustment prior to synchronizing throttle and ignition timing as follows: Turn throttle grip so timing mark on stator plate cam is aligned with cam follower (22–Fig. C8-1) within 1/32 inch. Turn screw (21) so cam follower just contacts cam. Turn throttle grip several times and recheck adjustment.

REED VALVES. A vee type reed block is located between the carburetor and intake manifold. Inspect reed petals and renew petals if they are broken, cracked or bent. Never attempt to straighten a bent reed. Seating surface of reed block should be smooth and flat. Be sure seal (26–Fig. C8-1) is seated in groove around reed block before installing reed block.

FUEL PUMP. A diaphragm type fuel pump is mounted on the side of the cylinder block and ported to the upper crankcase. Pressure and vacuum pulsations from the crankcase are directed through port (1–Fig. C8-2) to the rear of diaphragm (2). When the power head piston moves upward in its cylinder, vacuum in the crankcase draws the diaphragm inward and fuel enters the pump through filter (6) and the inlet reed valve (4) in reed plate (3). When the piston moves down in cylinder, crankcase pressure increases and the fuel pump diaphragm is forced outward into fuel chamber, and fuel passes through the outlet reed valve into carburetor line (7).

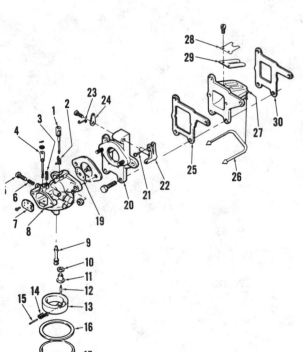

Fig. C8-1—Exploded view of carburetor and reed valve.

1. Throttle shaft
2. Spring
3. Spring
4. Choke shaft
5. Idle mixture screw
6. Spring
7. Choke plate
8. Carb body
9. Nozzle
10. Washer
11. Valve seat
12. Fuel inlet valve
13. Float
14. Spring
15. Float pin
16. Gasket
17. Float bowl
18. Drain plug
19. Throttle plate
20. Intake manifold
21. Screw
22. Cam follower
23. Throttle link
24. Throttle lever
25. Gasket
26. Seal
27. Reed valve body
28. Reed petals
29. Reed stop
30. Gasket

Defective or questionable parts should be renewed. Pump valves (3 – Fig. C8-3) should seat lightly and squarely on reed plate (4). Diaphragm should be renewed if air leaks or cracks are found, or if deterioration is evident.

IGNITION SYSTEM

Magnapower Models

These models are equipped with a breakerless, capacitor discharge ignition system. Refer to Fig. C8-4 for an exploded view of ignition components and to Fig. C8-5 for wiring diagram.

Full throttle and full advance should occur simultaneously. Full advance is limited by stator plate tab (T-Fig. C8-4) contacting a boss on the cylinder block. To check ignition timing, shift unit to forward gear and turn throttle grip to full throttle. Stator plate tab (T) should just contact cylinder block boss at full throttle. If not, adjust length of link (14 – Fig. C8-8). Recheck adjustment.

Tapered bore of flywheel and crankshaft end must be clean, dry and smooth before installing flywheel. Renew a chipped or cracked flywheel. Flywheel and crankshaft tapers may be cleaned by using fine valve grinding compound. Apply grinding compound to tapers and rotate flywheel back and forth approximately one quarter turn. Do not spin flywheel on crankshaft. Clean flywheel and crankshaft tapers thoroughly. Tighten flywheel nut to 40 ft.-lbs. torque.

If ignition malfunction occurs, use Chrysler tool T8953, plug adapter set T11201 and number 22 tester and refer to following trouble-shooting procedure:

Check and make sure ignition malfunction is not due to spark plug failure. If spark is absent at both cylinders, check condition of charge coil as follows:

Separate the blue wire connections between CD coil module and stator and attach single wire plug adapters to each

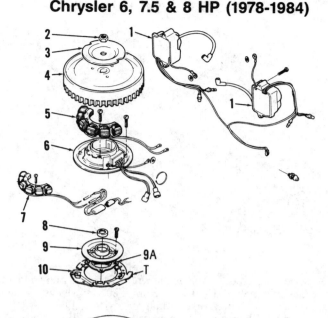

Fig. C8-4 — Exploded view of ignition components. Cam ring tab (T) is full advance stop.

1. CD coil module
2. Nut
3. Rope collar
4. Flywheel
5. Ignition stator
6. Stator plate
7. Alternator stator
8. Seal
9. Seal housing
9A. Gasket
10. Cam ring

Fig. C8-5 — Wiring diagram for models equipped with Magnapower ignition.

B. Black
Bl. Blue
G. Green
O. Orange
R. Red
W. White
Y. Yellow

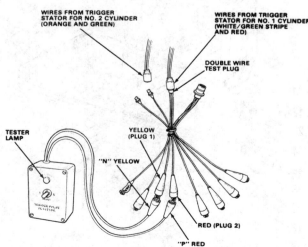

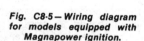

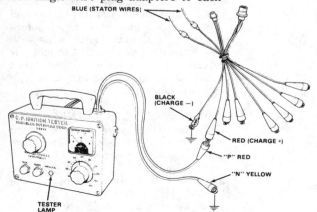

BLUE (STATOR WIRES)

BLACK (CHARGE −)

RED (CHARGE +)

"P" RED

"N" YELLOW

TESTER LAMP

Fig. C8-6 — Tester connections for checking voltage output of charge coils.

WIRES FROM TRIGGER STATOR FOR NO. 2 CYLINDER (ORANGE AND GREEN)

WIRES FROM TRIGGER STATOR FOR NO. 1 CYLINDER (WHITE/GREEN STRIPE AND RED)

DOUBLE WIRE TEST PLUG

TESTER LAMP

"N" YELLOW

YELLOW (PLUG 1)

RED (PLUG 2)

"P" RED

Fig. C8-7 — Tester connections for checking operation of trigger coil.

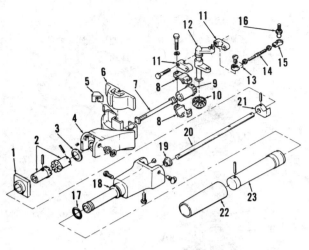

Fig. C8-8 — Exploded view of handle assembly.

1. Bushing
2. Gears
3. Wave washer
4. Steering arm
5. Bumper
6. Mount
7. Shaft
8. Bushings
9. Gear
10. Gear
11. Bushings
12. Towershaft
13. Link end
14. Link
15. Link end
16. Ball joint
17. Seal
18. Steering handle
19. Bushing
20. Shaft
21. Throttle stop
22. Sleeve
23. Grip

be 0.020 inch for each set of points, and can be adjusted after flywheel is removed. Both sets of points must be adjusted exactly alike. Place a mark on the high point of the breaker cam and set breaker point gap for both sets of breaker points with the mark aligned with the breaker point rub block.

The tapered bore in flywheel and tapered end of crankshaft must be clean, dry and smooth before installing flywheel. Tighten flywheel nut to 40 ft.-lbs. torque.

Spark plug electrode gap on all models should be 0.030 inch.

COOLING SYSTEM

WATER PUMP. All motors are equipped with a rubber impeller type water pump. When cooling system problems are encountered, check water inlet for plugging or partial stoppage. Remove lower unit gearcase and inspect water passages, water pump and sealing surfaces. To remove water pump, refer to LOWER UNIT section. Install water pump housing retaining stud in front hole and short (⅞ inch) cap screw in rear hole on all models except Sailor models.

POWER HEAD

R&R AND OVERHAUL. To remove power head, remove upper cover and disconnect linkage, fuel lines and wires which interfere with power head removal. Remove starter and carburetor. Unscrew eight screws on underside of motor leg flange and remove power head.

Remove flywheel and ignition components. Remove cylinder head. Drive out crankcase locating pins (7–Fig. C8-10), unscrew crankcase screws and separate crankcase from cylinder block. Crankshaft and piston assemblies are now accessible. Refer to appropriate paragraph for overhaul of power head components.

Inspect crankcase and cylinder mating surfaces for nicks, burrs or warpage. Use a suitable sealant on crankcase and cylinder block mating surfaces before assembly. Install crankshaft seals with lips towards crankcase. Assembly is reverse of disassembly. Drive shaft splines should be coated with a suitable anticorrosion substance.

PISTONS, PINS, RINGS AND CYLINDERS. Piston rings should be installed with the beveled inner edge toward closed end of piston.

Piston pin (13–Fig. C8-11) should be installed with closed end of pin (C) towards piston ring locating pins (P). Heat piston to approximately 200°F to aid in installation of piston pin. Sharp edge of snap rings (12) should be out.

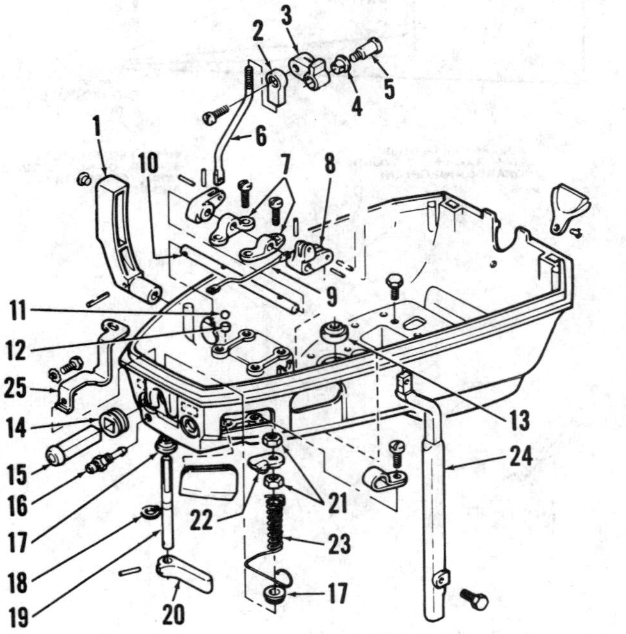

---

wire plug from stator as shown in Fig. C8-6. Attach red (P) lead from T8953 tester to red sleeved adapter wire marked Charge +. Attach yellow (N) lead of tester and black sleeved adapter wire marked Charge – to engine ground. Turn tester switch to position 45 and crank engine. If tester lamp does not light, high voltage windings of charge coil are defective and stator should be renewed. If lamp lights, charge coil operation is satisfactory and trigger coil circuits for each cylinder must be checked. Remove tester and plug adapter set, then reconnect blue wire plugs.

Separate the two wire connection with red and white/green colored wires between CD coil module for number one cylinder and trigger coil and attach double wire plug adapter to wire plug from trigger coil as shown in Fig. C8-7. Attach red (P) lead from tester number 22 to red sleeved adapter wire marked Plug

2 and yellow (N) lead of tester to yellow sleeved adapter wire marked Plug 1. Place switch of tester in number 1 position and crank engine. Trigger coil operation is satisfactory if tester lamp lights. Renew trigger housing if tester lamp does not light.

To check operation of number two cylinder trigger coil, repeat test procedure for number one cylinder trigger coil but attach double wire plug adapter to the two wire connection with orange and green colored wires.

If both stator and trigger coils are in satisfactory condition, then renewal of one or both CD coil modules may be required.

Magneto Models

All models not equipped with Magnapower ignition are equipped with breaker point, flywheel magneto ignition system. Breaker point gap should

Fig. C8-9 — View of lower motor cover and associated parts.

1. Gear shift handle
2. Rod end
3. Shift interlock lever
4. Bushing
5. Screw
6. Interlock shift rod
7. Shaft brackets
8. Shift lever
9. Interlock link
10. Shift shaft
11. Detent ball
12. Detent pad
13. Drive shaft seal
14. Grommet
15. Choke knob
16. Fuel fitting
17. Nyliner bushing
18. Snap ring
19. Latch rod
20. Latch handle
21. Nut
22. Latch cam
23. Spring
24. Upper shift rod
25. Choke link

Assemble piston to rod with piston ring locating pins (P) up and rod cap alignment marks (M) toward the right.

CONNECTING ROD, CRANKSHAFT AND BEARINGS. Assemble connecting rod on piston pin as outlined in previous section. Install rod and piston assembly in cylinder so alignment marks on rod are towards port side of engine. Connecting rod rides on a caged roller bearing with sixteen rollers. Be sure marks on rod and cap are correctly aligned. Tighten rod screws to 75-85 in.-lbs.

Upper crankshaft main bearing is not available separate from crankshaft. Center crankshaft main bearings consists of liner (15–Fig. C8-10) which forms outer race for 26 loose bearing rollers (20). A roller bearing is used on crankshaft lower end. Be sure to install center seal ring (23) around crankshaft prior to assembly.

MANUAL STARTER

All models are equipped with the manual starter shown in Fig. C8-12. Starter gear (11) engages the flywheel ring gear. Starter interlock (13) prevents starter gear rotation except when unit is in neutral.

To disassemble starter, remove starter interlock (13) and screw (12).

NOTE: Screw (12) locks pin (8) in place in starter shaft.

Thread the special "T" handle tool T2985 in threaded hole from which screw (12) was removed. Tighten the

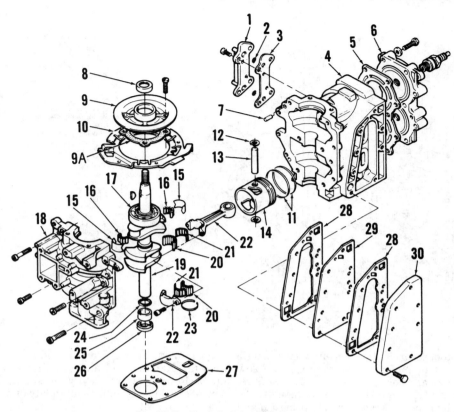

Fig. C8-10 — Exploded view of power head.

1. Cylinder drain cover	16. Main bearing rollers (26 per set)
2. Screen	17. Ball bearing
3. Gasket	18. Crankcase
4. Cylinder block	19. Crankshaft
5. Head gasket	20. Rod bearing rollers (16 per set)
6. Cylinder head	21. Bearing cage
7. Dowel pins (2)	22. Rod & cap
8. Oil seal	23. Center seal ring
9. Seal housing	24. Crankshaft inner seal
9A. Gasket	25. Bearing
10. Cam ring	26. Seal
11. Piston rings	27. Gasket
12. Pin retainer rings	28. Gasket
13. Piston pin	29. Exhaust plate
14. Piston	30. Exhaust cover
15. Main bearing liner	

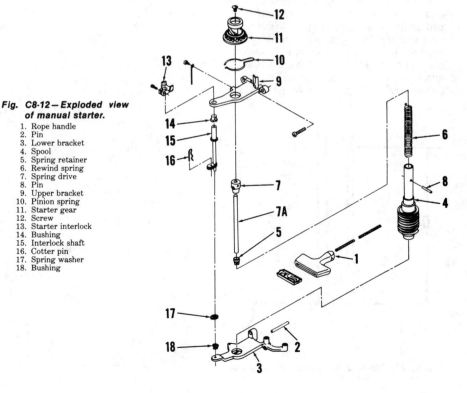

Fig. C8-12 — Exploded view of manual starter.

1. Rope handle
2. Pin
3. Lower bracket
4. Spool
5. Spring retainer
6. Rewind spring
7. Spring drive
8. Pin
9. Upper bracket
10. Pinion spring
11. Starter gear
12. Screw
13. Starter interlock
14. Bushing
15. Interlock shaft
16. Cotter pin
17. Spring washer
18. Bushing

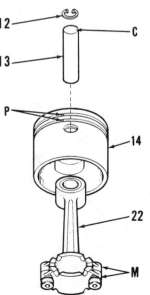
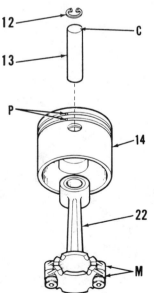

Fig. C8-11 — Assemble piston pin (13), piston (14) and rod (22) as shown. Refer to text.

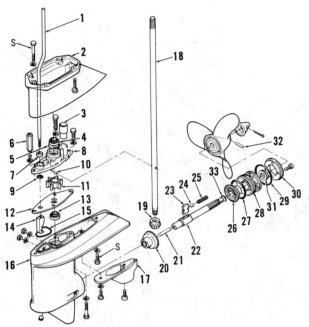

Fig. C8-13 — Exploded view of gear housing.

1. Shift rod
2. Motor leg extension
3. Water seal
4. Seal
5. Spacer
6. Stud
7. Seal
8. Water pump housing
9. Seal
10. Impeller pin
11. Impeller
12. Pump plate
13. Seal
14. Shift cam
15. Seal
16. Gear housing
17. Exhaust outlet
18. Drive shaft
19. Pinion gear
20. Forward gear & bearing
21. Shift pin
22. Propeller shaft
23. Shift dog
24. Pin
25. Spring
26. Reverse gear
27. "O" ring
28. Bearing & cage
29. "O" ring
30. Retainer
31. Seal
32. Thrust pin
33. Thrust washer

per shift rod to lower shift rod (1 – Fig. C8-13). Remove four screws retaining motor leg extension to motor leg and separate extension and gear housing from motor leg. Remove exhaust outlet (17). Unscrew screws (S) and separate extension (2) from gear housing.

To disassemble gear housing, unscrew lower shift rod (1). Remove screws and stud (6) retaining water pump and remove water pump (8), impeller pin (10) and plate (12). Withdraw drive shaft (18) and remove seal (13). Remove propeller and screws securing bearing cage retainer (30). Using Chrysler tool T8948-1 or suitable equivalent, pull bearing cage retainer (30) out of gear housing. Use same tool to withdraw bearing cage (28) from housing. Remove reverse gear (26) and thrust washer (33). Withdraw propeller shaft (22) and remove pinion gear (19) and forward gear (20). Depress pin (24) against spring (25) to release shift dog (23). Remove shift cam (14).

To reassemble lower unit, reverse disassembly procedure while noting following points: Install seal (31) in bearing carrier (28) with spring side of seal towards "O" ring groove. Seal must be flush with or 0.030 inch below face of bearing carrier. Shift cam (14) must be in forward (up) position when installing bearing carrier (28) or carrier will not seat properly. Install seal (13) with spring side towards water pump. Install shift rod seal (7) with raised bead facing out. Seal must be flush with or 0.010 inch below chamfer in seal bore. Install

tool securely, then carefully push pin (8) out of pinion and starter spool. Allow tool and spring drive (7) to turn until rewind spring (6) is unwound; then use the tool to withdraw rewind spring (6) and drive (7) from center of starter spool (4). Guide post (7A) and spring retainer (5) can be lifted out after rewind spring is removed.

Rewind spring, gear (11) or associated parts can be renewed at this time. To renew starter rope, remove brackets securing spool.

Thread the new rope through hole in end of spool and install rope retainer approximately ½ inch from end. Wind rope of spool and install spool, brackets and rope guide. Install rewind spring assembly and gear (11). Use "T" handle tool to wind rewind spring counterclockwise eight turns. Align holes in gear (11),

spool (4) and spring drive (7) and insert pin (8). Remove tool and install screw (12). Rewind spring cavity of starter spool should be filled with lubriplate or a similar grease.

LOWER UNIT

All Models Except Sailor

R&R AND OVERHAUL. To remove lower unit, remove screw securing up-

Fig. C8-15 — Exploded view of lower drive unit on Sailor models.

1. Intermediate shift rod
2. Locknut
3. Connector
4. Spring pin
5. Lower shift rod
6. Seal
7. Water seal
8. Water pump housing
9. Impeller
10. Back plate
11. Seal
12. Drive shaft
13. Impeller drive pin
14. Spring guide
15. Detent spring
16. Drive shaft housing
17. Shift seal
18. Drive shaft coupling
19. Screw
20. Pinion shaft & bearing
21. Pivot coupling
22. Pivot pin
23. Gearcase
24. Bearing cup
25. Forward gear & bearing
26. Shim
27. Shift coupling
28. Shift pin
29. Shift yoke
30. Shift shaft
31. Propeller shaft
32. Thrust washer
33. Reverse gear
34. Bushing
35. Shim
36. Bearing cone
37. Seal
38. Seal
39. Bearing cage
40. Propeller
41. Shear pin
42. Nut

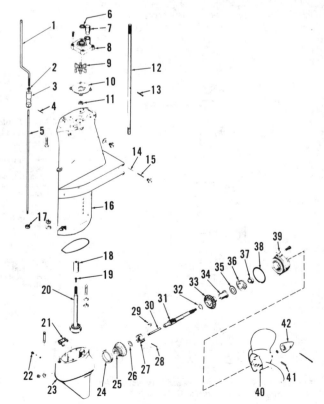

Fig. C8-14 — Distance (D) should be 5.76-6.56 inch. See text.

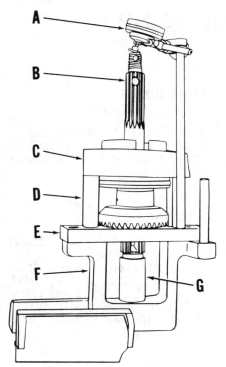

retaining screws and using a suitable puller remove bearing housing from gearcase. Remove detent plug, spring (15) and pin (14). Unscrew shift rod (5) from shift arm (21) by turning coupling (3) counterclockwise. Remove gearcase rear retaining stud nut by working through propeller shaft opening. Unscrew gearcase front retaining stud nut, then separate drive shaft housing (16) from gearcase (23).

Withdraw pinion shaft (20) and propeller shaft (31) assemblies from gearcase. When disassembling propeller shaft components, shims (26 and 35) should be marked so they may be returned to their original position.

Pinion shaft (20) and bearing are available only as an assembly as are forward gear and bearing (25). Install drive shaft seals (6 and 11) with lip towards power head, propeller shaft seal (37) with lip towards propeller and shift rod seal (17) with raised bead towards power head. Short splined end of drive shaft (12) is inserted into coupling (18).

Screw (19) must be adjusted to obtain desired engagement between crankshaft and drive shaft (12). With pinion shaft assembly (20) in gearcase (23), distance from top of screw (19) to gearcase mating surface should be 7⅜ inches.

To adjust reverse gear backlash, proceed as follows: Install thrust washer (32), reverse gear (33), bushing (34) and bearing (36) on propeller shaft (31). Bearing (36) must bottom against other components. Install bearing housing (39) without "O" ring (38) on propeller shaft and place propeller shaft assembly in Chrysler special tools shown in Fig. C8-16. Be sure all screws are tight. Propeller shaft end play should be 0.004-0.006 inch to obtain desired reverse gear backlash. Note end play, disassemble propeller shaft assembly and install shims (35 – Fig. C8-15) necessary to obtain desired end play.

Check propeller shaft end play after reverse gear backlash has been adjusted. Install components (24 through 39) except "O" ring (38) in gearcase and measure propeller shaft end play. Install shims (26) necessary to obtain 0.004-0.006 inch end play.

Adjust height of intermediate shift rod (1) by screwing rod in or out of connector (3). Turn shift rod so bend in rod is towards drive shaft as shown in Fig. C8-14. With gear housing shifted to neutral, distance from drive shaft housing surface to lower edge of shift rod screw hole should be 5.76-6.56 inch. See Fig. C8-14.

Fig. C8-16 — View of set-up for checking reverse gear backlash using Chrysler tools noted below.

A. Dial indicator
B. Propeller shaft
C. Bearing housing
D. Tool T8995
E. Tool T8982
F. Tool T8924-1
G. Tool T8982A

spacer (5) in water pump housing. Install seal (4) with spring side up and bottom seal against spacer (5).

Adjust height of lower shift rod (1) by screwing rod in or out of shift cam (14). Turn shift rod so bend in rod is towards drive shaft as shown in Fig. C8-14. With gear housing shifted to neutral, distance from motor leg extension surface to lower edge of shift rod screw hole should be 5.76-6.56 inch. See Fig. C8-14.

Sailor Models

R&R AND OVERHAUL. Refer to Fig. C8-15 for an exploded view of lower drive unit used on Sailor models. To remove lower drive unit, remove screw securing upper shift rod to intermediate shift rod (1). Remove four screws retaining drive shaft housing (16) to motor leg and separate housing assembly from motor leg. Detach intermediate shift rod (1) from lower shift rod (5). Remove water pump housing (8), impeller (9), drive shaft (12) with pin (13) and back plate (10). Remove propeller and drain lubricant. Unscrew bearing housing (39)

Fig. C8-17 — Exploded view of motor leg.

1. Bracket bolt
2. Pin
3. Starboard bracket
4. Handle
5. Screw
6. Wave washer
7. Tilt lock
8. Spacer
9. Spring
10. Port bracket
11. Lock bar
12. Handle
13. Kingpin
14. Shock mount covers
15. Pin
16. Bushing
17. Bracket
18. Reverse lock
19. Reverse lock spring
20. Reverse lock pin
21. Pin
22. Bushing
23. Reverse lock lever
24. Pin
25. Reverse lock arm
26. Reverse lock shaft
27. Washer
28. Swivel bracket
29. Seal
30. Water tube
31. Gasket
32. Motor leg
33. Idle relief baffle

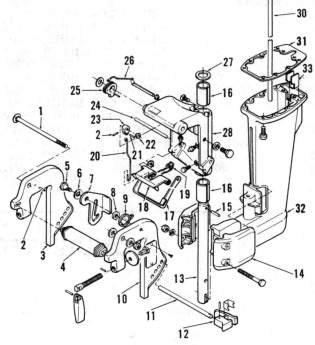

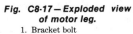

CHRYSLER 9.9, 10, 12, 12.9 AND 15 HP
(Incl. Sailor)

9.9 HP MODELS

Year Produced	Model
1969	907, 908, 917, 918, 923, 924, 933, 934
1970	92HA, 92BA, 93HA, 93BA, 94HA, 94BA, 95HA, 95BA
1971	92HB, 92BB, 93HB, 93BB, 94HB, 94BB, 95HB, 95BB
1972	92HD, 92BD, 93HD, 93BD, 94HD, 94BD, 95HD, 95BD
1973	92HE, 92BE, 93HE, 93BE, 94HE, 94BE, 95HE, 95BE
1979	91H9A, 91B9A, 92H9F, 92B9F, 93H9F, 93B9F, 98H9A, 98B9A, 99H9A, 99B9A
1980	91H0B, 91B0B, 92H0G, 92B0G, 93H0G, 93B0G, 95H0F, 95B0F
1981	92H1H, 92B1H, 95H1G, 95B1G, 98H1B, 98B1B
1982	92H2J, 92B2J, 95H2H, 95B2H, 98H2C, 98B2C
1983	91H3C, 91B3C, 92H3K, 92B3K, 95H3J, 95B3J
1984	91H4, 92H4, 95H4

10 HP MODELS

Year Produced	Model
1974	102HA, 102BA, 102HB, 102BB, 103HA, 103BA, 103HB, 103BB, 104HA, 104BA, 104HB, 104BB, 105HA, 105BA, 105HB, 105BB
1975	102HC, 102BC, 103HC, 103BC, 104HC, 104BC, 105HC, 105BC
1976	100HA (Sailor), 100BA (Sailor), 102HC, 102BC, 102HD, 102BD, 103HC, 103BC, 103HD, 103BD, 108HA, 108BA, 109HA, 109BA
1977	100HA (Sailor), 100BA (Sailor), 102HD, 102BD, 103HD, 103BD, 108HA, 108BA, 109HA, 109BA
1978	101H8A (Sailor), 101B8A (Sailor), 102H8E, 102B8E, 103H8E, 103B8E, 108H8B, 108B8B, 109H8B, 109B8B

12 HP MODELS

Year Produced	Model
1979	121H9A, 121B9A, 122H9E, 122B9E, 123H9E, 123B9E, 125H9E, 125B9E, 128H9A, 128B9A, 129H9A, 129B9A

12.9 HP MODELS

Year Produced	Model
1971	122HA, 122BA, 123HA, 123BA, 124HA, 124BA, 125HA, 125BA
1972	122HC, 122BC, 123HC, 123BC, 124HC, 124BC, 125HC, 125BC
1973	122HD, 122BD, 123HD, 123BD, 124HD, 124BD, 125HD, 125BD

15 HP MODELS

Year Produced	Model
1974	152HA, 152BA, 153HA, 153BA, 154HA, 154BA, 155HA, 155BA
1975	152HB, 152BB, 153HB, 153BB, 154HB, 154BB, 155HB, 155BB
1976	152HB, 152BB, 152HC, 152BC, 153HB, 153BB, 153HC, 153BC, 158HA, 158BA, 159HA, 159BA
1977	152HC, 152BC, 153HC, 153BC, 158HA, 158BA, 159HA, 159BA
1978	152H8D, 152B8D, 153H8D, 153B8D, 158H8B, 158B8B, 159H8B, 159B8B
1979	152H9E, 152B9E, 153H9E, 153B9E, 158H9C, 158B9C, 159H9C, 159B9C
1980	152H0F, 152B0F, 153H0F, 153B0F
1981	152H1G, 152B1G, 152H1H
1982	152H2H, 152B2H
1983	152H3J, 152B3J, 158H3D, 158B3D
1984	152H4, 158H4

CONDENSED SERVICE DATA

TUNE-UP	9.9 & 10 HP	12.9 HP	12 & 15 HP
Hp/rpm	9.9/4750 10/4750	12.9/5000	12/4750 15/5100
Bore – Inches	2-3/16	2-3/16	2¼
Stroke – Inches	1¾	1-13/16	1-15/16
Number of Cylinders	2	2	2
Displacement – Cu.-In.	13.15	13.62	15.41
Compression at Cranking Speed (average)	105-115†	120-130	125-135‡
Spark Plug: Champion	L4J	L4J	L4J
Electrode Gap – Inches	0.030	0.030	0.030

TUNE-UP (CONT.)	9.9 & 10 HP	12.9 HP	12 & 15 HP
Magneto:			
Point Gap—Inches	See Text	0.020	See Text
Timing	See Text	See Text	See Text
Carburetor:			
Make	See Text	See Text	See Text
Fuel:Oil Ratio			
Normal	50:1	50:1	50:1
Break-In & Severe Service	25:1	25:1	25:1

†Compression pressure for 10 hp HB, BB, HC and BC models is 115-125 psi.
‡Compression pressure for 15 hp 154, 155, 158 and 159 models is 90-100 psi.

*SIZES—CLEARANCES	9.9 HP	12 & 15 HP
Piston Rings:		
End Gap	0.006-0.016 in.	0.004-0.014 in.
Piston to Cylinder Clearance	0.0025-0.0040 in.	0.0025-0.0050 in.
Piston Pin:		
Diameter	0.50000-0.50015 in.	0.50000-0.50015 in.
Clearance (Rod)	Needle Bearing	Needle Bearing
Clearance (Piston)	0.00035 in. tight to	0.00035 in. tight to
	0.00010 in. loose	0.00010 in. loose
Crankshaft Journal Diameters:		
Upper Main	0.9849-0.9853 in.	0.9849-0.9853 in.
Center Main	0.8000-0.8005 in.	0.8000-0.8005 in.
Lower Main	0.7495-0.7500 in.	0.7495-0.7500 in.
Crankpin	0.7496-0.7501 in.	0.7496-0.7501 in.

*Size and clearance specifications are for 1979 and later models.

TIGHTENING TORQUES (All Values in Inch-Pounds)	9.9 & 10 HP	12.9 HP	12 & 15 HP
Armature Screw	300	300	300
Cylinder Head (1969-1978)	125	125	125
(1979-1982)	130	130	130
Flywheel Nut	600	600	600
Spark Plug	120-180	120-180	120-180
Connecting Rod Screws (1969-1978)	120	120	120
(1979-1982)	80	80	80
Standard Screws:			
No. 10-24	30	30	30
No. 10-32	35	35	35
No. 12-24	45	45	45
¼-20	70	70	70
5/16-18	160	160	160
⅜-16	270	270	270

LUBRICATION

The power head is lubricated by oil mixed with fuel. For normal service after break-in, mix 1/6 pint of two-stroke engine oil with each gallon of gasoline. The recommended ratio is one third (⅓) pint of oil per gallon of gasoline for severe service and break-in. Manufacturer recommends using no-lead automotive gasoline although regular or premium gasoline may be used if octane rating is 85 or higher. Gasoline and oil should be thoroughly mixed.

The lower unit gears and bearings are lubricated by oil contained in the gear case. Only a noncorrosive, leaded, EP90, outboard gear oil such as "Chrysler Outboard Gear Lube" should be used. The gearcase should be drained and refilled every 30 hours. Maintain fluid at level of upper (vent) plug.

To fill gearcase, have motor in upright position and fill through lower hole in side of gearcase until fluid reaches level of upper vent plug hole. Reinstall and tighten both plugs securely, using new gaskets if necessary, to assure a water tight seal.

FUEL SYSTEM

CARBURETOR. 9.9 hp motors prior to 1971 were equipped with Tillotson MD type carburetors shown in Fig. C5-1. 1982 through 1984 9.9 and 15 hp motors are equipped with Walbro LMB type carburetor shown in Fig. C5-2. All other models are equipped with Tillotson CO type carburetor shown in Fig. C5-3. Refer to appropriate following paragraph and exploded view for service.

Tillotson CO and MD carburetors are equipped with a pilot air screw which controls the idle mixture by determining the amount of air in the idle mixture. Initial setting of pilot air screw (Fig. C5-4) is one turn open. Turn pilot air screw clockwise to richen idle mixture or counterclockwise to lean idle mixture. Walbro LMB carburetors are equipped with an idle mixture screw that controls amount of idle mixture entering carburetor bore. Initial setting of idle mixture screw (C5-5) is one turn open. Turn idle mixture screw clockwise to lean idle mixture. Final carburetor adjustment should be made with engine at normal operating temperature and running in forward gear. Standard main jet size should be correct for operation below 3000 foot altitude. Refer to the following table for standard main jet sizes:

Carburetor Model No.	Main Jet Size
MD 144A	0.059
CO-3A	0.051
CO-5A	0.055
CO-7A	0.047

Carburetor Model No.	Main Jet Size
CO-7B, CO-7C	0.045
CO-8A	0.053
CO-10A, CO-10B	0.055
CO-11A	0.045
LMB-228	0.046
LMB-229	0.0625

End of float (10–Fig. C5-1) opposite pivot in MD type carburetors should be 1/64 inch below surface of float bowl (12) with float bowl inverted. Correct float height of CO type carburetor is 13/32 inch. Height is checked by inverting carburetor body and measuring

distance (A–Fig. C5-6) from bottom of float to gasket surface of carburetor body. Adjustment is accomplished by bending tang on float. Correct float height of LMB type carburetor is 1/8 inch. Height is checked by inverting carburetor body and measuring distance (A–Fig. C5-7) from top of float to gasket surface of carburetor body. Adjust by bending tang on float.

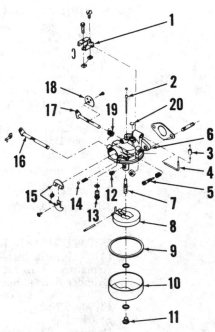

Fig. C5-3 — Exploded view of CO type carburetor.

1. Adjusting arm	11. Retaining screw
2. Bypass tube	12. Main jet
3. Throttle cam roller	13. Inlet valve
4. Throttle cam follower	14. Choke friction ball
5. Pilot air screw	15. Choke assy.
6. Throttle body	16. Choke shaft
7. Main nozzle	17. Throttle shaft
8. Float	18. Throttle plate
9. Gasket	19. Throttle return spring
10. Float bowl	20. Welch plug

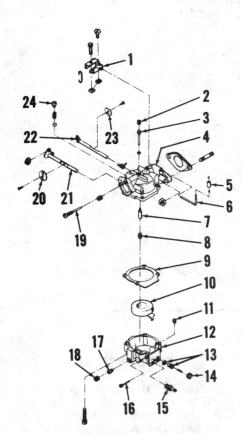

Fig. C5-1 — Exploded view of MD type carburetor.

1. Adjusting arm	13. Inlet valve
2. Idle plug screw	14. Plug
3. Idle tube	15. Fuel connector
4. Throttle body	16. Float pin
5. Throttle cam roller	17. Main jet
6. Throttle cam follower	18. Plug screw
7. Nozzle	19. Pilot air screw
8. Main nozzle plug	20. Choke plate
9. Gasket	21. Choke shaft
10. Float	22. Throttle shaft
11. Set screw	23. Throttle plate
12. Float bowl	24. Choke detent plug

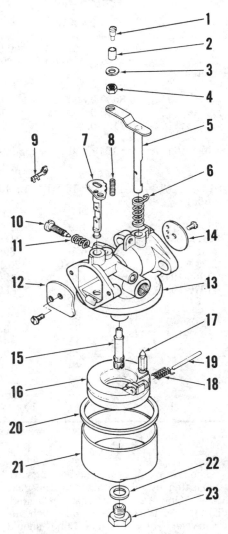

Fig. C5-2 — Exploded view of LMB type carburetor.

1. Adjusting screw	13. Throttle body
2. Throttle roller	14. Throttle plate
3. Washer	15. Main nozzle
4. Nut	16. Float
5. Throttle shaft	17. Inlet valve
6. Spring	18. Spring
7. Choke shaft	19. Float shaft
8. Spring	20. Gasket
9. Clip	21. Float bowl
10. Idle mixture screw	22. Gasket
11. Spring	23. Main jet assy.
12. Choke plate	

Fig. C5-4 — Initial setting for pilot air screw on MD and CO type carburetors is one turn out from a lightly seated position.

SPEED CONTROL LINKAGE. The speed control lever (or grip) is attached to the magneto stator plate and moving the speed control will advance or retard the ignition timing. Throttle linkage is synchronized to open the carburetor throttle as magneto timing is advanced. It is very important that the speed control linkage be properly synchronized for best performance. Adjust linkage with motor not running.

On models prior to 1982 adjustment is as follows: Adjust idle stop screw (Fig. C5-8) until pick-up mark (Fig. C5-9) is to left side of throttle roller (5 – Fig. C5-1 or 3 – Fig. C5-3) as viewed from front side of motor. Turn speed control handle slowly toward the fast position until throttle roller touches cam plate on magneto. Continue turning handle until throttle shaft just begins to move. Pick-up mark on throttle cam should be no more than 1/32 inch from throttle roller at this time. Turn adjusting screw (Fig. C5-9) to change point of throttle opening.

On 1982 through 1984 models, turn speed control handle slowly toward the fast position and observe pick-up mark

(Fig. C5-10) on throttle cam. Throttle shaft should just begin to move when pick-up mark is centered with throttle roller. Turn adjusting screw, if required, to change point of throttle opening.

Adjust idle speed with engine running at normal operating temperature and motor in forward gear. Idle stop screw location on models prior to 1982 is

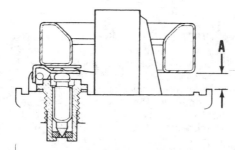

Fig. C5-7 – Float level (A) of LMB type carburetor should be ⅛ inch.

shown in Fig. C5-8 and on 1982 through 1984 models is shown in Fig. C5-11. Turn idle stop screw to obtain idle speed of 700 rpm.

REED VALVES. The inlet reed valves are located on reed plate between inlet manifold and crankcase. Reed petals should seat very lightly against reed plate throughout their entire length, with the least possible tension. Check seating visually. End of reed stops (1 – Fig. C5-12) should be 17/64 inch from reed plate (4).

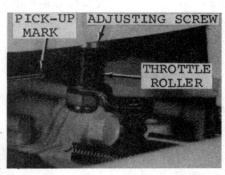

Fig. C5-10 – On motors equipped with LMB type carburetor, pick-up mark on throttle cam should be in the center of throttle roller when throttle shaft begins to move.

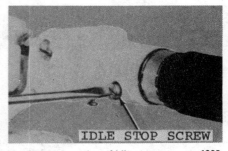

Fig. C5-11 – Location of idle stop screw on 1982 models.

Fig. C5-5 – Location of idle mixture screw on LMB type carburetor.

Fig. C5-8 – Idle stop screw should be adjusted with engine warm to obtain an idle speed of 700 rpm.

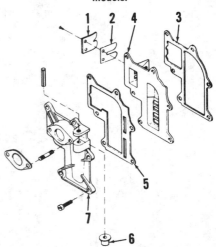

Fig. C5-12 – Exploded view of intake manifold and reed valve assembly.

1. Reed stop
2. Reed
3. Gasket
4. Reed plate

5. Gasket
6. Start rope pulley
7. Manifold

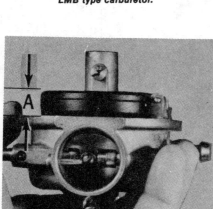

Fig. C5-6 – Float level (A) of CO type carburetor should be 13/32 inch.

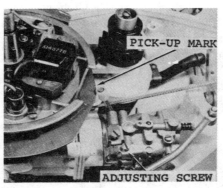

Fig. C5-9 – Pick-up mark on throttle cam should be no more than 1/32 inch from roller when throttle shaft begins to move.

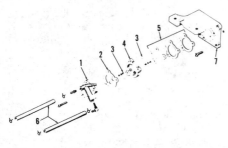

Fig. C5-13—Exploded view of diaphragm fuel pump used on models equipped with Magna-power ignition.

1. Pump cover
2. Gasket
3. Pump valve (2 used)
4. Plate
5. Diaphragm & gaskets
6. Fuel lines
7. Bracket

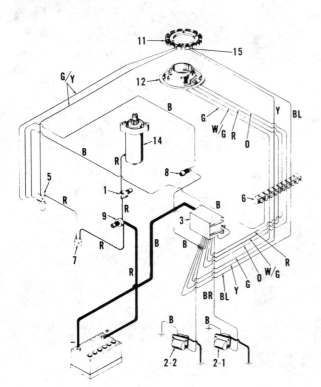

Fig. C5-14 — Exploded view of diaphragm fuel pump used on manual start models.

1. Pump cover
2. Gasket
3. Pump valve (2 used)
4. Plate
5. Diaphragm & gaskets
6. Fuel lines

Renew reeds if petals are broken, cracked, warped, rusted or bent. Never attempt to bend a reed petal or to straighten a damaged reed. Never install a bent or damaged reed. Seating surface of reed plate should be smooth and flat. When installing reeds or reed stop, make sure that petals are centered over the inlet holes in reed plate, and that the reed stops are centered over reed petals.

FUEL PUMP. A diaphragm type fuel pump is mounted on the side of power head cylinder block and ported to the upper crankcase.

Defective or questionable parts should be renewed. Pump valves should seat lightly and squarely on reed plate. Diaphragm should be renewed if air leaks or cracks are found, or if deterioration is evident.

IGNITION

Magnapower Models

These models are equipped with a Magnapower III breakerless, capacitor discharge ignition system. Note wiring diagram in Fig. C5-15. Ignition timing is not adjustable. Tapered bore in flywheel and crankshaft end must be clean, dry and smooth before installing flywheel. Tighten flywheel nut to 50 ft.-lbs. If ignition malfunction occurs, use Chrysler tool T8953 with load coil and number 22 tester from tool T8996 and refer to following trouble-shooting procedure:

Check and make sure ignition malfunction is not due to spark plug or ignition coil failure. If spark is absent at both cylinders, check condition of charge coil as follows: Locate blue wire from charge coils in stator, disconnect blue wire at engine terminal block and connect red (P) lead from tester number 22 to blue wire as shown in Fig. C5-16. Locate yellow lead from charge coil, disconnect yellow lead from engine terminal block and connect lead to ground terminal of terminal block. Connect

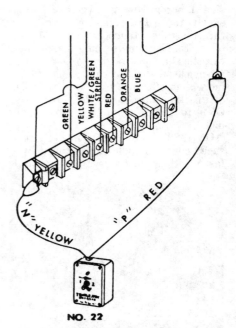

Fig. C5-16 — Tester connections for checking low voltage output of charge coils.

Fig. C5-15 — Wiring diagram of models equipped with Magnapower ignition.

1. Interlock switch
2-1. No. 1 cylinder ignition coil
2-2. No. 2 cylinder ignition coil
3. CD module
5. Rectifier
6. Engine terminal block
7. Circuit breaker
8. Stop switch
9. Starter switch
11. Stator
12. Trigger housing
14. Starter
15. Charge coils
B. Black
BL. Blue
BR. Brown
G. Green
O. Orange
R. Red
W. White
Y. Yellow

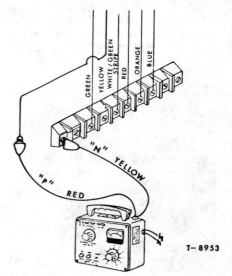

Fig. C5-17—Tester connections for checking high voltage output of charge coils.

yellow (N) lead of number 22 tester to ground terminal of terminal block. Place tester switch in number 2 position and crank engine. If tester lamp does not light, low voltage windings of charge coil are defective and stator should be renewed. If lamp lights, continue charge coil test by reconnecting blue charge coil lead to engine terminal block and connecting yellow charge coil lead to red (P) lead of T8953 tester as shown in Fig.

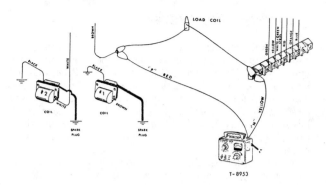

Fig. C5-20—View showing tester connections needed to check CD module output for number 1 cylinder.

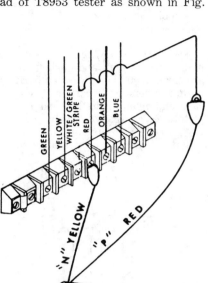

Fig. C5-18—Tester connections for checking operation of number 1 cylinder trigger coil.

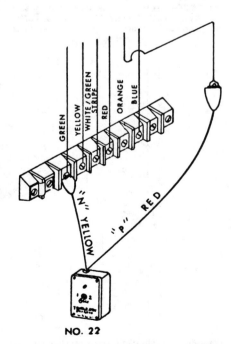

Fig. C5-19—Tester connections for checking operation of number 2 cylinder trigger coil.

C5-17. Connect yellow (N) lead of T8953 tester to ground terminal of engine terminal block. Turn tester switch to position 10 and crank engine. If tester lamp does not light, high voltage windings of charge coil are defective and stator should be renewed. If lamp lights, charge coil operation is satisfactory and trigger coil and CD module circuits for each cylinder must be checked.

To check number 1 cylinder trigger coil, disconnect white/green lead from trigger housing at engine terminal block and connect white/green lead to red (P) lead of number 22 tester. Connect yellow (N) lead of number 22 tester to red wire terminal of engine terminal block as shown in Fig. C5-18. Place switch of tester in number 1 position and crank engine. Trigger coil operation is satisfactory if tester lamp lights. Renew trigger housing if tester lamp does not light. Reconnect white/green lead to engine terminal block. To check operation of number 2 cylinder trigger coil, repeat above test procedure for number 1 cylinder trigger coil but connect red (P) lead of tester to orange wire from trigger housing and yellow (N) lead of tester to green wire terminal as shown in Fig. C5-19.

To check CD module performance for each cylinder, connect yellow (N) lead from tester T8953 to ground terminal of engine terminal block. Disconnect white (number 2 cylinder) or brown (number 1 cylinder) primary lead from ignition coil and connect red (P) lead of tester T8953 to primary lead. Connect leads to tester T8996 load coil to engine terminal block ground terminal and primary coil lead of cylinder being tested as shown in Fig. C5-20. Turn T8953 tester dial to number 50. Crank engine and tester lamp should light. Renew CD module if lamp does not light.

Magneto Models

All models not equipped with Magnapower III ignition are equipped with a breaker point, flywheel magneto ignition system. Breaker point gap should be 0.020 inch for each set of points, and

can be adjusted after flywheel is removed. Both sets of points must be adjusted exactly alike.

NOTE: High point of breaker cam coincides with location of flywheel key. Align key with the contact point rub block when adjusting points.

The tapered bore in flywheel and end of crankshaft must be clean, dry and smooth before installing flywheel. The flywheel nut for manual starting motors should be torqued to 600 in.-lbs. torque. Armature screw for electric starting motors should be tightened to 300 in.-lbs. torque. Spark plug electrode gap should be 0.030 inch.

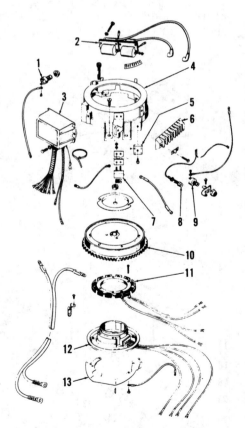

Fig. C5-21—Exploded view of Magnapower ignition components. Refer to Fig. C5-15 for identification except for: 4. Starter support; 10. Flywheel; 13. Throttle cam.

COOLING SYSTEM

WATER PUMP. All motors are equipped with a rubber impeller type water pump. When cooling system problems are encountered, first check the water inlet for plugging or partial stoppage, then if not corrected, remove the lower unit gearcase and check the condition of water pump, water passages and sealing surfaces.

Water pump may be disassembled in the following manner: Place motor on a suitable stand. Place motor in forward gear and remove four screws that secure upper gear housing gearcase to motor leg. Pull away from motor leg and remove screw securing lower end of upper shift rod. Pull gearcase free of motor leg. Refer to Fig. C5-22 or Fig. C5-32. Remove screws that secure pump body to gearcase and slide pump off drive shaft.

Top plate (8 – Fig. C5-22) is used only in pump assemblies that are secured with three screws.

Install impeller with slot in mesh with drive pin in drive shaft.

Water tube seal may be removed by depressing tabs on seal through holes in pump body and pulling on seal. Make certain that tabs are fully seated in holes when installing new seal. Drive shaft seals should be installed with spring loaded lip toward top.

Before reassembling all models except Sailor models, check shift rod adjustment. Center of screw hole in lower shift rod (2) must be 3/16 inch plus or minus 3/64 inch below surface of gear housing (or motor leg extension, if used), with unit in neutral. Refer to Fig. C5-24. Lubricate drive shaft splines and seal lips on all models with a good grade of silicone grease. Assemble upper and lower shift rods as shown in Fig. C5-25 to prevent leakage and damage to shift rod seal. Make certain that water tube is seated in seal and install screws that secure to gearcase motor leg.

POWER HEAD

R&R AND DISASSEMBLE. To overhaul the power head, clamp motor to a stand or support and remove engine cover (shroud), intake silencer and control panel. Remove flywheel, starter, magneto and carburetor. Remove all interfering wiring and linkage, and as many screws as possible retaining inlet manifold, exhaust covers, transfer port covers, cylinder head, etc., before detaching power head from lower unit.

Remove the screws which secure power head assembly to lower unit, and lift off the power head.

Crankshaft and pistons can be removed after removing retainer (28 – Fig. C5-26), then removing crankcase front

half. Exhaust cover (39 & 41), cylinder head (4), transfer port cover (7) and crankcase drain plate (8) should be removed for cleaning and inspection if major repairs are to be performed. Pry lugs are provided adjacent to the retaining dowels, for removing the crankcase front half.

Engine components are now accessible for removal and overhaul as outlined in the appropriate following paragraphs. Assemble as outlined in the ASSEMBLY paragraph.

ASSEMBLY. When reassembling, make sure all joint and gasket surfaces are clean, free from nicks and burrs and hardened cement or carbon. The crankcase and inlet manifold must be completely sealed against both vacuum and pressure. Exhaust manifold and cylinder head must be sealed against

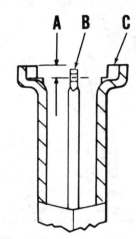

Fig. C5-24—Center of screw hole in lower shift rod (B) must be 3/16 inch (A) below surface of upper gearcase or motor leg extension (C) if installed.

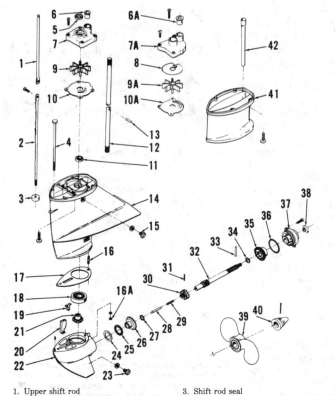

Fig. C5-22 — Exploded view of lower drive unit used on all models except Sailor.

5. Drive shaft seal
6. Water tube seal
6A. Water tube seal
7. Water pump housing
7A. Water pump housing
8. Top plate
9. Rubber impeller
9A. Rubber impeller
10. Bottom plate
10A. Bottom plate
11. Drive shaft seal
12. Drive shaft
13. Water pump drive pin
14. Upper gear housing
15. Vent plug
16. Stud
16A. Stud nut
17. Gasket
18. Ball bearing
19. Shift cam spring
20. Shift cam
21. Pinion gear
22. Lower gear housing
23. Drain plug
24. Bearing race
25. Thrust bearing
26. Forward bevel gear
27. Thrust washer
28. Shift pin
29. Shift pin spring
30. Clutch
31. Pin
32. Propeller shaft
33. Thrust pin
34. Thrust washer
35. Rear bevel gear
36. "O" ring
37. Bearing & cage
38. Seal
39. Propeller
40. Propeller nut
41. Motor leg extension
42. Water tube extension

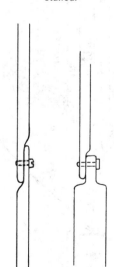

Fig. C5-25 — Upper can lower shift rods must be aligned as shown in view "A" for all models except Sailor or view "B" for Sailor models.

1. Upper shift rod
2. Lower shift rod
3. Shift rod seal
4. Bolt

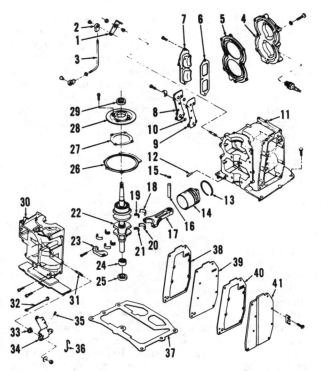

1. Interlock lever
2. Rod end
3. Interlock rod
4. Cylinder head
5. Gasket
6. Gasket
7. Transfer port cover
8. Cylinder drain cover
9. Gasket
10. Screen
11. Cylinder block
12. Locating pin
13. Piston ring
14. Piston
15. Pin retaining clip
16. Piston pin
17. Connecting rod
18. Main bearing liner
19. Main bearing rollers (26 per set)
20. Rod bearing liner
21. Rod bearing rollers (26 per set)
22. Crankshaft
23. Rod cap
24. Lower main bearing
25. Lower seal
26. Stator ring
27. Gasket
28. Retainer
29. Upper seal
30. Crankcase
31. Control lever pivot shaft
32. Throttle link
33. Control lever bearing
34. Control lever
35. Idle speed screw
36. Control link
37. Gasket

water leakage and pressure. Mating surfaces of exhaust area between power head and motor leg must form a tight seal.

Whenever power head is disassembled, it is recommended that all gasket surfaces and mating surfaces without gaskets, be carefully checked for nicks, burrs and warped surfaces which might interfere with a tight seal. The cylinder head, head end of cylinder block, and some mating surfaces of manifolds and crankcase may be checked, and lapped if necessary, to provide a smooth surface.

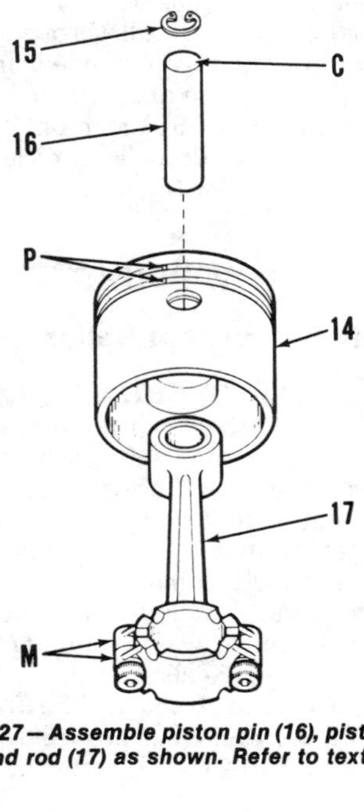

Do not remove any more metal than is necessary.

Mating surfaces of crankcase may be checked on the lapping block, and high spots or nicks removed, but the surface must not be lowered. If extreme care is used, a slightly damaged crankcase may be salvaged in this manner. In case of doubt, renew the crankcase assembly.

A heavy, nonfibrous grease should be used to hold loose needle bearings in position during assembly. All friction surfaces should be lubricated with new engine oil. Check frequently as power head is being assembled, for binding or locking. If encountered, remove the cause before proceeding with the assembly.

Gasket and sealing surfaces should be lightly and carefully coated with a non-hardening gasket cement. Make sure entire surface is coated, but avoid letting

excess cement squeeze out into crankcase, bearings, or other passages. Refer to Fig. C5-28 for cylinder head tightening sequence. When installing crankcase screws, tighten those next to the main bearings and dowels first. Crankshaft seals (29 & 25 – Fig. C5-26) should be renewed each time crankshaft is removed. Refer to CONDENSED SERVICE DATA table for tightening torques.

PISTONS, PINS, RINGS AND CYLINDERS. Piston rings should be installed with the beveled inner edge toward closed end of piston.

Piston pin (16 – Fig. C5-27) should be installed with closed end of pin (C) towards piston ring locating pins (P). Heat piston to approximately 200°F to aid in installation of piston pin. Sharp edge of snap rings (15) should be out.

Assemble piston to rod with piston ring locating pins (P) up and rod cap alignment marks (M) toward the left. When installing piston in cylinder, the long tapering side of piston head should be installed toward the exhaust port side of cylinder. All friction surfaces should be lubricated with new engine oil when assembling.

CONNECTING RODS, BEARINGS, AND CRANKSHAFT. Before detaching connecting rods from crankshaft, make certain that rod and cap are properly marked for correct assembly to each other and in the correct cylinder. The loose needle bearings at crankpin end of connecting rod should be kept with each assembly and not intermixed if reused.

The connecting rods contain 26 loose needle bearing rollers at crankpin end. When reassembling connecting rods make certain that marks (Fig. C5-27) on rod and rod cap are aligned.

Crankshaft upper main bearing is part of retainer (28 – Fig. C5-26). Center main bearing consists of 26 loose needle

Fig. C5-27 — Assemble piston pin (16), piston (14) and rod (17) as shown. Refer to text.

Fig. C5-28 — Tightening sequence for cylinder head screws.

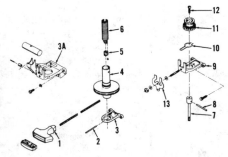

Fig. C5-29 — Exploded view of rewind starter used. Bracket (3A) is used on Autoelectric models. Interlock (13) is used on later models.

1. Pull handle
2. Spring pin
3 & 3A. Lower bracket
4. Spool
5. Spring retainer
6. Rewind spring
7. Spring arbor
8. Pinion pin
9. Upper bracket
10. Pinion spring
11. Starter pinion gear
12. Screw
13. Starter interlock

bearing rollers (19), which are contained in a split outer race (18). Lower main bearing (24) is a caged roller.

Oversize and undersize parts are not available. When assembling, follow the procedures outlined in the ASSEMBLY

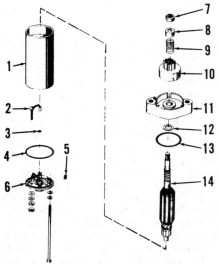

Fig. C5-30 — Exploded view of starter used on models with Magnapower ignition.

1. Starter housing	8. Pinion stop
2. Brushes	9. Spring
3. Disc	10. Pinion
4. Gasket	11. End cap
5. Brush springs	12. Washer
6. End plate	13. Gasket
7. Nut	14. Armature

paragraph. Tightening torques are listed in the CONDENSED SERVICE DATA table.

MANUAL STARTER

Figure C5-29 is an exploded view of the recoil starter assembly common to all manual start models. Unit used on electric start models is of similar construction. Starter pinion (11) engages starter ring gear on flywheel.

To disassemble the starter, first remove the engine cover and flywheel, then remove screw (12) in top of starter shaft.

NOTE: This screw locks pin (8) in place.

Thread the rewind key (Chrysler Special Tool TR2985) in threaded hole from which screw (12) was removed. Tighten the tool until it bottoms, then turn tool handle slightly counterclockwise to relieve recoil spring tension and push out pin (8). Allow the tool and drive arbor (7) to turn clockwise to unwind the recoil spring (6). Pull up on tool to remove the recoil spring and components. Pull rope and rewind spool (4) may be removed after removing top bracket (9). Wind new rope in spool counterclockwise as viewed from the top.

Rewind spring should be greased before installation. Assemble arbor (7), spring (6) and spring retainer (5) and in-

Fig. C5-31 — View of electric starter used on "Autoelectric" models.

1. Cover
2. Armature bolt
3. Starter housing
4. Starter relay
5. Armature
6. Rectifier diode
7. Circuit breaker
8. Woodruff key
9. Spacer
10. Bearing
11. Spacer
12. Starter support
13. Wiring harness
14. Flywheel
15. Condenser
16. Breaker points
17. Stator plate
18. Ignition coil assy.
19. Throttle cam plate
20. Interlock switch cam
21. Woodruff key
22. Point cam
23. Ground lead
24. Battery cable
25. Voltage regulator
26. Interlock switch

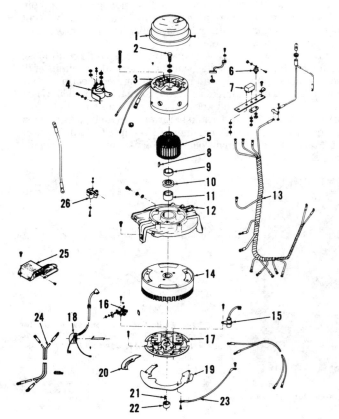

stall in spool. Grease inside of pinion gear (11) and install on top of arbor. Use rewind key to turn arbor and rewind spring 3½-4 turns counterclockwise as viewed from the top. Align holes in spool, arbor and slot in pinion gear and partially install pin (8). Remove rewind key while holding end of pin and then complete installation of pin. Install screw (12) in top of starter.

ELECTRIC STARTER

Sailor models and models with Magnapower ignition are equipped with the electric starter shown in Fig. C5-30. Autoelectric models are equipped with starter-generator shown in Fig. C5-31.

The armature of Autoelectric starter-generator is mounted directly on upper end of crankshaft. The 12 volt battery should be connected with negative terminal grounded. The positive terminal should be connected to the red battery lead. If battery is connected with wrong terminal grounded or if motor is operated without battery, the rectifier (6 – Fig. C5-31) or armature (5) may be damaged. Circuit breaker (7) will normally protect the electrical components.

The housing and field assembly (3) can be removed after disconnecting necessary wires and removing the six mounting screws. Housing (3) must be removed before armature (5) can be removed from crankshaft. Armature screw (2) should be tightened to 300 in.-lbs. torque.

PROPELLER

Both two and three blade propellers are used and are equipped with a thrust pin to prevent damage. Various pitch propellers are available and should be selected to provide full throttle operation within the recommended limits of 4250-5250 rpm on 9.9, 10 and 12 hp motors and 4600-5600 rpm on 12.9 and 15 hp motors. Propellers other than those designed for the motor should not be used.

LOWER UNIT

All Models Except Sailor

R&R AND OVERHAUL. Refer to Fig. C5-22. Attach motor to a suitable stand. Shift motor into forward gear and remove four screws that secure lower unit to motor leg. Pull lower unit away from motor leg far enough to remove screw holding shift rods (1 & 2) together. Pull lower unit free of motor leg. Disassemble water pump (7 or 7A) and remove drive shaft (12).

Propeller shaft bearing cage (37) is removed after removing propeller and installing two 10-24 x 1½ screw in tapped holes in cage to attach puller. Drain lubricant from gearcase and remove two screws that secure propeller shaft bearing cage to gearcase. Install puller and remove bearing cage. Seal (38) is removed by driving it out with a punch from inside the bearing cage.

NOTE: Two types of replacement seals are available. Seals cased in metal are installed with spring loaded lip toward gear housing. Rubber cased seals are installed with spring loaded lip toward propeller.

Internal gears and shaft mechanism may be serviced after removing lower gearcase (22). Disassemble gearcase in the following manner: Remove shift rod (2) by unscrewing it from shift cam (20). Use caution to prevent threads on shift rod from damaging seal (3) when sliding rod out of housing. Remove drive shaft bearing cage as previously described and remove nut (16A). Remove bolt (4) and separate upper and lower gearcase sections.

Shift rod seal (3) may be removed by screwing a 5/16 inch lag screw into seal from the top and then using a 1/4 inch diameter rod to drive lag screw and seal out from the bottom.

When reassembling, make certain that thrust bearing (25) and thrust bearing race (24) are installed as shown in Fig. C5-22. Rounded end of shift pin (28) must be toward shift cam (20). Clutch (30) must be installed so that engagement dogs with chamfered edges are

toward propeller.

Refer to WATER PUMP section for proper adjustment of shift rod (2) on reassembly. Backlash and mesh position of gears is not adjustable. Bottom of bolt head (4) should be coated with a heavy nonhardening sealer and torqued to 125 in.-lbs.

Sailor Models

R&R AND OVERHAUL. Refer to Fig. C5-32 for an exploded view of lower drive unit used on Sailor models. To disassemble lower drive, remove water pump as previously outlined. Withdraw drive shaft (12), remove propeller and drain lubricant. Unscrew bearing housing (39) retaining screws and using a suitable puller remove bearing housing from gearcase. Remove detent plug, spring (15) and pin (14). Unscrew shift rod (5) from shift arm (21) by turning coupling (3) counterclockwise. Remove gearcase rear retaining stud nut by working through propeller shaft opening. Unscrew gearcase front retaining stud nut, then separate drive shaft housing (16) from gearcase (23).

Withdraw pinion shaft (20) and propeller shaft (31) assemblies from gearcase. When disassembling propeller shaft components, shims (26 and 35) should be marked so they may be returned to their original position.

Pinion shaft (20) and bearing are available only as an assembly as are forward gear and bearing (25). Install drive

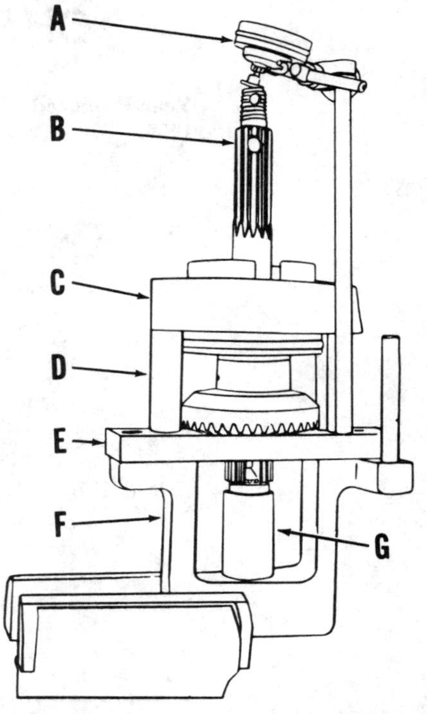

Fig. C5-32 — Exploded view of lower drive unit on Sailor models.

1. Spring pin
2. Upper shift rod
3. Connector
4. Spring pin
5. Lower shift rod
6. Seal
7. Water seal
8. Water pump housing
9. Impeller
10. Back plate
11. Seal
12. Drive shaft
13. Impeller drive pin
14. Spring guide
15. Detent spring
16. Drive shaft housing
17. Shift seal
18. Drive shaft coupling
19. Screw
20. Pinion shaft & bearing
21. Pivot coupling
22. Pivot pin
23. Gearcase
24. Bearing cup
25. Forward gear & bearing
26. Shim
27. Shift coupling
28. Shift pin
29. Shift yoke
30. Shift shaft
31. Propeller shaft
32. Thrust washer
33. Reverse gear
34. Bushing
35. Shim
36. Bearing cone
37. Seal
38. Seal
39. Bearing cage
40. Propeller
41. Shear pin
42. Nut

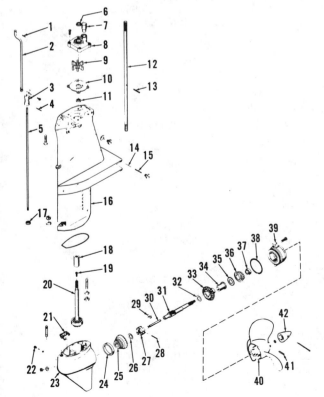

Fig. C5-33 — View of set-up for checking reverse gear backlash using Chrysler tools noted below.

A. Dial indicator
B. Propeller shaft
C. Bearing housing
D. Tool T8995
E. Tool T8982
F. Tool T8924-1
G. Tool T8982A

shaft seals (6 & 11) with lip towards power head, propeller shaft seal (37) with lip towards propeller and shift rod seal (17) with raised bead towards power head. Short splined end of drive shaft (12) is inserted into coupling (18).

Screw (19) must be adjusted to obtain desired engagement between crankshaft and drive shaft (12). With pinion shaft assembly (20) in gearcase (23), distance from top of screw (19) to gearcase mating surface should be 7 3/8 inches.

To adjust reverse gear backlash, proceed as follows: Install thrust washer (32), reverse gear (33), bushing (34) and bearing (36) on propeller shaft (31). Bearing (36) must bottom against other components. Install bearing housing (39) without "O" ring (38) on propeller shaft and place propeller shaft assembly in Chrysler special tools shown in Fig. C5-33. Be sure all screws are tight. Propeller shaft end play should be 0.004-0.006 inch to obtain desired reverse gear backlash. Note end play, disassemble propeller shaft assembly and install shims (35 — Fig. C5-32) necessary to obtain desired end play.

Check propeller shaft end play after reverse gear backlash has been adjusted. Install components (24 through 39) except "O" ring (38) in gearcase and measure propeller shaft end play. Install shims (26) necessary to obtain 0.004-0.006 inch end play.

CHRYSLER 20 HP (1969-1976)

Year Produced	Models
1969	2003, 2004, 2013, 2014
	*2023, *2024, *2033, *2034
1970	202HA, BA, 203HA, BA,
	*204HA, *BA, *205HA, *BA
1971	202HB, BB, 203HB, BB
	*204HB, *BB, *205HB, *BB
1972	202HD, BD, 203HD, BD,
	*204HD, *BD, *205HD, *BD
1973	202HD, 202BD, 202HE, 202BE,
	203HD, 203BD, 203HE, 203BE,
	*204HE, *204BE, *205HD, *205BD,
	*205HE, *205BE
1974	202HF, 202BF, 203HF, 203BF,
	*204HF, *204BF, *205HF, *205BF
1975 & 1976	202HG, 202BG, 203HG, 203BG,
	*204HG, *204BG, *205HG, *205BG

*Electric starting models.

CONDENSED SERVICE DATA

TUNE-UP

Hp/rpm	20/5000
Bore—Inches	2-7/16
Stroke—Inches	2-9/64
Number of Cylinders	2
Displacement—Cu. In.	19.96
Compression at Cranking Speed (average)	115-125 psi
Spark Plug:	
Champion	L4J
Electrode Gap	0.030 in.
Magneto:	
Point Gap	0.020 in.
Timing	See Text
Carburetor:	
Make	Tillotson
Model	MD
Fuel—Oil Ratio	**48:1

**Fuel:Oil ratio 24:1 for severe service.

SIZES—CLEARANCES (All Values in Inches)

Piston Rings:	
End Gap	0.003-0.008
Side Clearance	0.0025-0.0045
Piston to Cylinder Clearance	0.002-0.0035
Piston Pin:	
Diameter	0.56250-0.56265
Clearance (Rod)	Roller Bearing
Clearance (Piston)	0.0001-0.0006
Crankshaft Journal Diameters:	
Upper & Lower Main	0.8120-0.8124
Center Main	0.9295-0.9298
Crankpin	0.8101-0.8104
Crankshaft End Play	0.003-0.006
Rod Side Clearance	0.015-0.025

TIGHTENING TORQUES
(All Values in Inch-Pounds)

Armature Screw	300
Cylinder Head	120
Flywheel Nut	**540
Spark Plug	120-180
Standard Screws:	
No. 10-24	30
No. 10-32	35
No. 12-24	45
¼-20	70
5/16-18	160
3/8-16	270

**Armature screw for electric starting motors should be tightened to 300 inch-pounds torque.

LUBRICATION

The power head is lubricated by oil mixed with the fuel. For normal service after break-in, mix 1/6 pint of two-stroke engine oil with each gallon of gasoline. For severe service and during break-in, the recommended ratio is one third (⅓) pint of oil per gallon of gasoline. Manufacturer recommends no-lead automotive gasoline although regular or premium gasoline may be used if octane rating is 85 or higher. Gasoline and oil should be thoroughly mixed.

The lower unit gears and bearings are lubricated by oil contained in the gearcase. Only a non-corrosive, leaded, EP90, outboard gear oil such as "Chrysler Outboard Gear Lube" should be used. The gearcase should be drained and refilled every 100 hours or once each year, and fluid maintained at the level of the upper (vent) plug hole.

To fill the gearcase, have the motor in upright position and fill through the lower plug hole in the side of gearcase until fluid reaches level of upper vent plug hole. Reinstall and tighten both plugs securely, using new gaskets if necessary, to assure a water tight seal.

FUEL SYSTEM

CARBURETOR. Tillotson, type MD carburetors are used. Refer to Fig. C6-1. Normal initial setting is one turn open from the closed position for idle mixture needle (1). Carburetor must be readjusted under load, after motor is warm, for best low speed performance. The standard main jet (0.069 inch in 1971 and earlier models and 0.067 inch in 1972 and later models) should be correct below 5000 ft. altitude.

To adjust the float, remove and invert the fuel bowl assembly (13).

With bowl inverted and inlet needle valve closed, the lowest point of float at free end should project approximately 1/64-inch below gasket surface of bowl. Adjust by bending the vertical valve fork on float. Float must be

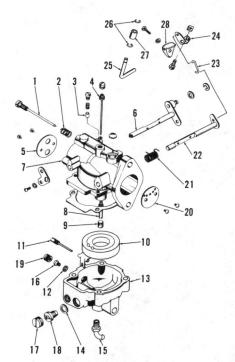

Fig. C6-1—Exploded view typical of Tillotson MD carburetor and cam follower linkage (23 through 28).

1. Idle mixture screw
2. Spring
3. Choke detent
4. Idle tube
5. Choke valve
6. Choke shaft
7. Body
8. Main nozzle
9. Plug
10. Float
11. Float shaft
12. Gasket
13. Body
14. Gasket
15. Fuel inlet fitting
16. Main (high speed) jet
17. Plug
18. Fuel inlet needle seat
19. Plug
20. Throttle plate
21. Spring
22. Throttle shaft
23. Link
24. Lever
25. Cam follower
26. Retaining rings
27. Roller
28. Bracket

removed to renew the inlet needle assembly (18). When installing float, make sure that slot in float lever engages groove in needle.

SPEED CONTROL LINKAGE. The speed control lever or grip is connected to the magneto stator plate to advance or retard the ignition timing. Throttle linkage is synchronized to open the throttle as magneto timing is advanced. It is very important that the throttle linkage be properly synchronized for best performance.

To synchronize the linkage, refer to Fig. C6-2. With the engine not running, loosen the clamping screw (S) in throttle control bellcrank. Move the speed control grip of lever until the scribe mark on throttle cam (2) is aligned with center of cam follower (1). Move cam follower until it just contacts cam at the scribe mark, then tighten screw (S). As speed control grip or lever is moved further to the "Fast" position, the throttle valve should start to open.

Fig. C6-2—View of speed control linkage. Cam (2) rotates with magneto armature plate and should begin to move follower (1) when scribed line on cam is aligned with center of cam follower (2).

The idle speed stop screw (IS—Fig. C6-3) should be adjusted to provide 800-1000 rpm in neutral. Throttle friction is adjusted by turning the inside nut (N) and adjustment is maintained by tightening locknut (L).

REED VALVES. The inlet reed valves are located on reed plate between inlet manifold and crankcase. The reed petals should seat very lightly against the reed plate throughout their entire length, with the least possible tension. Check seating visually. Reed stop setting should be 17/64-inch when measured as shown in Fig. C6-4.

Renew reeds if petals are broken, cracked, warped, rusted or bent. Never attempt to bend a reed petal or to straighten a damaged reed. Never install a bent or damaged reed. Seating surface of reed plate should be smooth and flat. When installing reeds or reed stop, make sure that petals are centered over the inlet holes in reed plate, and that the reed stops are centered over reed petals.

FUEL PUMP. A diaphragm type fuel pump is mounted on the side of power head cylinder block and ported to the upper crankcase. Pressure and vacuum pulsations from the crankcase are directed through the port (1—Fig. C6-4A) to the rear of diaphragm (2). When the powerhead piston moves upward in its cylinder, vacuum in the crankcase draws the diaphragm inward and fuel enters the pump through filter (6) and the inlet reed valve (4) in reed plate (3). As powerhead piston moves downward, pressure forces the diaphragm outward into fuel chamber, and fuel passes through the outlet reed valve into carburetor line (7).

Defective or questionable parts should be renewed. Reed valves (23—Fig. C6-7) should seat lightly and squarely on reed plate (24). Diaphragm should be renewed if air leaks or cracks are found, or if deterioration is evident.

IGNITION

Breaker point gap should be 0.020 inch for each set of points, and can be adjusted after the flywheel is removed.

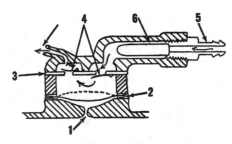

Fib. C6-4A—Schematic view of diaphragm type fuel pump. Check valves are of the reed type.

1. Pressure port
2. Diaphragm
3. Reed plate
4. Check valves
5. Inlet fitting
6. Filter
7. Outlet

Both sets of points must be adjusted exactly alike.

NOTE: High point of breaker cam coincides with location of flywheel key. Align key with the contact point rub block when adjusting points.

The tapered bore in flywheel and end of crankshaft must be clean, dry and smooth before installing flywheel. The flywheel nut for manual starting motors should be torqued to 540 in.-lbs. torque. Armature screw for electric starting motors should be tightened to 300 in.-lbs. torque.

COOLING SYSTEM

WATER PUMP. All motors are equipped with a rubber impeller type water pump. When cooling system problems are encountered, first check the water inlet for plugging or partial stoppage, then if not corrected, remove the lower unit gearcase and check the condition of water pump, water passages and sealing surfaces.

To detach the upper gearcase from the exhaust housing, proceed as follows: Remove covers (1—Fig. C6-5) and shift rod coupling (2—Fig. C6-6). Remove the four nuts (5—Fig. C6-5) and screws (6), then separate the gearcase from the exhaust housing. The water pump can be removed after removing screws (32 & 33—Fig. C6-12). Drive shaft seal (6) should be installed with spring loaded lip toward the top.

When reassembling pumps with three screws holding pump body, notice that screw (32) is 1-1/8 inches long and the two front screws (33) are 1-inch long. Screws are of equal length on pumps secured by four screws. Drive shaft spline seal (28) should be renewed if hard or cracked. Lubricate water tube

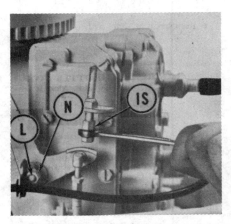

Fig. C6-3—Idle speed is adjusted at stop screw (IS) and throttle friction is adjusted by turning the inside nut (N). Tighten the outside locknut (L) to maintain the correct throttle friction.

Fig. C6-4—Reed stops should be 17/64 inch from seating surface of reed plate.

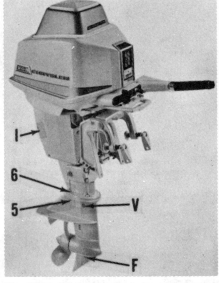

Fig. C6-5—View of 20 hp motor showing two of the screws (6) and nuts (5) that attach upper gearcase housing to motor leg (exhaust housing).

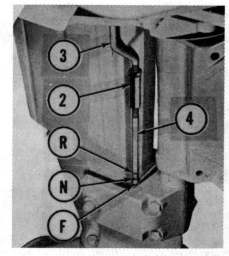

Fig. C6-6—Shift rod coupling (2) should be adjusted to provide equal travel in both directions (F & R) from neutral position (N).

seal (34) and splines on upper end of drive shaft (27). Carefully slide the housings together making certain that water tube enters seal (34). Install the four retaining screws and nuts. Nuts should be tightened to 256-275 in.-lbs. torque. Install shift rod coupling (2— Fig. C6-6) with right hand thread toward top. Shift to forward gear and mark shift rod (4) at (F) where it enters exhaust housing. Shift to neutral and mark the rod at the exhaust housing; then shift to reverse gear and again, mark the rod. Adjust the coupling so that marks for forward (F), neutral (N) and reverse (R) gears are equally spaced, then tighten the lock nut.

POWER HEAD

R&R AND DISASSEMBLE. To overhaul the power head, clamp the motor on a stand or support and remove the engine cover (shroud), intake silencer and control panel. Remove flywheel, starter, magneto and carburetor. Remove all interfering wiring and linkage, and as many screws as possible retaining inlet manifold, exhaust covers, transfer port covers, cylinder head, etc., before detaching power head from lower unit.

Remove the screws which secure the power head assembly to lower unit, and lift off the power head assembly.

Crankshaft and pistons can be removed after removing upper bearing cage (38—Fig. C6-8); then removing crankcase front half. Exhaust covers (3 & 4—Fig. C6-7), cylinder head (1), transfer port cover (26) and crankcase drain plate (16) should be removed for cleaning and inspection if major repairs are to be performed. Pry lugs are provided adjacent to the retaining dowels, for removing the crankcase front half.

Engine components are now accessible for removal and overhaul as outlined in the appropriate following paragraphs. Assemble as outlined in the ASSEMBLY paragraph.

ASSEMBLY. When reassembling, make sure all joint and gasket surfaces are clean, free from nicks and burrs and hardened cement or carbon. The crankcase and inlet manifold must be completely sealed against both vacuum and pressure. Exhaust manifold and cylinder head must be sealed against water leakage and pressure. Mating surfaces of exhaust areas between power head and motor leg must form a tight seal.

Whenever power head is disassembled, it is recommended that all gasket surfaces, and mating surfaces without

gaskets, be carefully checked for nicks and burrs and warped surfaces which might interfere with a tight seal. The cylinder head, head end of cylinder block, and some mating surfaces of manifolds and crankcase may be checked, and lapped if necessary, to provide a smooth surface. Do not remove any more metal than is necessary.

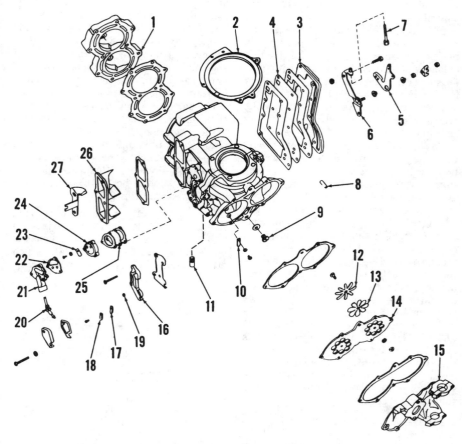

Fig. C6-7—Exploded view of cylinder and crankcase assembly. Refer to Fig. C6-8 for crankshaft and associated parts including the top main bearing cage (end cap).

1. Cylinder head	
2. Magneto stator ring	
3. Exhaust cover	8. Crankcase dowels
4. Exhaust plate	9. Plug
5. Magneto control lever	10. Reed (puddle drain)
6. Bracket	11. Water outlet
7. Idle speed stop screw	12. Reed stop
	13. Reed petals
	14. Reed plate

15. Inlet manifold and starter bracket	20. Fuel pump inlet and filter
16. Reed plate (cylinder drain)	21. Pump cover
17. Reed petal	22. Gasket
18. Reed stop	23. Fuel pump valve (2 used)
19. Screen	24. Plate
	25. Diaphragm
	26. Transfer port cover
	27. Idle stop switch cam

Fig. C6-8—Exploded view of crankshaft and connecting rod assembly. Later models are equipped with retainer (45) and seal (46).

28. Upper crankshaft seal
29. Top bearing
30. Connecting rod needles (30)
31A. Gasket
32. Crankshaft
33. Center main bearing outer race
34. Center main bearing needles (34)
35. Snap ring
36. Lower bearing
37. Lower seal
38. Bearing cage
39. Connecting rod
40. Piston
41. Piston pin
42. Retaining ring
43. Piston rings
45. Seal retainer
46. Seal

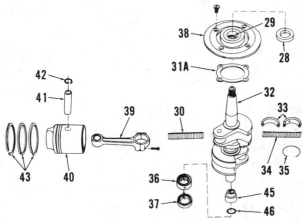

Mating surfaces of crankcase may be checked on the lapping block, and high spots or nicks removed, but the surface must not be lowered. If extreme care is used, a slightly damaged crankcase may be salvaged in this manner. In case of doubt, renew the crankcase assembly.

A heavy, non-fibrous grease should be used to hold loose needle bearings in position during assembly. All friction surfaces should be lubricated with new engine oil. Check frequently as power head is being assembled, for binding or locking. If encountered, remove the cause before proceeding with the assembly.

Gasket and sealing surfaces should be lightly and carefully coated with a non-hardening gasket cement. Make sure entire surface is coated, but avoid letting excess cement squeeze out into crankcase, bearings, or other passages. When installing crankcase screws, tighten those next to the main bearings and dowels first. Crankshaft seals (28 & 37—Fig. C6-8) should be renewed each time crankshaft is removed. Tighten cylinder head screws in sequence by starting at screws between cylinders and progressing in both directions. Refer to CONDENSED SERVICE DATA table for clearances and tightening torques.

Before attaching power head to lower unit, renew the drive shaft spline seal (28—Fig. C6-12) and coat the splines with grease.

PISTONS, PINS, RINGS AND CYLINDERS. Piston is fitted with three rings which should be installed with the beveled inner edge toward closed end of piston. Recommended ring end gap is 0.003-0.008 inch, with a maximum wear limit of 0.015 inch. Piston rings should have 0.0025-0.0045 inch side clearance in piston grooves, with a wear limit of 0.0055 inch.

Piston skirt clearance should be 0.002-0.0035 inch when measured at widest part of skirt at right angles to piston pin. Renew the piston if skirt clearance exceeds 0.005 inch. The maximum recommended out-of-round or taper for the cylinder is 0.002 inch.

The full floating piston pin should have 0.0001-0.0006 inch clearance in piston. Renew the parts if clearance exceeds 0.0016 inch in piston bosses.

When installing piston in cylinder, the long, tapering side of baffle on piston head should be installed toward the exhaust port side of cylinder. All friction surfaces should be lubricated with new engine oil when assembling.

CONNECTING RODS, BEARINGS AND CRANKSHAFT. Before detaching connecting rods from crankshaft, make certain that rod and cap are properly marked for correct assembly to each other and in the correct cylinder. The loose needle bearings at crankpin end of connecting rod should be kept with each assembly and not intermixed if reused.

The forged steel connecting rods contain 30 loose needle bearing rollers at crankpin end. Parting faces of rod and cap are not machined, but are fractured, to provide position location. When installing cap, make sure the correlation marks are aligned; then shift cap back and forth slightly while tightening, until fractured sections are in perfect mesh. When properly installed, the parting line is practically invisible. Rod side play on crankpin should be 0.015-0.025 inch, with a wear limit of 0.040 inch.

The crankshaft upper main bearing (29—Fig. C6-8) is a part of bearing cap (38). The center main bearing consists of 34 loose needle rollers (34), which are contained in a split outer race (33).

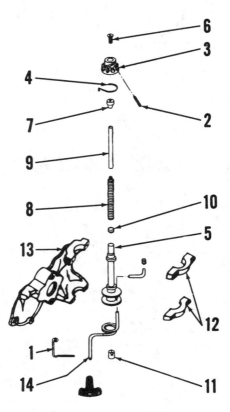

Fig. C6-9—Exploded view of recoil starter assembly. Pinion (3) meshes with teeth on magneto flywheel.

1. Rope guide	8. Recoil spring
2. Drive pin	9. Guide post
3. Pinion	10. Retainer
4. Pinion spring	11. Retainer extension
5. Starter spool	12. Bearing caps
6. Lock screw	13. Inlet manifold
7. Spring drive	14. Rope

The bearing race is separated by fracturing, and is held together by the retaining ring (35). When assembling, work the two halves of bearing race back and forth slightly until the fracture lines mesh, then install the retaining ring. The lower main bearing is of the caged roller type.

Recommended crankshaft end play is 0.003-0.006 inch, with a wear limit of 0.011 inch. Oversize and undersize parts are not available.

When assembling, follow the procedures outlined in the ASSEMBLY paragraph. Tightening torques are listed in the CONDENSED SERVICE DATA table.

MANUAL STARTER

Fig. C6-9 shows an exploded view of the recoil starter assembly. Starter pinion (3) engages a starter ring gear on the flywheel.

To disassemble the starter, first remove the engine cover, then remove screw (6—Fig. C6-9) in top of starter shaft.

NOTE: This screw locks pin (2) in place.

Thread the special "T" handle tool (T3139) in threaded hole from which screw (6) was removed. Tighten the tools until it bottoms; then turn tool handle slightly counterclockwise to relieve recoil spring tension, and push out pin (2). Allow the tool and spring drive (7) to turn clockwise to unwind the recoil spring (8). Pull up on tool to remove the recoil spring and components. Guide post (9) and spring retainer (10) can be lifted out after recoil spring is removed.

Recoil spring, pinion (3) or associated parts can be renewed at this time. To renew the starter rope, remove clamps (12) then remove the spool. Thread rope through hole in lower end of spool (5) and install the rope retainer approximately ½-inch from end of rope. Pull tight, then fully wind the rope onto spool and reinstall assembly. Make certain that retainer extension (11) is in place. With recoil spring and drive pinion (3) installed, use the "T" handle tool to wind the recoil spring counterclockwise eight turns. Align the holes in pinion (3), spool (5) and spring drive (7); then install the drive pin (2). Remove the tool and secure the pin with the locking screw (6). Recoil spring cavity should be partially filled with Lubriplate or similar grease when reassembling.

If tension of pinion spring (4) is incorrect, the pinion (3) may remain extended and prevent full speed operation.

ELECTRIC STARTER-GENERATOR

The combination starter and generator unit shown in Fig. C6-11 is used on "Autolectric" models. The armature (7) is mounted directly on upper end of crankshaft. The 12 volt battery should be connected with negative terminal grounded. The positive terminal should be connected to the red battery lead (18). If battery is connected with wrong terminal grounded or if motor is operated without battery, the rectifier (14) or armature (7) may be damaged. Circuit breaker (13) will normally protect the electric components.

The housing and field assembly (6) can be removed after disconnecting necessary wires and removing the six mounting screws. Housing (6) must be removed before armature (7) can be removed from crankshaft. Armature screw (2) should be tightened to 300 in.-lbs. torque.

LOWER UNIT

PROPELLER AND DRIVE PIN. A 3/16 x 1-5/16-inch stainless steel thrust pin is used on all 20 hp motors. The standard propeller is an 8½-inch diameter, 8½-inch pitch, right-hand rotating (clockwise), unit.

R&R AND OVERHAUL. Refer to Fig. C6-6. Loosen the locknut on the shift rod coupling (2) and remove coupling to disconnect the shift rod. Unbolt and remove the drive shaft housing (upper gearcase) from motor leg. Turn shift rod (1—Fig. C6-12) counterclockwise to clear the water pump housing; then disassemble and remove the water pump assembly.

Remove the propeller and thrust pin. Remove any burrs or rust from exposed end of propeller shaft. Remove snap ring (25), thread two screws in threaded holes of propeller shaft bearing cage (22) and remove the cage, using a puller.

To detach lower gearcase (12) from drive shaft housing (7), unscrew and remove shift rod (1). Housings are secured by a socket head cap screw at

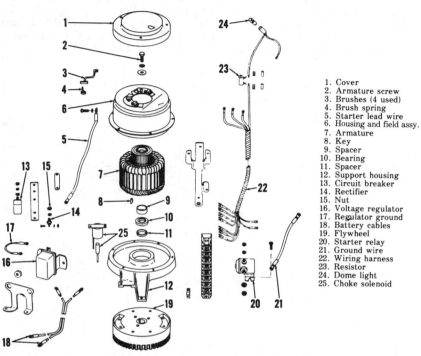

1. Cover
2. Armature screw
3. Brushes (4 used)
4. Brush spring
5. Starter lead wire
6. Housing and field assy.
7. Armature
8. Key
9. Spacer
10. Bearing
11. Spacer
12. Support housing
13. Circuit breaker
14. Rectifier
15. Nut
16. Voltage regulator
17. Regulator ground
18. Battery cables
19. Flywheel
20. Starter relay
21. Ground wire
22. Wiring harness
23. Resistor
24. Dome light
25. Choke solenoid

Fig. C6-11—Exploded view of electric starter-generator assembly for "Autolectric" models.

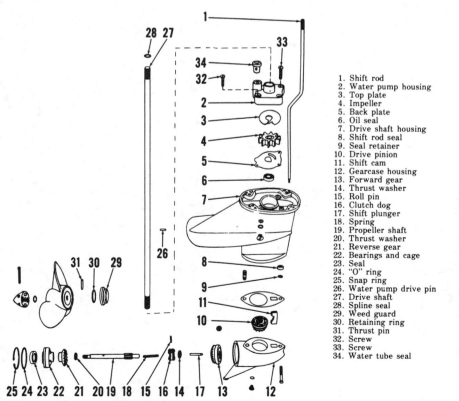

1. Shift rod
2. Water pump housing
3. Top plate
4. Impeller
5. Back plate
6. Oil seal
7. Drive shaft housing
8. Shift rod seal
9. Seal retainer
10. Drive pinion
11. Shift cam
12. Gearcase housing
13. Forward gear
14. Thrust washer
15. Roll pin
16. Clutch dog
17. Shift plunger
18. Spring
19. Propeller shaft
20. Thrust washer
21. Reverse gear
22. Bearings and cage
23. Seal
24. "O" ring
25. Snap ring
26. Water pump drive pin
27. Drive shaft
28. Spline seal
29. Weed guard
30. Retaining ring
31. Thrust pin
32. Screw
33. Screw
34. Water tube seal

Fig. C6-12—Exploded view of lower unit gearcase, drive shaft housing and associated parts. Top plate (3) is not used on models after 1969.

Fig. C6-13—Lower unit gearcase with propeller shaft bearing cage removed. Stud nut (arrow) must be removed before gearcase can be detached from drive shaft housing.

the front, and the stud nut INSIDE the case as shown by arrow, Fig. C6-13.

Propeller shaft, gears, bearings and shift mechanism can be removed after housings are separated. An internal expanding puller and slide hammer may be required to remove the front gear (13—Fig. C6-12). In some cases, gear may be removed by heating gearcase housing, then jarring open end on a block of wood to dislodge the gear and bearing assembly. When installing front gear and bearing assembly, assemble the bearing cage (22), without "O" ring (24) over rear of propeller shaft; install thrust washer (14) and gear assembly (13) on front of shaft, then use the propeller shaft as a piloted driver. Backlash and mesh position of the gears are not adjustable.

Assemble by reversing the disassembly procedure. Propeller shaft seal (23) should be installed with spring loaded lip toward inside. Drive shaft seal (6) should be installed with spring loaded lip toward top. With unit assembled, propeller shaft end play should be 0.003-0.028 inch. Backlash and mesh position are not adjustable. Refer to appropriate preceding paragraphs for water pump service cautions. Paragraph for water pump also includes adjustment of coupling (2 – Fig. C6-6).

CHRYSLER 20 (AFTER 1977) AND 25 HP

20 HP MODELS

Year Produced	Model
1978	202B8H, 202B8J, 203B8H, 203B8J, 206B8A, 207B8A
1979	202H9K, 202B9K, 203H9K, 203B9K, 206H9B, 206B9B, 207H9B, 207B9B
1980	202H0L, 202B0L, 203H0L, 203B0L
1981	202H1M, 202B1M, 203H1M, 203B1M, 206H1C, 206B1C, 207H1C, 207B1C
1982	202H2N, 202B2N

25 HP MODELS

Year Produced	Model
1973, 1974, 1975, 1976, 1977	252HA, 252BA, 252HB, 252BB, 253HA, 253BA, 253HB, 253BB, 254HA, 254BA, 254HB, 254BB, 255HA, 255BA, 255HB, 255BB, 256HA, 256BA, 257HA, 257BA
1978	252H8C, 252H8D, 253H8C, 253H8D, 256H8C, 257H8C
1981	252H1E, 252B1E
1982	252H2F, 252B2F
1983	252H3G, 252B3G, 257H3D, 257B3D
1984	252H4, 252B4

CONDENSED SERVICE DATA

TUNE-UP

Hp/rpm	20/4750
	25/5000
Bore – Inches	2.8125
Stroke – Inches	2.300
Number of Cylinders	2
Displacement – Cu. In.	28.57
Compression at Cranking Speed (Average)	95-105 psi
Spark Plug:	
Champion	L4J
Electrode Gap – In.	0.030
Magneto:	
Point Gap – Inches	†0.020
Timing	See Text
Carburetor:	
Make	Tillotson
Model	WB
Fuel: Oil Ratio	**50:1

†Breaker point gap is 0.015 inch for Models 256HA, 256HA, 257HA and 257BA.
**Fuel: Oil ratio should be 25:1 for break-in period.

SIZES – CLEARANCES

Piston Ring End Gap	0.007-0.017 in.
Piston to Cylinder Clearance	0.004-0.007 in.
Piston Pin Diameter	0.50000-0.50015 in.
Crankshaft Journal Diameters:	
Upper Main	1.3774-1.3780 in.
Center Main	1.3446-1.3451 in.
Lower Main	0.9849-0.9853 in.
Crankpin	1.1391-1.1395 in.

TIGHTENING TORQUES
(All Values in Inch-Pounds)

Cylinder Head	190
Flywheel Nut	720
Spark Plug	120-180
Connecting Rod Screws	180-190
Standard Screws:	
No. 10-24	30
No. 10-32	35
No. 12-24	45
1/4-20	70
5/16-18	160
3/8-16	270

LUBRICATION

The power head is lubricated by oil mixed with the fuel. For normal service after break-in, mix 1/6 pint of two-stroke engine oil with each gallon of gasoline. The recommended ratio is one third (1/3) pint of oil per gallon of gasoline for severe service and during break-in. Manufacturer recommends no-lead automotive gasoline although regular or premium gasoline may be used if octane rating is 85 or higher. Gasoline and oil should be thoroughly mixed.

The lower unit gears and bearings are lubricated by oil contained in the gear case. Only noncorrosive, leaded, EP90, outboard gear oil such as "Chrysler Outboard Gear Lube" should be used. The gearcase should be drained and refilled every 30 hours. Maintain fluid at level of upper (vent) plug.

To fill gearcase, have motor in upright position and fill through lower hole in side of gearcase until fluid reaches level of upper vent plug hole. Reinstall and tighten both plugs securely, using new gaskets if necessary, to ensure a water tight seal.

FUEL SYSTEM

CARBURETOR. A Tillotson WB type carburetor is used on all models. Refer to Fig. C7-1 for an exploded view of the carburetor.

Initial setting of idle mixture screw (10 – Fig. C7-1) is 1¼ turns out from a lightly seated position. Final adjustment of carburetor should be made with engine at normal operating temperature and running forward gear. Standard main jet size on 20 hp motors is 0.066 inch and on 25 hp motors is 0.064 inch which should be correct for operation below 1250 ft. altitude.

To check float level, remove float bowl and invert carburetor. Side of float nearest main jet should be parallel with gasket surface of carburetor. Adjust float level by bending float tang.

Install throttle plate (1 – Fig. C7-1) so that notch is up and chamfer is towards flange end of carburetor.

SPEED CONTROL LINKAGE. Ignition timing and throttle opening on all models must be synchronized so that throttle is opened as timing is advanced.

To synchronize linkage, first check ignition timing to be sure it is set correctly as outlined in IGNITION TIMING section. Disconnect link (L – Fig. C7-2) from throttle cam (C) and with throttle closed, turn eccentric screw (S) until roller (R) is exactly centered over mark (M) on throttle cam. Reconnect link (L) to magneto and rotate magneto stator ring until it is against full advance stop. Upper mark (AM) on throttle cam should now be aligned with roller (R). Disconnect link (L) and turn link ends to

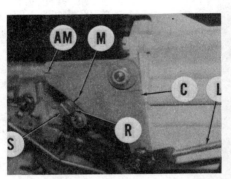

Fig. C7-2 — View of throttle cam and linkage. Refer to text for adjustment.

adjust length of link so that mark (AM) and roller are aligned when stator is at full advance. Turn throttle stop screw in steering handle shaft on models with manual starter so that screw provides a positive stop just as stator plate reaches full advance stop.

Idle speed in forward gear should be 550-650 rpm on manual start models. Adjust idle of manual start models by turning idle speed screw on side of steering handle. Idle speed in forward gear should be 650-750 rpm on electric start models. Adjust idle speed of electric start models by turning idle speed screw (I – Fig. C7-3) adjacent to exhaust port cover.

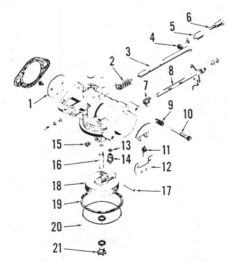

Fig. C7-1 — Exploded view of typical Tillotson model WB carburetor.

1. Throttle plate	
2. Spring	12. Choke plate
3. Throttle shaft	13. Gasket
4. Nut	14. Fuel inlet valve
5. Roller	15. High speed jet
6. Eccentric screw	16. Main nozzle
7. Spring	17. Float pin
8. Choke shaft	18. Float
9. Spring	19. Gasket
10. Idle mixture screw	20. Float bowl
11. Spring	21. Bowl retaining screw

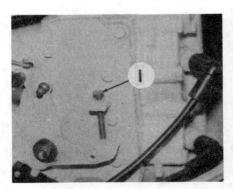

Fig. C7-3 — View of idle speed screw (I) used on models with electric starter. Idle speed should be 650-750 rpm with unit in forward gear.

REED VALVES. All models are equipped with a "V" type reed valve. The reed plate is located between the intake manifold and crankcase. Remove carburetor and intake manifold for access to reed valve.

Renew reeds if petals are broken, cracked, warped or bent. Never attempt to bend a reed petal in an effort to improve performance, nor attempt to straighten a damaged reed. Never install a bent or damaged reed. Seating surface of reed plate should be smooth and flat. Install reeds so that petals are centered over openings. Assembled reeds may stand open a maximum of 0.010 inch at tip end. Reed stop setting should be 9/32 inch when measured from tip of reed stop to reed plate.

PUDDLE DRAIN VALVE. Models prior to 1981 are equipped with a puddle drain valve located in the hose from the bottom of the crankcase cover to the bottom of the transfer port cover. The puddle valve is designed to remove puddled fuel from the crankcase, thus providing smooth operation at all speeds and lessening the possibility of spark plug fouling.

To check operation of puddle valve, disconnect hose ends and blow through each end of hose. Puddle valve should pass air when blowing through crankcase cover end of hose but not when blowing through transfer port end of hose. Remove puddle valve from hose if it does not operate correctly. Install new

puddle valve in hose approximately one inch from end of hose with small hole in puddle valve towards short end of hose. Attach hose to engine with puddle valve end of hose connected to crankcase cover.

FUEL PUMP. All models are equipped with a two stage diaphragm type fuel pump which is actuated by pressure and vacuum pulsations from the engine crankcases.

NOTE: Either stage of the fuel pump operating independently may permit the motor to run, but not at peak performance.

To remove fuel pump, disconnect fuel hoses to pump and unscrew six cap screws which retain fuel pump body. Check valves are renewable but be sure a new check valve is needed before removing old check valve as it will be damaged during removal. Unscrew the two retaining screws to remove center check valve. The two outer check valves must be driven out from below. Refer to Fig. C7-5 for view of correct check valve installation. Install check valves carefully to prevent damage. Inspect diaphragm and renew diaphragm if cracked, torn or badly distorted.

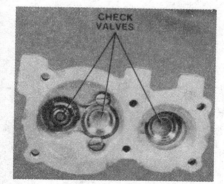

Fig. C7-4 — Exploded view of reed valve assembly.

1. Inlet manifold
2. Gasket
3. Adaptor plate
4. Gasket
5. Reed body
6. Reed petals
7. Reed stop

Fig. C7-5 — Fuel pump check valves must be installed as shown for proper operation of fuel pump.

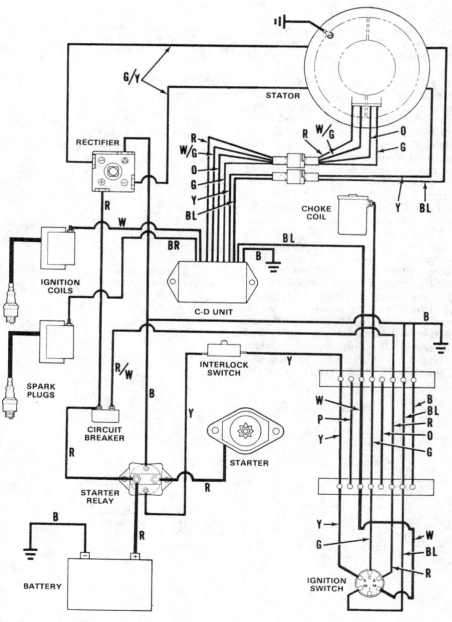

Fig. C7-6 — Wiring schematic for models equipped with Magnapower ignition.

B. Black			
BL. Blue	G. Green	P. Purple	W. White
BR. Brown	O. Orange	R. Red	Y. Yellow

IGNITION

Magnapower Models

These models are equipped with a breakerless, capacitor discharge ignition system. Note wiring diagram in Fig. C7-6. Tapered bore of flywheel and crankshaft end must be clean, dry and smooth before installing flywheel. Renew a chipped or cracked flywheel. Flywheel and crankshaft tapers may be cleaned by using fine valve grinding compound. Apply grinding compound to tapers and rotate flywheel back and forth approximately one quarter turn. Do not spin flywheel on crankshaft. Clean flywheel and crankshaft tapers thoroughly. Tighten flywheel nut to 45 ft.-lbs. torque.

If ignition malfunction occurs, use Chrysler tool T8953, plug adapter set T11201 and number 22 tester with load coil from tool T8996 and refer to following trouble-shooting procedure:

Check and make sure ignition malfunction is not due to spark plug or ignition coil failure. If spark is absent at both cylinders, check condition of charge coil as follows: Separate the blue and yellow wire connection between charge coil and CD module and attach double wire plug adapter to wire plug from charge coil as shown in Fig. C7-7. Attach red (P) lead from tester number 22 to red sleeved adapter wire marked Plug 2. Attach yellow (N) lead of number 22 tester and yellow sleeved adapter wire marked Plug 1 to engine ground. Place tester switch in number 2 position and crank engine. If tester lamp does not light, low voltage windings of charge coil are defective and stator should be renewed. If lamp lights, continue charge coil test by disconnecting yellow sleeved wire adapter from engine ground and attaching it to red (P) lead of T8953 tester as shown in Fig. C7-8. Attach yellow (N)

lead of T8953 tester to engine ground. Turn tester switch to position 10 and crank engine. If tester lamp does not light, high voltage windings of charge coil are defective and stator should be renewed. If lamp lights, charge coil operation is satisfactory and trigger coil and CD module circuits for each cylinder must be checked. Remove tester and plug adapter set, then reconnect blue and yellow wire plugs.

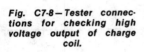

Fig. C7-8—Tester connections for checking high voltage output of charge coil.

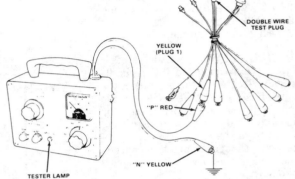

Separate the four wire connection between CD module and trigger coil and attach four wire plug adapter to wire plug from trigger coil as shown in Fig. C7-9. Attach red (P) lead from tester number 22 to red sleeved adapter wire marked Trigger 1 Pos. and yellow (N) lead to yellow sleeved adapter wire marked Trigger 1 Neg. Place switch of tester in number 1 position and crank engine. Trigger coil operation is

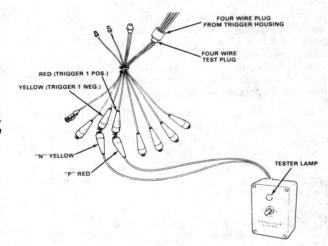

Fig. C7-9—Tester connections for checking operation of trigger coil.

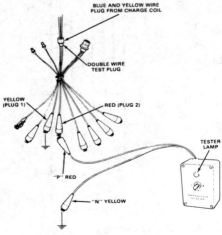

Fig. C7-7—Tester connections for checking low voltage output of charge coil.

Fig. C7-10—View showing tester connections needed to check CD module output.

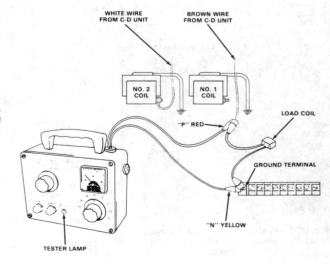

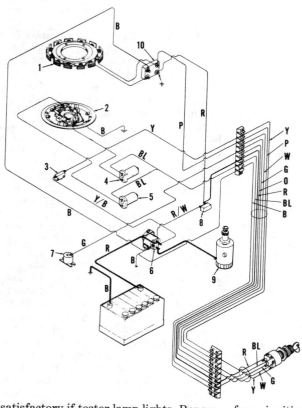

Fig. C7-11—Wiring schematic for breaker point models with battery ignition.

1. Alternator
2. Breaker plate
3. Neutral interlock switch
4. Top ignition coil
5. Bottom ignition coil
6. Starter relay
7. Choke solenoid
8. Circuit breaker
9. Electric starter motor
10. Rectifier
B. Black
BL. Blue
G. Green
O. Orange
P. Purple
R. Red
W. White
Y. Yellow

Breaker Point Models

Motors which are equipped with breaker points and an alternator have a battery ignition while all other motors with breaker points are equipped with a magneto ignition. Two breaker point sets are used on all models with each set of breaker points controlling ignition for one cylinder.

Breaker point gap should be 0.020 inch for each set of points except as noted in CONDENSED SERVICE DATA, and can be adjusted after the flywheel is removed. Both sets of points should be adjusted exactly alike. Place a mark on the high point of the breaker cam and set breaker point gap for both sets of breaker points with the mark aligned with the breaker point rub block.

The tapered bore in flywheel and tapered end of crankshaft must be clean, dry and smooth before installing flywheel. Tighten flywheel nut to 45 ft.-lbs.

Spark plug electrode gap on all models should be 0.030 inch. Recommended spark plug is Champion L4J.

COOLING SYSTEM

WATER PUMP. All motors are equipped with a rubber impeller type water pump. When cooling system problems are encountered, first check the water inlet for plugging or partial stoppage, then if not corrected, remove the lower unit gearcase and check the condition of water pump, water passages and sealing surfaces. Access to the water pump is possible after separating lower

---

satisfactory if tester lamp lights. Renew trigger housing if tester lamp does not light.

To check operation of number 2 cylinder trigger coil, repeat test procedure for number 1 cylinder trigger coil but connect red (P) lead of tester to red sleeved adapter wire marked Trigger 2 Pos. and yellow (N) lead to yellow sleeved adapter wire marked Trigger 2 Neg.

To check CD module performance for each cylinder, connect yellow (N) lead from tester T8953 to ground terminal of engine terminal block (Fig. C7-10). Disconnect white (number 2 cylinder) or brown (number 1 cylinder) primary lead

from ignition coil and connect red (P) lead of tester T8953 to primary lead. Connect leads of tester T8996 load coil to ground terminal of engine terminal block and primary coil lead of cylinder being tested. Turn T8953 tester dial to number 50. Crank engine and tester lamp should light. Renew CD module if lamp does not light.

Fig. C7-13—Exploded view of motor leg assembly used on early models.

1. Upper shift rod
2. Locknut
3. Coupler
4. Spacer plate
5. Water tube
6. Steering handle shaft
7. Throttle stop
8. Upper thrust mount
9. Kingpin plate
10. Steering handle
11. Bushing
12. Steering handle gear
13. Magneto control shaft gear
14. Bushing
15. Carrying handle
16. Exhaust gasket
17. Right motor leg cover
18. Left motor leg cover
19. Motor leg
20. Lower shock mount cover
21. Lower thrust pad

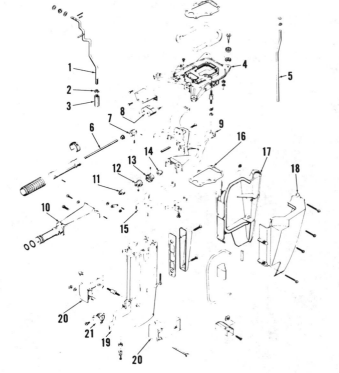

Fig. C7-12—View showing location of shift rod coupler (S).

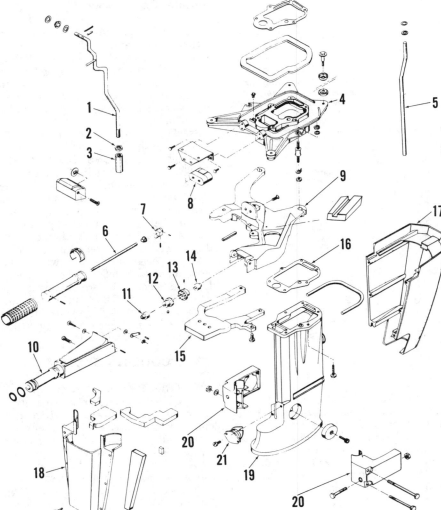

unit from motor leg and removing motor leg covers.

On models prior to 1979, unscrew shift rod coupler (S–Fig. C7-12). Separate lower unit from motor leg. Unbolt and remove water pump.

On 1979 and later models, unscrew fasteners securing drive shaft housing to motor leg and disconnect intermediate shift rod from lower shift rod by removing pin (11–Fig. C7-25). Separate lower unit from motor leg. Unbolt and remove water pump.

On all models, drive shaft seal (3–Fig. C7-24 or C7-25) should be installed with spring loaded lip towards top. Drive shaft spline seal should be renewed if hard or cracked. Lubricate water tube seal and splines on upper end of drive shaft.

On early models, carefully slide the housings together making certain that water tube enters seal. Install the water pump retaining screws and nuts. Shift lower unit into neutral and thread coupler (S–Fig. C7-12) onto shift rods. Position coupler so that shift knob indicates neutral and tighten locknut.

On late models, connect shift rods and carefully slide the housings together making certain that water tube enters seal. Install the water retaining screws and nuts.

POWER HEAD

R&R AND OVERHAUL. To remove the power head, mount the outboard motor on a stand and remove the engine cover. Disconnect choke rod from carburetor. Detach magneto control shaft gear (13–Fig. C7-13 or Fig. C7-14) from

Fig. C7-14—Exploded view of late model motor leg assembly.

1. Upper shift rod	7. Throttle stop	13. Magneto control shaft gear
2. Locknut	8. Upper thrust mount	14. Bushing
3. Coupler	9. Kingpin plate	15. Carrying handle
4. Spacer plate	10. Steering handle	16. Exhaust gasket
5. Water tube	11. Bushing	17. Rear motor leg cover
6. Steering handle shaft	12. Steering handle gear	
		18. Front motor leg cover
		19. Motor leg
		20. Lower shock mount cover
		21. Lower thrust pad

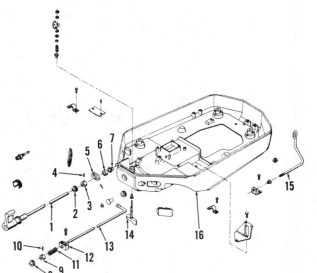

Fig. C7-15—Exploded view of manual start model support plate assembly.

1. Gear shift knob & shaft
2. Grommet
3. Collar
4. Set screw
5. Gear shift lever
6. Spacer
7. Bushing
8. Grommet
9. Retainer
10. Set screw
11. Spring
12. Bushing
13. Magneto control shaft
14. Latch pin
15. Choke rod
16. Support plate

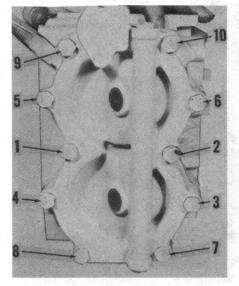

Fig. C7-16—Cylinder head cap screws should be tightened in the sequence shown above.

magneto control shaft (13–Fig. C7-15) on manual start models. Remove bushing (12) and detach magneto control shaft from control shaft link (31–Fig. C7-18). Loosen set screw in collar (3–Fig. C7-15) and remove gear shift knob and shaft (1) on manual start models. On electric start models, disconnect battery lead, red lead from upper terminal of starter relay and black lead from crankcase. On all models, unscrew nut retaining shift lever (20–Fig. C7-18) and detach gear shift linkage from lever.

On models prior to 1979, remove motor leg covers (17 and 18–Fig. C7-13), then unbolt and remove power head.

On 1979 and later models, remove lower shock mount covers (20–Fig. C7-14) and lower thrust pad (21) at front of motor leg. Remove the lower nuts on shocks between the kingpin plate (9) and spacer plate (4). Unscrew motor leg cover bolts and remove rear motor leg cover. Engage reverse lock and pull motor back enough to allow removal of front motor leg cover. Unscrew power head bolts and remove power head.

To disassemble power head, remove seal in bore of bottom end of crankshaft and remove starter and ignition assemblies from upper end of crankshaft. Unbolt and remove upper bearing cage and cylinder head. Remove reed valve assembly and transfer port cover. Unscrew cylinder to crankcase screws (two screws are in reed valve cavity) and using a suitable pry point separate cylinder and crankcase. Do not pry at machined mating surfaces between cylinder and crankcase.

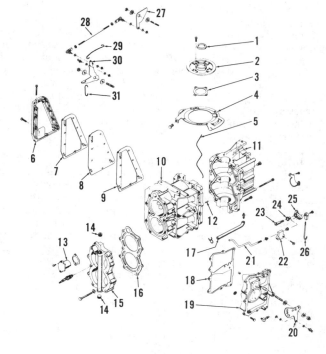

Fig. C7-18–Exploded view of cylinder block assembly.

1. Seal
2. Bearing cage
3. Gasket
4. Stator ring
5. Crankcase seal
6. Exhaust cover
7. Gasket
8. Exhaust plate
9. Gasket
10. Cylinder block
11. Lower crankcase
12. Dowel pin
13. Thermostat cover
14. Plug
15. Cylinder head
16. Gasket
17. Drain hose
18. Gasket
19. Transfer port cover
20. Gear shift lever
21. Starter interlock rod
22. Bushing retainer
23. Interlock lever pin
24. Bushing
25. Shift interlock lever
26. Shift interlock rod
27. Throttle cam
28. Throttle link
29. Magneto stator link
30. Magneto control lever
31. Magneto control link

Crankshaft, pistons and bearings are now accessible for removal and overhaul as outlined in the appropriate following paragraphs. Assemble as outlined in the ASSEMBLY paragraph.

ASSEMBLY. When reassembling, make sure all joint and gasket surfaces are clean, free from nicks and burrs, warped surfaces or hardened cement or carbon. The crankcase and inlet manifolds must be completely sealed against both vacuum and pressure. Exhaust manifold and cylinder head must be sealed against both vacuum and pressure. Exhaust manifold and cylinder head must be sealed against water leakage and pressure. Mating surfaces of exhaust areas between power head and motor leg must form a tight seal.

Sparingly apply a coating of sealant to mating surfaces of cylinder and crankcase. Tighten crankcase screws in a spiral pattern starting with center screws. Tighten cylinder head screws in sequence shown in Fig. C7-16. Install seal (6–Fig. C7-17) with "O" ring end inserted first until seal is flush with edge of bore. Install a new seal in bore of bottom end of crankshaft. Install long screw for transfer port cover in upper left hand hole as shown in Fig. C7-19. Complete remainder of assembly.

PISTONS, PINS, RINGS & CYLINDERS. Pistons are fitted with two piston rings which should be installed with the beveled inner edge (B–Fig. C7-20) toward closed end of piston. Rings are pinned in place to prevent rotation in ring grooves. Heat piston to

approximately 200°F to remove or install piston pin. Do not interchange pistons between cylinders. Pistons and rings are available in standard size and 0.010 and 0.030 inch oversizes.

When assembling piston, pin and connecting rod, match marks on connecting rod and cap must be aligned and long, tapering side of piston must be towards exhaust port.

CONNECTING RODS, BEARINGS AND CRANKSHAFT. Before detaching connecting rods from crankshaft, mark connecting rod and cap for correct reassembly to each other and in the correct cylinder. The needle rollers and cages at crankpin end of connecting rod should be kept with the assembly and not interchanged.

The bearing rollers and cages used in the connecting rods and the rollers and liners in the center main bearing are available only as a set for each bearing.

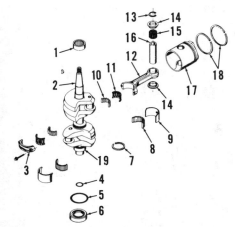

Fig. C7-17–Exploded view of crankshaft assembly.

1. Roller bearing
2. Crankshaft
3. Rod cap
4. Seal
5. "O" ring
6. Seal
7. Seal ring
8. Bearing rollers
9. Bearing liner
10. Bearing rollers
11. Bearing cage
12. Connecting rod
13. Snap ring
14. Spacer
15. Needle bearing
16. Piston pin
17. Piston
18. Piston rings
19. Ball bearing

Fig. C7-19–Install long cap screw (L) in upper left hole of transfer port cover.

Chrysler 20 (After 1977) & 25 HP

OUTBOARD MOTOR

The complete assembly should be installed whenever renewal is indicated. Connecting rod bearing cages have beveled notches which must be installed together and toward top (flywheel) end of crankshaft. Match marks on connecting rod and cap must be on same side as shown in Fig. C7-21. Connecting rod is fractured to provide an uneven surface between rod and cap. Be sure rod and cap are properly meshed before tightening rod screws.

Inspect condition of seal ring (7 – Fig. C7-17) and carefully install ring in crankshaft groove. Seal ring (7) must prevent leakage between cylinders and a defective seal will result in poor engine performance.

Before installing crankshaft in crankcase, install bearing liner (9) over dowel pin and place fourteen bearing rollers (8) in liner with a suitable grease to hold rollers in place. Install crankshaft and position remaining sixteen bearing rollers around crank journal. Place remaining bearing liner over rollers so that liner ends dovetail. Upper main bearing (1) should stand 1/8 inch higher than surface of crankcase.

MANUAL STARTER

Refer to Fig. C7-22 for an exploded view of manual starter. To disassemble starter, remove starter from engine, unscrew retainer (15) screws and remove retainer, shims (14), pawl plate (13) and spring (11). Remove rope handle, press

interlock lever and allow rope to rewind into starter housing. Press interlock lever and remove rope and pulley (10). If necessary, remove rewind spring.

Install rewind spring in housing with spring wound in counterclockwise direction from outer end of spring. Wind rope on pulley in counterclockwise direction as viewed with pulley in housing. Insert rope through slot of pulley with about nine inches of rope extending from slot. Install rope pulley in housing and place pawl spring (11) on rope pulley with ends pointing up. Install pawl plate (13) with pawl side toward pulley and engage slots with pawl spring (11) ends. Install three shims (0.006, 0.007 and 0.010 inch) and retainer (15). Turn rope pulley approximately two turns clockwise to preload rewind spring and pass end of rope through rope guide of starter housing. Attach rope handle and pull rope until it is fully extended. It should still be

possible to rotate rope pulley a slight amount after rope is extended to prevent damage to rewind spring.

PROPELLER

Propellers for normal use have three blades and are equipped with a thrust pin to prevent damage. Various pitch propellers are available and should be selected to provide full throttle operation within the recommended limits of 4250-5250 rpm on all models. Propellers other than those designed for the motor should not be used.

LOWER UNIT

Early Models

R&R AND OVERHAUL. Refer to WATER PUMP section for removal of lower unit. Turn shift rod (1–Fig. C7-24) counterclockwise to clear the water pump housing; then disassemble and remove the water pump assembly.

Remove the propeller and thrust pin. Remove any burrs or rust from exposed end of propeller shaft. Remove snap ring (25), thread two screws in threaded holes of propeller shaft bearing cage (22); and remove the cage, using a puller.

To detach lower gearcase (12) from drive shaft housing (7), unscrew and remove shift rod (1). Housings are secured by a socket head cap screw at the front, and the stud nut INSIDE the case.

Propeller shaft, gears, bearings and shift mechanism can be removed after housings are separated. An internal expanding puller and slide hammer may be required to remove the front gear (13). In some cases, gear may be removed by

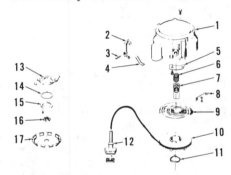

Fig. C7-22 – Exploded view of manual starter.

1. Starter housing
2. Interlock lever
3. Pin
4. Spring
5. Plate
6. Spring
7. Rope guide
8. Housing liner
9. Rewind spring
10. Rope & pulley
11. Spring
12. Handle
13. Pawl plate
14. Shims
15. Retainer
16. Flywheel nut
17. Starter cup

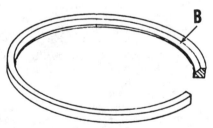

Fig. C7-20 – Install piston rings with bevel (B) to top.

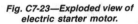

Fig. C7-23—Exploded view of electric starter motor.

1. Nut
2. Stop cup
3. Spring
4. Pinion cup
5. Sleeve
6. Pinion
7. Screw shaft
8. Washer
9. Cushion cup
10. Cushion
11. Thrust cup
12. End plate
13. Thrust washer
14. Shim
15. Armature
16. Thrust washer
17. Housing
18. Thrust washer
19. Spring
20. Brushes
21. Brush plate

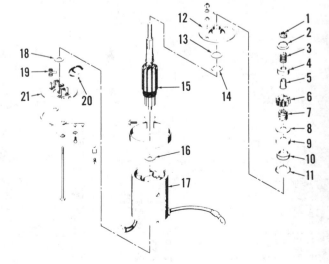

Fig. C7-21 – Match marks on connecting rod and rod cap must be on same side and towards flywheel end of crankshaft.

Illustrations Courtesy Chrysler

heating gearcase housing, then jarring open end on a block of wood to dislodge the gear and bearing assembly. When installing front gear and bearing assembly, assemble the bearing cage (22), without "O" ring (24) over rear of propeller shaft; install thrust washer (14) and gear assembly (13) on front of shaft; then use the propeller shaft as a piloted driver. Backlash and mesh position of the gears are not adjustable.

Assemble by reversing the disassembly procedure. Propeller shaft seal (23) should be installed with spring loaded lip toward inside. Drive shaft seal (6) should be installed with spring loaded lip toward top. With unit assembled, propeller shaft end play should be 0.003-0.028 inch. Backlash and mesh position are not adjustable. Refer to appropriate preceding paragraphs for water pump service cautions.

Late Models

R&R AND OVERHAUL. To remove the lower unit, refer to WATER PUMP section. Drain the gearcase and secure gearcase skeg in a vise. Disassemble and remove the drive shaft and water pump assembly. Remove propeller nut, pin (30 – Fig. C7-25) and propeller (29). Carefully clean exposed end of propeller shaft and remove the two screws securing propeller shaft bearing cage (27) to gearcase. Rotate the bearing cage approximately ½-turn until tabs are accessible from the sides; then using a soft hammer, gently tap the bearing cage rearward out of gearcase. Remove the gearcase rear retaining stud nut by working through propeller shaft opening. Unscrew gearcase front retaining stud nut, then lift off drive shaft housing (37).

Withdraw drive pinion (31) from top of gearcase and propeller shaft and associated parts through rear opening. Withdraw front and rear gears from propeller shaft. Remove spring pin (23), clutch dog (22) and shift pin (15).

The drive shaft seal (3) should be installed with spring loaded lip toward top (power head). Rubber coated side of shaft seal (28) should be installed with spring loaded lip toward outside of bearing cage (27). Sparingly apply Loctite 222 or 262 to outer diameter of shift rod seal (7).

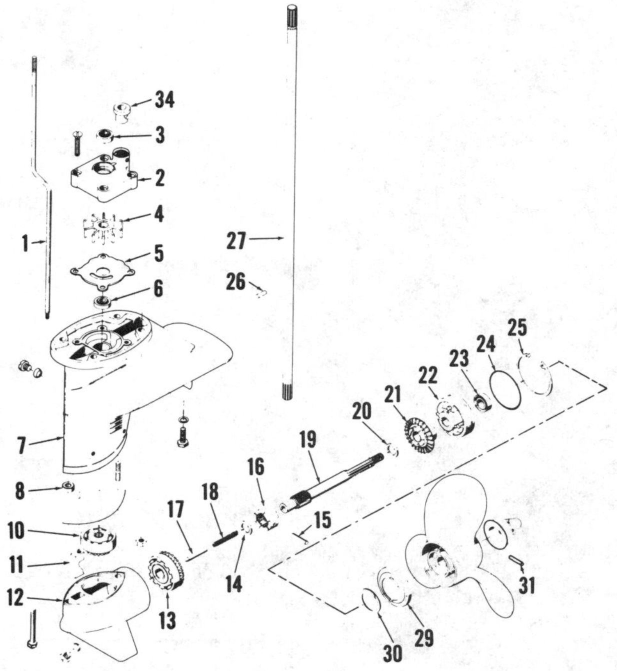

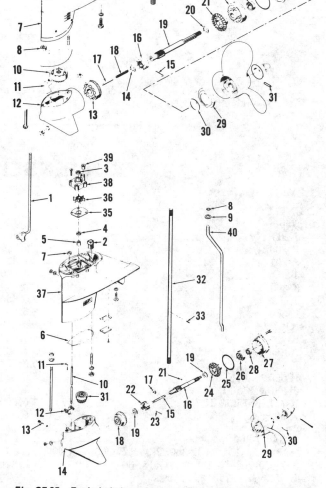

Fig. C7-24 — Exploded view of lower unit used on early models.

1. Shift rod
2. Water pump housing
3. Seal
4. Impeller
5. Back plate
6. Oil seal
7. Drive shaft housing
8. Shift rod seal
10. Drive pinion & bearing
11. Shift cam
12. Gearcase housing
13. Forward gear & bearing
14. Thrust washer
15. Roll pin
16. Clutch dog
17. Shift plunger
18. Spring
19. Propeller shaft
20. Thrust washer
21. Reverse gear
22. Bearings & cage
23. Seal
24. "O" ring
25. Snap ring
26. Water pump drive pin
27. Drive shaft
29. Weed guard
30. Retaining ring
31. Thrust pin
34. Water tube seal

1. Shift rod
2. Water screen
3. Drive shaft seal
4. Seal
5. Bushing
6. Gasket
7. Seal
8. Seal
9. Washer
10. Shift rod
11. Pin
12. Shift arm
13. Pivot pin
14. Gearcase
15. Shift pin
16. Propeller shaft
17. Yoke
18. Front gear & bushing
19. Thrust washer
21. Ball
22. Clutch dog
23. Spring pin
24. Rear gear
25. Cage seal
26. Bearing
27. Bearing cage
28. Seal
29. Propeller
30. Propeller pin
31. Drive pinion & bearing
32. Drive shaft
33. Water pump drive pin
35. Back plate
36. Impeller
37. Drive shaft housing
38. Pump body
39. Grommet
40. Water tube

Fig. C7-25 — Exploded view of lower unit used on late models.

Drive gear backlash and bearing preload are fixed and not adjustable. Assemble by reversing the disassembly procedure. Make sure that hole in clutch dog (22) is aligned with slot in propeller shaft (16) and hole in shift pin (15); then, insert spring pin (23).

CLINTON

**CLINTON ENGINES
CORPORATION
Maquoketa, Iowa 52060**

Year produced	Model
1969	AJ9, BJ9
1970	J-200, J-350, J-500, J-700
1971	J-300, J-350, J-500, J-700
1972	K-200, K-400, K-500, K-700
1973	K-200, K-400, K-500, K-700
1974	K-300, K-500, K-700, K-750
1975	K-300, K-500, K-700, K-750
1976	K-350, K-500, K-550, K-751, K-752, K-753
1977	K-201, K-350, K-550, K-751, K-753, K-900
1978, 1979, 1980	K-201, K-350, K-505, K-550, K-751, K-753, K-900

NOTE: Motors may be marked "CLINTON," or "CHIEF."

CONDENSED SERVICE DATA

TUNE-UP
Hp/rpm—
J-200	2/4000
K-200	2/3400
K-201	2/3800
J-300	3/4000
K-300	3/5000
J-350	3.5/6800
K-350	3.5/3800
BJ9	3.5/4800
K-400	4/6800
AJ9, J-500 & K-500	5/5600
K-505	5.5/5600
K-550	5.5/4500
J-700 & K-700	7/6000
K-751, K-752 & K-753	7.5/6000
K-900	9/6000

Bore—Inches:
J-200, J-300 & K-200	1-7/8
AJ9, BJ9, K-201, K-300, J-350, K-350 & K-400	2-1/8
J-500, J-700, K-500, K-505, K-550 & K-700	2-3/8
K-700* & K-750	2-7/16
K-751, K-752 & K-753	2½
K-900	2-5/8

Stroke—Inches:
K-900	1-7/8
K-505, K-550, J-700, K-700, K-750, K-751, K-752 & K-753	1¾
All other models	1-5/8

Number of Cylinders (All) 1

Displacement—Cu. In.:
J-200, K-200 & J-300	4.48
AJ9, BJ9, K-201, K-300, J-350, K-350 & K-400	5.76
J-500 & K-500	7.20
K-505, K-550, J-700 & K-700*	7.75
K-700* & K-750	8.17
K-751, K-752 & K-753	8.59
K-900	10.14

Spark Plug—Champion:
AJ9, BJ9 & K-201	J12J
K-500, K-505, K-700*, K-750, K-751, K-752, K-753 & K-900	J13Y
All other models	CJ8
Electrode Gap (All)	0.025
Magneto Point Gap	See Text
Fuel—Oil Ratio	See Text

*Model K-700 after 1973.

SIZES—CLEARANCES (All Values in Inches)
Piston Rings:
End Gap	0.010-0.015
Side Clearance	0.002-0.004

Piston Skirt Clearance:
Bore 1-7/8 Inches	0.0045-0.0065
Bore 2-1/8 Inches	0.0045-0.0070
Bore 2-3/8 Inches	0.0050-0.0070

Crankshaft Bearing Clearances:
Main Bearings—Bronze**	0.0015-0.0035
Connecting Rod—Bronze**	0.0021-0.0037

Piston Pin Bearing Clearances:
In Piston	0.0000-0.0002
In Rod**	0.0004-0.0011

Drive Shaft Clearance:#
Upper	0.002-0.0035
Lower	0.002-0.0035

Propeller Shaft Clearance:#
Front	0.0025-0.004
Rear	0.0025-0.004

**Clearances listed are applicable only to models with plain bearings. Most models are equipped with anti-friction (Ball or Roller) bearings.
#Applies to models with bushings.

Illustrations Courtesy Clinton

TIGHTENING TORQUES
(All Values in Inch-Pounds)

Connecting Rod:	
Aluminum	35-40
Steel	70-80
Crankcase Bearing Plate	75-95
Cylinder Head (J-500 & J-700)	140-160
Flywheel:	
Aluminum	400-450
Iron (with steel keyway insert)	375-400
(without insert)	180-200
Reed Plate & Carburetor	60-65
Spark Plug	230-270
Stator Plate	45-65

LUBRICATION

The power head is lubricated by oil mixed with the fuel. A high quality oil for outboard motors should be used. To each gallon of regular gasoline, add ½ pint of oil (16:1 ratio) for 4.48 and 5.76 cubic inch engines or 1/6 pint of oil (48:1 ratio) for all other engines. Add ¼ pint more oil to each gallon of fuel during break-in.

Lower unit gears and bearings are lubricated by oil contained in the gearcase. SAE 90 EP oil or a good quality outboard motor gear lubricant should be used. On models with fill (drain) and vent screws, insert fill tube into lower plug opening and fill unit until lubricant reaches vent plug opening. Note that plugs may be on same or opposite sides of gearcase. On models devoid of fill and vent plugs, invert unit, remove propeller and gearcase cover and fill gear cavity with lubricant. On Model K-201, gear oil is installed or drained through screw (S—Fig. CL1-13) hole in retainer (19).

Fig. CL1-2—Exploded view of carburetor typical of type used on some models. Refer to Fig. CL1-1 for parts identification.

FUEL SYSTEM

CARBURETOR. Several different carburetors have been used. On motors with Tillotson MT carburetor (Fig. CL1-1), initial setting is one turn open for high speed mixture needle (19) and ¾ turn open for idle mixture needle (16). High speed mixture on some carburetors is controlled by a drilled passage. On models with carburetor type shown in Fig. CL1-2, initial setting of idle needle (16) is 2 turns open and high speed needle (19) is 1½ turns open. Some models are equipped with idle speed stop screw (20) to adjust the minimum idling speed.

Final adjustment of the mixture needles must be accomplished with motor operating under load. On models with high speed needle, adjust high speed mixture first, then idle mixture. High speed mixture should be rechecked after adjusting idle mixture. Idle mixture should be set rich enough to allow smooth acceleration from idle to maximum speed.

The mixture adjustment knobs on control panel are designed so that the needles cannot be turned completely without removing the knobs. If a major adjustment is required, remove knobs. After adjustment is complete, reinstall knobs with indicators pointing horizontally outward away from each other. This position will allow the maximum of adjustment without removing knobs.

To adjust the float level on Tillotson MT carburetors (Fig. CL1-1), disconnect the fuel line and remove and invert bowl cover (9) with float (12) attached. Float setting is correct if the distance from gasket surface of cover to farthest edge of float is 1-13/32 inches. Adjust by removing float and bending float lever tang where it contacts inlet needle (10). Measurement should be made without the gasket and should not vary more than 1/64-inch from the given setting. Float must be removed to renew the inlet needle valve assembly (10).

To adjust the float level on carburetors shown in Fig. CL1-2, the carburetor should be removed. Remove the

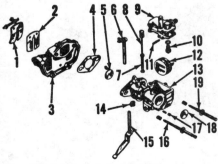

Fig. CL1-1—Exploded view of carburetor, intake manifold and reed valve assembly used on some motors.

1. Reed stop	10. Inlet needle valve assembly
2. Reed petals	11. Float pin
3. Inlet manifold and reed plate	12. Float
4. Gasket	13. Body assembly
5. Throttle valve	14. Spring
6. Throttle shaft	15. Choke shaft
7. Main nozzle	16. Idle adjustment needle
8. Idle tube	17. Friction pin
9. Bowl cover	18. Choke valve
	19. Main mixture needle

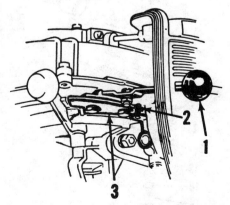

Fig. CL1-3—Speed control lever and synchronizing cam showing points of adjustment.

1. Lever
2. Cam follower
3. Synchronizing cam

fuel bowl (9) and invert the carburetor. Distance between outer rim of carburetor casting (bottom when inverted) and free end of float should be 1/8-inch. Float drop should be measured at the same place with the carburetor in normal position and should be 3/16-inch. Tabs are provided for adjusting float level and drop.

SPEED CONTROL LINKAGE. On most models, the speed control lever rotates the magneto stator plate to advance the magneto stator plate to advance or retard the timing. The throttle valve is synchronized with the plate to open throttle as timing is advanced. The high-speed position is fixed. Slow idle throttle setting can be adjusted as follows: Move speed control lever (1—Fig. CL2-3) against slow speed end of stop as shown. Loosen the two cap screws retaining speed control cam (3) to stator plate and move plate toward or away from throttle arm (2). Do not attempt to adjust slow speed by turning the slow speed MIXTURE needle. Check to make sure throttle valve is fully open when speed control lever is moved to "FAST" position.

REED VALVES. The inlet reed valve unit is located between carburetor and crankcase. The reed plate should be removed and reeds checked, whenever carburetor is removed for service. Reed petals should seat very lightly against reed plate. Do not attempt to straighten a bent reed or to bend a reed in an effort to alter performance. Reed petals should seat very lightly against reed plate. Do not attempt to straighten a bent reed or to bend a reed in an effort to alter performance. Reed petals should be handled and stored with the utmost care.

Seating surface of reed plate should be smooth and flat and the reed stop should not be twisted, bent or broken. On models with two petal reeds, the reed stop setting, measured at tip, should be approximately 0.280-inch from plate.

FUEL PUMP. Some models are equipped with a fuel pump which uses pressure and vacuum pulsations from power head crankcase to move pump diaphragm. The pump is mounted on carrying handle or under the motor lower shroud. Failure of diaphragm or check valve will prevent proper operation. Also check all connecting hoses for air and fuel leaks. The remote fuel tank filter must be clean to allow proper flow.

IGNITION

A solid-state ignition system is used on Models K-751, K-753 and K-900. No adjustment is necessary and faulty operation requires renewal of unit.

All models except K-751, K-753 and

K-900 are equipped with a flywheel magneto. Breaker point gap should be 0.020-inch.

Some models are equipped with an auxiliary electrical system which produces 42 watts of alternating current at rated speed.

Models with iron flywheel may have steel insert cast in center of flywheel. Note tightening torque in CONDENSED SERVICE DATA.

COOLING SYSTEM

All models are air cooled by a blower fan built into the flywheel. There is on all models except K-201, a coolant pump which supplies liquid cooling for the lower leg and exhaust gases. Coolant intake is located just below the anti-cavitation plate on each side of gearcase and coolant is pumped to exhaust deflector at upper part of lower unit where it cools the exhaust housing.

Coolant outlet consists of a series of holes arranged vertically on each side of the lower unit upper leg, just below the swivel bracket. If a spray of water does not emerge from outlet holes when motor is running, first check the coolant inlet for plugging, then if not corrected, remove gearcase from lower unit as outlined in LOWER UNIT section and overhaul the pump.

POWER HEAD

REMOVE AND REINSTALL. To remove the power head, first remove the engine shroud and disconnect fuel outlet line and impulse line from fuel pump. Remove the six cap screws

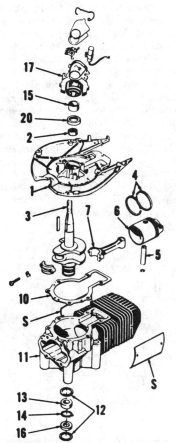

Fig. CL1-5—Exploded view of power head with closed end cylinder and plain bearing connecting rod. Refer to Fig. CL1-6 for legend.

Fig. CL1-6—Exploded view of power head with removable cylinder head and roller bearing connecting rod. Some models may be similar with closed end cylinder.

S. Shrouds
1. Bearing plate
2. Top main bearing
3. Crankshaft
4. Piston rings
5. Piston pin
6. Piston
7. Connecting rod
8. Bearing rollers
9. "O" ring
10. Gasket
11. Cylinder and crankcase
12. Retaining rings
13. Bottom main bearing
14. Snap ring
15. Ignition cam
16. Seal
17. Magneto coil
18. Advance bracket
19. Throttle cam
20. Seal
21. Seal retainer
22. Cylinder head
23. Gasket
24. Bearing insert
25. Piston pin bearing

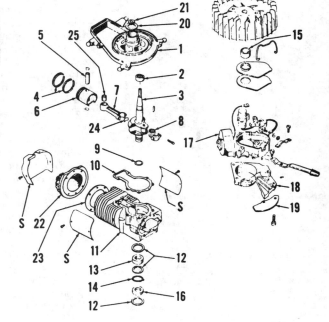

retaining power head to exhaust housing and lift the complete power head straight up off lower unit.

When reinstalling, use a new mounting gasket on each side of exhaust deflector and coat the drive shaft splines with a high melting-point grease before positioning the power head. Tighten the four front (5/16-inch) retaining cap screws to a torque of 90-120 in.-lbs.) and the two rear (¼-inch) screws to 80-100 in.-lbs.

DISASSEMBLE AND REASSEMBLE. If service is not required on the recoil starter assembly, remove starter and blower housing as a unit and remove control panel at the same time to avoid disconnecting the starter rope. Remove the flywheel, magneto assembly, shrouds (S—Fig. CL1-5 or CL1-6), carburetor and reed plate assembly, and spark plug.

On models so equipped, remove the cylinder head (22—Fig. CL1-6). Remove the connecting rod cap, needle rollers (8) and inserts (24), then push the connecting rod and piston unit out of cylinder.

On models with closed end cylinders (Fig. CL1-5), remove connecting rod cap and loose needle rollers (if so equipped). Push the connecting rod and piston unit to the closed end of cylinder. The piston and connecting rod can be removed after crankshaft is removed.

On all models, remove retaining ring (12—Fig. CL1-5 or CL1-6) from bottom of power head, then remove seal (16). Remove snap ring (14) from crankshaft, remove upper bearing plate (1), then withdraw crankshaft. On models with closed end cylinder, be careful not to damage connecting rod when removing crankshaft.

NOTE: On all models, seal (16) should be renewed when assembling.

Assemble by reversing the disassembly procedure. The sharp, vertical side of deflector on crown of piston must be installed toward intake transfer ports at top of power head as shown in Fig.

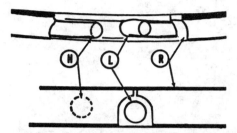

Fig. CL1-8—Piston rings are equipped with a retaining lock ring which fits on inside of ring in piston groove as shown. Locking tab is installed to right of locating hole in piston on upper and lower rings, and to left on center ring.

H. Locating hole (in piston)
L. Locking ring
R. Piston ring

CL1-7. Refer to CONDENSED SERVICE DATA table for tightening torques.

Crankshaft end play should be 0.000-0.002 inch. On some models, end play is controlled by the selected thickness of bearing plate gasket (10—Fig. CL1-5), which is available in a standard thickness of 0.030 inch and alternate thicknesses of 0.025 and 0.035 inch. Select the thinnest gasket which will not cause shaft to bind. On most models, end play is controlled by the ball type lower main bearing.

PISTON, PIN, RINGS & CYLINDER. A three ring piston is used on some models, while other motors use only two rings. On some models, each compression ring is provided with a lock ring which fits in the same groove. Refer to Fig. CL1-8. To install lock rings and piston rings, hold piston with sharp side of deflector (intake side) to right. Intall upper and lower locking rings with ring locating tab to right of locating hole (H) in piston and center locking ring with ring locating tab to left of locating hole. Install piston rings with cutout of ring gap surrounding locking tab as shown. Make sure ring gap will completely close before at-

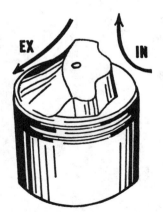

Fig. CL1-7—Long sloping side of piston deflector must be installed downward, toward exhaust ports.

EX. Exhaust flow
IN. Intake flow

Fig. CL1-9—Exploded view of recoil starter used on some motors.

1. Rope
2. Handle
3. Plug
4. Housing
5. Recoil spring
6. Retainer
7. Pulley
8. Wave washer
9. Washer
10. Snap ring
11. Pawl
12. Spring
13. Spacer
14. Plate
15. Flywheel

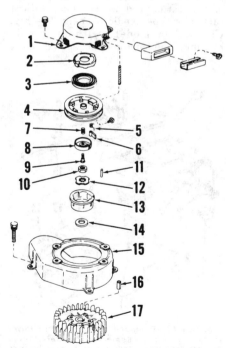

Fig. CL1-10—Exploded view of rewind starter used on some models.

1. Housing
2. Spring cup
3. Rewind spring
4. Rope pulley
5. Dog spring
6. Dog
7. Brake spring
8. Dog retainer
9. Screw
10. Nut
11. Pin
12. Washer
13. Starter cup
14. Washer
15. Shroud
16. Roll pin
17. Flywheel

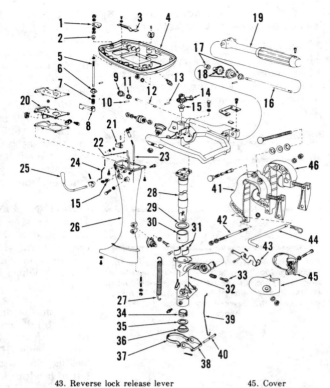

Fig. CL1-11—Exploded view of motor leg used on some later models.

1. Cam latch
2. Bushing
3. Detent spring
4. Lower shroud
5. latch rod
6. Bushing
7. Spring
8. Latch handle
9. Gear
10. Pin
11. Bushing
12. Speed control rod
13. Pin
14. Gear
15. Bushing
16. Speed control rod
17. Bushing
18. Gears
19. Steering & speed grip
20. Water deflector
21. Shift lever
22. Water tube
23. Upper shift rod
24. Shift limiter rod
25. Shift handle
26. Motor leg
27. Spring
28. Pivot shaft
29. Washer
30. Bushing
31. Friction liner
32. Swivel bracket
33. Friction screw
34. Bushing
35. Washer
36. Bushing
37. Outer reverse latch
38. Inner reverse latch
39. Reverse lock link
40. Reverse latch pin
41. Stern bracket
42. Rod
43. Reverse lock release lever
44. Tilt pin
45. Cover
46. Stern bracket

Make a visual check of block bore for excessive wear or scoring, and check for broken or damaged cooling fins. Broken cooling fins can cause power head to overheat.

CONNECTING ROD, CRANK-SHAFT AND BEARINGS. On most models, the lower end of crankshaft is carried by a ball type bearing and the upper end is by a cartridge type needle bearing. The connecting rod on some models is equipped with needle rollers and others use a cast-in bronze bushing at the crankpin end. Needle bearing connecting rods may be steel with needles riding directly on the crankpin and connecting rod or an aluminum rod with hardened inserts (24—Fig. CL1-6) to provide the outer race.

The crankshaft lower ball bearing (13—Fig. CL1-5 or CL1-6) is a slip fit on shaft. The bearing is retained in cylinder block by retaining ring (12) above and below outer race and is retained on shaft by the Tru-Arc snap ring (14) which fits into groove in shaft. Lower seal (16) must be removed before crankshaft can be removed, and will be damaged on removal. A new seal must be installed on reassembly.

Examine the crankshaft and bearing race of connecting rod bore for discoloration due to heat, or for wavy appearance due to damaged rollers, excess

tempting to install piston assembly.

On some models, the piston pin end of connecting rod is equipped with a cartridge type needle bearing (25—Fig. CL1-6). On models without needle bearing, the piston pin should have

0.004-0.0011 inch clearance in rod bore. On all models, piston pin should have 0.000-0.0002 inch clearance in piston bosses.

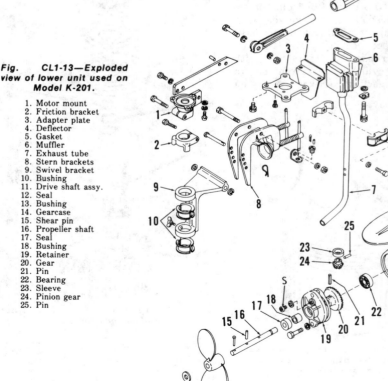

Fig. CL1-12—Exploded view typical of lower motor leg used on some early models. Some models may use a lower motor cover instead of carrying handle (10).

1. Lower motor leg
2. Reverse lock lug
3. Friction band
4. Swivel bracket cup
5. Set screw
6. Spacer ring
7. Gaskets
8. Exhaust deflector
9. Check valve
10. Carrying handle
11. Fuel pump body
12. Pump diaphragm
13. Washer
14. Pump spring
15. Steering handle
16. Shear pin holder
17. Swivel bracket
18. Stern brackets
19. Thrust bracket

Fig. CL1-13—Exploded view of lower unit used on Model K-201.

1. Motor mount
2. Friction bracket
3. Adapter plate
4. Deflector
5. Gasket
6. Muffler
7. Exhaust tube
8. Stern brackets
9. Swivel bracket
10. Bushing
11. Drive shaft assy.
12. Seal
13. Bushing
14. Gearcase
15. Shear pin
16. Propeller shaft
17. Seal
18. Bushing
19. Retainer
20. Gear
21. Pin
22. Bearing
23. Sleeve
24. Pinion gear
25. Pin

heat, or foreign material. If any such damage is found, both shaft (or rod) and bearings must be renewed. Lubricate parts thoroughly with new oil during assembly to provide initial lubrication.

MANUAL STARTER

Two types of rewind starters have been used. Refer to Fig. CL1-9 or CL1-10 for an exploded view of starter. Starter may be disassembled after removing starter from shroud. Care should be used when disassembling starter to prevent injury when removing rewind spring.

Install rewind spring in counter-clockwise direction. Wind rope around rope pulley in counter-clockwise direction as viewed from flywheel side of pulley. Renew starter pawls if worn or damaged.

LOWER UNIT

Model K-201

Refer to Fig. CL1-13 for an exploded view of lower unit used on model K-201. Service information was not available at time of publication.

Models K-550, K-750, K-653 and K-900

Refer to Fig. CL1-14 for exploded view of lower unit. Service information was not available at time of publication.

All Other Models

OVERHAUL. Most service on the lower unit can be performed by removing gearcase assembly from lower motor leg; or by removing gearcase housing lower cover (22—Fig. CL1-15). To remove the gearcase, remove spring cover (16) for access to front stud nut. The rear housing retaining cap screw is accessible inside exhaust outlet.

To remove the propeller shaft or disassemble gearcase, drive the gear retaining roll pin (7) a short distance into gear hub, rotate propeller shaft ½-turn and pull the roll pin with vise grip pliers. Gearcase must by completely sealed against water and grease leakage when reassembling.

Refer to CONDENSED SERVICE DATA TABLE for drive shaft bearing clearances. When installing gearcase to lower motor leg, tighten the (front) retaining stud nut to a torque of 50-60 in.-lbs. and the (rear) retaining screw to a torque of 75-90 in.-lbs.

Fig. CL1-14—Exploded view of lower unit used on Models K-550, K-750, K-753 and K-900.

1. Water pump housing	23. Gearcase cover
2. Pump impeller	24. Seal
3. Pin	25. Retainer
4. Plate	26. Gasket
5. Seal	27. Snap ring
6. Bearing	28. Thrust bearing races
7. Drive shaft	29. Thrust bearing
8. Snap ring	30. Shear pin
9. Bushing	31. Propeller shaft
10. Thrust bearing race	32. Retainer
11. Thrust bearing	33. Bearing
12. Pinion gear	34. Thrust bearing race
13. Snap ring	35. Thrust bearing
14. Cover	36. Reverse gear
15. Bearing	37. Shift clutch
16. Shift rod	38. Forward gear
17. Nut	39. Thrust bearing
18. Seal locator	40. Thrust bearing race
19. Seal	41. Bearing
20. Seal housing	42. Gearcase
21. Pin	43. Shift yoke assy.
22. Pin	

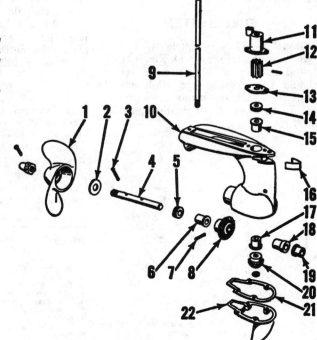

Fig. CL1-15—Exploded view of lower unit gearcase, water pump and associated parts used on all models except K-201, K-550, K-750, K-753 and K-900.

1. Propeller
2. Shaft washer
3. Shear pin
4. Propeller shaft
5. Oil seal
6. Shaft bushing
7. Roll pin
8. Propeller shaft gear
9. Drive shaft
10. Gearcase
11. Water pump body
12. Impeller
13. Pump cover
14. Oil seal
15. Shaft bushing
16. Snap-on cap
17. Shaft bushing
18. Spacer
19. Shaft bushing
20. Drive pinion
21. Gasket
22. Gearcase cover

CLINTON K-150 (1975-1978)

CONDENSED SERVICE DATA

TUNE-UP

Hp/rpm 1.5/5000
Bore—Inches 1.437
Stroke—Inches 1.250
Number of Cylinders 1
Displacement—Cu. In. 2.0

Spark Plug:
  Champion CJ6
  Electrode gap . . . . .0.025 in.

Magneto:
  Breaker point gap .0.015-0.018 in.

Carburetor:
  Make . . . . .Walbro
Fuel-Oil Ratio 32:1

SIZES—CLEARANCES

Piston Ring End Gap .0.067-0.077 in.
  Side Clearance . . . . .0.0015-0.0035 in.
Crankshaft Bearings:
  Upper main bearing . . . . .Roller bearing
  Lower main bearing . . . . .Ball bearing
  Crankpin .Loose roller bearing
  Number of rollers 28

TIGHTENING TORQUES
(All Values in Inch-Pounds)

Cylinder 50
Flywheel Nut 120
Spark Plug 100
Connecting Rod Screws 40-50

LUBRICATION

The power head is lubricated by oil mixed with the fuel. Recommended fuel:oil ratio is 32:1. Oil used should be a good quality outboard motor oil.

Lower unit gears and bearings are lubricated by oil contained in the gearcase. SAE 90 EP oil or a good quality outboard motor gear lubricant should be used. Gear oil is installed or drained through screw (S—Fig. CL2-1) hole in retainer.

FUEL SYSTEM

Model K-150 is equipped with float type carburetor shown in Fig. CL2-2. Initial position of idle mixture screw should be 2 turns open while initial position of high speed mixture screw is 1½ turns open. Normal idle speed is 2500 rpm.

To adjust float level, remove float bowl (12) and invert carburetor. Distance between outer rim of carburetor casting (bottom when inverted) and free end of float should be 1/8-inch. Float drop should be measured at the same place with carburetor in normal position and should be 3/16-inch.

REED VALVE. Model K-150 is equipped with a reed valve. Reed valve should be inspected for damage to reed valve petal or seat. Reed valve petal should seat flat with an allowable gap of 0.010 inch between petal and seat. Reed petals are not available separately. The notches form a passage for crankcase pulsations to the carburetor.

IGNITION

A flywheel type magneto is used. The breaker contact points are enclosed in a box under the flywheel and actuated by a cam on crankshaft. Armature and ignition coil are mounted outside flywheel. Refer to Fig. CL2-3.

To obtain access to breaker points, recoil starter assembly, blower housing

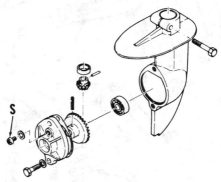

Fig. CL2-1—View showing location of gearcase fill screw (S).

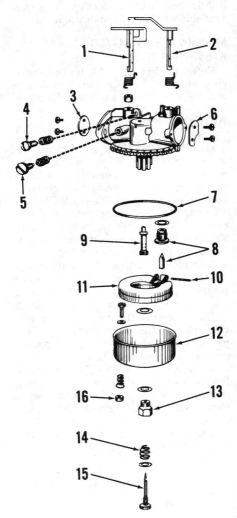

Fig. CL2-2—Exploded view of carburetor used on model K-150.

1. Throttle shaft	10. Float pin
2. Choke shaft	11. Float
3. Throttle plate	12. Float bowl
4. Idle speed screw	13. High speed mixture orifice
5. Idle mixture screw	14. Spring
6. Choke plate	15. High speed mixture screw
7. Gasket	
8. Fuel inlet valve	16. Bowl drain
9. Nozzle	

and flywheel must be removed. Tighten flywheel retaining nut to 120 in.-lbs.

Ignition timing is fixed. Breaker point gap should be 0.015-0.018 inch and must be correct, as incorrect point gap will affect ignition timing. Armature air gap should be 0.010 inch. Set air gap by loosening armature mounting screws and place 0.010 inch shim stock between armature and flywheel. Position armature against shim and tighten armature mounting screws. Remove shim stock.

POWER HEAD

PISTON, PIN, RINGS AND CYLINDER. The power head is equipped with a chrome plated cylinder. To remove cylinder, remove blower housing, flywheel and magneto back plate. Note position of exhaust so that cylinder may be reinstalled correctly depending on engine application.

Inspect cylinder for excessive wear or damage to chrome bore. Excessive wear may be checked by placing a new piston ring in cylinder bore and measuring ring end gap. If gap exceeds 0.077 inch, cylinder should be renewed. Remove, clean and inspect piston. Piston ring side clearance should be 0.0015-0.0035 inch. Piston ring end gap

should be 0.067-0.077 inch. Piston rings are non-directional. Install piston with piston ring locating pins towards flywheel side of engine. Tighten cylinder retaining nuts to 50 in.-lbs.

CONNECTING ROD. To remove connecting rod, remove cylinder and piston as previously outlined. Remove carburetor and reed valve assembly. Hold connecting rod cap (18—Fig. CL2-3) by placing a finger through intake port and remove rod cap screws. Remove connecting rod, being careful not to lose bearing rollers. Use a suitable press to remove and reinstall small end bearing.

Connecting rod is fractured and serrations of rod and cap must mesh during assembly. Rod and cap have match marks as shown in Fig. CL2-4 which must be aligned. To reinstall connecting rod, hold 14 bearing rollers in connecting rod cap with heavy grease and hold cap and rollers on crankshaft. New bearing rollers are on wax strips which may be used in place of grease. Place remaining 14 bearing rollers in rod with heavy grease, align match marks and serrations on rod and cap and install rod on crankshaft. Tighten connecting rod cap screws to 40-50 in.-lbs.

CRANKSHAFT AND CRANKCASE.

To remove crankshaft, remove connecting rod as previously outlined. Unscrew retaining screws and remove crankcase cover (3—Fig. CL2-3). Hold crankshaft while removing cover so that crankshaft does not fall against crankcase. Withdraw crankshaft being careful not to lose loose bearing rollers in bearing (8). Remove seal (43), heat crankcase and press bearing (8) race out of crankcase. Remove snap ring (6) and press bearing (5) out of cover.

Inspect components for wear or damage. Heat crankcase cover, press in bearing (5—CL2-3) and install snap ring (6). Heat crankcase and press in bearing (8) race so that letters on race are to inside of crankcase. Install 18 bearing rollers in race with grease to hold rollers in place. Install crankshaft, gasket and crankcase cover. Turn crankshaft and check for correct location of bearing (8) rollers and install seal (43). Reinstall remainder of engine components.

MANUAL STARTER

To disassemble starter, remove rope handle and allow rope to rewind into starter. Remove cover (42—Fig. CL2-3). Rewind spring (41) should remain in cover but care should be taken when removing cover as spring may uncoil and could cause injury. Remove remainder of starter assembly from engine.

To reassemble starter, install starter dogs as shown in view (A—Fig. CL2-5).

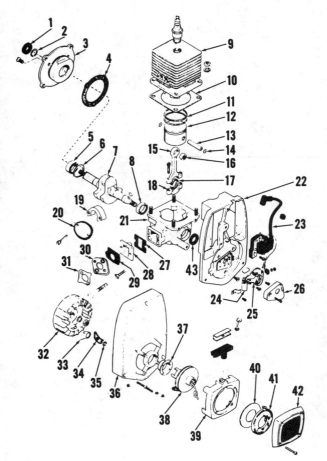

Fig. CL2-3—Exploded view of K-150 power head.

1. Seal
2. Snap ring
3. Cover
4. Gasket
5. Bearing
6. Snap ring
7. Crankshaft
8. Bearing
9. Cylinder
10. Gasket
11. Piston rings
12. Piston
13. Piston pin
14. Retainer
15. Connecting rod
16. Bearing
17. Bearing rollers (28)
18. Rod cap
19. Carb. silencer manifold
20. Crankcase
21. Crankcase
22. Magneto back plate
23. Armature & coil
24. Condenser
25. Breaker points
26. Cover
27. Gasket
28. Reed valve
29. Gasket
30. Carb. mounting plate
31. Gasket
32. Flywheel
33. Spring
34. Starter dog
35. "E" ring
36. Blower housing
37. Bushing
38. Rope pulley
39. Housing
40. Washer
41. Rewind spring
42. Cover
43. Seal

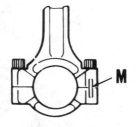

Fig. CL2-4—Connecting rod match marks (M) must be aligned during assembly.

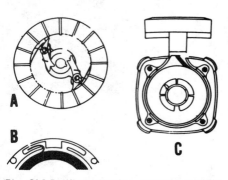

Fig. CL2-5—View showing correct assembly of starter dogs (A), rewind spring (B) and rope (C).

Place end of rope through hole in rope pulley and tie knot. Pass other end of rope through rope outlet in housing (39—Fig. CL2-3). Assemble components (32 through 39). Pull rope out of starter so that it is fully extended and attach rope handle so that there is 28 inches from starter housing to bottom of rope handle. Wind rope on pulley by turning pulley in direction that does not engage starter dogs. Install rewind spring in cover as shown in Fig. CL2-5. Lubricate spring with a suitable lubricant. To preload starter rope, install spring and cover so that inner hook of spring engages notch in rope pulley and turn cover 1-1½ turns in direction that will wind spring. Install cover screws.

LOWER UNIT

Refer to Fig. CL2-6 for an exploded view of lower unit used on model K-150. Service information was not available at time of publication.

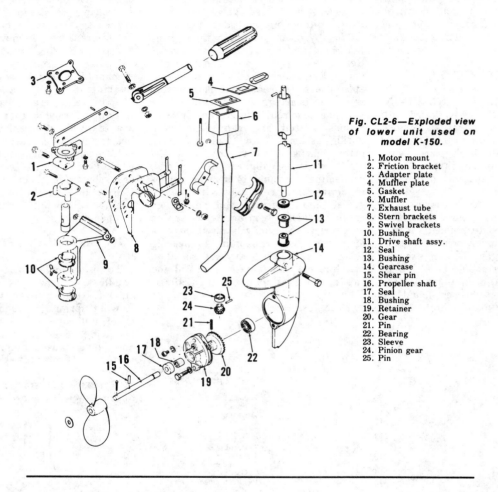

Fig. CL2-6—Exploded view of lower unit used on model K-150.

1. Motor mount
2. Friction bracket
3. Adapter plate
4. Muffler plate
5. Gasket
6. Muffler
7. Exhaust tube
8. Stern brackets
9. Swivel brackets
10. Bushing
11. Drive shaft assy.
12. Seal
13. Bushing
14. Gearcase
15. Shear pin
16. Propeller shaft
17. Seal
18. Bushing
19. Retainer
20. Gear
21. Pin
22. Bearing
23. Sleeve
24. Pinion gear
25. Pin

CRUISE 'N CARRY

HMC
20710 Alameda Street
Long Beach, California 90810

6500, 6600 AND 6700

CONDENSED SERVICE DATA

TUNE-UP

Hp/rpm:
6500	1.4/6500
6600	1.5/8000
6700	2.7/8000

Bore:
6500	1.22 in.
	(31 mm)
6600	1.25 in.
	(32 mm)
6700	1.57 in.
	(39.9 mm)

Stroke:
6500	1.18 in.
	(30 mm)
6600	1.18 in.
	(30 mm)
6700	1.30 in.
	(33 mm)

Number of cylinders 1

Displacement:
6500	1.38 cu. in.
	(22.6 cc)
6600	1.47 cu. in.
	(24.1 cc)
6700	2.5 cu. in.
	(41.5 cc)

Ignition Type:
6500	Breaker Point
6600	Breakerless
6700	Breakerless

Spark Plug:
6500
NGK	B8S
Electrode Gap	0.026 in.
	(0.6 mm)

6500 And 6700
Champion	CJ8
Electrode Gap	0.026 in.
	(0.6 mm)

Fuel:Oil Ratio 25:1

LUBRICATION

The power head is lubricated by oil mixed with the fuel. Recommended fuel:oil ratio is 25:1. Recommended oil is One-Mix or a BIA certified oil. Use only regular or unleaded grade gasoline.

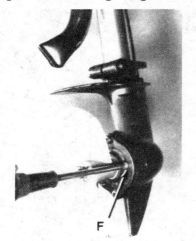

Fig. CC1-1 — View showing location of gearcase lubricant fill screw.

Lower unit is lubricated by oil contained in gearcase. To fill gearcase, remove fill screw (F-Fig. CC1-1) and fill gearcase with unit upright until lubricant flows out of fill screw hole. Use a 20W50 oil.

FUEL SYSTEM

CARBURETOR. Refer to Fig. CC1-2 for an exploded view of float type carburetor used. Air flow through carburetor is controlled by throttle slide (10). Jet needle (9) position in throttle slide is determined by clip (8). Jet needle (9) passes through needle jet (17) and alters fuel flow through main jet according to throttle slide movement. As the throttle slide is raised to admit more air through the carburetor, jet needle (9) will be withdrawn from the needle jet allowing more fuel to flow into carburetor bore. Relocating jet needle clip (8) on jet needle (9) will change fuel delivery. Moving the clip to a higher groove in the jet needle will lean the air:fuel mixture; placing the clip in a lower groove will richen the mixture.

NOTE: Examine spark plug core for determining proper location of jet needle clip (8) on jet needle (9).

Full throttle mixture is controlled by size of main jet (20).

To determine the float level, invert carburetor body (1) with needle valve (16), float arm (18), pin (19), needle jet (17), main jet (20) and float (21) installed. Place a straightedge across bottom of float (21). The bottom of float (21) should be level with bottom of main jet (20). Bend arms on float arm (18) evenly to adjust float level.

To adjust idle speed, start engine and allow to warm-up to normal operating temperature. Rotate throttle lever to idle position, shift into neutral position, then turn idle speed adjustment screw (13) clockwise to increase engine speed or counterclockwise to decrease engine speed. Recommended idle speed is 3500-3700 rpm with gearcase in neutral and propeller submerged in water on 6500 models and 4000 rpm with gearcase in neutral and propeller out of water on 6600 and 6700 models.

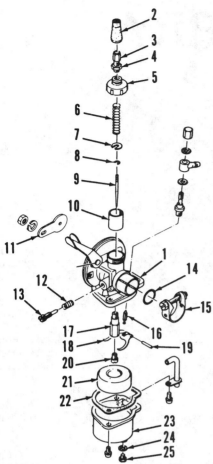

Fig CC1-2 — Exploded view of carburetor typical of the type used on all models. Fuel inlet fitting and idle speed screw (13) are on opposite side shown on Model 6700.

1. Body
2. Cover
3. Adjuster screw
4. Locknut
5. Gap
6. Spring
7. Clip retainer
8. Clip
9. Jet needle
10. Throttle slide
11. Choke plate
12. Spring
13. Idle speed screw
14. "O" ring
15. Clamp
16. Needle valve
17. Needle jet
18. Float arm
19. Pin
20. Main jet
21. Float
22. Gasket
23. Float bowl
24. Gasket
25. Drain plug

SPEED CONTROL LINKAGE. The engine speed is regulated by the position of the throttle lever on 6500 and 6600 models and by a twist grip on 6700 models. As throttle lever on twist grip is rotated, the carburetor throttle slide (10-Fig. CC1-2) is operated via a throttle cable. An engine kill switch is mounted on the tiller handle on 6500 and 6600 models and in the end of the twist grip on 6700 models.

IGNITION

The standard spark plug is NGK B8S with an electrode gap of 0.026 inch (0.6 mm) on 6500 models and Champion CJ8 with an electrode gap of 0.026 inch (0.6 mm) on 6600 and 6700 models.

On 6500 models, a breaker point ignition system is used. To check ignition timing, unplug breaker point wire from ignition coil connector. Connect one test lead of a suitable ohmmeter or point checker to terminal end of breaker point wire and the remaining test lead to a suitable engine ground. When the flywheel timing mark and the case timing mark are aligned as shown in Fig. CC1-3, the test meter should show the breaker points just starting to open. To adjust, remove the engine flywheel.

On 6600 and 6700 models, a breakerless ignition system is used. If

engine malfunction is noted and the ignition system is suspected, make sure the spark plug and all electrical wiring are in good condition before servicing breakerless ignition components.

COOLING SYSTEM

The power head is air-cooled by a fan built into the flywheel. The fan shroud must be in place and power head cooling fins must be clean and unbroken or engine may overheat.

POWER HEAD

OVERHAUL. Disassembly and reassembly of power head is evident after referral to Fig. CC1-4 and inspection of unit.

A closed end cylinder is used. Oversize pistons and rings are not available.

Connecting rod is one-piece which rides on bearing rollers around crankpin. Crankshaft halves are pressed on crankpin to retain connecting rod. Connecting rod, bearing, crankpin and crankshaft can be obtained as a unit only.

The crankshaft is supported at both ends by ball bearings. Bearing should be renewed if damaged or excessively worn.

Make sure all sealing surfaces are free of nicks and gouges.

Fig. CC1-4 — Exploded view of engine assembly typical of all models. Breakerless ignition system used on Model 6600 is shown.

1. Flywheel
2. Upper crankcase half
3. Seal
4. Ball bearing
5. Rod & crankshaft assy.
6. Lower crankcase half
7. Clip
8. Piston pin
9. Thrust washer
10. Needle bearing
11. Piston
12. Piston rings
13. Gasket
14. Cylinder head
15. Intake manifold
16. Insulator
17. Gaskets
18. Ignition coil
19. Module

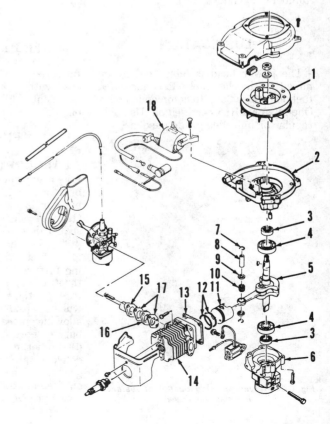

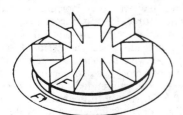

Fig. CC1-3 — Flywheel timing mark and case timing mark must be aligned when breaker points just start to open for proper ignition timing.

MANUAL STARTER

A pawl type rewind starter is used. Refer to Fig. CC1-5 for an exploded view of starter. Overhaul of starter is evident after inspection of unit and referral to exploded view. Rewind spring (2) must be wound in counterclockwise direction from outer end in starter housing (1). Starter rope (9) is wrapped around pulley (3) in a counterclockwise direction as viewed from flywheel side.

LOWER UNIT

Standard propeller on 6500 and 6600 models is two bladed with a diameter of 5¼ inches (133 mm) and a 95° pitch. Standard propeller on 6700 models is three bladed with a diameter of 5.7 inches (145 mm) and a pitch of 3.54 inches (90 mm).

Refer to Fig. CC1-7 for an exploded view of lower unit. Overhaul is evident after inspection of unit and referral to exploded view. Inspect components and renew any which are damaged or excessively worn.

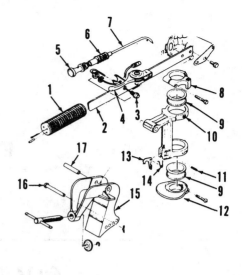

Fig. CC1-6 — Exploded view of mounting brackets, steering components, throttle components and gearcase shift cable used on 6500 and 6600 models. Model 6700 is similar with the exception a twist grip throttle control is used.

1. Rubber grip	10. Swivel bracket
2. Tiller handle	11. Pin
3. Kill switch	12. Tilt cam
4. Throttle lever	13. Reverse lock
5. Knob	14. Spring
6. Holder	15. Transom bracket
7. Shift cable	16. Tilt pin
8. Adjusting collar	17. Pivot pin
9. Cushion	

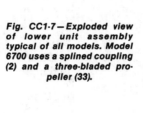

Fig. CC1-7 — Exploded view of lower unit assembly typical of all models. Model 6700 uses a splined coupling (2) and a three-bladed propeller (33).

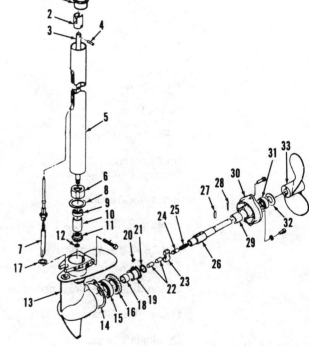

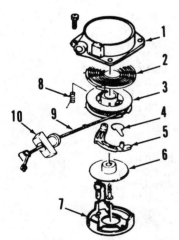

Fig. CC1-5 — Exploded view of rewind starter typical of all models. Housing (1) is square shaped on Model 6700.

1. Housing	6. Plate
2. Rewind spring	7. Drive plate
3. Pulley	8. Spring
4. Spring clip	9. Starter rope
5. Drive pawl	10. Handle

1. Bushing	10. Bushing	18. Bushing	26. Propeller shaft
2. Coupling	11. Pinion gear	19. Clutch	27. Shear pin
3. Drive shaft	12. Clip	20. Key	28. Cotter pin
4. Pin	13. Gearcase housing	21. Washer	29. Bushing
5. Drive shaft tube	14. Gasket	22. Plungers	30. Cap
6. Bushing	15. Bearing	23. Dog clutch	31. Seal
7. Shift cable	16. Gear	24. Guide	32. Washer
8. Gasket	17. Gasket	25. Spring	33. Propeller
9. Seal			

ESKA

THE ESKA COMPANY
2400 Kerper Blvd.
Dubuque, Iowa 52001

ESKA 1.2 AND 2.5 HP

Year Produced	1.2 hp	2.5 hp
1977............................	14048A	14089A
1978............................	.....	14089B
1979............................	.....	13089C

CONDENSED SERVICE DATA

TUNE-UP	1.2 hp	2.5 hp
Bore...........................	1.18 in.	1.61 in.
	(30 mm)	(41 mm)
Stroke..........................	1.18 in.	1.495 in.
	(30 mm)	(38 mm)
Number of Cylinders................	1	1
Displacement.....................	1.29 cu. in.	3.05 cu. in.
	(21.2 cc)	(50 cc)
Spark Plug:		
Champion.....................	RJ8J	RJ8J
Electrode Gap..................	0.025 in.	0.025 in.
	(0.6 mm)	(0.6 mm)
Ignition Timing...................	28° BTDC	28° BTDC
Breaker Point Gap.................	0.013 in.	0.013 in.
	(0.35 mm)	(0.35 mm)
Armature Air Gap.................	0.013 in.	0.013 in.
	(0.35 mm)	(0.35 mm)
Fuel:Oil Ratio.....................	32:1	32:1
SIZES—CLEARANCES		
Piston Ring End Gap................	0.002-0.010 in.	0.004-0.014 in.
	(0.05-0.25 mm)	(0.1-0.35 mm)
Piston Ring Side Clearance...........	0.002-0.003 in.	0.002-0.003 in.
	(0.045-0.08 mm)	(0.045-0.08 mm)
Piston Skirt Clearance—Max..........	0.005 in.	0.005 in.
	(0.12 mm)	(0.12 mm)
Crankshaft Bearings:		
Upper........................	Ball Bearing	Ball Bearing
Lower........................	Ball Bearing	Ball Bearing
Crankshaft End Play................	0.002-0.010 in.	0.002-0.010 in.
	(0.05-0.25 mm)	(0.05-0.25 mm)

LUBRICATION

The power head is lubricated by oil mixed with the fuel. Recommended fuel:oil ratio is 32:1. Oil should be BIA certified TC-W.

Lower unit is lubricated by oil contained in gearcase. To fill gearcase, remove fill screw (F. Fig. E1-1) and fill gearcase with unit upright until lubricant flows out of fill screw hole. Use a SAE 90 outboard gear lubricant.

FUEL SYSTEM

CARBURETOR. Refer to Fig. E1-2 or E1-3 for an exploded view of float type carburetor used. Air flow through carburetor is controlled by throttle slide (8). Jet needle (6) position in throttle slide is determined by clip (5). Recommended clip (5) position is third notch from the top on 1.2 hp models and second notch from the top on 2.5 hp models. Jet needle (6) passes through main jet

(11) or needle jet (17) and alters fuel flow through main jet according to throttle slide movement. As the throttle slide is raised to admit more air through the carburetor, the jet needle will be withdrawn from the main jet or needle jet allowing more fuel to flow into carburetor bore. Relocating the jet needle clip (5) on the jet needle (6) will change fuel delivery. Moving the clip to a higher groove in the jet needle will lean the air:fuel mixture; placing the clip in a

Fig. E1-1 – View showing location of lower unit lubricant fill screw. Drain lubricant by removing gear housing cover.

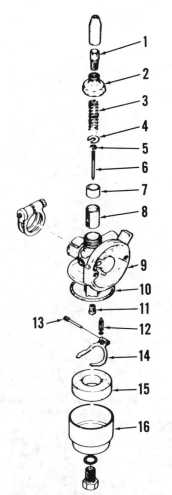

Fig. E1-2 – Exploded view of carburetor used on 1.2 hp models.

1. Cable guide	9. Body
2. Cap	10. Gasket
3. Spring	11. Main jet
4. Clip retainer	12. Fuel inlet valve
5. Clip	13. Float pin
6. Jet needle	14. Float arm
7. Throttle stop	15. Float
8. Throttle slide	16. Float bowl

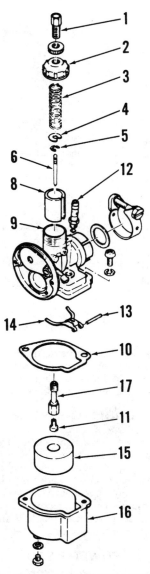

Fig. E1-3 – Exploded view of carburetor used on 2.5 hp models. Refer to Fig. E1-2 for parts identification except for: 17. Needle jet.

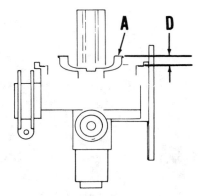

Fig. E1-4 – Carburetor float arm (A) on 1.2 hp models should be 0.138 inch (3.5 mm) (D) above gasket surface.

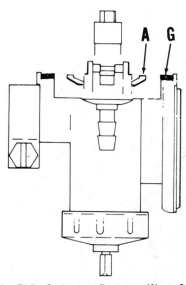

Fig. E1-5 – Carburetor float arm (A) on 2.5 hp models should be level with gasket (G).

Fig. E1-6 – View showing use of tool (T) to set air gap.

lower groove will richen the mixture. Full throttle mixture is controlled by size of main jet. Standard main jet is number 50 on 1.2 hp models and number 74 on 2.5 hp models.

Float arm on 1.2 hp models should be 0.138 inch (3.5 mm) above carburetor body measured as shown in Fig. E1-4. Float arm on 2.5 hp models should be level with the float bowl gasket as shown in Fig. E1-5.

IGNITION

Air gap between ignition coil legs and flywheel must be adjusted for optimum ignition output. Loosen coil mounting screws and install tool 95902 (1.2 hp) or 95903 (2.5 hp) in flywheel housing as shown in Fig. E1-6. Position ignition coil so legs contact tool and tighten ignition coil mounting screws. If special tool is not available, adjust armature air gap to 0.013 inch (0.35 mm).

Breaker point gap should be 0.013 inch (0.35 mm). The top of the flywheel magneto is marked with a T, for TDC,

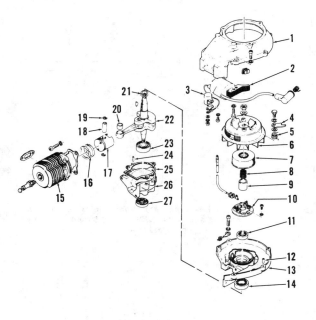

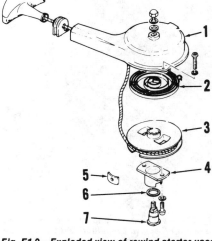

Fig. E1-7 — Exploded view of 1.2 hp engine.

1. Fan shroud
2. Ignition coil
3. Condenser
4. Starter pawl
5. Pawl spring
6. Flywheel
7. Cover
8. Spring
9. Breaker point cam
10. Breaker point plate assy.
11. Seal
12. Dowel pin
13. Upper crankcase half
14. Bearing
15. Cylinder
16. Piston rings
17. Piston
18. Piston pin
19. Pin retainers
20. Bushing
21. Shims
22. Crankshaft & rod assy.
23. Bearing
24. Dowel pin
25. Gasket
26. Lower crankcase half
27. Seal

Fig. E1-9 — Exploded view of rewind starter used on 1.2 hp models. Drive coupling (4) engages starter pawls (4 — Fig. E1-7).

1. Housing
2. Rewind spring
3. Rope pulley
4. Drive coupling
5. Rope guide
6. Washer
7. Pulley shaft

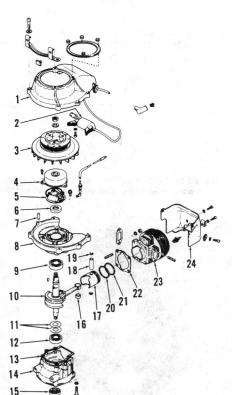

Fig. E1-8 — Exploded view of 2.5 hp engine.

1. Fan shroud
2. Ignition coil
3. Flywheel
4. Cover
5. Breaker point plate assy.
6. Seal
7. Dowel pin
8. Upper crankcase half
9. Bearing
10. Crankshaft & rod assy.
11. Shims
12. Bearing
13. Gasket
14. Lower crankcase half
15. Seal
16. Bushing
17. Piston
18. Piston pin
19. Pin retainers
20. Lower piston ring
21. Upper piston ring
22. Gasket
23. Cylinder
24. Shroud

and an M, for correct ignition timing. The breaker points must start to open when the M mark is aligned with the match mark on the crankcase.

COOLING SYSTEM

The power head is air-cooled by a fan built into the flywheel. The fan shroud must be in place and power head cooling fins must be clean and unbroken or engine may overheat. Manufacturer recommends renewing power head cylinder if 10 percent of cooling fins are missing or cracked.

POWER HEAD

DISASSEMBLY. To disassemble power head, remove cover, fuel tank, rewind starter, flywheel, muffler and carburetor. Unbolt power head from adapter plate and separate power head from lower unit.

Remove breaker point plate, cooling shroud and carrying handle. Pull drive adapter from crankshaft lower end. Unscrew cylinder base nuts or screws and separate cylinder from crankcase. Remove piston pin retainers, drive out piston pin and remove piston. Unscrew crankcase screws and separate crankcase halves. Remove crankshaft and rod assembly from crankcase half.

REASSEMBLY. To reassemble power head, reverse disassembly procedure. Crankcase and cylinder mating surfaces should be flat and free of nicks and gouges. Be sure piston rings are correctly positioned around piston ring locating pins in piston ring grooves when installing cylinder.

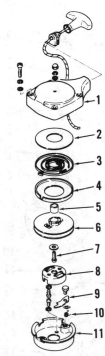

Fig. E1-10 — Exploded view of rewind starter used on 2.5 hp models.

1. Housing
2. Washer
3. Rewind spring
4. Spring case
5. Bushing
6. Rope pulley
7. Screw
8. Cover
9. Pawls
10. Pawl springs
11. Starter cup

PISTON, PIN, RINGS AND CYLINDER. All models are equipped with a closed end cylinder. Oversize pistons and rings are not available.

Piston rings are pinned in piston ring grooves. Piston rings on 1.2 hp models are interchangeable. On 2.5 hp models,

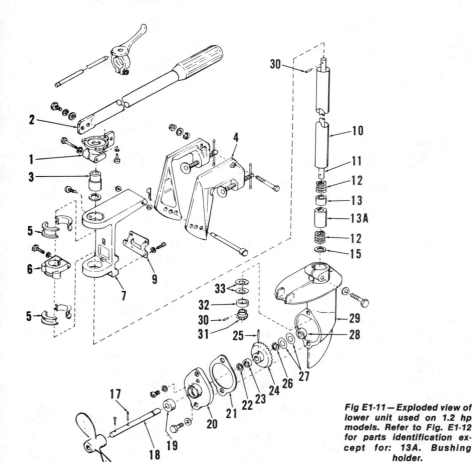

MANUAL STARTER

Both models are equipped with a pawl type rewind starter. Refer to Fig. E1-9 or E1-10 for an exploded view of starter. Overhaul of starter is evident after inspection of unit and referral to exploded view. Rewind spring on 1.2 hp models must be wound in counterclockwise direction from outer end in starter housing (1) while rewind spring on 2.5 hp models must be wound in clockwise direction in spring case (4 – Fig. E1-10). Rope is wrapped around pulley in counterclockwise direction as viewed from drive side on 1.2 hp models and clockwise direction on 2.5 hp models.

LOWER UNIT

Refer to Fig. E1-11 or E1-12 for an exploded view of lower unit. Overhaul is evident after inspection of unit and referral to exploded view. Be careful not to lose or damage shims during disassembly. Inspect components and renew any which are damaged or excessively worn.

Assembled backlash between pinion (31 – Fig. E1-11 or E1-12) and gear (24) should be 0.002-0.006 inch (0.05-0.15 mm). Vary thickness of shims (22 and 27) until backlash is within the recommended limits.

Fig E1-11 – Exploded view of lower unit used on 1.2 hp models. Refer to Fig. E1-12 for parts identification except for: 13A. Bushing holder.

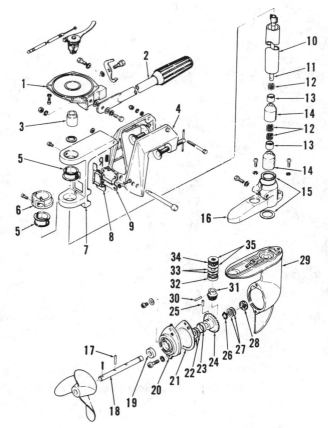

install cast iron ring in lower ring groove and chrome ring in upper ring groove.

Maximum piston skirt to cylinder wall clearance is 0.005 inch (0.12 mm).

CONNECTING ROD AND CRANK-SHAFT. Connecting rod is one-piece which rides on bearing rollers around crankpin. Crankshaft halves are pressed on crankpin to retain connecting rod. Connecting rod, bearing, crankpin and crankshaft may be obtained as a unit only.

The crankshaft is supported at both ends by ball bearings. Bearing should be renewed if damaged or excessively worn.

Crankshaft end play should be 0.002-0.010 inch (0.05-0.25 mm). Vary thickness of shims (21 – Fig. E1-7) on 1.2 hp models or (11 – Fig. E1-8) on 2.5 hp models to adjust crankshaft end play.

Fig. E1-12 – Exploded view of lower unit used on 2.5 hp models.

1. Adapter
2. Steering handle
3. Coupling
4. Bracket
5. Bushings
6. Tilt cam
7. Swivel bracket
8. Cam return guide
9. Cam plate
10. Drive shaft tube
11. Drive shaft
12. Springs
13. Bushing
14. Bushing holders
15. Gasket
16. Drive shaft housing
17. Pin
18. Propeller shaft
19. Seal
20. Cover
21. Gasket
22. Shims
23. Bushing
24. Gear
25. Pin
26. Snap ring
27. Shims
28. Bearing
29. Gearcase
30. Pin
31. Pinion
32. Bushing
33. Shims
34. Thrust bearing
35. Thrust washers

ESKA 3, 3.5, 4.5, 5, 5.5, 7
AND 7.5 HP (1969-1985)

Year Produced	Model No.	HP	Tecumseh Power Head	Year Produced	Model No.	HP	Tecumseh Power Head
1969	1188, 1700, 1703, 1703A, 1704, 1709, 1713, 1713A	3.5	AV-520	1975	1973A	3	AV-520
	1189, 1194, 1701, 1705, 1706, 1710, 1715	5	AV-600		1903C, 1941B, 1974A	4.5	AV-520
	1186, 1199, 1702, 1707, 1708, 1711, 1717	7	AV-750		1997A	5	AV-600
					1904A, 1904B, 1910A, 1969A, 1970A, 1975A	5.5	AV-600
1970	1188, 1703B, 1704B, 1709B, 1713B, 1723B	3.5	AV-520		1905C, 1909C, 1914C, 1944C, 1966C, 1967C, 1976A	7.5	AV-817
	1189B, 1194B, 1701B, 1705B, 1706B, 1715B, 1733B	5	AV-600	1976	1973B	3	AV-520
	1199, 1702B, 1707B, 1708B, 1717B, 1723B, 1734B	7	AV-750		1974B	4.5	AV-520
					1975B	5.5	AV-600
1971	1703C, 1713C, 1770A	3.5	AV-520		1944D, 1976B	7.5	AV-817
	1701C, 1705C, 1706C, 1715C, 1733C, 1766A, 1771A	5	AV-600	1977	1403B	3.5	AV-520
	1702C, 1708C, 1721A, 1727A, 1745A, 1747A, 1767A, 1772A, 1777A	7	AV-750		14035B, 14036B	5	AV-600
					14037B, 14038A, 14059A	7.5	AV-817
1972	1703D, 1713D, 1770B, 1788A, 1791A	3.5	AV-520	1978	14034C	3.5	AV-520
	1705D, 1706D, 1715D, 1766B, 1771B, 1784A, 1789A	5	AV-600		14035C, 14106A	5	AV-600
	1727B, 1746A, 1747B, 1756A, 1767B, 1772B, 1776A, 1790A	7	AV-817		14107A, 14108A	7.5	AV-817
				1979	14034D	3.5	AV-520
1973	1929A, 1945A	3.5	AV-520		14035D, 14106B	5	AV-600
	1903A	4.5	AV-520		14107B, 14108B	7.5	AV-817
	1705E, 1908A, 1913A, 1928A, 1930A	5	AV-600	1980	14139A	3.5	AV-520
	1747C, 1931A	7	AV-817		14140A	5	AV-600
	1905A, 1909A, 1914A, 1932A, 1966A	7.5	AV-817		14141A	7.5	AV-817
				1981	14178A, 14183A	3.5	AV-520
1974	1929B, 1945B	3.5	AV-520		14035E, 14140B, 14179B, 14189A	5	AV-600
	1903B	4.5	AV-520		14141B, 14180A	7.5	AV-817
	1705F, 1908B, 1913B, 1928B, 1930B	5	AV-600	1982	14178B, 14183B	3.5	AV-520
	1747D, 1931B	7	AV-817		14140C, 14179B	5	AV-600
	1905B, 1909B, 1914B, 1932B, 1944B	7.5	AV-817		14141C, 14180B	7.5	AV-817
				1983	14207	3.5	AV-520
					14208	5	AV-600
					14209	7.5	AV-817
				1984	14207	3.5	AV-520
					14208	5	AV-600
					14209	7.5	AV-817
				1985	14207	3.5	AV-520
					14208	5	AV-600
					14209	7.5	AV-817

These motors are also sold as Explorer, Federal, Golden-jet, Hanimex, Hiawatha, Pathfinder, Seaco, Seacruiser-Grant, Sea King, Sea Hawk, Sears, Skipper, Sportfisher and Wizard models.

Illustrations Courtesy Eska

CONDENSED SERVICE DATA

TUNE-UP	AV520	AV600	AV750	AV817
Bore	2.09 in.	2.09 in.	2.375 in.	2.437 in.
	(53 mm)	(53 mm)	(60.3 mm)	(61.9 mm)
Stroke	1.50 in.	1.76 in.	1.68 in.	1.75 mm
	(38.1 mm)	(44.7 mm)	(42.7 mm)	(44.4 mm)
Number of Cylinders	1	1	1	1
Displacement	5.16 cu. in.	6.05 cu. in.	7.50 cu. in.	8.17 cu. in.
	(84.6 cc)	(99.1 cc)	(122.9 cc)	(133.9 cc)
Spark Plug—				
Champion	J13Y*	J13Y*	J13Y*	J13Y*
AC	45S	45S	45S	45S
Electrode gap	0.030 in.	0.030 in.	0.030 in.	0.030 in.
	(0.76 mm)	(0.76 mm)	(0.76 mm)	(0.76 mm
Conventional Magneto—				
Breaker Point Gap	See Text	See Text	See Text	See Text
Piston Position Max.				
Advance Timing	See Text	See Text	See Text	See Text
Solid State Magneto—				
Max. Advance Timing	See Text	See Text	See Text	See Text
Fuel:Oil Ratio	See Text	See Text	See Text	See Text

SIZES—CLEARANCES				
Piston Rings—				
End gap	See Text	See Text	0.005-0.013 in.	0.007-0.017 in.
			(0.13-0.33 mm)	(0.18-0.43 mm)
Side clearance	See Text	See Text	See Text	See Text
Piston Pin Diameter	0.4997-0.4999 in.	0.4997-0.4999 in.	0.4997-0.4999 in.	0.4997-0.4999 in.
	(12.692-12.697 mm)	(12.692-12.697 mm)	(12.692-12.697 mm)	(12.692-12.697 mm)
Piston Skirt Clearance	0.005-0.007 in.	0.005-0.007 in.	0.0055-0.0075 in.	0.0058-0.0078 in.
	(0.13-0.18 mm)	(0.13-0.18 mm)	(0.14-0.19 mm)	(0.147-0.198 mm)
Crankshaft Clearance—				
Top main bearing	Ball or Needle	Ball or Needle	Needle	Needle
Bottom main bearing	Needle	Needle	Ball	Ball or Needle
Crankpin	See Text	See Text	Needle	Needle
End play	See Text	0.003-0.016 in.	Zero	Zero
		(0.07-0.40 mm)		

TIGHTENING TORQUES				
Connecting Rod—				
Plain bearing (Aluminum)	50-57 in.-lbs.	50-57 in.-lbs.	.....	50-57 in.-lbs.
	(5.6-6.4 N·m)	(5.6-6.4 N·m)		(5.6-6.4 N·m)
Needle bearing (Steel)	70-80 in.-lbs.	70-80 in.-lbs.	70-80 in.-lbs.	70-80 in.-lbs.
	(7.9-9 N·m)	(7.9-9 N·m)	(7.9-9 N·m)	(7.9-9 N·m)
Cylinder Head	80-100 in.-lbs.	80-100 in.-lbs.	80-100 in.-lbs.	80-100 in.-lbs.
	(9-11.3 N·m)	(9-11.3 N·m)	(9-11.3 N·m)	(9-11.3 N·m)
Flywheel	25 ft.-lbs.	25 ft.-lbs.	25 ft.-lbs.	25 ft.-lbs.
	(34 N·m)	(34 N·m)	(34 N·m)	(34 N·m)
Shroud Base to				
Crankcase	70-75 in.-lbs.	70-75 in.-lbs.	70-75 in.-lbs.	70-75 in.-lbs.
	(7.9-8.4 N·m)	(7.9-8.4 N·m)	(7.9-8.4 N·m)	(7.9-8.4 N·m)

*Recommended spark plug for models after 1976 is Champion RJ13Y.

The engine model number (AV-520, AV-600, AV-750 or AV-817) is for easy reference only to the general construction. If service parts are required, the type number MUST be used. The type number is stamped in the blower housing or on a tag attached to engine. A correct type number will usually consist of three numbers, a dash followed by two more numbers (such as 643-09). When servicing power head, make certain that identification tag is reinstalled.

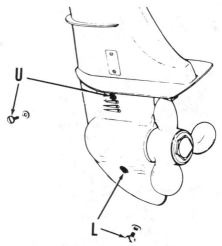

Fig. E2-1—View of gearcase showing upper (vent) plug (U) and lower (drain/fill) plug (L). Non-gear shift type units have drain/fill plug on opposite side of gearcase.

LUBRICATION

The power head is lubricated by oil mixed with regular grade gasoline. Recommended fuel to oil ratio is 16:1 for 1969 model motors. Oil used should be a good grade of oil intended for use in outboard motors. Fuel and oil should be mixed in a ratio of 24:1 for 1970 through 1973 model motors. Fuel:oil ratio of 32:1 may be used on 1974 and later models if oil used is BIA certified TC-W. If BIA certified TC-W oil is not available, use a good grade of outboard motor oil in a 24:1 fuel to oil mixture on 1974 and later models.

The lower unit gears and bearings are lubricated by oil contained in the gearcase. SAE 90 outboard gear lubricant

should be used. Lubricant should be checked at least every 20 hours of operation and maintained at level of the upper vent plug (U – Fig. E2-1), when motor is in upright position. The gearcase should be drained and filled with new oil at least once each season. Remove both plugs (U & L) and lay motor on side to drain the gearcase. If excessive water is noted when draining, seals and gaskets should be renewed as outlined in the LOWER UNIT section. Motor should be in upright position when filling gearcase with lubricant. Insert filler tube in lower plug (L) opening and fill until lubricant is at level of upper plug (U) opening. Install upper plug, then remove filler tube and install lower plug. Use new gaskets on plugs if necessary to provide a water tight seal.

FUEL SYSTEM

CARBURETOR. The Tecumseh float type carburetor is shown in Fig. E2-2. Idle mixture is adjusted at needle (L) and high speed mixture is adjusted at needle (H). Clockwise rotation of both needles leans the mixture. Initial setting is approximately 1 turn open for both needles.

Carburetor adjustments should only be made with motor in water so a load is placed on engine. Start and run motor until it reaches operating temperature, then adjust to provide smoothest operation in gear. The high speed mixture needle (H) should be adjusted first. Idle mixture (L) should be set rich enough to provide smooth acceleration from idle to high speed. Use caution when setting needles to prevent mixture from being too lean and causing engine damage.

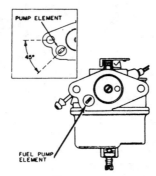

Fig. E2-3—Fuel pump element (4 – Fig. E2-2) should be installed at a 45° angle as shown.

CAUTION: Do not attempt to remove carburetor from AV750 models without removing the reed valve assembly.

NOTE: Several variations of this carburetor have been used and differences in servicing procedure will be noted.

Disassembly of carburetor will depend upon extent of service required. Parts (4, 13, 16, 20, 20L, 21, 25, 25D, 26, 26F and 26G) may be damaged by most commercial carburetor cleaning solvents and must be removed. The gravity feed inlet fitting (26F) and early type check valves (25 and 26) are pressed into carburetor body. The fitting (26 or 26F) should be pulled out of bore, then carefully drill outlet check valve (25) with a 9/64 inch (3.57 mm) drill to a depth of 1/8 inch (3.17 mm) as shown in Fig. E2-4.

CAUTION: Do not drill too far or carburetor body will be damaged.

Thread an 8-32 tap into the outlet check valve, then use the proper size nut and flat washer to convert tap into a puller as shown in Fig. E2-5. Pull check valve out by tightening nut.

Inlet needle (20 – Fig. E2-2) has a Viton tip that seats directly into carburetor body on some models or into a renewable Viton seat (20L) on later models. Seat (20L) may be removed by inserting a small wire hook through hole and pulling seat out of brass liner. Viton seat should be renewed if removed from carburetor body. New seat should be installed with grooved side toward carburetor body, away from needle (20).

On all models, install throttle plate (3) with stamped lines facing out (toward engine) and at 12 and 3 o'clock positions. If the choke plate (9) is provided with stamped mark, the mark should be toward inside of carburetor and flat should be toward fuel inlet fitting (26, 26F or 26L). If choke plate is not marked, the flat side should be down toward float bowl. Float setting should

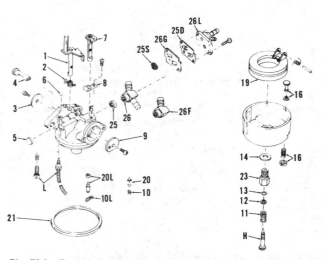

H.	High speed mixture needle
L.	Idle mixture needle
1.	Throttle shaft
2.	Throttle spring
3.	Throttle plate
4.	Pumping element
5.	Welch plug
6.	Lead shot
7.	Choke shaft
8.	Detent
9.	Choke plate
10.	Spring
10L.	Clip
11.	Spring
12.	Washer
13.	"O" ring
14.	Washer
16.	Bowl drain
19.	Float
20.	Inlet needle
20L.	Inlet needle & seat
21.	Seating ring
23.	Bowl retainer
25.	Outlet check valve
25D.	Check valves
25S.	Screen
26.	Inlet check valve & fitting
26F.	Inlet fitting
26G.	Gasket
26L.	Inlet cover

Fig. E2-2 — Exploded view of Tecumseh carburetor. On gravity feed models, fitting (26F) is used. On early fuel pump models, pumping element (4), outlet check valve (25), inlet check valve and fitting (26) are used. On latest models with fuel pump, check valves (25D), inlet cover (26L) and screen (25S) are used.

Illustrations Courtesy Eska

be 0.200-0.220 inch (5.08-5.58 mm), measured with body and float assembly inverted, between free end of float and rim of carburetor body. Preferred method for checking float level is to place a number 4 drill bit shank (0.209 inch or 5.30 mm) between float and carburetor body (Fig. E2-6). When installing fuel bowl, the flat under side should be located below the fuel inlet (26, 26F or 26L – Fig. E2-2).

The fuel pumping element (4) is a rubber boot which expands and contracts due to changes in crankcase pressure. The pumping element should be installed at 45° angle as shown in Fig. E2-3. Incorrect installation may interfere with pumping action.

On AV750 models, coat threads of carburetor retaining screws with "Loctite" before assembling.

SPEED CONTROL LINKAGE. The ignition timing is advanced by the speed control lever and the throttle is operated by a cam attached to the magneto stator plate. The ignition timing and throttle opening must be synchronized to provide correct operation. Refer to the appropriate following paragraphs for timing the ignition and synchronizing the throttle opening.

MODELS WITH BREAKER POINT MAGNETO. Before attempting to set ignition timing, make certain that breaker points are in good (or new) condition and gap at maximum opening is correct as described in the IGNITION paragraphs. The flywheel must be removed and wires from coil and condenser must be disconnected from breaker point terminal (1 – Fig. E2-7 or E2-8).

On models with fuel inlet fitting pressed into carburetor (26 & 26F – Fig. E2-2), check throttle pickup as follows:

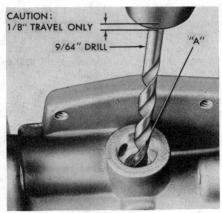

Fig. E2-4 — View showing method of removing early type check valve (25 – Fig. E2-2).

Fig. E2-5 — The 8-32 tap can be used as a puller to remove the outlet check valve from early fuel pump carburetors.

Move speed control lever until side is aligned with edge of shroud base (2 – Fig. E2-7). The follower (F) should be almost touching the cam.

NOTE: There should be slight clearance (thickness of paper) between cam and follower.

If clearance between follower and cam is incorrect, loosen screw (3), move idle end of cam as required, then tighten screw (3). Make certain that there is only a slight amount of clearance.

On models with fuel inlet fitting on carburetor plate (26L – Fig. E2-2), check the throttle pickup as follows: Set the piston at 0.003 inch **After** Top Dead Center as described in Fig. E2-9. Attach a timing light with battery (B – Fig. E2-8) or continuity meter to the breaker point terminal (1) and to magneto stator (ground). Move the speed control lever to starboard (clockwise) until the timing light glows (continuity exists through breaker points). Move the speed control lever toward fast position until the breaker points just open (light goes out).

NOTE: Do not move speed control lever too far. The cam follower (F) should just contact cam as the timing light goes out (breaker points open). If follower contacts cam before breaker points open or if there is clearance between follower and cam when breaker points open, loosen screw (3) and move the idle end of cam as required, then tighten screw (3).

On all models, refer to the following table and locate piston at correct timing position:

Fig. E2-6 — Float level may be checked by placing a number 4 drill bit (0.209 inch or 5.30 mm) between float and carburetor body.

TYPE NUMBER	TIMING BTDC
639-06	0.095 in. (2.41 mm)
640-12 thru 640-19A	0.115 in. (2.92 mm)
642-01 thru 642-07B	0.100 in. (2.54 mm)
642-07C	0.085 in. (2.15 in.)
642-08	0.110 in. (2.79 mm)
642-08A thru 642-10	0.100 in. (2.54 mm)
642-13 thru 642-16C	0.085 in. (2.15 mm)
642-16D	0.078 in. (1.98 mm)
642-17 thru 642-19	0.085 in. (2.15 mm)
642-19A	0.078 in. (1.98 mm)
642-20	0.085 in. (2.15 mm)
642-20A thru 642-22	0.078 in. (1.98 mm)
642-23	0.085 in. (2.15 mm)
642-24	0.085 in. (2.15 mm)
642-25	0.078 in. (1.98 mm)
642-26	0.085 in. (2.15 mm)
642-27 thru 642-28A	0.078 in. (1.98 mm)
642-29	0.085 in. (2.15 mm)
642-30 thru 642-35	0.078 in. (1.98 mm)
643-01 thru 643-14	0.090 in. (2.28 mm)
643-14A, 643-14B, 643-14C	0.085 in. (2.15 mm)
643-15	0.090 in. (2.28 mm)
643-15A thru 643-32A	0.085 in. (2.15 mm)

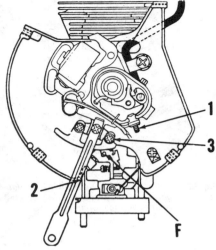

Fig. E2-7 — View showing speed controls and points of adjustment for motors with pressed in fuel inlet type carburetors and breaker point magneto. Refer to text.

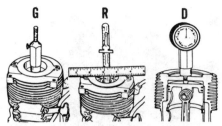

Fig. E2-9 — Piston position can be measured through the spark plug opening using the timing gage (G) available from Tecumseh Products Co. (part number 670124), a ruler (R) or dial indicator (D). After determining top dead center, turn crankshaft counterclockwise to set piston before top dead center (BTDC). Crankshaft should be turned clockwise to set piston after top dead center (ATDC).

Refer to Fig. E2-9. Attach a timing light with battery (B – Fig. E2-10) or continuity meter to the breaker point terminal (1) and to magneto stator plate (ground). Move the speed control lever clockwise until the timing light glows (breaker points closed). Move the speed control lever toward fast position (counterclockwise) until the breaker points just open (light goes out).

NOTE: It may be necessary to loosen the stop bracket (4) in order to allow enough movement to open breaker points. Also, make certain that follower (F) is not binding against cam.

The speed control lever should contact stop bracket (4) just as breaker points open. If incorrect, loosen the retaining screw and reposition stop bracket (4).

After the maximum advance stop (4) is correctly set, move the speed control lever against stop bracket (4) and check the cam follower (F). The follower should have opened the throttle com-

pletely, but make certain that cam and follower are not binding. If throttle is not completely open or if follower is binding, loosen screw (5), reposition the high speed end of cam as required then tighten screw (5).

The low speed (throttle pickup) adjustments should be checked again after setting the high speed adjustments. Changes at either end of the throttle cam will affect the location of the other end slightly. Position of cam is correct only after both low and high speed ends check satisfactory.

MODELS WITH SOLID STATE MAGNETOS. The flywheel must be removed and a special tool (part number 670236A for AV600 and AV750 models and part number 670238A for AV817 models) available from Tecumseh Products Co. must be used.

To set the maximum ignition advance, refer to following table and set the piston to the proper BTDC position as per instructions in Fig. E2-9.

MODEL NUMBER	TIMING BTDC
AV600	0.085 in. (2.15 mm)
AV750	0.095 in. (2.41 mm)
AV817	
Type 640-02 thru 640-06B	0.118 in. (2.99 mm)
Type 640-07 thru 640-21	0.115 in. (2.92 mm)

Position the proper Tecumseh special tool over the flywheel key in crankshaft as shown in Fig. E2-11, then move controls to maximum speed position (counterclockwise). The run trigger (R) should be aligned with edge "1" of special tool as shown in the inset. If incorrect, loosen stop bracket (4) and reposition as necessary to stop movement of speed control when run trigger is aligned with edge "1". After stop (4) is correctly positioned, check the cam follower (F) with controls in maximum speed position. The follower should have opened throttle completely, but make certain that cam and follower are not binding. If throttle is not completely open or if follower is binding, loosen screw (5), reposition the high speed end of cam as required then tighten screw (5).

To check the throttle pickup point, set the piston to the same BTDC position as for high speed adjustment (see previous ignition timing table). Move the speed control until the run trigger (R – Fig. E2-12) is aligned with the "2" mark on the special tool for AV750 models or the

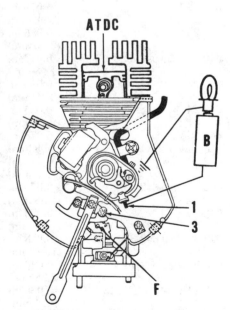

Fig. E2-8 — View showing speed controls and points of adjustments for motors with fuel inlet located on cover plate and breaker point magneto. Piston position (ATDC) should be set as described in Fig. E2-9.

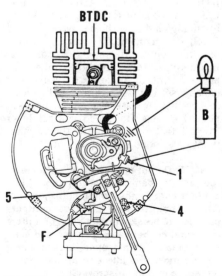

Fig. E2-10 — View showing controls and points of adjustment for adjusting maximum ignition advance and maximum throttle opening. The cam and/or carburetor may be damaged if cam attempts to open throttle further than possible.

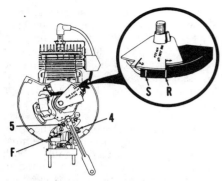

Fig. E2-11 — Refer to text for adjustment of controls. View shows high speed position. Insert shows location of starting trigger (S) and run trigger (R) in relation to the special tool.

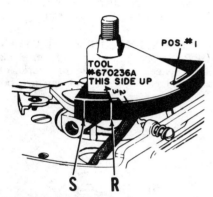

Fig. E2-12 — Refer to text for adjustment of the idle pickup. Changing the position of idle speed end of cam will affect high speed adjustment which should be rechecked.

"4" mark on the tool for AV600 models. Special tool 670238A, used to check AV817 models, has only "2" mark for throttle pickup point check. With speed control in this position, the cam should be just touching the follower (F – Fig. E2-11). Make certain that throttle has not yet moved, but is touching cam. If incorrect loosen screw and reposition the idle speed end of cam as required.

The throttle cam should be rechecked for full throttle opening after adjusting idle pickup. Changes at either end of cam will affect the location of the other end slightly. Position of cam is correct only after both low and high speed ends check satisfactorily.

After the high speed stop and throttle cam are accurately adjusted, move the speed control lever clockwise until lever is past the shroud bracket (2 – Fig. E2-13). Turn the ground (stop) screw (1) in until it contacts the stop plate on stator. The ignition will be grounded and motor will stop when the stop plate touches screw (1).

REED VALVES. The reed valves are located between the carburetor and the crankcase and should be checked each time the carburetor is removed for service.

On AV520, AV600 and AV817 models, the carburetor may be removed before removing reed valves. Reeds and reed plates may be renewed separately on most models but must be renewed as an assembly on certain early models. Check reeds for proper seating and damage. Reed petals should not bend away from plate more than 0.010 inch (0.25 mm).

On AV750 models, the reed valve assembly and carburetor must be removed as a unit by removing four screws that secure reed plate (6 – Fig. E2-15). Removal of the carburetor and disassembly of the reed valve can be accomplished by removing the two screws (5) and nuts (12). The reed petals can be renewed without renewing reed plate (6); however, make certain that seating surface is not damaged. The rough edge of reed petals must be away from reed plate. New reed petals (3) are marked on the smooth side and the marked surface should be against the reed plate (6). When assembling, coat threads of screw (5) with Loctite and tighten to 50-60 in.-lbs. (5.6-6.7 N·m) torque.

IGNITION

Solid state, breakerless magnetos and conventional, breaker-point timed, magnetos are used on these motors. Refer to the appropriate following paragraphs for service.

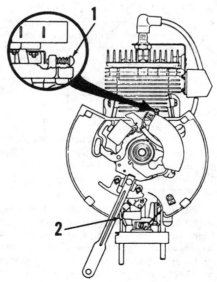

Fig. E2-13 — The stop (ground) screw (1) should be adjusted as described in text to stop motor after lever is past shroud bracket (2).

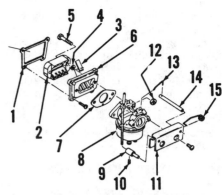

Fig. E2-15 — Exploded view of the reed valve used on AV750 models. Carburetor and reed valve must be removed and installed as a unit.

1. Gasket	8. Carburetor
2. Reed stop	9. Idle adjustment knob
3. Reed petals	10. Set screw
4. Washer	11. Bracket
5. Carburetor attaching	12. Nut
screw	13. Choke link
6. Reed plate	14. Choke rod
7. Gasket	15. Stop spring

BREAKER POINT MAGNETO. Breaker point gap should be 0.018 inch (0.45 mm) for type numbers 642-01 through 642-07B, 642-08A through 642-10, 643-01 through 643-05A, 643-06 through 643-09, and 643-15. Breaker point gap for all other engines should be 0.020 inch (0.5 mm). It is important that breaker point gap is correct and breaker points are in good (or new) condition before adjusting the speed control linkage. Ignition timing and throttle opening must be synchronized correctly to provide best operation. Refer to SPEED CONTROL LINKAGE paragraphs in the FUEL SYSTEM section for checking ignition timing.

If the magneto mounting plate must be removed, loosen friction screw then lift assembly off. When installing, apply a small amount of grease to friction screw, then install and tighten screw to 12-15 in.-lbs. (1.3-1.7 N·m) torque. Make certain that cam follower (F – Fig. E2-10) is on outside of cam.

SOLID STATE MAGNETO. The Tecumseh solid state magneto does not use breaker points. The only moving part of the system is the rotating flywheel with the magnets. Refer to Fig. E2-16. Refer to the SPEED CONTROL LINKAGE paragraphs in the FUEL SYSTEM section for synchronizing ignition timing to carburetor opening.

If the system fails to produce a spark at the spark plug, first check the condition of wire terminals and ground connections. Check condition of high tension lead (5) and if questionable, renew pulse transformer (4) and lead (5). Make certain that low tension lead (3) is not shorted against motor and renew if insulation is faulty. The ignition charging coil (1), electronic triggering system and mounting plate are available only as an assembly. If the mounting plate must be removed, loosen friction screw, then lift assembly off. When installing, apply a small amount of grease to friction screw, then install and tighten screw to 12-15 in.-lbs. (1.3-1.7 N·m) torque. Make certain that cam follower (F) is on outside of cam.

COOLING SYSTEM

The power head is air-cooled by a fan built into the flywheel. Make sure the shroud is in place and that cooling fins are kept clean.

The lower motor leg and exhaust gases are water-cooled. All models with more than 3 hp are equipped with a water pump. Coolant intake is located just below the antiventilation plate on each side of gearcase, and coolant is pumped to exhaust deflector at upper part of lower unit where it cools the exhaust housing.

Motors not equipped with a water pump use a coolant tube to aid in cooling motor leg. An open end of the coolant tube is located below antiventilation plate, facing forward. Forward motion and propeller wash force water up coolant tube to motor adapter plate. Make sure that coolant tube is free of obstructions.

Coolant outlet consists of a series of holes arranged vertically on each side of the lower unit upper leg, just below the

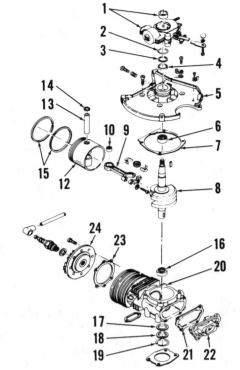

Fig. E2-20 — Exploded view typical of Tecumseh AV520 and AV600 models. Early models were equipped with plain bearings at connecting rod large end.

1. Magneto
2. Snap ring
3. Retainer
4. Seal
5. Shroud bracket
6. Top main bearing
7. Gasket
8. Crankshaft
9. Connecting rod
10. Needle bearing
12. Piston
13. Piston pin
14. Snap ring
15. Piston rings
16. Lower main bearing
17. Seal
18. Retainer
19. Snap ring
20. Crankcase & cylinder
21. Gasket
22. Reed valve
23. Gasket
24. Cylinder head

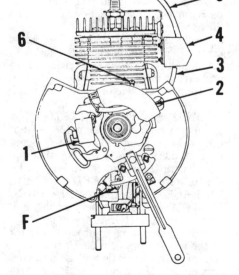

Fig. E2-16 — View of the solid state ignition components with flywheel removed.

1. Charging coil
2. Trigger system
3. Low-tension lead
4. Pulse transformer
5. High tension lead
6. Ground (stop) screw

swivel bracket. If a spray of water does not emerge from outlet holes when motor is running, first check coolant inlet for plugging, then if not corrected, remove gearcase from lower unit and overhaul the pump.

POWER HEAD

DISASSEMBLY. Unbolt and remove cylinder shroud, flywheel, magneto, cylinder head, reed valve and covers. Remove connecting rod cap and push the rod and piston unit out through top of cylinder.

NOTE: On AV520 and AV600 models with plain rod bearing, lock tab must be bent away from connecting rod screws before loosening. On other models, make certain that bearing needles are not lost in crankcase. On all models, it may be necessary to remove ridge from top of cylinder before pushing piston and connecting rod assembly out.

The crankshaft can be removed from all models after removing shroud base (5—Fig. E2-20, Fig. E2-21 or Fig. E2-22). On AV750 (and ball bearing lower main AV817 models), it may be necessary to bump crankshaft out of lower main bearing (16—Fig. E2-21 or Fig. E2-22).

ASSEMBLY. Because of the two-stroke cycle design, the crankcase must be completely sealed against both pressure and vacuum. It is recommended that all gasket surfaces be carefully cleaned and checked for burrs, nicks or warped surfaces which may interfere with a tight seal.

Refer to the appropriate paragraphs for inspection and reassembly of power head components. Refer to the CONDENSED SERVICE DATA table for recommended tightening torques.

PISTON, PIN, RINGS AND CYLINDER. Before detaching rod from crankshaft, check the correlation marks on rod and cap. If rod and cap are not

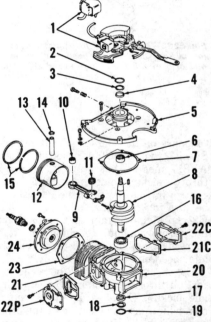

Fig. E2-21 — Exploded view typical of AV750 models. Some models may have breaker point type magneto.

1. Solid state magneto
2. Snap ring
3. Retainer
4. Seal
5. Shroud bracket
6. Top main bearing
7. Gasket
8. Crankshaft
9. Connecting rod
10. Needle bearing
11. Needle bearing
12. Piston
13. Piston pin
14. Snap ring
15. Piston ring
16. Lower main bearing
17. Seal
18. Retainer
19. Snap ring
20. Crankcase & cylinder
21. Gasket
21C. Gasket
22C. Cover
22P. Cover
23. Gasket
24. Cylinder head

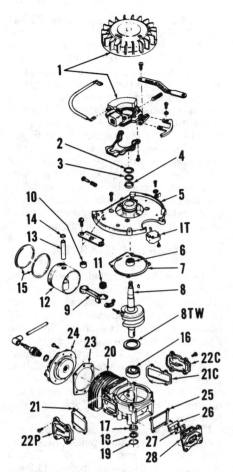

Fig. E2-22 — Exploded view of typical AV817 engine. All models are equipped with a solid state magneto.

1. Magneto assy.	16. Lower main bearing
1T. Magneto transformer	(ball or roller)
2. Snap ring	17. Seal
3. Retainer	18. Retainer
4. Seal	19. Snap ring
5. Shroud bracket	20. Crankcase
6. Top main bearing	21. Gasket
7. Gasket	21C. Gasket
8. Crankshaft	22C. Cover
8TW. Thrust washer	22P. Cover
9. Connecting rod	23. Head gasket
10. Needle bearing	24. Cylinder head
11. Needle rollers	25. Gasket
12. Piston	26. Reed stop
13. Piston pin	27. Reed
14. Snap ring	28. Reed plate
15. Piston rings	

marked, scribe a line to indicate proper assembly. Refer to the following specification data:

AV520 AND AV600
Cylinder bore
   diameter . . . . .2.093-2.094 in.
   (53.16-53.18 mm)
Piston-cylinder
   clearance. . . . . .0.005-0.007 in.
   (0.13-0.18 mm)
Ring end gap:
   Type nos. 642-01 thru
   642-07B, 642-08A thru
   642-10, 643-01 thru
   643-14 and 643-15 . . . .0.007-0.017 in.
   (0.18-0.43 mm)

All other type nos. . . . .0.006-0.016 in.
   (0.15-0.40 mm)
Ring side clearance:
   Top ring . . . . .0.003-0.005 in.
   (0.07-0.13 mm)
   Bottom ring . . . . .0.002-0.004 in.
   (0.05-0.10 mm)
Piston pin diameter . . .0.4997-0.4999 in.
   (12.692-12.697 mm)

AV750
Cylinder bore
   diameter . . . . .2.375-2.376 in.
   (60.32-60.35 mm)
Piston-cylinder
   clearance. . . . . .0.0055-0.0075 in.
   (0.139-0.190 mm)
Ring end gap . . . . .0.005-0.013 in.
   (0.13-0.33 mm)
Ring side clearance:
   Top ring . . . . .0.003-0.005 in.
   (0.07-0.13 mm)
   Bottom ring . . . . .0.002-0.004 in.
   (0.05-0.10 mm)
Piston pin diameter . . .0.4997-0.4999 in.
   (12.692-12.697 mm)

AV817
Cylinder bore
   diameter . . . . .2.437-2.438 in.
   (61.89-61.92 mm)
Piston-cylinder
   clearance. . . . . .0.0058-0.0078 in.
   (0.147-0.198 mm)
Ring end gap . . . . .0.007-0.017 in.
   (0.18-0.43 mm)
Ring side clearance:
   Top ring . . . . .0.003-0.005 in.
   (0.07-0.13 mm)
   Bottom ring . . . . .0.002-0.004 in.
   (0.05-0.10 mm)
Piston pin diameter . . .0.4997-0.4999 in.
   (12.692-12.697 mm)

Piston, rings and piston pin are available in standard size only. Piston rings should be installed on piston with beveled inside edge toward top of piston. The piston pin should be a press fit in heated piston on models with needle bearing in rod upper end. On models without needle bearing in rod upper end, the piston pin should be a palm push fit in piston and thumb push fit in rod. When assembling piston in connecting rod, observe the following. Open end of piston pin must be down, toward exhaust. The lubrication hole inside of connecting rod must be toward top of engine. On AV520 and AV600 models equipped with offset piston, make certain that "V" mark or "1111" mark stamped on top of piston is toward the right side as shown in Fig. E2-23.

A piston ring compressor should be used when installing piston in cylinder. Make certain that rings do not catch in recess at top of cylinder. The cylinder head retaining screws should be tightened to the torque listed in the CON-

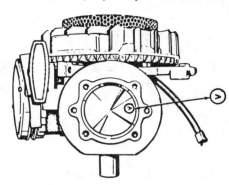

Fig. E2-23 — The "V" mark or "1111" mark on top of piston must be toward side shown. Lubrication hole in side of rod must also be toward top.

DENSED SERVICE DATA table. Refer to the CONNECTING ROD paragraphs for installation of connecting rods.

CONNECTING ROD AND BEARINGS. Several types of connecting rods are used and it is important that the correct rod is installed.

On models with an aluminum connecting rod and plain bearing at crankpin end, clearance on crankpin should be 0.0011-0.0020 inch (0.0028-0.051 mm). Crankpin journal should be 0.6857-0.6865 inch (17.416-17.437 mm). Crankshaft should be renewed if crankpin taper or out-of-round exceeds 0.001 inch (0.02 mm). Only standard size parts are available.

On models with aluminum connecting rod with steel liners and bearing needles at crankpin, observe the following: Crankpin journal standard diameter is 0.8442-0.8450 inch (21.442-21.463 mm) on AV600 engines or 0.6919-0.6927 inch (17.574-17.594 mm) on AV817 engines. Be sure that none of the 74 bearing rollers are lost and that ends of liners correctly engage when match marks on rod and cap are aligned. Piston pin diameter is 0.4997-0.4999 (12.692-12.697 mm) inch and rides in cartridge needle bearing that is pressed into piston end of connecting rod.

All models with steel connecting rod are provided with loose needle rollers at crankpin end of connecting rod and a cartridge needle bearing at piston pin end. Standard crankpin journal diameter is 0.6259-0.6266 inch (15.897-15.915 mm). Model AV750 uses 33 needle rollers in the 0.7588-0.7592 inch (19.273-19.283 mm) diameter connecting rod bore. Model AV817 uses 66 short (half length) needle rollers placed in two rows in the 0.7588-0.7592 inch (19.273-19.283 mm) diameter connecting rod bore.

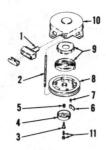

Fig. E2-26 — Exploded view of starter. Refer to Fig. E2-27 for installation of parts (5, 6 & 7).

1. Handle
2. Rope
3. Retainer screw
4. Retainer housing
5. Brake spring
6. Starter dog
7. Dog return spring
8. Pulley
9. Spring & keeper
10. Housing
11. Centering pin

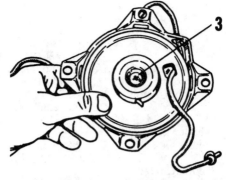

Fig. E2-28 — Refer to text when removing or installing rope. Retainer screw (3) should be torqued to 45-55 in.-lbs. (5-6 N·m).

On models with short (half length) needle rollers, bearing needles are placed in two rows around crankpin with flat ends together toward center of crankpin. On all models equipped with needle bearing at crankpin, rollers should be renewed only as a set. Renew bearing set if any roller is damaged. If rollers are damaged, check condition of crankpin and connecting rod carefully and renew if bearing races are damaged. New rollers are serviced in a strip and can be installed by wrapping the strip around crankpin. After new needle rollers and connecting rod cap are installed, force lacquer thinner into needles to remove the beeswax, then lubricate bearings with SAE 30 oil.

On all models, make certain that match marks on rod and cap are aligned. Some AV520 and AV600 models are stamped with "V" or "1111" mark on piston as shown in Fig. E2-23. On models so equipped, make certain that mark stamped on top of piston is toward the right side as shown. On all models with aluminum connecting rod, tighten rod cap retaining screws to 40-50 in.-lbs. (4.5-5.6 N·m) torque and lock with the tab washer. On all models with a steel connecting rod, tighten the rod cap retaining screws (self locking) to 70-80 in.-lbs. (7.9-9 N·m) torque.

CRANKSHAFT. Crankshaft main bearings may be either ball type or cartridge needle roller. If ball type main bearings are used, it should be necessary to bump the crankshaft out of the bearing inner races. Ball and roller bearing outer races should be a tight fit in bearing bores. If new ball bearings are to be installed, heat the crankcase when removing old bearings and installing new ones.

NOTE: Do not use an open flame.

On all models, bearings should be installed with printed face on race toward center of engine.

If the crankshaft is equipped with thrust washers at ends, make certain that they are installed when assembling.

Crankshaft end play should be ZERO for all AV750 and AV817 models. Crankshaft end play should be 0.003-0.016 inch (0.07-0.40 mm) for Models AV520 and AV600 equipped with two needle roller main bearings.

It is important to exercise extreme care when renewing crankshaft seals to prevent their being damaged during installation. If a protector sleeve is not available, use tap to cover any splines, keyways, shoulders or threads over which the seal must pass during installation. Seals should be installed so lip of the lower seal is towards outside (bottom) and the top (magneto end) seal is towards inside (center) of engine.

MANUAL STARTER

The rope for the recoil starter can be renewed without disassembling the starter. Remove the starter assembly from motor, pull rope out fully and hold pulley to prevent rewinding. Refer to Fig. E2-28. Remove old rope and install new rope, making certain that the inner knot is in pocket on underside of pulley. If the old rope was broken, preload the recoil spring by turning the pulley approximately 6 turns before installing new rope.

If the starter does not engage immediately when rope is pulled, make certain that retainer screw (3 – Fig. E2-26) is tightened to 44-55 in.-lbs. (4.9-6.2 N·m) torque.

To overhaul the starter, first remove the rope, then allow the pulley (8) to un-

Fig. E2-29 — Exploded view of lower motor leg typical of models with neutral clutch. Lever (12) is attached to shift shaft (9) with spirol pin.

1. Lower motor leg
2. Neutral speed advance stop rod
3. Neutral shift cam
4. Swivel bracket cap
5. Flat washers
6. Brass collar
7. Gaskets
8. Spring washer
9. Shift shaft
10. Carrying handle
11. Neutral clutch knobs
12. Lever
15. Steering handle
16. Shear pin holder
17. Swivel bracket
18. Stern clamps
19. Thrust bracket
20. Springs
21. Brass liner
22. Lower adapter plate
22D. Exhaust deflector plate
23. Upper adapter plate
24. Exhaust port gasket
25. Power head mount gasket
26C. Neutral clutch

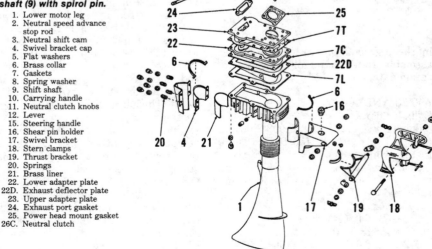

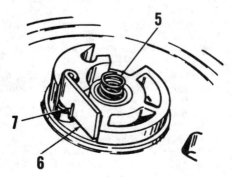

Fig. E2-27 — When assembling, make certain that parts (5, 6 & 7) are assembled as shown. End of dog return spring (7) should pull dog in.

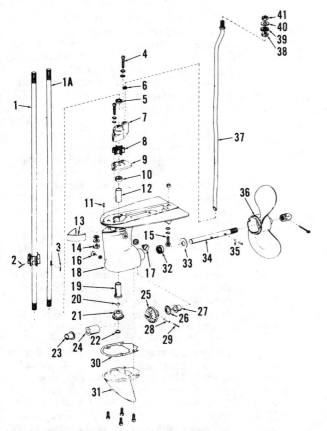

1. Drive shaft
1A. Drive shaft
2. Roll pin
3. Needle pin
4. Screw
5. Seal
6. "O" ring
7. Water pump housing
8. Impeller
9. Base plate
10. Seal
11. Roll pin
12. Sleeve
13. Clip
14. Stud nut
15. Screw
16. Fill/drain plug
17. Vent plug
18. Gearcase
19. Bushing
20. Snap ring
21. Pinion gear
22. Snap ring
23. Bushing
24. Spacer
25. Drive gear
26. Shim
27. Bushing
28. Roll pin (large)
29. Roll pin (small)
30. Gasket
31. Lower cover
32. Seal
33. Washer
34. Propeller shaft
35. Shear pin
36. Propeller
37. Water tube
38. Nut
39. Sealing washer
40. Washer
41. Nut

Fig. E2-30 — Exploded view of typical, nongear shift, lower unit. Note that water pump impeller may be driven with a needle (3) or a roll pin (2). Water tube (37) extends through exhaust opening on motors without water pump.

wind slowly. Remove retainer screw (3), then lift parts out of housing (10).

NOTE: Spring and keeper (9) are available only as a unit.

When assembling, grease spring (9) lightly then position spring and keeper (9) and pulley (8) in housing (10). Install brake spring (5), starter dog return spring (7) and starter dog (6) as shown in Fig. E2-27. Install retainer screw (3 – Fig. E2-26) and tighten to 45-55 in.-lbs. (5-6.2 N·m) torque. Preload the recoil spring by turning the pulley approximately six turns counterclockwise before installing the rope. Refer to Fig. E2-28.

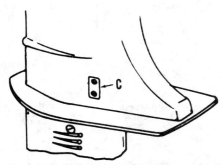

Fig. E2-31 — Remove inspection cover (C) for access to shift linkage screw.

PROPELLER

A three-blade propeller is used on 7 and 7.5 hp motors. All others are equipped with a two-blade unit. Various diameter and pitch propellers have been used. Steel shear pin, part 96284, is used on propeller of models not equipped with a forward/neutral or full gear shift lower unit. Models with forward/neutral lower unit use shear pin 95718. Motors equipped with full gear shift lower unit (Fig. E2-32) use shear pin part 96683.

LOWER UNIT

Three types of lower units are used. Some motors are equipped with a non-shifting lower unit (Fig. E2-30) while others are equipped with a full gear shift lower unit (Fig. E2-33) or forward/neutral lower unit (Fig. E2-36). Refer to the appropriate following paragraphs for servicing procedure.

Non-Shifting Lower Unit

R&R AND OVERHAUL. Most service on the lower unit can be performed by removing gearcase assembly from lower motor leg; or by removing gear-

case housing lower cover (31 – Fig. E2-30). To remove the gearcase, remove clip (13); then remove gearcase retaining nut and screw. The front gearcase retaining stud nut (14) is behind clip (13) and the rear gearcase housing cap screw is accessible from inside exhaust outlet. On later models, the front stud nut is located at front of motor leg.

To remove the propeller shaft or disassemble gearcase, drive the gear retaining roll pins (28 & 29) a short distance into gear hub, rotate propeller shaft ½-turn and pull the roll pins out with vise grip pliers. Gearcase must be completely sealed against water or grease leakage when reassembling.

Drive shaft should have a diametral clearance of 0.002-0.0035 inch (0.05-0.088 mm) in bushings (12 & 19). Propeller shaft should have a clearance of 0.0025-0.004 inch (0.063-0.10 mm) in bushings (23 & 27). Renew any parts which are worn or damaged. Backlash and mesh position of gears is fixed and not adjustable. If backlash is excessive, renew the worn parts. Renew seals (5 & 32) whenever unit is disassembled or whenever water or grease leaks are apparent.

Gear (25) is secured to propeller shaft by a small diameter roll pin (29) pressed into roll pin (28). A steel shear pin (35), part number 96284 should be used. When assembling gearcase to motor lower leg, make certain that water tube is correctly installed and not damaged. Tighten the (front) retaining stud nut to a torque of 50-60 in.-lbs. (5.6-6.7 N·m) and the (rear) retaining screw to a torque of 75-90 in.-lbs. (8.4-10.1 N·m).

Full Gear Shift Lower Unit

R&R AND OVERHAUL. To remove lower unit from motor leg, remove inspection cover (Fig. E2-31) and shift linkage screw (2 – Fig. E2-33). Be

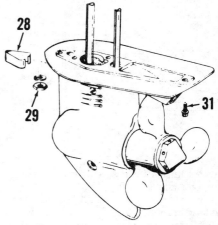

Fig. E2-32 — Lower unit may be removed from motor leg after removal of nut (29) and screw (31).

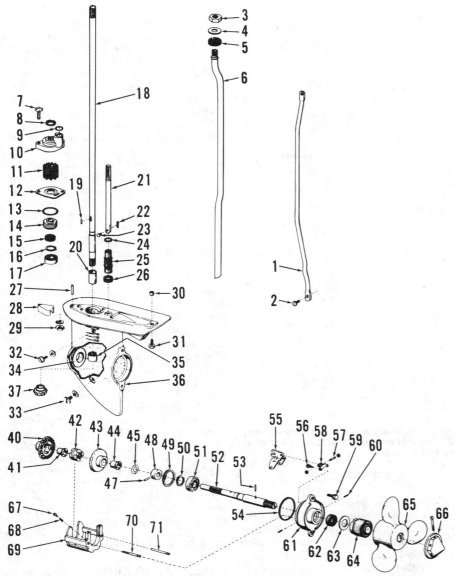

Fig. E2-33 — Exploded view of full gear shift lower unit. When assembling lower unit, use petroleum jelly to lubricate water pump impeller (11) and water tube seal (9).

1. Shift link	18. Drive shaft	35. Needle bearing	55. Fork lever
2. Screw	19. Pin	36. Gearcase	56. Screw
3. Nut	20. Spacer	37. Pinion gear	57. Pin
4. Washer	21. Shift rod	40. Forward gear	58. Lever bracket
5. Seal	22. Cotter pin	41. Bushing	59. Screw
6. Water tube	23. Clevis pin	42. Shift dog	60. Roll pin
7. Screw	24. "O" ring	43. Reverse gear	61. Cover
8. Seal	25. Rubber boot	44. Bushing	62. Seal
9. Seal	26. Seal	45. Shim washer	63. Washer
10. Pump body	27. Roll pin	47. Roll pin	64. Cushion hub
11. Impeller	28. Clip	48. Collar	65. Propeller
12. Base plate	29. Stud nut	49. Snap ring	66. Nut
13. "O" ring	30. Pilot bushing	50. Snap ring	67. Detent
14. Retainer plate	31. Screw	51. Ball bearing	68. Spring
15. Seal	32. Vent	52. Propeller shaft	69. Shifter bracket
16. Snap ring	33. Drain fill plug	53. Shear pin	70. Left guide pin
17. Shielded ball bearing	34. Bushing	54. "O" ring	71. Right guide pin

(61). Detent (67) and spring (68) will be released as bracket is pulled away.

Remove screws (56) securing fork lever bracket (58) to cover. Remove large snap ring (49) then gently tap propeller shaft (52) out of cover. Small roll pins (60) secure left (70) and right (71) shift bracket guide pins in cover (61). To remove bearing (51) from propeller shaft, clamp collar (48) in vise jaws, drive roll pin (47) out then remove collar and snap ring (50). Place propeller shaft in a vise so that inner race of ball bearing (51) is supported but jaws are not touching propeller shaft. Use a soft faced hammer to drive shaft out of bearing.

To remove drive shaft (18), remove retainer plate (14) and snap ring (16). Hold onto drive shaft and use a soft faced hammer to drive gearcase off shaft. Remove drive pinion (37) and forward gear (40). Ball bearing (17) may be removed from drive shaft by placing shaft in a vise so inner race of bearing is supported but jaws are not touching shaft. Use a soft faced hammer to drive shaft out of bearing. When installing ball bearing (17), make sure that shielded side of bearing is facing water pump.

Needle bearing (35) and bushing (34) should only be serviced with proper tools as improper service procedures may damage gearcase. A combination removal/installation tool for drive shaft needle bearing (35) may be constructed using drawing in Fig. E2-34.

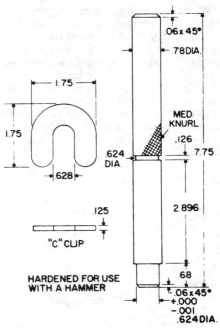

Fig. E2-34 — Drawing of a special tool that should be used for removal and installation of needle bearing (35 — Fig. E2-33).

careful not to drop screw in motor leg. Remove clip (28 – Fig. E2-32). Remove screw (31) and stud nut (29). Pull lower unit from motor leg.

Shift lower unit into neutral position. Remove water pump assembly. Be careful not to lose impeller drive pin (19 – Fig. E2-33). Remove propeller, shear pin and screw (59) that secure gear cover (61). Pull propeller shaft assembly from gear box while pulling up lightly on shift rod (21). Place thumb over detent hole in shifter bracket (69) while pulling bracket away from cover

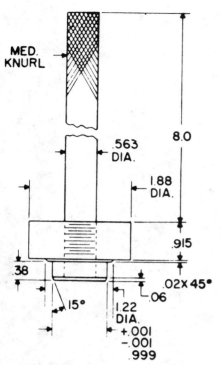

MED.
KNURL

8.0

.563
DIA.

1.88
DIA.

.915

.38

.02 X 45°

.06

15°

1.22
DIA.
+.001
−.001
.999

Fig. E2-35 — Drawing of special tool which may be used to install bushing (34 — Fig. E2-33) in gearcase.

To remove bearing (35 – Fig. E2-33), place tool, without "C" clip, in bearing from top of gearcase and pound on end of tool. To install bearing (35), place "C" clip on tool so that new bearing will be properly positioned in bore when driven in from top of gearcase.

A blind hole bearing puller should be used to pull propeller shaft bushing (34). A special driver (Fig. E2-35) should be used to install new bushing.

Bushings (41 & 44 – Fig. E2-33) may be removed and reinstalled with the aid of an arbor press.

When reassembling lower unit, make sure that oil seals (15, 26 and 62) are installed with lips facing inside of gearcase. Shift bracket guide pin (70) with detent grooves must be installed on left. Shift shaft (21) is installed with flat on end facing left side. Install retainer plate (14) so notches align with cutouts in water pump base plate (12).

When assembling gearcase to motor leg, use a flashlight to observe through exhaust outlet that water tube (6) is properly seating in water pump. Install washer and stud nut (29) before installing screw (31). Check shift mechanism for proper engagement. Detents in shift mechanism in lower units should be felt when operating shift lever.

Forward/Neutral Lower Unit

R&R AND OVERHAUL. Refer to Fig. E2-36 for an exploded view of lower unit. To remove lower unit from motor leg, remove inspection cover (Fig. E2-31) and shift linkage screw (2 – Fig. E2-36). Be careful not to drop screw in

motor leg. Remove retaining screw (10) and stud nut in front edge of motor leg and separate lower unit from motor leg. Drain lubricant and remove propeller and shear pin. Remove water pump assembly. Remove lower cover (32). Remove propeller shaft assembly and disassemble as required. Detach snap ring (30) and withdraw drive shaft (35).

Inspect components and renew any which are excessively worn or damaged. Backlash and mesh position are fixed and not adjustable. If backlash is excessive, renew the worn parts.

Reverse disassembly procedure when assembling lower unit. Be sure clutch lever (21) properly engages clutch (25) flange.

Fig. E2-36 — Exploded view of forward/neutral lower unit used on some models. Spacer (27A) is used on later models.

1. Shift link
2. Screw
3. Shift rod
4. Clevis pin
5. Cotter pin
6. "O" ring
7. Rubber boot
8. Seal
9. Pilot bushing
10. Screw
11. Nut
12. Cotter pin
13. Propeller
14. Cushion hub
15. Shear pin
16. Washer
17. Seal
18. Propeller shaft
19. Vent plug
20. Pin
21. Clutch lever
22. Shim
23. Washer
24. "E" ring
25. Clutch
26. Snap ring
27. Gear
27A. Spacer
28. Needle bearing
29. Pinion gear
30. Snap ring
31. Gasket
32. Lower cover
33. Gearcase
34. Water tube
35. Drive shaft
36. Pin
37. Seal
38. Seal
39. Pump body
40. Impeller
41. Base plate
42. Seal
43. Needle bearing
44. Stud
45. Roll pin

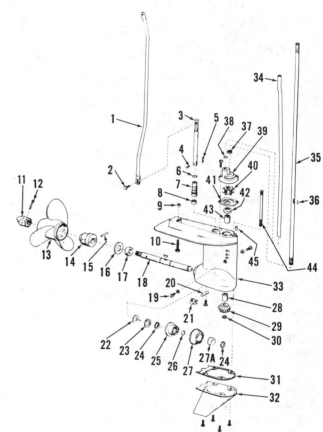

ESKA TWO-CYLINDER
MODELS (1973-1985)

Year Produced	Model No.	HP
1973	1925A	9.5
	1906A, 1911A, 1916A,	
	1933A, 1967A	9.9
	1926A, 1934A	14.0
	1907A, 1912A, 1917A, 1968A	15.0
1974	1925B	9.5
	1960B, 1911B, 1916B, 1933B	9.9
	1926B	14.0
	1907B, 1912B, 1917B, 1967A	15.0
1975	1906C, 1906D, 1978A, 1978B	9.9
	1907C, 1968C, 1979A	15.0
1976	1978C	9.9
	1979C	15.0
1977	14039	9.9
	14040	15.0
1978	14109A	9.9
	14110A	15.0
1979	14109B, 14136B	9.9
	14110B, 14137B	15.0
1980	14152A	9.9
	14153A	15.0
1981	14152B, 14181B	9.9
	14153B, 14182A	15.0
1982	14152C, 14181A, 14199A, 14204A	9.9
	14153C, 14182C	15.0
1983	14210	9.9
	14211	15.0
1984	14210	9.9
	14211	15.0
1985	14210	9.9
	14211	15.0

These motors are also sold as Explorer, Hanimex, Seaco, Seacruiser-Grant, Sea Hawk, Sears and Wizard models.

CONDENSED SERVICE DATA

TUNE-UP

Bore . . . . 2.37 in.
(60.3 mm)
Stroke . . . . 1.68 in.
(42.7 mm)
Number of Cylinders 2
Displacement . . . . 14.82 cu. in.
(242.8 cc)
Spark Plug:
  Champion J13Y*
  AC 45S
  Electrode Gap . . . . 0.030 in.
(0.76 mm)
Ignition Type . . . . Solid State
Max. Advance Timing – BTDC . . . . 0.125 in.
(3.18 mm)
Fuel:Oil Ratio . . . . 50:1†

SIZES – CLEARANCES

Piston Rings:
  End Gap . . . . 0.005-0.013 in.
(0.13-0.33 mm)

SIZES – CLEARANCES CONT.

Side Clearance –
  Top Ring . . . . 0.003-0.005 in.
(0.07-0.13 mm)
  Lower Ring . . . . 0.002-0.004 in.
(0.05-0.10 mm)
Piston Skirt Diameter . . . . 2.371-2.372 in.
(60.223-60.248 mm)
Piston Pin Diameter . . . . 0.4997-0.4999 in.
(12.692-12.697 mm)
Crankshaft Diameter:
  Top Main . . . . 0.9995-1.000 in.
(25.387-25.4 mm)
  Lower Main . . . . 0.9841-0.9845 in.
(24.996-25.006 mm)
  Crankpin . . . . 0.7522-0.7530 in.
(19.105-19.126 mm)
Crankpin Needle Diameter . . . . 0.0944-0.0945 in.
(2.397-2.400 mm)

TIGHTENING TORQUES

Carburetor Mounting Stud Nuts . . . . .65-75 in.-lbs.
(7.3-8.5 N·m)

Connecting Rod Bolts . . . . .70-80 in.-lbs.
(7.9-9 N·m)

Crankcase Screws . . . . .70-80 in.-lbs.
(7.9-9 N·m)

Cylinder Head Cover Screws . . . . .70-80 in.-lbs.
(7.9-9 N·m)

Exhaust Cover Screws . . . . .70-80 in.-lbs.
(7.9-9 N·m)

Flywheel Nut . . . . .30-35 ft.-lbs.
(40.8-47.6 N·m)

Lower Bearing Cap Screws . . . . .40-50 in.-lbs.
(4.5-5.6 N·m)

Starter Bracket Nuts . . . . .70-80 in.-lbs.
(7.9-9 N·m)

Stator Screws . . . . .40-50 in.-lbs.
(4.5-5.6 N·m)

TIGHTENING TORQUES CONT.

Spark Plugs . . . . .18-22 ft.-lbs.
(24.5-29.9 N·m)

Transformer Coil Screws . . . . .40-50 in.-lbs.
(4.5-5.6 N·m)

*Recommended spark plug for models after 1976 is Champion RJ13Y.

†Fuel:oil ratio should be increased to 32:1 if BIA certified TC-W oil is not used.

The engine model number, BV-1500, indicates basic engine configuration and displacement; B-Two cylinder, V-vertical crankshaft, 1500-15.00 cubic inch displacement. If service parts are required, the type number MUST be used. The type number is on a metal tag attached to one of the exhaust cover screws. Typical type numbers are 380 or 380A. When servicing power head, make certain that identification tag is reinstalled.

LUBRICATION

The power head is lubricated by oil mixed with regular grade, leaded, gasoline. Recommended fuel to oil ratio is 50:1 when using oils that are BIA certified TC-W. If BIA certified TC-W oil is not available, use a good grade of oil intended for use in outboard motors mixed in a 32:1 ratio with regular grade gasoline.

The lower unit gears and bearings are lubricated by approximately 6 oz. (177 mL) of oil contained in gearcase. SAE90 outboard gear lubricant should be used. Lubricant should be maintained at level of (vent) plug (U – Fig. E3-1) when motor is in upright position. The gearcase should be drained and filled with new lubricant at least once each year. Remove both plugs (U and L) to drain gearcase. If excessive water is noted when draining, seals and gaskets should be renewed as outlined in LOWER UNIT section. Motor should be in upright position when refilling gearcase. Insert filler tube in fill/drain plug opening (L) and squeeze tube until lubricant reaches level of vent plug opening (U). Install and tighten upper plug then remove filler tube and install lower plug. Make sure that gaskets on plugs are in good condition.

FUEL SYSTEM

CARBURETOR. Tecumseh float type carburetors (Fig. E3-2) with fixed high speed jet are used on all models. Carburetors used on all engines except type 381, 381A, 381B and 381C have a built in type fuel pump (4, 21, 22 and 23). Carburetors used on type 381, 381A, 381B and 381C engines use a separate fuel pump assembly (Fig. E3-3). Differences in service procedures will be noted when necessary.

Carburetor adjustments should be made with engine at normal operating temperature. Do not run engine unless lower unit is in water. Water pump is easily damaged by dry operation. To adjust idle mixture, press star wheel (11 – Fig. E3-2) in and hold it in this position while adjusting screw (12). Turn mixture screw (12) in until it is lightly seated then back out one turn. Hold star wheel (11) in and turn it so projection is on 12 o'clock position (straight up) then let it out to engage screw (12). Start and run motor until operating temperature is reached. Place motor in forward gear

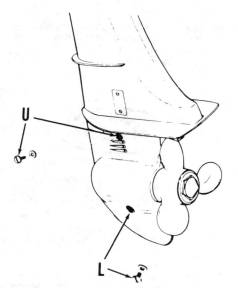

Fig. E3-1 — View of gearcase showing upper (vent) plug (U) and lower (drain/fill) plug (L).

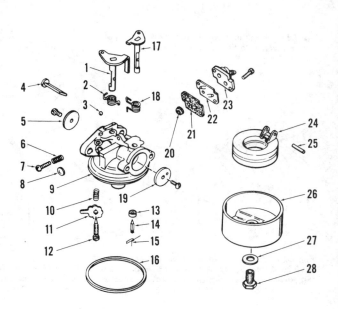

Fig. E3-2 — Exploded view of carburetor typical of unit used on type 380 engines. Fuel pump components (4, 21, 22 and 23) are not used on carburetors for type 381 engines.

1. Throttle shaft
2. Return spring
3. Lead shot
4. Pump element
5. Throttle shutter
6. Spring
7. Idle speed screw
8. Welch plug
9. Throttle body
10. Spring
11. Star wheel
12. Mixture needle
13. Viton needle seat
14. Inlet needle
15. Clip
16. Gasket
17. Choke shaft
18. Return spring
19. Choke shutter
20. Screen
21. Gasket
22. Check valve
23. Cover
24. Float
25. Pin
26. Float bowl
27. Gasket
28. Main jet

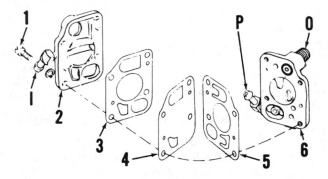

Fig. E3-3 — Exploded view of fuel pump assembly used on type 381 engines.

I. Fuel Inlet
O. Fuel Outlet
P. Crankcase pressure line
1. Screw
2. Cover
3. Gasket
4. Diaphragm
5. Check valve
6. Body

and turn speed control grip fully to slow speed position. Turn star wheel, without pushing in, slowly out (counterclockwise) until engine speed decreases from rich mixture. Turn star wheel back until engine is idling smoothly. Adjust idle speed screw (7 – Fig. E3-4) to obtain slowest possible smooth idle speed (approximately 750-1000 rpm). Mixture should be rich enough to provide smooth acceleration from idle to full throttle and not misfire when decelerating.

To adjust fast idle speed, shift motor to neutral and turn speed control grip until throttle bracket is touching locknut

lever (L – Fig. E3-5). Engine speed should be 2500-3500 rpm. If engine speed is not within limits, loosen set screw and reposition lever (A).

When disassembling carburetor for service note location of identification marks on choke shutter (19 – Fig. E3-2) and throttle shutter (5). Carburetors may be cleaned in commercial solvents after complete disassembly and removal of all rubber or nylon parts and gaskets. After cleaning, all passages should be cleared with compressed air.

Viton inlet needle seat (13) should not be removed unless renewal is intended. To remove seat (13), fashion a small hook from a paper clip, insert hook through seat and pull seat out of brass sleeve (Fig. E3-6). Do not try to remove brass sleeve. New Viton inlet needle seat may be driven into brass sleeve with a 5/32 inch (3.9687 mm) flat punch after lubricating sleeve with a drop of light oil. Seat must be installed with grooved side (G – Fig. E3-7) down. Make sure the needle seat is completely seated in brass sleeve (S).

Float setting should be 0.185-0.235 inch (4.70-5.97 mm) for carburetors used on type 380 through 380C and 382 through 382D engines and 0.155-0.217 inch (3.94-5.51 mm) for carburetors used on type 381 through 381C, 383 through 383C and 385 engines. Preferred method for checking float setting is to place an appropriate size drill bit between carburetor body and float assembly (Fig. E3-8). Recommended drill bit sizes are number 4 (0.209 inch or 5.308 mm) for carburetor used on type 380 through 380C and 382 through 382D engines and number 13 (0.185 inch or 4.699 mm) for carburetor used on type 381 through 381C, 383 through 383C and 385 engines.

When installing carburetor with built-in fuel pump, make sure that hole in mount gasket is correctly positioned over pump element (4 – Fig. E3-2). When installing fuel pump on carburetor of units with separate fuel pump (Fig. E3-3), coat pipe threads of fuel pump outlet with an antiseize compound.

SPEED CONTROL LINKAGE

Speed control grip operates carburetor throttle linkage only. A centrifugal ignition advance mechanism is used.

Fig. E3-7 — Use a 5/32 inch (3.9687 mm) flat punch to install new inlet needle seat. Install seat with grooved side (G) down.

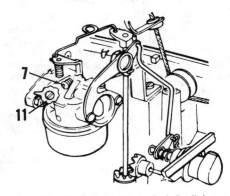

Fig. E3-4 — View of throttle and choke linkage. Refer to Fig. E3-2 for legend.

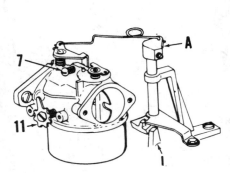

Fig. E3-5 — Maximum speed in neutral should be 2500-3500 rpm. Speed is adjusted by repositioning lever (A) when throttle bracket is against lockout lever (L).

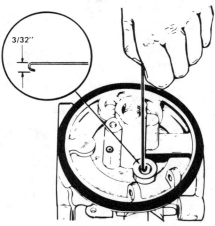

Fig. E3-6 — Viton inlet needle seat (13 – Fig. E3-2) may be removed by pushing a small hook through seat and pulling.

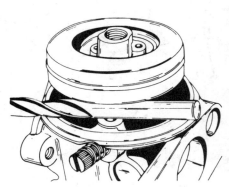

Fig. E3-8 — Float level should be checked by placing an appropriate size drill bit between float and carburetor body. Refer to text for proper size drill bit.

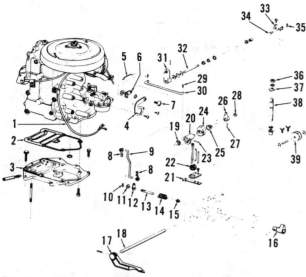

Fig. E3-11—View of gear shift and choke control linkage typical of all models.

1. Stop button leads
2. Gasket
3. Top adapter plate
4. Choke link bracket
5. Link
6. Lever
7. Shoulder screw
8. Clips
9. Choke link
10. Pin
11. Flat washer
12. Lever
13. Shaft
14. Spring
15. Nylon bushing
16. Knob
17. Shift lever
18. Shaft
19. Flanged bushing
20. Lever
21. Detent spring
22. Shear pin holder
23. Spirol pin
24. Detent cam
25. Flanged bushing
26. Lockout lever
27. Spirol pin
28. Bushing
29. Clip
30. Link
31. Lever
32. Shaft
33. Lever
34. Pin
35. Cotter pin
36. Nut
37. Hood lock
38. Shaft
39. Rope guide pulley

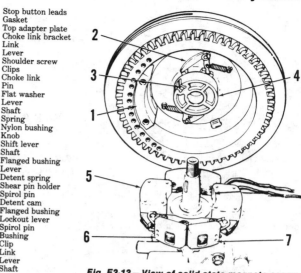

Fig. E3-13—View of solid state magneto assembly typical of all models.

1. Magnet
2. Flyweight
3. Trigger magnet
4. Sleeve assy.
5. Ignition module
6. High speed coil
7. Low speed coil

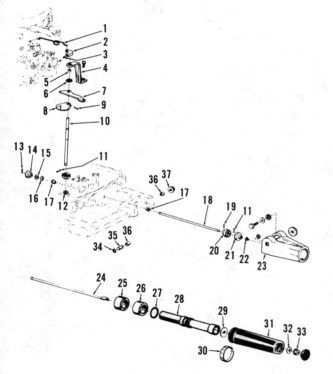

Fig. E3-12—View of throttle control linkage.

1. Link wire
2. Lever
3. Set screw
4. Bracket
5. Bushing
6. Retaining clip
7. Throttle stop
8. Throttle bracket
9. Spirol pin
10. Shaft
11. Pin
12. Bushing
13. Pin
14. Gear
15. Flat washer
16. Spring washer
17. Flanged bushing
18. Rod
19. Spirol pin
20. Gear
21. Gear
22. Nylon bushing
23. Bracket
24. Shaft
25. Rubber bushing
26. Rubber bushing
27. "O" ring
28. Handle
29. Special flat washer
30. Decal
31. Twist grip
32. Flat washer
33. Flanged nut

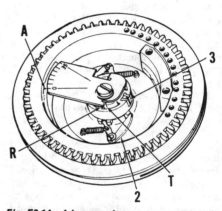

Fig. E3-14—Advancer sleeve movement may be checked with special tool. Refer to text for inspection procedure.

If control linkage has been disassembled, note that word "START" on twist grip decal should be aligned with arrow on bracket (23—Fig. E3-12) with motor in Neutral and grip turned counterclockwise as far as it will go. Linkage should be set as described to install a new decal (30).

IGNITION

A solid state, magnetically triggered magneto is used on all models. Magneto consists of one permanent magnet in flywheel, a small trigger magnet and sleeve assembly in center of flywheel, two ignition modules in stator assembly, two high speed ignition coils in stator, two low speed ignition coils in stator, two ignition transformer coils mounted on cylinder head and two spark plugs. Trigger magnet and sleeve assembly is linked to flywheel with a set of centrifugal advance weights so increasing engine speed will advance ignition timing.

Ignition timing should not change through normal use; however, if stator is removed without being marked for re-installation or if stator, flywheel, ad-

vance weights or trigger magnet assembly are renewed, it will be necessary to retime ignition.

Flywheel must be removed to adjust ignition timing. Two special tools, available from Tecumseh Products Company, should be used to properly time ignition. Full movement range of advancer mechanism must be checked first. Position special tool, Tecumseh part number 670243, in trigger sleeve assembly in flywheel. Tabs (T—Fig. E3-14) of tool should engage ribs (R) in trigger sleeve. Place a pencil mark (A) on flywheel adjacent to "O" degree mark on tool. Grasp advancer mechanism flyweights (2) and pull them out fully against their stop. Do not use tool to

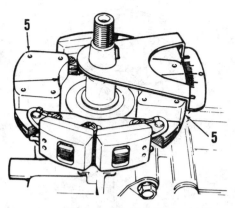

Fig. E3-15 — Stator assembly is timed using special tool. Refer to text for proper timing procedure.

turn trigger assembly. Observe and record degree mark on special tool adjacent to pencil mark on flywheel.

To adjust position of stator assembly, set number one (top) piston to 0.125 inch (3.175 mm) BTDC. Position special tool, Tecumseh part number 670244, on crankshaft. Make sure tool is fully seated on crankshaft and Woodruff key (Fig. E3-15). Make sure that crankshaft is not moved from desired position during timing operation. Refer to degree measurement taken in previous paragraph. If trigger sleeve assembly movement was 30°, set stator so mark on ignition module is aligned with 0° mark on tool. If trigger sleeve movement was greater than 30°, turn stator **clockwise** past 0° mark, the number of degrees that trigger sleeve assembly moved more than 30. For example; if trigger sleeve movement was 33°, stator should be turned clockwise until 3° mark on timing tool is aligned with mark on ignition module. If trigger sleeve movement was only 28°, turn stator 2° counterclockwise from point when line on ignition module and 0° mark on timing tool align.

When assembling components, put a small amount of EP lithium grease on portion of crankshaft adjacent to trigger sleeve assembly. Make sure that no grease is on crankshaft taper when reassembling unit. Tighten flywheel nut to 30-35 ft.-lbs. (40.8-47.6 N·m) torque.

COOLING SYSTEM

All models are equipped with a rubber impeller type water pump. Pump is mounted on top of lower unit gearbox, between gearbox and motor leg. Water inlet holes are forward, on each side of gearbox, just below antiventilation plate.

When cooling system problems are encountered, first check the water inlet for plugging or partial stoppage; then if not

corrected, remove the lower unit as outlined in the appropriate section and check the condition of the water pump, water passages, gasket and sealing surfaces.

POWER HEAD

R&R AND DISASSEMBLE. Mount motor on a convenient support and remove the hood. Tie a slip knot in starter rope at starter and remove pull handle. Disconnect fuel line, choke linkage, throttle linkage and wiring to STOP switch. Remove the six screws securing engine to base assembly.

Remove stud nut from bottom of base assembly, near carrying handle. Remove engine assembly. Remove six Allen head screws securing base plate to engine.

Remove recoil starter assembly. Remove flywheel, mark stator for reinstallation and remove stator assembly. Lower main bearing cap (28 – Fig. E3-17) must be removed before crankcase cover (43) can be removed. Remove screws securing crankcase cover to crankcase. Three pry points (P – Fig. E3-18) are provided to aid in separating the crankcase cover from crankcase. Do not pry at any other points as mating surfaces will be damaged and crankcase

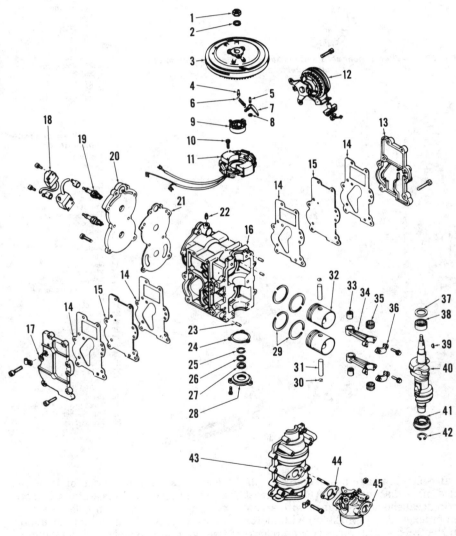

Fig. E3-17 — Exploded view of power head assembly.

1. Nut	24. Gasket	35. Bearing needles (28 each rod)
2. Lockwasher	25. Snap ring	36. Connecting rod cap
3. Flywheel	26. Retaining ring	37. Seal
4. Anchor pin	27. Seal	38. Needle bearing cartridge
5. Pivot pin	28. Bearing cup	39. Woodruff key
6. Spring	29. Piston rings	40. Crankshaft
7. Flyweight	30. Piston pin clip	41. Main bearing
8. Clip	31. Piston pin	42. Snap ring
9. Advancer sleeve	32. Piston	43. Crankcase cover
10. Screw	33. Needle bearing cartridge	44. Gasket
11. Stator	34. Connecting rod	45. Carburetor
12. Recoil starter		
13. Exhaust/transfer cover		
14. Gaskets		
15. Plates		
16. Crankcase/cylinder block		
17. Exhaust/transfer cover		
18. Transformer coil		
19. Spark plug		
20. Cylinder head cover		
21. Gasket		
22. Pipe plug		
23. Dowel		

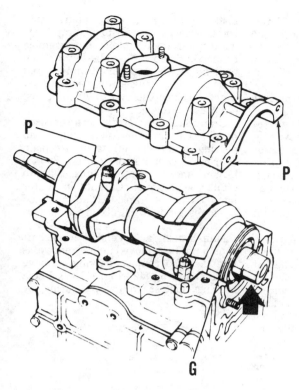

Fig. E3-18 — Pry only at three points (P) indicated when removing crankcase cover. Crankshaft should be broken loose from crankcase by tapping with a soft faced hammer in direction of large arrow.

cover may be bent or fractured. Crankcase cover and crankcase are a matched set and cannot be purchased separately.

Crankshaft may be removed with or without connecting rods and pistons. If pistons are to remain in cylinders, use caution to prevent loss of bearing needles when connecting rod caps are removed. Identify rod caps so they can be reinstalled in original location. To remove crankshaft, use a mallet or soft faced hammer to tap up on **pto end** of crankshaft (Fig. E3-18). Do not tap magneto end of crankshaft up first as pto bearing lock ring groove (G) in crankcase may be damaged. After crankshaft has been broken loose from crankcase, lift each end evenly to remove crankshaft without damaging components.

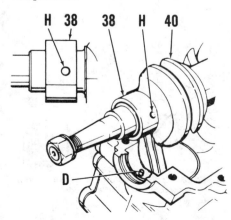

Fig. E3-19 — Hole (H) in magneto end main bearing case (38) must be positioned over dowel (D) in crankcase.

Refer to the appropriate following paragraphs for overhaul or repair procedures.

REASSEMBLE. Because of the two-stroke design, crankcase and transfer port covers must be completely sealed against both vacuum and pressure. Exhaust covers, engine base plate and cylinder head cover must be sealed against water leakage and pressure. Mating surfaces of water intake and exhaust areas between power head and lower unit must form a tight seal.

Whenever the power head is disassembled, it is recommended that all gasket surfaces and the mating surface of the crankcase and crankcase cover be carefully checked for nicks and burrs or warped surfaces which might interfere with a tight seal. The mating surfaces on crankcase and covers may be checked and lapped, if necessary, to provide a smooth surface. For lapping, use a regular lapping block or a sufficiently large piece of smooth glass. Lay a sheet of No. 00 emery cloth on the lapping plate then place the surface to be lapped on the emery cloth. Apply a very light pressure and use a figure eight motion, checking frequently to determine progress. Do not remove any more metal than is necessary. Finish lap using lapping compound or worn emery cloth. Thoroughly clean the parts with new oil on a clean, soft rag then wash with soap suds and clean rags.

Mating surface between crankcase and crankcase cover must not be

lowered by lapping. Both portions of crankcase must be renewed if either is damaged beyond repair.

Bronze liner cast in center of crankcase sections acts as a seal between cylinders and as a center main bearing. Crankcase sections should be renewed if bronze center bearing is heavily scored or otherwise damaged.

Burrs caused by staking crankshaft seal in place at magneto end of crankcase should be removed before reassembling crankcase sections.

Make sure that hole (H – Fig. E3-19) in top main bearing (38) is correctly positioned over dowel pin (D) in crankcase.

A nonhardening type gasket sealer should be used between crankcase and crankcase cover. Apply sealer in a thin bead, making sure that entire length of crankcase is sealed. Sealer should be kept at least ½ inch (12.7 mm) away from center main bearing liner to prevent excess sealer from squeezing into bearing when crankcase cover is installed. Install crankcase cover and tighten screws using torque sequence shown in Fig. E3-20. Screws should be tightened to 70-80 in.-lbs. (7.9-9 N·m) torque in increments of 20 in.-lbs. (2.3 N·m).

Magneto end crankshaft seal (37 – Fig. E3-17) may be installed after crankcase sections are assembled. Seal should be pressed into crankcase, using an appropriate size driver, until it is flush or no more than 1/32 inch (0.79 mm) below end of crankcase (Fig. E3-21). Crankcase should be staked to help retain seal.

Lower bearing cap seal (27 – Fig. E3-17) may be renewed after removal of snap ring (25) and retaining ring (26). Seal (27) should be installed with lip facing down (Fig. E3-22).

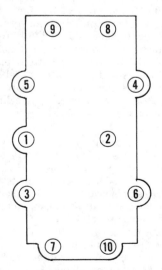

Fig. E3-20 — Crankcase cover screws should be tightened to 70-80 in.-lbs. (7.9-9 N·m) torque in increments of 20 in.-lbs. (2.3 N·m) using sequence shown.

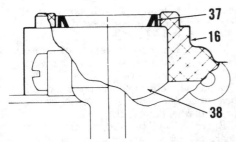

Fig. E3-21 — Seal (37) at magneto end of crankcase (16) should be pressed in until it is flush or no more than 1/32 inch (0.8 mm) below surface. Refer to Fig. E3-19 for proper installation of bearing (38).

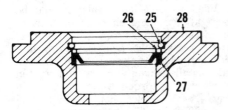

Fig. E3-22 — Lower main bearing cap seal (27) must be installed with lip down, away from main bearing. Refer to Fig. E3-17 for legend.

PISTONS, PINS, RINGS AND CYLINDERS. Before removing connecting rod caps, make certain that caps and rods are marked for reinstallation in original position. Use caution to prevent loss of crankpin bearing needles as rod cap is removed.

Standard piston skirt diameter is 2.371-2.372 inch (60.22-60.25 mm). Piston ring end gap should be 0.005-0.013 inch (0.13-0.33 mm). Side clearance of piston rings in grooves should be 0.003-0.005 inch (0.07-0.13 mm) for top piston ring and 0.002-0.004 inch (0.05-0.10 mm) for bottom piston ring. Pistons and rings are available in standard size only. If cylinder bores are damaged or worn excessively, cylinder block/crankcase assembly must be renewed.

When installing pistons, arrow on dome should point to port (left) side of engine. Match marks (MM – Fig. E3-24) on rod and rod cap should be toward magneto end of crankcase. Closed end of piston pin should also be facing magneto end of crankcase. Make certain that ring end gaps remain at locating pins (LP) as pistons are placed in cylinder bores. Rod cap screws should be tightened to 70-80 in.-lbs. (7.9-9 N·m) torque.

Components should be lubricated with two-stroke engine oil while being assembled.

CONNECTING RODS, BEARINGS AND CRANKSHAFT. Crankshaft may be removed with connecting rods attached or by removing rod caps and allowing pistons to remain in cylinder bores. Before removing rod caps, make certain that rods and caps are marked for reinstallation in original position.

After crankcase cover has been removed, crankshaft may be removed by tapping pto end of crankshaft up, out of crankcase (Fig. E3-18). Do not tap on magneto end of crankshaft as snap ring groove (G) at pto end of crankcase may be damaged. Once crankshaft has been broken loose from crankcase, it should be lifted straight up, out of engine.

Connecting rods use an encased needle bearing pressed into piston pin end and have 28 loose bearing needles at crankpin end. Inspect bearing surface in large end of connecting rod for scoring. Check rod for cracks and for discoloration caused by overheating. Piston pin and small end needle bearings should be renewed if piston pin appears worn in bearing contact area.

To assemble piston and connecting rod, install piston pin retaining clip on side of piston with ring locating pins (LP – Fig. E3-24). Heat piston in a container of oil, to approximately 300° F. Install piston pin, closed end first, with connecting rod positioned so that match mark (MM) is toward same side of piston as ring locating pins (LP). Install second piston pin retaining clip.

To install used bearing needles at crankpin, use a light, nonfibrous grease to hold half of the bearings in connecting rod. Position crankshaft in rod and use grease to hold remaining bearing needles on crankpin. Install rod cap. To

install new bearing needles at crankpin, leave beeswax on bearings. Wrap bearing strip around crankpin and assemble connecting rod. Flush beeswax from bearing with lacquer thinner and lubricate with two-stroke engine oil. Tighten rod-cap screws to 70-80 in.-lbs. (7.9-9 N·m) torque.

Crankshaft is supported by an encased needle bearing at magneto end, a ball bearing at pto end and a bronze plain bearing at center main journal. Bronze bearing liner for center main is cast into crankcase sections. Cutouts in center main journal of crankshaft act as timed passages for fuel:air mixture from carburetor.

Main bearing at pto end of crankshaft should not be removed unless renewal is intended. To remove bearing, remove small snap ring (42 – Fig. E3-17). Use a bearing splitter to grasp bearing by

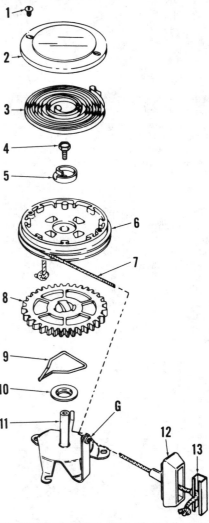

Fig. E3-24 — Closed end (C) of piston pin should be on same side of piston as ring locating pins (LP). Connecting rod should be assembled to piston with match mark (MM) on same side of piston as ring locating pins. Arrow on piston dome should be toward port (left) side of engine. Closed end (C) of piston pin will be toward top.

Fig. E3-26 — Exploded view of recoil starter assembly typical of all models.

G. Rope guide	7. Rope
1. Screw	8. Gear
2. Cover	9. Drag clip
3. Rewind spring	10. Thrust washer
4. Screw	11. Mount bracket
5. Spring anchor	12. Handle
6. Pulley	13. Rope anchor

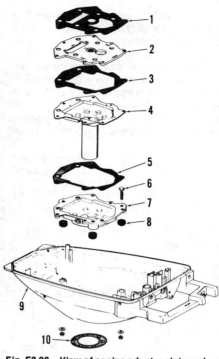

large snap ring then use an appropriate puller to remove bearing from crankshaft. Bearing is distorted by this removal method. Once bearing is removed, it is considered ruined and must be renewed.

To install new pto end main bearing, place crankshaft in a vise with pto end up. Heat new bearing, in a container of oil, to approximately 300°F. Bearing should be supported in container so it is not laying in bottom, next to the heat source. Once bearing is removed from oil it should be installed as quickly as possible. Make sure that bearing is fully seated on crankshaft.

When installing magneto end main bearing (38) note that locating hole in bearing case is not centered. Bearing should be installed with side closest to locating hole toward crank throw (Fig. E3-19).

MANUAL STARTER

The majority of recoil starter service required may be done with starter still attached to power head; however, starter may be removed as an assembly if engine work is to be performed.

To remove recoil starter assembly, tie a slip knot in rope next to guide (G — Fig.

Fig. E3-28 — View of engine adapter plate and exhaust separator.

1. Gasket
2. Water tube adapter plate
3. Gasket
4. Exhaust separator plate
5. Gasket
6. Screw
7. Adapter housing
8. Mount grommet
9. Mount base
10. Gasket

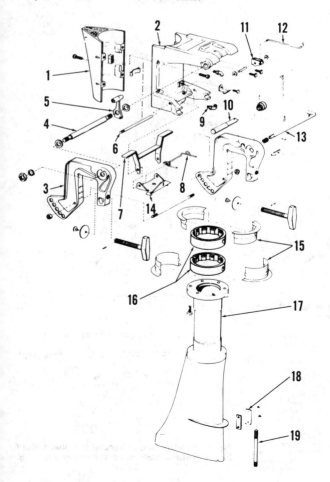

Fig. E3-29 — Exploded view of motor leg and stern bracket assembly.

1. Swivel bracket cap
2. Swivel bracket
3. Stern bracket
4. Tilt lock pin
5. Release lever
6. Pivot pin
7. Shallow drive prop bracket
8. Torsion spring
9. Grease fitting
10. Tilt lock pin
11. Lever
12. Link
13. Pin
14. Reverse tilt lock plate
15. Cushion liners
16. Cushion rings
17. Motor leg
18. Inspection cover
19. Stud

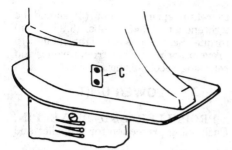

Fig. E3-31 — Remove inspection cover (C) for access to shift linkage screw.

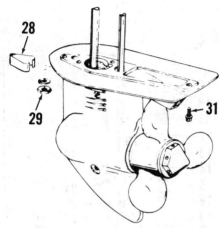

Fig. E3-32 — Lower unit gearbox may be removed from motor leg after removal of nut (29) and screw (31). On later models, stud nut (29) is located at front edge of motor leg.

E3-26) on starter bracket. Remove pull handle then remove screws securing mount bracket (11) to power head.

Stator should installed so teeth of starter gear are at least 1/16 inch (1.59 mm) below base of flywheel teeth. If starter is installed too close to flywheel, gears will bind and starter will be damaged by engine operation. Test installation of starter with spark plugs removed to be sure gears disengage completely. Starter mount bracket has a slotted hole to allow gear engagement adjustment.

To disassemble recoil starter for service, remove pull handle and allow rope to be pulled onto starter so rewind spring tension is relieved. Remove cover (2) only after spring tension has been released. Recoil spring can be renewed at this point. To remove pulley wheel (6), remove screw and spring hub (5).

Standard size pull rope is 5/32 inch (3.97 mm) in diameter and 69 inches (175.3 cm) in length.

Before assembling starter, lubricate both sides of thrust washer (10), axle portion of bracket (11) and pulley spirol with an EP lithium grease. Screw used to retain spring anchor (5) should be tightened to 35-45 in.-lbs. (3.9-5 N·m) torque. Screw must be tight enough to prevent spring anchor from turning and releasing recoil spring tension.

LOWER UNIT

PROPELLER AND DRIVE PIN.
Cushioning protection for propeller and lower unit is provided by a cushion hub (64 – Fig. E3-33) and by shear pin (53). Shear pin, Eska part 96683, should be used.

R&R AND OVERHAUL. To remove lower unit from motor leg, remove inspection cover (C – Fig. E3-31) and shift linkage screw (2 – Fig. E3-33). Be careful not to drop screw in motor leg. On early models, remove clip (28 – Fig. E2-32), screw (31) and stud nut (29). On later models, unscrew stud nut at front edge of motor leg and screw (31 – Fig. E2-32). Pull lower unit from motor leg.

Shift lower unit into neutral position. Remove water pump assembly. Be careful not to lose impeller drive pin (19 – Fig. E3-33). Remove propeller, shear pin and screws (59) that secure

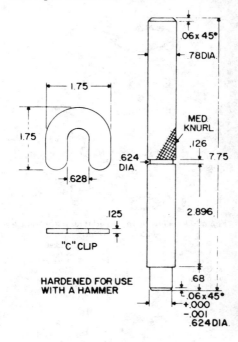

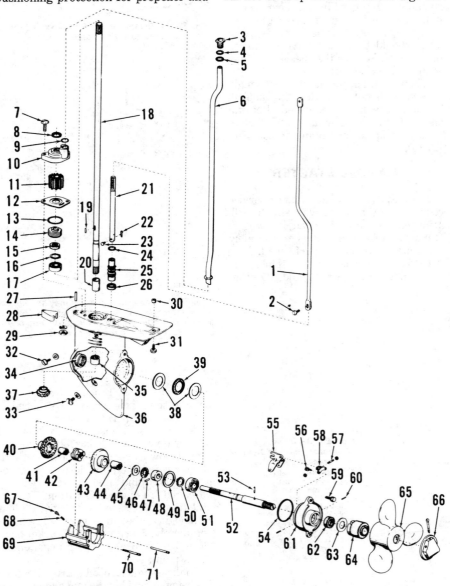

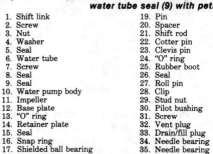

Fig. E3-33 – Exploded view of lower unit gearbox assembly. Lubricate water pump impeller (11) and water tube seal (9) with petroleum jelly when reassembling.

1. Shift link	19. Pin	37. Pinion gear	54. "O" ring
2. Screw	20. Spacer	38. Thrust washers	55. Fork lever
3. Nut	21. Shift rod	39. Thrust bearing	56. Screw
4. Washer	22. Cotter pin	40. Forward gear	57. Pin
5. Seal	23. Clevis pin	41. Bearing	58. Lever bracket
6. Water tube	24. "O" ring	42. Shift dog	59. Screw
7. Screw	25. Rubber boot	43. Reverse gear	60. Roll pin
8. Seal	26. Seal	44. Bearing	61. Cover
9. Seal	27. Roll pin	45. Washer	62. Seal
10. Water pump body	28. Clip	46. Thrust bearing	63. Washer
11. Impeller	29. Stud nut	47. Roll pin	64. Cushion
12. Base plate	30. Pilot bushing	48. Collar	65. Propeller
13. "O" ring	31. Screw	49. Snap ring	66. Nut
14. Retainer plate	32. Vent plug	50. Snap ring	67. Detent
15. Seal	33. Drain/fill plug	51. Ball bearing	68. Spring
16. Snap ring	34. Needle bearing	52. Propeller shaft	69. Shifter bracket
17. Shielded ball bearing	35. Needle bearing	53. Shear pin	70. Left guide pin
18. Drive shaft	36. Gearcase		71. Right guide pin

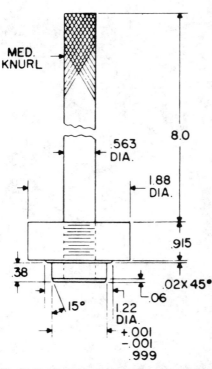

Fig. E3-35 – Drawing of special tool that should be used to install needle bearing (34 – Fig. E3-33).

gear cover (61). Pull propeller shaft assembly from gear box while pulling up lightly on shift rod (21). Place thumb over detent hole in shifter bracket (69) while pulling bracket away from cover (61). Detent (67) and spring (68) will be released as bracket is pulled away.

Remove screws (56) securing fork lever bracket (58) to cover. Remove large snap ring (49) then gently tap propeller shaft (52) out of cover. Small roll pins (60) secure left (70) and right (71) shift bracket guide pins in cover (61). To remove bearing (51) from propeller shaft, clamp collar (48) in vise jaws, drive roll pin (47) out then remove collar and snap ring (50). Place propeller shaft in a vise so that inner race of ball bearing (51) is supported but jaws are not touching propeller shaft. Use a soft faced hammer to drive shaft out of bearing.

To remove drive shaft (18), remove retainer plate (14) and snap ring (16). Hold onto drive shaft and use a soft faced hammer to drive gearcase off shaft. Remove drive pinion (37) and forward gear (40). Ball bearing (17) may be removed from drive shaft by placing shaft in a vise so inner race of bearing is supported but jaws are not touching shaft. Use a soft faced hammer to drive shaft out of bearing. When installing ball bearing (17), make sure that shielded side of bearing is facing water pump.

Needle bearings (34 and 35) should only be serviced with proper tools as improper service procedures may damage gearcase. A combination removal/installation tool for drive shaft needle bearing (35) may be constructed using drawing in Fig. E3-34.

To remove bearing (35 – Fig. E3-33), place tool, without "C" clip, in bearing from top of gearcase and pound on end of tool. To install bearing (35), place "C" clip on tool so new bearing will be properly positioned in bore when driven in from top of gearcase.

A blind hole bearing puller should be used to pull propeller shaft needle bearing (34). A special driver (Fig. E3-35) should be used to install new bearing.

Needle bearings (41 & 44 – Fig. E3-33) may be removed and reinstalled with the aid of an arbor press.

When reassembling lower unit, make sure that oil seals (15, 26 & 62) are installed with lips facing inside of gearcase. Shift bracket guide pin (70) with detent grooves must be installed on left side. Shift shaft (21) is installed with flat on end facing left side. Install retainer plate (14) so notches align with cutouts in water pump base plate (12).

When assembling gearcase to motor leg, use a flashlight to observe through exhaust outlet that water tube (6) is properly seating in water pump. Install washer and stud nut which retain lower unit to motor leg before installing screw (31). Check shift mechanism for proper engagement. Detents in shift mechanism in lower units should be felt when operating shift lever.

OUTBOARD MOTOR CORP.

EVINRUDE MOTORS
4143 N. 27th Street
Milwaukee, Wisconsin 53216

JOHNSON MOTORS
200 Sea-Horse Drive
Waukegan, Illinois 60085

EVINRUDE 1½ AND 2 HP

Year Produced	1½ hp	2 hp
1969.............	1902	.....
1970.............	1002	.....
1971.............	.....	2102
1972.............	.....	2202
1973.............	.....	2302
1974.............	.....	2402
1975.............	.....	2502
1976.............	.....	2602
1977.............	.....	2702
1978.............	.....	2802
1979.............	.....	2902
1980.............	.....	E2RCS
1981.............	.....	E2RCIB
1982.............	.....	E2RCNE
1983.............	.....	E2RCTD
1984.............	.....	E2RCRS
1985.............	.....	E2RCOC
1986.............	.....	EJR-CDR
1987.............	.....	EJRCU
1988.............	.....	EJRCC
1989.............	.....	EJRCE

JOHNSON 1½ AND 2 HP

Year Produced	1½ hp	2 hp
1969.............	1R-69	.....
1970.............	1R-70	.....
1971.............	.....	2R71
1972.............	.....	2R72
1973.............	.....	2R73
1974.............	.....	2R74
1975.............	.....	2R75
1976.............	.....	2R76
1977.............	.....	2R77
1978.............	.....	2R78
1979.............	.....	2R79
1980.............	.....	2RCS
1981.............	.....	J2RCIB
1982.............	.....	J2RCNE
1983.............	.....	J2RCTD
1984.............	.....	J2RCRS
1985.............	.....	J2RCOC
1986.............	.....	JCO-CDR
1987.............	.....	JCOCU
1988.............	.....	JCOCC
1989.............	.....	JCOCE

CONDENSED SERVICE DATA

TUNE-UP
Hp/rpm:
  1969-1970 ....1-1/2/4000
  1971-1982 ....2/4500
  1983 ....2/4200-4800
  1984 ....2/4000-5500
  1985 ....2/4000-5000
  1986-1989 ....2/4500-5500
Bore:
  Prior to 1989 ....1.567 in.
                                      (39.80 mm)
  1989 ....1.565 in.
                                      (39.75 mm)
Stroke:
  Prior to 1989.........................1.374 in.
                                      (34.90 mm)
  1989 ....1.375 in.
                                      (34.93 mm)
Number of Cylinders 1
Displacement ....2.64 cu. in.
                                      (43 cc)
Spark Plug-Champion:
  1969-1970 ....J4J
  1971-1984 ....J6J
  1985-1989 ....RJ6J

TUNE—UP CONT.
Electrode Gap ....0.030 in.
                                      (0.76 mm)
Breaker Point Gap.......................0.020 in.
                                      (0.51 mm)
Carburetor Make ....OMC
Idle Speed (In Forward Gear):
  Prior to 1989 ....650-700 rpm*
  1989................................625-675 rpm*
Gearcase Oil Capacity ....1.2 oz.
                                      (38 mL)

*For optimum results when adjusting idle speed, boat
should be in the water with the correct propeller installed.
Engine should be running in forward gear at normal
operating temperature with boat movement unrestrained.

SIZES—CLEARANCES
Piston Rings:
  End Gap ....0.015-0.025 in.
                                      (0.38-0.64 mm)
  Side Clearances (1969-1970) ....0.0010-0.0035 in.
                                      (0.025-0.089 mm)
  Side Clearances (1971-1984) ....0.0020-0.0040 in.
                                      (0.051-0.102 mm)

SIZES—CLEARANCES CONT.

Side Clearance (1985-1989) . . . . .0.004 in. Max.
(0.10 mm)

Piston Skirt Clearance
(1969-1984) . . . . .0.0043-0.0055 in.
(0.109-0.140 mm)

Standard Cylinder Bore
Diameter:
(1985-1988) . . . . .1.5668-1.5675 in.
(39.797-39.814 mm)
(1989). . . . . .1.5643-1.5650 in.
(39.733-39.751 mm)

Standard Piston Diameter:
(1985-1988) . . . . .1.5610-1.5635 in.
(39.649-39.713 mm)
(1989) . . . . .1.5620-1.5625 in.
(39.675-39.687 mm)

Crankshaft Main Journal Diameter:
(1969-1988) .0.7497-0.7502 in.
(19.042-19.055 mm)
(1989):
Upper . . . . .0.7497-0.7502 in.
(19.042-19.055 mm)
Lower . . . . .0.6691-0.6695 in.
(16.995-17.005 mm)

Crankshaft Crankpin Diameter:
(1969-1978) . . . . .0.6685-0.6690 in.
(16.980-16.993 mm)
(1979-1989) . . . . .0.6695-0.6700 in.
(17.005-17.018 mm)

Piston Pin Diametral Clearance In
Connecting Rod (Prior to 1980). . . . . .0.0004-0.0011 in.
(0.010-0.028 mm)

Drive Shaft Bearing Diametral
Clearance (1969-1984) . . . . .0.0010-0.0028 in.
(0.025-0.071 mm)

Propeller Shaft Diametral
Clearance (1969-1984):
Rear Bearing . . . . .0.0007-0.0022 in.
(0.018-0.056 mm)

SIZES—CLEARANCES CONT.

Propeller . . . . .0.0022-0.0057 in.
(0.056-0.145 mm)

TIGHTENING TORQUES
Connecting Rod . . . . .60-70 in.-lbs.
(6.8-7.9 N·m)
Cylinder Head. . . . . .60-84 in.-lbs.*
(6.8-9.5 N·m)
Flywheel . . . . .264-300 in.-lbs.
(29.8-33.9 N·m)
Inlet Manifold . . . . .60-84 in.-lbs.
(6.8-9.5 N·m)
Lower Main Bearing Housing. . . . . .60-84 in.-lbs.
(6.8-9.5 N·m)
Spark Plug. . . . . .216-240 in.-lbs.
(24.4-27.1 N·m)
Standard Screws:
No. 6 . . . . .7-10 in.-lbs.
(0.8-1.2 N·m)
No. 8 . . . . .15-22 in.-lbs
(1.6-2.4 N·m)
No. 10 . . . . .25-35 in.-lbs.
(2.8-4.0 N·m)
No. 12 . . . . .35-40 in.-lbs.
(4.0-4.6 N·m)
1/4 inch . . . . .60-80 in.-lbs.
(7-9 N·m)
5/16 inch . . . . .120-140 in.-lbs.
(14-16 N·m)
3/8 inch . . . . .220-240 in.-lbs.
(24-27 N·m)
7/16 inch . . . . .340-360 in.-lbs.
(38-40 N·m)

*Cylinder head and spark plug should be retightened to correct torque after motor has been test run and allowed to cool.

LUBRICATION

The power head is lubricated by oil mixed with the fuel. The recommended fuel is regular leaded or unleaded gasoline with a minimum octane rating of 67 on models produced after 1980 and 86 on models produced prior to 1981. If the recommended fuel is not available, gasoline containing not more than ten percent ethanol alcohol, or, gasoline containing not more than five percent methanol alcohol with five percent co-solvent additives may be used. Do not use gasoline exceeding the specified alcohol content regardless of octane rating.

The recommended oil is Evinrude or Johnson Outboard Lubricant or a suitable equivalent NMMA (formerly known as BIA) certified TC-W or TC-WII engine oil. The recommended fuel:oil ratio for normal service and during engine break-in is 50:1.

NOTE: OMC service bulletin 2211 issued September 1988, recommends using a 50:1 fuel:oil ratio on all recreational outboard motors which were previously recommended for a 100:1 fuel:oil mixture. For 1989, Accumix and Accumix R fuel and oil mixing systems have been changed to a 50:1 ratio.

On models so recommended, a 100:1 fuel:oil mixture may be used if an approved oil is used and if the engine is completely broken-in and motor is used on a frequent basis. Do not use a 100:1 mixture if motor is used infrequently and during nonuse the motor is stored in areas of high humidity or wide-scale temperature changes, or if motor is operated at constant high speeds.

The lower unit gears and bearings are lubricated by oil contained in the gearcase. The recommended oil is OMC HI-VIS Gearcase Lube. The gearcase oil capacity is 1.28 ounces (38 mL). Gearcase oil level should be checked after every 50 hours of operation and gearcase should be drained and filled with new oil every 100 hours or once each season, whichever occurs first. The gearcase is drained and filled through the same plug port.

To drain old oil, remove plug from starboard side of gearcase and turn motor starboard side down to allow oil to drain completely. To refill, position motor with starboard side up and fill gearcase until oil is at level of plug hole.

NOTE: Fill slowly, allowing air to escape.

FUEL SYSTEM

CARBURETOR. The carburetor is equipped with adjustment needles for both low and high speed mixture. Initial setting is 1-1/4 turns open for low speed mixture needle (L—Fig. OM1-1) and 1/2 to 1 turn open for high speed mixture needle (H). Needle should be adjusted after motor reaches normal operating temperature to provide best operation at idle speed. The high speed needle (H) should be adjusted for best operation at high speed before adjusting needle (L) for best operation at idle speed. Turning both needles clockwise leans the fuel mixture.

To check float level, remove float chamber (6) and invert carburetor. Place OMC float gage 324891 on carburetor body so legs of float gage rest on gasket mating surface as shown in Fig. OM1-2. Top of float should be even with float gage as shown. Be sure float gage is not pressing down on float. Carefully bend float arm to adjust.

To check float drop, position carburetor upright and allow float to hang as shown in Fig. OM1-3. Float drop (D) should be 1-1/8 to 1-1/2 inches (28.6-38.1 mm). Bend tang (T) to adjust.

SPEED CONTROL LINKAGE. The speed control lever rotates the magneto armature plate to advance the ignition timing. A cam attached to bottom

of armature plate is used to open carburetor throttle as ignition timing is advanced. The cam must be synchronized to open throttle the correct amount in relation to ignition timing. The throttle and ignition cannot be properly synchronized if the cam is bent. Also, check the cam follower and linkage for wear.

To synchronize speed controls, remove the motor cover and move speed control from stop position until carburetor throttle just begins to open. On models prior to 1978, the flat (port side) edge of the cam follower should be aligned with mark on cam (Fig. OM1-4). If incorrect, loosen throttle cam retaining screws and adjust throttle cam.

On models after 1977, cam follower roller (25—Fig. OM1-5) should be centered between marks on cam (15) just as carburetor throttle opens. Note that on some models after 1987, only one

mark is on throttle cam. On such models, single mark on cam should be aligned with center of roller (25). To adjust, turn cam follower adjusting screw (24—Fig. OM1-1) as necessary to center roller between marks or align roller with single mark depending on model being serviced.

REED VALVES. The inlet reed valve unit is located between carburetor and crankcase. Reed petals should seat lightly against reed plate throughout their entire length, with the least possible tension. Check seating visually and by blowing and drawing air through carburetor port. Renew reed petals if broken, cracked, warped, rusted or bent. A broken reed is sometimes caused by a bent or damaged reed stop. Seating surface of plate should be smooth and flat.

Reed stop setting should be 1/4 inch (6.35 mm) when measured between end of reed stop and reed plate as shown at (R—Fig. OM1-6).

IGNITION

Breaker point gap should be 0.020 inch (0.51 mm) on used points and 0.022 inch (0.56 mm) on new breaker points. Ignition timing may be checked by connecting a timing light to spark plug lead

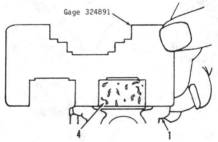

Fig. OM1-2—To check float level, place OMC float gage 324891 on carburetor body (1) as shown. Top of float (4) should be between gage notches.

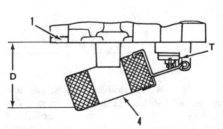

Fig. OM1-3—Float drop (D) should be 1-1/8 to 1-1/2 inches (28.6-38.1 mm) measured from carburetor body (1) to float (4) as shown. Bend tang (T) to adjust.

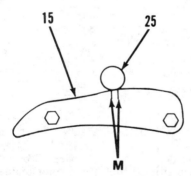

Fig. OM1-5—On models after 1977, cam follower roller (25) should be centered between marks (M) on cam (15) just as carburetor throttle opens. Note that some models have only one mark (M) which should be aligned with center of roller (25). Refer to text.

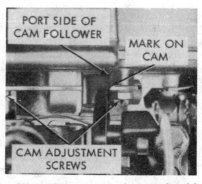

Fig. OM1-4—Refer to text when synchronizing speed control linkage on models prior to 1978.

Fig. OM1-6—View of reed plate with reed petals and reed stops installed. Reed stop should be ¼ inch (6.35 mm) above reed plate as shown at (R).

Fig. OM1-1—Exploded view of carburetor used on all models. Do not attempt to clean float (4) in solvent. Follower adjusting screw (24) and follower roller (25) are used on models after 1977.

H. High speed mixture needle	12. Choke shaft
L. Low speed mixture needle	13. Choke plate
	14. Shoulder screw
1. Carburetor body	15. Washer
2. Fuel inlet needle & seat	16. Cam follower
	17. Link
3. Needle to float clip	18. Throttle shaft
4. Float	19. Return spring
5. Pivot	20. Throttle plate
6. Float chamber	21. Washer
7. Packing	22. Throttle shaft retainer
8. Packing nut	23. Gasket
9. High speed nozzle	24. Follower adjusting screw
10. Gasket	25. Roller
11. Choke return spring	

and running engine at 1000 rpm. Ignition timing is correct if flywheel mark (F—Fig. OM1-7) is centered between timing marks (M) on magneto armature plate.

To remove the magneto armature plate, remove flywheel nut and on early models, the rope starter pulley. Then, use a suitable puller to remove flywheel. Disconnect ground wire (19—Fig. OM1-8), remove screw (8) and spring (9), then lift armature plate from power head. Remainder of disassembly is evident.

If bushing (17) is removed, the curved edge of tab (C—Fig. OM1-9) must be down and the raised boss in bushing

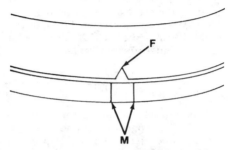

Fig. OM1-7—Ignition timing is correct if flywheel mark (F) is centered between timing marks (M) on magneto armature plate. Refer to text.

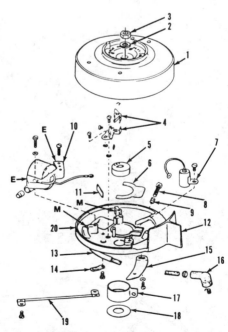

Fig. OM1-8—Exploded view of the magneto assembly.

1. Flywheel
2. Lockwasher
3. Nut
4. Breaker point assy.
5. Cam
6. Gasket
7. Condenser
8. Tension screw
9. Spring
10. Coil assy.
11. Oiler wick
12. Speed control lever
13. Spark plug lead
14. Clip
15. Throttle cam
16. Spark plug boot
17. Bushing
18. Washer
19. Ground wire
20. Magneto armature plate

must completely engage groove in crankcase. Lubricate bushing lightly before installing. Oil wick (11—Fig. OM1-8) must be installed before coil. The two ends (E) of the laminated coil core should be flush with machined edge of mounting bosses (M) after coil assembly is installed. A locating ring (4.472 inch ID × 5/8 inch thick) can be used to align coil. The spark plug (high tension) wire can be removed from coil. Screw (8) should be tightened enough to maintain a selected speed; however, it should be possible to move the speed control (armature plate) without excessive effort. Make certain that wire (19) is properly grounded. The flywheel drive key should be installed with edge of key parallel with crankshaft centerline. Taper on crankshaft and in flywheel bore must be clean and dry. Tighten the flywheel nut to 264-300 in.-lbs. (29.8-33.9 N·m).

COOLING SYSTEM

WATER PUMP. The water pump is accessible for service after removing the gearcase as outlined in the LOWER UNIT section. To remove the water tube, the power head must be separated from the drive shaft housing.

When cooling system problems are encountered, first check the water inlet for plugging or partial stoppage. Then, if not corrected, remove the gearcase and check water pump. The correct installation of the upper end of the water tube is shown in Fig. OM1-20.

POWER HEAD

REMOVE AND REINSTALL. The power head can be removed after removing six screws (6—Fig. OM1-11). Before reinstalling, coat the drive shaft upper splines lightly with water-

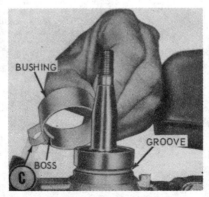

Fig. OM1-9—The bushing must be installed with curved edge (C) down. Boss must mesh with groove.

resistant grease. Carefully lower the power head into position and align drive shaft and crankshaft splines.

NOTE: Turn crankshaft in normal direction of rotation (flywheel clockwise) only when aligning splines.

DISASSEMBLY. Removal of engine covers, flywheel, magneto, carburetor and reed valves is usually easier before power head is detached from drive shaft housing.

Refer to Fig. OM1-14. Remove reed plate (2) and cylinder head (1). Remove connecting rod screws, remove cap (6), liners (9) and thirty bearing rollers (10). The connecting rod (7) and piston assembly can now be withdrawn. On models prior to 1989, the crankshaft can be removed after removing the lower bearing housing (12). On 1989 models, remove crankshaft and bearing housing as an assembly. Remove bearing housing from crankshaft by compressing snap ring located between lower main bearing and crankshaft web and sliding housing off main bearing.

ASSEMBLY. When assembling, the crankcase, reed plate and lower main bearing plate must be completely sealed against both pressure and vacuum. The exhaust cover and cylinder head must be sealed against water leakage and pressure. All mating surfaces must be smooth and clean to provide a tight seal. It is recommended that all gasket surfaces be checked for nicks and burrs or warped surfaces which might interfere with a tight seal. If necessary, surfaces may be lapped to provide a smooth surface; however, do not remove any more metal than necessary.

Refer to the specific service sections when assembling the crankshaft, con-

Fig. OM1-11—The power head is attached to the drive shaft housing with cap screws (6).

necting rod and piston. Recommended torque values are listed in the CONDENSED SERVICE DATA table. The cylinder head should be retorqued after motor is test run and allowed to cool.

PISTON, PIN, RINGS AND CYLINDER. The piston is fitted with two interchangeable rings. Maximum allowable cylinder bore taper is 0.002 inch (0.05 mm). Maximum allowable cylinder bore out-of-round is 0.003 inch (0.08 mm). Cylinder should be renewed or bored if excessively tapered or out-of-round or if bore diameter is oversize in excess of 0.002 inch (0.05 mm) from standard bore diameter. Refer to CONDENSED SERVICE DATA. Piston and rings are available in 0.030 inch (0.76 mm) oversize. Refer to CONDENSED SERVICE DATA for standard piston diameter. Renew piston if worn in excess of 0.002 inch (0.05 mm). Measure piston diameter 1/8 inch (3.2 mm) up from bottom of skirt.

Maximum allowable cylinder head warpage is 0.004 inch (0.10 mm). Renew head or lap mating surface if warpage exceeds specified amount.

One piston pin bore in piston is a press fit while other bore is a slip fit. The loose-fit bore can be identified by the mark "L" on bottom side of piston. When removing and installing piston pin, piston should be supported on press fit side to prevent damage to piston. Drive pin out toward press fit side. Reinstall pin in loose side first. Be sure to properly support piston on press fit side. Renew piston pin retainer clips during reassembly. Piston must be assembled to connecting rod with the long tapered side of piston crown facing toward exhaust side of cylinder and the oil hole

(H—Fig. OM1-15) in connecting rod facing up. Thoroughly lubricate all friction surfaces during reassembly.

CONNECTING ROD, CRANKSHAFT AND BEARINGS. The crankshaft upper main bearing (14—Fig. OM1-14) should be pressed into bore in crankcase until bearing is recessed 1/16 inch (1.6 mm) from thrust surface of crankcase. The bearing should be pressed into position by pressing against lettered side of bearing from lower opening in crankcase. Lip of upper seal (15) should be facing down toward bearing (14). On models prior to 1989, lower main bearing and seal are available only as an assembly with housing (12).

On 1989 models, lower main bearing and seal are available separately from bearing housing. Lower main bearing is a press fit on crankshaft. A snap ring located between bearing and crankshaft web secures bearing housing to main bearing. Crankshaft assembly must be removed from engine to remove bearing housing from crankshaft. Lower main bearing should be pressed on crankshaft from lettered side of bearing with crankshaft properly supported.

Refer to Fig. OM1-15 when assembling the piston and connecting rod. Position

the rod and piston in the cylinder. On early models make certain that both dowels (8—Fig. OM1-14) are installed. Insert one half of liner (9) in connecting rod. Coat liner with "OMC Needle Bearing Grease" (Part Number 378642) or equivalent and position 14 of the rollers (10) in connecting rod. Position the crankshaft (11) in crankcase, being careful not to damage seal (15) or the 14 connecting rod bearing rollers. Move the connecting rod against crankshaft crankpin, coat the crankpin with grease and position the remaining 16 bearing rollers. Position the other half of liner (9) over crankpin, then install rod cap (6) making certain that alignment marks (M—Fig. OM1-15) are together. Tighten the connecting rod screws. On early models, bend tabs on lock plates (16—Fig. OM1-14) over screws. Refer to the CONDENSED SERVICE DATA table for recommended torque values.

STARTER

The manual rewind starter assembly is an integral part of the engine cover. To overhaul the manual starter, proceed as follows: Remove the engine cover. Check pawl (9—Fig. OM1-17) for freedom of movement and excessive wear

Fig. OM1-15—The long sloping side of piston head (E) should be toward exhaust ports and oil hole (H) in rod should be up. Alignment marks (M) on rod and cap must be aligned.

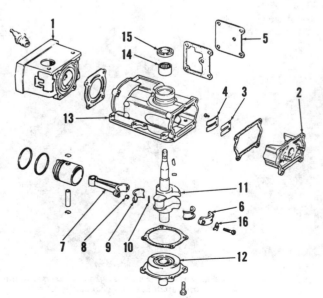

Fig. OM1-14—Exploded view of power head typical of all models prior to 1989. On 1989 models, lower main bearing and seal is separate from housing (12). Refer to text.

1. Cylinder head
2. Reed plate
3. Reed petals
4. Reed stop
5. Exhaust cover
6. Connecting rod cap
7. Connecting rod
8. Dowels
9. Bearing liners
10. Bearing rollers (30 used)
11. Crankshaft
12. Bearing housing
13. Cylinder & crankcase
14. Top main bearing
15. Top seal
16. Lock plate

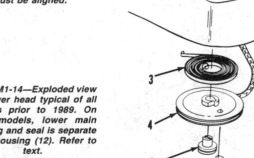

Fig. OM1-17—Exploded view of manual rewind starter used on later models.

1. Screw
2. Lockwasher
3. Rewind spring
4. Pulley
5. Starter rope
6. Spindle
7. Friction spring
8. Links
9. Drive pawl
10. Clip
11. Handle
12. Cover

of engagement area and damage. Renew or lubricate pawl (9) with OMC TRIPLE-GUARD GREASE or Lubriplate 777 and return starter to service if no other damage is noted.

To disassemble, remove clip (10) and withdraw pawl (9), links (8) and friction spring (7). Untie starter rope (5) at handle (11) and allow the rope to wind into the starter. Remove screw (1) and lockwasher (2), then withdraw spindle (6). Carefully lift pulley (4) with starter rope (5) from cover (12). BE CAREFUL when removing pulley (4) as rewind spring (3) may be dislodged. Remove rope (5) from pulley (4) if renewal is required. To remove rewind spring (3) from cover (12), invert cover so it sits upright on a flat surface, then tap the cover top until rewind spring (3) falls free and uncoils.

Inspect all components for damage and excessive wear and renew if needed.

To reassemble, first apply a coating of OMC TRIPLE-GUARD GREASE or Lubriplate 777 to rewind spring area of cover (12). Install rewind spring (3) in cover (12) so spring coils wind in a counterclockwise direction from the outer end.

NOTE: Lubricate all friction surfaces with OMC TRIPLE-GUARD GREASE or Lubriplate 777 during reassembly.

Install pulley (4) in cover (12). Make sure pulley hub properly engages hook on rewind spring (3). Wind starter rope (5) onto pulley (4) in a counterclockwise direction as viewed from the flywheel side. Install spindle (6). Spray screw (1) threads with OMC Locquic Primer and apply OMC Screw Lock on screw threads, then install screw (1) with lockwasher (2) and securely tighten.

Turn pulley (4) 3-1/2 turns clockwise when viewed from the flywheel side. Secure pulley position, then thread starter rope (5) through cover (12) opening and handle (11) and secure with a knot.

NOTE: Do not apply any more tension on rewind spring (3) than what is required to draw starter handle (11) back into the proper released position.

Install friction spring (7), links (8), pawl (9) and clip (10).

Remount engine cover (12).

LOWER UNIT

PROPELLER AND DRIVE PIN.
Drive pin protection is carefully en-

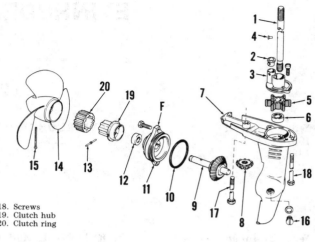

Fig. OM1-19—Exploded view of the gearcase and associated parts. Refer to Fig. OM1-21 for exploded view of the drive shaft housing. Models prior to 1973 are not equipped with clutch hub (19) or ring (20).

1. Drive shaft
2. Water tube seal
3. Pump cover
4. Impeller drive pin
5. Impeller
6. Seal
7. Gearcase
8. Drive pinion
9. Propeller shaft & gear
10. "O" ring
11. Gearcase head
12. Seal
13. Propeller drive pin
14. Propeller
15. Cotter pin
16. Drain plug
17. Screws
18. Screws
19. Clutch hub
20. Clutch ring

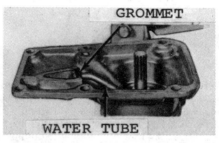

Fig. OM1-20—View of upper end of drive shaft housing with power head removed showing installation of water tube and grommet.

gineered and other pins must not be substituted. Protection depends on pin material as well as size. The propeller is retained to propeller shaft by cotter pin (15—Fig. OM1-19). Standard propeller diameter and pitch is 7-1/4 × 4-1/2 (184 × 114 mm). Propellers other than those designed for the motor should not be used.

R&R AND OVERHAUL. The gearcase can be removed after removing the two screws (17 and 18—Fig. OM1-19). Disassembly is evident after removing water pump cover (3) and gearcase head (11).

Inspect all parts for wear or damage. The gearcase (7) must be renewed if bearing bores or water pump bore is damaged. Clean all old sealer from parts before assembling.

Assembly procedure is self-evident. All screws should be coated with "OMC Gasket Sealing Compound" or equivalent before installing. Flat end (F) of gearcase head must be toward top. Apply a thin coat of grease to the drive shaft upper splines and coat water tube seal (2) with liquid soap before installing gearcase assembly. The flywheel can be turned in normal direction of rotation while aligning water tube and drive shaft. Refer to CONDENSED SERVICE DATA table for recommended torque values.

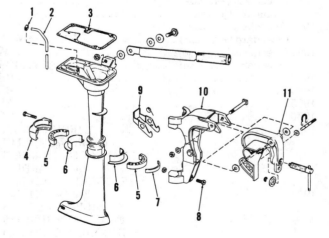

Fig. OM1-21—Exploded view of the drive shaft housing. Cap (4), vibration dampener (5) and pivot bearing (6) are also used for upper bearing.

1. Grommet
2. Water tube
3. Gasket
4. Cap
5. Vibration dampener
6. Pivot bearing
7. Steering tension brake
8. Steering tension screw
9. Reverse lock
10. Swivel bracket
11. Clamp

EVINRUDE AND JOHNSON

2.5 HP

Year Produced	EVINRUDE Models	Year Produced	JOHNSON Models
1987	E3RCU	1987	J3RCU
1988	E3RCC	1988	J3RCC

3 HP

Year Produced	EVINRUDE Models	Year Produced	JOHNSON Models
1989	E3BRCE	1989	J3BRCE

4 HP

Year Produced	EVINRUDE Models	Year Produced	JOHNSON Models
1970 (Weedless Gearcase)	4006	1970 (Weedless Gearcase)	4W70
(Standard Gearcase)	4036	(Standard Gearcase)	4R70
1971 (Weedless Gearcase)	4106	1971 (Weedless Gearcase)	4W71
(Standard Gearcase)	4136	(Standard Gearcase)	4R71
1972 (Weedless Gearcase)	4206	1972 (Weedless Gearcase)	4W72
(Standard Gearcase)	4236	(Standard Gearcase)	4R72
1973 (Weedless Gearcase)	4306	1973 (Weedless Gearcase)	4W73
(Standard Gearcase)	4336	(Standard Gearcase)	4R73
1974 (Weedless Gearcase)	4406	1974 (Weedless Gearcase)	4W74
(Standard Gearcase)	4436	(Standard Gearcase)	4R74
1975 (Weedless Gearcase)	4506	1975 (Weedless Gearcase)	4W75
(Standard Gearcase)	4536	(Standard Gearcase)	4R75
1976 (Weedless Gearcase)	4606	1976 (Weedless Gearcase)	4W76
(Standard Gearcase)	4636	(Standard Gearcase)	4R76
1977 (Weedless Gearcase)	4706	1977 (Weedless Gearcase)	4W77
(Standard Gearcase)	4736	(Standard Gearcase)	4R77
1978 (Weedless Gearcase)	4806	1978 (Weedless Gearcase)	4W78
(Standard Gearcase)	4836, 4837	(Standard Gearcase)	4R78, 4RL78
1979 (Weedless Gearcase)	4904	1979 (Weedless Gearcase)	4W79
(Standard Gearcase)	4932, 4933	(Standard Gearcase)	4R79, 4RL79
1980 (Weedless Gearcase)	4WCS	1980 (Weedless Gearcase)	4WCS
(Standard Gearcase)	4RLCS	(Standard Gearcase)	4RLCS
1981 (Weedless Gearcase)	4WCI	1981 (Weedless Gearcase)	4WCI
(Standard Gearcase)	4BRCI	(Standard Gearcase)	4BRCI
1982 (Weedless Gearcase)	4W	1982 (Weedless Gearcase)	4W
(Standard Gearcase)	4BR	(Standard Gearcase)	4BR
1983	4BR	1983	4BR
1984	4BR	1984	4BR
1985	4BR	1985	4BR
1986	4BR, 4RD	1986	4BR, 4RD
1987	E4RCU, E4RLCU	1987	J4RCU, J4RLCU
	E4BRCU, E4BRLCU		J4BRCU, J4BRLCU
	E4BRHCU, E4BRHLCU		J4BRHCU J4BRHLCU
	E4RDCU, E4RDLCU		J4RDCU, J4RDLCU
	E4RDHCU, E4RDHLCU		J4RDHCU, J4RDHLCU
1988	E4RCC, E4RLCC	1988	J4RCC, J4RLCC
	E4BRCC, E4BRLCC		J4BRCC, J4BRLCC
	E4BRHCC, E4BRHLCC		J4BRHCC, J4BRHLCC
	E4RDHCC, E4RDHLCC		J4RDHCC, J4RDHLCC
1989	E4RCE, E4RLCE	1989	J4RCE, J4RLCE
	E4BRHCE, E4BRHLCE		J4BRHCE, J4BRHLCE
	E4RDHCE, E4RDHLCE		J4RDHCE, J4DHLCE

4.5 HP

Year Produced	EVINRUDE Models	Year Produced	JOHNSON Models
1980 . . . . 5RCS		1980 . . . . 5RCS	
1981 . . . . 5RCI		1981 . . . . 5RCI	
1982 . . . . 5RH		1982 . . . . 5RH	
1983 . . . . 5RHCT		1983 . . . . 5RHCT	

CONDENSED SERVICE DATA

TUNE-UP

Hp/rpm 2.5/4000-5000
(1.9 kW)
3/4500-5500
(2.2 kW)
4/4500-5500*
(3.0 kW)
4.5/4500-5500
(3.4 kW)

Bore . . . . .1.565 in.
(39.75 mm)

Stroke . . . . .1.374 in.
(34.90 mm)

Number of Cylinders 2

Displacement . . . . .5.28 cu. in.
(86.5 cc)

Spark Plug—Champion:
2.5 Hp Models—
1987-1988 . . . . .QL77JC4
Electrode Gap . . . . .0.040 in.
(1.0 mm)

3 Hp Models—
1989 . . . . .RL82C
Electrode Gap . . . . .0.030 in.
(0.76 mm)

4 Hp Models—
1970 . . . . .J4J
Electrode Gap . . . . .0.020 in.
(0.51 mm)

1971-1976 . . . . .J6J
Electrode Gap . . . . .0.030 in.
(0.76 mm)

1977-1980 . . . . .L77J4
Electrode Gap . . . . .0.040 in.
(1.0 mm)

1981-1986
Breaker Point Ignition .L86
Electrode Gap . . . . .0.030 in.
(0.76 mm)
CD Ignition QL77JC4
Electrode Gap . . . . .0.040 in.
(1.0 mm)

1987
Breaker Point Ignition RL86C
Electrode Gap . . . . .0.030 in.
(0.76 mm)
CD Ignition QL77JC4
Electrode Gap . . . . .0.040 in.
(1.0 mm)

TUNE-UP CONT.

1988-1989
Breaker Point Ignition RL82C
Electrode Gap . . . . .0.030 in.
(0.76 mm)
CD Ignition QL77JC4
Electrode Gap . . . . .0.040 in.†
(1.0 mm)

4.5 Hp Models—
1980-1983 . . . . .QL77J4
Electrode Gap . . . . .0.040 in.
(1.0 mm)

Ignition Type:
2.5 Hp Models—
1987-1988 . . . . .CDI
3 Hp Models—
1989 . . . . .Breaker Point
4 Hp Models—
1970-1976 . . . . .Breaker Point
1977-1980 . . . . .CDI
1981-1985 . . . . .Breaker Point
1986-1989 . . . .‡
4.5 Hp Models . . . . .CDI
Breaker Point Gap:
Models So Equipped . . . . .0.020 in.
(0.51 mm)

Carburetor Make . . . . .OMC

Idle Speed (In Gear):
2.5 Hp Models—
1987 . . . . .600-650 rpm
1988 . . . . .775-825 rpm
3 Hp Models—
1989 . . . . .600-650 rpm
4 Hp Models—
Prior to 1987 . . . . .600 rpm
1987-1989 (including Deluxe) . . . . .600-650 rpm
4 Hp Excel & Ultra—
1987 . . . . .600-650 rpm
1988-1989 . . . . .725-775 rpm

Fuel:Oil Ratio . . . . .See Text

*On models prior to 1985, full throttle engine speed range is 4000-5000 rpm.

† On 1989 models, electrode gap should be 0.030 in. (0.76 mm).

‡ CD ignition is used on 1986-1989 4 hp Deluxe, Excel and Ultra models. Other 4 hp models are equipped with breaker point ignition.

CONDENSED SERVICE DATA (CONT.)

SIZES—CLEARANCES

POWER HEAD
Piston Rings End Gap:
  All Models . . . . .0.005-0.015 in.
  　　　　　　　　　　　　　　　　　　　(0.13-0.38 mm)

Piston Rings Side Clearance:
  1970-1984 . . . . .0.002-0.004 in.
  　　　　　　　　　　　　　　　　　　　(0.05-0.10 mm)
  1985-1989 . . . . .0.004 in. Max.
  　　　　　　　　　　　　　　　　　　　(0.10 mm)

Piston Skirt Clearance:
  1970 . . . . .0.0020-0.0040 in.
  　　　　　　　　　　　　　　　　　　　(0.051-0.102 mm)
  1971-1979 . . . . .0.0008-0.0020 in.
  　　　　　　　　　　　　　　　　　　　(0.020-0.051 mm)
  1980-1984 . . . . .0.0018-0.0030 in.
  　　　　　　　　　　　　　　　　　　　(0.046-0.076 mm)
  1985-1989 . . . .*
Standard Cylinder Diameter:
  All Models—
  1985-1989 . . . . .1.5643-1.5650 in.
  　　　　　　　　　　　　　　　　　　(39.733-39.751 mm)

Max. Allowable Cylinder Taper:
  All Models . . . . .0.002 in.
  　　　　　　　　　　　　　　　　　　　(0.05 mm)

Max. Allowable Cylinder Out-of-Round:
  Prior to 1987 . . . . .0.002 in.
  　　　　　　　　　　　　　　　　　　　(0.05 mm)
  1987-1989 . . . . .0.003 in.
  　　　　　　　　　　　　　　　　　　　(0.08 mm)

Standard Piston Diameter:
  Prior to 1988 . . . .†
  1988 Models . . . . .1.5610-1.5635 in.
  　　　　　　　　　　　　　　　　　　(39.649-39.713 mm)
  1989 . . . . .1.5625-1.5631 in.
  　　　　　　　　　　　　　　　　　　(39.686-39.703 mm)

Crankshaft Journal Diameters—
  1970-1977 Models:
  Top Main Journal . . . . .0.7515-0.7520 in.
  　　　　　　　　　　　　　　　　　(19.088-19.101 mm)
  Center Main Journal . . . . .0.6849-0.6854 in.
  　　　　　　　　　　　　　　　　　(17.396-17.409 mm)
  Bottom Main Journal . . . . .0.6849-0.6854 in.
  　　　　　　　　　　　　　　　　　(17.396-17.409 mm)
  Crankpin . . . . .0.6250-0.6255 in.
  　　　　　　　　　　　　　　　　　(15.875-15.888 mm)
  1978-1988 Models:
  Top Main Journal . . . . .0.7506-0.7510 in.
  　　　　　　　　　　　　　　　　　(19.065-19.075 mm)
  Center Main Journal . . . . .0.6685-0.6690 in.
  　　　　　　　　　　　　　　　　　(16.980-16.993 mm)
  Bottom Main Journal . . . . .0.7498-0.7502 in.
  　　　　　　　　　　　　　　　　　(19.045-19.055 mm)
  Crankpin . . . . .0.6695-0.6700 in.‡
  　　　　　　　　　　　　　　　　　(17.005-17.018 mm)
  1989 Models:
  Top Main Journal . . . . .0.7515-0.7520 in.
  　　　　　　　　　　　　　　　　　(19.088-19.101 mm)
  Center Main Journal . . . . .0.6685-0.6690 in.
  　　　　　　　　　　　　　　　　　(16.980-16.993 mm)
  Bottom Main Journal . . . . .0.6691-0.6695 in.
  　　　　　　　　　　　　　　　　　(16.995-17.005 mm)
  Crankpin . . . . .0.6695-0.6700 in.
  　　　　　　　　　　　　　　　　　(17.005-17.018 mm)

*The manufacturer does not specify piston-to-cylinder bore clearance on 1985-1989 models. If cylinder bore and piston are within specifications, piston clearance should be correct. To determine cylinder bore oversize diameter, add piston oversize dimension to standard bore diameter.
† The manufacturer does not specify standard piston diameter on models produced prior to 1988. To determine if piston is excessively worn, measure piston diameter 1/8 to 1/4 inch up from bottom of skirt. Take two measurements 90 degrees apart. If the difference between the two measurements exceeds 0.002 inch (0.05 mm), piston is excessively worn or out-of-round and should be renewed.
‡ Crankpin diameter on 1978 models is 0.6685-0.6690 inch (16.980-16.993 mm).

WEEDLESS LOWER UNIT
Drive Shaft Diametral Clearance . . . . .0.001-0.003 in.
  　　　　　　　　　　　　　　　　　(0.025-0.076 mm)
Propeller Shaft Diametral Clearance—
  Rear Bearing . . . . .0.0005-0.0015 in.
  　　　　　　　　　　　　　　　　　(0.013-0.038 mm)
Propeller Hub to Shaft (1969-1970) . . . . . .0.003-0.0065 in.
  　　　　　　　　　　　　　　　　　(0.076-0.165 mm)
Propeller Hub to Shaft (1971-1982) . . . . . .0.002-0.0053 in.
  　　　　　　　　　　　　　　　　　(0.051-0.135 mm)

STANDARD LOWER UNIT
Drive Gear to Housing Diametral Clearance:
  1969 . . . . .0.0010-0.0025 in.
  　　　　　　　　　　　　　　　　　(0.025-0.064 mm)
  1970-1980 . . . . .0.0005-0.0018 in.
  　　　　　　　　　　　　　　　　　(0.013-0.046 mm)
Propeller Shaft Diametral Clearance—
  1969-1970:
  Rear Bearing . . . . .0.0005-0.0020 in.
  　　　　　　　　　　　　　　　　　(0.013-0.051 mm)
  Front Bearing . . . . .0.0008-0.0020 in.
  　　　　　　　　　　　　　　　　　(0.020-0.051 mm)
Propeller Shaft Diametral Clearance—
  1971-1980:
  Rear Bearing . . . . .0.0007-0.0022 in.
  　　　　　　　　　　　　　　　　　(0.018-0.056 mm)
  Front Bearing . . . . .0.0007-0.0022 in.
  　　　　　　　　　　　　　　　　　(0.018-0.056 mm)
Propeller Hub to Shaft Diametral Clearance:
  Prior to 1974 . . . . .0.003-0.0055 in.
  　　　　　　　　　　　　　　　　　(0.076-0.140 mm)
  1974-1984 . . . . .0.0022-0.0067 in.
  　　　　　　　　　　　　　　　　　(0.056-0.170 mm)

TIGHTENING TORQUES
Connecting Rod . . . . .60-70 in.-lbs.
  　　　　　　　　　　　　　　　　　(6.8-7.9 N·m)
Crankcase Halves . . . . .60-84 in.-lbs.
  　　　　　　　　　　　　　　　　　(6.8-9.5 N·m)
Cylinder Head . . . . .60-84 in.-lbs.
  　　　　　　　　　　　　　　　　　(6.8-9.5 N·m)
Exhaust Cover . . . . .60-84 in.-lbs.
  　　　　　　　　　　　　　　　　　(6.8-9.5 N·m)
Flywheel . . . . .30-40 ft.-lbs.
  　　　　　　　　　　　　　　　　　(40.7-54.2 N·m)
Intake Manifold . . . . .60-84 in.-lbs.
  　　　　　　　　　　　　　　　　　(6.8-9.5 N·m)
Spark Plug . . . . .216-240 in.-lbs.
  　　　　　　　　　　　　　　　　　(24.4-27.1 N·m)

CONDENSED SERVICE DATA (CONT.)

TIGHTENING TORQUES CONT.

Standard Screws:

No. 6	7-10 in.-lbs.
	(0.8-1.2 N·m)
No. 8	15-22 in.-lbs.
	(1.6-2.4 N·m)
No. 10	25-35 in.-lbs.
	(2.8-4.0 N·m)
No. 12	35-40 in.-lbs.
	(4.0-4.6 N·m)
¼ Inch	60-80 in.-lbs.
	(7-9 N·m)
5/16 Inch	120-140 in.-lbs.
	(14-16 N·m)
⅜ Inch	220-240 in.-lbs.
	(24-27 N·m)
7/16 Inch	340-360 in.-lbs.
	(38-40 N·m)

LUBRICATION

The power head is lubricated by oil mixed with the fuel. The recommended fuel is regular leaded or unleaded gasoline with a minimum octane rating of 67 on models produced after 1980 and 86 on models produced prior to 1981. If the recommended fuel is not available, gasoline containing not more than ten percent ethanol alcohol, or gasoline containing not more than five percent methanol alcohol with five percent co-solvent additives may be used. Do not use gasoline exceeding the specified alcohol content regardless of octane rating. Discontinue the use of alcohol extended gasoline if fuel system problems are encountered.

The recommended oil is Evinrude or Johnson Outboard Lubricant or a suitable equivalent NMMA (formerly known as BIA) certified TC-W or TC-WII engine oil. Oil certified TC-WII is preferred on 1989 models. The recommended fuel:oil ratio for normal service and during engine break-in is 50:1.

NOTE: OMC service bulletin 2211 issued September 1988, recommends using a 50:1 fuel:oil ratio on all recreational outboard motors which were previously recommended for a 100:1 fuel and oil mixture. For 1989, Accumix and Accumix R fuel and oil mixing systems have been changed to a 50:1 ratio.

On models so recommended, a 100:1 fuel:oil mixture may be used if an approved oil is used and if the engine is completely broken-in and motor is used on a frequent basis. Do not use a 100:1 mixture if motor is used infrequently and during nonuse the motor is stored in areas of high humidity or wide-scale temperature changes, or if motor is operated at constant high speeds.

The lower unit gears and bearings are lubricated by oil contained in the gearcase. The recommended oil is OMC HI-VIS Gearcase Lube. The gearcase oil level should be checked after every 50 hours of operation and the gearcase should be drained and filled with new oil every 100 hours or once each season, whichever occurs first.

On early 4 hp models, the gearcase is drained and filled through the same plug port. To drain the oil, remove oil plug from gearcase housing. Lay the motor with the plug opening down and allow the lubricant to drain into a suitable container.

To fill the gearcase with oil, lay the motor with the plug opening up. Add oil through plug opening until the oil begins to overflow, then reinstall oil plug with a new gasket and tighten.

On 2.5 hp, 3 hp, late 4 hp, 4.5 hp and all weedless models, the gearcase oil is drained and filled through the same plug port. An oil level (vent) port is used to indicate the full level and to ease draining and refilling.

To drain the oil, place the outboard motor in a vertical position. Remove drain plug and oil level plug and allow the lubricant to drain into a suitable container.

To fill the gearcase with oil, place the outboard motor in a vertical position. Add oil through drain plug opening with an oil feeder until the oil begins to overflow from oil level plug port. Reinstall oil level plug with a new gasket, if needed, and tighten. Remove oil feeder, then reinstall drain plug with a new gasket, if needed, and tighten.

FUEL SYSTEM

CARBURETOR. All models are equipped with a carburetor of the type shown in Fig. OM2-1.

On models prior to 1978, the carburetor is equipped with adjustment needles for both low and high speed mixture. Initial setting is 1-1/4 turns out from a lightly seated position for low speed mixture needle (L) and 1/2 to 1 turn out from a lightly seated position for high speed mixture needle (H). Needle should be adjusted after motor reaches normal operating temperature to provide best operation at idle and high speed. The high speed needle (H) should be adjusted for best operation at high speed before adjusting needle (L) for best operation at idle speed. Turning both needles clockwise leans the fuel mixture.

On models after 1977, carburetor is equipped with adjustable low speed mixture and a fixed high speed jet. High speed air:fuel mixture is adjustable only by changing orifice size of the high speed jet. Initial setting of low speed mixture needle (L) is one turn out from a lightly seated position. On models equipped with fixed high speed jet, a fuel shut off valve is installed in place of high speed needle (H).

Refer to CONDENSED SERVICE DATA for recommended idle speed specifications for all models. Engine should be in gear at normal operating temperature when adjusting idle speed.

NOTE: For optimum results, check and adjust idle speed with boat in the water with the correct propeller installed. Engine should be running in gear at normal operating temperature with boat movement unrestrained.

To set carburetor float level, first unbolt and remove the carburetor. Refer to Fig. OM2-1 and unscrew and remove float chamber (6). Invert the carburetor body (1) and check position of float while carburetor is inverted. Upper surface of float (4—Fig. OM2-2) (lower when assembly is inverted) should be level and flush with gasket surface of carburetor body (1). If it is not, carefully bend float lever (F). Be sure that float does not bind or rub.

To check float drop, position carburetor upright and allow float to hang as shown in Fig. OM2-3. Float drop (D) should be 1-1/8 to 1-1/2 inches (28.6-38.1 mm). Bend tang (T) to adjust.

NOTE: During carburetor service on models after 1979, the manufacturer does not recommend submerging the parts in carburetor or parts cleaning solutions. An aerosol type carburetor cleaner is recommended. The float and other components made of plastic and rubber should not be subjected to some cleaning solutions. Safety eyewear and solvent resistant gloves are recommended.

SPEED CONTROL LINKAGE. The speed control lever rotates the magneto armature plate to advance the ignition timing. A cam (Fig. OM2-4) attached to the bottom of the magneto armature

Fig. OM2-2—With fuel inlet needle closed, float (4) should be level and flush with gasket surface of carburetor body (1). Bend float lever (F) to adjust.

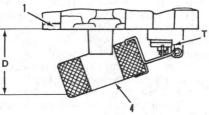

Fig. OM2-3—Float drop (D) on all models should be 1-1/8 to 1-1/2 inches (28.6-38.1 mm) measured from carburetor body (1) to float (4) as shown. Bend tang (T) to adjust.

Fig. OM2-4—View of typical ignition and throttle synchronizing components on models prior to 1978. Refer to text for adjusting procedures.

plate is used to open the carburetor throttle valve as the timing is advanced. The cam must be synchronized to open the throttle the correct amount in relation to the ignition timing. The throttle and ignition can not be synchronized properly if the cam is bent or damaged. Check condition of cam follower, link and spring.

To synchronize speed controls, remove the motor cover and move speed control from stop position until carburetor throttle just begins to open. On models prior to 1978, move the speed control so throttle cam just contacts cam follower as shown in Fig. OM2-4. Mark on cam should be directly behind the starboard edge of cam follower. If adjustment is incorrect, loosen the two cam mounting screws and relocate throttle cam as required.

On models after 1977, cam follower roller (25—Fig. OM2-5) should be centered between marks (M) on throttle cam (C) just as carburetor throttle opens. Turn cam follower adjusting screw (24—Fig. OM2-1) to center roller on marks. Note that some late models have one single mark on cam (C). On those models single mark should be aligned with center of roller (25).

REED VALVES. The inlet reed valve unit is located between crankcase and intake manifold. Reed valves should be inspected whenever the carburetor is removed from engine. Refer to Fig. OM2-6.

Reed petals should seat very lightly against reed plate (1) throughout their entire length, with the least possible tension. Check seating visually and by blowing and drawing air through ports. Renew reed petals if broken, cracked, warped, rusted or bent. Never attempt to straighten bent reed petals. Seating surface of plate (1) should be smooth and flat. Apply OMC Screw Lock or a suitable equivalent thread locking com-

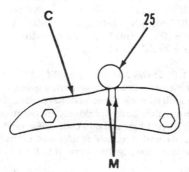

Fig. OM2-5—On models after 1977, cam follower roller (25) should be centered between marks (M) on cam (C) just as carburetor throttle opens. Some models are equipped with a single mark (M) which should be aligned with center of roller (25) when throttle begins to open. Refer to text.

Fig. OM2-1—Exploded view of carburetor typical of all models. Follower adjusting screw (24) and follower roller (25) are used on models after 1977. Note that late models are equipped with a fixed high speed jet. On models equipped with fixed high speed jet, high speed mixture needle (H) is replaced with a fuel shut-off valve.

H. High speed mixture needle	12. Choke shaft
L. Low speed mixture needle	13. Choke plate
1. Carburetor body	14. Shoulder screw
2. Fuel inlet needle & seat	15. Washer
3. Clip	16. Cam follower
4. Float	17. Link
5. Pivot	18. Throttle shaft
6. Float chamber	19. Return spring
7. Packing	20. Throttle plate
8. Packing nut	21. Washer
9. High speed nozzle	22. Throttle shaft retainer
10. Gasket	23. Gasket
11. Choke return spring	24. Follower adjusting screw
	25. Roller

pound to screws (4) and tighten screws (4) to 25-35 in.-lbs. (3-4 N·m).

Reed stop setting should be 1/4 inch (6.35 mm) for all models, when measured between end of stop and reed plate as shown at (A). Reed petals should be centered around alignment marks (M).

FUEL PUMP. Early motors are equipped with integral fuel tank; however, later motors are equipped with a fuel pump and use a remote fuel tank. Some of the earlier motors may be optionally equipped with a fuel pump and use remote tank.

The diaphragm type fuel pump attaches to side of cylinder block and is actuated by pressure and vacuum pulsations in upper crankcase. On early models, the fuel pump is available only as an assembly.

If fuel pump problems are encountered, first remove and clean the filter and blow through fuel lines to be sure they are open and clean; then, if trouble is not corrected, overhaul or renew the fuel pump assembly.

BREAKER POINT IGNITION

Breaker contact point gap should be 0.020 inch (0.51 mm) if points are being reused, or 0.022 inch (0.56 mm) if points are renewed. Both sets of points must be adjusted exactly alike. The flywheel must be removed to set breaker point gap. If OMC timing fixture 383603 (on models equipped with alternator, use timing fixture 554640) is available, set breaker point gap so points just open when pointer on timing fixture is between the two timing marks (TM—Fig. OM2-7) on armature plate. End of timing fixture marked (T) is for top cylinder, (B) is for bottom cylinder.

Taper on crankshaft and in flywheel should be clean and dry prior to installing flywheel. Flywheel retaining nut should be tightened to 30-40 ft.-lbs. (40.7-54.2 N·m). Check breaker point setting using a suitable timing light connected at each spark plug lead. Timing mark on flywheel should be centered between marks on armature plate at 1000 rpm.

Except for the permanent magnet built into the flywheel, the ignition system consists of a separate coil, condenser, point set and wiring for each cylinder. When ignition malfunction is encountered, check breaker point condition and gap adjustment, check for loose or corroded connections, damaged insulation and broken or shorted wires. The three ends of the laminated coil core should be flush with machined bosses on armature plate as shown at (F). Proper location of ignition coils on armature plate can be simplified by using OMC Locating Ring 317001. Place locating ring on armature plate, push ignition coils out to contact locating ring and tighten coil mounting screws. The flywheel drive key must be installed as shown in Fig. OM2-8. Breaker point cam should be installed with side marked TOP facing upward.

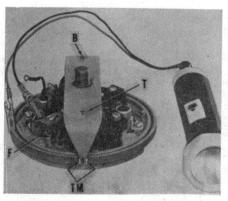

Fig. OM2-7—Breaker points should just open when pointer on timing fixture is between marks (TM). Use end marked (B) for setting points for bottom cylinder.

CD2 IGNITION SYSTEM

OPERATION. Four hp standard models 1977-1980, 1986-1988 4 hp Deluxe, 1987 and 1988 2.5 hp models, Excel 4, Ultra 4 and 4.5 hp models are equipped with a breakerless capacitor discharge ignition system. A charge coil and sensor coil are located under the flywheel. Two magnets in the flywheel induce a current in the charge coil which is rectified and directed to the capacitor inside the power pack for storage. The two flywheel magnets also induce current in the sensor coil to provide a positive charge on the gate of one of two silicon controlled rectifiers (SCR's). The positive charge opens the SCR and allows the charged capacitor to discharge through the SCR and primary circuit of the ignition coil. The rapid coil field buildup induces a secondary voltage which fires the spark plug. Diodes, SCR's and capacitor are contained in the power pack assembly and are not available individually.

Ignition timing is not adjustable on models with breakerless capacitor discharge ignition systems. However, backfiring and popping can occur if wires are not connected properly. Note wiring schematic in Fig. OM2-9.

Models Prior to 1989 (Except 2.5 hp, Excel 4 and Ultra 4)

TROUBLE-SHOOTING. On models prior to 1985, the 4-wire connector plugs connect the charge and sensor coil leads to the power pack. The 3-wire connector plugs connect the power pack and ignition coils. On models after 1984, a 5-wire connector is used between the power pack and armature plate. No timing adjustments are required with a CD2 ignition. Correct timing will be maintained as long as the wires are properly positioned in the connectors. On models prior to 1985, check to make sure the white/black wire in the 4-wire connector is positioned in connector terminal B. Also check to make sure the number 1 coil wire is in the 3-wire connector B terminal and that it connects with the power pack orange/blue wire in the other connector B terminal. On models after 1984, check to make sure the white/black wire in the 5-wire connector is positioned in connector terminal B of both connector halves. Also check to make sure the orange/blue power pack lead is connected to the number 1 ignition coil.

NOTE: Outer edges of charge coil and sensor coil must be flush with machined surface of armature plate to provide the proper clearance between coils and flywheel magnets. OMC locating ring 317001 may be used to simplify this procedure. Place locat-

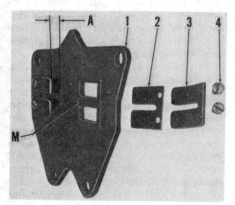

Fig. OM2-6—Exploded view of reed valves and reed plate.

1. Reed plate
2. Reed petals
3. Reed stop
4. Screws

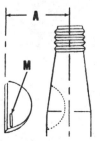

Fig. OM2-8—When installing breaker point cam and flywheel drive key, make certain that the upset mark (M) is down as shown.

ing ring over machined bosses on armature plate, push coil out against locating ring and tighten mounting screws.

To check charge coil output, use Merc-O-Tronic Model 781, Stevens Model CD77 or a suitable peak voltage tester. Disconnect connector between armature plate and power pack. Connect black tester lead to stator lead connector terminal A and red tester lead to terminal D. Turn tester knobs to Negative and 500. Crank engine while observing tester. If tester reading is below 230 volts, check condition of charge coil wiring and connectors, and verify pin location in connector. If wiring and connectors are in acceptable condition, check charge coil resistance as follows: Connect an ohmmeter to terminals A and D (Fig. OM2-9) in stator plate lead connector. Renew charge coil if resistance is not 500-650 ohms on models prior to 1986 or 550-600 ohms on 1986-1988 models. Connect negative ohmmeter lead to stator plate (ground) and positive ohmmeter lead to connector terminal A, then to connector terminal D. Infinite resistance should exist between A terminal and stator plate and D terminal and stator plate. If not, charge coil or charge coil lead is shorted to ground.

To check sensor coil, connect an ohmmeter to terminals B and C in stator plate lead connector. Renew sensor coil if resistance is not 30-50 ohms. Connect negative ohmmeter lead to stator plate (ground) and positive ohmmeter lead to connector terminal B, then to connector terminal C. Infinite resistance should exist between B terminal and stator

plate and C terminal and stator plate. If not, sensor coil or sensor coil lead is shorted to ground. To check sensor coil output, use Merc-O-Tronic Model 781, Stevens Model CD77 or a suitable peak voltage tester. Connect black tester lead to stator lead connector terminal C and red tester lead to terminal B. On Merc-O-Tronic Model 781, turn knobs to Positive and 5, and on Stevens Model CD77, turn knobs to S and 5. Crank engine while observing tester. Renew sensor coil if meter reads below 2 volts.

To check power pack output, first reconnect connector between armature plate and power pack. Use Merc-O-Tronic Model 781, Stevens Model CD77 or a suitable peak voltage tester. Connect black tester lead to a suitable engine ground. Connect red tester lead to

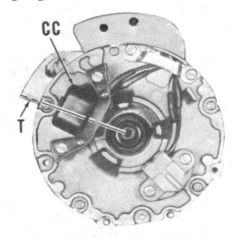

Fig. OM2-10—On 1977 and 1978 models, install stator plate so center of charge coil (CC) is aligned with stop (T) on cam plate.

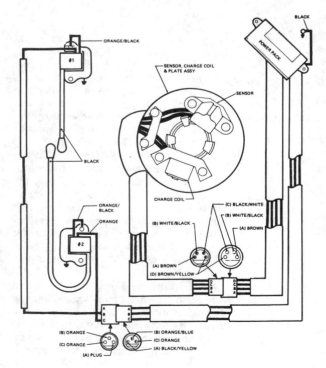

Fig. OM2-9—Typical wiring schematic for models equipped with breakerless CD2 capacitor discharge ignition (CDI) system. On models after 1984, a 5-wire connector is used between armature plate and power pack in place of 4-wire connector.

wire leading to either ignition coil. Turn tester knobs to Negative and 500. Crank engine while observing tester. Repeat test on other lead. Renew power pack if readings are not at least 180 volts or higher on models prior to 1985 or 200 volts or higher on models after 1984.

To test ignition coils, disconnect high tension lead at ignition coil. On models prior to 1985, disconnect 3-wire connector and insert a jumper lead in terminal B of the ignition coil end of connector. Connect ohmmeter positive lead to the B terminal jumper wire and ohmmeter negative lead to a good engine ground. On models after 1984, disconnect coil primary wire at coil and connect ohmmeter positive lead to coil primary terminal and negative lead to a good engine ground or to coil ground tab. Ignition coil primary resistance should be 0.05-0.15 ohm on all models. To check coil secondary resistance, move ohmmeter negative lead to the high tension terminal. Secondary resistance should be 225-325 ohms on models prior to 1986 and 250-300 ohms on models after 1985. Repeat procedure on number 2 ignition coil.

2.5 Hp Models, Excel 4 and Ultra 4

TROUBLE-SHOOTING. Connect a suitable spark tester to spark plug leads. Adjust tester spark gap to 3/8 inch (9.5 mm) and crank engine while observing spark tester. If spark is weak or nonexistent, proceed as follows: Disconnect black lead at the power pack and crank engine. If no spark is noted with black lead disconnected, test sensor coil as described in this section. If spark is noted at only one spark gap, test power pack as described in this section. If alternating spark is noted at both spark gaps, connect an ohmmeter between the disconnected black lead and engine ground. Ohmmeter should show an infinity reading with stop button not depressed and continuity reading when stop button is depressed. If not, renew stop button and harness.

To perform sensor coil ground test, disconnect black wire with white tracer and white wire with black tracer from the power pack. Using a Stevens CD77 or a suitable peak reading voltmeter, connect meter red lead to one sensor wire and the meter black lead to engine ground. Set meter switches to S and 5. Crank engine and note meter reading. Move meter red lead to the other sensor coil wire, crank engine and note meter reading. A voltage reading at either sensor coil wire indicates a grounded sensor coil or wires. Locate ground and repair as necessary. If sensor coil or wires are not grounded, renew sensor coil. Test sensor coil output by connecting CD voltmeter between sensor coil wires (black wire with white tracer and white wire with black tracer). Set CD voltmeter switches to S and 5. Crank engine and note meter reading. Reverse CD voltmeter leads, crank engine and note meter reading. If meter reading is four volts or more, test power pack as described in this section. If reading is less than four volts on either test, check for faulty sensor coil wiring or connectors. If sensor coil wiring and connectors are acceptable, check sensor coil resistance as follows: Connect a suitable ohmmeter between sensor coil wires (black wire with white tracer and white wire with black tracer). Renew sensor coil if resistance is not within 85-115 ohms. Next, connect ohmmeter black lead to engine ground and alternately connect ohmmeter red lead to each sensor coil lead. If ohmmeter shows continuity between either of the sensor coil wires and ground, check for grounded sensor coil or sensor coil wires and repair as necessary. If coil or wires are not grounded, renew sensor coil.

To perform power pack output test, disconnect ignition coil primary wires, install suitable terminal extenders (to allow test meter connection) and reconnect coil primary wires. Set CD voltmeter switches to Negative and 500. Connect voltmeter black test lead to engine ground and red test lead to terminal extender installed on number 1 coil primary terminal. Crank engine and note meter reading. CD voltmeter should indicate 125 volts or more. If not, remove coil primary wire from terminal extender and connect red tester lead directly to primary wire (not to coil) and crank engine. If voltmeter indicates 125 volts or more, test ignition coil as described in this section. If reading is less than 125 volts, inspect condition of primary wire and spring clip connector inside boot. If primary wire and spring clip connector are acceptable, renew power pack assembly. Repeat power pack test procedure on number 2 ignition coil. Be sure to remove terminal extender after test. Be sure orange wire with blue tracer (primary wire) is connected to number 1 ignition coil.

Check ignition coil primary resistance by connecting ohmmeter between coil primary terminal and coil ground. Primary resistance should be 0.05-0.15 ohm. Check secondary resistance by connecting ohmmeter between primary terminal and high tension terminal. Secondary resistance should be 250-300 ohms. Renew ignition coil if resistance is not as specified. Check coil output and surface leakage using a suitable CD ignition analyzer. Follow analyzer manufacturer's instructions for testing coil.

CD2U Ignition System

Four hp Deluxe models after 1988 are equipped with CD2U ignition system. Except for the ignition coils, all CD2U components are located under the flywheel indicated by the "U" in the model designation. Ignition system model number is printed on top of ignition module located under flywheel. The power pack and sensor coil are integrated into a single ignition module assembly instead of separate components as in earlier CD2 systems.

TROUBLE-SHOOTING. Disconnect spark plug leads from spark plugs and connect a suitable spark tester. Set tester spark gap to 1/2 inch (12.7 mm). On models so equipped, install emergency ignition cutoff clip and lanyard. Crank engine and observe spark tester. If an acceptable spark is noted at each spark gap, perform RUNNING OUTPUT TEST. If spark is noted at only one spark gap, perform IGNITION PLATE OUTPUT TEST as described in this section. If no spark is noted at either spark gap, perform STOP CIRCUIT TEST.

NOTE: If acceptable spark is noted at each spark gap during spark output test but engine pops and backfires during starting or running, ignition system may be out of time. Be sure orange/blue primary wire is connected to number 1 ignition coil, spark plug high tension leads are properly connected, flywheel is properly located on crankshaft and speed control linkage is properly adjusted.

STOP CIRCUIT TEST. Remove spark plug leads from spark plugs and connect a suitable spark tester. Disconnect stop circuit connector (Fig. OM2-11). Make sure ignition emergency cutoff clip and

Fig. OM2-11—View showing approximate location of one-pin stop circuit connector. Appearance of stop circuit connector is the same on all models but location may vary. Refer to text.

lanyard are installed on models so equipped. Crank engine and observe spark tester. If no spark is noted, perform IGNITION PLATE OUTPUT TEST. If normal spark is noted, connect ohmmeter between engine ground and the one-pin stop circuit connector (Fig. OM2-11) leading to tiller handle. Ohmmeter should show infinite resistance. If meter shows continuity, repair short in wiring or renew stop button. Depress stop button or remove emergency cutoff clip and note ohmmeter. If ohmmeter does not indicate continuity, repair open in wiring or renew stop button.

IGNITION PLATE OUTPUT TEST. Disconnect spark plug leads to prevent accidental starting. Remove primary leads from ignition coils. Connect number 1 ignition coil primary lead to the red lead of Stevens load adapter PL-88 and black lead of load adapter to engine ground.

NOTE: If Stevens load adapter is not available, fabricate load adapter using a 10 ohm, 10 watt resistor (Radio Shack part 271-132) or equivalent.

Connect red test lead of CD77 or equivalent peak reading voltmeter to red lead of Stevens load adapter PL-88 and black test lead to engine ground. Set CD voltmeter to Positive and 500. Crank engine and note meter. Repeat test procedure on number 2 ignition coil primary lead. If CD voltmeter indicates 175 volts or higher on both tests, perform IGNITION COIL TESTS. If one primary lead shows no output, renew ignition module. If both tests indicate no output, perform CHARGE COIL RESISTANCE TEST.

CHARGE COIL RESISTANCE TEST. Remove manual starter and flywheel. Remove two ignition module mounting screws and disconnect module brown and brown/yellow bullet connectors. Connect ohmmeter between brown and brown/yellow charge coil connectors. Renew charge coil if resistance is not within 535-585 ohms. Connect one ohmmeter lead to engine ground and connect other ohmmeter lead to brown charge coil lead, then to brown/yellow charge coil lead. Renew charge coil if ohmmeter shows continuity between engine ground and either wire. If charge coil tests acceptable, renew ignition module.

NOTE: When installing charge coil or ignition module, use OMC Locating Ring 334994 to properly position components on armature plate. Place ring over machined surfaces on armature plate, push compo-

nents outward against locating ring and tighten mounting screws to 30-40 in.-lbs. (3.4-4.5 N·m).

RUNNING OUTPUT TEST. Remove propeller and install the correct test wheel, then mount outboard motor in a suitable test tank. Remove ignition coil primary wires and install suitable terminal extenders (Stevens TS-77 or equivalent) on coil primary terminals, then install primary wires on terminal extenders. Connect peak reading voltmeter red test lead to number 1 coil terminal extender and black test lead to engine ground. Set voltmeter to Positive and 500. Start engine and run at rpm where ignition malfunction is evident while noting meter. Repeat test procedure on number 2 ignition coil. If either cylinder shows less than 200 volts, perform CHARGE COIL RESISTANCE TEST. If charge coil test results are acceptable, renew ignition module.

IGNITION COIL RESISTANCE TEST. To check ignition coil primary resistance, connect ohmmeter between primary terminal and coil ground. Resistance should be 0.05-0.15 ohm. To check secondary resistance, connect ohmmeter between coil high tension terminal and primary terminal. Resistance should be 250-300 ohms. Renew coil if resistance is not as specified.

COOLING SYSTEM

WATER PUMP. All models are equipped with a rubber impeller type water pump. Impeller is mounted on and driven by the drive shaft in the lower unit. Refer to Fig. OM2-30, OM2-31, OM2-33 or OM2-35. Water enters the lower unit through openings in the forward, side or rear of gearcase.

When cooling system problems are encountered, first check the water inlet for plugging or partial stoppage; then, if not corrected, remove the lower unit as outlined in the appropriate section and check the condition of the water pump, water passages, gaskets and sealing surfaces.

POWER HEAD

REMOVE AND REINSTALL. Refer to the appropriate following paragraph for method of removing and reinstalling power. Procedure varies depending upon type of construction.

Models Prior To 1979

To remove the power head, remove the four screws attaching drive shaft

housing to power head (lower engine cover). Then lift the power head and lower engine cover from exhaust housing and drive shaft.

NOTE: On models prior to 1978, the water tube is attached to lower engine cover with sleeve nut (29—Fig. OM2-13). On all models, detach water tube, then remove screws (S) and separate power head from lower engine cover.

To install the power head, it is necessary to remove the gearcase in order to correctly position lower end of water tube. The gearcase is attached to drive shaft housing with four screws. Assemble the power head, lower engine cover and water tube, then assemble the drive shaft and exhaust housing to the lower engine cover (and power head). Check condition of "O" ring at top of drive shaft and renew if damaged. Coat the drive shaft splines and lower end of water tube lightly with water-resistant grease. Install gearcase, carefully aligning drive shaft with splines in crankshaft and lower end of water tube with grommet in water pump.

NOTE: Use caution when inserting water tube into grommet. If tube is bent or improperly installed, the power head may overheat.

4 Hp Models 1979-1989 (Except Deluxe) And 3 Hp

To remove power head, remove choke knob and low speed adjustment knob. Remove lower engine cover. On models equipped with integral fuel tank, disconnect and plug hose at carburetor. Remove manual starter. Remove two retainers securing fuel tank and remove tank. Remove five screws securing power head-to-drive shaft housing (four

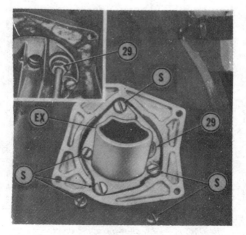

Fig. OM2-13—View of models prior to 1979 with exhaust housing (EX). Screws (S) attach exhaust housing and lower motor cover to power head.

screws on weedless models) and lift power head off drive shaft housing.

Prior to installing power head on weedless models, gearcase should be removed to be sure lower end of water tube is properly located in water pump grommet. On all models, apply OMC Moly Lube or a suitable water-resistant grease to drive shaft splines, install a new gasket on drive shaft housing and place power head into position. Apply a suitable gasket sealant to power head mounting screws and tighten screws to 60-80 in.-lbs. (6.8-9.0 N·m). Complete remainder of installation by reversing removal procedure.

4 Hp Deluxe and 4.5 Hp

To remove power head, remove fuel tank, disconnect ignition and electrical connectors, spark plugs, ignition coils and remove flywheel. On models prior to 1987, remove carburetor, reed valve assembly and intake manifold. Starter may be allowed to remain attached to crankcase if starter does not require service. Remove six screws securing power head to drive shaft housing and lift power head off housing. Remove exhaust tube from power head.

To reinstall power head, remove lower unit gearcase from drive shaft housing. Secure water tube to exhaust tube using a suitable rubber band. Lubricate end of water tube and splines of drive shaft with a suitable water-resistant grease. Install power head and tighten power head mounting screws to 60-84 in.-lbs. (6.8-9.5 N·m). Reinstall lower gearcase assembly on drive shaft housing making sure water tube is properly located in water pump grommet. Apply OMC Gasket Sealing Compound or a suitable equivalent to gearcase screws and tighten to to 60-84 in.-lbs. (6.8-9.5 N·m). Complete remainder of installation by reversing removal procedure.

2.5 Hp, Excel 4 HP and Ultra 4 Hp

To remove power head, remove upper and lower engine covers, carburetor and manual starter. Remove flywheel, ignition components and any component that will interfere with power head removal. Remove five screws securing power head to drive shaft housing and lift off power head.

Apply OMC Moly Lube or a suitable water-resistant grease to drive shaft splines. Install a new gasket on drive shaft housing, reinstall power head. Apply a suitable gasket sealing compound to power head mounting screws and tighten screws to 60-84 in.-lbs. (6.8-9.5 N·m). Complete remainder of installation by reversing removal procedure.

Coat threads of manual starter screws with a suitable thread locking compound and tighten screws to 60-84 in.-lbs. (6.8-9.5 N·m).

DISASSEMBLY. Removal of the starter, engine covers, flywheel, magneto, carburetor and manifold is usually easier before the power head is detached from the drive shaft housing.

Refer to Fig. OM2-15 or OM2-16 for exploded view of engine. Remove armature plate support and retainer. Remove cylinder head and taper pin(s) (12). Remove lower flange (31 or 32—Fig. OM2-16) on models after 1978. Unbolt and separate the crankcase halves.

NOTE: Make certain that screws (S—Fig. OM2-15 or OM2-16) are removed before attempting to separate crankcase halves.

Pistons, rods and crankshaft are now accessible for removal and overhaul as outlined in the appropriate following paragraphs.

When reassembling, follow the procedures outlined in ASSEMBLY paragraphs.

ASSEMBLY. Before assembling, make certain that all sealing surfaces are clean, smooth and flat. The crankcase and inlet manifold must be completely sealed against both vacuum and pressure; the exhaust manifold and cylinder must be sealed against water and exhaust leakage. Alignment of crankcase halves is accomplished with tapered dowels (12—Fig. OM2-15 or OM2-16). Make certain that the dowel pins are not bent, nicked or distorted, and that dowel holes are clean and true. When installing dowel pins, make sure they are fully seated, but do not use excessive force.

The mating surfaces of crankcase halves must be sealed during assembly by using a nonhardening cement such as OMC Gel-Seal or equivalent. Do not use sealers which will harden and prevent contact between crankcase mating surfaces. Make sure that all old cement is removed and that surfaces are flat and free from nicks and burrs. Apply cement sparingly and evenly to cylinder half of crankcase only; then immediately install front half. Install and tighten the crankcase screws equally to a torque of 60-84 in.-lbs. (6.8-9.5 N·m).

The boss (B—Fig. OM2-14) on cylinder head and gasket must be aligned and toward top. Tighten cylinder head screws in sequence shown to a torque of 60-84 in.-lbs. (6.8-9.5 N·m). Retorque cylinder head after motor has been test run and cooled.

When installing gaskets, check to make sure correct gasket is used and

that ALL water passage holes are open and not covered. Tightening torques are given in the CONDENSED SERVICE DATA section.

PISTONS, PINS, RINGS AND CYLINDERS. Before detaching connecting rods from crankshaft, make certain rod and cap are properly marked for correct assembly to each other and in the correct cylinder.

Mark pistons prior to removal for reference during reassembly. Each aluminum piston is fitted with two rings which are interchangeable and may be installed either side up. Oversize pistons and rings for 1978 and 1979 models are available in 0.020 inch (0.51 mm) and 0.030 inch (0.76 mm). On all models after 1979, oversize pistons and rings are only available in 0.030 inch (0.76 mm). Refer to CONDENSED SERVICE DATA for engine service specifications. On models prior to 1987, maximum allowable cylinder taper and out-of-round is 0.002 inch (0.05 mm). On 1987 and later models, maximum allowable taper is

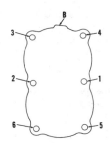

Fig. OM2-14—When installing cylinder head, make certain that boss (B) is toward top of gasket and head. Tighten retaining cap screws in sequence shown.

Fig. OM2-16—Typical view of power head used on models after 1977. Note location of crankcase screws (S). Flange (31) is used on 1981 and later standard lower unit models, while flange (32) is used on weedless models and some early standard models.

  9. Exhaust passage cover
10. Cylinder head
11. Cylinder & crankcase
12. Taper pins
13S. Gasket
14. Snap ring
15. Snap ring
15L. Seal
17. Crankshaft
17B. Bearing
18. Piston pin
19. Piston rings
20. Piston
21. Retaining rings
22. Connecting rod
23. Bearing cage
24. Bearing rollers
25. Bearing cage
26. Bearing rollers
27. Ball bearing
28. Seal
29. Plug
30. Roller bearing
31. Flange (standard)
32. Flange (weedless)

0.002 inch (0.05 mm) and maximum allowable out-of-round is 0.003 inch (0.08 mm). To check pistons for excessive wear, measure piston diameter 1/8 inch (3.2 mm) up from bottom of skirt, in two locations 90 degrees apart. Renew piston if difference between measurements exceeds 0.002 inch (0.05 mm). After 1985 models, the manufacturer does not specify piston-to-cylinder bore clearance. To determine the correct dimension for reboring cylinder oversize, add oversize amount to standard

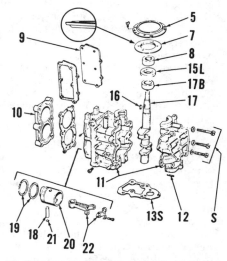

Fig. OM2-15—Exploded view of power head used on models prior to 1978. Lip of seal (15L) should be down.

5. Support	15L. Seal
7. Retainer	16. Woodruff key
8. Cam	17. Crankshaft
9. Exhaust passage cover	17B. Bearing
10. Cylinder head	18. Piston pin
11. Cylinder & crankcase	19. Piston rings
12. Taper pin	20. Piston
13S. Gasket	21. Retaining rings
	22. Connecting rod

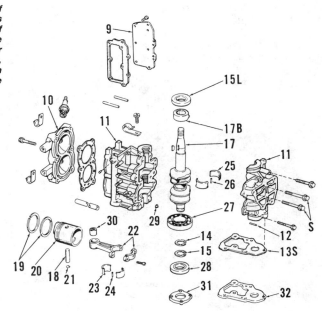

cylinder bore diameter (CONDENSED SERVICE DATA).

Piston pin rides directly in connecting rod small end on models prior to 1978 while 1978 and later models are equipped with a needle bearing in connecting rod small end.

One piston pin boss in piston is a press fit while the other boss is a slip fit to prevent distortion of piston as motor warms up. The loose pin boss is indicated by an embossed "L" as shown in Fig. OM2-17. When removing piston pin, remove both retaining rings and drive the pin out toward the unmarked boss of piston. Install pin through loose boss first. Piston should be installed with long tapering side of piston head toward exhaust port side of cylinder and lubrication holes in rod toward top of power head. When installing connecting rods, tighten the cap screws to 60-70 in.-lbs. (6.8-7.9 N·m). Thoroughly lubricate all friction surfaces during assembly.

CONNECTING RODS, BEARINGS AND CRANKSHAFT. Before detaching connecting rods from crankshaft, make sure rod and cap are properly marked for correct assembly to each other and in the correct cylinder.

The top main bearing (17B—Fig. OM2-15 or OM2-16) on all models is of the needle bearing type. Rollers may be held in place with grease during installation. Bottom and center main bearings on models prior to 1978 are bronze bushings cast into the crankcase halves. Center main bearing on models after 1977 consists of 30 caged bearing rollers while a ball bearing is used on crankshaft lower end.

Connecting rod on 1978 and later models rides on a caged roller bearing with 30 rollers. Connecting rod on all other models rides directly on crankshaft crankpin.

CAUTION: When assembling, make certain that all loose bearing rollers are in place.

Refer to the CONDENSED SERVICE DATA table for dimensional data and recommended torque values. If bearing

surface of rod and cap is rough, scored, worn, or shows evidence of overheating, renew the connecting rod. Inspect crankpin and main bearing journals. If scored, out-of-round, or worn, renew the crankshaft. All bearings and friction surfaces should be lubricated during assembly. The connecting rod must be assembled to piston so long sloping side of piston head is toward exhaust side of engine and lubrication holes in rod are toward top when power head is assembled. The connecting rod caps must be installed with rounded corners aligned on rod and cap.

NOTE: Rod caps should never be interchanged.

MANUAL STARTER

4 Hp Models Prior to 1979, 4.5 Hp Models And 4 Hp "DELUXE"

The recoil starter used on these models is shown in Fig. OM2-19 and rotates the flywheel via gear teeth on pulley (3), idler (9) and lower edge of flywheel (12). Refer to the following paragraphs for removal, installation and adjustment.

To remove the starter, remove handle (1) and allow starter to unwind slowly, pulling rope in.

NOTE: Hold pulley (3) to permit starter to unwind slowly and prevent damage.

Pull end of recoil spring out rear slot as shown in Fig. OM2-20 as far as possible, remove screws (10 and 11), then remove the starter assembly.

After cleaning, all metal parts should be wiped with an oil dampened cloth. Bushings (5—Fig. OM2-19) should be lightly coated with OMC TRIPLE-GUARD GREASE.

Insert rope through hole in pulley (3) with knot inside the gear and wind rope clockwise in groove as viewed from gear side of pulley. Hold rope in groove with rubber band or tape and locate end of spring on pulley as shown in Fig. OM2-21. Position the washer (13—Fig. OM2-19) on cup (6), then assemble pulley, rope and spring to the cup with end of spring protruding from slot in cup as shown in Fig. OM2-22. Install idler gear (9—Fig. OM2-19) on shaft of idler gear arm (8), then assemble spring (7), idler gear (9) and arm (8) to the pulley and cup.

NOTE: The idler arm must be located between stops on cup as shown in Fig. OM2-23.

With complete starter unit assembled as described, attach to power head with the shoulder bolt (11—Fig. OM2-19) and screw (10). Make certain that washer (13) has not slipped and shoulder bolt

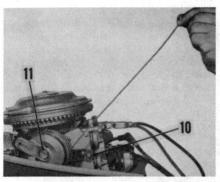

Fig. OM2-20—Recoil spring should be withdrawn as shown before removing starter assembly.

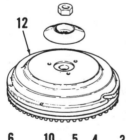

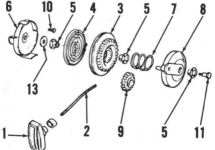

Fig. OM2-19—Exploded view of starter used on 4 hp models prior to 1979, 4.5 hp and Deluxe models.

1. Handle	
2. Rope	
3. Pulley	8. Idler arm
4. Recoil spring	9. Idler gear
5. Bushings	10. Adjusting screw
6. Cup	11. Shoulder bolt
7. Spring	12. Flywheel
	13. Washer

Fig. OM2-17—View of lower side of piston showing the "L" marking which indicates "Loose" piston pin boss.

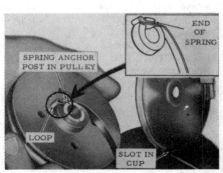

Fig. OM2-21—View showing installation of recoil spring inner end. Outer end catches on slot in cup.

(11) is through the washer. To draw the spring into housing, engage idler gear with flywheel gear and turn flywheel in clockwise direction until spring is drawn into cup. Refer to Fig. OM2-24. Disengage idler gear from flywheel to relax spring, then engage idler gear again and turn flywheel two turns clockwise to correctly preload the recoil spring. Release the starter rope, locate rope through guide and install handle.

To adjust idler gear engagement, hold idler gear into flywheel teeth and make certain that stop (S—Fig. OM2-25) is against the idler gear arm. With stop contacting the arm, tighten the adjustment screw and the shoulder bolt.

4 Hp Models After 1978 (Except Deluxe), 2.5 Hp, 3 Hp, Excel 4 and Ultra 4 Models

The manual rewind starter assembly is an integral part of the engine cover on 4 hp models after 1978 (except Deluxe) and 3 hp models. Refer to Fig. OM2-26 for exploded view of starter used on 3 hp and 4 hp models. Starter assembly is separate from engine cover on 2.5 hp, Excel 4 and Ultra 4 models. Refer to Fig. OM2-27.

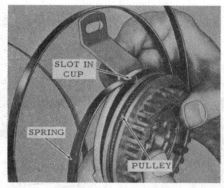

Fig. OM2-22—View showing assembly of pulley and cup with recoil spring coming through slot in cup.

Fig. OM2-23—Idler arm must be between stops on cup as shown.

To remove starter assembly on 3 hp and 4 hp models, remove lower engine cover, remove four upper cover mounting screws from underside of cover and lift cover and starter assembly from power head.

To remove starter on 2.5 hp, Excel 4 and Ultra 4 models, disconnect throttle cable (18—Fig. OM2-27) from armature plate and remove two screws (15) and one nut (20) securing starter assembly to power head. Remove starter assembly from power head. Disconnect throttle cable (18) from starter housing by removing screws (17) and rotating cable (18) counterclockwise to unscrew cable from throttle knob (14).

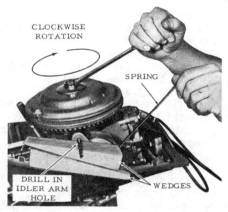

Fig. OM2-24—Refer to text for method of rewinding and preloading the recoil spring.

Fig. OM2-25—Refer to text for adjusting starter mesh with flywheel gear.

Fig. OM2-27—Exploded view of manual starter housing and related components used on 2.5 hp, Excel 4 and Ultra 4 models. Refer to components (3-10—Fig. OM2-26) for remainder of starter components.

1. Screw
11. Rope handle
13. Housing
14. Throttle control knob
15. Screw
16. Washer
17. Screw
18. Throttle cable assy.
19. Washer
20. Nut
21. Idle stop screw
22. Idle stop nut
23. "E" ring

On all models, check drive pawl (9—Fig. OM2-26) for freedom of movement, excessive wear or other damage. Renew or lubricate pawl (9) with OMC Triple-Guard Grease or Lubriplate 777 and return starter to service if no other damage is noted.

To disassemble starter, remove clip (10) and withdraw pawl (9), links (8) and friction spring (7). Untie starter rope (5) at handle (11) and allow rope to wind into the starter. Remove screw (1—Fig. OM2-26 or OM2-27) and lockwasher, then withdraw spindle (6). Carefully lift pulley (4) with starter rope (5) from cov-

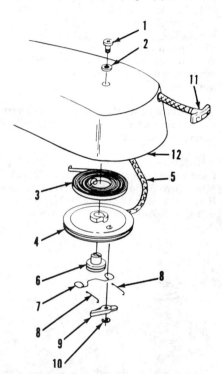

Fig. OM2-26—Exploded view of manual rewind starter used on 4 hp models after 1978. Starter used on 2.5 hp, 3 hp, Excel 4 and Ultra 4 is similar except housing (13—Fig. OM2-27).

1. Screw
2. Lockwasher
3. Rewind spring
4. Pulley
5. Starter rope
6. Spindle
7. Friction spring
8. Links
9. Drive pawl
10. Clip
11. Handle
12. Cover

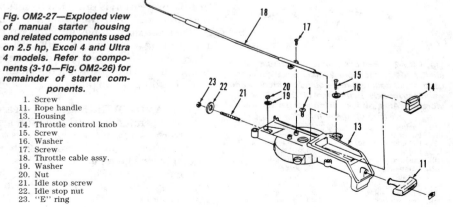

er (12—Fig. OM2-26) or from housing (13—Fig. OM2-27). BE CAREFUL when removing pulley (4) as rewind spring (3) may be dislodged. Remove rope (5) from pulley (4) if renewal is required. To remove rewind spring (3) from cover (12) or housing (13), invert cover or housing, lay upright on a flat surface and tap cover or housing until rewind spring falls free and uncoils.

Inspect all components for excessive wear or damage and renew as necessary. New rope length should be 59-1/2 inches (151 cm).

To reassemble, first apply a coating of OMC Triple-Guard Grease or Lubriplate 777 to rewind spring area of cover (12—Fig. OM2-26) or housing (13—Fig. OM2-27). Install rewind spring (3) into cover or housing so spring coils wind in a counterclockwise direction from the outer end.

NOTE: Lubricate all friction surfaces with OMC Triple-Guard Grease or Lubriplate 777 during reassembly.

Install pulley (4) into cover (12—Fig. OM2-26) or housing (13—Fig. OM2-27). Make sure pulley hub properly engages hook on rewind spring (3). Wind starter rope (5) onto pulley (4) in a counter-

clockwise direction as viewed from the flywheel side. Install spindle (6). Spray screw (1) threads with OMC Locquic Primer and apply OMC Screw Lock on screw threads, then install screw (1) and tighten securely.

Turn pulley (4) 3-1/2 turns counterclockwise as viewed from the flywheel side. Secure pulley position, then thread starter rope (5) through cover (12—Fig. OM2-26) or housing (13—Fig. OM2-27) opening and handle (11) and secure with a suitable knot.

NOTE: Do not apply more tension on rewind spring (3) than necessary to draw starter handle (11) into the proper released position.

Install friction spring (7), links (8), pawl (9) and clip (10). On 3 hp and 4 hp models, reinstall cover and starter assembly on power head and install lower engine cover to complete reassembly. On 2.5, Excel 4 and Ultra 4 models, install throttle cable (18—Fig. OM2-27) through guide in housing (13) and thread cable (18) into knob (14). Install screws (17) and tighten securely. Place starter assembly into position on power head, apply OMC Screw Lock to threads of screws (15) and nut (20) and tighten screws and nut to 60-80 in.-lbs. (7-9 N·m). To adjust throttle cable (18), proceed as follows: Back-off idle speed nut (22) completely and install cable (18) into armature plate. Push knob (14) in until knob contacts housing (13). Rotate armature plate fully clockwise, then adjust trunnion on cable (18) so trunnion will fit in retaining bracket without disturbing position of armature plate or knob (14). Adjust idle speed as necessary. Refer to CONDENSED SERVICE DATA for correct idle speed specification.

STANDARD LOWER UNIT

4 Hp Models Prior to 1981

PROPELLER AND DRIVE PIN. Lower unit protection is provided by a rubber ring built into the propeller hub. Service consists of renewing rubber protection ring (27—Fig. OM2-30). Optional propellers are available, however, only propellers designed for use on specific model should be installed.

R&R AND OVERHAUL. Gearcase may be separated from drive shaft housing after unscrewing two cap screws on gearcase underside. The propeller shaft assembly may be removed after detaching end cap (22—Fig. OM2-30). Withdraw drive shaft after removing water pump assembly.

When assembling gearcase, install end cap (22) so retaining screw hole with flat (F) is up.

4 Hp After 1980 (Except Deluxe), 2.5 Hp, 3 Hp, Excel 4 and Ultra 4

PROPELLER AND DRIVE PIN. Lower unit protection is provided by a rubber ring built into the propeller hub. Service consists of renewing rubber protection ring (27—Fig. OM2-31). Optional propellers are available. Select a propeller that will allow the engine to operate within the full throttle speed of 4000-5000 rpm on 1981-1986 4 hp models (except Deluxe) and 2.5 hp models and 4500-5500 rpm on 4 hp models after 1986, 3 hp, Excel 4 and Ultra 4 models.

R&R AND OVERHAUL. Gearcase can be separated from drive shaft housing after unscrewing two cap screws on gearcase underside. The propeller shaft assembly can be removed after detaching end cap (22—Fig. OM2-31). Withdraw drive shaft after removing water pump assembly.

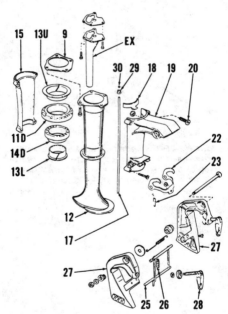

Fig. OM2-28—Exploded view of exhaust (drive shaft) housing, stern bracket and associated parts used on all constant-drive standard models and weedless models. Dampeners (11D & 14D) isolate vibration. Also, notice the inner exhaust housing (EX) on these models.

9. Gasket	20. Friction adjusting
11D. Dampener	screw
12. Exhaust housing	22. Reverse lock
13L. Bushing	23. Spring
13U. Bushing	25. Tilting lever
14D. Dampener	26. Spring
15. Clamp	27. Stern clamp
17. Water tube	28. Clamp screw
18. Friction block	29. Compression nut
19. Swivel bracket	30. Sleeve

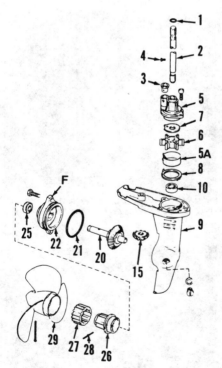

Fig. OM2-30—Exploded view of constant-drive gearcase used on 4 hp models prior to 1981.

1. "O" ring	10. Seal
2. Drive shaft	14. Seal
3. Grommet	15. Pinion gear
4. Impeller drive pin	20. Propeller shaft &
5. Water pump	gear
housing	21. "O" ring
5A. Liner	22. End cap
6. Impeller	25. Seal
7. Plate	26. Clutch hub
8. Ring	27. Clutch ring
9. Gearcase	28. Drive pin
	29. Propeller

When assembling propeller shaft (50) to drive gear (48), install spring clutch with tang end facing drive gear. Install screen (39) in gearcase (9) with tabs facing up.

4 Hp "DELUXE" Models And 4.5 Hp Models

PROPELLER AND SHEAR PIN. Shear pin (72—Fig. OM2-33) is used to provide lower unit protection. Optional propellers are available. Select a propeller that will allow the engine to operate within the range of 4500-5500 rpm at wide-open throttle.

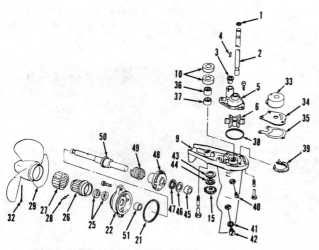

1. "O" ring	34. Plate
2. Drive shaft	35. Gasket
3. Grommet	36. Bearing
4. Impeller drive key	37. Bearing
5. Water pump housing	38. "O" ring
6. Impeller	39. Screen
9. Gearcase	40. Level plug
10. Seals	41. Gasket
15. Pinion gear	42. Drain plug
21. "O" ring	43. Thrust washer
22. End cap	44. Thrust bearing
25. Seals	45. Bearing
26. Clutch hub	46. Thrust washer
27. Clutch ring	47. Thrust bearing
28. Drive pin	48. Drive gear
29. Propeller	49. Spring clutch
32. Cotter pin	50. Propeller shaft
33. Liner	51. Bearing

Fig. OM2-31—Exploded view of gearcase used on 4 hp models after 1980 (except Deluxe), 2.5 hp, 3 hp, Excel 4 and Ultra 4 models.

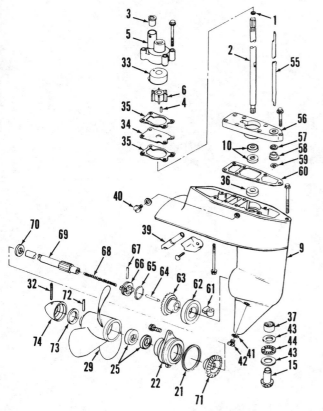

1. "O" ring	43. Thrust washers
2. Drive shaft	44. Thrust bearing
3. Grommet	55. Lower shift rod
4. Impeller drive key	56. Bearing housing
5. Water pump housing	57. "O" ring
6. Impeller	58. Guide
9. Gearcase	59. Retainer
10. Seals	60. Gasket
15. Pinion gear	61. Shift cam
21. "O" ring	62. Bearing
22. End cap	63. Forward gear
25. Seals	64. Plunger
29. Propeller	65. Retainer
32. Cotter pin	66. Dog clutch
33. Liner	67. Pin
34. Plate	68. Spring
35. Gaskets	69. Propeller shaft
36. Bearing	70. Thrust washer
37. Bearing	71. Reverse gear
39. Screen	72. Shear pin
40. Level plug	73. Washer
41. Gasket	74. Spinner
42. Drain plug	

Fig. OM2-33—Exploded view of gearcase used on 4.5 hp models and 4 hp "DELUXE" models.

R&R AND OVERHAUL. Gearcase can be separated from drive shaft housing after first placing shift lever in "Forward" position, then removing two cap screws on gearcase underside and one cap screw below drive shaft housing's lower pivot point. The propeller shaft assembly can be removed after detaching end cap (22—Fig. OM2-33). Withdraw drive shaft after removing water pump assembly and upper bearing housing (56).

Install dog clutch (66) on propeller shaft (69) with the stamping "PROP END" facing toward propeller end. Install thrust washers (43) with inside chamfer on lower washer facing down and outside chamfer on upper washer facing up.

WEEDLESS LOWER UNIT

PROPELLER AND DRIVE PIN. Lower unit protection is provided by a rubber ring built into the propeller hub. Service consists of renewing rubber protection ring (27—Fig. OM2-35). Optional propellers are available, however, only propellers designed for use on a specific model should be installed.

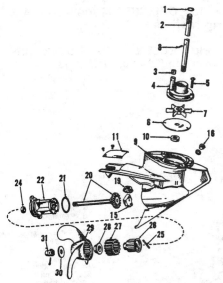

Fig. OM2-35—Exploded view of weedless gearcase, propeller and water pump assembly. "O" ring (1) seals upper drive shaft splines.

1. "O" ring	19. Pinion gear
2. Drive shaft	20. Propeller shaft
3. Grommet	21. "O" ring
4. Pump housing	22. Carrier
5. Screw	24. Seal
6. Plate	25. Drive pin
7. Impeller	26. Hub
8. Impeller drive pin	27. Ring
9. Gearcase	28. Bushing
10. Oil seal	29. Propeller
11. Cover	30. Washer
15. Thrust bearing	31. Nut

R&R AND OVERHAUL. To remove gearcase, unscrew four retaining screws and separate gearcase from drive shaft housing. The propeller shaft assembly (20—Fig. OM2-35) may be removed after detaching carrier (22), and drive shaft (2) may be withdrawn after removing water pump assembly.

Inspect components and renew if damaged or excessively worn. Renew all "O" rings and seals. Reverse the disassembly procedure for reassembly. Align marks on gearcase and carrier as shown in Fig. OM2-36.

Fig. OM2-36—Weedless models are provided with marks on gearcase and carrier for correct alignment of bushing oil hole.

EVINRUDE AND JOHNSON
6 HP (1969-1979)

Year Produced	EVINRUDE Models	Year Produced	JOHNSON Models
1969	6902, 6903	1969	6R69, 6RL69
1970	6002, 6003	1970	6R70, 6RL70
1971	6102, 6103	1971	6R71, 6RL71
1972	6202, 6203	1972	6R72, 6RL72
1973	6302, 6303	1973	6R73, 6RL73
1974	6402, 6403	1974	6R74, 6RL74
1975	6504, 6505	1975	6R75, 6RL75
1976	6604, 6605	1976	6R76, 6RL76
1977	6704, 6705	1977	6R77, 6RL77
1978	6804, 6805	1978	6R78, 6RL78
1979	6904, 6905	1979	6R79, 6RL79

CONDENSED SERVICE DATA

TUNE-UP

Hp/rpm	6/4500
Bore – Inches	1-15/16
Stroke – Inches	1½
Number of Cylinders	2
Displacement – Cu. In.	8.84

Spark Plug – 1969-1970:
- Champion ... J4J
- AC ... M42K
- Autolite ... A21X
- Electrode Gap ... 0.030 in.

Spark Plug – 1971-1976:
- Champion ... J6J
- AC ... M44C
- Autolite ... A3X
- Electrode Gap ... 0.030 in.

Spark Plug – 1977:
- Champion ... L77J4
- AC ... M40FFX
- Electrode Gap ... 0.040 in.

Spark Plug – 1978-1979:
- Champion ... L78V
- AC ... V40FFK
- Electrode Gap ... Surface Gap

Magneto:
- Point Gap* ... 0.020 in.

TUNE-UP CONT.

Carburetor:
- Make ... Own

Fuel:Oil Ratio ... 50:1

*1977, 1978 and 1979 models have a pointless ignition system.

SIZES – CLEARANCES

Piston Rings:
- End Gap ... 0.005-0.015 in.
- Side Clearance ... 0.001-0.0035 in.

Piston Skirt Clearance ... 0.0018-0.0030 in.

Crankshaft Journal Diameter:
- Top Main (1969) ... 0.808-0.8085 in.
- (1970-1979) ... 0.8075-0.8080 in.
- Center Main (All) ... 0.8075-0.8080 in.
- Bottom Main (1979) ... 0.808-0.8085 in.
- (1970-1979) ... 0.8075-0.8080 in.
- Crankpin (All) ... 0.6685-0.6690 in.

Crankshaft Bearings – Diametral Clearances:
- Top Main ... 0.0015-0.0025 in.
- Center Main (All) ... 0.0015-0.0025 in.
- Bottom Main ... 0.0015-0.0025 in.
- Crankpin (All) ... Roller Bearing

Crankshaft End Play ... 0.002-0.010 in.

Piston Pin – Diametral Clearance In Rod ... 0.0003-0.001 in.

TIGHTENING TORQUES
(All Values in Inch-Pounds)

Connecting Rod	60-66
Crankcase Halves	60-80
Cylinder Head	60-80
Exhaust Cover	24-36
Flywheel Nut	480-540
Intake Manifold	24-36
Spark Plug	210-246

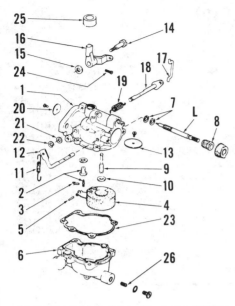

Fig. OM3-1 – Exploded view of typical carburetor used on all models. Follower adjusting screw (24) and follower roller (25) are used on models after 1977.

L. Low speed mixture	
needle	14. Shoulder screw
1. Carburetor body	15. Washer
2. Fuel inlet needle &	16. Cam follower
seat	17. Link
3. Needle to float clip	18. Throttle shaft
4. Float	19. Return spring
5. Pivot	20. Throttle plate
6. Float bowl	21. Washer
7. Packing	22. Throttle shaft
8. Packing nut	retainer
9. High speed nozzle	23. Gasket
10. Gasket	24. Follower adjusting
11. Choke return spring	screw
12. Choke shaft	25. Roller
13. Choke plate	26. Main jet

LUBRICATION

The power head is lubricated by oil mixed with the fuel. The recommended fuel is regular leaded or unleaded gasoline with a minimum octane rating of 85. The recommended oil is Evinrude or Johnson Outboard Lubricant or a suitable equivalent NMMA certified TC-W or TC-WII engine oil. The recommended fuel:oil ratio is 50:1. Make certain that oil and gasoline are thoroughly mixed before filling tank.

The lower unit gears and bearings are lubricated by oil contained in the gearcase. Special OMC HI-VIS Gearcase Lube should be used. This lubricant is supplied in a tube and filling procedures are as follows: Remove lower plug from gearcase and attach tube. Remove upper (vent) plug from case and, with motor in an upright position, fill gearcase until lubricant reaches level of upper (vent) plug hole. Reinstall vent plug; then remove lubricant tube and reinstall lower plug. Tighten both plugs securely, using new gaskets if necessary, to ensure a water-tight seal. Lower gear

lubricant should be maintained at level of vent plug, and drained and renewed every 100 hours of operation.

FUEL SYSTEM

CARBURETOR. A float type carburetor is used; refer to Fig. OM3-1 for exploded view. Normal initial setting for slow speed mixture needle (L) is 1½ turns open from closed position. Clockwise rotation of needle leans the mixture. Make final adjustment after motor has reached operating temperature. High speed mixture is controlled with a fixed jet (26) and is not adjustable. Hole diameter in fixed jet (26) should be 0.048 inch for 1969-1973 models; 0.044 inch for 1974-1975 models; 0.052 inch for 1976 models; 0.041 inch for 1977 models; 0.042 inch for 1978 and 1979 models.

To set the carburetor float level, first remove the carburetor, then unbolt and remove float bowl (6). Invert carburetor body (1) and check natural position of float with body inverted. Upper surface of float (4) (lower surface with body inverted) should be level and flush with gasket surface of carburetor body. If it is not, carefully bend float lever; then check after assembly to be sure float does not bind or rub.

Refer to Fig. OM3-1 when disassembling or reassembling the carburetor. High speed nozzle (9) can be removed with a blade screwdriver after float bowl (6) is removed. Renew all gaskets and packing whenever carburetor is disassembled.

SPEED CONTROL LINKAGE. The speed control lever rotates the magneto armature plate to advance the timing. The throttle valve is synchronized with the plate to open the throttle the proper amount as timing is advanced.

To synchronize speed controls, remove the motor cover and move speed control from stop position until carburetor throttle just begins to open. On models prior to 1978, move the speed

control so throttle cam just contacts cam follower as shown in Fig. OM3-2. Mark on cam should be directly behind the starboard edge of cam follower. If adjustment is incorrect, loosen the two cam mounting screws and relocate throttle cam as required. On models after 1977, cam follower roller (25–Fig. OM3-1) should be centered between marks on throttle cam just as carburetor throttle opens. Turn cam follower adjusting screw (24–Fig. OM3-1) to center roller on marks.

REED VALVES. The reed valve unit is located between intake manifold and crankcase. Refer to Fig. OM3-3.

Leaf petals (3) should seat very lightly against leaf plate (2) throughout their entire length with the least possible tension. Seating surface of plate (2) should be smooth and flat. Make sure that leaf stop (4) is not bent or otherwise damaged. Do not attempt to straighten a bent valve leaf nor bend a leaf in an attempt to improve performance; if a valve leaf is bent or damaged, renew the leaf.

The crankcase bleeder valve on early models can be checked as in the following paragraphs after leaf plate (2–Fig. OM3-3) is removed.

CRANKCASE BLEEDER VALVE. Early model motors are equipped with a crankcase bleeder valve (LV–Fig. OM3-4), designed to remove any liquid fuel or oil which might build up in the crankcase. The bleeder valve thus provides smoother operation at all speeds and lessens that possibility of spark plug fouling during slow-speed operation. The bleeder valve is covered by intake manifold and may be inspected when inlet leaf valves are being serviced.

A small passage leads from the bottom of each crankcase half to the bleeder valve. Any fuel that accumulates in the bleeder pocket is blown into the exhaust passage during the downward stroke of the piston.

Fig. OM3-2 – View of throttle cam index mark aligned with starboard side of cam follower on models prior to 1978.

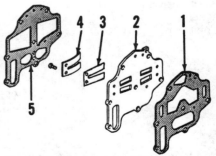

Fig. OM3-3 – Exploded view of reed valve plate and associated parts.

1. Gasket	
2. Leaf plate	
3. Leaf petal	4. Leaf stop
	5. Gasket

When engine is overhauled, bleed passages should be blown out with compressed air. The valve leaf (LV) should exert slight pressure against its seat. Seating surface on crankcase should be smooth and flat. Valve leaf should be renewed if broken, cracked, warped, rusted or bent. Clearance between stop (RS) and leaf valve (LV) should be 0.023-0.039 inch. Stop (RS) should be bent to set the correct clearance.

FUEL PUMP AND FILTER. The diaphragm type fuel pump (Fig. OM3-5) attaches to side of cylinder block and is actuated by pressure and vacuum pulsations to upper crankcase. The fuel pump is available only as an assembly and includes the filter unit.

If fuel pump problems are encountered, first remove and clean the filter and blow through fuel lines to be sure they are open and clean; then, if trouble is not corrected, renew the fuel pump assembly.

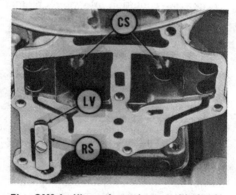

Fig. OM3-4 — View of crankcase with intake manifold removed. On models so equipped, the reed-type crankcase bleeder valve (LV) and stop (RS) can be removed for service, with manifold off. The two center main bearing screws (CS) must be removed before crankcase can be disassembled.

EARLY

LATE

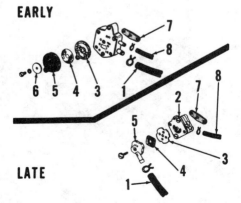

Fig. OM3-5 — Fuel pump, fuel filter and associated parts. Early type pump is shown at top.

1. Inlet fuel line	5. Cover
2. Fuel pump	6. Washer
3. Gasket	7. Gasket
4. Filter	8. Outlet fuel line

IGNITION SYSTEM

Models Prior to 1977

Breaker point gap should be 0.020 inch and both sets of points should be set to open exactly 180 degrees apart. Flywheel must be removed for breaker point adjustment or inspection.

The recommended method of breaker point adjustment is by using the special timing fixture (OMC Tool 383602) as shown in Fig. OM3-6 and a timing test light. Any test light or meter which indicates an open and closed circuit is satisfactory.

To adjust the points using the special tools, disconnect condenser and magneto coil leads from both points and install the timing fixture (TF—Fig. OM3-6) over crankshaft and flywheel key. Turn crankshaft until either end of pointer is aligned midway between the timing marks (TM) and armature plate. Attach the test light or meter to a suitable ground and to the terminal on the opening set of points; then adjust the gap until the points just open as indicated by test lamp going out. Turn crankshaft 180 degrees until opposite leg of pointer is midway between timing marks (TM) on armature plate and adjust the other set of points in the same manner.

To adjust the points without the special tools, adjust each gap to exactly 0.020 inch when flywheel key is aligned with rub block on movable point.

Except for the permanent magnet built into the flywheel, the ignition system consists of a separate coil, condenser, point set and wiring for each cylinder. When ignition troubles are encountered, check point condition and gap adjustment; check also for loose or corroded connections, damaged insulation and broken wires. The three ends of the laminated coil core should be flush with machined bosses on armature

Fig. OM3-6 — View of motor with timing fixture (TF) installed. Breaker points should just open when pointer is centered between timing marks (TM) on armature plate.

(stator) plate. The side of ignition cam marked "TOP" should face up. The cam and flywheel key should be installed with upset mark down as shown in Fig. OM3-6A.

Models After 1976

OPERATION. Models after 1976 are equipped with pointless capacitor discharge ignition system. A charge coil and sensor coil are located under flywheel. Two magnets in flywheel induce a current in the charge coil which is rectified and directed to a capacitor. The two flywheel magnets also induce current in the sensor coil to provide a positive charge on the gate of one of two silicon controlled rectifiers (SCR's). The positive charge opens the SCR and allows the charged capacitor to discharge through the SCR and primary circuit of the ignition coil. The rapid coil field buildup induces a secondary voltage which fires the spark plug. Diodes, SCR's and capacitor are contained in power pack assembly and are not available individually.

Ignition timing is not adjustable on models with pointless capacitor discharge ignition systems. However, backfiring and popping can occur if wires are not connected properly. Note wiring schematic in Fig. OM3-7.

TROUBLESHOOTING. If ignition malfunction occurs, use the following procedure to determine faulty component: Using testers or component replacement, be sure spark plugs and ignition coils function properly. To check charge coil, disconnect four-wire connector and connect an ohmmeter to terminals A and D in stator plate lead connector. Renew charge coil if resistance is not 500-650 ohms. Connect positive ohmmeter lead to connector terminal A and negative ohmmeter lead to stator plate (ground) to check for a short to ground. Infinite resistance should exist

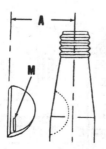

Fig. OM3-6A — When installing breaker point cam and flywheel drive key, make certain that the upset mark (M) is down as shown.

between A terminal and stator plate, if not, charge coil or charge coil lead is shorting to ground. To check charge coil output, connect Merc-O-Tronic M-80, M-90 or S-80 neon tester to stator lead connector terminals A and D and turn tester switch to No. 2. Push tester button B while cranking engine. Tester light should flash. Renew charge coil if tester light does not flash.

To check sensor coil, disconnect four-wire connector and connect an ohmmeter to terminals B and C in stator plate lead connector. Renew sensor coil if resistance is not 30-50 ohms. Connect positive ohmmeter lead to connector terminal C and negative ohmmeter lead to stator plate (ground) to check for a short to ground. If infinite resistance does not exist between terminal C and stator plate, sensor coil or sensor coil lead is shorting to ground. Merc-O-Tronic M-80, M-90 or S-80 may be used to check sensor coil output. A 1½ volt battery adapter must be used (negative end of adapter connected to black tester lead) with M-80 or S-80 tester. Measure battery voltage of tester with a voltmeter connected to tester leads (connect voltmeter to battery adapter and blue tester lead). Turn M-80 or S-80 tester switch to position 3 and M-90 tester switch to position 4. Minimum voltage reading should be 2½ volts when button B is pressed on tester. Disconnect four-wire connector and install a jumper wire between A terminals of male and female connector ends and another jumper wire between D terminals. Connect blue lead of tester to terminal B in power pack end of connector. Connect positive end

of battery adapter on M-80 or S-80 testers or black lead of M-90 tester to terminal C in power pack end of connector. Attach a spark gap tester to each ignition coil spark plug lead. Turn switch to position 3 on M-80 and S-80 testers or to position 4 on M-90 tester. Crank engine while tapping button B on tester. Spark should occur at spark gap tester connected to No. 2 cylinder ignition coil. If spark occurs at both coils, renew power pack. Reverse connections to B and C connector terminals and repeat test. If spark occurs at spark gap tester for No. 1 cylinder ignition coil, sensor coil is defective and must be renewed. If no spark was present at spark gap tester for either cylinder, or spark was present for one cylinder but not the other, proceed to power pack output check. Reconnect four-wire connector.

Proceed as follows for power pack output test: Disconnect three-wire connector between power pack and ignition coils and connect a jumper wire between C terminals of male and female connector ends. Ground blue lead of Merc-O-Tronic M-80, S-80 or M-90 tester to engine. Connect black lead of tester to B terminal of power pack connector end. Turn tester switch to No. 1 position. Push tester button A while cranking engine a note if tester lamp lights. Reverse position of jumper wire and black tester lead so jumper wire is in B terminals and tester lead is connected to C terminal of power pack connector end. Crank engine again while pushing tester button A. If tester lamp does not light during both tests, power pack is defective and must be renewed.

IGNITION ASSEMBLY. Install sensor coil and charge coil on stator plate so outside edges are flush with machined bosses on stator plate. Apply OMC Sea-Lube Moly Lube or equivalent to crankcase pilot boss for stator plate. Position stator plate so center of charge coil is aligned with cam plate as shown in Fig. OM3-7A and tighten stator plate screws. Crankshaft and flywheel tapers must be clean and dry. Tighten flywheel nut to 40-45 ft.-lbs.

COOLING SYSTEM

WATER PUMP. All motors are cooled by a rubber impeller type water pump which is mounted on and driven by the lower unit drive shaft.

When cooling system problems are encountered, first check water inlet for plugging or partial stoppage. Check the thermostat on models so equipped. If the difficulty is not thus corrected, remove the lower unit gearcase as outlined in the appropriate section and check the condition of water pump, water passages, gaskets, and sealing surfaces. Refer to Fig. OM3-17. The main water inlet is located in the lower unit gearcase housing below th antiventilation plate.

THERMOSTAT. All models are equipped with a thermostat which controls engine temperature.

The thermostat is calibrated to control coolant temperature within the range of 145°-150° F. Thermostat can be removed for inspection or renewal by first removing upper motor cover; then removing thermostat housing cover located on upper side of cylinder head. Refer to Fig. OM3-11 for exploded view of power head castings showing thermostat and associated parts.

Fig. OM3-7 — Wiring schematic for models after 1976. Stop button is not used on 1977 models.

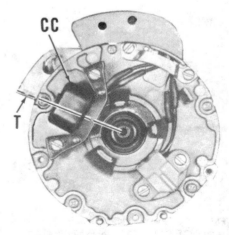

Fig. OM3-7A — Install stator plate so center of charge coil (CC) is aligned with stop (T) on cam plate.

POWER HEAD

R&R AND DISASSEMBLE. To overhaul the power head, clamp the motor on a stand, remove the upper motor cover and disconnect choke control. Remove the starter assembly as outlined in the STARTER section. Disconnect armature link from speed control shaft (22 – Fig. OM3-11), remove clamp from upper end of shaft and lift shaft (22) and pin (23) out of lower cover. Remove the seven cap screws (S – Fig. OM3-9) attaching power head to exhaust housing. Lift power head straight up off lower unit.

Intake manifold and carburetor can be removed as an assembly. Remove flywheel, breaker point cam and key from crankshaft. After the four screws (X – Fig. OM3-10) are removed, the magneto armature plate can be lifted off. Remove support (17 – Fig. OM3-11) and armature plate retainer (16). Remove cylinder head (10) and exhaust covers (19 & 21). Tap out the tapered crankcase aligning pins (1), working from cylinder side of crankcase flange. Remove the cap screws securing front crankcase housing (5) to cylinder (6) and separate the crankcase halves.

NOTE: Center main bearing cap screws (CS – Fig. OM3-4) are accessible through intake ports and must first be removed.

Pistons, rods and crankshaft are now accessible for removal and overhaul as outlined in the appropriate following paragraphs. When reassembling, follow the procedures outlined in ASSEMBLY paragraph.

ASSEMBLY. When reassembling, the crankcase and intake manifold must be completely sealed against both vacuum and pressure. Exhaust manifold and cylinder head must be sealed against water leakage and pressure. Mating surfaces of water intake and exhaust areas between power head and lower unit must form a tight seal.

Whenever the power head is disassembled, it is recommended that all gasket surfaces and the mating surfaces of crankcase halves be carefully checked for nicks and burrs or warped surfaces which might interfere with a tight seal. The cylinder head, head end of cylinder block, or mating surfaces of manifold and crankcase may be checked and lapped, if necessary, to provide a smooth surface. Do not remove any more metal than is necessary.

Mating surfaces of crankcase halves may be checked on the lapping block, and high spots or nicks removed, but surface must not be lowered. If extreme care is used, a slightly damaged crankcase may be salvaged in this manner. In case of doubt, renew the crankcase assembly.

Remove crankcase bleeder valve (4 – Fig. OM3-11) on models so equipped, oil line (8) and blow out oil passages while crankcase is disassembled.

The crankcase halves are positively located during assembly by the use of two tapered dowel pins (1). Check to make sure that the dowels are not bent, nicked or distorted, and that dowel holes are clean and true. When installing dowel pins, make sure they are fully seated, but do not use excessive force.

The mating surfaces of crankcase halves must be seated during assembly by using a non-hardening cement such as OMC Adhesive "M" or OMC Gel Seal. Make sure that surfaces are flat and free from nicks and burrs. Apply cement sparingly and evenly to cylinder half of crankcase only; then immediately install front half. Install the locating dowel pins; then install the crankcase screws. Tighten screws evenly to a torque of 60-80 inch-pounds.

When installing gaskets, check to make sure correct gasket is used and that ALL water passage holes are open and unobstructed. All gasket surfaces must be sealed, using a non-hardening cement such as OMC Gasket Sealing Compound. Use the non-hardening sealer on all screw threads and tighten to the torques given in CONDENSED SERVICE DATA table or in table given in SERVICE FUNDAMENTALS section in front of manual.

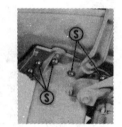

Fig. OM3-9 – The power head is attached to lower unit with seven cap screws (S). Two of the screws are on other side.

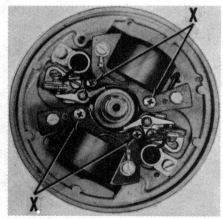

Fig. OM3-10 – The magneto armature plate can be lifted off after removing the four screws (X).

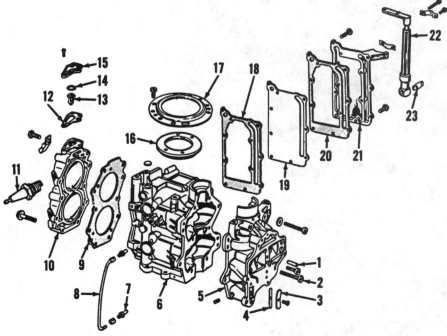

Fig. OM3-11 – Exploded view of power head of the type used.

1. Tapered pin	7. Nipple	13. Thermostat
2. Cap screw	8. Oil line	14. Seal
3. Leaf stop	9. Head gasket	15. Cover
4. Bleeder valve	10. Cylinder head	16. Retainer
5. Crankcase front half	11. Spark plug	17. Support
6. Cylinder block	12. Gasket	18. Gasket

19. Inner cover
20. Gasket
21. Exhaust cover
22. Speed control shaft
23. Pin

Lip of seal (13 – Fig. OM3-13) should be down. On all models, install armature plate retainer (16 – Fig. OM3-11) with flat side up and tapered side down.

Thoroughly lubricate all friction surfaces during assembly. Refer to Fig. OM3-13 for exploded view of crankshaft, piston and associated parts.

PISTONS, RINGS, PINS AND CYLINDERS.

Before detaching connecting rod caps from crankshaft, make certain that rod and cap are properly marked for correct assembly to each other and in the correct cylinder.

Piston on early models has three piston rings while piston on later models has two piston rings. Piston rings are interchangeable and may be installed either side up. Pistons and rings are available in standard size and one oversize. The recommended piston ring end gap, ring to groove clearance and piston to cylinder wall clearance are listed in the CONDENSED SERVICE DATA table. The piston pin is a loose fit in piston boss marked "L" (refer to Fig. OM3-12) and a tight fit in other boss.

When assembling, observe the following: Piston should have long, sloping side of head (EX – Fig. OM3-12) toward exhaust side of cylinder and oil hole (H)

in connecting rod should be up. Piston pin should be installed from the loose (L) side of piston. Ends of piston rings must engage pins (P) in grooves.

NOTE: Only two pins are shown, pin for center ring is on other side of piston.

CONNECTING RODS, BEARINGS AND CRANKSHAFT.

Before detaching connecting rod from crankshaft, make sure that rod and cap are properly marked for correct assembly to each other and in the proper cylinder.

The crankshaft end of each connecting rod contains 30 loose needle rollers which ride in a renewable split race in connecting rod and use the hardened, machined crankpin as the inner race. Piston end of connecting rod is unbushed; the rod should be renewed if clearance is excessive. If clearance is excessive between crankshaft main journals and bores in crankcase renew crankshaft and/or crankcase. Refer to CONDENSED SERVICE DATA table for recommended clearances and torque values.

When reassembling models prior to 1975, make certain dowels (4 – Fig. OM3-13) are correctly positioned. On all models, 30 bearing needles (6) are in

each race. Marks (M – Fig. OM3-12) on connecting rod and cap should be aligned on models prior to 1975. Marks on rod and cap of later models will be on same side but will not be aligned. All friction surfaces should be lubricated during assembly.

Fig. OM3-14 — The starter pinion can be blocked up as shown for removing starter rope.

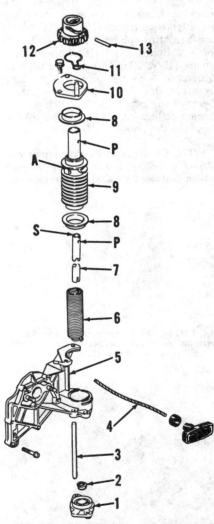

Fig. OM3-15 — Exploded view of typical rewind starter and associated parts. Intake manifold (5) contains the mounting bracket for starter unit.

1. Retainer plate	9. Spool
2. Bushing	10. Bearing head
3. Rope guide	11. Spring
4. Rope	12. Pinion
5. Intake manifold	13. Roll pin
6. Recoil spring	A. Attaching lug
7. Retainer	P. Pin hole
8. Bushing	S. Slot

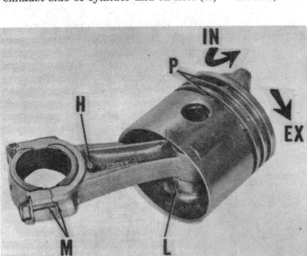

Fig. OM3-12 — Piston must be correctly assembled to rod with long, sloping side of piston head toward exhaust (EX) and oil hole (H) in rod up. When installing rod cap, make certain that marks (M) on rod and cap are located adjacent.

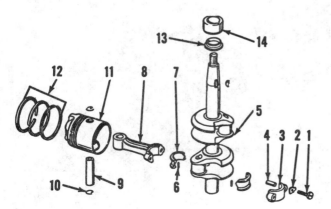

Fig. OM3-13 — Exploded view of crankshaft assemblies. Dowels (4) are not used on later models.

1. Cap screw
2. Lock
3. Rod cap
4. Dowel
5. Crankshaft
6. Bearing needle
7. Bearing race
8. Connecting rod
9. Piston pin
10. Retainer
11. Piston
12. Piston rings
13. Seal
14. Breaker cam

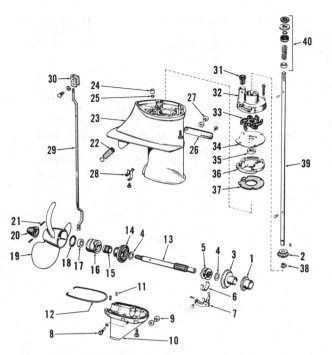

1. Bushing
2. Pinion
3. Forward gear
4. Thrust washer
5. Dog clutch
6. Cradle
7. Shift fork
8. Pivot screw
9. Drain plug
10. Lower gearcase
11. Dowel
12. Seal strip
13. Propeller shaft
14. Reverse gear
15. Bushing
16. Gearcase head
17. Seal
18. "O" ring
19. Propeller
20. Nut
21. Drive pin
22. Inlet strainer
23. Upper gearcase
24. Bushing
25. "O" ring
26. Cover
27. Vent plug
28. Detent
29. Shift rod
30. Connector
31. Grommet
32. Pump housing
33. Impeller
34. Plate
35. Seal
36. Bearing housing
37. Gasket
38. Snap ring
39. Drive shaft
40. Seal assembly

Fig. OM3-17 — Exploded view of lower unit gearcase, water pump and associated parts.

MANUAL STARTER

Refer to Fig. OM3-15 for an exploded view of starter assembly. Starter mounts on intake manifold as shown, and rope (4) extends through lower motor cover. The suggested procedure for rope renewal differs slightly from that required for other service; proceed as outlined for the type of service contemplated.

R&R STARTER ROPE. To renew a worn but still usable starter rope, remove upper motor cover and disconnect both spark plug high tension leads. Pull starter rope until almost fully extended. With rope-end in spool (9 – Fig. OM3-15) accessible, block pinion into engagement with flywheel, thus locking the recoil mechanism. Refer to Fig. OM3-14. With starter securely locked, disconnect from rubber grip and lug (A – Fig. OM3-15). Install a new rope by reversing the removal procedure. With rope secured at both ends, remove the wedge and allow starter to rewind. If rope is broken or disconnected, assemble as outlined for service removal.

To disconnect starter rope for removal of starter, pull out starter rope about a foot and tie a slip knot in rope to prevent complete rewind. Pry rope anchor from grip and remove the grip. Remove knot and allow rope to slowly enter hole in cover until rewind spring is fully unwound. Starter can now be removed.

To renew a broken rope or reconnect starter rope after service, proceed as follows: Insert a heavy-duty screwdriver

or brace with screwdriver bit through top of pinion (12 – Fig. OM3-15) and spool (9) and into slot (S) in top of spring retainer (7). Turn screwdriver or brace counterclockwise approximately 16½ turns on models prior to 1975 or 12½ turns on models after 1974 until anchor (A) in

Fig. OM3-19 — Exploded view of exhaust housing, stern clamps and associated parts typical of all models.

1. Stern clamp
2. Reverse lock arm
3. Adjusting screw
4. Reverse lock
5. Tilting lever
6. Thrust washer
7. "O" ring
8. Bushing
9. Stern bracket
10. Swivel bracket
11. Locking lever
12. Shift rod
13. Water tube
14. Lower mount
15. Liner
16. Friction block
17. Thrust washer
18. Pilot shaft
19. Rubber mount
20. Exhaust housing
21. Shift lever
22. Lever
23. Cover plate
24. Gear & shaft
25. Gear
26. Gear
27. Bushing
28. Gear & shaft
29. Steering bracket
30. Lower mount

spool is easily accessible. Then engage pinion (12) in teeth in flywheel ring gear and lock the assembly by inserting a suitable block or wedge between pinion and upper bearing head. Refer to Fig. OM3-14. Thread the rope through hole in anchor (A – Fig. OM3-15) making sure rope is properly positioned behind the rope guide (3); then reinstall the grip. Remove the previously installed locking block and allow starter to slowly rewind.

OVERHAUL. To overhaul the starter, first disconnect starter rope as previously outlined for service, and allow rewind spring to unwind. Remove the two cap screws securing upper bearing head (10 – Fig. OM3-15) to intake manifold (5) and lift off items (6 through 13) as a unit. Drive out roll pin (13) and separate the components.

Wash the parts in a suitable solvent and renew any which are worn, damaged, or questionable. When assembling the starter, lubricate rewind spring (6) with a light grease. Pinion gear (12) and spool (9) should not be lubricated, but installed dry to prevent dust accumulation. Align holes (P) in spring retainer (7) and spool (9) and slots in pinion gear (12), and tap the pin (13) through the holes and slots. Upper bearing head (10), spring (11) and upper bushing (8) must be properly positioned before installing pinion. Make sure slot in lower end of spring retainer (7) engages inner end of

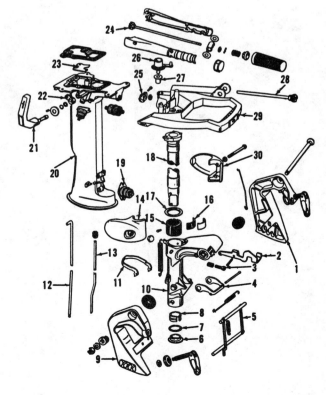

rewind spring (6) and enters bushing (2). Install rope and adjust rewind spring tension as outlined in the previous paragraph.

LOWER UNIT

PROPELLER AND DRIVE PIN. Cushioning protection of propeller and drive unit is built into propeller hub. Service consists of renewing propeller on models with cushioning hub.

Optional propellers are available, however, only propellers designed for these outboard models should be used.

REMOVE AND REINSTALL. Most service on the lower unit can be performed by detaching the gearcase housing from exhaust housing. Refer to Fig. OM3-17 for an exploded view of gearcase and associated parts and to Fig. OM3-19 for an exploded view of drive shaft housing and support assembly equipped with a full gear shift.

The propeller shaft (13 – Fig. OM3-17) and drive gears (3 & 14) can be removed after first draining lubricant from gear housing, removing pivot screw (8), then unbolting and removing gearcase lower housing (10).

To separate gearcase assembly from exhaust housing, place the gear shift lever in "Forward" position and remove the gearcase retaining cap screws. Separate gearcase from exhaust housing far enough to remove either connector screw from shift lever clamp (30); then withdraw the gearcase and drive as an assembly.

When assembling gearcase, use new seals, gaskets and "O" rings. Install new seal strip (12) in lower gearcase (10), and trim ends with a sharp knife to extend approximately 1/32-inch beyond ends of groove and form a tight butt-joint against gearcase head (16). Use a small amount of non-hardening sealer (such as OMC Adhesive "M") on each end of sealing strip (12) and a thin line of sealer on housing flange. Install immediately after sealer is applied. Use a non-hardening thread sealant on all cap screw threads.

EVINRUDE AND JOHNSON
7.5 HP (1980-1983)
6 & 8 HP (1984-1989)

EVINRUDE MODELS

Years Produced	6 Hp	7.5 Hp	8 Hp
1980	....	8RCS	....
1981	....	8RCI	....
1982	....	8RCN	....
1983	....	8RCT	....
1984	6RCR	....	8RCR
1985	6RCO	....	8RCO
1986	6RCD	....	8RCD
1987	E6BACU, E6BALCU	....	E8BACU, E8BALCU
	E6BFCU, E6BFLCU	....	E8RCU, E8RLCU
	E6RCU, E6RLCU	....	E8SRLCU
	E6SLCU		
1988	E6BACC, E6BALCC	....	E8BACC, E8BALCC
	E6DRCC, E6DRLCC	....	E8RCC, E8RLCC
	E6RCC, E6RLCC	....	E8SRLCC
	E6SLCC		
1989	E6BACE, E6BALCE	....	E8BACE, E8BALCE
	E6DRCE, E6DRLCE	....	E8RCE, E8RLCE
	E6RCE, E6RLCE	....	E8SRLCE
	E6SLCE		

JOHNSON MODELS

Year Produced	6 Hp	7.5 Hp	8 Hp
1980	....	8RCS	....
1981	....	8RCI	....
1982	....	8RCN	....
1983	....	8RCT	....
1984	6RCR	....	8RCR
1985	6RCO	....	8RCO
1986	6RCD	....	8RCD
1987	J6BACU, J6BALCU	....	J8BACU, J8BALCU
	J6BFCU, J6BFLCU	....	J8RCU, J8RLCU
	J6RCU, J6RLCU	....	J8SRLCU
	6SLCU		
1988	J6BACC, J6BALCC	....	J8BACC, J8BALCC
	J6DRCC, J6DRLCC	....	J8RCC, J8RLCC
	J6RCC, J6RLCC	....	J8SRLCC
	J6SLCC		
1989	J6BACE, J6BALCE	....	J8BACE, J8BALCE
	J6DRCE, J6DRLCE	....	J8RCE, J8RLCE
	J6RCD, J6DRLCE	....	J8SRLCE
	J6SLCE		

CONDENSED SERVICE DATA

TUNE-UP

Hp/rpm 6/4500-5500
(4.5 kW)
7.5/4500-5500
(5.6 kW)
8/5000-6000
(6.0 kW)
Bore . . . . .1.94 in.
(49.3 mm)
Stroke . . . . .1.70 in.
(43.2 mm)
Number of Cylinders 2
Displacement . . . . .10 cu. in.
(164 cc)
Spark Plug—Champion:
1980-1985 . . . . .L77J4*
1986-1989 . . . . .QL77JC4*
Electrode Gap . . . . .0.040 in.
(1.0 mm)
Ignition Type . . . . .CDI
Carburetor Make . . . . .OMC
Idle Speed (in gear):
Prior to 1987 . . . . .650 rpm
1987-1989 . . . . .650-700 rpm†
Fuel:Oil Ratio . . . . .See Text

*For sustained high speed operation, the manufacturer recommends using QL78V on 6 and 8 hp models prior to 1989, or QL16V on models after 1988. Renew surface gap spark plug if center electrode is worn in excess of 1/32 inch (0.79 mm) below flat surface of plug end.
†On Sailmaster and Yachtwin (6SL and 8SRL) models, idle speed should be 850-900 rpm in gear.

SIZES—CLEARANCES

Piston Ring End Gap . . . . .0.005-0.015 in.
(0.13-0.38 mm)
Piston Ring Side Clearance . . . . .0.004 in. Max.
(0.10 mm)
Standard Cylinder Bore
Diameter . . . . .1.9373-1.9380 in.
(49.207-49.225 mm)
Max. Allowable Taper .0.002 in.
(0.05 mm)
Max. Allowable Out-of-Round:
Prior to 1987 . . . . .0.002 in.
(0.05 mm)
After 1986 . . . . .0.003 in.
(0.08 mm)
Piston-to-Cylinder Clearance . . . . .See Text
Crankshaft Journal Diameters—
Top Main Journal:
Prior to 1988 . . . . .0.8723-0.8773 in.
(22.156-22.283 mm)
1988 . . . . .0.8745-0.8750 in.
(22.212-22.225 mm)

SIZES—CLEARANCES CONT.

1989 . . . . .0.8762-0.8767 in.
(22.255-22.268 mm)
Center Main Journal:
Prior to 1988 .0.8104-0.8155 in.
(20.584-20.714 mm)
1988 . . . . .0.8127-0.8130 in.
(20.643-20.650 mm)
1989 . . . . .0.8127-0.8132 in.
(20.643-20.655 mm)
Bottom Main Journal:
Prior to 1988 .0.7498-0.7562 in.
(19.045-19.207 mm)
1988 . . . . .0.6693-0.6695 in.
(17.000-17.005 mm)
1989 . . . . .0.6691-0.6695 in.
(16.995-17.005 mm)
Crankpin:
All Models . . . . .0.6695-0.6700 in.
(17.005-17.018 mm)

TIGHTENING TORQUES

Connecting Rod . . . . .60-70 in.-lbs.
(6.8-7.9 N·m)
Crankcase Halves . . . . .144-168 in.-lbs.
(16-19 N·m)
Cylinder Head . . . . .144-168 in.-lbs.
(16-19 N·m)
Exhaust Cover . . . . .60-84 in.-lbs.
(6.8-9.5 N·m)
Flywheel . . . . .40-50 ft.-lbs.
(54-70 N·m)
Intake Manifold . . . . .60-84 in.-lbs.
(6.8-9.5 N·m)
Spark Plug . . . . .216-240 in.-lbs.
(24.4-27.1 N·m)
Standard Screws:
No. 6 . . . . .7-10 in.-lbs.
(0.8-1.2 N·m)
No. 8 . . . . .15-22 in.-lbs.
(1.6-2.4 N·m)
No. 10 . . . . .25-35 in.-lbs.
(2.8-4.0 N·m)
No. 12 . . . . .35-40 in.-lbs.
(4.0-4.6 N·m)
¼ inch . . . . .60-80 in.-lbs.
(7-9 N·m)
5/16 inch . . . . .120-140 in.-lbs.
(14-16 N·m)
3/8 inch . . . . .220-240 in.-lbs.
(24-27 N·m)
7/16 inch . . . . .340-360 in.-lbs.
(38-40 N·m)

LUBRICATION

The power head is lubricated by oil mixed with the fuel. The recommended fuel is regular leaded or unleaded gasoline with a minimum octane rating of 67 on models produced after 1980, or octane rating of 86 on models produced prior to 1981. If the recommended fuel is not available, gasoline containing not more than ten percent ethanol alcohol, or gasoline containing not more than five percent methanol alcohol with five percent co-solvent additives may be used. Do not use gasoline exceeding the specified alcohol content regardless of octane rating. Discontinue the use of alcohol extended gasoline if fuel system problems are encountered.

The recommended oil is Evinrude or Johnson Outboard Lubricant or a suitable equivalent NMMA (formerly known as BIA) certified TC-W or TC-WII engine oil. The manufacturer recommends using oil certified TC-WII on 1989 models. The recommended fuel:oil ratio for normal service and during engine break-in is 50:1.

NOTE: OMC service bulletin 2211 issued September 1988, recommends using a 50:1 fuel:oil ratio on all recreational outboard motors which were previously recommended

for a 100:1 fuel:oil mixture. For 1989, Accumix and Accumix R fuel and oil mixing systems have been changed to a 50:1 ratio.

On models so recommended, a 100:1 fuel:oil mixture may be used if an approved oil is used and if the engine is completely broken-in and motor is used on a frequent basis. Do not use a 100:1 mixture if motor is used infrequently and during nonuse the motor is stored in areas of high humidity or wide-scale temperature changes, or if motor is operated at constant high speeds.

The lower unit gears and bearings are lubricated by oil contained in the gearcase. The recommended oil is OMC Hi-Vis Gearcase Lubricant. If OMC Hi-Vis gear lube is not available, OMC Premium Blend gearcase lube may be substituted. Gearcase oil level should be checked after every 50 hours of operation and drained and refilled with new oil after every 100 hours of operation or seasonally, whichever occurs first.

The gearcase oil should be drained and filled through the drain plug hole. An oil level (vent) port is used to indicate the full oil level and to vent gearcase to ease draining and refilling. Gearcase should be in the normal operating position when draining and refilling. Tighten drain and vent plugs to 60-84 in.-lbs. (7-9.5 N·m) after refilling gearcase with oil.

FUEL SYSTEM

CARBURETOR. All models prior to 1986 are equipped with the carburetor shown in Fig. OM4-1. All models after

1985 are equipped with the carburetor shown in Fig. OM4-2. Initial setting of low speed mixture needle (L—Fig. OM4-1) on models prior to 1986 is one turn out from a lightly seated position. Initial setting of low speed mixture needle (L—Fig. OM4-2) on 1986 and later models is 2-1/2 turns out from a lightly seated position. Turning slow speed needle clockwise leans the fuel mixture. Engine should be at normal operating temperature and in forward gear when performing final idle mixture and speed adjustments. Refer to SPEED CONTROL LINKAGE for final adjustment procedure.

A fixed high speed jet (2—Fig. OM4-1 or Fig. OM4-2) is used to regulate the high speed air:fuel mixture. Recommended high speed jet sizes for normal service are as follows:

1980-1982	
7.5 Hp	#35
1982	
7.5 Hp (SRL)	#33
1983	
7.5 Hp	#35
7.5 Hp (SRL)	#33
1984	
6 Hp	#35
6 Hp (SL)	#33
8 Hp (SRL)	#33
1985	
6 Hp	#32
6 Hp (BF)	#35
8 Hp	#36

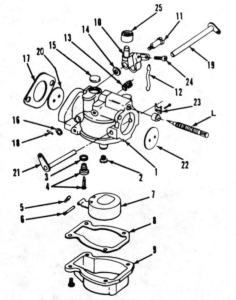

Fig. OM4-1—Exploded view of carburetor used on models prior to 1986.

L.	Low speed mixture needle
1.	Body
2.	High speed jet
3.	Gasket
4.	Needle & seat
5.	Clip
6.	Pin
7.	Float
8.	Gasket
9.	Float bowl
10.	Cam follower
11.	Shoulder screw
12.	Link
13.	Spring
14.	Washer
15.	Plug
16.	Washer
17.	Gasket
18.	Pin
19.	Throttle shaft
20.	Throttle plate
21.	Choke shaft
22.	Choke plate
23.	Retainer
24.	Follower adjusting screw
25.	Roller

Fig. OM4-2—Exploded view of carburetor used on 1986-1989 models. On 1988 and 1989 models, low speed mixture needle (L) is located on the top starboard side of carburetor.

L.	Low speed mixture needle
1.	Body
2.	High speed jet
3.	Gasket
4.	Needle & seat
6.	Pin
7.	Float
8.	Gasket
9.	Float bowl
10.	Cam follower
11.	Shoulder screw
12.	Link
13.	Spring
14.	Washer
16.	Washer
17.	Gasket
18.	Pin
19.	Throttle shaft
20.	Throttle plate
24.	Follower adjusting screw
25.	Roller
26.	Top cover
27.	Gasket
30.	Nozzle well
31.	Gasket
32.	Gasket
33.	Primer nozzle
34.	Idle speed screw
35.	Spring

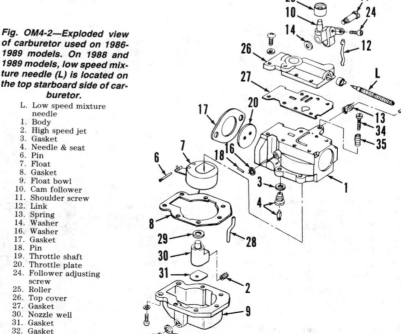

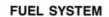

1986-1989

6 Hp . . . . #32
8 Hp . . . . #40

Recommended idle speed is 650 rpm on models prior to 1987, 650-700 rpm on 1987-1989 models and 850-900 rpm on Sailmaster and Yachtwin models.

NOTE: For optimum results, make final idle speed adjustment with boat in the water with the correct propeller installed. Engine should be running in gear at normal operating temperature with boat movement unrestrained.

To check float level, remove float bowl and invert carburetor. Place OMC Float Gage 324891 on float bowl gasket surface as shown in Fig. OM4-3. Use notch marked 2 thru 6 for 8 hp models prior to 1986 and all 7.5 hp models. Use notch marked 9.9 & 15 for all models after 1985. Make sure float gage is not pushing down on float. Float should be between specified notches on gage. Carefully bend float arm to adjust. If OMC float gage 324891 is not available, adjust so float is level and parallel with float bowl gasket surface. To check float drop, hold carburetor upright and allow float to hang by its own weight. Measure from float bowl mating surface to bottom of float 180 degrees from inlet needle. Float drop on models prior to 1986 should be 1-1/8 to 1-1/2 inches (28.6-38.1 mm) and 1 to 1-3/8 inches (25.4-34.9 mm) on 1986 and later models. Bend float tang (adjacent to inlet needle) to adjust float drop. Apply a suitable thread locking compound to float bowl screws during reassembly.

NOTE: The manufacturer does not recommend submerging the parts in carburetor or parts cleaning solutions. An aerosol type carburetor cleaner is recommended. The float and other components made of plastic and rubber should not be subjected to some cleaning solutions. Safety eyewear and solvent resistant gloves are recommended.

SPEED CONTROL LINKAGE. (Models Prior to 1986). The speed control linkage rotates the armature plate to advance the ignition timing. The throttle cam attached to the bottom of the armature plate is used to open the carburetor throttle as the ignition is advanced. The throttle opening and ignition timing cannot be properly synchronized if the throttle cam and related components are worn or damaged in any way. Renew components if needed.

To synchronize speed controls, first remove the engine cover. Move the speed control from the stop position until the carburetor throttle just begins to open. At this point, the cam follower roller (25—Fig. OM4-4) should be centered between marks (M) on cam (C). If not, turn cam follower adjusting screw (24—Fig. OM4-1) to center roller on marks when throttle plate starts to open.

(Models after 1985). Shift into neutral position. Use a dial indicator or

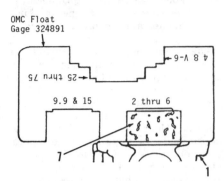

Fig. OM4-3—To check float level, invert carburetor and place OMC gage 324891 on carburetor body (1) as shown. On 8 hp models prior to 1986 and 7.5 hp models, float (7) should be between notches marked 2 through 6. On 1986 and later models, float (7) should be between notches marked 9.9 and 15. Bend float arm to adjust.

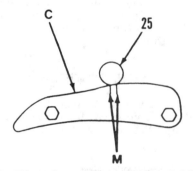

Fig. OM4-4—On models prior to 1986, cam follower roller (25) should be centered between marks (M) on cam (C) just as carburetor throttle plate starts to open.

suitable tool and verify number 1 piston is at TDC, then align timing pointer (P—Fig. OM4-5) with TDC mark on flywheel. Turn tiller handle idle speed knob completely counterclockwise. Remove cap screw (C) noting washer under bracket. Connect a suitable power timing light and tachometer to engine. Start engine and adjust idle speed screw (34—Fig. OM4-6) so engine will idle. Push stator plate to slow position and adjust stop bracket (B—Fig. OM4-5) so timing is 8-10 degrees ATDC. Stop engine and adjust bracket (D) so throttle cable and linkage is preloaded toward throttle closed position by approximately one rotation of bracket (D). Loosen follower adjusting screw (24—Fig. OM4-6) so roller (25) does not contact throttle cam.

Start engine and allow to warm to normal operating temperature. Make sure twist grip is in the full closed position. Engine should idle at approximately 700 rpm. Adjust low speed mixture screw (L—Fig. OM4-2) until the highest consistent rpm is obtained, then an additional 1/8 turn counterclockwise to prevent a too lean mixture at slow speeds. Adjust carburetor idle speed screw (34—Fig. OM4-6) so engine idles at the specified rpm (CONDENSED SERVICE DATA) in gear. Adjust follower adjusting screw (24) so roller (25) just contacts throttle cam, then back off 1/8 turn. Stop engine and rotate twist grip to wide open position. Adjust screw (W) as necessary to position throttle shaft pin (18) in a vertical position.

REED VALVES. The inlet reed valve unit is located between carburetor and crankcase, and should be checked whenever the carburetor is removed for service. Refer to Fig. OM4-7.

Reed petals (4) should seat very lightly against reed plate (5) throughout their

Fig. OM4-5—View of speed control linkage components used on 1986 and later models. Refer to text for adjustment procedures.

  B. Stop bracket
  C. Cap screw
  D. Bracket
  P. Timing pointer

entire length, with the least possible tension. Check seating visually and by blowing and drawing air through ports. Renew reed petals (4) if broken, cracked, warped, rusted or bent. A broken reed petal is sometimes caused by a bent or damaged reed stop (3). Seating surface of plate (5) should be smooth and flat.

FUEL PUMP. The diaphragm type fuel pump attaches to side of cylinder block and is actuated by crankcase pulsations. Fuel pump is available only as an assembly.

If fuel delivery problems are noted, first remove and clean fuel filter located under fuel pump cover. Install filter with lip of element facing away from pump cover. Remove and blow through fuel lines to ensure lines are clean and open. Test fuel lines and remote tank installation using a suitable vacuum pump and gage. If over 4 inches Hg (13.5 kPa) vacuum is required to draw fuel from tank, check for restrictions in fuel tank and lines. Note that remote fuel tank must not be more than 24 inches (61 cm) below fuel pump.

To test fuel pump, install a suitable pressure gage between fuel pump and carburetor and start engine. Fuel pump pressure should be 2.5 psi (17 kPa) at 4500 rpm. Fuel pump mounting screws should be treated with OMC Nut Lock or a suitable equivalent thread locking compound and tightened to 24-36 in.-lbs. (3-4 N·m). Tighten fuel pump cover screws to 10-15 in.-lbs. (1-2 N·m).

IGNITION

CD2 Ignition System

OPERATION. Models prior to 1989 are equipped with CD2 breakerless capacitor discharge ignition system. Refer to Fig. OM4-8 for wiring schematic. A charge coil and sensor coil are located under the flywheel. Two magnets in flywheel induce a current in the charge coil which is rectified and directed to a capacitor for storage. The two flywheel magnets also induce current in the sensor coil to provide a positive charge on the gate of one of two silicon controlled rectifiers (SCR'S). The positive charge opens the SCR and allows the charged capacitor to discharge through the SCR and primary circuit of the ignition coil. The rapid coil field buildup induces a secondary voltage which fires the spark plug. Diodes, SCR'S and capacitor are contained in the power pack assembly and are not available individually.

NOTE: Eight horsepower models with power pack marked "CDL" has a built-in device to limit engine speed to 6200 rpm.

Refer to previous SPEED CONTROL LINKAGE section for adjustment of ignition timing.

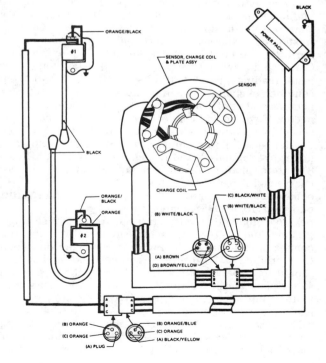

Fig. OM4-6—View of speed control linkage components used on 1986 and later models. Refer to text for adjustment procedures.
W. Screw
18. Pin
24. Follower adjusting screw
25. Roller
34. Carburetor idle speed screw

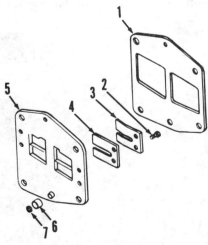

Fig. OM4-7—Exploded view of reed valve assembly typical of all models. Three retaining screws (2) per reed set are used on 8 hp models.

1. Gasket	
2. Screw	5. Reed plate
3. Reed stop	6. Check valve
4. Reed petals	7. Screen

Fig. OM4-8—Wiring schematic on models equipped with CD2 capacitor discharge ignition. Models after 1984 are equipped with a five-wire connector in place of four-wire connector.

TROUBLE-SHOOTING. On models prior to 1985, the 4-wire connector plugs connect the charge and sensor coil leads to the power pack. The 3-wire connector plugs connect the power pack and ignition coils. On models after 1984, a 5-wire connector is used between the power pack and armature plate. No timing adjustments are required with a CD2 ignition. Correct timing will be maintained as long as the wires are properly positioned in the connectors. On models prior to 1985, check to make sure the white/black wire in the 4-wire connector is positioned in connector terminal B. Also check to make sure the number 1 coil wire is in the 3-wire connector B terminal and that it connects with the power pack orange/blue wire in the other connector B terminal. On models after 1984, check to make sure the white/black wire in the 5-wire connector is positioned in connector terminal B of both connector halves. Also check to make sure the orange/blue power pack lead is connected to the number 1 ignition coil.

NOTE: Outer edges of charge coil and sensor coil must be flush with machined surface of armature plate to provide the proper clearance between coils and flywheel magnets. OMC locating ring 317001 may be used to simplify this procedure. Place locating ring over machined bosses on armature plate, push coil out against locating ring and tighten mounting screws.

To check charge coil output, use Merc-O-Tronic Model 781, Stevens Model CD77 or a suitable peak voltage tester. Disconnect connector between armature plate and power pack. Connect black tester lead to stator lead connector terminal A and red tester lead to terminal D. Turn tester knobs to Negative and 500. Crank engine while observing tester. If tester reading is below 230 volts, check condition of charge coil wiring and connectors, and verify pin location in connector. If wiring and connectors are in acceptable condition, check charge coil resistance as follows: Connect an ohmmeter to terminals A and D (Fig. OM4-8) in stator plate lead connector. Renew charge coil if resistance is not 500-650 ohms on models prior to 1986 or 550-600 ohms on 1986-1988 models. Connect negative ohmmeter lead to stator plate (ground) and positive ohmmeter lead to connector terminal A, then to connector terminal D. Infinite resistance should exist between A terminal and stator plate and D terminal and stator plate. If not, charge coil or charge coil lead is shorted to ground.

To check sensor coil, connect an ohmmeter to terminals B and C in stator plate lead connector. Renew sensor coil

if resistance is not 30-50 ohms. Connect negative ohmmeter lead to stator plate (ground) and positive ohmmeter lead to connector terminal B, then to connector terminal C. Infinite resistance should exist between B terminal and stator plate and C terminal and stator plate. If not, sensor coil or sensor coil lead is shorted to ground. To check sensor coil output, use Merc-O-Tronic Model 781, Stevens Model CD77 or a suitable peak voltage tester. Connect black tester lead to stator lead connector terminal C and red tester lead to terminal B. On Merc-O-Tronic Model 781, turn knobs to Positive and 5, and on Stevens Model CD77, turn knobs to S and 5. Crank engine while observing tester. Renew sensor coil if meter reads below 2 volts.

To check power pack output, first reconnect connector between armature plate and power pack. Use Merc-O-Tronic Model 781, Stevens Model CD77 or a suitable peak voltage tester. Connect black tester lead to a suitable engine ground. Connect red tester lead to wire leading to either ignition coil. Turn tester knobs to Negative and 500. Crank engine while observing tester. Repeat test on other lead. Renew power pack if readings are not at least 180 volts or higher on models prior to 1985 or 200 volts or higher on models after 1984.

To test ignition coils, disconnect high tension lead at ignition coil. On models prior to 1985, disconnect 3-wire connector and insert a jumper lead in terminal B of the ignition coil end of connector. Connect ohmmeter positive lead to the B terminal jumper wire and ohmmeter negative lead to a good engine ground. On models after 1984, disconnect coil primary wire at coil and connect ohmmeter positive lead to coil primary terminal and negative lead to a good engine ground or to coil ground tab. Ignition coil primary resistance should be 0.05-0.15 ohm on all models. To check coil secondary resistance, move ohmmeter negative lead to the high tension terminal. Secondary resistance should be 225-325 ohms on models prior to 1986 and 250-300 ohms on models after 1985. Repeat procedure on number 2 ignition coil.

CD2U Ignition System

Models after 1988 are equipped with CD2UL ignition system. Except for the ignition coils, all CD2U components are located under the flywheel indicated by the "U" in the model designation. Ignition system model number is printed on top of ignition module located under flywheel. The power pack and sensor coil are integrated into a single ignition module assembly instead of separate components as in earlier CD2 systems.

TROUBLE-SHOOTING. Disconnect spark plug leads from spark plugs and connect a suitable spark tester. Set tester spark gap to 1/2 inch (12.7 mm). On models so equipped, install emergency ignition cutoff clip and lanyard. Crank engine and observe spark tester. If an acceptable spark is noted at each spark gap, perform RUNNING OUTPUT TEST. If spark is noted at only one spark gap, perform IGNITION PLATE OUTPUT TEST as described in this section. If no spark is noted at either spark gap, perform STOP CIRCUIT TEST.

NOTE: If acceptable spark is noted at each spark gap during spark output test but engine pops and backfires during starting or running, ignition system may be out of time. Be sure orange/blue primary wire is connected to number 1 ignition coil, spark plug high tension leads are properly connected, flywheel is properly located on crankshaft and speed control linkage is properly adjusted.

STOP CIRCUIT TEST. Remove spark plug leads from spark plugs and connect a suitable spark tester. Disconnect stop circuit connector (Fig. OM4-9). Make sure ignition emergency cutoff clip and lanyard are installed on models so equipped. Crank engine and observe spark tester. If no spark is noted, perform IGNITION PLATE OUTPUT TEST. If normal spark is noted, connect ohmmeter between engine ground and the one-pin stop circuit connector (Fig. OM4-9) leading to tiller handle. Ohmmeter should show infinite resistance. If meter shows continuity, repair short in wiring or renew stop button. Depress stop button or remove emergency cutoff clip and note ohmmeter. If ohmmeter does not indicate continuity, re-

Fig. OM4-9—View showing approximate location of one-pin stop circuit connector. Appearance of stop circuit connector is the same on all models but location may vary. Refer to text.

pair open in wiring or renew stop button.

IGNITION PLATE OUTPUT TEST. Disconnect spark plug leads to prevent accidental starting. Remove primary leads from ignition coils. Connect number 1 ignition coil primary lead to the red lead of Stevens load adapter PL-88 and black lead of load adapter to engine ground.

NOTE: If Stevens load adapter is not available, fabricate load adapter using a 10 ohm, 10 watt resistor (Radio Shack part 271-132) or equivalent.

Connect red test lead of CD77 or equivalent peak reading voltmeter to red lead of Stevens load adapter PL-88 and black test lead to engine ground. Set voltmeter to Positive and 500. Crank engine and note meter. Repeat test procedure on number 2 ignition coil primary lead. If voltmeter indicates 175 volts or higher on both tests, perform IGNITION COIL TESTS. If one primary lead shows no output, renew ignition module. If both tests indicate no output, perform CHARGE COIL RESISTANCE TEST.

CHARGE COIL RESISTANCE TEST. Remove manual starter and flywheel. Remove two ignition module mounting screws and disconnect module brown and brown/yellow bullet connectors. Connect ohmmeter between brown and brown/yellow charge coil connectors. Renew charge coil if resistance is not within 535-585 ohms. Connect one ohmmeter lead to engine ground and connect other ohmmeter lead to brown charge coil lead, then to brown/yellow charge coil lead. Renew charge coil if ohmmeter shows continuity between engine ground and either wire. If charge coil tests acceptable, renew ignition module.

NOTE: When installing charge coil or ignition module, use OMC Locating Ring 334994 to properly position components on armature plate. Place ring over machined surfaces on armature plate, push components outward against locating ring and tighten mounting screws to 30-40 in.-lbs. (3.4-4.5 N·m).

RUNNING OUTPUT TEST. Remove propeller and install the correct test wheel, then mount outboard motor in a suitable test tank. Remove ignition coil primary wires and install suitable terminal extenders (Stevens TS-77 or equivalent) on coil primary terminals, then install primary wires on terminal extenders. Connect peak reading voltmeter red test lead to number 1 coil terminal extender and black test lead to engine ground. Set voltmeter to Positive and 500. Start engine and run at rpm where ignition malfunction is evident while noting meter. Repeat test procedure on number 2 ignition coil. If either cylinder shows less than 200 volts, perform CHARGE COIL RESISTANCE TEST. If charge coil test results are acceptable, renew ignition module.

IGNITION COIL RESISTANCE TEST. To check ignition coil primary resistance, connect ohmmeter between primary terminal and coil ground. Resistance should be 0.05-0.15 ohm. To check secondary resistance, connect ohmmeter between coil high tension terminal and primary terminal. Resistance should be 250-300 ohms. Renew coil if resistance is not as specified.

LIGHTING COIL. On models equipped with an alternator, disconnect three pin connector leading from armature plate. Connect an ohmmeter between yellow wire with gray tracer and yellow wire. Renew stator if resistance is not within 0.81-0.91 ohm. Next, connect ohmmeter between yellow wire with gray tracer and yellow wire with blue tracer. Renew stator if resistance is not within 1.19-1.23 ohms. Connect ohmmeter between engine ground and each pin in three pin connector (yellow, yellow/gray and yellow/blue). If ohmmeter does not indicate infinity between ground and each pin, inspect for shorted stator or stator wires and repair or renew as necessary.

COOLING SYSTEM

WATER PUMP. All models are equipped with a rubber impeller type water pump. Impeller is mounted on and driven by the drive shaft in the lower unit. Refer to Fig. OM4-16. Water enters the lower unit gearcase through an opening in the rear of the antiventilation plate.

If cooling system malfunction occurs, first check the water inlet for plugging or partial restriction. Then, remove lower unit as outlined in the appropriate section and inspect condition of the water pump, water passages, gaskets and sealing surfaces.

THERMOSTAT. The thermostat is located behind thermostat cover on top front of cylinder head. Refer to Fig. OM4-10. Engine operating temperature can be checked using Thermomelt Stiks. Start engine and run at 3000 rpm for approximately five minutes. Reduce engine speed to 900 rpm and mark cylin-

der block (near cylinder head) with a 100° F (37° C) Thermomelt stik and a 163° F (73° C) Thermomelt stik. The 100° F (37° C) stik should melt but not the 163° F (73° C) stik. If underheating or overheating condition is evident, inspect cooling system and repair as necessary.

POWER HEAD

REMOVE AND REINSTALL. Remove top engine cover. Remove starter, carburetor and fuel inlet hose. Remove speed control cable. Remove flywheel and stator plate components. Disconnect any components that will interfere with power head removal. Unscrew drive shaft housing to power head screws and separate power head from drive shaft housing.

Reinstall power head by reversing removal procedure. Refer to SPEED CONTROL LINKAGE section for adjustment of speed control cable.

DISASSEMBLY. Refer to Fig. OM4-10 for exploded view of power head. Remove armature plate support and retainer. Remove cylinder head and taper pin (22).

NOTE: Taper pin (22) must be driven out from cylinder head side toward intake manifold side. Use caution not to damage taper pin bore.

Unbolt and separate crankcase from cylinder block. Pistons, rods and crankshaft are now accessible for removal and overhaul as outlined in the appropriate following paragraphs.

REASSEMBLY. Prior to reassembly, make certain all sealing surfaces are clean, smooth and flat. The crankcase and inlet manifold must be completely sealed against both vacuum and pressure. The exhaust manifold and cylinder head must be sealed against water and exhaust leakage. Make certain that the taper pin (22—Fig. OM4-10) is not bent, nicked or distorted, and that pin hole is clean and true.

The mating surfaces of crankcase halves must be sealed during reassembly by using a nonhardening compound such as OMC Gel-Seal II or equivalent. Do not use sealers which will harden and prevent contact between crankcase mating surfaces. Make sure all old gasket compound is removed and that surfaces are flat and free from nicks and burrs. Prior to applying Gel-Seal, treat mating surfaces with OMC Locquic Primer and allow to dry. If not treated with Locquic Primer, allow Gel-Seal to cure at least 24 hours before returning unit to service. Apply Gel-Seal sparingly and evenly to cylinder half of crankcase only, then immediately install front half. Install and tighten the crankcase screws equally to 144-168 in.-lbs. (16.3-19 N·m). Tighten cylinder head screws in sequence shown in Fig. OM4-11 to 144-168 in.-lbs. (16.3-19 N·m). Retighten cylinder head screws after motor has been test run and allowed to cool.

PISTONS, PINS, RINGS AND CYLINDERS. Prior to detaching connecting rods from crankshaft, make certain rod and cap and pistons are marked for reference during reassembly.

Each aluminum piston is fitted with two rings which are interchangeable and may be installed either side up. Standard size and 0.030 inch (0.76 mm) oversize pistons and rings are available for all models. Refer to CONDENSED SERVICE DATA for service specifications. Maximum allowable cylinder bore taper is 0.002 inch (0.05 mm) on all models. Maximum allowable cylinder out-of-round is 0.002 inch (0.05 mm) on models prior to 1987 and 0.003 inch (0.08 mm) on 1987 and later models. To determine oversize bore diameter, add 0.030 inch (0.76 mm) to standard cylinder bore diameter. Refer to CONDENSED SERVICE DATA.

Measure piston diameter in two locations, 90 degrees apart, 1/8 inch (3.2 mm) up from bottom of skirt. Renew piston if difference between the two measurements exceeds 0.002 inch (0.05 mm).

On models prior to 1987, one piston pin bore in piston is a press fit while the other bore is a slip fit. The loose pin bore is indicated by the mark ''L'' cast into piston as shown in Fig. OM4-12. When removing piston pin, remove both retaining rings and drive the pin out toward the unmarked side of piston. Install pin through loose side first. Be sure to properly support press fit side of piston to prevent damage when removing and reinstalling piston pin.

On 1987 and later models, piston pin is a press fit in both bores in piston (without ''L'' Fig. OM4-12). Heat piston to 200°-400° F (93°-205° C) when removing or reinstalling pin on models after 1986. Renew piston pin retaining rings during reassembly on all models.

Piston should be installed into cylinder with long tapering side of piston crown toward exhaust port side of cylinder. On models with one hole in side of connecting rod (view A—Fig. OM4-13), install rod with oil hole facing up. On models with two oil holes in rod small end (B), rod may be installed with either side facing up. When installing connecting rods, tighten rod cap screws to 60-70 in.-lbs. (6.8-7.9 N·m). Thoroughly lubricate all friction surfaces with an approved engine oil during reassembly.

CONNECTING RODS, BEARINGS AND CRANKSHAFT. Prior to detaching connecting rods from crankshaft, make sure rod and cap are marked for correct assembly to each other and in the correct cylinder.

The top main bearing (2—Fig. OM4-10) is a caged needle bearing type and should be installed with lettered end facing up. Center main bearing (5) and connecting rod big end bearings (30) are loose needle bearings and contain 30 needle rollers each. Use a suitable needle bearing assembly grease to hold needle rollers in place during reassembly.

NOTE: During reassembly, make sure all loose bearing rollers are in place and not intermixed. Center main bearing and crankpin bearings contain 30 rollers each.

Refer to CONDENSED SERVICE DATA for service specifications and recommended tightening torques. Inspect rods and caps and renew if bearing sur-

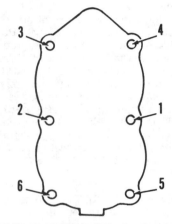

Fig. OM4-11—Tighten cylinder head screws following the sequence shown to 144-168 in.-lbs. (16-19 N·m).

Fig. OM4-12—View of lower side of piston showing the ''L'' mark indicating loose piston pin bore.

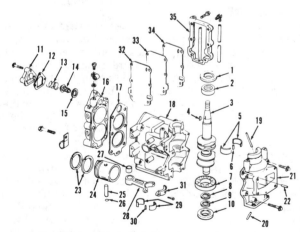

Fig. OM4-10—Exploded view of power head assembly.

1. Seal	13. Spring
2. Bearing	14. Thermostat
3. Crankshaft	15. Seal
4. Key	16. Cylinder head
5. Bearing cage	17. Cylinder head gasket
6. Bearing rollers	18. Cylinder block
7. Ball bearing	19. Drain tube
8. Snap ring	20. Drain tube
9. Snap ring	21. Crankcase
10. Seal	22. Taper pin
11. Thermostat housing	23. Piston rings
12. Gasket	

24. Piston
25. Piston pin
26. Retaining rings
27. Roller bearing
28. Connecting rod
29. Bearing cage
30. Bearing rollers
31. Rod cap
32. Gasket
33. Exhaust plate
34. Gasket
35. Exhaust cover

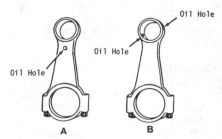

Fig. OM4-13—On connecting rod with one oil hole (view A), install rod with oil hole facing up. On rod with two holes in small end (view B), rod may face either direction.

faces are rough, scored, worn, or show evidence of overheating. Inspect crankpin and main bearing journals for excessive wear, scoring or out-of-round. Connecting rods must be assembled to pistons so long sloping side of piston crown is toward exhaust port side of cylinder block. On models equipped with connecting rod (A—Fig. OM4-13), oil hole in side of rod should face up. On models equipped with rod (B), connecting rod may be installed either side up. Connecting rod caps must be installed on rods with marks on cap and rod aligned.

NOTE: Rod caps and crankpin bearing rollers should never be interchanged.

MANUAL STARTER

The manual starter mounts on intake manifold (5—Fig. OM4-14) and starter rope (4) extends through the lower motor cover. A lockout lever mounted on

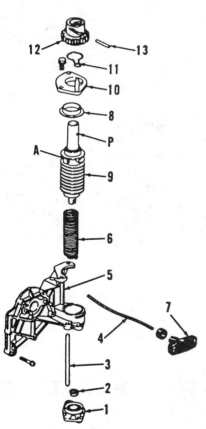

Fig. OM4-14—Exploded view of the manual rewind starter and related components. Intake manifold (5) contains mounting bracket for the starter assembly. Refer to text.

A. Attaching lug
P. Pin hole
1. Retainer plate
2. Bushing
3. Rope guide
4. Starter rope
5. Intake manifold
6. Rewind spring
7. Handle
8. Bushing
9. Spool
10. Bearing head
11. Spring
12. Pinion
13. Roll pin

top of bearing head (10) is used to prevent engagement of pinion gear (12) when throttle control lever is advanced past the START position. The recommended procedure for starter rope (4) renewal differs slightly from that required for starter overhaul; refer to the appropriate following sections for the recommended service procedures.

R&R WORN STARTER ROPE. To renew worn starter rope (4—Fig. OM4-14), first remove engine top cover and disconnect spark plug high tension leads. Pull starter rope (4) until almost fully extended and rope end is accessible in spool (9). Insert a small punch through pin (13) or block pinion (12) into engagement with flywheel as shown in Fig. OM4-15, locking the rewind mechanism. With starter securely locked, disconnect starter rope (4—Fig. OM4-14)) from handle (7) and lug (A). Install new rope (4) by reversing removal procedure. Note that new rope length should 59-1/2 inches (151 cm). While pulling rope (4) taut with handle (7), release pinion (12) and allow rope to slowly rewind. If rope is broken or disconnected, refer to the following section.

R&R BROKEN STARTER ROPE. To renew a broken starter rope (4—Fig. OM4-14), or to reconnect rope after service, proceed as follows: Insert a heavy-duty flat blade screwdriver or other suitable tool through top of pinion (12) and into slot in top of spool (9). Turn screwdriver or suitable tool counterclockwise until lug (A) in spool (9) is accessible. Insert a small punch through pin (13) or lock rewind mechanism as shown in Fig. OM4-15. With starter securely locked, install new rope (4—Fig. OM4-14). Note that new rope should be 59-1/2 inches (151 cm) long.

OVERHAUL. Pull out starter rope (4—Fig. OM4-14) approximately one foot (30 cm), tie a slip knot in rope to prevent rewinding and remove handle (7). Untie knot and allow the rope to slowly wind onto spool (9) until tension on

Fig. OM4-15—The starter pinion can be blocked into engagement with flywheel as shown, thus locking rewind mechanism allowing removal of the starter rope.

rewind spring (6) is fully released. Remove the two cap screws securing upper bearing head (10) to intake manifold (5) and lift off components (6 and 8 through 13) and separate the components.

Inspect all components for excessive wear or other damage and renew as necessary. When reassembling starter, lubricate rewind spring (6) with a light grease. To prevent dirt accumulation, do not lubricate pinion (12) or spool (9). Note the following during reassembly: Align hole (P) in spool (9) with slots in pinion (12), then tap pin (13) through hole and slots. Upper bearing head (10), spring (11) and upper bushing (8) must be properly positioned before installing pinion (12). Make sure slot in lower end of spool (9) engages inner end of rewind spring (6) and enters bushing (2).

LOWER UNIT

PROPELLER AND SHEAR PIN. Shear pin (72—Fig. OM4-16) is used to provide lower unit protection. Optional propellers are available from the manufacturer. Select a propeller that will allow a properly tuned and adjusted engine to operate within the range of 4500-5500 rpm at wide open throttle on 6 and 7.5 hp models and 5000-6000 rpm at wide open throttle on 8 hp models.

R&R AND OVERHAUL. Drain lower unit, remove propeller and shift lower unit into forward gear. Remove three screws securing gearcase and separate gearcase from drive shaft housing. Anode under antiventilation plate may require removal for access to gearcase screws. Place gearcase into a suitable holding fixture. Remove water pump screws and slide housing (5—Fig. OM4-16), impeller (6), key (4) and plate (34) up and off drive shaft (2). Remove three screws and lift bearing housing (56) off drive shaft (2) and lower shift rod (55). Pull drive shaft (2) and shift rod (55) out of gearcase. Remove two screws securing end cap (22). To remove end cap, lightly tap end cap ears with a wooden dowell and hammer so end cap is rotated in gearcase approximately 15 degrees. Using a soft-face mallet, carefully tap ears alternately on each side until end cap is free, then remove end cap and propeller shaft assembly.

To disassemble propeller shaft on models prior to 1988, remove and discard retainer (65). Insert OMC Spring Depressor 390766 into propeller shaft, compress spring (68) and push out pin (67). Slide dog clutch off propeller shaft (69). Remove forward gear (63) by inserting disassembled propeller shaft into gear. Bump shaft toward antiventilation plate with the palm of your hand to pop gear free. Remove forward gear (63), shift cam (61), pinion gear (15), thrust washers (43) and bearing (44).

On 1988 and later models, slide reverse gear (71) and thrust washer (70) off shaft then remove plunger (64—Fig. OM4-17), spring (68) and four detent balls (75). Remove forward gear (63—Fig. OM4-16), shift cam (61), pinion gear (15), thrust washers (43) and bearing (44).

On all models, remove bearings (36 and 37) and forward gear bearing race using a suitable slide-hammer puller.

NOTE: Do not remove bearings (36 and 37) or forward gear bearing race unless renewal is required. Forward gear bearing and race are available only as an assembly.

Inspect all components for excessive wear or other damage and renew as necessary. Renew all seals, "O" rings and gaskets during reassembly. Renew dog clutch retainer (65) on models prior to 1988.

Coat metal case of seals (25) with OMC Gasket Sealing Compound. Install narrow seal into end cap (22) first with lip facing away from propeller. Then install wide seal into end cap with lip facing propeller end. Coat metal case of seals (10) with OMC Gasket Sealing Compound and install back-to-back into housing (56). Pack cavity between seals (25) and (10) with OMC Triple-Guard Grease. Install shift cam (61) into gearcase with the flat side of inside diameter facing port side. On 1988 and later models, install shift cam with "UP" marking facing top of gearcase.

On models prior to 1988, install dog clutch on propeller shaft with end marked "PROP" facing propeller end of gearcase. Compress spring (68) with OMC Spring Depressor 390766 and install pin (67).

On 1988 and later models, install thrust washer (70) with beveled outer diameter toward shoulder on propeller shaft. Slide reverse gear on propeller shaft up to detent ball openings, then install spring (68—Fig. OM4-17) and plunger (64) into shaft (69). Depress plunger to align ramps in plunger with openings in propeller shaft. Install detent balls in openings adjacent to reverse gear, then slide reverse gear over detent balls to retain balls and plunger in propeller shaft. While holding reverse gear in position, install detent balls into

forward gear openings of propeller shaft and install propeller shaft into forward gear. Tighten end cap (22—Fig. OM4-16) screws to 60-84 in.-lbs. (6.8-9.5 N·m).

Complete remainder of reassembly by reversing disassembly procedure. Pressure check gearcase at 3-6 psi (21-41 kPa), then if no leakage is noted, to 16-18 psi (110-124 kPa). Vacuum check gearcase to 3-5 inches HG (10-17 kPa), then if no leakage is noted, to 15 inches HG (51 kPa). If pressure and vacuum

checks indicate no leakage, refill gearcase with recommended lubricant. Apply OMC Moly Lube to drive shaft splines. Do not allow lubricant on top of drive shaft as proper seating of drive shaft in crankshaft may not be possible. Apply OMC Nut Lock or a suitable thread locking compound to gearcase-to-drive shaft housing screws and tighten front screw to 120-144 in.-lbs. (13.5-16.3 N·m) and two rear screws to 60-84 in.-lbs. (6.8-9.5 N·m).

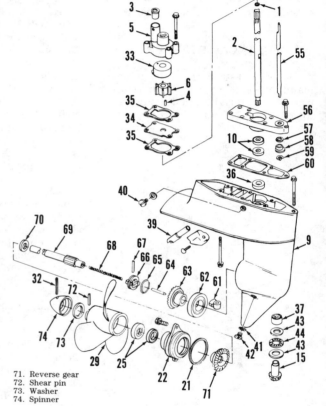

Fig. OM4-16—Exploded view of gearcase assembly. On 1988 and later models, dog clutch is replaced by four detent balls. Refer to Fig. OM4-17.

1. "O" ring
2. Drive shaft
3. Grommet
4. Impeller drive key
5. Water pump housing
6. Impeller
9. Gearcase
10. Seals
15. Pinion gear
21. "O" ring
22. End cap
25. Seals
29. Propeller
32. Cotter pin
33. Liner
34. Plate
35. Gaskets
36. Bearing
37. Bearing
39. Screen
40. Level plug
41. Gasket
42. Drain plug
43. Thrust washers
44. Thrust bearing
55. Lower shift rod
56. Bearing housing
57. "O" ring
58. Guide
59. Retainer
60. Gasket
61. Shift cam
62. Bearing
63. Forward gear
64. Plunger
65. Retainer
66. Dog clutch
67. Pin
68. Spring
69. Propeller shaft
70. Thrust washer
71. Reverse gear
72. Shear pin
73. Washer
74. Spinner

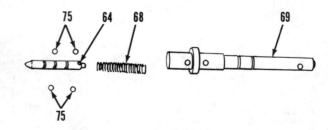

Fig. OM4-17—View of propeller shaft and related components on 1988 and later models. Refer to Fig. OM4-16 for component identification except detent balls (75).

EVINRUDE AND JOHNSON
9½ HP (1969-1973)

Year Produced	EVINRUDE Models	Year Produced	JOHNSON Models
1969	9922, 9923	1969	9R69, 9RL69
1970	9022, 9023	1970	9R70, 9RL70
1971	9122, 9123	1971	9R71, 9RL71
1972	9222, 9223	1972	9R72, 9RL72
1973	9322, 9323	1973	9R73, 9RL73

CONDENSED SERVICE DATA

TUNE-UP

Hp/rpm	9.5/4500
Bore—Inches	2-5/16
Stroke—Inches	1-13/16
Number of Cylinders	2
Displacement—Cu. In.	15.2

Spark Plug:

AC	M42K
Champion	J4J
Auto-Lite	A21X
Electrode Gap	0.030 in.

Magneto:

Point Gap	0.020 in.

Carburetor:

Make	Own
Fuel:Oil Ratio	50:1

SIZES—CLEARANCES (All Values in Inches)
POWER HEAD

Piston Pins:

End Gap	0.007-0.017
Side Clearance	0.001-0.0035
Piston Skirt Clearance	0.0035-0.005

Crankshaft Journal—Diameter:

Top Main Bearing	0.8120-0.8125
Center Main Bearing	0.8127-0.8132

SIZES—CLEARANCES
POWER HEAD CONT.

Lower Main Bearing	0.8120-0.8125
Crankpin	0.8127-0.8132
Diametral Clearance (All)	Roller Bearing
Piston Pin Diametral Clearance in Rod	Roller Bearing

LOWER UNIT

Drive Shaft Bearing Diametral Clearance:

Upper	0.0003-0.002
Lower	0.0013-0.003

Propeller Shaft Diametral Clearance:

Front Gear to Bearing	0.001-0.0022
Front Gear Bushing to Shaft	0.0005-0.0015
Rear Gear to Bushing	0.0005-0.002
Rear Gear Bushing to Shaft	0.0005-0.0015
Gearcase Head to Shaft	0.001-0.002
Propeller to Shaft	0.007-0.009

TIGHTENING TORQUES
(All Values in Inch-Pounds)

Connecting Rod	90-100
Crankcase Halves	120-145
Cylinder Head	96-120
Flywheel	480-540
Spark Plug	210-246

LUBRICATION

The power head is lubricated by mixing oil with the fuel. Recommended oil is BIA certified TC-W outboard oil mixed with the fuel at a ratio of 50:1. In emergencies, two stroke oil other than TC-W outboard oil may be used if mixed at a ratio of 24:1. The amount of oil should be doubled for new or rebuilt motors. Manufacturer recommends using lead free or low lead gasoline with octane rating on pump greater than 85 octane. Regular gasoline may be used in place of lead free or low lead gasoline if octane rating is greater than 85 octane. Make certain that oil and gasoline are thoroughly mixed before filling tank.

The lower unit gears and bearings are lubricated by oil contained in the gearcase. Special OMC Sea-Lube Premium Blend Gearcase Lube should be used. This lubricant is supplied in a tube and filling procedures are as follows: Remove lower plug from gearcase and attach tube. Remove upper (vent) plug from case and, with motor in an upright position, fill gearcase until lubricant reaches level of upper (vent) plug hole. Reinstall vent plug, then remove lubricant tube and reinstall lower plug. Tighten both plugs securely, using new gaskets if necessary, to assure a water-tight seal. Lower gear lubricant should be maintained at level of vent plug, and drained and renewed every 100 hours of operation.

FUEL SYSTEM

CARBURETOR. A float type carburetor is used; refer to Fig. OM5-1 for exploded view.

Normal initial setting for slow speed mixture needle (26) is ¾ turn open from closed position. On all models, the high speed mixture is controlled by a fixed jet (29) and is not adjustable. Orifice of jet (29) should be 0.048 inch diameter.

To set the carburetor float level, first remove the carburetor; then unbolt and remove float chamber (11). Invert carburetor body (13) and check the natural position of float with body inverted. Farthest edge of float should be parallel with carburetor body and measure 13/16-inch from gasket surface of body. With carburetor body in operating position, and float valve open, farthest corner of float should measure 1-7/16 inches from gasket surface. Adjust closed position by carefully bending float arm and open position by

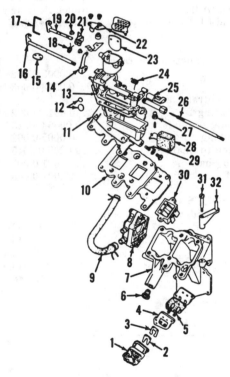

Fig. OM5-1—Exploded view of carburetor, intake manifold and associated parts typical of all 9½ hp models.

1. Cover	17. Link
2. Leaf stop	18. Spring
3. Crankcase valve	19. Choke shaft
4. Valve plate	20. Retainer
5. Screen	22. Bellcrank
6. Bumper	23. Choke plate
7. Intake manifold	24. Spring
8. Fuel pump	25. Throttle lever
9. Fuel line	26. Idle mixture needle
10. Base plate	27. Float valve
11. Float chamber	28. Float
12. Expansion plugs	29. High-speed jet
13. Throttle body	30. Leaf valve assy.
14. Throttle arm	31. Pivot screw
15. Throttle plate	32. Cam follower
16. Throttle shaft	

bending stop tab. Check to be sure float does not bind or rub.

Threaded ends of choke and throttle plate attaching screws are staked during factory assembly. The manufacturer recommends that these shafts and valve plates not be removed when carburetor is cleaned and that a new carburetor body be installed if parts are damaged or worn.

SPEED CONTROL LINKAGE. The speed control lever rotates the magneto armature plate to advance the timing. The throttle valve is synchronized with the plate to open throttle the proper amount as timing is advanced.

To synchronize the linkage, remove top motor cover and move speed control grip until center of cam follower is aligned with index mark on armature plate cam as shown in Fig. OM5-2. The cam, follower, and nylon roller on throttle lever should all be in contact and throttle valve (15—Fig. OM5-1) should be completely closed. If clearance exists or if throttle valve has started to open, loosen the adjustment screw (shown in Fig. OM5-2) and move the throttle lever until slack is removed and throttle is closed. Hold throttle shaft and lever and retighten screw, making sure adjustment is maintained. To further check the adjustment, turn speed control grip to "FAST" position and check to make sure that throttle valve is fully open.

LEAF (REED) VALVES. The inlet leaf valve units (30—Fig. OM5-1) attach to plate (10) located between carburetor body and intake manifold (7).

Leaf petals should seat against "vee" body very lightly throughout their entire length with the least possible tension. Seating surface of body should be smooth and flat.

Valve leaves are available only as an assembly which includes the leaf valves, stops and "V" body for one cylinder as shown at (30). Leaves and leaf stops may be removed for inspection or

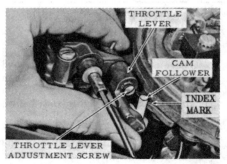

Fig. OM5-2—The index mark on cam should be aligned with center of cam follower when adjusting speed control linkage. The throttle lever adjustment screw holds lever to throttle shaft.

cleaning. When reinstalling, make sure leaves center on alignment marks (A—Fig. IM5-3). If valve leaf, stop or body are damaged, renew the assembly. Never attempt to repair a damaged leaf.

CRANKCASE BLEEDER VALVE. The motor is equipped with a crankcase bleeder valve (3—Fig. OM5-1), designed to remove any liquid fuel or oil which might build up in crankcase. The bleeder valve thus provides smoother operation at all speeds and lessens the possibility of spark plug fouling during slow-speed operation. The crankcase bleeder valves and screens (5) should be checked, and cleaned if necessary, whenever motor is disassembled. Clearance between seated valves and leaf stop (2) should be 0.040 inch; bend stop if necessary, if adjustment is required.

FUEL PUMP AND FILTER. The diaphragm type fuel pump (8—Fig. OM5-1) attaches to side of intake manifold and is actuated by pressure and vacuum pulsations in upper crankcase. The fuel pump is available only as an assembly which contains the filter unit components (3 through 6—Fig. OM5-4).

If fuel pump problems are encountered, first remove and clean the filter

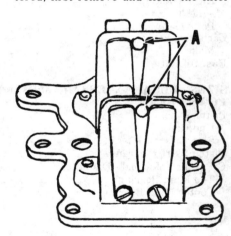

Fig. OM5-3—Inlet leaf valve units should be centered on alignment marks (A) when valves are assembled.

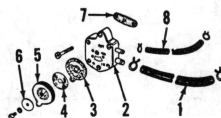

Fig. OM5-4—Fuel pump, fuel filter and associated parts typical of type used.

1. Inlet fuel line	5. Cover
2. Fuel pump	6. Washer
3. Gasket	7. Gasket
4. Filter	8. Outlet fuel line

and blow through fuel lines to be sure they are open and clean; then, if trouble is not corrected, renew the fuel pump assembly.

IGNITION SYSTEM

Breaker point gap should be 0.020 inch and both sets of points should be set to open exactly 180 degrees apart. Flywheel must be removed for breaker point adjustment or inspection.

The recommended method of breaker point adjustment is by using the special timing fixture (OMC Tool 383602) as shown in Fig. OM5-5; and a timing test light. Any test light or meter which indicates an open and closed circuit is satisfactory.

To adjust the points using the special tools, disconnect condenser and magneto coil leads from both sets of points and install the timing fixture over crankshaft and flywheel key as shown in Fig. OM5-5. Turn crankshaft until either end of pointer is aligned midway between the two lugs (TM) on armature plate. Attach the test light or meter to a suitable ground and to the terminal on the opening set of points; then adjust the gap until the points just open as indicated by test lamp going out. Turn crankshaft 180° until opposite end of pointer is midway between timing lugs (TM) and adjust the other set of points in the same manner.

To adjust the points without the special tools, adjust each gap to exactly 0.020 inch when flywheel key is aligned with rub block on moveable point.

Except for the permanent magnet built into the flywheel, the ignition systems consists of a separate coil, condenser, point set and wiring for each cylinder. When ignition troubles are encountered, check point condition and gap adjustment; check also for loose or corroded connections, damaged insulation and broken wires. The three ends of the laminated coil core should be flush with machined bosses on armature plate (F—Fig. OM5-5).

If crankshaft key has been removed while motor is disassembled, make sure that upset mark (M—Fig. OM5-6) is installed in end of slot nearest to crankcase as shown; and that outer flat surface of key is aligned with crankshaft centerline as shown at (A). DO NOT align edge of key with crankshaft taper. Use a suitable non-oily solvent and carefully clean all oil and grease from mating tapered surfaces of flywheel and crankshaft before flywheel installation, to prevent movement and wear of key and keyways after assembly. The breaker point cam should be installed with side marked "TOP" facing up.

COOLING SYSTEM

WATER PUMP. The motor is equipped with a rubber impeller type water pump which is mounted on and driven by the lower unit drive shaft. At slow speeds the flexible impeller blades follow the contour of the eccentric housing and the pump delivers cooling water by the displacement principle. As speed increases, the blades curve backward and coolant delivery becomes partially centrifugal, thus maintaining a relatively constant coolant flow regardless of engine speed.

When cooling problems are encountered, first check the water inlet for plugging or partial stoppage, then check the thermostat for proper operation. If the difficulty is not thus corrected, remove the lower unit gearcase as outlined in the appropriate section and check the condition of water pump, water passages, gaskets and sealing surfaces. The main water inlet is located below the exhaust outlet, above and behind the propeller, and a secondary inlet is located in the cover on port side of gearcase housing just above the anticavitation plate.

THERMOSTAT. A thermostat is used to regulate operating temperature. The thermostat is calibrated to control temperature within the range

of 145°-150°. Thermostat can be removed for inspection or renewal by first removing upper motor cover; then removing thermostat housing cover located on upper side of cylinder head. Refer to Fig. OM5-12 or OM5-13 for exploded view of power head castings showing thermostat (19) and associated parts.

POWER HEAD

REMOVE AND REINSTALL. To remove the power head, first remove upper motor cover, carburetor and flywheel. Disconnect inlet fuel line from pump and hose (4—Fig. OM5-11) from exhaust cover. Remove the four screws (X—Fig. OM5-7), disconnect speed control linkage and remove magneto armature plate. Shift to "Forward" position and remove cap screws securing gearcase to exhaust housing. Separate gearcase from exhaust housing far enough to remove shift rod clamp lower screw shown in Fig. OM5-19; then withdraw

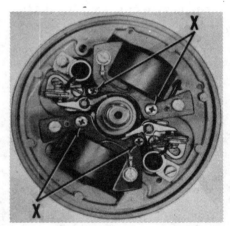

Fig. OM5-7—The magneto armature plate can be removed after disconnecting speed control linkage and removing the four screws (X).

Fig. OM5-9—On all models, one lower cover attaching screw is in position shown. Detent screw (22) is also shown in Fig. OM5-11.

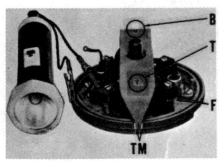

Fig. OM5-5—Breaker points should just open when pointer on timing fixture is between marks (TM). Use end marked (B) for setting other points for bottom cylinder.

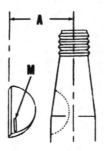

Fig. OM5-6—Flywheel key must be installed with outer flat edge parallel with crankshaft center line as shown at (A). Make sure upset mark (M) is toward cylinders to assure correct magneto timing.

gearcase and drive shaft assembly. Remove detent screw (22—Fig. OM5-9) and withdraw gear shift lever. Remove the lower cover attaching screw shown in Fig. OM5-9 and the five screws (A—Fig. OM5-10). Remove the two screws (B) securing steering friction plate to both lower covers. Remove nut (C) and cap screw (D) and lift off starboard cover (14). Loosen the two exhaust cover screws retaining port side stabilizer (31—Fig. OM5-13) to power head. Slide stabilizer in slotted holes and away from the two exhaust cover screws. Remove cap nut (E—Fig. OM5-10) and the two screws (F) and lift power head and exhaust housing off cover, swivel bracket and stern bracket assembly. Remove cotter pins and washer securing shift link (18—Fig. OM5-11) to upper shift rod (25); remove attaching cap screws, and separate power head and exhaust housing (8).

Install by reversing the removal procedure.

DISASSEMBLE AND REASSEMBLE. To disassemble the removed power head, refer to Fig. OM5-13. Remove the cap screws securing armature plate support (23) to crankcase; and lift off support and retaining ring (24). Remove cylinder head (12), exhaust covers (26 through 30) and intake manifold. Tap out the two taper pins (6), by working from cylinder block side of crankcase. Remove the retaining cap screws and separate the crankcase halves. Pistons, rods, crankshaft and bearings are now accessible for removal and overhaul as outlined in the appropriate following paragraphs.

The crankcase and intake manifold must be completely sealed against vacuum and pressure during reassembly. Exhaust manifold and cylinder head must be sealed against pressure and water leakage. Mating surfaces of

water intake and exhaust passages between power head and exhaust housing must form a tight seal.

Whenever the power head is disassembled, it is recommended that all gasket surfaces and the mating surfaces of crankcase halves be carefully checked for nicks, burrs or warped surfaces which might interfere with a tight seal. The cylinder head, head end of cylinder block, or mating surfaces of manifolds and crankcase may be lapped, if necessary, to provide a smooth surface. Do not remove any more metal than is necessary. Mating surfaces of crankcase halves may be checked on the lapping block, and high spots or nicks removed, but surface must not be lowered. If extreme care is used, a slightly damaged crankcase may be salvaged in this manner. In case of doubt, renew the crankcase assembly.

The crankcase halves are positively located during assembly by the use of two tapered dowel pins (6). Check to make sure that the dowels are not bent, nicked or distorted, and that dowel holes are clean and true. When installing dowel pins, make sure they are fully seated, but do not use excessive force. Upper and lower main bearings are positively located in their bores by dowels (8) which enter a hole in bearing race. Make sure holes are aligned with dowels when reassembling.

The mating surfaces of crankcase halves must be sealed during assembly by using a non-hardening cement such as OMC Adhesive "M". Make sure that all old cement is removed and that surfaces are flat and free from nicks

Fig. OM5-11—Exploded view of lower motor covers, exhaust housing and associated parts.

1. Port cover	17. Clamp screw
2. Clamp	18. Link
3. Clamp	19. Shift arm
4. Exhaust relief	20. Shift bracket
5. Rubber mount	21. Detent
6. Bumper	22. Detent screw
7. Lower mount	23. Link
8. Exhaust housing	24. Interlock arm
9. Shift rod boot	25. Shift rod
10. Plate	26. Seal
11. Bumper	27. Guide
12. Rubber mount	28. Pilot ring
13. Bumper	29. Seal retainer
14. Starboard cover	30. Seal clamp
15. Shift lever	31. Seal
16. Bushing	

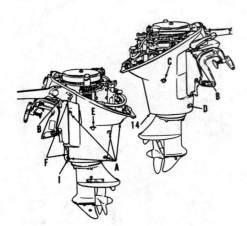

Fig. OM5-10—Port and starboard views of motor showing removal sequence for lower motor covers. Refer to text.

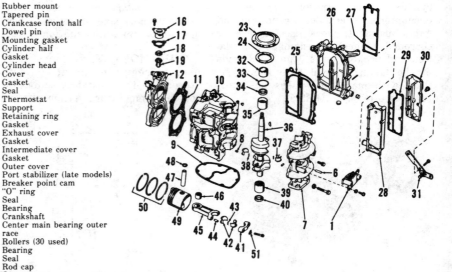

1. Rubber mount	
6. Tapered pin	
7. Crankcase front half	
8. Dowel pin	
9. Mounting gasket	
10. Cylinder half	
11. Gasket	
12. Cylinder head	
16. Cover	
17. Gasket	
18. Seal	
19. Thermostat	
23. Support	
24. Retaining ring	
25. Gasket	
26. Exhaust cover	
27. Gasket	
28. Intermediate cover	
29. Gasket	
30. Outer cover	
31. Port stabilizer (late models)	
32. Breaker point cam	
33. "O" ring	
34. Seal	
35. Bearing	
36. Crankshaft	
37. Center main bearing outer race	
38. Rollers (30 used)	
39. Bearing	
40. Seal	
41. Rod cap	
42. Outer race	
43. Rollers (30 each rod)	
44. Dowel (2 each rod)	
45. Connecting rod	

46. Bearing	48. Retainer	50. Ring set
47. Piston pin	49. Piston	51. Lock plate

Fig. OM5-13—Exploded view of typical power head assembly.

and burrs. Apply cement sparingly and evenly to cylinder half of crankcase only; then immediately install front half. Install the locating dowel pins; then install the crankcase screws. Tighten retaining cap screws to a torque of 120-145 inch-pounds. Temporarily install flywheel or other suitable tool and check for binding or misassembly by turning crankshaft.

Install cylinder head and tighten retaining cap screws to a torque of 96-120 inch-pounds, using the sequence shown in Fig. OM5-14. Cap screws should be retightened, using the same torque and sequence, after motor has been run-in and allowed to cool.

Reinstall magneto armature support (23—Fig. OM5-13) and retaining ring (24). Complete the assembly by reversing the disassembly procedure.

PISTONS, PINS, RINGS AND CYLINDERS. Before detaching connecting rod caps from crankshaft, make certain that rod and cap are properly marked for correct assembly to each other and in the correct cylinder.

Each aluminum piston is fitted with three rings which are pinned to prevent rotation in grooves. Pistons and rings are available in standard size and oversizes. The recommended piston end gap, ring to groove clearance and piston to cylinder wall clearance is listed in the CONDENSED SERVICE DATA table. Renew pistons, rings and/or cylinder if clearances are excessive.

The piston pin is a loose fit in one piston boss and a press fit in other boss. The loose piston pin boss is stamped "LOOSE." When removing or installing piston pin, work from side of piston having the loose pin boss. Pin end of connecting rod contains a needle roller bearing.

When reassembling, long tapering side of piston head must go toward exhaust port side of cylinder; and the side of rod containing the oil hole and "UP" marking should be toward flywheel end of crankshaft. Refer to Fig. OM5-15.

CONNECTING RODS, BEARINGS AND CRANKSHAFT. Before detaching connecting rods from crankshaft, make sure that rods and caps are properly marked for correct assembly to each other and in the proper cylinder.

Crankshaft end of connecting rods contain loose needle rollers which ride in renewable split races in connecting rods and use the hardened, machined crankpins as inner races. Piston end of connecting rod contains a caged needle roller bearing (46—Fig. OM5-13).

Upper and lower main crankshaft journals ride in caged needle bearings (35 & 39) which also contain the bore for crankshaft seals (34 & 40). The center main bearing uses 30 needle rollers (38) which ride directly on the crankshaft center journal and split outer races (37). Upper and lower main bearings contain a locating hole to accept a dowel pin (8) in cylinder half of crankcase. Connecting rod must be installed on crankshaft with "UP" marking and oil hole toward flywheel end of shaft.

All friction surfaces must be lubricated during assembly. Tighten connecting rod cap screws to a torque of 90-100 inch-pounds and lock in place by bending a corner of lock plate (51).

MANUAL STARTER

Refer to Fig. OM5-17 for an exploded view of starter assembly. Starter mounts on inner exhaust cover (14) and rope (13) extends through lower motor cover, necessitating removal of starter rope before power head can be removed. The suggested procedure for rope renewal differs slightly from that required for power head removal or starter service; proceed as outlined for the type of service contemplated.

R&R STARTER ROPE. To renew the starter rope, first remove upper motor cover and remove and ground the spark plug wires. Pull rope until almost fully extended, with rope-end in spool (7—Fig. OM5-17) accessible. Insert a suitable block or wedge between upper bearing head (11) and pinion (9), to hold pinion in engagement with

Fig. OM5-16—The starter pinion can be wedged up as shown for removing or installing rope.

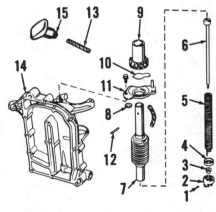

Fig. OM5-17—Exploded view of recoil starter and associated parts. Starter mounts on brackets are cast into exhaust cover.

1. Set screw	
2. Retainer	
3. Bushing	9. Pinion
4. Outer bearing	10. Spring
5. Recoil spring	11. Bearing head
6. Retainer	12. Roll pin
7. Spool	13. Rope
8. Gasket	14. Exhaust cover
	15. Grip

Fig. OM5-14—When installing cylinder head, tighten retaining cap screws to a torque of 96-120 inch-pounds using the sequence shown.

Fig. OM5-15—Side of connecting rod with "UP" marking contains an oil hole and should be installed toward flywheel end of crankshaft.

flywheel ring gear and prevent starter recoil. Refer to Fig. OM5-16. With starter thus secured, remove the rope. Install a new rope by reversing the removal procedure. With rope secured at both ends, remove the wedge and allow starter to recoil. If rope is broken or disconnected, assemble as outlined for service removal.

To disconnect starter rope for service removal of starter, pull out starter rope about a foot and tie a slip knot in rope to prevent complete recoil. Remove grip (15), then untie the temporary knot and allow rope to slowly enter hole in lower motor cover until recoil spring is fully unwound. Starter can now be removed.

To reconnect starter rope after service, proceed as follows: Insert a heavy-duty screwdriver or brace with screwdriver bit through top of pinion (9) and into slot in top of upper spring retainer (6). Turn screwdriver or brace counterclockwise approximately 20½ turns until rope anchor in spool (7) is easily accessible; then engage pinion (9) in teeth of flywheel ring gear. Lock the assembly by inserting a suitable wedge between pinion and upper bearing head. Refer to Fig. OM5-16. Thread the rope through anchor hole in spool (7—Fig. OM5-17) and hole in lower

motor cover. Anchor inner end with a knot and install grip (15) on outer end. With both ends of rope secured, remove the previously installed locking block and allow starter to slowly recoil.

OVERHAUL. To overhaul the starter, first disconnect starter rope as previously outlined for service, and allow recoil spring to unwind. Remove the two cap screws securing upper bearing head (11—Fig. OM5-17) to exhaust cover and lift off the starter assembly.

Drive out the roll pin (12) and remove set screw (1), then separate the starter components. Wash the parts in a suitable solvent and renew any which are worn, damaged or questionable.

When assembling the starter, lubricate the recoil spring (5) with a light grease. Pinion (9) and spool (7) should not be lubricated, but installed dry to prevent dust accumulation. Place outer bearing (4), bushing (3) and lower spring retainer (2) on lower end of recoil spring (5) and lock the assembly by tightening set screw (1). Assemble pinion (9), spring (10), and bearing head (11) over upper end of spool. Inset upper spring retainer (6); align pin holes in spring retainer (6) and spool (7) with engaging slots in pinion (9), then insert roll pin (12). Split in roll pin

should be horizontal to prevent binding in pinion engaging slots. Assemble upper and lower starter components with a twisting motion to engage upper end of spring with retainer (6), and install by reversing the removal procedure. Install rope and adjust recoil spring as outlined in the previous paragraph.

LOWER UNIT

PROPELLER AND DRIVE PIN. Cushioning protection of propeller and drive unit is built into propeller hub. Service consist of renewing the propeller.

Propeller clutch can be tested using a torque wrench and a suitable holding fixture and adapter. The cushioning clutch should slip at a torque of 80-120 ft.-lbs. An 8¼-inch diameter, 8-inch pitch or 8-1/8-inch diameter, 8-inch pitch, three-blade propeller is used. Drive pin (25—Fig. OM5-18) should be 3/16 x 1-25/64 inch stainless steel.

REMOVE AND REINSTALL. Most service on the lower unit can be performed by detaching the gearcase housing from exhaust housing. When servicing lower unit, pay particular attention to water pump and water tubes with respect to air or water leaks. Leaky connections may interfere with proper cooling of the motor.

Refer to Fig. OM5-18 for an exploded view of gearcase and associated parts and to Fig. OM5-20 for an exploded view of suspension units.

The propeller shaft (17—Fig. OM5-18) and drive gears (7 and 20) can be removed after first draining lubricant from gear housing, removing pivot screw (12), then unbolting and removing gearcase lower housing (14).

To separate the gearcase assembly from exhaust housing, place gear shift lever in "FORWARD" position and remove the gearcase retaining cap screws. Separate gearcase from exhaust housing far enough to remove the connector screw from shift lever clamp (3); then withdraw the gearcase and drive

Fig. OM5-18—Exploded view of lower unit gearcase and associated parts used on 9½ horsepower models. Items (42 through 45) are used on "Long" models only.

1. "O" ring
2. Shaft
3. Connector
4. Shift rod
5. Detent unit
6. Bushing
7. Forward gear
8. Thrust washer
9. Clutch dog
10. Cradle
11. Shift lever
12. Pivot pin
13. Plug
14. Gearcase half
15. Seal strip
16. Dowel
17. Propeller shaft
18. Drive pinion
19. Thrust washer
20. Reverse gear
21. Bushing
22. Gearcase head
23. "O" ring
24. Seal
25. Drive pin
26. Propeller
27. Nut
28. Screen
29. Gearcase
30. Inlet cover
31. Plug
32. Gasket
33. Plug
34. Bearing housing
35. Seal
36. Plate
37. Impeller
38. Housing
39. Washer
40. Seal
41. Grommet
42. Spacer
43. Extension
44. Seal
45. "O" ring

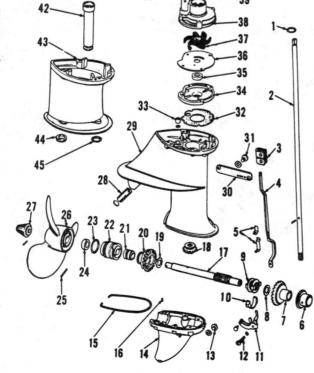

Fig. OM5-19—When removing the gearcase, the shift rod coupling must be disconnected by removing the lower coupling screw.

shaft as an assembly. Refer to Fig. OM5-19.

When reinstalling gearcase on exhaust housing, coat bore of water pump housing grommet (41—Fig. OM5-18) with oil or liquid soap to act as a lubricant. Install a new "O" ring (1) in groove in upper end of drive shaft. Carefully guide water tube into position in pump housing as parts are assembled. Turn propeller shaft, if necessary, to align drive shaft upper splines; however, make sure drive shaft turns only in a forward (clockwise) direction to keep from damaging water pump impeller. Reconnect shift rod, then secure gearcase to exhaust housing using a non-hardening sealer on screw threads.

OVERHAUL. Refer to CONDENSED SERVICE DATA tables for clearance specifications of gears and bushings and to Fig. OM5-18 for components location.

Clean all parts in a suitable solvent and examine for scoring, wear or other damage. Use new seals, gaskets and "O" rings when reassembling. Fit sealing strip (15) in groove in lower gearcase housing and cut ends squarely, 1/32-inch beyond ends of grooves, to assure a good seal. Apply a thin coat of non-hardening cement such as OMC Adhesive "M" to joints between gearcase halves, and use a non-hardening thread sealer on cap screw threads.

Check for free operation of gears and shift mechanism and refill lower unit gearcase with OMC Sea-Lube Premium Blend Gearcase Lube following the procedure outlined in LUBRICATION paragraph.

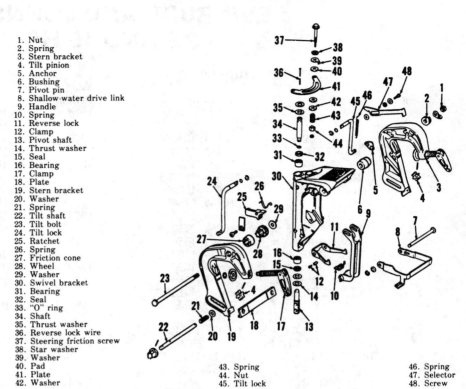

1. Nut
2. Spring
3. Stern bracket
4. Tilt pinion
5. Anchor
6. Bushing
7. Pivot pin
8. Shallow-water drive link
9. Handle
10. Spring
11. Reverse lock
12. Clamp
13. Pivot shaft
14. Thrust washer
15. Seal
16. Bearing
17. Clamp
18. Plate
19. Stern bracket
20. Washer
21. Spring
22. Tilt shaft
23. Tilt bolt
24. Tilt lock
25. Ratchet
26. Spring
27. Friction cone
28. Wheel
29. Washer
30. Swivel bracket
31. Bearing
32. Seal
33. "O" ring
34. Shaft
35. Thrust washer
36. Reverse lock wire
37. Steering friction screw
38. Star washer
39. Washer
40. Pad
41. Plate
42. Washer
43. Spring
44. Nut
45. Tilt lock
46. Spring
47. Selector
48. Screw

Fig. OM5-20—Exploded view of stern bracket, swivel bracket and associated parts used on 9½ horsepower models.

ADJUSTMENTS. Shift mechanism adjustment is fixed, however, shift lever can be repositioned with relation to symbols on lower motor housing by loosening the clamp screw (17—Fig. OM5-11) and repositioning lever (15).

Steering friction can be adjusted by turning friction screw (37—Fig. OM5-20) after removing upper motor cover. Tilting friction can be adjusted by tightening or loosening pivot bolt nut (1) on outside of port stern bracket.

EVINRUDE AND JOHNSON
9.9 AND 15 HP

EVINRUDE MODELS			JOHNSON MODELS		
Year Produced	**9.9 hp**	**15 hp**	**Year Produced**	**9.9 hp**	**15 hp**
			1974......	10R74, 10RL74	15R74, 15RL74
				*10E74, *10EL74	*15E74, *15EL74
1974......	10424, 10425	15404, 15405	1975......	10R75, 10RL75	15R75, 15RL75
	*10454, *10455	*15454, *15455		*10E75, *10EL75	*15E75, *15EL75
1975......	10524, 10525	15504, 15505	1976......	10R76, 10RL76	15R76, 15RL76
	*10554, *10555	*15554, *15555		*10E76, *10EL76	*15E76, *15EL76
1976......	10624, 10625	15604, 15605	1977......	10R77, 10RL77	15R77, 15RL77
	*10654, *10655	*15654, *15655		*10E77, *10EL77	*15E77, *15EL77
1977......	10724, 10725	15704, 15705	1978......	10R78, 10RL78	15R78, 15RL78
	*10754, *10755	*10754, *15755		*10EL78, *10SEL78	*15E78, *15EL78
1978......	10824, 10825	15804, 15805	1979......	10R79, 10RL79	15R79, 15RL79
	*10835, *10855	*15854, *15855		*10EL79, *10SEL79	*15E79, *15EL79
1979......	10924, 10925	15904, 15905	1980......	10RCS, 10RLCS	15RCS, 15RLCS
	*10935, *10955	*15954, *15955		*10ELCS,	*15ECS, *15ELCS
1980......	10RCS, 10RLCS	15RCS, 15RLCS		*10SELCS	
	*10ELCS,	*15ECS, *15ELCS	1981......	10RCI, 10RLCI,	15RCI, 15RLCI
	*10ELCS			*10ELCI	*15ECI
1981......	10RCI, 10RLCI	15RCI, 15RLCI		*10SELCI	
	*10ELCI, *10SELCI	*15ECI	1982......	10RCN, 10RLCN	15RCN, 15RLCN
1982......	10RCN, 10RLCN	15RCN, 15RLCN		*10ELCN,	*15ECN
	*10ELCN,	*15ECN		*10SELCN	
	*10SELCN		1983......	10RCT, 10RLCT	15RCT, 15RLCT
1983......	E10RCT, E10RLCT	E15RCT, E15RLCT		*10SELCT	*15ECT, *15ELCT
	*E10SELCT	*E15ECT, *E15ELCT	1984......	10RCR, 10RLCR	15RCR, 15RLCR
1984......	E10RCR, E10RLCR	E15RCR, E15RLCR		*10ELCR	*15ECR, *15ELCR
	*E10ELCR	*E15ECR, *E15ELCR	1985......	10RCO, 10RLCO	15RCO, 15RLCO
1985......	E10RCO, E10RLCO	E15RCO, E15RLCO		*10ECO, *10ELCO	*15ECO, *15ELCO
	*E10ECO, *E10ELCO	*E15ECO, *E15ELCO	1986......	J10RCD, J10RLCD	J15RCD, J15RLCD
1986......	E10RCD, E10RLCD	E15RCD, E15RLCD		*J10ECD, *J10ELCD	*J15ECD, *J15ELCD
	*E10ECD, *E10ELCD	*E15ECD, *E15ELCD	1987......	J10RCU, J10RLCU	J15RCU, *J15ECU
1987......	E10RCU, E10RLCU	E15RCU, *E15ECU		J10BACU, J10BALCU	J15RLCU, *J15ELCU
	E10BACU, E10BALCU	E15RLCU, *E15ELCU		*J10ECU, *J10ELCU	J15BACU, J15BALCU
	*E10ECU, *E10ELCU	E15BACU, E15BALCU		*J10SELCU	
	*E10SELCU		1988......	J10RCC, J10RLCC	J15RCC, *J15ECC
1988......	E10RCC, E10RLCC	E15RCC, *E15ECC		J10BACC, J10BALCC	J15RLCC, *J15ELCC
	E10BACC, E10BALCC	E15RLCC, *E15ELCC		*J10ECC, *J10ELCC	J15BACC, J15BALCC
	*E10ECC, *E10ELCC	E15BACC, E15BALCC		*J10SELCC	
	*E10SELCC		1989......	J10RCE, J10RLCE	J15RCE, *J15ECE
1989......	E10RCE, E10RLCE	E15RCE, *E15ECE		J10BACE, J10BALCE	J15RLCE, *J15ELCE
	E10BACE, E10BALCE	E15RLCE, *E15ELCE		*J10ECE, *J10ELCE	J15BACE, J15BALCE
	*E10ECE, *E10ELCE	E15BACE, E15BALCE		*J10SELCE	J15SPLCE
	*E10SELCE	E15SPLCE			

*Electric start models.

CONDENSED SERVICE DATA

TUNE-UP

Hp/rpm—
  9.9 Hp:
    Prior to 1989.....................9.9/5000-6000
                                            (7.4 kW)
    1989 ....9.9/5500-6500
                                            (7.4 kW)
  9.9 Hp SEL (1989) 9.9/5000-6000
                                            (7.4 kW)
  15 Hp 15/5500-7000
                                            (11.2 kW)
Bore ....2.188 in.
                                            (55.58 mm)

TUNE-UP CONT.

Stroke ....1.760 in.
                                            (44.70 mm)
Number of Cylinders...........................2
Displacement.........................13.2 cu. in.
                                            (216.3 cc)
Spark Plug—Champion:
  1974-1976.................................UL4J
    Electrode Gap ....0.030 in.
                                            (0.76 mm)
  1977-1989............................QL77JC4*
    Electrode Gap ....0.040 in.
                                            (1.0 mm)

CONDENSED SERVICE DATA CONT.

TUNE-UP CONT.

Ignition Type:
1974-1976 . . . . .Breaker Point
   Breaker Point Gap .0.020 in.
                                        (0.51 mm)
1977-1989 . . . . .Capacitor Discharge
Carburetor Make . . . . .OMC
Idle Speed (in gear) . . . . .650-700 rpm†
Fuel:Oil Ratio . . . . .See Text

*Champion QL78V surface gap spark plug is recommended for models used at sustained high speeds. Renew surface gap spark plug if center electrode is more than 1/32 inch (0.79 mm) below flat surface of spark plug end.
†For optimum results, check and adjust idle speed with boat in the water with the correct propeller installed. Engine should be running in gear at normal operating temperature with boat movement unrestrained.

SIZES—CLEARANCES

Piston Ring End Gap . . . . .0.005-0.015 in.
                                    (0.13-0.38 mm)
Lower Piston Ring Side Clearance:
1974-1984 . . . . .0.0025-0.0035 in.
                               (0.064-0.089 mm)
1985-1989 . . . . .0.004 in. Max.
                                     (0.10 mm)
Piston Skirt Clearance:
1974-1978 . . . . .0.0025-0.0053 in.
                               (0.064-0.135 mm)
1979-1984 . . . . .0.0025-0.0038 in.
                               (0.064-0.096 mm)
After 1984 . . . .*
Standard Cylinder Bore Diameter . . . . .2.1875-2.1883 in.
                               (55.562-55.583 mm)
Wear Limit . . . . .0.002 in.
                                     (0.05 mm)
Max. Allowable Taper:
Prior to 1985 . . . . .0.003 in.
                                     (0.08 mm)
1985-1989 . . . . .0.002 in.
                                     (0.05 mm)
Max. Allowable Out-of-Round:
Prior to 1985 . . . . .0.003 in.
                                     (0.08 mm)
1985-1986 . . . . .0.002 in.
                                     (0.05 mm)
1987-1989 . . . . .0.003 in.
                                     (0.08 mm)
Crankshaft Journal Diameters—
Top Main:
1974 . . . . .0.8120-0.8125 in.
                              (20.625-20.637 mm)
1975 . . . . .0.8752-0.8757 in.
                              (22.230-22.243 mm)
1976-1989 .0.8757-0.8762 in.
Center Main: (22.243-22.255 mm)
1974-1989 . . . . .0.8120-0.8125 in.
                              (20.625-20.637 mm)
Bottom Main:
1974-1984 . . . . .0.8120-0.8125 in.
                              (20.625-20.637 mm)
1985-1989 . . . . .0.7870-0.7874 in.
                              (19.990-20.000 mm)

SIZES—CLEARANCES CONT.

Crankpin:
1974-1979 . . . . .1.0630-1.0635 in.
                            (27.000-27.013 mm)
1980-1981 . . . . .0.8120-0.8125 in.
                            (20.625-20.637 mm)
1982 . . . . .1.0630-1.0635 in.
                            (27.000-27.013 mm)
1983 . . . . .0.8120-0.8125 in.
                            (20.625-20.637 mm)
1984 . . . . .0.7870-0.7874 in.
                            (19.990-20.000 mm)
1985-1989 . . . . .0.8120-0.8125 in.
                            (20.625-20.637 mm)

*The manufacturer does not specify piston skirt clearance on models after 1984. If cylinder bore and piston are within tolerance, piston clearance should be acceptable. Refer to text.

TIGHTENING TORQUES

Connecting Rod:
1974-1985 . . . . .48-60 in.-lbs.
                                   (5.4-6.8 N·m)
1986-1989 . . . . .60-70 in.-lbs.
                                   (6.8-7.9 N·m)
Crankcase-to-Cylinder Block:
1974-1985 . . . . .145-170 in.-lbs.
                                 (16.4-19.2 N·m)
1986-1989:
  Small Screws . . . . .60-84 in.-lbs.
                                 (6.8-9.5 N·m)
  Large Screws . . . . .144-168 in.-lbs.
                                 (16.3-19.0 N·m)
Cylinder Head:
1974-1977 . . . . .145-170 in.-lbs.
                                 (16.4-19.2 N·m)
1978-1989 . . . . .216-240 in.-lbs.
                                 (24.4-27.1 N·m)
Flywheel . . . . .45-50 ft.-lbs.
                                 (61.0-67.8 N·m)
Spark Plug:
1974-1985 . . . . .210-246 in.-lbs.
                                 (23.7-27.8 N·m)
1986-1989 . . . . .216-240 in.-lbs.
                                 (24.4-27.1 N·m)
Standard Screws:
No. 6 . . . . .7-10 in.-lbs.
                                   (0.8-1.1 N·m)
No. 8 . . . . .15-22 in.-lbs.
                                   (1.7-2.5 N·m)
No. 10 . . . . .25-35 in.-lbs.
                                   (2.8-4.0 N·m)
No. 12 . . . . .35-40 in.-lbs.
                                   (4.0-4.5 N·m)
1/4 inch . . . . .60-80 in.-lbs.
                                   (6.8-9.0 N·m)
5/16 inch . . . . .120-140 in.-lbs.
                                 (13.6-15.8 N·m)
3/8 inch . . . . .18-20 ft.-lbs.
                                 (24.4-27.1 N·m)
7/16 inch . . . . .28-30 ft.-lbs.
                                 (38.0-40.7 N·m)

LUBRICATION

The power head is lubricated by oil mixed with the fuel. The recommended fuel is regular leaded or unleaded gasoline with a minimum octane rating of 67 on models produced after 1980, or octane rating of 86 on models prior to 1981. If the recommended fuel is not available, gasoline containing not more than ten percent ethanol alcohol, or gasoline containing not more than five percent methanol alcohol with five percent co-solvent additives may be used. Do not use gasoline exceeding the specified alcohol content regardless of octane rating. Discontinue the use of alcohol extended gasoline if fuel system problems are encountered.

The recommended oil is Evinrude or Johnson Outboard Lubricant or a suitable equivalent NMMA (formerly known as BIA) certified TC-W or TC-WII engine oil. The manufacturer recommends using only oil certified TC-WII on 1989 models. The recommended fuel:oil ratio for normal service and during engine break-in is 50:1.

NOTE: OMC service bulletin 2211 issued September 1988, recommends using a 50:1 fuel:oil ratio on all recreational outboard motors which were previously recommended for a 100:1 fuel:oil mixture. For 1989, Accumix and Accumix R fuel and oil mixing systems have been changed to a 50:1 ratio.

On models so recommended, a 100:1 fuel:oil mixture may be used if an approved oil formulated for 100:1 mixture is used and if the engine is completely broken-in and motor is used on a frequent basis. Do not use a 100:1 mixture if motor is used infrequently and during nonuse the motor is stored in areas of high humidity or wide-scale temperature changes, or if motor is operated at constant high speeds.

The lower unit gears and bearings are lubricated by oil contained in the gearcase. The recommended oil is OMC HI-VIS Gearcase Lube. The gearcase oil level should be checked after every 50 hours of operation and the gearcase should be drained and filled with new oil every 100 hours or once each season, whichever occurs first.

The gearcase oil is drained and filled through the same plug port. An oil level (vent) port is used to indicate the full level of the gearcase with oil and to ease oil drainage.

To drain oil, place the outboard motor in a vertical position. Remove drain plug and oil level plug and allow the lubricant to drain into a suitable container.

To fill the gearcase with oil, place the outboard motor in a vertical position.

Add oil through drain plug opening with an oil feeder until the oil begins to overflow from oil level plug port. Reinstall oil level plug with a new gasket, if needed, and tighten. Remove oil feeder, then reinstall drain plug with a new gasket, if needed, and tighten.

FUEL SYSTEM

CARBURETOR. Models prior to 1987 and some late production 1986 models are equipped with the carburetor shown in Fig. OM6-1. Refer to Fig. OM6-2 for exploded view of carburetor used on later models.

NOTE: The manufacturer does not recommend submerging carburetor components in carburetor or parts cleaning solutions. An aerosol type carburetor cleaner is recommended to clean carburetor. The float and other components made of plastic and rubber should not be subjected to some cleaning solutions. Safety eyewear and hand protection are recommended when working with solvent.

Initial setting of low speed mixture needle is one turn out from a lightly seated position on models equipped with carburetor shown in Fig. OM6-1 and 2-1/2 turns out from a lightly seated

position on models equipped with carburetor shown in Fig. OM6-2. Make final idle mixture adjustment with engine running in gear at normal operating temperature. High speed air:fuel mixture is metered by fixed high speed jet (2—Fig. OM6-1 or Fig. OM6-2). Idle speed should be 650-700 rpm on all models. For optimum results when adjusting idle speed, boat should be in the water with the correct propeller installed. Engine should be running in forward gear at normal operating temperature with boat movement unrestrained.

To check float level, remove float bowl and invert carburetor. Place OMC Float Gage 324891 on float bowl gasket surface as shown in Fig. OM6-3. Use notch marked 9.9 and 15. Make sure float gage is not pushing down on float. Float should be between specified notches on gage. Carefully bend float arm to adjust. If OMC float gage 324891 is not available, adjust so float is level and parallel with float bowl gasket surface. To check float drop, hold carburetor upright and allow float to hang by its own weight. Measure from float bowl mating surface to bottom of float 180 degrees from inlet needle. Float drop should be 1-1/8 to 1-1/2 inches (28.6-38.1 mm) on models equipped with carburetor shown in Fig. OM6-1 and 1 to 1-3/8 inches (25.4-34.9 mm) on models equipped with carbure-

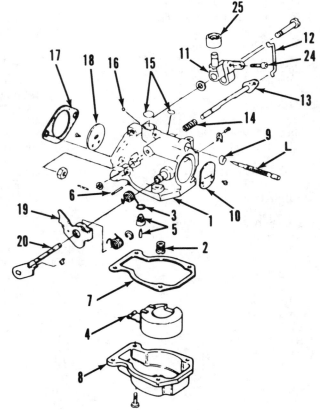

Fig. OM6-1—Exploded view of carburetor typical of the type used on models prior to 1987.

- L. Low speed mixture needle
- 1. Body
- 2. Main jet
- 3. Gasket
- 4. Float
- 5. Fuel inlet needle & seat
- 6. Pin
- 7. Gasket
- 8. Float bowl
- 9. Retainer
- 10. Choke plate
- 11. Cam follower
- 12. Link
- 13. Throttle shaft
- 14. Spring
- 15. Welch plugs
- 16. Lead ball
- 17. Gasket
- 18. Throttle plate
- 19. Choke lever
- 20. Choke shaft
- 24. Follower adjusting screw
- 25. Roller

tor shown in Fig. OM6-2. Bend float tang (adjacent to inlet needle) to adjust float drop. Apply a suitable thread locking compound to float bowl screws during reassembly.

SPEED CONTROL LINKAGE. The speed control linkage rotates the armature plate to advance the ignition timing. The throttle cam attached to the armature plate is used to open the carburetor throttle as the ignition is advanced. The throttle opening and ignition timing cannot be properly synchronized if the throttle cam and related components are excessively worn or damaged. Renew components as necessary.

To adjust cam follower pickup point, slowly rotate twist grip from the closed position until throttle just begins to open. At this point, cam follower roller

(25—Fig. OM6-1) should be centered on "V" mark on cam plate on models prior to 1979. On models after 1978, cam follower roller (25—Fig. OM6-4) should be centered between marks (M) on cam (C) when throttle begins to open. Note that on late models only one mark is present on cam (C). If adjustment is required, turn cam follower adjusting screw (24—Fig. OM6-1 or Fig. OM6-2) as necessary to center roller on marks (one mark on late models) when throttle plate just begins to open.

(1988 and 1989 Models) To adjust wide open throttle stop, shift into forward gear (engine off) and rotate twist grip to wide open throttle. Throttle shaft roll pin (39—Fig. OM6-2) should be in a vertical position with throttle wide open. Turn hex-head screw on throttle cam to adjust.

(All Models) With boat in the water, running at normal operating temperature, with the correct propeller installed and boat movement unrestrained, adjust slow speed mixture needle to obtain highest possible engine speed. After highest speed is obtained, open slow speed needle (counterclockwise) an additional 1/8 turn to prevent a too-lean condition at slow speeds. Adjust idle speed to 650 rpm in forward gear. Operate engine at full throttle for one minute, then rapidly return to idle. Engine should run smoothly at idle speed. If engine stalls, pops or backfires, idle mixture is most likely too lean. Open slow speed mixture screw in 1/16 turn increments until engine idles smoothly (after full throttle operation).

REED VALVES. All models are equipped with reed valve plate (Fig. OM6-5) located between intake manifold and power head.

Reed petals (11) must lay perfectly flat against reed plate (6) throughout entire length of reed and be centered over ports in reed plate. Renew reeds which are cracked, broken, warped or bent. Never attempt to repair damaged reed petals. Check reed plate for warpage, unevenness or excessive wear. Apply a suitable thread locking compound to threads of reed petal mounting screws during reassembly.

Fuel recirculating valve (12) is located in reed plate (6) to remove excess fuel in the crankcase. Valve and screen should be cleaned of any residue. Valve disc must be intact and free to move inside recirculation valve.

FUEL PUMP. The diaphragm type fuel pump attaches to side of cylinder block and is actuated by crankcase pulsations. Fuel pump is available only as an assembly.

If fuel delivery problems are noted, first remove and clean fuel filter located under fuel pump cover. Install filter with lip of element facing away from pump cover. Remove and blow through fuel lines to ensure lines are clean and open. Test fuel lines and remote tank installation using a suitable vacuum pump and gage. If over 4 inches Hg (13.5 kPa) vacuum is required to draw fuel from tank, check for restrictions in fuel tank and lines. Note that remote fuel tank must not be more than 24 inches (61 cm) below fuel pump.

To test fuel pump, install a suitable pressure gage between fuel pump and carburetor and start engine. Fuel pump pressure should be 2.5 psi (17 kPa) at 4500 rpm. Fuel pump mounting screws should be treated with OMC Nut Lock or a suitable equivalent thread locking compound and tightened to 24-36 in.-

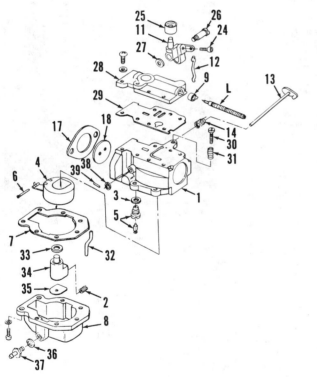

Fig. OM6-2—Exploded view of carburetor used on 1987-1989 models and some late production 1986 models.

L. Low speed mixture needle
1. Body
2. High speed jet
3. Gasket
4. Float
5. Inlet needle & seat
6. Pin
7. Gasket
8. Float bowl
9. Retainer
11. Cam follower
12. Link
13. Throttle shaft
14. Spring
17. Gasket
18. Throttle plate
24. Follower adjusting screw
25. Roller
26. Shoulder screw
27. Washer
28. Cover
29. Gasket
30. Idle speed screw
31. Spring
32. Tube
33. Gasket
34. Nozzle well
35. Gasket
36. Gasket
37. Nozzle
38. Washer
39. Pin

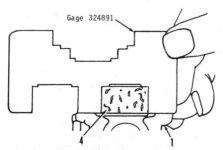

Fig. OM6-3—To check float level, place OMC float gage 324891 on carburetor body (1) as shown. Top of float (4) should be between notches on side of gage marked 9.9 and 15 Hp.

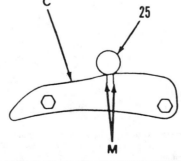

Fig. OM6-4—On models after 1978, cam follower roller (25) should be centered between marks (M) on cam (C) just as carburetor throttle opens.

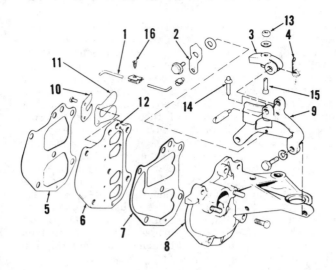

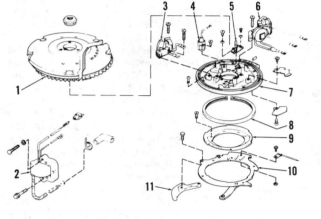

Fig. OM6-5—Exploded view of manual starter interlock assembly used on some models and reed valve used on all models. Link (1), cam (2) and rod (14) are not used on models after 1974.

1. Interlock link
2. Interlock cam
3. Pawl
4. Spring
5. Gasket
6. Reed plate
7. Gasket
8. Intake manifold
9. Interlock bracket
10. Reed stop
11. Reed petals
12. Fuel recirculating valve
13. Locknut
14. Rod
15. Adjusting screw
16. Link clamp screw

Fig. OM6-6—Exploded view of magneto assembly. Alternator coil (6) is used only on electric start models.

1. Flywheel
2. Ignition coil
3. Magneto coil
4. Condenser
5. Breaker points
6. Alternator coil
7. Armature plate
8. Ring
9. Plate support
10. Plate retainer
11. Speed control cam

crankshaft until fixture pointer rests midway between the two embossed armature plate timing marks shown in Fig. OM6-7. Adjust gap until points just open when timing fixture pointer is between the two marks (TM) on armature plate. Turn the crankshaft exactly one half turn until opposite pointer of timing fixture is aligned, then adjust other set of points.

NOTE: Timing fixture pointer legs are marked "T" and "B" to indicate upper and lower cylinders respectively.

Side of breaker point cam marked "Top" should face up. Face of coil shoes should be flush with machined surfaces on armature plate. One of the three points is shown at (F). The flywheel drive key and cam should be installed with marked end down and edge parallel with center of crankshaft.

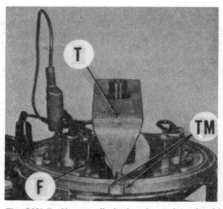

Fig. OM6-7—Upper cylinder breaker points should just open when mark at (T) end of timing fixture is between timing marks (TM).

lbs. (3-4 N·m). Tighten fuel pump cover screws to 10-15 in.-lbs. (1-2 N·m).

and to a suitable engine ground. Bulb should light when points are closed and go out when points are opened. Turn

IGNITION

Models Prior to 1977

Breaker point gap should be 0.020 inch (0.51 mm), and both sets of points should be synchronized so they open exactly 180 degrees apart. "Set" mark on breaker point cam indicates highest point of cam for setting breaker point gap. The manufacturer provides a timing fixture (OMC part 386636) for adjusting and synchronizing breaker points. The fixture is installed on crankshaft in place of flywheel as shown in Fig. OM6-7, and is used in combination with a timing light (with battery) or continuity meter or light.

To synchronize breaker points using the timing fixture and light, remove flywheel and install timing fixture, making sure fixture is properly fitted over flywheel key. Disconnect condenser and magneto coil leads from both sets of breaker points. Attach test light or meter to the opening set of breaker points

Fig. OM6-8—Wiring schematic for models prior to 1977. Electric starting circuit also applies to 1977 and 1978 models. Manual start models are not equipped with battery and electric start circuits.

1. Ignition coils
2. Starter motor
3. Kill switch
4. Rectifier
5. Neutral start switch
6. Start switch
7. Armature plate assy.
B. Black
BL. Blue
G. Gray
R. Red
W. White
Y. Yellow

CD2 Ignition System

OPERATION. Models produced 1977-1988 are equipped with CD2 breakerless capacitor discharge ignition system. Refer to Fig. OM6-9 for wiring schematic. A charge coil and sensor coil are located under the flywheel. Two magnets in flywheel induce a current in the charge coil which is rectified and directed to a capacitor for storage. The two flywheel magnets also induce current in the sensor coil to provide a positive charge on the gate of one of two silicon controlled rectifiers (SCR'S). The positive charge opens the SCR and allows the charged capacitor to discharge through the SCR and primary circuit of the ignition coil. The rapid coil field buildup induces a secondary voltage which fires the spark plug. Diodes, SCR'S and capacitor are contained in the power pack assembly and are not available individually.

TROUBLE-SHOOTING. On models prior to 1985, the 4-wire connector plugs connect the charge and sensor coil leads to the power pack. The 3-wire connector plugs connect the power pack and ignition coils. On models after 1984, a 5-wire connector is used between the power pack and armature plate. No timing adjustments are required with a CD2 ignition. Correct timing will be maintained as long as the wires are properly positioned in the connectors. On models prior to 1985, check to make sure the white/black wire in the 4-wire connector is positioned in connector terminal B. Also check to make sure the number 1 coil wire is in the 3-wire connector B terminal and that it connects with the power pack orange/blue wire in the other connector B terminal. On models after 1984, check to make sure the white/black wire in the 5-wire connector is positioned in connector terminal B of both connector halves. Also check to make sure the orange/blue power pack lead is connected to the number 1 ignition coil.

NOTE: Outer edges of charge coil and sensor coil must be flush with machined surface of armature plate to provide the proper clearance between coils and flywheel magnets. OMC locating ring 317001 may be used to simplify this procedure. Place locating ring over machined bosses on armature plate, push coil out against locating ring and tighten mounting screws.

To check charge coil output, use Merc-O-Tronic Model 781, Stevens Model CD77 or a suitable peak voltage tester. Disconnect connector between armature plate and power pack. Connect black tester lead to stator lead connector terminal A and red tester lead to terminal D.

Turn tester knobs to Negative and 500. Crank engine while observing tester. If tester reading is below 230 volts, check condition of charge coil wiring and connectors, and verify pin location in connector. If wiring and connectors are in acceptable condition, check charge coil resistance as follows: Connect an ohmmeter to terminals A and D in stator plate lead connector. Renew charge coil if resistance is not 500-650 ohms on models prior to 1986 or 550-600 ohms on 1986-1988 models. Connect negative ohmmeter lead to stator plate (ground) and positive ohmmeter lead to connector terminal A, then to connector terminal D. Infinite resistance should exist between A terminal and stator plate and D terminal and stator plate. If not, charge coil or charge coil lead is shorted to ground.

To check sensor coil, connect an ohmmeter to terminals B and C in stator plate lead connector. Renew sensor coil if resistance is not 30-50 ohms. Connect negative ohmmeter lead to stator plate (ground) and positive ohmmeter lead to connector terminal B, then to connector terminal C. Infinite resistance should exist between B terminal and stator plate and C terminal and stator plate. If not, sensor coil or sensor coil lead is shorted to ground. To check sensor coil output, use Merc-O-Tronic Model 781, Stevens Model CD77 or a suitable peak voltage tester. Connect black tester lead to stator lead connector terminal C and red tester lead to terminal B. On Merc-O-Tronic Model 781, turn knobs to Positive and 5, and on Stevens Model CD77, turn knobs to S and 5. Crank engine

while observing tester. Reverse tester leads and repeat test. Sensor coil output on both tests should be 2 volts or more on models prior to 1987 and 1.5 volts or more on 1987 and 1988 models. Renew sensor coil if output is not as specified.

To check power pack output, first reconnect connector between armature plate and power pack. Use Merc-O-Tronic Model 781, Stevens Model CD77 or a suitable peak voltage tester. Connect black tester lead to a suitable engine ground. Connect red tester lead to wire leading to either ignition coil. Turn tester knobs to Negative and 500. Crank engine while observing tester. Repeat test on other lead. Renew power pack if readings are not at least 180 volts or higher on models prior to 1985 or 200 volts or higher on models after 1984.

To test ignition coils, disconnect high tension lead at ignition coil. On models prior to 1985, disconnect 3-wire connector and insert a jumper lead in terminal B of the ignition coil end of connector. Connect ohmmeter positive lead to the B terminal jumper wire and ohmmeter negative lead to a good engine ground. On models after 1984, disconnect coil primary wire at coil and connect ohmmeter positive lead to coil primary terminal and negative lead to a good engine ground or to coil ground tab. Ignition coil primary resistance should be 0.05-0.15 ohm on all models. To check coil secondary resistance, move ohmmeter negative lead to the high tension terminal. Secondary resistance should

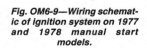

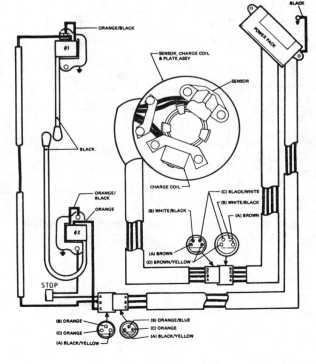

Fig. OM6-9—Wiring schematic of ignition system on 1977 and 1978 manual start models.

be 225-325 ohms on models prior to 1986 and 250-300 ohms on models after 1985. Repeat procedure on number 2 ignition coil.

CD2U Ignition System

Models after 1988 are equipped with CD2UL ignition system. Except for the ignition coils, all CD2U components are located under the flywheel indicated by the "U" in the model designation. Ignition system model number is printed on top of ignition module located under flywheel. The power pack and sensor coil are integrated into a single ignition module assembly instead of separate components as in earlier CD2 systems. Refer to Fig. OM6-10 for wiring schematic.

TROUBLE-SHOOTING. Disconnect spark plug leads from spark plugs and connect a suitable spark tester. Set tester spark gap to 1/2 inch (12.7 mm). On models so equipped, install emergency ignition cutoff clip and lanyard. Crank engine and observe spark tester. If an acceptable spark is noted at each spark gap, perform RUNNING OUTPUT TEST. If spark is noted at only one spark gap, perform IGNITION PLATE OUTPUT TEST as described in this section. If no spark is noted at either spark gap, perform STOP CIRCUIT TEST.

NOTE: If acceptable spark is noted at each spark gap during spark output test but engine pops and backfires during starting or running, ignition system may be out of time. Be sure orange/blue primary wire is connected to number 1 ignition coil, spark plug high tension leads are properly connected, flywheel is properly located on crankshaft and speed control linkage is properly adjusted.

STOP CIRCUIT TEST. Remove spark plug leads from spark plugs and connect a suitable spark tester. Disconnect stop circuit connector (Fig. OM6-11). Make sure ignition emergency cutoff clip and lanyard are installed on models so equipped. Crank engine and observe spark tester. If no spark is noted, perform IGNITION PLATE OUTPUT TEST. If normal spark is noted, connect ohmmeter between engine ground and the one-pin stop circuit connector (Fig. OM6-11) leading to tiller handle. Ohmmeter should show infinite resistance. If meter shows continuity, repair short in wiring or renew stop button. Depress stop button or remove emergency cutoff clip and note ohmmeter. If ohmmeter does not indicate continuity, repair open in wiring or renew stop button.

IGNITION PLATE OUTPUT TEST. Disconnect spark plug leads to prevent accidental starting. Remove primary leads from ignition coils. Connect number 1 ignition coil primary lead to the

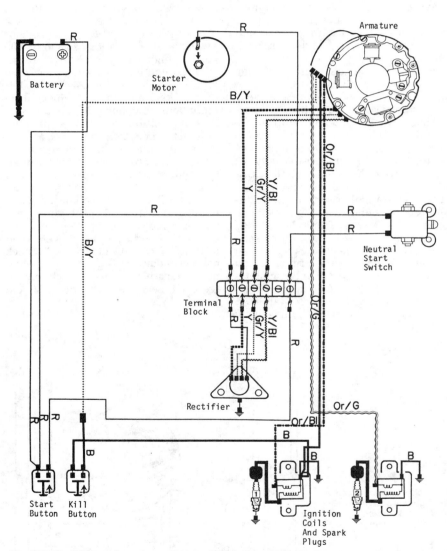

Fig. OM6-10—Wiring schematic on 1989 models equipped with CD2U ignition and electric start.

B. Black
R. Red
Y. Yellow
B/Y. Black with yellow tracer
Y/Bl. Yellow with blue tracer
Or/G. Orange with green tracer
Gr/Y. Gray with yellow tracer
Or/Bl. Orange with blue tracer

Fig. OM6-11—View showing approximate location of one-pin stop circuit connector. Appearance of stop circuit connector is the same on all models but location may vary. Refer to text.

red lead of Stevens load adapter PL-88 and black lead of load adapter to engine ground.

NOTE: If Stevens load adapter is not available, fabricate load adapter using a 10 ohm, 10 watt resistor (Radio Shack part 271-132) or equivalent.

Connect red test lead of CD77 or equivalent peak reading voltmeter to red lead of Stevens load adapter PL-88 and black test lead to engine ground. Set CD voltmeter to Positive and 500. Crank engine and note meter. Repeat test procedure on number 2 ignition coil primary lead. If CD voltmeter indicates 175 volts or higher on both tests, perform IGNITION COIL TESTS. If one primary lead shows no output, renew ignition module. If both tests indicate no output, perform CHARGE COIL RESISTANCE TEST.

CHARGE COIL RESISTANCE TEST. Remove manual starter and flywheel. Remove two ignition module mounting screws and disconnect module brown and brown/yellow bullet connectors. Connect ohmmeter between brown and brown/yellow charge coil connectors. Renew charge coil if resistance is not within 535-585 ohms. Connect one ohmmeter lead to engine ground and connect other ohmmeter lead to brown charge coil lead, then to brown/yellow charge coil lead. Renew charge coil if ohmmeter shows continuity between engine ground and either wire. If charge coil tests acceptable, renew ignition module.

NOTE: When installing charge coil or ignition module, use OMC Locating Ring 334994 to properly position components on armature plate. Place ring over machined surfaces on armature plate, push components outward against locating ring and tighten mounting screws to 30-40 in.-lbs. (3.4-4.5 N·m).

RUNNING OUTPUT TEST. Remove propeller and install the correct test wheel, then mount outboard motor in a suitable test tank. Remove ignition coil primary wires and install suitable terminal extenders (Stevens TS-77 or equivalent) on coil primary terminals, then install primary wires on terminal extenders. Connect peak reading voltmeter red test lead to number 1 coil terminal extender and black test lead to engine ground. Set voltmeter to Positive and 500. Start engine and run at rpm where ignition malfunction is evident while noting meter. Repeat test procedure on number 2 ignition coil. If either cylinder shows less than 200 volts, perform CHARGE COIL RESISTANCE

TEST. If charge coil test results are acceptable, renew ignition module.

IGNITION COIL RESISTANCE TEST. To check ignition coil primary resistance, connect ohmmeter between primary terminal and coil ground. Resistance should be 0.05-0.15 ohm. To check secondary resistance, connect ohmmeter between coil high tension terminal and primary terminal. Resistance should be 250-300 ohms. Renew coil if resistance is not as specified.

COOLING SYSTEM

WATER PUMP. All models are equipped with a rubber impeller type water pump which is mounted on and driven by the lower unit drive shaft. If cooling system malfunction occurs, first check water inlet for plugging or partial restriction, and check thermostat for proper operation. If necessary, remove lower unit gearcase as outlined in LOWER UNIT section and inspect condition of water pump, water passages, gaskets and sealing surfaces. Refer to Fig. OM6-24.

Install seal (4) into housing (5) with lip facing down. Rotate drive shaft in a clockwise direction when placing housing (5) over impeller (7) to set impeller vanes in the proper direction. Avoid turning drive shaft in opposite direction after water pump is reassembled to prevent impeller damage. Apply OMC Nut Lock or a suitable thread locking compound to threads of housing screws and tighten to 60-80 in.-lbs. (6.8-9.0 N·m).

THERMOSTAT. All models are equipped with a thermostat (5—Fig. OM6-12) located in cylinder head to ensure the proper engine operating temperature. Check thermostat operation by using Thermomelt Stiks. To check thermostat operation, install the correct test wheel and place outboard motor in a suitable test tank. Start engine and run at 3000 rpm for five minutes, then reduce engine speed to 900 rpm. Mark side of cylinder head with 125° F (52° C) and 163° F (73° C) Thermomelt Stiks. The 125° F (52° C) "Stik" should melt, but not the 163° F (73° C) "Stik." Increase engine speed to 5000 rpm and note the 163° F (73° C) mark. It should remain unmelted. Renew thermostat and inspect condition of water pump, water passages, gaskets and sealing surfaces if engine does not maintain correct operating temperature.

POWER HEAD

REMOVE AND REINSTALL. To remove power head, remove shift lock lever screw and swing lever aside. Disconnect fuel inlet hose from fuel pump. Disconnect stop switch (and ignition module on 1989 models) and ground wires at ignition coil mounting screw. Disconnect throttle cable. On models equipped with CD2 ignition, separate stop switch wire from E cavity of five-wire connector or A cavity of four-wire connector. On models equipped with CD2U ignition, disconnect one-pin stop switch connector (Fig. OM6-11). Remove

Fig. OM6-12—Exploded view of power head typical of all models.

1. Cylinder head cover
2. Gasket
3. Cylinder head
4. Gasket
5. Thermostat
6. Cylinder block
7. Dowel pin
8. Gasket
9. Transfer port cover
10. Main bearing dowel
11. Crankcase
12. Taper pin
13. Rectifier
14. Outer exhaust cover
15. Gasket
16. Inner exhaust cover
17. Neutral start switch (elec. start models)
18. Shift lock stop
19. Shift plate
20. Shift link
21. Shift detent

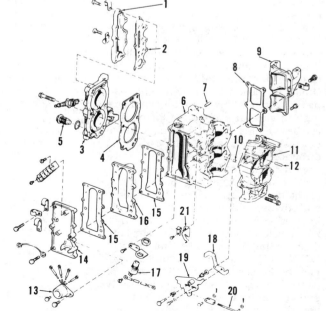

low speed adjustment knob, air silencer cover and air silencer, choke knob and manual starter. Remove electric starter on models so equipped. Remove any accessory connection that will prevent power head removal. Remove three lower cover screws. Remove six power head-to-drive shaft housing screws and lift power head off drive shaft housing.

NOTE: The upper main bearing oil seal can be renewed without power head removal or disassembly. With flywheel and armature plate removed, remove old seal using OMC tool 386629 on models prior to 1980 or 391060 on 1980 and later models. Install new seal using tool 319872 on models prior to 1980 or 391060 on 1980 and later models.

When reinstalling power head, remove lower unit gearcase to ease installation of water tube into water pump grommet. Make sure drive shaft and crankshaft splines are clean and free of corosion. On models prior to 1987, apply OMC Gasket Sealing Compound or a suitable sealant to power head-to-drive shaft housing gasket. On models after 1986, install gasket dry. Apply Permatex No. 2 or equivalent to machined outer diameter of lower crankcase seal housing. Tighten power head mounting screws to 60-84 in.-lbs. (6.8-9.5 N·m). Complete remainder of installation by reversing order of removal.

DISASSEMBLY AND REASSEMBLY. Refer to Fig. OM6-12. Remove lower seal housing, cylinder head cover, thermostat, cylinder head bypass cover, intake manifold and reed valve assembly. Carefully drive out taper pin (12). Note that taper pin (12) must be removed toward intake manifold. Use caution not to damage taper pin bore. Remove four crankcase flange screws and six main bearing screws. Tap flywheel end of crankshaft with a soft-face mallet to separate crankcase from cylinder block. Pistons, rods and crankshaft are now accessible for removal. Cylinder head should be loosely reinstalled to prevent pistons from falling out when connecting rod caps are removed. Piston and rod assemblies and all wearing components should be marked for location and direction for reference during reassembly.

Prior to reassembling power head, check all sealing surfaces of crankcase and covers making certain that all sealing surfaces are clean, smooth and flat. Small nicks or burrs may be polished out on a lapping plate, but sealing surfaces MUST NOT be lowered. Cylinder head may be lapped if warped in excess of 0.004 inch (0.10 mm). Remove only enough material to true head. Refer to specific service sections when assem-

bling crankshaft, connecting rods and pistons. Thoroughly lubricate all friction surfaces with a recommended engine oil during reassembly. Apply Locquic Primer to mating surface of crankcase and allow to dry, then apply OMC Gel-Seal II to mating surface of cylinder block. Do not allow Gel-Seal to contact labyrinth seals or bearings.

NOTE: If Locquic Primer is not available, allow Gel-Seal to cure a minimum of 24 hours before returning power head to service.

Install crankcase on cylinder block immediately after Gel-Seal application. Install retaining screws finger tight, then install taper pin. Make sure taper pin is seated solidly. Strike lower end of crankshaft to seat main bearings. Tighten six main bearing screws (large screws) to 144-168 in.-lbs. (16.3-19.0 N·m). Tighten remainder of crankcase screws (smaller screws) in a spiral sequence to 60-84 in.-lbs. (6.8-9.5 N·m). Rotate crankshaft during reassembly to check for binding or unusual noise. If binding or noise is noted, power head must be disassembled to determine cause and repaired. Starting with one center screw, tighten cylinder head screws in a spiral pattern to 216-240 in.-lbs. (24.4-27.1 N·m). Note that cylinder head screws should be retightened after engine has been run and allowed to cool.

PISTONS, RINGS AND CYLINDER. Each piston is fitted with two piston rings. Top ring is semi-keystone shape. Refer to CONDENSED SERVICE DATA for piston ring service specifications. Cylinder must be rebored or renewed if excessive taper or out-of-round is evident. It is acceptable practice to install one or more oversize pistons. Refer to CONDENSED SERVICE DATA for cylin-

der bore service specifications. Piston and rings are available in 0.030 inch (0.76 mm) oversize. Add 0.030 inch (0.76 mm) to standard cylinder bore diameter to determine oversize cylinder dimension. To determine piston wear, measure in two locations, 90 degrees apart, 1/8 inch (3 mm) up from bottom of skirt. Renew piston if difference between measurements exceeds 0.002 inch (0.05 mm). The manufacturer does not specify piston skirt clearance on models after 1984. If cylinder bore and piston are within tolerance, piston clearance should be acceptable.

On models prior to 1982, one piston pin bore is press fit while other bore is a loose fit. The loose fit bore is marked with an "L" cast into underside of piston. When removing piston pin, remove and discard retaining rings (2—Fig. OM6-13), and press pin from piston toward press fit side. Install pin through loose side first. On models after 1981, heat piston to approximately 200°-400° F (93°-204° C) when removing or reinstalling piston pin. Be sure to properly support piston when removing or reinstalling pin to prevent piston damage. Always renew pin retainers (2) upon reassembly. Piston must be installed with long tapered side of piston crown facing exhaust ports.

CONNECTING RODS, BEARINGS AND CRANKSHAFT. Prior to detaching connecting rods from crankshaft, make sure that rod, cap and piston are marked for reference during reassembly. Keep rod bearings with their respective rods to prevent intermixing bearings upon reassembly.

The small end of connecting rod is fitted with a caged needle bearing (4—Fig. OM6-13) on models prior to 1984. On models after 1983, connecting rod small end is fitted with 22 loose needle bearing rollers with washers located on each

Fig. OM6-13—Exploded view of crankshaft, piston and rod assemblies typical of all models. Piston pin bearing (4) consists of 22 loose needle bearing rollers with washers on models after 1983.

1. Piston rings
2. Pin retainers
3. Piston pin
4. Needle bearing
5. Connecting rod
6. Rollers & cage
7. Breaker point cam
8. Seal
9. Roller bearing
10. Crankshaft
11. Outer bearing race
12. Rollers & cage
13. Bearing retaining ring
14. Outer bearing race
15. Rod cap
17. "O" ring
18. Seal
19. Crankcase head
20. Bearing
21. Snap ring

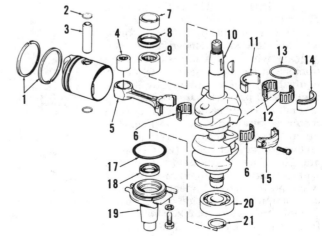

side of rod. Crankpin end of connecting rod uses split cage bearings with 14 bearing rollers.

The crankshaft is supported by three main bearings. Snap ring (21) must be removed prior to pulling roller bearing (20) from crankshaft. Do not remove bearing (20) unless renewal is required. Center main bearing (11, 12 and 14) is secured to crankshaft by retaining ring (13). Note that on 1984 and later models, center main bearing consists of 23 loose bearing rollers and races (11 and 14). Top main bearing (9) will slide off crankshaft for inspection. Install bearing (9) with lettered side facing flywheel end of power head. When installing crankshaft assembly into cylinder block, be sure main bearings properly engage dowel pins in bearing bores.

Connecting rod and cap must be installed on crankshaft so raised dots on rod and cap are aligned as shown in Fig. OM6-14. Joint between connecting rod is fractured and not machined. Install

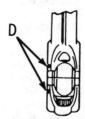

Fig. OM6-14—Dots (D) must be aligned when assembling connecting rod and cap.

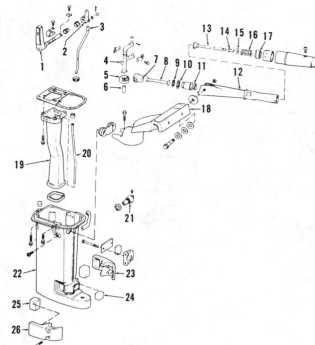

Fig. OM6-16—Exploded view of exhaust housing assembly. Tiller handle for models prior to 1986 is shown. A throttle cable type tiller handle is used on 1986 and later models. On models prior to 1986, raised arrow on vertical gear (5) and dot on inner gear (7) must be aligned during assembly.

1. Gear shift lever
2. Shift bellcrank
3. Upper shift rod
4. Tower shaft
5. Vertical gear
6. Pin
7. Inner gear
8. Shaft
9. Snap ring
10. Washer
11. Gear
12. Steering handle
13. Gear & shaft
14. Bushing
15. Washer
16. Spring
17. Friction block
18. Steering bracket
19. Exhaust tube
20. Water tube
21. Electric start switch
22. Exhaust housing
23. Left pivot tube bracket
24. Thrust block
25. Mounting block
26. Right pivot tube bracket

rod caps and nuts finger tight and check cap-to-rod alignment using a pencil or other suitable tool. Separation line between rod and cap should be nearly invisible when properly aligned. Renew connecting rod assembly if the proper alignment cannot be obtained. Refer to CONDENSED SERVICE DATA for recommended tightening values.

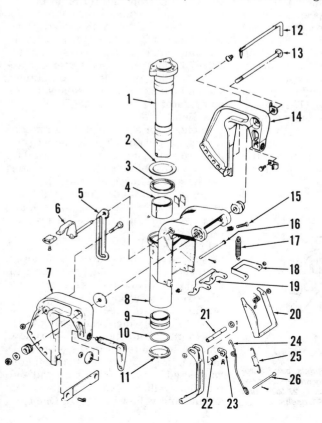

Fig. OM6-15—Exploded view of swivel bracket assembly.

1. Pivot tube
2. Thrust washer
3. Seal
4. Bushing
5. Tilt lock
6. Tilt lever
7. Right stern bracket
8. Swivel bracket
9. Bushing
10. "O" ring
11. Thrust washer
12. Thrust rod
13. Tilt bolt
14. Left stern bracket
15. Friction adjusting screw
16. Link pin
17. Reverse lock spring
18. Reverse lock lever
19. Reverse lock link
20. Shallow water link
21. Bushing
22. Spring
23. Reverse lock bellcrank
24. Release wire
25. Spring
26. Pin

MANUAL STARTER

To disassemble manual starter, remove rope handle and allow rope to wind into starter. Unscrew starter bolt (1—Fig. OM6-17) and remove starter. Be careful to keep starter assembly intact to prevent rewind spring from escaping. Remove pinion (3) and spring (4). Insert a putty knife or similar tool between rope pulley and rewind spring and lift rope pulley off spring cup. Care should be exercised if rewind spring is removed as uncontrolled unwinding of rewind spring could cause personal injury.

Lubricate rewind spring area of spring cup with OMC Triple-Guard grease or Lubriplate 777. Install rewind spring in spring cup with spring wound in counterclockwise direction from outer spring end. New rope length should be 65 inches (165 cm) on models after 1987 and 68.5 inches (174 cm) on all other models. Wind rope around rope pulley in counterclockwise direction as viewed from pinion end of pulley. Be sure inner end of rewind spring engages spring anchor of rope pulley when pulley and spring are assembled. Complete remainder of reassembly and tighten starter bolt (1) to 24-26 ft.-lbs. (33-35 N·m).

Three types of starter interlocks have been used. On 1974 models, the starter interlock is designed to allow manual starter operation only when the outboard motor is in neutral gear. To adjust interlock on 1974 models, place outboard in neutral, loosen locknut (13—Fig. OM6-18) and turn cam screw (15) until gap (G) between starter interlock

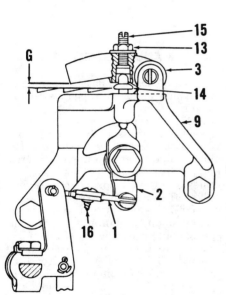

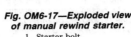

Fig. OM6-17—Exploded view of manual rewind starter.

1. Starter bolt
2. Washer
3. Pinion
4. Spring
5. Upper pulley half
6. Rope
7. Lower pulley half
8. Rewind spring
9. Washer
10. Spring cup

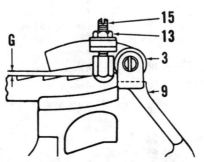

Fig. OM6-18—On 1974 models, gap (G) between upper edge of rope pulley and end of pawl (3) should be 0.070-0.100 inch (1.78-2.54 mm) when lower unit is in neutral.

pawl (3) and rope pulley is 0.070-0.100 inch (1.78-2.54 mm).

NOTE: If cam (2) lobe is not centered on cam follower rod (14), shift linkage should be adjusted before adjusting starter interlock. Refer to LOWER UNIT.

On 1975-1978 models, the starter interlock is designed to allow manual starter operation only when throttle is in START position. To adjust interlock, outboard should be in neutral and throttle in stop position. Loosen locknut (13—Fig. OM6-19) and turn adjusting screw (15) until gap (G) between start-

er interlock pawl (3) and rope pulley is 0.050-0.110 inch (1.27-2.79 mm).

On models after 1978, a pawl located on the throttle tower shaft prevents manual starter operation except when throttle control is in start position.

ELECTRIC STARTER

Some models are equipped with the electric starter motor shown in Fig. OM6-20. Starter no-load speed should be 7000-9200 rpm. Maximum current draw is 7 amps at 12-12.4 volts. Alignment marks for reassembly are located on housing (9), brush plate (13) and end cap (5). Tighten starter through-bolts to 30-40 in.-lbs. (3.4-4.5 N·m). Tighten pinion nut (1) to 150-170 in.-lbs. (17-19 N·m). Tighten starter motor assembly mounting screws to 10-12 ft.-lbs. (13.6-16.3 N·m).

On models equipped with electric start, battery must maintain a minimum

Fig. OM6-19—On 1975-1978 models, gap (G) between upper edge of rope pulley and end of pawl (3) should be 0.050-0.110 inch (1.27-2.79 mm) when throttle is in START position.

of 9.6 volts under cranking load for 15 seconds. If not, battery must be charged or renewed.

AC LIGHTING COIL

Manual Start Models

To test lighting coil, disconnect three pin connector leading from armature plate. Connect a suitable ohmmeter between yellow wire with gray tracer and yellow wire. Renew lighting coil if resistance is not within 0.81-0.91 ohm. Next, connect ohmmeter between yellow wire with gray tracer and yellow wire with blue tracer. Renew lighting coil if resistance is not within 1.19-1.23 ohms. Connect ohmmeter between engine ground and alternately to each pin in three pin connector (yellow, yellow/gray and yellow/blue). Ohmmeter should read infinity at each connection. If not, inspect for shorted lighting coil or coil wires.

BATTERY CHARGING SYSTEM

Electric Start Models

To test alternator output, connect a suitable ammeter in series with the red rectifier lead and red wiring harness lead. At 5500 rpm, alternator output should be approximately 4.5 amps. If not, proceed as follows: Disconnect battery cables from battery. Disconnect all stator leads from the terminal board. Using a suitable ohmmeter, connect red tester lead to stator yellow lead. Connect black tester lead to stator yellow/blue lead. Resistance should be 0.22-0.32 ohm. Move red tester lead to stator yellow/gray lead. Resistance should be 0.22-0.32 ohm. Renew or repair stator if resistance is not as specified.

To check for shorted stator or stator wiring, connect black tester lead to engine ground. Connect red tester lead to stator yellow/blue lead, then to stator yellow and yellow/gray leads. If ohmmeter does not read infinity at all connections, stator or stator wiring is shorted to ground and must be repaired or renewed.

To test rectifier, disconnect battery cables at battery and proceed as follows: Connect ohmmeter black test lead to engine ground and red test lead to rectifier yellow/gray lead. Note ohmmeter reading, then reverse tester lead connections. A very high reading should result in one connection and a very low reading should result in the other connection. Repeat test with ohmmeter connected between engine ground and rectifier yellow lead, then between ground and yellow/blue lead. One connection should show high resistance, the other low resistance. Next, connect ohmmeter between rectifier red lead and yellow/gray lead. Note reading and reverse tester connections. Repeat test between rectifier red lead and yellow lead, then red lead and yellow/blue lead. As before, one connection should show high resistance and the other low resistance. Renew rectifier if not as specified.

LOWER UNIT

PROPELLER. Protection for the propeller and drive unit is provided by a cushion propeller hub. Several propellers are available from the manufacturer. Select a propeller that will allow a properly tuned and adjusted engine to operate within the specified rpm range at wide-open throttle. Refer to CONDENSED SERVICE DATA for recommended operating ranges.

Propeller hub slippage can be checked using a torque wrench and a suitable holding fixture with adapter. Propeller hub is acceptable if no slippage is noted at 100 ft.-lbs. (135.6 N·m).

SHIFT LINKAGE ADJUSTMENT (1974 Models). To adjust shift linkage,

first remove the fuel pump. Loosen screws retaining detent spring plate to side of engine. Spring plate is located adjacent to shift plate (P—Fig. OM6-21). Loosen shift plate pivot bolt (B) and detach shift link clevis (C) from shift plate (P). Retighten pivot bolt and rotate shift plate (P) clockwise until plate contacts stop on intake manifold. Move detent so it is positioned in reverse (R) position on shift plate (P), then tighten detent screws. Rotate shift plate (P) counterclockwise until detent is in neutral notch. Push in firmly on propeller shaft to remove end play and center outer shift lever in neutral position. Turn clevis (C) on shift link (L) until clevis pin can be inserted easily into hole in shift plate (P). Reinstall fuel pump.

Check for proper engagement of forward (F), neutral (N) and reverse (R) and propeller rotation by turning the propeller.

WARNING: Disconnect and ground spark plug leads prior to performing any propeller service to prevent serious personal injury due to accidental starting.

Place outboard motor in neutral and note position of interlock rod (14—Fig. OM6-18) on cam (2). If rod is not centered on highest point of cam, loosen link coupling screw (16) and adjust length of link (1) so rod is centered. Shift outboard motor to forward and back to neutral and check adjustment.

(1976-1981 Models). Remove fuel hose from carburetor inlet. Remove cotter pin and washer from end of shift lever link (L—Fig. OM6-22) and detach link from shift lever. Position shift lever and shift plate (P) in reverse (R) position. Without exerting pressure on shift lever, adjust link (L) to align with hole in shift lever. Then shorten link (L) one full turn on 1976-1978 models and two full turns on 1979-1981 models. Install link (L) into shift lever and complete reassembly by reversing disassembly.

Check for proper engagement of forward (F), neutral (N) and reverse (R) positions and propeller rotation by turning the propeller.

WARNING: Disconnect and ground spark plug leads prior to performing any propeller service to prevent serious personal injury due to accidental starting.

(1982-1989 Models). Remove fuel hose from carburetor inlet. Remove the cotter pin and washer from end of shift lever link (L—Fig. OM6-23).

WARNING: Disconnect and ground spark plug leads prior to performing any propeller service to prevent serious personal injury due to accidental starting.

Move the directional shift lever to the forward (F) position and rotate the propeller shaft until dog clutch lugs engage drive gear lugs. Then slowly move the directional control lever toward the neutral position and note the position of detent (D) on shift plate (P) when the lugs disengage. Repeat the procedure with the directional shift lever in the reverse position.

Detach link (L) from the shift lever and adjust link (L) until detent (D) is positioned at equal points on shift plate forward and reverse ramps when lugs disengage. Install link (L) in shift lever and complete reassembly.

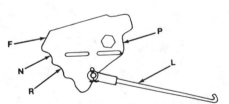

Fig. OM6-22—View showing shift plate (P) used on 1976-1981 models. Refer to text for adjustment procedures.

F. Forward notch	
L. Shift link	P. Shift plate
N. Neutral notch	R. Reverse notch

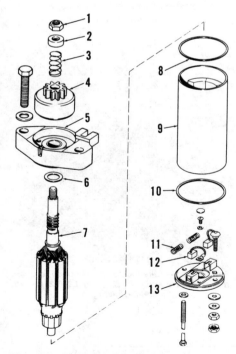

Fig. OM6-20—Exploded view of electric starter motor.

1. Nut	
2. Spacer	8. Gasket
3. Spring	9. Housing
4. Pinion	10. Gasket
5. End cap	11. Brush spring
6. Washer	12. Brush
7. Armature	13. Brush plate

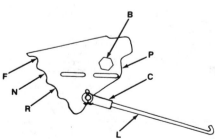

Fig. OM6-21—View showing shift plate (P) used on 1974 models. Refer to text for adjustment procedures.

B. Pivot bolt	
C. Clevis	
F. Forward notch	N. Neutral notch
L. Shift link	P. Shift plate
	R. Reverse notch

Fig. OM6-23—View showing shift plate (P) used on 1982 and later models. Refer to text for adjustment procedures.

D. Detent	N. Neutral notch
F. Forward position	P. Shift plate
L. Shift link	R. Reverse position

R&R AND OVERHAUL. To separate gearcase from drive shaft housing, unscrew six screws between housing and gearcase and separate housing and gearcase until there is sufficient clearance to detach upper shift rod from shift rod coupler (16—Fig. OM6-24). Separate gearcase from drive shaft housing. Drain gearcase lubricant and remove water pump assembly. Unscrew lower shift rod (17) from shift lever and yoke (25). Remove propeller and thrust bushing (42). Using a suitable puller, remove bearing housing (38) from gearcase. Withdraw propeller shaft and reverse gear (35) being careful not to lose detent balls (32) and spring (33). Unscrew pivot pin (22) and withdraw drive shaft (10). Remove dog clutch (27), pinion gear assembly (28 through 31), forward gear (24), clutch cradle (26), shift lever and yoke (25) and bearing (23). If necessary, remove bearing (23) cup from gearcase. To remove shift rod bushing (18), "O" ring (19) and

washer (20), insert a 1/4 inch (6 mm) threaded rod approximately 15 inches (38.1 cm) long through aforementioned components and screw a nut, which has been ground down to clear casting on end of rod. Attach a slide hammer to upper end of rod and pull out shift rod bushing, "O" ring and washer. Remove remaining bearings, seals and sleeve (14).

Inspect all components for excessive wear or other damage. Press or pull against lettered end of bearing when installing bearings (13, 15, 36 and 39). Install seals (12 and 40) with lip toward gears and seals (11 and 41) with lip away from gears. To reassemble lower unit, reverse disassembly procedure. Before installing shift lever and yoke (25), thread end of OMC yoke locator 319991 into shift rod hole of shift lever and pass end of yoke locator wire up through shift rod hole in gearcase. Grooves on dog clutch (27) must face reverse gear (35). Use a

suitable grease to hold detent balls (32) and spring (33) in position while installing propeller shaft. Apply OMC Gasket Sealing Compound to bearing housing screws. Apply OMC Gasket Sealing Compound to threads of pivot pin (22), and after propeller shaft and drive shaft components have been installed, move yoke locator wire as shown in Fig. OM6-25. until pivot pin (22—Fig. OM6-24) can be installed into hole in shift lever and yoke (25). Unscrew yoke locator wire and install shift rod (17). Screw shift rod into shift lever and yoke, then back out shift rod until bent upper portion of rod is forward and flat side of coupler (16) is toward drive shaft. Shift lower unit to neutral and measure from top of coupler to mating surface of gearcase. Distance should be approximately 13/32 to 7/16 inch (10.3-11.1 mm) and may be obtained by turning shift rod.

To install gearcase on exhaust housing, pull up on shift rod so lower unit is in reverse gear and move shift lever on motor to reverse position. Apply OMC Adhesive M to exhaust tube area of gearcase and lubricate water pump housing grommet (3) with oil. Apply a suitable antiseizing compound to splines of drive shaft and OMC Nut Lock to gearcase retaining screws.

Refer to SHIFT LINKAGE ADJUSTMENT section and adjust shift linkage. It may be necessary to readjust height of lower shift rod if shift linkage adjustment is not satisfactory.

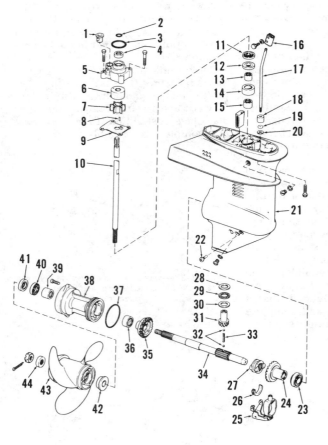

Fig. OM6-24—Exploded view of lower unit assembly. Propeller and bushing (43) are separate on later models.

1. Grommet
2. "O" ring
3. "O" ring
4. Seal
5. Water pump housing
6. Impeller cup
7. Impeller
8. Pin
9. Impeller plate
10. Drive shaft
11. Seal
12. Seal
13. Bearing
14. Sleeve
15. Bearing
16. Coupler
17. Lower shift rod
18. Bushing
19. "O" ring
20. Washer
21. Gearcase
22. Pivot pin
23. Bearing
24. Forward gear
25. Shift lever & yoke
26. Clutch cradle
27. Dog clutch
28. Thrust washer
29. Thrust bearing
30. Thrust washer
31. Drive pinion
32. Detent balls
33. Detent spring
34. Propeller shaft
35. Reverse gear
36. Bearing
37. "O" ring
38. Bearing housing
39. Bearing
40. Seal
41. Seal
42. Thrust bushing
43. Propeller & bushing
44. Thrust washer

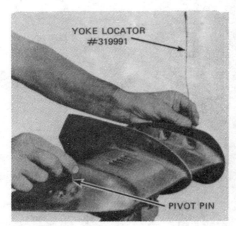

Fig. OM6-25—Yoke locator wire is used to position shift lever and yoke (25—Fig. OM6-24) when installing pivot pin.

EVINRUDE AND JOHNSON
18, 20, 25 AND 28 HP

EVINRUDE MODELS

Year Produced	18 hp	20 hp	25 hp	28 hp
1969	18902, 18903	....	25902, 25903	....
1970	18002, 18003	....	25002, 25003	....
1971	18102, 18103	....	25102, 25103	....
1972	18202, 18203	....	25202, 25203 *25252, *25253	....
1973	....	....	25302, 25303 *25352, *25353	....
1974	....	....	25402, 25403 *25452, *25453	....
1975	....	....	25502, 25503 *25552, *25553	....
1976	....	....	25602, 25603 *25652, *25653	....
1977	....	....	25702, 25703 *25752, *25753	....
1978	....	....	25802, 25803 *25852, *25853	....
1979	....	....	25904, 25905 *25952, *25953	....
1980	....	....	25RCS, 25RLCS *25TECS, 25TELCS	....
1981	....	....	25RCI, 25RLCI 25WCI, 25WLCI *25ECI, *25ELCI *25TECI, *25TELCI	....
1982	....	....	25RCN, 25RLCN 25WCN, 25WLCN *25ECN, *25ELCN *25TECN, *25TELCN	....
1983	....	....	25RCT, 25RLCT *25ECT, *25ELCT *25TECT, *25TELCT 25RWCT, 25RWLCT	....
1984	....	....	25RCR, 25RLCR *25TECR, *25TELCR	....
1985	....	20CRCO, 20CRLCO *20ECO, *20ELCO	25RCO, 25RLCO *25ECO, *25ELCO *25TECO, *25TELCO 25WRCO, 25RWLCO	....
1986	....	20CRCD, 20CRLCD *20ECD, *20ELCD	25RCD, 25RLCD *25ECD, *25ELCD *25TECD, *25TELCD 25RWCD, 25RWLCD	....
1987	....	E20RCU, E20BFCU E20RLCU, E20BFLCU *E20ECU, *E20TECU *E20ELCU	E25KCW, E25BACU E25KLCW, E25BALCU E25RCU, E25RACU E25RLCU, E25RALCU E25IRCU, *E25TECU E25IRLCU, *E25TELCU *E25IECU, E25RWCU *E25IELCU, E25WLCU E25RSM, *E25ECU E25RSLM, *E25ELCU E25RSYM	*E28ESLCU
1988	....	E20CRCC, E20BFCC E20CRLCC, E20BFLCC *E20ECC, *E20TECC *E20ELCC	E25RCC, E25RLCC E25BACC, E25BALCC E25IRCC, E25IRLCC *E25IECC, *E25IELCC E25RACC, E25RALCC *E25TECC, *E25TELCC *E25ECC, *E25ELCC	*E28ESLCC

EVINRUDE MODELS CONT.

Year Produced	18 hp	20 hp	25 hp	28 hp
1989	....	E20CRCE, E20BFCE E20CRLCE, E20BFLCE *E20ECE, *E20TECE *E20ELCE, *E20TELCE	E25RCE, E25RLCE E25BACE, E25BALCE E25IRCE, E25IRLCE *E25IECE, *E25IELCE E25RACE, E25RALCE *E25TECE, *E25TELCE *E25ECE, *E25ELCE *E25SECE, *E25SELCE	*E28ESLCE

*Electric start models.

JOHNSON MODELS

Year Produced	20 hp	25 hp	28 hp
1969	20R69, 20RL69	25R69, 25RL69	....
1970	20R70, 20RL70	25R70, 25RL70	....
1971	20R71, 20RL71	25R71, 25RL71	....
1972	20R,72, 20RL72	25R72, 25RL72 *25E72, *25EL72	....
1973	....	25R73, 25RL73 *25E73, *25EL73	....
1974	....	25R74, 25RL74 *25E74, *25EL74	....
1975	....	25R75, 25RL75 *25E75, *25EL75	....
1976	....	25R76, 25RL76 *25E76, *25EL76	....
1977	....	25R77, 25RL77 *25E77, *25EL77	....
1978	....	25R78, 25RL78 *25E78, *25EL78	....
1979	....	25R79, 25RL79 *25E79, *25EL79	....
1980	....	25RCS, 25RLCS *25TECS, *25TELCS	....
1981	....	25RCI, 25RLCI 25RWCI, 25RWLCI *25ECI, *25ELCI 25TECI, *25TELCI	....
1982	....	25RCN, 25RLCN 25RWCN, 25RWLCN *25ECN, *25ELCN *25TECN, *25TELCN	....
1983	....	25RCT, 25RLCT *25ECT, *25ELCT *25TECT, *25TELCT 25RWCT, 25RWLCT	....
1984	....	25RCR, 25RLCR *25TECR, *25TELCR	....
1985	20CRCO, 20CRLCO *20ECO, *20ELCO	25RCO, 25RLCO *25ECO, *25ELCO *25TECO, *25TELCO 25RWCO, 25RWLCO	....
1986	20CRCD, 20CRLCD *20ECD, *20ELCD	25RCD, 25RLCD *25ECD, *25ELCD *25TECD, *25TELCD 25RWCD, 25RWLCD	....

JOHNSON MODELS CONT.

Year Produced	20 hp	25 hp	28 hp
1987	J20RCU, J20BFCU J20RLCU, J20BFLCU *J20ECU, *J20TECU *J20ELCU	J25KCW, J25BACU J25KCLW, J25BALCU J25RCU, J25RACU J25RLCU, J25RALCU J25IRCU, *J25TECU J25IRLCU, *J25TELCU *J25IECU, J25RWCU *J25IELCU, J25RWLCU J25RSM, *J25ECU J25RSLM, *J25ELCU J25RSYM	*J28ESLCU
1988	J20CRCC, J20BFCC J20CRLCC, J20BFLCC *J20ECC, *J20TECC *J20ELCC	J25RCC, J25RLCC J25IRCC, J25IRLCC *J25IECC, *J25IELCC J25BACC, J25BALCC J25RACC, J25RALCC *J25TECC, *J25TELCC *J25ECC, *J25ELCC	*J28ESLCC
1989	J20CRCE, J20BFCE J20CRLCE, J20BFLCE *J20ECE, *J20TECE *J20ELCE, *J20TELCE	J25RCE, J25RLCE J25IRCE, J25IRLCE *J25IECE, *J25IELCE J25BACE, J25BALCE J25RACE, J25RALCE *J25TECE, *J25TELCE *J25ECE, *J25ELCE *J25SECE, *J25SELCE	*J28ESLCE

*Electric start models.

CONDENSED SERVICE DATA

TUNE-UP

Hp/rpm	18/4000-5000
	20/4500-5500*
	25/4500-5500†
	28/4500-5500

Bore:
Models Prior to 1977 ....2.500 in.
(63.5 mm)
Models After 1976 ....3.000 in.
(76.2 mm)
Stroke ....2.250 in.
(57.15 mm)
Number of Cylinders 2
Displacement:
Models Prior to 1977 ....22.0 cu. in.
(361 cc)
Models After 1976 ....31.8 cu. in.
(521 cc)
Spark Plug—Champion:
1969-1976 ....J4J
Electrode Gap ....0.030 in.
(0.76 mm)
1977-1989 ....QL77JC4‡
Electrode Gap ....0.040 in.
(1.0 mm)
Ignition Type:
1969-1976 ....Breaker Point
Breaker Point Gap ....0.020 in.
(0.51 mm)
1977-1989 ....CDI

TUNE-UP CONT.

Carburetor Make ....OMC
Idle Speed (in gear):
Prior to 1987 ....650 rpm
After 1986 ....650-700 rpm
Fuel:Oil Ratio ....See Text

*Johnson 1969-1972 20 hp models are rated at 4000-5000 rpm.
†All 1969-1976 25 hp models are rated at 5000-6000 rpm.
‡Champion QL78V surface gap spark plug is recommended when operated at sustained high speeds. Renew surface gap spark plug if center electrode is more than 1/32 inch (0.79 mm) below flat surface of plug end.

SIZES—CLEARANCES

Piston Ring End Gap ....0.007-0.017 in.
(0.18-0.43 mm)
Lower Piston Ring Side Clearance:
1969-1984 ....0.0015-0.0040 in.
(0.038-0.102 mm)
1985-1989 ....0.004 in. Max.
(0.10 mm)
Piston Skirt Clearance:
1969-1978 ....0.0030-0.0050 in.
(0.076-0.127 mm)
1979-1982 ....0.0035-0.0065 in.
(0.089-0.165 mm)
1983-1984 ....0.0024-0.0044 in.
(0.061-0.112 mm)
After 1984 ....See Text

CONDENSED SERVICE DATA CONT.

SIZES—CLEARANCES CONT.

Standard Cylinder Bore Diameter:
Prior to 1977 . . . . .2.450-2.550 in.
(62.23-64.77 mm)
Wear Limit. . . . . .0.003 in.
(0.08 mm)
After 1976. .2.9995-3.0005 in.
(76.187-76.213 mm)
Max. Allowable Out-of-Round . . . . .0.003 in.
(0.08 mm)
Max. Allowable Taper. . . . . .0.002 in.
(0.05 mm)

Crankshaft Journal Diameters—
Top Main:
1969-1976 . . . . .0.9995-1.0000 in.
(25.387-25.400 mm)
1977 . . . . .1.2495-1.2500 in.
(31.737-31.750 mm)
1978-1989 . . . . .1.2510-1.2515 in.
(31.775-31.788 mm)
Center Main:
1969-1977 . . . . .0.9995-1.0000 in.
(25.387-25.400 mm)
1978-1982 . . . . .1.1805-1.1810 in.
(29.985-29.997 mm)
1983-1989 . . . . .1.1833-1.1838 in.
(30.056-30.068 mm)
Bottom Main:
1969-1976 . . . . .0.9995-1.0000 in.
(25.387-25.400 mm)
1977-1989 . . . . .0.9842-0.9846 in.
(24.999-25.009 mm)
Crankshaft End Play:
1969-1976. . . . . .0.009-0.023 in.
(0.23-0.58 mm)
1977-1978 . . . . .0.003-0.011 in.
(0.08-0.28 mm)
1979-1984 .0.000-0.025 in.
(0.00-0.63 mm)
Lower Unit Diametral Clearances:
(1969-1977)
Propeller Shaft to Bushings
in Gears. . . . . .0.0005-0.0015 in.
(0.013-0.038 mm)
Propeller Shaft to Gearcase Head . . . . . .0.001-0.002 in.
(0.025-0.051 mm)
Drive Shaft Pinion to Gearcase . . . . . .0.0011-0.0023 in.
(0.028-0.058 mm)
Forward Gear to Gearcase Bushing. . .0.0045-0.0060 in.
(0.114-0.152 mm)
Bushing to Reverse Gear . . . . .0.0005-0.0020 in.
(0.013-0.051 mm)
(1978-1984)
Propeller Shaft to Forward
Gear Bushing . . . . .0.0010-0.0020 in.
(0.025-0.051 mm)

SIZES—CLEARANCES CONT.

Propeller Shaft to Reverse
Gear Bushing . . . . .0.0005-0.0015 in.
(0.013-0.038 mm)
Bushing to Reverse Gear . . . . .0.0005-0.0020 in.
(0.013-0.051 mm)

TIGHTENING TORQUES

Connecting Rod:
Prior to 1977 . . . . .180-186 in.-lbs.
(20.3-21.0 N·m)
1977-1987 . . . . .29-31 ft.-lbs.
(39.3-42.0 N·m)
1988-1989 . . . . .30-32 ft.-lbs.
(40.7-43.4 N·m)
Crankcase Halves:
Prior to 1977. . . . . .120-130 in.-lbs.
(14-15 N·m)
After 1976 (Six Main Bearing Screws) . . . .168-192 in.-lbs.
(19-22 N·m)
(Eight Outer Screws) . . . . .60-84 in.-lbs.
(7-9 N·m)
Cylinder Head:
Prior to 1977 . . . . .96-120 in.-lbs.
(11-14 N·m)
After 1976 . . . . .216-240 in.-lbs.
(24-27 N·m)
Flywheel:
Prior to 1977 . . . . .40-45 ft.-lbs.
(54-61 N·m)
After 1976. . . . . .100-105 ft.-lbs.
(136-143 N·m)
Spark Plug. . . . . .216-240 in.-lbs.
(24-27 N·m)
Standard Screws:
No. 6 . . . . .7-10 in.-lbs.
(0.8-1.2 N·m)
No. 8 . . . . .15-22 in.-lbs.
(1.6-2.4 N·m)
No. 10 . . . . .25-35 in.-lbs.
(2.8-4.0 N·m)
No. 12 . . . . .35-40 in.-lbs.
(4.0-4.6 N·m)
¼ Inch. . . . . .60-80 in.-lbs.
(7-9 N·m)
5/16 Inch . . . . .120-140 in.-lbs.
(14-16 N·m)
⅛ Inch. . . . . .220-240 in.-lbs.
(24-27 N·m)
7/16 Inch . . . . .340-360 in.-lbs.
(38-40 N·m)

LUBRICATION

The power head is lubricated by oil mixed with the fuel. The recommended fuel is regular leaded or unleaded gasoline with a minimum octane rating of 67 on models produced after 1980, or minumum octane rating of 86 on models prior to 1981. If the recommended fuel is not available, gasoline containing not more than ten percent ethanol alcohol, or gasoline containing not more than five percent methanol alcohol with five percent co-solvent additives may be used. Do not use gasoline exceeding the specified alcohol content regardless of octane rating. Discontinue the use of alcohol extended gasoline if fuel system problems are encountered.

The recommended oil is Evinrude or Johnson Outboard Lubricant or a suitable equivalent NMMA (formerly known as BIA) certified TC-W or TC-WII engine oil. The manufacturer recommends using only oil certified TC-WII on models after 1988. The recommended fuel:oil ratio for normal service and during engine break-in is 50:1.

NOTE: OMC service bulletin 2211 issued September 1988, recommends using a 50:1 fuel:oil ratio on all recreational outboard motors which were previously recommended for a 100:1 fuel:oil mixture. For 1989, Accumix and Accumix R fuel and oil mixing systems have been changed to a 50:1 ratio.

On models so recommended, a 100:1 fuel:oil mixture may be used if an approved oil formulated for 100:1 mixture is used and if the engine is completely broken-in and motor is used on a frequent basis. Do not use a 100:1 mixture if motor is used infrequently and during nonuse the motor is stored in areas of high humidity or wide-scale temperature changes, or if motor is operated at constant high speeds.

The lower unit gears and bearings are lubricated by oil contained in the gearcase. The recommended oil is OMC HI-VIS Gearcase Lube. The gearcase oil level should be checked after every 50 hours of operation and the gearcase should be drained and filled with new oil every 100 hours or once each season, whichever occurs first.

The gearcase oil is drained and filled through the same plug port. An oil level (vent) port is used to indicate the full level of the gearcase with oil and to ease oil drainage.

To drain the oil, place the outboard motor in a vertical position. Remove drain plug and oil level plug and allow the lubricant to drain into a suitable container.

To fill the gearcase with oil, place the outboard motor in a vertical position.

Add oil through drain plug opening with an oil feeder until the oil begins to overflow from oil level plug port. Reinstall oil level plug with a new gasket, if needed, and tighten. Remove oil feeder, then reinstall drain plug with a new gasket, if needed, and tighten.

FUEL SYSTEM

CARBURETOR. Refer to Fig. OM9-1 for view of carburetor typical to 18, 20 and 25 hp models prior to 1989, and all 28 hp models. Carburetor used on 1989 20 and 25 models is similar. Refer to Fig. OM9-2.

NOTE: The manufacturer does not recommend submerging carburetor components in carburetor or parts cleaning solutions. An aerosol type carburetor cleaner is recommended to clean carburetor. The float and other components made of plastic and rubber should not be subjected to some cleaning solutions. Safety eyewear and hand protection are recommended when working with solvent.

Initial setting of low speed needle (5—Fig. OM9-1 or OM9-2) is one turn open from a lightly seated position on models prior to 1977, 1-1/4 turns open on 1977-1986 models, one turn open on 1987 and 1988 models and 1-3/4 turns open on 1989 models. Make final idle mixture adjustment with engine running in gear at normal operating temperature. High speed fuel mixture is metered by fixed high speed jet (23). Note that 1989 20 and 25 hp models are equipped with intermediate jet (I—Fig. OM9-2). Idle speed should be 650 rpm on models prior to 1987 and 650-700 rpm on all other models. For optimum results when adjusting idle speed, boat should

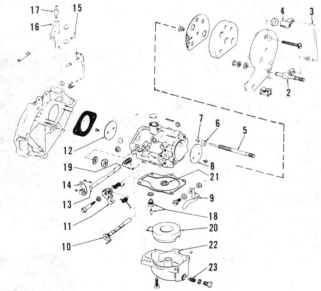

Fig. OM9-1—Exploded view of carburetor typical of all models. Carburetor used on 1989 20-25 hp models differs slightly. Refer to Fig. OM9-2.

2. Idle mixture shaft
3. Link
4. Lever
5. Idle mixture needle
6. Retainer
7. Bearing
8. Choke plate
9. Choke lever
10. Choke shaft
11. Choke bellcrank
12. Throttle plate
13. Throttle shaft
14. Throttle lever
15. Link
16. Follower
17. Follower roller
18. Inlet valve
19. Float pivot
20. Float
21. Nozzle gasket
22. Float chamber
23. Main jet

Fig. OM9-2—View of carburetor used on 1989 20 and 25 hp models. Refer to Fig. OM9-1 for component identification except intermediate jet (I).

be in the water with the correct propeller installed. Engine should be running in forward gear at normal operating temperature with boat movement unrestrained.

To check float level, remove float bowl and invert carburetor. Place OMC Float Gage 324891 on float bowl gasket surface as shown in Fig. OM9-3. Make sure float gage is not pushing down on float. Float should be between notches on side of float gage marked 25 THRU 75 HP. Carefully bend float arm to adjust level. If float gage 324891 is not available, adjust float so float is level and parallel with float bowl gasket surface. To check float drop, hold carburetor upright and allow float to hang by its own weight. Measure from float bowl gasket surface to bottom of float 180 degrees from inlet needle. Carefully bend tang on float arm (adjacent to inlet needle) to set float drop to 1-1/8 to 1-5/8 inches (28.6-41.3 mm) on 1989 20 and 25 hp models and 1-1/8 to 1-1/2 inches (28.6-38.1 mm) on all other models. Apply a suitable thread locking compound to float bowl screws upon reassembly.

SPEED CONTROL LINKAGE. The speed control lever rotates the magneto armature plate, and the carburetor throttle valve is synchronized to open as ignition timing is advanced. A cam attached to the bottom of the armature plate moves cam follower (16 and 17—Fig. OM9-1) which opens the throttle plate (12), via link (15) and lever (14). Ignition timing and throttle plate opening must be properly synchronized to obtain satisfactory operation.

Prior to adjusting speed control linkage, make certain that roller (17) is contacting the cam and that choke linkage (on models so equipped) is not holding throttle partially open. Turn speed control grip until cam follower roller is centered between the two index marks as shown in Fig. OM9-4. On models prior to 1973, loosen set screw (Fig. OM9-5), hold throttle up, then retighten set screw. On 1973-1976 models, loosen throttle link (15—Fig. OM9-1), hold throttle closed and retighten link (15) screw. On models after 1976, loosen throttle shaft screw (S—Fig. OM9-6), hold throttle closed and retighten screw (S). Check to make certain that throttle begins to open as marks on cam (Fig. OM9-4) align with roller (17—Fig. OM9-1). Adjust throttle control rod on models after 1976 by shifting unit to forward gear, then advance throttle so throttle lever is against cylinder stop. Push throttle control rod (R—Fig. OM9-7) to full open position and move collar (C) so collar is against pivot block (B). Retighten collar screw. Note that offset on pivot block (B) must face toward front of engine for proper operation. Refer to IGNITION section and check/adjust maximum timing advance.

The idle speed stop screw (Fig. OM9-8) should be adjusted to approximately 650 rpm on models prior to 1987 and 650-700 rpm on 1987 and later models. For optimum results when adjusting idle speed, boat should be in the water with the correct propeller installed. Engine should be running in forward gear at normal operating temperature with boat movement unrestrained.

REED VALVES. The reed type inlet valves (6—Fig. OM9-9) and reed stops (7) are attached to reed plate (5). Reed plate assembly is attached to power head with screw (3).

Fig. OM9-6—Loosen throttle shaft screw (S) to adjust linkage as outlined in text.

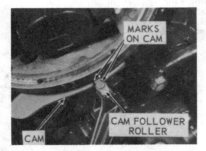

Fig. OM9-4—Refer to text when checking speed control linkage.

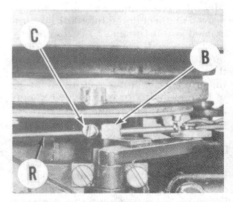

Fig. OM9-7—Collar (C) should touch pivot block (B) when throttle control rod (R) is in full forward position. Refer to text.

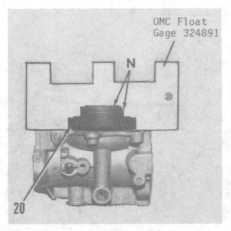

Fig. OM9-3—To check float level, invert carburetor and place OMC Float Gage 324891 on carburetor body as shown. Make sure float gage is not pushing down on float (20). Float should be between notches (N) on side of gage marked 25 THRU 75 HP. Bend float arm to adjust.

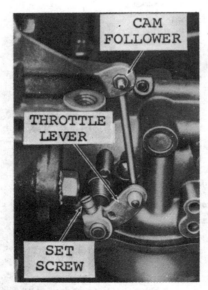

Fig. OM9-5—Throttle lever is attached to carburetor throttle shaft with a set screw on models prior to 1973. Refer to text for adjustment procedure.

Fig. OM9-8—Idle speed stop screw should be set to provide an idle speed of approximately 650 rpm on models prior to 1987 and 650-700 rpm on 1987 and later models.

Reed petals (6) should seat very lightly against reed plate (5) throughout entire length of reed, with the least possible tension. Renew reed petals if broken, cracked, warped or bent. Never attempt to repair damaged reed petals. Seating surface of reed plate (5) must be smooth and flat and reeds must be centered over inlet holes in plate. Check flatness of reed plate and intake manifold using a straightedge and feeler gage. Renew reed plate and/or intake manifold if warped in excess of 0.003 in. (0.08 mm). Alignment recesses are provided at one location for each set of reed petals to assist in centering reed petals. Make certain reed stops (7) are not damaged and that stops are centered behind reed petals.

Oil drain reed (4) should be centered over hole on outside of reed plate. Check petal and seating surface of reed plate (5) carefully and make certain that hole is clean and open. Threads of screw (3) should be coated with OMC Gel-Seal II during reassembly.

FUEL PUMP. The diaphragm type fuel pump (15—Fig. OM9-17) attaches to side of cylinder block and is actuated by crankcase pulsations. Fuel pump is available only as an assembly.

If fuel delivery problems are noted, first remove and clean fuel filter located under fuel pump cover. Install filter with lip of element facing away from pump cover. Remove and blow through fuel lines to ensure lines are clean and open. Test fuel lines and remote tank installation using a suitable vacuum pump and gage. If over 4 inches Hg (13.5 kPa) vacuum is required to draw fuel from tank, check for restrictions in fuel tank and lines. Note that remote fuel tank must not be more than 24 inches (61 cm) below fuel pump.

To test fuel pump, install a suitable pressure gage between fuel pump and carburetor and start engine. Fuel pump pressure should be 2.5 psi (17 kPa) at 4500 rpm. Fuel pump mounting screws should be treated with OMC Nut Lock or a suitable equivalent thread locking compound and tightened to 24-36 in.-lbs. (3-4 N·m). Tighten fuel pump cover screws to 10-15 in.-lbs. (1-2 N·m).

IGNITION

Models Prior to 1977

Breaker point gap should be 0.020 inch (0.51 mm), and both sets of points should be synchronized so they open exactly 180 degrees apart. The manufacturer provides a timing fixture (OMC tool 383602) to be used for adjusting and synchronizing breaker points. The fixture is installed on crankshaft in place of the flywheel as shown in Fig. OM9-10, and is used in combination with a timing light (battery powered) or ohmmeter.

To synchronize breaker points using timing fixture and light, remove flywheel and install timing fixture, making sure fixture is properly located over flywheel key. Disconnect condenser and magneto coil leads from both sets of breaker points. Attach test light or meter to the opening set of breaker points and to suitable engine ground. Test light bulb should go out or ohmmeter should indicate no continuity when points are opened. Turn crankshaft until end of fixture pointer marked T rests midway between the two embossed armature plate timing marks (TM—Fig. OM9-10). Adjust gap until points just open when timing fixture pointer is between the two marks (TM) on armature plate. Turn crankshaft exactly one half turn until the opposite pointer (marked B) of timing fixture is aligned with marks (TM) and adjust other breaker point set.

NOTE: Timing fixture pointers are marked T and B to indicate upper and lower cylinders respectively.

Side of breaker point cam marked TOP should face up. Face of coil shoes should be flush with machined surfaces (F) on armature plate. Flywheel drive key should be installed with marked end down and outer edge parallel with center of crankshaft.

CD2 Ignition System

OPERATION. Models produced 1977-1988 are equipped with CD2 breakerless

capacitor discharge ignition system. Refer to Fig. OM9-14 for wiring schematic. A charge coil and sensor coil are located under the flywheel. Two magnets in flywheel induce a current in the charge coil which is rectified and directed to a capacitor for storage. The two flywheel magnets also induce current in the sensor coil to provide a positive charge on the gate of one of two silicon controlled rectifiers (SCR'S). The positive charge opens the SCR and allows the charged capacitor to discharge through the SCR and primary circuit of the ignition coil. The rapid coil field buildup induces a secondary voltage which fires the spark plug. Diodes, SCR'S and capacitor are contained in the power pack assembly and are not available individually.

Models after 1988 are equipped with CD2USL ignition system. Except for the ignition coils, all CD2U components are located under the flywheel. Refer to Fig. OM9-15 for wiring schematic. The breakdown of the CD2USL model number is as follows: CD-capacitor discharge; 2-two cylinders; U-under flywheel ignition; L-engine speed limiter; S-S.L.O.W. (speed limiting overheat warning) function. The S.L.O.W. function limits engine speed to approximately 2000 rpm if engine temperature exceeds 180° F (82° C). Ignition system model number is printed on top of ignition module located under flywheel. The power pack and sensor coil are integrated into a single ignition module assembly instead of separate components as in earlier CD2 systems.

All Models

IGNITION TIMING. To check the ignition timing, first mount the outboard motor on a boat or a suitable test tank and immerse the lower unit. Connect a suitable timing light to the top cylinder (No. 1) spark plug lead. Start the engine and adjust the speed control until the

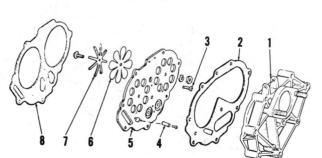

Fig. OM9-9—Exploded view of early reed valve and intake manifold. Later models are similar. Manifold is also shown in Fig. OM9-1.

1. Inlet manifold
2. Manifold-to-plate gasket
3. Plate retaining screw
4. Oil drain valve
5. Reed plate
6. Reed petals
7. Reed stop
8. Crankcase-to-plate gasket

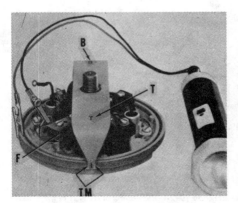

Fig. OM9-10—View showing timing fixture and test light attached. Refer to text for setting breaker point gap.

engine is running at full throttle. On manual rewind start models, timing mark (TM—Fig. OM9-11) should align with the flywheel 34 degree mark on models prior to 1982, 30-31 degree mark on 1982-1985 models and 29-31 degree mark on 1986 and later models. On electric start models, timing mark (TM—Fig. OM9-12) should align with the flywheel 34 degree mark on models prior to 1982, 30-31 degree mark on 1982-1985 models and 29-31 degree mark on 1986 and later models.

NOTE: Two sets of timing grids are located on flywheel. Use grid marked "CD" for rope start models and grid marked "ELEC CD" for models equipped with electric start.

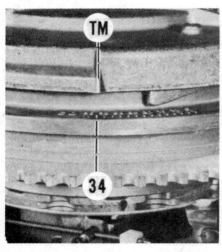

Fig. OM9-11—On manual rewind start models, timing mark (TM) should align with the flywheel 34 degree mark on models prior to 1982, 30-31 degree mark on 1982-1985 models and 29-31 degree mark on 1986 and later models. Thirty-four degree mark is identified. Turn screw (S—Fig. OM9-13) to adjust timing.

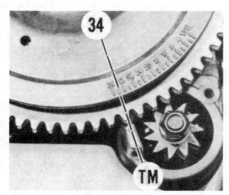

Fig. OM9-12—On electric start models, timing mark (TM) should align with the flywheel 34 degree mark on models prior to 1982, 30-31 degree mark on 1982-1985 models and 29-31 degree mark on 1986 and later models. Thirty-four degree mark is identified. Turn screw (S—Fig. OM9-13) to adjust timing.

To adjust timing on all models, turn timing stop screw (S—Fig. OM9-13). Each complete turn is equivalent to approximately one degree. Turning screw (S) clockwise advances ignition timing. Backfiring and popping may be due to improperly connected wiring. Refer to wiring schematic in Fig. OM9-14 and OM9-15.

CD2 Ignition

TROUBLE-SHOOTING. On models prior to 1985, the 4-wire connector plugs connect the charge and sensor coil

Fig. OM9-13—View of ignition timing adjusting screw.

Fig. OM9-14—Wiring schematic of CD2 ignition circuit on 1977-1988 models. Electric start models are equipped with a key switch in place of STOP button.

leads to the power pack. The 3-wire connector plugs connect the power pack and ignition coils. On models after 1984, a 5-wire connector is used between the power pack and armature plate. On models prior to 1985, check to make sure the white/black wire in the 4-wire connector is positioned in connector terminal B. Also check to make sure the number 1 coil wire is in the 3-wire connector B terminal and that it connects with the power pack orange/blue wire in the other connector B terminal. On models after 1984, check to make sure the white/black wire in the 5-wire connector is positioned in connector terminal B of both connector halves. Also check to make sure the orange/blue power pack lead is connected to the number 1 ignition coil.

NOTE: Outer edges of charge coil and sensor coil must be flush with machined surface of armature plate to provide the proper clearance between coils and flywheel magnets. OMC locating ring 317001 may be used to simplify this procedure. Place locating ring over machined bosses on armature plate, push coil out against locating ring and tighten mounting screws.

To check charge coil output, use Merc-O-Tronic Model 781, Stevens Model CD77 or a suitable peak voltage tester. Disconnect connector between armature plate and power pack. Connect black tester lead to stator lead connector terminal A and red tester lead to terminal D. Turn tester knobs to Negative and 500.

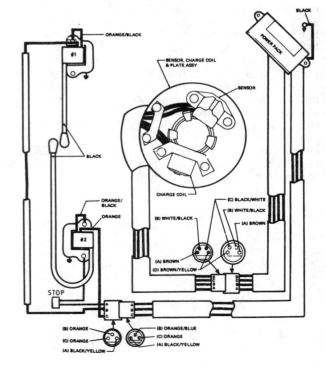

Crank engine while observing tester. If tester reading is below 230 volts, check condition of charge coil wiring and connectors, and verify pin location in connector. If wiring and connectors are in acceptable condition, check charge coil resistance as follows: Connect an ohmmeter to terminals A and D in stator plate lead connector. Renew charge coil if resistance is not 500-650 ohms on models prior to 1986 or 550-600 ohms on 1986-1988 models. Connect negative ohmmeter lead to stator plate (ground) and positive ohmmeter lead to connector terminal A, then to connector terminal D. Infinite resistance should exist between A terminal and stator plate and between D terminal and stator plate. If not, charge coil or charge coil lead is shorted to ground.

To check sensor coil, connect an ohmmeter to terminals B and C in stator plate lead connector. Renew sensor coil if resistance is not 30-50 ohms. Connect negative ohmmeter lead to stator plate (ground) and positive ohmmeter lead to connector terminal B, then to connector terminal C. Infinite resistance should exist between B terminal and stator plate and between C terminal and stator plate. If not, sensor coil or sensor coil lead is shorted to ground. To check sensor coil output, use Merc-O-Tronic Model 781, Stevens Model CD77 or a suitable peak voltage tester. Connect black tester lead to stator lead connector terminal C and red tester lead to terminal B. On Merc-O-Tronic Model 781, turn knobs to Positive and 5, or on Stevens Model CD77, turn knobs to S and 5. Crank engine while observing tester. Reverse tester leads and repeat test. Sensor coil output on both tests should be 2 volts or more on models prior to 1987 and 1.5 volts or more on 1987 and 1988 models. Renew sensor coil if output is not as specified.

To check power pack output, first reconnect connector between armature plate and power pack. Use Merc-O-Tronic Model 781, Stevens Model CD77 or a suitable peak voltage tester. Connect black tester lead to a suitable engine ground. Connect red tester lead to wire leading to either ignition coil. Turn tester knobs to Negative and 500. Crank engine while observing tester. Repeat test on other lead. Renew power pack if readings are not at least 180 volts or higher on models prior to 1985 or 200 volts or higher on models after 1984.

To test ignition coils, disconnect high tension lead at ignition coil. On models prior to 1985, disconnect 3-wire connector and insert a jumper lead in terminal B of the ignition coil end of connector. Connect ohmmeter positive lead to the B terminal jumper wire and ohmmeter negative lead to a good engine ground.

On models after 1984, disconnect coil primary wire at coil and connect ohmmeter positive lead to coil primary terminal and negative lead to a good engine ground or to coil ground tab. Ignition coil primary resistance should be 0.05-0.15 ohm on all models. To check coil secondary resistance, move ohmmeter negative lead to the high tension terminal. Secondary resistance should be 225-325 ohms on models prior to 1986 and 250-300 ohms on models after 1985. Repeat procedure on number 2 ignition coil.

CD2USL Ignition System

TROUBLE-SHOOTING. Disconnect spark plug leads from spark plugs and connect a suitable spark tester. Set tester spark gap to 1/2 inch (12.7 mm). On models so equipped, install emergency ignition cutoff clip and lanyard. Crank engine and observe spark tester. If an acceptable spark is noted at each spark gap, perform RUNNING OUTPUT TEST. If spark is noted at only one spark gap, perform IGNITION PLATE OUTPUT TEST as described in this section. If no spark is noted at either spark gap, perform STOP CIRCUIT TEST.

NOTE: If acceptable spark is noted at each spark gap during spark output test but engine pops and backfires during starting or running, ignition system may be out of time.

Be sure orange/blue primary wire is connected to number 1 ignition coil, spark plug high tension leads are properly connected, flywheel is properly located on crankshaft and speed control linkage is properly adjusted.

STOP CIRCUIT TEST. Remove spark plug leads from spark plugs and connect a suitable spark tester. Disconnect stop circuit connector (Fig. OM9-16). Make sure ignition emergency cutoff clip and lanyard are installed on models so

Fig. OM9-16—View showing location of single-pin stop circuit connector on models equipped with CD2USL ignition system.

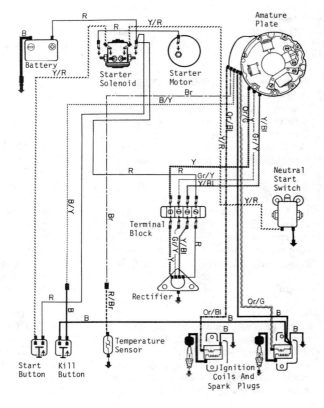

Fig. OM9-15—Wiring schematic of 1989 models equipped with CD2USL ignition and electric start.
B. Black
R. Red
Y. Yellow
Br. Brown
Y/R. Yellow with red tracer
R/Br. Red with brown tracer
R/Or. Red with orange tracer
Y/Bl. Yellow with blue tracer
Or/G. Orange with green tracer
Gr/Y. Gray with yellow tracer
Or/Bl. Orange with blue tracer

equipped. Crank engine and observe spark tester. If no spark is noted, perform IGNITION PLATE OUTPUT TEST. If normal spark is noted, connect ohmmeter between engine ground and the one-pin stop circuit connector (Fig. OM9-16). Ohmmeter should show infinite resistance. If meter shows continuity, repair short in wiring or renew stop button. Depress stop button or remove emergency cutoff clip and note ohmmeter. If ohmmeter does not indicate continuity, repair open in wiring or renew stop button.

IGNITION PLATE OUTPUT TEST. Disconnect spark plug leads to prevent accidental starting. Remove primary leads from ignition coils. Connect number 1 ignition coil primary lead to the red lead of Stevens load adapter PL-88 and black lead of load adapter to engine ground.

NOTE: If Stevens load adapter is not available, fabricate load adapter using a 10 ohm, 10 watt resistor (Radio Shack part 271-132) or equivalent.

Connect red test lead of CD77 or equivalent peak reading voltmeter to red lead of Stevens load adapter PL-88 and black test lead to engine ground. Set CD voltmeter to Positive and 500. Crank engine and note meter. Repeat test procedure on number 2 ignition coil primary lead. If CD voltmeter indicates 175 volts or higher on both tests, perform IGNITION COIL TESTS. If one primary lead shows no output, renew ignition module. If both tests indicate no output, perform CHARGE COIL RESISTANCE TEST.

CHARGE COIL RESISTANCE TEST. Remove manual starter and flywheel. Remove two ignition module mounting screws and disconnect module brown and brown/yellow bullet connectors. Connect ohmmeter between brown and brown/yellow charge coil connectors. Renew charge coil if resistance is not within 535-585 ohms. Connect one ohmmeter lead to engine ground and connect other ohmmeter lead to brown charge coil lead, then to brown/yellow charge coil lead. Renew charge coil if ohmmeter shows continuity between engine ground and either wire. If charge coil tests acceptable, renew ignition module.

NOTE: When installing charge coil or ignition module, use OMC Locating Ring 334994 to properly position components on armature plate. Place ring over machined surfaces on armature plate, push components outward against locating ring and

tighten mounting screws to 30-40 in.-lbs. (3.4-4.5 N·m).

RUNNING OUTPUT TEST. Remove propeller and install the correct test wheel, then mount outboard motor in a suitable test tank. Remove ignition coil primary wires and install suitable terminal extenders (Stevens TS-77 or equivalent) on coil primary terminals, then install primary wires on terminal extenders. Connect peak reading voltmeter red test lead to number 1 coil terminal extender and black test lead to engine ground. Set voltmeter to Positive and 500. Start engine and run at rpm where ignition malfunction is evident while noting meter. Repeat test procedure on number 2 ignition coil. If either cylinder shows less than 200 volts, perform CHARGE COIL RESISTANCE TEST. If charge coil test results are acceptable, renew ignition module.

IGNITION COIL RESISTANCE TEST. To check ignition coil primary resistance, connect ohmmeter between primary terminal and coil ground. Resistance should be 0.05-0.15 ohm. To check secondary resistance, connect ohmmeter between coil high tension terminal and primary terminal. Resistance should be 250-300 ohms. Renew coil if resistance is not as specified.

S.L.O.W. (Speed Limiting Overheat Warning). To test S.L.O.W. function, place outboard motor in a suitable test tank with the correct test wheel, or place boat in the water. Start engine and run at 3500 rpm. Disconnect brown temperature sensor lead and touch lead to engine ground. Engine speed should slow to approximately 2000 rpm when brown sensor lead is grounded. If not, inspect wiring harness or renew ignition module.

COOLING SYSTEM

WATER PUMP. All models are equipped with a rubber impeller type water pump which is mounted on and driven by the lower unit drive shaft. If cooling system malfunction occurs, first check water inlet for plugging or partial restriction, and check thermostat for proper operation.

To remove water pump, refer to LOWER UNIT section and remove the gearcase assembly. Water pump is located at top of gearcase as shown in Figs. OM9-30 and OM9-32. Make sure water passages and tubes are not damaged or restricted. Turn impeller in clockwise direction when installing impeller into housing. Sharp side of impeller drive key is the leading edge of key. Be sure key

is installed with sharp side facing toward clockwise direction.

THERMOSTAT. The thermostat is located under cover (1—Fig. OM9-17) on 22 cu. in. (361 cc) models and behind cylinder head cover (1—Fig. OM9-18) on 31.8 cubic inch (521 cc) models. Check thermostat operation by using Thermomelt Stiks. To check thermostat operation, install the correct test wheel and place outboard motor in a suitable test tank. Start engine and run at 3000 rpm for five minutes, then reduce engine speed to 900 rpm. Mark side of cylinder head with 125° F (52° C) and 163° F (73° C) Thermomelt Stiks. The 125° F (52° C) "Stik" should melt but not the 163° F (73° C) "Stik." Increase engine speed to 5000 rpm and note the 163° F (73° C) mark. It should remain unmelted. Renew thermostat and inspect condition of water pump, water passages, gaskets and sealing surfaces if engine does not maintain correct operating temperature.

POWER HEAD

R&R AND DISASSEMBLE. It is usually desirable, depending upon work to be performed, to remove the rewind starter (electric starter motor if so equipped), magneto assembly, carburetor, intake manifold, reed valves, fuel pump and covers prior to removing the power head. Remove the port and starboard starter mounting brackets, remove the power head attaching screws, then lift power head off drive shaft housing.

Remove cylinder head (5—Fig. OM9-17 or OM9-18) and drive out taper pin(s) toward front (carburetor) side of motor. Use caution not to damage taper pin bore. Remove armature support (10) and retainer (11), then remove crankcase half (44).

NOTE: Two crankcase screws are accessible through intake passages in front of crankcase.

Separate crankcase and cylinder block by tapping flywheel end of crankshaft (toward crankcase side) with a soft-face mallet. DO NOT pry between crankcase and cylinder block.

Pistons, rods and crankshaft are now accessible for removal and overhaul as outlined in the appropriate following paragraphs. Make sure all components are marked for reference during reassembly.

ASSEMBLY. Prior to reassembly, check sealing surfaces of crankcase and covers making certain that all are clean, smooth and flat. Small nicks or burrs may be polished out on a lapping plate, but sealing surfaces MUST NOT be lowered. Cylinder head may be lapped if warped in excess of 0.004 inch (0.10 mm). Cylinder head should be renewed if more than 0.010 inch (0.25 mm) is required to true head.

Refer to specific service sections when assembling crankshaft, connecting rods and pistons. Thoroughly lubricate all friction surfaces with a recommended engine oil during reassembly. Apply a thin even bead of OMC Gel-Seal II or equivalent to the crankcase sealing surface of cylinder block. Position crankcase half (44—Fig. OM9-17 or OM9-18) over cylinder block and install retaining screws finger tight. Drive taper pin(s) (43) into position toward cylinder block. Be sure taper pin is firmly seated. Re-

fer to Fig. OM9-19 for cylinder head tightening sequence. Cylinder head screws should be retightened after motor has been test run and allowed to cool.

Installation is the reverse of removal. Lubricate drive shaft splines with OMC Moly Lube. Make sure the ''O'' ring is installed in lower end of crankshaft. Apply Permatex No. 2 or equivalent to both sides of power head-to-exhaust housing gasket. Apply a liberal bead of a suitable RTV sealant around outer diameter of lower seal housing (54—Fig. OM9-18). Tighten power head retaining screws to 16-18 ft.-lbs. (21.7-24.4 N·m).

PISTONS, RINGS AND CYLINDERS. Mark pistons, connecting rods and caps for reassembly in original location. Each

piston is fitted with two piston rings. Top ring is semi-keystone shape. Refer to CONDENSED SERVICE DATA for piston ring service specifications. Pistons are equipped with locating pins to prevent ring rotation.

Refer to CONDENSED SERVICE DATA for piston skirt-to-cylinder clearance on models prior to 1985. The manufacturer does not specify piston skirt clearance on models after 1984. If cylinder bore and piston are within tolerance, piston-to-cylinder clearance should be acceptable. Pistons and rings are available in 0.030 inch (0.76 mm) oversize for all models.

On models prior to 1983, measure piston diameter 1/8 inch (3.2 mm) up from bottom of skirt. Take one measurement parallel to piston pin bore and another at 90 degrees to pin bore. Renew piston if difference between measurements exceeds 0.002 inch (0.05 mm).

Models produced 1983-1988 are equipped with cam ground pistons. To check wear on cam ground piston, proceed as follows: Measure piston diameter 90 degrees to piston pin bore 1/8 to 1/4 inch (3.2-6.3 mm) up from bottom of skirt. This dimension is the major piston diameter. Renew piston if major diameter is less than 2.9940 inch (76.048 mm) on standard size piston or 3.0240 inch (76.810 mm) for oversize piston. Next, measure piston skirt diameter parallel to piston pin bore. This measurement is the minor diameter. Renew piston if difference between major and minor diameters exceeds 0.0045 inch (0.114 mm), or if minor diameter is larger than major diameter.

On 1989 models, two piston designs are used. Refer to Fig. OM9-20 to visually identify pistons. Both piston designs are cam ground. On both designs, measure piston at a point 1/8 to 1/4 inch (3.2-6.3 mm) up from bottom of skirt. Measure piston at 90 degrees to pin bore (major diameter) and parallel to pin bore (minor diameter). Subtract minor diameter from major diameter to obtain piston cam dimension. Cam dimension should be 0.0015-0.0025 inch (0.038-0.063 mm) on Art type piston and 0.005-0.007 inch (0.13-0.18 mm) on Zollner type piston. Renew piston if cam dimension is not as specified.

Refer to CONDENSED SERVICE DATA for standard cylinder bore diameter. Maximum allowable cylinder bore out-of-round is 0.003 inch (0.08 mm) for all models. Maximum allowable cylinder bore taper is 0.002 inch (0.05 mm) for models after 1976 and 0.003 inch (0.08 mm) for all earlier models. To determine cylinder bore oversize diameter when reboring cylinder block, add piston oversize dimension (0.030 inch [0.76 mm]) to standard cylinder bore diameter.

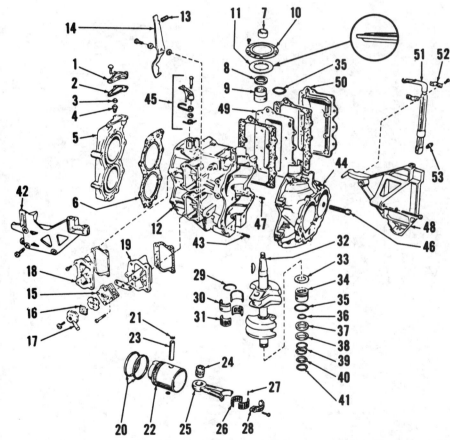

Fig. OM9-17—Exploded view of power head typical of 22 cu. in. (361 cc) models. On some models, fuel pump (15) is mounted on top transfer port cover (18). Flat side of magneto retainer (11) should face up.

1. Cover	15. Fuel pump	29. Retaining ring	41. Snap ring
2. Gasket	16. Fuel filter	30. Center bearing	42. Starter bracket
3. Seal	17. Cover	outer race	43. Taper pin
4. Thermostat	18. Transfer port cover	31. Center main bearing	44. Crankcase front half
5. Cylinder head	19. Transfer port cover	& cage halves	45. Lockout assy.
6. Gasket	20. Piston rings	32. Crankshaft	46. Crankcase screw
7. Magneto cam	21. Retaining rings	33. Thrust washer	47. Bearing retaining
8. Upper seal	22. Piston	34. Lower main bearing	dowel
9. Top main bearing	23. Piston pin	35. ''O'' ring	48. Starter bracket
10. Support	24. Needle bearing	36. Carbon ring	49. Exhaust inner cover
11. Retainer	25. Connecting rod	37. Lower bearing seal	50. Outer cover
12. Cylinder	26. Bearing cage	38. Inner washer	51. Speed control shaft
13. Spring	27. Roller	39. Spring	52. Clamp
14. Shift lock	28. Rod cap	40. Outer washer	53. Pin

On models prior to 1978, one pin bore is press fit while the other bore is a slip fit. The loose fit bore is marked on underside of piston. Piston pin must be removed from piston toward press fit side and reinstalled in loose fit side first. Be sure to properly support piston when removing or installing pin to prevent damage to piston. Piston may be heated to ease pin removal and installation. On later models, piston pin is loose fit on both piston bores and rides on 28 loose needle bearing rollers. Always renew piston pin retaining rings if removed. On all models, piston must be assembled to connecting rod with the long tapered side of piston crown facing exhaust ports. On models so equipped, oil hole (Fig. OM9-21) in connecting rod must face top of engine. Connecting rod with two holes in rod small end has no specific directional orientation but if reused should be installed in same direction as removed.

CONNECTING RODS, BEARINGS AND CRANKSHAFT. Prior to detaching connecting rods from crankshaft, make sure that rod, cap and piston are marked for correct location during reassembly.

Connecting rod small end is fitted with caged needle bearing on models prior to 1985 and with 28 loose bearing rollers and washers on 1985 and later models. Install washers with flat surface facing outward.

Crankshaft is supported by three main bearings. Refer to Figs. OM9-17 and OM9-18. Top main bearing (9) will slide off crankshaft for inspection. Do not remove lower main bearing (34—Fig. OM9-18) unless bearing renewal is required. Renew thrust washer (33—Fig. OM9-17) on 22 cu. in. (361 cc) engine if crankshaft end play exceeds 0.023 inch (0.58 mm). Install thrust washer (33) with bronze surface facing crankshaft.

When assembling main bearings and seals to crankshaft on models prior to 1977, observe the following: Position center main bearing rollers (31) around crankshaft journal and install bearing outer race halves (30) with retaining ring groove facing down. Make sure retaining ring (29) is properly installed in groove. Install thrust washer (33) with bronze surface toward crankshaft (up). Install lower bearing (34) on crankshaft with groove facing up and install "O" ring (35) around bearing (34). Refer to Figs. OM9-17 and OM9-22 to install lower crankshaft seal assembly. Lip of top seal (8—Fig. OM9-17) should face down. Be sure bearings properly engage dowel pins when installing crankshaft in cylinder block.

When assembling crankshaft and bearings on 1977 and later models, press

against lettered side of bearing when installing lower bearing (34—Fig. OM9-18) on crankshaft. Make sure snap ring (41) is properly seated in groove of crankshaft. Install upper bearing (9) on crankshaft with lettered end of bearing facing down. Install seal (8) with lip facing down. Install center main bearing rollers (31) around crankshaft journal and install outer race with retaining ring facing down. Lubricate "O" ring (56) with OMC Moly Lube and install in lower end of crankshaft. Apply OMC Gasket Sealing Compound to outer diameter of seal (37) and press into housing (54) until seated. Make sure lip of seal (37) faces upward. Make sure dowel pin on bearing (9) properly engages notch in cylinder block and dowel (47) properly engages center main bearing outer race.

Note that center main bearing alignment dowel (47) may be renewed if damaged or loose in cylinder block.

Joint between connecting rod and cap is fractured and not machined. When assembling connecting rods to crankpins, first determine if engine is equipped with hand-sanded or precision-ground connecting rods by referring to Fig. OM9-23. On models equipped with hand-sanded connecting rods (some 1985 and all earlier models), install rod cap making sure match marks on rod and cap are aligned and tighten cap screws finger tight. Check cap-to-rod alignment by running a pencil point or similar tool over joint between rod and cap. Align cap by carefully tapping with a suitable mallet. If rod and cap are properly aligned, joint between rod and

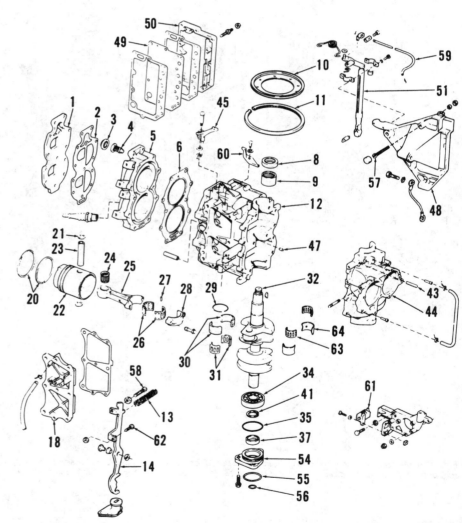

Fig. OM9-18—Exploded view of power head typical of the type used on models after 1976. Components (29, 30 and 31) are used on 1977 models while bearing (63) and races (64) are used on models after 1977. Refer to Fig. OM9-17 for identification of components except for the following.

54. Seal housing
55. "O" ring
56. "O" ring
57. Ignition timing adjusting screw
58. Shifter lock adjusting screw
59. Throttle control rod
60. Lockout lever
61. Electric start safety switch
62. Safety switch adjusting screw
63. Bearing
64. Bearing race

cap should be nearly invisible. When proper alignment is obtained, tighten cap screws to the recommended value (CONDENSED SERVICE DATA). If acceptable alignment cannot be obtained, rod and cap assembly should be renewed.

Models equipped with precision ground connecting rods (Fig. OM9-23) require the use of OMC Rod Cap Alignment Fixture 396749 to assembly rod and cap assemblies. Follow instructions provided with special tool and refer to Fig. OM9-24. Make sure rod and cap match marks are aligned. When rod and cap are correctly aligned, tighten cap screws using OMC Socket 331638. Refer to CONDENSED SERVICE DATA for recommended torque value.

On all models, be certain of the following: All bearing rollers are installed; oil hole (Fig. OM9-21) on models so equipped is facing up; long sloping side of piston crown is toward exhaust ports and match marks on rod and cap are aligned.

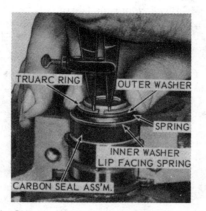

Fig. OM9-22—View of lower crankshaft seal on 22 cu. in. (361 cc) models. Refer to components (36 through 41—Fig. OM9-17).

STARTER

MANUAL REWIND STARTER. Figure OM9-25 shows an exploded view of the manual starter typical of all models. Starter can be removed from power head after removing three mounting screws and detaching starter lockout cable from starter housing if so equipped.

To disassemble starter, remove rope handle (13) and allow pulley (4) to unwind until all tension is removed from rewind spring (3). Remove nut on top of housing and withdraw screw, spindle

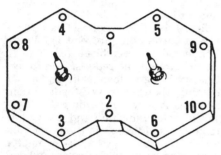

Fig. OM9-19—Follow sequence shown when tightening cylinder head bolts on all models.

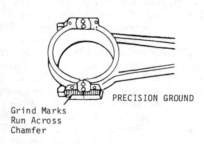

PRECISION GROUND

Grind Marks Run Across Chamfer

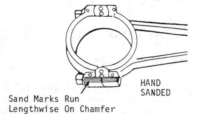

HAND SANDED

Sand Marks Run Lengthwise On Chamfer

Fig. OM9-23—To identify precision ground connecting rod, note direction of grind marks on chamfered edge of rod. Precision ground rods have grind marks running across chamfer as shown. Refer to text.

Fig. OM9-25—Exploded view of manual rewind starter typical of the type used on all models. Late model type starter is equipped with two drive pawls (7). A spring washer, friction ring, friction plate, shim and bushing are located between spindle (9) and pulley (4) on later models.

1. Housing
2. Rope
3. Recoil spring
4. Pulley
5. Spring
6. Link
7. Pawl
8. Retainer
9. Spindle
10. Clamp
11. Cover
12. Cover
13. Handle
14. Anchor

Fig. OM9-20—To identify Art or Zollner pistons used on 1989 models, view top of piston crown. Art piston will have half-circle in center of deflector as shown. Refer to text for piston measuring procedure.

Art   Zollner

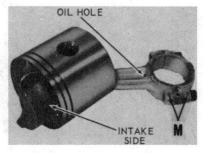

Fig. OM9-21—The piston and connecting rod must be assembled to each other with long sloping side of deflector facing exhaust side of cylinder block. On models so equipped, oil hole in connecting rod must face up and match marks on rod and cap must be aligned. Connecting rods with two holes in piston pin bore may be installed either direction. If reusing original rods, always reinstall in same direction as removed.

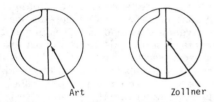

Fig. OM9-24—View showing OMC Rod Cap Alignment Fixture properly assembled on connecting rod. Follow instructions provided with special tool.

OMC Rod Cap Alignment Fixture 396749

and on later models, spring washer and friction ring (not shown). Remove retainers (8), pawls (7) and links (5). To remove pulley (4) and rewind spring (3), hold housing (1) upright and strike housing against a bench or other suitable flat surface to dislodge pulley and spring.

Inspect all components for excessive wear or other damage and renew as necessary. Reassemble starter by reversing disassembly. Apply OMC Triple-Guard grease or Lubriplate 777 to rewind spring, spindle and spindle area in housing. Wind rewind spring into housing in counterclockwise direction starting with outer coil. Preload rewind spring by winding pulley (4) counterclockwise until rewind spring is tight, back off pulley 1/2 to one full turn, then allow rewind spring to wind rope into housing. Apply a suitable thread locking compound to starter assembly mounting screws and tighten to 96-120 in.-lbs. (10.8-13.6 N·m). Starter lockout mechanism should prevent manual starter operation if shift handle is in forward or reverse gear position.

ELECTRIC STARTER. Electric starter motor used on early models is shown in OM9-26. Later models are equipped with the starter motor shown in OM9-27. On early model starter, no-load motor speed should be a minimum of 8000 rpm with maximum current draw of 60 amps at 10 volts. On late model starter, no-load speed should be 6500-7500 rpm with maximum current draw of 30 amps at 12-12.4 volts.

Seal the joints between starter frame, brush holder and head assembly with OMC Black Neoprene Dip or equivalent. Tighten through-bolts to 95-110 in.-lbs. (10.7-12.4 N·m). Nut (1) should be renewed if removed and tightened to 20-25 ft.-lbs. (27-34 N·m).

On models equipped with electric start, battery must maintain a minimum of 9.6 volts under cranking load for 15 seconds. If not, battery must be charged or renewed.

AC LIGHTING COIL

Manual Start Models

To test lighting coil, disconnect three pin connector leading from armature plate. Connect a suitable ohmmeter between yellow wire with gray tracer and yellow wire. Renew lighting coil if resistance is not within 0.81-0.91 ohm. Next, connect ohmmeter between yellow wire with gray tracer and yellow wire with blue tracer. Renew lighting coil if resistance is not within 1.19-1.23 ohms. Connect ohmmeter between engine ground and alternately to each pin in three pin connector (yellow, yellow/gray and yellow/blue). Ohmmeter should read infinity at each connection. If not, inspect for shorted lighting coil or coil wires.

BATTERY CHARGING SYSTEM

Electric Start Models

To test alternator output, connect a suitable ammeter in series with the red rectifier lead and red wiring harness lead. At 5500 rpm, alternator output should be approximately 4.5 amps. If not, proceed as follows: Disconnect battery cables from battery. Disconnect all stator leads from the terminal board. Using a suitable ohmmeter, connect red tester lead to stator yellow lead. Connect black tester lead to stator yellow/blue lead. Resistance should be 0.22-0.32 ohm. Move red tester lead to stator yellow/gray lead. Resistance should be 0.22-0.32 ohm. Renew or repair stator if resistance is not as specified.

To check for shorted stator or stator wiring, connect black tester lead to engine ground. Connect red tester lead to stator yellow/blue lead, then to stator yellow and yellow/gray leads. If ohmmeter does not read infinity at all connections, stator or stator wiring is shorted to ground and must be repaired or renewed.

To test rectifier, disconnect battery cables at battery and proceed as follows: Connect ohmmeter black test lead to engine ground and red test lead to rectifier yellow/gray lead. Note ohmmeter reading, then reverse tester lead connections. A very high reading should result in one connection and a very low reading should result in the other connection. Repeat test with ohmmeter connected between engine ground and rectifier yellow lead, then between ground and yellow/blue lead. One connection should show high resistance, the other low resistance. Next, connect ohmmeter between rectifier red lead and yellow/gray lead. Note reading and reverse tester connections. Repeat test between rectifier red lead and yellow lead, then red lead and yellow/blue lead. As before, one connection should show high resistance and the other low resis-

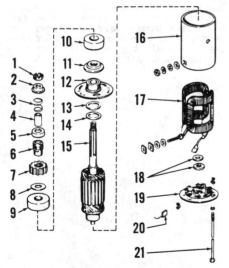

Fig. OM9-26—Exploded view of electric starter motor used on early models so equipped.

1. Stop nut	11. Cushion retainer
2. Pinion stop	12. Head assy.
3. Antidrift spring	13. Thrust washer
4. Spring sleeve	14. Thrust washer
5. Screwshaft cup	15. Armature
6. Screwshaft	16. Frame
7. Drive pinion	17. Field coil
8. Thrust washer	18. Thrust washers
9. Cushion grip	19. Brush holder
10. Starter drive	20. Brush
cushion	21. Through-bolt

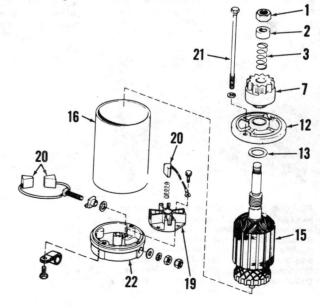

Fig. OM9-27—Exploded view of electric starter used on later models. Refer to Fig. OM9-26 for components identification except for end cap (22).

tance. Renew rectifier if not as specified.

LOWER UNIT

PROPELLER AND HUB. Protection for the propeller and drive unit is provided by a cushioning and slip clutch built into the propeller hub. Service consists of renewing propeller.

Various propellers are available. Select a propeller that will allow a properly tuned and adjusted outboard motor to operate at the specified rpm range (CONDENSED SERVICE DATA) at wide open throttle.

R&R AND OVERHAUL. Most service on the lower unit can be performed by detaching the gearcase housing from drive shaft and exhaust housing. When servicing lower unit, pay particular attention to water pump and water tubes with respect to air or water leaks. Leaky connections may interfere with proper cooling of the motor. Water leaks may also permit the inside of drive shaft casing to fill with water which can eventually find its way into motor and/or gearcase.

Refer to the appropriate exploded views when overhauling lower unit assembly. All gasket surfaces must be smooth, free from nicks and burrs and assembled using a nonhardening type sealer such as OMC Gasket Sealing Compound. All joints without gaskets must be smooth, free from nicks, burrs and sealant.

Propeller shaft (18—Fig. OM9-30) and drive gears can be removed after first draining lubricant from gearcase, removing pivot screw (4) and removing gearcase lower housing (7).

To separate gearcase from the exhaust housing, it is necessary to remove cover (10—OM9-28 or OM9-29) and loosen the shift rod clamp screw.

Pinion gear (32—Fig. OM9-30) to gearcase clearance on 1969-1977 models should be 0.0011-0.0023 inch (0.028-0.058 mm). If clearance between pinion gear and gearcase is excessive, gearcase must be renewed. On later models, pinion gear rides in a roller bearing (38) while forward gear (16) is supported by roller bearing (46).

During reassembly, install bearing (30) with lettered side up. Early models are equipped with a single drive shaft seal (29) while later models are equipped with two seals. Internal bevel on thrust washer (31) should be toward gear (32). External bevel on thrust washer (39) should be toward top of gearcase. Seal strip (8) should be trimmed to allow 1/32 inch (0.79 mm) to extend into each side of gearcase head bore. Apply OMC Adhesive M or a suitable equivalent to mating surfaces of gearcase and lower housing (7), locate strip (8) in groove, then apply sealer to strip, especially at ends. Check for free rotation and correct gear shifting prior to installing gearcase. The shift linkage adjustment should be checked after reassembly.

WARNING: Spark plug leads should be disconnected from spark plugs and properly grounded prior to performing any propeller service to prevent accidental starting and severe personal injury.

To check and adjust gear shift linkage on models prior to 1981, set shift lever in neutral and make certain that propeller turns freely. Rotate the propeller by hand while moving the shift lever (8—OM9-28 or OM9-29) slowly in each direction to the point where lower unit dog clutch contacts the drive gear lugs. Mark shift lever location on shroud at point of contact. Travel should be the same distance each side of neutral position to point of contact. If not, loosen clamp screw and adjustment screw (Fig. OM9-31) and move shift lever as necessary and retighten screws.

To adjust shift rod on models after 1980, move shift lever to neutral position and rotate propeller to be sure unit is in neutral. If propeller does not rotate freely, loosen screws securing shift rod clamp (37—Fig. OM9-30) and move lower shift rod so gearcase is in neutral, then retighten clamp screws. Check adjustment by moving shift lever to all three shift positions and rotating propeller.

Models After 1984

PROPELLER AND HUB. Protection for propeller and drive unit is provided by a cushioning hub built into the propeller. Service consists of propeller renewal if hub is damaged.

Fig. OM9-28—Exploded view of stern bracket, exhaust housing, drive shaft housing and related components on early models.

1. Shift rod retainer	18. Spring	33. Pilot shaft
2. Shift lever	19. Throttle shaft	34. Thrust washer
3. Shift rod	20. Bushing	35. Liner
4. Exhaust plate	21. Gear cover	36. Spacer
5. Exhaust housing	22. Drive shaft tube	37. Plate
6. Shifter shaft	23. Steering handle	38. Stern bracket
7. "O" ring	24. Spring	39. Clamp
8. Shift handle	25. Friction block	40. Lever arm
9. Rubber mount	26. Throttle grip	41. Friction adjusting
10. Cover plate	27. Throttle shaft	screw
11. Lower mount	28. Throttle pinion	42. Link
12. Lower mount	29. Throttle gear	43. Link
13. "O" ring	30. Idle speed adjusting	44. Tilt lever
14. "O" ring	screw	45. Swivel bracket
15. Spring	31. Bushing	46. Bushing
16. Stern bracket	32. Steering bracket	47. Thrust washer
17. Reverse lock		48. "O" ring

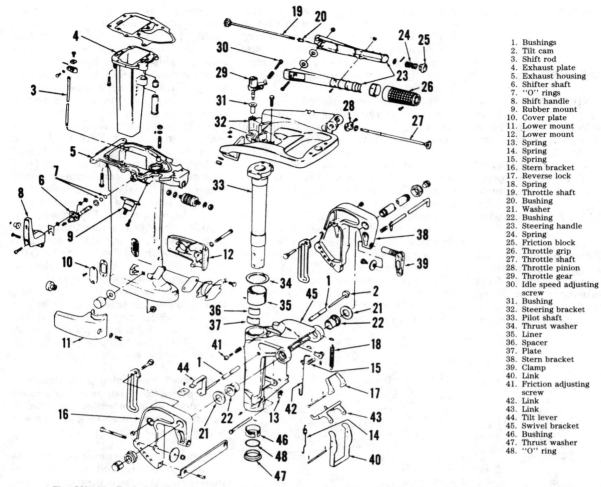

1. Bushings
2. Tilt cam
3. Shift rod
4. Exhaust plate
5. Exhaust housing
6. Shifter shaft
7. "O" rings
8. Shift handle
9. Rubber mount
10. Cover plate
11. Lower mount
12. Lower mount
13. Spring
14. Spring
15. Spring
16. Stern bracket
17. Reverse lock
18. Spring
19. Throttle shaft
20. Bushing
21. Washer
22. Bushing
23. Steering handle
24. Spring
25. Friction block
26. Throttle grip
27. Throttle shaft
28. Throttle pinion
29. Throttle gear
30. Idle speed adjusting screw
31. Bushing
32. Steering bracket
33. Pilot shaft
34. Thrust washer
35. Liner
36. Spacer
37. Plate
38. Stern bracket
39. Clamp
40. Link
41. Friction adjusting screw
42. Link
43. Link
44. Tilt lever
45. Swivel bracket
46. Bushing
47. Thrust washer
48. "O" ring

Fig. OM9-29—Exploded view of stern bracket, exhaust housing, drive shaft housing and related components used on later models.

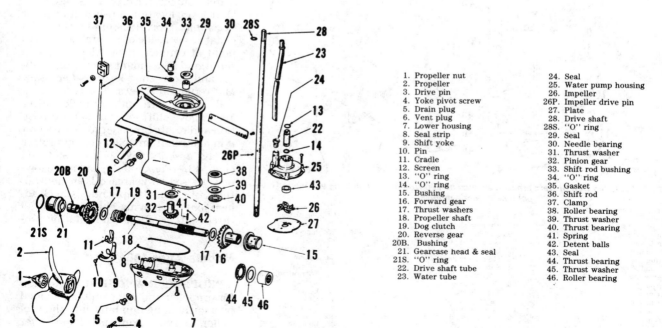

1. Propeller nut
2. Propeller
3. Drive pin
4. Yoke pivot screw
5. Drain plug
6. Vent plug
7. Lower housing
8. Seal strip
9. Shift yoke
10. Pin
11. Cradle
12. Screen
13. "O" ring
14. "O" ring
15. Bushing
16. Forward gear
17. Thrust washers
18. Propeller shaft
19. Dog clutch
20. Reverse gear
20B. Bushing
21. Gearcase head & seal
21S. "O" ring
22. Drive shaft tube
23. Water tube

24. Seal
25. Water pump housing
26. Impeller
26P. Impeller drive pin
27. Plate
28. Drive shaft
28S. "O" ring
29. Seal
30. Needle bearing
31. Thrust washer
32. Pinion gear
33. Shift rod bushing
34. "O" ring
35. Gasket
36. Shift rod
37. Clamp
38. Roller bearing
39. Thrust washer
40. Thrust bearing
41. Spring
42. Detent balls
43. Seal
44. Thrust bearing
45. Thrust washer
46. Roller bearing

Fig. OM9-30—Exploded view of gearcase assembly used on models prior to 1985.

Various propellers are available. Select a propeller that will allow a properly tuned and adjusted motor to operate within the recommended speed range (CONDENSED SERVICE DATA) at full throttle.

REMOVE AND REINSTALL. If water pump or gearcase service is required, remove engine cover and disconnect four wire connector. Drain lubricant and remove propeller if gearcase disassembly is necessary. Detach water inlet screens on both gearcase sides and unscrew upper shift rod connector (56—OM9-32). Note that keeper under nut may be dislodged when gearcase is removed. Unscrew fasteners retaining gearcase to exhaust housing and separate gearcase from exhaust housing.

To install gearcase, reverse removal procedure. Coat drive shaft splines with OMC Moly Lube or suitable equivalent. Do not apply lubricant to top of drive shaft or shaft may not fully seat inside engine crankshaft. Coat gearcase retaining screws with sealing compound.

WARNING: Spark plug leads should be disconnected from spark plugs and properly grounded prior to performing any propeller service to prevent accidental starting and severe personal injury.

Check shift mechanism to be sure gearcase and shift control lever are properly adjusted. Adjust shift mechanism by adjusting shift control lever position so neutral in gearcase is synchronized with neutral on shift control detent plate.

OVERHAUL. If OMC special tools are not available, note exact position of seals and bearings during disassembly for reference during reassembly.

Remove water pump and withdraw drive shaft. Remove screws which retain housing (34—OM9-32), then use OMC tool 378103 or suitable equivalent puller to withdraw bearing housing (34) from gearcase. Remove snap ring (38) and re-

tainer plate (39). Unscrew and remove shift rod (18). Remove shift yoke (44) and unscrew pivot pin (24). Withdraw propeller shaft assembly. Remove shift lever (46), pinion gear (28), thrust bearing (26), thrust washers (25 and 27), forward gear (50) and bearing (52). Using a suitable puller, remove seals (13), bearing (15) and housing (14). Drive bearings (16) into propeller shaft cavity of gearcase and remove bearings. Use a suitable puller to remove shift rod washer (21), "O" rings (20 and 55) and bushing (19). Using suitable pullers, remove bearing (52) cup from gearcase, seals (32)

and bearings (33 and 36) from bearing housing (34).

Inspect all components for excessive wear or damage. Chipped or excessively rounded engagement surfaces of dog clutch (48) or gears (41 and 50) may cause shifting malfunction. Be sure gearcase and exhaust housing mating surfaces are flat and free of nicks.

To reassemble gearcase, proceed as follows: Use OMC Gasket Sealing Compound or suitable equivalent around outer diameter of seals. Lubricate bearings, shafts and gears with recommended lubricant prior to assembly. In-

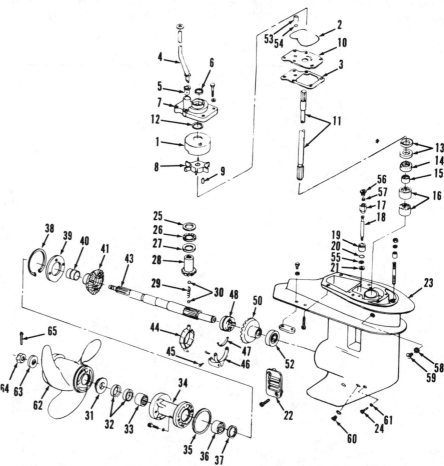

Fig. OM9-32—Exploded view of gearcase assembly used on 1985-1989 models.

1. Liner	22. Water inlet screen	44. Shift yoke
2. Seal	23. Gearcase	45. Pin
3. Gasket	24. Pivot pin	46. Shift lever
4. Water tube	25. Thrust washer	47. Collar
5. Grommet	26. Thrust bearing	48. Dog clutch
6. "O" ring	27. Thrust washer	50. Forward gear
7. Impeller housing	28. Pinion gear	52. Bearing
8. Impeller	29. Spring	53. Bushing
9. Cam	30. Detent balls	54. "O" ring
10. Plate	31. Spacer	55. "O" ring
11. Drive shaft	32. Seals	56. Connector
12. Seal	33. Bearing	57. Keeper
13. Seals	34. Bearing housing	58. Gasket
14. Bearing housing	35. "O" ring	59. Level plug
15. Bearing	36. Bearing	60. Drain plug
16. Bearings	37. Thrust washer	61. "O" ring
17. Nut	38. Snap ring	62. Propeller & drive hub
18. Shift rod	39. Retainer	63. Spacer
19. Bushing	40. Bushing	64. Nut
20. "O" ring	41. Reverse gear	65. Cotter pin
21. Washer	43. Propeller shaft	

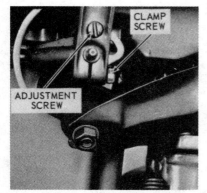

Fig. OM9-31—Refer to text to adjust shift linkage.

CLAMP SCREW

ADJUSTMENT SCREW

stall shift rod washer (21), "O" rings (20 and 55) and bushing (19) using OMC Tool 304515. Install pinion bearings (16) into gearcase to correct depth with lettered end of bearings facing up. Use OMC Tool 391257 with correct size spacer to install pinion bearings. Pinion bearings are at correct depth when plate bottoms against gearcase. Press bearing (15) into housing (14) so bearing is flush with housing. Using OMC Tool 322923, drive housing (14) into gearcase until plate bottoms against gearcase. Install seals (13) back-to-back in housing (14). Drive bearing (33) into bearing housing (34) with OMC Tool 321429 until tool abuts housing. Install seals (32) so inner seal lip is toward inside of bearing housing and outer seal lip is toward outside of housing. Drive bearing (36) into bearing housing with OMC Tool 321428 until tool abuts housing. Install bearing and cup (52) into gearcase. Place lower thrust washer (27) on pinion gear (28) with inner bevel toward gear. Install thrust bearing (26) and thrust washer (25) on pinion gear (28). External bevel on thrust washer (25) should be toward top of gearcase. Install pinion gear assembly into gearcase. Install forward gear (50) and shift lever (46) into gearcase. Place detent spring (29) and detent balls (30) into propeller shaft (43) and slide dog clutch (48) with groove toward propeller end of shaft onto shaft while making sure detent grooves in clutch are aligned with detent balls. Grease cradle (47) and install on clutch (48). Install propeller shaft and clutch assembly into gearcase with slots in cradle (47) facing shift lever (46). Engage shift lever (46) fingers into cradle slots. Install reverse gear (41).

Install shift yoke (44) with open end of hook toward gears and engage hook with shift lever pin (45). Thread shift rod (18) into yoke (44). Install pivot pin (24) into shift lever (46) hole by moving shift rod (18). Remainder of assembly is evident after inspection of unit and referral to Fig. OM9-32. Install impeller drive key with flat side against drive shaft and sharp edge pointing in a clockwise direction. Install water pump, attach gearcase to exhaust housing and fill gearcase with a recommended lubricant.

FORCE

BRUNSWICK MARINE POWER
1939 Pioneer Road
Fond du lac, Wisconsin 54935

4.0 AND 5.0 HP MODELS

Year Produced	4.0 Model	5.0 Model
1984	42F4A, 42FC4A	
1985	42F5A, 42FC5A	
1986	42F6A, 42FC6A	
1987	42F7, 43F7	
1988		52F8, 53F8
1989		52F9, 53F9

CONDENSED SERVICE DATA

TUNE-UP

Hp/rpm 4.0/5250
(3.0 Kw)
5.0/5250
(3.7 Kw)
Bore . . . . .2 in.
(50.8 mm)
Stroke . . . . .1-19/32 in.
(39 mm)
Number of Cylinders 1
Displacement . . . . .5.0 cu. in.
(81.9 cc)
Compression at Cranking Speed
(Average, with Recoil Starter) . . . . .110-125 psi
(759-862 kPa)
Spark Plug:
Champion .L86 (Canada RL86)
Electrode Gap . . . . .0.030 in.
(0.76 mm)
Breaker Point Gap . . . . .0.020 in.
(0.51 mm)
Fuel:Oil Ratio 50:1

SIZES—CLEARANCES

Piston Ring End Gap . . . . .0.006-0.011 in.
(0.15-0.28 mm)
Piston to Cylinder Clearance . . . . .0.0035-0.005 in.
(0.09-0.13 mm)
Piston Pin:
Diameter . . . . .0.43750-0.43765 in.
(11.112-11.116 mm)
Clearance at Piston . . . . .0.00035 in. (0.0089 mm)
tight to 0.0001 in.
(0.0025 mm) loose

SIZES—CLEARANCES CONT.

Crankshaft Journal Diameters:
Lower Main . . . . .0.7874-0.7878 in.
(20.000-20.010 mm)
Upper Main . . . . .0.8125-0.8130 in.
(20.637-20.650 mm)
Crankpin . . . . .0.7493-0.7496 in.
(19.032-19.040 mm)

TIGHTENING TORQUES

Connecting Rod . . . . .75-85 in.-lbs.
(8.5-9.6 N·m)
Cylinder Head . . . . .130 in.-lbs.
(14.7 N·m)
Flywheel Nut . . . . .204 in.-lbs.
(23 N·m)
Crankcase . . . . .70 in.-lbs.
(7.9 N·m)
Spark Plug . . . . .120-180 in.-lbs.
(13.6-20.3 N·m)
Standard Screws:
6-32 . . . . .9 in.-lbs.
(1 N·m)
10-24 . . . . .30 in.-lbs.
(3.4 N·m)
10-32 . . . . .35 in.-lbs.
(4 N·m)
12-24 . . . . .45 in.-lbs.
(5.1 N·m)
¼-20 . . . . .70 in.-lbs.
(7.9 N·m)
5/16-18 . . . . .160 in.-lbs.
(18.1 N·m)
⅜-16 . . . . .270 in.-lbs.
(30.5 N·m)

LUBRICATION

The power head is lubricated by oil mixed with the fuel. One-sixth (1/6) pint of a two-stroke engine oil should be mixed with each gallon of gasoline. Manufacturer recommends use of no-lead, regular or premium grade gasoline having an octane rating of 85 or higher. Recommended oil is Quicksilver Premium Blend 2-Cycle Outboard oil or a NMMA certified TC-W engine oil. Gasoline and oil should be thoroughly mixed.

The lower unit gears and bearings are lubricated by oil contained in the gearcase. Manufacturer recommends Quicksilver Premium Blend Outboard Gear Lube or an EP 90 outboard gear lube for use in gearcase. The gearcase should be drained and refilled every 100 hours or once each year. Maintain fluid at the level of the upper (vent) plug hole.

FUEL SYSTEM

CARBURETOR. All models are equipped with the single-barrel float-type carburetor shown in Fig. F1-1. Initial setting of idle mixture screw (7) is one turn out from lightly seated position. High speed mixture is controlled by high speed jet (17) and is nonadjustable. Idle speed should be 800-1200 rpm on 4.0 hp models and 800-1000 rpm on 5.0 hp models.

Adjust float level so float is parallel to float bowl gasket surface. Be sure float

support spring (11) is installed so spring pressure helps float close fuel inlet valve (10). Adjust float drop so a distance of 5/16 inch (7.9 mm) is between end of float (opposite inlet valve) and flange of carburetor body (5). Install throttle plate (4) so stamped letter is toward engine and holes in throttle plate (4) are on carburetor idle mixture screw side. Install choke plate (8) so stamped number is toward carburetor front and oblong slot is on fuel inlet side.

SPEED CONTROL LINKAGE. The speed control lever is connected to the magneto base plate to advance or retard ignition timing. Throttle linkage is synchronized to open the throttle as magneto timing is advanced.

To check speed control linkage, turn speed control lever until throttle cam (C—Fig. F1-2) contacts cam follower (F).

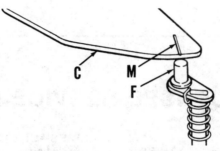

Fig. F1-2—Cam follower (F) should be centered on mark (M) when throttle cam (C) contacts follower.

Mark (M) on throttle cam should be in center of cam follower when cam contacts follower. If mark (M) is not aligned when cam contacts follower (F), loosen throttle cam (C) retaining screw and relocate cam. Recheck synchronization after relocating cam.

REED VALVE. Reed stop (21—Fig. F1-1) and reed petals (20) are attached directly to engine side of intake manifold (19). Inspect reed petals and renew if broken, cracked or bent. Never attempt to straighten a bent reed. Tip of reed petal must not stand open more than 0.006 inch (0.15 mm) from contact surface. Reed stop opening should be 0.24-0.26 inch (6.1-6.6 mm).

IGNITION

Breaker points are accessible after flywheel is removed. Breaker point gap should be 0.020 inch (0.51 mm) when index mark on breaker cam is aligned with breaker point rubbing block.

Tapered bore of flywheel and crankshaft end must be clean, dry and smooth before installing flywheel. Flywheel and crankshaft tapers can be cleaned by using fine valve grinding compound. Turn flywheel back and forth approximately one quarter turn. Do not spin flywheel on crankshaft. Clean flywheel and crankshaft tapers thoroughly. Renew chipped or cracked flywheels.

COOLING SYSTEM

All models are equipped with a rubber impeller water pump. When cooling system problems are encountered, first check the water inlet for plugging or partial stoppage. Then if not corrected, remove the lower unit gearcase and check the condition of water pump, water passages and sealing surfaces.

To detach gearcase from drive shaft housing, remove shift coupling cover and loosen shift coupling screw (S—Fig. F1-4). Remove the two cap screws securing gearcase to drive shaft housing and remove gearcase. Remove impeller cover (4—Fig. F1-8), impeller (5), impeller pin (14) and water pump body (8).

NOTE: When removing impeller pin (14), do not raise drive shaft (13) any higher than necessary to remove pin. Pinion gear (18) may fall out of position if drive shaft is raised too high.

Be sure impeller correctly engages drive pin (14) during assembly. Apply a suitable sealant to gearcase. Pull lower shift rod (3) up as far as possible and

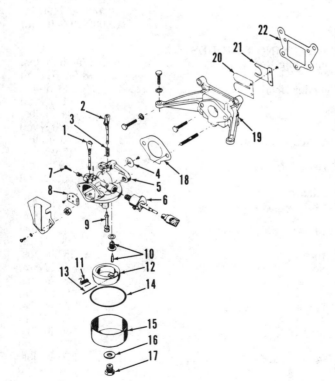

Fig. F1-1—Exploded view of carburetor used on early models. Carburetor used on later models is similar except fuel valve (6) is absent.

1. Choke shaft
2. Throttle shaft
3. Spring
4. Throttle plate
5. Body
6. Fuel valve
7. Idle mixture screw
8. Choke plate
9. Nozzle
10. Fuel inlet valve
11. Float spring
12. Float
13. Float pin
14. Gasket
15. Float bowl
16. Gasket
17. High speed jet
18. Gasket
19. Intake manifold
20. Reed petals
21. Reed stop
22. Gasket

move gear shift lever to neutral position (horizontal). Align shift rod with coupling (1) and water tube with seal (6), then mate gearcase with drive shaft housing. Tighten shift coupling screw (S—Fig. F1-4) and install cover.

POWER HEAD

R&R AND OVERHAUL. To remove power head, remove upper and lower engine covers, starter, fuel tank, flywheel, magneto base plate and carburetor. Disconnect stop switch leads. Unscrew two cap screws securing handle support plate to power head and remove plate. Unscrew six cap screws and separate power head from drive shaft housing.

Remove cylinder head. Drive out crankcase locating pins, unscrew crankcase screws and separate crankcase from cylinder block. Crankshaft and piston assemblies are now accessible. Re-

fer to appropriate paragraph for overhaul of power head components.

Inspect crankcase and cylinder block mating surfaces for nicks, burrs or warpage. Use a suitable sealant on crankcase and cylinder block mating surfaces before reassembly. Install crankshaft seals with lips toward crankcase. Be sure locating ring around crankshaft lower main bearing is seated in grooves in cylinder block and crankcase. Tighten crankcase screws to 70 in.-lbs. (7.9 N·m). Complete reassembly in reverse order of disassembly. Drive shaft splines should be coated with a suitable anticorrosion substance.

PISTON, PIN, RINGS AND CYLINDER. When properly assembled, connecting rod match marks will be toward port side of engine, piston pin open end and piston ring locating pins will be toward flywheel. See Fig. F1-6. The piston is equipped with two piston rings which must be installed so beveled inner edge is toward piston crown.

CONNECTING ROD, CRANKSHAFT AND BEARINGS. Assemble connecting rod, piston and pin as outlined in previous section. Install rod and piston assembly in cylinder so alignment mark on rod is toward port side of engine. Connecting rod (13—Fig. F1-5) rides on a caged roller bearing (4) with sixteen rollers (5). Be sure marks on rod and cap are correctly aligned. Tighten rod screws to 75-85 in.-lbs. (8.5-9.6 N·m).

Crankshaft upper main bearing is a needle roller bearing while a ball bearing is used on lower end of crankshaft. Retainer ring (9), bearing (10) and crankshaft (8) are available as a unit assembly only.

MANUAL STARTER

The manual starter is mounted on the fuel tank and is accessible after remov-

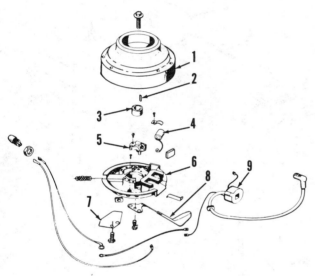

Fig. F1-3—Exploded view of ignition components.

1. Flywheel
2. Key
3. Breaker cam
4. Condenser
5. Breaker points
6. Magneto base plate
7. Throttle cam
8. Speed control lever
9. Ignition coil

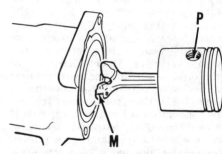

Fig. F1-6—Install piston assembly so open end of piston pin (P) is toward flywheel and connecting rod match mark (m) is toward port side of engine.

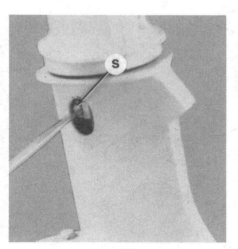

Fig. F1-4—View identifying shift coupling screw (S).

Fig. F1-5—Exploded view of crankcase, cylinder block and crankshaft assembly.

1. Crankcase
2. Dowel pin
3. Connecting rod cap
4. Bearing cage
5. Rollers (16)
6. Seal
7. Bearing
8. Crankshaft
9. Retainer ring
10. Bearing
11. Seal
12. Seal
13. Connecting rod
14. Piston
15. Clip
16. Piston pin
17. Piston rings
18. Cylinder block
19. Gasket
20. Cylinder head
21. Gasket

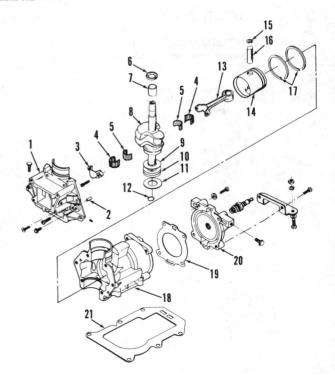

ing the upper engine cover. Refer to Fig. F1-7 for an exploded view of the starter.

To disassemble starter, remove starter from fuel tank, detach starter rope (4) from anchor (6) and allow rope to rewind into starter. Note location of sharp edges on friction shoes (9) and remove components (7 through 11). Lift pulley (3) with rope (4) out of housing (1) being careful not to dislodge rewind spring (2). If damaged, carefully remove rewind spring from housing.

Install lightly lubricated rewind spring into housing in counterclockwise direction from spring outer end. Wind a 48 inch (122 cm) long rope on pulley (3) in clockwise direction as viewed from rewind spring side of pulley. Lightly lubricate pulley bore and install pulley (3) into housing (1) making certain that inner and outer ends of spring are hooked in pulley and housing. Turn pulley (3) three turns clockwise to preload rewind spring (2), pass rope end through housing and tie a slip knot in the rope. Pull starter rope (4) out as far as possible, then try to turn pulley (3) counterclockwise. Pulley (3) should turn an additional 1/8 to 3/8 turn before bottoming out rewind spring (2). Check sharp end of friction shoes (9) and sharpen or renew as necessary. Install components (7 through 11). Make certain that friction shoe assembly is installed properly. If properly installed, sharp ends of friction shoes will extend when rope is pulled. Release slip knot and install starter rope (4) end through handle (5) and secure in anchor (6).

LOWER UNIT

R&R AND OVERHAUL. Refer to Fig. F1-8 for exploded view of lower unit.

Fig. F1-8—Exploded view of gearcase and water pump assemblies.
1. Shift coupling
2. Pin
3. Shift rod
4. Cover
5. Impeller
6. Water tube seal
7. Shift rod seal
8. Water pump body
9. Plug
10. Shift cam
11. Seal
12. "O" ring
13. Drive shaft
14. Impeller pin
15. Gearcase
16. Shift pin
17. Bevel gear
18. Pinion gear
19. Clutch
20. Clutch guide pin
21. Spring
22. Propeller shaft
23. Spacer
24. Bearing housing
25. Seal
26. "O" ring
27. Retainer

Remove water pump as previously outlined. Remove spinner, then drive out shear pin and remove propeller. Remove any burrs or rust from exposed end of propeller shaft. Remove four screws holding retainer (27) to bearing housing (24). Install two screws in threaded holes of retainer (27) and using a suitable puller, remove retainer. Propeller shaft assembly can be withdrawn after removal of retainer (27). Remove pinion gear (18) and bevel gear (17).

Assemble by reversing disassembly procedure. Shift rod seal (7) should have

raised bead up. Shift pin (16) is installed in propeller shaft with round end toward shift cam (10). Install bevel gear (17) and pinion gear (18). Pinion gear (18) is secured with drive shaft (13). Install propeller seal (25) with lip toward propeller.

Pressurize gear housing through drain plug hole to 10 psi (69 kPa). To prevent damage to gear housing seals do not exceed 10 psi (69 kPa). Housing should hold pressure for approximately five minutes. If not, determine location of leakage and repair as necessary.

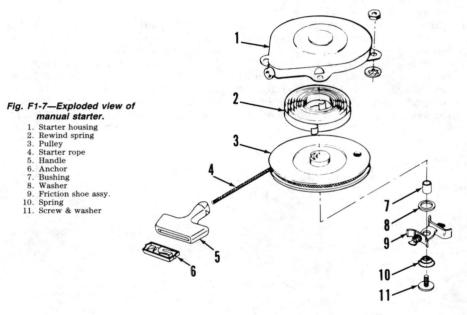

Fig. F1-7—Exploded view of manual starter.
1. Starter housing
2. Rewind spring
3. Pulley
4. Starter rope
5. Handle
6. Anchor
7. Bushing
8. Washer
9. Friction shoe assy.
10. Spring
11. Screw & washer

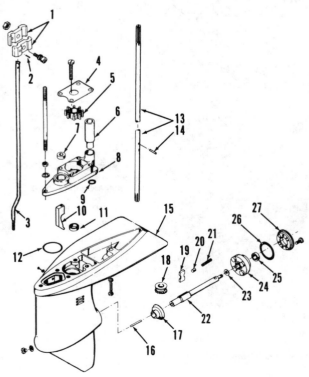

FORCE 9.9 AND 15 HP MODELS

Year Produced	9.9 Model	15 Model
1984	92F4A, 92F4B, 92FC4B	152F4A, 152FC4A
1985	92F5B, 92FC5B	152F5A, 152FC5A
1986	92F6B, 92FC6B	152F6A, 152FC6A
1987	92F7	152F7
1988	92F8	152F8
1989	92F9	152F9

CONDENSED SERVICE DATA

TUNE-UP   **9.9 and 15 HP**
Hp/rpm 9.9/5100
(7.4 kW)
15/5250
(11.2 kW)
Bore . . . . .2.25 in.*
(57.1 mm)
Stroke. . . . . .1.94 in.†
(49.3 mm)
Number of Cylinders 2
Displacement . . . . .15.41 cu. in.‡
(252.5 cc)
Compression at Cranking
Speed . . . . .125-135 psi§
(862-931 kPa)
Spark Plug . . . . .Champion L82C
Electrode Gap . . . . .0.030 in.
(0.76 mm)
Breaker Point Gap . . . . .0.020 in.
(0.51 mm)
Idle Speed in Gear .600-700 rpm
Recommended Operating
Range:
9.9 Hp Models . . . . .4600-5600 rpm
15 Hp Models. . . . . .4750-5750 rpm
Fuel:Oil Ratio 50:1

*Bore on 9.9 hp models manufactured before 1985 is 2.19 inches (55.6 mm).
†Stroke on 9.9 hp models manufactured before 1985 is 1-3/4 inches (44.4 mm).
‡Displacement on 9.9 hp models manufactured before 1985 is 13.15 cu. in. (2167 cc).
§Compression on 9.9 hp models before 1985 is 115-125 psi (793-862 kPa).

SIZES—CLEARANCES
Piston Ring End Gap . . . . .0.004-0.014 in.*
(0.10-0.36 mm)
Piston to Cylinder
Clearance . . . . .0.0035-0.004 in.†
(0.089-0.102 mm)
Piston Pin Diameter . . . . .0.50000-0.50015 in.
(12.700-12.704 mm)
Clearance at Piston . . . . .0.00035 in. (0.0089 mm) tight
to 0.0001 in. (0.0025 mm) loose
Crankshaft Journal
Diameter:
Lower Main . . . . .0.7495-0.7500 in.
(19.037-19.050 mm)
Center Main . . . . .0.8000-0.8005 in.
(20.320-20.333 mm)

SIZES—CLEARANCES (CONT.)
Upper Main . . . . .0.9849-0.9853 in.
(25.016-25.027 mm)
Crankpin . . . . .0.7496-0.7501 in.
(19.040-19.052 mm)
*On 9.9 hp models manufactured before 1985, piston ring end gap should be 0.006-0.016 inch (0.15-0.41 mm).
†Piston-to-cylinder clearance should be 0.0025-0.004 inch (0.063-0.10 mm) on 9.9 hp models before 1985.

TIGHTENING TORQUES
Connecting Rod . . . . .95 in.-lbs.
(10.7 N·m)
Cylinder Head . . . . .130 in.-lbs.
(14.7 N·m)
Exhaust Cover . . . . .90 in.-lbs.
(10.2 N·m)
Flywheel Nut . . . . .50 ft.-lbs.
(67.8 N·m)
Fuel Pump Screws . . . . .30 in.-lbs.
(3.4 N·m)
Gear Housing to
Drive Shaft Housing
Screws . . . . .130 in.-lbs.
(14.7 N·m)
Main Bearing Bolts .160 in.-lbs.
(18.1 N·m)
Shift Arm Pin . . . . .30 in.-lbs.
(3.4 N·m)
Transfer Port Cover . . . . .90 in.-lbs.
(10.2 N·m)
Upper to Lower Gear
Housing Nuts and
Screws . . . . .120 in.-lbs.
(13.6 N·m)
Standard Screws:
6-32 . . . . 9 in.-lbs.
(1.0 N·m)
8-32 . . . . .20 in.-lbs.
(2.3 N·m)
10-24 . . . . .30 in.-lbs.
(3.4 N·m)
10-32 . . . . .35 in.-lbs.
(4.0 N·m)
12-24 . . . . .45 in.-lbs.
(5.1 N·m)
1/4-20 . . . . .70 in.-lbs.
(7.9 N·m)
5/16-18 . . . . .160 in.-lbs.
(18.1 N·m)
3/8-16 . . . . .270 in.-lbs.
(30.5 N·m)

LUBRICATION

The power head is lubricated by oil mixed with fuel. For normal service after break-in, mix 1/6 pint of two-stroke engine oil with each gallon of gasoline. The recommended ratio is one-third (1/3) pint of oil per gallon of gasoline for severe service and break-in. Manufacturer recommends using no-lead, regular or premium gasoline having an octane rating of 85 or higher. Recommended oil is Quicksilver Premium Blend 2-Cycle Outboard Oil or a NMMA certified TC-W engine oil. Gasoline and oil should be thoroughly mixed.

The lower unit gears and bearings are lubricated by oil contained in the gearcase. Manufacturer recommends Quicksilver Premium Blend Outboard Gear Lube or an EP 90 outboard gear lube for use in gearcase. The gearcase should be drained and refilled every 100 hours or once each year. Maintain fluid at the level of the upper (vent) plug hole.

To fill gearcase, have the outboard motor in an upright position and fill through lower hole in side of gearcase until fluid reaches level of upper vent plug hole. Reinstall and tighten both plugs securely, using new gaskets if necessary, to ensure a water tight seal.

FUEL SYSTEM

CARBURETOR. Models are equipped with Walbro LMB (Fig. F2-1) or Tillotson CO (Fig. F2-2) carburetor. Initial setting of idle mixture screw (10—Figs. F2-1 and F2-2) is one turn open from a lightly seated position on all models. Turn idle screw clockwise to lean idle mixture. Final carburetor adjustment should be made with engine at normal operating temperature and running in forward gear. Standard main jet (23—Fig. F2-1) size on Walbro carburetor is 0.046 inch (1.17 mm) on 9.9 hp models and 0.0625 inch (1.59 mm) on 15 hp models. Standard main jet (23—Fig. F2-2) size on Tillotson carburetor is 0.055 inch (1.40 mm) on 9.9 hp models and 0.063 inch (1.60 mm) on 15 hp models.

Correct float level (L—Fig. F2-3) is 1/8 inch (3.17 mm) on Walbro LMB carburetor. On Tillotson CO carburetor, float should be parallel with flange of carburetor body.

SPEED CONTROL LINKAGE. The speed control twist grip is attached to the magneto base plate via control linkage. Turning the speed control twist grip will advance or retard the ignition timing. Throttle linkage is synchronized to open the carburetor throttle as magneto timing is advanced. The speed control linkage must be properly synchronized for best performance. Adjust linkage with motor not running.

To adjust speed control on models equipped with Walbro LMB carburetor, turn speed control twist grip slowly toward the fast position and observe pickup mark (Fig. F2-4) on throttle cam. Throttle shaft should just begin to move when pickup mark is centered with throttle roller. Turn adjusting screw, if required, to change point of throttle opening.

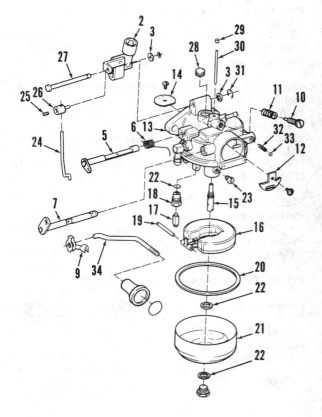

Fig. F2-3—Float level (L) should be 1/8 inch (3.17 mm) on Walbro carburetor. On Tillotson carburetor, float should be parallel with flange of carburetor body. Bend tang (A) to adjust.

Fig. F2-1—Exploded view of Walbro LMB carburetor used on some models.

1. Adjusting screw	
2. Throttle roller	
3. Washer	13. Body
4. Nut	14. Throttle plate
5. Throttle shaft	15. Main nozzle
6. Spring	16. Float
7. Choke shaft	17. Needle valve
8. Spring	18. Spring
9. Clip	19. Float pin
10. Idle mixture screw	20. Gasket
11. Spring	21. Float bowl
12. Choke plate	22. Gasket
	23. Main jet

Fig. F2-2—Exploded view of Tillotson CO carburetor used on some models.

2. Throttle roller
3. Washer
5. Throttle shaft
6. Spring
7. Choke shaft
9. Clip
10. Idle mixture screw
11. Spring
12. Choke plate
13. Body
14. Throttle plate
15. Main nozzle
16. Float
17. Inlet needle
18. Inlet seat
19. Float pin
20. Gasket
21. Float bowl
22. Gasket
23. Main jet
24. Throttle link
25. Screw
26. Swivel
27. Shaft
28. Plug
29. Plug
30. Bypass tube
31. "E" ring
32. Spring
33. Ball
34. Rod

To adjust speed control on models equipped with Tillotson CO carburetor, back-out idle speed screw so throttle plate is completely closed. Loosen set screw in throttle swivel (Fig. F2-5). Advance speed control twist grip toward fast position until pickup mark on throttle cam is aligned with throttle roller. Tighten set screw. Note that throttle shaft must move at the same time throttle linkage begins to move. If not, repeat adjustment procedure.

Adjust idle speed with engine running at normal operating temperature and outboard motor in forward gear. Turn idle stop screw (I—Fig. F2-6) to obtain idle speed of 600-750 rpm on models equipped with Walbro carburetor or 600-700 rpm on models equipped with Tillotson carburetor.

REED VALVES. The inlet reed valves are located on reed plate (4—Fig. F2-7) between intake manifold (7) and crankcase. Reed petals (2) should seat lightly against reed plate (4) throughout entire length. Reed petals (2) must not stand open more than 0.006 inch (0.15 mm).

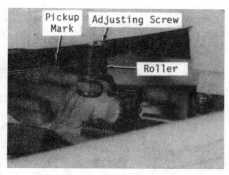

Fig. F2-4—On models equipped with Walbro LMB carburetor, pickup mark on throttle cam should be in center of throttle roller when throttle shaft begins to move. Rotate adjusting screw to change point of throttle shaft movement.

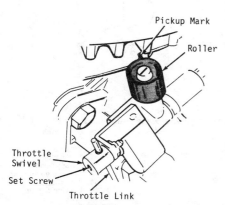

Fig. F2-5—On models equipped with Tillotson CO carburetor, pickup mark on throttle cam should be aligned with throttle roller then throttle shaft begins to move. Refer to text for adjustment procedure.

Renew reeds (2) if petals are broken, cracked, warped, rusted or bent. Never attempt to bend a reed petal. Seating surface of reed plate (4) should be smooth and flat. When installing reed (2) or reed stop (1), make sure that petals overlap reed plate inlet holes 0.030 inch (0.76 mm) and that reed stops are centered over reed petals.

Reed stop (1) opening must be 0.054-0.070 inch (1.37-1.78 mm) on 9.9 hp models and 0.200-0.220 inch (5.08-5.59 mm) on 15 hp models.

FUEL PUMP. A diaphragm type fuel pump is mounted on the side of power head cylinder block ported to the upper crankcase.

Defective or questionable parts should be renewed. Reed valves (3—Fig. F2-8) should seat lightly and squarely on reed plate (4). Diaphragm (6) should be renewed if air leaks or cracks are noted, or if deterioration is evident.

Fig. F2-6—View of idle speed screw (I) on models equipped with Walbro carburetor. Idle speed screw on Tillotson carburetor is similar.

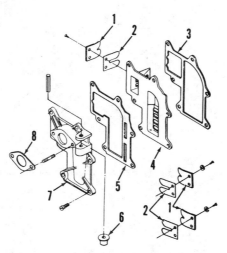

Fig. F2-7—Exploded view of intake manifold and reed valve assembly.

1. Reed stop
2. Reed
3. Gasket
4. Reed plate
5. Gasket
6. Starter rope pulley
7. Manifold
8. Gasket

IGNITION

All models are equipped with a breaker-point flywheel magneto ignition system. Breaker-point gap should be 0.020 inch (0.51 mm) for each set of points, and can be adjusted after fly-

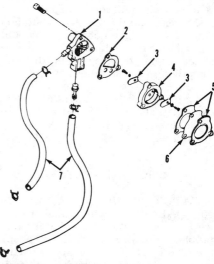

Fig. F2-8—Exploded view of diaphragm fuel pump.

1. Pump cover
2. Gasket
3. Reed valves
4. Reed plate
5. Gaskets
6. Diaphragm
7. Fuel lines

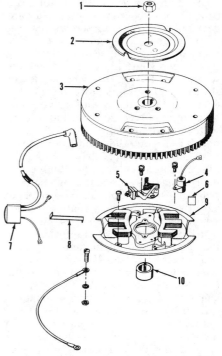

Fig. F2-9—Exploded view of breaker-point ignition system.

1. Nut
2. Rope pulley half
3. Flywheel
4. Condenser
5. Breaker point set
6. Felt
7. Ignition coil
8. Clip
9. Magneto base plate
10. Breaker point cam

wheel is removed. Both sets of points must be adjusted exactly alike.

NOTE: High point of breaker cam coincides with location of flywheel key. Align key with the contact point rub block when adjusting points.

Primary ignition coil resistance should be 0.7-0.9 ohms. Secondary ignition coil resistance should be 13,500-16,500 ohms. Renew coil if not to specification.

The tapered bore in flywheel and end of crankshaft must be clean, dry and smooth before installing flywheel. The flywheel nut should be torqued to 45-50 ft.-lbs. (61-68 N·m). Spark plug electrode gap should be 0.030 inch (0.76 mm). Torque spark plugs to 120-180 in.-lbs. (13.5-20.3 N·m).

COOLING SYSTEM

WATER PUMP. All motors are equipped with a rubber impeller type water pump. When cooling system problems are encountered, first check the water inlet for plugging or partial stoppage. If cooling system problem is not corrected, remove the lower unit gearcase and check the condition of water pump, water passages and sealing surfaces.

Water pump may be disassembled using the following procedure: Place outboard motor on a suitable holding fixture. Shift outboard motor into forward gear and remove four screws that secure upper gearcase housing to drive shaft housing. Pull gearcase housing from drive shaft housing and remove screw (40—Fig. F2-10) securing lower shift rod (2) to upper shift rod (1). Pull gearcase housing free of drive shaft housing. Remove screws that secure water pump housing (6) to gearcase housing (10) and slide pump housing (6) with impeller (7) off drive shaft (11). Water tube seal (4) can be removed by depressing tabs on seal through holes in pump housing and pulling on seal. Make sure that tabs are fully seated in holes when installing new seal.

Drive shaft seals (5 and 9) should be installed with spring loaded lip toward top. Rotate impeller (7) counterclockwise when installing in pump housing (6). Be sure impeller (7) correctly engages drive pin (12) during assembly.

Before reassembling, check shift rod adjustment. Center of screw hole in lower shift rod (2) must be 9/64 to 15/64 inch (3.57-5.95 mm) below surface of gear housing with unit in neutral. Refer to Fig. F2-11. Lubricate drive shaft splines and seal lips with a good grade of silicone grease. Assemble upper and lower shift rods as shown in Fig. F2-12

to prevent leakage and damage to shift rod seal (3—Fig. F2-10). Make certain that water tube is seated in seal and install screws that secure upper gearcase housing to drive shaft housing.

POWER HEAD

R&R AND DISASSEMBLE. To overhaul the power head, place the outboard motor on a suitable holding fixture and remove engine cover. Disconnect choke rod from choke plate lever, stop switch wires and fuel line from carryon tank connector. Remove manual starter handle and allow starter rope to slowly wind onto starter spool. Remove magneto control lever and disconnect starter interlock components to allow engine removal. Remove six cap screws retaining engine to drive shaft housing and lift off engine assembly.

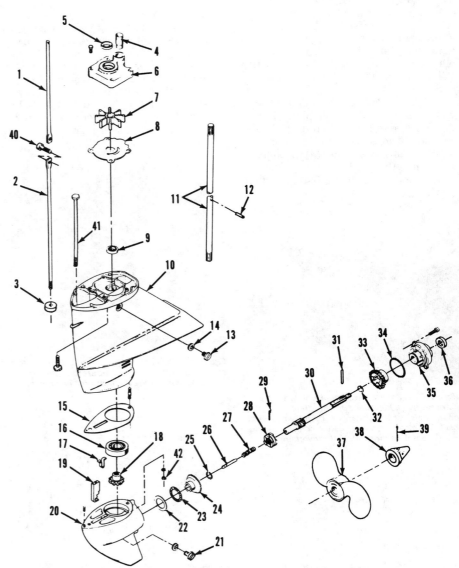

Fig. F2-10—Exploded view of gearcase and water pump assemblies.

1. Upper shift rod	15. Gasket	28. Dog clutch
2. Lower shift rod	16. Ball bearing	29. Pin
3. Seal	17. Shift cam spring	30. Propeller shaft
4. Seal	18. Pinion gear	31. Shear pin
5. Seal	19. Shift cam	32. Thrust washer
6. Pump housing	20. Lower gearcase	33. Reverse bevel gear
7. Impeller	housing	34. "O" ring
8. Plate	21. Fill plug	35. Bearing & cage
9. Seal	22. Bearing race	36. Seal
10. Upper gearcase	23. Thrust bearing	37. Propeller
housing	24. Forward bevel gear	38. Spinner
11. Drive shaft	25. Thrust washer	39. Cotter pin
12. Drive pin	26. Shift pin	40. Screw
13. Vent plug	27. Spring	41. Cap screw
14. Gasket		42. Nut

Remove carburetor, intake manifold, reed plate, fuel pump, flywheel, magneto base plate, manual starter, exhaust covers, cylinder head, transfer port cover and cylinder drain cover. Remove four 5/16 inch diameter screws and eight 1/4 inch diameter screws securing crankcase to cylinder block. Drive out two locating dowel pins and use pry lugs located adjacent to dowel pin holes to separate components.

Engine components are now accessible for removal and overhaul as outlined in the appropriate following paragraphs. Assemble as outlined in the following ASSEMBLY section. Reinstall engine in the reverse order of removal. Tighten six cap screws securing engine assembly to drive shaft housing to 155-165 in.-lbs. (17.5-18.6 N·m).

ASSEMBLY. When reassembling, make sure all joint and gasket surfaces are clean, free from nicks and burrs and hardened cement or carbon. The crankcase and intake manifold must be completely sealed against both vacuum and pressure. Exhaust manifold and cylinder head must be sealed against water leakage and pressure. Mating surfaces of exhaust area between power head and drive shaft housing must form a tight seal.

Whenever power head is disassembled, it is recommended that all gasket surfaces and mating surfaces without gaskets be carefully checked for nicks, burrs and warped surfaces which might interfere with a tight seal. The cylinder head, cylinder block, and some mating surfaces of manifolds and crankcase should be checked, and lapped if necessary, to provide a smooth surface. Do not remove any more metal than is necessary. Renew cylinder head if warped in excess of 0.012 inch (0.30 mm).

Mating surfaces of crankcase may be checked on the lapping block and high spots or nicks removed, but the surface must not be lowered. If extreme care is used, a slightly damaged crankcase may be salvaged using this procedure. In case of doubt, renew crankcase and cylinder block assembly.

A heavy nonfibrous grease should be used to hold loose needle bearings in position during assembly. All friction surfaces should be lubricated with new engine oil. During assembly, check power head frequently for binding or locking. If binding or locking is noted, determine and repair cause before proceeding with reassembly.

Gasket and sealing surfaces should be lightly and carefully coated with a nonhardening gasket sealing compound. Make sure entire surface is coated, but

Fig. F2-11—Center of screw hole in lower shift rod (2) must be 9/64 to 15/64 inch (3.57-5.95 mm) (dimension A) below surface of upper gearcase housing (10) with unit in neutral.

Fig. F2-12—Upper and lower shift rods must be aligned as shown for proper assembly.

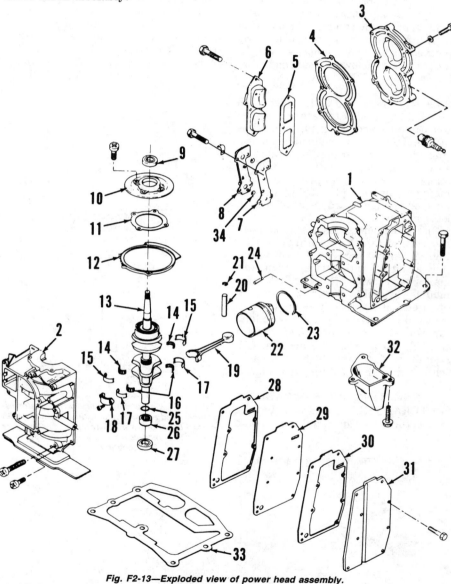

Fig. F2-13—Exploded view of power head assembly.

1. Cylinder block	13. Crankshaft	23. Piston ring
2. Crankcase	14. Bearing rollers	24. Dowel pin (2)
3. Cylinder head	(26 per set)	25. Seal
4. Gasket	15. Main bearing liner	26. Lower main bearing
5. Gasket	16. Rod bearing rollers	27. Seal
6. Transfer port cover	(26 per set)	28. Gasket
7. Gasket	17. Rod bearing liner	29. Inner exhaust cover
8. Cylinder drain cover	18. Rod cap	30. Gasket
9. Seal	19. Connecting rod	31. Outer exhaust cover
10. Retainer	20. Piston pin	32. Exhaust tube
11. Gasket	21. Clip	33. Gasket
12. Magneto ring	22. Piston	34. Screen

avoid excess compound squeezing into crankcase, bearings or other passages. Refer to Fig. F2-14 for cylinder head tightening sequence. When installing crankcase screws, tighten those next to the main bearings and dowel pins first. Crankshaft seals (9 and 27—Fig. F1-13) should be renewed each time crankshaft is removed. Refer to CONDENSED SERVICE DATA table for tightening torques.

PISTONS, PINS, RINGS AND CYLINDERS.

NOTE: Note position of open side of piston pin during disassembly. On early models, open side of piston pin must face away from piston ring locating pins in ring grooves. On later models, open side of piston pin must face toward piston ring locating pins.

Piston rings should be installed with beveled inner edge toward top of piston. On some models, top piston ring has more bevel and must be installed in top ring groove. Piston may be heated to ease piston pin installation. Install pin on early models with open side of pin facing away from piston ring locating pins, or facing toward locating pins on later models.

On early models, assemble piston to rod with piston ring locating pins (P—Fig. F2-15) and closed end (C) of piston pin facing up and rod cap alignment marks (M) toward the left. On later models, assemble piston to rod with open end of piston pin facing up.

Install piston into cylinder with long tapering side of piston crown toward the exhaust port side of cylinder. All friction surfaces should be lubricated with clean engine oil during reassembly.

CONNECTING RODS, BEARINGS AND CRANKSHAFT. Before detaching connecting rods from crankshaft, make certain that rod and cap are properly marked for correct assembly to each other and in the correct cylinder. The loose needle bearings at crankpin end of connecting rod should be kept with each assembly and not intermixed if reused.

NOTE: Do not use a magnet to retrieve bearing rollers that have fallen into cylinder block. Magnetized bearing rollers will attract metal shavings and lead to bearing failure.

Connecting rods contain 16 bearing rollers at each crankpin on early models. Later models are equipped with 52 bearing rollers at each crankpin. Center main bearing contains 26 bearing rollers on all models. When installing crankshaft assembly into cylinder block, make sure lower main bearing is positioned as shown in Fig. F2-16.

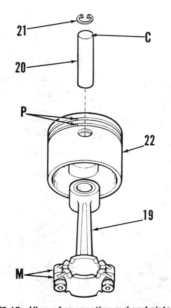

Fig. F2-15—View of connecting rod and piston assembly used on early models. Install pin (20) with closed (C) end toward piston ring locating pins (P). On later models, open end of piston pin must face locating pins (P).

Cylinder block should be renewed if cylinder bore wear exceeds 0.002 inch (0.051 mm). Bottom crankshaft seal (27—Fig. F2-13) should be staked in place after installation using a suitable center punch.

Oversize and undersize parts are not available. When reassembling, follow the procedures outlined in the ASSEMBLY paragraph. Tightening torques are listed in the CONDENSED SERVICE DATA table.

MANUAL STARTER

Early Models

Refer to Fig. F2-17 for exploded view of the manual rewind starter assembly used on early models. Starter pinion (2) engages starter ring gear on flywheel.

To disassemble starter, remove engine cover and flywheel, then remove screw (1) in top of starter shaft.

NOTE: This screw locks pin (9) in place.

Thread the rewind key (Special Tool 2985) into threaded hole from which screw (1) was removed. Tighten tool until it bottoms, then turn tool handle slightly counterclockwise to relieve rewind spring tension and push out pin (9). Allow the tool and drive arbor (8) to turn clockwise to unwind rewind spring (10). Pull up on tool to remove the rewind spring and components. Starter rope and rewind spool (13) can be removed after removing top bracket (4). Wind new rope in spool counterclockwise as viewed from top.

Rewind spring (10) should be greased before installation. Assemble arbor (8), spring (10) and spring retainer (11) and install into spool. Grease inside of pinion gear (2) and install on top of arbor. Use rewind key to turn arbor and rotate rewind spring 3-1/2 to 4 turns counterclockwise as viewed from top. Align holes in spool, arbor and slot in pinion

Fig. F2-16—When installing crankshaft into cylinder block, position lower main bearing 1/16 to 3/16 inch (1.59-4.76 mm) from edge of block as shown.

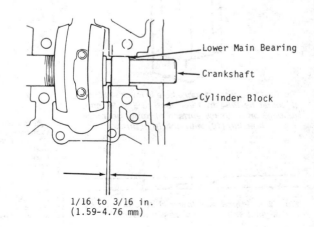

1/16 to 3/16 in. (1.59-4.76 mm)

gear and partially install pin (9). Remove rewind key while holding end of pin and then complete installation of pin. Install screw (1) in top of starter.

Late Models

Refer to Fig. F2-18 for exploded view of rewind starter used on late models. To disassemble starter, remove three screws and one nut securing starter housing (1) to power head. Disconnect interlock link (19) while lifting housing. Remove rope handle (13) and carefully allow rope to wind onto pulley (6). Remove three retainers (8) and lift pulley (6) from housing (1). Push rewind spring and cartridge assembly (3) from housing with a screwdriver or other suitable tool, through openings in top of housing.

Install rewind spring assembly (3) with tab (T) engaging notch in housing (1). Wind rope around pulley (6) in counterclockwise direction as viewed from engine side of pulley. Place rope into notch in outer periphery of pulley to prevent rope from unwinding. Install pulley into housing and rotate pulley counterclockwise until notch in pulley is aligned with front of housing. Hold

pulley in place and install three retainers (8). Apply a light coat of grease (Rykon #2EP or equivalent) to starter shaft and install starter assembly on power head. Make sure interlock link (19) is properly connected.

ADJUST NEUTRAL SPEED LIMITER. Mark (M—Fig. F2-19) on speed limiter lever (18) should align with tip of speed limiter arm (16) when unit is shifted to neutral. If not, remove screw (S) and turn connector (14) on rod (15) as necessary to align mark and tip of arm.

PROPELLER

Both two and three blade propellers are used and are equipped with a shear pin to prevent damage. Various pitch propellers are available and should be selected to provide full throttle operation within the recommended engine speed limits. Refer to CONDENSED SERVICE DATA for recommended operating range. Propellers other than those designed for the motor should not be used.

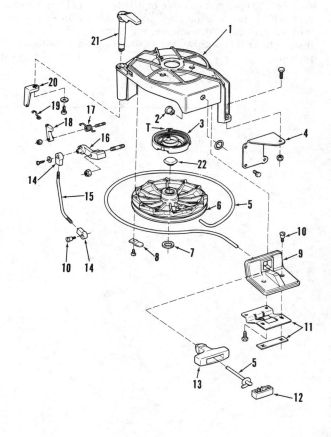

Fig. F2-18—Exploded view of rewind starter used on late models.

1. Housing
2. Spacer
3. Rewind spring & cartridge assy.
4. Bracket
5. Rope
6. Rope pulley
7. Spacer
8. Retainer
9. Rope guide
10. Shoulder screw
11. Bracket
12. Rope anchor
13. Rope handle
14. Joint & bearing assy.
15. Rod
16. Speed limiter arm
17. Spring
18. Speed limiter lever
19. Interlock link
20. Interlock arm
21. Interlock stop
22. Plug

Fig. F2-17—Exploded view of manual rewind starter used on early models.

1. Screw
2. Pinion gear
3. Pinion spring
4. Upper bracket
5. Starter interlock
6. Interlock detent ball (2)
7. Interlock detent spring (2)
8. Arbor
9. Pin
10. Rewind spring
11. Spring retainer
12. Spring end
13. Spool
14. Lower bracket
15. Anchor
16. Handle
17. Starter rope
18. Spring pin

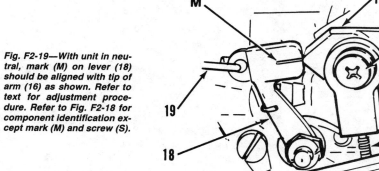

Fig. F2-19—With unit in neutral, mark (M) on lever (18) should be aligned with tip of arm (16) as shown. Refer to text for adjustment procedure. Refer to Fig. F2-18 for component identification except mark (M) and screw (S).

LOWER UNIT

R&R AND OVERHAUL. Refer to Fig. F2-10. Attach outboard motor to a suitable holding fixture. Shift motor into forward gear and remove four screws securing lower unit to drive shaft housing. Pull lower unit away from drive shaft housing far enough to remove screw (40) holding shift rods (1 and 2) together. Pull lower unit free of drive shaft housing. Disassemble water pump and remove drive shaft (11).

Drain lubricant from gearcase and remove propeller (37). Remove two screws securing propeller shaft bearing cage (35) to gearcase, then use puller assembly T8948-1 or a suitable equivalent and withdraw bearing cage (35). Seal (36) is removed by driving seal out from inside bearing cage with a suitable punch.

NOTE: Two types of replacement seals are available. Seals cased in metal are installed with spring loaded lip toward gear housing. Rubber cased seals are installed with spring loaded lip toward propeller.

Internal gears and shaft mechanism may be serviced after removing lower gearcase housing (20). Disassemble gearcase in the following manner: Remove shift rod (2) by unscrewing from shift cam (19). Use caution to prevent threads on shift rod from damaging seal (3) when sliding rod out of housing. Remove propeller shaft bearing cage as previously outlined. Remove cap screw (41) and nut (42), then separate upper and lower gearcase sections.

Shift rod seal (3) may be removed by screwing a 5/16 inch lag screw into seal from the top and using a 1/4 inch diameter rod to drive lag screw and seal out from the bottom.

When reassembling, make certain that thrust bearing (23) and thrust bearing race (22) are installed as shown in Fig. F2-10. Rounded end of shift pin (26) must be toward shift cam (19). Renew shift pin (26) if worn to less than 1.706 inches (43.3 mm) long. Clutch spring (27) free length should be 2-7/16 inches (62 mm) on 1984-1986 models and 2-1/4 inches (57.1 mm) on 1987 and later models. Dog clutch (28) must be installed so engagement dogs with chamfered edges are toward propeller.

Refer to water pump section for proper adjustment of shift rod (2). Backlash and mesh position of bevel drive gears are not adjustable. Bottom of cap screw (41) head should be coated with non-hardening sealant and tightened to 125 in.-lbs. (14 N·m).

MARINER

BRUNSWICK MARINE POWER
1939 Pioneer Road
Fond du Lac, Wisconson 54935

MARINER 2 HP (1977-1989)

CONDENSED SERVICE DATA

NOTE: Metric fasteners are used throughout outboard motor.

TUNE-UP

Hp/rpm 2/5000
Bore . . . . .39 mm
                                       (1.54 in.)
Stroke . . . . .36 mm
                                       (1.42 in.)
Displacement . . . . .43 cc
Number of Cylinders 1
                                    (2.62 cu. in.)
Spark Plug—NGK:
  Prior to Serial No. 6A1-011601 . . . . B6HS
  Electrode Gap . . . . .0.5-0.6 mm
                              (0.020-0.024 in.)
  After Serial No. 6A1-011600 . . . . B5HS
  Electrode Gap . . . . .0.6 mm
                                  (0.024 in.)
Breaker Point Gap:
  Prior to Serial No. 6A1-000101 . . . . . . .0.25-0.45 mm
                              (0.010-0.018 in.)
  After Serial No. 6A1-000100 . . . . .0.30-0.40 mm
                              (0.012-0.016 in.)
Ignition Timing . . . . .See Text
Carburetor Make . . . . .TK
Idle Speed:
  Prior to Serial No. 6A1-000101 . . . . .900-1100 rpm
  After Serial No. 6A1-000100 . . . . .1150-1250 rpm
Fuel:Oil Ratio 50:1
Gearcase Capacity . . . . .1.5 oz.
                                       (45 mL)

SIZES—CLEARANCES

Piston Ring End Gap:
  Prior to Serial No. 6A1-000101 . . . . .0.15-0.35 mm
                              (0.006-0.014 in.)
  After Serial No. 6A1-000100 . . . . .0.1-0.3 mm
                              (0.004-0.012 in.)

SIZES—CLEARANCES CONT.

Piston Skirt Clearance:
  Prior to Serial No. 6A1-000101 . . . . . . .0.030-0.035 mm
                              (0.0012-0.0014 in.)
  After Serial No. 6A1-000100 . . . . .0.030-0.040 mm
                              (0.0012-0.0016 in.)
Max. Connecting Rod Side Clearance . . . . .0.5 mm
                                    (0.012 in.)
Lower Unit Gear Backlash . . . . .0.08-0.3 mm
                                (0.003-0.012 in.)

TIGHTENING TORQUES

Crankcase . . . . .9.8 N·m
                                    (7 ft.-lbs.)
Cylinder Head . . . . .9.8 N·m
                                    (7 ft.-lbs.)
Flywheel:
  Prior to Serial No. 6A1-000101 . . . . .30-34 N·m
                              (22-25 ft.-lbs.)
  After Serial No. 6A1-000100 . . . . .39-49 N·m
                              (29-36 ft.-lbs.)
Standard Screws:
  4 mm . . . . .2.0 N·m
                                  (1.5 ft.-lbs.)
  5 mm . . . . .4.9-5.9 N·m
                              (3.6-4.3 ft.-lbs.)
  6 mm . . . . .7.8-9.8 N·m
                                (5.7-7 ft.-lbs.)
  7 mm . . . . .14.7-19.6 N·m
                            (10.8-14.4 ft.-lbs.)
  10 mm . . . . .29.4 N·m
                                (21.6 ft.-lbs.)

LUBRICATION

The power head is lubricated by oil mixed with the fuel. Fuel should be regular leaded, low lead or unleaded gasoline with a minimum octane rating of 86. Recommended oil is Quicksilver Premium Blend 2-Cycle Outboard Oil or a suitable equivalent NMMA certified TC-WII engine oil. Fuel:oil ratio is 50:1 for normal service and 25:1 during break-in of a new or rebuilt engine.

Lower unit gears and bearings are lubricated by oil contained in the gearcase. Recommended oil is Quicksilver Premium Blend Gear Lube.

FUEL SYSTEM

CARBURETOR. A TK type carburetor is used. Standard main jet (27—Fig. MR1-1) size is number 64 for normal operation. Jet needle clip (12) should be in third from top groove in jet needle (13). Inserting clip (12) in a higher groove will lean midrange mixture while insertion in a lower groove will richen midrange mixture. Throttle valve (14) cutaway is 0.5 mm (0.02 in.). Needle jet (26) diameter is 2.085 mm (0.083 in.). To determine float level, invert carburetor body (25—Fig. MR1-2) and measure distance (D) from gasket surface of body to float pads (P) of float arm. Distance (D) should be 3.5-4.5 mm (0.14-0.18 in.).

When installing carburetor on spigot of flange (11—Fig. MR1-4), place "O" ring inside carburetor bore then install carburetor on flange spigot. Lightly push carburetor toward flange so spigot end is seated against "O" ring and tighten carburetor retaining clamp. Be sure carburetor is in a vertical position. Adjust idle speed screw (20—Fig. MR1-1) so engine idles at 900-1100 rpm on models prior to serial number 6A1-000101 and 1150-1250 rpm on models with serial number 6A1-000101 and above with engine at normal operating temperature.

SPEED CONTROL LINKAGE. (Models prior to Serial No. 6A1-000101). Refer to MAGNETO section and be sure magneto stop plate (4—Fig. MR1-3) is properly located. Loosen swivel screw (1) so throttle link (9) is free in swivel and loosen adjuster plate screw (2). Rotate magneto base plate counterclockwise until stop plate (4) contacts throttle bracket (10) tang. Note that adjuster plate tang (T) contacts carburetor throttle arm (28—Fig. MR1-1). With magneto base plate held in full advance position as previously described, position adjuster plate (6—Fig. MR1-3) so carburetor throttle valve is open fully then tighten adjuster plate screw (2). Move speed control lever to full throttle position and tighten swivel screw (1). Adjust clamp screw (3) so 19.6-24.5 newtons (4.4-5.5 lbs.) are required to move end of speed control lever (8).

Models After Serial No. 6A1-000100). The engine speed is regulated by the position of the throttle lever. As the throttle lever is raised or lowered, the carburetor's throttle valve (14—Fig. MR1-1) is operated via throttle rod (1).

REED VALVES. The inlet reed valve unit is located between carburetor and crankcase and should be checked whenever the carburetor is removed. Reed petals (12—Fig. MR1-4) should seat very lightly against reed plate (11) throughout their entire length. Renew petals if broken, cracked, warped, rusted or bent. Seating surface on plate (11) must be smooth and flat.

IGNITION

Breaker point gap should be 0.25-0.45 mm (0.010-0.018 in.) on models prior to serial number 6A1-000101 and 0.30-0.40 mm (0.012-0.016 in.) on models with serial number 6A1-000101 and after. Breaker point gap is adjustable through opening in flywheel (22—Fig. MR1-5). The flywheel must be removed for breaker point renewal. When installing flywheel, make sure crankshaft and flywheel taper is perfectly clean and dry. Tighten flywheel nut to 30-34 N·m (22-25 ft.-lbs.) on models prior to serial number 6A1-000101 and 39-49 N·m (29-36 ft.-

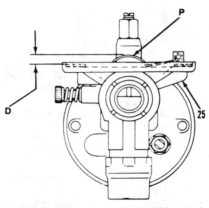

Fig. MR1-1—Exploded view of a typical TK carburetor used on all models.

D. Drain plug	18. Fuel inlet seat
P. Float pad	19. Fuel inlet valve
1. Throttle rod	20. Idle speed screw
2. Cover	21. Spring
3. Nut	22. Choke valve
4. Cotter pin	23. Choke shaft
5. Clevis pin	24. Cap screw
6. Bracket	25. Body
7. Washer	26. Main nozzle
8. Washer	27. Main jet
9. Cap nut	28. Throttle arm
10. Spring	29. Float arm
11. Retainer	30. Float pin
12. Clip	31. Gasket
13. Jet needle	32. Float bowl
14. Throttle valve	33. Spring
15. Nut	34. Gasket
16. Fuel inlet	35. Plug
17. Washers	36. Float

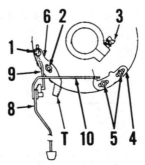

Fig. MR1-3—Diagram showing speed control linkage used on models prior to serial number 6A1-000101. Refer to text for adjustment.

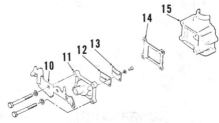

Fig. MR1-2—With carburetor body (25) inverted as shown, distance (D) from the body's gasket surface to float pads (P) should be 3.5-4.5 mm (0.14-0.18 inch).

Fig. MR1-4—Exploded view of reed valve.

10. Throttle bracket	13. Reed stop
11. Reed plate	14. Gasket
12. Reed petals	15. Crankcase half

lbs.) on models with serial number 6A1-000101 and after.

Use the following procedure to obtain correct ignition timing on models prior to serial number 6A1-000101. Check and adjust breaker point gap to correct specification. Install a suitable degree wheel on flywheel or a dial indicator in spark plug hole. Loosen magneto stop plate (4—Fig. MR1-3) and move speed control lever to full throttle position. Ignition timing should occur at 18-24 degrees before top dead center or 1.2-2.0 mm (0.047-0.079 in.) BTDC. Rotate flywheel so flywheel and piston are properly positioned before top dead center then rotate magneto base so breaker points just begin to open (use a suitable continuity tester to determine breaker point opening). Without disturbing magneto base, position stop plate (4) tab against bracket (10) stop tab and tighten screws (5). Recheck ignition timing then adjust speed control linkage as previously outlined.

To obtain the correct ignition timing on models with serial number 6A1-000101 and above, proceed as follows: Install a suitable dial indicator in the spark plug hole and place piston at TDC. Properly synchronize indicator face with piston position. Disconnect the white wire leading to the stop switch at the connector located below the magneto base plate. Using a suitable continuity tester, connect one tester lead to the white wire leading to the breaker point assembly and the other tester lead to an engine ground. Rotate the flywheel counterclockwise until the continuity tester indicates the breaker points just close, then note the dial indicator. The dial indicator should read between 0.99 and 1.23 mm (0.039 and 0.049 in.). If not, adjust the breaker point gap. If indicator reads less than 0.99 mm (0.039 in.), increase breaker point gap. If indicator reads more than 1.23 mm (0.049 in.), decrease breaker point gap.

COOLING SYSTEM

WATER PUMP. A rubber impeller type water pump is located in the gearcase and mounted on and driven by the lower unit drive shaft.

When cooling system problems are encountered, first check the water inlet for plugging or partial stoppage, then if not corrected, remove the gearcase and overhaul pump. Refer to Fig. MR1-6 for an exploded view of water pump. Apply water-resistant grease to seals (1 and 3) and oil seal (7).

POWER HEAD

REMOVE AND REINSTALL. To remove power head, remove power head cover, unscrew six screws securing power head to drive shaft housing and separate power head from drive shaft housing. Before reinstalling power head, apply water-resistant grease to ends of crankshaft and upper drive shaft. Install new gaskets between power head, exhaust plate and drive shaft housing.

DISASSEMBLY. Disconnect fuel line and remove fuel tank. Disconnect stop switch leads and remove control panel assembly. Remove carburetor, flywheel and magneto components shown in Fig. MR1-5. Detach reed plate (11—Fig. MR1-4), then remove cylinder head (49—Fig. MR1-7). Unscrew two crankcase screws, separate crankcase half (15) from cylinder block and remove crankshaft assembly from cylinder block. Disassemble crankshaft assembly as required for service.

Refer to the following section for assembly procedure.

ASSEMBLY. Refer to specific service sections when reassembling crankshaft, connecting rod and piston. Install crankshaft assembly into cylinder block being sure clips in outer races of main bearings are properly seated in holes in cylinder block as shown in Fig. MR1-8. Be certain crankcase and cylinder block mating surfaces are thoroughly clean. Apply Loctite Master Gasket Sealer part 92-72592-1 to crankcase half mating surface in a continuous 1.6 mm (1/16 in.) bead and position crankcase half on cylinder block. Install two side crankcase screws finger tight. Install reed plate with bracket (10—Fig. MR1-4) and four screws. Tighten six crankcase screws (two at side and four at reed plate) using sequence shown in Fig. MR1-9 to 4.9 N·m (43 in.-lbs.), then to 9.8 N·m (87 in.-lbs.). Apply Loctite 271 or a suitable equivalent thread locking compound to cylinder head screws. Install gasket and cylinder head. Tighten cylinder head screws in a crossing pattern to 4.9 N·m (43 in.-lbs.), then to 9.8 N·m (87 in.-lbs.). Complete remainder of reassembly by reversing disassembly procedure.

PISTON, PIN, RINGS AND CYLINDER. The piston is fitted with two piston rings. Piston ring end gap should be 0.15-0.35 mm (0.006-0.014 in.) on models prior to serial number 6A1-000101 and 0.1-0.3 mm (0.004-0.012 in.) on models after serial number 6A1-000100. The piston pin is fully floating and secured by retaining rings (39—Fig. MR1-7). Piston-to-cylinder bore clearance should be 0.030-0.035 mm (0.0012-0.0014 in.) on models prior to serial number 6A1-000101 and 0.030-0.040 mm (0.0012-0.0016 in.) on models after serial number 6A1-000100. Measure piston diameter at right angle to piston pin bore approximately 8.5 mm (0.34 inch) from

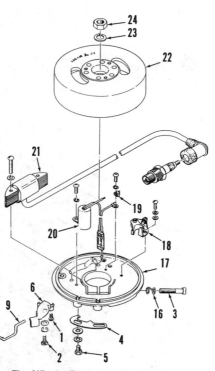

Fig. MR1-5—Exploded view of magneto.

1. Screw	18. Ignition breaker
2. Screw	points
3. Screw	19. Felt
4. Stop plate	20. Condenser
5. Screw	21. Ignition coil
6. Adjuster plate	22. Flywheel
9. Link	23. Lockwasher
16. Spring	24. Nut
17. Base plate	

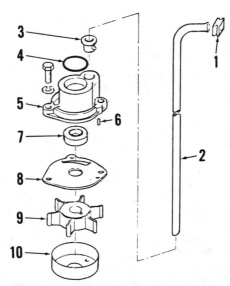

Fig. MR1-6—Exploded view of water pump.

1. Seal	6. Dowel pin
2. Water tube	7. Oil seal
3. Seal	8. Plate
4. "O" ring	9. Impeller
5. Pump housing	10. Liner

bottom of skirt. Piston and rings are available in standard size and 0.25 mm (0.010 in.) and 0.50 mm (0.020 in.) oversizes. On early models, install piston on connecting rod so arrow on piston crown will point toward exhaust port. On later models, stamped mark "UP" on piston crown must face toward flywheel side of crankshaft.

CONNECTING ROD, CRANKSHAFT AND CRANKCASE. The connecting rod rides on a roller bearing around the crankpin. Crankshaft, crankpin, bearing and connecting rod are available only as a unit assembly. Maximum allowable side clearance between rod and crankshaft is 0.5 mm (0.020 in.). Determine rod bearing wear by moving small rod end from side to side as shown in Fig. MR1-10. Normal side to side movement is 1.0 mm (0.04 in.) or less; renew crankshaft assembly if side movement exceeds 2.0 mm (0.08 in.).

Use a suitable press to remove and install main bearings (28 and 35—Fig. MR1-7). Install bearings so bearing side with outer race locating clip is toward crankshaft end. Install seals (27 and 37) with open side toward bearing.

MANUAL STARTER

The manual starter must be disassembled to renew starter rope (2—Fig. MR1-11) or any other internal starter component.

To overhaul the manual starter, proceed as follows: Remove the engine's bottom and side covers. Remove the screws securing the manual starter to the power head and withdraw.

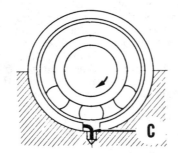

Fig. MR1-8—Retaining clip (C) in main bearing outer race must engage hole in cylinder block. Note crankshaft rotation when installing clip.

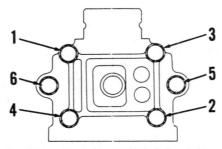

Fig. MR1-9—Use sequence shown when tightening crankcase screws.

To disassemble, untie starter rope (2) at handle (10) and allow the rope to wind into the starter. Invert the manual starter and remove cap screw (8), then withdraw plate (7), spring clip (6), drive pawl return spring (9) and drive pawl (5). Lift pulley (4) with starter rope (2) from starter housing (1). BE CAREFUL when removing pulley (4) as rewind spring (3) may be dislodged.

NOTE: Should pulley (4) not lift free from rewind spring (3), insert a suitable screwdriver blade through hole in pulley (4) to hold rewind spring (3) securely in housing (1).

Untie starter rope (2) and remove rope from pulley (4) if renewal is required. To remove rewind spring (3), use suitable hand protection and extract rewind spring (3) from housing (1). Allow rewind spring to uncoil in a safe area.

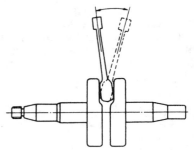

Fig. MR1-10—Move small connecting rod end side to side as shown to determine rod, bearing and crankpin wear. Refer to text.

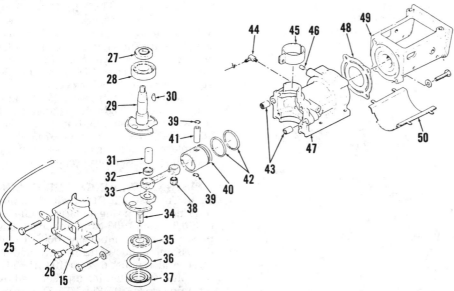

Fig. MR1-7—Exploded view of power head components. Bleeder hose (25) is routed to a passage at top of crankcase half (15) on later models.

15. Crankcase half	33. Connecting rod	42. Piston rings
25. Bleeder hose	34. Crankshaft half	43. Dowel pins
26. Crankcase bleeder valve	35. Bearing	44. Bleeder fitting
27. Oil seal	36. Spacer	45. Magneto bushing
28. Bearing	37. Oil seal	46. Plug
29. Crankshaft half	38. Bearing	47. Cylinder block
30. Key	39. Retaining rings	48. Gasket
31. Crankpin	40. Piston	49. Cylinder head
32. Bearing	41. Piston pin	50. Cover

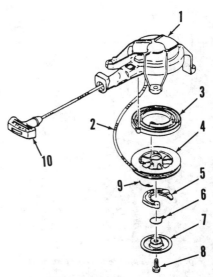

Fig. MR1-11—Exploded view of manual rewind starter.

1. Starter housing	6. Spring clip
2. Rope	7. Plate
3. Rewind spring	8. Cap screw
4. Pulley	9. Return spring
5. Drive pawl	10. Handle

Inspect all components for excessive wear or any other damage and renew if needed.

To reassemble, first apply a coating of a suitable water-resistant grease to rewind spring area of housing (1). Install rewind spring (3) in housing (1) so spring coils wind in a counterclockwise direction from the outer end. Make sure the spring's outer hook is properly secured in starter housing. Wind starter rope (2) onto pulley (4) approximately 3 turns counterlockwise when viewed from the flywheel side. Direct remaining starter rope (2) length through notch in pulley (4).

NOTE: Lubricate all friction surfaces with a suitable water-resistant grease during reassembly.

Assemble pulley (4) to starter housing making sure that slot in pulley's drum properly engages hook end in rewind spring (3). Thread starter rope (2) through housing (1) and handle (10) and

secure. Install drive pawl (5), return spring (9), spring clip (6) and plate (7). Apply a suitable thread fastening solution on cap screw (8) threads and securely tighten. Turn pulley (4) 2-3 turns counterclockwise when viewed from the flywheel side, then release starter rope (2) from pulley (4) notch and allow rope to slowly wind onto pulley.

NOTE: Do not apply any more tension on rewind spring (3) than is required to draw starter handle (10) back into the proper released position.

LOWER UNIT

PROPELLER AND SHEAR PIN. Lower unit protection is provided by a shear pin (16—Fig. MR1-13). Be sure correct shear pin is installed for maximum protection to lower unit.

Standard propeller size is 184 mm (7-1/4 in.) diameter with a 114 mm (4-1/2 in.) pitch with clockwise rotation. An optional propeller is offered with 184 mm (7-1/4 in.) diameter and 140 mm (5-1/2 in.) pitch.

R&R AND OVERHAUL. To remove gearcase, unscrew two screws securing gearcase to drive shaft housing and separate gearcase from drive shaft housing. Unscrew drain plug and drain gear lubricant. Detach cotter pin (21—Fig. MR1-13) and remove propeller. Remove water pump. Unscrew and remove shaft carrier (18) then detach "E" ring (8). Withdraw drive shaft (1) while simultaneously removing pinion gear (7), thrust washer (6) and shims (5). Remove propeller shaft (15) and shims (14). If necessary, use a suitable puller and remove bearing (13) and two bushings (4).

Inspect all components for excessive wear or other damage. If removed, install two bushings (4) and bearing (13). To check gear mesh position and backlash, make a trial assembly with components (1, 5, 6, 7, 8, 14 and 15). Mesh position is adjusted using shims (5) while shims (14) are used to adjust gear backlash. Gear backlash should be 0.08-0.3 mm (0.003-0.012 in.) on models prior to serial number 6A1-000101 and 0.1-0.3 mm (0.004-0.012 in.) on models after serial number 6A1-000100. Complete reassembly by reversing disassembly procedure.

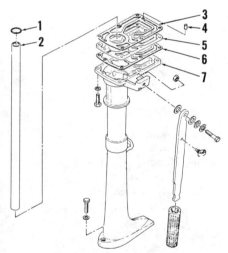

Fig. MR1-12—Exploded view of drive shaft housing.

1. "O" ring
2. Drive shaft tube
3. Gasket
4. Dowel pin
5. Exhaust plate
6. Gasket
7. Drive shaft housing

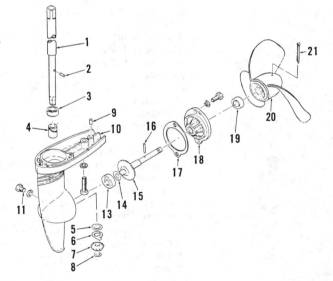

Fig. MR1-13—Exploded view of gearcase.

1. Drive shaft
2. Pin
3. Oil seal
4. Bushing (2)
5. Shim
6. Thrust washer
7. Pinion gear
8. "E" ring
9. Dowel pin
10. Gearcase
11. Drain/fill plug
13. Bearing
14. Shim
15. Prop shaft & gear
16. Shear pin
17. Gasket
18. Carrier
19. Oil seal
20. Propeller
21. Cotter pin

MARINER 3½ HP (1977-1981)

CONDENSED SERVICE DATA

NOTE: Metric fasteners are used throughout outboard motor.

TUNE-UP

Hp/rpm	3.5/4500
Bore	45 mm
Stroke	40 mm
Number of Cylinders	1
Displacement	63 cc
Spark Plug – NGK	B7HS
Electrode Gap	0.6-0.7 mm
Breaker Point Gap	0.3-0.45 mm
Ignition Timing	See text
Carburetor:	
Make	Mikuni
Model	BV18-14
Idle Speed	1250-1350 rpm
Fuel:Oil Ratio	50:1
Gearcase Oil Capacity	80 cc

SIZES – CLEARANCES

Piston Ring End Gap	0.15-0.35 mm
Piston Ring Side Clearance:	
Top Ring	0.04-0.08 mm
Bottom Ring	0.03-0.07 mm
Piston Skirt Clearance	0.050-0.055 mm
Crankshaft Journal Diameter	20.0 mm
Crankshaft Runout – Max.	0.0025 mm
Connecting Rod Small End Shake:	
Standard	0.8-1.0 mm
Limit	2.0 mm
Lower Unit Gear Backlash	0.10-0.25 mm

TIGHTENING TORQUES
(All values are in newton meters.)

Crankcase	9.8
Cylinder Head	9.8
Flywheel	29.4-34.3
Standard Screws:	
4 mm	2.0
5 mm	4.9-5.9
6 mm	7.8-9.8
8 mm	14.7-19.6
10 mm	29.4

LUBRICATION

The power head is lubricated by oil mixed with the fuel. Fuel should be regular leaded, low lead or unleaded gasoline with a minimum pump octane rating of 86. Recommended oil is Quicksilver Formula 50-D Outboard Lubricant. Normal fuel:oil ratio is 50:1; during engine break-in, fuel:oil ratio should be 25:1.

Lower unit gears and bearings are lubricated by oil contained in the gearcase. Recommended oil is Mariner Super Duty Gear Lube. Lubricant is drained by removing vent and drain plugs in gearcase. Refill through drain plug hole until oil has reached level of top (vent) plug hole.

FUEL SYSTEM

CARBURETOR. Refer to Fig. MR2-1 for exploded view of carburetor. Normal position of pilot air screw (9) is

1⅛ turns open from a lightly seated position. Final adjustment should be made with motor running and at normal operating temperature. Set idle speed at 1250-1350 rpm. Main fuel mixture is controlled by a number 75 fixed main jet (15).

To check fuel level adjustment, press float bowl drain (29) with fuel petcock "ON" and hold drain line up. Fuel level in drain tube should be 23 mm below center of carburetor throttle bore. Float level may be adjusted by bending tang on float (21). Check condition of inlet valve (17) before changing float setting.

SPEED CONTROL LINKAGE. Engine speed is controlled by position of throttle linkage. No ignition advance is used. A twist grip at the steering handle is used to control throttle settings.

REED VALVES. Reed petals and reed stopper are mounted on the reed valve assembly located between the carburetor and the crankcase. Height (A – Fig. MR2-2) of reed stopper should

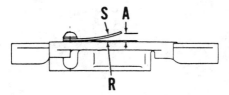

Fig. MR2-2 — Reed stopper (S) should curve smoothly to height of 6.5 mm (A) from reed petal (R) laying flat on reed plate.

be 6.5 mm. Do not attempt to straighten bent or distorted reed petals or stopper. Reed petals should seat lightly and evenly on valve body with the least possible tension.

IGNITION

Breaker point gap should be set at 0.3-0.45 mm at point of maximum opening. Adjustment may be accomplished through holes in flywheel. Magneto base plate is fixed to engine with tapered screws and no timing adjustment is possible other than varying the breaker point gap. Breaker points should open when piston is 0.96-1.2 mm (16°-18°) BTDC. Flywheel must be removed to

renew breaker points, coil or condenser. Tighten flywheel nut to 29.4-34.3 N·m.

COOLING SYSTEM

The power head is air cooled by a fan built into the flywheel. Make sure that cooling fins are unobstructed and shroud (1 – Fig. MR2-5) is in place. Do not attempt to run motor without outer cover.

POWER HEAD

R&R AND OVERHAUL. To remove and disassemble power head for overhaul, proceed as follows: Remove engine cover and fuel tank. Disconnect throttle cable and remove flywheel and magneto base plate. Unscrew six screws holding fuel tank brackets to power head. Remove induction assembly and fuel petcock. Remove four screws that secure reed valve assembly to crankcase. Remove cooling shroud around cylinder and unscrew hardware securing cylinder head. Cylinder and crankcase assembly may be lifted from motor leg after removal of exhaust manifold (7 – Fig. MR2-5) and four bolts (3 – Fig. MR2-10). Crankshaft and piston assembly may be withdrawn after removal of two screws holding crankcase halves together.

Engine components are now available for overhaul as outlined in the appropriate following paragraphs. Assemble as outlined in the ASSEMBLY paragraphs following.

ASSEMBLY. When reassembling, make sure that all joint and gasket surfaces are clean, free from nicks and burrs and hardened cement or carbon.

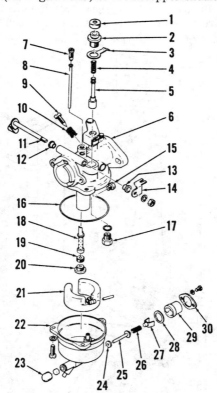

Fig. MR2-1 — Exploded view of Mikuni BV18-14 carburetor.

1. Cover	16. Gasket
2. Plunger cap	17. Inlet valve
3. Start lever plate	18. Main nozzle
4. Spring	19. Nozzle holder
5. Start plunger	20. Plug
6. Throttle body	21. Float
7. Pilot jet	22. Float chamber
8. Pipe	23. Cap
9. Pilot air screw	24. Packing
10. Spring	25. Drain valve
11. Starter lever	26. Spring
12. Bushing	27. Spring guide
13. Bushing	28. Gasket
14. Lever	29. Drain cup
15. Main jet	30. Plate

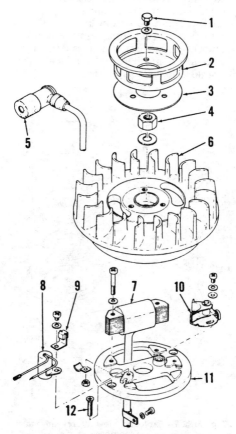

Fig. MR2-3 — Exploded view of flywheel magneto unit.

1. Screw	7. Ignition coil
2. Starter pulley	8. Condenser
3. Plate	9. Lubrication felt
4. Flywheel nut	10. Breaker points
5. Spark plug cap	11. Base plate
6. Flywheel	12. Screw

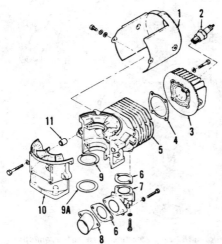

Fig. MR2-5 — Exploded view of crankcase and cylinder assembly.

1. Cooling shroud	7. Exhaust manifold
2. Spark plug	8. Exhaust guide
3. Cylinder head	9. Bearing retainer
4. Head gasket	9A. Bearing retainer
5. Cylinder	10. Crankcase half
6. Gasket	11. Dowel

Mating surfaces of crankcase, cylinder head, exhaust and intake manifolds may be checked on a lapping block, and high spots or nicks removed. Do not remove any more metal than necessary to obtain a smooth surface.

All friction surfaces should be thoroughly lubricated with two cycle engine oil during reassembly. Coat mating surfaces with a nonhardening type gasket sealer. Refer to CONDENSED SERVICE DATA table for recommended torque values.

PISTON, PIN, RINGS AND CYLINDER. Measure cylinder bore in several locations to determine if an out-of-round or taper is present. Total difference between maximum and minimum cylinder bore diameter should be no more than 0.07 mm. Cylinder should be bored to accept next oversize piston if worn beyond limits. Piston and rings are available in standard and two oversizes. Recommended piston skirt to cylinder clearance is 0.050-0.055 mm measured at a point 10 mm from bottom of piston skirt at a right angle to the piston pin hole. Piston ring end gap should be 0.15-0.35 mm. Recommended side clearance for top piston ring is 0.04-0.08 mm and 0.03-0.07 mm for bottom piston ring.

When assembling, make sure that rings are installed with chrome ring in top groove and markings on both rings toward top of piston. Install piston with

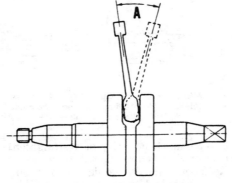

Fig. MR2-7 — Maximum small end shake (A) is 2.0 mm.

arrow pointing toward exhaust port. Renew piston pin retaining clips (9 – Fig. MR2-6) on each reassembly.

CRANKSHAFT, ROD AND BEARINGS. The built-up crankshaft assembly may be dismantled if necessary to renew individual parts. Maximum side shake (A – Fig. MR2-7) at small end of connecting rod is 2.0 mm. If side shake at small end is excessive, it is usually necessary to renew rod (7 – Fig. MR2-6), bearing (6) and crankpin (3). Connecting rod side shake should be within limits of 0.8-1.0 mm when rebuilding unit. Standard limit of crankshaft runout is 0.0025 mm measured at bearing surfaces with crankshaft ends supported.

Square drive end of crankshaft should be inspected when power head is removed. Width across flats should be 10.83-10.93 mm. Diagonal measurement should be 12.40-13.45 mm. Renew crankshaft if drive end measures less than specified.

Install main bearings (2 and 14) on crankshaft with markings next to seals (1 and 15).

Bearing retaining ring may be of one-piece construction (9A – Fig. MR2-5) or two-piece (9). Install retainer between bearing (14 – Fig. MR2-6) and seal (15).

MANUAL STARTER

Refer to Fig. MR2-9 for exploded view of manual starter used. Starter must be disassembled to renew rope. Starter may be disassembled as follows: Remove motor top cowl and then remove single remaining screw securing starter assembly to motor. Untie rope at start handle and allow rope to wind into starter. Invert unit and press on drive plate (14) to ease removal of snap ring (16) and thrust washer (15). Remove drive plate, pawls (13), pawl return

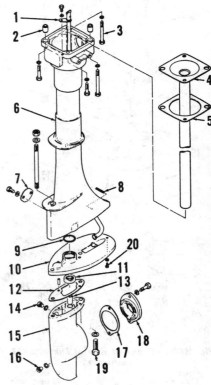

Fig. MR2-10—Exploded view of drive shaft housing and gear housing assembly.

1. Water tube	11. Seal
2. Dowel	12. Gasket
3. Bolt	13. Bushing
4. Drive shaft casing	14. Vent plug
5. Gasket	15. Gearcase
6. Drive shaft housing	16. Drain plug
7. Cover	17. Gasket
8. Spring pin	18. Case cap
9. "O" ring	19. Cap screw
10. Cavitation plate	20. Cap screw

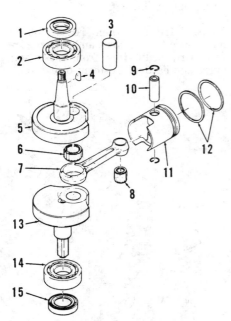

Fig. MR2-6 — Exploded view of crankshaft, piston and related parts.

1. Seal	
2. Ball bearing	9. Piston pin clip
3. Crankpin	10. Piston pin
4. Woodruff key	11. Piston
5. Crank half	12. Piston rings
6. Needle bearing	13. Crank half
7. Connecting rod	14. Ball bearing
8. Needle bearing	15. Seal

Fig. MR2-9 — Exploded view of rewind starter assembly.

1. Collar	9. Lubricator
2. Cover	10. Thrust washer
3. Case	11. Spring
4. Anchor	12. Pawl return spring
5. Guide	13. Pawls
6. Snap ring	14. Drive plate
7. Recoil spring	15. Thrust washer
8. Drum & pulley	16. Snap ring

spring (12), drive plate spring (11), thrust washer (10) and lubricator (9). Turn drum (8) clockwise until rewind spring (7) is disengaged and remove drum. Use caution when removing drum to prevent possible injury from rewind spring. Wind start rope onto drum counterclockwise viewed from the bottom. Leave approximately 16 inches of starter rope extending from notch in drum (8) and turn drum 4-5 full turns counterclockwise. Thread rope through guide (5), handle and anchor (4), then knot end of rope. Install pawls, lubricator pad and springs. Hook one end of pawl return spring (12) in hole in drum and other end in slot of drive plate (14). Turn the drive plate 30-50 degrees clockwise and position it in assembly. Install thrust washer and snap ring (16).

LOWER UNIT

PROPELLER AND SHEAR PIN. A shear pin is used to provide protection for the propeller and lower unit. Some units are equipped with a rubber cushion hub for further protection. Propellers are available in two and three blade designs with diameters of 180 and 190 mm and pitches of 100 and 142 mm.

R&R AND OVERHAUL. Refer to Fig. MR2-11 for an exploded view of lower unit. The following procedure may be used to remove and disassemble unit for overhaul.

Remove vent and drain plugs in gear case (15 – Fig. MR2-10). Remove stud nut on top forward side of cavitation plate, the 5 mm screw (20) and the 8 mm screw (19), then pull gearcase assembly from motor leg. Remove propeller and shear pin. Remove two screws securing case cap (18) and use a soft faced hammer to dislodge and remove cap. Remove snap ring (6 – Fig. MR2-11), pinion gear (5), thrust washers (3 and 4) and clip (2) so that drive shaft may be pulled from case. Propeller shaft with drive gear may now be pulled from gearcase.

Backlash and mesh position of drive and pinion gear may be adjusted by varying thickness and number of thrust washers (3) and shims (8).

All seals, gaskets and "O" rings should be renewed on each reassembly to limit the possibility of leakage.

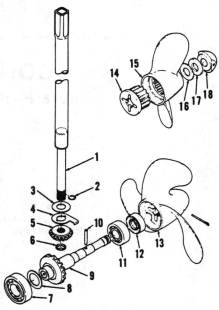

Fig. MR2-11 — Exploded view of drive shaft and lower unit gears.

1. Drive shaft
2. Clip
3. Thrust washer
4. Thrust washer
5. Pinion gear
6. Snap ring
7. Ball bearing
8. Shim
9. Propeller shaft
10. Shear pin
11. Ball bearing
12. Seal
13. Propeller
14. Rubber damper
15. Propeller
16. Washer
17. Washer
18. Cap

MARINER 5 HP (1977-1981)

CONDENSED SERVICE DATA

NOTE: Metric fasteners are used throughout outboard motor.

TUNE-UP

Hp/rpm	5/5000
Bore	50 mm
Stroke	47 mm
Number of cylinders	1
Displacement	92 cc
Spark plug—NGK	B-7HS
Electrode gap	0.5-0.6 mm
Breaker point gap	0.30-0.40 mm
Ignition timing	See text
Idle speed	1550-1650 rpm
Fuel:oil ratio	50:1
Gearcase oil capacity	80 cc

SIZES—CLEARANCES

Piston ring end gap	0.15-0.35 mm
Piston skirt clearance	0.035-0.040 mm
Crankshaft journal diameter	20.0 mm
Crankshaft runout—max.	0.03 mm
Connecting rod small end shake—	
Standard	0.8 mm
Limit	2.0 mm
Lower unit gear backlash	0.1-0.3 mm

TIGHTENING TORQUES
(All values are in newton meters.)

Crankcase	10.8-12.7
Cylinder head	10.8-12.7
Flywheel	39.2-49
Standard screws	
5 mm	4.9-5.8
6 mm	7.9-9.8
8 mm	14.7-19.6

LUBRICATION

The power head is lubricated by oil mixed with the fuel. Fuel should be regular leaded, low lead or unleaded gasoline with a minimum pump octane rating of 86. Recommended oil is Quicksilver Formula 50-D Outboard Lubricant. Normal fuel:oil ratio is 50:1; during engine break-in, fuel:oil ratio should be 25:1.

Lower unit gears and bearings are lubricated by oil contained in the gearcase. Recommended oil is Mariner Super Duty Gear Lube. Lubricant is drained by removing vent and drain plugs in gearcase. Refill through drain plug hole until oil has reached level of top (vent) plug hole.

FUEL SYSTEM

CARBURETOR. Refer to Fig. MR3-1 for an exploded view of carburetor. Normal position of pilot air screw (3) is 1⅜ turns open from lightly seated position. Final adjustment should be made with engine running and at normal operating temperature. Set idle speed at 1550-1650 rpm by turning idle speed screw (4). Main jet (24) size for normal operation is number 82 for early models and number 80 for later models.

To check fuel level in float bowl, connect a clear tube to float bowl drain as shown in Fig. MR3-2. Run engine at idle speed for a few minutes then stop engine. Measure height of fuel level in tube from center of carburetor bore.

Fuel level (L) should be 27-31 mm. Adjust fuel level by bending float arm pads (P—Fig. MR3-1).

SPEED CONTROL LINKAGE. No ignition advance is used. Engine speed is controlled by position of throttle. Check linkage to make certain that throttle plate opens and closes fully according to throttle control setting.

FUEL PUMP. An exploded view of diaphragm type fuel pump is shown in Fig. MR3-3. Defective or questionable parts should be renewed. Petals of check valve (5) should seat lightly and squarely on plate (4). Diaphragm (3) should be renewed if air leaks or cracks are found, or if deterioration is evident.

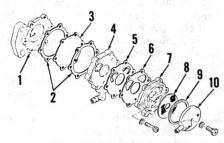

Fig. MR3-1—Exploded view of carburetor.

1. Top cover	17. Choke shaft
2. Gasket	18. Snap ring
3. Pilot air screw	19. Gasket
4. Idle speed screw	20. Fuel inlet valve
5. Springs	21. Gasket
6. Low speed jet	22. Main fuel nozzle
7. Low speed air jet	23. Gasket
8. Main air jet	24. Main jet
9. Washer	25. Float pin
10. Cable connector	26. Float pivot arm
11. Throttle shaft screw	27. Float
12. Carburetor body	28. Gasket
13. Throttle cable plate	29. Float bowl
14. Choke plate	30. Drain plug
15. Main nozzle screw	31. Spring
16. Spring	32. "O" ring

IGNITION

The ignition system is shown in Fig. MR3-4. Breaker point gap may be adjusted through opening in flywheel. However, flywheel must be removed to renew breaker points or condenser. Breaker point gap should be 0.30-0.40 mm.

Ignition timing should occur at 1.05-1.85 mm (15½°-20½°) BTDC and is not adjustable. Be sure breaker point gap is correct, otherwise, ignition timing will be affected.

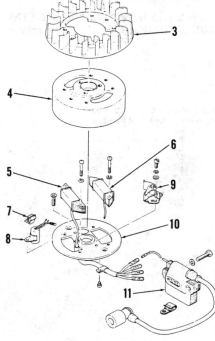

Fig. MR3-3—Exploded view of fuel pump.

1. Base	6. Gasket
2. Gasket	7. Body
3. Diaphragm	8. Screen
4. Body	9. Gasket
5. Check valve	10. Inlet

To check ignition coil located on air shroud, connect one ohmmeter lead to metal laminations, then connect remaining ohmmeter lead alternately to primary and secondary ignition coil leads. Resistance reading for primary wire connection should be approximately 1.0 ohm while secondary wire connection resistance reading should be approximately 5900 ohms.

COOLING SYSTEM

The power head is air cooled by a fan built into the flywheel. Make sure cylinder cooling fins are free of debris and air shrouds (1 and 2 – Fig. MR3-5) are in place.

A water tube in the drive shaft housing directs water through the lower unit to cool exiting exhaust gases. Check water tube for blockage when servicing unit.

POWER HEAD

R&R AND OVERHAUL. Cylinder head, cylinder and piston may be serviced without removing power head. To remove power head for service, proceed as follows: Disconnect control cables, fuel lines and stop wire. Remove carburetor, air shroud, magneto assembly and exhaust manifold. Unscrew four

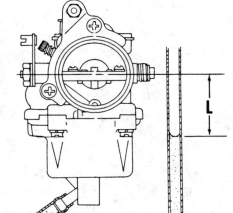

Fig. MR3-2 – Fuel level (L) should be 27-31 mm from carburetor bore center.

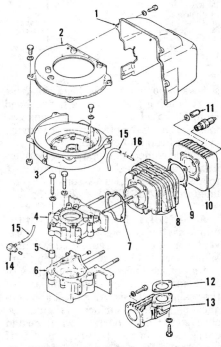

Fig. MR3-5 – Exploded view of crankcase and cylinder assembly.

1. Air shroud	
2. Air shroud	10. Cylinder head
3. Flywheel housing	11. Nut
4. Upper crankcase half	12. Gasket
5. Dowel	13. Exhaust manifold
6. Lower crankcase half	14. Crankcase bleeder
7. Gasket	valve
8. Cylinder	15. Hose
9. Gasket	16. Fitting

Fig. MR3-4—View of magneto.

1. Nut	7. Felt
2. Lockwasher	8. Condenser
3. Fan	9. Breaker points
4. Flywheel	10. Base plate
5. Lighting coil	11. High tension
6. Ignition coil	ignition coil

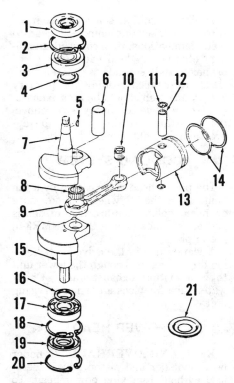

Fig. MR3-6 — Exploded view of crankshaft assembly. On later models, oil slinger (21) is used in place of snap ring (18) and snap rings (2, 18 and 20) are not used.

1. Oil seal	
2. Snap ring	12. Piston pin
3. Bearing	13. Piston
4. Shim	14. Piston rings
5. Key	15. Crank half
6. Crankpin	16. Shim
7. Crank half	17. Bearing
8. Needle bearing	18. Snap ring
9. Connecting rod	19. Bearing
10. Needle bearing	20. Snap ring
11. Piston pin clip	21. Oil slinger

rings and cylinder should be thoroughly lubricated when assembling. Apply a suitable nonhardening gasket sealer to crankcase mating surfaces. Apply heat resistant gasket sealer to exhaust manifold gaskets. Refer to CONDENSED SERVICE DATA for tightening torques.

CYLINDER, PISTON AND RINGS. Cylinder should be checked in several locations to determine if an out-of-round or tapered condition exists. Cylinder should be bored to fit an oversize piston and ring set if out-of-round or taper is beyond limit of 0.07 mm. Pistons and rings are available in oversizes of 0.25 mm and 0.50 mm.

Recommended piston skirt to cylinder clearance is 0.035-0.040 mm. Piston should be measured at a point 10 mm from the bottom at a right angle from the pin hole for cylinder clearance check.

Piston ring end gap should be 0.15-0.35 mm. Side clearance for top piston ring should be 0.04-0.08 mm and side clearance for bottom piston ring should be 0.03-0.07 mm. Piston pin diameter should be 11.996-12.000 mm.

Thoroughly lubricate small end needle bearing, piston pin, piston rings, piston and cylinder with engine oil when reassembling. Piston should be installed with arrow on dome toward exhaust port of cylinder. Piston pin slips (11 – Fig. MR3-6) should be renewed on each reassembly.

CRANKSHAFT, CONNECTING ROD AND BEARINGS. Maximum run-

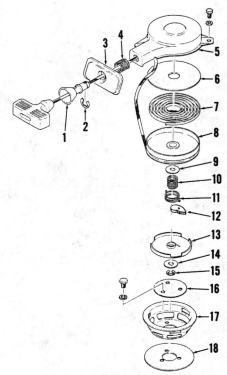

Fig. MR3-7 — Exploded view of rewind starter.

1. Rope guide	10. Spring
2. "E" ring	11. Pawl return spring
3. Guide plate	12. Pawls
4. Spring	13. Drive plate
5. Housing	14. Washer
6. Plate	15. "E" ring
7. Spring	16. Plate
8. Pulley	17. Starter cup
9. Washer	18. Plate

screws securing power head to drive shaft housing and separate power head from drive shaft housing. Crankcase may be disassembled after removing cylinder head and cylinder.

Engine components may now be overhauled as outlined in the appropriate following paragraphs. Assemble as outlined in the ASSEMBLY section.

ASSEMBLY. It is important that the crankcase be completely sealed to prevent leakage of pressure and vacuum. When reassembling, make certain there are no nicks, burrs or accumulations of hardened cement or carbon on any of the sealing surfaces. All gasket and non-gasket mating surfaces should be checked for nicks, burrs or warpage and corrected on a lapping plate if necessary. Do not remove any more metal than is necessary to obtain a smooth surface.

All seals and gaskets should be renewed to reduce the possibility of leakage. Lubricate crankcase seals with a nonfibrous heat resistant grease during reassembly. Bearings, piston, piston

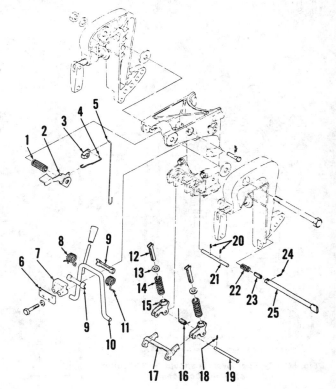

Fig. MR3-8 — Exploded view of reverse lock mechanism.

1. Spring
2. Release lever
3. Reverse lock cam
4. Link
5. Link
6. Plate
7. Bracket
8. Spring
9. Bushing halves
10. Tilt lever
11. Spring
12. Spring guide
13. Spring seat
14. Spring
15. Arm
16. Spring
17. Hook
18. Cotter pin
19. Shaft
20. Cotter pins
21. Shaft
22. Spring
23. Arm
24. Pin
25. Lockpin

MANUAL STARTER

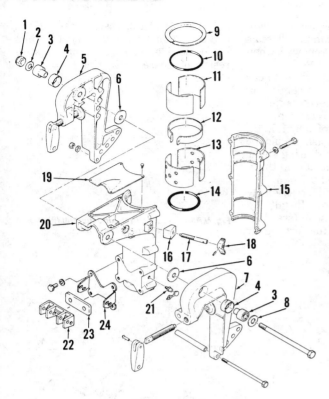

Movement of pulley (8–Fig. MR3-7) causes starter pawls (12) to swing out and engage starter cup (17) which is secured to the flywheel.

Starter assembly may be dismounted by removing three screws securing unit to air shroud. To disassemble, remove "E" ring (15) and pull drive plate (13) away from pulley. Disconnect rope handle from rope and allow rope to wind onto pulley. Carefully lift pulley out of starter. Use caution to prevent injury from rewind spring flying out of housing.

Wind new rope onto pulley in counter-clockwise direction as viewed from pawl side. Make sure that rewind spring is hooked in starter housing and in pulley notch when placing pulley in housing. Grasp end of starter rope and wind pulley 4 to 5 turns clockwise as viewed from pawl side. Thread rope through housing guide and attach rope handle. Install thrust washer (9), springs (10 and 11) and pawls (12). Hook one end of return spring (11) in drive plate (13), then turn plate 30-50 degrees clockwise and position it in assembly. Install thrust washer (14) and "E" ring (15).

Fig. MR3-9 — Exploded view of swivel bracket.
1. Nut
2. Lockwasher
3. Pilot bushing
4. Bushing
5. Stern bracket
6. Washer
7. Stern bracket
8. Washer
9. Thrust collar
10. "O" ring
11. Upper bushing halves
12. Clamp
13. Lower bushing halves
14. "O" ring
15. Rear swivel bracket section
16. Rubber seal
17. Clamp adjusting screw
18. Screw head
19. Cover
20. Front swivel bracket section
21. Grease fitting
22. Thrust flange
23. Rubber spacer
24. Thrust bracket

out of crankshaft is 0.02 mm with crankshaft supported between lathe centers. Maximum side to side shake measured at small end of connecting rod is 3.0 mm. If side to side shake is beyond limits, renew crankshaft assembly or defective parts. Crankshaft should only be disassembled if the proper tools are available to correctly realign the assembly.

If crankshaft has been disassembled; if crankshaft is being renewed or if bearings have been removed from crankcase, proceed as follows: Install snap ring (2–Fig. MR3-6) on early models so that lubrication hole in crankcase is in open end of snap ring. Press ball bearing (3) into case so that lettered side will be toward inside of crankcase. Depth from mating surface of crankcase halves to bearing should be 22.0-22.2 mm. Install snap ring (18) and press ball bearing (17) into case with lettered side toward inside of crankcase. Depth from mating surface of crankcase to ball bearing (17) should be 22.0-22.2 mm. Assembled width of crankshaft assembly excluding shims (4 and 16) should be 42.90-42.95 mm. Add the appropriate thicknesses of shims (4 and 16) to obtain axial play of 0.30-0.40 mm with crankcase and crankshaft assembled. Shims are available in six different thicknesses ranging from 0.3 mm to 0.8 mm.

When reassembling, follow procedures outlined in the ASSEMBLY section and refer to CONDENSED SERVICE DATA table for tightening torques.

Fig. MR3-10 — Exploded view of drive shaft housing.
1. Drive shaft tube
2. Gasket
3. Grease fitting
4. Cover
5. Gasket
6. Pin
7. Bushing
8. Shift body
9. Gasket
10. Water tube
11. Dowel pin
12. Gasket (later model)
13. Gasket (early model)
14. Exhaust tube
15. Gasket
16. Drive shaft housing
17. Sleeve
18. Cover
19. Pin

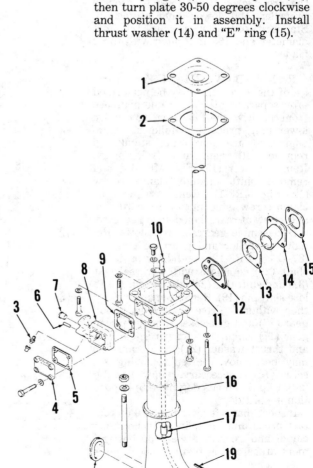

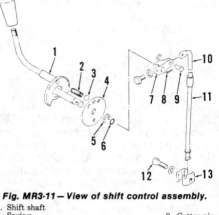

Fig. MR3-11 — View of shift control assembly.

1. Shift shaft
2. Spring
3. Ball
4. Detent plate
5. "E" ring
6. "O" ring
7. Arm
8. Cotter pin
9. Pin
10. Shift rod
11. Sleeve
12. Screw
13. Coupler

LOWER UNIT

PROPELLER AND SHEAR PIN. A shear pin as well as a rubber cushion in the propeller hub are used to provide propeller and lower unit protection. Standard propeller size is 184 mm diameter and 165 mm pitch with three blades.

R&R AND OVERHAUL. Most service of the lower unit may be performed after separating the lower unit gearcase from the drive shaft housing. To remove lower unit, proceed as follows: Clamp engine to an appropriate stand and remove both vent and drain plugs. Remove cover (18–Fig. MR3-10) and remove shift linkage clamp screw (12–Fig. MR3-11). Remove water tube clamp screw, stud nut on forward side and screw at rear, then detach gearcase.

Disassemble gearcase as follows: Remove propeller and gearcase end cap (37–Fig. MR3-12). Withdraw propeller shaft (29) complete with reverse gear (32) and shift dog (24). Be careful not to lose shift pin (19). Remove snap ring (18) then withdraw drive shaft from pinion gear (17) and gearcase. Remove pinion gear (17), shim (16), forward gear (22) and thrust washer (21). Shift cam (10) may be removed after removing set screw (12). If necessary, remove bearing (20). Clip (26) holds dog pin (25) in position in shift dog.

Inspect shafts for wear on seal lip contact areas and on splines. Inspect dog clutch and gears for wear on engagement areas of dog teeth. Inspect gears

for wear and damage. Inspect shift cam for excessive wear on ramp. All seals and "O" rings should be renewed when unit is reassembled.

To check gear mesh pattern and gear backlash, make a trial assembly using original shims. Mesh pattern is adjusted using pinion gear shim (16) which is available in thicknesses of 0.8, 1.0, 1.2 and 1.4 mm. Gear backlash should be 0.1-0.3 mm and is adjusted using shims (21 and 33) which are available in thicknesses of 0.4, 0.5, 0.6 and 0.7 mm.

Reverse disassembly for reassembly while noting the following: Install dog clutch so "F" marked side (see Fig. MR3-13) is towards forward gear

(22–Fig. MR3-12). Install seals (35) in end cap so innermost seal is 0.4-0.6 mm below bore of end cap. Apply water-resistant grease to "O" ring (36).

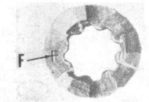

Fig. MR3-13—Dog clutch side marked (F) should be toward forward gear.

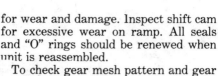

Fig. MR3-12—Exploded view of gearcase.

1. Drive shaft
2. "O" ring
3. Oil seal
4. Thrust washer
5. Plate
6. Shift rod boot
7. Bushing
8. Gasket
9. Dowel pin
10. Shift cam
11. Vent plug
12. Shift cam stopper
13. Drain plug
14. Bushing
15. Anode
16. Shim
17. Pinion gear
18. Snap ring
19. Shift pin
20. Bearing
21. Shim
22. Forward gear
23. Thrust washer
24. Clutch
25. Clutch pin
26. Clip
27. Spring guide
28. Spring
29. Propeller shaft
30. Shear pin
31. Thrust washer
32. Reverse gear
33. Shim
34. Bearing
35. Oil seals
36. "O" ring
37. End cap

MARINER 4 AND 5 HP (1982-1989)

CONDENSED SERVICE DATA

NOTE: Metric fasteners are used throughout outboard motor.

TUNE-UP

Hp/rpm	4/5000
	5/5000
Bore:	
4 hp	50 mm
	(1.98 in.)
5 hp	54 mm
	(2.14 in.)
Stroke:	
4 hp	42 mm
	(1.67 in.)
5 hp	45 mm
	(1.79 in.)
Number of Cylinders	1
Displacement:	
4 hp	83 cc
	(5 cu. in.)
5 hp	103 cc
	(6.3 cu. in.)
Spark Plug	NGK B7HS
Electrode Gap	0.5-0.6 mm
	(0.020-0.024 in.)
Ignition type	CDI
Idle Speed (in gear)	950-1050 rpm
Fuel:Oil Ratio	50:1
Gearcase Oil Capacity	105 mL
	(3.5 oz.)

SIZES—CLEARANCES

Piston Ring End Gap	0.15-0.35 mm
	(0.006-0.014 in.)
Piston Skirt Clearance	0.030-0.035 mm
	(0.0012-0.0014 in.)
Crankshaft Journal Diameter	20 mm
	(0.787 in.)
Crankshaft Runout—Max	0.03 mm
	(0.0012 in.)
Connecting Rod Small End Shake:	
Standard	0.8 mm
	(0.0315 in.)
Limit	2.0 mm
	(0.0787 in.)

TIGHTENING TORQUES

Crankcase	11.2 N·m
	(100 in.-lbs.)
Cylinder Head Cover	8.5 N·m
	(75 in.-lbs.)
Exhaust Cover	8.5 N·m
	(75 in.-lbs.)
Flywheel	40.7-47.5 N·m
	(30-35 ft.-lbs.)
Spark Plug	27.1 N·m
	(20 ft.-lbs.)

TIGHTENING TORQUES CONT.

Standard Screws:

4 mm	2 N·m (18 in.-lbs.)
5 mm.	3.4-5.1 N·m (30-45 in.-lbs.)
6 mm	5.9-9 N·m (53-80 in.-lbs.)
8 mm	14.9-21.7 N·m (11-16 ft.-lbs.)
10 mm.	28.5-44.7 N·m (21-33 ft.-lbs.)
12 mm.	35.3-50.2 N·m (26-37 ft.-lbs.)

LUBRICATION

The power head is lubricated by oil mixed with the fuel. Fuel should be regular leaded, low lead or unleaded gasoline with a minimum pump octane rating of 86. Recommended oil is Quicksilver Formula 50-D Outboard Lubricant or a BIA certified TC-W motor oil. The recommended fuel:oil ratio for normal operation is 50:1. During engine break-in, the fuel:oil ratio should be increased to 25:1.

Lower unit gears and bearings are lubricated by oil contained in the gearcase. Recommended oil is Mariner Super Duty Gear Lube or a suitable EP 90 outboard gear oil. Lubricant is drained by removing vent and drain plugs in gearcase. Refill through drain plug hole until oil has reached level of top (vent) plug hole.

FUEL SYSTEM

CARBURETOR. The fuel pump and carburetor are a complete unit. Use the standard carburetor jet sizes as recommended by the manufacturer for normal operation when used at altitudes of 2500 feet (760 mm) and less. Main jet (12 – Fig. MR4-1) size should be reduced from standard recommendation by one size for altitudes of 2500 to 5000 feet (760 to 1525 m), two sizes for altitudes 5000 to 7500 feet (1525 to 2285 m) and three sizes for altitudes of 7500 feet (2285 m) and up. Initial adjustment of idle mixture screw (5) is 1½ to 2 turns out from a lightly seated position on 4 hp models and 1 to 1½ turns out from a lightly seated position on 5 hp models. Recommended idle speed is 950-1050 rpm in gear with the engine at normal operating temperature.

To determine the float level, invert carburetor body (3 – Fig. MR4-2) with needle valve (10 – Fig. MR4-1) and float lever (13 – Fig. MR4-2) installed. Measure distance (D) from carburetor body sealing surface to top of float lever hump. Distance should be 1.5-2.5 mm (0.06-0.10 in.) and is adjusted by bending the arms of float lever (13).

FUEL PUMP. A diaphragm type fuel pump is mounted on the side of the carburetor. The fuel pump is operated by crankcase pulsations transferred through passageways in the crankcase, reed valve plate and carburetor body. Passageways must be clear of obstructions or fuel pump will not operate properly. Refer to Fig. MR4-1 for an exploded view of fuel pump.

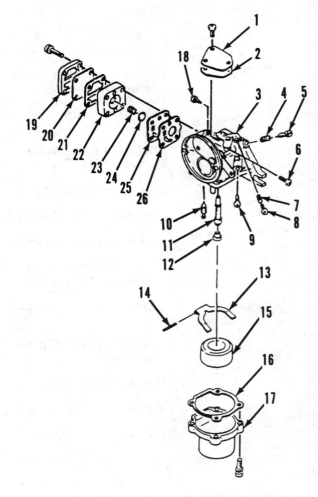

Fig. MR4-1 – Exploded view of carburetor/fuel pump assembly.

1. Cover plate
2. Gasket
3. Carburetor body
4. Spring
5. Idle mixture screw
6. Screw
7. Spring
8. Idle speed screw
9. Pilot jet
10. Needle valve
11. Main nozzle
12. Main jet
13. Float lever
14. Pin
15. Float
16. Gasket
17. Float bowl
18. Guide screw
19. Fuel pump cover
20. Diaphragm
21. Gasket
22. Pump body
23. Spring
24. Spring plate
25. Diaphragm
26. Gasket

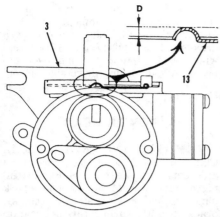

Fig. MR4-2 — With carburetor body (3) inverted, check float level by measuring distance (D) from carburetor body sealing surface to top of float lever (13) hump. Distance should be 1.5-2.5 mm (0.06-0.10 in.) and is adjusted by bending the arms of float lever (13).

SPEED CONTROL LINKAGE. The engine speed is regulated by the position of the carburetor's throttle plate. The throttle plate is controlled by the twist grip via a control cable. When the twist grip is placed in the "FAST" position, stopper (TS – Fig. MR4-3) on the carburetor's throttle arm should contact carburetor stop (CS). If not, reposition the control cable inner wire (W) length until the correct positioning is obtained.

REED VALVE. A reed valve plate is mounted between the carburetor and crankcase. Reed petals should seat squarely and smoothly along their entire length and should be free of cracks, nicks, tears or burrs. Do not attempt to straighten or repair bent or damaged reeds. If reed stop (S – Fig. MR4-4) is removed, install new retaining screws and apply Loctite 271 or 290 on screw threads. Reed stop height (H) should be 6.8-7.2 mm (0.27-0.29 in.). Bend reed stop (S) to adjust height (H).

IGNITION

The standard spark plug on both the 4 and 5 hp models is NGK B7HS with an electrode gap of 0.5-0.6 mm (0.020-0.024 in.).

Both the 4 and 5 hp models are equipped with a capacitor discharge ignition (CDI) system. If engine malfunction is noted and the ignition system is suspected, make sure the spark plug and all electrical wiring are in good condition and all electrical connections are tight before proceeding to trouble-shooting the CD ignition system.

Proceed as follows to test CDI system components: Refer to Fig. MR4-5. To test ignition coil, disconnect black wire with white tracer (B/W) at connector and spark plug boot from spark plug.

Remove ignition coil from mounting bracket. Use a suitable ohmmeter and connect red tester lead to black wire with white tracer (B/W) and black tester lead to black wire (B). The primary winding resistance reading should be 0.2-0.3 ohms. Leave black tester lead connected to black wire (B). Connect red tester lead to terminal end in spark plug boot. The secondary winding resistance reading should be 7500-9500 ohms. Use a suitable coil tester or tester Model 9800 Magneto Analyzer to perform a power test. Connect tester leads as outlined in tester's handbook. A steady spark should jump a 5 mm (13/64 in.) gap when a current value of 1.7 amperes is applied. A surface insulation test can be performed using a suitable coil tester or tester Model 9800 Magneto Analyzer and following tester's handbook.

To check source (charge) coil, first remove engine flywheel. Disconnect black wire (B), brown wire (Br), white wire with red tracer (W/R) and white wire with green tracer (W/G) at connectors leading from magneto base plate. Use a suitable ohmmeter and connect red tester lead to brown wire (Br) and black tester lead to black wire (B). The ohmmeter should read 250-300 ohms.

To check low speed pulser (trigger) coil, remove engine flywheel and disconnect wires as outlined under source (charge) coil. Use a suitable ohmmeter and connect red tester lead to white wire with green tracer (W/G) and black tester lead to black wire (B). The ohmmeter should read 280-340 ohms.

To check high speed pulser (trigger) coil, remove engine flywheel and disconnect wires as outlined under source (charge) coil. Use a suitable ohmmeter and connect red tester lead to white wire with red tracer (W/R) and black tester lead to black wire (B). The ohmmeter should read 30-36 ohms.

To test CDI module, first disconnect all wires at connectors and remove CDI module from outboard motor. Use a suitable ohmmeter and refer to Fig. MR4-6. With reference to chart, perform CDI module resistance tests.

Renew any components that are not within the manufacturer's recommended limits.

COOLING SYSTEM

WATER PUMP. A rubber impeller type water pump is mounted between the drive shaft housing and gearcase. The impeller is driven by a dowel pin in the drive shaft.

Whenever cooling problems are encountered, check water inlet for plugging or partial stoppage. If cooling problems persist, remove gearcase as outlined under LOWER UNIT section and check condition of the water pump, water passages and sealing surfaces.

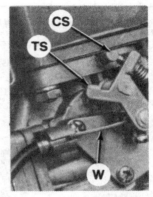

Fig. MR4-3 — View depicting control cable inner wire (W), carburetor stop (CS) and throttle arm stop (TS). Refer to text.

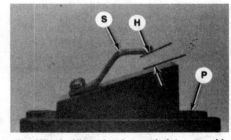

Fig. MR4-4 — View showing reed plate assembly (P). Reed stop height (H) should be 6.8-7.2 mm (0.27-0.29 in.). Bend reed stop (S) to adjust height (H).

Fig. MR4-5 — View identifying CDI system components.

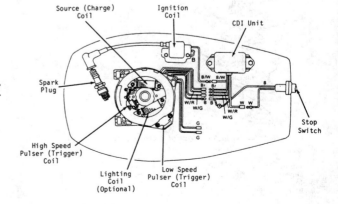

Red Ohmmeter Lead	Black Ohmmeter Lead	CDI UNIT LEADS					
		Stop	Charge	Pulser High Speed	Pulser Low Speed	Earth (Ground)	Ignition
		W	Br	W/R	W/G	B	B/W
Stop	W		A	B	B	B	H
Charge	Br	A		B	B	B	H
Pulser High Speed	W/R	C	C		B	E	H
Pulser Low Speed	W/G	C	C	D		F	H
Earth (Ground)	B	G	G	E	B		H
Ignition	B/W	H	H	H	B	H	

Fig. MR4-6—Use chart and values listed below to test condition of CD ignition module. Before making test (H), connect CDI module's black wire and black wire with white tracer together. Then disconnect wires and perform desired test.

A. Zero
B. Infinity
C. 12,000-28,000 ohms
D. 16,000-36,000 ohms
E. 7,500-17,500 ohms
F. 4,500-14,500 ohms
G. 2,200-6,200 ohms
H. Tester needle should show 200,000-500,000 ohms then return to infinity.

When water pump is disassembled, check condition of impeller (5–Fig. MR4-7), lining (3) and plate (6). Turn drive shaft clockwise (viewed from top) while placing pump housing over impeller. Avoid turning drive shaft in opposite direction when water pump is assembled.

POWER HEAD

REMOVE AND REINSTALL. Clamp outboard motor to suitable stand and remove engine top cowl. Remove integral fuel tank (4 hp models), spark plug, manual rewind starter, tool kit bracket and carburetor/fuel pump assembly. Remove starter cup and flywheel as a complete unit. Withdraw flywheel key from crankshaft slot. Remove two magneto base mounting screws, detach wires at connectors and lift magneto base from power head.

NOTE: Magneto base contains upper crankshaft seal and "O" ring. Renewal is required prior to magneto base installation.

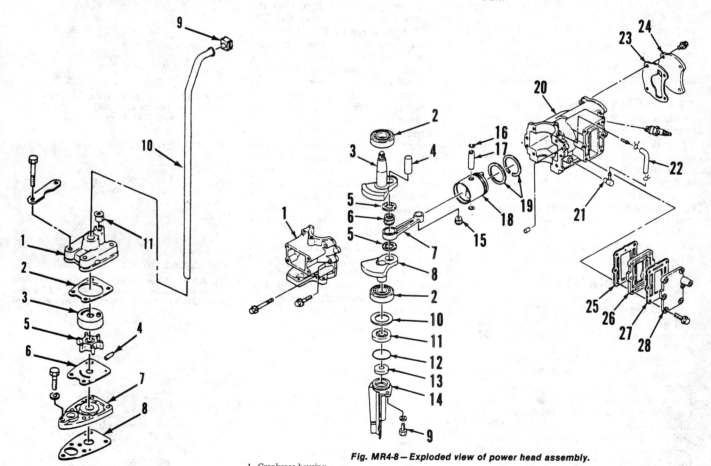

Fig. MR4-7—Exploded view of water pump.

1. Body
2. Gasket
3. Lining
4. Dowel pin
5. Impeller
6. Plate
7. Base
8. Gasket
9. Seal
10. Water tube
11. Grommet

Fig. MR4-8—Exploded view of power head assembly.

1. Crankcase housing
2. Ball bearing
3. Crankshaft half
4. Crankpin
5. Thrust washer
6. Roller bearing
7. Connecting rod
8. Crankshaft half
9. Cap screw
10. Washer
11. Seal
12. "O" ring
13. Seal
14. Lower crankshaft seal housing
15. Needle bearing
16. Piston pin clips
17. Piston pin
18. Piston
19. Piston rings
20. Cylinder block
21. Check valve
22. Recirculation hose
23. Gasket
24. Cylinder head cover
25. Gasket
26. Inner cover
27. Gasket
28. Exhaust cover

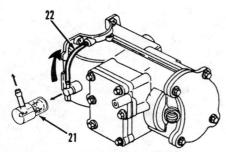

Fig. MR4-9 — View showing check valve (21) and recirculation hose (22) for crankcase breather system.

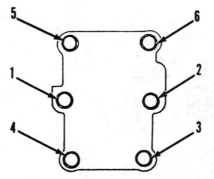

Fig. MR4-11 — Use sequence shown when tightening exhaust cover screws.

0.0014 in.). Recommended piston ring end gap is 0.15-0.35 mm (0.006-0.014 in.) for both rings. The bottom (square) piston ring should have a side clearance of 0.03-0.07 mm (0.0012-0.0027 in.). The top piston ring is semi-keystone shaped. Make sure piston rings properly align with locating pins in ring grooves.

When reassembling, install new piston pin retaining clips (16 – Fig. MR4-8) and make sure that "UP" on dome of piston is towards flywheel end of engine. Coat bearings, piston, rings and cylinder bore with engine oil during assembly.

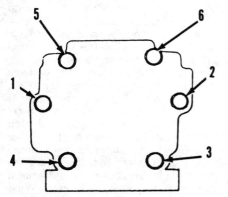

Fig. MR4-10 — Use sequence shown when tightening crankcase screws.

On 5 hp models, disconnect starter lockout rod from cable's actuating lever located on engine's starboard side. Remove seven cap screws retaining power head to drive shaft housing and lift off power head.

Installation is reverse order of removal. Install a new gasket between power head and drive shaft housing. Coat both sides of the gasket with a thin coating of "Perfect Seal" or a suitable equivalent. Securely tighten power head retaining screws. Tighten flywheel nut to 40.7-47.5 N·m (30-35 ft.-lbs.) and spark plug to 27.1 N·m (20 ft.-lbs.).

DISASSEMBLY. Remove the two reed plate retaining screws and withdraw the reed plate assembly. Remove the six exhaust cover retaining screws and withdraw exhaust cover (28 – Fig. MR4-8), outer cover gasket (27), inner cover (26) and inner cover gasket (25). Remove cap screw (9), then tap lower crankshaft seal housing (14) with a rubber mallet to remove. Remove recirculation hose (22). Remove six cap screws securing crankcase housing (1) to cylinder block (20). While being careful, pry crankcase housing from cylinder block. Lift crankshaft and piston assembly from cylinder block. Remove the four cylinder head cover retaining

screws and withdraw cylinder head cover and gasket.

ASSEMBLY. When reassembling, make sure all joints and gasket surfaces are clean and free from nicks and burrs. All friction surfaces and bearings must be lubricated with engine oil during reassembly. Make sure locating pins on crankshaft ball bearings fit into the slots in cylinder block. Check frequently as power head is being assembled for binding of working parts. If binding or locking is encountered, correct cause before proceeding with assembly.

Cylinder block and crankcase cover mating surfaces must be thoroughly cleaned prior to reassembly. Apply Loctite Master Gasket Sealer part 92-12564-1 to mating surface of crankcase cover in a continuous 1.6 mm (1/16 in.) bead. All other gasket and sealing surfaces should be lightly and evenly coated with a nonhardening sealing compound. Avoid excess application. Tighten crankcase screws to 11.2 N·m (100 in.-lbs.) following sequence shown in Fig. MR4-10. Tighten exhaust cover screws to 8.5 N·m (75 in.-lbs.) following sequence shown in Fig. MR4-11. Tighten cylinder head cover screws to 8.5 N·m (75 in.-lbs.) following the sequence shown in Fig. MR4-12. Complete remainder of reassembly by reversing disassembly procedure.

CYLINDER, RINGS AND PISTON. Cylinder bore should be measured in several different locations to determine if an out-of-round or tapered condition exists. Inspect cylinder wall for scoring. If minor scoring is noted, use number 600 grit sandpaper to smooth out cylinder wall.

NOTE: Cylinder sleeve and cylinder head are cast into the cylinder block. If cylinder is out-of-round or tapered, or if excessive scoring is noted, the cylinder block must be renewed.

Recommended piston skirt to cylinder clearance is 0.030-0.035 mm (0.0012-

CRANKSHAFT, BEARINGS AND ROD. The connecting rod rides on a roller bearing around the crankpin. Crankshaft, crankpin, bearing and connecting rod are available only as a unit assembly. Maximum allowable side clearance between rod and crankshaft is 0.30 mm (0.012 in.). Maximum runout of crankshaft is 0.03 mm (0.0012 in.) with crankshaft ends supported. Determine rod, rod bearing and crankpin wear by moving small rod end from side to side

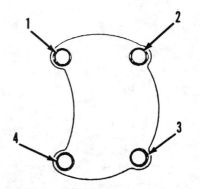

Fig. MR4-12 — Use sequence shown when tightening cylinder head screws.

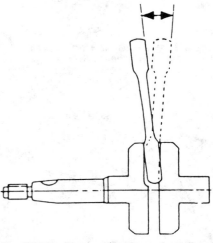

Fig. MR4-13 — Move connecting rod small end side to side as shown to determine rod, rod bearing and crankpin wear. Refer to text.

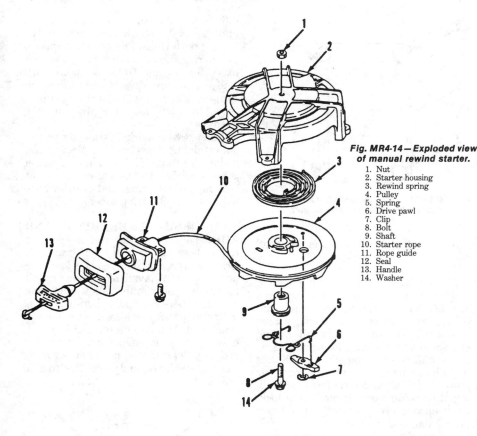

Fig. MR4-14 — Exploded view of manual rewind starter.

1. Nut
2. Starter housing
3. Rewind spring
4. Pulley
5. Spring
6. Drive pawl
7. Clip
8. Bolt
9. Shaft
10. Starter rope
11. Rope guide
12. Seal
13. Handle
14. Washer

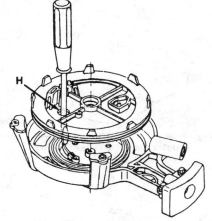

Fig. MR4-15 — Pulley hole (H) is used during pulley withdrawal. Refer to text.

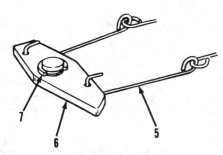

Fig. MR4-16 — View showing proper installation of pawl spring (5), drive pawl (6) and clip (7).

resistant grease and return starter to service if no other damage is noted.

To disassemble, remove clip (7) and withdraw pawl (6) and pawl spring (5). Untie starter rope (10) at handle (13) and allow the rope to wind into the starter. Remove bolt (8), washer (14) and shaft (9), then place a suitable screwdriver blade through hole (H – Fig. MR4-15) to hold rewind spring (3 – Fig. MR4-14) securely in housing (2). Carefully lift pulley (4) with starter rope (10) from housing (2). BE CAREFUL when removing pulley (4) as the rewind spring may be dislodged. Untie starter rope (10) and remove rope from pulley (4) if renewal is required. To remove rewind spring (3) from housing (2), invert housing so it sits upright on a flat surface, then tap the housing top until rewind spring (3) falls free and uncoils.

Inspect all components for damage and excessive wear and renew if needed.

To reassemble, first apply a coating of a suitable water-resistant grease to rewind spring area of housing (2). Install rewind spring (3) in housing (2) so spring coils wind in a counterclockwise direction from the outer end. Make sure the spring's outer hook is properly secured over starter housing (2) pin. Wind starter rope (10) onto pulley (4) approximately 2½ turns counterclockwise when viewed from the flywheel side. Direct remaining starter rope (10) length through notch in pulley (4).

NOTE: Lubricate all friction surfaces with a suitable water-resistant grease during reassembly.

Assemble pulley (4) to starter housing making sure that pulley's pin engages hook end in rewind spring (3). Install shaft (9), washer (14) and bolt (8). Apply Loctite 271 or 290 or an equivalent thread fastening solution on bolt (8) threads and install nut (1) and securely tighten.

Thread starter rope (10) through starter housing (2), rope guide (11) and handle (13) and secure with a knot. Turn pulley (4) two turns counterclockwise when viewed from the flywheel side, then release starter rope (10) from pulley notch and allow rope to slowly wind onto pulley.

NOTE: Do not apply any more tension on rewind spring (3) than is required to draw starter handle (13) back into the proper released position.

Install spring (5), pawl (6) and clip (7) as shown in Fig. MR4-16. Remount manual starter assembly.

Adjust starter lockout assembly by turning adjusting nuts at cable end so starter will engage when gear shift lever

as shown in Fig. MR4-13. Normal side to side movement is 0.8 mm (0.0315 in.) or less; renew crankshaft assembly if side movement exceeds 2.0 mm (0.0787 in.).

Protect crankshaft end and use a suitable press to remove and install main ball bearings (2 – Fig. MR4-8).

MANUAL STARTER

A starter lockout assembly is used to prevent starter engagement when the gear shift lever is in the forward or reverse position.

The manual starter must be disassembled to renew starter rope (10 – Fig. MR4-14) and rewind spring (3).

To overhaul the manual starter, proceed as follows: Remove the engine's top cowl. Remove the screws retaining the manual starter to the engine. Remove the starter lockout cable at the starter housing. Note plunger and spring located at cable end, care should be used not to lose the components should they fall free. Withdraw the starter assembly.

Check pawl (6) for freedom of movement, excessive wear of engagement area and any other damage. Renew or lubricate pawl (6) with a suitable water-is in "Neutral" position, but will not engage when gear shift lever is in "Forward" or "Reverse" position.

LOWER UNIT

PROPELLER AND SHEAR PIN. A shear pin is used to provide protection for the propeller and lower unit. The standard propeller on 4 hp models has three blades, a diameter of 190 mm (7-1/2 in.) and a pitch of 203 mm (8 in.). The standard propeller on 5 hp models has three blades, a diameter of 184 mm (7-1/4 in.) and a pitch of 210 mm (8-1/4 in.). Optional propellers are available. Select a propeller that will allow the engine at full throttle to reach maximum operating rpm range (4500-5500).

R&R AND OVERHAUL. Clamp outboard motor to an appropriate stand and remove gearcase drain plug and vent plug. Allow gearcase lubricant to drain into a suitable container. Remove cover (2–Fig. MR4-17) and LOOSEN shift linkage clamp screw (9). Remove the two cap screws retaining gearcase housing to drive shaft housing and withdraw gearcase housing.

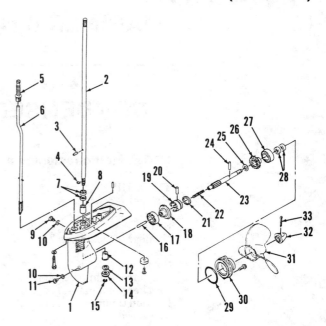

Fig. MR4-18 — Exploded view of lower unit gearcase assembly.

1. Gearcase housing
2. Drive shaft
3. Dowel pin
4. Clip
5. Boot
6. Shift rod
7. Seals
8. Bushing
9. Vent plug
10. Gasket
11. Drain plug
12. Bushing
13. Thrust washer
14. Pinion
15. Snap ring
16. Shift plunger
17. Ball bearing
18. Forward gear
19. Dog clutch
20. Pin
21. Clip
22. Spring
23. Propeller shaft
24. Shear pin
25. Thrust washer
26. Reverse gear
27. Ball bearing
28. Seals
29. "O" ring
30. Gearcase housing cover
31. Propeller
32. Spinner
33. Cotter pin

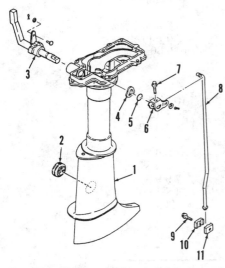

Fig. MR4-17 — View of drive shaft housing and gear shift linkage.

1. Drive shaft housing	7. Cap screw
2. Cover	8. Upper shift rod
3. Shift handle	9. Screw
4. Wave washer	10. Clamp half
5. "O" ring	11. Clamp half
6. Shift lever	

Disassemble gearcase as follows: Remove cotter pin (33–Fig. MR4-18), spinner (32), propeller (31) and shear pin (24). Remove water pump assembly (Fig. MR4-7). Withdraw shift rod (6–Fig. MR4-18). Remove two cap screws retaining gearcase housing cover (30). Extract cover (30) with components (16 and 19 through 29). Pry snap ring (15) from end of drive shaft and withdraw drive shaft from gearcase. Remove pinion (14) and thrust washer (13). Withdraw forward gear (18) from gearcase housing. Detach retainer clip (21) and drive out pin (20) to remove shift plunger (16), dog clutch (19) and spring (22).

Inspect shafts for wear on seal lip contact areas and on splines. Inspect dog clutch and gears for wear on engagement areas of dog teeth. Inspect gears for excessive wear and damage. Inspect shift cam for excessive wear on ramp. All seals and "O" ring should be renewed when unit is reassembled.

NOTE: No adjustment of gear mesh pattern and gear backlash is provided. The parts were machined at very close tolerances and require no shimming when in good condition and are properly assembled.

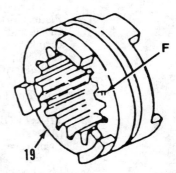

Fig. MR4-19 — Install dog clutch (19) so "F" mark (F) is towards forward gear.

Reverse disassembly for reassembly while noting the following: Install dog clutch (19) with "F" marked side (Fig. MR4-19) toward forward gear (18–Fig. MR4-18). Apply a water-resistant grease to the lip surfaces of all seals.

Adjust shift linkage by depressing shift rod (6) downward to bottom stop. Make sure lower unit is in reverse gear. Move shift handle (3–Fig. MR4-17) to "Reverse" and tighten clamp screw (9).

MARINER 8 HP (PRIOR TO 1979)

CONDENSED SERVICE DATA

NOTE: Metric fasteners are used throughout outboard motor.

TUNE-UP
Hp/rpm	8/5000
Bore	50 mm
Stroke	42 mm
Number of cylinders	2
Displacement	164 cc
Spark plug – NGK	B-7HS
Electrode gap	0.5-0.6 mm
Breaker point gap	0.30-0.40 mm
Ignition timing	See text
Idle speed	1150-1250 rpm
Fuel:oil ratio	50:1
Gearcase oil capacity	230 mL

SIZES – CLEARANCES
Piston ring end gap	0.15-0.35 mm
Piston skirt clearance	0.030-0.045 mm
Crankshaft journal diameter	20.0 mm
Crankshaft runout – max.	0.03 mm
Connecting rod small end shake –	
Standard	0.8 mm
Limit	2.0 mm
Lower unit gear backlash	0.10-0.30 mm

TIGHTENING TORQUES
(All values are in newton meters.)
Crankcase	10.8-12.7
Cylinder head	10.8-12.7
Flywheel	29.4-34.3
Standard screws:	
4 mm	2.0
5 mm	4.9-5.8
6 mm	7.9-9.8
8 mm	14.7-19.6
10 mm	29.4

LUBRICATION

The power head is lubricated by oil mixed with the fuel. Fuel should be regular leaded, low lead or unleaded gasoline with a minimum pump octane rating of 86. Recommended oil is Quicksilver Formula 50-D Outboard Lubricant. Normal fuel:oil ratio is 50:1; during engine break-in, fuel:oil ratio should be 25:1.

Lower unit gears and bearings are lubricated by oil contained in the gearcase. Recommended oil is Mariner Super Duty Gear Lube. Lubricant is drained by removing vent and drain plugs in gearcase. Refill through drain plug hole until oil has reached level of top (vent) plug hole.

FUEL SYSTEM

CARBURETOR. Refer to Fig. MR6-1 for an exploded view of carburetor. Initial setting of pilot air screw (15) is one turn out from a lightly seated position. Set idle speed to 1150-1250 rpm with motor running in gear at normal operating temperature.

Float arm pivot pin (10) is staked in carburetor top (1). Restake pin during assembly to prevent fluctuating fuel level. To set fuel level, invert top (1) and measure height of float arm as shown in Fig. MR6-2 with gasket (12 – Fig. MR6-1) installed on top (1). Float arm height should be 0.5-1.5 mm and is adjusted by bending float arm evenly. Start plunger (16) should be adjusted to just clear starter bleed hole in bottom of carburetor body (13) when starter knob is pulled. Adjustment is accomplished by turning screw (20).

Standard main jet size is number 86.

SPEED CONTROL LINKAGE.

Movement of the speed control handle is transferred by flexible cables to linkage at the magneto stator plate. A cam ramp is incorporated in part of the magneto control linkage to operate the carburetor throttle. Refer to Fig. MR6-3 for exploded view of linkage.

NOTE: Hole for top mount screw in bracket (13) extends into crankcase cavity. Screw must be coated with a locking compound to prevent leakage if bracket is disturbed.

Adjustment of the throttle cam (2) should only be made after ignition timing has been checked and adjusted if necessary. When speed control grip is moved completely against the high speed stop, the carburetor throttle should be fully opened. Make sure that carburetor throttle is not reaching the full open stop before ignition is fully advanced.

REED VALVES. Reed valve plates (7 and 11 – Fig. MR6-5) are secured to the intake manifold. Two sets of reeds are used, one for top cylinder and one for lower cylinder. Height of reed stop (A – Fig. MR6-6) should be 6.4-6.9 mm. Both reed stops should be set alike. Reed petals should seat squarely and smoothly along their entire length and should be free of cracks, nicks, tears and burrs.

Do not attempt to straighten or repair bent or damaged reeds. Reed petals, plates and stops are available only as an assembly.

Hole for screw (14 – Fig. MR6-5) extends into crankcase cavity. To prevent leakage, screw must be coated with a locking compound on reassembly.

Reed plate gaskets (8 and 10) are composed of a special material that requires no gasket sealer during assembly. All other manifold gaskets should be coated with a nonhardening type gasket sealer.

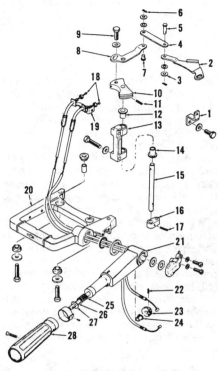

Fig. MR6-3 — View of speed control linkage components.

1. Base plate stopper	15. Shaft
2. Throttle cam	16. End piece
3. Washer	17. Spring pin
4. Link	18. Control cables
5. Pivot pin	19. Bracket
6. Clip	20. Handle bracket
7. Pivot pin	21. Steering lever
8. Link	22. Spring pin
9. Screw	23. Pulley
10. Pulley	24. Bushing
11. Spring pin	25. Spring
12. Bushing	26. Shaft
13. Bracket	27. Washer
14. Bushing	28. Grip

Fig. MR6-1—View of carburetor.

1. Top	14. Throttle stop screw
2. Main nozzle	15. Pilot air screw
3. Pilot jet	16. Starter plunger
4. Screw	17. Spring
5. Main nozzle plug	18. Plunger cap
6. Emulsion jet	19. Nut
7. Main jet	20. Adjustment fitting
8. Inlet valve	21. Throttle shaft screw
9. Float lever	22. Throttle shaft
10. Float lever pin	23. Roller
11. Float	24. Snap ring
12. Gasket	25. Starter jet
13. Main body	26. Drain screw

Fig. MR6-5 — Exploded view of intake manifold and exhaust cover assembly with reed valves. Hole for screw (14) extends into crankcase for lower cylinder. Screw must be coated with a locking compound to prevent leakage.

1. Cover
2. Carburetor
3. Gaskets
4. Insulator
5. Plate
6. Gasket
7. Reed valve assy.
8. Gasket
9. Manifold
10. Gasket
11. Reed valve assy.
12. Gasket
13. Cover
14. Screw

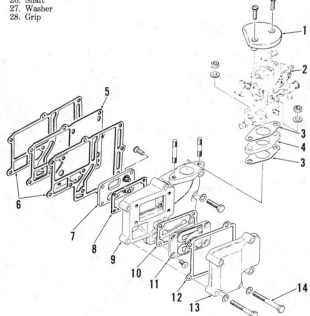

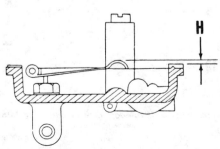

Fig. MR6-2 — With carburetor top inverted, float arm height (H) above gasket should be 0.5-1.5 mm.

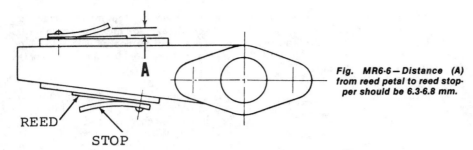

Fig. MR6-6 – Distance (A) from reed petal to reed stopper should be 6.3-6.8 mm.

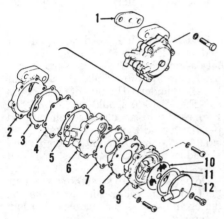

Fig. MR6-7 – Exploded view of diaphragm fuel pump.

1. Gasket
2. Base
3. Gasket
4. Diaphragm
5. Gasket
6. Body

7. Gasket
8. Check valve
9. Body
10. Screen
11. Gasket
12. Inlet fitting

FUEL PUMP. A diaphragm type fuel pump (Fig. MR6-7) is mounted on port side of power head. Pressure and vacuum pulsations in the crankcase are channeled through a passage in pump base (2). Vacuum in the crankcase draws diaphragm (4) inward and fuel is drawn from the fuel tank through inlet fitting (12). Pressure in the crankcase forces the fuel out through pump body (6). Check valves (8) prevent reverse flow.

When inspecting pump, pay particular attention to condition of diaphragm (4) and check valve (8). Any deformation or deterioration of these parts is cause for renewal. Make sure that filter screen (10) has been cleaned. Gasket (1) should be coated with a nonhardening type gasket sealer to ensure a leak proof installation. Use caution to prevent excess cement from squeezing into pressure hole.

IGNITION

Breaker point gap should be set to 0.30-0.40 mm. Adjustment may be accomplished through holes in flywheel

after removing motor top cowl and flywheel hole cover (2 – Fig. MR6-9)

Recommended spark plug electrode gap is 0.5-0.6 mm.

Ignition timing may be checked and adjusted as follows: Attach a point checker or an ohmmeter to grey wire coming from the magneto (top cylinder primary lead) and check for breaker point opening at maximum advance when top piston is 2.1-2.8 mm BTDC. Timing pointer (1 – Fig. MR6-3) will align with mark on flywheel when piston is in this position. Adjust full advance timing by moving magneto base plate stopper (10 – Fig. MR6-9). Cylinder head should be removed and piston position checked with a dial indicator if pointer (1 – Fig. MR6-3) has been disturbed. Attach point checker or ohmmeter to orange wire from magneto (lower cylinder primary lead) and check for breaker point opening at full advance when lower piston is 2.1-2.8 mm BTDC. Adjust lower cylinder full advance timing by varying breaker point gap.

COOLING SYSTEM

WATER PUMP. A rubber impeller type water pump is mounted between the drive shaft housing and gearcase. On later models the impeller is driven by a Woodruff key in the drive shaft, while on early models, collar (1 – Fig. MR6-18) is secured to the drive shaft by spring pin (2) and collar key (4) drives the water pump impeller.

Whenever cooling problems are encountered, check water inlet for plug-

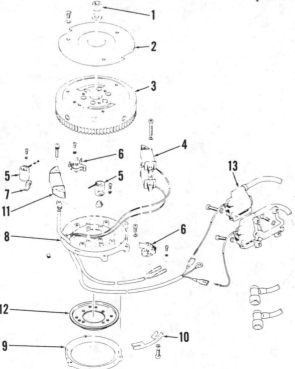

Fig. MR6-9 – View of component parts of ignition system.

1. Nut
2. Cover
3. Flywheel
4. Primary coils
5. Condensers
6. Breaker points
7. Felt oiler
8. Base plate
9. Base plate retainer
10. Base plate stopper
11. Lighting coil
12. Retainer
13. Secondary coil

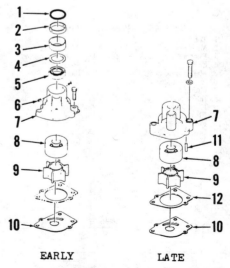

EARLY   LATE

Fig. MR6-10 – Exploded view of early and late water pumps.

1. "O" ring
2. Retainer
3. Spacer
4. Spacer
5. Seal
6. Spring pins

7. Pump housing
8. Liner
9. Impeller
10. Lower plate
11. Dowel
12. Gasket

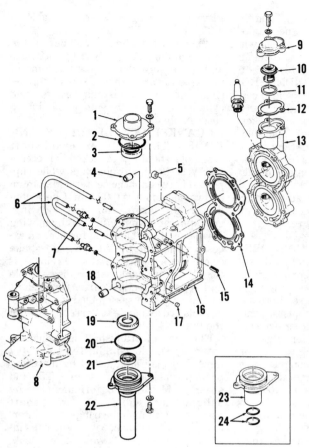

Fig. MR6-11 — Exploded view of crankcase and cylinder head. End cap (23) and "O" rings (24) were used on early models in place of end cap (22).

1. Oil seal housing
2. "O" ring
3. Ball bearing
4. Dowel
5. Coil mount damper
6. Bleeder hose
7. Crankcase bleeder valves
8. Crankcase half
9. Thermostat cover
10. Thermostat
11. Spacer
12. Gasket
13. Cylinder head
14. Gasket
15. Roll pin
16. Cylinder block
17. Plug
18. Dowel
19. Oil seal
20. "O" ring
21. Oil seal
22. End cap (later models)
23. End cap (early models)
24. "O" rings (early models)

vided to aid in separating the crankcase halves. Use caution to prevent any damage to crankcase mating surfaces.

Engine components are now accessible for removal and overhaul as outlined in the appropriate following paragraphs. Assemble as outlined in the ASSEMBLY paragraphs.

ASSEMBLY. When reassembling, make sure all joints and gasket surfaces are clean, free from nicks and burrs and hardened cement or carbon. The crankcase and inlet manifold must be completely sealed against water leakage and pressure. Mating surfaces of water intake and exhaust areas between power head and lower unit must form a tight seal.

Whenever power head is disassembled, it is recommended that all gasket surfaces and mating surfaces without gaskets be carefully checked for nicks, burrs and warped surfaces which might interfere with a tight seal. Cylinder head, head end of cylinder block, and some mating surfaces of manifold and crankcase should be checked on a surface plate, and lapped if necessary, to provide a smooth surface. Do not remove any more metal than is necessary.

All friction surfaces and needle bearings should be lubricated with engine oil during reassembly. Seals should be filled with a nonfibrous grease. "O" rings (24 – Fig. MR6-11) on early models are made with a special heat resistant

ging or partial stoppage, then if not corrected, remove gearcase and check condition of the water pump, water passages and sealing surfaces.

When water pump is disassembled, check condition of impeller (9 – Fig. MR6-10), lining (8) and plate (10). On early models, inspect seal (5) and collar spring pin (2 – Fig. MR6-18). On all models, turn drive shaft clockwise (viewed from top) while placing pump housing over impeller. Avoid turning drive shaft in opposite direction when water pump is assembled.

POWER HEAD

R&R AND OVERHAUL. The power head may be removed for disassembly and overhaul as follows: Clamp motor to a suitable stand and remove engine top cowl. Remove flywheel, rewind starter assembly and fuel system. Disconnect speed control linkage cables. Remove magneto base plate and high tension ignition coils. Remove cylinder head and top oil seal housing (1 – Fig. MR6-11). Remove seven screws securing power head to drive shaft housing and lift power head away. Remove lower oil seal housing (22 or 23), exhaust cover and lower crankcase half. Pry slots are pro-

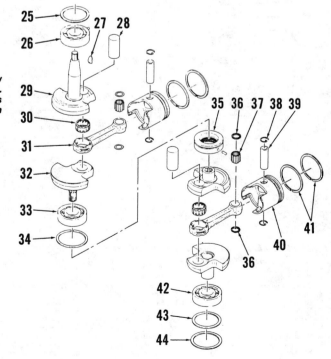

Fig. MR6-12 — Exploded view of crankshaft assembly. Twenty-eight bearing rollers are used in each piston pin bearing (37).

25. Shim
26. Ball bearing
27. Key
28. Crankpin
29. Crank half
30. Needle bearing
31. Connecting rod
32. Crank half
33. Ball bearing
34. Locating ring
35. Labyrinth seal
36. Washer
37. Needle bearing
38. Piston pin clip
39. Piston pin
40. Piston
41. Piston rings
42. Ball bearing
43. Shim
44. Spacer

material that is red in color. Red "O" rings must be installed in lower grooves as shown. Check frequently as power head is being assembled for binding of the working parts. If binding or locking is encountered, remove the cause before proceeding with the assembly.

Gasket and sealing surfaces should be lightly and evenly coated with a non-hardening gasket cement. Make sure entire surface is coated, but avoid letting excess amount squeeze out into crank-

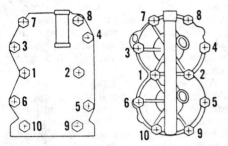

Fig. MR6-13—Tighten crankcase and cylinder head screws in sequence shown above. Refer to text for tightening torques.

case, bearing or other passages. Tighten the cylinder head screws and the crankcase screws in the sequences shown (Fig. MR6-13) first to 6 N·m, then in same sequence to a final torque of 10.8-12.7 N·m. Refer to CONDENSED SERVICE DATA table for clearances and standard torques.

Holes for top mount screw in bracket (13 – Fig. MR6-3) and intake manifold screw (14 – Fig. MR6-5) extend into crankcase. These screws must be coated with a locking compound during assembly to prevent leakage.

Before attaching power head to lower unit, make certain that splines are clean and then coated with light grease.

CYLINDERS, RINGS AND PISTONS. Cylinder bores should be measured in several different locations to determine if an out-of-round or tapered condition exists. Bore and hone cylinder to fit an oversize piston and ring set if out-of-round or taper exceeds 0.07 mm. Be sure to chamfer edges of ports in cylinder after boring to prevent rings from hanging up on sharp edges.

Recommended piston skirt to cylinder clearance is 0.030-0.045 mm. Recommended piston ring end gap is 0.15-0.35 mm for both rings and the maximum limit is 0.6 mm. Top piston ring is chrome plated and has semi-keystone shape. Install piston rings with manufacturer's markings toward top of piston.

Pistons and ring sets are available in 0.25 mm and 0.50 mm oversizes.

When reassembling, install new piston pin retaining clips (38 – Fig. MR6-12) and make sure that arrow on dome of piston is toward exhaust side of engine. Coat bearings, pistons, rings and cylinder bores with engine oil during reassembly.

CRANKSHAFT, BEARINGS AND RODS. The built-up crankshaft assembly should be checked for eccentricity at the main bearings while supported between lathe centers. Maximum allowable runout is 0.03 mm. Check condition of large end rod bearing, crankpin, and connecting rod by moving small end of rod back and forth. If an excessive amount of side to side shake (more than approximately ⅛ inch) is found, renew crankshaft or disassemble and renew defective parts. Crankshaft should only be disassembled if the proper tools are available to correctly realign the unit.

End play of crankshaft in crankcase assembly should be adjusted to 0.1-0.7 mm. End play is adjusted by installing proper thickness of shims (25 and 43 – Fig. MR6-12). Determine play by subtracting width of crankshaft assembly with main bearings from internal width of crankcase with end caps installed. Shims are available in thicknesses of 0.2, 0.3 and 0.5 mm and should be installed to obtain correct end play.

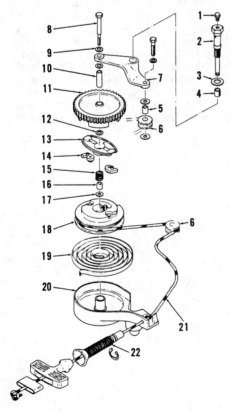

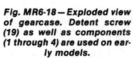

Fig. MR6-15—Exploded view of rewind starter assembly.

1. Grease fitting	12. Thrust washer
2. Pivot bolt	13. Drive plate
3. Thrust washer	14. Pawl
4. Bushing	15. Spring
5. Bushing	16. Collar
6. Roller	17. Washer
7. Lever	18. Sheave drum
8. Bolt	19. Recoil spring
9. Washer	20. Housing
10. Distance collar	21. Cable
11. Starter gear	22. Guide

Fig. MR6-18 – Exploded view of gearcase. Detent screw (19) as well as components (1 through 4) are used on early models.

1. Drive shaft collar
2. Spring pin
3. "O" ring
4. Key
5. Boot
6. Bushing
7. Shift rod
8. Drive shaft
9. Key
10. Seals
11. Bushing
12. Bearing housing
13. Collar
14. Gasket
15. Gearcase
16. Vent plugs
17. Dowel
18. Water inlet
19. Detent screw
20. Drain plug
21. Washer
22. Anode
23. Screen
24. Bushing
25. Thrust washer
26. Shim
27. Pinion gear
28. Snap ring
29. Shift plunger
30. Bearing
31. Shims
32. Forward gear
33. Thrust washer
34. Clip
35. Clutch
36. Pin
37. Spring guide
38. Spring
39. Shear pin
40. Propeller shaft
41. Thrust washer

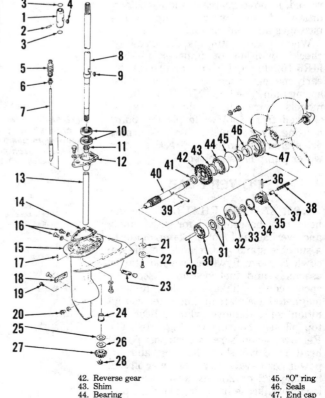

42. Reverse gear	45. "O" ring
43. Shim	46. Seals
44. Bearing	47. End cap

When installing crankshaft, lubricate seals with a heat resistant nonfibrous grease and use engine oil on pistons, rings, cylinders and bearings. Use sequences shown in Fig. MR6-13 to tighten cylinder head screws and crankcase screws. Torque cylinder head and crankcase screws first to 6 N·m, then repeat sequence, torquing screws to 10.8-12.7 N·m final torque. Refer to CONDENSED SERVICE DATA for general torquing specifications.

MANUAL STARTER

Refer to Fig. MR6-15 for exploded view of recoil starter assembly used. Movement of starter handle causes starter assembly to pivot on its mount and engage teeth on starter gear (11) with teeth on flywheel. Pulling start handle also causes the pawls (14) to swing away from the rope pulley (18) and engage in slots in lower side of gear (11). Further movement of handle causes pulley, starter gear and finally the flywheel to turn.

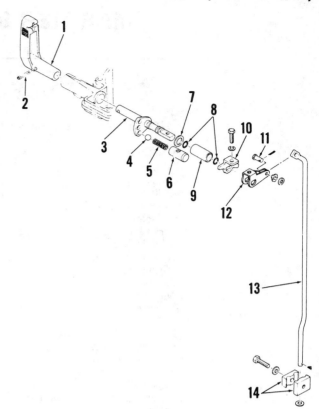

Fig. MR6-20 — Exploded view of shift control assembly. Clamp (14) connects shift rod (13) with gearcase shift rod (7 — Fig. MR6-18).

1. Shift handle
2. Roll pin
3. Shaft
4. Detent ball
5. Spring
6. Spring guide
7. Washer
8. "O" ring
9. Collar
10. Stop
11. Pin
12. Lever
13. Shift rod
14. Clamp

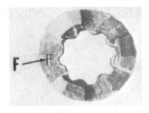

Fig. MR6-19 — Install a clutch so end marked (F) is towards forward gear.

Starter may be disassembled for repair or renewal of defective parts as follows: Remove pull handle and allow cable to slowly wind onto pulley. Starter assembly may be lifted from power head after removal of pivot bolt (2). Remove lever (7) and starter gear (11). Drive plate and starter pawls may be serviced at this point. Lift pulley (18) from starter housing using caution to prevent injury from rewind spring flying out.

When reassembling, make sure that rewind spring is correctly hooked in housing (20) and in pulley. Main pivot bolt (2) should be installed before tightening bolt through roller (6) and bolt (8) through gear.

LOWER UNIT

PROPELLER AND SHEAR PIN. A shear pin is used to provide shock protection for lower unit gears and shafts.

Three bladed propellers are used. Standard propeller has a diameter of 229 mm and a pitch of 229 mm. A 229 mm diameter propeller with 178 or 190 mm pitch is optionally available.

R&R AND OVERHAUL. Most service of lower unit can be performed after removal of lower unit gearcase from the drive shaft housing. Gearcase may be removed as follows: Clamp motor to an appropriate work stand, remove propeller and drain gearcase lubricant. Remove circular cover on starboard side of drive shaft housing and loosen shift rod clamp screw. Remove four screws securing gearcase to drive shaft housing. If a drive shaft housing extension is installed, remove gearcase and extension as an assembly and then separate them. Remove water pump assembly (Fig. MR6-10) and gearcase cap (47 – Fig. MR6-18). Extract propeller shaft and reverse gear assembly. Pry snap ring (28) from end of drive shaft and withdraw drive shaft from gearcase. Remove thrust washer (25), shim (26), pinion gear (27), forward gear (32) and shims (31). Detach retainer clip (34) and drive out pin (36) to remove clutch (35), spring guide (37) and spring (38) from propeller shaft. Unscrew de-

tent screw (19), if so equipped, and remove shift rod (7).

Inspect shafts for wear on seal lip contact areas and on splines. Inspect clutch and gears for wear on engagement areas of dog teeth. Inspect gears for wear and damage. Inspect shift cam for excessive wear on ramp. All seals and "O" rings should be renewed when unit is reassembled.

To check gear mesh pattern and gear backlash, make a trial assembly using original shims. Mesh pattern is adjusted by using pinion gear shim (26) which is available in thicknesses of 0.8, 1.0, 1.2 and 1.4 mm. Gear backlash should be 0.1-0.3 mm and is adjusted using shims (31 and 43) which are available in thicknesses of 0.1, 0.3 and 0.5 mm.

Reverse disassembly for reassembly while noting the following: Install clutch to "F" marked side (see Fig. MR6-19) is towards forward gear (32 – Fig. MR6-18). Install seals (46) in end cap so innermost seal is 0.4-0.6 mm below bore of end cap. Apply water-resistant grease to "O" ring (45).

Adjust shift linkage by depressing shift rod (7) downward to bottom stop. Make sure lower unit is in reverse gear. Move shift handle (1–Fig. MR6-20) to "Reverse" and tighten clamp (14) screw.

MARINER 8 HP (1979-1984)

CONDENSED SERVICE DATA

NOTE: Metric fasteners are used throughout outboard motor.

TUNE-UP

Hp/rpm	8/5000
Bore	50 mm
Stroke	42 mm
Number of cylinders	2
Displacement	164 cc
Spark plug – NGK	B-7HS
Electrode gap	0.5-0.6 mm
Breaker point gap	0.30-0.40 mm
Ignition timing	See text
Idle speed	1150-1250 rpm
Fuel:oil ratio	50:1
Gearcase oil capacity	230 mL

SIZES – CLEARANCES

Piston ring end gap	0.15-0.35 mm
Piston skirt clearance	0.030-0.035 mm
Crankshaft journal diameter	20.0 mm
Crankshaft runout – max.	0.03 mm
Connecting rod small end shake –	
Standard	0.8 mm
Limit	2.0 mm
Lower unit gear backlash	0.10-0.30 mm

TIGHTENING TORQUES
(All values are in newton meters.)

Crankcase	9.8-12.7
Cylinder head	9.8-12.7
Flywheel	39.2-49.0
Standard screws:	
4 mm	2.0
5 mm	4.9-5.8
6 mm	7.9-9.8
8 mm	14.7-19.6
10 mm	29.4

LUBRICATION

The power head is lubricated by oil mixed with the fuel. Fuel should be regular leaded, low lead or unleaded gasoline with a minimum pump octane rating of 86. Recommended oil is Quicksilver Formula 50-D Outboard Lubricant. Normal fuel:oil ration is 50:1; during engine break-in, fuel:oil ratio should be 25:1.

Lower unit gears and bearings are lubricated by oil contained in the gearcase. Recommended oil is Mariner Super Duty Gear Lube. Lubricant is drained by removing vent and drain plugs in gearcase. Refill through drain plug hole until oil has reached level of top (vent) plug hole.

FUEL SYSTEM

CARBURETOR. Refer to Fig. MR7-2 for an exploded view of carburetor. Initial setting of idle mixture screw (8) is 1⅞-2⅜ turns open from a lightly seated position. Adjust idle speed with outboard in forward gear at normal engine operating temperature so engine idles smoothly at lowest engine speed.

To set fuel level, invert carburetor and measure from carburetor body to float

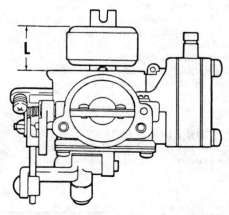

Fig. MR7-1—Float level (L) should be 20.5-22.5 mm.

as shown in Fig. MR7-1. Float level (L) should be 20.5-22.5 mm and is adjusted by bending float arms evenly. Standard main jet size is number 78 for operation at altitudes less than 2500 ft.

SPEED CONTROL LINKAGE. To synchronize ignition and throttle control linkage, first be sure ignition timing is correct then proceed as follows: Turn twist grip to "FAST" position and turn cable bracket nuts (N – Fig. MR7-3) so there is approximately 1-2 mm slack in loose cable. Release twist grip. Move magneto base to full retard position and adjust slow cable adjuster (A) so "SLOW" position on twist grip is aligned with pointer on handle. Move magneto base to full advance position and adjust fast cable adjuster (A) so "FAST" position on twist grip is aligned with pointer on handle. With twist grip in "FAST" position, the center of throttle roller (R – Fig. MR7-4) should be aligned with throttle cam full advance mark (A). Loosen screws (S) and reposition cam (C) if mark is not aligned.

REED VALVE. A pyramid type reed valve is mounted between the carburetor and crankcase. Reed petals should seat squarely and smoothly along their entire length and should be free of cracks, nicks, tears and burrs. Do not attempt to straighten or repair bent or damaged reeds. Reed petals are available. Reed petal ends should not stand open more than 0.2 mm. Reed stop height (H – Fig. MR7-6) should be 1.35-1.65 mm.

FUEL PUMP. A diaphragm type fuel pump is mounted on the side of the carburetor. The fuel pump is operated by crankcase pulsations transferred through passageways in the crankcase, reed valve plate and carburetor body. Passageways must be clear of obstructions or fuel pump will not function properly.

Refer to Fig. MR7-2 for an exploded view of fuel pump. Fuel pump components (22 through 28) are used on later models while components (29 through 35) were used on early models.

IGNITION

Breaker point gap should be set to 0.30-0.40 mm. Adjustment may be accomplished through holes in the flywheel after removing outboard top cover, rewind starter and flywheel cover.

Recommended spark plug is NGK B-7HS with an electrode gap of 0.5-0.6 mm.

Ignition timing may be checked and adjusted as follows: Connect a point checker or ohmmeter to gray wire

Fig. MR7-3 – Speed control cables are adjusted as outlined in text.

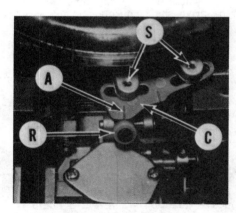

Fig. MR7-4 – View of throttle pickup cam (C). Adjust speed control linkage as outlined in text.

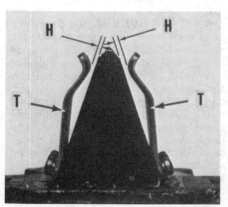

Fig. MR7-6 – View of reed valve assembly. Height (H) of reed valve stops (T) should be 1.35-1.65 mm.

Fig. MR7-2—Exploded view of carburetor. Fuel pump (22 through 29) is used on later models; fuel pump (29 through 35) was used on early models.

1. Cover	10. Idle speed screw	19. Float bowl	28. Gasket
2. Gasket	11. Spring	20. Gasket	29. Fuel pump cover
3. Rod end	12. Gasket	21. Main jet	30. Diaphragm
4. Throttle rod	13. Fuel inlet valve	22. Fuel pump cover	31. Diaphragm
5. Screw	14. Main nozzle	23. Diaphragm	32. Pump body
6. Pilot jet	15. Pin	24. Gasket	33. Diaphragm
7. Spring	16. Float arm	25. Check valve	34. Diaphragm
8. Idle mixture screw	17. Float	26. Pump body	35. Gasket
9. Carburetor body	18. Gasket	27. Diaphragm	

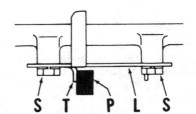

Fig. MR7-8 — Diagram showing magneto in full advance position. Refer to text for ignition timing adjustment.

leading from magneto (top cylinder primary lead). Remove spark plugs and install a dial indicator in top cylinder's spark plug hole. Set top piston at 2.1-2.7 mm before top dead center. Magneto base plate tang (T – Fig. MR7-8) should contact magneto stop (P) just as the breaker points open. Loosen screws (S) and reposition plate (L) to adjust ignition timing. Adjust lower cylinder full advance timing by varying breaker point gap.

COOLING SYSTEM

WATER PUMP. A rubber impeller type water pump is mounted between the drive shaft housing and gearcase. The impeller is driven by a Woodruff key in the drive shaft.

Whenever cooling problems are encountered, check water inlet for plugging or partial stoppage,, then if not corrected, remove gearcase and check condition of the water pump, water passages and sealing surfaces.

When water pump is disassembled, check condition of impeller (9 – Fig. MR7-10), lining (8) and plate (11). Turn drive shaft clockwise (viewed from top) while placing pump housing over impeller. Avoid turning drive shaft in opposite direction when water pump is assembled.

POWER HEAD

R&R AND OVERHAUL. The power head may be removed for disassembly and overhaul as follows: Clamp outboard to a suitable stand and remove top cowl. Remove rewind starter, flywheel and fuel system. Disconnect speed control cables. Remove magneto base plate and ignition coils. Remove seven screws securing power head to drive shaft housing and lift off power head. Remove cylinder head and top oil seal housing (20 – Fig. MR7-13). Remove lower oil seal housing (41) and exhaust cover, then disconnect crankcase breather hoses. Carefully remove crankcase half (1 – Fig. M7-12) while being careful not to damage mating surfaces.

Engine components are now accessible for removal and overhaul as outlined in the appropriate following paragraphs. Assemble as outlined in the ASSEMBLY paragraphs.

ASSEMBLY. When reassembling, make sure all joints and gasket surfaces are clean, free from nicks and burrs and hardened cement or carbon. The crankcase and inlet manifold must be completely sealed against water leakage and pressure. Mating surfaces of water intake and exhaust areas between power head and drive shaft housing must form a tight seal.

Whenever the power head is disassembled, it is recommended that all gasket surfaces and mating surfaces without gaskets be carefully checked for nicks, burrs and warped surfaces which might interfere with a tight seal. Cylinder head, head end of cylinder block and some mating surfaces of manifold and crankcase should be checked on a surface plate and lapped if necessary to provide a smooth surface. Do not remove any more metal than is necessary.

All friction surfaces and needle bearings should be lubricated with engine oil during reassembly. Seals should be filled with a nonfibrous grease. Check frequently as power head is being assembled for binding of working parts. If binding or locking is encountered, correct cause before proceeding with assembly.

Gasket and sealing surfaces should be lightly and evenly coated with a nonhardening gasket cement. Make sure entire surface is coated, but avoid an excess application as cement may be squeezed into crankcase, bearings or

passages. Tighten crankcase screws using tightening sequence in Fig. MR7-14 and cylinder head screws using tightening sequence in Fig. MR7-15. Tighten crankcase and cylinder head screws to 9.8-12.7 N·m.

Before attaching power head to drive shaft housing, make certain drive shaft splines are clean then coat them with a light coating of grease. Tighten power head retaining screws to 9.8-12.7 N·m.

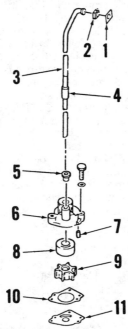

Fig. MR7-10 — Exploded view of water pump.

1. Plate	7. Dowel pin
2. Seal	8. Lining
3. Water tube	9. Impeller
4. Sleeve	10. Gasket
5. Seal	11. Plate
6. Water pump body	

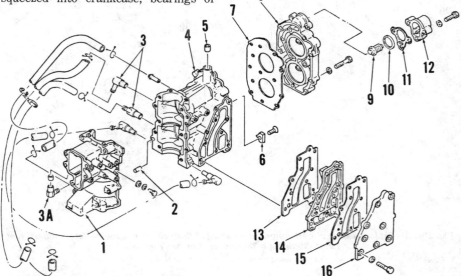

Fig. MR7-12 — Exploded view of crankcase and cylinder block assemblies.

1. Crankcase	5. Dowel pin	9. Thermostat	13. Gasket
2. Dowel pin	6. Anode	10. Washer	14. Plate
3. & 3A. Breather valves	7. Gasket	11. Gasket	15. Gasket
4. Cylinder block	8. Cylinder head	12. Thermostat housing	16. Exhaust cover

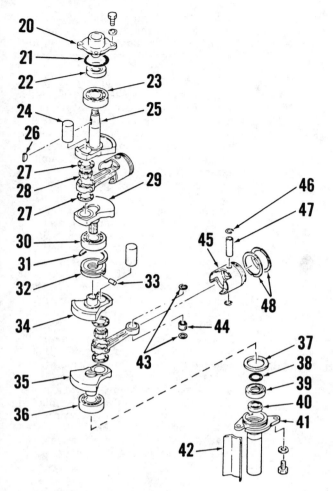

CRANKSHAFT, BEARINGS AND RODS. The built-up crankshaft assembly should be checked for eccentricity at the main bearings while supported between lathe centers. Maximum allowable runout is 0.03 mm. Check condition of large end rod bearing, crankpin and connecting rod by moving small end of rod back and forth. If an excessive amount of side to side shake (more than approximately 2 mm) is found, renew crankshaft or disassemble and renew defective parts. Crankshaft should only be disassembled if the proper tools are available to correctly realign the unit.

When installing crankshaft, lubricate seals with a heat resistant nonfibrous grease and use engine oil on pistons, rings, cylinders and bearings. Use sequences shown in Figs. MR7-14 and MR7-15 to tighten cylinder head screws and crankcase screws. Tighten cylinder head and crankcase screws to 9.8-12.7 N·m. Refer to CONDENSED SERVICE DATA for general torquing specifications.

Fig. MR7-13 — Exploded view of crankshaft assembly.

20. Oil seal housing
21. "O" ring
22. Oil seal
23. Ball bearing
24. Crankpin
25. Crankshaft
26. Key
27. Thrust washer
28. Roller bearing
29. Crankshaft
30. Ball bearing
31. Snap ring
32. Seal
33. Pin
34. Crankshaft
35. Crankshaft
36. Ball bearing
37. Washer
38. "O" ring
39. Oil seal
40. Oil seal
41. Oil seal housing
42. Seal
43. Thrust washer
44. Bearing rollers
45. Piston
46. Pin retainer
47. Piston pin
48. Piston rings

STARTER

Starter may be disassembled for overhaul or renewal of individual components as follows: Remove engine top cowl and three bolts securing starter assembly to power head. Check pawl (10 – Fig. MR7-17) for wear of engagement area and freedom of movement. Renew or grease as necessary. Remove rope handle and allow rope to wind onto rope pulley (7). Remove screw (15) and shaft (13), then carefully lift rope pulley out of housing. Use caution when removing pulley to prevent injury if rewind spring is dislodged from housing.

CYLINDERS, RINGS AND PISTONS. Cylinder bores should be measured in several different locations to determine if an out-of-round or tapered condition exists. Bore and hone cylinder to fit an oversize piston and ring set if out-of-round or taper exceeds 0.07 mm. Be sure to chamfer edges of ports in cylinder after boring to prevent rings from hanging up on sharp edges.

Recommended piston skirt to cylinder clearance is 0.030-0.035 mm. Recommended piston ring end gap is 0.15-0.35 mm for both rings. Top piston ring is chrome plated and has semi-keystone shape. Install piston rings with manufacturer's markings toward top of piston. Pistons and ring sets are available in 0.25 mm and 0.50 mm oversizes.

When reassembling, install new piston pin retaining clips (46 – Fig. MR7-13) and make sure that "UP" on dome of piston is towards flywheel end of engine. Coat bearings, pistons, rings and cylinder bores with engine oil during reassembly.

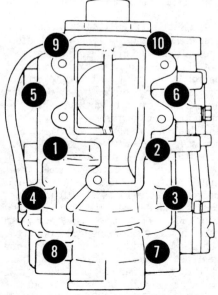

Fig. MR7-14 — Use above sequence when tightening crankcase screws.

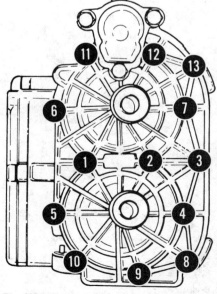

Fig. MR7-15 — Use above sequence when tightening cylinder head screws.

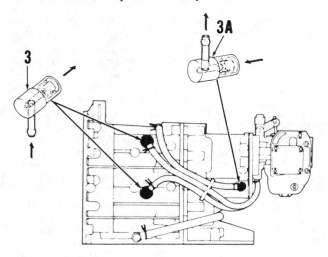

Fig. MR7-16 — View showing location of crankcase breather valves (3 and 3A). Note difference in flow through valves.

screw (16) and remove shift rod (2). Unscrew seal housing (8) and pry housing from gearcase. Remove sleeve (9) and drive bushing (10) down into gear cavity for removal.

Inspect shafts for wear on seal lip contact areas and on splines. Inspect clutch and gears for wear on engagement areas of dog teeth. Inspect gears for wear and damage. Inspect shift cam for excessive wear ramp. All seals and "O" rings should be renewed when unit is reassembled.

To check gear mesh pattern and gear backlash, make a trial assembly using original shims. Mesh pattern is adjusted using pinion gear shim (11) which is available in thicknesses of 0.8, 1.0, 1.2 and 1.4 mm. Install shims between washer (6) and bushing (7) to obtain minimum drive shaft end play. Gear backlash should be 0.1-0.3 mm and is adjusted using shims (22 and 35) which are available in thicknesses of 0.1, 0.3 and 0.5 mm.

Reverse disassembly for reassembly while noting the following: Install bushing (7) so groove in bushing top is towards oil hole in seal housing (8). Install seals (5) with lips toward water pump. Install clutch (27) so "F" marked side (see Fig. MR7-22) is towards forward gear (24 – Fig. MR7-20). Install seals (28) so seal lips are towards propeller. Apply water-resistant grease to "O" ring (37).

With gearcase installed, adjust shift linkage by depressing shift rod (2) downward to bottom stop. Make sure lower unit is in reverse gear. Move shift control handle to "REVERSE" and tighten shift rod clamp screw (S – Fig. MR7-21).

Broken rewind spring or rope may be renewed at this point. Rewind spring should be hooked in housing with coil winding counterclockwise from outer end. Wind rope onto pulley counterclockwise as viewed from bottom. Hook end of rope through notch in pulley leaving enough rope to attach rope handle. Assemble pulley to starter housing making sure that pin in drum engages eye in end of rewind spring. Install shaft (13)

and retaining screw (15). Install spring (9) and pawl (10) as shown in Fig. MR7-18. Grasp end of rope and turn pulley three or four turns counterclockwise. Thread rope through starter housing and attach rope handle. All friction surfaces should be greased.

Adjust starter safety cable by turning adjusting nuts at cable end so starter will operate with outboard in neutral but not in forward or reverse gear.

LOWER UNIT

PROPELLER AND SHEAR PIN. A shear pin is used to protect lower unit gears and shafts. Three-bladed propellers are used. Standard propeller has a nine-inch diameter and seven-inch pitch. Optional propellers are available and should be selected so full throttle engine speed is 4500-5500 rpm.

R&R AND OVERHAUL. Most lower unit service can be performed after separation of gearcase from drive shaft housing. The gearcase may be removed as follows: Clamp outboard to an appropriate work stand, remove propeller and drain gearcase lubricant. Remove circular cover on starboard side of drive shaft housing and loosen shift rod clamp screw (S – Fig. MR7-21). Remove four screws securing gearcase to drive shaft housing and separate gearcase from drive shaft housing. Remove water pump assembly (Fig. MR7-10) and gearcase cap (39 – Fig. MR7-20). Extract propeller shaft and reverse gear assembly. Pry snap ring (13) from drive shaft end and withdraw drive shaft from gearcase. Remove pinion gear (12), shim (11), forward gear (24) and shims (22). Detach spring clip (26) and drive out pin (28) to remove clutch (27) and spring (30) from propeller shaft. Unscrew detent

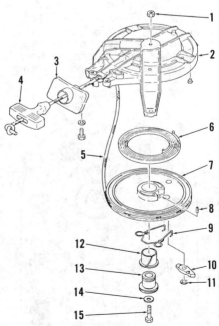

Fig. MR7-17 — Exploded view of starter.

1. Nut
2. Starter housing
3. Rope guide
4. Rope handle
5. Rope
6. Rewind spring
7. Rope pulley
8. Pin
9. Pawl spring
10. Pawl
11. "E" ring
12. Bushing
13. Shaft
14. Washer
15. Screw

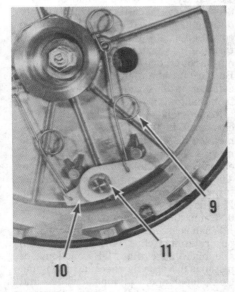

Fig. MR7-18 — View showing proper installation of pawl spring (9), pawl (10) and "E" ring (11).

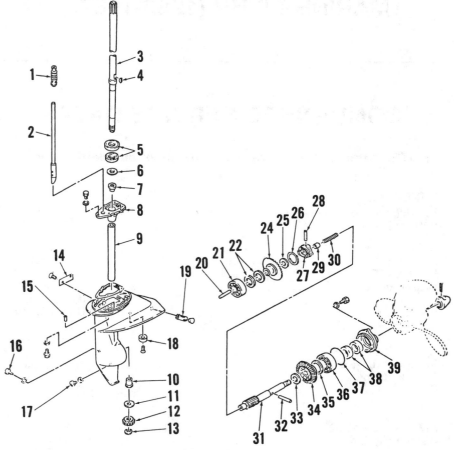

Fig. MR7-20 — Exploded view of gearcase.

1. Boot	11. Shim	21. Ball bearing	31. Propeller shaft
2. Shift rod	12. Pinion gear	22. Shims	32. Shear pin
3. Drive shaft	13. Snap ring	24. Forward gear	33. Thrust washer
4. Key	14. Water inlet cover	25. Thrust washer	34. Reverse gear
5. Oil seals	15. Dowel pin	26. Spring clip	35. Shim
6. Washer	16. Detent screw	27. Clutch	36. Ball bearing
7. Bushing	17. Drain screw	28. Pin	37. "O" ring
8. Seal housing	18. Anode	29. Spring guide	38. Oil seals
9. Sleeve	19. Water inlet screen	30. Spring	39. Cap
10. Bushing	20. Shift pin		

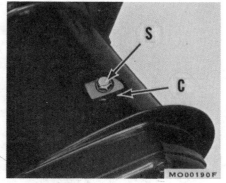

Fig. MR7-21 — View showing location of shift rod clamp (C) and screw (S).

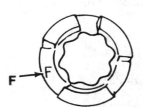

Fig. MR7-22 — Install clutch so (F) mark is towards forward gear.

MARINER 8 HP (1985-1987)

CONDENSED SERVICE DATA

NOTE: Metric fasteners are used throughout outboard motor.

TUNE-UP

Hp/rpm	8/5500
Bore	50 mm
	(1.98 in.)
Stroke	42 mm
	(1.67 in.)
Number of Cylinders	2
Displacement	165 cc
	(10.01 cu. in.)
Spark Plug	NGK B7HS-10
Electrode Gap	1.0 mm
	(0.040 in.)
Ignition Type	CDI
Idle Speed (in gear)	750-850 rpm
Fuel:Oil Ratio	50:1
Gearcase Oil Capacity	160 mL
	(5.4 oz.)

SIZES—CLEARANCES

Piston Ring End Gap	0.15-0.35 mm
	(0.006-0.014 in.)
Piston Skirt Clearance	0.05-0.10 mm
	(0.002-0.004 in.)
Crankshaft Runout—Max.	0.03 mm
	(0.0012 in.)
Connecting Rod Small End Shake—Max.	2.0 mm
	(0.0787 in.)
Connecting Rod Side Clearance	0.2-0.7 mm
	(0.008-0.028 in.)

TIGHTENING TORQUES

Crankcase/Intake Manifold	12 N·m
	(106 in.-lbs.)
Cylinder Head Cover	10 N·m
	(89 in.-lbs.)
Exhaust Cover	8 N·m
	(70 in.-lbs.)
Flywheel	43.4 N·m
	(32 ft.-lbs.)
Power Head	8 N·m
	(70 in.-lbs.)
Spark Plug	19 N·m
	(14 ft.-lbs.)
Standard Screws:	
5 mm	4 N·m
	(36 in.-lbs.)
6 mm	8 N·m
	(70 in.-lbs.)
8 mm	18 N·m
	(13 ft.-lbs.)
10 mm	36 N·m
	(26 ft.-lbs.)
12 mm	42 N·m
	(31 ft.-lbs.)

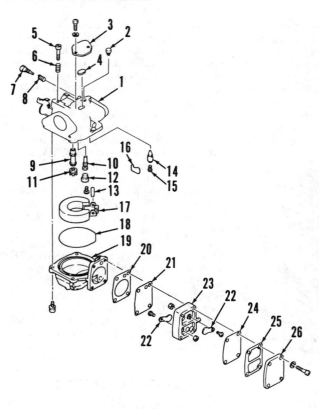

Fig. MR8-1—Exploded view of carburetor/fuel pump assembly.

1. Body
2. Plug
3. Cover
4. Packing
5. Idle speed screw
6. Spring
7. Idle mixture screw
8. Spring
9. Main nozzle
10. Low speed idle jet
11. Main jet
12. Plug
13. Pin
14. Needle valve
15. Pin
16. Clip
17. Float
18. Seal
19. Float bowl
20. Gasket
21. Diaphragm
22. Check valve
23. Pump body
24. Diaphragm
25. Gasket
26. Pump outer cover

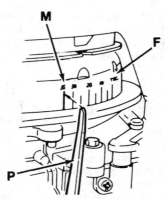

Fig. MR8-3—Align timing pointer (P) with 35° BTDC mark (M) on flywheel (F) during adjustment of speed control linkage. Refer to text.

LUBRICATION

The power head is lubricated by oil mixed with the fuel. Fuel should be regular leaded, low lead or unleaded gasoline with a minimum pump octane rating of 86. Recommended oil is Quicksilver Formula 50-D Outboard Lubricant or a BIA certified TC-W motor oil. The recommended fuel:oil ratio for normal operation and engine break-in is 50:1.

Lower unit gears and bearings are lubricated by oil contained in the gearcase. Recommended oil is Quicksilver Super-Duty Gear Lubricant or a suitable EP 90 outboard gear oil. Lubricant is drained by removing vent and drain plugs in gearcase. Refill through drain plug hole until oil has reached level of top (vent) plug hole.

FUEL SYSTEM

CARBURETOR. The fuel pump and carburetor are a complete unit. Standard main jet (11–Fig. MR8-1) size is 0.98 mm (0.039 in.). Main jet (11) size should be reduced from standard recommendation by 0.05 mm (0.002 in.) for altitudes of 2500 to 5000 feet (760 to 1525 m), 0.10 mm (0.004 in.) for altitudes of 5000 to 7500 feet (1525 to 2285 m) and 0.15 mm (0.006 in.) for altitudes of 7500 feet (2285 m) and up. Initial adjustment of idle mixture screw (7) is 1¼ turns out from a lightly seated position. Recommended idle speed is 750-850 rpm in gear with the engine at

normal operating temperature. Rotate screw (5) to adjust idle speed.

To determine the float level, invert carburetor body (1) with float bowl (19) and seal (18) removed. Measure float height as shown in Fig. MR8-2. Distance from carburetor body sealing surface to top of float should be 14 mm (9/16 in.). Bend tang on float arm to adjust.

FUEL PUMP. The fuel pump is an integral part of the carburetor. Refer to Fig. MR8-1 for an exploded view of fuel pump assembly. Note that fuel pump assembly can be overhauled without carburetor removal.

SPEED CONTROL LINKAGE. To synchronize ignition timing and throttle

Fig. MR8-2—View showing procedure for checking float level. Refer to text.

opening, proceed as follows: Remove both spark plugs and install a dial indicator in the number 1 (top) cylinder. Use the dial indicator to verify when piston is at TDC. With piston at TDC, timing pointer (P–Fig. MR8-3) must align with TDC mark on flywheel (F).

Disconnect magneto base plate control rod (R–Fig. MR8-4) from magneto base plate control lever (L). Rotate flywheel to align 35° BTDC mark (M–Fig. MR8-3) on flywheel with timing pointer (P). Loosen cap screw (S–Fig. MR8-5) and rotate magneto base plate until timing pointer (T) on magneto base plate is aligned with mark stamped on base of flywheel (F). Move stop bracket (B) until light contact is made with stop tab on timing pointer (T). Tighten cap screw (S).

Rotate twist grip to wide-open throttle (WOT), then adjust maximum advance throttle cable (A–Fig. MR8-6) until carburetor throttle lever (C–Fig. MR8-4) is in contact with WOT stop (W). Adjust idle throttle cable (I–Fig. MR8-6) to remove cable slack. With timing at maximum advance position as previously outlined and carburetor throttle lever (C–Fig. MR8-4) against WOT stop (W), adjust ball socket at end of magneto base plate control rod (R) to slide over ball joint on magneto base plate control lever (L).

REED VALVE. A reed valve plate is mounted between the intake manifold and crankcase. Reed petals should seat squarely and smoothly along their entire length and should be free of cracks, nicks, tears and burrs. Do not attempt to straighten or repair bent or damaged reeds. If reed stop (S–Fig. MR8-7) is removed, install new retaining screws and apply Loctite 271 or 290 on screw threads. Reed stop height should be 4.76 mm (3/16 in.). To check reed stop height, insert a 3/16 inch drill bit (B) between reed petals and reed stop as shown in Fig. MR8-7. Bend reed stop (S) to adjust reed stop height.

IGNITION

The standard spark plug is NGK B7HS-10 with an electrode gap of 1.0 mm (0.040 in.).

Models are equipped with a capacitor discharge ignition (CDI) system. If engine malfunction is noted and the ignition system is suspected, make sure the spark plugs and all electrical wiring are in good condition and all electrical connections are tight before proceeding to trouble-shooting the CD ignition system.

Proceed as follows to test CDI system components: Refer to Fig. MR8-8. To test ignition coil, disconnect black wire (B) and orange wire (Or) at connectors and spark plug boots from spark plugs. Use a suitable ohmmeter and connect black tester lead to black wire (B) and red tester lead to orange wire (Or). The resistance reading should be 0.12-0.18 ohms. Connect one tester lead to terminal end in one of the spark plug boots and the other tester lead to the terminal end in the other spark plug boot. The resistance reading should be 2800-4200

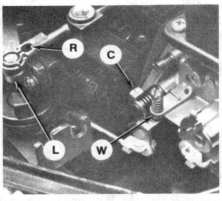

Fig. MR8-4—View identifying carburetor throttle lever (C), magneto base plate control lever (L), magneto base plate control rod (R) and WOT stop (W).

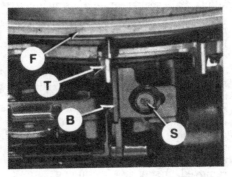

Fig. MR8-5—Cap screw (S) retains stop bracket (B). Timing pointer (T) should align with mark stamped on base of flywheel (F) when timing is at maximum advance position.

ohms. Use a suitable coil tester or tester Model 9800 Magneto Analyzer to perform a power test. Connect tester leads as outlined in tester's handbook. A steady spark should jump a 5 mm (13/64 in.) gap when a current value of 1.7 to 2.1 amperes is applied. A surface insulation test can be performed using a suitable coil tester or tester Model 9800 Magneto Analyzer and following tester's handbook.

Fig. MR8-6—Loosen jam nuts (N) to adjust maximum advance throttle cable (A) and idle throttle cable (I).

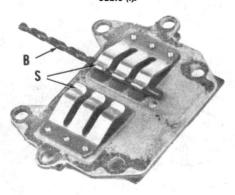

Fig. MR8-7—View showing reed valve plate assembly. Use a 3/16 inch drill bit (B) inserted between reed petals and reed stop (S) to check reed stop height. Refer to text.

Fig. MR8-8 — View identifying CDI system components. Wires are identified as follows.

B. Black
G. Green
W. White
Br. Brown
Or. Orange
W/R. White wire with red tracer

To check source (charge) coil, first remove engine flywheel. Disconnect black wire (B) and brown wire (Br) at connectors leading from magneto base plate. Use a suitable ohmmeter and connect red tester lead to brown wire (Br) and black tester lead to black wire (B). The ohmmeter should read 81-99 ohms.

To check trigger coil, remove engine flywheel and disconnect black wire (B) and white wire with red tracer (W/R) at connectors leading from magneto base plate. Use a suitable ohmmeter and connect red tester lead to white wire with red tracer (W/R) and black tester lead to black wire (B). The ohmmeter should read 92-112 ohms.

To test CDI module, first disconnect all wires at connectors and remove CDI module from outboard motor. Use a suitable ohmmeter and refer to Fig. MR8-9. With reference to chart, perform CDI module resistance tests.

Renew any components that are not within the manufacturer's recommended limits.

COOLING SYSTEM

WATER PUMP. A rubber impeller type water pump is mounted between the drive shaft housing and gearcase. The impeller is driven by a Woodruff key in the drive shaft.

Whenever cooling problems are encountered, check water inlets for plugging or partial stoppage. If cooling problems persist, remove gearcase as out-

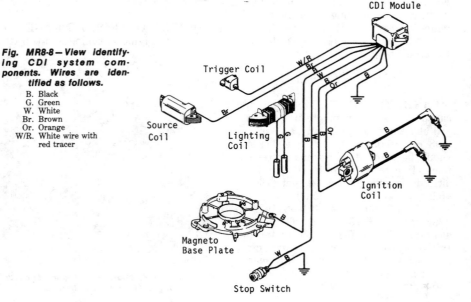

TESTER LEADS	CDI MODULE LEADS				
− BLACK / + RED	W	B	Br	W/R	Or
C D I M O D U L E L E A D S W		A	A	A	A
B	A		H	A	G
Br	A	C		A	G
W/R	D	E	F		G
Or	A	A	G	A	

Fig. MR8-9—Use chart and values listed below to test condition of CD ignition module. Wires are identified in Fig. MR8-8. Before making test (G), connect CDI module's black wire and orange wire together. Then disconnect wires and perform desired test.

- A. Infinity
- C. 63,000-95,000 ohms
- D. 8,000-14,000 ohms
- E. 14,000-22,000 ohms
- F. 30,000-46,000 ohms
- G. Tester needle swings once then returns to infinity.
- H. 7,000-12,000 ohms

flywheel, tool kit and bracket and carburetor/fuel pump assembly. Withdraw flywheel key from crankshaft slot. Disconnect speed control linkage. Remove CDI module and ignition coil. Remove three magneto base plate mounting screws, detach wires at connectors and lift magneto base plate from power head. Remove six cap screws retaining power head to drive shaft housing and lift off power head.

Installation is reverse order of removal. Install a new gasket between power head and drive shaft housing. Coat both sides of the gasket with a thin coating of "Perfect Seal" or a suitable equivalent. Tighten power head retaining screws to 8 N·m (70 in.-lbs.). Tighten flywheel nut to a torque of 43.4 N·m (32 ft.-lbs.).

DISASSEMBLY. Remove lower oil seal housing (20 – Fig. MR8-11), exhaust manifold, (22) and gasket (21). Remove three friction plate (8) cap screws and

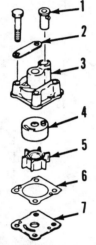

Fig. MR8-10—Exploded view of water pump assembly.

1. Seal
2. Plate (2)
3. Housing
4. Liner
5. Impeller
6. Gasket
7. Plate

lined under LOWER UNIT section and check condition of the water pump, water passages and sealing surfaces.

When water pump is disassembled, check condition of impeller (5 – Fig. MR8-10), lining (4) and plate (7). Turn drive shaft clockwise (viewed from top) while placing pump housing over impeller. Avoid turning drive shaft in opposite direction when water pump is assembled. Tighten water pump housing retaining screws to 8 N·m (70 in.-lbs.).

POWER HEAD

REMOVE AND REINSTALL.

Clamp outboard motor to a suitable stand and remove engine top cowl. Remove manual rewind starter,

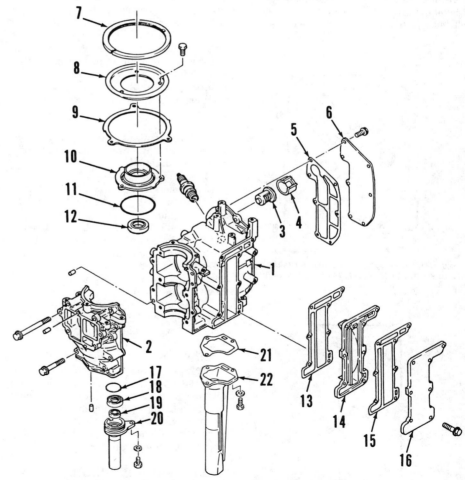

Fig. MR8-11—Exploded view of crankcase and cylinder block assembly.

1. Cylinder block
2. Crankcase cover
3. Thermostat
4. Nylon spacer
5. Gasket
6. Cylinder head cover
7. Nylon ring
8. Friction plate
9. Retaining ring
10. Upper oil seal housing
11. "O" ring
12. Seal
13. Gasket
14. Inner exhaust cover
15. Gasket
16. Outer exhaust cover
17. "O" ring
18. Seal
19. Seal
20. Lower oil seal housing
21. Gasket
22. Exhaust manifold

withdraw friction plate (8), nylon ring (7) and retaining ring (9). Remove six intake manifold cap screws and withdraw intake manifold and reed valve plate assembly. Remove upper oil seal housing (10). Remove cylinder head cover (6) and withdraw nylon spacer (4) and thermostat (3). Remove seven exhaust cover cap screws and separate outer exhaust cover (16) from inner exhaust cover (14). Remove four remaining crankcase cover cap screws and separate crankcase cover (2) from cylinder block (1) while being careful not to damage mating surfaces.

Engine components are now accessible for removal and overhaul as outlined in the appropriate service paragraphs.

ASSEMBLY. When reassembling, make sure all joints and gasket surfaces are clean and free from nicks and burrs. All friction surfaces and bearings must be lubricated with engine oil during reassembly. Make sure locating pins on crankshaft ball bearings and labyrinth seal fit into the slots in cylinder block. Check frequently as power head is being

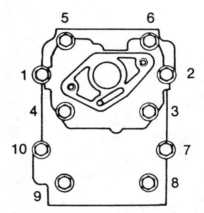

Fig. MR8-12—Tighten crankcase/intake mani-fold screws to 12 N·m (106 in.-lbs.) in sequence shown.

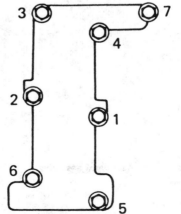

Fig. MR8-13—Tighten exhaust cover screws to 8 N·m (70 in.-lbs.) in sequence shown.

assembled for binding of working parts. If binding or locking is encountered, correct cause before proceeding with assembly.

Apply a continuous bead of Loctite Master Gasket Sealant to sealing surface of crankcase cover (2–Fig. MR8-11). Make sure entire surface is coated, but avoid an excess application as sealant may be squeezed into crankcase, bearings or passages.

Install reed valve plate assembly and intake manifold with new gaskets. Tighten the crankcase/intake manifold screws to 12 N·m (106 in.-lbs.) following the sequence shown in Fig. MR8-12. Tighten the exhaust cover screws to 8 N·m (70 in.-lbs.) following the sequence shown in Fig. MR8-13. Tighten the cylinder head cover screws to 10 N·m (89 in.-lbs.) following the sequence shown in Fig. MR8-14, then complete reassembly.

CYLINDERS, RINGS AND PISTONS. Cylinder bores should be measured in several different locations to determine if an out-of-round or tapered condition exists. Inspect cylinder walls for scoring. If cylinder bore is out-of-round more than 0.076 mm (0.003 in.) or excessive scoring is noted, cylinder block (1–Fig. MR8-11) and crankcase cover (2) must be renewed.

NOTE: To deglaze cylinder walls, lightly hone following hone manufacturer's recommendations.

Recommended piston skirt to cylinder clearance is 0.05-0.10 mm (0.002-0.004 in.). Recommended piston ring gap is 0.15-0.35 mm (0.006-0.014 in.) for both rings. The top (semi-keystone) piston ring should have a side clearance of 0.02-0.06 mm (0.0008-0.0024 in.) and the bottom (square) piston ring should have a side clearance of 0.04-0.08 mm (0.0016-0.0032 in.). Make sure piston rings properly align with locating pins in ring grooves and identifying letter faces up.

When reassembling, install new piston pin retaining clips (11–Fig. MR8-15) and make sure that pistons are installed with sharp vertical side of deflector toward intake side and long sloping side will be toward exhaust port in cylinder. Coat bearings, pistons, rings and cylinder bores with engine oil during assembly.

CRANKSHAFT, BEARINGS AND RODS. The connecting rods ride on a roller bearing around the crankpin. Crankshaft, crankpins, bearings and connecting rods are available only as a unit assembly. Maximum allowable side clearance between rod and crankshaft is

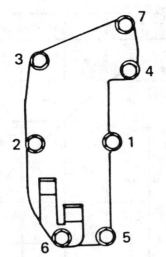

Fig. MR8-14—Tighten cylinder head cover screws to 10 N·m (89 in.-lbs.) in sequence shown.

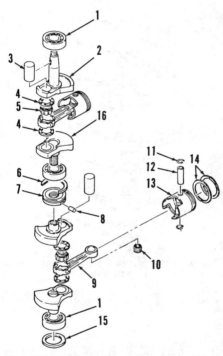

Fig. MR8-15—Exploded view of crankshaft assembly.

1. Ball bearings	9. Connecting rod
2. Crank half	10. Roller bearing
3. Crankpin	11. Retaining clip
4. Thrust washers	12. Piston pin
5. Roller bearing	13. Piston
6. Snap ring	14. Piston rings
7. Labyrinth seal	15. Washer
8. Pin	16. Crank half

0.2-0.7 mm (0.008-0.028 in.). Maximum runout of crankshaft is 0.03 mm (0.0012 in.) with crankshaft ends supported. Determine rod, rod bearing and crankpin wear by moving small rod end from side to side as shown in Fig. MR8-16. Renew crankshaft assembly if side movement exceeds 2.0 mm (0.0787 in.).

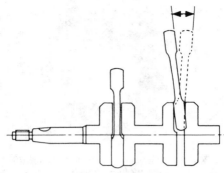

Fig. MR8-16—Move connecting rod small end side to side as shown to determine rod, rod bearing and crankpin wear. Refer to text.

Protect crankshaft end and use a suitable press to remove and install main ball bearings (1 – Fig. MR8-15).

MANUAL STARTER

A starter lockout assembly is used to prevent starter engagement when the gear shift lever is in the forward or reverse position.

The manual starter must be disassembled to renew starter rope (11 – Fig. MR8-17) and rewind spring (3).

To overhaul the manual starter, proceed as follows: Remove the engine's top cowl. Remove the screws retaining the manual starter to the engine. Remove the starter lockout cable at the starter housing. Note plunger and spring located at cable end, care should be used not to lose components should they fall free. Withdraw the starter assembly.

Check pawl (7) for freedom of movement, excessive wear of engagement area and any other damage. Renew or lubricate pawl (7) with a suitable water-resistant grease and return starter to service if no other damage is noted.

To disassemble, remove clip (8) and withdraw pawl (7) and pawl spring assembly (6). Remove cover (15) and untie starter rope (11) at handle (14) and allow the rope to wind into the starter. Remove bolt (10), washer (9) and shaft (5), then place a suitable screwdriver blade through hole (H – Fig. MR8-18) to hold rewind spring (3 – Fig. MR8-17) securely in housing (2). Carefully lift pulley (4) with starter rope (11) from housing (2). BE CAREFUL when removing pulley (4) as the rewind spring may be dislodged. Untie starter rope (11) and remove rope from pulley (4) if renewal is required. To remove rewind spring (3) from housing (2), invert housing so it sits upright on a flat surface, then tap the housing top until rewind spring (3) falls free and uncoils.

Inspect all components for damage and excessive wear and renew if needed.

To reassemble, first apply a coating of a suitable water-resistant grease to rewind spring area of housing (2). Install rewind spring (3) in housing (2) so spring coils wind in a counterclockwise direction from the outer end. Make sure the spring's outer hook is properly secured over starter housing (2) pin. Wind starter rope (11) onto pulley (4) approximately 1½ turns counterclockwise when viewed from the flywheel side. Direct remaining starter rope (11) length through notch in pulley (4).

NOTE: Lubricate all friction surfaces with a suitable water-resistant grease during reassembly.

Assemble pulley (4) to starter housing making sure that pulley's pin engages hook end in rewind spring (3). Install shaft (5), washer (9) and bolt (10). Apply Loctite 271 or 290 or an equivalent thread fastening solution on bolt (10) threads and install nut (1) and tighten to 8 N·m (70 in.-lbs.).

Thread starter rope (11) through starter housing (2), rope guide (12) and handle (14) and secure with a knot. Install cover (15). Turn pulley (4) three turns counterclockwise when viewed from the flywheel side, then release starter rope (11) from pulley notch and allow rope to slowly wind onto pulley.

NOTE: Do not apply any more tension on rewind spring (3) than is required to draw starter handle (14) back into the proper released position.

Install spring assembly (6), pawl (7) and clip (8). Remount manual starter assembly.

Fig. MR8-17—Exploded view of manual rewind starter.

1. Nut
2. Housing
3. Rewind spring
4. Pulley
5. Shaft
6. Pawl spring assy.
7. Pawl
8. Clip
9. Washer
10. Bolt
11. Starter rope
12. Rope guide
13. Seal
14. Handle
15. Cover

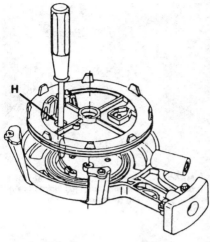

Fig. MR8-18—Pulley hole (H) is used during pulley withdrawal. Refer to text.

Adjust starter lockout assembly by turning adjusting nuts at cable end so starter will engage when gear shift lever is in "Neutral" position, but will not engage when gear shift lever is in "Forward" or "Reverse" position.

LOWER UNIT

PROPELLER AND DRIVE HUB. Lower unit protection is provided by a cushion type hub in the propeller. The standard propeller has three blades with a 216 mm (8½ in.) diameter and a pitch of 190.5 mm (7½ in.). Optional propellers are available. Select a propeller that will allow the engine to reach maximum engine speed of 4500-5500 rpm.

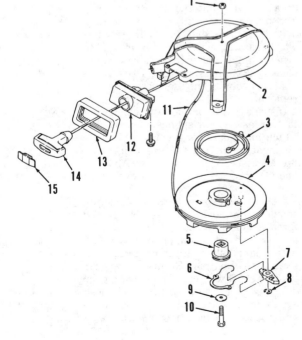

Fig. MR8-19—Loosen cap screw (S) so lower shift rod slides freely in clamp (C) before removing gearcase.

varying thickness of shim (19). Gear backlash should be 0.25-0.75 mm (0.01-0.03 in.) and is adjusted by shims (21 and 32).

Reassemble gearcase by reversing disassembly procedure while noting the following: Install seals (7) in water pump base (9) so lips are towards top of housing. Install seals (37) in bearing carrier (36) so lips are towards propeller. Install dog clutch (26) so "F" marked side (see Fig. MR8-21) is toward forward gear (23 – Fig. MR8-20). Apply a light coat of water-resistant grease to drive shaft up-

Fig. MR8-21—Install dog clutch so "F" mark (F) is toward forward gear.

per splines. Tighten gearcase to drive shaft housing screws to 8 N·m (70 in.-lbs.).

With gearcase assembled and installed, synchronize gear engagement with shift lever. Tighten cap screw (S – Fig. MR8-19) to secure shift rods in clamp (C).

R&R AND OVERHAUL. Most lower unit service can be performed after removing lower unit gearcase from the drive shaft housing. Remove gearcase as follows: Clamp outboard motor to a suitable stand, remove propeller and drain lubricant. Place shift lever in "Reverse" and tilt outboard motor to full up position. Loosen cap screw (S – Fig. MR8-19) so lower shift rod slides freely in clamp (C). Remove four cap screws retaining gearcase to drive shaft housing. Withdraw gearcase assembly. Remove water pump assembly.

Remove two cap screws securing bearing carrier (36 – Fig. MR8-20), then extract bearing carrier (36) with propeller shaft assembly. Separate propeller shaft assembly from bearing carrier (36). Remove spring clip (28) and push out pin (27) to remove dog clutch (26). Lift out shim (30), reverse gear (31) and shim (32) from bearing carrier (36). Use suitable pullers to extract bearing (33) and seals (37). Remove water pump base (9) and lower shift rod (2). Remove clip (6), pinion gear (20) and shim (19). Withdraw drive shaft (4). Withdraw forward gear (23) with cone of bearing (22). Use a suitable puller to withdraw cup of bearing (22) and shim (21). Drive bushing (18) down into gear cavity for removal.

Inspect shafts for wear on seal lip contact areas and on splines. Inspect dog clutch and gears for wear and damage on engagement areas. Inspect shift cam for excessive wear on ramp. All seals and "O" rings should be renewed when unit is assembled.

Gear backlash and mesh position should be checked on reassembly. Install forward gear (23) with original shim (21) in gearcase. Position pinion gear (20) with original shim (19) in gearcase then install drive shaft (4). Secure pinion gear (20) to drive shaft with clip (6). Forward gear (23) and pinion gear (20) should mesh evenly when drive shaft (4) is pulled up and rotated. Adjust mesh position by

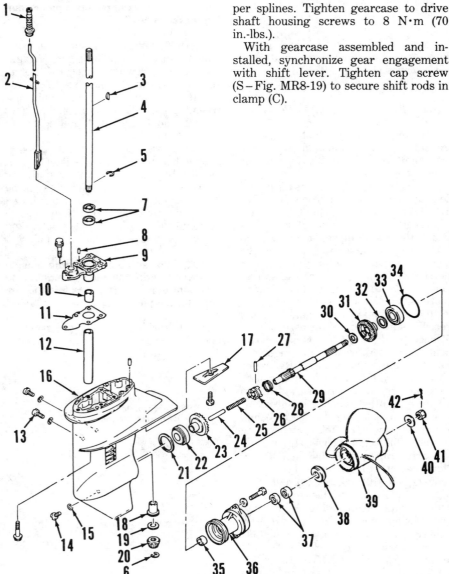

Fig. MR8-20—Exploded view of gearcase.

1. Boot	12. Sleeve	22. Bearing	32. Shim
2. Lower shift rod	13. Level plug	23. Forward gear	33. Bearing
3. Key	14. Drain plug	24. Shift pin	34. "O" ring
4. Drive shaft	15. Gasket	25. Spring	35. Bushing
5. Clip	16. Housing	26. Dog clutch	36. Bearing carrier
6. Clip	17. Anode	27. Pin	37. Seals
7. Seals	18. Bushing	28. Spring clip	38. Thrust hub
8. Dowel pin	19. Shim	29. Propeller shaft	39. Propeller
9. Water pump base	20. Pinion gear	30. Thrust washer	40. Washer
10. Bushing	21. Shim	31. Reverse gear	41. Nut
11. Gasket			42. Cotter pin

MARINER 9.9 HP (1979-1986) AND 15 HP (1979-1988)

CONDENSED SERVICE DATA

NOTE: Metric fasteners are used throughout outboard motor.

TUNE-UP

Hp/rpm	9.9, 15/5500
Bore	56 mm
	(2.205 in.)
Stroke	50 mm
	(1.968 in.)
Number of cylinders	2
Displacement	246 cc
	(15 cu. in.)
Spark plug	See Text
Ignition type	See Text
Idle speed (in gear)	600-700 rpm
Fuel:oil ratio	50:1

SIZES—CLEARANCES

Piston ring end gap	0.15-0.35 mm
	(0.006-0.014 in.)
Piston skirt clearance	0.035-0.040 mm
	(0.0014-0.0016 in.)
Crankshaft runout—max.	0.03 mm
	(0.0012 in.)
Connecting rod small end shake—	
Standard	0.8 mm
	(0.031 in.)
Limit	2.0 mm
	(0.078 in.)
Lower unit gear backlash	0.1-0.3 mm
	(0.004-0.012 in.)

TIGHTENING TORQUES

Crankcase—	
M6	10.8-12.7 N·m
	(8-9 ft.-lbs.)
M8	27.4-31.4 N·m
	(20-23 ft.-lbs.)
Cylinder head	14.7-18.6 N·m
	(11-14 ft.-lbs.)
Flywheel	68.6-78.4 N·m
	(50-58 ft.-lbs.)
Standard screws—	
5 mm	4.9-5.8 N·m
	(43-51 in.-lbs.)
6 mm	7.9-9.8 N·m
	(70-87 in.-lbs.)
8 mm	14.7-19.6 N·m
	(11-14 ft.-lbs.)
10 mm	27.4-44.1 N·m
	(20-32 ft.-lbs.)
12 mm	34.3-49.0 N·m
	(25-36 ft.-lbs.)

LUBRICATION

The power head is lubricated by oil mixed with the fuel. Fuel should be regular leaded, low lead or unleaded gasoline with a minimum pump octane rating of 86. Recommended oil is Quicksilver Premium Blend 2-Cycle Outboard Oil. Normal fuel:oil ratio is 50:1; during engine break-in fuel:oil ratio should be 25:1.

Lower unit gears and bearings are lubricated by oil contained in the gearcase. Recommended oil is Quicksilver Premium Blend Gear Lube. Lubricant is drained by removing vent and drain plugs in the gearcase. Refill through drain plug hole until oil has reached level of top (vent) plug hole.

FUEL SYSTEM

CARBURETOR. Refer to Fig. MR10-2 for an exploded view of carburetor. Initial setting of idle mixture screw (8) is $1\frac{7}{8}$-$2\frac{3}{8}$ turns open from a lightly seated position. Adjust idle speed with outboard in forward gear at normal engine operating temperature so engine idles smoothly at lowest engine speed.

To set fuel level, invert carburetor and measure from carburetor body to float as shown in Fig. MR10-1. Float level (L) should be 20.5-22.5 mm (13/16-57/64 in.) and is adjusted by bending float arms evenly.

SPEED CONTROL LINKAGE. Before synchronizing throttle control and ignition, ignition timing should be

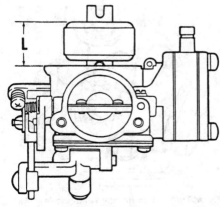

Fig. MR10-1 — Float level (L) should be 20.5-22.5 mm (13/16-57/64 in.).

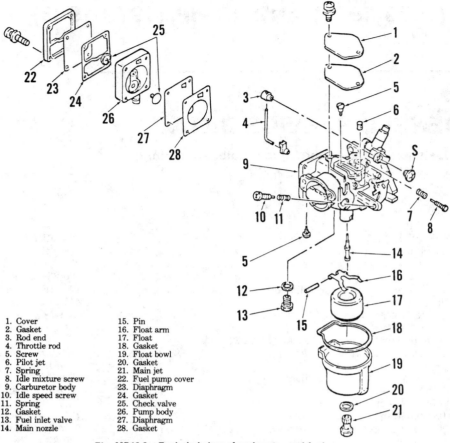

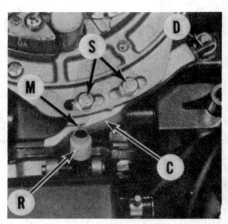

Fig. MR10-4 — View of magneto base plate and throttle cam.

C. Throttle cam
D. Idle ignition timing
   adjustment screw

M. Mark
R. Roller
S. Screws

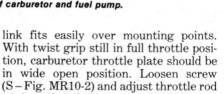

1. Cover	15. Pin
2. Gasket	16. Float arm
3. Rod end	17. Float
4. Throttle rod	18. Gasket
5. Screw	19. Float bowl
6. Pilot jet	20. Gasket
7. Spring	21. Main jet
8. Idle mixture screw	22. Fuel pump cover
9. Carburetor body	23. Diaphragm
10. Idle speed screw	24. Gasket
11. Spring	25. Check valve
12. Gasket	26. Pump body
13. Fuel inlet valve	27. Diaphragm
14. Main nozzle	28. Gasket

Fig. MR10-2 — Exploded view of carburetor and fuel pump.

checked and adjusted if required. Disconnect adjustable link between tower shaft and magneto base plate. Turn twist grip to "FAST" position and note if marks (M – Fig. MR10-3) are aligned. If marks do not align, remove gears and reinstall with marks properly aligned. With twist grip in "FAST" position, rotate magneto to full advanced position then install adjustable link between magneto base plate and tower shaft; adjust length of link as required so

link fits easily over mounting points. With twist grip still in full throttle position, carburetor throttle plate should be in wide open position. Loosen screw (S – Fig. MR10-2) and adjust throttle rod (4) in rod end (3) to obtain wide open throttle, then retighten screw (S).

All models are equipped with reverse gear throttle limiting linkage to prevent full throttle when outboard is in reverse gear. To adjust linkage, shift outboard to reverse gear and turn twist grip so throttle roller (R – Fig. MR10-4) is aligned with throttle cam mark (M). Loosen stop bolt (B – Fig. MR10-5) and move stop plate (P) so it contacts lever (L), then retighten bolt (B).

REED VALVE. A pyramid type reed valve is mounted between the carburetor and crankcase. Reed petals should seat squarely and smoothly along their entire length and should be free of cracks, nicks, tears and burrs. Do not attempt to straighten or repair bent or damaged reeds. Reed petals are available. Reed petal ends should not stand open more than 0.2 mm (0.008 in.). Reed stop height (H – Fig. MR10-7) should be 1.37-1.65 mm (0.054-0.065 in.) on 9.9 hp models manufactured for use in the U.S.A. and Australia and 2.9-3.1 mm (0.114-0.122 in.) on 9.9 hp models manufactured for use in all other countries or 3.9-4.1 mm (0.154-0.161 in.) on 15 hp models.

FUEL PUMP. A diaphragm type fuel pump is mounted on the side of the carburetor. The fuel pump is operated by crankcase pulsations transferred through passageways in the crankcase, reed valve plate and carburetor body. Passageways must be clear of obstructions or fuel pump will not operate properly. Refer to Fig. MR10-2 for an exploded view of fuel pump.

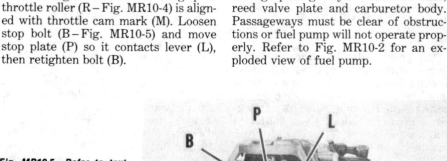

Fig. MR10-3 — With throttle twist grip in "FAST" position, control gear marks (M) should be aligned.

Fig. MR10-5 — Refer to text for adjustment of reverse gear throttle stop plate (P).

IGNITION

Breaker Point Models

Breaker point gap should be 0.3-0.4 mm (0.012-0.016 in.). Adjustment may be accomplished through holes in the flywheel after removing outboard top cover, rewind starter and flywheel cover.

Recommended spark plug is NGK B7HS with an electrode gap of 0.5-0.6 mm (0.020-0.024 in.).

Ignition timing may be checked and adjusted as follows: Connect a point checker or ohmmeter to gray wire leading from magneto (top cylinder primary lead). Rotate magneto base plate to full advanced position so boss on throttle cam (C–Fig. MR10-4 contacts stop. Rotate flywheel clockwise and breaker points should open at 23½°-26½° before top dead center. Adjust full advance ignition timing by loosening screws (S) and repositioning throttle cam (C). Adjust lower cylinder full advance ignition timing by varying breaker point gap.

To adjust idle speed ignition timing, rotate magneto base plate to full retard position and check breaker point opening while turning flywheel clockwise. Idle speed ignition timing should be 3°-5° after top dead center. Adjust idle speed ignition timing by turning screw (D).

If flywheel timing marks or timing pointer location is questioned, full advance ignition timing may be determined using a dial indicator. Remove spark plugs and install a dial indicator in top cylinder's spark plug hole. Set top piston at 2.7-3.1 mm (0.011-0.012 in.) before top dead center. Adjust full advance ignition timing as previously described.

After adjusting ignition timing, recheck carburetor and speed control linkage adjustments.

Fig. MR10-8 — View identifying CDI system components. Wires are identified as follows.

- B. Black
- G. Green
- W. White
- Br. Brown
- Or. Orange
- W/R. White wire with red tracer

Fig. MR10-9 — Use chart and values listed below to test condition of CD ignition module. Wires are identified in Fig. MR10-8. Before making test (G), connect CDI module's black wire and orange wire together. Then disconnect wires and perform desired test.

- A. Infinity
- C. 63,000-95,000 ohms
- D. 8,000-14,000 ohms
- E. 14,000-22,000 ohms
- F. 30,000-46,000 ohms
- G. Tester needle swings once then returns to infinity
- H. 7,000-12,000 ohms

TESTER LEADS −BLACK / +RED	CDI MODULE LEADS				
	W	B	Br	W/R	Or
W		A	A	A	A
B	A		H	A	G
Br	A	C		A	G
W/R	D	E	F		G
Or	A	A	G	A	

CDI Models

The standard spark plug is NGK B7HS-10 with an electrode gap of 1.0 mm (0.040 in.). If engine malfunction is noted and the ignition system is suspected, make sure the spark plugs and all electrical wiring are in good condition and all electrical connections are tight before proceeding to trouble-shooting the CD ignition system.

Proceed as follows to test CDI system components: Refer to Fig. MR10-8. To test ignition coil, disconnect black wire (B) and orange wire (Or) at connectors and spark plug boots from spark plugs. Use a suitable ohmmeter and connect black tester lead to black wire (B) and red tester lead to orange wire (Or). The resistance reading should be 0.12-0.18 ohms. Connect one tester lead to terminal end in one of the spark plug boots and the other tester lead to the terminal end in the other spark plug boot. The resistance reading should be 2800-4200 ohms. Use a suitable coil tester or tester Model 9800 Magneto Analyzer to perform a power test. Connect tester leads as outlined in tester's handbook. A steady spark should jump a 5 mm (13/64 in.) gap when a current value of 1.7 to 2.1 amperes is applied. A surface insulation test can be performed using a suitable coil tester or tester Model 9800 Magneto Analyzer and following tester's handbook.

To check source (charge) coil, first remove engine flywheel. Disconnect

Fig. MR10-7 — View of reed valve assembly. Refer to text for specifications of height (H) of reed valve stops (T).

black wire (B) and brown wire (Br) at connectors leading from magneto base plate. Use a suitable ohmmeter and connect red tester lead to brown wire (Br) and black tester lead to black wire (B). The ohmmeter should read 81-99 ohms.

To check trigger coil, remove engine flywheel and disconnect black wire (B) and white wire with red tracer (W/R) at connectors leading from magneto base plate. Use a suitable ohmmeter and connect red tester lead to white wire with red tracer (W/R) and black tester lead to black wire (B). The ohmmeter should read 92-112 ohms.

To test CDI module, first disconnect all wires at connectors and remove CDI module from outboard motor. Use a suitable ohmmeter and refer to Fig. MR10-9. With reference to chart, perform CDI module resistance tests.

Renew any components that are not within the manufacturer's recommended limits.

Ignition timing can be checked and adjusted as follows: Remove both spark plugs and install a dial indicator in the number 1 (top) cylinder. Use the dial indicator to verify when piston is at TDC. With piston at TDC, timing pointer (P–Fig. MR10-10) must align with TDC mark on flywheel (F).

Disconnect adjustable link between tower shaft and magneto base plate. Rotate flywheel to align 30 degree BTDC mark (D) on flywheel with timing pointer (P). Place shift lever in "Forward" position. Loosen two cap screws (S—Fig. MR10-4) securing throttle cam to magneto base plate. Position magneto base plate (B—Fig. MR10-10) so timing mark (M) aligns with triangle shaped timing mark (T) on flywheel. Place throttle cam (C—Fig. MR10-4) so magne-

to stop on base of cam is in contact with stop on cylinder block. Retighten two cap screws (S).

Rotate flywheel to align 5 degree BTDC mark on flywheel with timing pointer. Rotate magneto base plate until idle ignition timing adjustment screw (D) is in contact with stop on cylinder block. Adjust screw (D) to align timing mark (M–Fig. MR10-10) on magneto base plate with triangle shaped timing mark (T) on flywheel.

After adjusting ignition timing, recheck carburetor and speed control linkage adjustments.

COOLING SYSTEM

WATER PUMP. A rubber impeller type water pump is mounted between the drive shaft housing and gearcase. The impeller is driven by a Woodruff key in the drive shaft.

Whenever cooling problems are encountered, check water inlet for plugging or partial stoppage and thermostat in cylinder head for proper operation. If cooling problem persists, remove gearcase and check condition of the water pump, water passages and sealing surfaces.

When water pump is disassembled, check condition of impeller (7–Fig. MR10-12), lining (6) and plate (9). Turn drive shaft clockwise (viewed from top) while placing pump housing over im-

peller. Avoid turning drive shaft in opposite direction when water pump is assembled.

POWER HEAD

R&R AND OVERHAUL. The power head may be removed for disassembly and overhaul as follows: Clamp outboard to a suitable stand and remove engine top cowl. Remove manual starter and, if so equipped, electric starter. Remove fuel system, flywheel, magneto base plate and ignition coil or coils, then disconnect speed control linkage. Remove six screws securing power head to drive shaft housing and lift off power head. Disconnect crankcase breather hoses then remove cylinder head, lower oil seal housing (20–Fig. MR10-14) and exhaust cover. Carefully remove crankcase half while being careful not to damage mating surfaces.

Assemble as outlined in the ASSEMBLY paragraphs.

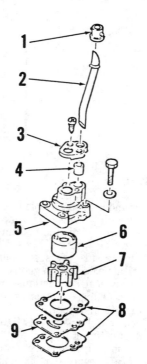

Fig. MR10-10—Refer to text for setting ignition timing.

B. Magneto base plate
D. 30° BTDC mark
F. Flywheel
M. Magneto base plate timing mark
P. Timing pointer
T. Triangle shaped timing mark

Fig. MR10-12—Exploded view of water pump.

1. Seal
2. Water tube
3. Cover
4. Seal
5. Water pump body
6. Lining
7. Impeller
8. Gaskets
9. Plate

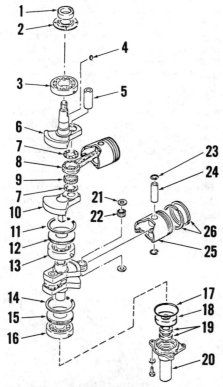

Fig. MR10-14—Exploded view of crankshaft assembly.

1. Seal
2. Plate
3. Ball bearing
4. Key
5. Crankpin
6. Crankshaft
7. Thrust washer
8. Connecting rod
9. Roller bearing
10. Crankshaft
11. Snap ring
12. Seal
13. Ball bearing
14. Snap ring
15. Seal
16. Ball bearing
17. "O" ring
18. Seal
19. Seals
20. Seal housing
21. Thrust washers
22. Needle bearing (25)
23. Piston pin clips
24. Piston pin
25. Piston
26. Piston rings

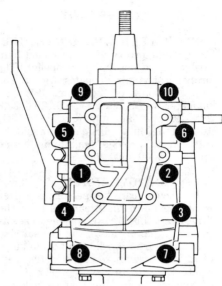

Fig. MR10-15 — Tighten crankcase screws in sequence shown above.

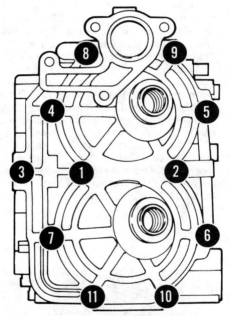

Fig. MR10-16 — Tighten cylinder head screws in sequence shown above.

ASSEMBLY. When reassembling, make sure all joints and gasket surfaces are clean, free from nicks and burrs and hardened cement or carbon. The crankcase and inlet manifold must be completely sealed against water leakage and pressure. Mating surfaces of water intake and exhaust areas between power head and drive shaft housing must form a tight seal.

Whenever the power head is disassembled, it is recommended that all gasket surfaces and mating surfaces without gaskets be carefully checked for nicks, burrs and warped surfaces which

might interfere with a tight seal. Cylinder head, cylinder block and crankcase should be checked on a surface plate and lapped if necessary to provide a smooth surface. Do not remove any more metal than is necessary.

All friction surfaces and needle bearings should be lubricated with engine oil during reassembly. Seals should be filled with a nonfibrous grease. Check frequently as power head is being assembled for binding of working parts. If binding or locking is encountered, correct cause before proceeding with assembly.

Cylinder block and crankcase cover mating surfaces must be thoroughly cleaned prior to reassembly. Apply a 1.6 mm (1/16 in.) bead of Loctite Master Gasket Sealer part 92-12564-1 to crankcase cover mating surface. All other gasket and sealing surfaces should be lightly and evenly coated with a suitable nonhardening gasket compound. Make sure entire surface is coated but avoid excess application. Tighten crankcase screws in sequence shown in Fig. MR10-15 and cylinder head screws in sequence shown in Fig. MR10-16. Tighten M6 crankcase screws to 10.8-12.7 N·m (8-9 ft.-lbs.) and M8 crankcase screws to 27.4-31.4 N·m (20-23 ft.-lbs.). Tighten cylinder head screws to 14.7-18.6 N·m (11-14 ft.-lbs.).

Before attaching power head to drive shaft housing, make certain drive shaft splines are clean then coat splines with a light coating of water-resistant grease. Tighten power head retaining screws to 13.7-21.5 N·m (10-16 ft.-lbs.).

CYLINDERS, RINGS AND PISTONS. Cylinder bores should be measured in several different locations to determine if an out-of-round or tapered condition exists. Bore and hone cylinder to fit an oversize piston and ring set if out-of-round or taper exceeds 0.07 mm (0.003 in.). Be sure to chamfer edges of ports in cylinder after boring to prevent rings from hanging up on sharp edges.

Recommended piston skirt to cylinder clearance is 0.035-0.040 mm (0.0014-

0.0016 in.). Recommended piston ring end gap is 0.15-0.35 mm (0.006-0.014 in.) for both rings. Top piston ring is chrome plated and has semi-keystone shape. Install piston rings with manufacturer's markings toward top of piston. Pistons and ring sets are available in 0.25 mm (0.010 in.) and 0.50 mm (0.020 in.) oversizes.

When reassembling, install new piston pin retaining clips (23—Fig. MR10-14) and make sure that "UP" on dome of piston is toward flywheel end of engine. Coat bearings, pistons, rings and cylinder bores with engine oil during reassembly.

CRANKSHAFT, BEARINGS AND RODS. The built-up crankshaft assembly should be checked for eccentricity at the main bearings while supported between lathe centers. Maximum allowable runout is 0.03 mm (0.0012 in). Check condition of large end rod bearing, crankpin and connecting rod by moving small end of rod back and forth. If an excessive amount of side to side shake (more than approximately 2 mm (0.078 in.) is found, renew crankshaft or disassemble and renew defective parts. Crankshaft should only be disassembled if the proper tools are available to correctly realign the unit.

When installing crankshaft, lubricate seals with a heat resistant nonfibrous grease and use engine oil on pistons, rings, cylinders and bearings. Use sequences shown in Figs. MR10-15 and MR10-16 to tighten cylinder head screws and crankcase screws. Tighten M6 crankcase screws to 10.8-12.7 N·m (8-9 ft.-lbs.) and M8 crankcase screws to 27.4-31.4 N·m (20-23 ft.-lbs.). Tighten cylinder head screws to 14.7-18.6 N·m (11-14 ft.-lbs.).

STARTER

MANUAL STARTER. Starter may be disassembled for overhaul or renewal of individual components as follows: Re-

Fig. MR10-17 — Diagram of crankcase breather system. Note difference in check valves which should be installed so flow through valve is as shown.

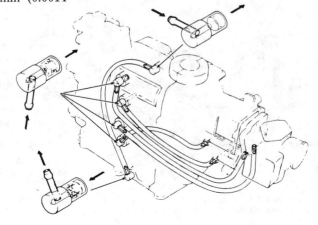

move engine top cowl and three bolts securing starter assembly to power head. Check pawl (10 – Fig. MR10-18) for wear of engagement area and freedom of movement. Renew or grease as necessary. Remove rope handle and allow rope to wind onto rope pulley (7). Remove screw (15) and shaft (13), then carefully lift rope pulley out of housing. Use caution when removing pulley to prevent injury from rewind spring flying out of housing. Broken rewind spring or

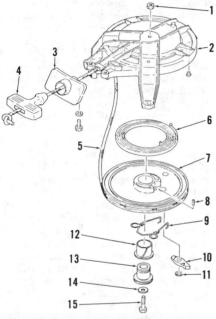

Fig. MR10-18 — Exploded view of manual starter.

1. Nut
2. Starter housing
3. Rope guide
4. Rope handle
5. Rope
6. Rewind spring
7. Rope pulley
8. Pin
9. Pawl spring
10. Pawl
11. "E" ring
12. Bushing
13. Shaft
14. Washer
15. Screw

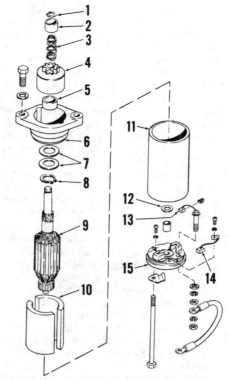

Fig. MR10-20 — Exploded view of electric starter used on some models.

1. Snap ring
2. Collar
3. Spring
4. Starter drive
5. Bushing
6. End frame
7. Washers
8. Snap ring
9. Armature
10. Magnets
11. Housing
12. Washer
13. Positive brush
14. Negative brush
15. End cap

rope may be renewed at this point. Rewind spring should be hooked in housing with coil winding clockwise from outer end. Wind rope onto pulley counterclockwise as viewed from bottom. Hook end of rope through notch in pulley leaving enough rope to attach rope handle. Assemble pulley to starter housing making sure that pin in drum engages eye in end of rewind spring. Install shaft (13) and retaining screw (15). Install spring (9) and pawl (10) as shown in Fig. MR10-19. Grasp end of rope and turn pulley three or four turns counterclockwise. Thread rope through starter housing and attach rope handle. All friction surfaces should be greased.

Adjust starter safety cable by turning adjusting nuts at cable end so starter will operate with outboard in neutral but not in forward or reverse gear.

ELECTRIC STARTER. Some models are equipped with the 12-volt electric starter shown in Fig. MR10-20.. Normal no-load current draw is 35 amperes. Minimum brush wear limit is 9.5 mm (3/8 in.).

LOWER UNIT

PROPELLER AND DRIVE HUB. Lower unit protection is provided by a cushion type hub in the propeller. The propeller has three blades with a 235 mm (9¼ in.) or 241 mm (9½ in.) diameter and a pitch of 165, 203, 229, 248, 267, or 305 mm (6½, 8, 9, 9¾, 10½ or 12 in.). Propeller should be selected to provide maximum engine speed of 4500-5500 rpm.

R&R AND OVERHAUL. Most lower unit service can be performed after removing lower unit gearcase from the drive shaft housing. Remove gearcase as follows: Clamp motor to a suitable stand, remove propeller and drain lubricant. Loosen shift rod locknut (N – Fig. MR10-21) and unscrew coupler (C) to disconnect upper shift rod from lower shift rod (3). Unscrew four screws and separate gearcase from drive shaft housing. Remove water pump assembly. Unscrew two cap screws securing bearing carrier (39 – Fig. MR10-22) then withdraw bearing carrier and propeller shaft assembly. Separate propeller shaft from bearing carrier. To remove clutch (28), detach spring clip (30) and drive out pin (29). Use a suitable puller to separate reverse gear (35) and bearing (37) from bearing carrier. Detach snap ring (22), remove pinion gear (21) and pull drive shaft (5) out of gearcase. Forward gear (27) may now be removed. Pry seal housing (9) free and remove along with sleeve (10). Drive bushing (19) down into gear cavity for removal. Unscrew retainer (1) and withdraw shift rod and cam (3).

Fig. MR10-19 — View showing proper installation of pawl spring (9), pawl (10) and "E" ring (11).

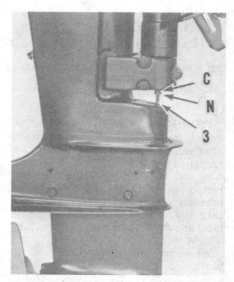

Fig. MR10-21 — Loosen locknut (N) and unscrew coupler (C) from lower shift rod (3) before removing gearcase.

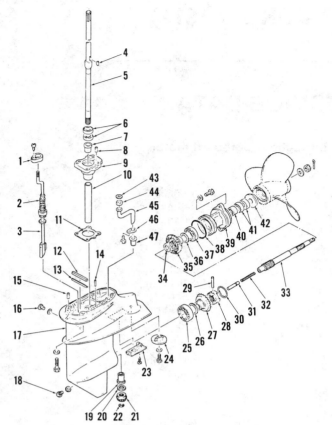

Fig. MR10-22 — Exploded view of gearcase.

1. Retainer
2. Boot
3. Shift rod & cam
4. Key
5. Drive shaft
6. Seals
7. Bushing
8. Dowel pin
9. Seal housing
10. Sleeve
11. Gasket
12. Seal
13. Retainer
14. Dowel pin
15. Dowel pin
16. Vent plug
17. Gearcase
18. Drain plug
19. Bushing
20. Shim
21. Pinion gear
22. Snap ring
23. Water inlet
24. Anode
25. Ball bearing
26. Shim
27. Forward gear
28. Clutch
29. Pin
30. Spring clip
31. Shift pin
32. Spring
33. Propeller shaft
34. Thrust washer
35. Reverse gear
36. Shim
37. Ball bearing
38. "O" ring
39. Bearing carrier
40. Needle bearing
41. Seals
42. Thrust hub

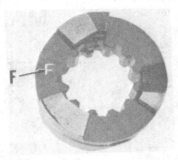

Fig. MR10-23 — Install clutch (28 — Fig. MR10-22) so (F) mark is towards forward gear.

Inspect shafts for wear on seal lip contact areas and on splines. Inspect dog clutch and gears for wear on engagement areas of dog teeth. Inspect gears for wear and damage. Inspect shift cam for excessive wear on ramp. All seals and "O" rings should be renewed when unit is assembled.

Gear backlash and mesh position should be checked on reassembly. Install forward gear (27) with original shim (26) in gearcase. Position pinion gear (21) with original shim (20) in gearcase then install drive shaft (5). Secure pinion gear to drive shaft with snap ring (22). Forward gear (27) and pinion gear (21) should mesh evenly when drive shaft (5) is pulled up and rotated. Adjust mesh position by varying thickness of shim (20). Gear backlash should be 0.1-0.3 mm (0.004-0.012 in.) and is adjusted using shims (26 and 36).

Reassemble gearcase by reversing disassembly procedure while noting the following: Install seals (6) in seal housing (9) so lips are towards top of housing. Install seals (41) in bearing carrier (39) so lips are towards propeller. Install clutch (28) so "F" marked side (see Fig. MR10-23) is toward forward gear. Apply a light coat of water-resistant grease to drive shaft upper splines.

With gearcase assembled and installed, synchronize gear engagement with gear selector handle by turning shift rod coupler (C – Fig. MR10-21), then tighten locknut (N) against coupler.

MARINER 15 HP (PRIOR TO 1979)

CONDENSED SERVICE DATA

NOTE: Metric fasteners are used throughout outboard motor.

TUNE-UP

Hp/rpm	15/5500
Bore	56 mm
Stroke	50 mm
Number of cylinders	2
Displacement	246 cc
Spark plug – NGK	B-7HS
Electrode gap	0.5-0.6 mm
Breaker point gap	0.3-0.4 mm
Ignition timing	See text
Idle speed	900-1000 rpm
Fuel:oil ratio	50:1

SIZES – CLEARANCES

Piston ring end gap	0.15-0.35 mm
Piston skirt clearance	0.030-0.035 mm
Crankshaft runout – max.	0.03 mm
Connecting rod small end shake –	
Standard	1.0 mm
Limit	2.0 mm
Lower unit gear backlash	0.1-0.3 mm

TIGHTENING TORQUES
(All values are in newton meters.)

Crankcase	
M6	10.8-12.7
M8	27.4-31.4
Cylinder head	
M6	10.8-12.7
M8	27.4-31.4
Flywheel	68.6-78.4
Standard screws	
5 mm	4.9-5.8
6 mm	7.9-9.8
8 mm	14.7-19.6

LUBRICATION

The power head is lubricated by oil mixed with the fuel. Fuel should be regular leaded, low lead or unleaded gasoline with a minimum pump octane rating of 86. Recommended oil is Quicksilver Formula 50-D Outboard Lubricant. Normal fuel:oil ratio is 50:1; during engine break-in fuel:oil ratio should be 25:1.

Lower unit gears and bearings are lubricated by oil contained in the gearcase. Recommended oil is Mariner Super Duty Gear Lube. Lubricant is drained by removing vent and drain plugs in the gearcase. Refill through drain plug hole until oil has reached level of top (vent) plug hole.

FUEL SYSTEM

CARBURETOR. An exploded view of carburetor is shown in Fig. MR9-1. Initial setting of pilot air screw (7) is 1¼ turns out from a lightly seated position. Set idle speed to 900-1000 rpm by turning idle speed screw (10) with motor running in gear at normal operating temperature.

Fuel level is checked by attaching a clear hose to the drain fitting in bottom of float bowl with outboard in an upright position. Run engine at idle speed for a few minutes then stop engine. Measure height of fuel level in hose from center of carburetor bore. Fuel level (L – Fig. MR9-2) should be 26-30 mm or approximately level with boss (B) on carburetor. Adjust fuel level by bending float arm.

SPEED CONTROL LINKAGE. The speed control is connected by cables to a pulley adjacent to the engine. Pulley movement is transferred by linkage to rotate the magneto base plate and actuate the carburetor throttle so ignition timing is advanced as the throttle opens.

Before adjusting speed control linkage, be sure ignition timing is correct as indicated in IGNITION section.

To adjust speed control linkage on early models, proceed as follows: Loosen lockscrew securing throttle link (22 – Fig. MR9-4) in arm (23) and back out idle speed screw (10 – Fig. MR9-1) until clearance exists between screw and throttle lever on carburetor. Turn idle speed screw (10) in until screw contacts lever, then turn screw an additional 2½ turns. With speed control handle completely in "Slow" speed position, tighten lockscrew to secure throttle link (22 – Fig. MR9-4) in arm (23). Adjust idle speed as outlined in CARBURETOR section.

To adjust speed control linkage on later models, proceed as follows: Turn control cable adjusters (11 – Fig. MR9-5) so control cable slack is 1-2 mm. Move speed control handle to full throttle position and rotate pulley (10) against stop of bracket (13), then adjust full throttle stop screw in speed control handle so bracket stop and speed control handle stop are contacted simultaneously at full throttle. With speed control handle in full throttle position, loosen lockscrew (17) and move carburetor throttle lever to full throttle position, then retighten lockscrew (17). Adjust idle speed as outlined in CARBURETOR section.

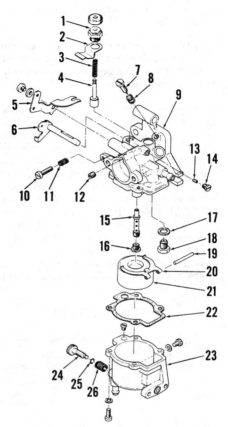

Fig. MR9-1 — Exploded view of carburetor.

1. Nut	14. Guide screw
2. Plate	15. Main nozzle
3. Spring	16. Main jet
4. Choke plunger	17. Gasket
5. Choke lever	18. Fuel inlet valve
6. Throttle shaft	19. Float arm pin
7. Pilot air screw	20. Float arm
8. Spring	21. Float
9. Body	22. Gasket
10. Idle speed screw	23. Float bowl
11. Spring	24. Drain screw
12. Low speed air jet	25. "O" ring
13. Low speed jet	26. Spring

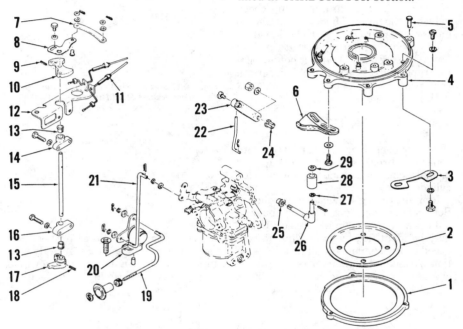

Fig. MR9-4 — View of speed control components used on early models.

1. Base plate retainer	9. Pin	16. Stay	23. Throttle arm
2. Retainer	10. Pulley	17. Neutral throttle stop	24. Bushing
3. Stop plate	11. Control cables	18. Pin	25. Bushing
4. Magneto base plate	12. Bracket	19. Starter control rod	26. Throttle spindle
5. Pivot pin	13. Bushing	20. Bellcrank	27. "E" ring
6. Throttle cam	14. Stay	21. Link	28. Roller
7. Link	15. Shaft	22. Throttle link	29. Washer
8. Lever			

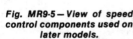

Fig. MR9-5 — View of speed control components used on later models.

1. Base plate retainer
2. Retainer
3. Stop plate
4. Magneto base plate
5. Nut
6. Swivel
7. Magneto control rod
8. Nut
9. Rod end
10. Pulley
11. Control cables
12. Bushing
13. Bracket
14. Sleeve
15. Throttle arm
16. Throttle link
17. Lockscrew
18. Swivel
19. Starter control rod
20. Bellcrank
21. Link

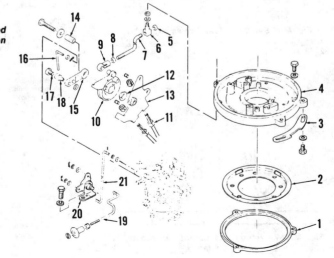

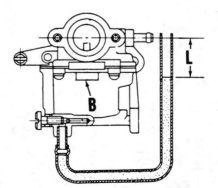

Fig. MR9-2 — Fuel level (L) should be 26-30 mm which is approximately even with boss (B).

REED VALVE. The reed valve assembly is located between the carburetor and crankcase. Inspect reed petals for cracks or signs of distortion. Do not attempt to straighten bent reed petals or reed stops. Reed stop height (A–Fig. MR9-7) should be 6.4-6.8 mm for all reed stops. Reed valve assembly (3–Fig. MR9-6) is available only as a unit assembly.

FUEL PUMP. The diaphragm type fuel pump is fitted to the port side of the power head. Refer to Fig. MR9-8 for an exploded view of fuel pump. Alternating pressure and vacuum in the crankcase actuates the diaphragm and check valves in the pump. Make certain that all gaskets, diaphragms and check valves are in good condition when reassembling unit. Coat gasket (1) with a nonhardening type gasket sealer making certain that passage in center is not plugged with gasket sealer.

IGNITION

A flywheel magneto is used with separate breaker points, condenser, primary coil and secondary coil for each cylinder.

Ignition timing is checked as follows: Set breaker point gap of top cylinder to 0.3-0.4 mm–top cylinder breaker points may be identified by gray wire. Rotate speed control handle to full throttle position. Attach an ohmmeter or continuity checker to gray wire of top cylinder

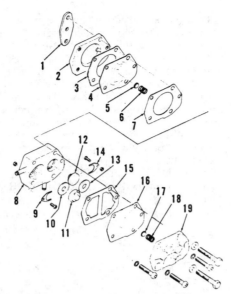

Fig. MR9-8—Exploded view of fuel pump. Diaphragms (4 and 16) are identical.

1. Gasket
2. Base
3. Gasket
4. Pump diaphragm
5. Spring plate
6. Spring
7. Gasket
8. Body
9. Retainer
10. Gasket
11. Outlet check valve
12. Inlet check valve
13. Gasket
14. Retainer
15. Gasket
16. Damper diaphragm
17. Spring plate
18. Spring
19. Cover

breaker points and note flywheel position when points open. Be sure flywheel timing mark for number 1 (top) cylinder is used. Flywheel timing mark should be

aligned with forward edge of stop bracket (8–Fig. MR9-14 or MR9-15). Adjust position of stop plate (3–Fig. MR9-4 or MR9-5) to adjust top cylinder ignition timing. Rotate flywheel so flywheel timing mark for number 2 (bottom) cylinder is aligned with stop bracket and adjust bottom cylinder timing by varying breaker point gap within range of 0.3-0.4 mm.

NOTE: Replacement flywheels do not have timing marks and must be marked according to piston position as outlined in following paragraph.

If ignition timing marks are questioned or a new flywheel is installed, piston position must be determined. Remove spark plugs and install a dial indicator in top cylinder's spark plug hole. Set top piston at 2.50 mm BTDC and mark flywheel adjacent to forward edge of stop bracket (8–Fig. MR9-14 or MR9-15). Attach dial indicator to bottom cylinder and mark flywheel in same manner with bottom piston at 2.50 mm BTDC.

When timing adjustment is completed, check speed control linkage adjustment as previously outlined.

COOLING SYSTEM

WATER PUMP. The water pump is mounted between the drive shaft housing and gearcase. Water pump impeller (7–Fig. MR9-10) is driven by a key in

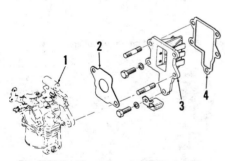

Fig. MR9-6 – View of read valve assembly.

1. Carburetor
2. Gasket
3. Reed valve assy.
4. Gasket

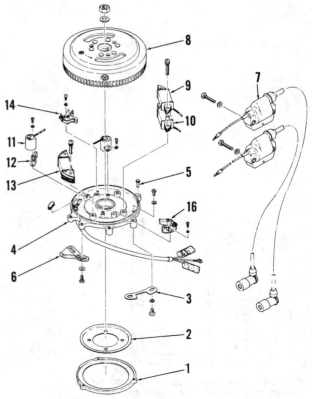

Fig. MR9-9—Exploded view of early type magneto. Later models are similar.

1. Base plate retainer
2. Retainer
3. Stop plate
4. Magneto base plate
5. Pivot pin
6. Throttle cam
7. Secondary coils
8. Flywheel
9. Primary coil–top cyl.
10. Primary coil–bottom cyl.
11. Condenser
12. Felt
13. Lighting coil
14. Breaker points–top cyl.
15. Breaker points–bottom cyl.

Fig. MR9-7 – Reed stop height (A) should be 6.4-6.8 mm.

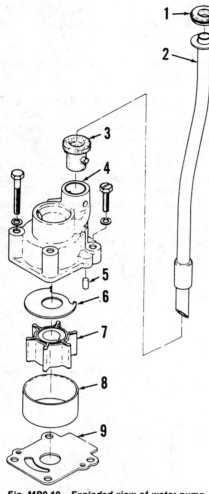

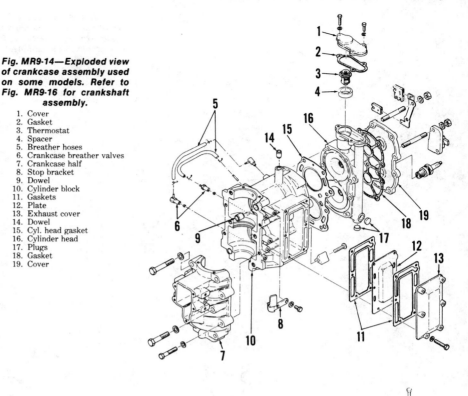

Fig. MR9-14—Exploded view of crankcase assembly used on some models. Refer to Fig. MR9-16 for crankshaft assembly.

1. Cover
2. Gasket
3. Thermostat
4. Spacer
5. Breather hoses
6. Crankcase breather valves
7. Crankcase half
8. Stop bracket
9. Dowel
10. Cylinder block
11. Gaskets
12. Plate
13. Exhaust cover
14. Dowel
15. Cyl. head gasket
16. Cylinder head
17. Plugs
18. Gasket
19. Cover

Fig. MR9-10—Exploded view of water pump.

1. Grommet
2. Water tube
3. Seal
4. Pump housing
5. Pin
6. Plate
7. Impeller
8. Liner
9. Plate

Fig. MR9-15—Exploded view of crankcase assembly used on some models. Refer to Fig. MR9-14 for parts identification. Refer to Fig. MR9-17 for view of crankshaft assembly.

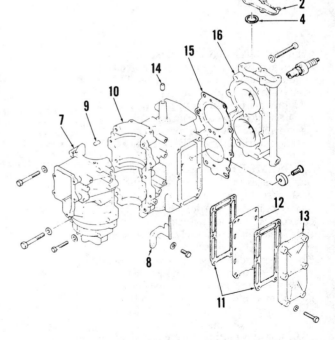

the drive shaft. Some early models and all later models are equipped with a thermostat (3 – Fig. MR9-14) located in the cylinder head.

When cooling system problems are encountered, first check water inlet for plugging or partial stoppage. On engines so equipped, be sure thermostat operates properly. If the water pump is suspected defective, separate gearcase from drive shaft housing and inspect pump. Impeller height should be 22 mm while impeller diameter should be 40 mm. Maximum axial clearance between impeller and pump housing is 0.33 mm. Apply nonhardening gasket sealer to mating surfaces of pump housing and plate (9 – Fig. MR9-10).

POWER HEAD

R&R AND OVERHAUL. The power head may be removed for service as follows: Remove engine cover and re-

wind starter assembly. Unscrew flywheel nut and use a suitable puller to remove flywheel. Disconnect speed control link from magneto base plate (4 – Fig. MR9-9) and remove magneto base plate assembly. Disconnect speed control cables from pulley (10 – Fig. MR9-4 or MR9-5). Remove carburetor, reed valve, fuel pump, fuel filter and ignition coils. Remove six screws securing

power head then separate power head from lower unit.

To disassemble power head, proceed as follows: Remove retainer (2 – Fig. MR9-4 and MR9-5) and base plate retainer (1). Unscrew nine stud nuts and remove cylinder head (16 – Fig. MR9-14 and MR9-15) and cover (19), if so equipped. Unscrew ten screws and separate crankcase half (7) from

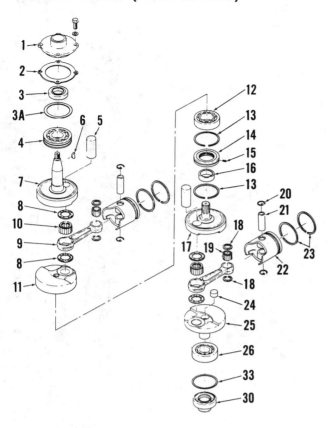

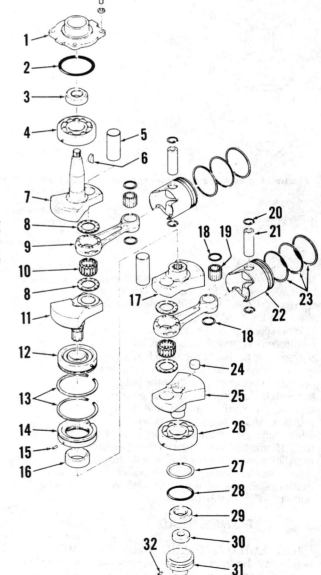

Fig. MR9-16—View of crankshaft used on some models. Refer to Fig. MR9-14 for crankcase assembly.

1. Seal housing
2. Gasket
3. Seal
3A. Shim
4. Bearing
5. Crankpin
6. Key
7. Crank half
8. Thrust washer
9. Connecting rod
10. Needle bearing
11. Crank half
12. Bearing
13. Snap ring
14. Seal
15. Pin
16. Collar
17. Crank half
18. Thrust washer
19. Needle bearing
20. Pin retainer clip
21. Piston pin
22. Piston
23. Piston rings
24. Plug
25. Crank half
26. Bearing
30. Seal
33. Shim

sequence to the final torque of 10.8-12.7 N·m for M6 screws and 27.4-31.4 N·m for M8 screws.

Coat drive shaft splines with water-resistant grease before installing assembled power head.

PISTONS, PINS, RINGS AND CYLINDERS. The engine may be equipped with pistons equipped with two or three piston rings depending on engine model. Piston ring end gap for all rings should be 0.15-0.35 mm with a maximum allowable piston ring end gap of 0.8 mm.

Piston skirt to cylinder clearance should be 0.030-0.035 mm. Measure piston diameter perpendicular to piston pin and approximately 10 mm from bottom of piston skirt.

cylinder block (10). Crankshaft and piston assembly may now be removed. If required, remove exhaust cover (13) and crankcase breather hoses.

Components may now be overhauled as outlined in the appropriate following paragraphs. Assemble power head as outlined in the ASSEMBLY paragraph.

ASSEMBLY. When reassembling power head make sure all joint and gasket surfaces are clean and free of nicks, burrs or hardened cement and carbon. All mating surfaces must form a tight seal on reassembly. All gaskets, seals and "O" rings should be renewed. Check cylinder head, cylinder head cover, if so equipped, and exhaust port cover for warpage on a surface plate and lap to smooth if warpage is detected. Do not remove any more metal than is necessary to obtain a smooth surface.

Gasket and mating surfaces should be coated with a nonhardening type gasket sealer. Avoid squeezing excess sealer into crankcase, bearing and water passages.

Tighten cylinder head and crankcase screws using sequences shown in Figs. MR9-18 and MR9-19. Tighten cylinder head and crankcase screws first to a torque that is half the desired final torque, and then repeat the tightening

Fig. MR9-17—View of crankshaft assembly used on some models with crankcase assembly shown in Fig. MR9-15. Refer to Fig. MR9-16 for parts identification except for:

27. Snap ring
28. "O" ring
29. Seal
31. Seal housing
32. Pin

Cylinders should be bored if tapered or out-of-round more than 0.07 mm. Pistons and piston rings are available in standard size and oversizes of 0.25 and 0.50 mm.

Piston pin diameter should be 15.995-16.000 mm while piston pin bore diameter should be 15.996-16.015 mm. Piston pin should be a snug fit in piston at room temperature.

Install piston so "UP" on piston crown is towards flywheel.

CONNECTING RODS, CRANK-SHAFT AND BEARINGS. The built-up crankshaft assembly should only be disassembled if the necessary tools and experience are available.

Maximum crankshaft runout measured at bearing outer races with crankshaft ends supported in lathe centers is 0.03 mm. Maximum connecting rod big end side clearance is 0.5 mm and maximum side to side shake measured at rod small end is 2.0 mm.

Crankshaft, connecting rods and center section components are available only as a unit assembly. Outer main bearings (4 and 26 – Fig. MR9-16 and MR9-17) are available individually.

Twenty-eight bearing rollers (19) are used in each connecting rod small end. Rollers may be held in place with petroleum jelly while installing piston.

Lubricate bearings, pistons, rings and cylinders with engine oil prior to installation. Tighten cylinder head screws in sequence shown in Fig. MR9-18 first to a torque that is half the desired final torque, and then repeat the tightening sequence to the final torque of 10.8-12.7 N·m for M9 screws and 27.4-31.4 N·m for M8 screws.

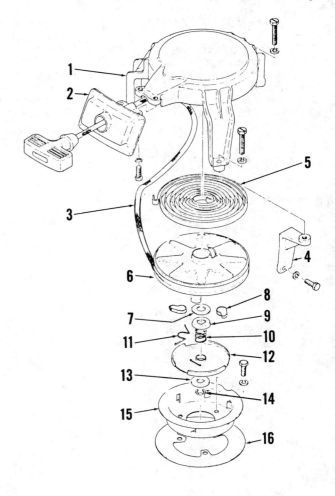

Fig. MR9-20—Exploded view of starter.

1. Housing
2. Rope guide
3. Rope
4. Bracket
5. Rewind spring
6. Rope pulley
7. Thrust washer
8. Pawls
9. Thrust washer
10. Drive plate spring
11. Pawl return spring
12. Drive plate
13. Washer
14. Snap ring
15. Starter cup
16. Cover

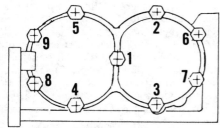

Fig. MR9-18—Tighten cylinder head screws in sequence shown above.

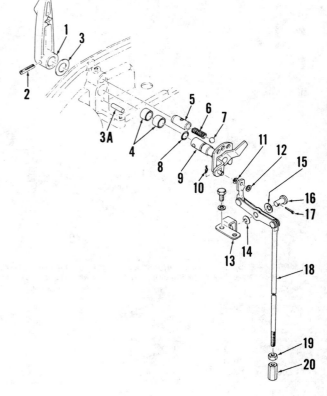

Fig. MR9-21—Exploded view of shift control linkage.

1. Handle
2. Pin
3. Washer
3A. Stop pin
4. Bushings
5. Spring guide
6. Spring
7. Detent ball
8. "O" ring
9. Lever
10. Clip
11. Wave washer
12. Washer
13. Bracket
14. Washer
15. Washer
16. Pin
17. Cotter pin
18. Upper shift rod
19. Locknut
20. Coupler

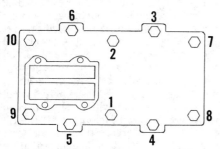

Fig. MR9-19—Tighten crankcase screws in sequence shown above.

MANUAL STARTER

Refer to Fig. MR9-20 for exploded view of rewind starter common to all models. Cover (16) and pulley (15) are bolted to the magneto flywheel.

Starter may be disassembled as follows: Remove starter housing (1) from power head and untie rope in starter handle. Slowly, allow rope to wind onto rope pulley (6). Turn housing upside down and remove snap ring (14) and thrust washer (13). Lift drive plate (12) and remove pawls (8) and pawl return springs (11). Carefully remove rope pulley assembly (6) to prevent re-wind spring (5) flying out of housing. Any part of the starter may be serviced or renewed at this point.

Reassemble as follows: Install rewind spring (5) in housing (1) beginning with outside coil of spring. Wind rope on pulley (6) two turns counterclockwise as viewed from bottom and bring rope through notch in pulley. Turn pulley five turns counterclockwise as viewed from bottom then feed end of rope through starter housing and attach handle. Assemble parts (7 through 11) and hook drive plate (12) in return springs (11). Turn drive plate approximately ½-turn counterclockwise and position it on rope pulley. Install thrust washer (13) and snap ring (14).

LOWER UNIT

PROPELLER AND SHEAR PIN. A shear pin as well as a rubber cushion in the propeller hub are used to provide protection for the lower unit. Standard propeller is a three bladed, right-hand rotation propeller with 234 mm diameter and 286 mm pitch. Optional propellers are available.

R&R AND OVERHAUL. Most service of the lower unit can be performed after removing lower unit gearcase from the drive shaft housing. Remove gearcase as follows: Clamp motor to a suitable stand, remove propeller and drain lubricant. Loosen shift rod locknut (19 – Fig. MR9-21) and unscrew coupler (20) to disconnect upper shift rod (18) from lower shift rod (3 or 3B – Fig. MR9-22) or connector (4). Unbolt gearcase from drive shaft housing and separate units. Remove water pump assembly. Unscrew three cap screws securing end cap (47) and bump cap with a soft faced hammer to remove. Pull propeller shaft (39) from gearcase if not removed with end cap. Detach snap ring (28), remove pinion gear (27) and pull drive shaft (9) from gearcase. Forward gear (32) may now be removed.

Unscrew shift rod retainer (1 or 5) on models so equipped, then unscrew detent screw (20) on all models. Withdraw shift rod cam (3, 3A and 3B).

Inspect bearings, splines, gears, clutch dogs and shaft surfaces. Bushings (14 and 25) should be inspected and renewed if worn or damaged. All seals and "O" rings should be renewed and coated with waterproof grease on reassembly.

Gear backlash and mesh position should be checked on reassembly. Install forward gear (32) with a shim (31) in gearcase. Position pinion gear (27) with shims (26) in gearcase then install drive shaft (9). Secure pinion gear to drive shaft with snap ring (28). Forward gear (32) and pinion gear (27) should mesh

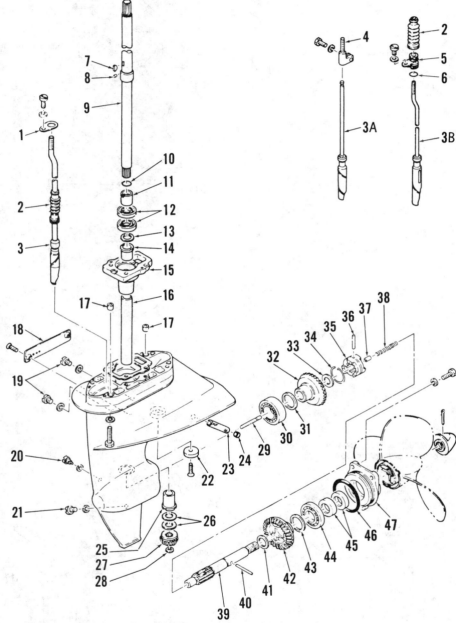

Fig. MR9-22 — Exploded view of gearcase. Note different types of lower shift rods (3, 3A and 3B) which have been used. Components (8, 10 and 11) are used on early models.

1. Retainer	12. Seals	24. Plug	36. Pin
2. Boot	13. Shim	25. Bushing	37. Spring guide
3, 3A & 3B. Lower shift rod	14. Bushing	26. Shims	38. Spring
4. Connector	15. Bushing housing	27. Pinion gear	39. Propeller shaft
5. Retainer	16. Tube	28. Snap ring	40. Shear pin
6. "O" ring	17. Dowel	29. Shift plunger	41. Thrust washer
7. Key	18. Water inlet cover	30. Bearing	42. Reverse gear
8. Pin	19. Vent plugs	31. Shim	43. Shim
9. Drive shaft	20. Detent screw	32. Forward gear	44. Bearing
10. "O" ring	21. Fill plug	33. Thrust washer	45. Seals
11. Sleeve	22. Anode	34. Clip	46. "O" ring
	23. Screen	35. Clutch dog	47. End cap

evenly when drive shaft (9) is pulled up and rotated. Adjust mesh position by varying thickness of shims (26). Gear backlash may be checked by running a piece of lead wire between pinion gear and forward gear while pulling up on drive shaft. Backlash is equal to twice thickness of crushed portion of lead wire. Forward gear backlash should be 0.1-0.3 mm and is adjusted by varying thickness of shim (31). Place thrust washers (33 and 41) and reverse gear (42) on propeller shaft. Use lead wire to determine backlash between pinion gear (27) and reverse gear (42) with end cap (47) torqued in position. Use shims (43) as required to set reverse gear backlash to 0.1-0.3 mm. Install shims (13) as re-

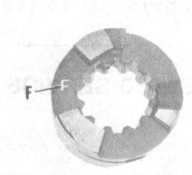

Fig. MR9-23 — Install clutch dog so (F) mark is towards forward gear.

quired so drive shaft end play is 0.5 mm or less.

Install seals (12) in bushing housing (15) so lips are toward top of housing. Install seals (45) in end cap (47) so lips are toward propeller side. Install clutch dog (35) so "F" marked side (see Fig. MR9-23) is toward forward gear (32 – Fig. MR9-22). Shift plunger (29) is installed with round end towards shift cam (3, 3A or 3B). Apply water-resistant grease to drive shaft upper splines.

With gearcase assembled and installed, synchronize gear engagement with gear selector handle by turning shift rod coupler (20 – Fig. MR9-21), then tighten locknut (19) against coupler.

MARINER 8 (1988 & 1989), 9.9 (1987-1989) AND 15 (1989) HP

CONDENSED SERVICE DATA

TUNE-UP

Hp/rpm 8/4500-5500
(11.2 kW)
9.9/5000-6000
(7.4 kW)
15/5000-6000
(11.2 kW)
Bore:
  8 and 9.9 Hp . . . . .2.125 in.
(53.97 mm)
  15 Hp . . . . .2.375 in.
(60.32 mm)
Stroke. . . . . .1.800 in.
(45.72 mm)
Number of Cylinders 2
Displacement:
  8 and 9.9 Hp . . . . .12.8 cu. in.
(209.7 cc)
  15 Hp . . . . .16.0 cu. in.
(262.2 cc)
Spark Plug:
  8 and 9.9 Hp . . . . .Champion L82YC*
    Electrode Gap . . . . .0.040 in.
(1.0 mm)
  15 Hp .NGK BP8HS*
    Electrode Gap . . . . .0.060 in.
(1.5 mm)
Ignition Type . . . . .CDI
Idle Speed (in gear) . . . . .700-750 rpm†
Fuel:Oil Ratio 50:1
Gearcase Oil Capacity . . . . .6.5 oz.
(200 mL)

*Models equipped with standard ignition coils only. Recommended spark plug for models equipped with high energy ignition coils is NGK BUHW surface gap spark plug.
†On models not equipped with idle speed screw, carburetor is factory calibrated to maintain 600-700 rpm idle speed in forward gear.

SIZES—CLEARANCES

Max. Allowable Cylinder Bore
  Out-of-Round . . . . .0.004 in.
(0.10 mm)
Max. Allowable Cylinder Bore
  Taper. . . . . .0.004 in.
(0.10 mm)
Standard Piston Diameter:
  8 and 9.9 Hp . . . . .2.123 in.
(53.92 mm)
  15 Hp . . . . .2.373 in.
(60.27 mm)

TIGHTENING TORQUES

Connecting Rod Cap . . . . .100 in.-lbs.
(11.3 N·m)
Crankcase Cover . . . . .200 in.-lbs.
(22.6 N·m)
Cylinder Block Cover . . . . .60 in.-lbs.
(6.8 N·m)
Exhaust Cover . . . . .60 in.-lbs.
(6.8 N·m)
Flywheel Nut. . . . . .50 ft.-lbs.
(67.8 N·m)
Flywheel Ring Gear (electric
  start models) . . . . .65 in.-lbs.
(7.3 N·m)
Power Head-to-Drive Shaft Housing
  Nuts and Screws . . . . .100 in.-lbs.
(11.3 N·m)
Reed Block . . . . .60 in.-lbs.
(6.8 N·m)
Transfer Port Cover . . . . .60 in.-lbs.
(6.8 N·m)

LUBRICATION

The power head is lubricated by oil mixed with the fuel. Recommended fuel is regular leaded or unleaded gasoline. Recommended oil is Quicksilver Premium Blend 2-Cycle Outboard Oil or a suitable NMMA certified TC-W or TC-WII engine oil. Fuel:oil ratio for normal service is 50:1.

Lower unit gears and bearings are lubricated by oil contained in the gearcase. Recommended oil is Quicksilver Premium Blend Gear Lube. Lower unit lubricant is drained by removing vent and drain plugs in the gearcase. Refill gearcase through drain plug hole until oil reaches level of vent plug hole. Gearcase capacity is approximately 6.5 ounces (200 mL).

FUEL SYSTEM

CARBURETOR. All models are equipped with the carburetor shown in Fig. MR11-1. Carburetor is equipped with integral fuel pump and diaphragm type primer system.

Standard main jet (3) size for normal service (sea level to 2500 feet [762 m] above sea level) is 0.046 inch (1.17 mm) on 8 hp models, 0.056 inch (1.42 mm) for 9.9 hp models and 0.066 inch (1.68 mm) for 15 hp models. Various jets are available for higher elevations or special conditions.

Initial setting of idle mixture screw (28) is 1-1/2 turns out from a lightly seated position. Perform final idle mixture adjustment with primer knob pushed fully in, engine running at operating temperature and in forward gear. On models so equipped, remove plug in air intake cover for access to idle mixture screw. On models equipped with idle speed screw (16), adjust idle speed to 700-750 rpm in forward gear. On models without idle speed screw, carburetor is calibrated at the factory to provide 600-700 rpm idle speed.

To check float level, remove float bowl (4) and invert carburetor. Measure from boss on carburetor body to top of float as shown in Fig. MR11-2. Bend float arm (9) to adjust distance (D) to one inch (25.4 mm).

FUEL PUMP. Refer to Fig. MR11-1 for exploded view of integral fuel pump assembly and Fig. MR11-3 for view of later design fuel pump. Renew pump gaskets and diaphragm if pump is dis-

assembled. If performing carburetor service, do not disassemble fuel pump unless pump service is necessary. Note that fuel pump assembly can be overhauled without carburetor removal.

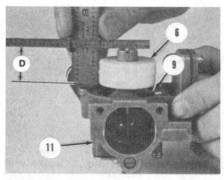

Fig. MR11-2—With carburetor body (1) inverted, distance (D) should be one inch (25.4 mm) when measured as shown. Bend float arm (9) to adjust float (6) height.

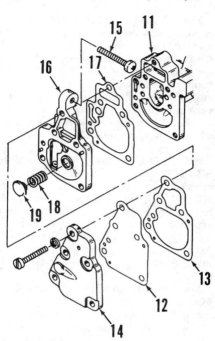

Fig. MR11-3—Exploded view of second design fuel pump.

11. Carburetor body	
12. Diaphragm	
13. Gasket	16. Pump body
14. Cover	17. Gasket
15. Maximum advance	18. Spring
adjustment screw	19. Cap

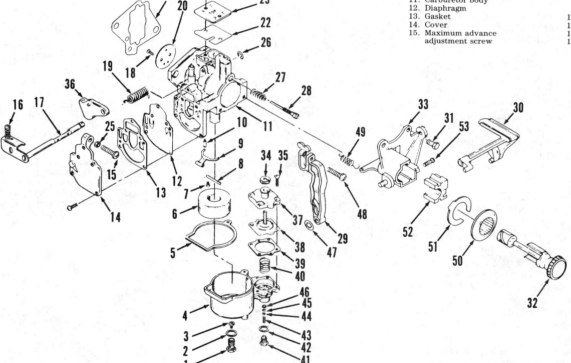

Fig. MR11-1—Exploded view of carburetor with integral fuel pump and primer system used on all models. Note that idle speed screw (16) is absent on some models.

1. Float bowl retainer	15. Maximum spark advance adjustment screw	26. Retaining clip
2. Gasket		27. Spring
3. Main jet	16. Idle speed screw (models so equipped)	28. Low speed mixture screw
4. Float bowl		29. Fast idle cam
5. Gasket	17. Throttle shaft	30. Primer lever
6. Float	18. Screw	31. Screw
7. Screw	19. Spring	32. Primer knob
8. Pin	20. Throttle valve	33. Bracket
9. Float arm	21. Gasket	34. Seal
10. Inlet needle	22. Gasket	35. Screw
11. Body	23. Cover	36. Throttle cam
12. Check valve diaphragm	24. Screw	37. Cover
13. Gasket	25. Nut	38. Primer diaphragm
14. Cover		39. Gasket

40. Spring
41. Plug
42. Gasket
43. Spring
44. Check ball
45. Retainer
46. Seat
47. Retainer
48. Screw
49. Spring
50. Bezel
51. Retainer
52. Cam block
53. Screw

FUEL FILTER. A fuel filter assembly is connected between fuel supply line and fuel pump inlet fitting. With engine stopped, occasionally unscrew fuel filter cup from filter base and withdraw rubber washer and filter element. Clean cup and filter element in a suitable solvent and dry with compressed air. If excessive filter element blockage or damage is noted, renew element.

REED VALVE. Reed valve assembly is located between the carburetor and crankcase/intake manifold (1—Fig. MR11-4). Renew cracked, warped, chipped or bent reed petals (8). Do not attempt to straighten or repair bent or damaged reed petals. Never turn used reed petals over for reuse. Do not remove reed petals unless renewal is required.

Reed petals should seat smoothly against reed block along their entire length but not be preloaded against reed block or stand open more than 0.007 inch (0.18 mm). Reed stop opening (O— Fig. MR11-5) should be 7/32 inch (5.6 mm) on 8 and 9.9 hp models and 19/64 inch (7.5 mm) on 15 hp models. Check reed stop opening by inserting an appropriate size drill bit between tip of stops and reed block. Carefully bend reed stops to adjust.

When reassembling reed valve assembly, tighten screws (6) to 20 in.-lbs. (2.3 N·m). Seal ends (S) of rubber seal (5) with Quicksilver RTV part 91-91600-1 or a suitable equivalent sealant. Lubricate rubber seal (5) with a suitable needle bearing assembly grease and tighten reed block mounting screws (10—Fig. MR11-4) to 60 in.-lbs. (6.8 N·m).

SPEED CONTROL LINKAGE. To synchronize ignition timing and throttle opening, proceed as follows: Mount outboard motor on a boat or a suitable test tank and immerse lower unit. Check tiller handle cable adjustment in forward and reverse gears. Adjust cable jam nuts to remove any slack in cable. On models equipped with an idle speed screw, back off screw so throttle valve is completely closed. Turn idle screw back in until screw contacts throttle cam, then an additional 1/2 turn clockwise. To check maximum advance timing, connect a suitable timing light to number 1 (top) spark plug lead. With outboard motor in forward gear running at wide open throttle, timing pointer (Fig. MR11-6) should be aligned with three dots (36 degrees BTDC) on flywheel. To adjust maximum advance, turn screw (1—Fig. MR11-7) as necessary to align three dots with timing pointer at full throttle. To adjust idle speed timing, push primer knob fully in and rotate knob fully counterclockwise.

With engine running at idle speed in forward gear, timing pointer should be aligned with two dots (6 degrees BTDC) on flywheel. Turn screw (3) as necessary to adjust.

To adjust idle wire, push primer knob in and rotate knob fully counterclockwise. Shift into neutral and turn screw (4) until all clearance is removed between idle wire (5) and CDI trigger assembly. Adjust idle speed screw (on models so equipped) so engine idles at 700-750 rpm in forward gear.

IGNITION

All models are equipped with an alternator driven, capacitor discharge ignition (CDI) system. Major components include the flywheel, stator assembly, trigger coil, switch box, ignition coils and spark plugs.

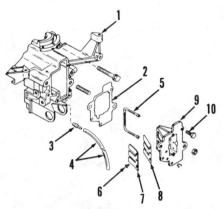

Fig. MR11-4—Exploded view of crankcase/intake manifold, reed valve assembly and related components.

1. Crankcase/intake manifold
2. Gasket
3. Check valve
4. Bleed hose
5. Rubber seal
6. Screw
7. Reed stop
8. Reed petals
9. Reed block
10. Screw

The flywheel contains two sets of magnets (Fig. MR11-8). The outer magnets induce voltage into the low and high speed charge coils in the stator assembly. This voltage charges and is stored in the capacitor located in the switch box. The low speed charge coil operates at engine speeds up to approximately 1700-1800 rpm, and the high speed charge coil begins operation at speeds of approximately 1800 rpm and above. The inner flywheel magnets induce voltage into the trigger coil which actuates the SCR switches (silicon controlled rectifier) inside the switch box. The SCR switches trigger the capacitor to discharge the stored voltage to the primary windings of the ignition coils. The ignition coils then amplify this voltage to a value sufficient to jump the spark plug gap. Ignition timing is advanced or retarded by rotating the trigger coil in relation to the inner flywheel magnets. The engine is shut down by shorting stator output to ground by the stop or ignition switch. The components

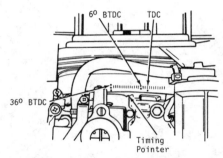

Fig. MR11-6—View of timing pointer and flywheel timing marks. Three dots on flywheel is 36 degrees BTDC (maximum advance), two dots is 6 degrees BTDC (idle speed timing) and single dot is TDC. Note that each increment on flywheel equals 2 degrees.

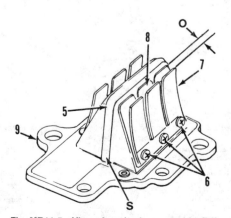

Fig. MR11-5—View of reed valve assembly. Refer to Fig. MR11-4 for component identification. Reed stop opening (O) should be 7/32 inch (5.6 mm) on 8 and 9.9 hp models and 19/64 inch (7.5 mm) on 15 hp model. Refer to text.

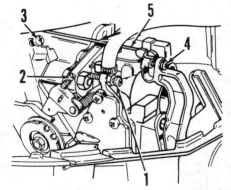

Fig. MR11-7—Refer to text to adjust speed control linkage.

1. Maximum advance screw
2. Idle speed screw
3. Idle speed timing screw
4. Idle wire screw
5. Idle wire

contained in the switch box are not serviceable separately. If switch box malfunction is evident, switch box must be renewed.

If engine malfunction is noted, and the ignition system is suspected, make sure the spark plugs and all electrical wiring are in acceptable condition and all electrical connections are clean and tight prior to trouble-shooting the CDI system.

To properly test the switch box and ignition coils require the use of Quicksilver Multi-Meter DVA Tester part 91-99750 or a suitable voltmeter capable of measuring a minimum of 400 DC volts used with Quicksilver Direct Voltage Adaptor (DVA) part 91-89045. Follow instructions provided by tester manufacturer when performing tests. If these testers are not available, a process of elimination must be used when testing the ignition system. Stator and trigger assemblies can be effectively tested using a suitable ohmmeter.

NOTE: All tests that involve cranking or running the engine must be performed with lead wires connected. Switch box case must be grounded to engine for all tests or switch box may be damaged.

To test ignition system, proceed as follows:

IGNITION COILS. Connect DVA red test lead to ignition coil negative (–) terminal and black test lead to coil positive (+) terminal. Position tester selector switch to 400 VDC. Tester should read 100-250 volts at cranking or idle speed (300-1000 rpm) and 150-300 volts at 1000-4000 rpm. If voltage readings are below specified reading, refer to SWITCH BOX STOP CIRCUIT test. If readings are within specifications, connect a suitable spark tester to ignition coil high tension lead, crank engine and

note spark. If weak or no spark is noted, renew ignition coil(s). If normal spark is noted, renew spark plugs. If malfunction is still evident after renewing spark plugs, check ignition timing. If ignition timing is erratic, inspect trigger advance linkage for excessive wear or damage and inner flywheel magnets (shifted position or other damage). If timing is within specifications, problem is not in ignition system.

SWITCH BOX STOP CIRCUIT. Connect DVA red test lead to engine ground and black test lead to black/yellow switch box terminal. Refer to Fig. MR11-9. Set DVA selector switch to 400 VDC. Voltage reading at cranking and all running speeds should be 200-360 volts. If reading is within specifications, refer to STATOR tests. If reading is above specified voltages, connect a suitable ohmmeter between trigger brown/yellow and brown/white leads. Trigger resistance should be 650-850 ohms. If not, renew trigger assembly. If trigger resistance is acceptable, renew switch box and repeat SWITCH BOX STOP CIRCUIT test. If SWITCH BOX STOP CIRCUIT test reading is below specified voltage, disconnect ignition switch, stop switch and mercury switch from black/yellow switch box terminal (orange switch box terminal on early models). Note that black/yellow stator lead must remain connected to switch box. With stop switch, ignition switch and mercury switch isolated, repeat SWITCH BOX STOP CIRCUIT test. If reading is now within specification, ignition switch, stop switch or mercury switch is defective. If reading remains below specification refer to STATOR test.

STATOR. Connect DVA red lead to engine ground and black lead to black/yellow switch box terminal. Set

DVA selector switch to 400 VDC. Voltage reading should be 200-360 volts at all speeds (cranking speed to 4000 rpm). Switch DVA black test lead to black/white switch box terminal. Leave red test lead connected to engine ground. Voltage reading should be 10-100 volts at cranking or idle speeds and 100-300 volts at 1000-4000 rpm.

If either STATOR test is not to specification, proceed as follows: Connect a suitable ohmmeter between black/white stator lead and engine ground. Make sure stator is properly grounded to engine. Resistance should be 120-180 ohms. Connect ohmmeter between black/yellow stator lead and engine ground. Resistance should be 3200-3800 ohms. Connect ohmmeter between black/yellow and black/white stator leads. Resistance should be 3100-3700 ohms. Renew stator if resistance is not as specified. If stator resistance is as specified, renew switch box and repeat STATOR tests.

IGNITION COILS. Disconnect wires and high tension lead from coil. Connect a suitable ohmmeter between coil positive (+) and negative (–) terminals. Resistance should be 0.02-0.04 ohm. Connect ohmmeter between coil high tension terminal and negative (–) terminal. Resistance should be 800-1100 ohms. Renew ignition coil(s) if resistance is not as specified.

NOTE: Ignition coil resistance tests can only detect open or shorted windings. If coil resistance is within specification and still suspected as defective, coil must be tested using DVA meter as previously outlined in IGNITION COIL test. If DVA meter is not available, substitute a known good ignition coil and run engine to test.

B/W. Black with white tracer
B/Y. Black with yellow tracer
G/W. Green with white tracer
G/Y. Green with yellow tracer
Br/W. Brown with white tracer
Br/Y. Brown with yellow tracer

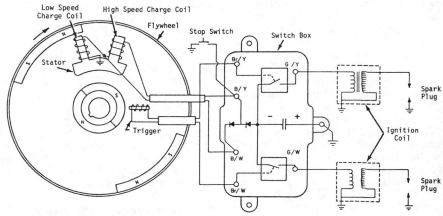

Fig. MR11-8—View identifying CDI ignition system components and wiring.

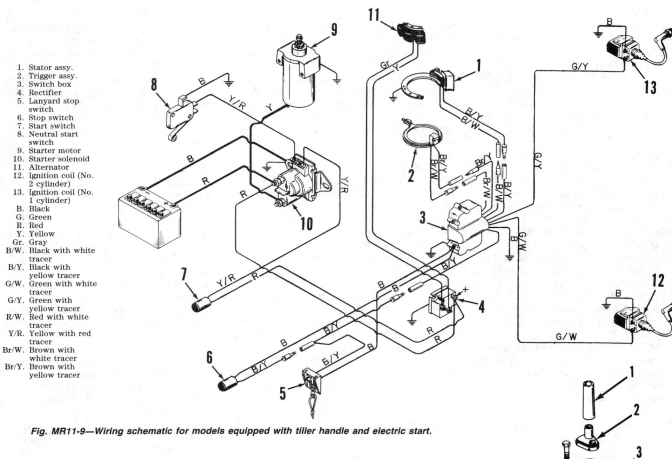

1. Stator assy.
2. Trigger assy.
3. Switch box
4. Rectifier
5. Lanyard stop switch
6. Stop switch
7. Start switch
8. Neutral start switch
9. Starter motor
10. Starter solenoid
11. Alternator
12. Ignition coil (No. 2 cylinder)
13. Ignition coil (No. 1 cylinder)
B. Black
G. Green
R. Red
Y. Yellow
Gr. Gray
B/W. Black with white tracer
B/Y. Black with yellow tracer
G/W. Green with white tracer
G/Y. Green with yellow tracer
R/W. Red with white tracer
Y/R. Yellow with red tracer
Br/W. Brown with white tracer
Br/Y. Brown with yellow tracer

Fig. MR11-9—Wiring schematic for models equipped with tiller handle and electric start.

COOLING SYSTEM

WATER PUMP. A rubber impeller type water pump is mounted between the drive shaft housing and gearcase. Water pump impeller (4—Fig. MR11-10) is driven by key (5).

If cooling system malfunction is encountered, first inspect water inlets for plugging or partial restriction. Check thermostat (if so equipped) for proper operation. Remove lower unit gearcase to inspect water pump assembly. Note that cover (3) secures drive shaft in gearcase. Make sure all seals and mating surfaces are in good condition and water passages are unobstructed. Inspect plate (6), impeller (4) and cover (3) for excessive wear. The manufacturer recommends renewing impeller (4) if removed.

Install seal (9) into base (11) with lip facing down and seal (8) with lip facing up. Lubricate seals (15, 12, 2) and inside of housing (3) with Quicksilver 2-4-C Marine Lubricant during reassembly. Rotate drive shaft clockwise when installing cover (3) over impeller (4). Avoid turning drive shaft in opposite direction after reassembly. Apply Loctite 271 to threads of cover (3) screws and tighten screws (3) to 40 in.-lbs. (4.5 N·m).

THERMOSTAT. Some models are equipped with a thermostat (20—Fig. MR11-11) located under cover (23). Thermostat should begin to open at approximately 120° F (49° C). Renew thermostat if it fails to fully open at the specified temperature.

POWER HEAD

REMOVE AND REINSTALL. To remove power head, remove rewind starter and electric starter if so equipped. Using a suitable puller, remove flywheel and ignition components that will interfere with power head removal. Disconnect speed control cables, remove carburetor and reed valve assembly. Remove four screws and two nuts securing power head to drive shaft housing, remove power head and place on a bench or mount on a suitable holding fixture.

Renew gasket (12—Fig. MR11-11) when reinstalling power head. Apply Loctite 680 retaining compound to threads of power head mounting screws and studs and tighten to 120 in.-lbs. (13.6 N·m). Complete remainder of reassembly by reversing removal procedure.

DISASSEMBLY. Remove thermostat cover (23—Fig. MR11-11) and ther-

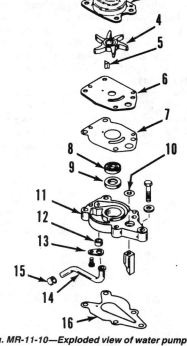

Fig. MR-11-10—Exploded view of water pump assembly.

1. Water tube guide
2. Seal
3. Cover
4. Impeller
5. Key
6. Plate
7. Plate
8. Seal
9. Seal
10. "O" ring
11. Base
12. Seal
13. Retainer
14. Pickup tube
15. Seal
16. Gasket

mostat (20) on models so equipped. Remove cylinder block cover (19), outer exhaust cover (1), inner exhaust cover (4) and transfer port cover (17). Remove six screws securing crankcase (5) to cylinder block (15). Break crankcase seal by tapping crankcase with a soft-face mallet and lift off crankcase. Crankshaft assembly can now be removed for overhaul. Mark all wearing components for location and direction for reference during reassembly. Refer to the appropriate service sections when reassembling crankshaft, pistons and connecting rods.

REASSEMBLY. Renew all seals and gaskets during reassembly. The manufacturer recommends renewing connecting rod bearings and rod cap screws during reassembly. Make sure all joints and gasket surfaces are clean and free from nicks and burrs. Note that crankcase and cylinder block are a matched set and if necessary, must be renewed as an assembly. All friction surfaces should be lubricated with a recom-

mended engine oil during reassembly. Apply Loctite 271 or a suitable thread locking compound to threads of all fasteners securing moving or rotating components, and to outer diameter of all metal-cased seals. Check crankshaft rotation frequently during reassembly for binding or unusual noise. If binding or noise is noted, power head must be disassembled and repaired prior to proceeding with reassembly.

Crankcase and cylinder block mating surfaces must be thoroughly cleaned using Loctite Primer T, lacquer thinner or acetone. Do not clean with petroleum based solvent. Apply a continuous 1/16 inch (1.6 mm) bead of Loctite Master Gasket Sealer part 92-12564-1 to crankcase mating surface. Sealer should be run on inside of all screw holes. Tighten all fasteners in three progressive steps. Refer to CONDENSED SERVICE DATA for final torque specifications. Refer to Figs. MR11-13, MR11-14 and MR11-15 for recommended fastener tightening sequences on crankcase, exhaust cover and cylinder block cover.

CYLINDERS, RINGS AND PISTONS. Make sure all wearing components are marked for location and direction prior to reassembly. Measure cylinder bore at top, center and bottom of piston ring travel. Take two measurements at each location 90 degrees to each other. Renew cylinder block and crankcase assembly if cylinder bore is tapered or out-of-round in excess of 0.004 inch (0.10 mm). Refer to CONDENSED SERVICE DATA for standard bore diameter.

NOTE: Cylinder sleeves and cylinder heads are cast into the cylinder block. If a cylinder is out-of-round or tapered more than 0.004 inch (0.10 mm), or if excessive scoring is noted, the cylinder block and crankcase must be renewed.

Measure piston diameter 0.10 inch (2.5 mm) up from bottom of skirt at a right angle to piston pin bore. Piston-to-cylinder bore clearance should be 0.002-0.005 inch (0.05-0.13 mm). Refer to CONDENSED SERVICE DATA for standard piston diameter. Piston and pin are available as an assembly only. Renew piston pin retainers (20—Fig. MR11-12) during reassembly. Piston pin rides on 24 loose bearing rollers (18). Install piston on connecting rod so long sloping side of crown will face toward exhaust ports.

Install piston rings with end gaps 180 degrees apart and aligned with piston pin bore.

CRANKSHAFT, BEARINGS AND CONNECTING RODS. All wearing components must be installed in same location and direction as removed. The manufacturer recommends renewing connecting rod bearings (5 and 6—Fig. MR11-12) and rod cap screws (9) if removed. Apply Loctite 271 to threads of screws (9). Do not remove bearing (10) unless renewal is required. Lubricate rod and main bearings with Quicksilver Needle Bearing Assembly Grease during reassembly. Install connecting rods on crankshaft so lobe side of rod faces flywheel (up). Tighten rod cap screws (9) to 100 in.-lbs. (11.3 N·m). Chamfered side of retaining ring (12) should face away from bearing (10).

On 15 hp models, install center main bearing outer race (25) with retainer ring groove toward flywheel end of engine. Make sure retaining ring (24) overlaps both race fracture lines. When installing crankshaft assembly into cylinder block, make sure hole in center main bearing race properly engages pin in cylinder block.

On all models, make sure alignment boss on upper bearing (2) properly engages notch in cylinder block. On 8 and

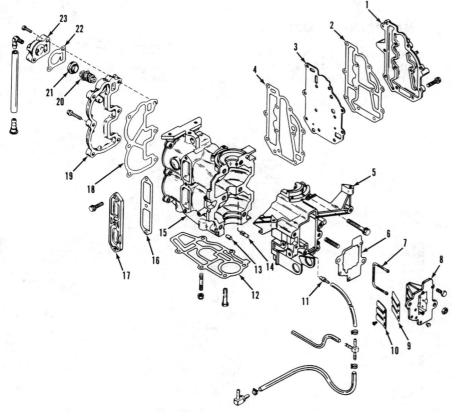

Fig. MR11-11—Exploded view of cylinder block, crankcase and related components.

1. Exhaust cover
2. Gasket
3. Exhaust manifold
4. Gasket
5. Crankcase/intake manifold
6. Gasket
7. Seal
8. Reed block
9. Reed petals
10. Reed stop
11. Check valve
12. Gasket
13. Dowel pin
14. Groove pin (15 hp models only)
15. Cylinder block
16. Gasket
17. Transfer port cover
18. Gasket
19. Cylinder block cover
20. Thermostat
21. Grommet
22. Gasket
23. Thermostat cover

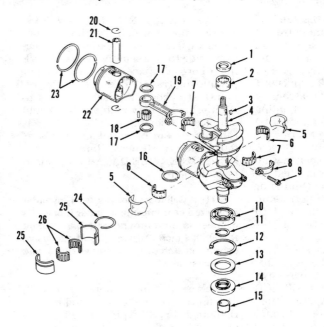

Fig. MR11-12—Exploded view of crankshaft, connecting rods and pistons assembly.

1. Seal
2. Upper main bearing
3. Key
4. Crankshaft
5. Bearing sleeve (except 15 hp models)
6. Center main bearing half
7. Connecting rod bearing half
8. Connecting rod cap
9. Screw
10. Lower main bearing
11. Snap ring
12. Retaining ring
13. Stuffer washer
14. Seal
15. Coupling seal
16. Seal ring
17. Washer
18. Needle rollers
19. Connecting rod
20. Retaining ring
21. Piston pin
22. Piston
23. Piston rings
24. Retaining ring (15 hp models)
25. Bearing race (15 hp models)
26. Center main bearing (15 hp models)

remove three screws and lift starter assembly from power head.

To renew starter rope, pull out rope approximately one foot (30.5 cm) and secure with a knot. Remove retainer (12) and handle (11). Extend rope completely and hold pulley (9) securely. Invert starter and pull out remainder of rope from pulley side of starter. Cut new rope to a length of 66 inches (168 cm) and affix handle (11) and retainer (12) to end of rope. Rotate pulley (9) counterclockwise until rewind spring (7) is wound tight, then carefully allow pulley to back off until knot recess (19) is aligned with rope hole in housing (1).

9.9 hp models, make sure split lines of center main bearing sleeves (5) are aligned when installing crankcase.

MANUAL STARTER

To remove starter, pry fuel filter from rope handle support (2—Fig. MR11-16), disconnect interlock rod from arm (15),

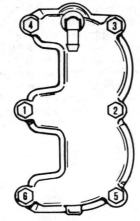

Fig. MR11-15—Tighten cylinder block cover screws in sequence shown.

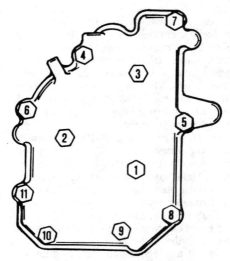

Fig. MR11-13—Tighten crankcase screws in sequence shown.

Fig. MR11-16—Exploded view of manual rewind starter.

1. Housing
2. Handle support
3. Bushing
4. Retainer ring
5. Rope guide
6. Support plate
7. Rewind spring & case assy.
8. Cap
9. Rope pulley
10. Rope
11. Handle
12. Rope retainer
13. Lock lever
14. Washer
15. Arm
16. Cover
17. Tab
18. Screw
19. Knot recess

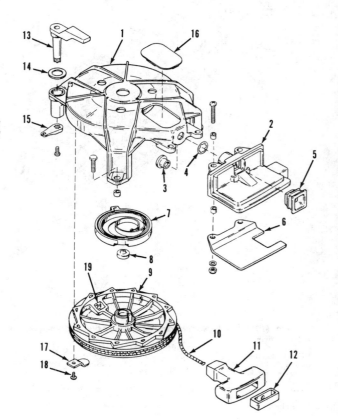

Fig. MR11-14—Tighten outer exhaust cover screws in sequence shown.

Thread new rope through housing (1), pulley (9), secure with a suitable knot and pull knot into recess (19). Slowly allow rope to rewind onto pulley (9).

To overhaul starter, remove rope as previously outlined. With rope removed, slowly allow pulley (9) to unwind relieving rewind spring (7) tension. Loosen three screws to allow retainer tabs (17) to rotate away from pulley (9). Carefully lift pulley (9) out of housing (1). Insert a suitable tool into hole in top of housing and push rewind spring and case (7) from housing (1). Insert a punch into pulley center hole and drive out cap (8). Pry oil seal (not shown) from pulley (9) center hole.

Inspect all components for excessive wear or damage. If starter operation was erratic or excessively noisy, inspect starter clutch for lack of lubrication, excessive wear or other damage. Note that pulley (9) and clutch are available as a unit assembly only.

Reassemble by reversing order of disassembly. Lubricate rewind spring with a suitable low-temperature grease. Install rope as previously outlined.

ELECTRIC STARTER

Some models are equipped with a 12-volt electric starter. Armature and drive components are shown in Fig. MR11-17. Disassembly is evident after inspection of unit. Minimum brush length is 3/16 inch (4.8 mm). Lightly lubricate helical threads on armature shaft and drive end bushing with SAE 10W oil during reassembly.

The recommended battery for electric start models is 12 volts with a minimum of 180 cold cranking amps and 35 minutes reserve capacity. Charge or renew battery if voltage drops below 9.5 volts under cranking load.

CHARGING SYSTEM

Alternator output should be 3.5-4.5 amperes measured at battery. To test alternator, disconnect gray and yellow alternator leads at rectifier. Refer to Fig. MR11-9. Connect a suitable ohmmeter between gray and yellow leads. Resis-

tance should be approximately 0.65 ohm. Connect ohmmeter between ground (or alternator frame if removed) and gray lead then yellow lead. No continuity should exist between gray or yellow alternator leads and ground.

Rectifier can be tested without removal from power head. Disconnect all leads from rectifier terminals. Calibrate ohmmeter to R × 1000 ohms scale. To test rectifier, connect ohmmeter between ground (D—Fig. MR11-18) and terminal (A) then terminal (B). Reverse ohmmeter leads and retest. Ohmmeter should show continuity in one test and no continuity in other test. Next, connect ohmmeter between terminal (C) and alternately to terminals (A and B). Note reading then reverse leads and repeat test. Ohmmeter should show continuity on one test and no continuity in other test.

LOWER UNIT

PROPELLER AND DRIVE HUB. Lower unit protection is provided by a cushion type hub in the propeller. The standard propeller is three bladed with diameter of nine inches (228.6 mm). Standard propeller pitch is 9 inches (228.6 mm) on 8 and 9.9 hp models and 10.5 inches (266.7 mm) on 15 hp models. Optional propellers are available. Select a propeller that will allow a properly tuned and adjusted engine to operate within the specified rpm range at full throttle. Refer to CONDENSED SERVICE DATA for recommended full throttle rpm range.

NOTE: The manufacturer recommends propping outboard motor to operate at or near the high end of the recommended rpm range at full throttle.

R&R AND OVERHAUL. Mount outboard motor in a suitable holding fixture. Disconnect and ground spark plug leads, shift motor into forward gear and tilt motor to full up position. Refer to Fig. MR11-20 and disconnect shift shaft (3). Remove reverse lock actuator (4—Fig. MR11-19) and remove three screws securing gearcase assembly to drive shaft housing. Secure gearcase into a

suitable holding fixture and drain lower unit lubricant. Unscrew bearing carrier (26) using Tool 91-13664. Note that carrier has left-hand threads.

NOTE: The four slots in Tool 91-13664 must be widened by 1/8 inch (3.2 mm) to function properly on these models. Original width of slots is 5/16 inch (7.9 mm) and should be enlarged to 7/16 inch (11.1 mm) wide.

If Bearing Carrier Tool 91-13664 is not available, separate cap (31) from thrust hub (30) with a hammer. Install thrust hub on shaft and tighten to unscrew bearing carrier (26). Pull propeller shaft (24) with components (19 through 29) from gearcase. Take care not to dislodge cam follower (19) from propeller shaft (24). Pry retainer ring (20) off dog clutch (21), remove pin (22) and slide dog clutch (21) off propeller shaft (24). Remove water pump cover, impeller and drive key, then lift drive shaft (2) out top of gearcase. Remove water pump plate and base along with shift shaft (3). Reach into gear cavity and remove pinion gear (14), thrust washer (13) and forward gear (18). Do not remove bearing (16) from forward gear (18) or bearing race (15) from gearcase (1) unless bearing or race require renewal. Do not remove bushing (7), bushing holder (8) or bushing (12) unless renewal is required. Use a suitable slide hammer puller to remove bushing (7) and holder (8) if necessary. If bushing (12) must be removed, pull lubrication sleeve (9) from gearcase and drive bushing down into gear cavity using the proper pilot and driver rod from Drive Shaft Bushing Removal Tool 91-13657A1 or equivalent.

Inspect all components for excessive wear or damage and renew as necessary. Maximum allowable propeller shaft runout is 0.006 inch (0.15 mm). Renew all seals and gaskets. The manufacturer recommends renewing water pump impeller once pump is disassem-

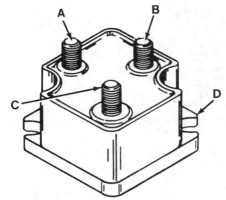

Fig. MR11-17—View showing electric starter armature and drive components.

1. Nut
2. Spacer
3. Spring
4. Drive assy.
5. End frame
6. Armature

Fig. MR11-18—Refer to text to test rectifier.

bled regardless of impeller condition. Apply Loctite 271 or equivalent to outer diameter of metal-cased seals.

NOTE: No adjustment of gear mesh pattern and gear backlash is provided. Make sure all parts are in good condition and properly assembled.

To reassemble, reverse disassembly procedure while noting the following: Install dog clutch (21) with short side toward forward gear (18). Apply Quicksilver 2-4-C Marine Grease or a suitable equivalent to the lip surfaces of all seals. Rotate carrier assembly (26) counterclockwise to tighten. Tighten carrier (26) to 60 ft.-lbs. (81 N·m). Install cap (31) on thrust hub (30) and assemble with thrust hub ears facing propeller (32). Tighten propeller nut (34) to 70 in.-lbs. (8 N·m).

If shift linkage components were disassembled, refer to the following: Measure distance (D—Fig. MR11-21) from water pump base to center of hole (H) in shift shaft (3). Distance (D) should be 16.5 inches (419 mm) on models with a short drive shaft, 22 inches (559 mm) on models with a long drive shaft and 27.5 inches (698 mm) on models with an extra long drive shaft. Rotate shift shaft (3) clockwise to decrease distance (D) and counterclockwise to increase distance (D).

Install gearcase housing assembly to drive shaft housing and tighten gearcase housing retaining screws to 180 in.-lbs. (20 N·m). With shift lever in the neutral position, reverse lock actuator (4—Fig. MR11-19) should just contact reverse lock hook on outboard motor mid-section.

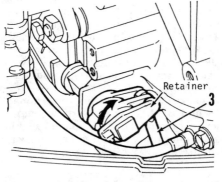

Fig. MR11-20—Rotate shift shaft retainer in direction of arrow to disconnect shift shaft (3).

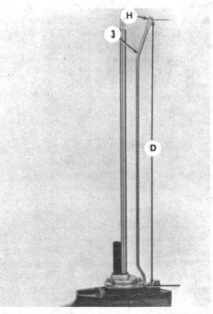

Fig. MR11-21—Refer to text to adjust shift shaft (3).

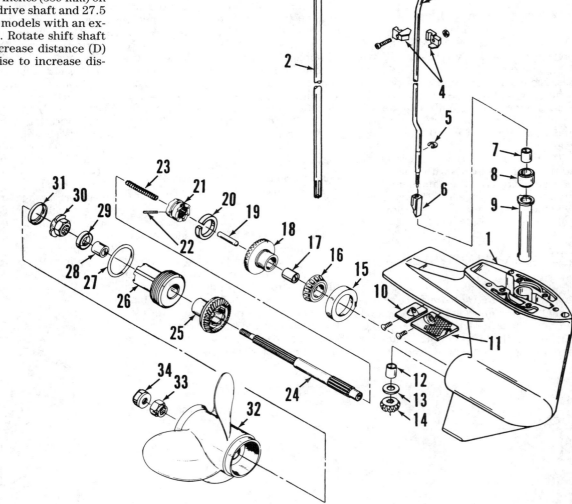

1. Housing
2. Drive shaft
3. Shift shaft
4. Reverse lock actuator
5. Clip
6. Shift cam
7. Bushing
8. Bushing holder
9. Lubrication sleeve
10. Anode
11. Water inlet cover
12. Bushing
13. Thrust washer
14. Pinion gear
15. Bearing race
16. Bearing
17. Bushing
18. Forward gear
19. Cam follower
20. Retainer ring
21. Dog clutch
22. Pin
23. Spring
24. Propeller shaft
25. Reverse gear
26. Bearing carrier
27. "O" ring
28. Bushing
29. Seal
30. Thrust hub
31. Cap
32. Propeller
33. Thrust hub
34. Nut

Fig. MR11-19—Exploded view of lower unit gearcase assembly.

MARINER 20 (PRIOR TO 1980), 25 (1980-1984) AND 28 HP

CONDENSED SERVICE DATA

NOTE: Metric fasteners are used throughout outboard motor.

TUNE-UP

Hp/rpm	20/4500-5500
	25/4500-5500*
	28/4500-5500
Bore:	
20 hp	64 mm
	(2.52 in.)
25 & 28 hp	67 mm
	(2.64 in.)
Stroke	61 mm
	(2.40 in.)
Number of Cylinders	2
Displacement:	
20 hp	392 cc
	(24 cu. in.)
25 & 28 hp	430 cc
	(26.2 cu. in.)
Spark Plug – NGK:	
20 hp	B6HS
25 & 28 hp	B7HS
Electrode Gap	0.5-0.6 mm†
	(0.020-0.024 in.)
Ignition	See Text
Idle Speed:	
20 & 25 hp (early)	650-700 rpm
	(in gear)
25 hp (late)	650-750 rpm
	(in gear)
28 hp	1000-1100 rpm
Fuel:Oil Ratio	50:1

*For early 25 hp models, full throttle rpm range is 4700-5700.
†For 20 hp and early 25 hp models, electrode gap should be 0.6-0.7 mm (0.024-0.027 in.).

SIZES—CLEARANCES

Piston Ring End Gap:	
20 & 25 hp (early)–	
Top Ring	0.3-0.5 mm
	(0.012-0.020 in.)
Bottom Ring	0.25-0.45 mm
	(0.010-0.018 in.)
25 hp (late) & 28 hp – Both Rings	0.3-0.5 mm
	(0.012-0.020 in.)
Piston Skirt Clearance:	
All Models Except Late 25 hp	0.030-0.045 mm
	(0.0012-0.0018 in.)
Late 25 hp	0.040-0.045 mm
	(0.0016-0.0018 in.)
Crankshaft Runout – Max.	0.03 mm
	(0.0012 in.)
Connecting Rod Small End Shake:	
Standard	0.8-1.0 mm
	(0.03-0.04 in.)
Limit	2.0 mm
	(0.08 in.)

SIZES—CLEARANCES CONT.
Lower Unit Gear Backlash:
20 & 25 hp (early) . . . . 0.1-0.3 mm
(0.004-0.012 in.)

28 hp . . . . 0.15-0.25 mm
(0.006-0.010 in.)

25 hp (late) . . . . See Text

TIGHTENING TORQUES
(All Models Except Late 25 hp)
Crankcase . . . . 27.4-29.4 N·m
(20-22 ft.-lbs.)

Cylinder Head . . . . 27.4-29.4 N·m
(20-22 ft.-lbs.)

Flywheel . . . . 68.6-78.4 N·m
(50-58 ft.-lbs.)

Standard Screws:
5 mm . . . . 4.9-5.8 N·m
(3.6-4.3 ft.-lbs.)

6 mm . . . . 7.9-9.8 N·m
(5.8-7.2 ft.-lbs.)

8 mm . . . . 14.7-19.6 N·m
(10.8-14.4 ft.-lbs.)

10 mm . . . . 29.4 N·m
(22 ft.-lbs.)

(Late 25 hp)
Crankcase . . . . 24.5-34 N·m
(18-25 ft.-lbs.)

Cylinder Head . . . . 24.5-34 N·m
(18-25 ft.-lbs.)

Flywheel . . . . 95.2-108.8 N·m
(70-80 ft.-lbs.)

Standard screws:
4 mm . . . . 2.3 N·m
(20 in.-lbs.)

5 mm . . . . 4.3-6.6 N·m
(38-58 in.-lbs.)

6 mm . . . . 6.6-10.8 N·m
(58-96 in.-lbs.)

8 mm . . . . 13.6-21.8 N·m
(10-16 ft.-lbs.)

10 mm . . . . 27.2-44.9 N·m
(20-33 ft.-lbs.)

12 mm . . . . 35.4-50.3 N·m
(26-37 ft.-lbs.)

LUBRICATION

The power head is lubricated by oil mixed with the fuel. Fuel should be regular leaded, low lead or unleaded gasoline with a minimum pump octane rating of 86. Recommended oil is Quicksilver Formula 50-D Outboard Lubricant. Normal fuel:oil ratio is 50:1; during engine break-in fuel:oil ratio should be 25:1.

Lower unit gears and bearings are lubricated by oil contained in the gearcase. Recommended oil is Mariner Super Duty Gear Lube. Lubricant is drained by removing vent and drain plugs in the gearcase. Refill through drain plug hole until oil has reached level of vent plug hole.

FUEL SYSTEM

CARBURETOR. Refer to Fig. MR12-1 for an exploded view of carburetor. On 20 hp and early 25 hp models under normal operation, the following jet sizes are the standard recommendation: main jet (8—Fig. MR12-1) #140 and pilot jet (2) #60. On late 25 hp and 28 hp models, use the standard carburetor jet sizes as recommended by the manufacturer for normal operation when used at altitudes of 2500 feet (750 m) and less. Main jet (8) size should be reduced from standard recommendation by one size for altitudes of 2500 to 5000 feet (750 to 1500 m), two sizes for altitudes of 5000 to 7500 feet (1500 to 2250 m) and three sizes for altitudes of 7500 feet (2250 m) and up. Initial adjustment of idle mixture screw (19) is 1-1½ turns out from a lightly

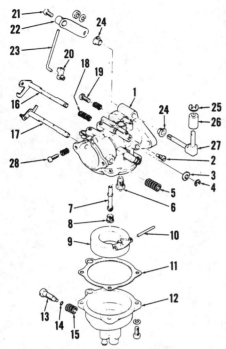

Fig. MR12-1 — Exploded view of carburetor. Components 13, 14 and 15 are not used on late 25 hp models.

1. Body	15. Spring
2. Pilot jet	16. Throttle shaft
3. Washer	17. Choke shaft
4. Clip	18. Spring
5. Spring	19. Idle mixture screw
6. Fuel inlet valve	20. Link keeper
7. Main nozzle	21. Screw
8. Main jet	22. Throttle arm
9. Float	23. Link
10. Pin	24. Bushing
11. Gasket	25. Clip
12. Float bowl	26. Cam follower roller
13. Drain valve	27. Cam follower
14. "O" ring	28. Idle speed screw

seated position on 20 hp and early 25 hp models, 1¼ to 1¾ turns out from a lightly seated position on 28 hp models and 1-3/8 to 2 turns out from a lightly seated position on late 25 hp models. Recommended idle is 650-700 rpm (in gear) on 20 hp and early 25 hp models, 650-750 rpm (in gear) on late 25 hp models and 1000-1100 on 28 hp models with the engine at normal operating temperature.

To check carburetor fuel level on 20 hp, early 25 hp and 28 hp models, proceed as follows: Remove the engine cowl and position the outboard motor in an upright position. Connect a clear vinyl tube to the float bowl drain nozzle and hold the drain tube up. Open the float bowl drain plug. Run the engine at idle speed for a few minutes, then stop the engine. Fuel level (L–Fig. MR12-2) should be 29-33 mm (1.13-1.31 in.). If fuel level is incorrect, float bowl (12–Fig. MR12-1) must be removed and inlet valve (6) renewed if excessively worn or tab on float (9) adjusted until the proper setting is obtained.

To determine the float level on late 25 hp models, remove the carburetor and float bowl (12). Invert carburetor body (1) and slowly raise float (9). Note whether float (9) is parallel with surface of carburetor body when needle of fuel inlet valve (6) just breaks contact with float (9) tang. If not, adjust float (9) tang until proper float level is obtained.

FUEL FILTER. A fuel filter assembly (1–Fig. MR12-3) is connected between fuel supply line (2) and fuel

pump inlet line (3). With the engine stopped, periodically unscrew fuel filter cup (7) from filter base (4) and withdraw filter element (6), "O" ring (5) and gasket (8) if applicable. Clean cup (7) and filter element (6) in a suitable solvent and blow dry with clean compressed air. Inspect filter element (6). If excessive blockage or damage is noted, renew element.

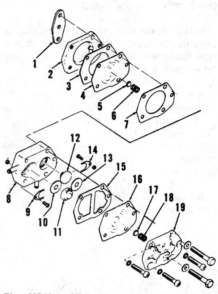

Fig. MR12-4 — View showing early type fuel pump assembly. Late type fuel pump assembly can be indentified by ribs on the inlet and outlet nozzle. Late type fuel pump uses reed valve type check valves instead of umbrella type check valves (11 and 12) as used on early type fuel pump.

1. Gasket	
2. Base	11. Outlet check valve
3. Gasket	12. Inlet check valve
4. Diaphragm	13. Gasket
5. Spring plate	14. Retainer
6. Spring	15. Gasket
7. Gasket	16. Diaphragm
8. Body	17. Spring plate
9. Retainer	18. Spring
10. Gasket	19. Cover

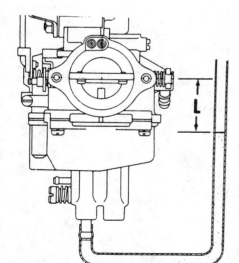

Fig. MR12-2 — On 20 hp, early 25 hp and 28 hp models, fuel level (L) should be 29-33 mm (1.13-1.31 in.) below center of carburetor bore when viewed through a clear vinyl tube. Refer to text.

Fig. MR12-3 — View showing fuel filter assembly, mounting bracket and fuel hoses. Both assemblies have been used.

1. Fuel filter assy.
2. Fuel supply line
3. Fuel pump inlet line
4. Filter base
5. "O" ring
6. Filter element
7. Cup
8. Gasket

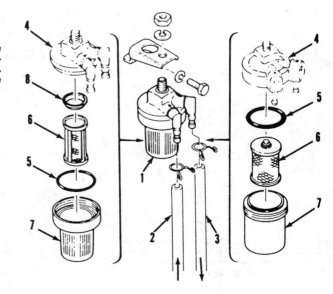

Reassembly is reverse order of disassembly. Renew "O" ring (5) and gasket (8), if applicable, during reassembly.

FUEL PUMP. The diaphragm type fuel pump is located on the port side of the engine. Refer to Fig. MR12-4 for an exploded view of fuel pump. Alternating pressure and vacuum pulsations in the crankcase actuates the diaphragm and check valves in the pump.

NOTE: Early type fuel pump assembly uses umbrella type check valves and late type fuel pump assembly uses reed valve type check valves.

Make certain that all gaskets, diaphragms and check valves are in good condition when reassembling unit. Coat gasket (1) with a nonhardening type gasket sealer making certain that passage in center is not blocked with gasket sealer.

REED VALVE. The reed valve assembly is located between the intake

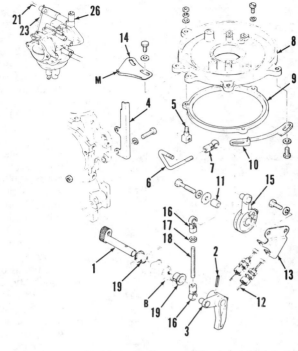

Fig. MR12-7 — View of speed control components used on 28 hp models. Other models are similar.

1. Shaft
2. Pin
3. Throttle blockout lever
4. Stop bracket
5. Swivel
6. Link
7. Rod end
8. Magneto base plate
9. Retainer
10. Bracket
11. Sleeve
12. Control cables
13. Bracket
14. Throttle cam
15. Pulley
16. Rod end
17. Locknut
18. Link
19. Bushing
21. Screw
23. Link
26. Roller

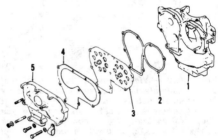

Fig. MR12-5 — Exploded view of reed valve and intake manifold assembly.

1. Crankcase half
2. Gasket
3. Reed valve assy.
4. Gasket
5. Intake manifold

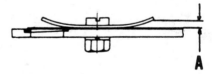

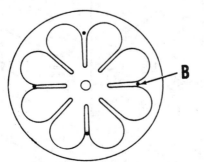

Fig. MR12-6 — Height (A) of reed stop should be 5.0-5.5 mm (0.20-0.22 in.). Make sure marks (B) are aligned between reed petals when reassembling unit. Refer to text.

manifold and crankcase. Refer to Fig. MR12-5 for a view of reed valve assembly.

Cracked, warped, chipped or bent reed petals will impair operation and should be renewed. Do not attempt to straighten or repair bent or damaged reed petals. Reed petals should seat smoothly against reed plate along their entire length. Reassemble reed stops and reed petals on chamfered side of reed plate (3). Position reed petals so index marks (B – Fig. MR12-6) are showing between petals. Note that index mark consists of two dots on later models. On early models, height (A) of reed stop should be 5.0-5.5 mm (0.20-0.22 in.). On later models, the manufacturer does not recommend the adjustment of reed stop height (A). Renew reed stop if height adjustment is questioned or damage is noted.

SPEED CONTROL LINKAGE (All Models Except Late 25 Hp). To synchronize ignition and throttle control linkage, first make sure the ignition timing has been correctly adjusted. Turn twist grip to full throttle position. Loosen locknut and turn control cable (12 – Fig. MR12-7) adjuster so control cable slack is 1-2 mm (0.039-0.079 in.) on the cable opposite the pull cable, then tighten locknut. Remove rod end (7) from pulley (15). With the twist grip held in the full throttle position, push magneto base plate (8) to full advance position. Adjust rod end (7) on magneto control rod (6) until rod end (7) aligns with ball joint on pulley (15), then snap into position. Loosen locknut (17) and adjust rod end (16) on link (18) so throt-

tle blockout lever (3) contacts bottom cowling stopper (B) when twist grip is turned to the full throttle position. Tighten locknut (17).

With twist grip in the full throttle position, mark on tab (M) of throttle cam (14) should be aligned with center of cam follower roller (26). To adjust, loosen retaining screws and reposition throttle cam (14) to center mark on roller (26). With twist grip in full throttle position, loosen lockscrew (21) and move carburetor throttle lever (23) to wide open position, then retighten lockscrew (21).

Fig. MR12-8 — View of blockout lever control rod (1), blockout lever (2) and magneto base plate control rod (3) used on late 25 hp models. Locknuts (N) and adjuster (A) are used to adjust cable slack. Refer to text.

(Late 25 Hp Models). To synchronize ignition and throttle control linkage, first make sure the ignition timing has been correctly adjusted. Detach magneto base plate control rod (3 – Fig. MR12-8) and blockout lever control rod (1). Measure length of magneto base plate control rod from joint center to joint center and adjust to a length of 69.2-70.0 mm (2.58-2.90 in.), then reconnect control rod. Position gear shift lever in "NEUTRAL."

Turn twist grip to full throttle position. Loosen locknuts (N) and turn control cable adjustment (A) until cable slack is 1-2 mm (0.039-0.079 in.), then tighten locknuts.

With the twist grip held in the full throttle position, push magneto base plate to full advance position. Measure length of blockout lever control rod (1) from joint center to joint center and adjust to a length of 91.5 mm (3.6 in.), then reconnect control rod. Blockout lever (2) should contact bottom cowling stopper when twist grip is turned to the full throttle position with the magneto base plate fully advanced and the gear shift lever is in "NEUTRAL" position. If not, readjust blockout lever control rod (1) until the proper adjustment is obtained.

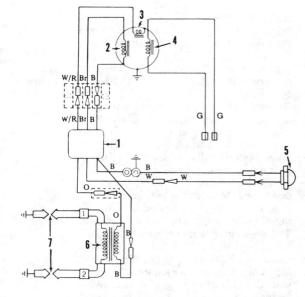

Fig. MR12-10 – View identifying CDI system components.

1. CDI module
2. Charge coil
3. Pulser coil
4. Lighting coil
5. Stop switch
6. Ignition coil
7. Spark plugs

IGNITION

Breaker Point Models

On 20 hp, early 25 hp, 28 hp and some late 25 hp models, a flywheel magneto ignition system is used with separate breaker points, condenser, primary coil and secondary coil for each cylinder.

Ignition timing may be checked and adjusted as follows: Remove engine cowl and starter assembly. Remove flywheel covers (17 and 20 – Fig. MR12-9), then set breaker point gap of top cylinder breaker points (top cylinder breaker

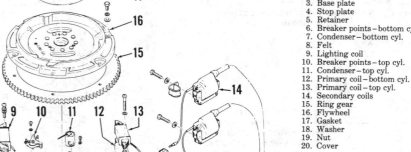

Fig. MR12-9 – Exploded view of magneto. Ring gear (15) is used on 28 hp models with electric start.

1. Throttle cam
2. Stator plate
3. Base plate
4. Stop plate
5. Retainer
6. Breaker points – bottom cyl.
7. Condenser – bottom cyl.
8. Felt
9. Lighting coil
10. Breaker points – top cyl.
11. Condenser – top cyl.
12. Primary coil – bottom cyl.
13. Primary coil – top cyl.
14. Secondary coils
15. Ring gear
16. Flywheel
17. Gasket
18. Washer
19. Nut
20. Cover

points can be identified by gray wire) to 0.25-0.45 mm (0.010-0.018 in.). Rotate speed control handle to full throttle position. Attach an ohmmeter or continuity checker to gray wire of top cylinder breaker points and note flywheel position when points open. Be sure flywheel timing mark for number 1 (top) cylinder is used. Flywheel timing mark should be aligned with forward edge of stop bracket (4 – Fig. MR12-7). Adjust position of stop plate (10) to adjust top cylinder ignition timing. Rotate flywheel so flywheel timing mark for number 2 (bottom) cylinder is aligned with stop bracket and adjust bottom cylinder timing by varying breaker point gap within range of 0.25-0.45 mm (0.010-0.018 in.).

NOTE: Replacement flywheels do not have timing marks and must be marked according to piston position as outlined in following paragraph.

If ignition timing marks are questioned or a new flywheel is installed, piston position must be determined. Remove cylinder head and install a dial indicator to determine number 1 (top) piston position. Set top piston at 3.35 mm (0.132 in.) BTDC and mark flywheel adjacent to forward edge of stop bracket (4). Attach dial indicator to bottom of cylinder and mark flywheel in same manner with bottom piston at 3.35 mm (0.312 in.) BTDC.

When timing adjustment is completed, check speed control linkage adjustment as previously outlined.

CDI Models

Some late 25 hp models are equipped with a capacitor discharge ignition (CDI) system. If engine malfunction is noted and the ignition system is suspected, make sure the spark plugs and all electrical connections are tight before proceeding to troubleshooting the CD ignition system.

Proceed as follows to test CDI system components: Refer to Fig. MR12-10. To test ignition coil, disconnect black wire (B) and orange wire (O) at connectors and spark plug boots from spark plugs. Use a suitable ohmmeter and connect red tester lead to orange wire (O) and black tester lead to black wire (B). The primary winding resistance reading should be 0.08-0.10 ohms. Connect red tester lead to terminal end in one spark plug boot and black tester lead to terminal end in remaining spark plug boot. The secondary winding resistance reading should be 3,475-4,025 ohms. Use a suitable coil tester or tester Model 9800 Magneto Analyzer to perform a power test. Connect tester leads as outlined in tester's handbook. A steady spark should jump a 5 mm (13/64 in.) gap when a current value of 1.7-2.1 amperes is applied. A surface insulation test can be performed using a suitable coil tester or tester Model 9800 Magneto Analyzer and following tester's handbook.

To check source (charge) coil, disconnect black wire (B) and brown wire (Br) at connectors leading from magneto base plate. Use a suitable ohmmeter and connect red tester lead to brown wire (Br) and black tester lead to black wire (B). DO NOT rotate flywheel while making test. The ohmmeter should read 121-147 ohms. Reconnect wires after completing test.

To check pulser (trigger) coil, disconnect white wire with red tracer (W/R) at connector leading from magneto base plate and black wire (B) at back of CDI unit. Use a suitable ohmmeter and connect red tester lead to white wire with red tracer (W/R) and black tester lead to black wire (B). DO NOT rotate flywheel while making test. The ohmmeter should read 12.6-15.4 ohms.

To test CDI module, first disconnect all wires at connectors and remove CDI module from outboard motor. Use a

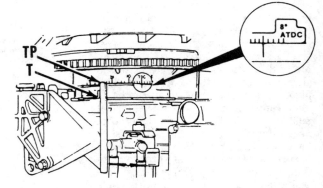

Fig. MR12-12—Full advance occurs when stop bracket tab (T) contacts timing pointer (TP). Refer to text for ignition timing adjustment.

suitable ohmmeter and refer to Fig. MR12-11. With reference to chart, perform CDI module resistance tests.

Renew any components that are not within the manufacturer's recommended limits.

To check ignition timing, rotate flywheel so timing pointer (TP – Fig. MR12-12) is aligned with 25° BTDC mark on flywheel. Rotate stator plate so stop bracket tab (T) is against timing pointer. The stamped mark on the stator plate should be aligned with 0° (TDC) mark on flywheel. Adjust timing by loosening stop bracket retaining screws and relocating bracket.

COOLING SYSTEM

WATER PUMP. A rubber impeller type water pump is mounted between the drive shaft housing and gearcase. Water pump impeller (6 – Fig. MR12-13 or MR12-14) is driven by a key in the drive shaft.

When cooling system problems are encountered, first check water inlet for plugging or partial stoppage. Be sure

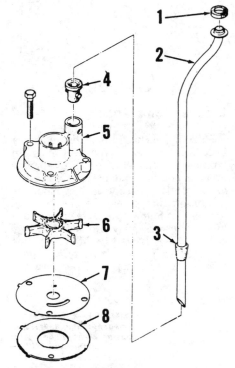

Fig. MR12-13—Exploded view of early type water pump assembly. Gasket (8) is not used on some models.

1. Grommet	5. Pump housing
2. Water tube	6. Impeller
3. Sleeve	7. Plate
4. Seal	8. Gasket

Red Test Lead \ Black Test Lead	CDI UNIT LEADS				
	White	Black	Brown	White w/Red	Orange
C D I U N I T L E A D S White	A	B	B	B	B
Black	C	A	D	B	J
Brown	E	F	A	B	J
White w/Red	G	H	I	A	J
Orange	B	B	B	B	A

Fig. MR12-11—Use chart and values listed below to test condition of CD ignition module. Before making test (J), connect CDI module's orange wire and black wire together. Then disconnect wires and perform desired test.

A. Zero
B. Infinity
C. 9,000-19,000 ohms
D. 2,000-6,000 ohms
E. 80,000-160,000 ohms
F. 70,000-150,000 ohms
G. 33,000-63,000 ohms
H. 7,000-17,000 ohms
I. 15,000-35,000 ohms
J. Tester needle should show deflection then return toward infinite resistance

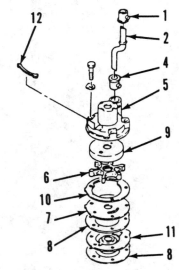

Fig. MR12-14—Exploded view of later type water pump assembly.

1. Seal	8. Gasket
2. Water tube	9. Liner
4. Seal	10. Gasket
5. Pump housing	11. Base
6. Impeller	12. Spacer
7. Plate	

thermostat located in cylinder head operates properly. If the water pump is suspected defective, separate gearcase from drive shaft housing and inspect pump. Make sure all seals and mating surfaces are in good condition and water passages are unobstructed. Check impeller (6) and plate (7) for excessive wear. When reassembling, coat gasket surfaces with a thin coating of Perfect Seal.

POWER HEAD

R&R AND OVERHAUL. The power head can be removed for disassembly and overhaul as follows: Clamp outboard motor to a suitable stand and remove engine cowl and starter assembly. Disconnect speed control cables, fuel line and any wiring that will interfere with power head removal. Remove or disconnect any component that will interfere with power head removal.

Remove six screws securing power head to drive shaft housing and lift power head free. Remove flywheel, ignition components, carburetor, intake manifold and reed valve assembly. Remove screws retaining exhaust cover (14 – Fig. MR12-15) and withdraw. Crankcase halves can be separated after removal of ten screws securing crankcase half (21) to cylinder block. Crankshaft and pistons are now accessible for removal and overhaul as outlined in the appropriate following paragraphs.

ASSEMBLY. Two-stroke engine design dictates that intake manifold and crankcase are completely sealed against both vacuum and pressure. Exhaust manifold and cylinder head must be sealed against water leakage and pressure. Mating surfaces of water intake and exhaust areas between power head and drive shaft housing must form a tight seal.

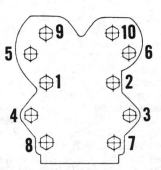

Fig. MR12-16 — Tighten crankcase screws on all models except late 25 hp models in sequence shown above.

Whenever the power head is disassembled, it is recommended that all gasket surfaces of crankcase halves be carefully checked for nicks, burrs or warped surfaces which might interfere with a tight seal. The cylinder head, head end of cylinder block, and the mating surfaces of manifolds and crankcase may be checked and lapped, if necessary to provide a smooth surface. Do not remove any more metal than is necessary to obtain a smooth finish. Thoroughly clean the parts with new oil on a clean, soft rag, then wash with soapsuds and clean rags.

Mating surface of crankcase halves may be checked on the lapping block, and highs spots or nicks removed, but surfaces must not be lowered. If extreme care is used, a slightly damaged crankcase can be salvaged in this manner. In case of doubt, renew the crankcase assembly.

The crankcase halves are positively located during assembly by the use of two dowel pins. Check to make sure that dowel pins are not bent, nicked or distorted and that dowel holes are clean and true. When installing pins, make certain they are fully seated, but do not use excessive force.

The mating surfaces of the crankcase halves must be sealed during reassembly using a nonhardening type of gasket sealer. Make certain that surfaces are thoroughly cleaned of oil and old sealer before making a fresh application. Apply sealer evenly and use sparingly, so excess does not squeeze into crankcase cavity. Cylinder head, gasket (11 – Fig. MR12-15) and exhaust manifold gasket (12) should be coated with a good grade of heat resistant gasket sealer.

Tighten the crankcase screws on all models except late 25 hp models to 27.4-29.4 N·m (20-22 ft.-lbs.) following the sequence shown in Fig. MR12-16. Tighten the crankcase screws on late 25 hp models to 24.5-34 N·m (18-25 ft.-lbs.)

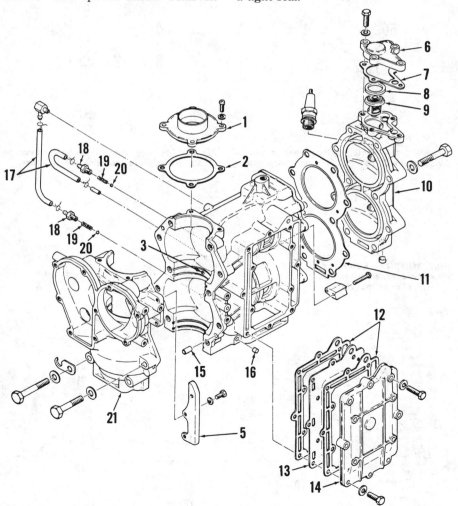

Fig. MR12-15 — Exploded view of crankcase assembly used on 20 and early 25 hp models. Crankcase on late 25 and 28 hp models is similar. Breather valve (20) is used on early models while valve (3) is used on later models.

1. Oil seal housing	7. Gasket	12. Gaskets	17. Breather hoses
2. Gasket	8. Spacer	13. Plate	18. Fitting
3. Check valve	9. Thermostat	14. Exhaust cover	19. Spring
5. Stop bracket	10. Cylinder head	15. Dowel	20. Breather valve ball
6. Thermostat cover	11. Gasket	16. Plug	21. Crankcase half

following the sequence shown in Fig. MR12-17. Tighten the cylinder head screws on 20 and early 25 hp models to 27.4-29.4 N·m (20-22 ft.-lbs.) following the sequence shown in Fig. MR12-18. Tighten the cylinder head screws on late 25 hp models to 24.5-34 N·m (18-25 ft.-lbs.) following the sequence shown in Fig. MR12-19. Tighten the cylinder head screws on 28 hp models to 27.4-29.4 N·m (20-22 ft.-lbs.) following the sequence shown in Fig. MR12-20. Refer to CONDENSED SERVICE DATA section for general torquing specifications.

PISTONS, PINS, RINGS AND CYLINDERS. (All Models Except late 25 Hp). The pistons are equipped with two piston rings each. Piston ring end gap should be 0.3-0.5 mm (0.012-0.020 in.) with a maximum limit of 0.9 mm (0.036 in.).

Piston clearance should be 0.030-0.045 mm (0.0012-0.0018 in.). Measure piston diameter at a point approximately 10 mm (0.394 in.) from bottom of skirt perpendicular to piston pin bore. Cylinder must be bored to oversize if out-of-round or taper exceeds 0.07 mm (0.003 in.). Pistons and rings are available in standard size and oversizes of 0.25 and 0.50 mm (0.010 and 0.020 in.).

Install piston so arrow on piston crown points towards exhaust side. Use new piston pin retaining clips (22–Fig. MR12-21) during assembly and thoroughly coat piston, pin and rings with oil.

(Late 25 Hp). Cylinder bore should be measured in several different locations to determine if an out-of-round or tapered condition exists. Inspect cylinder wall for scoring. If minor scoring is noted, cylinders should be honed to smooth out cylinder wall.

NOTE: Cylinder sleeves are cast into the cylinder block. If cylinder is out-of-round or tapered more than 0.54 mm (0.021 in.), or if excessive scoring is noted, the cylinder block must be removed.

Recommended piston skirt to cylinder clearance is 0.040-0.045 mm (0.0016-0.0018 in.). Recommended piston ring end gap is 0.3-0.5 mm (0.012-0.020 in.) for both rings. The top piston ring is semi-keystone shaped. Make sure piston rings properly align with locating pins in ring grooves.

When reassembling, install new piston pin retaining clips (22–Fig. MR12-21) and make sure that "UP" on dome of piston is towards flywheel end of engine. Coat bearings, pistons, rings and cylinder bores with engine oil during assembly.

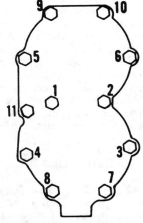

Fig. MR12-19—Tighten cylinder head screws on late 25 hp models in sequence shown above.

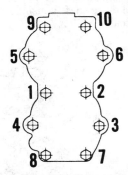

Fig. MR12-18—Tighten cylinder head screws on 20 and early 25 hp models in sequence shown above.

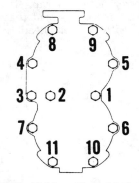

Fig. MR12-20—Tighten cylinder head screws on 28 hp models in sequence shown above.

Fig. MR12-21—Exploded view of crankshaft assembly typical of all models.

1. Oil seal
2. Bearing
3. Key
4. Crankpin
5. Crank half
6. Thrust washer
7. Connecting rod
8. Needle bearing
9. Crank half
10. Bearing
11. Snap ring
12. Seal
13. Crank half
14. Crank half
15. Bearing
16. "O" ring
17. Washer
18. Oil seal
19. Oil seal
20. Washer
21. Needle bearing
22. Clips
23. Piston pin
24. Piston
25. Piston rings

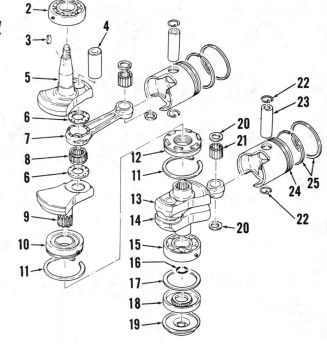

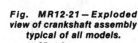

Fig. MR12-17—Tighten crankcase screws on late 25 hp models in sequence shown above.

CONNECTING RODS, CRANK-SHAFT AND BEARINGS. The built-up crankshaft assembly should only be disassembled if the necessary tools and experience are available to service this type of crankshaft.

Maximum crankshaft runout measured at bearing outer races with crankshaft ends supported in lathe centers is 0.03 mm (0.0012 in.). Maximum connecting rod big end side clearance is 0.3 mm (0.012 in.) on 20 and early 25 hp models, 0.4-0.8 mm (0.016-0.032 in.) on 28 hp models and less than 0.8 mm (0.032 in.) on late 25 hp models. Standard side to side shake of connecting rod small end measured as shown in Fig. MR12-22 should be 0.8-1.0 mm (0.03-0.04 in.) with a maximum of 2.0 mm (0.08 in.).

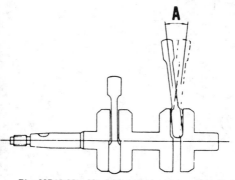

Fig. MR12-22 — Maximum shake at small end of connecting rod (A) should be less than 2.0 mm (0.08 in.).

Crankshaft, connecting rods and center section components are available only as a unit assembly. Outer main bearings (2 and 15 – Fig. MR12-21) are available individually.

Thirty-one bearing rollers (21) are used in each connecting rod small end. Rollers may be held in place with petroleum jelly while installing piston.

Lubricate bearings, pistons, rings and cylinders with engine oil prior to installation. Tighten crankcase and cylinder head screws as outlined in ASSEMBLY section.

STARTER

MANUAL STARTER. Refer to Fig. MR12-23 for an exploded view of rewind starter. When starter rope handle is pulled, rope pulley (12) rotates and pawl (14) moves out to engage magneto flywheel which is secured to crankshaft. Safety plunger (5) engages lugs on pulley (12) when outboard motor is shifted to forward or reverse gear.

Starter may be disassembled for overhaul or renewal of individual components as follows: Remove engine top cowl and three bolts securing starter assembly to power head. Check pawl (14) for wear of engagement area and

freedom of movement. Renew or grease as necessary. Remove rope handle and allow rope to wind onto rope pulley (12). Remove screw (18) and shaft (16), then carefully lift rope pulley out of housing. Use caution when removing pulley to prevent injury from rewind spring flying out of housing. Broken rewind spring or rope may be renewed at this point. Rewind spring should be hooked in housing with coil winding counterclockwise from outer end. Wind rope onto pulley counterclockwise as viewed from bottom. Hook end of rope through notch in pulley leaving enough rope to attach rope handle. Assemble pulley to starter housing making sure that pin in pulley engages eye in end of rewind spring. Install shaft (16) and retaining screw (18). Grasp end of rope and turn pulley three or four turns counterclockwise. Thread rope through starter housing and attach rope handle. All friction surfaces should be greased.

Adjust starter safety cable by turning adjusting nuts (1) so plunger (5) end is recessed 1 mm when outboard motor is in neutral gear.

ELECTRIC STARTER. Some 28 hp engines are equipped with a Hitachi S108-36 electric starter motor. Refer to Fig. MR12-24 for an exploded view of starter motor. Motor operates on 12 volts with a rated output of 0.6 kw. Minimum brush length is 9.5 mm. (3/8 in.).

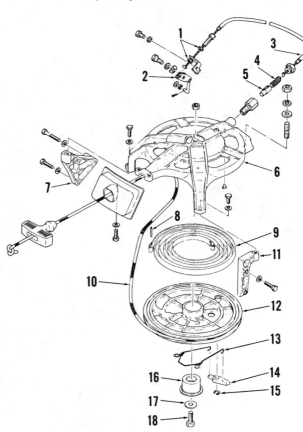

Fig. MR12-23 — Exploded view of rewind starter used on all models.

1. Adjusting nuts
2. Lever & link
3. Starter lockout cable
4. Spring
5. Plunger
6. Starter housing
7. Bracket
8. Pin
9. Rewind spring
10. Rope
11. Bracket
12. Pulley
13. Pawl spring
14. Pawl
15. "E" ring
16. Shaft
17. Washer
18. Screw

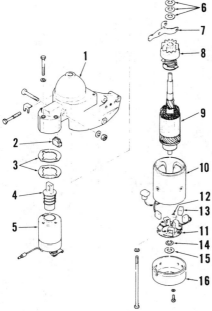

Fig. MR12-24 — Exploded view of electric starter used on some 28 hp models.

1. End frame	9. Armature
2. Dampener	10. Frame
3. Washers	11. Brush plate
4. Plunger	12. Spring
5. Solenoid	13. Brush
6. Washers	14. Washer
7. Fork	15. Washer
8. Drive assy.	16. Cover

Some late 25 hp models are equipped with an electric starter motor. Refer to Fig. MR12-25 for an exploded view of the starter motor. Commutator undercut should be 0.5-0.8 mm (0.02-0.03 in.) with a minimum limit of 0.2 mm (0.008 in.). Minimum brush length is 10 mm (0.394 in.).

During reassembly, adjust shims so armature end play is 1.5-2.0 mm (0.06-0.08 in.).

LOWER UNIT

20 Hp And Early 25 Hp Models

PROPELLER AND SHEAR PIN. Lower unit protection is provided by a shear pin. Standard propeller rotates clockwise, has three blades and measures 241 mm (9½ in.) in diameter and 292 mm (11½ in.) in pitch. Optional propellers are available.

R&R AND OVERHAUL. Most lower unit service may be performed after separating the gearcase from the drive shaft housing. The gearcase may be removed and disassembled as follows: Attach outboard motor to a suitable stand and remove both vent and drain plugs in gearcase to allow lubricant to drain. Loosen locknut (20 – Fig. MR12-27) and remove coupler nut (19). Remove four bolts securing gearcase to drive shaft housing and carefully separate gearcase

from drive shaft housing. Remove water pump using caution to prevent loss of key (8 – Fig. MR12-26). Remove propeller and unscrew the six screws securing lower gearcase cover (25). Propeller shaft (40), complete with gears and bearings, may now be removed. Use caution

to prevent loss of shift pin (30). Spring clip (35) retains drive pin (36) in propeller shaft. Drive shaft may be removed from gearcase after removal of snap ring (23). Do not lose collar pin (9). Shift rod (4) may be removed after removal of retainer (2).

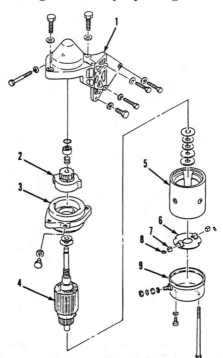

Fig. MR12-25 — Exploded view of electric starter assembly used on late 25 hp models.

1. End frame
2. Drive assy.
3. Frame cover
4. Armature
5. Frame
6. Brush plate
7. Brush
8. Brush spring
9. End cover

Fig. MR12-26 — Exploded view of gearcase used on 20 hp and early 25 hp models.

1. Boot
2. Retainer
3. "O" ring
4. Lower shift rod
5. Water inlet cover
6. Vent plug
7. Stop pin
8. Key
9. Pin
10. Drive shaft
11. Oil seals
12. Collar
13. "O" ring
14. Bushing
15. Dowel
16. Sealing strip
17. Shim
18. Needle bearing
19. Shim
20. Thrust washer
21. Thrust bearing
22. Pinion gear
23. Snap ring
24. Drain plug
25. Lower gearcase cover
26. Gearcase
27. Screen
28. Plug
29. Anode
30. Shift plunger
31. Bearing
32. Shim
33. Forward gear
34. Thrust washer
35. Spring clip
36. Pin
37. Clutch
38. Spring guide
39. Spring
40. Propeller shaft
41. Shear pin
42. Thrust washer
43. Reverse gear
44. Shim
45. Bearing
46. Oil seals
47. Bearing housing
48. Pin
49. "O" ring
50. Nut
51. Cotter pin

Inspect gears for wear on teeth and in engagement dogs. Inspect clutch (37) for wear on engagement surfaces. Inspect shafts for wear on splines and on friction surfaces of gears and oil seals. Check shift cam for excessive wear on shift ramps. All seals and "O" rings should be renewed on each reassembly.

Backlash between pinion gear (22) and drive gears (33 and 43) should be 0.1-0.3 mm (0.004-0.012 in.) and is adjusted by varying thickness of shims (32 and 44). Adjust gear mesh position by varying thickness of shim (19).

End play of drive shaft (10) should be 0.5 mm (0.020 in.) or less. Drive shaft end play is adjusted by varying number of 0.4 mm (0.016 in.) thick thrust washer (17).

When reassembling gearcase, make sure all case mating surfaces are clean and free of nicks or burrs. Coat mating surfaces with a nonhardening type gasket sealer. Sealing strip (16) should be cut so it extends approximately 0.8 mm (0.032 in.) beyond end of groove on each side.

Shift linkage is set by pressing lower shift rod (4) down until cam is against stopper pin (7) then adjusting coupler (19 – Fig. MR12-27) so shift control lever is in "REVERSE" position.

28 Hp And Later 25 Hp Models

PROPELLER AND DRIVE HUB. Lower unit protection is provided by a cushion type hub in the propeller. Standard propeller rotates clockwise, has three blades and measures 251 mm (9⅞ in.) in diameter and 267 mm (10½ in.) in pitch. Optional propellers are available. Propeller should be selected to provide maximum engine speed of 4500-5500 rpm.

R&R AND OVERHAUL. Most service on lower unit can be performed after detaching gearcase from drive shaft housing. To remove gearcase, attach outboard motor to a suitable stand and remove vent and drain plugs in gearcase to allow lubricant to drain. Loosen locknut (21 – Fig. MR12-29) and remove coupler nut (20). Remove four bolts securing gearcase to drive shaft housing and carefully separate gearcase from drive shaft housing. Remove water pump being careful not to lose impeller key (10 – Fig. MR12-28). Remove propeller.

Disassemble gearcase by bending back locking tab of lockwasher (41), then remove nut (42) and lockwasher (41). Using a suitable puller attached to propeller shaft, extract components (24 through 40) from gearcase. Disassemble propeller shaft assembly as required being careful not to lose shims (33). Detach

spring clip (26) and pin (25) to remove clutch (24), spring guide (28) and spring (29). Use a suitable puller to separate ball bearing (36) from reverse gear (32).

To remove drive shaft, unscrew pinion gear nut (19) and withdraw drive shaft (11). Forward gear (23) and bearing (22) cone may now be removed. Use a suitable puller to extract bearing cup; do not lose shims (21). Pull oil seals (12) and bearing (13) out of gearcase being careful not to lose shims (14). Remove drive shaft tube (15) then drive bearing (16) down into gear cavity. Lower shift rod (4) may be removed after unscrewing retainer (2).

Inspect gears for wear on teeth and in engagement dogs. Inspect clutch (24) for wear on engagement surfaces. Inspect shafts for wear on splines and on friction surfaces of gears and oil seals. Check shift cam for excessive wear on shift ramps. All seals and "O" rings should be renewed on each reassembly.

Assemble gearcase by reversing disassembly procedure. Install oil seals (12) with lips away from bearing (13). Install thrust washer (17) with grooved side facing pinion gear (18).

NOTE: Replacement propeller shaft (30—Fig. MR12-28) produced after 1987 for use in earlier models may not require the use of spring guide (28). Measure depth of hole in front side of propeller shaft (30) to determine if spring guide (28) is required. If hole is 3-1/8 inches (79.4 mm) deep, do not install guide (28). If hole is 3-7/8 inches (98.4 mm) deep, guide (28) must be installed. Also note that thrust washer (17) is not used on late model replacement gearcase. Thrust washer must fit into recess machined into gearcase if required. If pinion gear (18) surface of gearcase if machined flat, thrust washer (17) is not required.

On 28 hp models and 25 hp models equipped with early type water pump, tighten pinion gear nut (19) to 24.5-34.3 N·m (18-25 ft.-lbs.). Adjust gear mesh position by varying thickness of shim (14) which is available in thicknesses of 0.05, 0.08, 0.12, 0.30 and 0.50 mm. Backlash between pinion gear (18) and gears (23 and 32) should be 0.15-0.25 mm (0.006-0.010 in.) and is adjusted by varying thickness of shims (21 and 33) which are available in thicknesses of 0.05, 0.08, 0.12, 0.30, and 0.50 mm.

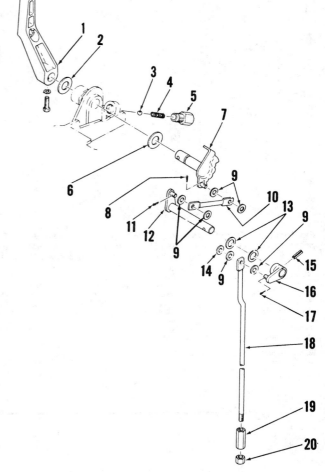

Fig. MR12-27 — View of shift control linkage used on 20 hp and early 25 hp models.
1. Shift control handle
2. Washer
3. Detent ball
4. Spring
5. Guide
6. Washer
7. Cam
8. Cotter pin
9. Washer
10. Link
11. Cotter pin
12. Shaft
13. Washer
14. Washer
15. Roll pin
16. Arm
17. Cotter pin
18. Upper shift rod
19. Coupler nut
20. Locknut

On 25 hp models equipped with late type water pump, forward gear backlash should be 0.2-0.5 mm (0.008-0.020 in.) and reverse gear backlash should be 0.7-1.0 mm (0.028-0.039 in.).

Install clutch (24) so "F" marked side (see Fig. MR12-30) is toward forward gear (23—Fig. MR12-28). Shift plunger (27) is installed with round end toward shift cam (4). Apply water-resistant grease to drive shaft upper splines.

With gearcase assembled and installed, synchronize gear engagement with gear selector handle by turning shift rod adjusting coupler nut (20—Fig. MR12-29), then tighten locknut (21).

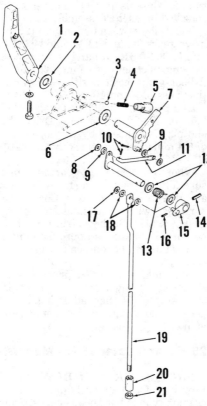

Fig. MR12-29—Exploded view of shift control linkage.

1. Shift control handle	12. Washers
2. Washer	13. Spring
3. Detent ball	14. Pin
4. Spring	15. Arm
5. Guide	16. Cotter pin
6. Washer	17. Washer
7. Cam	18. Washers
8. Washer	19. Upper shift rod
9. Washer	20. Coupler nut
10. Pins	21. Locknut
11. Link	

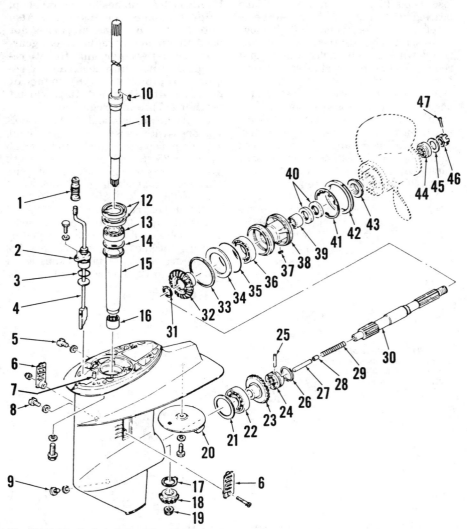

Fig. MR12-28—Exploded view of gearcase used on 28 hp and later 25 hp models. Note that on later propeller shaft (30), spring guide (28) may not be required. Also note that thrust washer (17) is not used on later replacement gearcase. Refer to text.

1. Boot	13. Bearing	25. Pin	37. Key
2. Retainer	14. Shim	26. Spring clip	38. Bearing housing
3. "O" ring	15. Drive shaft tube	27. Shift plunger	39. Needle bearing
4. Lower shift rod	16. Needle bearing	28. Spring guide	40. Oil seals
5. Vent plug	17. Thrust washer	29. Spring	41. Tab washer
6. Water inlet cover	18. Pinion gear	30. Propeller shaft	42. Nut
7. Dowel	19. Nut	31. Thrust washer	43. Spacer
8. Oil level plug	20. Trim tab	32. Reverse gear	44. Spacer
9. Drain plug	21. Shim	33. Shim	45. Washer
10. Key	22. Taper roller bearing	34. Thrust washer	46. Nut
11. Drive shaft	23. Forward gear	35. "O" ring	47. Cotter pin
12. Oil seals	24. Clutch	36. Ball bearing	

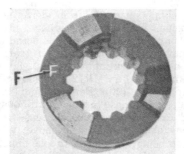

Fig. MR12-30—Install clutch dog so (F) mark is towards forward gear.

MARINER 20 AND 25 HP (1985-1989)

CONDENSED SERVICE DATA

TUNE-UP

Hp/rpm	20/4500-5500
	25/5000-6000
Bore.	2.56 in.
	(65 mm)
Stroke	2.36 in.
	(60 mm)
Number of Cylinders.	2
Displacement	24.4 cu. in.
	(400 cc)
Spark Plug	See Text
Idle Speed (in gear).	600-700
Fuel:Oil Ratio.	50:1
Gearcase Oil Capacity.	7.6 oz.
	(225 mL)

SIZES—CLEARANCES

Cylinder Bore Out-Of-Round – Max.	0.003 inch
	(0.076 mm)
Connecting Rod Alignment – Max. Bend.	0.002 inch
	(0.051 mm)
Thrust Washers and Crankshaft Clearance.	0.030 inch
	(0.762 mm)

TIGHTENING TORQUES

Connecting Rod Cap.	150 in.-lbs.
	(16.9 N·m)
Crankcase.	30 ft.-lbs.
	(40.7 N·m)
Exhaust Cover.	80 in.-lbs.
	(9 N·m)
Transfer Port Cover.	30 in.-lbs.
	(3.4 N·m)
Cylinder Block Cover.	80 in.-lbs.
	(9 N·m)
Carburetor Adpater Plate	30 in.-lbs.
	(3.4 N·m)
Flywheel	50 ft.-lbs.
	(67.8 N·m)
Carburetor Mounting Nuts.	180 in.-lbs.
	(20.3 N·m)
Power Head to Drive Shaft Housing.	200 in.-lbs.
	(22.6 N·m)

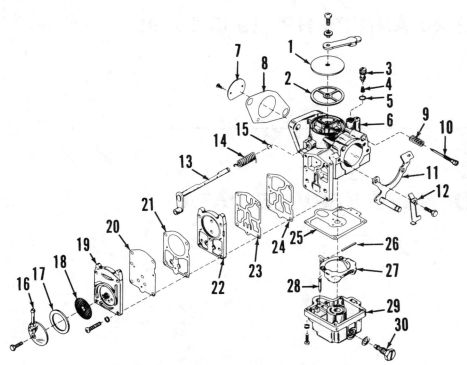

Fig. MR13-1 – Exploded view of "BC" type carburetor.

1. Cover	9. Spring	14. Spring
2. Gasket	10. Idle mixture	15. Snap ring
3. Enrichment valve	screw	16. Inlet cover
4. Spring	11. Plate	17. Gasket
5. Gasket	12. Choke knob	18. Strainer
6. Body	detent	19. Fuel pump cover
7. Throttle plate	13. Throttle shaft	20. Diaphragm
8. Gasket	roller	21. Gasket

22. Pump body
23. Check valves
24. Gasket
25. Gasket
26. Float pin
27. Float
28. Fuel inlet valve
29. Float bowl
30. Main jet

Fig. MR13-2 – View showing carburetor enrichment system used on "BC"-type carburetor. Refer to text for adjustment procedures.

A. Enrichment arm
C. Enrichment valve cover
R. Enrichment rod
T. Enrichment valve stem

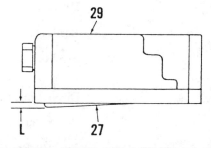

Fig. MR13-3 – With float bowl (29) inverted as shown level (L) of float (27) should be even with or less than 1/32 inch (0.8 mm) below float bowl edge.

LUBRICATION

The power head is lubricated by oil mixed with the fuel. Fuel should be regular leaded, low lead or unleaded gasoline with minimum pump octane rating of 86. Recommended oil is Quicksilver Formula 50-D Outboard Lubricant. Normal fuel:oil ratio is 50:1.

Lower unit gears and bearings are lubricated by oil contained in the gearcase. Recommended oil is Quicksilver Super-Duty Gear Lubricant. Lubricant is drained by removing vent and drain plugs in the gearcase. Refill through drain plug hole until oil has reached level of vent plug hole.

FUEL SYSTEM

CARBURETOR (Models With "BC" Type Carburetor). The fuel pump and carburetor are a complete unit. Standard main jet (30–Fig. MR13-1) size is 0.067 inch (1.70 mm). Other main jet (30) sizes are available for adjusting the air:fuel mixture for altitude or other

special conditions. Initial adjustment of idle mixture screw (10) is 1¼ turns out from a lightly seated position. Recommended idle speed is 600-700 rpm with engine at normal operating temperature and in gear.

All models are equipped with an enrichment valve (3) to enrichen the fuel mixture for cold starting. Raise enrichment valve cover (C–Fig. MR13-2) if so equipped. With the choke knob turned fully clockwise, arm (A) should depress valve stem (T). Bend rod (R) to adjust position of arm (A).

To determine the float level, invert carburetor float bowl (29–Fig. MR13-1) with fuel inlet valve (25) and float (27) installed. With float (27) hanging down as shown in Fig. MR13-3, float end (L) should be even with or less than 1/32 inch (0.8 mm) below float bowl (29) edge. Bend float arm tang to adjust.

(Models With "WMC" Type Carburetor). The fuel pump and carburetor are a complete unit. Standard main jet (30–Fig. MR13-4) size is 0.046 inch

(1.17 mm) on 20 hp models and 0.080 inch (2.03 mm) on 25 hp models. Other main jet (30) sizes are available for adjusting the air:fuel mixture for altitude or other special conditions. Initial adjustment of idle mixture screw (6) is 1¼ turns out from a lightly seated position. Recommended idle speed is 600-700 rpm with engine at normal operating temperature and in gear.

To determine the float level, invert carburetor body (1–Fig. MR13-5) with fuel inlet valve (25–Fig. MR13-4), float arm (26–Fig. MR13-5) and float (28) installed. Measure distance (D) as shown in Fig. MR13-5. Distance (D) should be 1 inch (25.4 mm). Bend float arm (26) to adjust.

FUEL FILTER. A fuel filter assembly is connected between fuel supply line and carburetor/fuel pump inlet line. With the engine stopped, occasionally unscrew fuel filter cup (4–Fig. MR13-6) from filter base (1) and withdraw sealing ring (3) and filter element (2). Clean cup (4) and filter element (2) in a suitable solvent and blow dry with clean compressed air. Inspect filter element (2). If excessive blockage or damage is noted, renew element.

Reassembly is reverse order of disassembly. If needed, renew sealing ring (3) during reassembly.

A strainer (18–Fig. MR13-7) positioned behind inlet cover (16) on "BC" type carburetors, is used to provide additional filtering of foreign contaminants. To inspect, remove inlet cover (16) and strainer (18). Clean strainer (18) in a suitable solvent and blow dry with clean compressed air. Inspect strainer (18). If excessive blockage or damage is noted, then renew strainer (18). If needed, renew gasket (17).

FUEL PUMP. On "BC" and "WMC" type carburetors, the fuel pump is an integral part of the carburetor. Refer to Fig. MR13-1 for and exploded view of fuel pump assembly used on "BC" type carburetors and Fig. MR13-4 for an ex-

ploded view of fuel pump assembly used on "WMC" type carburetors. Note that fuel pump assembly can be overhauled without carburetor removal.

REED VALVE. The reed valve assembly is located between the carburetor adapter plate and crankcase. Refer to Fig. MR13-8 for a view of reed valve assembly.

Cracked, warped, chipped or bent reed petals will impair operation and should be renewed. Do not attempt to straighten or repair bent or damaged reed petals. Reed petals should seat smoothly against reed block along their entire length. Reed petal ends should not stand open more than 0.007 inch (0.178 mm). Tighten reed retaining screws to 25 in.-lbs. (28. N·m).

SPEED CONTROL LINKAGE. The speed control twist grip, through the use of linkage, operates the stator plate to advance or retard the ignition timing.

The carburetor throttle plate is synchronized to open as the timing is advanced.

(Models With "BC" Type Carburetor And "BCIA" Stamped On Carburetor Flange). To synchronize ignition timing and throttle opening, proceed as follows:

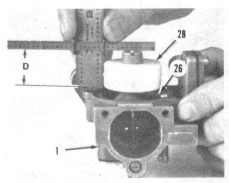

Fig. MR13-5 — With carburetor body (1) inverted, distance (D) should be 1 inch (25.4 mm) when measured as shown. Bend float arm (26) to adjust position of float (28).

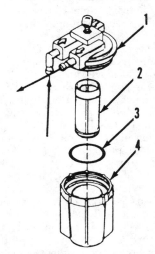

Fig. MR13-6 — Exploded view of reusable type fuel filter.

1. Filter base
2. Filter element
3. Sealing ring
4. Filter cup

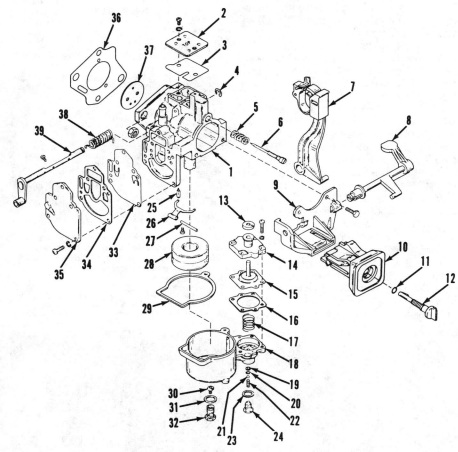

Fig. MR13-4 — Exploded view of "WMC" type carburetor.

1. Carburetor body	11. "O" ring	21. Check ball	31. Gasket
2. Cover	12. Fast idle knob	22. Spring	32. Plug
3. Gasket	13. Seal	23. Gasket	33. Diaphragm
4. Clip	14. Cover	24. Plug	34. Gasket
5. Spring	15. Enrichment diaphragm	25. Inlet needle	35. Cover
6. Idle mixture screw	16. Gasket	26. Float arm	36. Gasket
7. Neutral rpm ratchet	17. Spring	27. Float pin	37. Throttle plate
8. Enrichment lever	18. Float bowl	28. Float	38. Spring
9. Enrichment bracket	19. Seat	29. Gasket	39. Throttle shaft
10. Enrichment knob	20. Retainer	30. Main jet	

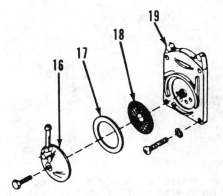

Fig. MR13-7 — On "BC" type carburetor, view showing fuel strainer (18) located behind fuel pump inlet cover (16). Gasket (17) is used to seal between inlet cover (16) and pump cover (19).

Fig. MR13-8—View showing reed valve assembly.

1. Block
2. Petals
3. Stop
4. Screw

plunger is fully depressed when the engine is idling at the recommended rpm.

(Models With "WMC" Type Carburetor). To synchronize ignition timing and throttle opening, proceed as follows: Mount the outboard motor on a boat or a suitable test tank and immerse the lower unit. Remove the engine cover. Connect a power timing light to the top cylinder

Mount the outboard motor on a boat or a suitable test tank and immerse the lower unit. Remove the engine cover. Connect a power timing light to the top cylinder spark plug lead. With the outboard motor in the "Forward" gear and the engine running at full throttle, three timing dots (D—Fig. MR13-9) should be aligned with timing mark (M) on starter housing. To adjust full advance ignition timing, stop the engine and adjust length of link (K) by disconnecting and turning link end. Lengthening link will advance ignition timing. Recheck full throttle ignition timing, then stop engine.

Disconnect throttle rod (T) from throttle cam, loosen screw (W—Fig. MR13-10) and move throttle cam (C) so mark (L) is aligned with roller (R) and cam just touches roller. Retighten screw (W). Start the engine, then advance throttle lever (V—Fig. MR13-11) until two timing dots (B) on flywheel are aligned with timing mark (M). Adjust length of throttle rod (T) so when rod is attached to throttle cam (C), mark (L) is in contact with roller (R).

Idle speed is adjusted at stop screw (IS). Recommended idle speed is 600-700 rpm with engine at normal operating temperature and in gear. Adjust position of dashpot (P) so dashpot plunger is fully depressed when the engine is idling at the recommended rpm.

(Models With "BC" Type Carburetor And "BCIB" Or "BCIC" Stamped On Carburetor Flange). To synchronize ignition timing and throttle opening, proceed as follows: Mount the outboard motor on a boat or a suitable test tank and immerse the lower unit. Remove the engine cover. Connect a power timing light to the top cylinder spark plug lead. With the outboard motor in "Forward" gear and the engine running at full throttle, three timing dots (D—Fig. MR13-9) should be aligned with timing mark (M) on starter housing. To adjust full advance ignition timing, stop the engine and adjust length of link (K) by disconnecting and turning link end. Lengthening link will advance ignition timing. Recheck full throttle ignition timing, then stop engine.

Disconnect throttle rod (T) from throttle cam, loosen screw (W—Fig. MR13-10) and move throttle cam (C) so mark (L) is aligned with roller (R) and cam just touches roller. Retighten screw (W). Start the engine, then advance throttle lever (V—Fig. MR13-12) until four timing dots (F) on flywheel are aligned with timing mark (M). Adjust length of throttle rod (T) so when rod is attached to throttle cam (C), mark (L) is in contact with roller (R).

Idle speed screw is adjusted at stop screw (IS). Recommended idle speed is 600-700 rpm with engine at normal operating temperature and in gear. Adjust position of dashpot (P) so dashpot

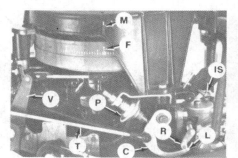

Fig. MR13-11—View showing speed control linkage components used on models with "BC" type carburetor and "BCIA" stamped on carburetor flange.

B. Timing dots
C. Throttle cam
L. Throttle cam mark
M. Timing mark
P. Dashpot
R. Roller
T. Throttle rod
V. Throttle lever
IS. Idle speed stop screw

Fig. MR13-12—View showing speed control linkage components used on models with "BC" type carburetor and "BCIB" or "BCIC" stamped on carburetor flange.

C. Throttle cam
F. Timing dots
L. Throttle cam mark
M. Timing mark
P. Dashpot
R. Roller
T. Throttle rod
V. Throttle lever
IS. Idle speed stop screw

Fig. MR13-9—On models with "BC" type carburetor, at full throttle the ignition timing is at full advance when three dots (D) align with timing mark (M) on starter housing. Refer to text for adjustment of speed control link (K) and throttle rod (T).

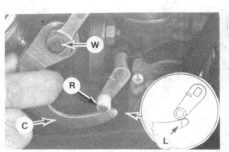

Fig. MR13-10—View showing throttle cam (C), throttle cam mark (L), throttle shaft roller (R) and screw (W) used on models with "BC" type carburetor. Refer to text for speed control linkage adjustment procedures.

MR13-13—On models with "WMC" type carburetor, at full throttle the ignition timing at full advance when three dots (D) align with timing mark (M) on starter housing. Refer to text for adjustment of speed control link (K).

spark plug lead. With the outboard motor in the "Forward" gear and the engine running at full throttle, three timing dots (D–Fig. MR13-13) should be aligned with timing mark (M) on starter housing. To adjust full advance ignition timing, stop the engine and adjust length of link (K) by disconnecting and turning link end. Lengthening link will advance ignition timing. Recheck full throttle ignition timing, then stop engine.

With the engine stopped, loosen screw (W–Fig. MR13-14) and move throttle cam (C) so mark (L) is aligned with roller (R) and cam just touches roller.

NOTE: Adjust idle speed screw (IS—Fig. MR13-15), dashpot (P) and neutral rpm ratchet (N—Fig. MR13-16) if needed to obtain desired setting.

Retighten screw (W–Fig. MR13-14). Start the engine, then advance throttle lever (V–Fig. MR13-15) until the 2° ATDC timing mark (H) (one mark to the right of single dot) is aligned with timing mark (M). Adjust length of throttle rod (T) so when rod is attached to throttle

Fig. MR13-14 — View showing throttle cam (C), throttle cam mark (L), throttle shaft roller (R) and screw (W) used on models with "WMC" type carburetor. Refer to text for speed control linkage adjustment procedures.

Fig. MR13-15 — View showing speed control linkage components used on models with "WMC" type carburetor.

C. Throttle cam
H. Flywheel timing mark
L. Throttle cam mark
M. Starter housing timing mark

P. Dashpot
R. Roller
T. Throttle rod
V. Throttle lever
IS. Idle speed screw

cam (C), mark (L) is in contact with roller (R).

Idle speed is adjusted at stop screw (IS). Recommended idle speed is 600-700 rpm with engine at normal operating temperature and in gear. Adjust position of dashpot (P) so dashpot plunger is fully depressed when the engine is idling at the recommended rpm.

With a suitable tachometer attached, start the engine and rotate the throttle control to the "SLOW" position. Position the primer/fast idle knob (B–Fig. MR13-16) in the middle detent position and adjust ratchet (N) until 1400-1700 rpm is obtained.

Fig. MR13-16 — View showing neutral rpm ratchet (N) and prime/fast idle knob (B) used on models with "WMC" type carburetor.

Fig. MR13-17 — View showing ground plate (P) attached to the negative ignition coil terminal.

IGNITION

On models with ground plate (P–Fig. MR13-17) attached to the negative ignition coil terminal, the standard spark plug is Champion L77J4. A Champion QL77J4 is recommended by the manufacturer should radio frequency interference suppression be required. Spark plug electrode gap should be 0.040 inch (1.02 mm). On models that are equipped with a ground wire attached to the negative ignition coil terminal, the standard spark plug is Champion L76V. A Champion QL76V is recommended by the manufacturer should radio frequency interference suppression be required. Renew surface gap spark plug if center electrode is more than 1/32 inch (0.79 mm) below the flat surface of the plug end.

A capacitor discharge ignition (CDI) system is used on all models. If engine malfunction is noted and the ignition system is suspected, make sure the spark plugs and all electrical wiring are in good and all electrical connections are tight before proceeding to troubleshooting the CD ignition system.

Proceed as follows to test CDI system components: Refer to Fig. MR13-18. To test stator assembly, first make sure stator assembly is grounded to engine. Disconnect black wire with yellow tracer (B/Y) and black wire with white tracer (B/W) from switch box. Use a suitable ohmmeter and perform the following tests. Connect black tester lead to engine ground and red tester lead to black wire with white tracer (B/W) from stator assembly. The resistance reading should be 120-180 ohms. Leave black tester lead connected to engine ground and connect red tester lead to black wire with yellow tracer (B/Y) from stator assembly. The resistance reading should be 3200-3800 ohms. Connect tester leads between black wire with yellow tracer

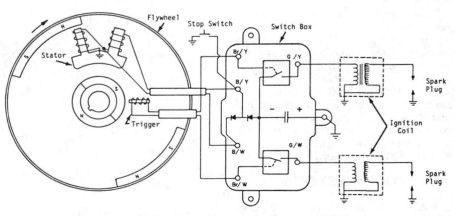

Fig. MR13-18 — View identifying CDI system components and wiring.

B/W. Black wire with white tracer
B/Y. Black wire with yellow tracer

G/W. Green wire with white tracer
G/Y. Green wire with yellow tracer

Br/W. Brown wire with white tracer
Br/Y. Brown wire with yellow tracer

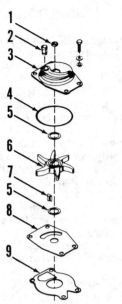

Fig. MR13-19 — Exploded view of water pump assembly.

1. Rubber seal
2. Outlet tube
3. Cover
4. "O" ring
5. Fiber washer
6. Impeller
7. Key
8. Plate
9. Gasket

When cooling system problems are encountered, first check water inlets for plugging or partial stoppage. If the water pump is suspected defective, separate gearcase from drive shaft housing and inspect pump. Make sure all seals and mating surfaces are in good condition and water passages are unobstructed. Check impeller (6) and plate (8) for excessive wear. When reassembling, tighten cover (3) securing screws evenly, but DO NOT overtighten screws as the four plastic isolators may be damaged.

POWER HEAD

R&R AND OVERHAUL. The power head can be removed for disassembly and overhaul as follows: Clamp outboard motor to a suitable stand and remove top and bottom engine cowl. Detach spark plug leads from spark plugs and remove spark plugs from power head. Remove manual starter assembly. Disconnect speed control cables, fuel line and any wiring that will interfere with power head removal. Remove or disconnect any component that will interfere with power head removal. Remove six

screws securing power head to drive shaft housing and lift power head free. Remove flywheel, ignition components, carburetor, carburetor adapter plate and reed valve assembly. Remove screws retaining exhaust cover (9 – Fig. MR13-20) and withdraw. Remove screws retaining cylinder block cover (4) and withdraw. Remove screws retaining six transfer port covers and withdraw. Crankcase halves can be separated after removal of six screws securing crankcase half (1) to cylinder block (2). Crankshaft and pistons are now accessible for removal and overhaul as outlined in the appropriate following paragraphs.

ASSEMBLY. When reassembling, make sure all joints and gasket surfaces are clean and free from nicks and burrs. All friction surfaces and bearings must be lubricated with engine oil during reassembly. Make sure crankshaft's center main bearing dowel opening properly aligns with dowel pin in cylinder block. Make sure locating pins on crankshaft roller bearings fit into the slots in cylinder block. Check frequently as power head is being assembled for binding of working parts. If binding or lock-

(B/Y) and black wire with white tracer (B/W) from stator assembly. The resistance reading should be 3100-3700 ohms.

To test trigger assembly, disconnect brown wire with yellow tracer (Br/Y) and brown wire with white tracer (Br/W) from switch box. With engine at room temperature (68°F/20°C), use a suitable ohmmeter and connect tester leads between brown wire with yellow tracer (Br/Y) and brown wire with white tracer (Br/W) from trigger assembly. The resistance reading should be 650-850 ohms.

To test ignition coil assembly, disconnect wires and spark plug lead from coil assembly. Use a suitable ohmmeter and connect tester leads between positive (+) and negative (−) coil terminals. The resistance reading should be 0.02-0.04 ohms. Leave the one tester lead connected to the negative (−) coil terminal and connect the remaining tester lead to the spark plug lead's terminal end in the coil tower. The resistance reading should be 800-1100 ohms.

COOLING SYSTEM

WATER PUMP. A rubber impeller type water pump is mounted between the drive shaft housing and gearcase. Water pump impeller (6 – Fig. MR13-19) is driven by a key in the drive shaft.

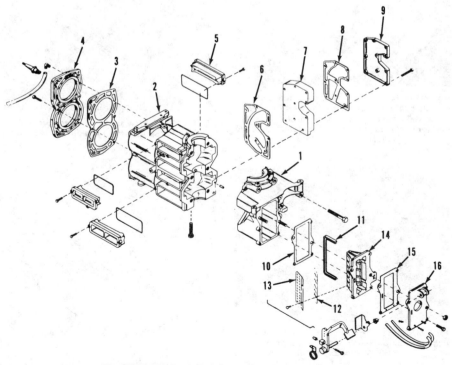

Fig. MR13-20 — Exploded view of crankcase assembly.

1. Crankcase half
2. Cylinder block
3. Gasket
4. Cylinder block cover
5. Transfer port cover
6. Gasket
7. Exhaust manifold
8. Gasket
9. Exhaust cover
10. Gasket
11. Seal
12. Reed petals
13. Reed stop
14. Reed block
15. Gasket
16. Adapter plate

ing is encountered, correct cause before proceeding with assembly.

Apply a continuous 1/16 inch (1.6 mm) bead of Loctite 514 to sealing surface of crankcase half (1 – Fig. MR13-20). Make sure entire surface is coated, but avoid an excess application as sealant may be squeezed into crankcase, bearings or passages.

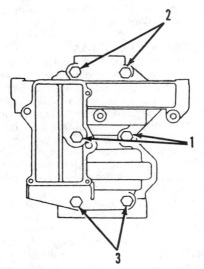

Fig. MR13-21 – Tighten crankcase screws in sequence shown above.

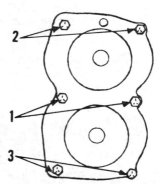

Fig. MR13-22 – Tighten cylinder block cover screws in sequence shown above.

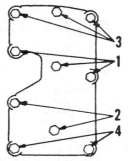

Fig. MR13-23 – Tighten exhaust cover screws in sequence shown above.

Refer to CONDENSED SERVICE DATA for final torque specifications. Tighten screws in three progressive steps. Refer to Fig. MR13-21 for crankcase screws tightening sequence. Refer to Fig. MR13-22 for cylinder block cover screws tightening sequence. Refer to Fig. MR13-23 for exhaust cover screws tightening sequence.

CYLINDERS, RINGS AND PISTONS. Cylinder bores should be measured halfway between top of cylinder and exhaust ports. Measurements should be taken every 45° of the cylinder bore to determine if an out-of-round condition exists. If cylinder bore is out-of-round more than 0.003 inch (0.076 mm), cylinder block (2 – Fig. MR13-20) and crankcase (1) must be renewed. If chrome surface of cylinder bore has been penetrated, excessively scored or is flaking, the cylinder block (2) and crankcase (1) must be renewed.

Measure diameter of pistons 0.010 inch (2.54 mm) from base of piston skirt and at a right angle (90°) to piston pin. Pistons should measure 2.554-2.559 inches (64.87-64.99 mm). If not, renew piston or pistons. Make sure piston rings properly align with locating pins in ring grooves.

When reassembling, install new piston pin retaining clips (12 – Fig. MR13-24) and make sure that "UP" on inside of piston is towards flywheel end of engine. Coat bearings, pistons, rings and cylinder bores with engine oil during assembly.

CRANKSHAFT, BEARINGS AND RODS. The connecting rods ride on a roller bearing around the crankpins. Maximum allowable assembled clearance between thrust washers (16 – Fig. MR13-24) and crankshaft is 0.030 inch

(0.762 mm). Maximum allowable bend of connecting rod (9) is 0.002 inch (0.051 mm). Note that the manufacturer only recommends using crocus cloth to clean-up bearing surfaces of crankshaft journals and connecting rod surfaces.

STARTER

MANUAL STARTER. A starter lockout assembly is used to prevent starter engagement when the gear shift control is in the "Forward" or "Reverse" position.

To overhaul the manual starter, proceed as follows: Remove the engine cover. Detach fuel filter assembly from starter housing by pulling filter assembly straight down. Remove the three starter housing retaining screws and withdraw the starter assembly.

To disassemble, remove clips (13 – Fig. MR13-25) and withdraw pawls (12) and springs (11). Untie starter rope (10) at anchor (19) and allow the rope to wind into the starter. Remove screw (16), cam (14) and spring (15). Carefully lift pulley (9) with starter rope (10) from housing (1). BE CAREFUL when removing pulley (9) as the rewind spring in case (8) may be dislodged. Remove starter rope (10) from pulley (9) if renewal is required. Separate rewind spring and case (8) from pulley (9). If renewal of rewind spring is required, use extreme caution when removing rewind spring from spring case (8).

Inspect all components for damage and excessive wear and renew if needed.

To reassemble, first apply a coating of a suitable water-resistant grease to rewind spring area of spring case (8). Install rewind spring in spring case (8) so spring coils wind in a clockwise direction from the outer end. Make sure the spring's outer hook is properly secured.

Fig. MR13-24 – Exploded view of crankshaft assembly, connecting rods and piston assemblies.

1. Seal
2. Bearing
3. Key
4. Crankshaft assy.
5. Crankshaft carrier
6. Connecting rod cap
7. Bearing cage half
8. Roller bearings (12)
9. Connecting rod
10. Washer
11. Needle bearings (27)
12. Clip
13. Piston pin
14. Piston
15. Piston rings
16. Thrust washer half
17. Bearing half
18. Bearing race half
19. Spring clip

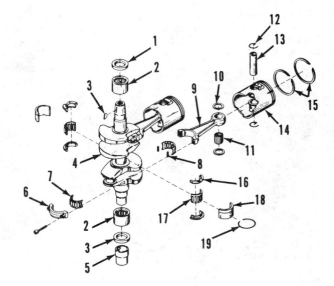

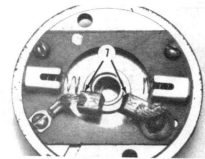

Fig. MR13-25 — Exploded view of manual rewind starter.

1. Starter housing
2. Cover
3. Lockout lever
4. Spring
5. Pin
6. Pulley lock lever
7. Felt pad
8. Rewind spring & case
9. Pulley
10. Starter rope
11. Spring
12. Pawl
13. Clip
14. Cam
15. Spring
16. Screw
17. Rope guide
18. Handle
19. Anchor

PROPELLER AND DRIVE HUB.

Lower unit protection is provided by a cushion type hub in the propeller. The standard propeller is three bladed with a diameter of 10-3/8 inches (264 mm) and a pitch of 13 inches (330 mm). Optional propellers are available. Select a propeller that will allow the engine at full throttle to reach maximum operating rpm range (4500-5500 on 20 hp models and 5000-6000 on 25 hp models).

R&R AND OVERHAUL.

Clamp outboard motor to an appropriate stand and remove gearcase drain plug and vent plug. Allow gearcase lubricant to drain into a suitable container. Detach shift rod from actuator at top of motor leg. Note the flat washer located at top of shift rod. Remove the four cap screws retaining gearcase housing to drive shaft housing and withdraw gearcase housing. Do not lose shift rod washer during disassembly.

Disassemble gearcase as follows: Remove locknut (44 – Fig. MR13-29), propeller (43) and thrust hub (42). Remove water pump assembly (Fig. MR13-19). Remove screws securing retaining plate (41 – Fig. MR13-29) and withdraw plate and "O" ring (40). Remove cap from around thrust hub (42). Install thrust hub (42) on propeller shaft (34) with the hub's three ears facing toward carrier assembly (36). Install propeller (43) and secure with locknut (44). Place a suitable tool on hex head hub of propeller and turn propeller CLOCKWISE to unscrew carrier as-

Install rewind spring and case (8) into pulley (9). Wind starter rope (10) onto pulley (9) counterclockwise when viewed from the flywheel side. Assemble pulley (9) to starter housing (1) making sure rewind spring end properly engages notch in starter housing center shaft. When pulley (9) is seated properly, pulley bushing will be flush with end of starter housing shaft. Install spring (15), cam (14) and secure with screw (16). Install springs (11), pawls (12) and clips (13) as shown in Fig. MR13-26.

Rotate pulley (9 – Fig. MR13-25) counterclockwise until starter rope (10) end is aligned with starter housing rope outlet. Thread starter rope (10) through starter housing (1), rope guide (17) and handle (18) and secure in anchor (19). Pull starter rope (10) out to full length while checking for freedom of travel,

then allow starter rope (10) to rewind onto pulley (9). Starter handle (18) should be drawn back into the proper released position. If not, release starter rope (10) from handle (18) and rotate pulley (9) one complete turn counterclockwise (flywheel side) and reassemble.

NOTE: Do not apply any more tension on rewind spring (8) than is required to draw starter handle (18) back into the proper released position.

Remount manual starter assembly and complete reassembly.

ELECTRIC STARTER.

Some models are equipped with a 12 volt electric starter. The armature and drive components are shown in Fig. MR13-27. Normal no-load current draw is 15 amperes and load current draw is 60 amperes. Minimum brush (7 – Fig. MR13-28) wear limit is 3/16 inch (4.8 mm).

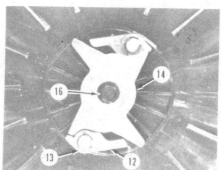

Fig. MR13-26 — View showing correct installation of pawls (12), clips (13), cam (14) and screw (16).

Fig. MR13-27 — View showing electric starter armature and drive components.

1. Locknut
2. Spacer
3. Spring
4. Starter drive
5. End frame
6. Armature

Fig. MR13-28 — Minimum electric starter brush (7) wear limit is 3/16 inch (4.8 mm).

sembly (36). When carrier assembly (36) is completely unthreaded, remove locknut (44), propeller (43) and thrust hub (42) from propeller shaft (34). Withdraw propeller shaft (34) with components (29 through 39). Remove cap screw (25) and withdraw pinion gear (24) and bearing (23). Withdraw forward gear (28) and tapered roller bearing (26). If needed, remove shift linkage components.

Inspect shafts for wear on seal lip contact areas and on splines. Inspect dog clutch and gears for wear on engage-

ment areas of dog teeth. Inspect gears for excessive wear and damage. Inspect shift cam for excessive wear on ramp. All seals and "O" rings should be renewed when unit is reassembled.

NOTE: No adjustment of gear mesh pattern and gear backlash is provided. Make sure all parts are in good condition and properly assembled.

Reverse disassembly for reassembly while noting the following: Install dog clutch (32) with "F" marked side toward forward gear (28). Apply a water-resistant grease to the lip surfaces of all seals. Rotate carrier assembly (36) **counterclockwise** to tighten. Install cap on thrust hub (42) and assemble with thrust hub ears facing propeller (43).

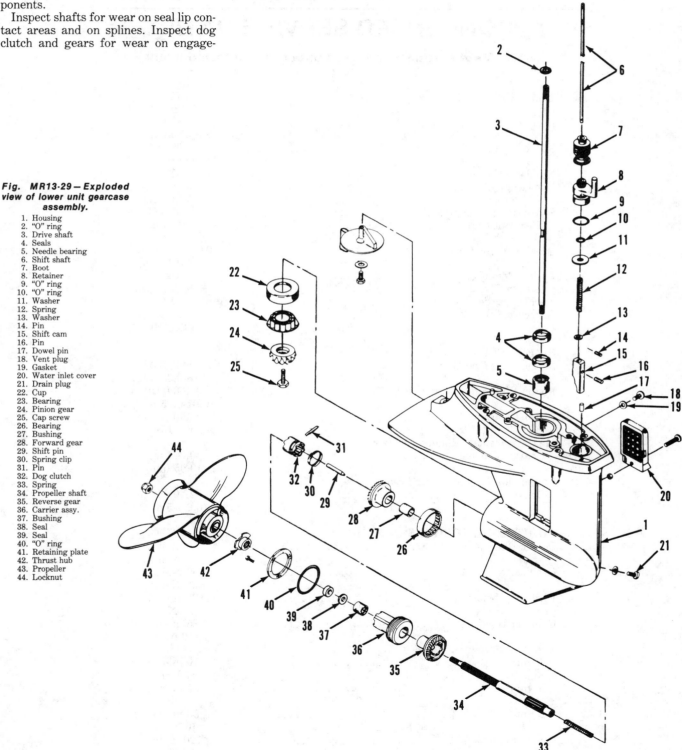

Fig. MR13-29 — Exploded view of lower unit gearcase assembly.

1. Housing
2. "O" ring
3. Drive shaft
4. Seals
5. Needle bearing
6. Shift shaft
7. Boot
8. Retainer
9. "O" ring
10. "O" ring
11. Washer
12. Spring
13. Washer
14. Pin
15. Shift cam
16. Pin
17. Dowel pin
18. Vent plug
19. Gasket
20. Water inlet cover
21. Drain plug
22. Cup
23. Bearing
24. Pinion gear
25. Cap screw
26. Bearing
27. Bushing
28. Forward gear
29. Shift pin
30. Spring clip
31. Pin
32. Dog clutch
33. Spring
34. Propeller shaft
35. Reverse gear
36. Carrier assy.
37. Bushing
38. Seal
39. Seal
40. "O" ring
41. Retaining plate
42. Thrust hub
43. Propeller
44. Locknut

MERCURY

BRUNSWICK MARINE POWER
1939 Pioneer Road
Fond du Lac, Wisconsin 54935

MERC 2.2

CONDENSED SERVICE DATA

NOTE: Metric fasteners are used throughout outboard motor.

TUNE-UP

Hp	2.2
Bore	1.85 in.
	(47 mm)
Stroke	1.69 in.
	(43 mm)
Number Of Cylinders	1
Displacement	4.5 cu. in.
	(74.6 cc)
Spark Plug—Champion	RL87YC
Electrode Gap	0.040 in.
	(1 mm)
Breaker Point Gap	0.012-0.016 in.
	(0.3-0.4 mm)
Ignition Timing	Fixed
Idle Speed	900-1000 rpm
Fuel:Oil Ratio	50:1
Gearcase Oil Capacity	3 oz.
	(90 mL)

SIZES—CLEARANCES

Piston Ring End Gap	0.006-0.012 in.
	(0.18-0.33 mm)
Piston Ring Side Clearance	0.0003-0.0010 in.
	(0.01-0.05 mm)
Piston Clearance	0.002-0.005 in.
	(0.06-0.15 mm)
Max. Crankshaft Runout At Main Bearing Journal	0.001 in.
	(0.05 mm)
Connecting Rod Small End Side Shake	0.022-0.056 in.
	(0.6-1.5 mm)

TIGHTENING TORQUES

Power Head Mounting Screws	50 in.-lbs.
	(6 N·m)
Crankcase	50 in.-lbs.
	(6 N·m)
Flywheel Nut	30 ft.-lbs.
	(41 N·m)
Cylinder Head	85 in.-lbs.
	(10 N·m)
Standard Screws:	
4 mm	10 in.-lbs.
	(1 N·m)
5 mm	25 in.-lbs.
	(3 N·m)
6 mm	50 in.-lbs.
	(6 N·m)
8 mm	120 in.-lbs.
	(14 N·m)

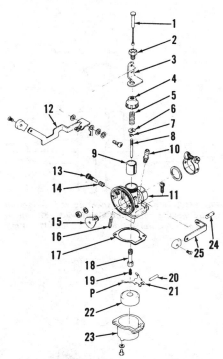

Fig. M1-1—Exploded view of TK type carburetor.

1. Throttle wire	14. Spring
2. Guide screw	15. Choke plate
3. Bracket	16. Fuel inlet valve
4. Cap	17. Gasket
5. Spring	18. Main nozzle
6. Retainer	19. Main jet
7. Clip	20. Float arm pin
8. Jet needle	21. Float arm
9. Throttle slide	22. Float
10. Fuel inlet	23. Float bowl
11. Body	24. Shaft
12. Throttle lever	25. Choke lever
13. Idle speed screw	

LUBRICATION

The power head is lubricated by oil mixed with the fuel. Recommended oil is Quicksilver Premium Blend Outboard Lubricant mixed at a fuel:oil ratio of 50:1.

Lower unit gears and bearings are lubricated by oil contained in the gearcase. Recommended oil is Quicksilver Premium Blend Gear Lubricant. The gearcase should be refilled periodically and the lubricant renewed after every 30 days.

FUEL SYSTEM

CARBURETOR. The TK type carburetor shown in Fig. M1-1 is used. Standard main jet (19) size for normal operation is number 94. Normal position of clip (7) is second groove from top. Inserting clip in a higher groove will lean midrange mixture while insertion in a lower groove will richen midrange mixture.

To determine the float level, invert carburetor body (11 – Fig. M1-2) and measure distance (D) from top of carburetor bowl gasket (17) to base of float

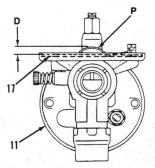

Fig. M1-2 — Float level is measured by inverting carburetor body (11) and measuring distance (D) from top of carburetor bowl gasket (17) to base of float arm pad (P). Bend float arms evenly to adjust.

arm pad (P). Distance should be 0.090 inch (2.3 mm) and is adjusted by bending float arm pads (P) evenly until the correct distance is obtained.

Adjust idle speed screw (13) so engine idles at 900-1000 rpm with engine at normal operating temperature.

REED VALVE. The reed valve is located on inside of crankcase. Inspect reed valve (4 – Fig. M1-5) and renew if cracked, bent or otherwise damaged. Do not attempt to straighten reed valve. Reed valve stop height (H – Fig. M1-3) should be 0.236-0.244 inch (6.0-6.2 mm).

SPEED CONTROL LINKAGE. Engine speed is regulated by position of throttle lever (12 – Fig. M1-1). As throttle lever (12) is raised or lowered, carburetor throttle slide (9) is operated via throttle wire (1).

IGNITION

Refer to Fig. M1-4 for an exploded view of ignition components. Breaker point gap should be 0.012-0.016 inch (0.3-0.4 mm) and is adjustable through opening in flywheel. The flywheel must be removed for breaker point renewal. Tighten flywheel nut to 30 ft.-lbs. (41 N·m).

Magneto base plate (5) is fixed to the engine with tapered screws and no timing adjustment is possible other than varying the breaker point gap between the recommended 0.012-0.016 inch (0.3-0.4 mm) tolerance.

To check ignition coil (6), primary circuit resistance reading should be 0.81-1.09 ohms while the secondary circuit resistance reading should be 4250-5750 ohms.

COOLING SYSTEM

WATER PUMP. A rubber impeller type water pump is located in the gearcase and mounted on and driven by the propeller shaft.

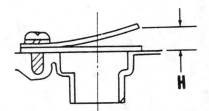

Fig. M1-3 — Reed valve stop height (H) should be 0.236-0.244 inch (6.0-6.2 mm).

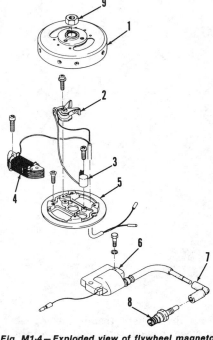

Fig. M1-4 — Exploded view of flywheel magneto unit.

1. Flywheel	
2. Breaker point assy.	
3. Condenser	6. Ignition coil
4. Exciter coil	7. Spark plug boot
5. Magneto base plate	8. Spark plug
	9. Nut

When cooling system problems are encountered, first check the water inlet for plugging or partial stoppage, then if not corrected, remove propeller and gearcase cap for access to pump impeller. Refer to Fig. M1-8 for an exploded view of water pump.

POWER HEAD

REMOVE AND REINSTALL. To remove power head, remove motor covers, fuel tank and manual starter. Remove starter cup, unscrew flywheel nut and remove flywheel using a suitable puller. Disconnect ignition wires and remove ignition assembly. Remove carburetor. Unscrew the six screws securing power head and separate power head from drive shaft housing.

Reverse removal procedure when installing power head. Apply water resistant grease to ends of crankshaft and

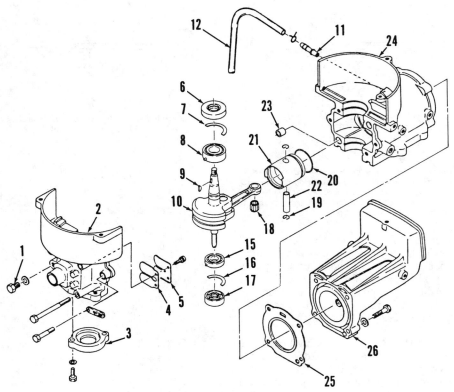

Fig. M1-5 — Exploded view of engine.

1. Plug	7. Locating ring	15. Ball bearing	21. Piston
2. Crankcase	8. Ball bearing	16. Locating ring	22. Piston pin
3. Head plate	9. Key	17. Seal	23. Dowel
4. Reed valve	10. Crankshaft assy.	18. Roller bearing	24. Cylinder block
5. Reed valve stop	11. Fitting	19. Clip	25. Head gasket
6. Seal	12. Hose	20. Piston ring	26. Cylinder head

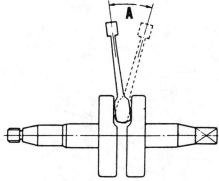

Fig. M1-6 — Measure connecting rod deflection (A) by moving small end side-to-side. Maximum allowable rod deflection is 0.056 inch (1.5 mm).

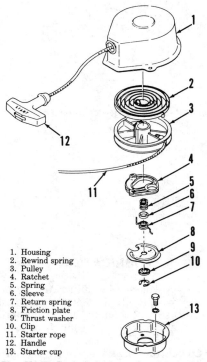

1. Housing
2. Rewind spring
3. Pulley
4. Ratchet
5. Spring
6. Sleeve
7. Return spring
8. Friction plate
9. Thrust washer
10. Clip
11. Starter rope
12. Handle
13. Starter cup

Fig. M1-7 — Exploded view of manual starter assembly.

upper drive shaft. Install a new gasket between power head and drive shaft housing.

DISASSEMBLY. To disassemble power head, detach cylinder head (26 – Fig. M1-5) and head plate (3). Unscrew six screws securing crankcase (2) to cylinder block (24) and separate crankcase from cylinder block. Crankshaft assembly is now accessible and can be removed from cylinder block (24). Refer to specific service sections for overhaul.

ASSEMBLY. All friction surfaces and bearings must be lubricated with engine oil during reassembly. Install piston on connecting rod so arrow on piston crown points towards flywheel end of crankshaft. Insert piston in cylinder block while being sure piston ring properly engages locating pin in piston ring groove. Install crankshaft assembly in cylinder block with locating rings (7 and 16 – Fig. M1-5) properly positioned in grooves of cylinder block (24). Check frequently as power head is being assembled for binding of working parts. If binding or locking is encountered, correct cause before proceeding with assembly.

Apply a continuous 1/16 inch (1.6 mm) bead of Loctite Master Sealer part 92-12564-1 to crankcase (2) mating surface. Make sure sealer bead is continuous but avoid excess application. Install crankcase half (2) on cylinder block while being sure locating pins in bearings (8 and 15) properly engage notches in cylinder block (24). Install head plate (3).

PISTON, PIN, RING AND CYLINDER. The standard cylinder bore is 1.850 inches (47 mm) with a maximum wear limit of 1.852 inches (47.05 mm). Bore cylinder to 0.020 inch (0.5 mm) oversize if maximum wear limit is exceeded or cylinder bore is tapered or out-of-round more than 0.002 inch (0.05 mm). Piston and piston ring are available in standard size and 0.020 inch (0.5 mm) oversize.

The piston pin is retained by clips (19—Fig. M1-5) which should be renewed if removed. The piston pin rides in a roller bearing in rod small end. Install piston on connecting rod so arrow on piston crown points toward flywheel end of crankshaft.

Recommended piston ring end gap is 0.006-0.012 inch (0.18-0.33 mm). Recommended piston ring side clearance is 0.0003-0.0010 inch (0.01-0.05 mm).

CRANKSHAFT AND CONNECTING ROD. Crankshaft, connecting rod, crankpin and bearing are assembled as a pressed-together unit. Renew crankshaft assembly as a complete unit.

Determine connecting rod deflection (A – Fig. M1-6) by moving small rod end from side-to-side. Normal side-to-side movement is 0.022-0.056 inch (0.6-1.5 mm). Renew crankshaft assembly if side movement exceeds 0.056 inch (1.5 mm).

MANUAL STARTER

To overhaul the manual starter, proceed as follows: Remove the screws retaining the engine's port and starboard side covers, then withdraw covers.

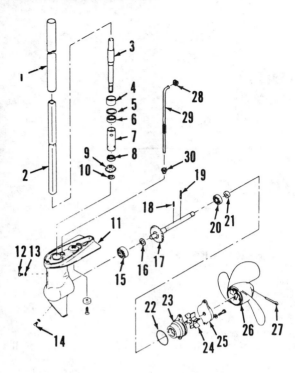

1. Tube
2. Upper drive shaft
3. Lower drive shaft
4. Seal
5. Snap ring
6. Ball bearing
7. Sleeve
8. Ball bearing
9. Pinion gear
10. Clip
11. Gearcase
12. Vent (level) plug
13. Gasket
14. Drain plug
15. Ball bearing
16. Thrust washer
17. Propeller shaft
    with gear
18. Impeller drive pin
19. Shear pin
20. Ball bearing
21. Seal
22. "O" ring
23. Water pump housing
24. Impeller
25. Cap
26. Propeller
27. Cotter pin
28. Grommet
29. Water tube
30. Seal

wind spring (2) by engaging starter rope (11) in pulley (3) notch and turning pulley counterclockwise, then release starter rope (11) from pulley notch.

NOTE: Do not apply more tension on rewind spring (2) than is required to draw starter handle (12) back into the proper released position.

Check starter action, then remount manual starter assembly and engine's side covers to complete reassembly.

LOWER UNIT

PROPELLER AND SHEAR PIN. Lower unit protection is provided by a shear pin (19 – Fig. M1-8). Be sure correct shear pin is installed for maximum protection to lower unit.

Standard propeller is two-bladed on 1984 models and three-bladed on 1985 and 1986 models. Standard propeller diameter is 7.4 inches (188 mm) and pitch is 4.5 inches (114 mm). Propeller rotation is clockwise.

R&R AND OVERHAUL. To remove gearcase, unscrew two screws securing gearcase to drive shaft housing and separate. Unscrew drain plug (14 – Fig. M1-8) and vent (level) plug (12) and allow lubricant to drain into a suitable container. Remove cotter pin (27) and withdraw propeller (26). Remove cap (25), water pump impeller (24), pin (18) and water pump housing (23). Remove clip (10) and withdraw lower drive shaft (3). Remove pinion gear (9) and withdraw propeller shaft with gear (17). If necessary, remove remaining bearings from gearcase.

Inspect all components for excessive wear and damage and renew if needed. Reassembly is reverse order of disassembly. Fill gearcase with lubricant until lubricant begins to overflow from vent (level) plug (12) port.

Remove the screws retaining the manual starter assembly to the power head and withdraw.

To disassemble, untie starter rope (11 – Fig. M1-7) at handle (12) and allow rope to wind into the starter. Invert the unit and remove clip (10), then withdraw thrust washer (9), friction plate (8), return spring (7), sleeve (6), spring (5) and ratchet (4). Remove pulley (3) while being careful not to dislodge rewind spring (2). Remove starter rope (11) from pulley (3) if renewal is required. If rewind spring (2) must be removed, care must be used to prevent spring from uncoiling dangerously.

Reassembly is the reverse order of disassembly. Apply a water-resistant grease to rewind spring area of starter housing (1). Install rewind spring (2) with coils wrapped in a counterclockwise direction from outer spring end. Wrap starter rope (11) around pulley (3) in a counterclockwise direction when viewed from the bottom side. Install pulley (3) in starter housing (1) making sure pulley properly engages rewind spring (2). Thread rope end through starter housing (1) and secure on handle (12).

NOTE: Lubricate all friction surfaces with a suitable water-resistant grease during reassembly.

Install ratchet (4) so ratchet tooth points counterclockwise when viewed from the bottom side. Assemble remaining components. Apply tension to re-

MERCURY

MERC 4 (1979-1981)
MERC 40 (1976-1978)

CONDENSED SERVICE
DATA

TUNE-UP
Rated Horsepower 4.0
Full Throttle Rpm Range. 4300-4700
Bore – Inches 1.562
Stroke – Inches 1.437
Number of Cylinders. 2
Displacement – Cu. In. 5.5
Spark Plug:
  Type. . . . . .Champion L7J
  Electrode 0.050
Ignition . . . . Breakerless
Carburetor:
  Make. . . . . .Own
Fuel:Oil Ratio. . . . . .See Text

SIZES – CLEARANCES
Piston Rings:
  End Gap. . . . .*
  Side Clearance . . . .*
Piston Clearance. . . . . .See Text
Crankshaft Bearings:
  Upper Main Bearing. . . . . .Roller
  Lower Main Bearing. . . . . .Ball
  Crankpin. . . . . .Loose Rollers
Piston Pin Bearing In Rod. . . . . .Loose Rollers

*Publication not authorized by manufacturer.

TIGHTENING TORQUES
(All Values Given In Inch-Pounds)
Connecting Rod. 75
Crankcase-to-Cylinder Block. 90
Flywheel Nut. 240
Spark Plug. 240
Power Head Retaining Nuts. 80

LUBRICATION

The engine is lubricated by oil mixed with the fuel. Fuel should be regular leaded, low lead or unleaded gasoline with a minimum pump octane rating of 86. Premium gasoline may be used if desired regular gasoline is not available. Recommended oil is Quicksilver Premium Blend 2-Cycle Oil. A good quality NMMA certified TC-W oil may be used if Premium Blend 2-Cycle Oil is not available.

Fuel:oil ratio when using the recommended oil is 50:1 for normal operation. Follow fuel:oil ratio recommended by oil manufacturer if the recommended oil is not used.

When breaking in a new or overhauled engine, do not operate engine above half throttle (2500-3500 rpm) for first two hours. Avoid sustained full throttle operation for first ten hours of operation.

Lower unit gears and bearings are lubricated by oil in the gearcase. Recommended oil is Quicksilver Premium Blend Gear Lubricant. Remove vent plug and fill gearcase through fill plug opening in lower end of gearcase until oil is expelled from vent plug opening. Gearcase oil capacity is 2-3/4 fl. ozs.

FUEL SYSTEM

CARBURETOR. Refer to Fig. M2-1 for an exploded view of Mercarb carburetor used on Merc 4 and 40. Standard main jet (13) size is 0.041 at elevations below 2500 ft. Initial setting of idle mixture screw (4) is 1-1/2 turns open. Float level should be 0.078-0.100 inch measured from carburetor body to edge of float as shown in Fig. M2-2. Do not measure from gasket surface.

Some models are equipped with a remote idle mixture control. Idle mixture

lever (14—Fig. M2-1) should be pressed over idle mixture screw (4) so lever points in 10 o'clock direction. Do not disturb idle mixture screw setting.

SPEED CONTROL LINKAGE. The throttle twist grip is connected to the throttle lever (13—Fig. M2-3) by two control cables (AC & RC—Fig. M2-4). Throttle cam (14—Fig. M2-3) is attached to throttle lever (13) and contacts carburetor cam follower. Ignition lever (10) rests on throttle lever (13) and both are supported by shoulder bolt (17). Rod (6) connects ignition lever (10) to trigger ring (5) and spring (12) attaches to ignition lever (10) and throttle lever. When the throttle twist grip is rotated for more speed, advance control cable (left cable) is pulled which rotates lever (13) on shoulder bolt. Spring (12) forces ignition lever (10) to rotate with throttle lever (13) until ignition lever contacts maximum advance screw (11). Rod (6) forces trigger ring (5) to rotate as ignition lever rotates thereby changing ignition timing.

Before adjusting throttle pickup point, refer to IGNITION TIMING section and check ignition timing. To adjust throttle pickup point, connect an ignition timing light to number 1 spark plug. Run engine and note ignition timing when carburetor cam follower contacts throttle cam. Ignition timing should be 12-16 degrees ATDC. Loosen throttle cam screw (15—Fig. M2-3) and adjust throttle cam position to obtain desired pickup point.

REED VALVES. The inlet reed valve unit is located between carburetor and crankcase. Refer to Fig. M2-5 for an exploded view of reed valve assembly. Reed petals (4) should seat very lightly against reed block (5) throughout their entire length with least possible tension. Renew petals if cracked, warped, pitted or bent. Seating surface of reed block must be perfectly smooth and flat. Gap between tips of reed stop plates (3) and reed valve block should be 0.154 inch.

IGNITION SYSTEM

SPARK PLUG. Recommended spark plug is Champion L7J. Electrode gap should be 0.050 inch.

IGNITION. All models are equipped with a Thunderbolt CD breakerless ignition system. Refer to Fig. M2-4A for wiring schematic. Stator coils (S) and flywheel magnets charge capacitor in switch box (B). Electric charge in capacitor is released through ignition coil (IC) when trigger module (T) sends an impulse to switch box.

IGNITION TIMING. The following ignition timing procedure must be followed from start to finish or incorrect timing may result.

Place twist grip in full retard position. Gap between throttle cam (14—Fig. M2-3) and carburetor cam follower should be 0.005-0.015 inch. If not, loosen cam screw (15), move cam, then retighten screw. Loosen nuts and turn retard cable fitting (RF—Fig. M2-4) so 3-4 threads are exposed on cable housing end of fitting. Retighten nuts. Hold twist against

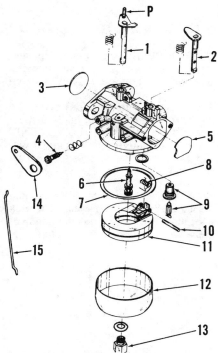

Fig. M2-1—Exploded view of carburetor. Remote idle mixture lever (14) and link (15) are used on later models.

P. Pickup arm
1. Throttle shaft
2. Choke shaft
3. Throttle plate
4. Idle mixture screw
5. Choke plate
6. Nozzle
7. Gasket
8. Spring
9. Fuel inlet valve
10. Float pin
11. Float
12. Float bowl
13. Main jet
14. Remote idle mixture lever
15. Link

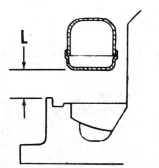

Fig. M2-2—Float level (L) should be 0.078-0.100 inch.

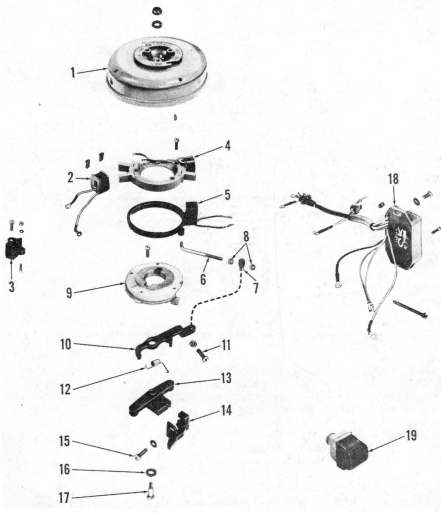

Fig. M2-3—Exploded view of ignition system.

1. Flywheel
2. Stator coil
3. Terminal block
4. Stator
5. Trigger ring
6. Trigger ring rod
7. Swivel bolt
8. Nuts
9. Stator bracket
10. Ignition lever
11. Maximum advance screw
12. Spring
13. Throttle lever
14. Throttle cam
15. Throttle cam screw
16. Washer
17. Shoulder bolt
18. Switch box
19. Ignition coils

Refer to SPEED CONTROL LINKAGE section and adjust carburetor throttle pickup point.

TROUBLE-SHOOTING. The following test specifications should be used to isolate faulty component if ignition system malfunctions. Resistance between yellow stator lead and ground should be 1500-2000 ohms. Resistance between yellow and white stator wires should be 750-950 ohms. Resistance between two trigger module leads should be 140-160 ohms. Ignition coils may be checked using a suitable ignition oil tester. Replace switch box with a switch box known to be good if malfunction is suspected.

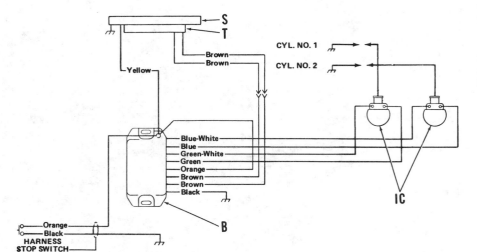

Fig. M2-4—Refer to text for speed control and ignition timing adjustments.

COOLING SYSTEM

WATER PUMP. An impeller type water pump is located in gearcase housing and is mounted on and driven by drive shaft.

If cooling system problems occur, be sure water inlet is not plugged or partially obstructed. Refer to LOWER UNIT section and remove gear housing if water pump, water tube or seals must be examined.

NOTE: During disassembly of water pump mark impeller so it can be installed in original location. Reversing original rotation of impeller will cause premature failure.

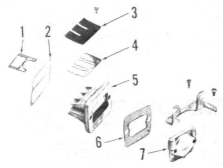

Fig. M2-4A—Wiring schematic for Merc 4 and 40. Trigger module has two brown leads on models prior to 1978 and a brown lead and a white lead on models after 1977.

Fig. M2-5—Exploded view of reed valve assembly. Filler block was used on early models.

1. Filler block
2. Gasket
3. Reed stop
4. Reed petal
5. Reed block
6. Gasket
7. Intake manifold

idle stop and adjust advance cable fitting (AF) to just remove slack in advance cable (AC). Immerse lower unit in water and connect a power timing light to number 1 (top) spark plug. Start and run engine until warm. With unit in gear, run engine at 1000-1500 rpm then quickly close throttle while noting ignition timing. Timing should momentarily retard to 18-20 degrees ATDC at idle speed of 600 rpm. Turn link rod nuts (N—Fig. M2-6) so ignition timing is 2 degrees below advance reading. For instance, if timing fully retards to 18 degrees ATDC then advances to 15 degrees ATDC at 600 rpm, set ignition timing at idle at 17 degrees ATDC.

Maximum ignition timing should be 22-26 degrees BTDC and is adjusted by turning maximum advance screw (M).

Fig. M2-6—View showing location of maximum advance screw (M) and trigger rod nut (N).

POWER HEAD

R&R AND DISASSSEMBLE. Remove top cover and remove spark plugs. Remove intake silencer box from carburetor. Detach advance and retard control cables and choke cable. Remove idle mixture lever from idle mixture screw. Disconnect electrical wires which will interfere with power head removal. Disconnect fuel line and remove fuel tank. Unscrew rewind starter retaining screws and hang starter over side of lower cover. Unscrew six nuts on under side of drive shaft housing. Carefully lift straight up while holding bottom cover down and separate power head from bottom cover. There are gaskets between power head and bottom cover and between bottom cover and drive shaft housing. The lower gasket must be renewed if bottom cover separates from drive shaft housing. Drive shaft may bind in crankshaft during power head removal and disengage drive shaft key from water pump impeller. Note distance required to push drive shaft down so it bottoms in gearcase. If drive shaft moves more than 1/4 inch, drive shaft key must be reinstalled in pump impeller. Refer to LOWER UNIT section.

Remove flywheel, flywheel key, ignition switch box, stator assembly, carburetor and reed valve assembly. If so equipped, remove filler plate (1—Fig. M2-5). Remove cylinder block cover (26—Fig. M2-7) and exhaust cover (2). Unscrew crankcase-to-cylinder block screws and separate crankcase from cylinder block while being careful not to lose loose needle bearing rollers in center main bearing. Remove center main bearing rollers (31).

Refer to appropriate following sections to service engine components. Assemble by following procedure outlined in ASSEMBLY paragraph.

ASSEMBLY. Make sure all joint and gasket surfaces are clean, free from nicks, burrs and hardened cement or carbon. Crankcase and intake manifold must be completely sealed against vacuum and pressure. Exhaust cover and cylinder block cover must be sealed against water leakage and pressure.

Crankcase and cylinder block are machined as a unit and must be serviced as a unit assembly. Cylinder block bores are chrome plated. Cylinder block bore and crankcase must be renewed if chrome on cylinder bores is flaking, scored, scratched or worn through to base metal. Cylinders may be lightly honed with a 45 degrees to 64 degrees pattern to remove metal transferred from pistons. Thoroughly clean

cylinders and check for out-of-round condition after honing.

To assemble power head, assemble components (3 through 24—Fig. M2-7), except seal (14), as outlined in appropriate paragraphs. Thoroughly lubricate pistons, rings and cylinder bores and make sure that piston ring gaps are properly positioned around locating pins in piston ring grooves. Two special Mercury ring compressors should be used to compress rings into grooves. Position crankshaft assembly in cylinder block by inserting pistons into ends of cylinders. Install the center main bearing liner (30) that has a hole in it in the cylinder block with "V" end of liner toward exhaust cover side of block. Ap-

ply a thin bead of Loctite 271 around outer circumference of seal (21), then seat crankshaft in cylinder block. Rotate snap ring (19) so end gap is aligned with bleed groove in cylinder block mating surface as shown in Fig. M2-8. Push oil seal (21—Fig. M2-7) up tightly against snap ring (19). Lubricate center main bearing rollers (31) with a suitable needle bearing assembly grease. Push rollers around center bearing journal then place remainder on journal until 25 rollers are installed. Install remaining bearing liner (30) in crankcase so ends of liner will dovetail with previously installed liner in cylinder block.

Apply a continuous 1/16 inch bead of Loctite Master Gasket Sealer part 92-

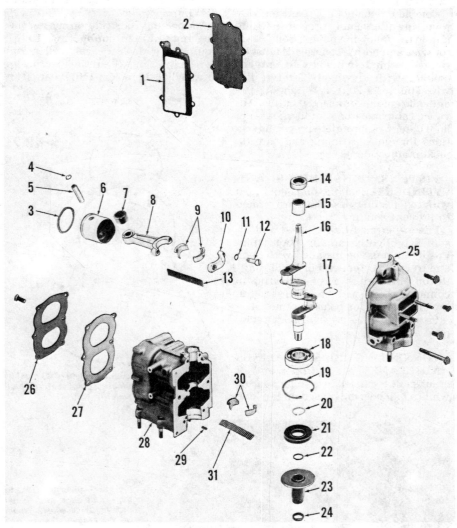

Fig. M2-7—Exploded view of power head.

1. Gasket	12. Rod screw	23. Coupler &
2. Exhaust cover	13. Bearing rollers (25)	counterweight
3. Piston rings (2)	14. Oil seal	24. Seal & retainer
4. Pin retainer	15. Roller bearing	25. Crankcase
5. Piston pin	16. Crankshaft	26. Cylinder block
6. Piston	17. Seal	cover
7. Roller bearing	18. Ball bearing	27. Gasket
8. Connecting rod	19. Snap ring	28. Cylinder block
9. Bearing liner	20. Snap ring	29. Dowel pins (2)
10. Rod cap	21. Oil seal	30. Bearing liners
11. Tab washer	22. "O" ring	31. Bearing rollers (25)

12564-1 to crankcase (25) mating surface. Make sure sealer bead is continuous but do not allow sealer in bleed groove (G—Fig. M2-8). Be sure oil seal (21—Fig. M2-7) is tight against snap ring (19). Install crankcase on cylinder block and insert screws. Note that two lower screws are two inches long, two center screws are 5/8 inch long and two upper screws are 7/8 inch long. Tighten screws evenly to 90 in.-lbs. in three steps. Rotate crankshaft and check for binding. Direct compressed air through bleed hole to blow excess sealer out of bleed groove. Apply a thin bead of Loctite 271 to outer circumference of upper oil seal (14), then drive oil seal over crankshaft with metal side up. Install cylinder block cover and tighten screws to 30 in.-lbs.

Complete remainder of reassembly by reversing disassembly procedure while noting the following points: Yellow stator wire and both trigger leads must be rotated behind switchbox to prevent contact with flywheel. Tighten flywheel nut to 17-20 ft.-lbs. Tighten power head retaining nuts to 80 in.-lbs. Advance cable must be routed under fuel line. Refer to appropriate preceding sections for ignition timing and throttle pickup adjustments.

PISTONS, PINS, RINGS AND CYLINDERS. Each piston is equipped with two piston rings which are pinned to prevent rotation.

Piston pin may be removed and installed by lightly tapping against pin. Piston pin must be installed with open end toward bottom end of crankshaft. Piston pin rides in a roller bearing in connecting rod small end. Refer to following section for bearing removal.

Pistons and rings are available in standard size only.

CONNECTING RODS, BEARINGS AND CRANKSHAFT. Upper end of crankshaft is carried by a roller bearing while a ball bearing is used on the lower end. The center main bearing consists of 25 bearing rollers which should be installed as outlined in ASSEMBLY section.

To assemble components of bottom end of crankshaft, proceed as follows: Press ball bearing (18—Fig. M2-7) on crankshaft and install snap ring (20). Lay snap ring (19) on bearing and install oil seal (21) with lip toward splines. Lubricate "O" ring (22) and position against crankshaft shoulder. Note counterweight on coupler (23) and press coupler on crankshaft so counterweight is aligned with number 1 connecting rod journal and 180 degrees from number 2 connecting rod journal as shown in Fig. M2-9. Be sure coupler is over "O" ring (22—Fig. M2-7) and against crankshaft shoulder. Press seal and retainer (24) into coupler.

Connecting rods ride on loose roller bearings. Each connecting rod is equipped with 25 bearing rollers and two bearing lines (9). Install bearing liner with hole in rod cap (10). Bearing liner ends must dovetail and connecting rod alignment marks must match when assembling rod. Tighten rod screws to 75 in.-lbs.

MANUAL STARTER

To remove starter, remove hood, detach starter rope handle and allow rope to wind into starter. Unscrew starter retaining screws and remove starter. To disassemble starter, remove center screw (1—Fig. M2-10) which has left-hand threads. Remove components (2 through 8). Hold pulley (10) and spring housing (12) together and rotate starter gear (9) off pulley (10) helix. Separate pulley (10) from spring housing (12) while detaching spring end from back of pulley. If necessary, carefully dislodge rewind spring (11) from spring housing (12) so spring uncoils away from body. Pins in rope pulley (10) must be driven out for rope removal.

Lubricate rewind spring with multipurpose grease and attach outer end to post (P—Fig. M2-11). Pass spring around guide (G) and coil spring in housing in counterclockwise direction. To install rope on pulley, retain end loop with pin nearest hub and stake pin.

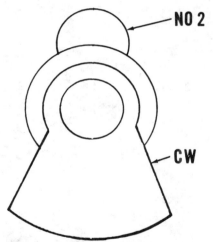

Fig. M2-9—Coupler counterweight (CW) must be 180 degrees from number 2 crankshaft rod journal. Refer to text.

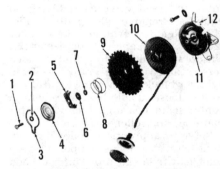

Fig. M2-10—Exploded view of manual starter.

1. Screw	7. Washer
2. Washer	8. Spring
3. Spring	9. Starter gear
4. Spring retainer	10. Rope pulley
5. Spring holder	11. Rewind spring
6. Shoulder washer	12. Housing

Fig. M2-8—Snap ring (19) end gap must align with bleed groove (G). Oil seal (21) must be tight against snap ring (19).

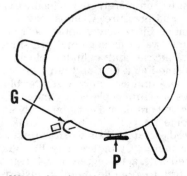

Fig. M2-11—Attach rewind spring to housing as outlined in text.

Wrap rope twice around pulley in counterclockwise direction as viewed from helix end. Insert and stake second pin in pulley. Install rope pulley on starter housing post and engage inner end of rewind spring with slot in pulley. Lubricate helix with multipurpose grease and install starter gear (9—Fig. M2-10).

Install shoulder washer (6) and spring holder (5) on starter gear and measure distance from spring holder cutout to face of starter gear as shown in Fig. M2-12. Distance must be at least 1/16 inch. If not, install washers (7—Fig. M2-10) behind or ahead of shoulder washer (6) so correct distance is obtained. Remove spring holder and assemble components (1 through 8). Tighten screw (1) to 30 in.-lbs. Preload starter so there is sufficient spring tension so rope rewinds freely and rope handle is snug against cowl.

LOWER UNIT

PROPELLER AND DRIVE CLUTCH.
Protection for motor is provided by a special cushioning clutch built into the propeller hub. Propeller is splined to the shaft. Propeller should be selected to provide maximum engine speed of 4300-4700 rpm.

R&R AND OVERHAUL.
To remove gear housing, unscrew nut adjacent to exhaust outlet and nut in drive shaft housing. Separate gear housing from drive shaft housing.

Drain lubricant from gear housing. Unscrew and remove water pump cover (7—Fig. M2-13). Remove face plate (8). Withdraw drive shaft while holding pump impeller in housing. Unscrew and remove water pump housing (14).

NOTE: Mark impeller so it will turn in same direction after installation. Reversing original rotation will cause premature failure.

Fig. M2-12—Distance (D) between spring holder cutout and face of starter gear should be at least 1/16 inch. Refer to text.

Unscrew cover nut (38) using Cover Nut Tool (C-91-74588) or other suitable tool. Remove washer (37), if so equipped. Hold propeller shaft in a vise and bump against gear housing to dislodge propeller shaft assembly from housing. Be careful not to lose the key (43). Remove pinion gear (23), thrust bearing (22) and thrust washer (21).

To disassemble propeller shaft assembly, remove bearing carrier (34) and spacer (32). Do not remove roller bearing (35) from bearing carrier (34) unless renewal is required. Unscrew gear nut (24) and remove gear (26) by turning gear against direction of spring coils. If bearing (29) must be renewed, remove nut (30) with tool C-91-74589 or equivalent and press gear out of bearing.

Use tool C-91-77644 or equivalent to pull bearings (18 and 20) out of gear housing. Coupler (19) is located between bushings and will be removed along with bushings.

To determine required thickness of shim (28), install pinion gear bearing (20) in gear housing. Refer to Fig. M2-14 and insert Gage Rod Adapter C-23-75484 in gear housing. Insert Gage Rod C-91-74585 through Gage Rod Adapter and pinion gear bushing. Position Gage Adapter C-91-74586 in propeller shaft

so it bottoms in gear housing. Using a depth micrometer, measure distance (D) from Gage Rod to face of Gage Adapter. Subtract measured distance (D) from 3.691 inches to obtain desired thickness of shim (28—Fig. M2-13).

To assemble gear housing, proceed as follows: Drive bearing (20) into gear housing using tool C-91-77548. Bearing is properly located when tool bottoms against gear housing. Install coupler (19). Drive bearing (18) into gear housing following same procedure used when installing bearing (20). Press bearing (29) onto gear (26) so bearing is tight against gear. Apply Loctite 271 to threads of nut (30) and tighten nut on gear to 30 ft.-lbs. using tool C-91-74589 or equivalent. Assemble gear, clutch spring (27) and propeller shaft (31). Install slotted washer (25) on shaft. Screw a new locknut (24) onto shaft until tight, then back nut off so there is 0.005-0.010 inch clearance between washer (25) and locknut (24).

Press bearing (35) into bearing carrier (34). Apply Loctite 271 to outer edge of seal (36), then press seal into bearing carrier (34) so seal lip is toward bearing. Install pinion gear (23) in bearing (20). Install shim (28) in gear housing. Insert propeller shaft and gear assem-

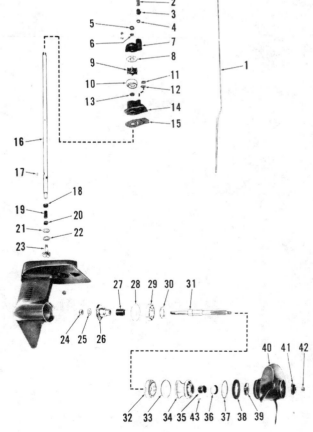

Fig. M2-13—Exploded view of lower unit.

1. Shift shaft
2. Water tube sleeve
3. Seal
4. Washer
5. Rubber ring
6. Oil seal
7. Pump cover
8. Face plate
9. Impeller
10. Liner
11. Quad seal
12. Washer
13. Oil seal
14. Water pump housing
15. Gasket
16. Drive shaft
17. Impeller key
18. Roller bearing
19. Coupler
20. Roller bearing
21. Thrust washer
22. Thrust bearing
23. Pinion gear
24. Nut
25. Washer
26. Gear
27. Clutch spring
28. Shim
29. Ball bearing
30. Nut
31. Propeller shaft
32. Spacer
33. "O" ring
34. Bearing carrier
35. Roller bearing
36. Oil seal
37. Washer
38. Nut
39. Thrust hub
40. Propeller
41. Thrust hub
42. Nut
43. Key

bly in gear housing. Install spacer assembly in gear housing. Install spacer (32) so shift shaft holes (H—Fig. M2-15) in spacer and gear housing are aligned and alignment bosses (B) are toward prop end of shaft. Lubricate and install "O" ring (33—Fig. M2-13) on spacer. Apply a suitable sealant to outer circumference of bearing carrier (34) and install bearing carrier so alignment tab is inserted between bosses (B—Fig. M2-15) on spacer. Install key (43—Fig. M2-13) into grooves in bearing carrier and gear housing. Thread cover nut (38) into gear housing so words "OFF-ON" are facing out and tighten nut to 40 ft.-lbs.

using Cover Nut Tool C-91-74588 or equivalent.

To install water pump, reverse removal procedure. Install seals (6 and 13) with lips toward top. Be sure tabs on liner (10) and plate (8) mate with slots in water pump housing. Tighten water pump cover nuts to 20 in.-lbs.

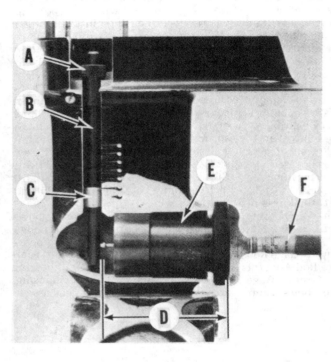

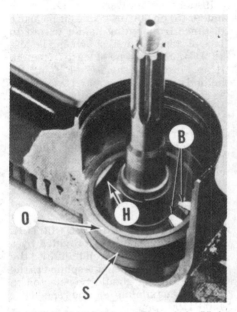

Fig. M2-14—Assemble gage tools as shown to determine shim thickness.

A. Gage rod adapter C-23-75484
B. Gage rod C-91-74585
C. Roller bearing
D. Measured distance
E. Gage adapter C-91-74586
F. Depth micrometer

Fig. M2-15—Install spacer (S) so hole (H) is aligned with shift shaft hole in gear housing. Note position of "O" ring land (O) and alignment bosses (B).

MERCURY
MERC 3.5, 3.6 AND 4.5
MERC 4 (1986 AND 1987)
MERC 40 (1969-1974) AND 45

Year Produced

1969	Merc 40
1970	Merc 40
1971	Merc 40
1972	Merc 40
1973	Merc 40
1974	Merc 40
1975	Merc 45
1976	Merc 45
1977	Merc 45
1978	Merc 45
1979	Merc 4.5
1980	Merc 4.5
1981	Merc 3.6, Merc 4.5
1982	Merc 3.6, Merc 4.5
1983	Merc 3.5, Merc 4.5
1984	Merc 3.5, Merc 4.5
1985	Merc 3.5, Merc 4.5
1986	Merc 4*
1987	Merc 4*

*Merc 4 hp model (1986 and 1987) is a later version of the earlier 4.5 hp model. Refer to 4.5 hp model when servicing 1986 and 1987 4 hp outboard motor.

CONDENSED SERVICE DATA

TUNE-UP

Hp/rpm	3.5/4500-5000
	3.6/4500-5000
	4.0/4500-5000
	4.5/4500-5500
Bore	2 in.
	(50.8 mm)
Stroke	1¾ in.
	(44.45 mm)
Number of Cylinders	1
Displacement	5.5 cu. in.
	(90.1 cc)
Spark plug:	
Type	See Text
Electrode Gap	See Text
Ignition	See Text
Idle Speed	See Text
Fuel:Oil Ratio	50:1
Fuel Pump:	
Discharge Pressure at WOT	2 psi
	(14 kPa)
Gearcase Oil Capacity	See Text

SIZES—CLEARANCES

Piston Rings:	
End Gap	*
Side Clearance	*
Piston Skirt Clearance	*
Crankshaft Bearings:	
Upper Main Bearings	Ball & Roller
Lower Main Bearing	Ball Bearings
Crankpin	Loose Rollers
No. of Rollers	29
Crankshaft End Play	0.004-0.012 in.
	(0.102-0.305 mm)
Piston Pin Bearing in Rod	Loose Rollers
No. of Rollers	20

*Publication not authorized by manufacturer.

TIGHTENING TORQUES

Connecting Rod	180 in.-lbs.
	(20.3 N·m)
Flywheel Nut	35 ft.-lbs.
	(41.5 N·m)
Spark Plug	20 ft.-lbs.
	(27.2 N·m)
Power Head to Drive Shaft Housing	80 in.-lbs.
	(9 N·m)

LUBRICATION

The engine is lubricated by oil mixed with the fuel. Fuel should be regular leaded, low lead or unleaded gasoline with a minimum pump octane rating of 86. Premium gasoline may be used if desired regular gasoline is not available. Recommended oil is Quicksilver Premium Blend 2-Cycle Oil. A good quality NMMA certified TC-W oil may be used. Fuel:oil ratio should be 50:1 when using the recommended oil. Follow fuel:oil ratio recommended by oil manufacturer if the recommended oil is not used.

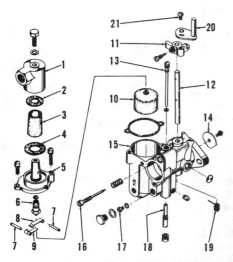

Fig. M3-4 — With bowl cover (5) upright, distance (D) between primary lever (8) and end of secondary lever (9) should be ¼ inch (6.4 mm). Bend tab (T) to adjust.

Fig. M3-1 — Exploded view of Tillotson KB type carburetor.

1. Strainer cover	12. Throttle shaft
2. Gasket	13. Idle tube
3. Strainer	14. Throttle valve
4. Gasket	15. Body
5. Bowl cover	16. Idle needle
6. Inlet needle & seat	17. High speed jet
7. Shaft	18. Main nozzle
8. Primary lever	19. Spring
9. Secondary lever	20. Follower lever
10. Float	21. Screw
11. Throttle lever	

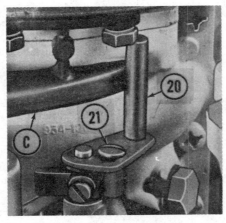

Fig. M3-5 — On motors before serial number 2693144, the speed control linkage should be adjusted so that follower lever (20) just contacts cam (C) at 1000 rpm.

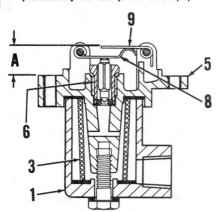

Fig. M3-2 — Idle speed should be adjusted to approximately 650-700 rpm at screw (IS).

Fig. M3-6 — View of speed control cam (C) and follower (20) for motors serial number 2771622 and above except Merc 3.5 and 3.6. Refer to text for adjustment.

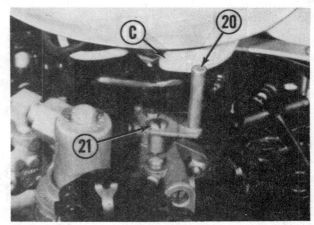

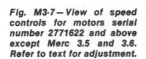

Fig. M3-3 — Schematic view of float mechanism showing points of adjustment. Refer to text.

Fig. M3-7 — View of speed controls for motors serial number 2771622 and above except Merc 3.5 and 3.6. Refer to text for adjustment.

To break in new or overhauled motors, observe the following: If Quicksilver Premium Blend 2-Cycle Oil is used, the amount of oil should be doubled for the first tank. Motor should not be operated above 1/2 throttle (2500-3500 rpm) for the first 2 hours. Avoid sustained full throttle operation for the first 10 hours of operation.

The lower unit gears and bearings are lubricated by oil contained in the gearcase. Only Quicksilver Premium Blend Gear Lubricant should be used. Gearcase is filled through the drain plug hole on starboard side of case, with motor in an upright position. The vent plug (fill plug) should be removed when filling. Lubricant should be maintained at level of vent plug.

FUEL SYSTEM

Merc 4.5, 40 And 45

CARBURETOR. A Tillotson KB-10A carburetor is used. Standard size main jet (17 – Fig. M3-1) is 0.036 inch (0.91 mm). Other main jet sizes are available for adjusting the calibration for altitude or other special conditions. Initial setting for idle mixture needle (16) is one turn open. Idle mixture adjustment should be accomplished with motor operating under load, at slow speed (approximately 500 rpm), after it has reached normal operating temperature. Turning the idle mixture needle clockwise leans the mixture.

The idle fuel mixture must be correctly set before adjusting idle speed. Run the motor until it reaches normal operating temperature, loosen locknut and turn idle speed screw (IS – Fig. M3-2 or M3-7) to provide 650-700 rpm in forward gear, under normal load.

To adjust the fuel level, remove bowl cover (5 – Fig. M3-1) and invert cover assembly. Measure distance (A – Fig. M3-3) between primary lever (8) and gasket surface of bowl cover (5) with inlet valve (6) closed. This distance (A) should be 13/32 inch (10.32 mm). If setting is incorrect, bend curved end of secondary lever (9). Turn bowl cover (5 – Fig. M3-4) upright and measure distance (D) between primary lever (8) and end of secondary lever (9). Distance (D) should be ¼ inch (6.4 mm). Bend tab (T) to adjust. The contact spring located in center of float (10 – Fig. M3-1) should extend 3/32 inch (2.38 mm) above top of float. Check to see if spring has been stretched or damaged.

SPEED CONTROL LINKAGE. The speed control grip moves the magneto stator plate to advance or retard the ignition timing. The carburetor throttle valve is synchronized to open as the timing is advanced. Before attempting to synchronize throttle opening to the ignition advance, the idle fuel mixture and point gap must be correctly set.

On motors before serial number 2693114, run motor until it reaches normal operating temperature, engage forward gear, then turn the speed control handle until engine is operating at 1000 rpm. With controls set as outlined, the control cam (C – Fig. M3-5), attached to magneto stator plate, should just contact the throttle follower lever (20). Adjust by loosening screw (21) and moving throttle follower (20). Make certain that carburetor throttle valve is not slightly open.

On motors serial number 2771622 and above, move the speed control to maximum speed position (in forward gear with motor NOT running) and check play between throttle follower (20 – Fig.

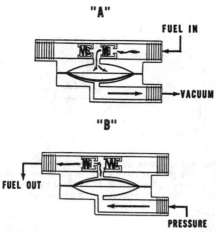

Fig. M3-9—Schematic view of diaphragm type fuel pump showing method of operation. Vacuum-Pressure line attaches to the crankcase. When power head piston moves upward in cylinder, vacuum in crankcase draws diaphragm out and fuel in as shown in view "A". Crankcase pressure resulting from power stroke forces diaphragm in and fuel out as shown in view "B".

M3-6) and cam (C). The follower should have almost completely opened the throttle with approximately 0.050 inch (1.27 mm) play remaining. If incorrect, loosen screw (21) and reposition throttle follower (20). To position cam for correct throttle pickup, rotate crankshaft until piston is exactly 0.005 inch (0.13 mm) ATDC. Attach continuity meter to the white wire from contact points and to motor ground. Move the speed control lever from fast toward slow position until the continuity meter shows that contact points just close. With crankshaft and speed controls set as described, the cam (C – Fig. M3-7) should be just touching follower (20). If cam and follower are not touching or if throttle is partially open, loosen the two screws attaching cam (C) and reposition cam as required. Very little adjustment is normally necessary; however, the maximum throttle opening should be rechecked.

REED VALVES. The inlet reed valve unit is located between carburetor and crankcase, and should be checked whenever the carburetor is removed for service. Refer to Fig. M3-8. Reed petals (10) should seat very lightly against reed block (9) throughout their entire length with the least possible tension. Check seating visually and by blowing and drawing air through port. Renew petals (10) if broken, cracked, warped, rusted or bent. Seating surface of reed block (9) must be perfectly smooth and flat. Reed petals should be installed with notches (N) at upper right and lower left as shown. On late models, the reed retainers are similarly marked. Rounded edge of retainers should be toward inside as shown in the inset of Fig. M3-8.

FUEL PUMP. A diaphragm type fuel pump is used, and is operated by pressure and vacuum pulsations in the crankcase as shown in Fig. M3-9. Vacuum in the crankcase draws the diaphragm down, pulling fuel past the inlet check valve as shown in view "A". Crankcase pressure forces the diaphragm out and the trapped fuel enters the carburetor line past the outlet check valve as shown in view "B".

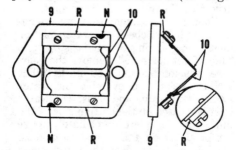

Fig. M3-8—View of reed valve used. Side of retainers (R) with rounded edge should be toward inside as shown in the inset at right.

N. Notches
R. Retainers
9. Reed block
10. Reed petals

Fig. M3-10—Exploded view of Mikuni VM-16 carburetor.

1. Body
2. Cap
3. Gasket
4. Spring
5. Throttle stud
6. Retainer
7. Clip
8. Jet needle
9. Throttle slide
10. Gasket
11. Fuel inlet valve
12. Float pin
13. Float
14. Pilot jet
15. Nozzle
16. Main jet
17. Gasket
18. Float bowl
19. Springs
20. Idle speed screw
21. Idle mixture screw
22. Plunger
23. Spring
24. Nut
25. Clip
26. Cap
27. Choke lever

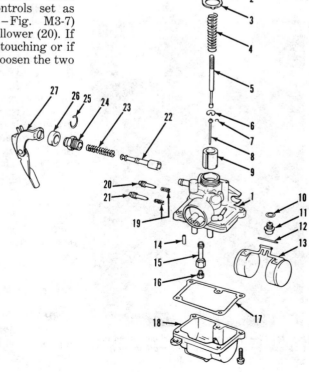

All defective or questionable parts should be renewed. Check valves must be installed to allow passage of fuel as shown in Fig. M3-9.

Merc 3.5 And 3.6

CARBURETOR. Merc 3.5 and 3.6 models are equipped with a Mikuni VM-16, sliding valve, float type carburetor. Refer to Fig. M3-10 for an exploded view of carburetor.

Initial setting of idle mixture screw (I – Fig. M3-11) is 2 turns out from a lightly seated position. Idle mixture screw regulates an idle air passage and will lean the idle mixture when turned counterclockwise. Adjust idle mixture and idle speed after engine reaches normal operating temperature. Loosen locknut (N) and ramp follower (F) prior to idle speed adjustment, then turn idle speed screw (S) so engine idles at 750-850 rpm. Refer to SPEED CONTROL LINKAGE section after idle speed adjustment and follow throttle synchronization procedure.

High speed mixture is controlled by main jet (16 – Fig. M3-10) Midrange mixture is controlled by the position of clip (7) in notches on jet needle (8). Leanest mixture is obtained by inserting clip in top jet needle notch while richest mixture results from inserting clip in bottom notch. Inserting clip in fourth notch from top of jet needle will provide best mixture for normal operation.

To determine the float level, invert carburetor body (1 – Fig. M3-12) and measure distance (D) from carburetor body surface to top of float (13).

Fig. M3-11 – View of carburetor and speed control lever on Merc 3.5 and 3.6 models. Refer to text for adjustment.

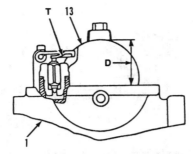

Fig. M3-12 – With carburetor body (1) inverted, distance (D) from carburetor body surface to top of float (13) should be ⅞ to 31/32 inch (22.2-24.6 mm). Adjust distance (D) by bending float arm tang (T).

Distance (D) should be ⅞ to 31/32 inch (22.2-24.6 mm). Adjust distance (D) by bending float arm tang (T).

SPEED CONTROL LINKAGE. The ignition is advanced as the speed control lever attached to the magneto base plate is moved towards full throttle position. The carburetor throttle slide is pulled upwards as ramp follower (F – Fig. M3-11) rides up speed control lever ramp.

To synchronize throttle opening with speed control lever movement, be sure idle speed is adjusted; then position speed control lever at lowest idle position with engine stopped. Loosen locknut (N) and adjust ramp follower (F) so follower just touches ramp on speed control lever. Do not rotate throttle slide stud. Tighten locknut (N). Throttle slide should rise just as speed control lever moves from idle position.

REED VALVES. The inlet reed valve unit is located between carburetor and crankcase, and should be checked whenever the carburetor is removed for service. Refer to Fig. M3-8. Reed petals (10) should seat very lightly against reed block (9) throughout their entire length with the least possible tension. Check seating visually and by blowing and drawing air through port. Renew petals (10) if broken, cracked, warped, rusted or bent. Seating surface of reed block (9) must be perfectly smooth and flat. Reed petals should be installed with notches (N) at upper right and lower left as shown. On late models, the reed retainers are similarly marked. Rounded edge of retainers should be toward inside as shown in the inset of Fig. M3-8.

IGNITION SYSTEM

Merc 4.5, 40 And 45

SPARK PLUG. Motors from serial number 2498136 to 2693114 should be equipped with ½ inch reach Champion L9J or AC type M45FF spark plug.

Electrode gap for these motors should be 0.030 inch (0.76 mm).

Motor serial number 2771622 and above use AC surface gap V40FFK spark plug. Renew surface gap plug if center electrode is more than 1/32 inch (0.79 mm) below flat surface of plug end.

MAGNETO. All models are equipped with a magneto ignition; however, late models (serial number 2771622 and above) are equipped with a maker point, electronic ignition magneto.

Point gap should be 0.020 inch (0.51 mm) at maximum opening for all models and can be adjusted after removing flywheel. Ignition maximum advance timing is not adjustable. The cam for ignition points is keyed to the crankshaft and should be installed with arrow up and indicating direction of rotation.

Merc 3.5 And 3.6

SPARK PLUG. Recommended spark plug is Champion L81Y or Autolite AE22. Champion QL81Y may be used if radio frequency interference suppression is required. Spark plug electrode gap should be 0.035 inch (0.89 mm).

MAGNETO. Merc 3.5 and 3.6 models are equipped with a breakerless, capacitor discharge ignition system. Remove flywheel for access to ignition module. Note that puller jaws should be placed adjacent to flywheel magnets to prevent flywheel breakage when pulling flywheel off crankshaft.

The engine is stopped when contact is made between the ignition module tab and a ground tab secured by an end cap (12 – Fig. M3-13) retaining screw. With speed control lever in stop position, tabs should make sufficient contact to stop engine. Bend ground tab if necessary.

Ignition timing is not adjustable.

COOLING SYSTEM

WATER PUMP. The rubber impeller type water pump is located in the gearcase housing and is mounted on and driven by the lower unit drive shaft.

When cooling system problems are encountered, first check the water inlet or inlets for plugging or partial stoppage. Then if not corrected, remove the gearcase housing as outlined in LOWER UNIT section and examine the water pump, water tube and seals. The water inlet is located on the bottom side of the antiventilation plate immediately above the propeller on 4.5, 40 and 45 models. On 3.5 and 3.6 models, the water inlets are located on the port and starboard sides of the lower unit.

When assembling, make certain that water pump retaining nuts are tighten-

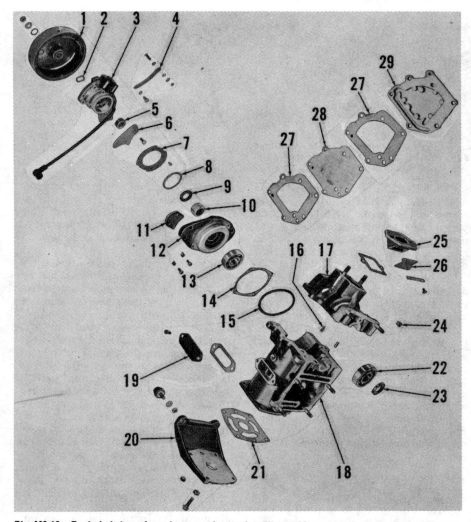

Fig. M3-13 — Exploded view of crankcase and associated parts. Magneto unit shown is type used on motors before serial number 2771622. Refer to Fig. M3-14 for view of late type ignition unit used on Merc 4.5, 40 and 45.

1. Flywheel
2. Wave washer
3. Armature plate
4. Speed control link
5. Ignition cam
6. Throttle synchronizer cam
7. Retainer ring
8. Shims (0.015 in.)
9. Seal
10. Roller bearing
11. Clamp for item 7
12. End cap
13. Ball bearing
14. Shims
15. "O" ring
16. Dowels
17. Front crankcase half
18. Cylinder & crankcase half
19. Transfer port cover
20. Cylinder cover
21. Gasket
22. Ball bearing
23. Seal
24. Crankcase check valve
25. Reed block
26. Reed petals
27. Gaskets
28. Baffle plate
29. Exhaust cover

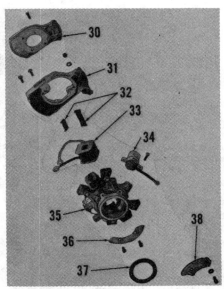

Fig. M3-14 — View of maker-point ignition unit used on serial number 2771622 and later models except Merc 3.5 and 3.6.

30. Cover
31. Ignition module
32. Coil retaining clips
33. Coil
34. Condenser
35. Stator assy.
36. Stator hold down plate
37. Stator plate shim
38. Throttle cam

ASSEMBLY. When assembling the crankcase must be completely sealed against both vacuum and pressure. Exhaust manifold and water passages must be sealed against pressure leakage. Whenever power head is disassembled, it is recommended that all gasket surfaces and machined joints without gaskets be carefully checked for nicks and burrs which might interfere with a tight seal.

Completely assemble the crankshaft, lower bearing, connecting rod, piston and rings and install assembly in cylinder (18 – Fig. M3-13). If special Mercury ring compressor is not available, use extreme care to prevent damage especially to piston and rings. Thoroughly lubricate piston, rings and bearings using new engine oil and make certain that ring end gaps are aligned with locating pins in ring grooves. After crankshaft is installed, turn the shaft until each ring appears in the exhaust and transfer ports and check for damage during assembly.

Assemble the upper main bearing cap (12) using the shim pack (14) which was removed. Install and tighten two screws which retain cap to cylinder block, tap the crankshaft back and forth using a soft mallet, then measure the gap between bearing (13) and crankshaft. The clearance should be 0.004-0.012 inch (0.102-0.305 mm). If incorrect, remove end cap and vary the thickness of shim pack (14) until the proper end play is obtained. Shims are available in thicknesses of 0.002, 0.003, 0.005 and 0.0010 inch.

ed to 30 in.-lbs. (3.4 N·m) on all models. If nuts are incorrectly tightened, the water pump may be damaged.

POWER HEAD

R&R AND DISASSEMBLE. To remove the power head assembly, first remove the top cowl and, on models so equipped, disconnect stop switch wire, speed control linkage and choke linkage. Remove fuel valve and nuts or screws securing power head to lower unit; then lift off the complete power head assembly.

Place the unit on power head stand or equivalent, and remove fuel pump, if so equipped, carburetor, flywheel and magneto. Exhaust manifold cover plates (28 & 29 – Fig. M3-13), cylinder block cover plate (20) and transfer port cover (19) should be removed for cleaning and inspection.

Remove the cap screws which retain upper end cap (12) to power head, then unbolt and remove crankcase front half (17). Carefully separate halves using extra care not to spring the parts or to mar the machined mating surfaces. Crankcase half (17) and cylinder (18) are matched and align bored, and are available only as an assembly.

The crankshaft and bearings assembly, with piston and connecting rod attached, can now be lifted out for service as outlined in the appropriate following paragraphs. Assemble by following the procedures outlined in the ASSEMBLY paragraph.

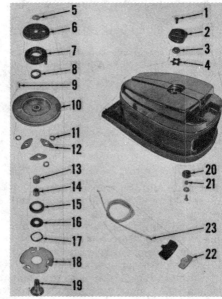

1. Piston rings
2. Snap ring
3. Piston
4. Piston pin
5. Bearing rollers
6. Bearing washers
7. Connecting rod
8. Bearing rollers
9. Rod cap
10. Crankshaft

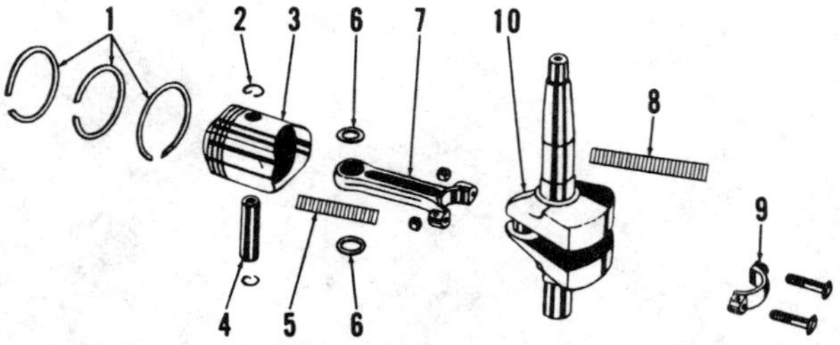

Fig. M3-15 — Exploded view of crankshaft, connecting rod and piston. Piston pin end of rod is fitted with 20 loose rollers (5); crankshaft end is fitted with 29 rollers (8). Three piston rings (1) are used on 4.5, 40 and 45 models, and two piston rings are used on 3.5 and 3.6 models.

Remove the end cap to cylinder block screws, withdraw cap and install "O" ring (15). Coat mating surfaces of crankcase halves lightly with sealer and assemble. Slide end cap (12) into position before tightening crankcase halves. Tighten crankcase cap screws by working each way from the center, to prevent distortion. Ignition ground tab must be properly located and secured by an end cap screw on Merc 3.5 and 3.6 models.

Turn the crankshaft several revolutions before installing power head to make certain that parts are free and do not bind.

PISTON, PIN, RINGS & CYLINDER. Before detaching the connecting rod from the crankshaft, make sure that rod and cap are properly marked for correct assembly to each other.

The piston on 4.5, 40 and 45 models is fitted with three rings which are pinned to prevent rotation in grooves. The piston on 3.5 and 3.6 models is fitted with two rings which are pinned to prevent rotation in grooves.

The piston pin is pressed in piston bosses and secured with retaining rings. Piston end of connecting rod is fitted with loose needle bearings which use connecting rod bore and piston pin as bearing races. Install bearing washers (6 – Fig. M3-15) and 20 loose rollers (5) in piston end of connecting rod using light nonfibrous grease and a suitable piston pin tool to hold them in place. Piston must be installed so sharp vertical side of deflector will be toward intake side (transfer port) and long sloping side of piston head will be toward exhaust port in cylinder. Thoroughly lubricate all friction surfaces during assembly.

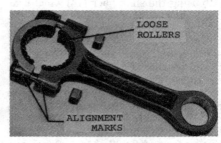

Fig. M3-16 — Marks on connecting rod and cap must be aligned as shown.

CONNECTING ROD, BEARINGS AND CRANKSHAFT. Upper end of crankshaft is carried by a ball bearing plus a caged needle bearing. The lower main bearing is a ball bearing which is interchangeable with the upper ball bearing.

The connecting rod rides on loose needle rollers at both ends. The piston pin end has 20 rollers and crankpin end has 29. Check rod for alignment, using Mercury Alignment tool (C-91-28442A2), or by placing rod on surface plate and checking with a light. When installing connecting rod on crankshaft, make certain that alignment marks (Fig. M3-16) are both on same side. If bearing surface of rod and cap is rough, scored, worn or shows evidence of overheating, renew the connecting rod. If crankpin or main bearing journals are scored, out-of-round or worn, renew the crankshaft.

Fig. M3-17 — Exploded view of the rewind starter assembly used on Merc 4.5, 40 and 45.

1. Screw
2. Trim cap
3. Nut
4. Lockwasher
5. Washer
6. Retainer washer
7. Rewind spring
8. Spring guide bushing
9. Rope retainer pin
10. Sheave
11. Wave washers
12. Pawls
13. Nylon bushing
14. Spacer
15. Retainer
16. Washer
17. Wave washer
18. Pawl retainer plate
19. Sheave shaft
20. Pulley
21. Spacer
22. Anchor
23. Rope

MANUAL STARTER

Merc 4.5, 40 And 45

Refer to Fig. M3-17. To disassemble the starter, remove the top cowl; then remove screw (1) and trim cap (2). Insert a screwdriver in slot in top of sheave shaft (19) and loosen the left-hand thread nut (3). Allow screwdriver and shaft (19) to turn clockwise until recoil spring unwinds. Pry anchor (22) out of starter handle and remove anchor and handle. Remove nut (3), invert the assembly and remove parts, making sure that recoil spring (7) remains in recess as sheave (10) is removed. Protect hands with gloves or cloth, remove recoil spring (7) and allow it to unwind slowly.

Lubricate the parts with a suitable low temperature grease and assemble by reversing the disassembly procedure. Install spring guide bushing (8) on hub of sheave (10) with chamfered end of bushing toward sheave. Be sure that pawls (12) are all installed the same way, with radius toward outside and identification mark away from the sheave (10). Install wave washer retainer (15) with cup end out and position washer (16) and wave washer (17) in cup. Make certain that tang on spring retainer (6) engages slot in sheave shaft (19). Position starter with end of shaft (19) through cowl and install lockwasher (4) and nut (3). Pull free end of recoil rope through cowl and install handle. Turn sheave shaft (19) counterclockwise until handle is pulled against top cowl, plus an additional 1¼ turns; then tighten nut (3). Pull cord out to full length and check for sticking.

Fig. M3-18 — With pulley hole (H) aligned with cover hole, insert rope through pulley and cover holes and pull rope until knot (K) is seated in rope pulley. Refer to text for starter rope installation.

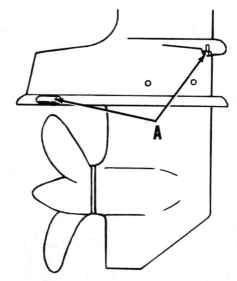

Fig. M3-20 — To remove the lower unit gearcase assembly, remove the attaching stud nuts at (A).

Merc 3.5 And 3.6 Models

Merc 3.5 and 3.6 models are equipped with a rewind starter. Individual starter components are not available and starter must be serviced as a unit assembly, except for starter rope renewal using the following procedure:

To renew starter rope, remove top cowl and starter. If rope is not broken, remove rope handle and allow rope to wind into starter. Unwind rope from rope pulley. Tie a knot in end of new rope. As viewed from pulley side of starter, rotate rope pulley in counter-clockwise direction (against spring tension) until pulley stops. Slowly allow pulley to rotate clockwise until rope hole in pulley and starter cover are adjacent. Thread unknotted end of rope through rope pulley and starter cover as shown in Fig. M3-18 so knot is seated in rope pulley. Hold rope taut, release rope pulley and allow approximately one foot of rope to wind into starter and install rope handle.

When installing starter, note that slotted mounting ear slides under fuel tank mounting tab. Before tightening starter retaining nuts, pull starter rope so starter dogs engage starter cup thereby centering starter, then tighten nuts while maintaining tension on rope.

LOWER UNIT

Merc 4.5, 40 And 45

PROPELLER AND DRIVE CLUTCH. Protection for the motor is provided by a special cushioning clutch built into the propeller hub. Propeller is splined to the shaft. No adjustment of the propeller or cushioning clutch is

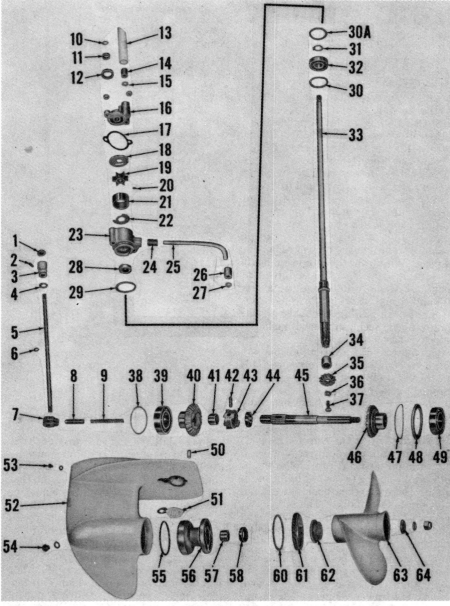

Fig. M3-21 — Exploded view of full gear shift type gearcase assembly used on all Merc 4.5, 40 and 45.

1. Oil seal	16. Water pump cover	32. Ball bearing
2. Bushing retainer screw	17. Gasket	33. Drive shaft
3. Bushing	18. Plate	34. Roller bearing
4. "O" ring	19. Impeller	35. Drive pinion
5. Shift shaft	20. Key	36. Lockplate
6. Snap ring	21. Insert	37. Cap screw
7. Shift cam	22. Plate	38. Shim
8. Cam follower	23. Pump housing	39. Ball bearing
9. Spring	24. Tube seal	40. Forward gear
10. "O" ring	25. Inlet tube	41. Roller bearing
11. Rubber ring (slinger)	26. Tube seal	42. Cross pin
12. Oil seal	27. Nylon washer	43. Dog clutch
13. Guide sleeve	28. Oil seal	44. Retaining ring
14. Seal	29. "O" ring	45. Propeller shaft
15. Nylon washer	30. & 30A. Shims	46. Reverse gear
	31. Snap ring	47. Shim

48. Thrust washer	
49. Ball bearing	
50. Hollow dowel	
51. Inlet screen	
52. Gear housing	
53. Vent screw	
54. Filler screw	
55. "O" ring	
56. Bearing carrier	
57. Roller bearing	
58. Oil seal	
60. Washer	
61. Gear housing cover nut	
62. Guide collar	
63. Propeller	
64. Spline spacer	

possible. Various pitch propellers are available and should be selected for best performance under applicable conditions. With speed control linkage correctly adjusted, propeller should be selected to provide maximum engine speed of 4500-5500 rpm. Propellers other than those designed for the motor must not be used.

R&R AND OVERHAUL. Most service on the lower unit can be performed by detaching the gearcase housing from the drive shaft housing. To remove the housing, remove the two stud nuts (A – Fig. M3-20) and withdraw the lower unit gearcase assembly.

Remove the housing plugs and drain the housing, then secure the gearcase in a vise between two blocks of soft wood, with propeller up. Wedge a piece of wood between propeller and antiventilation plate, remove the propeller nut, then remove the propeller.

Check the backlash of the propeller drive gears before disassembly by pulling out on the drive shaft and pushing in on the propeller shaft, then rotating drive shaft lightly while noting backlash by feel. No more than 0.003-0.005 inch (0.076-0.127 mm) backlash should exist if gears are properly adjusted.

Disassemble the gearcase by removing the gearcase housing cover nut (61 – Fig. M3-21). Nut is secured with left-hand thread. Clamp the outer end of propeller shaft in a soft jawed vise and remove the gearcase by tapping with a rubber mallet. Forward gear (40) will remain in housing. Withdraw the propeller shaft from bearing carrier (56) and reverse gear (46). Remove and save the shims (47) and thrust washer (48) from inside of gear housing. Shims should be reinstalled if gear backlash was within limits before disassembly.

Clamp the bearing carrier (56) in a soft jawed vise and remove reverse gear (46) and bearing (49) with an internal expanding puller and slide hammer. Remove and discard the propeller shaft rear seal (58).

To remove dog clutch (43) from propeller shaft, insert the cam follower (8) in hole in shaft and apply only enough pressure on end of cam follower to remove the spring pressure. Remove retaining ring (44), then push out the pin (42) with a small punch. The pin passes through drilled holes in dog clutch and operates in slotted hole in propeller shaft.

To disassemble the drive shaft and associated parts, reposition gearcase in vise with drive shaft projecting upward, remove the rubber slinger (11) from upper end of shaft; then unbolt and remove water pump (16). Remove the face plate (18); then remove impeller (19) and impeller drive pin. Withdraw the remainder of the water pump parts. Clamp upper end of drive shaft in a soft jawed vise, remove pinion retaining cap screw (37); then tap gearcase off drive shaft and bearing. Note the position and thickness of shims (30 and 30A) on drive shaft upper bearing. Mesh position of pinion is controlled by shims (30) placed underneath the bearing, while shaft end play is controlled by total shim pack thickness. The shims are identical but should not be interchanged or mixed, except to adjust the mesh position of drive pinion.

After drive shaft has been removed the forward gear (40) and bearing (39) can usually be dislodged by jarring open end of gearcase against a block of soft

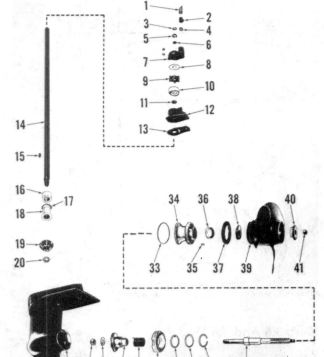

Fig. M3-22 — Exploded view of gearcase used on Merc 3.6 models. Gearcase used on Merc 3.5 models is similar.

1. Sleeve
2. Water tube seal
3. "O" ring
4. Spacer
5. Rubber ring
6. Oil seal
7. Water pump cover
8. Plate
9. Impeller
10. Lining
11. Oil seal
12. Water pump body
13. Gasket
14. Drive shaft
15. Key
16. Bushing
17. Shim
18. Bushing
19. Pinion gear
20. Nut
23. Gearcase
24. Nut
25. Washer
26. Drive gear
27. Clutch spring
28. Spacer
29. Washer
30. Shim
31. Snap ring
32. Propeller shaft
33. "O" ring
34. Carrier
35. Key
36. Oil seal
37. Nut
38. Thrust hub
39. Propeller
40. Thrust hub
41. Nut

wood. Remove and save the shim pack (38).

Shift shaft (5) can be removed after removing set screw (2) retaining bushing (3). When installing, make sure that long shaft splines are on upper end, and that shift cam (7) is installed with the notches (detents) toward rear.

Increasing the thickness of shim pack (38) DECREASES the backlash of forward gear (40). Increasing the thickness of shim pack (47) INCREASES the backlash of reverse gear (46). The number and thickness of shims (30) controls mesh position of drive pinion. Shims are available in thicknesses of 0.002, 0.003, 0.005 and 0.010 inch.

When renewing gearcase housing, or when correcting backlash and mesh of drive gear train, first install drive shaft (33), bearing (32), shims (30 and 30A) and water pump housing (23). Adjust total thickness of shims (30) so that water pump will seat on housing with no shaft end play. Remove the shaft and lay shims (30) aside for reinstallation during assembly. Make a trial assembly of forward gear (40) and bearing (39) using the removed shims (38). Install drive shaft (33), bearing (32) and shims (30). Install drive pinion (35) and install and tighten locking screw (37). Coat gears with bearing blue then check mesh pattern by pressing drive shaft down and turning clockwise to rotate the gears. If pressure is heavy on lower end of pinion tooth, remove one shim from pack (30).

Place the removed shim with pack (30A) to retain end play adjustment. Reverse the procedure if pressure is heavy on upper end of tooth. After adjusting mesh position, check and adjust backlash to 0.003-0.005 inch (0.076-0.127 mm) by adding or removing shims (38). Install reverse gear (46) and bearing (49) in bearing carrier (56); then install assembled parts in gearcase without propeller shaft. Adjust to minimum backlash without binding, by adding or removing shims (47).

When assembling, nuts securing water pump and cover (16) to gear housing should be tightened to 30 in.-lbs. (3.4 N·m). Incorrect tightening may damage pump.

Before attaching gearcase housing to the drive shaft housing, make certain that both the shift cam (7) and the shift lever (on starboard side of motor) are in forward gear position. Shift shaft (5) should be in counterclockwise position (viewed from top end of shaft) and shift lever should be pulled up. Complete assembly by reversing disassembly procedure.

Merc 3.5 And 3.6

PROPELLER AND DRIVE CLUTCH. Motor protection is provided by a special cushioning clutch hub in the propeller. Optional propellers are available and should be selected to provide maximum engine speed of 4500-5500 rpm. Propellers other than those designed for the motor should not be used.

R&R AND OVERHAUL. Most lower unit service can be performed by detaching the gearcase from the drive shaft housing. To remove the gearcase, remove the two stud nuts (A – Fig. M3-20) and separate gearcase from drive shaft housing.

Drain lubricant and place gearcase in a soft-jawed vise with drive shaft in a vertical position. Remove propeller. Remove water pump cover (7 – Fig. M3-22), plate (8), impeller (9) and drive key (15). Carefully pry up and remove water pump body (12). Unscrew nut (37) and place propeller shaft in a soft-jawed vise, then tap on gearcase to separate gearcase from propeller shaft assembly. To remove drive shaft, unscrew pinion gear nut (20), withdraw drive shaft (14) and remove pinion gear (19).

To disassemble propeller shaft components, grip propeller end of shaft in a soft-jawed vise and unscrew gear retaining nut (24). Discard nut (24). While turning counterclockwise, pull gear assembly off shaft. Unwind spring (27) from shaft. Detach snap ring (31) and remove washer (30), shims (29) and spacer (28) from gear.

To remove lower drive shaft bushing (18), drive bushing down into gear cavity while being careful not to lose any shims (17) on 3.6 models. Pull bushing (16) upward for removal. When installing new bushing (18) on 3.6 models place original shims (17) on bushing flange or a 0.005 inch shim if original shims cannot be used. Install upper bushing (16) so upper end is flush with gearcase bore.

Reverse disassembly procedure to assemble gearcase components while noting the following: Install new seals and "O" rings. Tighten pinion gear nut (20) to 80 in.-lbs. (9 N·m). Lubricate shaft surfaces of gear (26) prior to mating with spacer (28). With components (26, 28, 29, 30 and 31) assembled, there should be 0.002-0.010 inch (0.051-0.254 mm) gear end play in spacer. Add or delete shims (30) as required to obtain desired end play. Install clutch spring (27) so extended end is towards gear end of propeller shaft (32). Tighten drive gear retaining nut (24) to 180 in.-lbs. (20.3 N·m) on Merc 3.6. On Merc 3.5 models, tighten nut (24) until seated against washer (25). Then loosen nut (24) until a clearance of 0.005-0.010 inch (0.127-0.254 mm) exists between nut (24) and washer (25). Apply a light coat of Perfect Seal to mating circumference of carrier (34). Install propeller shaft assembly so notch in spacer (28) inner diameter is downward towards skeg, then install carrier (34) so tab meshes with spacer notch. Be sure to install key (35) in carrier and gearcase grooves. Tighten nut (37) to 40 ft.-lbs. (54.2 N·m).

Install oil seal (11) in water pump body (12) so seal lip is towards pump impeller cavity. If old impeller is to be reused, install impeller so original rotation is retained. Rotate drive shaft clockwise during impeller installation and do not reverse drive shaft rotation after impeller installation. Install oil seal (6) with lip facing away from pump cover (7). Tighten water pump retaining nuts to 30 in.-lbs. (3.4 N·m).

MERCURY

MERC 4 HP (Serial Number A818721 And Above) AND 5 HP (Serial Number 819951 And Above)

CONDENSED SERVICE DATA

NOTE: Metric fasteners are used throughout outboard motor.

TUNE-UP

Hp/rpm	4/4500-5500
	(3 kW)
	5/4500-5500
	(3.7 kW)
Bore	2.165 in.
	(55 mm)
Stroke	1.693 in.
	(43 mm)
Number of Cylinders	1
Displacement	6.2 cu. in.
	(102 cc)
Ignition Type	CDI
Spark Plug	NGK BP7HS-10
Electrode Gap	0.040 in.
	(1.0 mm)
Idle Speed (in gear)	900-1000 rpm
Fuel:Oil Ratio	50:1
Gearcase Oil Capacity	6.6 oz.
	(195 mL)

SIZES—CLEARANCES

Max. Allowable Cylinder Out-of-Round	0.003 in.
	(0.08 mm)
Max. Allowable Cylinder Taper	0.003 in.
	(0.08 mm)
Standard Piston Diameter	2.164 in.
	(54.97 mm)
Piston Skirt Clearance	0.0012-0.0024 in.
	(0.030-0.061 mm)
Piston Ring End Gap	0.008-0.016 in.
	(0.20-0.41 mm)

SIZES—CLEARANCES CONT.

Piston Ring Side Clearance:	
Top	0.0012-0.0023 in.
	(0.030-0.058 mm)
Second	0.0008-0.0024 in.
	(0.020-0.061 mm)
Connecting Rod Side Clearance	0.005-0.015 in.
	(0.13-0.38 mm)
Max. Allowable Crankshaft Runout	0.002 in.
	(0.05 mm)

TIGHTENING TORQUES

Crankcase	91 in.-lbs.
	(10.3 N·m)
Cylinder Head	216 in.-lbs.
	(24.4 N·m)
Flywheel	40 ft.-lbs.
	(54.2 N·m)
Lower Oil Seal Housing	70 in.-lbs.
	(8 N·m)
Spark Plug	168 in.-lbs.
	(19 N·m)
Standard Screws:	
8 mm	36 in.-lbs.
	(4.1 N·m)
10 mm	70 in.-lbs.
	(8.0 N·m)
12 mm	13 ft.-lbs.
	(17.6 N·m)
14 mm	26 ft.-lbs.
	(35.2 N·m)
17 mm	31 ft.-lbs.
	(42.0 N·m)

LUBRICATION

The power head is lubricated by oil mixed with the fuel. The recommended fuel is unleaded or low lead automotive gasoline with minimum octane rating of 87. The recommended oil is Quicksilver Premium Blend 2-Cycle Outboard Oil. Fuel:oil ratio for normal service including engine break-in is 50:1.

Lower unit gears and bearings are lubricated by oil contained in the gear-case. Recommended gearcase lubricant is Quicksilver Premium Blend Gear Lube. Gearcase lubricant is drained by removing vent and drain plugs in the gearcase. Refill through drain plug hole until oil reaches level of vent plug hole.

FUEL SYSTEM

CARBURETOR. Refer to Fig. M3A-1 for exploded view of the carburetor with integral fuel pump used on all models. Initial setting of low speed mixture screw (3) is 1-1/2 turns out from a lightly seated position. Make final idle mixture adjustment with engine running at normal operating temperature. Adjust slow speed mixture so optimum idle speed is obtained and engine accelerates cleanly without hesitation. Adjust idle speed screw (5) to obtain 900-1000 rpm with motor in forward gear.

Standard main jet size (11) for normal service (under 2500 feet [762 m] above sea level) is #78 on 4 hp models and #80 on 5 hp models. Reduce main jet (11) size by 0.002 inch (0.05 mm) for operation at 2500-5000 feet (762-1524 m) above sea level, 0.004 inch (0.10 mm) at 5000-7500 feet (1524-2286 m) above sea level and 0.006 inch (0.15 mm) for operation at elevations of 7500 feet (2286 m) and higher.

To measure float level, remove float bowl (17) and invert carburetor. Float level should be 1/2 inch (12.7 mm) measured as shown in Fig. M3A-2. Bend float tang to adjust float level.

Fuel pump is an integral part of carburetor and can be serviced without carburetor removal. Check valves (22—Fig. M3A-1) should be centered over valve seats and free of nicks, cracks, bends or other damage.

REED VALVE. The reed valve is attached on inside of crankcase. Do not disassemble reed valve assembly unless renewal is required. Inspect reed petals and renew if cracked, bent or damaged. Never attempt to straighten or repair damaged reed petals. Tighten reed securing screws to 9 in.-lbs. (1.0 N·m).

NOTE: On 4 hp models, one reed stop is flattened against reed petal to prevent reed petal from opening.

Reed stop opening (H—Fig. M3A-3) should be 0.240-0.248 inch (6.1-6.3 mm). Carefully bend reed stop to adjust.

IGNITION

A breakerless capacitor discharge ignition (CDI) system is used. Major components are the flywheel, CDI module, charge coil, trigger coil, ignition coil and

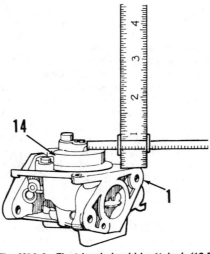

Fig. M3A-2—Float level should be ½ inch (12.7 mm) measured from body (1) to float (14) as shown.

spark plug. Stop switch (4—Fig. M3A-4) grounds trigger coil (1) output to stop engine.

TROUBLE-SHOOTING. To test charge coil (2—Fig. M3A-4), disconnect charge coil at bullet connectors. Connect a suitable ohmmeter between white lead and brown lead with red tracer. Charge coil resistance should be within 93-142 ohms. To renew charge coil, remove flywheel using a suitable puller. Do not strike flywheel with a hammer. Apply Loctite 271 to threads of charge coil screws and tighten to 14 in.-lbs. (1.6 N·m) during reassembly.

To test trigger coil (1), disconnect trigger coil red lead with white tracer and trigger coil ground lead. Note that ground lead is located under trigger coil mounting screw. Connect ohmmeter between trigger coil leads. Resistance should be 80-115 ohms. Renew trigger coil if not as specified.

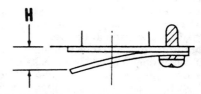

Fig. M3A-3—Reed stop opening (H) should be 0.240-0.248 inch (6.1-6.3 mm). Bend reed stop to obtain correct opening.

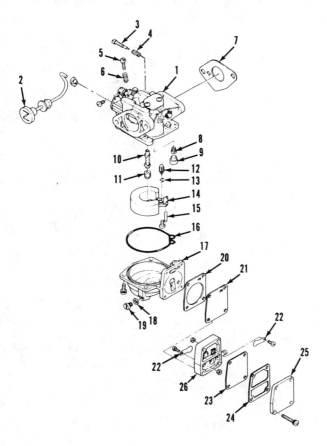

Fig. M3A-1—Exploded view of carburetor used.
1. Body
2. Choke rod assy.
3. Low speed mixture screw
4. Spring
5. Idle speed screw
6. Spring
7. Gasket
8. Low speed jet
9. Plug
10. Main nozzle
11. Main jet
12. Inlet needle
13. Clip
14. Float
15. Pin
16. Seal
17. Float bowl
18. Gasket
19. Drain plug
20. Gasket
21. Diaphragm
22. Check valve
23. Diaphragm
24. Cover
25. Cover
26. Pump body

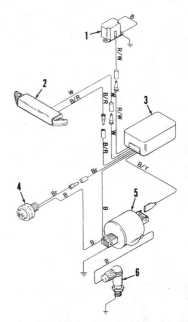

Fig. M3A-4—Diagram of ignition system components.

1. Trigger coil
2. Charge coil
3. CDI module
4. Stop switch
5. Ignition coil
6. Spark plug
B. Black
W. White
Br. Brown
B/R. Black with red tracer
B/Y. Black with yellow tracer
R/W. Red with white tracer

To test ignition coil (5), connect a suitable spark tester to coil high tension lead and engine ground. Crank engine and note spark. If weak or no spark is noted, proceed as follows: Disconnect coil leads and connect a suitable ohmmeter between coil primary terminal and coil laminations (ground). Primary winding resistance should be 0.02-0.38 ohm. Next, check secondary resistance by connecting ohmmeter between coil primary terminal and spark plug end of high tension lead. Secondary winding resistance should be 3000-4400 ohms. Renew coil if resistance is not as specified.

CDI module can only be effectively tested using a volt meter capable of measuring 400 DC volts or more used with Direct Voltage Adapter (DVA) part 91-99045, or a suitable Multi-Meter with built-in DVA. Follow instructions provided with tester to trouble-shoot CDI module.

IGNITION TIMING. Use a dial indicator to ensure that TDC mark is aligned with crankcase mating surfaces (S—Fig. M3A-5) with piston at top dead center.

Ignition timing is electronically advanced as engine speed is increased. No timing adjustments are provided. If ignition timing is not as specified, refer to TROUBLE-SHOOTING section to test for defective ignition system components.

Using a suitable timing light, 5 degrees BTDC timing mark (I) should align with crankcase mating surfaces (S) at idle speed. At full throttle, 30 degrees BTDC mark (F) should align with crankcase mating surfaces (S).

COOLING SYSTEM

A rubber impeller type water pump is mounted between the drive shaft housing and gearcase. The impeller is driven by a key in the drive shaft.

In the event cooling system malfunction is noted, inspect water inlet for plugging or partial restriction. If necessary, remove lower unit gearcase to check condition of water pump, water passages and sealing surfaces.

When water pump is disassembled, inspect condition of impeller (5—Fig. M3A-11), liner (4) and plate (7). Rotate drive shaft clockwise (viewed from top) while placing pump housing over impeller. Avoid turning drive shaft in opposite direction after water pump is reassembled.

POWER HEAD

REMOVE AND REINSTALL. Remove rewind starter, flywheel, CDI module and ignition coil. Remove carburetor, fuel tank and throttle linkage. Remove six screws securing power head to drive shaft housing and lift off power head.

Renew power head-to-drive shaft housing gasket when reinstalling power head. Tighten six power head mounting screws to 70 in.-lbs. (8.0 N·m). Remainder of installation is reverse of removal procedure.

DISASSEMBLY. Remove lower seal housing (25—Fig. M3A-6). Remove cylinder head (18) and gasket (17). Remove six crankcase screws and carefully pry at tab locations (each side of crankcase/cylinder block assembly) to sepa-rate crankcase half (22) from cylinder block (16). Crankshaft assembly is now accessible for removal from cylinder block. Do not remove bearings (3 and 6) unless bearing renewal is required. Refer to specific service sections to overhaul.

REASSEMBLY. Prior to reassembling power head, be sure all joints and gasket surfaces are clean, free from nicks and burrs and gasket sealer or carbon. Cylinder block and crankcase cover are only available as a unit assembly.

All friction surfaces and bearings should be thoroughly lubricated with engine oil during reassembly. Renew all gaskets and seals. Apply a continuous bead of Loctite Master Gasket Sealant to mating surface of crankcase cover. Make sure bead is continuous but avoid excess application. Tighten crankcase screws to 91 in.-lbs. (10.3 N·m) in sequence shown in Fig. M3A-7. Tighten cylinder head screws to 215 in.-lbs. (24.3 N·m) in sequence shown in Fig. M3A-8. Lubricate lip of seal (24—Fig. M3A-6) with Quicksilver 2-4-C Marine Lubricant. Install housing (25) and tighten housing screws to 70 in.-lbs. (8 N·m).

PISTON, PIN, RINGS, CYLINDER AND HEAD. Cylinder liner is cast into the cylinder block and can not be renewed. Measure cylinder bore in several locations to determine if excessive

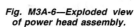

Fig. M3A-6—Exploded view of power head assembly.

1. Seal
2. Locating washer
3. Bearing
4. Key
5. Crankshaft & connecting rod assy.
6. Bearing
7. Locating ring
8. Seal
9. Piston
10. Retaining ring
11. Piston rings
12. Needle bearing
13. Piston pin
14. Reed petals
15. Reed stop
16. Cylinder block
17. Gasket
18. Cylinder head
19. Detent ball
20. Spring
21. Pin
22. Crankcase cover
23. Gasket
24. Seal
25. Seal housing

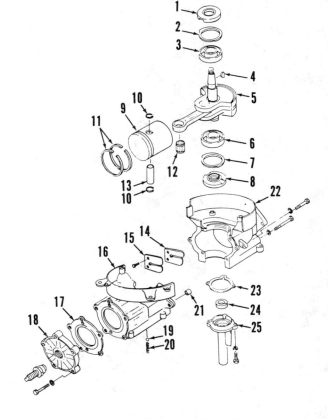

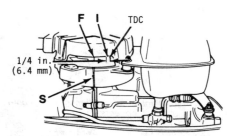

Fig. M3A-5—View identifying TDC mark, idle speed timing mark (I) and full throttle timing mark (F) and crankcase mating surfaces (S). Note that idle speed mark (I) is ¼ inch (6.4 mm) from TDC mark as shown. Refer to text.

out-of-round or taper exists. Refer to CONDENSED SERVICE DATA for service specifications. Piston and rings are available in 0.020 inch (0.5 mm) oversize. Measure piston diameter at a right angle to piston pin bore at a point 5/8 inch (16 mm) up from bottom of skirt. Piston skirt clearance should be 0.0012-0.0024 inch (0.030-0.061 mm).

Piston pin is retained by retaining rings (10—Fig. M3A-6) which should be renewed if removed. Piston pin rides in needle bearing (12) in connecting rod small end.

Refer to CONDENSED SERVICE DATA for piston ring service specifications. Make sure ring end gaps are properly located around ring locating pins in piston ring grooves. Install piston on connecting rod so "UP" mark on piston crown faces flywheel end of crankshaft.

Renew cylinder head if warpage exceeds 0.002 inch (0.05 mm). Remove small nicks or burrs by lapping head mating surface on a suitable flat surface.

CRANKSHAFT AND CONNECTING ROD. Crankshaft, connecting rod, crankpin and bearing are a unit assembly. Do not remove bearings (3 and 6— Fig. M3A-6) from crankshaft unless renewal is required. Crankshaft runout

should not exceed 0.002 inch (0.05 mm). Connecting rod side clearance should be within 0.005-0.015 inch (0.13-0.38 mm). The manufacturer recommends cleaning connecting rod small end bore with a suitable crocus cloth only.

When installing crankshaft assembly into cylinder block, make sure locating pins on bearings (3 and 6) properly engage notches in cylinder block. Install locating rings (2 and 7) with large diameter half engaged in grooves in cylinder block.

MANUAL STARTER

Refer to Fig. M3A-9 for an exploded view of manual starter. To overhaul manual starter, proceed as follows: Remove engine cover. Remove screws retaining manual starter to power head. Remove starter lockout rod (16) from rod retainer (15). Withdraw starter assembly.

Check pawl (27) for freedom of movement and excessive wear or damage of engagement area and renew if necessary. Lubricate pawl (27) with a suitable water-resistant grease.

To disassemble, remove "E" ring (28) and withdraw pawl (27) and pawl springs (25 and 26). Untie starter rope (3) at retainer (1) and allow the rope to

wind into the starter. Remove screw (24), washer (23) and bushing (22). Carefully lift pulley (30) with starter rope (3) from housing (5). Be careful not to dislodge rewind spring (20) when removing pulley (30). Remove starter rope (3) from pulley (30) if renewal is required. If renewal of rewind spring (20) is necessary, use extreme caution when removing rewind spring (20) from spring case (19).

Inspect all components for damage and excessive wear and renew as necessary.

To reassemble, first apply a coating of a suitable water-resistant grease to rewind spring area of spring case (19). Install rewind spring (20) in spring case so spring coils wind in a counterclockwise direction from the outer end. Make sure the spring outer hook is properly secured in slot of housing (19). Wind starter rope (3) onto pulley (30) 2-3 turns counterclockwise when viewed from flywheel side. Direct remaining starter rope length through notch in pulley (30).

NOTE: Lubricate all friction surfaces with a suitable water-resistant grease during reassembly.

Assemble pulley (30) to starter housing making sure that pulley hub proper-

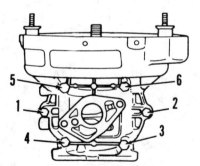

Fig. M3A-7—Tighten crankcase cover screws in sequence shown.

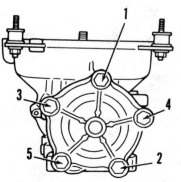

Fig. M3A-8—Tighten cylinder head screws in sequence shown.

Fig. M3A-9—Exploded view of manual rewind starter assembly.

1. Retainer
2. Handle
3. Rope
4. Rope guide
5. Housing
6. Nut
7. Starter lock
8. Sleeve
9. Spring
10. Washer
11. Screw
12. Cam
13. Wave washer
14. Shoulder screw
15. Rod retainer
16. Rod
17. Rod retainer
18. Guide plate
19. Spring case
20. Rewind spring
21. Plug
22. Bushing
23. Washer
24. Screw
25. Spring
26. Spring
27. Pawl
28. "E" ring
29. Washer
30. Rope pulley

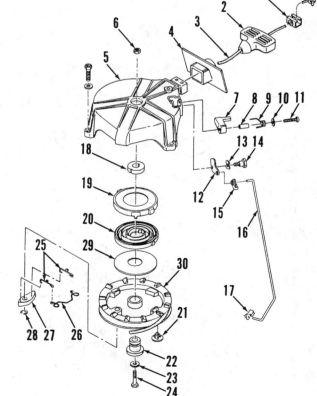

ly engages inner hook of rewind spring (20). Install spindle (22), washer (23) and screw (24). Apply a suitable thread locking compound to threads of screw (24), install nut (6) and tighten to 70 in.-lbs. (8 N·m).

Thread starter rope (3) through starter housing (5), rope guide (4), handle (2), retainer (1) and secure with a suitable knot. Turn pulley (30) 2-3 turns counterclockwise as viewed from flywheel side, then release starter rope from pulley notch and allow rope to slowly wind onto pulley.

NOTE: Do not apply any more tension on rewind spring (20) than necessary to draw starter handle (2) back to the properly released position.

Install springs (25 and 26), pawl (27) and clip (28) as shown in Fig. M3A-10. Remount starter assembly on power head. Tighten starter mounting screws to 70 in.-lbs. (8 N·m). Reconnect starter lockout rod (16—Fig. M3A-9) to retainer (15) and check for proper operation of starter lockout assembly.

LOWER UNIT

PROPELLER. Standard propeller has three blades with a diameter of 8-3/8 inches (212.7 mm) and pitch of 7 inches (177.8 mm). Various propellers are available from the manufacturer. Select a propeller that will allow a properly tuned and adjusted outboard motor to operate within 4500-5500 rpm at full throttle.

NOTE: The manufacturer recommends propping outboard motor to operate at or near the high end of rpm range.

R&R AND OVERHAUL. Note location and thickness of all shims for reference during reassembly. To remove gearcase, first place shift lever in the re-

verse position. Disconnect lower shift rod by removing plug in side of drive shaft housing and loosening cap screw (9—Fig. M3A-12). Remove screws securing gearcase to drive shaft housing and separate gearcase from drive shaft housing. Drain lubricant from gearcase. Remove cotter pin (42—Fig. M3A-11), nut (41), washer (40), propeller (39) and spacer (38). Remove bearing carrier (37) retaining screws and withdraw propeller shaft and carrier assembly. Remove pinion gear (29). Remove water pump assembly and retainer (13) screw. Remove water pump base (9), drive shaft (14) and lower shift rod assembly. Withdraw forward gear (24).

Inspect all components for excessive wear or damage and renew as necessary. Renew all gaskets and "O" rings. Lubricate all seal lips and "O" rings

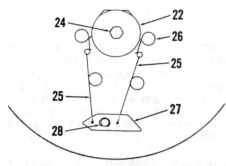

Fig. M3A-10—View showing proper installation of starter pawl (27) and springs (25 and 26). Refer to Fig. M3A-9 for complete identification of components.

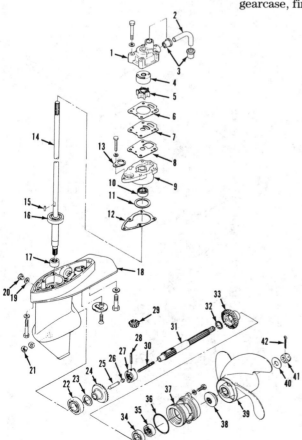

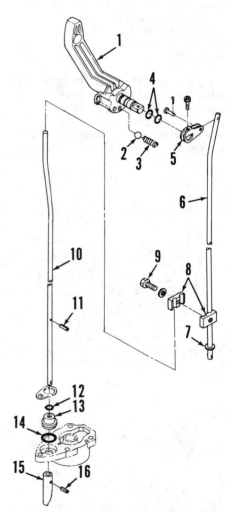

Fig. M3A-11—Exploded view of lower unit assembly.

1. Water pump housing
2. Pickup tube
3. Grommets
4. Liner
5. Impeller
6. Gasket
7. Plate
8. Gasket
9. Water pump base
10. Seal
11. Shim
12. Gasket
13. Retainer
14. Drive shaft
15. Key
16. Bearing
17. Bearing
18. Gearcase
19. Gasket
20. Vent plug
21. Drain plug
22. Bearing
23. Shim
24. Forward gear
25. Plunger
26. Spring holder
27. Dog clutch
28. Pin
29. Pinion gear
30. Spring
31. Propeller shaft
32. Thrust washer
33. Reverse gear
34. Bearing
35. Seal
36. "O" ring
37. Bearing carrier
38. Spacer
39. Propeller
40. Washer
41. Nut
42. Cotter pin

Fig. M3A-12—Exploded view of shift control components.

1. Shift lever
2. Detent ball
3. Spring
4. "O" rings
5. Lever
6. Upper shift rod
7. Washer
8. Clamp assy.
9. Screw
10. Lower shift rod
11. Pin
12. "O" ring
13. Bushing
14. "O" ring
15. Shift cam
16. Pin

with Quicksilver 2-4-C Marine Lubricant. Lubricant all bearings and friction surfaces with Quicksilver Gear Lube or equivalent.

Reverse disassembly procedure when reassembling gearcase. Install all shims in original location. All bearings that require driving or pressing into position should be driven or pressed from let-tered side of bearing. Taper on shift cam (15—Fig. M3A-12) should face away from bend in lower shift rod (10). Tighten water pump housing screws and bearing carrier screws to 70 in.-lbs. (8 N·m).

Gearcase and shift lever must be in reverse position for proper shift rod (10—Fig. M3A-12) alignment with clamp (8).

Push down on shift rod (10) while rotating propeller shaft to engage reverse gear. Lubricate drive shaft splines with Quicksilver 2-4-C or equivalent water resistant grease. Tighten propeller nut to 150 in.-lbs. (17 N·m). Tighten gearcase-to-drive shaft housing screws to 70 in.-lbs. (8 N·m). Securely tighten clamp screw (9).

MERCURY

MERC 6, 8, 9.9 AND 15 HP

CONDENSED SERVICE DATA

TUNE-UP

Hp/rpm	6/4000-5000
	(4.5 kW)
	8/4500-5500
	(6.0 kW)
	9.9/5000-6000
	(7.4 kW)
	15/5000-6000
	(11.2 kW)

Bore:
  6, 8 and 9.9 Hp ....2.125 in.
    (53.97 mm)
  15 Hp ....2.375 in.
    (60.32 mm)
Stroke ....1.800 in.
    (45.72 mm)
Number of Cylinders............................2
Displacement:
  6, 8 and 9.9 Hp ....12.8 cu. in.
    (209.7 cc)
  15 Hp ....16.0 cu. in.
    (262.2 cc)
Spark Plug:
  6, 8 and 9.9 Hp ....Champion L82YC*
    Electrode Gap.....................0.040 in.
    (1.0 mm)
  15 Hp ....NGK BP8HS*
    Electrode Gap.....................0.060 in.
    (1.5 mm)
Ignition Type ....CDI
Idle Speed (in gear) ....700-750 rpm†
Fuel:Oil Ratio 50:1
Gearcase Oil Capacity ....6.5 oz.
    (200 mL)

*Models equipped with standard ignition coils only. Recommended spark plug for models equipped with high energy ignition coils is NGK BUHW surface gap spark plug.
†On models not equipped with idle speed screw, carburetor is factory calibrated to maintain 600-700 rpm idle speed in forward gear.

SIZES—CLEARANCES

Max. Allowable Cylinder Bore
  Out-of-Round ....0.004 in.
    (0.10 mm)
Max. Allowable Cylinder Bore
  Taper ....0.004 in.
    (0.10 mm)
Standard Piston Diameter:
  6, 8 and 9.9 Hp ....2.123 in.
    (53.92 mm)
  15 Hp ....2.373 in.
    (60.27 mm)

TIGHTENING TORQUES

Connecting Rod Cap ....100 in.-lbs.
    (11.3 N·m)
Crankcase Cover ....200 in.-lbs.
    (22.6 N·m)
Cylinder Block Cover ....60 in.-lbs.
    (6.8 N·m)
Exhaust Cover ....60 in.-lbs.
    (6.8 N·m)
Flywheel Nut...........................50 ft.-lbs.
    (67.8 N·m)
Flywheel Ring Gear (electric
  start models) ....65 in.-lbs.
    (7.3 N·m)
Power Head-to-Drive Shaft Housing
  Nuts and Screws ....100 in.-lbs.
    (11.3 N·m)
Reed Block ....60 in.-lbs.
    (6.8 N·m)
Transfer Port Cover ....60 in.-lbs.
    (6.8 N·m)

LUBRICATION

The power head is lubricated by oil mixed with the fuel. Recommended fuel is regular leaded or unleaded gasoline with minimum octane rating of 87. Recommended oil is Quicksilver Premium Blend 2-Cycle Outboard Oil or a suitable NMMA certified TC-W or TC-WII engine oil. Fuel:oil ratio for normal service is 50:1.

Lower unit gears and bearings are lubricated by oil contained in the gearcase. Recommended oil is Quicksilver Premium Blend Gear Lube. Lower unit lubricant is drained by removing vent and drain plugs in the gearcase. Refill gearcase through drain plug hole until oil reaches level of vent plug hole. Gearcase capacity is approximately 1.5 ounces (45 mL).

FUEL SYSTEM

CARBURETOR. All models are equipped with the carburetor shown in

Fig. M4-1. Carburetor is equipped with integral fuel pump and diaphragm type primer system.

Standard main jet (19) size for normal service (sea level to 2500 feet [762 m] above sea level) is 0.046 inch (1.17 mm) on Merc 6 and 8 hp models, 0.056 inch (1.42 mm) on Merc 9.9 hp models and 0.066 inch (1.68 mm) on Merc 15 hp models. Main jet (19) size should be reduced from standard recommendation by 0.002 inch (0.05 mm) for elevations of 2500-5000 feet (760-1525 m), 0.004 inch (0.10 mm) for elevations of 5000-7500 feet (1525-2285 m) and 0.006 inch (0.15 mm) for elevations of 7500 feet (2285 m) and higher.

Initial setting of idle mixture screw (34) is 1-1/2 turns out from a lightly seated position. Perform final idle mixture adjustment with primer knob pushed fully in, engine running at operating temperature and in forward gear. On models so equipped, remove plug in air intake cover for access to idle mixture screw. On models equipped with idle speed screw, adjust idle speed to 700-750 rpm in forward gear. On models without idle speed screw, carburetor is calibrated at the factory to provide 600-700 rpm idle speed.

To determine the float level, invert carburetor body (1—Fig. M4-2) with fuel inlet valve (13—Fig. M4-1), float arm (14—Fig. M4-2) and float (16) installed. Measure distance (D) as shown in Fig. M4-2. Distance (D) should be one inch (25.4 mm). Bend float arm (14) to adjust.

FUEL FILTER. A fuel filter assembly is connected between fuel supply line and carburetor/fuel pump inlet line. With the engine stopped, occasionally unscrew fuel filter cup (4—Fig. M4-3) from filter base (1) and withdraw sealing ring (3) and filter element (2). Clean cup (4) and element (2) using a suitable solvent and dry with compressed air. Renew element (2) if excessive blockage or other damaged is noted. Reassembly is reverse order of disassembly.

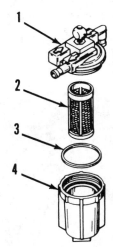

Fig. M4-2—With carburetor body (1) inverted, distance (D) should be 1 inch (25.4 mm) when measured as shown. Bend float arm (14) to adjust position of float (16).

FUEL PUMP. The fuel pump is an integral part of the carburetor. Refer to Fig. M4-1 for exploded view of carburetor and first design fuel pump. Second design pump is similar except pump check valve is part of pump body located between carburetor body (1) and pump cover (11). Renew pump gaskets and diaphragm if pump is disassembled. If performing carburetor service, do not disassemble fuel pump unless pump service is necessary. Note that fuel pump assembly can be overhauled without carburetor removal.

REED VALVE. Reed valve assembly is located between the carburetor and crankcase/intake manifold. Refer to Fig. M4-4 for view of reed valve assembly. Renew cracked, warped, chipped or bent reed petals. Do not attempt to straighten or repair bent or damaged reed petals. Never turn used reed petals over for reuse. Do not remove reed petals from reed block unless renewal is required.

Reed petals should seat smoothly against reed block along their entire length but not be preloaded against reed

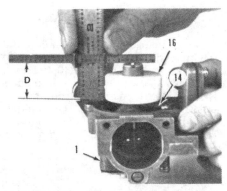

Fig. M4-1—Exploded view of carburetor and first design fuel pump assembly. Second design fuel pump is similar. Note that carburetor shown is not equipped with an idle speed screw.

1. Body
2. Gasket
3. Cover
4. Throttle plate
5. Gasket
6. Spring
7. Throttle lever
8. Throttle shaft
9. Diaphragm
10. Gasket
11. Cover
12. Maximum spark advance screw
13. Inlet valve
14. Float arm
15. Float pin
16. Float
17. Gasket
18. Float bowl
19. Main jet
20. Gasket
21. Plug
22. Seal
23. Cover
24. Enrichment diaphragm
25. Gasket
26. Spring
27. Seat
28. Retainer
29. Check ball
30. Spring
31. Gasket
32. Plug
33. Spring
34. Idle mixture screw

Fig. M4-3—Exploded view of fuel filter assembly.

1. Base
2. Element
3. Sealing ring
4. Cup

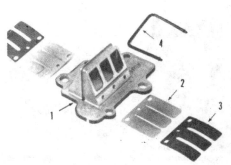

Fig. M4-4—View showing reed valve assembly.

1. Block
2. Petals
3. Stops
4. Seal

block or stand open more than 0.007 inch (0.18 mm). Reed stop opening should be 7/32 inch (5.6 mm) on 6, 8 and 9.9 hp models and 19/64 inch (7.5 mm) on 15 hp models. Check reed stop opening by inserting an appropriate size drill bit between end of stops (3) and reed block (1). Carefully bend reed stops to adjust.

When reassembling reed valve assembly, tighten screws to 20 in.-lbs. (2.3 N·m). Seal ends of rubber seal (4) with Quicksilver RTV part 91-91600-1 or a suitable equivalent sealant. Lubricate rubber seal (4) with a suitable needle bearing assembly grease and tighten reed block mounting screws to 60 in.-lbs. (6.8 N·m).

SPEED CONTROL LINKAGE. To synchronize ignition timing and throttle opening, proceed as follows: Mount the outboard motor on a boat or a suitable test tank and immerse the lower unit. Remove the engine cover. Connect a power timing light to the top cylinder spark plug lead. With the outboard motor in "FORWARD" gear and the engine running at full throttle, three timing dots (D—Fig. M4-5) should be aligned with timing pointer (P). Loosen jam nut (J—Fig. M4-6) and turn screw (E) to adjust.

To check idle speed timing, push primer knob fully "IN" and rotate knob completely counterclockwise. With the outboard motor in "FORWARD" gear and the engine running at idle speed, 6 degrees BTDC mark (or two dots on some models) (M—Fig. M4-5) should be aligned with timing pointer (P). Turn screw (I—Fig. M4-6) to adjust. After idle speed timing adjustment, loosen screw (S) and rotate cam follower (F) until contact is made with throttle cam (C). Tighten screw (S).

Leave primer knob pushed fully "IN" and rotated completely counterclockwise. Shift outboard motor to "NEUTRAL" position. Adjust screw (N—Fig. M4-7) until all clearance between idle wire (W) and CDI's trigger assembly is removed.

IGNITION SYSTEM

The standard spark plug on 6, 8 and 9.9 hp models is Champion L82YC with electrode gap of 0.040 inch (0.102 mm). Standard spark plug for 15 hp models is NGK BP8HS with electrode gap of 0.060 inch (1.52 mm). On models equipped with high-energy ignition coils, NGK BUHW surface gap spark

Fig. M4-7—Adjust screw (N) to remove clearance between idle wire (W) and CDI's trigger assembly. Refer to text.

plug is recommended. Renew surface gap spark plug if center electrode is more than 1/32 inch (0.79 mm) below flat surface of the plug end.

A capacitor discharge ignition (CDI) system is used on all models. If engine malfunction is noted and the ignition system is suspected, make sure the spark plugs and all electrical connections are tight before proceeding to trouble-shooting the CD ignition system.

Proceed as follows to test CDI system components: Refer to Fig. M4-8. To test stator assembly, first make sure stator assembly is grounded to engine. Disconnect black wire with yellow tracer (B/Y) and black wire with white tracer (B/W) from switch box. Use a suitable ohmmeter and perform the following tests. Connect black tester lead to engine ground and red tester lead to black wire with white tracer (B/W) from stator assembly. The resistance reading should be 120-180 ohms. Leave black tester lead connected to engine ground and connect red tester lead to black wire with yellow tracer (B/Y) from stator assembly. The resistance reading should be 3200-3800 ohms. Connect tester leads between black wire with yellow tracer (B/Y) and black wire with white tracer (B/W) from stator assembly. The resistance reading should be 3100-3700 ohms.

To test trigger assembly, disconnect brown wire with yellow tracer (Br/Y) and brown wire with white tracer (Br/W) from switch box. With engine at room temperature (68° F [20° C]), use a suitable ohmmeter and connect tester leads between brown wire with yellow tracer (Br/Y) and brown wire with white tracer (Br/W) from trigger assembly. The resistance reading should be 650-850 ohms.

To test ignition coil assembly, disconnect wires and spark plug lead from coil

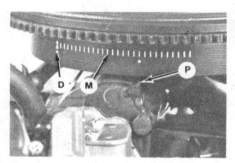

Fig. M4-5—View identifying three timing dots (D), 6 degrees BTDC mark (M) and pointer (P) for adjusting ignition timing. Refer to text.

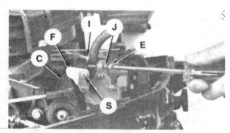

Fig. M4-6—View showing speed control linkage components. Refer to text for adjustment procedures.

C. Throttle cam
E. Screw
F. Cam follower
I. Screw
J. Jam nut
S. Screw

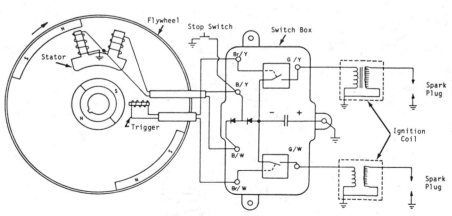

Fig. M4-8—View identifying CDI system components and wiring.

B/W. Black wire with white tracer
B/Y. Black wire with yellow tracer

G/W. Green wire with white tracer
G/Y. Green wire with yellow tracer

Br/W. Brown wire with white tracer
Br/Y. Brown wire with white tracer

assembly. Use a suitable ohmmeter and connect tester leads between positive (+) and negative (–) coil terminals. The resistance reading should be 0.02-0.04 ohm. Leave the one tester lead connected to the negative (–) coil terminal and connect the remaining tester lead to the spark plug leads's terminal end in the coil tower. The resistance reading should be 800-1100 ohms.

COOLING SYSTEM

WATER PUMP. A rubber impeller type water pump is mounted between the drive shaft housing and gearcase. Water pump impeller (4—Fig. M4-9) is driven by a key in the drive shaft.

When cooling system problems are encountered, first check water inlet for plugging or partial stoppage. If the water pump is suspected defective, separate gearcase from drive shaft housing and inspect pump. Make sure all seals and mating surfaces are in good condition and water passages are unobstructed. Check impeller (4) and plate (6) for excessive wear. When reassembling, coat the threads of cover (3) securing screws with Loctite 271 or 290 and tighten screws evenly to a final torque of 40 in.-lbs. (4.5 N·m).

POWER HEAD

R&R AND OVERHAUL. The power head can be removed for disassembly and overhaul as follows: Clamp outboard motor to a suitable stand and remove engine cowl. Detach spark plug leads from spark plugs and remove spark plugs from power head. Remove manual starter assembly. Disconnect speed control cables, fuel line and any wiring that will interfere with power head removal. Remove or disconnect any component that will interfere with power head removal. Remove four screws and two nuts securing power head to drive shaft housing and lift power head free. Remove flywheel, ignition components and carburetor. Remove screws retaining reed valve block (9—Fig. M4-10) and withdraw. Remove screws retaining exhaust cover (6) and withdraw. Remove screws retaining cylinder block cover (13) and withdraw. Remove screws retaining transfer port cover (16) and withdraw. Crankcase halves can be separated after removal of six screws securing crankcase half (1)

to cylinder block (2). Crankshaft and pistons are now accessible for removal and overhaul as outlined in the appropriate following paragraphs.

ASSEMBLY. When reassembling, make sure all joints and gasket surfaces are clean and free from nicks and burrs.

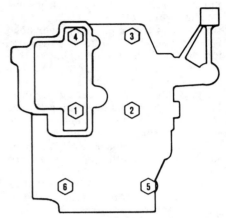

Fig. M4-11—Tighten crankcase screws in sequence shown above.

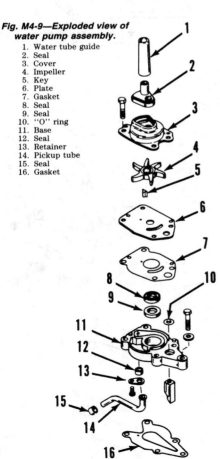

Fig. M4-9—Exploded view of water pump assembly.
1. Water tube guide
2. Seal
3. Cover
4. Impeller
5. Key
6. Plate
7. Gasket
8. Seal
9. Seal
10. ''O'' ring
11. Base
12. Seal
13. Retainer
14. Pickup tube
15. Seal
16. Gasket

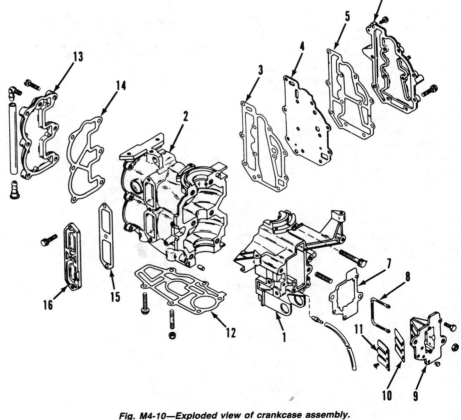

Fig. M4-10—Exploded view of crankcase assembly.
1. Crankcase half
2. Cylinder block
3. Gasket
4. Exhaust manifold
5. Gasket
6. Exhaust cover
7. Gasket
8. Seal
9. Reed valve block
10. Reed petals
11. Reed stops
12. Gasket
13. Cylinder block cover
14. Gasket
15. Gasket
16. Transfer port cover

All friction surfaces and bearings must be lubricated with engine oil during reassembly. Make sure crankshaft's center main bearing sleeves (5—Fig. M4-14) are properly positioned in cylinder block's crankcase and crankcase cover. Make sure locating pin on upper crankshaft roller bearing (12) fits into the slot in cylinder block. Properly seat retaining ring (11) in cylinder block groove during crankshaft assembly's installation. Check frequently as power head is being assembled for binding of working parts. If binding or locking is encountered, correct cause before proceeding with assembly.

Apply a continuous bead of Loctite Master Gasket Sealant to sealing surface of crankcase half (1—Fig. M4-10). Make sure entire surface is coated, but avoid an excess application as sealant may be squeezed into crankcase, bearings or passages.

Refer to CONDENSED SERVICE DATA for final torque specifications. Tighten screws in three progressive steps. Refer to Fig. M4-11 for crankcase screws tightening sequence. Refer to Fig. M4-12 for cylinder block cover screws tightening sequence. Refer to Fig. M4-13 for exhaust cover screws tightening sequence.

CYLINDERS, RINGS AND PISTONS. Cylinder bores should be measured in several different locations to determine if an out-of-round or tapered condition exists. Inspect each cylinder wall for scoring. If minor scoring is noted, lightly hone cylinder wall.

NOTE: Cylinder sleeves and cylinder heads are cast into the cylinder block. If a cylinder is out-of-round or tapered more than 0.004 inch (0.10 mm), or if excessive scoring is noted, the cylinder block and crankcase must be renewed.

Measure diameter of pistons 0.10 inch (2.5 mm) from base of piston skirt and at a right angle (90 degrees) to piston pin. Standard piston diameter is 2.123 inches (53.92 mm) on 6, 8 and 9.9 models and 2.373 inches (60.27 mm) on 15 hp models. Recommended piston skirt-to-cylinder bore clearance is 0.002-0.005 inch (0.05-0.13 mm).

The piston pin is pressed in piston bosses and secured with retaining clips. Install new retaining clips (16—Fig. M4-14) during assembly. Piston end of connecting rod is fitted with loose needle bearings which use connecting rod bore and piston pin as bearing races. Install bearing washers (19) and 24 loose needle bearing (20) in piston end of connecting rod using light nonfibrous grease and a suitable piston pin tool to hold them in place.

Install piston rings on each piston so ring gaps are 180 degrees apart on piston pin centerline. Pistons must be installed so sharp vertical side of deflector will be toward intake side (transfer port) and long sloping side of piston head will be toward exhaust port in cylinder. Coat bearings, pistons, rings and cylinder bores with engine oil during assembly.

CRANKSHAFT, BEARINGS AND RODS. The connecting rods ride on a roller bearing around the crankpins. Maximum allowable bend of connecting rod (21—Fig. M4-14) is 0.002 inch (0.051 mm). Note that the manufacturer only

recommends using crocus cloth to cleanup bearing surfaces of crankshaft journals and connecting rod surfaces. If a bearing half is noted as being defective, both halves must be renewed.

STARTER

MANUAL STARTER. A starter lockout assembly is used to prevent starter engagement when the gear shift control

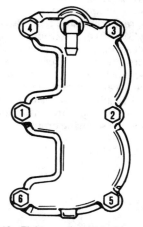

Fig. M4-12—Tighten cylinder block cover screws in sequence shown above.

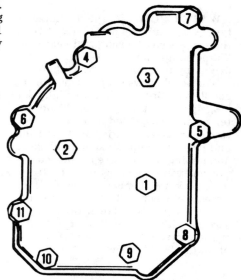

Fig. M4-13—Tighten exhaust cover screws in sequence shown above.

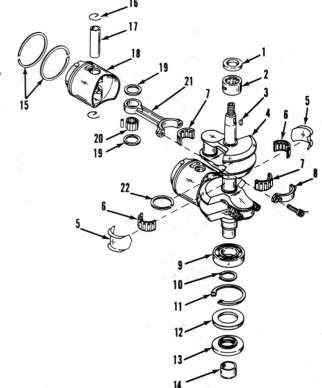

Fig. M4-14—Exploded view of crankshaft assembly used on 6, 8 and 9.9 hp models. Center main bearing assembly (5 and 6) differs slightly on 15 hp models.

1. Seal
2. Upper roller bearing
3. Key
4. Crankshaft
5. Sleeve half
6. Roller bearing half
7. Roller bearing half
8. Connecting rod cap
9. Ball bearing
10. Snap ring
11. Retaining ring
12. Special washer
13. Seal
14. Coupling seal
15. Piston rings
16. Clip
17. Piston pin
18. Piston
19. Washer
20. Needle bearings (24)
21. Connecting rod
22. Seal ring

is in the "FORWARD" or "REVERSE" position.

To overhaul the manual starter, proceed as follows: Remove the engine cowl. Detach fuel filter assembly from starter housing by pulling filter assembly straight down. Detach control rod from lower lockout lever (15—Fig. M4-15). Remove the three starter housing retaining screws and withdraw the starter assembly.

To disassemble, untie starter rope (10) at anchor (12) and allow the rope to wind into the starter. Loosen screws (18) and swing clips (17) clear of pulley (9). Carefully lift pulley (9) with starter rope (10) from housing (1). BE CAREFUL when removing pulley (9) as the rewind spring in case (7) may be dislodged. Remove starter rope (10) from pulley (9) if renewal is required. Separate rewind spring and case (7) from starter housing (1) by inserting a suitable size punch through the openings in starter housing (1).

Inspect all components for damage and excessive wear and renew if needed.

To reassemble, lubricate rewind spring area of starter housing (1) with a nonmetallic low temperature grease. Install rewind spring and case (7) into starter housing (1). Assemble pulley (9) to starter housing (1) making sure rewind spring end properly engages notch in pulley center shaft. Swing clips (17) over to secure pulley (9) and tighten screws (18).

Rotate pulley (9) counterclockwise until starter rope (10) end is aligned with starter housing rope outlet. Thread starter rope (10) through starter housing (1), bushing (3), rope guide (2), bushing (5) and handle (11) and secure in anchor (12). Pull starter rope (10) out to full length while checking for freedom of travel, then allow starter rope (10) to rewind onto pulley (9). Starter handle (11) should be drawn back into the proper released position. If not, release starter rope (10) from handle (11) and rotate pulley (9) one complete turn counterclockwise (flywheel side) and reassemble.

NOTE: Do not apply any more tension on rewind spring (7) than is required to draw starter handle (11) back into the proper released position.

Remount manual starter assembly and complete reassembly.

ELECTRIC STARTER. Some models are equipped with a 12 volt electric starter. The armature and drive components are shown in Fig. M4-16. Minimum brush (7—Fig. 4-17) wear limit is 3/16 inch (4.8 mm).

LOWER UNIT

PROPELLER AND DRIVE HUB. Lower unit protection is provided by a cushion type hub in the propeller. The standard propeller is three bladed with diameter of nine inches (228.6 mm). Standard propeller pitch is 9 inches (228.6 mm) on 6, 8 and 9.9 hp models and 10.5 inches (266.7 mm) on 15 hp models. Optional propellers are available. Select a propeller that will allow a properly tuned and adjusted engine to operate within the specified rpm range at full throttle. Refer to CONDENSED SERVICE DATA for recommended full throttle rpm range.

NOTE: The manufacturer recommends propping outboard motor to operate at or near the high end of the recommended rpm range at full throttle.

R&R AND OVERHAUL. Clamp outboard motor to an appropriate stand and remove gearcase drain plug and vent plug. Allow gearcase lubricant to drain into a suitable container. Detach shift shaft (3—Fig. M4-19) from upper actuating lever and remove reverse lock actuator (4) from shift shaft (3). Remove the three cap screws retaining gearcase housing to drive shaft housing and withdraw gearcase housing.

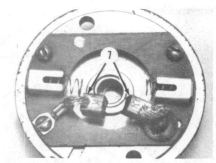

Fig. M4-17—Minumum electric starter brush (7) wear limit is 3/16 inch (4.8 mm).

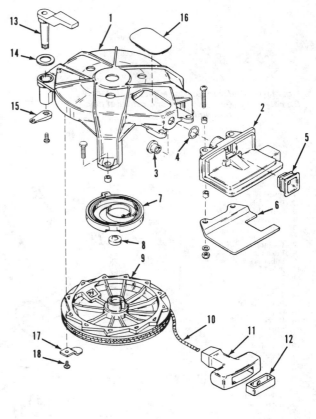

Fig. M4-15—Exploded view of manual rewind starter assembly.

1. Starter housing
2. Rope guide
3. Bushing
4. Lock ring
5. Bushing
6. Support
7. Rewind spring & case
8. Cap
9. Pulley
10. Starter rope
11. Handle
12. Anchor
13. Pulley lock lever
14. Washer
15. Lockout lever
16. Cover
17. Clip (3)
18. Screw (3)

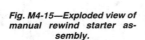

Fig. M4-16—View showing electric starter armature and drive components.

1. Locknut
2. Spacer
3. Spring
4. Starter drive
5. End frame
6. Armature

Disassemble gearcase as follows: Remove locknut (34), thrust hub (33), propeller (32) and thrust hub (30) with cap (31). Remove water pump assembly (Fig. M4-9).

NOTE: Use Mercury special tool 91-13664 to remove carrier assembly (26—Fig. M4-

19). The four slots in tool 91-13664 must be widened by 1/8 inch (3.2 mm) to function properly on these models. Original width of slots is 5/16 inch (7.9 mm) and should be enlarged to 7/16 inch (11.1 mm) wide. Rotate carrier assembly (26) clockwise to remove.

If Mercury special tool 91-13664 is not available, install thrust hub (30—Fig. M4-13) on propeller shaft (24) with the hub's three ears facing toward carrier assembly (26). Place a suitable tool on hex head of thrust hub (30) and turn tool CLOCKWISE to unscrew carrier assembly (26). Withdraw propeller shaft (24) with components (19 through 29). Withdraw drive shaft (2), then withdraw pinion gear (14) and thrust washer (13). Withdraw forward gear (8) and tapered roller bearing (6). If needed, remove shift linkage components.

Inspect shafts for wear on seal lip contact areas and on splines. Inspect dog clutch and gears for wear on engagement areas of dog teeth. Inspect gears for excessive wear and damage. Inspect shift cam for excessive wear on ramp. All seals and "O" rings should be renewed when unit is reassembled.

NOTE: No adjustment of gear mesh pattern and gear backlash is provided. Make sure all parts are in good condition and properly assembled.

Reverse disassembly for reassembly while noting the following: Install dog clutch (21) with short side toward forward gear (18). Apply Quicksilver 2-4-C Multi-Lube or a suitable equivalent to the lip surfaces of all seals. Rotate carrier assembly (26) COUNTERCLOCKWISE to tighten. Tighten carrier assem-

Fig. M4-18—Refer to text for adjusting distance (D) between water pump base and center of hole (H) in shift shaft (3).

1. Housing
2. Drive shaft
3. Shift shaft
4. Reverse lock actuator
5. Clip
6. Shift cam
7. Bushing
8. Bushing holder
9. Lubrication sleeve
10. Anode
11. Water inlet cover
12. Bushing
13. Thrust washer
14. Pinion gear
15. Cup
16. Bearing
17. Bushing
18. Forward gear
19. Shift pin
20. Retaining ring
21. Dog clutch
22. Pin
23. Spring
24. Propeller shaft
25. Reverse gear
26. Carrier assy.
27. "O" ring
28. Bushing
29. Seal
30. Thrust hub
31. Cap
32. Propeller
33. Thrust hub
34. Locknut

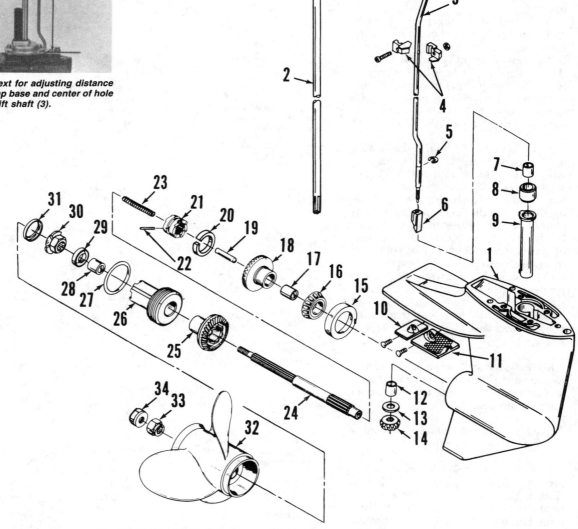

Fig. M4-19—Exploded view of lower unit gearcase assembly.

bly (26) to 60 ft.-lbs. (81 N·m). Install cap (31) on thrust hub (30) and assemble with thrust hub ears facing propeller (32). Tighten propeller nut (34) to 70 in.-lbs. (8 N·m).

If shift linkage components were disassembled refer to the following: Measure distance (D—Fig. M4-18) from water pump base to center of hole (H) in shift shaft (3). Distance (D) should be 16-1/2 inches (419 mm) on models with a short drive shaft, 22 inches (559 mm) on models with a long drive shaft and 27-1/2 inches (698 mm) on models with an extra long drive shaft. Rotate shift shaft (3) clockwise to decrease distance (D) and counterclockwise to increase distance (D).

Install gearcase housing assemble to drive shaft housing and tighten gearcase housing (1—Fig. M4-19) retaining screws to 180 in.-lbs. (20 N·m).

With shift lever in the "NEUTRAL" position, reverse lock actuator (4) should just contact reverse lock hook on outboard motor's midsection.

MERCURY

MERC 7.5 AND 9.8
MERC 75 AND 110

Year Produced

1969-1978	Merc 75	Merc 110
1979-1985	Merc 7.5	Merc 9.8

CONDENSED SERVICE DATA

	Merc 7.5, Merc 75	Merc 9.8, Merc 110
TUNE-UP		
Rated Horsepower	7.5	9.8
Maximum Rpm	4500-5500*	4500-5500*
Bore – Inches	2	2
Stroke – Inches	1¾	1¾
Number of Cylinders	2	2
Displacement – Cu.-In.	10.9	10.9
Compression at Cranking Speed	Not more than 15 psi variation between cylinders	
Spark Plug	See Text	See Text
Magneto – Point Gap:		
1969-1973	0.020 in.	0.020 in.
1974 and later	Breakerless Ignition	
Carburetor Make:		
1972 and earlier	Tillotson	Tillotson
1973 and later	Mercarb	Mercarb
Fuel:Oil Ratio	See Text	See Text
SIZES – CLEARANCES		
Piston Rings:		
End gap	†	†
Side clearance	†	†
Piston Skirt Clearance	†	†
Crankshaft Bearings:		
Upper main bearings	Ball & Roller	Ball & Roller
Center main bearing	Bushing	Bushing
Lower main bearing	Ball	Ball
Crankpin	Loose Rollers	Loose Rollers
No. of rollers (each rod)	29	29
Crankshaft End Play	0.004-0.012 in.	0.004-0.012 in.
Piston Pin Bearing In Rod	Loose Rollers	Loose Rollers
No. of rollers (each rod)	20	20

*Rated rpm on 7.5 models above serial number 5226934 and 9.8 models above serial number 5206549 is 5000-5800.
†Publication not authorized by manufacturer.

TIGHTENING TORQUES
(All Values in Inch-Pounds Unless Noted)

Center Main Bearing Lock Screw	40-45‡
Connecting Rod	180
Cylinder Cover	100
Exhaust Cover	90
Flywheel Nut	35 ft.-lbs.
Reed Stop Screws	20-25
Spark Plug	20 ft.-lbs.

‡15 ft.-lbs. after 1974

LUBRICATION

The engine is lubricated by oil mixed with the fuel. Fuel should be regular leaded, low lead or unleaded gasoline with a minimum pump octane rating of 86. Premium gasoline may be used if desired regular gasoline is not available. Recommended oil is Quicksilver Formula 50 or 50-D. A good quality BIA certified TC-W oil may be used. Fuel:oil ratio should be 50:1 when using Formula 50 or 50-D oil. Follow fuel:oil ratio recommended by oil manufacturer if Formula 50 or 50-D is not used.

To break in new or overhauled motors, observe the following: Motors should not be operated above ½ throttle (2500-3500 rpm) for the first 2 hours. Avoid sustained full throttle operation for the first 10 hours of operation.

The lower unit gears and bearings are lubricated by oil contained in the gearcase. Only "SUPER-DUTY Quicksilver Outboard Gear Lubricant" should be used. Gearcase is filled through the forward plug hole on starboard side of case, with motor in an upright position. The vent plug (located aft of fill plug) should be removed when filling. Lubricant should be maintained at level of vent plug.

FUEL SYSTEM

CARBURETOR. Tillotson, float type carburetors (Fig. M6-1) are used on 1972 and earlier models. Mercarb carburetors with built in fuel pump (Fig. M6-3) are used on 1973 and later motors. Refer to the following for carburetor application and standard main (high speed) jet size.

Merc 7.5
Carburetor Model . . . . Mercarb
Std. Size Main Jet 0.040

Merc 9.8
Carburetor Model . . . . Mercarb
Std. Size Main Jet 0.039

Merc 75 (Ser. No. 2529895-2721150)
Carburetor Model KB-9A
Std. Size Main Jet 0.034

Merc 75 (Ser. No. 2810637-3488152)
Carburetor Model KB-12A
Std. Size Main Jet 0.035

Merc 75 (Ser. No. 3588153-4131609)
Carburetor Model . . . . Mercarb
Std. Size Main Jet 0.034

Merc 75 (Ser. No. 4131610-4397536)
Carburetor Model . . . . Mercarb
Std. Size Main Jet 0.032

Merc 75 (Ser. No. 4397537 & up)
Carburetor Model . . . . Mercarb
Std. Size Main Jet 0.045

Merc 110 (Before Ser. No. 2475312)
Carburetor Model KB-5A
Std. Size Main Jet 0.049

Merc 110 (Ser. No. 2508759-2708898)
Carburetor Model KB-8A
Std. Size Main Jet 0.049

Merc 110 (Ser. No. 2798057-3482752)
Carburetor Model KB-11A
Std. Size Main Jet 0.047

Merc 110 (Ser. No. 3482753 & up)
Carburetor Model . . . . Mercarb
Std. Size Main Jet 0.041

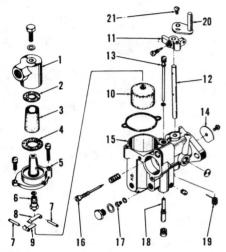

Fig. M6-1—Exploded view of Tillotson type carburetor used on early models.

1. Strainer cover
2. Gasket
3. Strainer
4. Gasket
5. Bowl cover
6. Inlet needle & seat
7. Shaft
8. Primary lever
9. Secondary lever
10. Float
11. Throttle lever
12. Throttle shaft
13. Idle tube
14. Throttle valve
15. Body
16. Idle needle
17. High speed jet
18. Main nozzle
19. Spring
20. Throttle follower
21. Screw

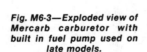

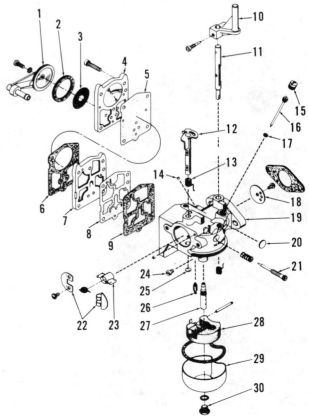

Fig. M6-3—Exploded view of Mercarb carburetor with built in fuel pump used on late models.

1. Inlet fitting
2. Gasket
3. Screen
4. Cover
5. Diaphragm
6. Gasket
7. Pump body
8. Check valve diaphragm
9. Gasket
10. Throttle lever
11. Throttle shaft
12. Choke shaft
13. Return spring
14. Plug
15. Screw plug
16. Idle tube
17. Gasket
18. Throttle plate
19. Throttle body
20. Welch plug
21. Idle mixture screw
22. Choke shutter plates
23. Boost venturi
24. Main jet
25. Welch plug
26. Inlet needle
27. Main nozzle
28. Float
29. Float bowl
30. Retaining screw

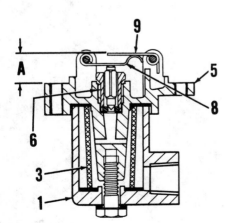

Fig. M6-2—Schematic view of fuel bowl and inlet assembly on Tillotson carburetor. Refer to text for setting float height.

All carburetors employ a fixed, high-speed jet (17–Fig. M6-1 or 24–Fig. M6-3), with optional sizes available for adjusting the calibration for altitude or other special conditions.

Initial setting for the idle adjustment needle (16–Fig. M6-1 or 21–Fig. M6-3) is one turn open. Adjustment should be accomplished with engine operating under load, at slow speed (650-750 rpm) after it has reached normal operating temperature.

On all Merc 110 models with KB-5A carburetor, turning idle mixture needle counterclockwise leans the mixture. On all Merc 7.5, 9.8 and 75 models and late Merc 110 models, turning the idle mixture needle clockwise leans the mixture.

The idle speed is adjusted at screw (IS–Fig. M6-7, M6-9 or M6-10). The idle fuel mixture must be correctly set before adjusting idle speed. Run the engine until it reaches normal operating temperature, loosen lock nut and turn screw (IS) to provide 650-750 rpm in forward gear. Do not attempt to adjust idle speed unless engine is under normal load.

Refer to the appropriate paragraphs in the SPEED CONTROL LINKAGE section for adjusting the remaining speed controls.

To adjust the fuel level on Tillotson type carburetor (Fig. M6-1), remove bowl cover (5) and invert the cover. Measure distance (A–Fig. M6-2) between primary lever (9) and gasket sur-face of bowl cover with inlet valve (6) closed. This distance should be 13/32 inch; if it is not, bend the curved tang on secondary lever (8) until correct measurement is obtained. After adjusting float height, bend the vertical tang on primary lever (9) to allow a maximum clearance of 0.040 inch between secondary lever (8) and inlet needle (6).

To adjust fuel level on Mercarb type carburetor (Fig. M6-3), remove carburetor from engine and remove float bowl. Invert carburetor body and measure distance from float to gasket surface (Fig. M6-4). Float level should be 5/64-7/64 inch. Adjust float level by bending float arm (A) resting on inlet needle. Turn carburetor right side up and check float drop measurement. Distance from lowest portion of float to highest point on main jet (MJ) should be 1/64-1/32 inch. Adjust float drop by bending tang (T) on float arm.

SPEED CONTROL LINKAGE. The speed control grip moves the magneto stator plate to advance or retard the ignition timing. The carburetor throttle valve is synchronized to open as the timing is advanced. Before attempting to synchronize throttle opening to the ignition advance, the idle fuel mixture must be correctly set. Several types of linkage are used. Refer to the appropriate following paragraphs for adjustment.

Merc 75 (Before Ser. No. 2810637) & Merc 110 (Ser. No. 1580203-2798056). The idle speed stop screw (IS–Fig. M6-7 or M6-9) should be adjusted to provide 650-750 rpm in forward gear. With motor at normal operating temperature and in forward gear, advance speed control to 1000-1100 rpm. With controls set as outlined, the throttle control cam (C–Fig. M6-5 or M6-8) should just contact the follower (20). If cam and follower are not touching or if throttle is partially open, loosen screw (21) and reposition follower (20) as required. The maximum advance stop screw (HS–Fig. M6-7) should be set so that threaded end of screw extends ¼ inch through control lever as shown at (A).

On later models, one of the cam attaching holes is slotted so that angle of cam is adjustable. Refer to Fig. M6-8. On these models, move speed control to maximum speed position and check for complete throttle opening. If the carburetor throttle is not completely open or if throttle is completely open and linkage is binding, the cam should be repositioned. If the position of cam is changed, it is necessary to recheck throttle pick-up at 1000-1100 rpm.

The neutral stop (Fig. M6-6) should be adjusted to provide maximum speed of 2400-2700 rpm in neutral. Stop can be moved as necessary after loosening screw (S). Start position on twist grip should be aligned at this setting.

Fig. M6-5—On early Merc 110 models, cam (C) should just contact follower (20) at 1000-1100 rpm.

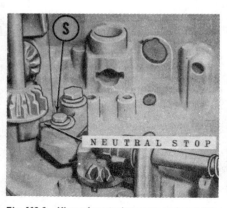

Fig. M6-6—View of neutral stop on early models. Later models are similar.

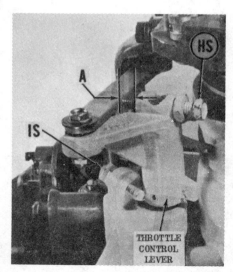

Fig. M6-7—View of speed control linkage used on some Merc 110 models. The idle speed stop screw (S) may be located as shown in Fig. M6-9 on some models.

Fig. M6-4—Float level on Mercarb carburetor should be 5/64-7/64 inch from float to throttle body basket surface. Bend float arm (A) to adjust float level. Refer to text for float drop adjustment.

Merc 75 (Ser. No. 2810637-3801457) and Merc 110 (Ser. No. 2798057-3795657). On these models, it is important for both sets of ignition points to be correctly gapped (0.020 inch) before checking the speed control linkage. Remove top spark plug and turn crankshaft until the top piston is 0.193 inch Before Top Dead Center. (Mercury dial indicator, part number C-9158222 can be used.) Attach a continuity meter to the white lead from contact points and to motor ground. Hold speed control handle against the maximum speed stop and adjust advance stop screw (HS – Fig. M6-9) until meter indicates that points **just** close.

With throttle set at maximum speed position, check play between follower (20 – Fig. M6-8) and cam (C). The follower should have almost opened the throttle completely with approximately 0.050 inch play remaining. If incorrect, loosen screw (21) and reposition throttle follower (20).

Throttle pick-up should occur 0.002 inch after top dead center on Merc 75 serial number 2810637-3488152 and Merc 110 serial number 2798057-3482752. Throttle pick-up should occur 0.007 inch after top dead center on Merc 75 serial number 3482752-3795657. To position cam for correct throttle pick-up, rotate crankshaft until top piston is in specified position. Move the speed control toward idle position until the continuity meter indicates that points just open. With crankshaft and speed controls set as described, the cam (C – Fig. M6-8) should be just touching follower (20). If cam and follower are not touching or if throttle is partially open, loosen the two screws attaching cam (C) and reposition cam as required. Very little adjustment is normally necessary; however, the maximum throttle opening should be rechecked.

Power timing light may be used to check ignition timing and throttle pick-up on models with degree markings on

cowl support bracket. Mount motor in test tank and attach power timing light to top spark plug wire. Full advance position for all motors is 34 degrees before top dead center. Adjust maximum advance stop if necessary. Move throttle toward stop position while observing flywheel timing mark with timing light. Stop moving speed control when timing mark is 2 degrees after top dead center on Merc 75 serial number 2810637-3488152 and Merc 110 serial number 2798057-3482752 or when mark is 6 degrees after top dead center on Merc 75 serial number 3488153-3801457 and Merc 110 serial number 3482753-3795657. Throttle control cam should be just touching throttle lever at this point. Adjust throttle pick-up screw if necessary.

The neutral stop (Fig. M6-6) should be adjusted to provide maximum speed of 2400-2700 rpm in neutral. Stop can be moved as necessary after loosening screw (S). The "START" position on twist grip should be aligned when at 2400-2700 rpm. If not, loosen the Allen screw in bottom of twist grip and reposition.

Merc 75 (Ser. No. 3801458 & Above) and Merc 110 (Ser. No. 379658 & Above). These motors are equipped with breakerless, electronic ignitions. It is not necessary to remove flywheel to adjust ignition timing. To adjust speed control linkage, place motor in forward gear, move speed control to full speed position. Timing mark (TM – Fig. M6-11) on trigger coil holder should be aligned with timing index mark (I) on crankcase end plate. Turn maximum advance stop screw (MA – Fig. M6-10) to align marks if necessary. Initial throttle pick-up point is not adjustable.

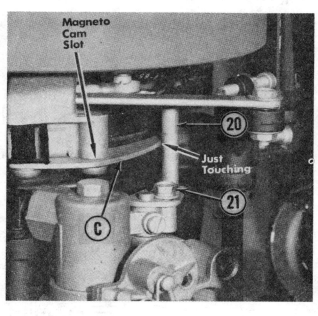

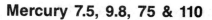

Fig. M6-8 – View of later type speed control linkage. One of the cam mounting screw holes is slotted for adjustment.

Fig. M6-9 – View of the speed control linkage typical of late models with point type magneto.

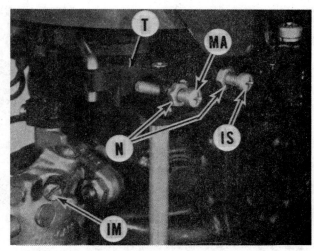

Fig. M6-10 – View of maximum advance stop screw (MA) and idle speed stop screw (IS). Idle mixture screw (IM) should be 1 turn out from a lightly seating position.

To check timing with a power timing light, place motor in a suitable test tank and attach timing light to top spark plug wire. Start engine and move speed control to full speed position. Timing mark on flywheel (M–Fig. M6-12) should align with 30° BTDC on timing decal of Merc 75 models after 1975 and 35° BTDC on other models prior to 1978. Models after 1977 are not equipped with timing decal so timing marks on flywheel and starter housing should be aligned. Adjust timing by turning maximum advance stop screw (Fig. M6-10). Be sure to tighten locknut on screw when adjustment is completed.

Adjust idle speed screw (IS–Fig. M6-10) to obtain 650-750 rpm with motor in forward gear.

The neutral stop (Fig. M6-6) should be adjusted to provide maximum speed of 2400-2700 rpm in neutral. Stop can be moved as necessary after loosening screw (S). The "START" position on twist grip should be aligned when at 2400-2700 rpm. If not, loosen Allen screw in bottom of twist grip and reposition.

Merc 7.5 and Merc 9.8. To adjust speed control mechanism, shift motor to forward gear and rotate speed control handle to full throttle position. Loosen control cable nuts (N–Fig. M6-13). Move throttle lever (T–Fig. M6-10) so timing mark on trigger coil holder (TM–Fig. M6-11) is aligned with timing mark (I) on crankcase end plate. Turn maximum advance screw (MA-Fig. M6-10) so screw contacts throttle lever (T) just as timing marks are aligned. With throttle lever contacting maximum advance screw, pull advance control cable (A–Fig. M6-13) toward speed control handle (do not use excessive force) and tighten control cable nuts (N). Remove slack from reverse control cable (R) using same procedure. Run engine until normal engine temperature is attained then obtain an idle speed of 650-750 rpm by turning idle speed screw (IS–Fig. M6-10). Stop engine, then with throttle lever (T) against idle speed screw (IS), adjust carburetor throttle lever (10–Fig. MR6-3) on throttle shaft (11) so pin in throttle lever just contacts throttle cam.

REED VALVES. The inlet reed valves are located on the crankshaft center main bearing assembly. The crankshaft must be removed before reed valves can be serviced.

Reed petals (2–Figs. M6-15 and M6-16) should be perfectly flat and have no more than 0.007 inch clearance between free end and seating surface of main bearing. The reed stop (1) must be carefully adjusted to provide correct clearance (A–Fig. M6-16) between end

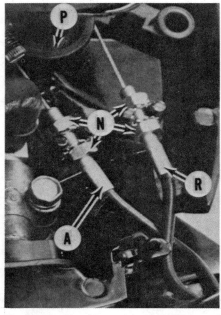

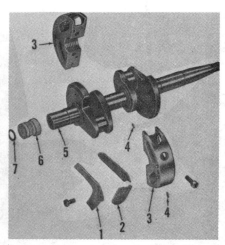

Fig. M6-13 – View of speed control cables used on Merc 7.5 and 9.8 models.

A. Advance cable   P. Pulley
N. Cable nuts   R. Retard cable

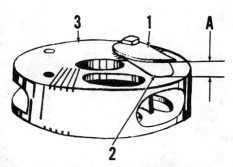

Fig. M6-16—Center main bearing showing inlet reed valves. Refer to text for adjustment.

Fig. M6-11—Timing mark (TM) on trigger coil housing should align with index mark (I) on crankcase end plate with motor in forward gear and speed control fully advanced. Use maximum advance stop screw (MA—Fig. M6-10) to adjust if necessary.

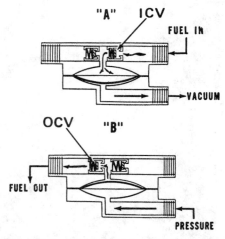

Fig. M6-18—Schematic view of diaphragm type fuel pump used on motors with Tillotson type carburetor. Vacuum-Pressure line attaches to lower crankcase. When power head piston moves upward in cylinder, vacuum in crankcase draws diaphragm out and fuel in as shown in view "A". Crankcase pressure resulting from power stroke forces diaphragm in and fuel out as shown in view "B".

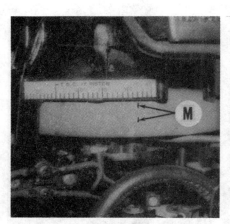

Fig. M6-12—Timing mark (M) on flywheel should appear aligned at 34½ degrees when checking full advance timing with a power timing light. A timing mark on starter housing is used in place of timing decal on models after 1977.

Fig. M6-15—Exploded view of crankshaft center main bearing and reed valves.

1. Reed stop
2. Reed petals
3. Bearing and reed block
4. Dowels
5. Crankshaft
6. Seal carrier
7. Seal

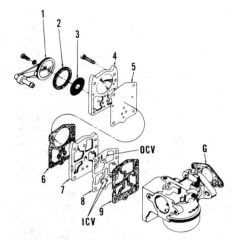

Fig. M6-19—View of diaphragm fuel pump portion of Mercarb carburetor. Make certain that vacuum passage hole in gasket (G) is correctly positioned over hole in crankcase when reassembling. Refer to Fig. M6-3 for legend.

of stop and seating surface of bearing. The recommended clearance is 5/32 inch. Seating surface of bearing must be smooth and flat, and may be refinished on a lapping plate after removing reed valves and dowels. Do not attempt to bend or straighten a reed petal and never install a bent petal. Lubricate the reed valve assembly before reassembling.

FUEL PUMP. A diaphragm type fuel pump is used which is operated by pressure and vacuum pulsations in the lower crankcase as shown in Fig. M6-18. Fuel pump (Fig. M6-19) is included in carburetor assembly of motors equipped with Mercarb carburetor. Vacuum in the crankcase draws the diaphragm in, pulling fuel past the inlet check valve (ICV). Crankcase pressure forces the diaphragm out and the trapped fuel enters the carburetor line past the outlet check valve (OCV).

All defective or questionable parts should be renewed.

IGNITION SYSTEM

SPARK PLUG. The correct spark must be selected for the specific motor. Refer to the following for spark plug application and electrode gap.

Merc 7.5 (Before Ser. No. 5226935)
Use special surface gap spark plug AC V40FFK or Champion L78V.

Merc 7.5 (After Ser. No. 5226934)
Use special surface gap spark plug Champion L77J4. Champion QL77J4 may be used if radio frequency interference suppression is needed.

Merc 9.8 (Before Ser. No. 5206550)
Use special surface gap spark plug AC V40FFK or Champion L78V.

Merc 9.8 (After Ser. No. 5206549)
Use special surface gap spark plug Champion L77J4. Champion QL77J4 may be used if radio frequency interference suppression is needed.

Merc 75 (Before Ser. No. 2810637)
Type . . . . Champion L7J
Thread Reach . . . . ½ inch
Electrode Gap . . . . 0.030 inch

Merc 75 (Ser. No. 2810637-3801457)
Use special surface gap AC type V40FFK, Champion type L78V or AC type VR40FF radio noise suppression spark plugs.

Merc 75 (After Ser. No. 3801457)
Use special surface gap AC type V40FFk, Champion type L77V or AC type VR40FF radio noise suppression spark plugs.

Merc 110 (Ser. No. 2508759-2708898)
Type . . . . Champion L4J
Thread Reach . . . . ½ inch
Electrode Gap . . . . 0.030 inch

Merc 110 (Ser. No. 2798057-3795657)
Use special surface gap AC type V40FFK, Champion type L78V or AC type VR40FF radio noise suppression spark plugs.

Merc 110 (After Ser. No. 3795657)
Use special surface gap AC type V40FFM, Champion type L77V or AC type VR40FF radio noise suppression spark plugs.

MAGNETO. Four different ignition systems have been used on these motors. Two different, breaker point timed, conventional magnetos; an electronic, maker point timed, magneto; and a breakerless, electronic magneto have all been used.

Point gap at maximum opening should be 0.020 inch for all later motors with breaker points or maker points.

The later, breaker point timed, magneto can be identified by the cover over the compartment which contains the contact points. Points can be synchronized on motors equipped with the later type conventional magneto to open at 180 degree intervals using special Mercury tool C-91-36445A1 shown in Fig. M6-21.

The maker point type magneto used on Merc 75 serial number 2810637-3801457 and Merc 110 serial number 2798057-3705657 uses two high tension coils mounted on a bracket at rear of motor in addition to the generating coils on the stator plate. Gap should be 0.020 inch at maximum opening for both sets of contact points. The high primary voltage of this ignition system will pit and darken contact points. Renewal of points should not be necessary unless points are broken or completely worn away.

The breakerless, electronic magneto used on Merc 75 after serial number 3801458, Merc 110 after serial number 3795658, Merc 7.5 and 9.8 uses a trigger coil, mounted close to flywheel to time ignition spark. Unit may be identified by switch box mounted on power head in addition to ignition coils. Check all wires and connections before troubleshooting ignition circuit. Resistance between yellow and white stator coil wires should be 750-1000 ohms while resistance between stator yellow wire and ground should be 1500-2000 ohms. Resistance between brown and white trigger module leads should be 140-160 ohms.

On all models, refer to the appropriate SPEED CONTROL LINKAGE paragraphs in the Fuel System section for adjusting controls.

COOLING SYSTEM

WATER PUMP. The rubber impeller type water pump is housed in the gearcase housing. The impeller is mounted on and driven by the lower unit drive shaft.

When cooling system problems are encountered, first check the water inlet for plugging or partial stoppage and check thermostat operation, then if not corrected, remove the gearcase housing as outlined in LOWER UNIT section and examine the water pump, water tubes and seals. The water inlet is located on the antiventilation plate immediately above the propeller.

Fig. M6-21—Synchronizing tool installed for adjusting magneto points. Early type magneto is shown; however, procedure is similar for later point type models.

DP. Degree plate   P. Pointer

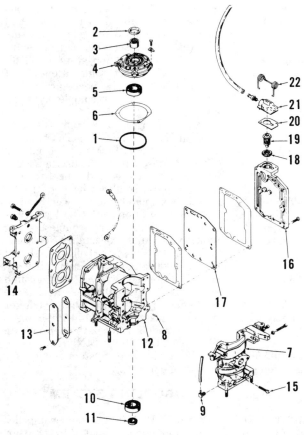

Fig. M6-23—Exploded view of Merc 9.8 power head crankcase and associated parts. Other models are similar.

1. "O" ring
2. Oil seal
3. Roller bearing
4. End cap
5. Ball bearing
6. Shim
7. Crankcase half
8. Dowel
9. Crankcase check valve
10. Ball bearing
11. Oil seal
12. Cylinder half
13. Transfer port cover
14. Cylinder cover
15. Center bearing screw
16. Exhaust cover
17. Baffle plate
18. Gasket
19. Thermostat
20. Gasket
21. Housing
22. Retainer

Thoroughly lubricate the pistons, rings and bearings using new engine oil and make sure that ring end gaps are aligned with the locating pins in ring grooves. After crankshaft is installed, turn the shaft until each ring appears in the exhaust and transfer ports and check for damage during assembly.

Make certain that center main bearing dowel is in place and that main bearing is properly located over dowel. Assemble the upper main bearing cap (4 – Fig. M6-23) and install over crankshaft using the shim pack (6) which was removed. Install and tighten the two cap screws which retain the cap to cylinder block, tap the crankshaft back and forth using a soft mallet, then measure the gap between bearing (5) and the crankshaft. The clearance should be 0.004-0.012 inch. If incorrect, remove the end cap and vary the thickness of shim pack (6) until the proper end play is obtained. Shims are available in thicknesses of 0.002, 0.003, 0.005 and 0.010 inch.

Remove the end cap to cylinder block screws, withdraw cap and install "O" ring (1). Coat mating surfaces of crankshaft halves lightly with sealer and assemble. Slide end cap (4) into position before tightening crankcase halves. Tighten crankcase cap screws by working each way from the center to prevent distortion.

Turn the crankshaft several revolutions before installation to make certain the parts are free and do not bind.

When assembling, make certain that water pump retaining nuts are tightened to 25-30 in.-lbs. torque. If nuts are incorrectly tightened, the water pump may be damaged.

POWER HEAD

R&R AND DISASSEMBLE. To remove the power head assembly, first remove the top cowl and disconnect stop switch wire, speed control linkage and choke shutter spring. Remove the screws which secure fuel line check unit to lower cowl and the nuts securing power head to lower unit; then lift off the complete power head assembly.

Place the unit on power head stand or equivalent and remove fuel pump, carburetor, flywheel and magneto. Exhaust manifold cover plate, cylinder block cover plate and transfer port cover should be removed for cleaning and inspection.

Remove the cap screws which retain upper end cap (4 – Fig. M6-23) to power head, remove center main bearing locking screw (15); then unbolt and remove crankcase front half (7).

NOTE: A special recess is located at the center on each side of crankcase half (7). Separate crankcase halves by carefully prying at these points ONLY with a screwdriver. Use extra care not to spring the

parts to mar the machined, mating surfaces. Crankcase half (7) and cylinder half (12) are matched and align bored, and are available only as an assembly.

The crankshaft and bearings assembly, with pistons and connecting rods attached, can now be lifted out of cylinder block for service and overhaul as outlined in the appropriate following paragraphs. Assemble by following the procedures outlined in the ASSEMBLY paragraph.

ASSEMBLY. When assembling, the crankcase must be completely sealed against both vacuum and pressure. Exhaust manifold and water passages must be sealed against pressure leakage. Whenever power head is disassembled, it is recommended that all gasket surfaces and machined joints without gaskets be carefully checked for nicks and burrs which might interfere with a tight seal.

Completely assemble the crankshaft, lower and center main bearings, connecting rods, pistons and rings and install the assembly by inserting pistons in lower ends of cylinders. Two special Mercury ring compressors should be used. If ring compressor kit is not available, two men must work together and use extreme care in installing the crankshaft and pistons assembly.

PISTONS, PINS, RINGS & CYLINDERS. Before detaching connecting rods from crankshaft assembly, make sure that rod and cap are properly identified for correct assembly to each other and in the correct cylinder.

Each piston is fitted with three interchangeable rings which are pinned to prevent rotation in the grooves.

Piston pin is pressed in piston bosses and secured with retaining rings. Piston end of connecting rod is fitted with 20 loose needle bearings which use the connecting rod bore and the piston pin as bearings races. Install bearing washers and needle bearings in piston end of connecting rod using light nonfibrous

Fig. M6-24—Alignment marks on connecting rod and cap should be on same side as shown.

grease to hold them in place, then install the piston pin. Piston must be installed so that sharp vertical side of deflector will be toward intake side and long sloping side of piston will be toward exhaust port in cylinder. Thoroughly lubricate all friction surfaces during assembly.

CONNECTING RODS, BEARINGS & CRANKSHAFT. Upper end of crankshaft is carried by a ball bearing plus a caged needle bearing. The unbushed center main bearing (3 – Fig. M6-15) also contains the inlet reed valves. Lower main bearing is interchangeable with the upper ball bearing.

Connecting rod rides in loose needle rollers at both ends with 20 loose rollers at piston end and 29 at crankpin. Check rod for alignment, using Mercury Alignment Tool (C-91-28441A2), or by placing rod on a surface plate and checking with a light. When installing connecting rods, make certain that alignment marks (Fig. M6-24) are both on same side.

If bearing surface of rod and cap is rough, scored, worn, or shows evidence of overheating, renew the connecting rod. Inspect crankpin and main bearing journals. If scored, out-of-round, or worn, renew the crankshaft. Check the crankshaft for straightness using a dial indicator and "V" blocks.

Inspect and adjust the reed valves as outlined in REED VALVE paragraph, and reassemble as outlined in ASSEMBLY paragraph.

MANUAL STARTER

Refer to Fig. M6-26 for a typical exploded view of rewind starter. To disassemble starter, remove cowl and starter from motor. Insert a screwdriver in slot in top of pulley shaft (19) and loosen the left-hand thread nut (3). Allow the screwdriver and shaft (19) to turn clockwise until recoil spring unwinds. Remove rope handle. Remove nut (3), invert the assembly and remove the parts, making sure that recoil spring (7) remains in housing recess as pulley (10) is removed. Protect hands with gloves or a cloth, grasp recoil spring (7), remove spring and allow it to unwind slowly.

Lubricate the parts with Multipurpose Lubricant, and assemble by reversing the disassembly procedure. Install spring guide bushing (8) with chamfered end of bushing toward sheave (10). Make sure that pawls (12) are all installed the same way, with radius to outside and identification mark away from pulley (10). Install retainer (15) with cup end out and position washer (16) and wave washer (17) in cup. Make certain that tang on spring retainer (6) engages slot in shaft (19). Position starter with end of

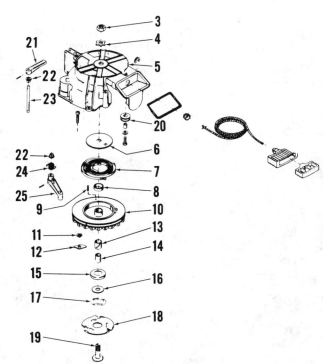

Fig. M6-26 — Exploded view of rewind starter. Components (21 through 25) prevent starter pulley rotation except in neutral.

3. Nut
4. Lockwasher
5. Starter housing
6. Retainer
7. Recoil spring
8. Bushing
9. Rope retainer pin
10. Sheave
11. Wave washers
12. Pawls
13. Nylon bushing
14. Spacer
15. Retainer
16. Washer
17. Wave washer
18. Plate
19. Sheave shaft
20. Rope guide
21. Pulley lock lever
22. Bushing
23. Shaft
24. Spring
25. Actuator

shaft (19) through starter housing (5) and install lockwasher (4) and nut (3). Pull free end of rope through starter housing and install rope handle. Turn shaft (19) counterclockwise until handle is pulled against starter housing, plus an additional 1¼ turns; then tighten nut (3). Pull cord out and check for sticking and full return.

LOWER UNIT

PROPELLER AND DRIVE CLUTCH. Protection for the motor is built into a special cushioning clutch in the propeller hub. No adjustment is possible on the propeller or clutch. Various pitch propellers are available and propeller should be selected for best performance under applicable conditions. With speed control linkage correctly adjusted, propeller should be selected to provide the correct maximum engine speed as listed in the CONDENSED SERVICE DATA table. Propellers other than those designed for the motor must not be used.

R&R AND OVERHAUL. Most service on the lower unit can be performed by detaching the gearcase from the drive shaft housing. To remove the gearcase, remove the two stud nuts (A – Fig. M6-28) and withdraw the lower unit gearcase assembly.

Remove the housing plugs and drain the housing, then secure the gearcase in a vise between two blocks of soft wood,

with propeller up. Wedge a piece of wood between propeller and antiventilation plate, remove the propeller nut, then remove the propeller.

Check the backlash of the propeller drive gears before disassembly by pulling out on the drive shaft and pushing in on the propeller shaft, then rotating drive shaft lightly while noting backlash by feel. No more than 0.003-0.005 inch backlash should exist if gears are properly adjusted.

Disassemble the gearcase by removing gearcase nut (61 – Fig. M6-29). Nut is secured with left-hand thread. Clamp the

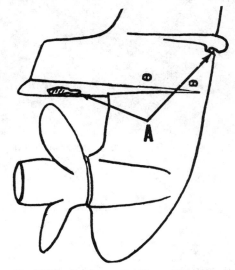

Fig. M6-28—To remove the lower unit gearcase assembly, remove the attaching stud nuts at (A).

outer end of propeller shaft in a soft jawed vise and remove the gearcase by tapping with a rubber mallet. Forward gear (40) will remain in housing. Withdraw the propeller shaft from bearing carrier (56) and reverse gear (46).

Remove and save the shims (47) and thrust washer (48) from inside of gear housing. Shims should be reinstalled if gear backlash was within limits before disassembly.

Clamp the bearing carrier (56) in a soft

jawed vise and remove reverse gear (46) and bearing (49) with an internal expanding puller and slide hammer. Remove and discard the propeller shaft rear seal (58).

To remove dog clutch (43) from propeller shaft, insert the shift plunger (8) in hole in shaft and apply only enough pressure on end of shift plunger to remove the spring pressure. Remove retaining ring (44), then push out the pin (42) with a small punch. The pin passes through drilled holes in dog clutch and operates in slotted hole in propeller shaft.

To disassemble the drive shaft and associated parts, reposition gearcase in vise with drive shaft projecting upward, then unbolt and remove water pump cover (16). Remove the face plate (18); then remove impeller (19) and impeller drive pin. Withdraw the remainder of the water pump parts. Clamp upper end of drive shaft in a soft jawed vise, remove pinion retaining cap screw (37); then tap gearcase off drive shaft and bearing. Note the position and thickness of shims (30 & 30A) on drive shaft upper bearing. Mesh position of pinion is controlled by shims (30) placed underneath the bearing, while shaft end play is controlled by total shim pack thickness. The shims are identical but should not be interchanged or mixed, except to adjust the mesh position of drive pinion.

After drive shaft has been removed, the forward gear (40) and bearing (39) can usually be dislodged by jarring open end of gearcase against a block of soft wood. Remove and save the shim pack (38).

Shift shaft (5) can be removed after removing set screw (2) retaining bushing (3). When installing, make sure that long shaft splines are on upper end, and that shift cam (7) is installed with the notches (detents) toward rear.

Increasing the thickness of shim pack (38) DECREASES the backlash of forward gear (40). Increasing the thickness of shim pack (47) INCREASES the backlash of reverse gear (46). The number and thickness of shims (30) controls mesh position of drive pinion. Shims are available in thicknesses of 0.002, 0.003, 0.005 and 0.010 inch.

When renewing gearcase, or when correcting backlash and mesh of drive train, first install drive shaft (33), bearing (32), shims (30 & 30A) and water pump housing (23). Adjust total thickness of shims (30) so that water pump will seat on housing with no shaft end play. Remove the shaft and lay shims (30) aside for reinstallation during assembly. Make a trial assembly of forward gear (40) and bearing (39) using the removed shims (38). Install drive shaft (33), bearing (32) and shims (30).

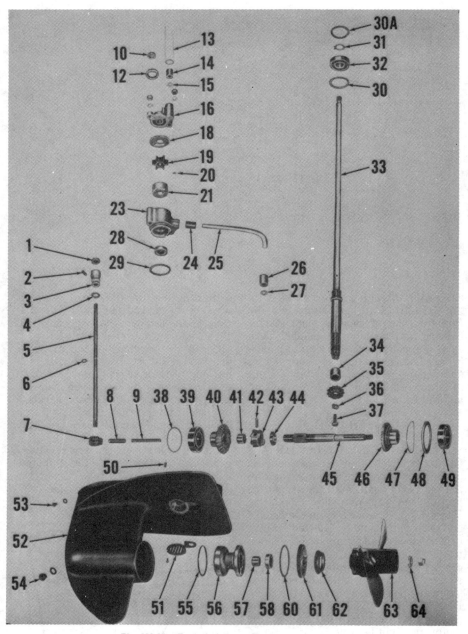

Fig. M6-29—Exploded view of gearcase assembly.

1. Oil seal
2. Bushing retainer screw
3. Bushing
4. "O" ring
5. Shift shaft
6. Tube seal
7. Shift cam
8. Shift plunger
9. Spring
10. "O" ring
12. Oil seal
13. Guide sleeve
14. Seal
15. Nylon washer
16. Water pump cover

18. Plate
19. Impeller
20. Key
21. Insert
23. Pump housing
24. Tube seal
25. Inlet tube
26. Tube seal
27. Nylon washer
28. Oil seal
29. "O" ring
30. & 30A. Shims
31. Snap ring
32. Ball bearing
33. Drive shaft

34. Roller bearing
35. Drive pinion
36. Lockplate
37. Cap screw
38. Shim
39. Ball bearing
40. Forward gear
41. Roller bearing
42. Cross pin
43. Dog clutch
44. Retaining ring
45. Propeller shaft
46. Reverse gear
47. Shim
48. Thrust washer

49. Ball bearing
50. Hollow dowel
51. Inlet screen
52. Gear housing
53. Vent screw
54. Filler screw
55. "O" ring
56. Bearing carrier
57. Roller bearing
58. Oil seal
60. Washer
61. Nut
62. Guide collar
63. Propeller
64. Splined spacer

Install drive pinion (35) and install and tighten locking screw (37). Coat gears with bearing blue then check mesh pattern by pressing drive shaft down and turning clockwise to rotate the gears. If pressure is heavy on lower end of pinion tooth, remove one shim from pack (30). Place the removed shim with pack (30A) to retain end play adjustment. Reverse the procedure if pressure is heavy on upper end of tooth. After adjusting mesh position, check and adjust backlash to 0.003-0.005 inch by adding or removing shims (38). Install reverse gear (46) and bearing (49) in bearing carrier (56); then install assembled parts in gearcase without propeller shaft. Adjust to minimum backlash without binding, by adding or removing shims (47).

When assembling, nuts securing water pump and cover (16) to gear housing should be tightened to 25-30 in.-lbs. torque. Incorrect tightening may damage pump.

Before attaching gearcase to the drive shaft housing, make certain that both the shift cam (7) and the shift lever (on starboard side of motor) are in forward gear position. Shift shaft (5) should be in counterclockwise position (viewed from top end of shaft) and shift lever should be pulled up. Complete assembly by reversing disassembly procedure.

MERCURY
MERC 18 AND 25
(Prior To Serial No. 6416713)

CONDENSED SERVICE DATA

NOTE: Metric and U.S. fasteners are used on outboard motor. Be sure correct fasteners and tools are used servicing motor.

TUNE-UP
Rated Horsepower/rpm	18/5000-5500
	25/5400-6000
Bore–Inches	2.56
Stroke–Inches	2.36
Number of Cylinders	2
Displacement–Cu.-In.	24.4
Spark Plug:	
Type	Champion L77J4
Electrode Gap	0.040 in.
Ignition	Breakerless
Carburetor:	
Make	Own
Fuel:Oil Ratio	50:1

SIZES–CLEARANCES
Piston Rings:	
End Gap	*
Side Clearance	*
Piston Clearance	See Text
Crankshaft Bearings:	
Main Bearings	Roller
Crankpin	Loose Rollers
Piston Pin Bearing In Rod	Loose Rollers

*Publication not authorized by manufacturer.

TIGHTENING TORQUES
(All Values Given In Inch-Pounds)
Carburetor Mount Plate:	
M5	30
M8	180
Connecting Rod	160
Crankcase-to-Cylinder Block	29 ft.-lbs.
Cylinder Cover	90
Exhaust Cover	90
Flywheel	50 ft.-lbs.
Power Head	200
Spark Plug	240
Transfer Port Cover	30

LUBRICATION

The engine is lubricated by oil mixed with the fuel. Fuel should be regular leaded, low lead or unleaded gasoline with a minimum pump octane rating of 86. Premium gasoline may be used if desired regular gasoline is not available. Recommended oil is Quicksilver Formula 50 or Formula 50-D. A good quality BIA certified TC-W oil may be used if Formula 50 or 50-D is not available.

Fuel:oil ratio when using Formula 50 or 50-D oil is 50:1 for normal operation. Follow fuel:oil ratio recommended by oil manufacturer if Formula 50 or 50-D is not used.

When breaking in a new or overhauled engine, operate at varied throttle settings for first hour of operation. Avoid sustained full throttle running and do not idle for prolonged periods in cold water. Normal operation is possible after break-in hour is completed.

FUEL SYSTEM

CARBURETOR. Merc 18 models are equipped with a Tillotson BC2A carburetor while Merc 25 models are equipped with a Tillotson BC1A or BC1B carburetor. Refer to Fig. M8-1 for an exploded view of carburetor.

Standard main jet size is 0.046 on Merc 18 and 0.067 on Merc 25. To check float level, invert float bowl so float is hanging down as shown in Fig. M8-2. Float end should be level with or less than 1/32 inch below float bowl edge. Initial setting of idle mixture screw (10–Fig. M8-3) is 1¼ turns from a lightly seated position.

All models are equipped with an enrichment valve (3–Fig. M8-1) to enrich the fuel mixture for cold start-

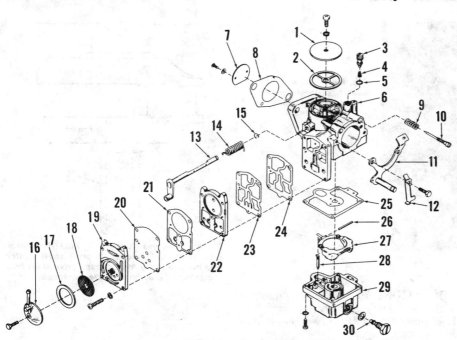

Fig. M8-1—Exploded view of Tillotson carburetor used on all models.

1. Cover	9. Spring	17. Gasket
2. Gasket	10. Idle mixture screw	18. Screen
3. Enrichment valve	11. Plate	19. Fuel pump cover
4. Spring	12. Choke knob detent	20. Diaphragm
5. Gasket	13. Throttle shaft	21. Gasket
6. Body	14. Spring	22. Pump body
7. Throttle plate	15. Snap ring	23. Check valves
8. Gasket	16. Fuel inlet	24. Gasket

25. Gasket
26. Float pin
27. Float
28. Fuel inlet valve
29. Float bowl
30. Main jet

Fig. M8-5—Ignition timing is at full advance when three flywheel dots (D) align with timing mark (M) at ignition. Refer to text for speed control linkage adjustment.

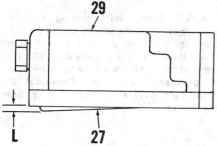

Fig. M8-2—With float bowl (29) inverted as shown, float (27) should be even with or less than 1/32 inch (L) below float bowl edge.

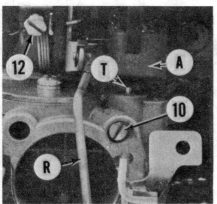

Fig. M8-3—View of carburetor. Refer to text for adjustment.

ing. With choke knob turned fully clockwise, arm (A – Fig. M8-3) should depress valve stem (T). Bend rod (R) to adjust position of arm (A).

SPEED CONTROL LINKAGE. To synchronize ignition timing and throttle opening, proceed as follows: Place motor in a test tank and connect a power timing light to number 1 (top) cylinder spark plug lead. With engine running at full throttle, three timing dots (D – Fig. M8-5) should be aligned with timing mark (M) on starter housing. To adjust full advance ignition timing, stop engine and adjust length of link (K) by disconnecting and turning link end. Lengthen-

ing link will advance ignition timing. Recheck full throttle ignition timing, then stop engine. Disconnect throttle rod (T) from throttle cam, loosen screw (W – Fig. M8-6) and move throttle cam so mark (L) is aligned with roller (R) and cam just touches roller. Retighten screw (W). Run engine and open speed control so two timing dots on flywheel are aligned with timing mark (M – Fig. M8-5). Adjust length of throttle rod (T) so when rod is attached to throttle cam, mark (L – Fig. M8-6) is within 1/16 inch of alignment with center of roller (R). Adjust position of dashpot (P) so dashpot plunger is fully depressed when roller (R) is located at end of throttle cam (C). Adjust idle speed screw (12 – Fig. M8-3) so engine idle speed is 600-700 rpm in forward gear.

REED VALVE. All models are equipped with the vee type reed valve assembly shown in Fig. M8-8. Reed petals should be flat and have no more than 0.007 inch clearance between free end of reed petal and seating surface of reed block. Do not attempt to bend or straighten a reed petal or turn reed petals around on reed block. Reed block

Fig. M8-4—View of throttle and shift linkage. Note location of shift detent ball (B) and spring (G).

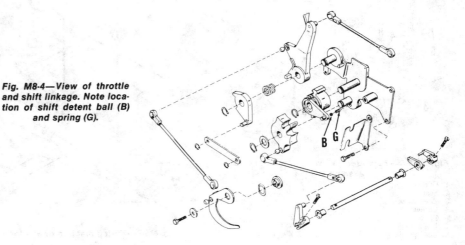

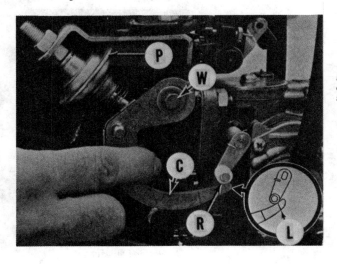

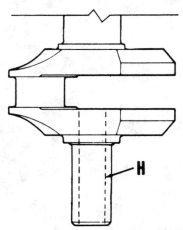

Fig. M8-6—View of throttle cam (C). Refer to text for speed control linkage adjustment.

Fig. M8-11—Drive shaft mating hole (H) in lower crankshaft end extends through shaft center and insertion of a long dummy drive shaft into crankshaft may contact the connecting rod.

seating surface must be flat. Reed block should be renewed if damaged or indented by reed petals.

FUEL PUMP. The fuel pump is an integral part of carburetor as shown in Fig. M8-1. Crankcase pulsations are channeled through carburetor mount and passages in carburetor to operate pump diaphragm (20) and check valves (23). Damaged or questionable components should be renewed. When installing carburetor, make sure that crankcase passage hole in gasket (8) is positioned over hole in carburetor mount plate.

IGNITION SYSTEM

SPARK PLUG. Recommended spark plug is Champion L77J4. Electrode gap should be 0.040 inch. Champion QL77J4 may be used if radio frequency interference suppression is required.

IGNITION. All models are equipped with a breakerless, capacitor discharge ignition system. Refer to Fig. M8-9 for a wiring diagram.

The following test specifications will assist in locating an ignition system malfunction: Resistance between stator black/white lead and ground should be 120-180 ohms. Resistance between stator black/yellow lead and ground should be 3200-3800 ohms. Resistance between stator black/white and black/yellow leads should be 3100-3700 ohms. Resistance between trigger module leads should be 650-850 ohms.

COOLING SYSTEM

WATER PUMP. The rubber impeller type water pump is located at top of gearcase and is mounted on and driven by the drive shaft.

When cooling system problems are encountered, first check the water inlet for plugging or partial stoppage, then if not corrected, remove the gearcase as outlined in LOWER UNIT section and examine the water pump, water tube and seals.

POWER HEAD

NOTE: Drive shaft mating hole in crankshaft extends into crankpin area of crankshaft. When using a power head stand that utilizes a dummy drive shaft to support the power head, be sure the dummy drive shaft does not extend past the crankshaft drive shaft mating hole. See Fig. M8-11.

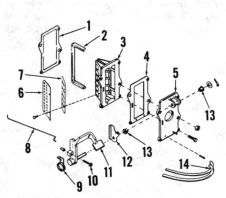

Fig. M8-8—Exploded view of reed valve assembly.

1. Gasket
2. Seal
3. Reed block
4. Gasket
5. Plate
6. Reed stop
7. Reed petals
8. Link
9. Spring
10. Idle speed screw
11. Lever
12. Plate
13. Bushing
14. Bleed hoses

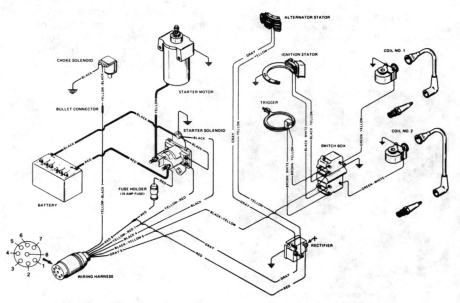

Fig. M8-9—Wiring diagram of electric start models. Manual start models are similar.

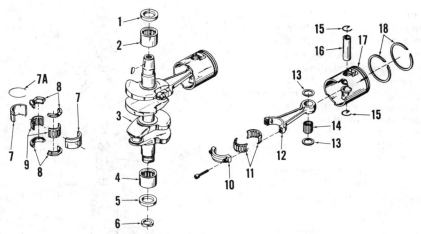

Fig. M8-12—Exploded view of crankshaft assembly.

Fig. M8-14—Install transfer port cover (24) so long side (L) is towards flywheel.

1. Oil seal	6. Seal	10. Rod cap
2. Roller bearing	7. Outer bearing race	11. Roller bearing
3. Crankshaft	7A. Retaining ring	12. Connecting rod
4. Roller bearing	8. Thrust spacer	13. Thrust washer
5. Oil seal	9. Roller bearing	14. Bearing rollers (27)
		15. Snap ring
		16. Piston pin
		17. Piston
		18. Piston ring

R&R AND DISASSEMBLE. To remove power head assembly, first remove top and bottom cowls and manual starter. Remove spark plugs, flywheel and ignition components. Disconnect shift and speed control mechanism. Disconnect lower unit shift shaft from coupler at engine crankcase. Unscrew six screws securing power head to drive shaft and lift off power head.

Remove carburetor and reed valve. Detach cylinder block cover (20 – Fig. M8-13), exhaust cover (32), exhaust manifold (30) and transfer port covers (24, 26 and 28). Unscrew six screws and remove crankcase (33). The crankshaft assembly can now be lifted out of cylinder block for service or overhaul as outlined in the appropriate following paragraphs. Assembly by following the procedures outlined in the ASSEMBLY paragraph.

ASSEMBLY. When assembling, the crankcase must be completely sealed against both vacuum and pressure. Exhaust manifold and water passages must be sealed against pressure leakage.

Whenever power head is disassembled, it is recommended that all gasket surfaces and machined joints without gaskets be carefully checked for nicks and burrs which might interfere with a tight seal.

Thoroughly lubricate pistons, rings and bearings with new engine oil and make sure ring end gaps are aligned with locating pins in ring grooves. Install crankshaft assembly by inserting pistons into lower end of cylinders while being sure locating pin (P – Fig. M8-13) properly mates with center main bearing outer race (7 – Fig. M8-12). Apply a thin coat of Loctite 514 to cylinder block and crankcase mating surfaces. Install crankcase and tighten screws to 29 ft.-lbs. by tightening center screws first and working outward. Rotate crankshaft and check for binding. Inspect piston rings through exhaust and transfer ports and check for ring damage during assembly. Complete remainder of assembly by reversing disassembly procedure. Apply Perfect Seal to exhaust cover screws and tighten to 90 in.-lbs. by tightening center screws first and work-

ing outward. Install port side transfer port covers (24 – Fig. M8-13) so long side is towards top of engine as shown in Fig. M8-14. Tighten cylinder cover screws to 90 in.-lbs. by tightening center screws first and working outward.

PISTON, PINS, RINGS AND CYLINDERS. Each piston is equipped with two piston rings which are pinned to prevent rotation. The piston pin may be driven out after removing pin retaining clips; pin is supported by 27 loose bearing rollers in rod small end.

Measure piston diameter at 0.10 inch above piston bottom at right angle to piston pin and then in line with piston pin. Thrust side diameter (right angle to pin) should be 0.000-0.004 inch greater than diameter in line with pin. Measure piston diameter just below bottom ring groove. Thrust side diameter should be 0.000-0.004 inch greater than diameter in line with pin. Thrust side diameter at bottom of piston should be 0.005 inch greater than thrust side diameter below bottom ring groove. Pistons and piston rings are available in standard size only.

When installing piston on rod, position piston so "E" on piston crown will be towards exhaust port.

CONNECTING RODS, BEARINGS AND CRANKSHAFT. The crankshaft is supported by roller bearings at both ends and at center. The center main bearing is held in place by a retaining ring (7A – Fig. M8-12). Maximum allowable side clearance between crankshaft and thrust spacers (8) is 0.030 inch. Renew bearing and/or crankshaft if side clearance is excessive.

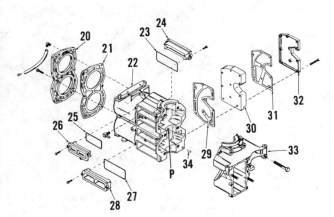

Fig. M8-13—Exploded view of cylinder block assembly.

20. Cylinder cover
21. Gasket
22. Cylinder block
23. "O" ring
24. Transfer port cover
25. "O" ring
26. Transfer port cover
27. "O" ring
28. Transfer port cover
29. Gasket
30. Exhaust manifold
31. Gasket
32. Exhaust cover
33. Crankcase
34. Dowel pin

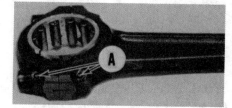

Fig. M8-15—Alignment marks (A) must be on same side of connecting rod and rod cap.

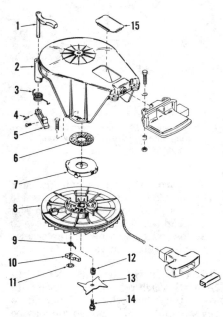

Fig. M8-17—Exploded view of rewind starter.

1. Lockout lever	
2. Starter housing	9. Spring
3. Spring	10. Pawl
4. Pin	11. "E" ring
5. Pulley lock lever	12. Spring
6. Felt pad	13. Cam
7. Rewind spring	14. Screw
8. Rope pulley	15. Cover

The connecting rod is equipped with roller bearings in both ends. Small end bearing has 27 loose bearing rollers while big end has 12 bearing rollers contained in a cage. Check rod for alignment by placing rod on a surface plate and attempt to insert a 0.002 inch feeler gage between rod machined surface and plate. If feeler gage can be inserted, discard rod.

Connecting rod bearing surface and crankshaft rod journals may be polished with number 320 grit emery cloth if slight chatter marks are evident. Do not remove excessive material.

If bearing surface of rod and cap is rough, scored, worn or shows signs of overheating, renew the connecting rod. If crankpin or main bearing journals are scored, out-of-round or worn, renew the crankshaft. Check crankshaft for straightness.

When installing connecting rods, be sure cap fits correctly on rod and alignment marks (A – Fig. M8-15) are on same side.

STARTER

MANUAL STARTER. To remove starter, remove top cowl and detach fuel filter from starter housing by pulling filter straight down. Unscrew starter housing retaining screws and lift off starter. Remove rope handle and allow rope to wind into starter housing. Remove screw (14 – Fig. M8-17), cam (13), spring (12) and rope pulley (8). If necessary, carefully dislodge rewind spring cartridge (7) from rope pulley. Clean and inspect components and renew any which are damaged or excessively worn.

To assemble starter, reverse disassembly procedure while noting the following: The rewind spring is wound in clockwise direction from outer end. When pulley is seated properly, pulley bushing will be flush with end of starter housing spindle. Wind starter rope in counterclockwise direction around rope pulley as viewed from pawl side of pulley. Note position of pawls and cam in Fig. M8-18.

ELECTRIC STARTER. Merc 25 models may be equipped with the electric starter shown in Fig. M8-19. Determine if starter solenoid or neutral start switch are operating properly before servicing starter.

Note location of negative and positive brushes in Fig. M8-20. Slot (S) in end cap should align with chisel mark on starter housing. Lightly lubricate bushings and armature helix with SAE 10W oil.

LOWER UNIT

PROPELLER AND DRIVE CLUTCH. Protection for the motor is provided by a special cushioning clutch built into the propeller hub. Propeller is splined to the shaft. No adjustment of propeller or cushioning clutch is possible. Optional propellers are available

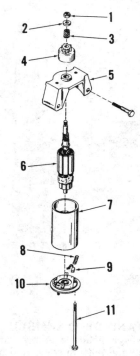

Fig. M8-19—Exploded view of electric starter.

1. Locknut	
2. Spacer	
3. Spring	7. Housing
4. Drive gear	8. Spring
5. End frame	9. Brush
6. Armature	10. End cap
	11. Cap screw

and should be selected for optimum performance with engine operating at maximum engine speed of 5000-5500 rpm on Merc 18 or 5400 rpm on Merc 25. Propellers other than those designed for the motor must not be used.

R&R AND OVERHAUL. Most service on the lower unit can be performed by detaching the gearcase from the drive shaft housing. To remove gearcase, remove top cowl and disconnect lower unit shift shaft from coupler at engine crankcase; on electric start models it will be necessary to pull away bottom cowl for access to coupler. Unscrew retaining screws and separate

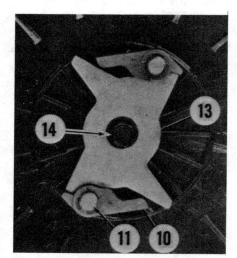

Fig. M8-18—View showing correct installation of pawls (10), "E" rings (11), cam (13) and screw (14).

Fig. M8-20—View showing proper installation of negative brush (N) and positive brush (P).

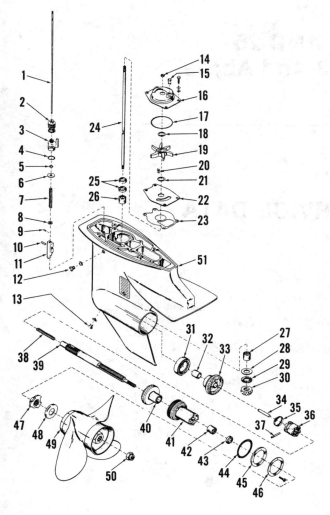

Fig. M8-23—Exploded view of gearcase.

1. Shift shaft
2. Boot
3. Retainer
4. "O" ring
5. "O" ring
6. Washer
7. Spring
8. Washer
9. Pin
10. Pin
11. Shift cam
12. Vent plug
13. Fill plug
14. Slinger
15. Seal
16. Water pump housing
17. "O" ring
18. Fiber washer
19. Impeller
20. Key
21. Fiber washer
22. Plate
23. Gasket
24. Drive shaft
25. Oil seals
26. Needle bearing
27. Needle bearing
28. Thrust washer
29. Thrust bearing
30. Pinion gear
31. Taper roller bearing
32. Bushing
33. Forward gear
34. Shift pin
35. Wire clip
36. Dog clutch
37. Pin
38. Spring
39. Propeller shaft
40. Reverse gear
41. Bearing carrier
42. Needle bearing
43. Oil seal
44. "O" ring
45. Retainer
46. Anode
47. Thrust hub
48. Cap
49. Propeller
50. Nut
51. Gearcase

(27) may be removed by driving bearing down into gear cavity.

Inspect components for damage and excessive wear. Renew all seals and "O" rings. Manufacturer recommends renewing water pump impeller (19) any time it is removed. If old impeller must be reused, install impeller so it will rotate in original direction. With propeller shaft supported at bearing surfaces in vee blocks, shaft runout should not exceed 0.006 inch as measured in area between threads and splines at rear of shaft.

To assemble gearcase, proceed as follows: Install bearing (31) cup and bearing (26). When installing lower bearing (27), pull bearing up into bore from gear cavity and mark puller so bearing is pulled into housing approximately ⅝ inch from initial contact. Install seals (25) so upper seal lip is pointing up and lower seal lip is pointing down. Upper seal should be ⅛ inch below top of gearcase bore. Assemble shift shaft components (1 through 11) and flatten both ends of pin (10) so they are flush with sides of shift cam (11). Install shift shaft assembly. Install forward gear (33) and bearing cone. Install thrust washer (28), thrust bearing (29) and pinion gear (30), then while holding pinion gear in position, insert drive shaft so splines fully engage gear. Place clutch (36) on propeller shaft so end nearer groove is towards forward gear. Install spring (38) and shift pin (34) into propeller shaft with rounded end of pin out. While forcing shift pin against spring, insert clutch pin (37) through clutch, propeller shaft and shift pin. Wrap wire clip (35) around clutch groove without overlapping coils. Install propeller shaft assembly in gearcase so it bottoms in forward gear (33) then slide reverse gear (40) onto shaft. Install bearing carrier (41) and carefully screw carrier (left-hand threads) into gearcase. Bearing carrier may be tightened by assembling same arrangement of hub (47), propeller and nut (50) used to loosen carrier. Install "O" ring (44), retainer (45) and anode (46). Install remainder of components by reversing disassembly procedure while noting that flange end of hub (47) must be adjacent to propeller. Do not overtighten water pump mount screws.

gearcase from drive shaft housing. Do not lift or support gearcase by drive shaft or shift shaft.

Secure the gearcase in a soft-jawed vise with drive shaft pointing up and drain lubricant. Remove slinger (14 – Fig. M8-23) while holding down drive shaft. Remove water pump housing (16), fiber washer (18), impeller (19), key (20), fiber washer (21) and plate (22).

Remove propeller, cap (48), thrust hub (47), anode ring (46), retainer (45) and "O" ring (44). Separate cap (48) from hub (47). Reinstall hub (47) so ears engage notches in bearing carrier (41) then install propeller and thread nut (50) onto

shaft so propeller is snug against hub (47). Engage hex head of propeller hub and turn propeller clockwise (left-hand threads) to unscrew bearing carrier and remove propeller shaft assembly. If bearing carrier cannot be unscrewed using the preceding procedure, Mercury tool number C-91-93843 may be used.

With propeller shaft assembly removed, withdraw drive shaft (24) and remove pinion gear (30) and forward gear (33). Remove shift assembly by pulling up shift shaft (1).

Remove wire clip (35), drive out pin (37) and slide dog clutch (36) off propeller shaft. Lower drive shaft bearing

MERCURY
MERC 18, 20 AND 25
(Serial No. 6416713 And Above)

CONDENSED SERVICE DATA

TUNE-UP
Hp/rpm...18,20/4500-5500
                                                     25/5000-6000
Bore...2.56 in.
                                                       (65 mm)
Stroke...2.36 in.
                                                       (60 mm)
Number of Cylinders.......................................2
Displacement......................................24.4 cu. in.
                                                      (400 cc)
Ignition Type ....Breakerless
Spark Plug....................................See Text
Idle Speed (in gear)...........................600-700
Fuel:Oil Ratio.....................................50:1
Gearcase Oil Capacity..............................7.6 oz.
                                                     (225 mL)

SIZES—CLEARANCES
Cylinder Bore Out-of-Round—Max....................0.003 inch
                                                     (0.076 mm)
Connecting Rod Alignment—Max. Bend................0.002 inch
                                                     (0.051 mm)
Thrust Washers and Crankshaft Clearance...........0.030 inch
                                                     (0.762 mm)

TIGHTENING TORQUES
Connecting Rod Cap...............................150 in.-lbs.
                                                   (16.9 N·m)
Crankcase..30 ft.-lbs.
                                                   (40.7 N·m)
Exhaust Cover......................................80 in.-lbs.
                                                    (9 N·m)
Transfer Port Cover................................30 in.-lbs.
                                                   (3.4 N·m)
Cylinder Block Cover...............................80 in.-lbs.
                                                    (9 N·m)
Carburetor Adapter Plate...........................30 in.-lbs.
                                                   (3.4 N·m)
Flywheel...50 ft.-lbs.
                                                   (67.8 N·m)
Carburetor Mounting Nuts..........................180 in.-lbs.
                                                   (20.3 N·m)
Power Head to Drive Shaft Housing.................200 in.-lbs.
                                                   (22.6 N·m)

LUBRICATION

The power head is lubricated by oil mixed with the fuel. Fuel should be regular leaded, low lead or unleaded gasoline with a minimum pump octane rating of 86. Recommended oil is Quicksilver Formula 50-D Outboard Lubricant. Normal fuel:oil ratio is 50:1.

Lower unit gears and bearings are lubricated by oil contained in the gearcase. Recommended oil is Quicksilver Super-Duty Gear Lubricant. Lubricant is drained by removing vent and drain plugs in the gearcase. Refill through drain plug hole until oil has reached level of vent plug hole.

FUEL SYSTEM

CARBURETOR. (Models With "BC" Type Carburetor). The fuel pump and carburetor are a complete unit. Standard main jet (30–Fig. M10-1) size is 0.067 inch (1.70 mm). Other main jet (30) sizes are available for adjusting the air:fuel mixture for altitude or other special conditions. Initial adjustment of idle mixture screw (10) is 1¼ turns out from a lightly seated position. Recommended idle speed is 600-700 rpm with engine at normal operating temperature and in gear.

All models are equipped with an enrichment valve (3) to enrichen the fuel

mixture for cold starting. Raise enrichment valve cover (C–Fig. M10-2) if so equipped. With the choke knob turned fully clockwise, arm (A) should depress valve stem (T). Bend rod (R) to adjust position of arm (A).

To determine the float level, invert carburetor float bowl (29–Fig. M10-1) with fuel inlet valve (28) and float (27) installed. With float (27) hanging down as shown in Fig. M10-3, float end (L) should be even with or less than 1/32 inch (0.8 mm) below float bowl (29) edge. Bend float arm tang to adjust.

(Models With "WMC" Type Carburetor). The fuel pump and carburetor are a complete unit. Standard main jet (30–Fig. M10-4) size is 0.046 inch (1.17 mm) on 20 hp models and 0.080 inch (2.03 mm) on 25 hp models. Other main jet (30) sizes are available for adjusting the air:fuel mixture for altitude or other special conditions. Initial adjustment of idle mixture screw (6) is 1¼ turns out from a lightly seated position. Recommended idle speed is 600-700 rpm with engine at normal operating temperature and in gear.

To determine the float level, invert carburetor body (1–Fig. M10-5) with fuel inlet valve (25–Fig. M10-4), float arm (26–Fig. M10-5) and float (28) installed. Measure distance (D) as shown in Fig. M10-5. Distance (D) should be 1

Fig. M10-2 – View showing carburetor enrichment system used on "BC" type carburetor. Refer to text for adjustment procedures.

A. Enrichment arm
C. Enrichment valve cover
R. Enrichment rod
T. Enrichment valve stem

inch (25.4 mm). Bend float arm (26) to adjust.

FUEL FILTER. A fuel filter assembly is connected between fuel supply line and carburetor/fuel pump inlet line. With the engine stopped, occasionally unscrew fuel filter cup (4–Fig. M10-6) from filter base (1) and withdraw sealing ring (3) and filter element (2). Clean cup (4) and filter element (2) in a suitable solvent and blow dry with clean compressed air. Inspect filter element (2). If excessive blockage or damage is noted, renew element.

Reassembly is reverse order of disassembly. If needed, renew sealing ring (3) during reassembly.

A strainer (18–Fig. M10-7) positioned behind inlet cover (16) on "BC" type carburetors, is used to provide additional filtering of foreign contaminants. To inspect, remove inlet cover (16) and strainer (18). Clean strainer (18) in a suitable solvent and blow dry with clean compressed air. Inspect strainer (18). If excessive blockage or damage is noted, then renew strainer (18). If needed, renew gasket (17).

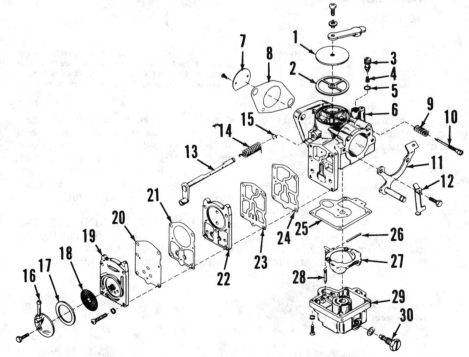

Fig. M10-1 – Exploded view of "BC" type carburetor.

1. Cover	9. Spring	16. Inlet cover	23. Check valves
2. Gasket	10. Idle mixture screw	17. Gasket	24. Gasket
3. Enrichment valve	11. Plate	18. Strainer	25. Gasket
4. Spring	12. Choke knob detent	19. Fuel pump cover	26. Float pin
5. Gasket	13. Throttle shaft roller	20. Diaphragm	27. Float
6. Body	14. Spring	21. Gasket	28. Fuel inlet valve
7. Throttle plate	15. Snap ring	22. Pump body	29. Float bowl
8. Gasket			30. Main jet

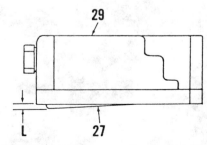

Fig. M10-3 – With float bowl (29) inverted as shown, float (27) level (L) should be even with or less than 1/32 inch (0.8 mm) below float bowl edge.

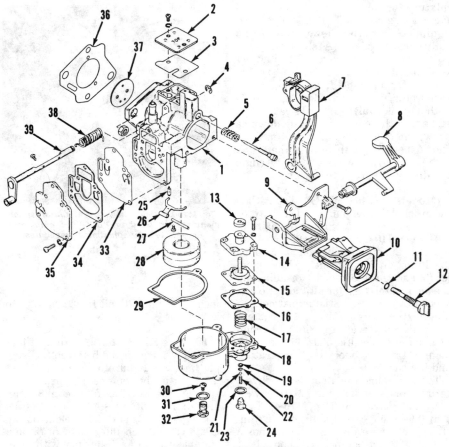

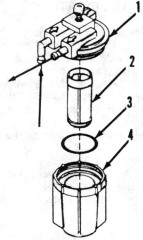

Fig. M10-6 — Exploded view of reusable type fuel filter.

1. Filter base
2. Filter element
3. Sealing ring
4. Filter cup

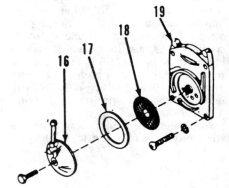

Fig. M10-4 — Exploded view of "WMC" type carburetor.

1. Carburetor body	12. Fast idle knob	21. Check ball
2. Cover	13. Seal	22. Spring
3. Gasket	14. Cover	23. Gasket
4. Clip	15. Enrichment	24. Plug
5. Spring	diaphragm	25. Inlet needle
6. Idle mixture screw	16. Gasket	26. Float arm
7. Neutral rpm ratchet	17. Spring	27. Float pin
8. Enrichment lever	18. Float bowl	28. Float
9. Enrichment bracket	19. Seat	29. Gasket
10. Enrichment knob	20. Retainer	30. Main jet
11. "O" ring		

31. Gasket	36. Gasket
32. Plug	37. Throttle plate
33. Diaphragm	38. Spring
34. Gasket	39. Throttle shaft
35. Cover	

Fig. M10-7 — On "BC" type carburetor, view showing fuel strainer (18) located behind fuel pump inlet cover (16). Gasket (17) is used to seal between inlet cover (16) and pump cover (19).

FUEL PUMP. On "BC" and "WMC" type carburetors, the fuel pump is an integral part of the carburetor. Refer to Fig. M10-1 for an exploded view of fuel pump assembly used on "BC" type carburetors and Fig. M10-4 for an exploded view of fuel pump assembly used on "WMC" type carburetors. Note that fuel pump assembly can be overhauled without carburetor removal.

REED VALVE. The reed valve assembly is located between the carburetor adapter plate and crankcase. Refer to Fig. M10-8 for a view of reed valve assembly.

Cracked, warped, chipped or bent reed petals will impair operation and should be renewed. Do not attempt to straighten or repair bent or damaged reed petals. Reed petals should seat smoothly against reed block along their entire length. Reed petal ends should not stand open more than 0.007 inch (0.178 mm). Tighten reed retaining screws to 25 in.-lbs. (2.8 N·m).

SPEED CONTROL LINKAGE. The speed control twist grip, through the use of linkage, operates the stator plate to advance or retard the ignition timing.

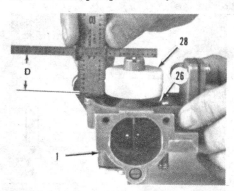

Fig. M10-5 — With carburetor body (1) inverted, distance (D) should be 1 inch (25.4 mm) when measured as shown. Bend float arm (26) to adjust position of float (28).

Fig. M10-8 — View showing reed valve assembly.
1. Block
2. Petals
3. Stop
4. Screw

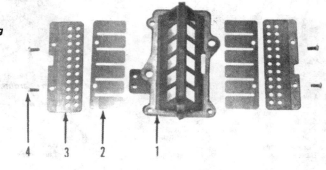

The carburetor throttle plate is synchronized to open as the timing is advanced.

(Models With "BC" Type Carburetor And "BCIA" Stamped On Carburetor Flange). To synchronize ignition timing and throttle opening, proceed as follows: Mount the outboard motor on a boat or a suitable test tank and immerse the lower unit. Remove the engine cover. Connect a power timing light to the top cylinder spark plug lead. With the outboard motor in the "Forward" gear and the engine running at full throttle, three timing dots (D–Fig. M10-9) should be aligned with timing mark (M) on starter housing. To adjust full advance ignition timing, stop the engine and adjust length of link (K) by disconnecting and turning link end. Lengthening link will advance ignition timing. Recheck full throttle ignition timing, then stop engine.

Disconnect throttle rod (T) from throttle cam, loosen screw (W–Fig. M10-10) and move throttle cam (C) so mark (L) is aligned with roller (R) and cam just touches roller. Retighten screw (W). Start the engine, then advance throttle lever (V–Fig. M10-11) until two timing dots (B) on flywheel are aligned with timing mark (M). Adjust length of throttle rod (T) so when rod is attached to

throttle cam (C), mark (L) is in contact with roller (R).

Idle speed is adjusted at stop screw (IS). Recommended idle speed is 600-700 rpm with engine at normal operating temperature and in gear. Adjust position of dashpot (P) so dashpot plunger is fully depressed when the engine is idling at the recommended rpm.

(Models With "BC" Type Carburetor And "BCIB" Or "BCIC" Stamped On Carburetor Flange). To synchronize ignition timing and throttle opening, proceed as follows: Mount the outboard motor on a boat or a suitable test tank and immerse the lower unit. Remove the engine cover. Connect a power timing light to the top cylinder spark plug lead. With the outboard motor in "Forward" gear and the engine running at full throttle, three timing dots (D–Fig. M10-9) should be aligned with timing mark (M) on starter housing. To adjust full advance ignition timing, stop the engine and adjust length of link (K) by disconnecting and turning link end. Lengthening link will advance ignition

timing. Recheck full throttle ignition timing, then stop engine.

Disconnect throttle rod (T) from throttle cam, loosen screw (W–Fig. M10-10) and move throttle cam (C) so mark (L) is aligned with roller (R) and cam just touches roller. Retighten screw (W). Start the engine, then advance throttle lever (V–Fig. M10-12) until four timing dots (F) on flywheel are aligned with timing mark (M). Adjust length of throttle rod (T) so when rod is attached to throttle cam (C), mark (L) is in contact with roller (R).

Idle speed is adjusted at stop screw (IS). Recommended idle speed is 600-700 rpm with engine at normal operating temperature and in gear. Adjust position of dashpot (P) so dashpot plunger is fully depressed when the engine is idling at the recommended rpm.

(Models With "WMC" Type Carburetor). To synchronize ignition timing and throttle opeing, proceed as follows: Mount the outboard motor on a boat or a suitable test tank and immerse the lower unit. Remove the engine cover. Connect a power timing light to the top cylinder spark plug lead. With the outboard motor in the "Forward" gear and the engine running at full throttle, three timing dots (D–Fig. M10-13) should be aligned with timing mark (M) on starter housing. To adjust full advance ignition timing, stop the engine and adjust length of link (K) by disconnecting and turning link end. Lengthening link will advance ignition timing. Recheck full throttle ignition timing, then stop engine.

With the engine stopped, loosen screw (W–Fig. M10-14) and move throttle cam (C) so mark (L) is aligned with roller (R) and cam just touches roller.

NOTE: Adjust idle speed screw (IS–Fig. M10-15), dashpot (P) and neutral rpm ratchet (N–Fig. M10-16) if needed to obtain desired setting.

Fig. M10-9–On models with "BC" type carburetor, at full throttle the ignition timing is at full advance when three dots (D) align with timing mark (M) on starter housing. Refer to text for adjustment of speed control link (K) and throttle rod (T).

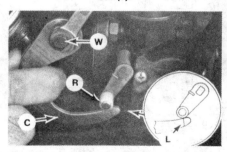

Fig. M10-10–View showing throttle cam (C), throttle cam mark (L), throttle shaft roller (R) and screw (W) used on models with "BC" type carburetor. Refer to text for speed control linkage adjustment procedures.

Fig. M10-11–View showing speed control linkage components used on models with "BC" type carburetor and "BCIA" stamped on carburetor flange.

B. Timing dots	R. Roller
C. Throttle cam	T. Throttle rod
L. Throttle cam mark	V. Throttle lever
M. Timing mark	IS. Idle speed stop screw
P. Dashpot	

Fig. M10-12–View showing speed control linkage components used on models with "BC" type carburetor and "BCIB" or "BCIC" stamped on carburetor flange.

C. Throttle cam	R. Roller
F. Timing dots	T. Throttle rod
L. Throttle cam mark	V. Throttle lever
M. Timing mark	IS. Idle speed stop screw
P. Dashpot	

Fig. M10-13–On models with "WMC" type carburetor, at full throttle the ignition timing is at full advance when three dots (D) align with timing mark (M) on starter housing. Refer to text for adjustment of speed control link (K).

Retighten screw (W–Fig. M10-14). Start the engine, then advance throttle lever (V–Fig. M10-15) until the 2° ATDC timing mark (H) (one mark to the right of single dot) is aligned with timing mark (M). Adjust length of throttle rod (T) so when rod is attached to throttle cam (C), mark (L) is in contact with roller (R).

Idle speed is adjusted at stop screw (IS). Recommended idle speed is 600-700 rpm with engine at normal operating temperature and in gear. Adjust position of dashpot (P) so dashpot plunger is fully depressed when the engine is idling at the recommended rpm.

With a suitable tachometer attached, start the engine and rotate the throttle control to the "SLOW" position. Position the primer/fast idle knob (B–Fig. M10-16) in the middle detent position and adjust ratchet (N) until 1400-1700 rpm is obtained.

IGNITION

On models with ground plate (P–Fig. M10-17) attached to the negative ignition coil terminal, the standard spark plug is Champion L77J4. A Champion

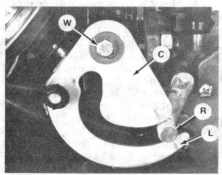

Fig. M10-14-View showing throttle cam (C), throttle cam mark (L), throttle shaft roller (R) and screw (W) used on models with "WMC" type carburetor. Refer to text for speed control linkage adjustment procedures.

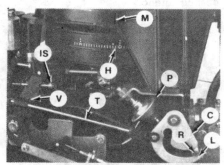

Fig. M10-15 – View showing speed control linkage components used on models with "WMC" type carburetor.

QL77J4 is recommended by the manufacturer should radio frequency interference suppression be required. Spark plug electrode gap should be 0.040 inch (1.02 mm). On models that are equipped with a ground wire attached to the negative ignition coil terminal, the standard spark plug is Champion L76V. A Champion QL76V is recommended by the manufacturer should radio frequency interference suppression be required. Renew surface gap spark plug if center electrode is more than 1/32 inch (0.79 mm) below the flat surface of the plug end.

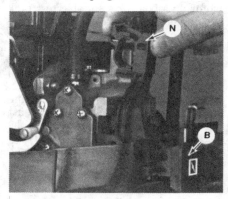

Fig. M10-16 – View showing neutral rpm ratchet (N) and primer/fast idle knob (B) used on models with "WMC" type carburetor.

Fig. M10-17 – View showing ground plate (P) attached to the negative ignition coil terminal.

A capacitor discharge ignition (CDI) system is used on all models. If engine malfunction is noted and the ignition system is suspected, make sure the spark plugs and all electrical wiring are in good condition and all electrical connections are tight before proceeding to troubleshooting the CD ignition system.

Proceed as follows to test CDI system components: Refer to Fig. M10-18. To test stator assembly, first make sure stator assembly is grounded to engine. Disconnect black wire with yellow tracer (B/Y) and black wire with white tracer (B/W) from switch box. Use a suitable ohmmeter and perform the following tests. Connect black tester lead to engine ground and red tester lead to black wire with white tracer (B/W) from stator assembly. The resistance reading should be 120-180 ohms. Leave black tester lead connected to engine ground and connect red tester lead to black wire with yellow tracer (B/Y) from stator assembly. The resistance reading should be 3200-3800 ohms. Connect tester leads between black wire with yellow tracer (B/Y) and black wire with white tracer (B/W) from stator assembly. The resistance reading should be 3100-3700 ohms.

To test trigger assembly, disconnect brown wire with yellow tracer (Br/Y) and brown wire with white tracer (Br/W) from switch box. With engine at room temperature (68°F/20°C), use a suitable ohmmeter and connect tester leads between brown wire with yellow tracer (Br/Y) and brown wire with white tracer (Br/W) from trigger assembly. The resistance reading should be 650-850 ohms.

To test ignition coil assembly, disconnect wires and spark plug lead from coil assembly. Use a suitable ohmmeter and connect tester leads between positive (+) and negative (−) coil terminals. The

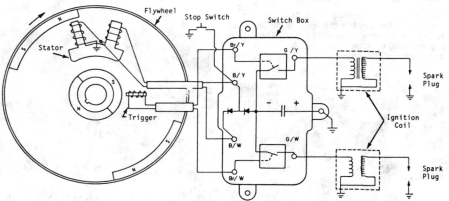

Fig. M10-18 – View identifying CDI system components and wiring.

C. Throttle cam	P. Dashpot	
H. Flywheel timing mark	R. Roller	
L. Throttle cam mark	T. Throttle rod	
M. Starter housing timing mark	V. Throttle lever	
	IS. Idle speed screw	

B/W. Black wire with white tracer	G/W. Green wire with white tracer
B/Y. Black wire with yellow tracer	G/Y. Green wire with yellow tracer

Br/W. Brown wire with white tracer
Br/Y. Brown wire with yellow tracer

resistance reading should be 0.02-0.04 ohms. Leave the one tester lead connected to the negative (−) coil terminal and connect the remaining tester lead to the spark plug lead's terminal end in the coil tower. The resistance reading should be 800-1100 ohms.

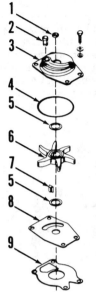

Fig. M10-19 — Exploded view of water pump assembly.

1. Rubber seal	
2. Outlet tube	6. Impeller
3. Cover	7. Key
4. "O" ring	8. Plate
5. Fiber washer	9. Gasket

COOLING SYSTEM

WATER PUMP. A rubber impeller type water pump is mounted between the drive shaft housing and gearcase. Water pump impeller (6 – Fig. M10-19) is driven by a key in the drive shaft.

When cooling system problems are encountered, first check water inlets for plugging or partial stoppage. If the water pump is suspected defective, separate gearcase from drive shaft housing and inspect pump. Make sure all seals and mating surfaces are in good condition and water passages are unobstructed. Check impeller (6) and plate (8) for excessive wear. When reassembling, tighten cover (3) securing screws evenly, but DO NOT overtighten screws as the four plastic isolators may be damaged.

POWER HEAD

R&R AND OVERHAUL. The power head can be removed for disassembly and overhaul as follows: Clamp outboard motor to a suitable stand and remove top and bottom engine cowl. Detach spark plug leads from spark plugs and remove spark plugs from power head. Remove manual starter assembly. Disconnect speed control cables, fuel line and any wiring that will interfere with power head removal. Remove or disconnect any component that will in-

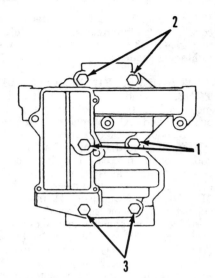

Fig. M10-21 — Tighten crankcase screws in sequence shown above.

terfere with power head removal. Remove six screws securing power head to drive shaft housing and life power head free. Remove flywheel, ignition components, carburetor, carburetor adapter plate and reed valve assembly. Remove screws retaining exhaust cover (9 – Fig. M10-20) and withdraw. Remove screws retaining cylinder block cover (4) and withdraw. Remove screws retaining six transfer port covers and withdraw. Crankcase halves can be separated after removal of six screws securing crankcase half (1) to cylinder block (2). Crankshaft and pistons are now accessible for removal and overhaul as outlined in the appropriate following paragraphs.

ASSEMBLY. When reassembling, make sure all joints and gasket surfaces are clean and free from nicks and burrs. All friction surfaces and bearings must be lubricated with engine oil during reassembly. Make sure crankshaft's center main bearing dowel opening properly aligns with dowel pin in cylinder block. Make sure locating pins on crankshaft roller bearings fit into the slots in cylinder block. Check frequently as power head is being assembled for binding of working parts. If binding or locking is encountered, correct cause before proceeding with assembly.

Apply a continuous 1/16 inch (1.6 mm) bead of Loctite 514 to sealing surface of crankcase half (1 – Fig. M10-20). Make sure entire surface is coated, but avoid an excess application as sealant may be squeezed into crankcase, bearings or passages.

Refer to CONDENSED SERVICE DATA for final torque specifications. Tighten screws in three progressive steps. Refer to Fig. M10-21 for crankcase screws tightening sequence.

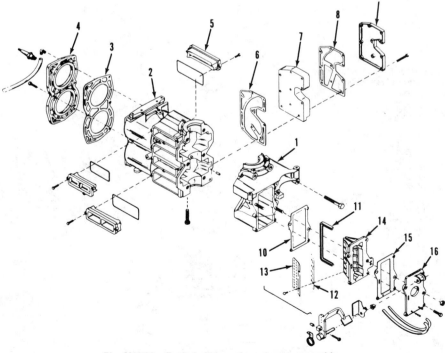

Fig. M10-20 — Exploded view of crankcase assembly.

1. Crankcase half	5. Transfer port cover	9. Exhaust cover	13. Reed stop
2. Cylinder block	6. Gasket	10. Gasket	14. Reed block
3. Gasket	7. Exhaust manifold	11. Seal	15. Gasket
4. Cylinder block cover	8. Gasket	12. Reed petals	16. Adapter plate

Refer to Fig. M10-22 for cylinder block cover screws tightening sequence. Refer to Fig. M10-23 for exhaust cover screws tightening sequence.

CYLINDERS, RINGS AND PISTONS.

Cylinder bores should be measured halfway between top of cylinder and exhaust ports. Measurements should be taken every 45° of the cylinder bore to determine if an out-of-round condition exists. If cylinder bore is out-of-round more than 0.003 inch (0.076 mm), cylinder block (2–Fig. M10-20) and crankcase (1) must be renewed. If chrome surface of cylinder bore has been penetrated, excessively scored or is flaking, the cylinder block (2) and crankcase (1) must be renewed.

Measure diameter of pistons 0.010 inch (2.54 mm) from base of piston skirt and at a right angle (90°) to piston pin. Pistons should measure 2.554-2.559 inches (64.87-64.99 mm). If not, renew piston or pistons. Make sure piston rings properly align with locating pins in ring grooves.

When reassembling, install new piston pin retaining clips (12–Fig. M10-24) and make sure that "UP" on inside of piston is towards flywheel end of engine. Coat bearings, pistons, rings and cylinder bores with engine oil during assembly.

CRANKSHAFT, BEARINGS AND RODS.

The connecting rods ride on a roller bearing around the crankpins. Maximum allowable assembled clearance between thrust washers (16–Fig. M10-24) and crankshaft is 0.030 inch (0.762 mm). Maximum allowable bend of connecting rod (9) is 0.002 inch (0.051 mm). Note that the manufacturer only recommends using crocus cloth to clean-up bearing surfaces of crankshaft journals and connecting rod surfaces.

STARTER

MANUAL STARTER. A starter lockout assembly is used to prevent starter engagement when the gear shift control is in the "Forward" or "Reverse" position.

To overhaul the manual starter, proceed as follows: Remove the engine cover. Detach fuel filter assembly from starter housing by pulling filter assembly straight down. Remove the three starter housing retaining screws and withdraw the starter assembly.

To disassemble, remove clips (13–Fig. M10-25) and withdraw pawls (12) and springs (11). Untie starter rope (10) at anchor (19) and allow the rope to wind into the starter. Remove screw (16), cam (14) and spring (15). Carefully lift pulley (9) with starter rope (10) from housing

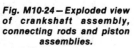

Fig. M10-24—Exploded view of crankshaft assembly, connecting rods and piston assemblies.

1. Seal
2. Bearing
3. Key
4. Crankshaft assy.
5. Crankshaft carrier
6. Connecting rod cap
7. Bearing cage half
8. Roller bearings (12)
9. Connecting rod
10. Washer
11. Needle bearings (27)
12. Clip
13. Piston pin
14. Piston
15. Piston rings
16. Thrust washer half
17. Bearing half
18. Bearing race half
19. Spring clip

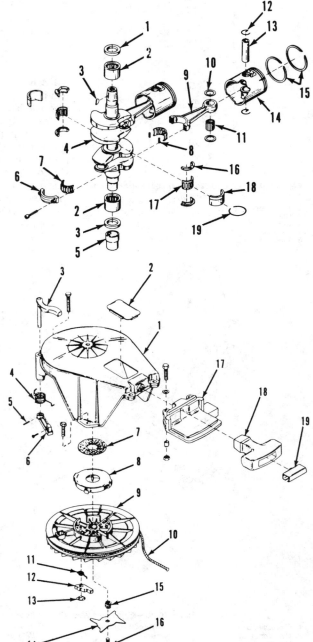

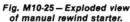

Fig. M10-25—Exploded view of manual rewind starter.

1. Starter housing
2. Cover
3. Lockout lever
4. Spring
5. Pin
6. Pulley lock lever
7. Felt pad
8. Rewind spring & case
9. Pulley
10. Starter rope
11. Spring
12. Pawl
13. Clip
14. Cam
15. Spring
16. Screw
17. Rope guide
18. Handle
19. Anchor

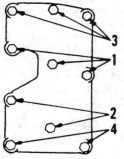

Fig. M10-22—Tighten cylinder block cover screws in sequence shown above.

Fig. M10-23—Tighten exhaust cover screws in sequence shown above.

(1). BE CAREFUL when removing pulley (9) as the rewind spring in case (8) may be dislodged. Remove starter rope (10) from pulley (9) if renewal is required. Separate rewind spring and case (8) from pulley (9). If renewal of rewind spring is required, use extreme caution when removing rewind spring from spring case (8).

Inspect all components for damage and excessive wear and renew if needed.

To reassemble, first apply a coating of a suitable water-resistant grease to rewind spring area of spring case (8). Install rewind spring in spring case (8) so spring coils wind in a clockwise direction from the outer end. Make sure the spring's outer hook is properly secured. Install rewind spring and case (8) into pulley (9). Wind starter rope (10) onto pulley (9) counterclockwise when viewed from the flywheel side. Assemble pulley (9) to starter housing (1) making sure rewind spring end properly engages notch in starter housing center shaft. When pulley (9) is seated properly, pulley bushing will be flush with end of starter housing shaft. Install spring (15), cam (14) and secure with screw (16). Install springs (11), pawls (12) and clips (13) as shown in Fig. M10-26.

Rotate pulley (9 – Fig. M10-25) counterclockwise until starter rope (10) end is aligned with starter housing rope outlet. Thread starter rope (10) through starter housing (1), rope guide (17) and handle (18) and secure in anchor (19). Pull starter rope (10) out to full length while checking for freedom of travel, then allow starter rope (10) to rewind onto pulley (9). Starter handle (18) should be drawn back into the proper released position. If not, release starter rope (10) from handle (18) and rotate pulley (9) one complete turn counterclockwise (flywheel side) and reassemble.

NOTE: Do not apply any more tension on rewind spring (8) than is required to draw starter handle (18) back into the proper released position.

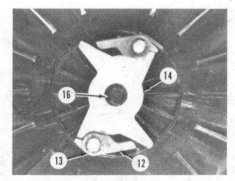

Fig. M10-26 – View showing correct installation of pawls (12), clips (13), cam (14) and screw (16).

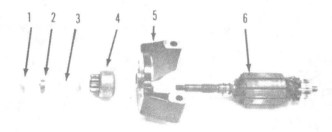

Fig. M10-27 – View showing electric starter armature and drive components.

1. Locknut
2. Spacer
3. Spring
4. Starter drive
5. End frame
6. Armature

Remount manual starter assembly and complete reassembly.

ELECTRIC STARTER. Some models are equipped with a 12-volt electric starter. The armature and drive components are shown in Fig. M10-27. Normal no-load current draw is 15 amperes and load current draw is 60 amperes. Minimum brush (7 – Fig. M10-28) wear limit is 3/16 inch (4.8 mm).

LOWER UNIT

PROPELLER AND DRIVE HUB. Lower unit protection is provided by a cushion type hub in the propeller. The standard propeller is three bladed with a diameter of 10-3/8 inches (264 mm) and a pitch of 13 inches (330 mm). Optional propellers are available. Select a propeller that will allow the engine at full throttle to reach maximum operating rpm range (4500-5500 on 20 hp models and 5000-6000 on 25 hp models).

R&R AND OVERHAUL. Clamp outboard motor to an appropriate stand and remove gearcase drain plug and vent plug. Allow gearcase lubricant to drain into a suitable container. Detach shift rod from actuator at top of motor leg. Note the flat washer located at top of shift rod. Remove the four cap screws retaining gearcase housing to drive shaft housing and withdraw gearcase housing. Do not lose shift rod washer during disassembly.

Disassemble gearcase as follows: Remove locknut (44 – Fig. M10-29), propeller (43) and thrust hub (42). Remove water pump assembly (Fig. M10-19). Remove screws securing retaining plate (41 – Fig. M10-29) and withdraw plate and "O" ring (40). Remove cap from around thrust hub (42). Install thrust hub (42) on propeller shaft (34) with the hub's three ears facing toward carrier assembly (36). Install propeller (43) and secure with locknut (44). Place a suitable tool on hex head hub of propeller and turn propeller CLOCKWISE to unscrew carrier assembly (36). When carrier

assembly (36) is completely unthreaded, remove locknut (44), propeller (43) and thrust hub (42) from propeller shaft (34). Withdraw propeller shaft (34) with components (29 through 39). Remove cap screw (25) and withdraw pinion gear (24) and bearing (23). Withdraw forward gear (28) and tapered roller bearing (26). If needed, remove shift linkage components.

Inspect shafts for wear on seal lip contact areas and on splines. Inspect dog clutch and gears for wear on engagement areas of dog teeth. Inspect gears for excessive wear and damage. Inspect shift cam for excessive wear on ramp. All seals and "O" rings should be renewed when unit is reassembled.

NOTE: No adjustment of gear mesh pattern and gear backlash is provided. Make sure all parts are in good condition and properly assembled.

Reverse disassembly for reassembly while noting the following: Install dog clutch (32) with "F" marked side toward forward gear (28). Apply a water-resistant grease to the lip surfaces of all seals. Rotate carrier assembly (36) COUNTERCLOCKWISE to tighten. Install cap on thrust hub (42) and assemble with thrust hub ears facing propeller (43).

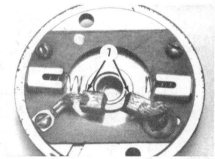

Fig. M10-28 – Minimum electric starter brush (7) wear limit is 3/16 inch (4.8 mm).

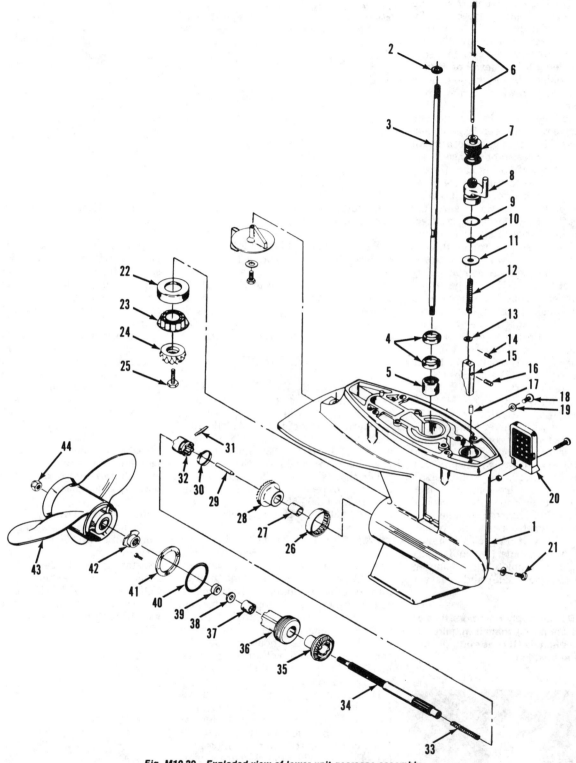

Fig. M10-29—Exploded view of lower unit gearcase assembly.

1. Housing	12. Spring	23. Bearing	34. Propeller shaft
2. "O" ring	13. Washer	24. Pinion gear	35. Reverse gear
3. Drive shaft	14. Pin	25. Cap screw	36. Carrier assy.
4. Seals	15. Shift cam	26. Bearing	37. Bushing
5. Needle bearing	16. Pin	27. Bushing	38. Seal
6. Shift shaft	17. Dowel pin	28. Forward gear	39. Seal
7. Boot	18. Vent plug	29. Shift pin	40. "O" ring
8. Retainer	19. Gasket	30. Spring clip	41. Retaining plate
9. "O" ring	20. Water inlet cover	31. Pin	42. Thrust hub
10. "O" ring	21. Drain plug	32. Dog clutch	43. Propeller
11. Washer	22. Cup	33. Spring	44. Locknut

MERCURY
MERC 20 (1979-1980)
MERC 200 (1969-1978)

Year Produced	20 hp	Year Produced	20 hp
1969	Merc 200	1975	Merc 200
1970	Merc 200	1976	Merc 200
1971	Merc 200	1977	Merc 200
1972	Merc 200	1978	Merc 200
1973	Merc 200	1979	Merc 20
1974	Merc 200	1980	Merc 20

CONDENSED SERVICE DATA

TUNE-UP

Rated Horsepower 20
Maximum Rpm 4800-5500
Bore – Inches 2-9/16
Stroke – Inches 2-1/8
Number of Cylinders 2
Displacement – Cu.-In. 22
Compression at Cranking Speed . . . . *
Spark Plug:
　　1969 . . . . .Champion L4J
　　1970 and later . . . . .AC V40FFK
Electrode Gap:
　　1969 . . . . .0.030 in.
　　1970 and later . . . . .Surface Gap
Magneto – Point Gap:
　　1969-1972 . . . . .0.020 in.
　　1973 and later . . . . .Breakerless Ignition
Carburetor Make:
　　1969-1972 . . . . .Tillotson
　　1973 and later . . . . .Mercarb
Fuel:Oil Ratio . . . . .See Text

SIZES – CLEARANCES

Piston Rings:
　　End gap . . . .*
　　Side clearance . . . .*
Piston Skirt Clearance . . . .*
Crankshaft Bearings:
　　Upper main bearings . . . . .Ball & Roller
　　Center main bearing . . . . .Bushing
　　Lower main bearing . . . . .Ball
　　Crankpin . . . . .Loose Rollers
　　　No. of rollers (each rod) 25
Crankshaft End Play .0.004-0.12 in.
Piston Pin Bearing in Rod . . . . .Loose Rollers
　　No. of rollers (each rod) . . . . .See Text

*Publication not authorized by manufacturer.

TIGHTENING TORQUES
(All Values in Inch-Pounds Unless Noted)

Center Main Bearing 120
Connecting Rod 180
Cylinder Cover 100
Flywheel Nut . . . .**35 ft.-lbs.
Reed Stop Screws 35-40
Spark Plug 240
Water Pump:
　　1/4-28 Stud nuts 25-30
　　5/16-24 Stud nuts 35-40

**65 ft.-lbs. on models prior to 1975.

LUBRICATION

The engine is lubricated by oil mixed with the fuel. Fuel should be regular leaded, low lead or unleaded gasoline with a minimum pump octane rating of 86. Premium gasoline may be used if desired regular gasoline is not available. Recommended oil is Quicksilver Formula 50 or 50-D. A good quality BIA certified TC-W oil may be used. Fuel:oil ratio should be 50:1 when using Formula 50 or 50-D oil. Follow fuel:oil ratio recommended by oil manufacturer if Formula 50 or 50-D is not used.

To break in new or overhauled motors, observe the following: Motors should not be operated above ½ throttle (2500-3500 rpm) for the first 2 hours. Avoid sustained full throttle operation for the first 10 hours of operation.

The lower unit gears and bearings are lubricated by oil contained in the gearcase. Only "SUPER-DUTY Quicksilver Gear Lubricant" should be used. Gearcase is filled through the lower filler hole, located on the starboard side of gearcase until lubricant reaches level of the upper (vent) plug hole. Lubricant should be maintained at level of upper vent plug.

FUEL SYSTEM

CARBURETOR. Tillotson float type carburetors are used on all models before 1973. Mercarb carburetors with integral fuel pump are used on 1973 and later models.

Refer to the following for standard size of main jet (17 – Fig. M7-1) used in Tillotson carburetors.

Carburetor Model	Std. Main Jet Size
KA-20A	0.061
KA-22A	0.059
KA-22B	0.063
KA-22C	0.065
KA-23A	0.063
KA-25A	0.059

Refer to Fig. M7-3 for exploded view of Mercarb carburetor used on Merc 200 after serial number 3537530. Standard size of main jet (24) is 0.057 on motors with serial number 3537531-4102789, 0.053 on motors with serial number 4102790-4351589 and 0.057 on motors with serial number 4351590 and later.

All carburetors employ a fixed, main (high speed jet) with optional sizes available for adjusting the calibration for altitude or other special conditions.

Initial setting for the idle adjustment needle is one turn open. Adjustment should be accomplished with engine operating under load, at slow speed (approximately 600-700 rpm), after it has reached normal operating temperature. Turning the idle needle clockwise will lean the mixture.

Idle speed is set at idle stop screw shown at (IS – Fig. M7-8A). Idle speed for all motors when operating in forward gear should be 550-600 rpm. The idle fuel mixture must be correctly set before adjusting idle speed.

To adjust the fuel level on Tillotson type carburetor, remove bowl cover (5 – Fig. M7-1) and invert the cover. Measure the distance (A – Fig. M7-2) between primary lever (9) and gasket surface of bowl cover with inlet valve (6) closed. This distance should be 13/32-inch. If incorrect, bend the curved tang on secondary lever (8) until correct measurement is obtained. After adjusting float height, bend the vertical tang on primary lever (9) to allow a maximum clearance of 0.040 inch between secondary lever (8) and inlet needle (6).

To adjust the fuel level on Mercarb type carburetor, remove float bowl (29 – Fig. M7-3) and invert carburetor assembly. Measure distance from float to gasket surface (Fig. M7-3A). Float level should be ¼ inch plus or minus 1/64 inch. Adjust float level by bending float arm (A) resting on inlet needle. Turn carburetor right side up and check float drop measurement. Distance from lowest portion of float to highest point on main jet (MJ) should be 1/64-1/32 inch. Adjust float drop by bending tang (T) on float arm.

SPEED CONTROL LINKAGE. Several types of linkage have been used and method of adjustment for each is different. On all models with ignition points, gap should be correctly set and opening time for both sets should be synchronized as outlined in the IGNITION paragraph before any change is made in speed control linkage. Before changing the idle speed or maximum neutral speed, the carburetor mixture should be checked and adjusted (if necessary).

To check and adjust the linkage, refer to the appropriate following paragraphs after determining which type of linkage is used.

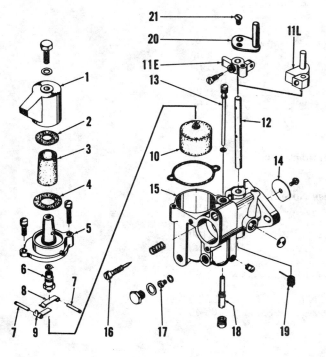

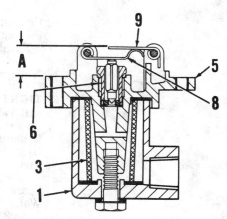

Fig. M7-2—Float height on Tillotson type carburetor is adjusted by bending secondary lever (8) until distance (A) is 13/32 inch with inlet valve (6) closed.

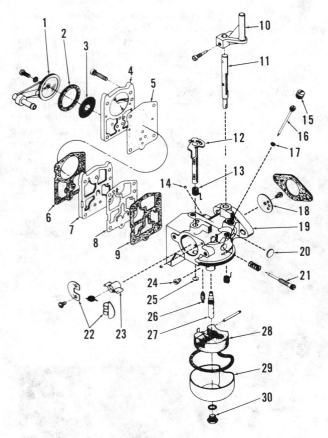

Fig. M7-3—Exploded view of Mercarb type carburetor used on 1973 and later models.

1. Inlet fitting
2. Gasket
3. Screen
4. Cover
5. Diaphragm
6. Gasket
7. Pump body
8. Check valve diaphragm
9. Gasket
10. Throttle lever
11. Throttle shaft
12. Choke shaft
13. Return spring
14. Plug
15. Screw plug
16. Idle tube
17. Gasket
18. Throttle plate
19. Throttle body
20. Welch plug
21. Idle mixture screw
22. Choke shutter plates
23. Boost venturi
24. Main jet
25. Welch plug
26. Inlet needle
27. Main nozzle
28. Float
29. Float bowl
30. Retaining screw

Make certain breaker point gap is correctly set before changing length of link rod (LR). Additional speed control linkage adjustments will not be accurate if length of rod (LR) is incorrect, but normally it will not be necessary to change link rod adjustment.

Turn crankshaft until the top piston is 0.235 inch BTDC. (A Mercury timing gage C-91-26916A1 can be used to position piston at 0.235 inch BTDC.) Twist the speed control grip to full throttle (fast) position and turn the high speed stop screw (F – Figs. M7-8A and M7-8B) in until the breaker points just close. Tighten locknut and recheck to make certain that points just start to open as lever touches stop screw (F).

Twist the speed control grip until lever is tight against stop screw (F) and turn screw (OS – Fig. M7-8B) in until carburetor throttle is completely open.

NOTE: If screw (OS) is turned in too far, linkage may be damaged and throttle opening will not be synchronized to ignition advance. With correct propeller, motor should accelerate smoothly to maximum rpm.

Idle speed is adjusted at stop screw (IS – Figs. M7-8A and M7-8B). Idle speed in Forward gear should be 500 rpm with motor at normal operating temperature. Do not attempt to adjust idle speed while in Neutral.

1970-1972 Models (Serial No. 2827677-3537530). The speed control linkage can be adjusted either with motor running or with motor stopped. Refer to the following paragraphs.

Motor Stopped. Make certain that both sets of ignition contact points are set to the proper (0.020 inch) gap at

1969 Models (Ser. No. 2550065-2827676). To check and adjust the complete speed control linkage, proceed as follows:

Remove the recoil starter assembly, flywheel and both spark plugs. Turn the crankshaft until the top piston is exactly 0.300 inch BTDC. Shift to forward gear and turn the speed control grip until the breaker points for the top cylinder just open. The pin (P – Fig. M7-8A) in the intermediate lever (IL) should be positioned exactly as shown in Fig. M7-8. If the position of pin (P) is not exactly correct, loosen nuts (N – Fig. M7-8A) and adjust length of link rod (LR) until pin (P) is in correct position when points open.

NOTE: Mercury timing gage C-91-39735A1 can be used to set piston at 0.300 inch BTDC and a timing light (with battery) or a continuity meter should be used to indicate points opening.

Fig. M7-8—Pin in the intermediate lever groove must be positioned exactly as shown when adjusting link rod. The magneto intermediate lever is shown at (IL—Fig. M7-8A).

Fig. M7-3A—Float level on Mercarb carburetor should be ¾ inch from float to throttle body gasket surface. Bend float arm (A) to adjust float level. Refer to text for float drop adjustment.

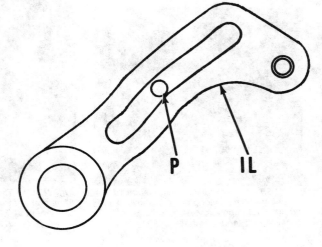

maximum opening. The high primary voltage of this ignition system will pit and darken contact points. Renewal of points should not be necessary unless points are broken or completely worn away. Remove the top spark plug and turn crankshaft until the top piston is 0.196 inch BTDC.

NOTE: A dial indicator such as Mercury tool number C-91-58222 can be used to position the piston.

Connect a timing light (with battery) or ohmmeter to the white wire from magneto stator and ground the other test lead. Shift to Forward gear and move speed control grip to maximum speed position. The points should just close when piston is at 0.196 inch BTDC. If incorrect, turn the two self-locking nuts (N – Fig. M7-9) to provide correct timing. Nuts should be tight against swivel post with adjustment complete.

Move the crankshaft until top piston is 0.002 inch BTDC and move speed control toward slow speed position until ignition points just close. Loosen locknut

and turn the throttle pick-up screw (P – Fig. M7-9A) until screw just touches the post on throttle follower.

Move speed controls to maximum speed position and check clearance of throttle follower. If the throttle follower post does not have 0.035-0.048 inch play, adjust the high speed stop screw (HS – Fig. M7-9B) until clearance (play) is correct.

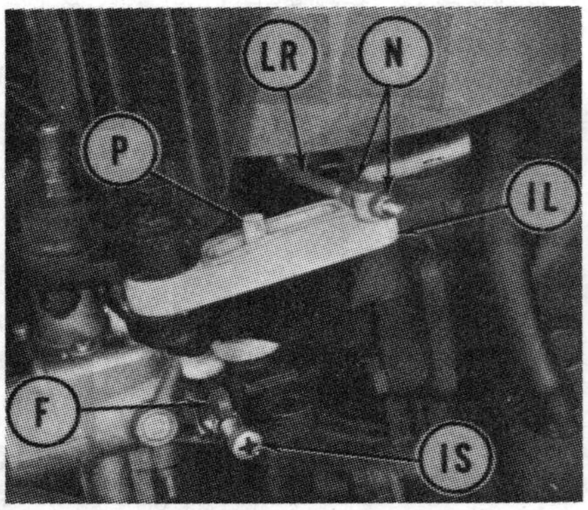

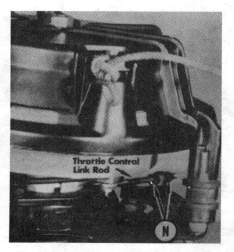

Fig. M7-9—Ignition maximum advance is adjusted on 1970 and later models by turning nuts (N). Refer to text.

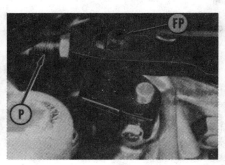

Fig. M7-9A – View of the throttle pick-up screw (P) just touching the throttle follower post (FP). Refer to text for adjusting throttle pick-up.

Motor Running. Before adjusting speed control linkage, make certain that both sets of contact points are set to proper (0.020 inch) gap.

Connect a power timing light (such as Mercury C-91-35507) to the top spark plug lead and to external power source. Start motor and operate at maximum advance setting. When timing light flashes, the flywheel timing mark should be located between the 32 and 34 degree marks on starter as shown in Fig. M7-10. If incorrect, turn the two self locking nuts (N – Fig. M7-9) to provide correct maximum advance timing. Nuts should be tight against swivel post with adjustment complete.

Move speed control toward slow speed position until the flywheel timing mark is between 1⅞ Before the TDC and the 4° After TDC marks as shown in Fig. M7-10A. The throttle pick-up screw (P – Fig. M7-9A) should just touch the post on throttle follower with timing set between 1° BTDC and 4° ATDC. If in-

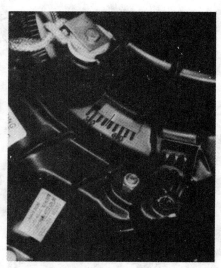

Fig. M7-10—The maximum advance timing should occur at 33 degrees BTDC on 1970 and later models.

Fig. M7-8A—View of 1969 magneto advance (speed control) linkage. Refer to text for method of adjusting.

F. High speed stop screw
IL. Intemediate lever
IS. Idle speed stop screw
LR. Link rod
N. Nuts
P. Pin

Fig. M7-9B—The high speed stop screw (HS) should stop movement of linkage when throttle follower post (FP) has 0.035-0.048 inch play. Idle speed stop screw is shown at (IS).

Fig. M7-10A—Throttle pickup (Fig. M7-9A) should occur when ignition timing is within range of 1° BTDC-4° ATDC on 1970-1972 motors and from 2° BTDC-2° ATDC on 1973 and later motors.

Fig. M7-8B—View of 1969 carburetor (speed control) linkage. Carburetor pick-up is shown at (CP) and maximum opening adjusting screw at (OS). Refer to text for method of adjusting linkage.

correct, loosen locknut and turn the throttle pick-up screw as required.

Stop motor and remove timing light. Adjust the high speed stop screw (HS–Fig. M7-9B) to provide 0.035-0.048 inch play at the throttle follower when speed control is in maximum speed position. The linkage may be damaged if follower has too much play. After stop screw (HS) is correctly set to open throttle completely, propeller should be selected to provide maximum speed within limits of 4800-5500 rpm.

Idle speed should be adjusted at screw (IS) to 550-600 rpm in Forward gear.

1973 and Later Models (Serial No. 3537531 & Up). Speed control linkage may be adjusted with motor running or stopped. Refer to appropriate following paragraph.

Motor Stopped. Remove engine cowl and recoil starter assembly. Shift motor into Forward gear and turn speed control grip to full speed position. Leading edge of trigger coil assembly (Fig. M7-11) should be aligned with full advance mark on stator bracket at this point. Adjust stop nuts on link rod to align trigger coil assembly with full advance mark if necessary.

Turn speed control grip as far as possible toward slow speed position. Observe trigger coil assembly while turning speed control back toward FAST position. Stop moving speed control when leading edge of trigger coil is aligned with pick-up mark on stator bracket. Throttle pick-up screw (P–Fig. M7-9A) should be just touching throttle follower at this point. Adjust pick-up screw if necessary and retighten jam nut.

Turn speed control to full speed position again and check clearance (play) between pick-up screw (P–Fig. M7-9A) and throttle follower. Play should be 0.010-0.015 inch and is adjusted by turning high speed stop screw (HS–Fig.

M7-9B). Be sure to tighten jam nut on screw when adjustment is completed.

Motor Running. Place motor in a suitable test tank and attach a power timing light to #1 (top) spark plug lead. Start engine and place motor in Forward gear. Turn speed control to full speed position and observe timing mark on flywheel with timing light. Timing mark should be aligned at 33° BTDC on grid marked on starter housing (Fig. M7-10), or full advance timing mark (Fig. M7-11) should align with timing pointer on models not equipped with degree marks. Full advance ignition timing is adjusted by turning the two self-locking stop nuts (Fig. M7-11) on throttle control link rod. Be sure that nuts are tight against swivel post when adjustment is completed.

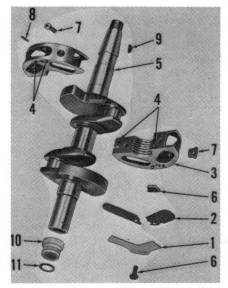

Fig. M7-12 — Exploded view of crankshaft, center main bearing and reed valves.

1. Reed stop
2. Reed petals
3. Bearing & reed block
4. Dowel pins
5. Crankshaft
6. Screw & nut
7. Screw & nut
8. Dowel
9. Flywheel key
10. Seal carrier
11. Seal

To check throttle pick-up turn speed control so flywheel mark is between 2° BTDC and 2° ATDC timing marks on models below serial number 4102799, between 3-7° BTDC timing marks on models above serial number 4102789, or pick-up timing mark (Fig. M7-11) is aligned with timing pointer on models not equipped with degree marks. Adjust screw (P–Fig. M7-9A) so screw just touches throttle follower post (FP).

Stop engine, move control grip to full speed position and check clearance (play) between pick-up screw (P–Fig. M7-9A) and throttle follower. Play should be 0.010-0.015 inch and is adjusted by turning high speed stop screw (HS–Fig. M7-9B). Be sure to tighten jam nut on screw when adjustment is completed.

Move speed control grip to slow speed position and adjust idle speed screw (IS–Fig. M7-9B) to obtain 550-650 rpm with motor in Forward gear.

Maximum speed in Neutral should be 2400-2700 rpm. Speed control grip should be adjusted so that START position on grip is aligned with arrow on tiller handle at this engine speed.

REED VALVES. The inlet reed valves are located on the crankshaft center main bearing assembly. The crankshaft must be removed before reed valves can be serviced.

Reed petals (2–Fig. M7-12 and M7-12A) should be perfectly flat and have no more than 0.007 inch clearance between free end and seating surface of main bearing. The reed stop (1) must be carefully adjusted to provide 3/16 inch clearance between end of stop and bearing surface as shown at (A–Fig. M7-12A). Seating surface of bearing must be smooth and flat, and may be

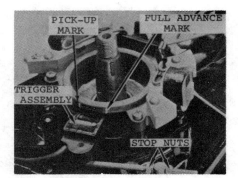

Fig. M7-11 — View of breakerless magneto stator assembly used on 1973 and later motors. Flywheel is removed for clarity, marks are visible with flywheel installed.

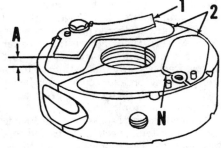

Fig. M7-12A — Center main bearing showing inlet reed valves. Reed petals (2) are right and left-hand units. When installing reed petals, place the reed with the cut-out notch (N) on the left as shown. Adjust free height (A) of reed stop (1) as outlined in text.

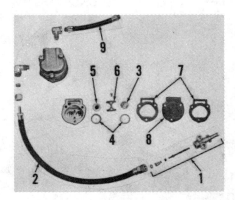

Fig. M7-13 — Exploded view of the fuel pump used on motors with Tillotson type carburetors. Check valves (3 & 5) are identical, but one is inverted.

1. Adapter
2. Inlet hose
3. Inlet check valve
4. Gasket
5. Outlet check valve
6. Retainer
7. Gaskets
8. Diaphragm
9. Outlet hose

refinished on a lapping plate after removing reed valves and dowels. Do not attempt to bend or straighten a reed petal and never install a bent petal. Lubricate the reed valve before assembly. The reed petals with extra notch (N – Fig. 7-12A) should be installed on left side as shown with other petals to the right.

FUEL PUMP. A diaphragm type fuel pump, operated by pressure and vacuum pulsations in the crankcase, is used. Fuel pump (Fig. M7-13) is mounted on crankcase of motors equipped with Tillotson type carburetors. Vacuum in the crankcase draws the diaphragm (8) in, pulling fuel from the tank past the inlet check valve (3). Crankcase pressure forces diaphragm out and the trapped fuel enters the carburetor line past the outlet valve (5). All questionable parts should be renewed.

Fuel pump is an integral part of Mercarb type carburetor (Fig. M7-3) used on late models. Crankcase vacuum is channeled through carburetor mount and passages in carburetor to outboard side of diaphragm (5 – Fig. M7-13A). Fuel is drawn through inlet check valves (ICV) from tank as vacuum pulls diaphragm (5) into cavity of cover (4). Crankcase pressure forces diaphragm inward (toward carburetor) and forces trapped fuel through outlet check valve (OCV) and into float bowl of carburetor. Damaged or questionable fuel pump components should be renewed. When installing carburetor, make sure that vacuum passage hole in gasket (G) is positioned over hole in crankcase.

IGNITION SYSTEM

SPARK PLUG. The correct spark plug must be selected for the specific motor. Refer to CONDENSED SERV-

ICE DATA for spark plug application and electrode gap.

MAGNETO. Three different point timed magnetos have been used. A breakerless, electronic ignition system is used on 1973 and later motors.

Point gap at maximum opening should be 0.020 inch for all later motors with contact points. The later type magneto can be identified by the cover over the compartment which contains the contact points. Points can be synchronized on motors with the later type conventional magneto to open at 180 degree intervals using special Mercury Tool C-91-3645A1.

The maker point magneto (used on 1970-1972 models) uses two high tension coils mounted on a bracket at rear of motor in addition to the generating coils on the stator plate. Gap should be 0.020 inch at maximum opening for both sets of contact points. The high primary voltage of this ignition system will pit and darken contact points. Renewal of points should not be necessary unless points are broken or completely worn away.

On all models, refer to appropriate SPEED CONTROL LINKAGE paragraphs in the FUEL SYSTEM section for adjusting controls.

To synchronize the point timing on models so equipped, using the special Mercury tool, proceed as follows: Remove the flywheel and install degree plate (DP – Fig. M7-14) and pointer (P). Set the contact points for top cylinder at exactly the correct maximum opening. Remove the spark plugs and disconnect coil leads from both sets of points. Install a test light or continuity meter by attaching one clip to insulated point connection and the other clip to a suitable ground. Turn the crankshaft clockwise (as viewed from top) slowly until breaker points just open as indicated by test light bulb going out. Turn the degree plate until the 0 degree mark is aligned with pointer; then attach the timing light or continuity meter to the other set of breaker points. Turn the crankshaft ½ turn until pointer is aligned with 180 degree mark on degree plate as shown in Fig. M7-14. Then, adjust the breaker points for the lower cylinder to just open. Recheck after adjusting to make certain that breaker points for lower cylinder open exactly 180 degrees after the points for top cylinder.

On models with breakerless, electronic ignition system, check all wires and connections before troubleshooting. Resistance between yellow and white stator coil wires should be 750-1000 ohms while resistance between stator yellow wire and ground should be 1500-2000 ohms. Resistance between brown and white

trigger module leads should be 140-160 ohms.

COOLING SYSTEM

WATER PUMP. The rubber impeller type water pump is housed in the gearcase housing. The impeller is mounted on and driven by the lower unit drive shaft.

When cooling system problems are encountered, first check the water inlet for plugging or partial stoppage, then if not corrected, remove the gearcase housing as outlined in LOWER UNIT section and examine the water pump, water tubes and seals.

When assembling, make certain that water pump retaining nuts are tightened to the correct torque listed in the CONDENSED SERVICE DATA table.

POWER HEAD

R&R AND DISASSEMBLE. To remove the power head assembly, first remove the top cowl and disconnect stop switch wire, speed control linkage and choke linkage. Remove the two screws which secure fuel line check unit to lower cowl and nuts securing power head to lower unit; then lift off the complete power head assembly.

Place the unit on power head stand or equivalent and remove fuel pump, carburetor, flywheel and magneto. Exhaust cover plate (19 – Fig. M7-16) cylinder block cover plate (13) and transfer port cover (14) should be removed for inspection and cleaning.

Remove the cap screws which retain upper end cap (6) to power head, remove center main bearing screw located at (S); then unbolt and remove crankcase front half (17).

NOTE: A special recess is located at the center on each side of crankcase half (17). Separate crankcase halves by carefully

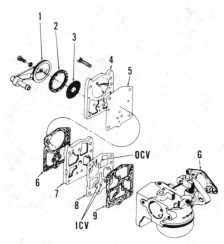

Fig. M7-14 – View of early type magneto with degree plate (DP) and pointer (P) installed for synchronizing breaker point opening. Procedure for later motors is similar.

prying at these points ONLY with a screwdriver. Use extra care not to spring the parts or to mar the machined, mating surfaces. Crankcase half (17) and cylinder (16) are matched and align bored, and are available only as an assembly.

The crankshaft and bearings assembly, with pistons and connecting rods attached can now be lifted out of cylinder block for service or overhaul as outlined in the appropriate following paragraphs. Assemble by following the procedures outlined in the ASSEMBLY paragraph.

ASSEMBLY. When assembling, the crankcase must be completely sealed against both vacuum and pressure. Exhaust manifold and water passages must be sealed against pressure leakage. Whenever power head is disassembled, it is recommended that all gasket surfaces and machined joints without gaskets be carefully checked for nicks and burrs which might interfere with a tight seal.

Completely assemble the crankshaft, lower and center main bearings, connecting rods, pistons, rings, lower seals (10 – Fig. M7-16) and spacer (11). Lip of all seals (4 & 10) should be down, toward lower unit. Install the crankshaft assembly by inserting pistons in lower end of cylinders. Two special Mercury ring compressors should be used. If ring compressor kit is not available, two men must work together and use extreme care in installing the crankshaft and

pistons assembly. Thoroughly lubricate the pistons, rings and bearings using new engine oil and make sure that ring end gaps are aligned with the locating pins in ring grooves. After crankcase is installed, turn the shaft until each ring appears in the exhaust and transfer ports and check for damage during assembly. Make certain the center main bearing dowel is in place and that main bearing is properly located over dowel. Assemble the upper main bearing (end) cap (6 or 6E) using the same shim pack (12) which was removed. Install end cap and tighten the retaining cap screw which retains that cap to cylinder (16). Tap the crankshaft back and forth using a soft mallet and measure gap between bearing (7) and the crankshaft. The clearance should be 0.004-0.012 inch. If incorrect, add or remove shims (12) behind bearing (7). Shims are available in thicknesses of 0.002, 0.003, 0.005 and 0.010 inch. If more than one shim is required, center the crankshaft by placing half the shim pack below the lower bearing (9).

Remove the end cap (6 or 6E) and install "O" ring (8). Coat mating surfaces of crankcase halves lightly with sealer and assemble. Slide end cap into position and start the retaining screws before tightening crankcase halves. Tighten the screws attaching crankcase halves together by working each way from the center to prevent distortion.

Turn the crankshaft several revolutions before installation to make certain that parts are free and do not bind.

PISTONS, PINS, RINGS & CYLINDERS.

Before detaching connecting rods from crankshaft assembly, make sure that rod and cap are properly identified for correct assembly to each other and in the correct cylinder.

Each piston if fitted with three interchangeable rings which are pinned to prevent rotation in the grooves.

Piston pin is pressed in piston bosses and secured with retaining rings. Piston end of connecting rod is fitted with loose bearing rollers which use the connecting rod bore and the piston pin as bearing races. The piston pin bearing contains 27 loose needle rollers. The bearing

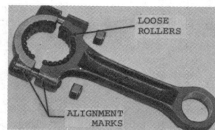

Fig. M7-17 – Alignment marks on connecting rod and cap should be on same side as shown.

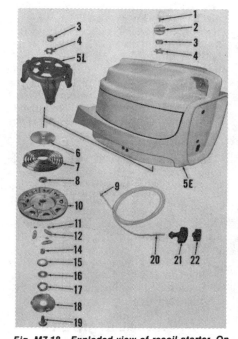

Fig. M7-18 – Exploded view of recoil starter. On early models, starter is mounted on cowl (5E), later motors have starter housing (5L).

1. Screw	10. Sheave	
2. Trim plug	11. Wave washers	
3. Nut	12. Pawls	
4. Lockwasher	14. Spacer	
5E. Cowl (early)	15. Retainer	
5L. Starter housing	16. Washer	
6. Retainer	17. Wave washer	
7. Recoil spring	18. Plate	
8. Bushing	19. Sheave shaft	
9. Rope retainer pin		

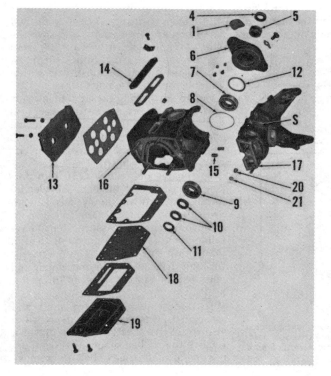

Fig. M7-16 – Exploded view of crankcase and associated parts typical of 1969 and later motors. Motors after 1969 do not have spacer (11) and have only one seal (10).

1. Clips
4. Seal
5. Roller bearing
6. End cap
7. Ball bearing
8. "O" ring
9. Ball bearing
10. Seals
11. Spacer
12. End play shims
13. Cylinder block cover
14. Transfer port cover
15. Dowels
16. & 17. Cylinder
18. Exhaust baffle
19. Exhaust cover
20. Check valve
21. Welch plug

washers between sides of rod and bosses in piston are of several thicknesses. Make certain that correct thickness is installed, depending upon the connecting rod used. Install bearing washers and needle bearings in piston end of connecting rod using light nonfibrous grease to hold them in place, then install the piston pin using Mercury tool (C-91-22803A1) for early models, C-91-52395A1 for later models). Piston must be installed so that sharp vertical side and long sloping side of piston will be toward exhaust port in cylinder. Thoroughly lubricate all friction surfaces during assembly.

CONNECTING ROD, BEARINGS & CRANKSHAFT. Upper end of crankshaft is carried by a ball bearing plus a caged needle bearing. The unbushed center main bearing also contains the inlet reed valves. Lower main bearing (9 – Fig. M7-16) is interchangeable with the upper ball bearing (7).

Each connecting rod rides on loose bearing rollers at piston pin end and at crankpin end. All models use 25 rollers at crankpin. The bearing washers between piston pin end of connecting rod and bosses in piston must be of correct thickness depending upon connecting rod used. Check rod for alignment, using Mercury Alignment Tool (C-91-28441A2), or by placing rod on a surface plate and checking with a light. When installing connecting rods, make certain that alignment marks (Fig. M7-17) are both on same side.

Bearing surface in connecting rods and rod journals on crankshaft may be polished with #320 grit emery cloth if slight chatter marks are evident. Inside diameters must not be increased nor outside diameters decreased by more than 0.001 inch.

If bearing surface of rod and cap is rough, scored, worn, or shows evidence of overheating, renew the connecting rod. Inspect crankpin and main bearing journals. If scored, out-of-round, or worn, renew the crankshaft. Check the crankshaft for straightness using a dial indicator and "V" blocks.

Inspect and adjust the reed valves as outlined in REED VALVE paragraph, and reassemble as outlined in ASSEMBLY paragraph.

MANUAL STARTER

Refer to Fig. M7-18. On early motors, the starter is mounted on the cowl (5E); later motors have a separate starter housing (5L) mounted on the power head under the cowl. To disassemble early type, remove screw (1), trim plug (2); then remove cowl (5E). On late motors, detach starter housing (5L) from top of

motor and remove recoil starter assembly. On all models, insert a screwdriver in slot in top of sheave shaft (19) and loosen the left-hand thread nut (3). Allow the screwdriver and shaft (19) to turn clockwise until recoil spring unwinds. Pry anchor (22) out of starter handle and remove anchor and handle from rope. Remove nut (3), invert the assembly and remove the parts, making sure that recoil spring (7) remains in housing recess as sheave (10) is removed. Protect hands with gloves or a cloth, grasp recoil spring (7), remove spring and allow it to unwind slowly.

Lubricate the parts with Multipurpose Lubricant, and assemble by reversing the disassembly procedure. Install spring guide bushing (8) with chamfered end toward sheave (10). Make sure that pawls (12) are all installed the same way, with radius to outside and identification mark away from sheave (10). Install retainer (15) with cup end out and position washer (16) and wave washer (17) in cup. Make certain that tang on spring retainer (6) engages slot in sheave shaft (19). Position starter with end of shaft (19) through cowl (5E) or housing (5L) and install lockwasher (4) and nut (3). Pull free end of recoil rope through cowl or starter housing and install handle (21) and anchor (22). Turn sheave shaft (19) counterclockwise until handle is pulled against cowl or starter housing, plus an additional 1¼ turns; then tighten nut (3). Pull cord out and check for sticking and full return.

LOWER UNIT

PROPELLER AND DRIVE CLUTCH. Protection for the motor is built into a special cushioning clutch in

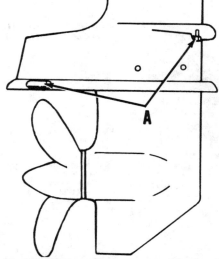

Fig. M7-19—To remove the lower unit gearcase assembly, remove the attaching stud nuts at (A). On later models, two stud nuts are located at rear.

the propeller hub. No adjustment is possible on the propeller or clutch. Various pitch propellers are available and propeller should be selected for best performance under applicable conditions. With speed control linkage correctly adjusted, propeller should be selected to provide maximum engine speed of 4800-5500 rpm. Propellers other than those designed for the motor must not be used.

R&R AND OVERHAUL. Most service on the lower unit can be performed by detaching the gearcase housing from the drive shaft housing. To remove the housing, remove the two or three stud nuts (A – Fig. M7-19) and withdraw the lower unit gearcase assembly.

Remove the housing plugs and drain the housing, then secure the gearcase in a vise between two blocks of soft wood, with propeller up. Wedge a piece of wood between propeller and antiventilation plate, remove the propeller nut, then remove the propeller.

Check the backlash of the propeller drive gears before disassembling by pulling out on the drive shaft and pushing in on the propeller shaft, then rotating drive shaft lightly while noting backlash by feel. No more than 0.003-0.005 inch backlash should exist if gears are properly adjusted.

Disassemble the gearcase by removing the gearcase housing cover nut (61 – Fig. M7-20). Nut is secured with left-hand thread. Clamp the outer end of propeller shaft in a soft jawed vise and remove the gearcase by tapping with a rubber mallet. Forward gear (40) will remain in housing. Withdraw the propeller shaft from bearing carrier (56) and reverse gear (46). Remove and save the shims (47) and thrust washer (48) from inside of gear housing. Shims should be reinstalled if gear backlash was within limits before disassembly.

Clamp the bearing carrier (56) in a soft jawed vise and remove reverse gear (46) and bearing (49) with an internal expanding puller and slide hammer. Remove and discard the propeller shaft rear seals (58 & 59).

To remove dog clutch (43) from propeller shaft, insert the cam follower (8) in hole in shaft and apply only enough pressure on end of cam follower to remove the spring pressure. Remove retaining ring (44), then push out the pin (42) with a small punch. The pin passes through drilled holes in dog clutch and operates in slotted hole in propeller shaft.

To disassemble the drive shaft and associated parts, reposition gearcase in vise with drive shaft projecting upward, remove the rubber slinger (11) from upper end of shaft; then unbolt and remove water pump cover (16). Remove impeller (19) and impeller drive pin. Withdraw the remainder of the water pump parts. Clamp upper end of drive shaft in a soft jawed vise, remove pinion retaining cap screw (37); then tap gearcase off drive shaft and bearing. Note the position and thickness of shims (30 & 30A) on drive shaft upper bearing. Mesh position of pinion is controlled by shims (30) placed underneath the bearing, while shaft end play is controlled by total shim thickness. The shims are identical but should not be interchanged or mixed, except to adjust the mesh position of drive pinion.

After drive shaft has been removed, the forward gear (40) and bearing (39) can usually be dislodged by jarring open end of gearcase against a block of soft wood. Remove and save the shim pack (38).

Shift shaft (5) can be removed after removing set screw (2) retaining bushing (3). When installing, make sure that long shaft splines are on upper end, and that shift cam (7) is installed with the notches (detents) toward rear.

Increasing the thickness of shim pack (38) DECREASES the backlash of forward gear (40). Increasing the thickness of shim pack (47) INCREASES the backlash of reverse gear (46). The number and thickness of shims (30) controls mesh position of drive pinion. Shims are available in thicknesses of 0.002, 0.003, 0.005 and 0.010 inch.

When renewing gearcase housing, or when correcting backlash and mesh of drive gear train, first install drive shaft (33), bearing (32), shims (30 & 30A) and water pump housing (23). Adjust total thickness of shims (30) so that water pump will seat on housing with no shaft end play. Remove the shaft and lay shims (30) aside for reinstallation during assembly. Make a trial assembly of forward gear (40) and bearing (39) using the removed shims (38). Install drive shaft (33), bearing (32) and shims (30). Install drive pinion (35) and install and tighten locking screw (37). Coat gears with bearing blue then check mesh pattern by pressing drive shaft down and turning clockwise to rotate the gears. If pressure is heavy on lower end of pinion tooth, remove one shim from pack (30). Place the removed shim with pack (30A) to retain end play adjustment. Reverse the procedure if pressure is heavy on upper end of tooth. After adjusting mesh position, check and adjust backlash to 0.003-0.005 inch by adding or removing shims (38). Install reverse gear (46) and bearing (49) in bearing carrier (56); then install assembled parts in gearcase without propeller shaft. Adjust to minimum backlash without binding, by adding or removing shims (47).

Before attaching gearcase housing to the drive shaft housing, make certain that both the shift cam (7) and the shift lever (on starboard side of motor) are in forward gear position. Shift shaft (5) should be in counterclockwise position (viewed from top end of shaft) and shift lever should be pulled up. Complete assembly by reversing disassembly procedure.

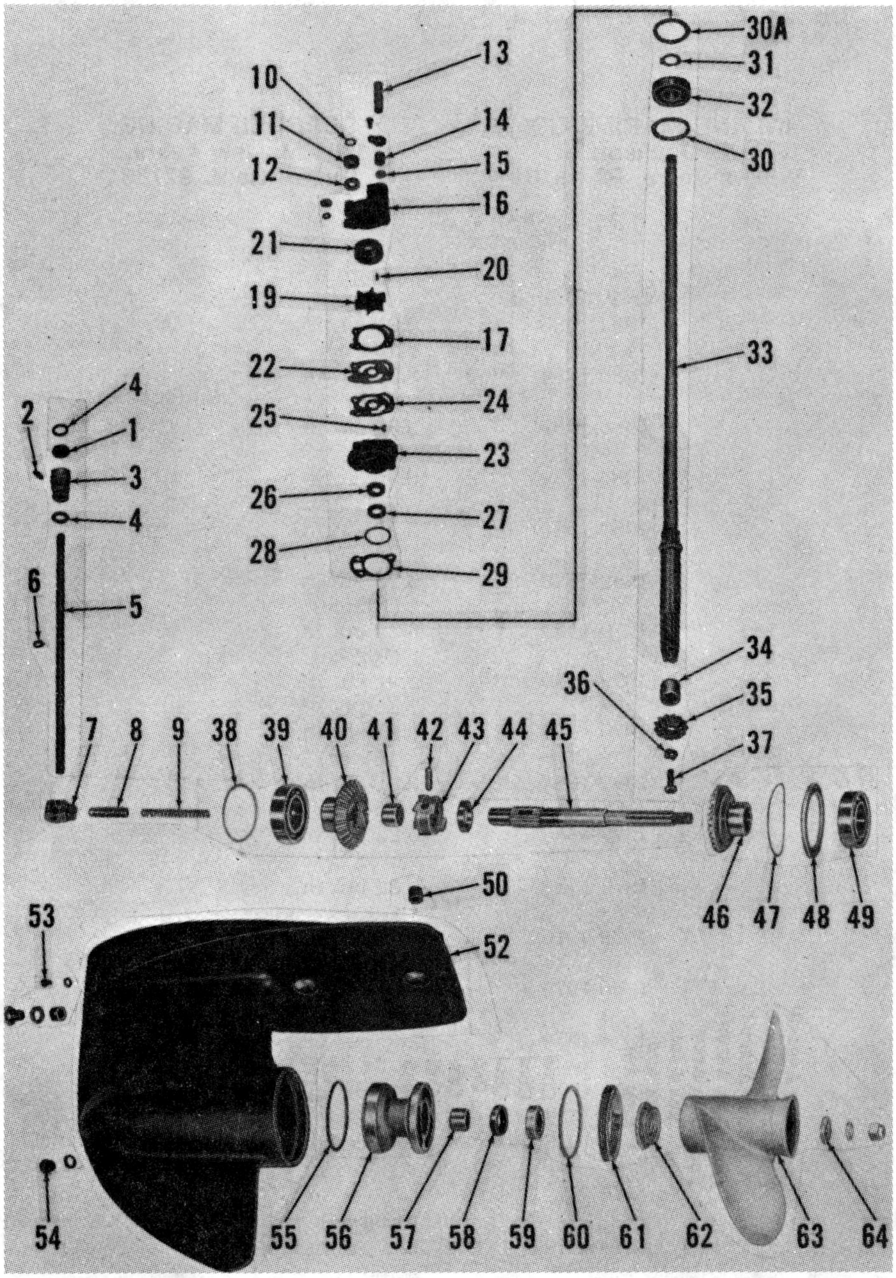

Fig. M7-20—Exploded view of late full gear shift type gearcase assembly. Early models are similar.

1. Oil seal	16. Water pump body	33. Drive shaft	49. Ball bearing
2. Bushing retainer screw	17. Gasket	34. Roller bearing	50. Hollow dowel
3. Bushing	19. Impeller	35. Drive pinion	52. Gear housing
4. "O" rings	20. Key	36. Lockplate	53. Vent screw
5. Shift shaft	21. Insert	37. Cap screw	54. Filler screw
6. Snap ring	22. Plate	38. Shim	55. "O" ring
7. Shift cam	23. Pump base	39. Ball bearing	56. Bearing carrier
8. Cam follower	24. Gasket	40. Forward gear	57. Roller bearing
9. Spring	25. Dowel	41. Roller bearing	58. Spring loaded oil seal
10. "O" ring	26. Oil seal	42. Cross pin	59. Oil seal
11. Rubber ring (slinger)	27. Spring loaded oil seal	43. Dog clutch	60. Washer
12. Oil seal	28. "O" ring	44. Retaining ring	61. Gear housing cover
13. Guide sleeve	29. Gasket	45. Propeller shaft	62. Guide collar
14. Seal	30 & 30A. Shims	46. Reverse gear	63. Propeller
15. Nylon washer	31. Snap ring	47. Shim	64. Spline spacer
	32. Ball bearing	48. Thrust washer	

SEAGULL

BRITISH SEAGULL LTD.
Unit 1, Newtown Business Park
Parkstone, Poole,
Dorset, England BH12 3LJ

IMTRA CORP.
30 Samuel Barnet Blvd.
New Bedford, MA 02745

INLAND MARINE CO.
79 E. Jackson St.
Wilkes-Barre, PA 18701

SEAGULL MARINE
1851 McGaw Avenue
Irvine, Calif. 92705

Model Code	Year Produced	Engine Displ.
AF	1984-1985	3.91 cu. in. (64 cc)
AFPC	1983-1984	3.91 cu. in. (64 cc)
EF	1985-1989	3.91 cu. in. (64 cc)
ENC	1984-1989	6.91 cu. in. (102 cc)
EFPW	1983-1989	3.91 cu. in. (64 cc)
EN	1982-1989	6.22 cu. in. (102 cc)
EFNR	1979-1989	6.22 cu. in. (102 cc)
EFPC	1979-1989	3.91 cu. in. (64 cc)
EFS	1979-1989	3.91 cu. in. (64 cc)
EGF	1982-1984	3.91 cu. in. (64 cc)
ESC	1979-1989	6.22 cu. in. (102 cc)
ESPC	1979-1989	6.22 cu. in. (102 cc)
F	1969-1976	3.86 cu. in. (64 cc)
FP	1969-1979	3.86 cu. in.* (64 cc)
FPC	1978-1979	3.86 cu. in.* (64 cc)
FS	1978-1979	3.86 cu. in.* (64 cc)
GF	1977-1978	3.86 cu. in. (64 cc)
GFP	1976-1979	3.86 cu. in.* (64 cc)
GFPC	1978-1979	3.86 cu. in.* (64 cc)
GFS	1978-1979	3.86 cu. in.* (64 cc)
S	1969	6.18 cu. in. (102 cc)
SP	1969	6.18 cu. in. (102 cc)
SPC	1969	6.18 cu. in. (102 cc)
W	1969-1973	6.18 cu. in. (102 cc)
WP	1969	6.18 cu. in. (102 cc)

Illustrations Courtesy British Seagull

Model Code	Year Produced	Engine Displ.
WPC	1969-1973	6.18 cu. in. (102 cc)
WS	1969-1979	6.18 cu. in.* (102 cc)
WSC	1978-1979	6.18 cu. in.* (102 cc)
WSPC	1969-1979	6.18 cu. in.* (102 cc)

*After 1978, 3.86 cu. in. (64 cc) and 6.18 cu. in. (102 cc) models are designated by the manufacturer as 3.91 cu. in. (64 cc) and 6.22 cu. in. (102 cc) respectively.

NOTE: Model designation may include suffix letter "L" to denote long shaft model.

CONDENSED SERVICE DATA

TUNE-UP	**Engine 3.86, 3.91 cu. in. (64 cc)**	**Displacement 6.18, 6.22 cu. in. (102 cc)**
Bore	1.77 in. (45 mm)	2.24 in. (56.9 mm)
Stroke...................	1.57 in. (39.9 mm)	1.57 in. (39.9 mm)
Displacement		
1969-1978	3.86 cu. in. (64 cc)	6.18 cu. in. (102 cc)
1979-On	3.91 cu. in. (64 cc)	6.22 cu. in. (102 cc)
Spark Plug—		
Champion	British, 8 Com. American, D16	British 8 Com. American, D16
Electrode Gap	0.020 in. (0.51 mm)	0.020 in. (0.51 mm)
Magneto—		
Make	See Text	See Text
Breaker Point Gap.........	0.020 in.* (0.51 mm)	0.020 in.* (0.51 mm)
Ignition Timing	Fixed	Fixed
Carburetor—		
Make	See Text	See Text
Fuel:Oil Ratio	See Text	See Text

*Later models are equipped with breakerless ignition system.

SIZES—CLEARANCES

Cylinder Diameter	1.770-1.771 in. (44.96-44.98 mm)	2.237-2.238 in. (56.82-56.84 mm)
Piston Diameter	1.768-1.769 in. (44.91-44.93 mm)	2.2335-2.2345 in. (56.731-56.756 mm)
Crankshaft Main Journal Diameter.................	0.6225-0.6235 in. (15.811-15.837 mm)	0.6225-0.6235 in. (15.811-15.837 mm)

CONDENSED SERVICE DATA CONT.

SIZES—CLEARANCES CONT.

Main Bearing Bushing
Inner Diameter . . . . 0.6245-0.6250 in.   0.6245-0.6250 in.
(15.862-15.875 mm)   (15.862-15.875 mm)

Connecting Rod Small End
Bushing Inner
Diameter. . . . . 0.438-0.439 in.   0.500-0.502 in.
(11.12-11.15 mm)   (12.70-12.75 mm)

Piston Pin Diameter . . . . 0.4370-0.4375 in.   0.4994-0.4998 in.
(11.100-11.112 mm)   (12.685-12.695 mm)

LUBRICATION

The power head is lubricated by mixing oil with the fuel. On models manufactured prior to 1978 the recommended fuel:oil ratio is 10:1 while the recommended fuel:oil ratio for models after 1977 is 25:1. Early GF and GFP series motors equipped with a Bing carburetor may use the 25:1 fuel:oil ratio. Early F and FP series motors may use the 25:1 fuel:oil ratio if equipped a Villiers carburetor and the tapered needle is changed to a number 2 needle. Early WS and WSPC series motors may use the 25:1 fuel:oil ratio if equipped with an Amal carburetor and power jet is changed to a number 40 power jet. A good quality outboard motor oil should be used.

Lower unit gears are lubricated by oil contained in the gearcase. Recommended lubricant for EFNR and ENS models is SAE 90 gear oil while SAE 140 gear oil should be used in all other models. Do not overfill gearcase of EFNR and ENS models; oil level must be no higher than oil fill plug hole with motor in an upright position. To fill gearcase on all other models, remove plug (19–Fig. SG17) and lay motor on floor with fuel tank down, then fill gearcase until oil is ½-inch above gear (11).

FUEL SYSTEM

CARBURETOR. Five different carburetors have been used. The Villiers concentric float chamber carburetor is shown in Fig. SG1. The Seamal with offset float chamber is shown in Fig. SG2. The Amal "Twin Jet" carburetor with removable float chamber is shown in Fig. SG3. The Amal "Concentric" carburetor is shown in Fig. SG4. The Bing carburetor is shown in Fig. SG5. Refer to the appropriate following paragraphs for servicing.

VILLIERS. Refer to Fig. SG1. Mixture is adjusted by turning screw in center of throttle slide as shown in Fig. SG1A. Normal setting is accomplished by turning screw until top of screw is flush with top of throttle slide; then turn screw out ½-1 turn above flush. Turning screw in will lean the mixture. Mixture should be adjusted to provide even running at high speed. Correct adjustment may cause idle mixture to be slightly rich.

To disassemble the carburetor, first disconnect fuel line banjo fitting by removing bolt (25–Fig. SG1). Throttle slide (10) and associated parts can be withdrawn after removing nut (4). Carburetor can be separated from cylinder after loosening clamp screw (26). To remove the jet (11), remove nut (32), washer (31), float bowl (30), float (29) and gasket (28); then, remove screw (13) and withdraw jet from carburetor body (17).

When reinstalling jet (11), make certain that screw (13) engages the cut away (C) on top of jet. With fuel inlet

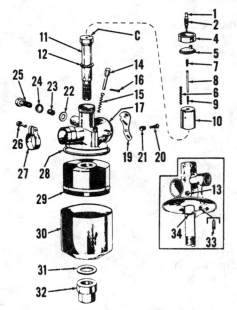

Fig. SG1—Exploded view of Villiers carburetor. Washer (22) has smaller inside diameter than washer (24).

1. Throttle cable	19. Choke
2. Cable adjuster	20. Pivot screw
5. Top cover	21. Spring
6. Throttle spring	22. Washer
7. Mixture adjuster	23. Filter
8. Taper needle	24. Washer
9. Needle spring	25. Banjo bolt
10. Throttle slide	26. Screw
11. Jet	27. Mounting clamp
12. Washer	28. Gasket
13. Jet locking screw	29. Float
14. Primer	30. Float bowl
15. Spring	31. Washer
16. Cotter pin	33. Inlet needle
17. Body	34. Lever

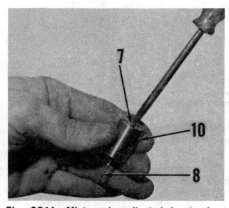

Fig. SG1A—Mixture is adjusted by turning screw (7) on Villiers carburetor. Refer to text.

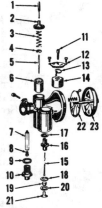

Fig. SG2—Exploded view of Seamal carburetor.

1. Cable	
2. Top screw cap	
3. Throttle spring	13. Primer spring
4. Clip	14. Float
5. Needle	15. Inlet needle
6. Throttle slide	16. Inlet seat
7. Jet tube	17. Gasket
8. Main jet	18. Banjo fitting gasket
9. Gasket	(large hole)
10. Bottom nut	19. Screen
11. Primer	20. Banjo fitting gasket
12. Float cover	(small hole)
	21. Union bolt

needle lever (34) correctly shaped, distance between top of float (29) and carburetor body (17) should be 7/32-inch with needle valve (33) seated.

SEAMAL. Refer to Fig. SG2. Mixture is adjusted by location of clip (4) on needle (5). Moving the clip to a higher groove on needle leans the mixture. Normal clip position is in center groove. Mixture should be adjusted to provide smooth even running at high speed. Correct adjustment may cause idle mixture to be slightly rich.

Disassembly procedure will be self-evident. Clip for attaching inlet needle (15) to float (14) is attached to top of float. Needle (15) should provide a tight seal against seat (16).

AMAL "TWIN JET." Refer to Fig. SG3. Mixture is not adjustable. Make certain that short jet (6) is toward power head end of carburetor and longer jet (7) is toward inlet (18) end. Jets do not use gaskets. The slot on side of throttle slide (5) should correctly engage screw in side of carburetor body. The fuel inlet needle (12) should provide a tight seal against seat (13). Seat is available only as part of

the fuel bowl (15) and should not be removed. The float chamber must be assembled to carburetor on side of carburetor away from fuel tank (nearest boat).

AMAL "CONCENTRIC". Refer to Fig. SG4 for an exploded view of Amal "Concentric" carburetor. High speed mixture is controlled by main jet (18). Intermediate speed mixture is controlled by taper needle (8) and the position of clip (7) in needle grooves. Normal position of clip in second groove from tapered end of needle. Moving clip to a higher groove will lean mixture while moving clip to a lower groove will richen the mixture.

Float bowl (20) is attached to carburetor body by screw threads. Fuel inlet valve seat is permanently fixed to carburetor body and is not renewable. Be sure throttle slide groove properly engages pin in throttle slide bore of carburetor during throttle slide installation.

BING. Refer to Fig. SG5 for an exploded view of Bing carburetor used on some models. High speed mixture is controlled by main jet (19). Intermediate

speed mixture is controlled by taper needle (9) and the position of clip (8) in needle grooves. Normal position of clip is in second groove from tapered end of needle. Moving clip to a higher groove will lean mixture while moving clip to a lower groove will richen mixture.

Float bowl (22) is attached to carburetor body by screw threads. Fuel inlet seat is permanently fixed to carburetor body and is not renewable. When installing needle retainer (7) position retainer end gap over "B" engraved on throttle slide (10). Be sure throttle slide groove properly engages pin in throttle slide bore of carburetor during throttle slide installation.

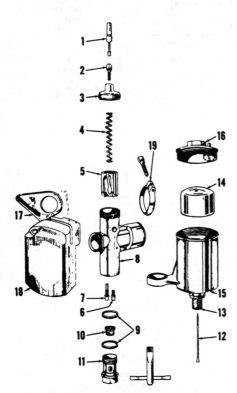

Fig. SG3 — Exploded view of Amal "Twin Jet" carburetor.

1. Cable		11.	Float chamber
2. Adjuster			holding bolt
3. Top screw cap		12.	Fuel inlet needle
4. Spring		13.	Seat
5. Throttle slide		14.	Float
6. Economy jet		15.	Float bowl
7. Power jet		16.	Cover
8. Body		17.	Choke
9. Gaskets		18.	Air intake
10. Screen		19.	Clamp ring

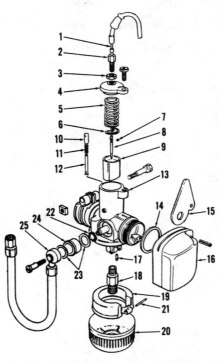

Fig. SG4 — Exploded view of Amal "Concentric" carburetor.

1. Throttle cable			
2. Cable adjuster		14.	Washer
3. Locknut		15.	Choke plate
4. Cap		16.	Air intake
5. Spring		17.	Inlet fuel valve
6. Retainer		18.	Main jet
7. Clip		19.	Float
8. Tapered needle		20.	Float bowl
9. Throttle slide		21.	Float pin
10. Primer button		22.	Filter
11. Spring		23.	Washer
12. Primer rod		24.	Spacer
13. Body		25.	Fuel fitting

Fig. SG5 — Exploded view of Bing carburetor.

1. Throttle cable		13.	Pin
2. Cable adjuster		14.	Choke lever
3. Locknut		15.	Choke plate
4. Cap		16.	Body
5. Spring		17.	Fuel inlet valve
6. Washer		18.	Jet holder
7. Retainer		19.	Main jet
8. Clip		20.	Float
9. Tapered needle		21.	Float pin
10. Throttle slide		22.	Float bowl
11. Primer button		23.	Filter
12. Spring		24.	Filter cover

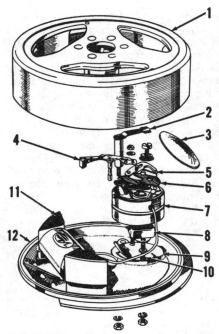

Fig. SG6 — Exploded view of Villiers magneto assembly. Retainer (2) holds cover (3).

1. Flywheel
2. Retainer
3. Cover
4. & 5. Breaker points
6. Insulator
7. Housing
8. Condenser
9. Gasket
10. Studs
11. Coil
12. Stator plate

IGNITION

Models EFS, EFPC, EFNR, EFPW, ENC, ENS And ESC

A breakerless, solid-state, capacitor discharge ignition system is used on Models EFS, EFPC, EFNR, EFPW, ENC, ENS and ESC. Ignition timing is fixed and the only service required is to renew damaged components.

If the flywheel must be removed, proceed as follows: Remove starter, if so equipped, flywheel nut, starter pulley, flywheel cover and spacer. Reinstall flywheel nut so crankshaft end does not protrude through nut. Remove spark plug and turn flywheel until piston is at bottom of stroke. Suspend motor by

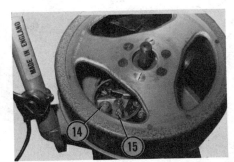

Fig. SG7 — Breaker point lock screw is shown at (14) and eccentric adjuster cam at (15).

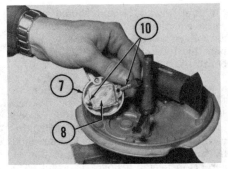

Fig. SG8 — Condenser (8) is retained in housing (7) by shoulder on studs (10).

holding flywheel, then bump flywheel nut until flywheel is loose on crankshaft. DO NOT use a puller to remove flywheel.

NOTE: It is important to have piston at bottom of stroke to prevent damage when dislodging flywheel.

The flywheel is equipped with two keyway grooves. Be sure the flywheel is installed with the correct groove engaging the crankshaft key. Tighten flywheel retaining nut to 20-22 ft.-lbs.

All Other Models

Two different breaker point type ignition systems have been used. The Villiers magneto (Fig. SG6) can be identified by the silver colored flywheel. The Wipac magneto (Fig. SG9) has a bronze flywheel. On both models, the flywheel can be removed as follows: Remove flywheel nut, washer and starter pulley, then reinstall flywheel nut finger tight. Remove spark plug and turn flywheel until piston is at bottom of stroke. Suspend motor above floor by holding flywheel, then bump the flywheel nut until flywheel is loose on crankshaft taper.

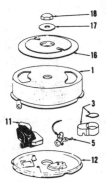

Fig. SG9 — Exploded view of Wipac magneto assembly. Condenser is molded inside the coil (11).

1. Flywheel
3. Breaker point cover
5. Breaker points
11. Coil
12. Stator plate
16. Pulley plate
17. Washer
18. Flywheel

Fig. SG10 — Breaker point lock screw is shown at (14) and eccentric adjuster cam at (15).

NOTE: It is important to have piston at bottom of stroke when bumping, to prevent damage.

The stator plate should be marked if removal is required so plate can be installed in original position. Note correct position of stator plate in Fig. SG11 if plate was not marked prior to removal.

Refer to the appropriate following paragraphs for servicing the magneto used.

VILLIERS MAGNETO. Breaker point gap should be 0.020 inch and can be adjusted through opening in flywheel after removing starter pulley, flywheel cover and cover (3 – Fig. SG6). Breaker point lock screw is shown at (14 – Fig. SG7) and adjuster cam at (15). Breaker point cam is on flywheel and flywheel

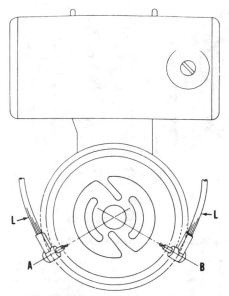

Fig. SG11 — The magneto stator plate must be installed so the high tension lead (L) is located at (A) on 3.86 cu. in. engines or at (B) on 6.18 cu. in. engines.

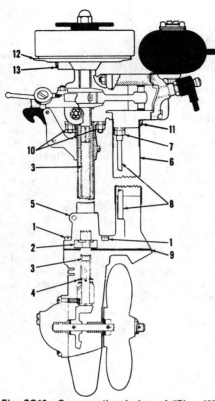

Fig. SG12—Cross-sectional view of "Plus 40" motor. Other models are similar.

2. Water pump impeller	7. Fitting
3. Drive shaft	8. Water tube
4. Washer	9. Gasket
5. Water pump housing	12. Magneto stator plate
6. Exhaust tube	13. Screw

should be seated firmly on crankshaft taper when adjusting breaker point gap. The condenser (8–Fig. SG6 and SG8) is retained in housing by shoulder on studs (10).

Ignition timing is fixed and not adjustable. Stator plate (12–Fig. SG6) is retained on crankcase with one screw (13–Fig. SG12) which must engage hole in crankcase shoulder for correct ignition timing.

NOTE: The crankshaft top main bearing may be damaged if screw (13) is over tightened.

When reinstalling flywheel, make certain that taper on crankshaft and flywheel bore are clean and dry.

WIPAC MAGNETO. Breaker point gap should be 0.020 inch and can be adjusted through opening in flywheel. Breaker point lock screw is shown at (14–Fig. SG10) and adjusting (cam) screw at (15). Breaker point cam is on flywheel and flywheel should be firmly seated on crankshaft taper when checking point gap. The condenser is molded in unit with the coil and cannot be renewed separately.

Ignition timing is fixed and not adjustable. The stator plate is retained on crankcase with one screw (13–Fig. SG12) which should engage the recess in crankcase shoulder for correct timing. Make certain that screw is aligned with hole before tightening.

NOTE: The crankcase top main bearing may be damaged if screw is over tightened.

Make certain that taper on crankshaft and bore in flywheel are clean and dry before installing flywheel.

COOLING SYSTEM

All motors are equipped with a centrifugal type water pump located directly above the gearcase housing. The water inlet is in leading edge of gearcase. Water pump on Model EFNR and ENS is accessible after gearcase removal as outlined in LOWER UNIT section. On all other models, remove the two screws (1–Fig. SG12) attaching gearcase to water pump housing (5) and remove gearcase. If impeller (2) is renewed on all models, make certain that side marked "TOP" (flanged center) is toward power head. Impeller should be heated in hot water before installing. Press impeller on lower end of drive shaft (3) just far enough to prevent impeller from contacting gasket (9) when lower end of drive shaft is resting against washer (4). If impeller is pressed onto drive shaft too far, impeller (2) may wear against top of bore in water pump housing (5). Some motors may have locating pin through water pump impeller and drive shaft.

To remove the water tube (8), first remove power head retaining nuts (10) then lift power head, exhaust tube (6) and water tube (8) from lower unit. Remove exhaust tube screw (11) or

clamp at upper end and remove exhaust tube. It may be necessary to heat the power head end of exhaust tube. Fitting (7) and water tube (8) can now be removed. When attaching power head to lower unit, make certain that lower end of water tube correctly enters hole in water pump housing (5).

When operating motor in test tank, propeller should be removed. When operating motor (on boat or in test tank) water level should be near top of water pump housing (5).

POWER HEAD

R&R AND DISASSEMBLE. To remove the power head, remove the two nuts (10–Fig. SG12) and lift power head from lower unit.

When disassembling, do not remove cylinder head unless a new copper head gasket is available.

Remove fuel tank, carburetor, flywheel, steering handle and spark plug. Remove the four cap screws (or stud nuts) attaching cylinder and head assembly to crankcase and slide the cylinder head, exhaust tube and cylinder off as a unit. Engine components are now accessible for overhaul as outlined in the appropriate following paragraphs.

ASSEMBLY. When reassembling, make sure all joint at gasket surfaces are clean, free of nicks, burrs and hardened cement or carbon. The crankcase should be completely sealed against both vacuum and pressure. Use a non-hardening sealer on cylinder to crankcase gasket and on threads of cylinder to crankcase screws.

When installing cylinder assembly over piston, use a new gasket and make certain that piston rings are properly positioned with relation to the ring groove pins. When installing magneto stator plate (12–Fig. SG12), make cer-

Fig. SG13—View of crankshaft, piston, connecting rod and associated parts. Deflector (D) on piston, open end of piston pin (3) and side of connecting rod (4) marked "SEAGULL" should be toward top.

1. Piston
2. Snap rings
3. Piston pin
4. Connecting rod
5., 6. & 7. Crankpin bearing assy.
8. Cap
9. Screws
10. Crankshaft
11. Piston pin bushing

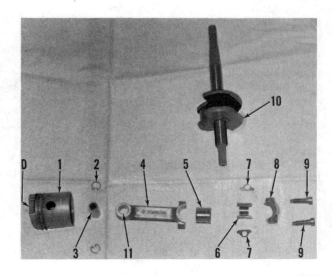
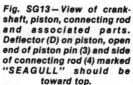

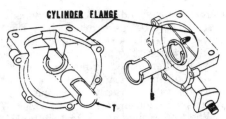

Fig. SG14—The crankshaft main bearing bushings should be pressed into crankcase halves with cut-away section toward cylinder as shown. Top bushing is shown at (T) and bottom bushing with thrust shoulder at (B).

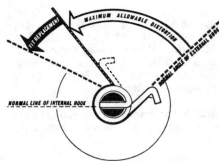

Fig. SG16—View showing distortion limits of propeller drive spring.

Fig. SG15—The long sloping side of piston should be down toward exhaust. When installing cylinder, make certain that ends of rings correctly engage pins (P). Other pin is on opposite side of piston.

on the rod, with no noticeable looseness. When installing piston on connecting rod make sure that long sloping side of piston head and the closed end of piston pin are both down (toward exhaust port and exhaust tube).

CONNECTING ROD, CRANK-SHAFT AND CRANKCASE. Before detaching connecting rod from crankshaft, carefully mark the connecting rod (4—Fig. SG13), cap (8) and bearing spacers (7) for correct assembly. Screws (9) are safety wired together around connecting rod (4). Piston pin bushing (11) and crankpin bearing assembly (5, 6 and 7) are not available separately. If crankpin bearing or piston pin bushing is damaged or worn excessively, connecting rod assembly must be renewed. Lubricating slot in piston pin bushing and end of rod must be perfectly aligned. Misalignment indicates loose fit in rod and connecting rod assembly should be renewed.

tain that screw (13) properly engages hole in crankcase shoulder. Refer to Fig. SG11 on breaker point models. Taper on crankshaft and bore in flywheel should be clean and dry when installing flywheel. Ignition cam is part of flywheel hub on breaker point models. Be careful not to damage breaker points when installing flywheel.

PISTON, PIN, RINGS AND CYLINDER. The piston can be removed after removing cylinder assembly. The piston is fitted with two rings which are interchangeable in the grooves. Rings are pinned to prevent rotation in ring grooves. Pins are in top part of grooves allowing installation of ring only with cut-away section of ring ends towards head of piston. Ring end gap should be 0.004 inch.

The head end of piston is provided with a steep deflector (D—Fig. SG13) which directs the flow of the incoming fuel charge for proper scavenging of the cylinder.

The full floating piston pin is a tight push fit in piston pin bosses and a slightly looser fit in rod bushing. Make certain that piston pin bushing is a tight fit in rod. If oil slot in bushing is not aligned with slot in end of connecting rod, renew rod and bearing assembly. Fit is correct when piston will rock of its own weight

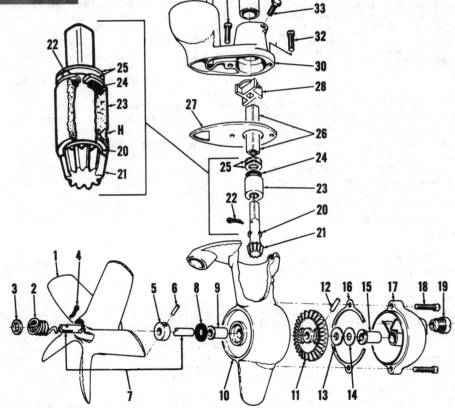

Fig. SG17—Exploded view of Forty Plus gearcase assembly. All except models with clutch are similar. Refer to Fig. SG12 for clutch type gearcase.

1. Propeller	9. Bushing	16. Gasket
2. Drive spring	10. Housing	17. End cap
3. Washer	11. Driven gear	19. Oil fill plug
4. Cotter pin	12. Drive pin	20. Hardened thrust
5. Collar	13. Shim washers	washer
6. Pin	14. Hardened thrust	21. Bevel pinion
7. Propeller shaft	washer	22. Cotter pin
8. Oil seal washer	15. Bushing	23. Bearing

24. Oil seal washer
25. Thrust washers
26. Drive shaft
27. Joint plate
28. Water pump impeller
29. Water pipe
30. Pump housing
31. Drive shaft tube

Fig. SG18—View of gearcase and cap removed for inspection.

Crankcase halves contain renewable main bearing bushings as shown in Fig. SG14. Bushings should be pressed into position with cut-away section toward cylinder as shown. Bushings must be line reamed to 0.6245-0.6255 inch after installation.

Check the mating surfaces of crankcase halves for flatness using a lapping block. Crankcase halves may be lapped to remove irregularities, but do not lower the surface.

Coat all friction surfaces with oil when reassembling. Install connecting rod with side marked "SEAGULL" toward top, making certain that cap (8 – Fig. SG13) and bearing (5, 6 and 7) are correctly positioned. Marks put on rod (4), bearing parts (5, 6 and 7) and cap (8) during disassembly will facilitate correct installation. Connecting rod screws should be tightened evenly; then, secure the screws together with lock wire around the connecting rod. Coat crankcase halves lightly with a thin, hardening sealer. Position crankcase halves over crankshaft and install through-bolts. Tighten through-bolts after perfectly aligning the cylinder flanges on crankcase halves. Piston must be installed on connecting rod with long sloping slide of piston head and closed end of piston pin down toward exhaust.

LOWER UNIT

All Models Except EFNR And ENS

PROPELLER AND DRIVE SPRING. All models are equipped with a propeller drive spring which also cushions propeller. The drive spring should be renewed if spring distortion has exceeded the maximum allowance shown in Fig. SG16. Later models are equipped with a weedless type propeller

which is also available as a replacement for early model propellers. The propeller should be removed when motor is operated in a test tank.

R&R AND OVERHAUL. Service on the lower unit can be performed by detaching gearcase housing (10 – Fig. SG17) from the water pump housing (30). Inspection of gearcase can be accomplished after removing propeller (1), pin (6), collar (5) and front cover (17).

If renewed, bushings (9 and 15) must be line reamed to 0.501-0.502 inch.

To remove the bevel pinion (21) and bushing (23), remove propeller, collar (5), front cover (17), then withdraw propeller shaft (7) and bevel gear (11). Remove the two attaching screws (32) and separate gearcase (10) from water pump housing (30). Thoroughly clean all oil from the gearcase housing (10) and bump the bevel pinion (21) and bushing out toward top. Pinion can be bumped out using a soft brass drift inserted at an angle through opening in the front of gearcase. It may be necessary to heat gearcase before bevel pinion can be removed.

The bevel pinion bushing (23) is located in housing with top screw (18). When pressing the bevel pinion and bushing into position, make certain that locating hole in bushing is aligned with threaded hole for the top screw. Shims (13) are used to adjust bevel gear backlash.

Some models are available with a clutch as shown in Fig. SG19. No adjustment is necessary. Service procedures are similar to other models. If clutch

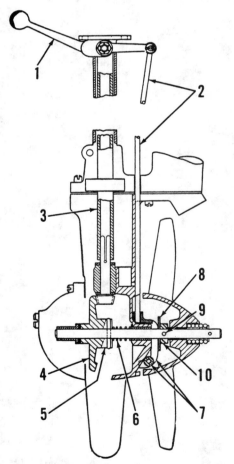

Fig. SG19—Cross-sectional view of clutch available on Century Plus and Silver Century Plus models.

1. Handle	6. Spring
2. Control rod	7. Roller & release arm
3. Drive shaft	8. Thrust washer
4. Bevel gear	9. Pin
5. Dog clutch	10. Collar

Fig. SG20—Exploded view of gearcase used on EFNR and ENS models. Propeller shaft is not shown.

1. Drive shaft
2. Thrust washer
3. Pinion gear
4. Seal retainer
5. Seal
6. Drive sleeve
7. Thrust washer
8. Upper shift rod
9. Locknut
10. Coupler nut
11. Lower shift rod
12. Spacer
13. Seal
14. Collar
15. Pin
16. Drive spring
17. Spring collar
18. Seal
19. Pin
20. Selector cover
21. Gasket
22. Dowel pin
23. Bushing
24. Selector
25. Pin
26. Selector body
27. Clevis pin
28. Gearcase
29. Thrust washer
30. Reverse gear
31. Dog clutch
32. Forward gear
33. Thrust washer
34. End cap
35. Gasket

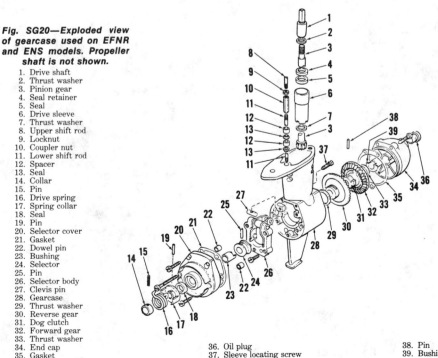

36. Oil plug	38. Pin
37. Sleeve locating screw	39. Bushing

engagement is erratic, check condition of ramp for roller (7), spring (6) and jaws on dog clutch (5) and bevel gear (4).

Model EFNR And ENS

PROPELLER AND DRIVE SPRING. A four-blade, 9½ inch diameter propeller is used. A drive spring is used to rotate the propeller as well as cushion the lower unit. The drive spring should be renewed if spring distortion has exceeded the maximum allowance shown in Fig. SG16.

R&R AND OVERHAUL. To remove gearcase, detach upper end of upper shift rod (8 – Fig. SG20) and unscrew coupler nut (10). Remove gearcase retaining screws and separate gearcase from water pump housing. Remove pin (15), collar (14) and propeller. Remove drive spring (16), then drive out pin (19) and remove spring carrier (17). Remove oil fill plug (36) and drain lubricant. While noting screw lengths, remove selector cover (20). Unscrew and remove lower shift rod (11). Remove selector body (26). Remove end cap (34); it may be necessary to tap on propeller shaft with a soft faced mallet to loosen end cap. Note that thrust washer (33) may adhere to end cap. Remove forward gear (32). Unscrew pinion sleeve locating screw (37), then using a suitable soft punch, drive against pinion gear (3) and force pinion gear and sleeve assembly out the top of the gearcase. It may be necessary to heat the gearcase area surrounding pinion gear sleeve when removing pinion gear assembly. Unscrew drive shaft (1) from pinion gear (3) and withdraw pinion gear from sleeve (6). Withdraw propeller shaft assembly. Drive out pins (25 and 38) if further disassembly of propeller shaft assembly is required. If necessary, remove remaining oil seals.

Inspect components and renew any which are damaged or excessively worn. Bushing in pinion sleeve (6) is not renewable.

Assemble gearcase by reversing disassembly procedure while noting the following points: Tighten pinion gear in drive shaft to 20 ft.-lbs. Install pinion gear assembly by driving against pinion sleeve, do not drive against drive shaft end. Be sure locating hole in side of pinion sleeve is aligned with index hole in gearcase. Apply sealer to gaskets (21 and 35) but do not apply sealer to upper surface of gearcase. After assembly, turn coupler nut (10) so gear engagement and shift control lever position are sychronized.

SEA KING

MONTGOMERY WARD
619 W. Chicago Ave.
Chicago, Illinois 60607

Some Sea King motors were manufactured for Montgomery Ward by Clinton Engines, Maquoketa, Iowa. Refer to the following Sea King sections for models not listed below.

Service procedures for models listed below will not differ greatly from those given for Clinton models. This does not mean, however, that parts are interchangeable. If parts are required, they should be ordered from Montgomery Ward.

Model	Year	Clinton Model
27002	1970	J-300
27003	1970, 1971	J-350
27005	1970, 1971	J-500
27007	1970, 1971	J-700
27402	1973	K-200
27404	1973	K-400
27405	1973	K-500
27407	1973	K-700
50415	1976	K-150
50435	1976	K-350
50475	1976	K-751
50505	1977, 1980	K-550
50507	1978, 1979	K-751
50520	1977, 1978, 1979, 1980	K-201
50535	1977, 1978, 1979, 1980	K-350
50575	1977, 1978, 1979	K-751
50576	1980	K-751
50577	1981, 1982, 1983, 1984	K-753
52202	1974	K-200
52203	1975	K-300
52205	1974	K-500
52207	1974	K-750
52235	1974	K-350
52250	1974	K-500
52257	1975	K-750
52259	1975	K-750
52275	1974	K-750
52277	1975	K-750
52307	1977, 1978	K-753
52309	1977, 1978, 1979	K-900
52319	1979	K-900
52329	1980	K-900
52350	1976	K-550
52370	1976	K-752
52375	1976	K-753

SEA KING 3.5 AND 4 HP

Year Produced	3.5 hp	4 hp
1978	....	52004
1979	....	52004A
1980	....	52004B
1981	52003	52004C
1982	....	52004D
1983	....	52004
1984	....	52004

CONDENSED SERVICE DATA

TUNE-UP

Hp/rpm	3.5/4500
	4/5250
Bore—Inches	2
Stroke—Inches	1-19/32
Number of Cylinders	1
Displacement—Cu. In.	5.0
Compression at Cranking Speed (Average, with recoil starter)	110-125 psi
Spark Plug:	
Champion	L86
Electrode gap	0.030
Magneto:	
Breaker point gap	0.020 in.
Fuel-Oil Ratio	50:1

TIGHTENING TORQUES
(All Values in Inch-Pounds)

Connecting Rod	75-85
Cylinder Head	130
Flywheel nut	204
Main Bearing Bolts	70
Spark Plug	120-180
Standard Screws:	
6-32	9
10-24	30
10-32	35
12-24	45
¼-20	70
5/16-18	160
⅜-16	270

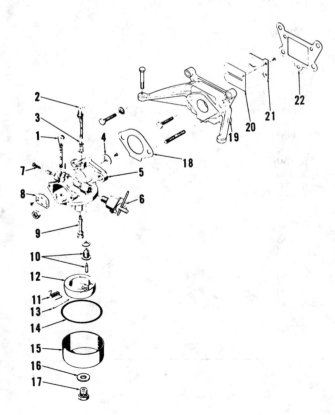

Fig. SK6-1 — Exploded view of carburetor.

1. Choke shaft
2. Throttle shaft
3. Spring
4. Throttle plate
5. Carb. body
6. Fuel valve
7. Idle mixture screw
8. Choke plate
9. Nozzle
10. Fuel inlet valve
11. Float spring
12. Float
13. Float pin
14. Gasket
15. Float bowl
16. Washer
17. High speed jet
18. Gasket
19. Intake manifold
20. Reed petals
21. Reed stop
22. Gasket

LUBRICATION

The power head is lubricated by oil mixed with the fuel. One-sixth (1/6) pint of two-stroke engine oil should be mixed with each gallon of gasoline. Manufacturer recommends use of no-lead automotive gasoline although regular or premium grade gasoline may be used if octane rating is 85 or higher. Gasoline and oil should be thoroughly mixed.

The lower unit gears and bearings are lubricated by oil contained in the gearcase. Manufacturer rcommends Chrysler Outboard Gear Lube for use in gearcase. The gearcase should be drained and refilled every 100 hours or once each year, and fluid maintained at the level of the upper (vent) plug hole.

FUEL SYSTEM

CARBURETOR. Refer to Fig. SK6-1 for an exploded view of carburetor. Initial setting of idle mixture screw (7) is one turn open. High speed mixture is controlled by high speed jet (17). Adjust idle speed so engine idles at 800-1200 rpm.

Adjust float level so float is parallel to float bowl gasket surface with carburetor inverted. Be sure float support spring (11) is installed so spring pressure helps float close fuel inlet valve. Install throttle plate so stamped letter is towards engine and holes in throttle plate are on same side as idle mixture screw. Install choke plate with stamped number towards carburetor front and oblong slot on fuel inlet side of carburetor.

SPEED CONTROL LINKAGE. The speed control lever is connected to the magneto stator plate to advance or retard ignition timing. Throttle linkage is synchronized to open the throttle as magneto timing is advanced.

To check speed control linkage, turn speed control lever until throttle cam shown in Fig. SK6-2 contacts cam follower (F). Mark (M) on throttle cam should be in center of cam follower when cam contacts follower. If mark is not aligned with cam follower centerline, loosen throttle cam retaining screw and relocate cam. Recheck synchronization after relocating cam.

REED VALVE. The reed valve is located on inside of intake manifold as shown in Fig. SK6-1. Inspect reed petals and renew any which are broken, cracked, bent or otherwise damaged. Never attempt to straighten a bent reed. Tip of reed petal should not stand open more than 0.006 inch from reed seat. Reed stop opening should be 0.24-0.26 inch.

IGNITION

Breaker points are accessible after flywheel is removed. Breaker point gap should be 0.020 inch when index mark on breaker cam is aligned with breaker point rubbing block.

Tapered bore of flywheel and crankshaft end must be clean, dry and smooth

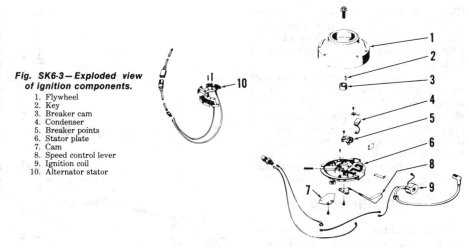

Fig. SK6-3 — Exploded view of ignition components.

1. Flywheel
2. Key
3. Breaker cam
4. Condenser
5. Breaker points
6. Stator plate
7. Cam
8. Speed control lever
9. Ignition coil
10. Alternator stator

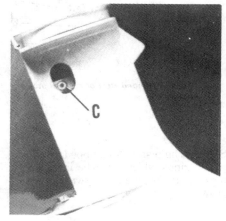

Fig. SK6-4 — View showing location of shift rod coupling (C).

before installing flywheel. Renew chipped or cracked flywheels. Flywheel and crankshaft tapers may be cleaned by using fine valve grinding compound. Apply grinding compound to tapers and rotate flywheel back and forth approximately one quarter turn. Do not spin flywheel on crankshaft. Clean flywheel and crankshaft tapers thoroughly.

COOLING SYSTEM

All models are equipped with a rubber impeller water pump. When cooling system problems are encountered, first check the water inlet for plugging or partial stoppage, then if not corrected, remove the lower unit gearcase and check the condition of water pump, water passages and sealing surfaces.

To detach gearcase from motor leg, remove shift coupling cover and loosen shift coupling screw shown in Fig.

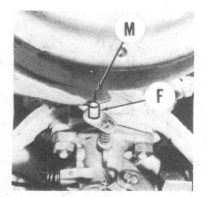

Fig. SK6-2 — Cam follower (F) should be centered on cam mark (M) when cam contacts follower.

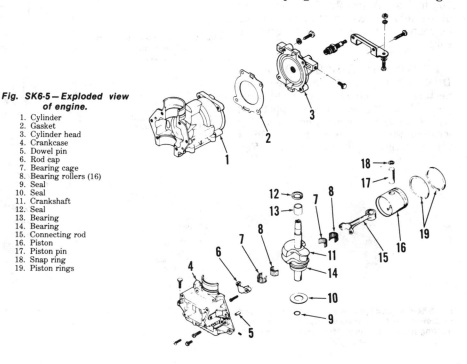

Fig. SK6-5 — Exploded view of engine.

1. Cylinder
2. Gasket
3. Cylinder head
4. Crankcase
5. Dowel pin
6. Rod cap
7. Bearing cage
8. Bearing rollers (16)
9. Seal
10. Seal
11. Crankshaft
12. Seal
13. Bearing
14. Bearing
15. Connecting rod
16. Piston
17. Piston pin
18. Snap ring
19. Piston rings

SK6-4. Remove the two screws securing gearcase to motor leg and remove gearcase. Remove impeller cover (4 – Fig. SK6-8), impeller (5) and water pump body (8).

Be sure impeller correctly engages drive pin (26) during assembly. Apply a suitable sealant to gearcase. Pull lower shift rod up as far as possible and move gear shift lever to neutral position (horizontal). Align shift rod with coupling and water line with seal and mate gearcase with motor leg. Tighten shift coupling screw and install cover.

POWER HEAD

R&R AND OVERHAUL. To remove power head, remove upper and lower engine covers, starter, fuel tank, flywheel, stator and carburetor. Disconnect stop switch leads. Unscrew two screws securing handle support plate to power head and remove plate. Unscrew six screws and separate power head from motor leg.

Remove cylinder head. Drive out crankcase locating pins, unscrew crankcase screws and separate crankcase from cylinder. Crankshaft and piston assemblies are now accessible. Refer to appropriate paragraph for overhaul of power head components.

Inspect crankcase and cylinder mating surfaces for nicks, burrs or warpage. Use a suitable sealant on crankcase and cylinder mating surfaces before assembly. Install crankshaft seals with lips towards crankshaft. Be sure locating ring around crankshaft lower main bearing is seated in grooves in cylinder and crankcase. Tighten crankcase screws to 70 in.-lbs. Assembly is reverse of disassembly. Drive shaft splines should be coated with a suitable anti-corrosion substance.

PISTON, PIN, RINGS AND CYLINDER. When properly assembled, connecting rod match marks will be towards port side of engine, piston pin open end will be towards flywheel and piston ring locating pins will be on same side of piston as piston pin open end. See Fig.

Fig. SK6-6 — Install piston assembly so open end of piston pin (P) is towards flywheel and connecting rod match mark (M) is towards port side of engine.

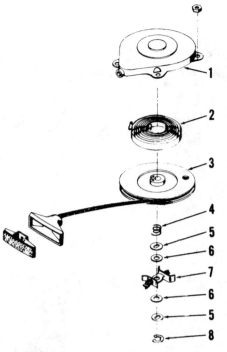

Fig. SK6-7 — Exploded view of manual starter.
1. Starter housing
2. Rewind spring
3. Rope pulley
4. Spring
5. Washer
6. Fiber washer
7. Friction shoe assy.
8. "E" ring

SK6-6. The piston is equipped with two piston rings which must be installed so beveled inner edge is towards piston crown.

Fig. SK6-8 — Exploded view of gearcase.
1. Shift coupling
2. Pin
3. Shift rod
4. Cover
5. Impeller
6. Water tube seal
7. Shift rod seal
8. Water pump body
9. Shift cam clutch
10. Seal
11. "O" ring
12. Gearcase
13. Clutch shift pin
14. Bevel gear
15. Pinion gear
16. Clutch
17. Clutch guide pin
18. Spring
19. Propeller shaft
20. Spacer
21. Bearing housing
22. Seal
23. "O" ring
24. Retainer
25. Drive shaft
26. Impeller pin
27. Nut
28. Thrust pin

CONNECTING ROD, CRANKSHAFT AND BEARINGS. Assemble connecting rod, piston and pin as outlined in previous section. Install rod and piston assembly in cylinder so alignment mark on rod is towards port side of engine. Connecting rod rides on a caged roller bearing with sixteen rollers. Be sure marks on rod and cap are correctly aligned. Tighten rod screws to 75-85 in.-lbs.

Crankshaft upper main bearing is a needle roller bearing while a ball bearing is used on lower end of crankshaft. Lower bearing and crankshaft are available as a unit assembly only.

MANUAL STARTER

The manual starter is mounted on the fuel tank and is accessible after removing the upper engine cover. Refer to Fig. SK6-7 for an exploded view of the starter.

To disassemble starter, remove starter from fuel tank and allow rope to rewind into starter. Note location of sharp edges on friction shoes and remove components (4 thru 8). Lift pulley and rope (3) out of housing (1), being careful not to dislodge rewind spring (2). If damaged, carefully remove rewind spring from housing.

Install lightly lubricated rewind spring in housing in counterclockwise direction from outer spring end. Wind rope 48

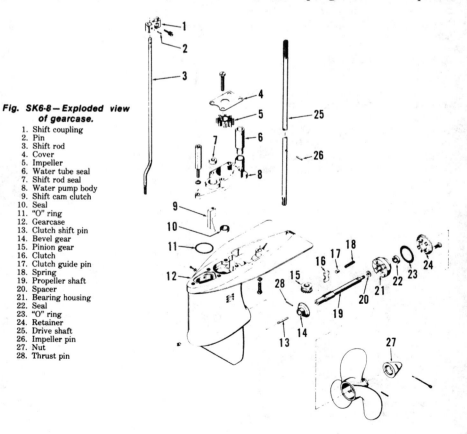

inches long on pulley in clockwise direction as viewed from rewind spring side of pulley. Lightly lubricate pulley bore and install pulley in housing making certain that inner and outer ends of spring are hooked in pulley and housing. Turn pulley three turns clockwise to preload rewind spring, pass rope end through housing and tie a knot in the rope. Pull rope out as far as possible and then try to turn pulley counterclockwise. Pulley should turn an additional $1/8$-$1/3$ turn before bottoming out rewind spring. Check sharp end of friction shoes (7) and sharpen or renew as necessary. Install components (4 thru 8). Make certain that friction shoe assembly is installed properly. If properly installed, sharp

ends of friction shoes will extend when rope is pulled.

LOWER UNIT

R&R AND OVERHAUL. Refer to Fig. SK6-8 for exploded view of lower unit. All 3.5 hp models are constant drive and do not use components (1, 2, 3, 9 and 13). On 3.5 hp models, propeller and propeller shaft (19) are splined and bevel gear (14) is secured to propeller shaft with a thrust pin (28) in place of components (16, 17 and 18).

Remove water pump as previously outlined. Remove propeller nut (27), then drive out propeller thrust pin and remove propeller. Remove any burrs or

rust from exposed end of propeller shaft. Remove four screws holding retainer (24) to bearing housing (21). Install two screws in threaded holes of retainer and using a suitable puller, remove retainer. Propeller shaft assembly may be withdrawn after removal of retainer. Remove pinion gear (15) and bevel gear (14).

Assemble by reversing disassembly procedure. Shift rod seal (7) should have raised bead up. Shift pin (13) is installed in propeller shaft with round end forward, towards cam (9). Install bevel gear (14) and pinion gear (15). Pinion gear is secured with drive shaft (25). Install propeller shaft seal (22) with lip towards propeller.

SEA KING 6 AND 9.2 HP
(1969-1972)

Year Produced	6 hp	9.2 hp
1969	27906	27909
		*27910
1970	27006	. . . . .
1971	27006	. . . . .
1972	27206	. . . . .

*Electric starting models.

CONDENSED SERVICE DATA

TUNE-UP	6 HP	9 HP
Hp/rpm.	6/4500	9.2/4750
Bore—Inches	2	2-1/8
Stroke—Inches	1-11/16	1-11/16
Number of Cylinders	2	2
Displacement—Cu. In.	10.60	11.97
Compression at Cranking Speed		
(Average, with recoil starter)	55-65 psi	75-90 psi
Spark Plug:		
Champion	H10J	J4J
Electrode Gap	0.030	0.030
Magneto:		
Breaker Point Gap	0.020	0.020
Carburetor:		
Make	Tillotson	Tillotson
Model	MT-91B	MT-97A
Fuel:Oil Ratio	24:1	24:1

SIZES—CLEARANCES (All Values In Inches)

Piston Rings:		
End Gap	0.006-0.011	0.006-0.011
Side Clearance.	0.0015-0.004	0.0015-0.004
Piston to Cylinder Clearance	0.002-0.003	0.002-0.003
Piston Pin:		
Diameter	0.500	0.500
Clearance (Rod).	Roller Bearing	Roller Bearing
Clearance (Piston)	0.00005-0.0005	0.00005-0.0005
Crankshaft Journal Diameters:		
Upper Main	0.8711-0.8715	0.8711-0.8715
Center Main.	0.8120-0.8125	0.8120-0.8125
Lower Main	0.7495-0.750	0.7495-0.750
Crankpin	0.7497-0.750	0.7497-0.750
Crankshaft Bearing Clearance:		
Upper Main	Roller Bearing	Roller Bearing
Center Main.	0.0025-0.0035	0.0025-0.0035
Lower Main	0.0015-0.0025	Roller Bearing
Crankpin.	Roller Bearing	Roller Bearing
Crankshaft End Play	0.002-0.006	0.002-0.006
Rod Side Clearance	0.015-0.025	0.015-0.025
Lower Unit:		
Drive Shaft Bearing Clearance	0.0009-0.0023	0.0009-0.0023
Propeller Shaft End Play	0.003-0.028	0.003-0.028

TIGHTENING TORQUES

(All Values in Inch-Pounds)	6 HP	9.2 HP
Connecting Rod:		
Aluminum	70	...
Steel	80	80
Cylinder Head	65	65
Flywheel Nut	480	**480
Spark Plug	120-180	120-180
Standard Screws:		
6-32	9	9
10-24	30	30
10-32	35	35
12-24	45	45
¼-20	70	70
5/16-18	160	160
3/8-16	270	270

**Armature screw for electric starting motors should be tightened to 240-300 inch-pounds torque.

LUBRICATION

The power head is lubricated by oil mixed with the fuel. One-half (½) pint of two-stroke engine oil should be mixed with each gallon of gasoline. Manufacturer recommends use of no-lead automotive gasoline although regular or premium grade gasoline may be used if octane rating is 85 or higher. Gasoline and oil should be thoroughly mixed.

The lower unit gears and bearings are lubricated by oil contained in the gearcase. Only a non-corrosive, leaded, EP90, outboard gear oil such as "Texaco EP90 Outboard Gear Oil" should be used. The gearcase should be drained and refilled every 100 hours or once each year, and fluid maintained at the level of the upper (vent) plug hole.

To fill the gearcase, have the motor in upright position and fill through the lower plug hole (F—Fig. SK1-13) in the side of gearcase until fluid reaches level of upper vent plug hole (V). Have both plugs removed while filling. Reinstall and tighten both plugs securely, using new gaskets if necessary, to assure a water tight seal.

FUEL SYSTEM

CARBURETOR. Tillotson, MT, float type carburetor shown in Fig. SK1-1 is used. Normal initial setting is one turn open from the closed position for both the high speed adjustment needle (11) and the idle mixture adjustment needle (15). Carburetor must be readjusted under load, after motor is warm, for best high speed and low speed performance.

After idle mixture needle (15) is set correctly, position the arm (13) on needle in horizontal position. Idle adjusting knob on instrument panel should be in center of travel.

To adjust the float, remove float bowl cover (1) with float attached. Invert the cover and adjust the float by bending tang (T) until farthest edge of float measures 1-7/64 inch from gasket surface of bowl cover.

It may be necessary to remove welch plug (P) and blow out idle passages if carburetor is badly plugged.

SPEED CONTROL LINKAGE. The speed control lever or grip is connected to the magneto stator plate to advance or retard the ignition timing. Throttle linkage is synchronized to open the throttle as magneto timing is advanced. It is very important that the throttle linkage be properly synchronized for best performance.

To check the linkage, turn the speed control grip unit until mark (M—Fig. SK1-2) is aligned with center line of roller (20). The carburetor throttle valve should just start to open. To adjust, align mark (M) with center of roller (20), loosen nut (N) and position roller stud so that roller is against cam with throttle still closed. Retighten nut (N) and recheck. Make certain that roller is against cam when mark (M) is aligned, but throttle must be fully closed.

The speed control grip should require 18-30 inch-pounds torque to turn. Fric-

Fig. SK1-1—Exploded view of Tillotson MT carburetor used on 6 and 9.2 hp motors. Knob on instrument panel moves idle mixture needle (15) via link (12) and arm (13).

P. Plug
T. Tang
1. Bowl cover
2. Float shaft
3. Inlet seat
4. Inlet needle
5. Float
6. Throttle body
7. Choke plate
8. Choke shaft
9. Packing
10. Main adjustment needle
11. Main adjustment needle
12. Link
13. Arm
14. Screw
15. Idle adjustment needle
16. Throttle plate
17. Spring
18. Throttle shaft
19. Follower stud
20. Follower roller
21. Idle tube
22. Main nozzle

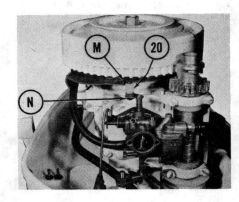

Fig. SK1-2—The carburetor throttle valve should just begin to open when mark (M) on cam is aligned with center of roller (20).

tion is adjusted by tightening the inside nut (1—Fig. SK1-3). After adjusting, tighten locknut (2) to maintain correct friction on lever.

REED VALVES. The inlet reed valves are located on reed plate between inlet manifold and crankcase. Reed petals should seat very lightly against the reed plate throughout their entire length, with the least possible tension. Check seating visually. Reed

Fig. SK1-3—The speed control grip should require 18-30 inch-pounds torque to turn. Refer to text for adjusting friction.

Fig. SK1-4—Reed stops should be 3/16-inch from seating surface of reed plate.

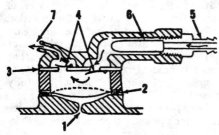

Fig. SK1-5—Schematic view of the diaphragm type fuel pump used on all models. Check valves are of the reed type.

1. Pressure port
2. Diaphragm
3. Reed plate
4. Check valves
5. Inlet fitting
6. Filter
7. Outlet

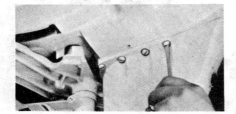

Fig. SK1-6—The power head is retained to lower unit with eight screws. Other four are similarly located on starboard side.

stop setting should be 3/16-inch when measured from free end of reed stop to seating surface on reed plate as shown in Fig. SK1-4. Renew reeds if petals are broken, cracked, warped, rusted or bent. Never attempt to bend a reed petal or to straighten a damaged reed. Broken petals are sometimes caused by a bent or damaged reed stop. Seating surface of reed plate should be smooth and flat.

FUEL PUMP. A diaphragm type fuel pump is attached to the transfer port cover for the upper crankcase. Pressure and vacuum pulsations from the crankcase are directed through the port (1—Fig. SK1-5) to the rear of diaphragm (2). When the power head piston moves upward in its cylinder, vacuum in the crankcase draws the diaphragm inward and fuel enters the fuel chamber through filter (6) and the inlet reed valve (4) in the reed plate (3). As power head piston moves downward, pressure forces the diaphragm outward into fuel chamber and fuel

passes through the outlet reed valve to carburetor line (7).

Defective or questionable parts should be renewed. Reeds (26—Fig. SK1-7) should seat lightly and squarely on reed plate (27). Diaphragm should be renewed if air leaks or cracks are found, or if deterioration is evident.

IGNITION

Breaker point gap should be 0.020 for each set of points, and can be adjusted after the flywheel is removed. Both sets of points should be adjusted exactly alike.

NOTE: High point of breaker cam coincides with location of flywheel key. Align key with rub block when adjusting each set of points.

The tapered bore in flywheel and end of crankshaft must be clean, dry and smooth before installing flywheel. Flywheel nut for manual start motors should be torqued to 480 inch-pounds. Armature screw for electric starting

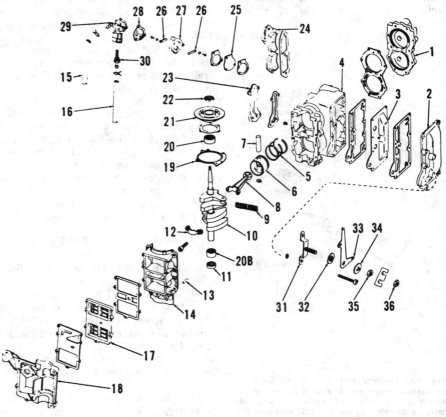

Fig. SK1-7—Exploded view of power head and associated parts. Bearing (20B) is used on 9.2 hp motors.

1. Cylinder head	11. Seal	20B. Needle bearing
2. Exhaust cover	12. Cap	(9.2 hp motors)
3. Exhaust cover	13. Dowel	21. Bearing cage
4. Cylinder half	14. Crankcase half	22. Seal
5. Piston rings	15. Pressure line to	23. Drain cover
6. Piston	carburetor	24. Transfer port
7. Piston pin	16. Inlet line	cover
8. Connecting rod	17. Reed plate	25. Pump diaphragm
9. Needle rollers	18. Intake manifold	26. Reed valve
10. Crankshaft	19. Stator ring	27. Reed plate
	20. Needle bearing	

28. Gasket
29. Pump cover
30. Inlet screen
31. Bracket
32. Bearing
33. Magneto control
lever
34. Washer
35. Friction adj. nut
36. Locknut

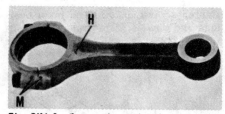

Fig. SK1-8—Connecting rod and cap are perfectly mated parts and the fractured joint should be invisible when correctly assembled. Marks (M) should be aligned and oil hole (H) and marks should be toward top of motor when connecting rod assembly is installed.

motors should be tightened to 240-300 inch-pounds torque. Spark plug electrode gap should be 0.030 inch.

COOLING SYSTEM

WATER PUMP. All motors are equipped with a rubber impeller water pump. When cooling system problems are encountered, first check the water inlet for plugging or partial stoppage, then if not corrected, remove the lower unit gearcase and check the condition of water pump, water passages and sealing surfaces.

To detach the upper gearcase from the exhaust housing, proceed as follows: Shift to Reverse gear, then remove the four nuts (1—Fig. SK1-13) and screws (2). Lower the gearcase and remove the two screws (8—Fig. SK-14) that attach the two sections of shift rod (7 & 9) together. The water pump can be removed after removing screws (31 & 32). Drive shaft seal (29) should be installed with spring loaded tip down.

When reassembling, notice that screw (31) is 1-1/8 inches long and the two front screws (32) are 1 inch long. Drive shaft spline seal (24) should be renewed if hard or cracked. Lubricate water tube seal (21) and splines on upper end of drive shaft (22). Position gearcase assembly so that shift rods (7 & 9) can be connected with screws (8). Carefully slide the housing together making

certain that water tube (18) enters seal (21) and install the four retaining screws (2—Fig. SK1-13) and nuts (1).

POWER HEAD

R&R AND OVERHAUL. To remove power head, clamp the motor on a stand or support, and remove the engine cover. The power head can be lifted off after removing the eight retaining screws (Fig. SK1-6) and dis-

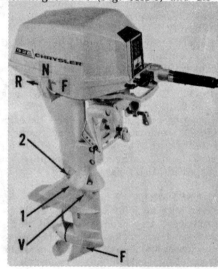

Fig. SK1-13—View of 9.2 hp motor showing two of the screws (2) and nuts (1) that attach upper gearcase housing to motor leg (exhaust housing).

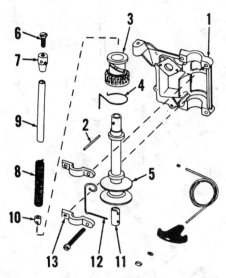

Fig. SK1-9—Exploded view of recoil starter assembly.

1. Inlet manifold	8. Recoil spring
2. Drive pin	9. Guide post
3. Drive pinion	10. Retainer
4. Pinion spring	11. Retainer extension
5. Starter spool	12. Rope guide
6. Locking screw	13. Bearing caps
7. Spring drive	

Fig. SK1-10—View of special "T" handle tool (No. T-3139) for removing and installing starter recoil spring assembly.

Fig. SK1-11—Exploded view of electric starter-generator assembly for electric start models.

1. Cover
2. Armature screw
3. Brushes (2 used)
4. Brush spring
5. Starter lead wire
6. Housing & field assembly
7. Armature
8. Key
9. Spacer
10. Bearing
11. Spacer
12. Support housing
13. Circuit breaker
14. Rectifier
15. Nut
16. Voltage regulator
17. Regulator ground
18. Battery cables
19. Flywheel
20. Starter relay
22. Wiring harness
23. Resistor
24. Dome light

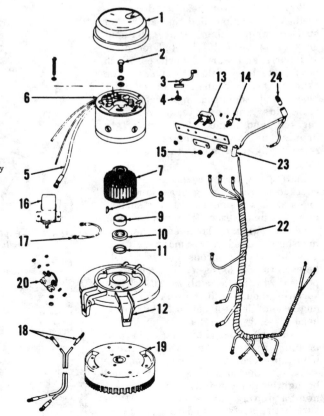

connecting the interfering wires, speed control linkage and fuel lines. If power head is to be serviced, it is usually easier to remove carburetor, magneto and starter before detaching power head from lower unit.

The crankshaft and pistons can be removed after removing cylinder head (1—Fig. SK1-7), intake manifold (18), reed plate (17), bearing cage (21) and crankcase front half (14). Parts (5, 6, 7, 8, 9 & 12) should be identified for correct assembly to the cylinder from which they were removed. The exhaust covers (2 & 3), transfer port cover (24) and drain cover (23) should be removed for cleaning and inspection if major repairs are to be performed. Pry lugs are provided adjacent to the retaining dowels for removing the crankcase front half.

Engine components are now accessible for removal and overhaul as outlined in the appropriate following paragraphs. Assemble as outlined in the ASSEMBLY paragraph.

ASSEMBLY. When reassembling, make sure all joint and gasket surfaces are clean, free from nicks and burrs and hardened cement or carbon. The crankcase and intake manifold must be completely sealed against water leakage and pressure. Mating surfaces of water intake, and exhaust areas between power head and lower unit must form a tight seal.

Whenever power head is disassembled, it is recommended that all gasket surfaces and mating surfaces without gaskets be carefully checked for nicks and burrs and warped surfaces which might interfere with a tight seal. The cylinder head, head end of cylinder block, and some mating surfaces of manifolds and crankcase may be checked, and lapped if necessary, to provide a smooth surface. Do not remove any more metal than is necessary.

Mating surface of crankcase may be checked on the lapping block, and high spots or nicks removed, but the surface must not be lowered. If extreme care is used, a slightly damaged crankcase may be salvaged in this manner.

A heavy, non-fibrous grease should be used to hold loose needle bearings in position during assembly. All friction surfaces should be lubricated with new engine oil. Check frequently as power head is being assembled, for binding of the working parts. If binding or locking is encountered, remove the cause before proceeding with the assembly.

Gasket and sealing surfaces should be lightly and carefully coated with a non-hardening gasket cement. Make sure entire surface is coated, but avoid

letting excess cement squeeze out into crankcase, bearing or other passages. When installing the crankcase screws, tighten screws next to the main bearings and dowels first. Crankshaft seals (11 & 22—Fig. SK1-7) should be

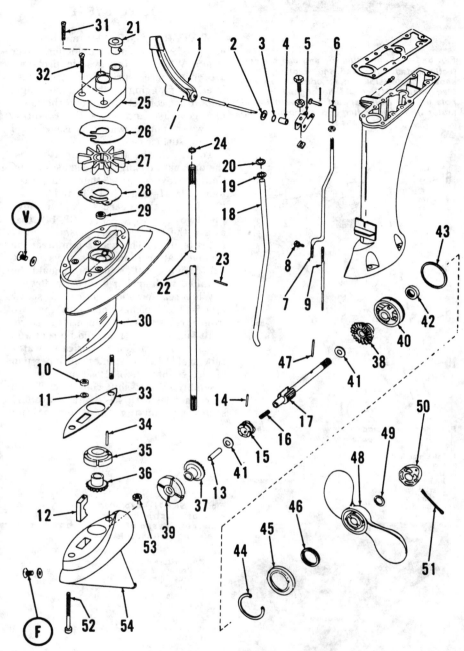

Fig. SK1-14—Exploded view of lower unit assembly. Spring (16) should be compressed in propeller shaft (17) while driving pin (14) through coupling (15) and shaft.

F. Filler plug	36. Bevel pinion
V. Vent (oil level) plug	37. Bevel gear
1. Shift handle	38. Bevel gear
2. Nylon washer	39. Bearing
3. Seal	40. Bearing & end cap
4. Spacer	41. Thrust washers
5. Lever arm	42. Seal
6. Coupling	43. Seal
7. Upper shift rod	44. Snap ring
8. Screws	45. Weed guard
9. Lower shift rod	46. Retaining ring
10. Shift rod seal	47. Shear pin
11. Seal retainer	48. Propeller
12. Shift cam	49. Seal
13. Shift plunger	50. Nut
14. Pin	51. Stainless steel cotter pin
15. Coupling (clutch)	52. Socket head screw
16. Spring	53. Nut
17. Propeller shaft	54. Lower gearcase
18. Water tube	
19. Stainless steel washer	
20. Seal	
21. Seal	
22. Drive shaft	
23. Water pump drive pin	
24. Spline seal	
25. Water pump body	
26. Top plate	
27. Impeller	
28. Bottom plate	
29. Drive shaft seal	
30. Upper gearcase (drive shaft)	
31. Screw (1-1/8 inch)	
32. Screws (1 inch)	
33. Gasket	
34. Spring pin	
35. Bevel pinion thrust bearing	

renewed each time crankshaft is removed. Refer to CONDENSED SERVICE DATA table for clearances and tightening torques.

Before attaching power head to lower unit, renew the drive shaft spline seal (24—Fig. SK1-14) and coat splines with grease.

PISTONS, PINS, RINGS AND CYLINDERS. Piston is fitted with three rings which should be installed with the beveled inner edge toward closed end of piston. Recommended ring end gap is 0.006-0.011, with a maximum wear limit of 0.016. Piston rings should have 0.0015-0.004 side clearance in piston grooves, with a wear limit of 0.005.

Piston skirt clearance should be 0.002-0.003 when measured at widest part of skirt at right angles to piston pin. Renew the piston if skirt clearance exceeds 0.005.

When installing piston on connecting rod and the rod and piston in cylinder, observe the following: The long, tapering side of piston head should be installed toward the exhaust ports and the oil hole (H—Fig. SK1-8) in connecting rod should be toward top of motor. All friction surfaces should be lubricated with new engine oil when assembling.

CONNECTING RODS, BEARINGS AND CRANKSHAFT. Before detaching connecting rods from crankshaft, make certain that rod and cap are properly marked for correct assembly to each other and in the correct cylinder. The loose needle bearings at crankpin end of connecting rod should be kept with each assembly and not intermixed if reused.

The forged steel connecting rods contain 28 loose needle rollers at crankpin end of rod and a caged needle bearing at piston end. Parting faces of rod and cap are not machined, but are fractured, to provide positive location. When installing cap, make sure the correlation marks (M—Fig. SK1-8) are aligned; then shift cap back and forth slightly while tightening, until fractured sections are in perfect mesh. When properly installed, the fractured parting line is practically invisible as shown. Rod side play on crankpin should be 0.015-0.025, with a wear limit of 0.035.

The crankshaft upper main needle bearing (20—Fig. SK1-7) is contained in the end cap (21) and the center main bearing is a bronze bushing cast into the crankcase halves. The lower main bearing is a cast-in bronze bushing for 6 hp motors and renewable needle

bearing (20B) for 9.2 hp motors. On all models, recommended diametral clearance is 0.0025-0.0035 for the center bearing and 0.0015-0.0025 for the lower bushing on 6 hp motors. Recommended crankshaft end play is 0.002-0.006. Oversize and undersize parts are not available.

When assembling, follow the procedures outlined in the ASSEMBLY paragraph. Tightening torques are listed in the CONDENSED SERVICE DATA table.

MANUAL STARTER

Fig. SK1-9 shows an exploded view of the recoil starter assembly. Starter pinion (3) engages a starter ring gear on the flywheel.

To disassemble the starter assembly, first remove the engine cover, then remove screw.

NOTE: This screw locks pin (2) in place in starter shaft.

Thread the special "T" handle tool (T3139) in threaded hole from which screw (6) was removed. Tighten the tool securely, then carefully push the pin (2) out of pinion and starter spool. Allow the tool and spring drive (7) to turn clockwise until recoil spring (8) is unwound; then use the tool to withdraw the recoil spring (8) and drive (7) from center of starter spool (5). Guide post (9) and spring retainer (10) can be lifted out after recoil spring is removed.

Recoil spring, pinion (3) or associated parts can be renewed at this time. To renew the starter rope, remove the bearing caps (13) retaining spool (5) to inlet manifold (1) and remove the spool.

NOTE: Bearing caps (13) should be reinstalled in the original location.

Thread the new rope through hole in end of spool (5) and install the retainer link approximately ½-inch from end. Pull secured end of rope into spool, then wind rope on spool and install spool. Rope guide (12) should be installed with end through hole in retainer extension (11) and attached by screw retaining the lower bearing cap. Install the recoil spring assembly, and drive pinion (3). Use the "T" handle tool to wind the recoil spring counterclockwise eight turns as shown in Fig. SK1-10. Align the holes in pinion (3—Fig. SK1-9), spool (5) and spring drive (7); then insert the drive pin (2). Remove the tool and reinstall the locking screw (6). Recoil spring cavity of starter spool (5) should be filled with lubriplate or a similar grease when reassembling.

If tension of pinion spring (4) is incorrect, the pinion (3) may prevent full throttle operation.

ELECTRIC STARTER-GENERATOR

The combination starter and generator unit shown in Fig. SK1-11 is used on electric start 9.2 hp motors. The armature (7) is mounted directly on upper end of crankshaft. The 12 volt battery should be connected with negative terminal grounded. The positive terminal should be connected to the red battery cable (18). If battery is connected with wrong terminal grounded or if motor is operated without battery, the rectifier (14) or armature (7) may be damaged. Circuit breaker (13) will normally protect the electric components.

The housing field assembly (6) can be removed after disconnecting necessary wires and removing the six mounting screws. Housing (6) must be removed before armature (7) can be removed from crankshaft. Armature screw (2) should be tightened to 240-300 inch-pounds torque.

LOWER UNIT

PROPELLER AND DRIVE PIN. Shear pin protection is carefully engineered for each unit. Protection depends on shear pin material as well as size. Although, in an emergency, the shear pin may be replaced by one of any available material, the correct shear pin should be installed as soon as possible to insure maximum performance and protection. Spare shear pins should always be carried.

All models use a 5/32 x 1-3/16 inch stainless steel shear pin. Six (6) hp motors use 7½ inch diameter, 7½ inch pitch propeller. Propeller used on 9.2 hp motors is 8 inch diameter, 8 inch pitch. Right hand rotating (clockwise), two bladed, aluminum propeller is standard for all models.

R&R AND OVERHAUL. To detach the upper gearcase from the exhaust housing, shift to Reverse gear, then remove the four nuts (1—Fig. SK1-13) and screws (2). Lower gearcase and remove the two screws (8—Fig. SK1-14) that attach the two sections of shift rod (7 & 9) together.

Remove the propeller and shear pin. Remove any burrs or rust from exposed end of propeller shaft. Remove snap ring (44), thread two screws in threaded holes of propeller shaft bearing cage (40); and remove the cage using a puller.

To detach lower gearcase (54) from drive shaft housing (30), unscrew and remove shift rod (9) from cam (12). Housings are secured by screw (52) at forward end and stud nut (53) INSIDE the case shown by arrow, Fig. SK1-15.

Propeller shaft, gears, bearings and shift mechanism can be removed after housings are separated. Front gear and bearing (37 & 39—Fig. SK1-14) can usually be dislodged from housing by jarring open end of housing on a block of wood. If trouble is encountered, heat gearcase to loosen bearing. When installing front gear (37) and bearing (39) in housing, assemble bearing cage (40), without the "O" ring (43) over rear of propeller shaft; install thrust washer (41), and gear assembly (37) on front of shaft; and use the shaft as a piloted driver.

Spring loaded lip of drive shaft seal (29) should be down. Spring loaded lip of propeller shaft seal (42) should be toward outside (rear). Grooved side of bearing (39) should be toward front (away from gear). With unit assembled, propeller shaft end play should be 0.003-0.028. Backlash and mesh position of gears are not adjustable.

Before installing the assembled gearcase to the drive shaft housing, renew drive shaft spline seal (24) and coat splines and lower end of water tube (18) with grease. Make certain that water tube correctly enters seal (21).

Fig. SK1-15—Lower unit gearcase with propeller shaft bearing cage removed, showing location of rear stud nut (53—Fig. SK1-14).

SEA KING 6 AND 8 HP
(1973-1977)

Year Produced	6 hp	8 hp
1973	27400	.....
	27406	
1974	52000	.....
	52006	
1975	52100	.....
	52106	
1976	52106	52175
1977	52106	52175

CONDENSED SERVICE DATA

TUNE-UP	6 HP	8 HP
Hp/rpm..........................	6/5000	8/5000
Bore—Inches	1-7/8	2
Stroke—Inches	1-5/8	1-5/8
Number of Cylinders	2	2
Displacement—Cu. In.	8.99	10.2
Compression at Cranking Speed		
(Average)	6 hp, 85-95 psi	8 hp, 100-110 psi
Spark Plug:		
Champion	L4J	L4J
Electrode Gap—Inch	0.030	0.030
Magneto:		
Point Gap—Inch	0.020	0.020
Timing..........................	See Text	See Text
Carburetor:		
Make	Tillotson	Tillotson
Model	CO	CO
Fuel:Oil Ratio	††50:1	††50:1
SIZES—CLEARANCES		
Piston Rings:		
End Gap	*	*
Side Clearance....................	*	*
Piston to Cylinder Clearance	*	*
Piston Pin:		
Diameter:	*	*
Clearance (Rod)....................	*	*
Clearance (Piston)	*	*
Crankshaft Bearings:		
Upper Main	Ball	Ball
Lower Main	Bushing or	Bushing or
	Caged Needle	Caged Needle
Crankpin........................	Loose Needles	Loose Needles
Center main	Loose Needles	Loose Needles
Rod Side Clearance	*	*
Crankshaft End Play	*	*

*Publication not authorized by manufacturer.

††Use a 24:1 fuel to oil ratio to break in a freshly overhauled engine.

TIGHTENING TORQUES (All Values in Inch-Pounds)	6 HP	8 HP
Flywheel Nut	480	480
Cylinder Head	125	125
Spark Plug	120-180	120-180
Connecting Rod Screws	90	90
Standard Screws:		
No. 10-24	30	30
No. 10-32	35	35
No. 12-24	45	45
¼-20	70	70
5/16-18	160	160
3/8-16	270	270

LUBRICATION

Power head is lubricated by oil mixed with the fuel. For normal service after break-in, mix 1/6 pint of two-stroke engine oil with each gallon of gasoline. For severe service and during break-in, the recommended ratio is one third (⅓) pint of oil per gallon of gasoline. Manufacturer recommends use of automotive no-lead gasoline although regular or premium gasoline may be used if octane rating is 85 or higher. Gasoline and oil should be thoroughly mixed.

The lower unit gears and bearings are lubricated by oil contained in the gearcase. Only a non-corrosive, leaded EP90, outboard gear oil should be used. The gearcase should be drained and refilled every 30 hours and fluid maintained at the level of the upper (vent) plug hole.

To fill the gearcase, have the motor in upright position and fill through the lower plug hole in the side of gearcase until fluid reaches level of upper plug hole. Reinstall and tighten both plugs securely, using new gaskets if necessary, to assure a water tight seal.

FUEL SYSTEM

CARBURETOR. Tillotson type CO carburetors are used. Refer to Fig. SK2-1. Initial setting of idle mixture screw (A—Fig. SK2-3) is one turn out from a lightly seated position. Final adjustment of carburetor must be made with engine at normal operating temperature and motor running with normal load. Standard main jet sizes should be correct for operation below 5000 ft. altitutde. Standard size main jet for 6 hp models is 0.037 inch with CO6A, 0.032 inch with CO6B and 0.033 inch with CO6C carburetor. Standard size main jet for 8 hp models is 0.049 inch with CO4A, 0.047 inch with CO4B and 0.045 inch with CO4C or CO4D carburetor.

Correct float height of CO type carburetor is 13/32 inch. Height is checked by inverting carburetor body and measuring distance from bottom of float to gasket surface of carburetor body. Refer to Fig. SK2-4. Adjustment is accomplished by bending tang on float.

SPEED CONTROL LINKAGE. The speed control lever or grip is connected to the magneto stator plate to advance or retard the ignition timing. Throttle linkage is synchronized to open the throttle as magneto timing is advanced. It is very important that the throttle linkage be properly synchronized for best performance.

Throttle pick-up point is adjusted in the following manner: With engine turned off, turn idle speed stop screw (14—Fig. SK2-6) until pick-up mark on throttle cam plate (Fig. SK2-5) is in approximate position shown. Turn speed control grip slowly until throttle cam touches roller on throttle cam follower. Continue to turn speed control grip until carburetor throttle shaft (17—Fig. SK2-1) begins to move. Pick-up mark on throttle cam should be even with or no more than 1/32 inch

Fig. SK2-1—Exploded view of CO type carburetor.

1. Adjusting arm	11. Retaining screw
2. By-pass tube	12. Main jet
3. Throttle cam roller	13. Inlet valve
4. Throttle cam follower	14. Choke friction ball
5. Idle screw	15. Choke assembly
6. Throttle body	16. Choke shaft
7. Main nozzle	17. Throttle shaft
8. Float	18. Throttle plate
9. Gasket	19. Throttle return spring
10. Float bowl	20. Welch plug

Fig. SK2-3—Final adjustment of idle mixture should be done with engine under load and at operating temperature.

Fig. SK2-4—Float level of CO type carburetor should be 13/32 inch measured at (A).

from roller at this time. Turn screw (A—Fig. SK2-5) to adjust throttle pick-up point. Make final adjustment of idle speed stop screw (14—Fig. SK2-6) with engine running to obtain idle speed of 700 rpm in forward gear.

REED VALVES. The inlet reed valves are located on reed plate between inlet manifold and crankcase. The reed petals should seat very lightly against the reed plate throughout their entire length, with the least possible tension. Check seating visually. End of reed stops (2—Fig. SK2-7) should be 17/64 inch from reed plate (4) when installed.

Renew reeds if petals are broken, cracked, warped, rusted or bent. Never attempt to bend a reed petal or to straighten a damaged reed. Seating surface of reed plate should be smooth and flat. When installing reeds or reed stop, make sure that petals are centered over the inlet holes in reed plate, and that the reed stops are centered over reed petals.

FUEL PUMP. A diaphragm type fuel pump is mounted on the side of power head cylinder block and ported to the upper crankcase. Pressure and vacuum pulsations from the crankcase are directed through the port (1—Fig. SK2-8) to the rear of diaphragm (2). When the power head piston moves upward in its cylinder, vacuum in the crankcase draws the diaphragm inward and fuel enters the pump through filter (6) and the inlet reed valve (4) in reed plate (3). As power head piston moves downward pressure forces the diaphragm outward into fuel chamber, and fuel passes through the outlet reed valve into carburetor line (7).

Defective or quesionable parts should be renewed. Pump valves (3—Fig. SK2-9) should seat lightly and squarely

on reed plate (4). Diaphragm should be renewed if air leaks or cracks are found, or if deterioration is evident.

IGNITION

Breaker point gap should be 0.020 inch for each set of points, and can be adjusted after the flywheel is removed. Both sets of points must be adjusted exactly alike.

NOTE: High point of breaker cam co-incides with location of flywheel key. Align key with the contact point rub block when adjusting points.

The tapered bore in flywheel and end of crankshaft must be clean, dry and smooth before installing flywheel. the flywheel nut should be torqued to 480 inch-pounds torque. Spark plug electrode gap should be set at 0.030 inch.

COOLING SYSTEM

WATER PUMP. All motors are equipped with a rubber impeller type water pump. When cooling system problems are encountered check the water inlet for plugging or partial stoppage. Remove lower unit gearcase and inspect water passages, water pump and sealing surfaces if previous check revealed nothing.

Water pump is removed in the following manner: Remove four screws that secure lower unit. Pull lower unit away from motor leg and remove shift rod screw (A—Fig. SK2-10). Pull lower unit free of motor. Remove screws holding water pump to lower unit and slide pump off drive shaft.

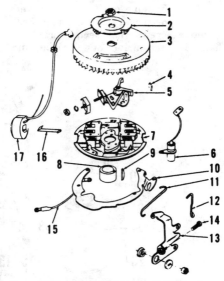

Fig. SK2-6—Exploded view of flywheel and breaker assembly base plate used.

1. Nut	10. Throttle cam
2. Starter collar	11. Throttle link
3. Flywheel	12. Speed control link
4. Felt wiper	13. Control lever
5. Breaker points	14. Idle stop screw
6. Condenser	15. Ground wire
7. Base plate	16. Wedge spring
8. Point cam	17. Coil/plug lead
9. Woodruff key	

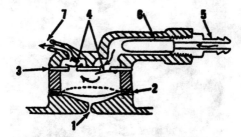

Fig. SK2-8—Schematic view of diaphragm type fuel pump used on all models. Check valves are of the reed type.

1. Pressure port	5. Inlet fitting
2. Diaphragm	6. Filter
3. Reed plate	7. Outlet
4. Check valve	

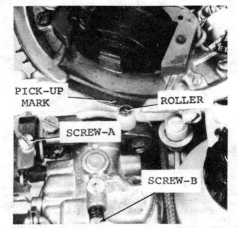

Fig. SK2-5—View of throttle pick-up point timing. Adjust pick-up point by turning screw (A). Refer to text for procedure.

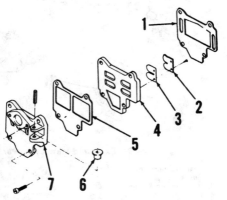

Fig. SK2-7—View of inlet manifold and reed plate assembly.

1. Gasket	5. Gasket
2. Reed stop	6. Start rope pulley
3. Reed petal	7. Manifold
4. Reed plate	

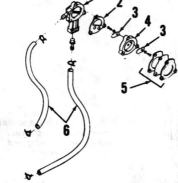

Fig. SK2-9—Exploded view of fuel pump assembly common to all models.

1. Pump cover	4. Plate
2. Gasket	5. Diaphragm & gaskets
3. Pump valve (2 used)	6. Fuel lines

When reassembling water pump, make certain that slot in impeller (10 – Fig. SK2-15) is down toward back plate (11). Water tube seal (8) may be removed by depressing tabs on seal through holes in pump body (9) while pulling on seal. Make certain tabs are fully seated in pump on reassembly. Make certain that all seals are in good condition and lubricated with a light grease on reassembly. Screws that secure pump body should be coated with an anti-seize compound before installation.

Center line of screw hole in lower shift rod (4) must be 3/16 inch (plus or minus 3/64 inch) below top of lower unit gearcase with unit in neutral. Same tolerance applies to top of motor leg extension (32), if used. A longer lower shift rod is used on these models.

Shift rods should be aligned as shown in Fig. SK2-11. If rods are assembled incorrectly, shift rod seal (5—Fig. SK2-15) will be damaged. Be sure that water tube is seated in seal (8) when assembling.

POWER HEAD

R&R AND DISASSEMBLY. Disassemble motor for overhaul as follows: Remove engine top cowl, tie a slip knot in starter rope at pulley and remove handle. Disconnect fuel line (at carburetor) and magneto control link, then remove magneto and starter assembly. Remove carburetor adapter flange/reed plate assembly, starter and upper crankshaft bearing cage (28—Fig. SK2-12). Remove the six screws securing power head to motor leg and lift power head off. Remove exhaust port covers, transfer port covers and cylinder head. Remove screws that secure crankcase half (30) and drive out locating pins between cases. A screwdriver may be used at pry points around the crankcase to aid in removal.

Engine components are now accessible for removal and overhaul as outlined in the appropriate following paragraphs. Assemble as outlined in the following section.

ASSEMBLY. When reassembling, make sure all joint and gasket surfaces are clean, free from nicks and burrs and hardened cement or carbon. The crankcase and inlet manifold must be completely sealed against both vacuum and pressure. Exhaust manifold and cylinder head must be sealed against water leakage and pressure. Mating surfaces of exhaust area between power head and motor leg must form a tight seal.

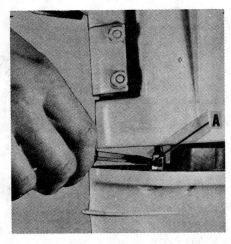

Fig. SK2-10—Remove shift rod screw (A) to free lower unit. Socket head screws are used on late models.

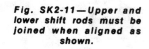

Fig. SK2-11—Upper and lower shift rods must be joined when aligned as shown.

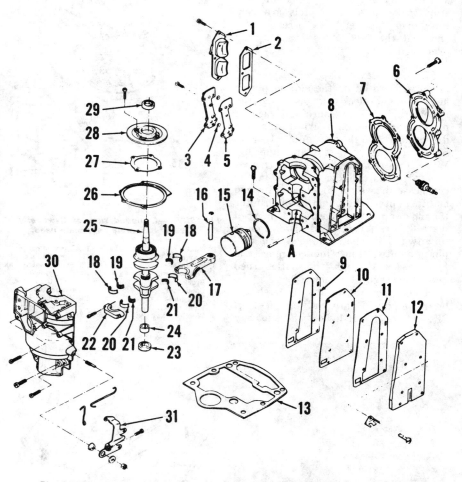

Fig. SK2-12—Exploded view of power head. Construction is similar to all models.

1. Transfer port cover
2. Gasket
3. Drain cover & check valves
4. Drain screens
5. Gasket
6. Cylinder head
7. Head gasket
8. Cylinder block
9. Exhaust cover & gasket
10. Exhaust plate
11. Exhaust cover gasket
12. Exhaust cover
13. Gasket
14. Piston rings
15. Piston
16. Piston pin
17. Connecting rod
18. Main bearing liner
19. Main bearing rollers
   (26 per set)
20. Rod bearing liner
21. Rod bearing rollers
   (24 per set)
22. Rod cap
23. Crankshaft seal
24. Lower main bearing
25. Crankshaft
26. Stator ring
27. Bearing cage gasket
28. Bearing cage
29. Crankshaft seal
30. Crankcase half
31. Speed control lever

Whenever power head is disassembled, it is recommended that all gasket surfaces, and mating surfaces without gaskets, be carefully checked for nicks and burrs and warped surfaces which might interfere with a tight seal. The cylinder head, head end of cylinder block, and some mating surfaces of manifolds and crankcase may be checked, and lapped if necessary, to provide a smooth surface. Do not remove any more metal than is necessary.

Make certain that all mating surfaces are clean and then coated with a non-hardening type sealer, such as Loctite "Fit-All", before installing crankcase cover. Coat all screws with a non-hardening type sealer and install in case cover. Screws around main bearings (5/16 inch) should be torqued to 155-165 inch-pounds torque. Apply a coating of light grease between the lips of a new lower main seal (23) and install seal on crankshaft with spring loaded lip toward outside of crankcase. Drive seal into bore until fully seated then stake engine case in two places with a center punch. Punch marks should be 180° apart and about 1/8 inch from mating surfaces of cylinder block and crankcase cover. Marks should be placed 1/16 inch from seal bore and should force material a minimum of 0.005 inch out over seal backing.

Oversize or undersize parts are not available.

PISTON, PINS, RINGS AND CYLINDERS. Piston rings are installed with beveled edge toward dome (top) of piston. Pistons should be heated before attempting to remove or reinstall piston pins. If pistons are to be reused, they must be reinstalled in the original position. Apply a light coating of SAE 30 motor oil to pistons and rings. Install pistons with long sloping side of dome toward exhaust port side of cylinder.

Oversize pistons and rings are not available.

CONNECTING RODS, BEARINGS AND CRANKSHAFT. Before detaching connecting rods from crankshaft, make certain that rod and rod cap are properly marked for correct assembly to each other and in the cylinder. The loose needle bearings at crankpin end of connecting rod should be kept with each assembly and not intermixed if they are to be reused.

The cast aluminum connecting rods have two steel bearing liners and 24 loose rollers each. Use light grease to hold rollers in position on reassembly. Make certain the correlation marks on the rod and the rod cap are aligned and torque rod cap bolts to 85-95 inch-pounds torque.

Upper crankshaft main bearing is not available as a spare part. Crankshaft and bearing may be returned to manufacturer in exchange for a rebuilt assembly. Center crankshaft main bearing consists of liner (18—Fig. SK2-12) which forms outer race and 26 loose needle rollers (19). To assemble center main bearing, place one half of liner in cylinder block with a light coating of grease and install 12 rollers. Install crankshaft, remaining 14 rollers and other half of bearing liner. Position lower main bearing on crankshaft 1/16-3/16 inch from top of bearing bore in cylinder block (A—Fig. SK2-12). Lower main seal (23) is installed after assembling crankcase cover (30) to cylinder block.

MANUAL STARTER

Refer to Fig. SK2-14 for exploded view of recoil starter assembly common to all models.

To disassemble, remove motor top cowl and flywheel. Remove screw (12—Fig. SK2-14) and install rewind key (Tool #2985) in top of spring arbor (7) where screw (12) was installed. Tighten rewind key and then apply a slight amount of counter-clockwise force so that pinion pin (8) may be removed. Use caution as rewind spring (6) is now free to unwind and will spin the arbor (7) and the rewind key. Slowly allow rewind key to turn and unwind the recoil spring. Pinion, arbor and spring may be lifted free of starter at this time.

Starter rope may be removed after removing upper bracket (9) and starter spool (4). Wind rope in spool counter-clockwise as viewed from top of spool.

Rewind spring should be greased before reinstallation. Assemble arbor

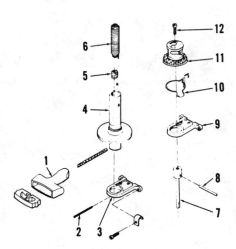

Fig. SK2-14—View of recoil starter components.

1. Pull handle
2. Spring pin
3. Lower bracket
4. Start spool and shaft
5. Spring retainer
6. Rewind spring
7. Spring arbor
8. Pinion pin
9. Upper bracket
10. Pinion spring
11. Starter pinion gear
12. Screw

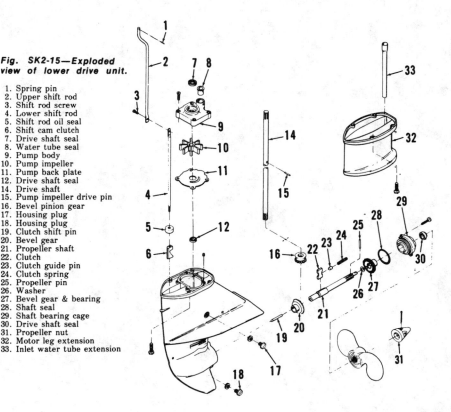

Fig. SK2-15—Exploded view of lower drive unit.

1. Spring pin
2. Upper shift rod
3. Shift rod screw
4. Lower shift rod
5. Shift rod oil seal
6. Shift cam clutch
7. Drive shaft seal
8. Water tube seal
9. Pump body
10. Pump impeller
11. Pump back plate
12. Drive shaft seal
13. Drive shaft
14. Drive shaft
15. Pump impeller drive pin
16. Bevel pinion gear
17. Housing plug
18. Housing plug
19. Clutch shift pin
20. Bevel gear
21. Propeller shaft
22. Clutch
23. Clutch guide pin
24. Clutch spring
25. Propeller pin
26. Washer
27. Bevel gear & bearing
28. Shaft seal
29. Shaft bearing cage
30. Drive shaft seal
31. Propeller nut
32. Motor leg extension
33. Inlet water tube extension

(7), spring (6) and spring retainer (5) and install in spool. Grease inside of pinion gear (11) and install on top of arbor. Use rewind key to turn arbor and rewind spring 3½-4 turns counterclockwise as viewed from the top. Align holes in spool, arbor and slot in pinion gear and partially install pin (8). Remove rewind key while holding end of pin and then complete installation of pin. Install screw (12) in top of starter.

LOWER UNIT

PROPELLER AND THRUST PIN. A 5/32 x 1-3/16 inch thrust pin is used in all motors. Standard propeller on 6 hp motors is a 7 inch diameter, 4¾ inch pitch aluminum unit. Standard propeller on 8 hp motors is a 7½ inch diameter, 6¼ inch pitch aluminum unit. Propellers on all models are two bladed and have right hand (clockwise) rotation.

R&R AND OVERHAUL. Refer to Fig. SK2-15. Remove fill and vent plugs from lower unit and drain all lubricant. Remove four screws that secure lower unit to motor leg. Remove gear shift rod screw (A—Fig. SK2-10) and separate lower unit from motor leg. Remove screws securing water pump body (9—Fig. SK2-15). Remove pump body and drive shaft. Remove propeller and thrust pin. Remove any burrs or rust from exposed end of propeller shaft. Remove two screws holding bearing cage (29) to gear housing. Install two 10-24 x 1½ screws in threaded holes on inside of bearing cage and attach a suitable puller to remove bearing cage.

Shaft seal (30) is not renewable. Propeller shaft (21) may be pulled from unit after removal of bearing cage (29). Remove pinion gear (16) and then forward bevel gear (20) after removing propeller shaft. Shift pin (19) is installed in propeller shaft with round end out (forward). Shift cam (6) may be removed by pulling lower shift rod (4) up and removing seal (5) with shift cam.

Assemble by reversing disassembly procedure. Lower shift rod seal (5) should have outside coated with a non-hardening sealer, such as Loctite "Fit-All", before installation. Install bevel gear (20) and pinion gear (16). Pinion gear is secured with drive shaft (14). Install propeller shaft, thrust washer (if used) and rear bevel gear (27). Propeller shaft seal (30) is installed with spring loaded lip toward propeller. Backlash and mesh position are not adjustable.

SEA KING 7.5 HP (1979-1982)

Year Produced	7.5 hp
1979	52179
1980	52179A
1981	52179B
1982	52179C

CONDENSED SERVICE DATA

TUNE-UP

Hp/rpm	7.5/4750
Bore–Inches	2.0
Stroke–Inches	1.584
Number of Cylinders	2
Displacement–Cu. In.	10.0
Compression at Cranking Speed (Average, with recoil starter)	115-130 psi
Spark Plug:	
Champion	L86
Electrode gap	0.030 in.
Magneto:	
Breaker point gap	Breakerless
Fuel:Oil Ratio	50:1

TIGHTENING TORQUES
(All Values in Inch-Pounds)

Connecting Rod	75-85
Cylinder Head	130
Flywheel Nut	204
Main Bearing Bolts	70
Spark Plug	120-180
Standard Screws:	
6-32	9
10-24	30
10-32	35
12-24	45
1/4-20	70
5/16-18	160
3/8-16	270

LUBRICATION

The power head is lubricated by oil mixed with the fuel. One-sixth (1/6) pint of two-stroke engine oil should be mixed with each gallon of gasoline. Manufacturer recommends use of no-lead automotive gasoline although regular or premium grade gasoline may be used if octane rating is 85 or higher. Gasoline and oil should be thoroughly mixed.

The lower unit gears and bearings are lubricated by oil contained in the gearcase. A good quality gear lube should be used in gearcase. The gearcase should be drained and refilled every 100 hours or once each year, and fluid maintained at the level of the upper (vent) plug hole.

FUEL SYSTEM

CARBURETOR. All models are equipped with the single barrel float type carburetor shown in Fig. SK7-1. Initial idle mixture screw (5) setting is one turn open. Refer to following table for recommended main jet sizes:

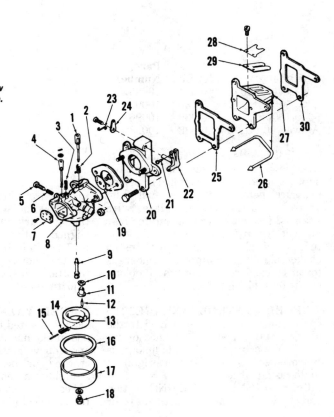

Fig. SK7-1 — Exploded view of carburetor and reed valve.

1. Throttle shaft
2. Spring
3. Spring
4. Choke shaft
5. Idle mixture screw
6. Spring
7. Choke plate
8. Carb body
9. Nozzle
10. Washer
11. Valve seat
12. Fuel inlet valve
13. Float
14. Spring
15. Float pin
16. Gasket
17. Float bowl
18. Drain plug
19. Throttle plate
20. Intake manifold
21. Screw
22. Cam follower
23. Throttle link
24. Throttle lever
25. Gasket
26. Seal
27. Reed valve body
28. Reed petals
29. Reed stop
30. Gasket

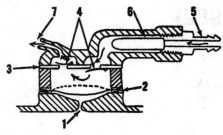

Fig. SK7-2 — Schematic view of diaphragm type fuel pump. Check valves are of the reed type.

1. Pressure port
2. Diaphragm
3. Reed plate
4. Check valves
5. Inlet fitting
6. Filter
7. Outlet

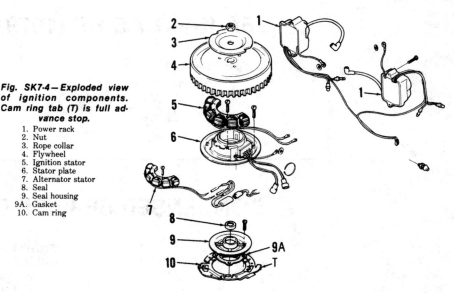

Fig. SK7-4 — Exploded view of ignition components. Cam ring tab (T) is full advance stop.

1. Power rack
2. Nut
3. Rope collar
4. Flywheel
5. Ignition stator
6. Stator plate
7. Alternator stator
8. Seal
9. Seal housing
9A. Gasket
10. Cam ring

Fig. SK7-3 — Exploded view of fuel pump.

1. Pump housing
2. Gasket
3. Pump valve (2 used)
4. Plate
5. Diaphragm & gaskets
6. Fuel lines

Fig. SK7-5 — Wiring diagram for models equipped with Magnapower ignition.

B. Black
R. Red
O. Orange
G. Green
Y. Yellow
W. White
BL. Blue

Altitude	Jet Size	Part Number
Sea Level-3000 ft.	0.041	10089
3000-5000 ft.	0.040	10097
5000-7000 ft.	0.039	10096
Above 7000 ft.	0.038	10093

Adjust float level so float is parallel to float bowl gasket surface. Be sure float support spring (14) is installed so spring pressure helps float close fuel inlet valve. Install throttle plate with stamped letter towards carburetor rear and with throttle plate hole on idle mixture screw side of carburetor. Install choke plate so stamped number is towards carburetor front and oblong slot is on fuel inlet side.

SPEED CONTROL LINKAGE. The speed control lever is connected to the ignition stator plate to advance or retard ignition timing. Throttle linkage is synchronized to open throttle as ignition timing is advanced.

Refer to IGNITION TIMING section and check full advance adjustment prior to synchronizing throttle and ignition timing as follows: Turn throttle grip so timing mark on stator plate cam is aligned with cam follower (22 – Fig. SK7-1) within 1/32 inch. Turn screw (21) so cam follower just contacts cam. Turn throttle grip several times and recheck adjustment.

REED VALVES. A vee type reed block is located between the carburetor and intake manifold. Inspect reed petals and renew petals if they are broken, cracked or bent. Never attempt to straighten a bent reed. Seating surface of reed block should be smooth and flat. Be sure seal (26 – Fig. SK7-1) is seated

in groove around reed block before installing reed block.

FUEL PUMP. A diaphragm type fuel pump is mounted on the side of the cylinder block and ported to the upper crankcase. Pressure and vacuum pulsations from the crankcase are directed through port (1 – Fig. SK7-2) to the rear of diaphragm (2). When the power head piston moves upward in its cylinder, vacuum in the crankcase draws the diaphragm inward and fuel enters the pump through filter (6) and the inlet reed valve (4) in reed plate (3). When the piston moves down in cylinder, crankcase pressure increases and the fuel

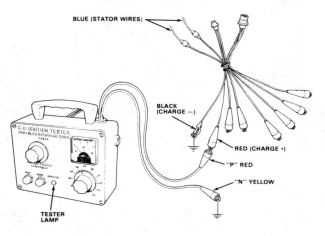

BLUE (STATOR WIRES)

BLACK (CHARGE —)

RED (CHARGE +)

"P" RED

"N" YELLOW

TESTER LAMP

Fig. SK7-6 — Tester connections for checking voltage output of charge coils.

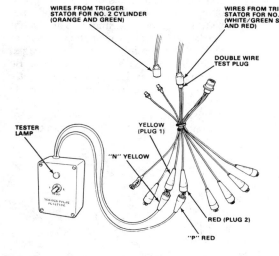

WIRES FROM TRIGGER STATOR FOR NO. 2 CYLINDER (ORANGE AND GREEN)

WIRES FROM TRIGGER STATOR FOR NO. 1 CYLINDER (WHITE/GREEN STRIPE AND RED)

DOUBLE WIRE TEST PLUG

TESTER LAMP

YELLOW (PLUG 1)

"N" YELLOW

RED (PLUG 2)

"P" RED

Fig. SK7-7 — Tester connections for checking operation of trigger coil.

number 22 tester and refer to following troubleshooting procedure:

Check and make sure ignition malfunction is not due to spark plug failure. If spark is absent at both cylinders, check condition of charge coil as follows:

Separate the blue wire connections between CD coil module and stator and attach single wire plug adapters to each wire plug from stator as shown in Fig. SK7-6. Attach red (P) lead from T8953 tester to red sleeved adapter wire marked "Charge +". Attach yellow (N) lead of tester and black sleeved adapter wire marked "Charge —" to engine ground. Turn tester switch to position 45 and crank engine. If tester lamp does not light, high voltage windings of charge coil are defective and stator should be renewed. If lamp lights, charge coil operation is satisfactory and trigger coil circuits for each cylinder must be checked. Remove tester and plug adapter set, then reconnect blue wire plugs.

Separate the two-wire connection with red and white/green colored wires between CD coil module for number one cylinder and trigger coil and attach double wire plug adapter to wire plug from trigger coil as shown in Fig. SK7-7. Attach red (P) lead from tester number 22 to red sleeved adapter wire marked "Plug 2" and yellow (N) lead of tester to yellow sleeved adapter wire marked "Plug 1." Place switch of tester in number 1 position and crank engine. Trigger coil operation is satisfactory if tester lamp lights. Renew trigger housing if tester lamp does not light.

To check operation of number two cylinder trigger coil, repeat test procedure for number one cylinder trigger coil but attach double wire plug adapter to the two wire connection with orange and green colored wires.

If both stator and trigger coils are in satisfactory condition, then renewal of one of both CD coil modules may be required.

pump diaphragm is forced outward into fuel chamber, and fuel passes through the outlet reed valve into carburetor line (7).

Defective or questionable parts should be renewed. Pump valves (3 – Fig. SK7-3) should seat lightly and squarely on reed plate (4). Diaphragm should be renewed if air leaks or cracks are found, or if deterioration is evident.

IGNITION SYSTEM

These models are equipped with a breakerless, capacitor discharge ignition system. Refer to Fig. SK7-4 for an exploded view of ignition components and Fig. SK7-5 for wiring diagram.

Full throttle and full advance should occur simultaneously. Full advance is limited by stator plate tab (T – Fig. SK7-4) contacting a boss on the cylinder block. To check ignition timing, shift unit to forward gear and turn throttle grip to full throttle. Stator plate tab (T) should just contact cylinder block boss at full throttle. If not, adjust length of link (14 – Fig. SK7-8). Recheck adjustment.

Tapered bore of flywheel and crankshaft end must be clean, dry and smooth before installing flywheel. Renew a

chipped or cracked flywheel. Flywheel and crankshaft tapers may be cleaned by using fine valve grinding compound. Apply grinding compound to tapers and rotate flywheel back and forth approximately one quarter turn. Do not spin flywheel on crankshaft. Clean flywheel and crankshaft tapers thoroughly. Tighten flywheel nut to 45 ft.-lbs. torque.

If ignition malfunction occurs, use tool T8953, plug adapter set T11201 and

Fig. SK7-8 — Exploded view of handle assembly.
1. Bushing
2. Gears
3. Wave washer
4. Steering arm
5. Bumper
6. Mount
7. Shaft
8. Bushings
9. Gear
10. Gear
11. Bushings
12. Towershaft
13. Link end
14. Link
15. Link end
16. Ball joint
17. Seal
18. Steering handle
19. Bushing
20. Shaft
21. Throttle stop
22. Sleeve
23. Grip

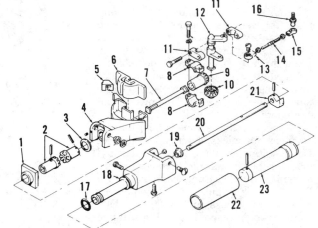

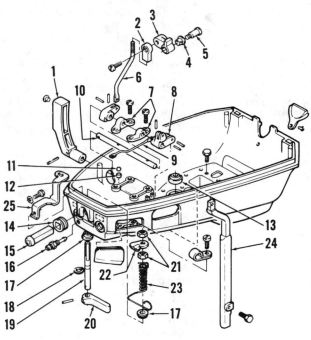

Fig. SK7-9 — View of lower motor cover and associated parts.

1. Gear shift handle
2. Rod end
3. Shift interlock lever
4. Bushing
5. Screw
6. Interlock shift rod
7. Shaft brackets
8. Shift lever
9. Interlock link
10. Shift shaft
11. Detent ball
12. Detent pad
13. Drive shaft seal
14. Grommet
15. Choke knob
16. Fuel fitting
17. Nyliner bushing
18. Snap ring
19. Latch rod
20. Latch handle
21. Nut
22. Latch cam
23. Spring
24. Upper shift rod
25. Choke link

COOLING SYSTEM

WATER PUMP. All motors are equipped with a rubber impeller type water pump. When cooling system problems are encountered, check water inlet for plugging or partial stoppage. Remove lower unit gearcase and inspect water passages, water pump and sealing surfaces. To remove water pump, refer to LOWER UNIT section. Install water pump housing retaining stud in front hole and short (⅞ inch) capscrew in rear hole.

POWER HEAD

R&R AND OVERHAUL. To remove power head, remove upper cover and disconnect linkage, fuel lines and wires which interfere with power head removal. Remove starter and carburetor. Unscrew eight screws on underside of motor leg flange and remove power head.

Remove flywheel and ignition components. Remove cylinder head. Drive out crankcase locating pins (7 – Fig. SK7-10), unscrew crankcase screws and separate crankcase from cylinder block. Crankshaft and piston assemblies are now accessible. Refer to appropriate paragraph for overhaul of power head components.

Inspect crankcase and cylinder mating surfaces for nicks, burrs or warpage. Use a suitable sealant on crankcase and cylinder block mating surfaces before assembly. Install crankshaft seals with lips towards crankcase. Assembly is reverse of disassembly. Drive shaft splines should be coated with a suitable anti-corrosion substance.

PISTONS, PINS, RINGS AND CYLINDERS. Piston rings should be installed with the beveled inner edge toward closed end of piston.

Piston pin (13 – Fig. SK7-11) should be installed with closed end of pin (C) towards piston ring locating pins (P). Heat piston to approximately 200 degrees F. to aid in installation of piston pin. Sharp edge of snap rings (12) should be out.

Assemble piston to rod with piston ring locating pins (P) up and rod cap alignment marks (M) toward the right.

CONNECTING ROD, CRANK-SHAFT AND BEARINGS. Assemble connecting rod on piston pin as outlined in previous section. Install rod and piston assembly in cylinder so alignment marks on rod are towards port side of engine. Connecting rod rides on a caged roller bearing with sixteen rollers. Be sure marks on rod and cap are correctly aligned. Tighten rod screws to 75-85 in.-lbs.

Upper crankshaft main bearing is not available separate from crankshaft.

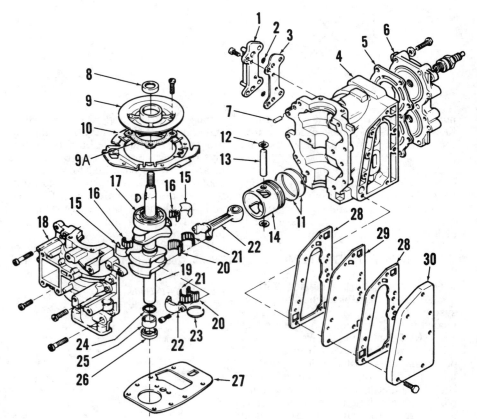

Fig. SK7-10 — Exploded view of power head.

1. Cylinder drain cover	9. Seal housing	16. Main bearing rollers (26 per set)
2. Screen	9A. Gasket	17. Ball bearing
3. Gasket	10. Cam ring	18. Crankcase
4. Cylinder block	11. Piston rings	19. Crankshaft
5. Head gasket	12. Pin retainer rings	20. Rod bearing rollers (16 per set)
6. Cylinder head	13. Piston pin	21. Bearing cage
7. Dowel pins (2)	14. Piston	22. Rod & Cap
8. Oil seal	15. Main bearing liner	23. Center seal ring
		24. Crankshaft inner seal
		25. Bearing
		26. Seal
		27. Gasket
		28. Gasket
		29. Exhaust plate
		30. Exhaust cover

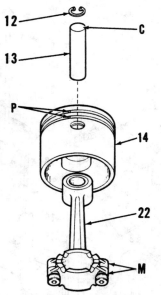

Fig. SK7-11—Assemble piston pin (13), piston (14) and rod (22) as shown. Refer to text.

Fig. SK7-12— Exploded view of manual starter.
1. Rope handle
2. Pin
3. Lower bracket
4. Spool
5. Spring retainer
6. Rewind spring
7. Spring drive
8. Pin
9. Upper bracket
10. Pinion spring
11. Starter gear
12. Screw
13. Starter interlock
14. Bushing
15. Interlock shaft
16. Cotter pin
17. Spring washer
18. Bushing

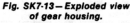

Center crankshaft main bearings consists of liner (15–Fig. SK7-10) which forms outer race for 26 loose bearing rollers (20). A roller bearing is used on crankshaft lower end. Be sure to install center seal ring (23) around crankshaft prior to assembly.

MANUAL STARTER

All models are equipped with the manual starter shown Fig. SK7-12. Starter gear (11) engages the flywheel ring gear. Starter interlock (13) prevents starter gear rotation except when unit is in neutral.

To disassemble starter, remove starter interlock (13) and screw (12).

NOTE: Screw (12) locks pin (8) in place in starter shaft.

Thread the special "T" handle tool T2985 in threaded hole from which screw (12) was removed. Tighten the tool securely, then carefully push pin (8) out of pinion and starter spool. Allow tool and spring drive (7) to turn until rewind spring (6) is unwound; then use the tool to withdraw rewind spring (6) and drive (7) from center of starter spool (4). Guide post (7A) and spring retainer (5) can be lifted out after rewind spring is removed.

Rewind spring, gear (11) or associated parts can be renewed at this time. To renew starter rope, remove brackets securing spool.

Thread the new rope through hole in end of spool and install rope retainer ap-

proximately ½ inch from end. Wind rope on spool and install spool, brackets and rope guide. Install rewind spring assembly and gear (11). Use "T" handle tool to wind rewind spring counterclockwise eight turns. Align holes in gear (11), spool (4) and spring drive (7) and insert pin (8). Remove tool and install screw (12). Rewind spring cavity of starter spool should be filled with lubriplate or a similar grease.

LOWER UNIT

R&R AND OVERHAUL. To remove lower unit, remove screw securing upper shift rod to lower shift rod (1–Fig. SK7-13). Remove four screws retaining motor leg extension to motor leg and separate extension and gear housing from motor leg. Remove exhaust outlet (17). Unscrew screws (S) and separate extension (2) from gear housing.

Fig. SK7-13— Exploded view of gear housing.
1. Shift rod
2. Motor leg extension
3. Water seal
4. Seal
5. Spacer
6. Stud
7. Seal
8. Water pump housing
9. Seal
10. Impeller pin
11. Impeller
12. Pump plate
13. Seal
14. Shift cam
15. Seal
16. Gear housing
17. Exhaust outlet
18. Drive shaft
19. Pinion gear
20. Forward gear & bearing
21. Shift pin
22. Propeller shaft
23. Shift dog
24. Pin
25. Spring
26. Reverse gear
27. "O" ring
28. Bearing & cage
29. "O" ring
30. Retainer
31. Seal
32. Thrust pin
33. Thrust washer

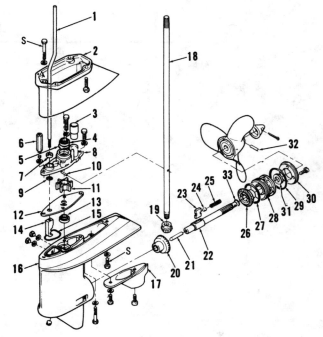

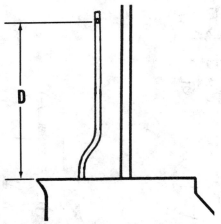

Fig. SK7-14 — Distance (D) should be 5.76-6.56 inch. See text.

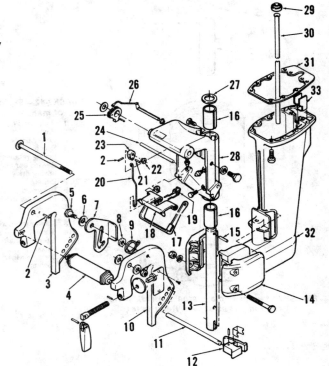

Fig. SK7-15 — Exploded view of motor leg.

1. Bracket bolt
2. Pin
3. Starboard bracket
4. Handle
5. Screw
6. Wave washer
7. Tilt lock
8. Spacer
9. Spring
10. Port bracket
11. Lock bar
12. Handle
13. Kingpin
14. Shock mount covers
15. Pin
16. Bushing
17. Bracket
18. Reverse lock
19. Reverse lock spring
20. Reverse lock link
21. Pin
22. Bushing
23. Reverse lock lever
24. Pin
25. Reverse lock arm
26. Reverse lock shaft
27. Washer
28. Swivel bracket
29. Seal
30. Water tube
31. Gasket
32. Motor leg
33. Idle relief baffle

To disassemble gear housing, unscrew lower shift rod (1). Remove screws and stud (6) retaining water pump and remove water pump (8), impeller pin (10) and plate (12). Withdraw drive shaft (18) and remove seal (13). Remove propeller and screws securing bearing cage retainer (30). Using tool number T8948-1 or suitable equivalent, pull bearing cage retainer (30) out of gear housing. Use same tool to withdraw bearing cage (28) from housing. Remove reverse gear (26) and thrust washer (33). Withdraw propeller shaft (22) and remove pinion gear (19) and forward gear (20). Depress pin (24) against spring (25) to release shift dog (23). Remove shift cam (14).

To reassemble lower unit, reverse disassembly procedure while noting following points: Install seal (31) in bearing carrier (28) with spring side of seal towards "O" ring groove. Seal must be flush with or 0.030 inch below face of bearing carrier. Shift cam (14) must be in forward (up) position when installing bearing carrier (28) or carrier will not seat properly. Install seal (13) with spring side towards water pump. Install shift rod seal (7) with raised bead facing out. Seal must be flush with or 0.010 inch below chamfer in seal bore. Install spacer (5) in water pump housing. Install seal (4) with spring side up and bottom seal against spacer (5).

Adjust height of lower shift rod (1) by screwing rod in or out of shift cam (14). Turn shift rod so bend in rod is towards drive shaft as shown in Fig. SK7-14. With gear housing shifted to neutral, distance from motor leg extension surface to lower edge of shift rod screw hole should be 5.76-6.56 inch. See Fig. SK7-14.

SEA KING 9.6, 9.9, 10 AND 15 HP

Year Produced	9.6 hp	9.9 hp	10 hp	15 hp
1970	27009	....	....	....
1971	27009	....	....	....
1972	27209	....	....	....
1973	27409	....	....	....
1974	....	....	52010	52015
1975	....	....	52110	52115
1976	....	....	52110	52115
1977	....	....	52110	52115
1978	....	....	....	52115
1979	....	....	....	52119
1980	....	52299	....	52119A
1981	....	52299A	....	52118
				52119B
1982	....	52299B	....	52118A
				52119B*
				52119C
1983	....	52299	....	52118
1984	....	52299	....	52118

*After serial number 24200.

CONDENSED SERVICE DATA

TUNE-UP

Hp/rpm	9.6/4750 9.9/4750 10/4750	15/5100
Bore – Inches	2-3/16	2¼
Stroke – Inches	1¾	1-15/16
Number of Cylinders	2	2
Displacement – Cu. In.	13.15	15.41
Spark Plug:		
Champion	L4J	L4J
Electrode Gap – Inches	0.030	0.030
Magneto:		
Point Gap – Inches	See Text	See Text
Timing	See Text	See Text
Carburetor:		
Make	See Text	See Text
Fuel:Oil Ratio:		
Normal.	50:1	50:1
Break-In & Severe Service	25:1	25:1

*SIZES – CLEARANCES	**9.9 hp**	**15 hp**
Piston Rings:		
End Gap	0.006-0.016 in.	0.004-0.014 in.
Piston to Cylinder Clearance	0.0025-0.0040 in.	0.0025-0.0050 in.
Piston Pin:		
Diameter	0.50000-0.50015 in.	0.50000-0.50015 in.
Clearance (Rod)	Needle Bearing	Needle Bearing
Clearance (Piston)	0.00035 in. tight to 0.00010 in. loose	0.00035 in. tight to 0.00010 in. loose
Crankshaft Journal Diameters:		
Upper Main	0.9849-0.9853 in.	0.9849-0.9853 in.
Center Main.	0.8000-0.8005 in.	0.8000-0.8005 in.
Lower Main	0.7495-0.7500 in.	0.7495-0.7500 in.
Crankpin	0.7496-0.7501 in.	0.7496-0.7501 in.

*Size and clearance specifications are for 1979 and later models. Earlier model specifications are not available.

TIGHTENING TORQUES (All Values in Inch-Pounds)	9.6, 9.9 & 10 hp	15 hp
Armature Screw	300	300
Cylinder Head (1969-1978)	125	125
Cylinder Head (1979-1982)	130	130
Flywheel Nut	600	600
Spark Plug	120-180	120-180
Connecting Rod Screws (1969-1978)	120	120
Connecting Rod Screws (1979-1982)	80	80
Standard Screws:		
No. 10-24	30	30
No. 10-32	35	35
No. 12-24	45	45
1/4-20	70	70
5/16-18	160	160
3/8-16	270	270

LUBRICATION

The power head is lubricated by oil mixed with fuel. For normal service after break-in, mix 1/6 pint of two-stroke engine oil with each gallon of gasoline. The recommended ratio is 1/3 pint of oil per gallon of gasoline for severe service and break in. Manufacturer recommends using no-lead automotive gasoline although regular or premium gasoline may be used if octane rating is 85 or higher. Gasoline and oil should be thoroughly mixed.

The lower unit gears and bearings are lubricated by oil contained in the gearcase. Only a non-corrosive, leaded, EP90, outboard gear oil should be used. The gearcase should be drained and refilled every 30 hours. Maintain fluid at level of upper (vent) plug.

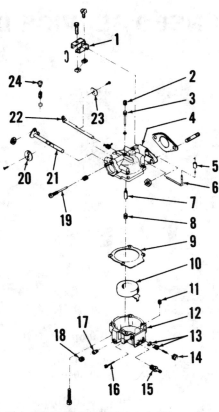

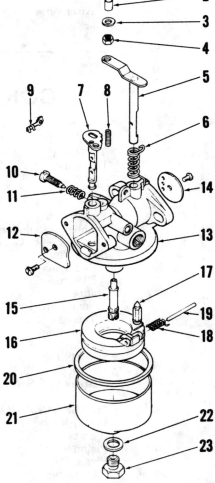

Fig. SK3-1 — Exploded view of CO type carburetor.

1. Adjusting arm
2. By-pass tube
3. Throttle cam roller
4. Throttle cam follower
5. Idle screw
6. Throttle body
7. Main nozzle
8. Float
9. Gasket
10. Float bowl
11. Retaining screw
12. Main jet
13. Inlet valve
14. Choke friction ball
15. Choke assembly
16. Choke shaft
17. Throttle shaft
18. Throttle plate
19. Throttle return spring
20. Welch plug

Fig. SK3-2 — Exploded view of MD type carburetor.

1. Adjusting arm
2. Idle plug screw
3. Idle tube
4. Throttle body
5. Throttle cam roller
6. Throttle cam follower
7. Nozzle
8. Main nozzle plug
9. Gasket
10. Float
11. Set screw
12. Float bowl
13. Inlet valve
14. Plug
15. Fuel connector
16. Float pin
17. Main jet
18. Plug screw
19. Idle screw
20. Choke plate
21. Choke shaft
22. Throttle shaft
23. Throttle plate
24. Choke detent plug

Fig. SK3-3 — Exploded view of LMB type carburetor.

1. Adjusting screw
2. Throttle roller
3. Washer
4. Nut
5. Throttle shaft
6. Spring
7. Choke shaft
8. Spring
9. Clip
10. Idle mixture screw
11. Spring
12. Choke plate
13. Throttle body
14. Throttle plate
15. Main nozzle
16. Float
17. Inlet valve
18. Spring
19. Float shaft
20. Gasket
21. Float bowl
22. Gasket
23. Main jet assembly

To fill gearcase, have motor in upright position and fill through lower hole, in side of gearcase until fluid reaches level of upper vent plug hole. Reinstall and tighten both plugs securely, using new gaskets if necessary, to assure a water tight seal.

FUEL SYSTEM

CARBURETOR. 9.9 hp motors prior to 1971 were equipped with Tillotson MD type carburetors shown in Fig. SK3-2, 1982 9.9 and 15 hp motors are equipped with Walbro LMB type carburetor shown in Fig. SK3-3. All other models are equipped with Tillotson CO type carburetor shown in Fig. SK3-1. Refer to appropriate following paragraph and exploded view for service.

Tillotson CO and MD carburetors are equipped with a pilot air screw which controls the idle mixture by determining the amount of air in the idle mixture. Initial setting of pilot air screw (Fig. SK3-4) is one turn open. Turn pilot air screw clockwise to richen idle mixture or counterclockwise to lean idle mixture.

Fig. SK3-4—Initial setting for pilot air screw is one turn out from a lightly seated position.

Fig. SK3-5—Location of idle mixture screw on LMB type carburetor.

Walbro LMB carburetors are equipped with an idle mixture screw that controls amount of idle mixture entering carburetor bore. Initial setting of idle mixture screw (Fig. SK3-5) is one turn open. Turn idle mixture screw clockwise to lean idle mixture. Final carburetor adjustment should be made with engine at normal operating temperature and running in forward gear. Standard main jet size should be correct for operation below 3000 foot altitude. Refer to the following table for standard main jet sizes:

Carburetor Model No.	Main Jet Size
MD 144A	0.059
CO-3A	0.051
CO-5A	0.055
CO-7A	0.047
CO-7B, CO-7C	0.045
CO-8A	0.053
CO-10A, CO-10B	0.055
CO-11A	0.045
LMB-228	0.046
LMB-229	0.0625

End of float (10 – Fig. SK3-2) opposite pivot in MD type carburetors should be 1/64-inch below surface of float bowl (12) with float bowl inverted. Correct float height of CO type carburetor is 13/32-inch. Height is checked by inverting carburetor body and measuring distance (A – Fig. SK3-6) from bottom of float to gasket surface of carburetor body. Adjustment is accomplished by bending tang on float. Correct float height of LMB type carburetor is ⅛-inch. Height is checked by inverting carburetor body and measuring distance (A – Fig. SK3-7) from top of float to gasket surface of carburetor body. Adjust by bending tang on float.

SPEED CONTROL LINKAGE. The speed control lever (or grip) is attached to the magneto stator plate and moving the speed control will advance or retard

Fig. SK3-6—Float level (A) of CO type carburetor should be 13/32-inch.

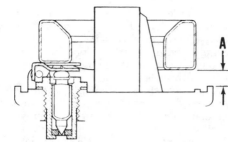

Fig. SK3-7—Float level (A) of LMB type carburetor should be ⅛-inch.

the ignition timing. Throttle linkage is synchronized to open the carburetor throttle as magneto timing is advanced. It is very important that the speed control linkage be properly synchronized for best performance. Adjust linkage with motor not running.

On models prior to 1982 adjustment is as follows: Adjust idle stop screw (Fig. SK3-8) until pick-up mark (Fig. SK3-9) is to left side of throttle roller (3 – Fig. SK3-1 or 5 – Fig. SK3-2) as viewed from front side of motor. Turn speed control handle slowly toward the fast position until throttle roller touches cam plate on magneto. Continue turning handle until throttle shaft just begins to move. Pick-up mark on throttle cam should be no more than 1/32-inch from throttle roller at this time. Turn adjusting screw (Fig. SK3-9) to change point of throttle opening.

On 1982 models, turn speed control handle slowly toward the fast position

Fig. SK3-8—Idle stop screw should be adjusted with engine warm to obtain an idle speed of 700 rpm.

and observe pick-up mark (Fig. SK3-10) on throttle cam. Throttle shaft should just begin to move when pick-up mark is centered with throttle roller. Turn adjusting screw, if required, to change point of throttle opening.

Adjust idle speed with engine running at normal operating temperature and motor in forward gear. Idle stop screw location on models prior to 1982 is shown in Fig. SK3-8 and on 1982 models is shown in Fig. SK3-11. Turn idle stop screw to obtain idle speed of 700 rpm.

REED VALVES. The inlet reed valves are located on reed plate between inlet manifold and crankcase. Reed petals should seat very lightly against

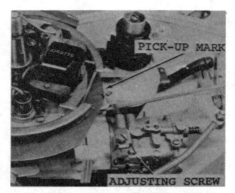

Fig. SK3-9 — Pick-up mark on throttle cam should be no more than 1/32-inch from roller when throttle shaft begins to move.

Fig. SK3-10 — On motors equipped with LMB type carburetor, pick-up mark on throttle cam should be in the center of throttle roller when throttle shaft begins to move.

Fig. SK3-11 — Location of idle stop screw on 1982 models.

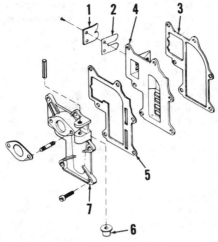

Fig. SK3-12 — Exploded view of intake manifold and reed valve assembly.

1. Reed stop
2. Reed
3. Gasket
4. Reed plate
5. Gasket
6. Start rope pulley
7. Manifold

Fig. SK3-13 — Diagram of fuel pump used on models with Magnapower ignition.

1. Pump cover
2. Gasket
3. Pump valve (2 used)
4. Plate
5. Diaphragm & gaskets
6. Fuel lines
7. Bracket

reed plate throughout their entire length, with the least possible tension. Check seating visually. End of reed stops (1 – Fig. SK3-12) should be 17/64-inch from reed plate (4).

Renew reeds if petals are broken, cracked, warped, rusted or bent. Never attempt to bend a reed petal or to straighten a damaged reed. Never install a bent or damaged reed. Seating surface of reed plate should be smooth and flat. When installing reeds or reed stop, make sure that petals are centered over the inlet holes in reed plate, and that the reed stops are centered over reed petals.

FUEL PUMP. A diaphragm type fuel pump is mounted on the side of power head cylinder block and ported to the upper crankcase.

Defective or questionable parts should be renewed. Pump valves should seat

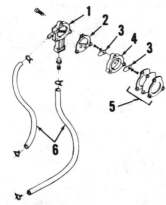

Fig. SK3-14 — Exploded view of diaphragm fuel pump used on early models.

1. Pump cover
2. Gasket
3. Pump valve (2 used)
4. Plate
5. Diaphragm & gaskets
6. Fuel lines

very lightly and squarely on reed plate. Diaphragm should be renewed if air leaks or cracks are found, or if deterioration is evident.

IGNITION

Breakerless Ignition Models

These models are equipped with a breakerless, capacitor discharge ignition system. Note wiring diagram in SK3-15. Ignition timing is not adjustable. Tapered bore in flywheel and crankshaft end must be clean, dry and smooth before installing flywheel. Tighten flywheel nut to 50 ft.-lbs. If ignition malfunction occurs, use tool T8953 with load coil and number 22 tester from tool T8996 and refer to following troubleshooting procedure:

Check and make sure ignition malfunction is not due to spark plug or ignition coil failure. If spark is absent at both cylinders, check condition of charge coil as follows: Locate blue wire from charge coils in stator, disconnect blue wire at engine terminal block and connect red (P) lead from tester number 22 to blue wire as shown in Fig. SK3-16. Locate yellow lead from charge coil, disconnect yellow lead from engine terminal block and connect lead to ground terminal of terminal block. Connect yellow (N) lead of number 22 tester to ground terminal of terminal block. Place tester switch in number 2 position and crank engine. If tester lamp does not light, low voltage windings of charge coil are defective and stator should be renewed. If lamp lights, continue charge coil test by reconnecting blue charge coil lead to engine terminal block and connecting yellow charge coil lead to red (P) lead of T8953 tester as shown in Fig. SK3-17. Connect yellow (N) lead of T8953 tester

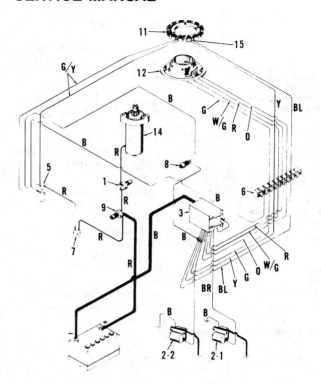

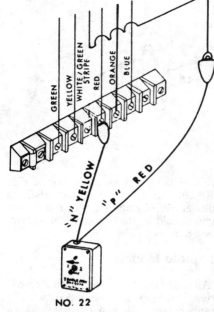

Fig. SK3-15 — Wiring diagram of models equipped with Magnapower ignition.

1. Interlock switch
2-1. No. 1 cyl. ign. coil
2-2. No. 2 cyl. ign. coil
3. CD module
5. Rectifier
6. Engine terminal block
7. Circuit breaker
8. Stop switch
9. Starter switch
11. Stator
12. Trigger housing
14. Starter
15. Charge coils
B. Black
BL. Blue
BR. Brown
G. Green
O. Orange
R. Red
W. White
Y. Yellow

Fig. SK3-18 — Tester connections for checking operation of No. 1 cylinder trigger coil.

to ground terminal of engine terminal block. Turn tester switch to position 10 and crank engine. If tester lamp does not light, high voltage windings of charge coil are defective and stator should be renewed. If lamp lights, charge coil operation is satisfactory and trigger coil and CD module circuits for each cylinder must be checked.

To check number 1 cylinder trigger coil, disconnect white/green lead from trigger housing at engine terminal block

and connect white/green lead to red (P) lead of number 22 tester. Connect yellow (N) lead of number 22 tester to red wire terminal of engine terminal block as shown in Fig. SK3-18. Place switch of tester in number 1 position and crank engine. Trigger coil operation is satisfactory if tester lamp lights. Renew trigger housing if tester lamp does not light. Reconnect white/green lead to engine terminal block. To check operation of number 2 cylinder trigger coil, repeat above test procedure for number 1 cylinder trigger coil but connect red (P) lead of tester to orange wire from trigger housing and yellow (N) lead of

tester to green wire terminal as shown in Fig. SK3-19.

To check CD module performance for each cylinder, connect yellow (N) lead from tester T8953 to ground terminal of engine terminal block. Disconnect white (number 2 cylinder) or brown (number 1 cylinder) primary lead from ignition coil and connect red (P) lead of tester T8953 to primary lead. Connect leads of tester T8996 load coil to engine terminal block ground terminal and primary coil lead of

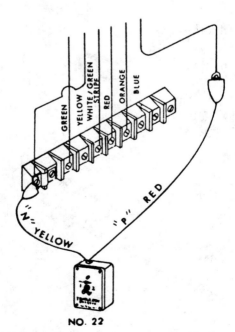

Fig. SK3-16 — Tester connections for checking low voltage output of charge coils.

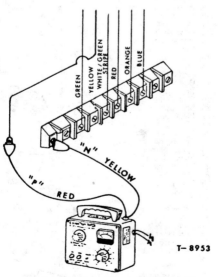

Fig. SK3-17 — Tester connections for checking high voltage output of charge coils.

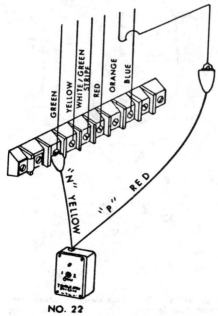

Fig. SK3-19 — Tester connections for checking operation of No. 2 cylinder trigger coil.

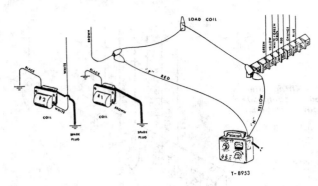

Fig. SK3-20 — View showing tester connections needed to check CD module output for No. 1 cylinder.

cylinder being tested as shown in Fig. SK3-20. Turn T8953 tester dial to number 50. Crank engine and tester lamp should light. Renew CD module if lamp does not light.

Magneto Models

All models not equipped with a breakerless ignition are equipped with a breaker point, flywheel magneto ignition system. Breaker point gap should be 0.020 inch for each set of points, and can be adjusted after flywheel is removed. Both sets of points must be adjusted exactly alike.

NOTE: High point of breaker cam coincides with location of flywheel key. Align key with the contact point rub block when adjusting points.

The tapered bore in flywheel and end of crankshaft must be clean, dry and smooth before installing flywheel. The flywheel nut for manual starting motors should be torqued to 600 in.-lbs. torque. Armature screw for electric starting motors should be tightened to 300 in.-lbs. torque. Spark plug electrode gap should be 0.030 inch.

COOLING SYSTEM

WATER PUMP. All motors are equipped with a rubber impeller type water pump. When cooling system problems are encountered, first check the water inlet for plugging or partial stoppage, then if not corrected, remove the lower unit gearcase and check the condition of water pump, water passages and sealing surfaces.

Water pump may be disassembled in the following manner: Place motor on a suitable stand. Place motor in forward gear and remove four screws that secure upper gear housing gearcase to motor leg. Pull away from motor leg and remove screw securing lower end of upper shift rod. Pull gearcase free of motor leg. Remove screws that secure pump body to gearcase and slide pump off drive shaft.

Top plate (8 – Fig. SK3-22) is used only in pump assemblies that are secured with three screws.

Install impeller with slot in mesh with drive pin in drive shaft.

Water tube seal may be removed by depressing tabs on seal through holes in pump body and pulling on seal. Make certain that tabs are fully seated in holes when installing new seal. Drive shaft seals should be installed with spring loaded lip toward top.

Before reassembling, check shift rod adjustment. Center of screw hole in lower shift rod (2) must be 3/16-inch plus or minus 3/64-inch below surface of gear housing (or motor leg extension, if used), with unit in neutral. Refer to Fig. SK3-23. Lubricate drive shaft splines and seal lips on all models with a good grade of silicone grease. Assemble upper and lower shift rods as shown in Fig. SK3-24 to prevent leakage and damage to shift rod seal. Make certain that water tube is seated in seal and install

Fig. SK3-21 — Exploded view of breakerless, solid-state ignition components. Refer to Fig. SK3-15 for identification except for: 4. Starter support; 10. Flywheel; 13. Throttle cam.

Fig. SK3-22 — Exploded view of lower drive unit.

1. Upper shift rod
2. Lower shift rod
3. Shift rod seal
4. Bolt
5. Drive shaft seal
6. & 6A. Water tube seal
7. & 7A. Water pump housing
8. Top plate
9. & 9A. Rubber impeller
10. & 10A. Bottom plate
11. Drive shaft seal
12. Drive shaft
13. Water pump drive pin
14. Upper gear housing
15. Vent plug
16. Stud
16A. Stud nut
17. Gasket
18. Ball bearing
19. Shift cam spring
20. Shift cam
21. Pinion gear
22. Lower gear housing
23. Drain plug
24. Bearing race
25. Thrust bearing
26. Forward bevel gear
27. Thrust washer
28. Shift pin
29. Shift pin spring
30. Clutch
31. Pin
32. Propeller shaft
33. Thrust pin
34. Thrust washer
35. Rear bevel gear
36. "O" ring
37. Bearing & cage
38. Seal
39. Propeller
40. Propeller nut
41. Motor leg extension
42. Water tube extension

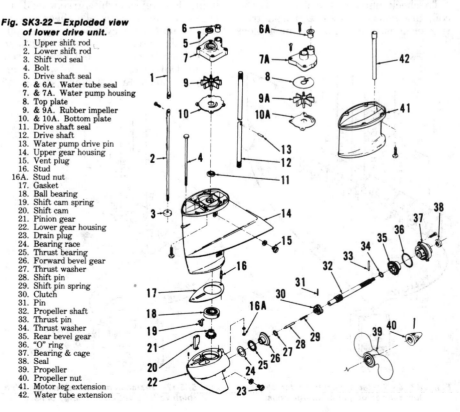

screws that secure to gearcase motor leg.

POWER HEAD

R&R AND DISASSEMBLE. To overhaul the power head, clamp motor to a stand or support and remove engine cover (shroud), intake silencer and control panel. Remove flywheel, starter, magneto and carburetor. Remove all interfering wiring and linkage, and as many screws as possible retaining inlet manifold, exhaust covers, transfer port covers, cylinder head, etc., before detaching power head from lower unit.

Remove the screws which secure power head assembly to lower unit, and lift off the power head.

Crankshaft and pistons can be removed after removing retainer (28 – Fig. SK3-25) then detaching crankcase front half. Exhaust cover (39 and 41), cylinder head (4), transfer port cover (7) and

crankcase drain plate (8) should be removed for cleaning and inspection if major repairs are to be performed. Pry lugs are provided adjacent to the retaining dowels, for removing the crankcase front half.

Engine components are now accessible for removal and overhaul as outlined in the appropriate following paragraphs. Assemble as outlined in the ASSEMBLY paragraph.

ASSEMBLY. When reassembling, make sure all joint and gasket surfaces are clean, free from nicks and burrs and hardened cement or carbon. The crankcase and inlet manifold must be completely sealed against both vacuum and pressure. Exhaust manifold and cylinder head must be sealed against water leakage and pressure. Mating surfaces of exhaust area between power head and motor leg must form a tight seal.

Whenever power head is disassembled, it is recommended that all gasket surfaces and mating surfaces without gaskets, be carefully checked for nicks, burrs and warped surfaces which might interfere with a tight seal. The cylinder head, head end of cylinder block, and some mating surfaces of manifolds and crankcase may be checked, and lapped if necessary, to provide a smooth surface. Do not remove any more metal than is necessary.

Mating surfaces of crankcase may be checked on the lapping block, and high

spots or nicks removed, but the surface must not be lowered. If extreme care is used, a slightly damaged crankcase may be salvaged in this manner. In case of doubt, renew the crankcase assembly.

A heavy, non-fibrous grease should be used to hold loose needle bearings in position during assembly. All friction surfaces should be lubricated with new engine oil. Check frequently as power head is being assembled, for binding or locking. If encountered, remove the cause before proceeding with the assembly.

Fig. SK3-26 — Tightening sequence for cylinder head screws.

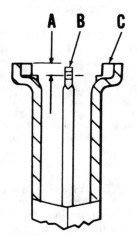

Fig. SK3-23 — Center of screw hole in lower shift rod (B) must be 3/16-inch (A) below surface of upper gear case or motor leg extension (C) if installed.

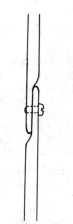

Fig. SK3-24 — Upper and lower shift rods (1 & 2 – Fig. SK3-22) must be joined with flat sides together.

Fig. SK3-25 — Exploded view of power head assembly.

1. Interlock lever
2. Rod end
3. Interlock rod
4. Cylinder head
5. Gasket
6. Gasket
7. Transfer port cover
8. Cylinder drain cover
9. Gasket
10. Screen
11. Cylinder block
12. Locating pin
13. Piston ring
14. Piston
15. Pin retaining clip
16. Piston pin
17. Connecting rod
18. Main bearing liner
19. Main bearing rollers (26 per set)
20. Rod bearing liner
21. Rod bearing rollers (26 per set)
22. Crankshaft
23. Rod cap
24. Lower main bearing
25. Lower seal
26. Stator ring
27. Gasket
28. Retainer
29. Upper seal
30. Crankcase half
31. Control lever pivot shaft
32. Throttle link
33. Control lever bearing
34. Control lever
35. Idle speed screw
36. Control link
37. Gasket
38. Gasket
39. Inner exhaust cover
40. Gasket
41. Outer exhaust cover

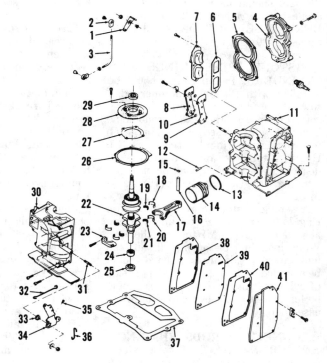

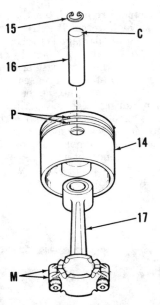

Fig. SK3-27—Assemble piston pin (16), piston (14) and rod (17) as shown. Refer to text.

make certain that rod and cap are properly marked for correct assembly to each other and in the correct cylinder. The loose needle bearings at crankpin end of connecting rod should be kept with each assembly and not intermixed if reused.

The connecting rods contain 26 loose needle bearing rollers at crankpin end. When reassembling connecting rods make certain that marks (Fig. SK3-27) on rod and rod cap are aligned.

Crankshaft upper main bearing is part of bearing cage (28—Fig. SK3-25). Center main bearing consists of 26 loose needle bearing rollers (19), which are contained in a split outer race (18). Lower main bearing (24) is a caged roller.

Oversize and undersize parts are not available. When assembling, follow the procedures outlined in the ASSEMBLY paragraph. Tightening torques are listed in the CONDENSED SERVICE DATA table.

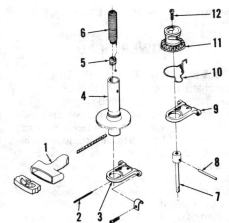

Fig. SK3-28—Exploded view of recoil starter used.

1. Pull handle	7. Spring arbor
2. Spring pin	8. Pinion pin
3. Lower bracket	9. Upper bracket
4. Spool	10. Pinion spring
5. Spring retainer	11. Starter pinion gear
6. Rewind spring	12. Screw

Gasket and sealing surfaces should be lightly and carefully coated with a non-hardening gasket cement. Make sure entire surface is coated, but avoid letting excess cement squeeze out into crankcase, bearings, or other passages. Refer to Fig. SK3-26 for cylinder head tightening sequence. When installing crankcase screws, tighten those next to the main bearings and dowels first. Crankshaft seals (29 and 25—Fig. SK3-25) should be renewed each time crankshaft is removed. Refer to CONDENSED SERVICE DATA table for tightening torques.

PISTONS, PINS, RINGS AND CYLINDERS. Piston rings should be installed with the beveled inner edge toward closed end of piston.

Piston pin (16—Fig. SK3-27) should be installed with closed end of pin (C) towards piston ring locating pins (P). Heat piston to approximately 200 degrees F. to aid in installation of piston pin. Sharp edge of snap rings (15) should be out.

Assemble piston to rod with piston ring locating pins (P) up and rod cap alignment marks (M) toward the left. When installing piston in cylinder, the long tapering side of piston head should be installed toward the exhaust port side of cylinder. All friction surfaces should be lubricated with new engine oil when assembling.

CONNECTING RODS, BEARINGS, AND CRANKSHAFT. Before detaching connecting rods from crankshaft,

MANUAL STARTER

Fig. SK3-28 is an exploded view of the recoil starter assembly common to all manual start models. Unit used on electric start models is of similar construction. Starter pinion (11) engages starter ring gear on flywheel.

To disassemble the starter, first remove the engine cover and flywheel, then remove screw (12) in top of starter shaft.

NOTE: This screw locks pin (8) in place.

Thread the rewind key (Tool #TR2985) in threaded hole from which screw (12) was removed. Tighten the tool until it bottoms; then turn tool handle slightly counterclockwise to relieve recoil spring tension and push out pin (8). Allow the tool and drive arbor (7) to turn clockwise to unwind the recoil spring (6). Pull up on tool to remove the recoil spring and components. Pull rope and rewind spool (4) may be removed after removing top bracket (9). Wind new rope in spool counterclockwise as viewed from the top.

Rewind spring should be greased before installation. Assemble arbor (7), spring (6) and spring retainer (5) and install in spool. Grease inside of pinion gear (11) and install on top of arbor. Use rewind key to turn arbor and rewind spring 3½-4 turns counterclockwise as viewed from the top. Align holes in spool, arbor and slot in pinion gear and partially install pin (8). Remove rewind key while holding end of pin and then complete installation of pin. Install screw (12) in top of starter.

LOWER UNIT

PROPELLER AND THRUST PIN. Both two and three blade propellers are used and are equipped with a thrust pin to prevent damage. Various pitch propellers are available and should be selected to provide full throttle operation within the recommended limits of 4250-5250 rpm on 9.6, 9.9 and 10 hp motors or 4600-5600 rpm on 15 hp motors. Propellers other than those designed for the motor should not be used.

R&R AND OVERHAUL. Refer to Fig. SK3-22. Attach motor to a suitable stand. Shift motor into forward gear and remove four screws that secure lower unit to motor leg. Pull lower unit away from motor leg far enough to remove screw holding shift rods (1 & 2) together. Pull lower unit free of motor leg. Disassemble water pump (7) and remove drive shaft (12).

Propeller shaft bearing cage (37) is removed after removing propeller and installing two 10-24 x 1½ screws in tapped holes in cage to attach puller. Drain lubricant from gearcase and remove two screws that secure propeller shaft bearing cage to gearcase. Install puller and remove bearing cage. Seal (38) is removed by driving it out with a punch from inside the bearing cage.

NOTE: Two types of replacement seals are available. Seals cased in metal are installed with spring loaded lip toward gear housing. Rubber cased seals are installed with spring loaded lip toward propeller.

Internal gears and shift mechanism may be serviced after removing lower gearcase (22). Disassemble gearcase in the following manner: Remove shift rod (2) by unscrewing it from shift cam (20). Use caution to prevent threads on shift rod from damaging seal (3) when sliding rod out of housing. Remove drive shaft bearing cage as previously described and remove nut (16A). Remove bolt (4) and separate upper and lower gearcase sections.

Shift rod seal (3) may be removed by screwing a 5/16-inch lag screw into seal from the top and then using a ¼-inch diameter rod to drive lag screw and seal out from the bottom.

When reassembling, make certain that thrust bearing (25) and thrust bearing race (24) are installed as shown in Fig. SK3-22. Rounded end of shift pin (28) must be toward shift cam (20). Clutch (30) must be installed so that engagement dogs with chamfered edges are toward propeller.

Refer to WATER PUMP section for proper adjustment of shift rod (2) on reassembly. Backlash and mesh position of gears is not adjustable. Bottom of bolt head (4) should be coated with a heavy non-hardening sealer and torqued to 125 inch-pounds.

SEA KING 20 HP

Year Produced	Model
1969	28920, 28921
1970	27020
1971	27020
1972	27220
1973	27420

CONDENSED SERVICE DATA

TUNE-UP

Hp/rpm	20/5000
Bore – Inches	2-7/16
Stroke – Inches	2-9/64
Number of Cylinders	2
Displacement – Cu. In.	19.96
Compression at Cranking Speed (Average)	115-125 psi

Spark Plug:

Champion	L4J
Electrode Gap	0.030

Magneto:

Point Gap	0.020
Timing	See Text

Carburetor:

Make	Tillotson
Model	MD
Fuel:Oil Ratio	**50:1

**Fuel:Oil ratio 24:1 for severe service.

SIZES – CLEARANCES

Piston Rings:

End Gap	0.003-0.008 in.
Side Clearance	0.0025-0.0045 in.
Piston to Cylinder Clearance	0.002-0.0035 in.

Piston Pin:

Diameter	0.56250-0.56265 in.
Clearance (Rod)	Roller Bearing
Clearance (Piston)	0.0001-0.0006 in.

Crankshaft Journal Diameters:

Upper & Lower Main	0.8120-0.8124 in.
Center Main	0.9295-0.9298 in.
Crankpin	0.8101-0.8104 in.
Crankshaft End Play	0.003-0.006 in.
Rod Side Clearance	0.015-0.025 in.

TIGHTENING TORQUES
(All Values in Inch-Pounds)

Armature Screw	300
Cylinder Head	120
Flywheel Nut	540
Spark Plug	120-180

Standard Screws:

No. 10-24	30
No. 10-32	35
No. 12-24	45
1/4-20	70
5/16-18	160
3/8-16	270

LUBRICATION

The power head is lubricated by oil mixed with fuel. For normal service after break-in, mix 1/6 pint of two-stroke engine oil with each gallon of gasoline. For severe service and during break-in, the recommended ratio is 1/3 pint of oil per gallon of gasoline. Manufacturer recommends no-lead automotive gasoline although regular or premium gasoline may be used if octane rating is 85 or higher. Gasoline and oil should be thoroughly mixed.

The lower unit gears and bearings are lubricated by oil contained in the gearcase. Only a non-corrosive, leaded, EP90, outboard gear oil should be used. The gearcase should be drained and refilled every 100 hours or once each year, and fluid maintained at the level of the upper (vent) plug hole.

To fill the gearcase, have the motor in upright position and fill through the lower plug hole in the side of gearcase until fluid reaches level of upper vent plug hole. Reinstall and tighten both plugs securely, using new gaskets if necessary, to assure a water tight seal.

FUEL SYSTEM

CARBURETOR. Tillotson, type MD carburetors are used. Refer to Fig. SK4-1. Normal initial setting is one turn open from the closed position for idle mixture needle (1). Carburetor must be readjusted under load, after motor is warm, for best low speed performance. The standard main jet (0.069 inch in 1971 and earlier models and 0.067 inch in 1972 and later models) should be correct below 5000 ft. altitude.

To adjust the float, remove and invert the fuel bowl assembly (13). With bowl inverted and inlet needle valve closed, the lowest point of float at free end should project approximately 1/64-inch below gasket surface of bowl. Adjust by bending the vertical valve fork on float. Float must be removed to renew the inlet needle assembly (18). When installing float, make sure that slot in float lever engages groove in needle.

SPEED CONTROL LINKAGE. The speed control lever or grip is connected to the magneto stator plate to advance or retard the ignition timing. Throttle linkage is synchronized to open the throttle as magneto timing is advanced. It is very important that the throttle linkage be properly synchronized for best performance.

To synchronize the linkage, refer to Fig. SK4-2. With the engine not running, loosen the clamping screw (S) in throttle control bellcrank. Move the speed control grip or lever until the scribe mark on throttle cam (2) is aligned with center of cam follower (1). Move cam follower until it contacts cam at the scribe mark, then tighten screw (S). As speed control grip or lever is moved further to the "Fast" position, the throttle valve should start to open.

The idle speed stop screw (IS – Fig. SK4-3) should be adjusted to provide 800-1000 rpm in neutral. Throttle friction is adjusted by turning the inside nut (N) and adjustment is maintained by tightening locknut (L).

REED VALVES. The inlet reed valves are located on reed plate between inlet manifold and crankcase. The reed petals should seat very lightly against the reed plate throughout their entire length, with the least possible tension.

Check seating visually. Reed stop setting should be 17/64-inch when measured as shown in Fig. SK4-4.

Renew reeds if petals are broken, cracked, warped, rusted or bent. Never attempt to bend a reed petal or to straighten a damaged reed. Never install a bent or damaged reed. Seating surface of reed plate should be smooth and flat. When installing reeds or reed stop, make sure that petals are centered over the inlet holes in reed plate, and that the reed stops are centered over reed petals.

FUEL PUMP. A diaphragm type fuel pump is mounted on the side of power head cylinder block and ported to the upper crankcase. Pressure and vacuum pulsations from the crankcase are directed through the port (1 – Fig. SK4-4A) to the rear of diaphragm (2). When the power head piston moves upward in its cylinder, vacuum in the crankcase draws the diaphragm inward and fuel enters the pump through filter (6) and the inlet reed valve (4) in reed plate (3). As power head piston moves downward, pressure forces the diaphragm outward into fuel chamber, and fuel passes through the outlet reed valve into carburetor line (7).

Defective or questionable parts should be renewed. Reed valves (23 – Fig. SK4-7) should seat lightly and squarely

Fig. SK4-2 — View of speed control linkage. Cam (2) rotates with magneto armature plate and should begin to move follower (1) when scribed line on cam is aligned with center of cam follower (2).

Fig. SK4-4 — Reed stops should be 17/64 inch from seating surface of reed plate.

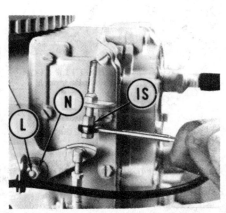

Fig. SK4-3 — Idle speed is adjusted at stop screw (IS) and throttle friction is adjusted by turning the inside nut (N). Tighten the outside lock nut (L) to maintain the correct throttle friction.

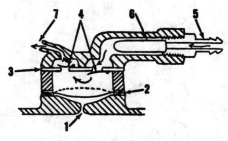

Fig. SK4-4A — Schematic view of diaphragm type fuel pump. Check valves are of the reed type.

1. Pressure port
2. Diaphragm
3. Reed plate
4. Check valves
5. Inlet fitting
6. Filter
7. Outlet

Fig. SK4-1 — Exploded view typical of Tillotson MD carburetor and cam follower linkage (23 through 28).

1. Idle mixture screw	15. Fuel inlet fitting
2. Spring	16. Main (high speed) jet
3. Choke detent	17. Plug
4. Idle tube	18. Fuel inlet needle seat
5. Choke valve	19. Plug
6. Choke shaft	20. Throttle plate
7. Body	21. Spring
8. Main nozzle	22. Throttle shaft
9. Plug	23. Link
10. Float	24. Lever
11. Float shaft	25. Cam follower
12. Gasket	26. Retaining rings
13. Body	27. Roller
14. Gasket	28. Bracket

on reed plate (24). Diaphragm should be renewed if air leaks or cracks are found, or if deterioration is evident.

IGNITION

Breaker point gap should be 0.020 inch for each set of points, and can be adjusted after the flywheel is removed. Both sets of points must be adjusted exactly alike.

NOTE: High point of breaker cam coincides with location of flywheel key. Align key with the contact point rub block when adjusting points.

The tapered bore in flywheel and end of crankshaft must be clean, dry and smooth before installing flywheel. The flywheel nut for manual starting motors should be torqued to 540 inch-pounds torque.

COOLING SYSTEM

WATER PUMP. All motors are equipped with a rubber impeller type water pump. When cooling system problems are encountered, first check the water inlet for plugging or partial stoppage, then if not corrected, remove the lower unit gearcase and check the condition of water pump, water passages and sealing surfaces.

To detach the upper gearcase from the exhaust housing, proceed as follows: Remove covers (1–Fig. SK4-5) and shift rod coupling (2–Fig. SK4-6). Remove the four nuts (5–Fig. SK4-5) and screws (6), then separate the gearcase from the exhaust housing. The water pump can be removed after removing screws (32 & 33–Fig. SK4-12). Drive shaft seal (6) should be installed with spring loaded lip toward the top.

When reassembling pumps with three screws holding pump body, notice that screw (32) is 1⅛ inches long and the two front screws (33) are one inch long.

Screws are of equal length on pumps secured by four screws. Drive shaft spline seal (28) should be renewed if hard or cracked. Lubricate water tube seal (34) and splines on upper end of drive shaft (27). Carefully slide the housing together making certain that water tube enters seal (34). Install the four retaining screws and nuts. Nuts should be tightened to 256-275 inch-pounds torque. Install shift rod coupling (2 – Fig. SK4-6) with right hand thread toward top. Shift to forward gear and mark shift rod (4) at (F) where it enters exhaust housing. Shift to neutral and mark the rod at the exhaust housing; then shift to reverse gear and again, mark the rod. Adjust the coupling so that marks for forward (F), neutral (N) and reverse (R) gears are equally spaced, then tighten the locknut.

POWER HEAD

R&R AND DISASSEMBLE. To overhaul the power head, clamp the

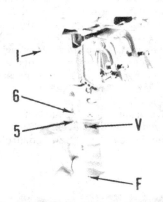

Fig. SK4-5 — View of 20 hp motor showing two of the screws (6) and nuts (5) that attach upper gearcase housing to motor leg (exhaust housing).

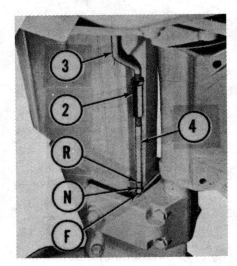

Fig. SK4-6 — Shift rod coupling (2) should be adjusted to provide equal travel in both directions (F & R) from neutral position (N).

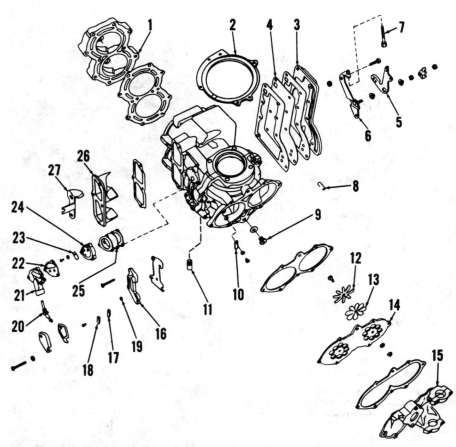

Fig. SK4-7 — Exploded view of cylinder and crankcase assembly. Refer to Fig. SK4-8 for crankshaft and associated parts including the top main bearing cage (end cap).

1. Cylinder head	9. Plug	16. Reed plate (cylinder
2. Magneto stator ring	10. Reed (puddle drain)	drain)
3. Exhaust cover	11. Water outlet	17. Reed petal
4. Exhaust plate	12. Reed stop	18. Reed stop
5. Magneto control lever	13. Reed petals	19. Screen
6. Bracket	14. Reed plate	20. Fuel pump inlet
7. Idle speed stop screw	15. Inlet manifold and	and filter
8. Crankcase dowels	starter bracket	21. Pump cover

22. Gasket
23. Fuel pump valve
(2 used)
24. Plate
25. Diaphragm
26. Transfer port cover
27. Idle stop switch cam

motor on a stand or support and remove the engine cover (shroud), intake silencer and control panel. Remove flywheel, starter, magneto and carburetor. Remove all interfering wiring and linkage, and as many screws as possible retaining inlet manifold, exhaust covers, transfer port covers, cylinder head, etc., before detaching power head from lower unit.

Remove the screws which secure the power head assembly to lower unit, and lift off the power head assembly.

Crankshaft and pistons can be removed after removing upper bearing cage (38 – Fig. SK4-8) then detaching crankcase front half. Exhaust covers (3 & 4 – Fig. SK4-7), cylinder head (1), transfer port cover (26) and crankcase drain plate (16) should be removed for cleaning and inspection if major repairs are to be performed. Pry lugs are provided adjacent to the retaining dowels, for removing the crankcase front half.

Engine components are now accessible for removal and overhaul as outlined in the appropriate following paragraphs. Assemble as outlined in the ASSEMBLY paragraph.

ASSEMBLY. When reassembling, make sure all joint and gasket surfaces are clean, free from nicks and burrs and hardened cement or carbon. The crankcase and inlet manifold must be completely sealed against both vacuum and pressure. Exhaust manifold and cylinder head must be sealed against water leakage and pressure. Mating surfaces of exhaust areas between power head and motor leg must form a tight seal.

Whenever power head is disassembled, it is recommended that all gasket surfaces be carefully checked for nicks and burrs and warped surfaces which might interfere with a tight seal. The cylinder head, head end of cylinder block, and some mating surfaces of manifolds and crankcase may be checked, and lapped if necessary, to provide a smooth surface. Do not remove any more metal than is necessary.

Mating surfaces of crankcase may be checked on the lapping block, and high spots or nicks removed, but the surface must not be lowered. If extreme ..re is used, a slightly damaged crankcase may be salvaged in this manner. In case of doubt, renew the crankcase assembly.

A heavy, non-fibrous grease should be used to hold loose needle bearings in position during assembly. All friction surfaces should be lubricated with new engine oil. Check frequently as power head is being assembled, for binding or locking. If encountered, remove the cause before proceeding with the assembly.

Gasket and sealing surfaces should be lightly and carefully coated with a non-hardening gasket cement. Make sure entire surface is coated, but avoid letting excess cement squeeze out into crankcase, bearings, or other passages. When installing crankcase screws, tighten those next to the main bearings and dowels first. Crankshaft seals (28 & 37 – Fig. SK4-8) should be renewed each time crankshaft is removed. Tighten cylinder head screws in sequence by starting at screws between cylinders and progressing in both directions. Refer to CONDENSED SERVICE DATA table for clearances and tightening torques.

Before attaching power head to lower unit, renew the drive shaft spline seal (28 – Fig. SK4-12) and coat the splines with grease.

PISTONS, PINS, RINGS AND CYLINDERS. Piston is fitted with three rings which should be installed with the beveled inner edge toward closed end of piston. Recommended ring end gap is 0.003-0.008 inch, with a maximum wear limit of 0.015 inch. Piston rings should have 0.0025-0.0045 inch side clearance in piston grooves, with a wear limit of 0.0055 inch.

Piston skirt clearance should be 0.002-0.0035 inch when measured at widest part of skirt at right angles to piston pin. Renew the piston if skirt clearance exceeds 0.005 inch. The maximum recommended out-of-round or taper for the cylinder is 0.002 inch.

The full floating piston pin should have 0.0001-0.0006 inch clearance in piston. Renew the parts if clearance exceeds 0.0016 inch in piston bosses.

When installing piston in cylinder, the long, tapering side of baffle on piston head should be installed toward the exhaust port side of cylinder. All friction

surfaces should be lubricated with new engine oil when assembling.

CONNECTING RODS, BEARINGS AND CRANKSHAFT. Before detaching connecting rods from crankshaft, make certain that rod and cap are properly marked for correct assembly to each other and in the correct cylinder. The loose needle bearings at crankpin end of connecting rod should be kept with each assembly and not intermixed if reused.

The forged steel connecting rods contain 30 loose needle bearing rollers at crankpin end. Install small rollers with flat ends butted together. Parting faces of rod and cap are not machined, but are fractured, to provide positive location. When installing cap, make sure the correlation marks are aligned; then shift cap back and forth slightly while tightening, until fractured sections are in perfect mesh. When properly installed, the parting line is practically invisible. Rod side play on crankpin should be 0.015-0.025 inch, with a wear limit of 0.040 inch.

The crankshaft upper main bearing (29 – Fig. SK4-8) is a part of bearing cap (38). The center main bearing consists of 34 loose needle rollers (34), which are contained in a split outer race (33). The bearing race is separated by fracturing, and is held together by the retaining ring (35). When assembling, work the two halves of bearing race back and forth slightly until the fracture lines mesh, then install the retaining ring. The lower main bearing is of the caged roller type.

Recommended crankshaft end play is 0.003-0.006 inch, with a wear limit of 0.011 inch. Oversize and undersize parts are not available.

When assembling, follow the procedures outlined in the ASSEMBLY paragraph. Tightening torques are listed in the CONDENSED SERVICE DATA table.

Fig. SK4-8 – Exploded view of crankshaft and connecting rod assembly. Early models are not equipped with retainer (45) and seal (46).

28. Upper crankshaft seal
29. Top bearing
30. Connecting rod needles (30)
31A. Gasket
32. Crankshaft
33. Center main bearing outer race
34. Center main bearing needles (34)
35. Snap ring
36. Lower bearing
37. Lower seal
38. Bearing cage
39. Connecting rod
40. Piston
41. Piston pin
42. Retaining ring
43. Piston rings
45. Seal retainer
46. Seal

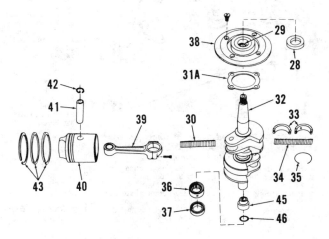

MANUAL STARTER

Fig. SK4-9 shows an exploded view of the recoil starter assembly. Starter pinion (3) engages a starter ring gear on the flywheel.

To disassemble the starter, first remove the engine cover, then remove screw (6–Fig. SK4-9) in top of starter shaft.

NOTE: This screw locks pin (2) in place.

Thread the special "T" handle tool (T3139) in threaded hole from which screw (6) was removed. Tighten the tool until it bottoms; then turn tool handle slightly counterclockwise to relieve recoil spring tension, and push out pin (2). Allow the tool and spring drive (7) to turn clockwise to unwind the recoil spring (8). Pull up on tool to remove the recoil spring and components. Guide post (9) and spring retainer (10) can be lifted out after recoil spring is removed.

Recoil spring, pinion (3) or associated parts can be renewed at this time. To renew the starter rope, remove clamps (12) then remove the spool. Thread rope through hole in lower end of spool (5) and install the rope retainer approximately ½-inch from end of rope. Pull tight, then fully wind the rope onto spool and reinstall assembly. Make certain that retainer extension (11) is in place. With recoil spring and drive pinion (3) installed, use the "T" handle tool to wind the recoil spring counterclockwise eight turns. Align the holes in pinion (3), spool (5) and spring drive (7); then install the drive pin (2). Remove the tool and secure the pin with the locking screw (6). Recoil spring cavity should be partially filled with lubriplate or similar grease when reassembling.

If tension of pinion spring (4) is incorrect, the pinion (3) may remain extended and prevent full speed operation.

LOWER UNIT

PROPELLER AND DRIVE PIN. A 3/16 x 1-5/16 inch stainless steel thrust pin is used on all 20 hp motors. The standard propeller is an 8½ inch diameter, 8½ inch pitch, right hand rotating (clockwise), unit.

R&R AND OVERHAUL. Refer to Fig. SK4-6. Loosen the locknut on the shift rod coupling (2) and remove coupling to disconnect the shift rod. Unbolt and remove the drive shaft housing (upper gearcase) from motor leg. Turn shift rod (1–Fig. SK4-12) counterclockwise to clear the water pump housing; then disassemble and remove the water pump assembly.

Remove the propeller and thrust pin. Remove any burrs or rust from exposed end of propeller shaft. Remove snap ring (25), thread two screws in threaded holes of propeller shaft bearing cage (22); and remove the cage, using a puller.

To detach lower gearcase (12) from drive shaft housing (7), unscrew and remove shift rod (1). Housing is secured by a socket head cap screw at the front, and the stud nut INSIDE the case as shown by arrow, Fig. SK4-13.

Propeller shaft, gears, bearings and shift mechanism can be removed after housings are separated. An internal expanding puller and slide hammer may be required to remove the front gear (13–Fig. SK4-12). In some cases, gear may be removed by heating gearcase housing, then jarring open end on a block of wood to dislodge the gear and bearing assembly. When installing front gear and bearing assembly, assemble the bearing cage (22), without "O" ring

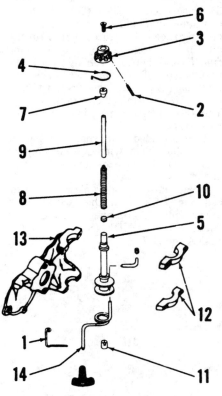

Fig. SK4-9 — Exploded view of recoil starter assembly. Pinion (3) meshes with teeth on magneto flywheel.

1. Rope guide	8. Recoil spring
2. Drive pin	9. Guide post
3. Pinion	10. Retainer
4. Pinion spring	11. Retainer extension
5. Starter spool	12. Bearing caps
6. Lock screw	13. Inlet manifold
7. Spring drive	14. Rope

1. Shift rod
2. Water pump housing
3. Top plate
4. Impeller
5. Back plate
6. Oil seal
7. Drive shaft housing
8. Shift rod seal
9. Seal retainer
10. Drive pinion
11. Shift cam
12. Gearcase housing
13. Forward gear
14. Thrust washer
15. Roll pin
16. Clutch dog
17. Shift plunger
18. Spring
19. Propeller shaft
20. Thrust washer
21. Reverse gear
22. Bearings & cage
23. Seal
24. "O" ring
25. Snap ring
26. Water pump drive pin
27. Drive shaft
28. Spline seal
29. Weed guard
30. Retaining ring
31. Thrust pin
32. Screw
33. Screw
34. Water tube seal

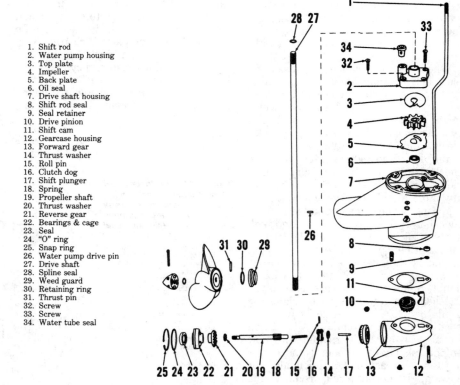

Fig. SK4-12 — Exploded view of lower unit gearcase, drive shaft housing and associated parts. Top plate (3) is not used on models after 1969.

(24) over rear of propeller shaft; install thrust washer (14) and gear assembly (13) on front of shaft; then use the propeller shaft as a piloted driver. Backlash and mesh position of the gears are not adjustable.

Assemble by reversing the disassembly procedure. Propeller shaft seal (23) should be installed with spring loaded lip toward inside. Drive shaft seal (6) should be installed with spring loaded lip toward top. With unit assembled, propeller shaft end play should be

0.003-0.028 inch. Backlash and mesh position are not adjustable. Refer to appropriate preceding paragraphs for water pump service cautions. Paragraph for water pump also includes adjustment of coupling (2 – Fig. SK4-6).

Fig. SK4-13 — Lower unit gearcase with propeller shaft bearing cage removed. Stud nut (arrow) must be removed before gearcase can be detached from driveshaft housing.

SEA KING 25 HP

Year Produced	Model
1974	52025
1975, 1976 & 1977	52125

CONDENSED SERVICE DATA

TUNE-UP

Hp/rpm	25/5000
Bore – Inches	2.8125
Stroke – Inches	2.300
Number of Cylinders	2
Displacement – Cu. In.	28.57
Compression at Cranking Speed (Average)	95-105 psi

Spark Plug:

Champion	L4J
Electrode Gap – Inches	0.030

Magneto:

Point Gap – Inches	†0.020
Timing	See Text

Carburetor:

Make	Tillotson
Model	WB
Fuel:Oil Ratio	**50:1

†Breaker point gap is 0.015 inch for models with battery ignition.

**Fuel:Oil ratio should be 24:1 for break-in period.

SIZES – CLEARANCES

Piston Ring End Gap & Side Clearance	*
Piston to Cylinder Clearance	*

Crankshaft Bearings:

Upper Main Bearing	Caged Needles
Center Main Bearing	Loose Rollers
Number of rollers	30
Lower Main Bearing	Ball
Crankpin	Loose Rollers
Number of rollers	16 (each rod)

*Publication not authorized by manufacturer.

TIGHTENING TORQUES
(All Values in Inch-Pounds)

Cylinder Head . . . . , ...	225
Flywheel Nut	540
Spark Plug	120-180
Connecting Rod Screws	165-175
No. 10-24	30
No. 10-32	35
No. 12-24	45
¼-20	70
5/16-18	160
3/8-16	270

LUBRICATION

The power head is lubricated by oil mixed with the fuel. For normal service after break-in, mix 1/6 pint of two-cycle engine oil with each gallon of gasoline. The recommended ratio is one third (⅓) pint of oil per gallon of gasoline for severe service and during break-in. Manufacturer recommends no-lead automotive gasoline although regular or premium gasoline may be used if octane rating is 85 or higher. Gasoline and oil should be thoroughly mixed.

The lower unit gears and bearings are lubricated by oil contained in the gearcase. Only non-corrosive, leaded, EP90, outboard gear oil should be used. The gearcase should be drained and refilled every 30 hours. Maintain fluid at level of upper (vent) plug.

To fill gearcase, have motor in upright position and fill through lower hole in side of gearcase until fluid reaches level of upper vent plug hole. Reinstall and tighten both plugs securely, using new gaskets if necessary, to assure a water tight seal.

FUEL SYSTEM

CARBURETOR. A Tillotson WB19B carburetor is used on 25 hp motors. Refer to Fig. SK5-1 for an exploded view of the carburetor.

Initial setting of idle mixture screw (10 – Fig. SK5-1) is 1¼ turns out from a lightly seated positon. Final adjustment of carburetor should be made with engine at normal operating temperature and running in forward gear. Standard main jet size is 0.064 inch which should be correct for operation below 1250 ft. altitude.

To check float level, remove float bowl and invert carburetor. Side of float nearest main jet should be parallel with gasket surface of carburetor. Adjust float level by bending float tang.

Install throttle plate (1 – Fig. SK5-1) so that notch is up and chamfer is towards flange end of carburetor.

SPEED CONTROL LINKAGE. Ignition timing and throttle opening on all models must be synchronized so that throttle is opened as timing is advanced.

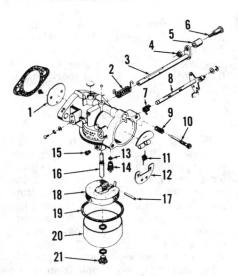

Fig. SK5-1 – Exploded view of typical Tillotson Model WB carburetor.

1. Throttle plate
2. Spring
3. Throttle shaft
4. Nut
5. Roller
6. Eccentric screw
7. Spring
8. Choke shaft
9. Spring
10. Idle mixture screw
11. Spring
12. Choke plate
13. Gasket
14. Fuel inlet valve
15. High speed jet
16. Main nozzle
17. Float pin
18. Float
19. Gasket
20. Float bowl
21. Bowl retaining screw

To synchronize linkage, first check ignition timing to be sure it is set correctly as outlined in the IGNITION TIMING section. Disconnect link (L–Fig. SK5-2) from throttle cam (C) and with throttle closed, turn eccentric screw (S) until roller (R) is exactly centered over mark (M) on throttle cam. Reconnect link (L) to magneto and rotate magneto stator ring until it is against full advance stop. Upper mark (AM) on throttle cam should now be aligned with roller (R). Disconnect link (L) and turn link ends to adjust length of link so that mark (AM) and roller are aligned when stator is at full advance. Turn throttle stop screw in steering handle shaft on models with manual starter so that screw provides a

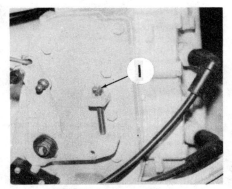

Fig. SK5-3 – View of idle speed screw (I) used on models with electric starter. Idle speed should be 650-750 rpm with unit in forward gear.

positive stop just as stator plate reaches full advance stop.

Idle speed in forward gear should be 550-650 rpm on manual start models. Adjust idle of manual start models by turning idle speed screw on side of steering handle. Idle speed in forward gear should be 650-750 rpm on electric start models. Adjust idle speed of electric start models by turning idle speed screw (I – Fig. SK5-3) adjacent to exhaust port cover.

REED VALVES. All models are equipped with a "V" type reed valve. The reed plate is located between the intake manifold and crankcase. Remove carburetor and intake manifold for access to reed valve.

Renew reeds if petals are broken, cracked, warped or bent. Never attempt to bend a reed petal in an effort to improve performance, nor attempt to straighten a damaged reed. Never install a bent or damaged reed. Seating surface of reed plate should be smooth and flat. Install reeds so that petals are centered over openings. Assembled reeds may stand open a maximum of 0.010 inch at tip end. Reed stop setting

should be 9/32 inch when measured from tip of reed stop to reed plate.

PUDDLE DRAIN VALVE. A puddle drain valve is located in the hose from the bottom of the crankcase cover to the bottom of the transfer port cover. The puddle valve is designed to remove puddled fuel from the crankcase, thus providing smooth operation at all speeds and lessening the possibility of spark plug fouling.

To check operation of puddle valve, disconnect hose ends and blow through each end of hose. Puddle valve should pass air when blowing through crankcase cover and end of hose but not when blowing through transfer port end of hose. Remove puddle valve from hose if it does not operate correctly. Install new puddle valve in hose approximately one inch from end of hose with small hole in puddle valve towards short end of hose. Attach hose to engine with puddle valve end of hose connected to crankcase cover.

FUEL PUMP. All models are equipped with a two-stage diaphragm type fuel pump which is actuated by pressure and vacuum pulsations from the engine crankcases.

NOTE: Either stage of the fuel pump operating independently may permit the motor to run, but not at peak performance.

To remove fuel pump, disconnect fuel hoses to pump and unscrew six cap screws which retain fuel pump body. Check valves are renewable but be sure new check valve is needed before removing old check valve as it will be damaged during removal. Unscrew the two retaining screws to remove center check valve. The two outer check valves must be driven out from below. Refer to Fig. SK5-5 for view of correct check valve installation. Install check valves carefully to prevent damage. Inspect diaphragm and renew diaphragm if cracked, torn or badly distorted.

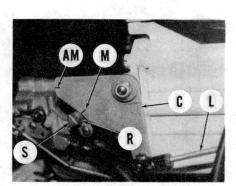

Fig. SK5-2 – View of throttle cam and linkage. Refer to text for adjustment.

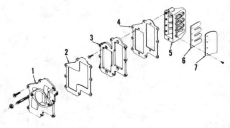

Fig. SK5-4 – Exploded view of reed valve assembly.

1. Inlet manifold
2. Gasket
3. Adaptor plate
4. Gasket
5. Reed body
6. Reed petals
7. Reed stop

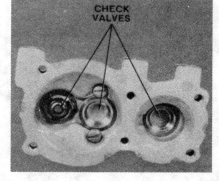

Fig. SK5-5 – Fuel pump check valves must be installed as shown for proper operation of fuel pump.

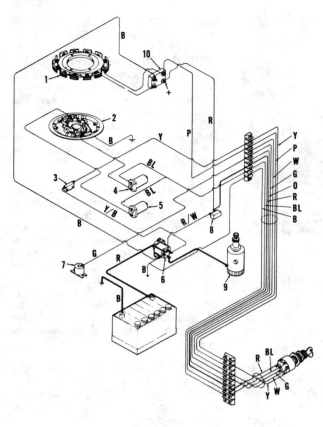

dry and smooth before installing flywheel. Tighten flywheel nut to 45 ft.-lbs.

Spark plug electrode gap should be 0.030 inch. Recommended spark plug is Champion L4J.

COOLING SYSTEM

WATER PUMP. All motors are equipped with a rubber impeller type water pump. When cooling system problems are encountered, first check the water inlet for plugging or partial stoppage, then if not corrected, remove the lower unit gearcase and check the condition of water pump, water passages and sealing surfaces.

Access to the water pump is possible after separating lower unit from motor leg. Remove motor leg covers. Unscrew shift rod coupler (S–Fig. SK5-7) and separate lower unit from motor leg. Unbolt and remove water pump.

Drive shaft seal (3–Fig. SK5-18) should be installed with spring loaded lip towards top. Drive shaft spline seal should be renewed if hard or cracked. Lubricate water tube seal and splines on upper end of drive shaft. Carefully slide the housing together making certain that water tube enters seal. Install the water pump retaining screws and nuts. Shift lower unit into neutral and thread coupler (S–Fig. SK5-7) onto shift rods. Position coupler

Fig. SK5-6 — Wiring schematic for models with battery ignition.

1. Alternator
2. Breaker plate
3. Neutral interlock switch
4. Top ignition coil
5. Bottom ignition coil
6. Starter relay
7. Choke solenoid
8. Circuit breaker
9. Electric starter model
10. Rectifier
B. Black
BL. Blue
G. Green
O. Orange
P. Purple
R. Red
W. White
Y. Yellow

IGNITION

Motors which are equipped with an alternator have a battery ignition while all other motors are equipped with a magneto ignition. Two breaker point sets are used on all models with each set of breaker points controlling ignition for one cylinder.

Breaker point gap should be as noted in CONDENSED SERVICE DATA and can be adjusted after the flywheel is removed. Both sets of points should be adjusted exactly alike. Place a mark on the high point of the breaker cam and set breaker point gap for both sets of

breaker points with the mark aligned with the breaker point rub block.

The tapered bore in flywheel and tapered end of crankshaft must be clean,

Fig. SK5-8 — Exploded view of motor leg assembly.

1. Upper shift rod
2. Locknut
3. Coupler
4. Spacer plate
5. Water tube
8. Upper thrust mount
9. Kingpin plate
15. Carrying handle
16. Exhaust gasket
17. Right motor leg cover
18. Left motor leg cover
19. Motor leg
20. Lower shock mount cover
21. Lower thrust pad

Fig. SK5-7 — View showing location of shift rod coupler (S).

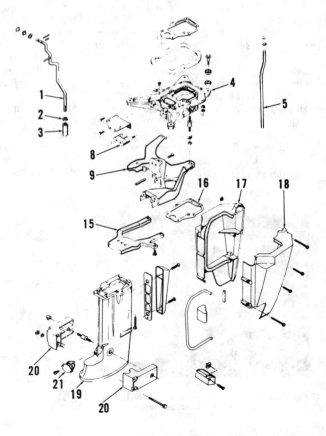

so that shift knob indicates neutral and tighten locknut.

POWER HEAD

R&R AND OVERHAUL. To remove the power head, mount the outboard motor on a stand and remove the engine cover. Disconnect battery leads, red lead from upper terminal of starter relay and black lead from crankcase. Unscrew nut retaining shift lever (1 – Fig. SK5-8) and detach gear shift linkage from lever. Remove motor leg covers, unbolt power head from motor leg and remove power head.

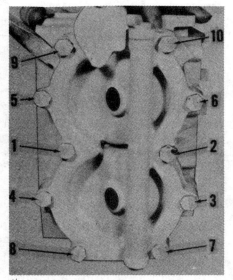

Fig. SK5-10 — Cylinder head cap screws should be tightened in the sequence shown above.

To disassemble power head, remove seal in bore of bottom end of crankshaft and remove starter and ignition assemblies from upper end of crankshaft. Unbolt and remove upper bearing cage and cylinder head. Remove reed valve assembly and transfer port cover. Unscrew cylinder to crankcase screws (two screws are in reed valve cavity) and using a suitable pry point separate cylinder and crankcase. Do not pry at machined mating surfaces between cylinder and crankcase.

Crankshaft, pistons and bearings are now accessible for removal and overhaul as outlined in the appropriate following paragraphs. Assemble as outlined in the ASSEMBLY paragraph.

ASSEMBLY. When reassembling, make sure all joint and gasket surfaces are clean, free from nicks and burrs, warped surfaces or hardened cement or carbon. The crankcase and inlet manifolds must be completely sealed against both vacuum and pressure. Exhaust manifold and cylinder head must be sealed against both vacuum and pressure. Exhaust manifold and cylinder head must be sealed against water leakage and pressure. Mating surfaces of exhaust areas between power head and motor leg must form a tight seal.

Sparingly apply a coating of sealant to mating surfaces of cylinder and crankcase. Tighten crankcase screws in a spiral pattern starting with center screws. Tighten cylinder head screws in sequence shown in Fig. SK5-10. Install seal (6 – Fig. SK5-11) with "O" ring end inserted first until seal is flush with edge

of bore. Install a new seal in bore of bottom end of crankshaft. Install long screw for transfer port cover in upper left hand hole as shown in Fig. SK5-13. Complete remainder of assembly.

PISTONS, PINS, RINGS & CYLINDERS. Pistons are fitted with two piston rings which should be installed with the beveled inner edge (B – Fig.

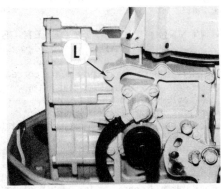

Fig. SK5-13 — Install long cap screw (L) in upper left hole of transfer port cover.

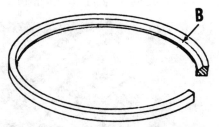

Fig. SK5-14 — Install piston rings with bevel (B) to top.

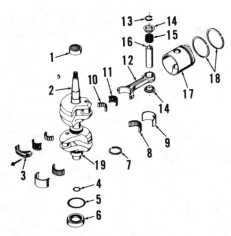

Fig. SK5-11 — Exploded view of crankshaft assembly.

1. Roller bearing
2. Crankshaft
3. Rod cap
4. Seal
5. "O" ring
6. Seal
7. Seal ring
8. Bearing rollers
9. Bearing liner
10. Bearing rollers
11. Bearing cage
12. Connecting rod
13. Snap ring
14. Spacer
15. Needle bearing
16. Piston pin
17. Piston
18. Piston rings
19. Ball bearing

Fig. SK5-12 — Exploded view of cylinder block assembly.

1. Seal
2. Bearing cage
3. Gasket
4. Stator ring
5. Crankcase seal
6. Exhaust cover
7. Gasket
8. Exhaust plate
9. Gasket
10. Cylinder block
11. Lower crankcase
12. Dowel pin
13. Thermostat cover
14. Plug
15. Cylinder head
16. Gasket
17. Drain hose
18. Gasket
19. Transfer port cover
20. Gear shift lever
21. Shift interlock rod
22. Bushing retainer
23. Interlock lever pin
24. Bushing
25. Shift interlock lever
26. Shift interlock rod
27. Throttle cam
28. Throttle link
29. Magneto stator link
30. Magneto control lever
31. Magneto control link

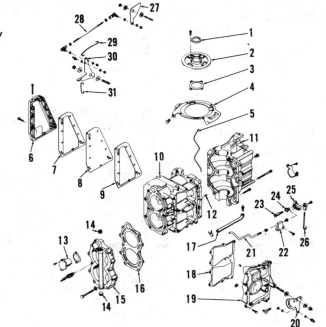

SK5-14) toward closed end of piston. Rings are pinned in place to prevent rotation in ring grooves. Heat piston to approximately 200°F. to remove or install piston pin. Do not interchange pistons between cylinders. Pistons and rings are available in standard size and 0.010 and 0.030 inch oversizes.

When assembling piston, pin and connecting rod, match marks on connecting rod and cap must be aligned and long, tapering side of piston must be towards exhaust port.

CONNECTING RODS, BEARINGS AND CRANKSHAFT. Before detaching connecting rods from crankshaft, mark connecting rod and cap for correct reassembly to each other and in the correct cylinder. The needle rollers and cages at crankpin end of connecting rod should be kept with the assembly and not interchanged.

The bearing rollers and cages used in the connecting rods and the rollers and liners in the center main bearing are available only as a set for each bearing. The complete assembly should be installed whenever renewal is indicated. Connecting rod bearing cages have beveled notches which must be installed

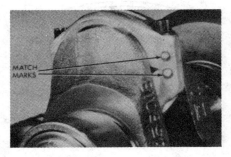

Fig. SK5-15 — Match marks on connecting rod and rod cap must be on same side and towards flywheel end of crankshaft.

together and toward top (flywheel) end of crankshaft. Match marks on connecting rod and cap must be on same side as shown in Fig. SK5-15. Connecting rod is fractured to provide an uneven surface between rod and cap. Be sure rod and cap are properly meshed before tightening rod screws.

Inspect condition of seal ring (7 – Fig. SK5-11) and carefully install ring in crankshaft groove. Seal ring (7) must prevent leakage between cylinders and a defective seal will result in poor engine performance.

Before installing crankshaft in crankcase, install bearing liner (9) over dowel pin and place 14 bearing rollers (8) in liner with a suitable grease to hold rollers in place. Install crankshaft and position remaining 16 bearing rollers around crank journal. Place remaining bearing liner over rollers so that liner ends dovetail. Upper main bearing (1) should stand ⅛ inch higher than surface of crankcase.

MANUAL STARTER

Refer to Fig. SK5-16 for an exploded view of manual starter. To remove starter from engine, unscrew retainer (15) screws and remove retainer, shims (14), pawl plate (13) and spring (11). Remove rope handle, press interlock lever and allow rope to rewind into starter housing. Press interlock lever and remove rope and pulley (10). If necessary, remove rewind spring.

Install rewind spring in housing with spring wound in counterclockwise direction from outer end of spring. Wind rope on pulley in counterclockwise direction as viewed with pulley in housing. Insert rope through slot of pulley with about nine inches of rope extending from slot. Install rope pulley in housing and place

pawl spring (11) on rope pulley with ends pointing up. Install pawl plate (13) with pawl side toward pulley and engage slots with pawl spring (11) ends. Install three shims (0.006, 0.007 and 0.010 inch) and retainer (15). Turn rope pulley approximately two turns clockwise to preload rewind spring and pass end of rope through rope guide of starter housing. Attach rope handle and pull rope until it is fully extended. It should still be possible to rotate rope pulley a slight amount after rope is extended to prevent damage to rewind spring.

PROPELLER

Propellers for normal use have three blades and are equipped with a thrust pin to prevent damage. Standard propeller has right hand rotation, 10 inch pitch and 8½ inch diameter.

LOWER UNIT

R&R AND OVERHAUL. Refer to WATER PUMP section for removal of lower unit. Turn shift rod (1 – Fig. SK5-18) counterclockwise to clear the water pump housing; then disassemble and remove the water pump assembly.

Remove the propeller and thrust pin. Remove any burrs or rust from exposed end of propeller shaft. Remove snap ring (25), thread two screws in threaded holes of propeller shaft bearing cage (22); and remove the cage, using a puller.

To detach lower gearcase (12) from drive shaft housing (7), unscrew and remove shift rod (1). Housings are secured by a socket head cap screw at the front, and the stud nut INSIDE the case.

Propeller shaft, gears, bearings and shift mechanism can be removed after

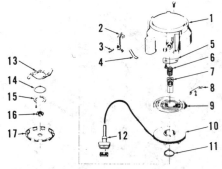

Fig. SK5-16 — Exploded view of manual starter.

1. Starter housing
2. Interlock lever
3. Pin
4. Spring
5. Plate
6. Spring
7. Rope guide
8. Housing liner
9. Rewind spring
10. Rope & pulley
11. Spring
12. Handle
13. Pawl plate
14. Shims
15. Retainer
16. Flywheel nut
17. Starter cup

Fig. SK5-17 — Exploded view of electric starter motor.

1. Nut
2. Stop cup
3. Spring
4. Pinion cup
5. Sleeve
6. Pinion
7. Screw shaft
8. Washer
9. Cushion cup
10. Cushion
11. Thrust cup
12. End plate
13. Thrust washer
14. Shim
15. Armature
16. Thrust washer
17. Housing
18. Thrust washer
19. Spring
20. Brushes
21. Brush plate

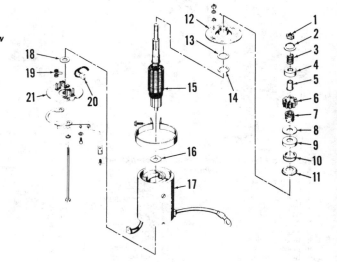

housings are separated. An internal expanding puller and slide hammer may be required to remove the front gear (13). In some cases, gear may be removed by heating gearcase housing, then jarring open end on a block of wood to dislodge the gear and bearing assembly. When installing front gear and bearing assembly, assemble the bearing cage (22), without "O" ring (24) over rear of propeller shaft; install thrust washer (14) and gear assembly (13) on front of shaft; then use the propeller shaft as a piloted driver. Backlash and mesh position of the gears are not adjustable.

Assemble by reversing the disassembly procedure. Propeller shaft seal (23) should be installed with spring loaded lip toward inside. Drive shaft seal (6) should be installed with spring loaded lip toward top. With unit assembled, propeller shaft end play should be 0.003-0.028 inch. Backlash and mesh position are not adjustable. Refer to appropriate preceding paragraphs for water pump service cautions.

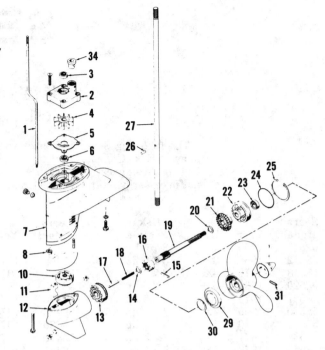

Fig. SK5-18 — Exploded view of lower unit.
1. Shift rod
2. Water pump housing
3. Seal
4. Impeller
5. Back plate
6. Oil seal
7. Drive shaft housing
8. Shift rod seal
10. Drive pinion & bearing
11. Shift cam
12. Gearcase housing
13. Forward gear & bearing
14. Thrust washer
15. Roll pin
16. Clutch dog
17. Shift plunger
18. Spring
19. Propeller shaft
20. Thrust washer
21. Reverse gear
22. Bearings & cage
23. Seal
24. "O" ring
25. Snap ring
26. Water pump drive pin
27. Drive shaft
29. Weed guard
30. Retaining ring
31. Thrust pin
34. Water tube seal

SEARS

SEARS, ROEBUCK & CO.
Sears Tower
Chicago, Illinois 60684

The following Sears outboards were manufactured for Sears, Roebuck & Company by Eska Company, Dubuque, Iowa. Service procedures for these Sears models will not differ greatly form those given for similar Eska models. However, parts are not necessarily interchangeable and should be obtained from Sears.

Sears Model	Year	HP	Eska Section
58511	1969	3.6	3-7.5 hp
58512	1969	3.6	3-7.5 hp
58513	1970	3.6	3-7.5 hp
58520	1969	5.0	3-7.5 hp
58521	1970	5.0	3-7.5 hp
58530	1969	7.0	3-7.5 hp
58531	1970	7.0	3-7.5 hp
58532	1971	7.0	3-7.5 hp
58540	1970	3.0	3-7.5 hp
58541	1971	3.0	3-7.5 hp
58543	1973	3.0	3-7.5 hp
58544	1974	3.0	3-7.5 hp
58550	1975	3.5	3-7.5 hp
58560	1972	3.5	3-7.5 hp
58561	1974	3.5	3-7.5 hp
58562	1975	3.5	3-7.5 hp
58563	1976	3.5	3-7.5 hp
58580	1970	4.0	3-7.5 hp
58610	1970	5.0	3-7.5 hp
58620	1970	5.0	3-7.5 hp
58710	1973	9.9	Two Cylinder
58711	1974	9.9	Two Cylinder
58720	1973	10.5	Two Cylinder
58721	1974	10.5	Two Cylinder
58760	1973	15.0	Two Cylinder
58761	1974	15.0	Two Cylinder
58820	1971	7.5	3-7.5 hp
58821	1971	7.5	3-7.5 hp
58830	1974	7.0	3-7.5 hp
58850	1974	7.5	3-7.5 hp
58870	1972	7.0	3-7.5 hp
58880	1972	7.5	3-7.5 hp
58881	1973	7.5	3-7.5 hp
58882	1974	7.5	3-7.5 hp
58890	1973	7.5	3-7.5 hp
58891	1973	7.5	3-7.5 hp
58960	1969	5.0	3-7.5 hp
58961	1969	5.0	3-7.5 hp
58962	1969	5.0	3-7.5 hp
58970	1969	4.8	3-7.5 hp
58971	1969	4.8	3-7.5 hp
58990	1970	5.0	3-7.5 hp
58991	1971	5.0	3-7.5 hp
58992	1971	5.0	3-7.5 hp
59310	1971	5.0	3-7.5 hp
59311	1972	5.0	3-7.5 hp
59430	1971	5.5	3-7.5 hp
59431	1972	5.5	3-7.5 hp
59432	1973	5.5	3-7.5 hp
59440	1971	7.0	3-7.5 hp
59450	1972	7.5	3-7.5 hp

Sears Model	Year	HP	Eska Section
59460	1971	4.5	3-7.5 hp
59461	1971	4.5	3-7.5 hp
59462	1972	4.5	3-7.5 hp
59463	1973	4.5	3-7.5 hp
59464	1974	4.5	3-7.5 hp
59480	1971	7.0	3-7.5 hp
59490	1973	7.5	3-7.5 hp
59491	1974	7.5	3-7.5 hp
59671	1969	5.0	3-7.5 hp
59672	1969	5.0	3-7.5 hp
59673	1970	5.0	3-7.5 hp
59680	1974	5.0	3-7.5 hp
59861	1969	3.5	3-7.5 hp
59862	1970	3.5	3-7.5 hp
59980	1974	5.5	3-7.5 hp
585120	1977, 1978	1.2	1.2-2.5 hp
585121	1978	1.2	1.2-2.5 hp
585122	1979	1.2	1.2-2.5 hp
585210	1975	3.0	3-7.5 hp
585211	1976	3.0	3-7.5 hp
585220	1976	3.0	3-7.5 hp
585230	1977	3.5	3-7.5 hp
585240	1978	3.5	3-7.5 hp
585241	1979	3.5	3-7.5 hp
585250	1976	4.0	3-7.5 hp
585270	1977	4.0	3-7.5 hp
585280	1980	3.5	3-7.5 hp
585281	1981	3.5	3-7.5 hp
585410	1975	5.0	3-7.5 hp
585411	1976	5.0	3-7.5 hp
585420	1977	5.0	3-7.5 hp
585430	1978	5.0	3-7.5 hp
585431	1979	5.0	3-7.5 hp
585440	1978	5.0	3-7.5 hp
585441	1979	5.0	3-7.5 hp
585460	1980	5.0	3-7.5 hp
585461	1981	5.0	3-7.5 hp
585470	1980	5.0	3-7.5 hp
585471	1981	5.0	3-7.5 hp
585510	1982	5.0	3-7.5 hp
585511	1983	5.0	3-7.5 hp
585710	1975	5.5	3-7.5 hp
585750	1982	7.5	3-7.5 hp
585751	1983	7.5	3-7.5 hp
585810	1978	7.5	3-7.5 hp
585811	1979	7.5	3-7.5 hp
585830	1978	7.5	3-7.5 hp
585831	1979	7.5	3-7.5 hp
585840	1980	7.5	3-7.5 hp

Sears Model	Year	HP	Eska Section
585841	1981	7.5	3-7.5 hp
585850	1977	7.5	3-7.5 hp
585860	1976	7.0	3-7.5 hp
585861	1976	7.0	3-7.5 hp
585870	1975	7.5	3-7.5 hp
585880	1976	7.5	3-7.5 hp
585890	1977	7.5	3-7.5 hp
585910	1975	7.5	3-7.5 hp
585911	1976	7.5	3-7.5 hp
585920	1977	7.5	3-7.5 hp
585930	1978	7.5	3-7.5 hp
585931	1979	7.5	3-7.5 hp
585932	1980	7.5	3-7.5 hp
585940	1981	7.5	3-7.5 hp
586110	1975	7.5	3-7.5 hp
586111	1976	7.5	3-7.5 hp
586120	1977	7.5	3-7.5 hp
586210	1975	9.9	Two Cylinder
586211	1976	9.9	Two Cylinder
586220	1977	9.9	Two Cylinder
586230	1978	9.9	Two Cylinder
586231	1979	9.9	Two Cylinder
586240	1980	9.9	Two Cylinder
586250	1981	9.9	Two Cylinder
586251	1982, 1983	9.9	Two Cylinder
586252	1984	9.9	Two Cylinder
586253	1984	9.9	Two Cylinder
586254	1984	9.9	Two Cylinder
586270	1982, 1983	9.9	Two Cylinder
586310	1975	15.0	Two Cylinder
586311	1976	15.0	Two Cylinder
586320	1977	15.0	Two Cylinder
586330	1978	15.0	Two Cylinder
586331	1979	15.0	Two Cylinder
586340	1980	15.0	Two Cylinder
586350	1981	15.0	Two Cylinder
586351	1982, 1983	15.0	Two Cylinder
586352	1984	15.0	Two Cylinder
586353	1984	15.0	Two Cylinder
586610	1984	5.0	3-7.5 hp
586611	1984	5.0	3-7.5 hp
586612	1984, 1985	5.0	3-7.5 hp
586750	1984	7.5	3-7.5 hp
586751	1984	7.5	3-7.5 hp
586752	1984, 1985	7.5	3-7.5 hp

SUZUKI

SUZUKI AMERICA CORPORATION
3251 E. Imperial Way
P.O. Box 1100
Brea, California 92621

SUZUKI DT2

To determine model and year of manufacture of Suzuki outboard motors, refer to numbers located on motor clamp bracket. The first six characters indicate the model and second six characters are motor serial number. The first character of serial number indicates year of manufacture. The years 1977, 1978 and 1979 are identified by the letters ''C,'' ''D'' and ''F'' respectively. Starting with 1980, the first number in serial number corresponds with model year. For example, if first number in serial number is 1, model year is 1981.

CONDENSED SERVICE DATA

NOTE: Metric fasteners are used throughout outboard motor.

TUNE-UP

Hp/rpm	2/4500
Bore	41.0 mm
	(1.614 in.)
Stroke	37.8 mm
	(1.488 in.)
Displacement	50 cc
	(3.05 cu. in.)
Spark Plug:	
NGK	BR5HS
Electrode gap	0.5-0.6 mm
	(0.020-0.023 in.)
Magneto:	
Breaker point gap	0.3-0.4 mm
	(0.012-0.016 in.)
Carburetor:	
Make	Mikuni
Model	VM-11-10
Fuel:Oil Ratio	See Text

SIZES—CLEARANCES

Piston Ring End Gap	0.10-0.25 mm
	(0.004-0.010 in.)
Piston to Cylinder	
Clearance	0.053-0.060 mm
	(0.0021-0.0024 in.)
Piston Pin Diameter	11.996-12.000 mm
	(0.4723-0.4724 in.)

SIZES—CLEARANCES CONT.

Crankshaft Runout at Main	
Bearing Journal (Max.)	0.03 mm
	(0.0012 in.)
Connecting Rod Small End	
Side Shake (Max.)	3.0 mm
	(0.118 in.)

TIGHTENING TORQUES

Cylinder Head	8-12 N·m
	(6-9 ft.-lbs.)
Crankcase	8-12 N·m
	(6-9 ft.-lbs.)
Reed Plate	0.5-0.75 N·m
	(4.5-6.6 in.-lbs.)
Flywheel Nut	40-50 N·m
	(30-37 ft.-lbs.)
Standard Screws:	
5 mm	2-4 N·m
	(18-36 in.-lbs.)
6 mm	4-7 N·m
	(36-62 in.-lbs.)
8 mm	10-16 N·m
	(89-141 in.-lbs.)
10 mm	22-35 N·m
	(195-310 in.-lbs.)

LUBRICATION

The power head is lubricated by oil mixed with the fuel. Fuel:oil ratio should be 30:1 during break-in of a new or rebuilt engine. Fuel:oil ratio for normal service is 50:1 on models prior to 1987 and 100:1 on 1987 and later models. Recommended oil is Suzuki Outboard Motor Oil or a good quality NMMA certified TC-W oil. When using any other type of two-stroke engine oil, fuel:oil ratios should be 20:1 during break-in and 30:1 for normal service. Manufacturer recommends regular or unleaded automotive gasoline having an 85-95 octane rating. Gasoline and oil should be thoroughly mixed.

The lower unit gears and bearings are lubricated with SAE 90 hypoid outboard gear oil. Lower unit capacity on models prior to 1987 is approximately 40 mL (1.3 oz.). Oil capacity on later models is approximately 70 mL (2.4 oz.) on short drive shaft models and 120 mL (4.1 oz.) on long drive shaft models. On early models (prior to 1987), lay motor on side to fill with oil. Later models are equipped with a vent/oil level check plug on side of gearcase. Reinstall plug securely using a new gasket if necessary to ensure a water tight seal.

FUEL SYSTEM

CARBURETOR. A Mikuni sliding valve float type carburetor is used. Refer to Fig. SZ1-1 for exploded view. Idle speed should be adjusted after motor has reached normal operating temperature. Move speed control to slow speed stop and adjust idle speed screw (14) to obtain idle speed of 800-900 rpm. Note that on 1987 and later models, carburetor is equipped with a pilot air screw (Fig. SZ1-2) for low speed mixture adjustment. Carburetor with pilot air screw can be identified by the presence of a float bowl drain plug. Initial setting of pilot air screw is two turns out from a lightly seated position. Final adjustment should be made with engine at operating temperature and running in forward gear. Adjust pilot air screw so engine idles smoothly and accelerates without hesitation.

Main fuel metering is controlled by main jet (20—Fig. SZ1-1). Standard main jet size is #95 for models through 1986 and #90 for 1987 and later models. Normal position for clip (9) on jet needle (10) is third notch from top of needle. If midrange mixture is too lean or too rich, minor fuel mixture adjustment can be accomplished by repositioning clip on jet needle. Moving clip down on needle richens fuel mixture while moving clip up on needle leans fuel mixture. Fuel

filter (17) should be cleaned after every 50 hours of operation.

To check float level, remove float bowl and invert carburetor. With float installed on float arm (23), float surface nearest main jet should be 19-21 mm (0.748-0.826 in.) away from carburetor gasket surface. Make certain float is level with gasket surface when measuring. Adjust float level by bending float arm tang.

When installing carburetor, renew "O" ring (13) as required.

IGNITION SYSTEM

Breaker point gap should be set to 0.3-0.4 mm (0.012-0.016 in.) at maximum opening. Adjustment may be accomplished through holes in flywheel. Flywheel must be removed to renew breaker points. Tighten flywheel nut to 40-50 N·m (30-37 ft.-lbs.).

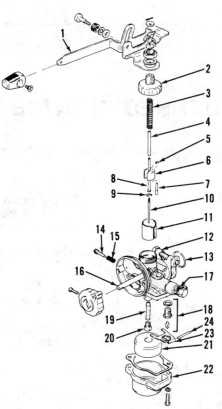

Fig. SZ1-1—Exploded view of carburetor used on models prior to 1987. On 1987 and later models, carburetor is equipped with a pilot air screw (Fig. SZ1-2) for low speed mixture adjustment.

1.	Speed control assy.	13.	"O" ring
2.	Cap nut	14.	Idle speed screw
3.	Spring	15.	Spring
4.	Tube	16.	Choke assy.
5.	Clip	17.	Fuel filter
6.	Spring seat	18.	Fuel inlet valve
7.	Seat pin	19.	Main nozzle
8.	Throttle rod	20.	Main jet
9.	Clip	21.	Float
10.	Jet needle	22.	Float bowl
11.	Throttle valve	23.	Float arm
12.	Body	24.	Pivot pin

After adjusting breaker points, check ignition timing using a dial indicator and an ohmmeter or continuity tester. Remove the spark plug and insert the dial indicator. Set piston position at TDC, then zero the dial indicator. Disconnect the black lead to stop button and connect the ohmmeter or continuity tester between lead from magneto and ground. Rotate the flywheel clockwise until meter or continuity tester indicates that points have just opened. Dial indicator should read 0.804 mm (0.032 in.). If ignition timing adjustment is required, remove the flywheel and loosen magneto base plate (7—Fig. SZ1-3) retaining screws. Rotating base plate clockwise retards ignition timing while rotating counterclockwise advances ignition timing.

COOLING SYSTEM

WATER PUMP. A rubber impeller type water pump is used to cool the

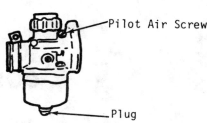

Fig. SZ1-2—Initial setting of pilot air screw on models so equipped is two turns out from a lightly seated position.

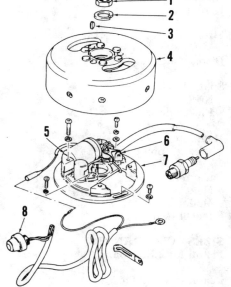

Fig. SZ1-3—Exploded view of magneto.

1.	Nut	5.	Ignition coil
2.	Lockwasher	6.	Ignition breaker points
3.	Key	7.	Base plate
4.	Flywheel	8.	Stop switch

power head and lower unit. Pump is located in the gearcase and driven by the propeller shaft.

Water inlet should be inspected for plugging or partial restriction if cooling system malfunction is noted. Refer to Fig. SZ1-9 for exploded view of water pump. To remove the impeller, remove propeller, propeller thrust pin and gearcase end cap (1), then withdraw the impeller (2). Inspect impeller for cracks or excessive wear or scoring. Power head should be separated from drive shaft housing and water passages thoroughly cleaned if large accumulations of foreign material are evident. Turn propeller shaft in a clockwise direction when inserting impeller in pump cavity.

POWER HEAD

REMOVE AND REINSTALL. To remove power head, remove power head cover, fuel tank, control panel assembly and carburetor. Remove recoil starter assembly, flywheel and magneto base plate assembly. Unscrew the six cap screws securing power head to drive shaft housing and separate power head from drive shaft housing.

Before reinstalling power head, inspect water inlet and outlet passages in drive shaft housing and remove any foreign material. Apply a coat of silicone sealer to mating surfaces of power head and drive shaft housing and install a new gasket. Assemble power head on drive shaft housing and tighten retaining cap screws to 6-10 N·m (53-88 in.-lbs.). Complete installation by reversing removal procedure.

DISASSEMBLY. Disassembly and inspection may be accomplished in the following manner: Remove cylinder head and clean carbon from combustion chamber and any foreign material accumulated in water passages. Detach crankcase half (1—Fig. SZ1-4) from cylinder block after removing six crankcase cap screws. Crankshaft and piston assembly may now be removed from cylinder block.

REASSEMBLY. Refer to specific service sections when assembling crankshaft, connecting rod, piston and reed valves. Make sure all joint and gasket surfaces are clean and free of nicks and burrs. Make sure all carbon, salt, dirt and sand are cleaned from the combustion chamber, exhaust port and water passages.

On early models place thrust rings (11—Fig. SZ1-5) in cylinder block (2—Fig. SZ1-4), then install crankshaft assembly. On later models, thrust rings are full-circle design and must be assembled on crankshaft prior to installing crank-

shaft. Press crankshaft seals flush against thrust rings. Install "O" ring (8) in cylinder block, then apply a suitable water resistant-grease to "O" ring and splined area of crankshaft. Apply a suitable sealer to cylinder block and crankcase half mating surfaces and position crankcase half on cylinder block. Using a crossing pattern, tighten six crankcase screws to 8-12 N·m (6-9 ft.-lbs.).

Do not use sealer when installing cylinder head gasket. Align water passage holes in cylinder block with holes in head gasket and install cylinder head. Tighten cylinder head bolts in a crossing pattern to 8-12 N·m (6-9 ft.-lbs.).

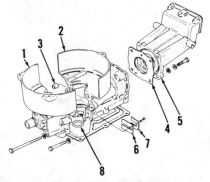

Fig. SZ1-4—Exploded view of crankcase and cylinder assembly.

1. Crankcase half	5. Cylinder head
2. Cylinder block	6. Reed petal
3. Dowel	7. Reed stop
4. Head gasket	8. "O" ring

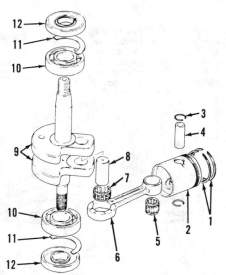

Fig. SZ1-5—Exploded view of crankshaft, piston and related components. On 1988 and later models, thrust rings (11) are full-circle design.

1. Piston rins	7. Bearing
2. Piston	8. Crankpin
3. Retainer ring	9. Crankshaft
4. Piston pin	10. Ball bearings
5. Bearing	11. Thrust rings
6. Connecting rod	12. Crankshaft seals

PISTON, PIN, RINGS AND CYLINDER. The piston is fitted with two piston rings. Piston ring end gap should be 0.10-0.25 mm (0.004-0.010 in.) with a maximum allowable ring end gap of 0.60 mm (0.024 in.). Piston rings are retained in position by locating pins. Piston-to-cylinder clearance should be 0.053-0.060 mm (0.0021-0.0024 in.). Pistons and rings are available in standard size as well as 0.25 mm (0.010) and 0.50 mm (0.020 in.) oversize. Cylinder should be bored to an oversize if cylinder is out of round or taper exceeds 0.10 mm (0.004 in.). Install piston on connecting rod so arrow on piston crown will point toward exhaust port.

CONNECTING ROD, BEARINGS AND CRANKSHAFT. Connecting rod, bearings and crankshaft are a press together unit. Crankshaft should be disassembled ONLY by experienced service personnel using appropriate service equipment.

Caged roller bearings are used at both large and small ends of the connecting rod. Determine rod bearing wear from side-to-side as shown in Fig. SZ1-6. Normal side-to-side movement is 3.0 mm (0.118 in.) or less. Maximum limit of crankshaft runout is 0.03 mm (0.0012 in.) measured at bearing surfaces with crankshaft ends supported.

Apply a suitable high temperature grease to lip area of crankshaft seals and install seals on crankshaft with open side toward bearings.

REED VALVE. The reed valve is located on the inside of crankcase (1—Fig. SZ1-4). Power head must be removed and crankcase separated from cylinder block as outlined in the POWER HEAD section to service reed valve assembly.

Renew reed (6) if petals are broken, cracked, warped or rusted. Tip of reed petal must not stand open in excess of 0.2 mm (0.008 in.) from contact surface. Reed stop opening should be 4.0 mm (0.160 in.). Reed petal should be in-

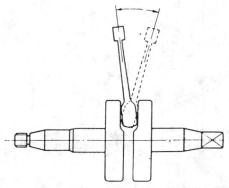

Fig. SZ1-6—Move connecting rod small end side-to-side as shown to determine rod, bearing and crankpin wear. Refer to text.

stalled in crankcase with beveled corner (C—Fig. SZ1-7) away from flywheel end of crankcase.

MANUAL STARTER

Refer to Fig. SZ1-8 for exploded view of manual starter assembly. Starter may be removed as a complete unit by removing three cap screws securing starter assembly to power head. To disassemble starter, proceed as follows: If rewind spring (3) remains under tension, pull starter rope and hold rope pulley (4) with notch in pulley adjacent to rope outlet. Pull rope back through outlet so rope engages notch in pulley and allow pulley to slowly unwind. Remove cap screw (8) and disassemble unit. Be careful when removing rewind spring (3) to prevent personal injury.

Rewind spring is wound in counterclockwise direction in starter housing. Rope is wound on rope pulley in counterclockwise direction as viewed with pulley in housing. Reassemble starter by reversing disassembly procedure making certain pin on starter pawl (5) is engaged between ends of spring clip (6). To place tension on rewind spring, pass rope through rope outlet in housing and install rope handle. Pull rope out and hold rope pulley so notch on pulley is adjacent to rope outlet. Pull rope back through outlet between notch in pulley and housing. Turn rope pulley counterclockwise six complete revolutions to place tension on spring. Do not place more tension on rewind spring than is necessary to draw rope handle snug against housing.

LOWER UNIT

PROPELLER AND SHEAR PIN. Propeller for normal use has three blades and is equipped with a shear pin to prevent damage. Standard propeller is 188

mm (7.4 in.) in diameter and has 115 mm (4.5 in.) pitch. Optional propellers are available from the manufacturer and should be selected to provide full throttle operation within the recommended limits of 4200-4800 rpm.

R&R AND OVERHAUL. To remove gearcase, unscrew drain plug and drain

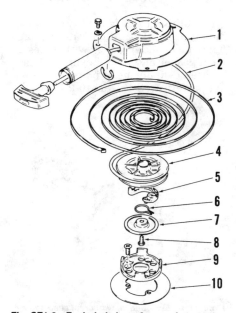

Fig. SZ1-8—Exploded view of manual starter assembly.

1. Housing	6. Spring clip
2. Rope	7. Plate
3. Recoil spring	8. Cap screw
4. Rope pulley	9. Drive plate
5. Starter pawl	10. Magneto insulator

gear lubricant. Remove propeller and shear pin. Remove cover (18—Fig. SZ1-9) and unscrew two retaining nuts, then separate gearcase (16) from drive shaft housing. Remove gearcase end cap (1), withdraw impeller (2), impeller drive pin (3) and pump housing (4). Pull drive shaft seal tube (25) from gearcase. Detach "E" ring (12) and withdraw drive shaft (26) while simultaneously removing pinion gear (13) and shims (14 and 15). Remove propeller shaft (9) and shims (10). If necessary, use a suitable puller to remove bearing (11).

Inspect all components for excessive wear or other damage. Apply a water resistant grease to lip area of all seals. If removed, install bearing (20) and check clearance between upper bearing and retaining ring (22). Clearance should not exceed 0.1 mm (0.004 in.) and can be adjusted by varying thickness of shims (19). Shims are available in 0.1 mm, 0.2 mm and 0.5 mm sizes. Install propeller shaft (9) with original shims (10). Reassemble pinion gear (13) with original shims (14 and 15) and drive shaft (26) in gearcase, then check mesh pattern of pinion gear and forward gear. Mesh pattern is adjusted by varying thickness of shims (14). Install water pump assembly, then check propeller shaft end play. Propeller shaft end play should be 0.05-0.50 mm (0.002-0.020 in.) and is adjusted using shims (10). Complete reassembly by reversing disassembly procedure. Fill gearcase with SAE 90 hypoid outboard gear oil.

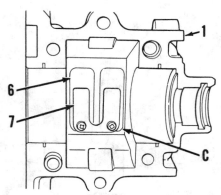

Fig. SZ1-7—Reed petal (6) should be installed with beveled corner (C) toward drive end of crankcase as shown.

Fig. SZ1-9—Exploded view of gearcase and water pump assembly. Note that drive shaft spacer (21) is redesigned on late models and must be installed with "up" mark facing top of gearcase.

1. Cap
2. Impeller
3. Pin
4. Pump housing
5. "O" ring
6. Seal
7. Bearing
8. Spacer
9. Propeller shaft
10. Shims
11. Bearing
12. "E" ring
13. Pinion gear
14. Shims
15. Shim
16. Gearcase
17. Drain plug
18. Cover
19. Shim
20. Bearing
21. Spacer
22. Snap ring
23. Seal
24. Bushing
25. Tube
26. Drive shaft
27. Bushing
28. Water tube
29. Grommet

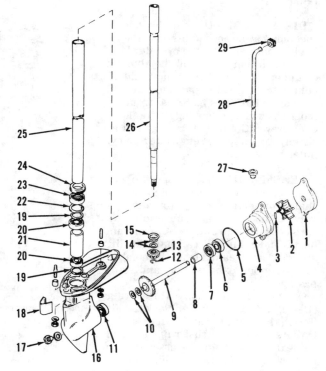

SUZUKI DT3.5

CONDENSED SERVICE DATA

NOTE: Metric fasteners are used throughout outboard motor.

TUNE-UP

Hp/rpm 3.5/4800-5300
Bore . . . . .46 mm
(1.81 in.)
Stroke . . . . .42 mm
(1.65 in.)
Displacement. . . . . .69.8 cc
(4.3 cu. in.)
Spark Plug:
NGK BP6HS
Electrode Gap . . . . .0.6-0.7 mm
(0.024-0.028 in.)
Ignition Type. . . . . .Breaker Point
Breaker Point Gap . . . . .0.3-0.4 mm
(0.012-0.016 in.)
Ignition Timing @ 5000 rpm . . . . .23.5° BTDC
Carburetor:
Make. . . . . .Mikuni
Model BV-18-15
Idle Speed (in gear) . . . . .900-1000 rpm
Fuel:Oil Ratio 50:1

SIZES—CLEARANCES

Piston Ring End Gap . . . . .0.15-0.35 mm
(0.006-0.014 in.)
Piston to Cylinder Clearance . . . . .0.052-0.067 mm
(0.0020-0.0026 in.)

SIZES—CLEARANCES CONT.

Piston Pin Diameter . . . . .11.996-12.000 mm
(0.4723-0.4724 in.)
Max. Crankshaft Runout at Main
Bearing Journal . . . . .0.03 mm
(0.0012 in.)
Max. Connecting Rod Small End
Side Shake . . . . .3.0 mm
(0.12 in.)

TIGHTENING TORQUES

Power Head Mounting Screws and Nuts . . . . . . .15-20 N·m
(11-14 ft.-lbs.)
Crankcase . . . . .8-12 N·m
(6-8 ft.-lbs.)
Flywheel Nut . . . . .40-50 N·m
(29-36 ft.-lbs.)
Standard Screws:
5 mm . . . . .2-4 N·m
(1-3 ft.-lbs.)
6 mm . . . . .4-7 N·m
(3-5 ft.-lbs.)
8 mm . . . . .10-16 N·m
(7-11 ft.-lbs.)
10 mm . . . . .22-35 N·m
(16-25 ft.-lbs.)

LUBRICATION

The power head is lubricated by oil mixed with the fuel. Fuel:oil ratios should be 30:1 during break-in of a new or rebuilt engine and 50:1 for normal service when using a BIA certified TC-W engine oil or Suzuki "CCI" oil. When using any other type of two-stroke engine oil, fuel:oil ratios should be 20:1 during break-in and 30:1 for normal service. Manufacturer recommends regular or no-lead automotive gasoline having an 85-95 octane rating. Gasoline and oil should be thoroughly mixed.

The lower unit gears and bearings are lubricated by approximately 85 mL (2.9 ozs.) of SAE 90 hypoid outboard gear oil. Reinstall vent and fill plugs securely using a new gasket, if necessary, to ensure a water tight seal.

FUEL SYSTEM

CARBURETOR. A Mikuni BV-18-15 carburetor is used. Refer to Fig. SZ2-1 for exploded view. Initial setting of pilot air screw (15) from a lightly seated position should be ¾-1¼ turns. Final carburetor adjustment should be made with engine at normal operating temperature and running in forward gear. Adjust throttle stop screw (12) so engine idles at approximately 900-1000 rpm. Adjust pilot air screw so engine idles smooth and will accelerate cleanly without hesitation. If necessary, readjust throttle stop screw to obtain 900-1000 rpm idle speed.

Main fuel metering is controlled by main jet (2). Standard main jet size for normal operation is #90. Standard pilot jet (14) size is #15.

To check float level, remove float bowl (7) and invert carburetor body (1). Base of float (6) should be 12-14 mm (0.47-0.55 in.) away from sealing ring surface of carburetor body with sealing ring (3) removed. Adjust float level by bending float tang.

FUEL PUMP. A diaphragm fuel pump (Fig. SZ2-2) is mounted on the side of power head cylinder block and is actuated by pressure and vacuum pulsations from the engine crankcase.

When servicing pump, defective or questionable parts should be renewed. Diaphragm should be renewed if air leaks or cracks are found, or if deterioration is evident.

REED VALVE. The reed valve is located in a reed plate that is located

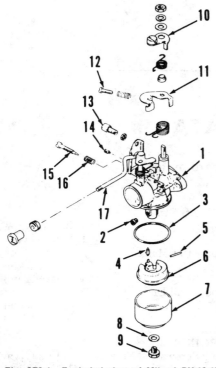

Fig. SZ2-1 – Exploded view of Mikuni BV-18-15 carburetor.

1. Body	10. Cable lever
2. Main jet	11. Throttle lever
3. Sealing ring	12. Throttle stop screw
4. Needle valve	13. Cable adjuster
5. Float pin	14. Pilot jet
6. Float	15. Pilot air screw
7. Float bowl	16. Spring
8. Gasket	17. Choke lever
9. Plug	

behind the intake manifold. The intake manifold must be removed in order to remove reed plate and service reed valve.

Renew reed valve (2–Fig. SZ2-3) if petals are broken, cracked, warped, rusted or bent. Tip of reed petal must not stand open more than 0.2 mm (0.008 in.) from contact surface. Reed stop opening should be 4.8-5.2 mm (0.19-0.20 in.).

SPEED CONTROL LINKAGE.
Engine speed is regulated by position of twist grip. As twist grip is rotated, the carburetor's throttle valve is operated via throttle cable. An engine kill switch is used to stop engine operation.

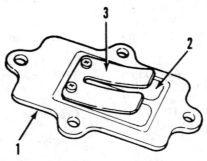

Fig. SZ2-3 – View showing reed plate (1), reed valve (2) and reed stop (3).

IGNITION SYSTEM

Breaker point gap should be set to 0.3-0.4 mm (0.012-0.016 in.) at maximum opening. Adjustment may be accomplished through holes in flywheel. Flywheel must be removed to renew breaker points. Tighten flywheel nut to 40-50 N·m (29-36 ft.-lbs.).

After adjusting breaker points, check ignition timing using a dial indicator and an ohmmeter or continuity tester. Remove the spark plug and insert the dial indicator. Set piston position at TDC, then zero the dial indicator. Unplug wire at connector leading from magneto base plate (11–Fig. SZ2-4) to kill engine switch. Connect red tester lead of ohmmeter or continuity tester to wire coming from magneto base plate (11). Connect the black tester lead to an engine ground. Rotate the flywheel clockwise until meter or continuity tester indicates that points have just opened. Dial indicator should read 2.52 mm (0.099 in.). If ignition timing adjustment is required, remove the flywheel and loosen magneto base plate (11) retaining screws. Rotating base plate clockwise retards ignition timing while rotating counterclockwise advances ignition timing.

COOLING SYSTEM

WATER PUMP. A rubber impeller type water pump is mounted between

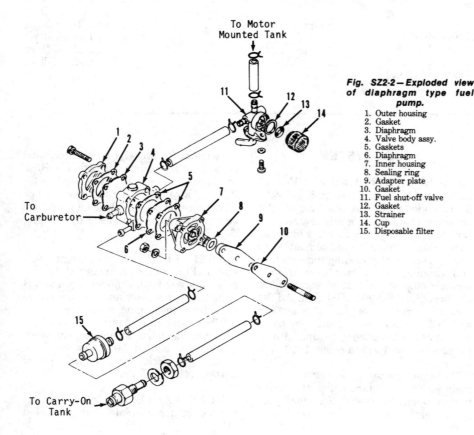

Fig. SZ2-2 – Exploded view of diaphragm type fuel pump.

1. Outer housing
2. Gasket
3. Diaphragm
4. Valve body assy.
5. Gaskets
6. Diaphragm
7. Inner housing
8. Sealing ring
9. Adapter plate
10. Gasket
11. Fuel shut-off valve
12. Gasket
13. Strainer
14. Cup
15. Disposable filter

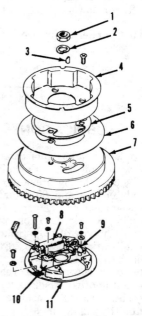

Fig. SZ2-4 – Exploded view of magneto components and starter cup.

1. Nut	
2. Lockwasher	
3. Key	7. Flywheel
4. Starter cup	8. Ignition coil
5. Insulator	9. Breaker points
6. Plate	10. Condenser
	11. Base plate

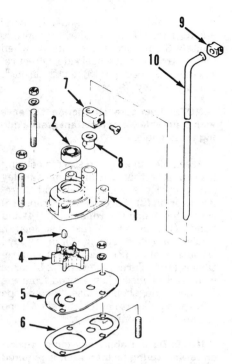

Fig. SZ2-5 — Exploded view of water pump assembly.

1. Pump housing	6. Gasket
2. Seal	7. Water tube guide
3. Impeller drive key	8. Grommet
4. Impeller	9. Grommet
5. Back plate	10. Water tube

the drive shaft housing and gearcase. A key in the drive shaft is used to turn the pump impeller. If cooling system problems are encountered, check water intakes for plugging or partial stoppage. If water intakes are clear, remove gearcase as outlined under LOWER UNIT and check condition of the water pump, water passages and sealing surfaces.

When water pump is disassembled, check condition of impeller (4–Fig. SZ2-5) and plate (5) for excessive wear. Turn drive shaft clockwise (viewed from top) while placing pump housing over impeller. Avoid turning drive shaft in opposite direction when water pump is assembled.

POWER HEAD

REMOVE AND REINSTALL. To remove the power head, first remove engine's top cover and shut-off fuel. Disconnect throttle cable, carburetor fuel inlet line and wires which will interfere with power head removal. Remove fuel tank and selector valve, carburetor, fuel pump, secondary ignition coil, rewind starter, starter cup, flywheel and key and magneto components. Remove four screws and two nuts which secure power head assembly to drive shaft housing and lift off power head.

Before installing power head, make certain drive shaft splines are clean then coat them with a light coating of water resistant grease. Apply a coat of silicone sealer to mating surfaces of power head and drive shaft housing and install a new gasket. Install power head on drive shaft housing and tighten retaining cap screws and nuts to 15-20 N·m (11-14 ft.-lbs.). The remainder of installation is the reverse of removal procedure.

DISASSEMBLY. Disassembly and inspection may be accomplished in the following manner. Remove cylinder head. Remove intake manifold and reed valve assembly from crankcase. Remove four crankcase cap screws, then separate crankcase from cylinder block. Lift crankshaft assembly with piston and connecting rod assembly from cylinder block.

Engine components are now accessible for overhaul as outlined in the appropriate following paragraphs. Clean carbon from cylinder head and combustion chamber and remove any foreign material accumulation in water passages. Inspect components for damage and renew if needed. Refer to the following section for assembly procedure.

ASSEMBLY. Refer to specific service sections when assembling the crankshaft, connecting rod, piston and reed valve. Make sure all joint and gasket surfaces are clean and free from nicks and burrs. Make sure all carbon, salt, dirt and sand are cleaned from the combustion chamber, exhaust port and water passages.

Lubricate crankpin bearing and cylinder wall of cylinder block with Suzuki "CCI" oil or a suitable BIA certified two-stroke engine oil. Install crankshaft assembly in crankcase. Make sure thrust ring (1–Fig. SZ2-7) fits properly in crankcase groove. Spread a coat of Suzuki Bond No. 4 or a suitable

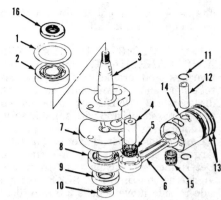

Fig. SZ2-7 — Exploded view of piston and crankshaft assembly.

1. Thrust ring	9. Seal
2. Ball bearing	10. Seal
3. Crank half	11. Retainer
4. Crank pin	12. Piston pin
5. Roller bearing	13. Piston rings
6. Connecting rod	14. Piston
7. Crank half	15. Roller bearing
8. Ball bearing	16. Seal

equivalent on the mating surfaces of the crankcase and the cylinder block. Position crankcase half on cylinder block and tighten the four crankcase screws to 8-12 N·m (6-8 ft.-lbs.) in the sequence shown in Fig. SZ2-6.

PISTON, PIN, RINGS AND CYLINDER. The piston is fitted with two piston rings. Piston ring end gap should be 0.15-0.35 mm (0.006-0.014 in.) with a maximum allowable ring end gap of 0.70 mm (0.028 in.). Piston rings are retained in position by locating pins. Install marked side of piston ring toward top of piston. Piston to cylinder wall clearance should be 0.052-0.067 mm (0.0020-0.0026 in.). Piston and rings are available in standard size as well as 0.25 mm (0.010 in.) and 0.50 mm (0.020 in.) oversizes. Cylinder should be bored to an oversize if cylinder is out-of-round or taper exceeds 0.10 mm (0.004 in.). Install piston on connecting rod so arrow

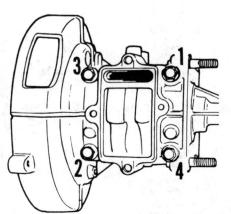

Fig. SZ2-6 — View showing tightening sequence of four crankcase screws.

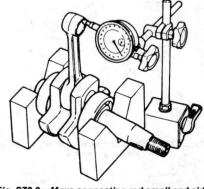

Fig. SZ2-8 — Move connecting rod small end side to side and measure with a dial indicator as shown to determine connecting rod, bearing and crank pin wear. Refer to text.

on piston crown points toward drive shaft end of crankshaft.

CONNECTING ROD, BEARINGS AND CRANKSHAFT. Connecting rod, bearings and crankshaft are a press together unit. Crankshaft should be disassembled ONLY by experienced service personnel and with suitable service equipment.

Cage roller bearings are used at both large and small ends of connecting rod. Determine rod bearing wear from side to side as shown in Fig. SZ2-8. Normal side to side movement is 3.0 mm (0.12 in.) or less. Maximum limit of crankshaft runout is 0.03 mm (0.0012 in.) measured at bearing surfaces with crankshaft ends supported.

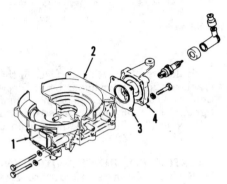

Fig. SZ-9 — Exploded view of cylinder block and crankcase assembly.

1. Crankcase	3. Gasket
2. Cylinder block	4. Cylinder head

Apply Suzuki Super Grease "A" or a suitable high temperature grease to lip portion of crankshaft seals prior to installation.

MANUAL STARTER

To overhaul the manual starter, proceed as follows: Remove the engine's top cover. Remove the screws securing the manual starter to the power head and withdraw.

To disassemble, untie starter rope (15 – Fig. SZ2-10) at handle (16) and allow the rope to wind into the starter. Invert the manual starter and remove retainer (10), washer (9), drive plate (8), drive pawl (7), return spring (6), spacer (5) and spring (4). Lift pulley (3) with starter rope (15) from starter housing (1). BE CAREFUL when removing pulley (3) to prevent possible injury from rewind spring (2).

Withdraw starter rope (15) from pulley (3) if renewal is required. To remove rewind spring (2), use suitable hand protection and extract rewind spring (2) from housing (1). Allow rewind spring to uncoil in a safe area.

Inspect all components for damage and excessive wear and renew if needed.

To reassemble, first apply a coating of a suitable water resistant grease to rewind spring area of housing (1). Install rewind spring (2) in housing (1) so spring coils wind in a counterclockwise direction from the outer end. Make sure the outer hook of rewing spring (2) is prop-

erly secured in starter housing. Wind starter rope (15) onto pulley (3) approximately 3 turns counterclockwise when viewed from the flywheel side. Direct remaining starter rope (15) length through notch in pulley (3).

NOTE: Lubricate all friction surfaces with a suitable water resistant grease during reassembly.

Assemble pulley (3) to starter housing making sure that slot in drum of pulley (13) properly engages hook end in rewind spring (2). Thread starter rope (15) through housing (1), rope guide (14) and handle (16) and secure. Install spring (4), spacer (5), return spring (6), drive pawl (7), drive plate (8), washer (9) and retainer (10). Turn pulley (3) 2-3 turns counterclockwise when viewed from the flywheel side, then release starter rope (15) from pulley (3) notch and allow rope to slowly wind onto pulley.

NOTE: Do not apply any more tension on rewind spring (2) than what is required to draw starter handle (16) back into the proper released position.

Remount manual starter assembly, then complete reassembly.

LOWER UNIT

PROPELLER AND SHEAR PIN. Propellers for normal use have three blades and are equipped with a shear pin

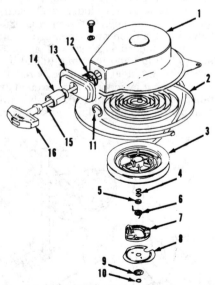

Fig. SZ2-10 — Exploded view of manual rewind starter assembly.

1. Housing	9. Washer
2. Rewind spring	10. Retainer
3. Pulley	11. Retainer
4. Spring	12. Spring
5. Spacer	13. Plate
6. Return spring	14. Rope guide
7. Drive pawl	15. Starter rope
8. Drive plate	16. Starter handle

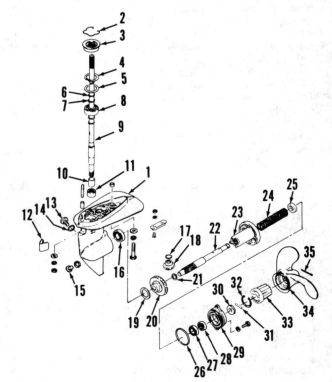

Fig. SZ2-11 — Exploded view of lower unit gearcase assembly.

1. Housing
2. Retainer
3. Oil seal
4. Snap ring
5. Shim
6. Snap ring
7. Washer
8. Bearing
9. Drive shaft
10. Bearing race
11. Bearing
12. Cover
13. Vent plug
14. Gasket
15. Drain plug
16. Bearing
17. Shim
18. Pinion gear
19. Shim
20. Forward gear
21. Shim
22. Propeller shaft
23. Dog clutch
24. Spring
25. Spacer
26. "O" ring
27. Bearing
28. Seal
29. Bearing housing
30. Stopper
31. Shear pin
32. Snap ring
33. Hub
34. Propeller
35. Cotter pin

to prevent damage. Standard propeller has a 190 mm (7½ in.) diameter and a 150 mm (5⅞ in.) pitch. Optional propellers are available from the manufacturer and should be selected to provide full throttle operation within the recommended limits of 4800-5300 rpm.

R&R AND OVERHAUL. Refer to Fig. SZ2-11 for exploded view of lower unit gearcase assembly. During disassembly, note the location of all shims and washers to aid in reassembly. To remove gearcase, first remove drain plug (15) and vent plug (13) and drain gear lubricant. Remove shift rod adjustment cover located at base of motor leg and loosen lower shift rod adjustment screw (10 – Fig. SZ2-12). Remove cotter pin (35 – Fig. SZ2-11), propeller (34) with hub (33) and shear pin (31). Remove cap screw and nut retaining lower unit gearcase and withdraw from drive shaft housing.

Remove stopper (30) and bearing housing (29) retaining screws. Being careful, pry bearing housing (29) from gearcase housing. Withdraw bearing housing with propeller shaft assembly. Refer to Fig. SZ2-4 and remove water pump assembly. Remove retainer (2 – Fig. SZ2-11), oil seal (3) and snap ring (4). Withdraw drive shaft assembly. Remove pinion gear (18) with shim (17). Remove forward gear (20) with shim (19). Use a suitable bearing puller to extract bearing (16) if needed.

Inspect all components for excessive wear aand damage. Apply a water resistant grease to lip portion of all seals. All seals and "O" rings should be renewed when unit is reassembled.

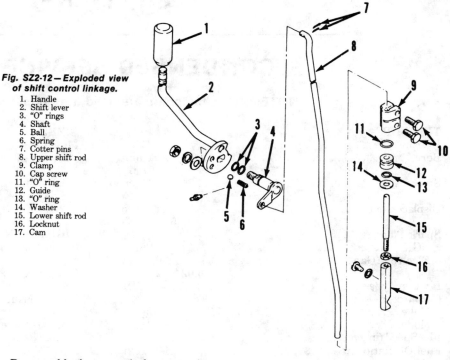

Fig. SZ2-12 — Exploded view of shift control linkage.
1. Handle
2. Shift lever
3. "O" rings
4. Shaft
5. Ball
6. Spring
7. Cotter pins
8. Upper shift rod
9. Clamp
10. Cap screw
11. "O" ring
12. Guide
13. "O" ring
14. Washer
15. Lower shift rod
16. Locknut
17. Cam

Reassemble lower unit by reversing disassembly procedure while noting the following: Check mesh pattern of pinion gear (18) and forward gear (20) to determine which shim or shims should be adjusted. Recomended backlash between pinion gear (18) and forward gear (20) is 0.1-0.2 mm (0.0039-0.0079 in.). Assembled propeller shaft end play should be 0.2-0.4 mm (0.008-0.016 in.). Adjust thickness of shim (21) until recommended end play is obtained. Apply silicone sealer to lower unit and drive shaft housing mating surfaces.

With lower unit installed, adjust shift linkage by first ensuring lower unit is in "Forward" position. Set shift control handle to "Forward" position, then tighten cap screw (10 – Fig. SZ2-12) to secure rod position. Install shift rod cover. Fill gearcase with approximately 85 mL (2.9 ozs.) of SAE 90 hypoid outboard gear oil.

SUZUKI DT4

CONDENSED SERVICE DATA

NOTE: Metric fasteners are used throughout outboard motor.

TUNE-UP

Hp/rpm	4/5000
Bore	50 mm
	(1.97 in.)
Stroke	46 mm
	(1.81 in.)
Displacement	90 cc
	(5.5 cu. in.)
Spark Plug:	
NGK	BP6HS
Electrode Gap	0.6-0.7 mm
	(0.024-0.028 in.)
Ignition Type	CDI
Carburetor:	
Make	Mikuni
Model	BV-18-15
Idle Speed (in gear)	850-900 rpm
Fuel:Oil Ratio	See Text

SIZES — CLEARANCES

Piston Ring End Gap	0.15-0.35 mm
	(0.006-0.014 in.)
Piston to Cylinder Clearance	0.052-0.067 mm
	(0.0020-0.0026 in.)
Piston Pin Diameter	11.995-12.000 mm
	(0.4722-0.4724 in.)

SIZES — CLEARANCES CONT.

Max. Crankshaft Runout at Main	
Bearing Journal	0.05 mm
	(0.002 in.)
Max. Connecting Rod Small End	
Side Shake	4.0 mm
	(0.16 in.)

TIGHTENING TORQUES

Power Head Mounting Screws	15-20 N·m
	(11-14 ft.-lbs.)
Crankcase	8-12 N·m
	(6-8 ft.-lbs.)
Flywheel Nut	45 N·m
	(32 ft.-lbs.)
Standard Screws:	
5 mm	2-4 N·m
	(1-3 ft.-lbs.)
6 mm	4-7 N·m
	(3-5 ft.-lbs.)
8 mm	10-16 N·m
	(7-11 ft.-lbs.)
10 mm	22-35 N·m
	(16-25 ft.-lbs.)

LUBRICATION

The power head is lubricated by oil mixed with the fuel. Fuel:oil ratios should be 30:1 during break-in of a new or rebuilt engine. For normal service, fuel:oil ratio should be 50:1 on models prior to 1986 and 100:1 on 1986 and later models when using Suzuki Outboard Motor Oil or a good quality NMMA certified TC-W engine oil. When using any other two-stroke oil, fuel:oil ratio should be 20:1 during break-in and 30:1 for normal service. Manufacturer recommends regular or unleaded automotive gasoline having an 85 minimum octane rating. Gasoline and oil should be thoroughly mixed.

The lower unit gears and bearings are lubricated by approximately 190 mL (6.4 ozs.) of SAE 90 hypoid outboard gear oil. Reinstall vent and fill plugs securely using a new gasket, if necessary, to ensure a water tight seal.

FUEL SYSTEM

CARBURETOR. A Mikuni BV-18-15 carburetor is used. Refer to Fig. SZ3-1 for exploded view. Initial setting of pilot air screw (6) should be 1 to 1-1/2

turns out from a lightly seated position. Final adjustment should be made with engine at normal operating temperature and running in forward gear. Adjust throttle stop screw (9) so engine idles at approximately 850-900 rpm. Adjust pilot air screw so engine idles smoothly and will accelerate cleanly without hesitation. If necessary, readjust throttle

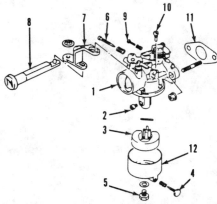

Fig. SZ3-1 — Exploded view of Mikuni BV-18-15 carburetor.

1. Body	7. Choke lever
2. Main jet	8. Choke knob
3. Float	9. Idle speed screw
4. Screw	10. Pilot jet
5. Plug	11. Gasket
6. Pilot air screw	12. Float bowl

stop screw to obtain 850-900 rpm idle speed.

Main fuel metering is controlled by main jet (2). Standard main jet size for normal operation is #97.5. Standard pilot jet (10) size is #45.

To check float level, remove float bowl (12) and invert carburetor body (1). Base of float (3) should be 12-14 mm (0.47-0.55 in.) away from gasket surface of carburetor body with float bowl gasket removed. Adjust float level by bending float tang.

FUEL PUMP. A diaphragm fuel pump (Fig. SZ3-2) is mounted on the side of power head cylinder block and is actuated by pressure and vacuum pulsations from the engine crankcase.

When servicing pump, defective or questionable parts should be renewed. Diaphragm should be renewed if air leaks or cracks are found, or if deterioration is evident.

SPEED CONTROL LINKAGE. Engine speed is controlled by position of throttle linkage. Ignition advance is electronically controlled. A twist grip at the steering handle is used to control throttle settings.

Illustrations Courtesy Suzuki America Corp.

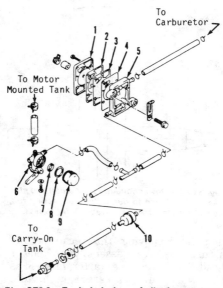

1. Inner housing
2. Gasket
3. Diaphragm
4. Check valve assy.
5. Outer housing
6. Fuel shut-off valve
7. Strainer
8. Gasket
9. Cup
10. Disposable filter

IGNITION

A breakerless, capacitor discharge ignition system is used. Refer to Fig. SZ3-3 for wiring diagram.

Full throttle and full ignition advance should occur simultaneously. Ignition timing is controlled by throttle position. As throttle opening is increased, ignition timing is electronically advanced.

If ignition malfunction occurs, check condition of spark plug, all wires and connections before trouble-shooting ignition circuit. Using Suzuki pocket tester 09900-25002 or a suitable ohmmeter, refer to the following test specifications and procedures to aid trouble-shooting.

Check condition of primary coil by separating black wire with red tracer and black wire (see Fig. SZ3-3) and connect a tester lead to each wire. Primary coil can be considered satisfactory if resistance reading is within the limits of 15-45 ohms at 20°C (68°F).

Check condition of pulser coil by separating white wire with red tracer and black wire (see Fig. SZ3-3) and connect a tester lead to each wire. Pulser coil can be considered satisfactory if resistance reading is within the limits of 12-18 ohms at 20°C (68°F).

Check condition of lighting coil by separating yellow wire and red wire (see Fig. SZ3-3) and connect a tester lead to each wire. Lighting coil can be considered satisfactory if resistance reading is within the limits of 0.5-1.5 ohms at 20°C (68°F). To check ignition coil, primary coil resistance should be 0.1-0.2 ohms at 20°C (68°F) and secon-

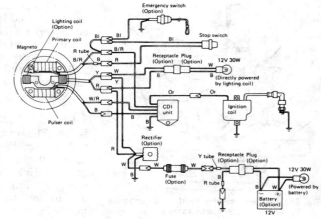

Fig. SZ3-3 — Wiring diagram of electrical system.

B. Black
R. Red
W. White
Y. Yellow
Bl. Blue
Or. Orange
B/R. Black with red tracer
W/R. White with red tracer

dary coil resistance should be 1500-2300 ohms at 20°C (68°F).

NOTE: Special Suzuki "CDI CHECKER" is required to test CDI unit.

COOLING SYSTEM

WATER PUMP. A rubber impeller type water pump is mounted between the drive shaft housing and gearcase. A key in the drive shaft is used to turn the pump impeller. If cooling system problems are encountered, check water intake for plugging or partial stoppage. If water intake is clear, remove gearcase as outlined under LOWER UNIT and check condition of the water pump, water passages and sealing surfaces.

When water pump is disassembled, check condition of impeller (4 – Fig. SZ3-4) and plate (5) for excessive wear. Turn drive shaft clockwise (viewed from top) while placing pump housing over impeller. Avoid turning drive shaft in opposite direction when water pump is assembled.

POWER HEAD

REMOVE AND REINSTALL. To remove the power head, first remove engine top cover and close fuel shut-off valve. Disconnect throttle cable, carburetor fuel inlet line and wires which will interfere with power head removal. Remove fuel tank and selector valve, carburetor, fuel pump, CDI unit, ignition coil, rewind starter, starter cup, flywheel and key. Remove six screws which secure power head assembly to drive shaft housing and lift off power head.

Before reinstalling power head, make certain drive shaft splines are clean, then apply a light coating of water-resistant grease to shaft splines. Apply a coat of silicone sealer to mating surfaces of power head and drive shaft housing, then install a new gasket. In-

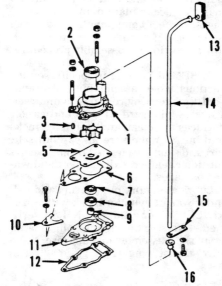

Fig. SZ3-4 — Exploded view of water pump assembly.

1. Pump housing
2. Seal
3. Impeller drive key
4. Impeller
5. Back plate
6. Gasket
7. Seal
8. Seal
9. Bushing
10. Shift rod clamp
11. Housing
12. Gasket
13. Grommet
14. Water tube
15. Water tube guide
16. Grommet

stall power head on drive shaft housing and tighten retaining cap screws to 15-20 N·m (11-14 ft.-lbs.). The remainder of installation is the reverse of removal procedure.

DISASSEMBLY. Disassembly and inspection may be accomplished in the following manner. Remove lubrication hose, rewind starter bracket, water jacket cover and gasket and cylinder head. Remove six crankcase cap screws, then separate crankcase from cylinder block. Lift crankshaft assembly with piston and connecting rod assembly from cylinder block.

Engine components are now accessible for overhaul as outlined in the appropriate following paragraphs. Clean carbon from cylinder head and combus-

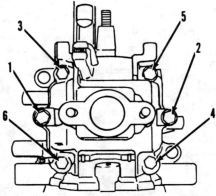

Fig. SZ3-5 — View showing tightening sequence of six crankcase screws.

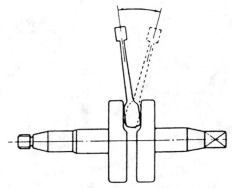

Fig. SZ3-7 — Move connecting rod small end side to side as shown to determine connecting rod, bearing and crank pin wear. Refer to text.

tion chamber and remove any foreign material accumulation in water passages. Inspect components for damage and renew if needed. Refer to the following section for assembly procedure.

ASSEMBLY. Refer to specific service sections when assembling the crankshaft, connecting rod, piston and reed valves. Make sure all joint and gasket surfaces are clean and free from nicks and burrs. Make sure all carbon, salt, dirt and sand are cleaned from the combustion chamber, exhaust port and water passages.

Lubricate crank pin bearing and cylinder wall of cylinder block with Suzuki "CCI" oil or a suitable NMMA certified two-stroke engine oil. Install crankshaft assembly in crankcase. Make sure thrust ring (2—Fig. SZ3-6) fits

properly in crankcase groove. Spread a coat of Suzuki Bond No. 4 or a suitable equivalent on the mating surfaces of the crankcase and the cylinder block. Position crankcase half on cylinder block and tighten the six crankcase screws in the sequence shown in Fig. SZ3-5 to 8-12 N·m (6-8 ft.-lbs.).

PISTON, PIN, RINGS AND CYLINDER. The piston is fitted with two piston rings. Piston ring end gap should be 0.15-0.35 mm (0.006-0.014 in.) with a maximum allowable ring end gap of 0.70 mm (0.028 in.). Piston rings are retained in position by locating pins. Install marked side of piston ring toward top of piston. Piston to cylinder wall clearance should be 0.052-0.067 mm (0.0020-0.0026 in.). Pistons and rings are available in standard size as well as 0.25 mm (0.010 in.) and 0.50 mm (0.020 in.) oversizes. Cylinder should be bored to an oversize if cylinder is out-of-round or taper exceeds 0.10 mm (0.004 in.) Install piston on connecting rod so arrow on piston crown points toward flywheel end of crankshaft.

CONNECTING ROD, BEARINGS AND CRANKSHAFT. Connecting rod, bearings and crankshaft are a press together unit. Crankshaft should be disassembled ONLY by experienced service personnel and with suitable service equipment.

Caged roller bearings are used at both large and small ends of the connecting rod. Determine rod bearing wear from side to side as shown in Fig SZ3-7. Normal side to side movement is 4.0 mm (0.16 in.) or less. Maximum limit of crankshaft runout is 0.05 mm (0.002 in.) measured at bearing surfaces with crankshaft ends supported.

Apply Suzuki Super Grease "A" or a suitable high temperature grease to lip portion of crankshaft seals prior to installation.

REED VALVE. The reed valve is located on the inside of crankcase (1—Fig. SZ3-8). Power head must be removed and crankcase separated from cylinder block as outlined in the POWER HEAD section in order to service reed valve.

Renew reed valve (10) if petals are broken, cracked, warped, rusted or bent. Tip of reed petal must not stand open more than 0.2 mm (0.008 in.) from contact surface. Reed stop opening should be 4.8-5.2 mm (0.19-0.20 in.).

MANUAL STARTER

Refer to Fig. SZ3-9 for an exploded view of manual starter assembly. Starter may be removed as a complete

unit by removing three cap screws securing starter assembly to power head. To disassemble starter, proceed as follows: Remove starter handle (11—Fig. SZ3-9) and allow starter rope (10) to slowly wind onto pulley (4). Invert starter housing (1) and remove cap screw (9). Withdraw ratchet (8), friction spring (7), friction plate (6) and return spring (5). Lift pulley (4) with starter rope (10) and rewind spring (3) from starter housing (1). Be careful when removing rewind spring (3); a rapidly uncoiling starter spring could cause serious injury.

To reassemble, coat rewind spring area of pulley (4) with a suitable water resistant grease. Install rewind spring (3) in pulley (4). Rewind spring (3) must wind in a counterclockwise direction from the outer end. Starter rope (10) must wrap around pulley (4) in a counterclockwise direction when viewed from the bottom side. Reassemble starter assembly by reversing disassembly procedure making certain rewind spring's inner hook properly

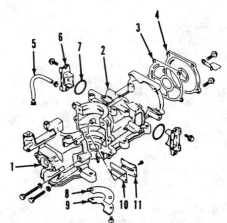

Fig. SZ3-8 — Exploded view of cylinder block and crankcase assembly.

1. Crankcase	7. "O" ring
2. Cylinder block	8. Gasket
3. Gasket	9. Water jacket cover
4. Cylinder head	10. Reed valve
5. Lubrication hose	11. Reed valve stop
6. Cover	

Fig. SZ3-6 — Exploded view of piston and crankshaft assembly.

1. Seal	9. Ball bearing
2. Thrust ring	10. Seal
3. Ball bearing	11. Seal
4. Crank half	12. Retainer
5. Connecting rod	13. Piston pin
6. Roller bearing	14. Roller bearing
7. Crank pin	15. Piston
8. Crank half	16. Piston rings

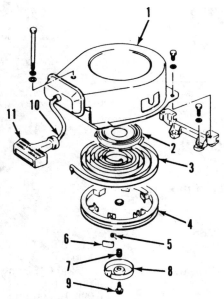

Fig. SZ3-9 — Exploded view of manual starter assembly.

1. Starter housing
2. Rewind spring case
3. Rewind spring
4. Pulley
5. Return spring
6. Friction plate
7. Friction spring
8. Ratchet
9. Cap screw
10. Starter rope
11. Starter handle

engages groove in starter housing. To place tension on rewind spring (3), pass starter rope (10) through rope outlet in housing (1) and install rope handle (11). With handle (11) against starter housing, grasp starter rope (10) on inside of housing and rotate pulley (4) two turns counterclockwise. Do not place more tension on rewind spring than is necessary to draw rope handle up against housing.

LOWER UNIT

PROPELLER AND SHEAR PIN. Propellers for normal use have three blades and are equipped with a shear pin to prevent damage to lower unit gears. Standard propeller has a 190.5 mm (7-1/2 in.) diameter and a 152.4 mm (6 in.) pitch. Optional propellers are available from the manufacturer and should be selected to provide full throttle operation within the recommended limits of 4500-5500 rpm.

R&R AND OVERHAUL. Refer to Fig. SZ3-10 for exploded view of lower unit gearcase assembly. During disassembly, note the location of all shims and washers to aid in reassembly.

To remove gearcase, first remove drain plug (8) and vent plug (6) and drain gear lubricant. Remove shift rod adjustment cover and loosen shift rod adjustment screw. Remove cotter pin (40), spinner (39), propeller (38) and shear pin (36). Remove two lower unit cap screws (41) and withdraw lower

Fig. SZ3-10 — Exploded view of lower unit gearcase.

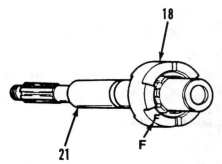

1. Housing
2. Drive shaft
3. Snap ring
4. Circlip
5. Bushing
6. Vent plug
7. Gasket
8. Drain plug
9. Gasket
10. Water filter
11. Roller bearing
12. Shim
13. Forward gear
14. Shim
15. Push rod
16. Push pin
17. Dog clutch return spring
18. Dog clutch
19. Pin
20. Spring
21. Propeller shaft
22. Shim
23. Reverse gear
24. Shim
25. Thrust washer
26. Washer
27. Pinion gear
28. "O" ring
29. Roller bearing
30. Roller bearing
31. Bearing housing
32. Washer
33. Seals
34. Seal protector
35. Washer
36. Shear pin
37. Propeller housing
38. Propeller
39. Spinner
40. Cotter pin
41. Cap screws

unit assembly from drive shaft housing.

Remove bearing housing (31) retaining screws. Carefully pry bearing housing (31) from gearcase housing. Withdraw bearing housing with propeller shaft assembly. If needed, remove pinion gear (27), washer (26) thrust washer (25) and forward drive gear (13) with shim (12).

Inspect components for excessive wear and damage and renew as necessary. Apply a water-resistant grease to lip portion of all seals. All seals and "O" rings should be renewed when unit is reassembled.

Reassemble lower unit by reversing disassembly procedure while noting the following: Install clutch (18) on propeller shaft (21) so "F" marked side (Fig. SZ3-11) is towards forward gear (13—Fig. SZ3-10). Clutch return spring (17) recommended free length is 69 mm (2.7 in.) and minimum length is 67 mm (2.6 in.). Tighten bearing housing (31) retaining cap screws to 6-10 N·m (5-7 ft.-lbs.). Assembled drive shaft end play should be 0.1-0.2 mm (0.004-0.008 in.). Adjust thickness of thrust washer (25), shim (12) or shim (24) until recommended end play is obtained. Check mesh pattern of pinion gear and forward gear to determine which shims or thrust washer should be adjusted. Assembled propeller shaft end play should be 0.2-0.4 mm (0.008-0.016 in.). Adjust thickness of shim (22) until recommended end play is obtained. Apply silicone sealer to lower unit and drive shaft housing mating surfaces.

With lower unit installed, adjust shift linkage by first ensuring lower unit is in "Forward" position. Set shift control handle to "Forward" position, then tighten cap screw (16—Fig. SZ3-12) to secure shift rod position. Install shift rod cover. Fill gearcase with approximately 190 mL (6.4 ozs.) of SAE 90 hypoid outboard gear oil.

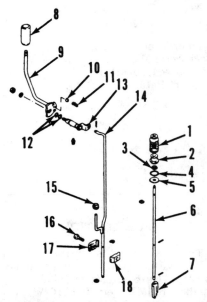

Fig. SZ3-11 — Install clutch (18) so "F" mark (F) is toward forward gear.

Fig. SZ3-12 — Exploded view of shift control linkage.

1. Boot
2. Guide
3. "O" ring
4. "O" ring
5. Washer
6. Lower shift rod
7. Cam
8. Handle
9. Shift lever
10. Ball
11. Spring
12. "O" ring
13. Shaft
14. Upper shift rod
15. Bushing
16. Cap screw
17. Bracket half
18. Bracket half

SUZUKI DT5, DT6 AND DT8

CONDENSED SERVICE DATA

NOTE: Metric fasteners are used throughout outboard motor.

TUNE-UP

Hp/rpm	5/4800-5500
	6/5200-5700
	8/5200-5700
Bore:	
5 Hp	43 mm
	(1.69 in.)
6 & 8 Hp	50 mm
	(1.97 in.)
Stroke:	
5 Hp	39 mm
	(1.54 in.)
6 & 8 Hp	42 mm
	(1.65 in.)
Number of Cylinders	2
Displacement:	
5 HP	113 cc
	(6.90 cu. in.)
6 & 8 Hp	165 cc
	(10.07 cu. in.)
Spark Plug:	
NGK	BP6HS
Electrode Gap	0.8-0.9 mm
	(0.031-0.035 in.)
Ignition Type	CDI
Carburetor Make	Mikuni
Idle Speed (in gear)	600-650 rpm
Fuel:Oil Ratio	See Text

SIZES—CLEARANCES

Piston Ring End Gap	0.10-0.30 mm
	(0.004-0.012 in.)
Piston to Cylinder Clearance	0.052-0.067 mm
	(0.0020-0.0026 in.)
Piston Pin Diameter	11.996-12.000 mm
	(0.4723-0.4724 in.)
Max. Crankshaft Runout at	
Main Bearing Journal	0.05 mm
	(0.002 in.)
Max. Connecting Rod Small	
End Side Shake	4.0 mm
	(0.160 in.)

TIGHTENING TORQUES

Power Head Mounting Screws	15-20 N·m
	(11-15 ft.-lbs.)
Crankcase	8-12 N·m
	(6-9 ft.-lbs.)
Flywheel Nut	60-70 N·m
	(44-52 ft.-lbs.)
Cylinder Head Screws	20-26 N·m
	(15-19 ft.-lbs.)
Standard Screws:	
5 mm	2-4 N·m
	(1-3 ft.-lbs.)
6 mm	4-7 N·m
	(3-5 ft.-lbs.)
8 mm	10-16 N·m
	(7-12 ft.-lbs.)
10 mm	22-35 N·m
	(16-26 ft.-lbs.)

LUBRICATION

The power head is lubricated by oil mixed with the fuel. Recommended oil is Suzuki Outboard Motor Oil or a good quality NMMA certified TC-W two-stroke engine oil. Fuel:oil ratio should be 30:1 during break-in of a new or rebuilt engine. For normal service, fuel:oil ratio should be 50:1 on models prior to 1986 and 100:1 for 1986 and later models. Manufacturer recommends regular or unleaded automotive gasoline having an 85-95 octane rating.

Gasoline and oil should be thoroughly mixed.

The lower unit gears and bearings are lubricated by approximately 240 mL (8.1 oz.) of SAE 90 hypoid outboard gear oil. Reinstall vent and fill plugs securely using a new gasket, if necessary, to ensure a water tight seal.

FUEL SYSTEM

CARBURETOR. A Mikuni BV-18-15 carburetor is used on DT5 models, Mikuni BV-18-14 is used on DT6 models and Mikuni BV-24-18 is used on DT8 models. Refer to Fig. SZ4-1 for exploded view. Initial setting of pilot air screw (13) should be 3/4 to 1-1/4 turns out from a lightly seated position on Models DT5 and DT8, and 1-3/4 to 2-1/4 turns out on Model DT6. Final carburetor adjustment should be performed with engine at normal operating temperature and running in forward gear. Adjust idle speed screw (11) so engine idles at approximately 600-650 rpm. Adjust pilot air screw (13) so engine idles smoothly and will accelerate cleanly without hesitation. If necessary, readjust idle speed screw (11) to obtain 600-650 rpm idle speed.

Main fuel metering is controlled by main jet (2). Standard main jet for normal operation is #100 on DT5 models, #115 on DT6 short shaft models, #120 on DT6 long shaft models, #95 on DT8 short shaft models and #100 on DT8 long shaft models. Standard pilot jet size

is #20 on DT5 and DT6 models and #50 on DT8 models.

To check float level, remove float bowl (7) and invert carburetor body (1). Base of float (4 – Fig. SZ4-2) should be a distance (D) of 13-15 mm (0.51-0.59 in.) away from top of carburetor body flange on DT5 and DT6 models and a distance (D) of 22-24 mm (0.87-0.94 in.) on DT8 models. Adjust float level by bending float tang.

FUEL PUMP. A diaphragm fuel pump (Fig. SZ4-3) is mounted on the side of power head cylinder block and is actuated by pressure and vacuum pulsations from the engine crankcase.

When servicing pump, defective or questionable parts should be renewed. Diaphragm should be renewed if air leaks or cracks are found, or if deterioration is evident.

REED VALVES. The reed valves are located in a reed plate that is located behind the intake manifold. The intake manifold must be removed in order to remove reed plate and service reed valves.

Renew reed valves (2 – Fig. SZ4-4 or SZ4-5) if petals are broken, cracked, warped, rusted or bent. Tip of reed petal must not stand open more than 0.2 mm (0.008 in.) from contact surface. Reed stop opening should be 3.8-4.2 mm (0.15-0.17 in.) on DT5 models and 4.1-4.5 mm (0.16-0.18 in.) on DT6 and DT8 models.

SPEED CONTROL LINKAGE. Engine speed is regulated by position of twist grip. As twist grip is rotated, the carburetor's throttle valve is operated and the ignition system's stator plate is rotated via throttle cables and mechanical linkage. An engine kill switch is used to stop engine operation.

Check and adjust, if needed, the ignition timing as outlined in the following IGNITION section prior to adjusting tension on throttle cables. Adjust throttle cables until all slack is removed from inner cables.

IGNITION

A breakerless, capacitor discharge ignition system is used. Refer to Fig. SZ4-6 for wiring diagram.

Full throttle and full ignition advance should occur simultaneously. The ignition timing is mechanically advanced and must be synchronized with throttle opening.

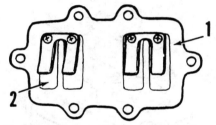

Fig. SZ4-3 – Exploded view of diaphragm type fuel pump.

1. Inner housing
2. Gaskets
3. Diaphragm
4. Outer housing

Fig. SZ4-4 — View showing reed plate (1) and reed valve (2) assembly used on DT5 models.

Fig. SZ4-5 — View showing reed plate (1) and reed valve (2) assembly used on DT6 and DT8 models.

Fig. SZ4-1 — Exploded view of Mikuni BV-18-15 carburetor used on DT5 models. Carburetors used on DT6 and DT8 models are similar.

1. Body
2. Main jet
3. Needle valve
4. Float
5. Float pin
6. Seal
7. Float bowl
8. Gasket
9. Plug
10. Spring
11. Idle speed screw
12. Air jet
13. Pilot air screw
14. Spring
15. Choke knob

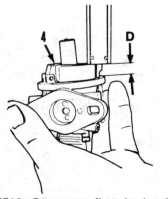

Fig. SZ4-2 — For proper float level, adjust distance (D) from top of carburetor body flange to base of float (4). Refer to text for specification.

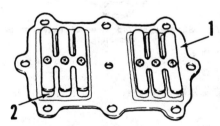

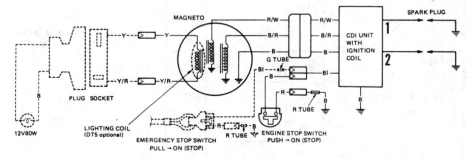

Fig. SZ4-6 — Wiring diagram typical of all models.

B. Black
G. Green
R. Red
Y. Yellow
Bl. Blue
B/R. Black with red tracer
R/W. Red with white tracer
Y/R. Yellow with red tracer

To check ignition timing, first immerse lower unit of outboard motor in water. Connect a suitable tachometer to the engine. Connect a power timing light to upper spark plug. Start engine and warm up to normal operating temperature. Shift into "Forward" gear and accelerate to 1000 rpm and note ignition timing. Cylinder center line should be aligned with mark adjacent to "T1" (0 degree) mark on flywheel. Loosen screws retaining stator plate stopper bracket and adjust bracket until ignition timing at 1000 rpm is as recommended. Maximum advance timing should be 23-27 degrees BTDC at 5000 rpm. Adjust length of stator rod to adjust maximum ignition timing advance.

If ignition malfunction occurs, check condition of spark plugs, all wires and connections before trouble-shooting ignition circuit. Using Suzuki pocket tester 09900-25002 or a suitable ohmmeter, refer to the following test specifications and procedures to aid trouble-shooting.

To check secondary coil resistance of CDI unit, detach spark plug wires at spark plugs. Connect a tester lead to terminal end of each spark plug wire. Secondary coil resistance should be 1272-1908 ohms at 20° C (68° F) on DT5 and DT8 models and 1350-1830 ohms at 20° C (68° F) on Model DT6.

Check condition of capacitor charge coil by separating connector between stator plate and CDI unit (see Fig. SZ4-6). Connect black tester lead to stator plate connector's black wire (B) and red tester lead to connector's black wire with red tracer (B/R). Capacitor charge coil can be considered satisfactory if resistance reading is within the limits of 257-314 ohms at 20°C (68°F). To test pulser coil, leave black tester lead connected to connector's black wire (B). Connect red tester lead to connector's red wire with white tracer (R/W). Pulser coil can be considered satisfactory if resistance reading is within the limits of 20.5-25.1 ohms at 20°C (68°F).

Check condition of lighting coil by separating yellow wire (Y) and yellow wire with red tracer (Y/R) at magneto and connect a tester lead to each wire. Lighting coil can be considered satisfactory if resistance reading is within the limits of 0.37-0.45 ohms at 20°C (68°F).

To check CDI unit, refer to chart shown in Fig. SZ4-7 and wiring diagram Fig. SZ4-6 for identification of wires.

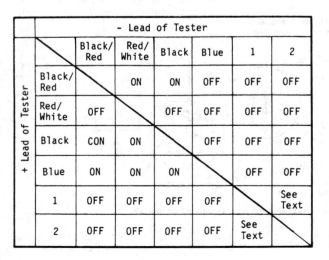

Fig. SZ4-8 — Exploded view of water pump assembly.

1. Case	7. Gasket
2. Grommet	8. Drive shaft bearing
3. Seal	housing
4. Key	9. Gasket
5. Impeller	10. Seal
6. Back plate	11. Snap ring

COOLING SYSTEM

WATER PUMP. A rubber impeller type water pump is mounted between the drive shaft housing and gearcase. A key in the drive shaft is used to turn the pump impeller. If cooling system problems are encountered, check water intakes for plugging or partial stoppage. If water intakes are clear, remove gearcase as outlined under LOWER UNIT and check condition of the water pump, water passages and sealing surfaces.

When water pump is disassembled, check condition of impeller (5—Fig. SZ4-8) and plate (6) for excessive wear. Turn drive shaft clockwise (viewed from top) while placing pump housing over impeller. Avoid turning drive shaft in opposite direction after water pump is reassembled.

POWER HEAD

REMOVE AND REINSTALL. To remove the power head, first remove engine's top cover. Disconnect throttle cables, carburetor fuel inlet line and wires which will interfere with power head removal. Remove air intake cover, carburetor, fuel pump, CDI unit, rewind starter, starter cup (if needed), flywheel and key. Remove stator plate assembly and upper crankcase oil seal housing. Remove six screws which secure power head assembly to drive shaft housing and lift off power head.

Before reinstalling power head, make certain drive shaft splines are clean, then coat splines with a light coat of a suitable water-resistant grease. Apply a coat of silicone sealer to mating surfaces of power head and drive shaft housing and install new gasket. Install power head on drive shaft housing and tighten retaining screws to 15-20 N·m (11-15 ft.-lbs.). The remainder of installation is the reverse of removal procedure.

	- Lead of Tester					
+ Lead of Tester		Black/Red	Red/White	Black	Blue	1	2
	Black/Red		ON	ON	OFF	OFF	OFF
	Red/White	OFF		OFF	OFF	OFF	OFF
	Black	CON	ON		OFF	OFF	OFF
	Blue	ON	ON	ON		OFF	OFF
	1	OFF	OFF	OFF	OFF		See Text
	2	OFF	OFF	OFF	OFF	See Text	

Fig. SZ4-7 — Use chart to test CDI unit and refer to Fig. SZ4-6.

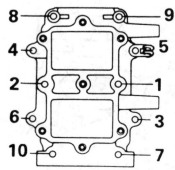

Fig. SZ4-9 — View shows DT6 and DT8 crankcase. DT5 crankcase is similar. Tighten crankcase screws to 8-12 N·m (6-8 ft.-lbs.) in the sequence shown.

DISASSEMBLY. Disassembly and inspection may be accomplished in the following manner. Remove cylinder head. Remove intake manifold and reed plate assembly from crankcase. Remove exhaust cover assembly and lower oil housing. Remove ten crankcase cap screws, then separate crankcase from cylinder block. Lift crankshaft assembly with piston and connecting rod assemblies from cylinder block.

Engine components are now accessible for overhaul as outlined in the appropriate following paragraphs. Clean carbon from cylinder head and combustion chambers and remove any foreign material accumulation in water passages. Inspect components for damage and renew if needed. Refer to the following section for assembly procedure.

ASSEMBLY. Refer to specific service sections when assembling the crankshaft, connecting rods, pistons and reed valves. Make sure all joint and gasket surfaces are clean and free from nicks and burrs. Make sure all carbon, salt, dirt and sand are cleaned from the combustion chambers, exhaust ports and water passages.

Lubricate crankpin bearings and cylinder walls with Suzuki "CCI" oil or a suitable NMMA certified TC-W engine oil. Install crankshaft assembly in crankcase. Make sure shim (1—Fig. SZ4-12) is properly placed on crankshaft. Apply a coat of Suzuki Bond No. 4 or suitable equivalent on mating surfaces of crankcase and cylinder block. Position crankcase half on cylinder block

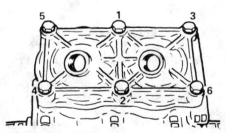

Fig. SZ4-10—On DT5 models, tighten cylinder head screws to 20-26 N·m (15-19 ft.-lbs.) in sequence shown.

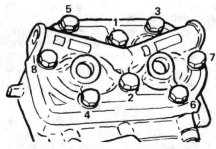

Fig. SZ4-11—On Models DT6 and DT8, tighten cylinder head screws to 20-26 N·m (15-19 ft.-lbs.) in sequence shown.

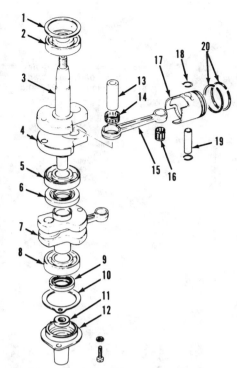

Fig. SZ4-12 — Exploded view of piston and crankshaft assembly.

1. Shim	11. Seal
2. Ball bearing	12. Lower oil seal housing
3. Crank half	13. Crankpin
4. Crank half	14. Roller bearing
5. Ball bearing	15. Connecting rod
6. Seal	16. Roller bearing
7. Lower crank assy.	17. Piston
8. Ball bearing	18. Retainer
9. Seal	19. Piston pin
10. Gasket	20. Piston rings

and tighten ten crankcase screws to 8-12 N·m (6-9 ft.-lbs.) in the sequence shown in Fig. SZ4-9. Tighten cylinder head screws to 20-26 N·m (15-19 ft.-lbs.) following sequence shown in Fig. SZ4-10 on DT5 models and sequence shown in Fig. SZ4-11 on Models DT6 and DT8 models.

PISTONS, PINS, RINGS AND CYLINDERS. Each piston is fitted with two piston rings. Upper piston ring is semi-keystone shaped. Piston ring end gap should be 0.10-0.30 mm (0.004-0.012 in.) with a maximum allowable ring end gap of 0.60 mm (0.024 in.). Piston rings are retained in position by locating pins. Install marked side of piston ring toward top of piston. Piston to cylinder wall clearance should be 0.052-0.067 mm (0.0020-0.0026 in.). Pistons and rings are available in standard size as well as 0.25 mm (0.010 in.) and 0.50 mm (0.020 in.) oversizes. Cylinders should be bored to an oversize if either of the cylinders is out-of-round or taper exceeds 0.10 mm (0.004 in.). Install pistons on connecting rods so arrow on piston crown points toward exhaust port side of cylinder bore.

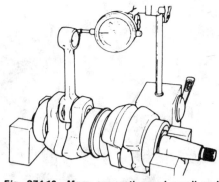

Fig. SZ4-13—Move connecting rod small end side to side to determine connecting rod, bearing and crank pin wear. See text.

CONNECTING RODS, BEARINGS AND CRANKSHAFT. Connecting rod, bearings and crankshaft are a press together unit. Crankshaft should be disassembled ONLY by experienced service personnel and with suitable service equipment.

Caged roller bearings are used at both large and small ends of the connecting rod. Determine rod bearing wear from side to side as shown in Fig. SZ4-13. Normal side to side movement is 4.0 mm (0.16 in.) or less. Maximum limit of crankshaft runout is 0.05 mm (0.002 in.) measured at bearing surfaces with crankshaft ends supported.

Apply Suzuki Super Grease "A" or a suitable high temperature grease to lip portion of crankshaft seals prior to installation.

MANUAL STARTER

The power head may be equipped with either an overhead type starter (Fig. SZ4-15) or a gear type starter (Fig. SZ4-16). Refer to following service sections.

OVERHEAD TYPE STARTER. On models equipped with an overhead type starter, starter may be disassembled for overhaul or renewal of individual components as follows: Remove engine's top cover and three cap screws securing starter assembly to power head. If starter spring remains under tension, pull starter rope and hold rope pulley (3 – Fig. SZ4-15) with notch in pulley adjacent to rope outlet. Pull rope back through outlet so rope engages notch in pulley and allow pulley to slowly unwind. Remove retainer (10) and disassemble unit. Be careful when removing rewind spring (2); a rapidly uncoiling starter spring could cause serious injury.

Rewind spring (2) is wound in a counterclockwise direction from the outer end. Rope (12) is wound on pulley (3) in a counterclockwise direction as viewed

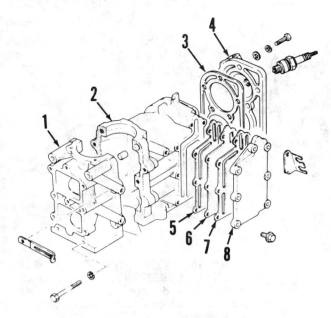

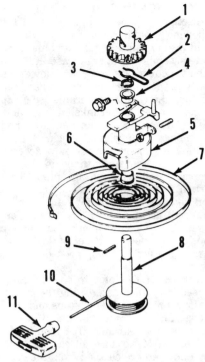

Fig. SZ4-14—Exploded view of cylinder block and crankcase assembly on DT6 and DT8 models. DT5 models are similar.

1. Crankcase
2. Cylinder block
3. Gasket
4. Cylinder head
5. Gasket
6. Exhaust plate
7. Gasket
8. Exhaust cover

from the flywheel side. Reassemble starter assembly by reversing disassembly procedure. To place tension on rewind spring (2), pass rope (12) through rope outlet in housing (1) and install rope handle (11). Pull rope (12) out and hold pulley (3) so notch on pulley is adjacent to rope outlet. Pull rope back through outlet between notch in pulley and housing. Turn pulley (3) counterclockwise six complete revolutions to place tension on rewind spring (2). Release starter rope (12) and allow rope to wind onto pulley (3). Do not place more tension on rewind spring than is necessary to draw rope handle up against housing.

GEAR TYPE STARTER. On models with gear type starter, starter may be removed and disassembled for overhaul or renewal of individual components as follows: Remove engine's top cover, then remove rope handle (11–Fig. SZ4-16) and allow starter rope (10) to wind onto starter reel (8). Remove the nut and cap screw securing starter assembly to power head and withdraw assembly. Use a suitable punch and drive out pin (9). Slide starter pinion (1) with spring clip (2) from starter reel (8). Remove snap ring (3), then carefully withdraw reel (8) from housing (5) so rewind spring (7) will not uncoil from housing; a rapidly uncoiling rewind spring could cause serious injury. Broken rewind spring or rope may be renewed at this point.

Rewind spring (7) is wound in clockwise direction into housing (5) as viewed from bottom side. Wind starter rope (10) onto starter reel (8) in a clockwise direction as viewed from bottom side. Insert reel (8) into housing, engaging eye in end of spring with notch at reel base. Install

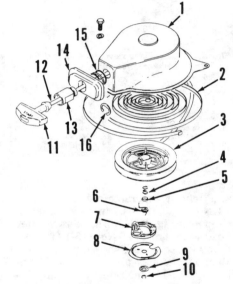

Fig. SZ4-15—Exploded view of overhead type manual starter.

1. Housing
2. Rewind spring
3. Pulley
4. Spring
5. Spacer
6. Return spring
7. Drive pawl
8. Drive plate
9. Washer
10. Retainer
11. Handle
12. Starter rope
13. Rope guide
14. Plate
15. Spring
16. Retainer

snap ring (3), then place starter pinion (1) with spring clip (2) on shaft. Make certain spring clip is centered over lug on housing. Install pin (9). Thread starter rope (10) through starter housing (5) and attach rope handle (11). Hold starter reel (8) so notch on starter reel pulley is adjacent to rope outlet. Pull a loop of rope back through outlet between notch in pulley and housing. While grasping rope, turn starter reel (8) one complete revolution clockwise as viewed from bottom side to place tension on rewind

Fig. SZ4-16 — Exploded view of gear type manual starter.

1. Starter pinion
2. Spring clip
3. Snap ring
4. Bushing
5. Housing
6. Bushing
7. Rewind spring
8. Starter reel
9. Pin
10. Starter rope
11. Handle

spring (7). Release starter rope (10) and allow rope to wind onto starter reel pulley. Do not place more tension on rewind spring than is necessary to draw rope handle (11) up against engine's bottom cover.

LOWER UNIT

PROPELLER AND SHEAR PIN. Propeller for normal use has three blades and is equipped with a shear pin to prevent damage to lower unit gears. Standard propeller has a 200 mm (7-7/8 in.) diameter on DT5 and DT6 models and 215 mm (8-1/2 in.) on Model DT8. Standard propeller has a pitch of 170 mm (6-3/4 in.) on Model DT5, 190 mm (7-1/2 in.) on Model DT6 and 180 mm (7-1/8 in.) on Model DT8. Optional propellers are available from the manufacturer and should be selected to provide full throttle operation within the recommended limits of 4800-5500 rpm on DT5 models and 5200-5700 rpm on Models DT6 and DT8.

R&R AND OVERHAUL. Refer to Fig. SZ4-17 for exploded view of lower unit gearcase assembly. During disassembly, note the location of all shims and washers to aid in reassembly. To remove gearcase, first remove drain plug (32) and vent plug and drain gear lubricant. Remove shift rod adjustment cover and loosen shift rod adjustment screw (10–Fig. SZ4-19). Remove cotter pin (31–Fig. SZ4-17), spinner (30), propeller (29) and shear pin (27). Remove four lower unit cap screws and withdraw lower unit assembly from drive shaft housing.

Remove bearing housing (25) retaining screws. Being careful, pry bearing housing (25) from gearcase housing. Withdraw bearing housing with propeller shaft assembly. If needed, remove pinion gear (12), shim (11) and forward drive gear (9) with shim (8).

Inspect all components for excessive wear and damage. Apply a water resistant grease to lip portion of all seals. All seals and "O" rings should be renewed when unit is reassembled.

Reassemble lower unit by reversing disassembly procedure while noting the following: Install dog clutch (16) on propeller shaft (18) so "F" marked side (see Fig. SZ4-18) is toward forward gear (9–Fig. SZ4-17). Securely tighten bearing housing (25) retaining cap screws. Check mesh pattern of pinion gear and forward gear to determine which shim

or shims should be adjusted. Recommended backlash between forward gear and pinion gear is 0.1-0.2 mm (0.0039-0.0079 in.). Assembled propeller shaft end play should be 0.05-0.50 mm (0.002-0.020 in.). Adjust thickness of shims (10 and 19) until recommended end play is obtained. Apply silicone sealer to lower unit and drive shaft housing mating surfaces. Tighten the four cap screws securing lower unit to drive shaft housing to 15-20 N·m (11-15 ft.-lbs.).

With lower unit installed, adjust shift linkage as follows: Make sure lower unit is in "Forward" position. Set shift con-

trol handle to "Forward" position, then tighten cap screw (10–Fig. SZ4-19) to secure shift rod position. Make sure "Neutral" and "Reverse" positions properly engage. Install shift rod cover. Fill gearcase with approximately 240 mL (8.1 oz.) of SAE 90 hypoid outboard gear oil.

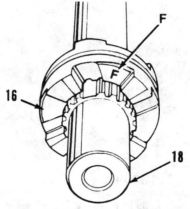

Fig. SZ4-18—Install dog clutch (16) on propeller shaft (18) so "F" mark (F) is toward forward gear.

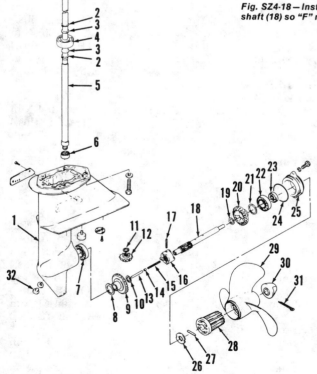

Fig. SZ4-17—Exploded view of lower unit gearcase assembly.

1. Housing
2. Snap ring
3. Washer
4. Ball bearing
5. Drive shaft
6. Roller bearing
7. Ball bearing
8. Shim
9. Forward gear
10. Pinion gear
11. Shim
12. Shim
13. Rod
14. Pin
15. Spring
16. Dog clutch
17. Pin
18. Propeller shaft
19. Shim
20. Reverse gear
21. Shim
22. Ball bearing
23. Seal
24. "O" ring
25. Bearing housing
26. Spacer
27. Shear pin
28. Thrust hub
29. Propeller
30. Spinner
31. Cotter pin
32. Drain plug

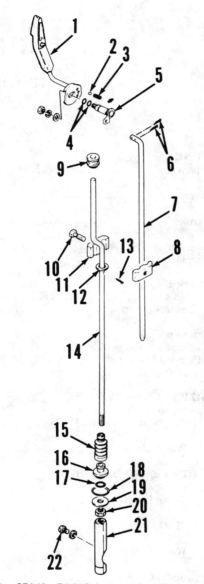

Fig. SZ4-19—Exploded view of shift control linkage.

1. Shift lever
2. Ball
3. Spring
4. "O" rings
5. Shaft
6. Cotter pins
7. Upper shift rod
8. Bracket half
9. Guide
10. Cap screw
11. Bracket half
12. Washer
13. Cotter pin
14. Lower shift rod
15. Boot
16. Guide
17. "O" ring
18. "O" ring
19. Washer
20. Nut
21. Shift cam
22. Retainer screw

SUZUKI DT9.9 & DT15 (1983-1987)
AND DT15C (1988)

CONDENSED SERVICE DATA

NOTE: Metric fasteners are used throughout outboard motor.

TUNE-UP

Hp/rpm 9.9/4500-5300
                                                15/4700-5500
Bore ....59 mm
                                                (2.32 in.)
Stroke ....52 mm
                                                (2.05 in.)
Number of Cylinders 2
Displacement ....284 cc
                                                (17.33 cu. in.)
Spark Plug:
  NGK BR7HS-10
  Electrode Gap ....0.9-1.0 mm
                                                (0.035-0.039 in.)
Ignition Type ....CDI
Carburetor Make ....Mikuni
Idle Speed (in gear) ....600-650 rpm
Fuel:Oil Ratio ....See Text

SIZES—CLEARANCES

Piston Ring End Gap:
  DT9.9 and DT15 (to 1987) ....0.15-0.35 mm
                                                (0.006-0.014 in.)
    Wear Limit ....0.7 mm
                                                (0.027 in.)
  DT9.9 and DT15 (1987) ....0.20-0.40 mm
                                                (0.008-0.016 in.)
    Wear Limit ....0.8 mm
                                                (0.031 in.)
  DT15C.............................0.10-0.25 mm
                                                (0.004-0.010 in.)
    Wear Limit ....0.8 mm
                                                (0.031 in.)
Piston-to-Cylinder
  Clearance:
  DT9.9 and DT15 ....0.052-0.067 mm
                                                (0.0020-0.0026 in.)
  DT15C........................0.042-0.062 mm
                                                (0.0016-0.0024 in.)
Piston Pin Diameter.............13.995-14.000 mm
                                                (0.5510-0.5512 in.)
Maximum Crankshaft Runout
  at Main Bearing Journal ....0.05 mm
                                                (0.002 in.)
Maximum Connecting Rod
  Small End Side Shake:
  DT9.9 and DT15 ....4.0 mm
                                                (0.157 in.)

SIZES—CLEARANCES CONT.

DT15C ....5.0 mm
                                                (0.197 in.)

TIGHTENING TORQUES

Power Head Mounting Screws ....15-20 N·m
                                                (11-15 ft.-lbs.)
Crankcase:
  6 mm ....8-12 N·m
                                                (6-9 ft.-lbs.)
  8 mm ....20-26 N·m
                                                (15-19 ft.-lbs.)
Cylinder Head Screws:
  DT9.9 and DT15 ....20-26 N·m
                                                (15-19 ft.-lbs.)
  DT15C ....21-25 N·m
                                                (16-18 ft.-lbs.)
Flywheel Nut ....80-90 N·m
                                                (59-66 ft.-lbs.)
Standard Screws—
  (Marked "4"):
  5 mm ....2-4 N·m
                                                (18-35 in.-lbs.)
  6 mm ....4-7 N·m
                                                (35-62 in.-lbs.)
  8 mm ....10-16 N·m
                                                (7-12 ft.-lbs.)
  10 mm ....22-35 N·m
                                                (16-26 ft.-lbs.)
  (Stainless Steel):
  5 mm ....2-4 N·m
                                                (18-35 in.-lbs.)
  6 mm ....6-10 N·m
                                                (53-88 in.-lbs.)
  8 mm ....15-20 N·m
                                                (11-15 ft.-lbs.)
  10 mm ....34-41 N·m
                                                (25-30 ft.-lbs.)
  (Marked "7"):
  5 mm ....3-6 N·m
                                                (26-53 in.-lbs.)
  6 mm ....8-12 N·m
                                                (71-106 in.-lbs.)
  8 mm ....18-28 N·m
                                                (13-21 ft.-lbs.)
  10 mm ....40-60 N·m
                                                (29-44 ft.-lbs.)

LUBRICATION

The power head is lubricated by oil mixed with the fuel. Recommended oil is Suzuki Outboard Motor Oil or a good quality NMMA certified TC-W two-stroke engine oil. Recommended fuel is no-lead or regular automotive gasoline having an 85-95 octane rating. Fuel and oil should be thoroughly mixed.

On all models except DT15C, fuel:oil ratio should be 30:1 during break-in of a new or rebuilt engine. On DT9.9 and DT15 models prior to 1986, fuel ratio after initial 15 hours of operation should be 50:1 when using a recommended oil. On 1986 and later DT9.9 and DT15 models, fuel ratio after initial 15 hours of operation should be 100:1 when using a recommended oil.

Model DT15C is equipped with automatic oil injection. When breaking-in a new or rebuilt engine, mix a recommended oil with the gasoline at a 50:1 ratio in combination with the oil injection system to ensure sufficient lubrication during break-in. Switch to straight gasoline after completion of the first tank of fuel.

Oil injection system on Model DT15C is equipped with a renewable oil filter between oil tank and oil pump. Renew filter after 50 hours of operation or after three months.

The lower unit gears and bearings are lubricated by approximately 170 mL (5.7 ozs.) of SAE 90 hypoid outboard gear oil. Reinstall vent and fill plugs securely using a new gasket, if necessary, to ensure a water tight seal.

FUEL SYSTEM

CARBURETOR. A Mikuni B24-15 carburetor is used on DT9.9 models and Mikuni B24-18 carburetor is used on DT15 and DT15C models. Refer to Fig. SZ6-1 for exploded view of carburetor. Initial setting of pilot air screw (2) from a lightly seated position should be 1-1/4 to 1-3/4 turns on DT9.9 and DT15 models prior to 1987, 1-1/8 to 1-5/8 turns on Model DT9.9 after 1986, 7/8 to 1-3/8 turns on DT15 models after 1986 and 1-1/2 to 2 turns on Model DT15C. Final carburetor adjustment should be made with engine running at normal operating temperature in forward gear. Adjust idle speed screw (4) so engine idles at approximately 600-650 rpm. Adjust pilot air screw so engine idles smoothly and will accelerate cleanly without hesitation. As adjustments affect each other, readjustment of idle speed may be necessary.

Main fuel metering is controlled by main jet (13). Standard main jet size for normal operation is #110 on DT9.9 models, #122.5 on early DT15 models (prior to 1987) and #125 on late DT15 and all DT15C models. Standard pilot jet (6) size is #52.5 on DT9.9 models, #57.5 on DT15 models and #65 on DT15C models.

To check float level, remove float bowl (10) and invert carburetor body (1). Base of float (9—Fig. SZ6-2) should

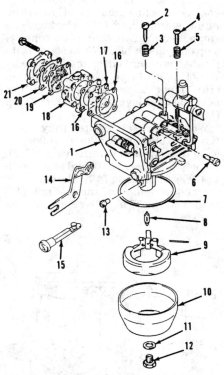

Fig. SZ6-1—Exploded view of Mikuni type carburetor and fuel pump.

1. Body	12. Screw
2. Pilot air screw	13. Main jet
3. Spring	14. Choke lever
4. Idle speed screw	15. Choke knob
5. Spring	16. Gasket
6. Pilot jet	17. Diaphragm
7. Gasket	18. Check valve assy.
8. Needle valve	19. Diaphragm
9. Float	20. Gasket
10. Float bowl	21. Cover
11. Gasket	

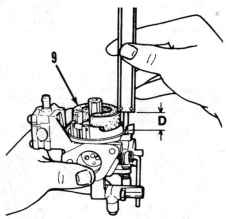

Fig. SZ6-2—For proper float level, base of float (9) should be a distance (D) of 23-25 mm (0.91-0.98 in.) away from top of carburetor body flange.

be a distance (D) of 23-25 mm (0.91-0.98 in.) from top of carburetor body flange on all models. Adjust float level by bending float tang.

FUEL FILTER. A fuel filter assembly mounted on engine port side is used to filter the fuel prior to entering the fuel pump assembly. Periodically unscrew cup (5—Fig. SZ6-3) from base (1) and withdraw filter element (4). Clean cup (5) and filter element (4) in a suitable solvent and blow dry with clean compressed air. Inspect filter element (4). If excessive blockage or damage is noted, then the element must be renewed.

Reassembly is reverse order of disassembly. Renew "O" ring (3) and, if needed, seal (2) during reassembly.

FUEL PUMP. The fuel pump is an integral part of the carburetor. The fuel pump assembly can be overhauled without carburetor removal, proceed as follows: Remove engine top cover and disconnect the fuel tank supply hose at the outboard motor connector. Disconnect the fuel supply hose at the fuel pump inlet.

With reference to Fig. SZ6-1, disassemble the fuel pump assembly. Inspect all components for damage and excessive wear and renew if needed. Clean components as needed with a suitable cleaning solution. Blow dry with clean compressed air. If compressed air is not available, use only lint-free cloths to

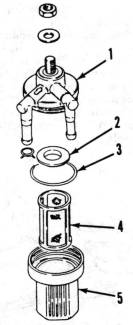

Fig. SZ6-3—Exploded view of fuel filter assembly.

1. Base
2. Seal
3. "O" ring
4. Element
5. Cup

wipe dry. Make sure all passages are clear of any obstruction.

With reference to Fig. SZ6-1, reassemble the fuel pump assembly with new gaskets. Securely tighten the retaining screws.

NOTE: Fuel pump and engine malfunction will result if the fuel pump and all connections are not airtight.

Complete reassembly.

REED VALVES. The reed valves are located in a reed plate that is located behind the intake manifold. The intake manifold must be removed in order to remove reed plate and service reed valves.

Renew reed valves (2—Fig. SZ6-4) if petals are broken, cracked, warped, rusted or bent. Tip of reed petal must not stand open more than 0.2 mm (0.008 in.) from contact surface. Reed stop opening should be 2.2-2.6 mm (0.09-0.10 in.) on early DT9.9 models (prior to 1987) and 5.5-5.9 mm (0.22-0.23 in.) on DT15 and DT15C models.

SPEED CONTROL LINKAGE. Models DT9.9 and DT15. Check and adjust, if necessary, the ignition timing as outlined in the following IGNITION section prior to speed control linkage adjustment.

With shift lever in "Neutral" position there should be zero clearance (C—Fig. SZ6-5) between throttle lever (1) and throttle limiter (2). If necessary, adjust ball nut (3) until zero clearance is obtained. Without disturbing position of throttle lever (1), adjust throttle cables (4) until all slack is removed from inner cables (5).

Shift into the "Forward" position. Loosen screw (6) retaining carburetor throttle rod (7). Rotate twist grip to the full throttle position. Move throttle rod (7) until carburetor throttle plate is at wide-open throttle and tighten screw (6). Rotate twist grip to full closed po-

sition. A small clearance between roller (8) and throttle cam (9) should be noted.

Model DT15C. Check and adjust, if necessary, the ignition timing as outlined in the following IGNITION section prior to speed control linkage adjustment.

Standard length of stator link rod (10—Fig. SZ6-6) is 85.5 mm (3.37 in.). To check stator link adjustment, rotate ignition stator plate fully clockwise so stopper bracket on stator plate contacts stop on cylinder block. With stator plate rotated as described, spark advance lever (12) should be against lever stop (16). If not, adjust stator link (10) as necessary so lever (12) contacts stop (16).

With stator plate rotated fully clockwise as described above, roller (8) should be against throttle cam (9). To adjust, loosen screw (6) and adjust roller (8) so throttle is fully closed.

Standard length of throttle link (11) is 75.5 mm (2.97 in.). To adjust throttle

link (11), rotate throttle control lever (15) clockwise until lever contacts throttle control lever stop (17) on cylinder block, then adjust throttle link (11) so carburetor valve is fully open.

NOTE: Throttle and spark advance must occur simultaneously. If not, readjust throttle link (11) as necessary to provide simultaneous throttle and spark advance.

Adjust throttle cables (4) so throttle control lever (15) contacts lever stop (17) at full throttle. Tension on throttle cables should not be excessively tight. Make sure throttle cable drum (14) is against throttle drum stop (13) with throttle in full closed position. If not, readjust throttle cables (4) as necessary.

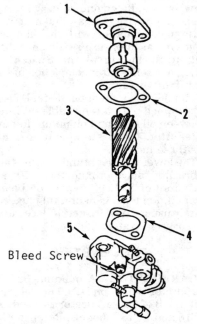

Fig. SZ6-7—View of oil pump assembly and related components.

1. Retainer
2. Gasket
3. Driven gear
4. Gasket
5. Oil pump assy.

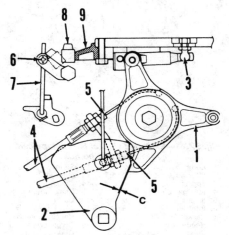

Fig. SZ6-5—View of speed control linkage on DT9.9 and DT15 models. Refer to text for adjustment procedures.

1. Throttle lever
2. Throttle limiter
3. Ball nut
4. Throttle cables
5. Inner cables
6. Screw
7. Throttle rod
8. Roller
9. Throttle cam

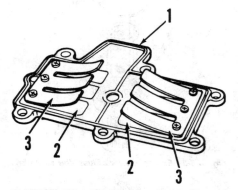

Fig. SZ6-4—View identifying reed plate (1), reed valves (2) and reed stops (3).

Fig. SZ6-6—View of speed control linkage. Refer to text for adjustment procedure.

1. Throttle lever
4. Throttle cables
5. Inner cables
6. Screw
8. Roller
9. Throttle cam
10. Stator link
11. Throttle link
12. Spark advance lever
13. Throttle drum stop
14. Throttle drum
15. Throttle control lever
16. Spark advance lever stop
17. Throttle control lever stop

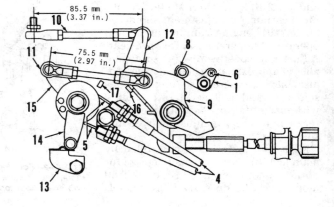

OIL INJECTION

BLEEDING PUMP. Air must be bled from oil injection system if oil pump, tank or oil lines have been removed from motor, or if motor has been in storage. Mix a recommended oil with the fuel at a 50:1 ratio to ensure proper lubrication while performing bleeding procedure. Remove plug (Fig. SZ6-8) and loosen bleed screw two or three turns with a screwdriver. Start engine and allow to run at idle speed (600-650 rpm) until all air is discharged from bleed screw. Make sure bleed screw is securely tightened after bleeding system.

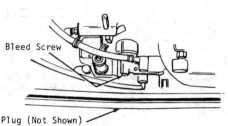

Fig. SZ6-8—To bleed oil injection system, remove plug (not shown) and insert screwdriver and loosen bleed screw. Refer to text.

CHECKING OIL PUMP OUTPUT. Start engine and allow to warm-up for approximately five minutes prior to checking oil pump output. Stop engine, remove oil tank and connect oil measuring gage 09900-21602 to oil supply line. Fill oil measuring gage with recommended oil until even with an upper reference mark. Start engine and run at 1500 rpm for five minutes. After five minutes, stop engine and note oil level in measuring gage. Oil consumption should be 1.5-2.5 mL (0.051-0.084 oz.) in five minutes at 1500 rpm. Renew oil pump assembly if oil consumption is not to specification.

IGNITION

Models DT9.9 and DT15

A breakerless capacitor discharge ignition system is used. Refer to Fig. SZ6-9 for wiring diagram.

Full throttle and full ignition timing advance should occur simultaneously. The ignition timing is mechanically advanced and must be synchronized with throttle opening.

To check ignition timing, first immerse lower unit of outboard motor in water. Connect a suitable tachometer to engine. Connect a power timing light to upper spark plug wire. Start the engine and warm up to normal operating temperature. Shift into "Forward" gear and note ignition timing. Refer to Fig. SZ6-10. On early Models DT9.9 and DT15 (prior to 1987), timing should be 0-4 degrees ATDC at 650 rpm. On 1987 and later DT9.9 and DT15 models, timing should be 0-2 degrees ATDC at 650 rpm. To adjust timing, loosen throttle cam (9—Fig. SZ6-11) mounting screws and adjust throttle cam until idle speed timing is as recommended. Maximum timing advance should be 16.5-20.5 degrees BTDC at 5000 rpm on early (prior to 1987) DT9.9 models and 23-27 degrees BTDC at 5000 rpm on later (1987 and after) DT9.9 and all DT15 models. On DT9.9 models, adjust cam stopper screw (S) to limit ignition timing maximum advance.

If ignition malfunction occurs, check condition of spark plugs, all wires and connections before trouble-shooting ig-

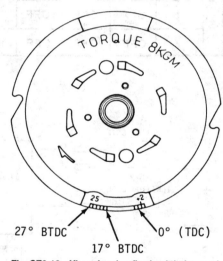

Fig. SZ6-10—View showing flywheel timing marks on Models DT9.9 and DT15. Each mark is a 2 degree increment.

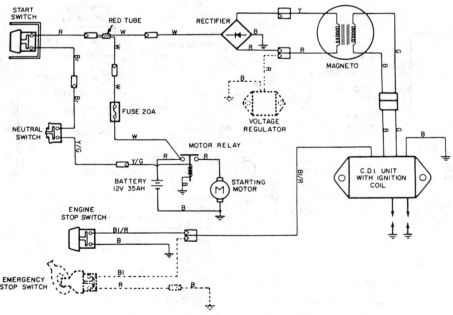

Fig. SZ6-9—Wiring diagram of electrical system on Models DT9.9 and DT15 equipped with electric starter.

B. Black
G. Green
R. Red
W. White
Y. Yellow
Bl. Blue
Br. Brown
Bl/r. Blue with red tracer
Y/G. Yellow with green tracer

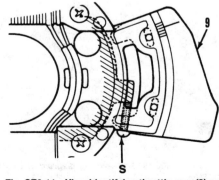

Fig. SZ6-11—View identifying throttle cam (9) on Models DT9.9 and DT15. On DT9.9 models, adjust cam stopper screw (S) to limit ignition timing maximum advance.

nition circuit. Using Suzuki pocket tester 09900-25002 or a suitable ohmmeter, refer to the following test specifications and procedures to aid trouble-shooting.

To check secondary coil resistance of CDI unit, detach spark plug wires at spark plugs. Connect a tester lead to terminal end of each spark plug wire. Secondary coil resistance should be 2000-3000 ohms at 20° C (68° F).

Check condition of primary coil by separating connector between primary coil and CDI unit. Refer to Fig. SZ6-9. Connect a tester lead to primary coil black wire (B) and gree wire (G). Primary coil resistance should be 240-306 ohms at 20° C (68° F). Check condition of battery charge coil by separating yellow wire (Y) and red wire (R) at magneto and connect a tester lead to each wire. Battery charge coil resistance should be 0.18-0.26 ohm at 20° C (68° F) on early models (prior to 1987) and 0.1-0.4 ohms at 20° C (68° F) on later models.

To check CDI unit, refer to chart shown in Fig. SZ6-12 and Fig. SZ6-13 for identification of wires.

Model DT15C

A breakerless, capacitor discharge ignition system is used. Refer to Fig. SZ6-14 for wiring diagram. Full throttle and full ignition timing advance must occur simultaneously for proper operation. Refer to SPEED CONTROL LINKAGE section.

Timing marks (Fig. SZ6-15) on stator and stator stopper must be aligned for

	⊖ lead of tester				
	Green	**Black**	**Blue/ Red**	**1**	**2**
Green		ON	OFF	OFF	OFF
Black	CON		OFF	OFF	OFF
Blue/ Red	ON	ON		OFF	OFF
1	OFF	OFF	OFF		2500 Ω
2	OFF	OFF	OFF	2500 Ω	

(⊕ lead of tester)

Fig. SZ6-12—Use chart to test CDI unit. Refer to Fig. SZ6-13.

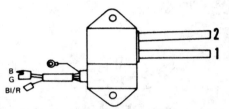

Fig. SZ6-13—View showing CDI unit. Refer to Fig. SZ6-12 for chart used in testing CDI unit.

1. No. 1 cylinder high tension lead
2. No. 2 cylinder high tension lead
B. Black
G. Green
Bl/R. Blue with red tracer

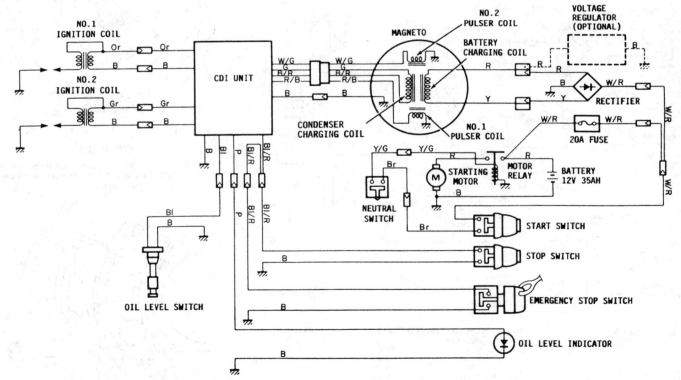

Fig. SZ6-14—Wiring diagram of electrical system on Model DT15C equipped with electric starter and optional voltage regulator.

B. Black	Bl. Blue	B/R. Blue with red tracer
G. Green	Br. Brown	R/B. Red with black tracer
P. Pink	Gr. Gray	
R. Red	Or. Orange	W/G. White with green tracer
Y. Yellow		W/R. White with red tracer

W/G. White with green tracer
W/R. White with red tracer

Y/G. Yellow with green tracer
Bl/R. Blue with red tracer

Illustrations Courtesy Suzuki America Corp.

correct ignition timing. Loosen screw securing stator stopper and adjust stopper as necessary to align marks. To check ignition timing, immerse lower unit of motor in water. Connect a suitable tachometer to engine. Connect a suitable timing light to upper spark plug lead, start engine and warm to normal operating temperature. Refer to Fig. SZ6-16. Timing should be 8-12 degrees ATDC at 650-700 rpm. Maximum timing advance should be 25-29 degrees BTDC at 2000 rpm or above.

If ignition malfunction occurs, check condition of spark plugs, all wires and connections prior to trouble-shooting ignition circuit. Use Suzuki CDI tester 09930-99830 and tester lead 09930-88910 to test capacitor discharge unit. Follow manufacturer's instructions when using tester.

Stevens Model CD-77 peak voltage tester may be used to test ignition and battery charging components. Refer to Fig. SZ6-18 when using Stevens peak voltage tester for test sequence and results.

Suzuki Pocket Tester 09900-25002 or a suitable ohmmeter may be used to test condenser charging coil, battery charging coil, pulser coils and ignition coils. Refer to Fig. SZ6-14. To test condenser charging coil, connect tester between green wire and black wire with red tracer. Resistance should be 170-250 ohms at 20° C (68° F).

To test battery charging coil on electric start models, connect tester leads between coil red and yellow wires. On manual start models, connect tester between yellow wire with red tracer and red wire, then between red wire and yellow wire. Resistance should be 0.2-0.5 ohms at 20° C (68° F).

To test number 1 pulser coil, connect tester between red wire with black tracer and engine ground. To test number 2 pulser coil, connect tester between white wire with black tracer and engine ground. Resistance for both coils should be 260-380 ohms at 20° C (68° F).

Primary ignition coil resistance should be 0.1-0.3 ohms at 20° C (68° F). Connect tester between orange wire and black wire on number 1 coil and gray wire and black wire on number 2 coil. Secondary ignition coil resistance should be 2600-3600 ohms at 20° C (68° F). Connect tester between orange wire and end of spark plug lead to test number 1 coil and gray wire and end of spark plug lead on number 2 coil.

To test battery charging coil rectifier, refer to Fig. SZ6-19 for wire identification and Fig. SZ6-20 for test sequence and results. Renew rectifier if not to specification.

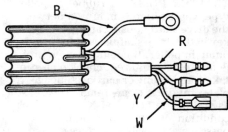

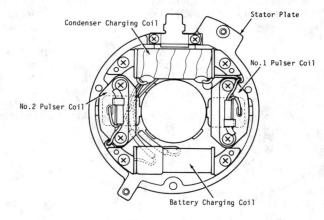

Fig. SZ6-19—View showing battery charging rectifier used on Model DT15C. Refer to Fig. SZ6-20 to test rectifier.

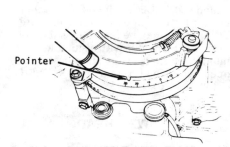

Fig. SZ6-16—View showing flywheel timing marks and timing pointer on Model DT15C.

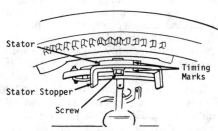

Fig. SZ6-15—On Model DT15C, timing marks on stator and stator stopper must be aligned for proper ignition timing. Loosen stopper screw and move stopper as necessary to adjust.

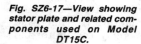

Fig. SZ6-17—View showing stator plate and related components used on Model DT15C.

TESTING SEQUENCE	TEST LEAD CONNECTION		PEAK VOLTAGE	TESTING RANGE	REMARKS
		RED LEAD	BLACK LEAD			
CDI Output	No.1	Orange	Black	50V or over	POS 500	Connect the Ignition Coil.
	No.2	Gray	Black			
Condenser Charging Coil Output	No.1	Green	Black/Red	82V or over	POS 500	Connect the CDI Unit.
Pulser Coil Output	No.1	White/Green	Black	1.8V or over	SEN 5	Connect the CDI Unit.
	No.2	Red/Black	Black			
Battery Charging Coil Output	Manual Starter	Red	Yellow	0.75V or over	POS 5	Disconnect the Rectifier.
		Yellow/Red	Yellow	1.8V or over		
	Electric Starter	Red	Yellow	1.8V or over		

Fig. SZ6-18—When using Stevens Model CD-77 peak voltage tester, refer to chart shown for test sequence and results. Refer to Fig. SZ6-14 for wiring diagram.

	⊕ PROBE OF TESTER TO:			
		Black	White	Yellow	Red
⊖ PROBE OF TESTER TO:	Black		5,500-8,500 Ω	2,200-3,200 Ω	2,200-3,200 Ω
	White	∞		∞	∞
	Yellow	∞	2,200-3,200 Ω		∞
	Red	∞	1,700-2,700 Ω	∞	

Fig. SZ6-20—Use chart shown when testing charging rectifier on Model DT15C. Refer to Fig. SZ6-19.

COOLING SYSTEM

WATER PUMP. A rubber impeller type water pump is mounted between the drive shaft housing and gearcase. A key in the drive shaft is used to turn the pump impeller. If cooling system problems are encountered, check water intake for plugging or partial stoppage. If water intake is clear, remove gearcase as outlined in LOWER UNIT and check condition of the water pump, water passages and sealing surfaces.

When water pump is disassembled, check condition of impeller (10—Fig. SZ6-21) and plate (14) for excessive wear. Turn drive shaft clockwise (viewed from top) while placing pump housing over impeller. Avoid turning drive shaft in opposite direction after water pump is reassembled.

Model DT15C is equipped with a thermostat located in exhaust cover plate. Thermostat may be tested by submersing in heated water with a suitable thermometer. Thermostat should start to open when water reaches 58°-62° C (136°-144° F).

POWER HEAD

REMOVE AND REINSTALL. To remove the power head on DT9.9 and DT15 models, first remove engine top cover. Disconnect throttle cable, neutral start cable, fuel pump inlet hose and wires which will interfere with power head removal. Label wires for later reference. Remove carburetor air intake cover, rewind starter, rectifier assembly, CDI unit, starter motor relay, electric starter motor, flywheel and key, fuel filter assembly, carburetor and fuel pump assembly and stator plate with battery charge coil and primary coil. Remove six screws securing power head to drive shaft housing and lift off power head.

To remove power head on Model DT15C, disconnect battery, remove rewind starter and electric parts holder cover. Disconnect any wires or hoses that interfere with power head removal. Remove electric parts holder and oil tank. Remove carburetor, disconnect throttle cables and remove idle speed adjustment knob. Remove six bolts securing power head to lower unit and lift off power head.

Before reinstalling power head on all models, make certain drive shaft splines are clean, then coat splines with a suitable water-resistant grease. Apply a coat of silicone sealant to mating surfaces of power head and drive shaft housing. Renew power head-to-drive shaft housing gasket. Coat threads of power head retaining screws with silicone sealant and tighten screws to 15-20 N·m (11-15 ft.-lbs.). Complete remainder of installation by reversing removal procedure. Refer to SPEED CONTROL LINKAGE for synchronizing throttle opening with ignition advance.

To disassemble power head on Models DT9.9 and DT15, remove electric starter bracket, intake manifold, reed valve plate, exhaust cover, exhaust plate and gasket and cylinder head. Remove ten crankcase cap screws, then separate crankcase from cylinder block. Lift crankshaft assembly with pistons and connecting rod assemblies from cylinder block.

To disassemble power head on Model DT15C, remove exhaust tube and oil seal housing. Remove CDI unit, starter motor, throttle control components, neutral switch, ignition coils and oil

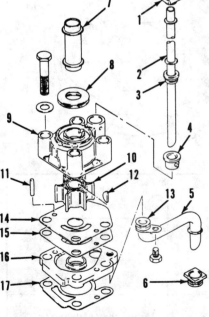

Fig. SZ6-21—Exploded view of water pump assembly used on all models.

1. Tube seal	10. Impeller
2. Water tube	11. Pin
3. Grommet	12. Key
4. Bushing	13. Grommet
5. Inlet tube	14. Back plate
6. Grommet	15. Gasket
7. Seal tube	16. Housing
8. Grommet	17. Gasket
9. Case	

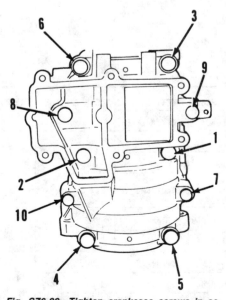

Fig. SZ6-22—Tighten crankcase screws in sequence shown on Models DT9.9 and DT15. Refer to text for correct torque value.

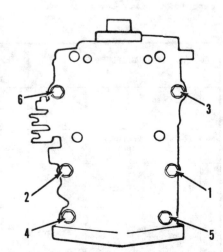

Fig. SZ6-23—On Model DT15C, tighten crankcase screws to 20-26 N·m (15-19 ft.-lbs.) in sequence shown.

pump. Remove flywheel using a suitable flywheel puller. Remove stator plate assembly, stator spacer, cylinder head, exhaust cover, thermostat cover and thermostat. Remove intake manifold and reed valve plate. Remove six crankcase screws, separate crankcase from cylinder block and lift out crankshaft assembly.

Engine components are now accessible for overhaul as outlined in the appropriate following paragraphs. Clean carbon from cylinder head and combustion chambers and remove any foreign material accumulation in water passages. Inspect components for damage and renew if needed. Refer to the following section for assembly procedure.

ASSEMBLY. Refer to specific service sections when reassembling crankshaft,

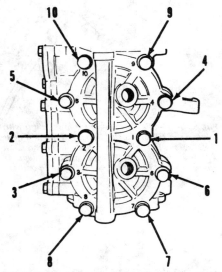

Fig. SZ6-24—Tighten cylinder head screws on all models in sequence shown to 20-26 N·m (15-19 ft.-lbs.).

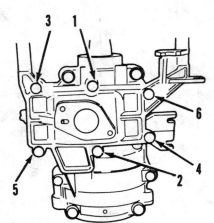

Fig. SZ6-25—On DT9.9 and DT15 models, securely tighten intake manifold screws in sequence shown. On Model DT15C, install screws marked "9" in upper (flywheel) end of manifold and screws marked "7" in lower side.

connecting rods, pistons and reed valves. Make sure all joint and gasket surfaces are clean and free from nicks and burrs. Make sure all carbon, salt, dirt and sand are cleaned from the combustion chambers, exhaust ports and water passages.

Lubricate crankpin bearings and cylinder walls with Suzuki Outboard Motor Oil or a suitable equivalent NMMA certified TC-W engine oil. Make sure flange of lower oil seal (9—Fig. SZ6-26) properly fits groove in crankcase. Apply a coat of Suzuki Bond No. 4 or a suitable equivalent on crankcase and cylinder block mating surfaces. Tighten crankcase screws in sequence shown in Fig. SZ6-22 or SZ6-23 to 8-12 N·m (6-8 ft.-lbs.) on 6 mm screws and 20-26 N·m (15-19 ft.-lbs.) on 8 mm screws. Tighten cylinder head screws in sequence shown in Fig. SZ6-24 to 20-26 N·m (15-19 ft.-lbs.). Tighten intake manifold screws in sequence shown in Fig. SZ6-25.

PISTONS, PINS, RINGS AND CYLINDERS. Each piston is fitted with two piston rings. Piston ring end gap on Models DT9.9 and DT15 should be 0.15-0.35 mm (0.006-0.014 in.) with a wear limit of 0.70 mm (0.028 in.). Piston ring end gap on Model DT15C should be 0.10-0.25 mm (0.004-0.010 in.) with a wear limit of 0.80 mm (0.031 in.). Piston rings are retained in position by locating pins. Install marked side of piston ring toward top of piston. Piston-to-

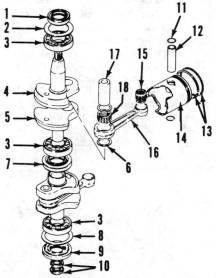

Fig. SZ6-26—Exploded view of piston and crankshaft assembly typical of all models.

1. Seal	10. Seals
2. Washer	11. Retainer
3. Ball bearings	12. Piston pin
4. Crank half	13. Piston rings
5. Crank half	14. Piston
6. Washer	15. Roller bearing
7. Seal	16. Connecting rod
8. Washer	17. Crankpin
9. Seal	18. Roller bearing

cylinder clearance should be 0.052-0.067 mm (0.0020-0.0026 in.) on DT9.9 and DT15 models, and 0.042-0.062 mm (0.0017-0.0024 in.) on Model DT15C. Pistons and rings are available in standard size as well as 0.25 mm (0.010 in.) and 0.50 mm (0.020 in.) oversizes. Cylinders should be bored to an oversize if either out-of-round or taper exceeds 0.10 mm (0.004 in.). Standard piston pin diameter is 13.995-14.000 mm (0.5510-0.5512 in.) on all models. Install pistons on connecting rods so arrow on piston crown points toward exhaust port side of cylinder.

CONNECTING RODS, BEARINGS AND CRANKSHAFT. Connecting rod, bearings and crankshaft are a press together unit. Crankshaft should be disassembled ONLY by experienced personnel using appropriate service equipment.

Caged roller bearings are used at both large and small ends of the connecting rods. Determine rod bearing wear from side-to-side movement as shown in Fig. SZ6-27. Normal side-to-side movement is 4.0 mm (0.16 in.) or less on DT9.9 and DT15 models, and 5.0 mm (0.20 in.) or less on Model DT15C. Maximum limit of crankshaft runout is 0.05 mm (0.002 in.) on all models, measured at bearing surfaces with crankshaft ends supported.

Apply Suzuki Super Grease "A" or a suitable high temperature grease to lip area of lower crankshaft seal prior to installation.

MANUAL STARTER

Refer to Fig. SZ6-29 for exploded view of manual starter assembly. Starter may be removed as a complete unit by detaching neutral start cable and removing three screws securing starter assembly to power head. To disassemble starter, proceed as follows: Remove starter handle (16) and allow rope (15)

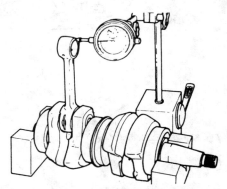

Fig. SZ6-27—Move connecting rod small end side-to-side to determine connecting rod, bearing and crankpin wear. Refer to text.

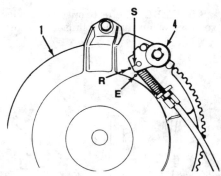

Fig. SZ6-28—Exploded view of cylinder block and crankcase assembly typical of all models.

1. Crankcase
2. Cylinder block
3. Gasket
4. Cylinder head
5. Gasket
6. Exhaust plate
7. Exhaust cover

Reinstall starter assembly on power head and reassemble neutral start cable and related components. With gear shift lever in "Neutral" position, slit (S—Fig. SZ6-31) in lever (4) must align with release dot (R) on housing (1). Adjust length of neutral start cable to obtain correct alignment. When gear shift lever is moved to "Forward" or "Reverse" position, slit (S) should align with engaged dot (E).

ELECTRIC STARTER

Some models are equipped with electric starter shown in Fig. SZ6-32. Disas-

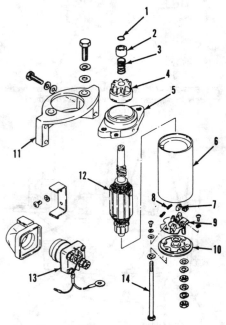

Fig. SZ6-31—Slit (S) in lever (4) must align with release dot (R) on starter housing (1) when gear shift lever is in the "Neutral" position, and align with the engaged dot (E) when gear shift lever is moved to the "Forward" or "Reverse" position.

to slowly wind onto pulley (8). Remove cotter pin (2), washer (3), lever (4) and spring (5). Invert starter housing (1) and remove screw (13). Withdraw plate (12) and spring (11).

Remove drive pawl (10) and return spring (9). Lift pulley (8) with starter rope (15) from starter housing. Remove pulley stop (6). Use suitable hand and eye protection and withdraw rewind spring (7) from housing (1). Be careful

when removing rewind spring to prevent personal injury.

To reassemble starter, coat rewind spring area of housing (1) with a suitable water-resistant grease. Install rewind spring (7) in housing (1). Rewind spring must wind in counterclockwise direction from the outer coil. Wrap starter rope (15) in clockwise direction 2-1/2 turns onto pulley (8) (viewed from flywheel side). Reassemble starter by reversing disassembly procedure making certain rewind spring inner hook properly engages groove in pulley (8). Apply water resistant grease to friction side of drive plate (12). Make sure slot (S—Fig. SZ6-30) in drive plate properly engages tab (T) on starter housing boss.

To preload rewind spring (7—Fig. SZ6-29), pass starter rope (15) through rope outlet in housing (1) and install handle (16). With rope (15) inserted in slot of pulley (8), rotate pulley four turns counterclockwise (viewed from flywheel side). Secure pulley (8), release rope (15) from slot in pulley and allow rope to slowly wind onto pulley. Do not place more tension on rewind spring than necessary to draw rope handle snug against housing.

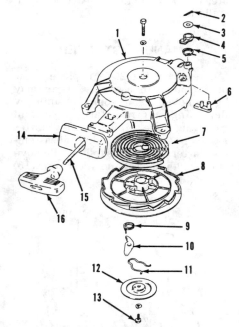

Fig. SZ6-29—Exploded view of manual starter assembly.

1. Housing
2. Cotter pin
3. Washer
4. Lever
5. Spring
6. Pulley stop
7. Rewind spring
8. Pulley
9. Return spring
10. Drive pawl
11. Spring
12. Plate
13. Cap screw
14. Rope guide
15. Starter rope
16. Handle

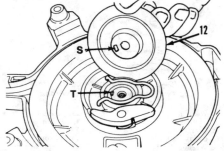

Fig. SZ6-30—Install drive plate (12) with tab (T) on housing boss inserted in slot (S).

Fig. SSZ6-32—Exploded view of electric starter motor.

1. Retainer
2. Stop
3. Spring
4. Drive
5. Frame head
6. Frame
7. Brush
8. Spring
9. Brush holder
10. Cover
11. Bracket
12. Armature
13. Starter solenoid
14. Through-bolt

sembly is evident after inspection of unit and referral to exploded view. Standard commutator outside diameter is 19.6 mm (0.77 in.). Renew armature if commutator outside diameter is worn to 19 mm (0.75 in.) or less. Renew starter brushes if worn to 4.5 mm (0.18 in.) or less.

During reassembly, make sure upper and lower alignment marks on frame (6—Fig. SZ6-32) align with marks on frame head (5) and brush cover (10). Starter assembly should be bench tested prior to installation on power head.

LOWER UNIT

PROPELLER AND RUBBER DAMPER. Rubber damper (36—Fig. SZ6-33) is used to provide shock protection for lower unit gears and shafts. Three-blade propeller is used. Standard propeller diameter is 234.9 mm (9-1/4 in.). Standard pitch is 279.4 mm (11 in.) on short shaft models and 254 mm (10 in.) on long shaft models. Optional propellers are available from the manufacturer and should be selected to provide full throttle operation within the recommended limits of 4500-5300 rpm on DT9.9 models and 4700-5500 rpm on Models DT15 and DT15C.

R&R AND OVERHAUL. Refer to Fig. SZ6-33 for exploded view of lower unit assembly. During disassembly, note location and size of all shims and washers for reference during reassembly.

Remove drain plug (11) and vent plug (9) and drain gearcase lubricant. Loos-en shift rod locknut (5—Fig. SZ6-35) and unscrew adjustment nut (6) until upper and lower shift rods are separated. Remove cotter pin (40—Fig. SZ6-33), nut (39), washer (38), spacer (37) and withdraw propeller (35) with thrust hub (36). Withdraw spacer (34). Remove four lower unit screws (12). Withdraw lower unit assembly from drive shaft housing.

Remove propeller shaft housing (31) retaining screws. Using a suitable slide hammer-type puller, carefully remove bearing housing along with propeller shaft assembly. Refer to Fig. SZ6-21 and disassemble and remove water pump. Remove snap ring (3—Fig. SZ6-33) and pull drive shaft (2) with bearing (4) from housing (1). Remove pinion (41), thrust washers and bearing (6 and 7) and shims (5).

Inspect all components for excessive wear or other damage. Renew all seals, "O" rings and gaskets. Apply a suitable water-resistant grease to lip of all seals.

Reassemble lower unit by reversing disassembly procedure while noting the following: Install clutch (21—Fig. SZ6-34) on propeller shaft (25) with side marked "F" facing forward gear. Clutch return spring (24—Fig. SZ6-33) free length should be 70 mm (2.755 in.). Renew spring (24) if free length is less than 68 mm (2.68 in.). Tighten water pump housing screws to 6-10 N·m (4-7 ft.-lbs.). Tighten propeller shaft housing screws to 6-10 N·m (4-7 ft.-lbs.). As-

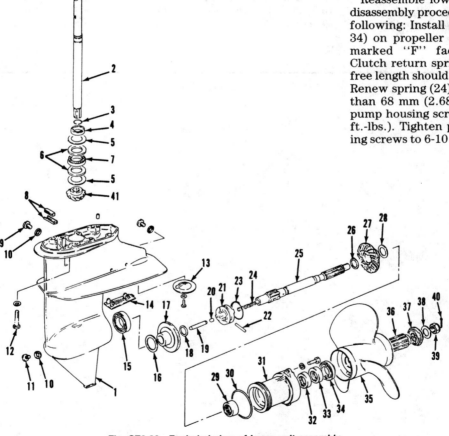

Fig. SZ6-33—Exploded view of lower unit assembly.

1. Housing	12. Cap screw	22. Pin
2. Drive shaft	13. Corrosion protector	23. Retainer
3. Snap ring	14. Water inlet cover	24. Spring
4. Bearing	15. Bearing	25. Propeller shaft
5. Shims	16. Shim	26. Shim
6. Thrust washers	17. Forward gear	27. Reverse gear
7. Needle roller	18. Shim	28. Shim
bearing	19. Rod	29. Bearing
8. Exhaust seal assy.	20. Pin	30. "O" ring
9. Vent plug	21. Dog clutch	
10. Gasket		
11. Drain plug		

31. Propeller shaft
housing
32. Seal
33. Seal
34. Spacer
35. Propeller
36. Thrust hub
37. Spacer
38. Washer
39. Nut
40. Cotter pin
41. Pinion

sembled drive shaft end play should be 0.05-0.30 mm (0.002-0.012 in.). Increase or decrease thickness of shims (5 or 16) to obtain recommended drive shaft end play. Check mesh pattern of pinion gear-to-forward gear to determine which shim(s) should be adjusted. Note final end play setting for reference dur-

ing reverse gear adjustment. Assembled propeller shaft end play should be 0.2-0.4 mm (0.008-0.016 in.). Adjust thickness of reverse gear shim washer (26) to obtain specified propeller shaft end play. At this time, recheck drive shaft end play. If drive shaft end play is the same as end play previously noted, proceed with reassembly. If drive shaft end play is less than previously noted, decrease thickness of reverse gear shim (28) so end play is the same as forward gear end play setting. Apply silicone sealant to lower unit-to-drive shaft housing mating surfaces. Tighten lower unit screws to 15-20 N·m (11-15 ft.-lbs.). Tighten propeller retaining nut to 50-60 N·m (37-44 ft.-lbs.).

Adjust shift rod nut (6—Fig. SZ6-35) until proper engagement of "Forward," "Neutral" and "Reverse" positions are obtained. The shift lever should have an equal angle of travel for both "Forward" and "Reverse" when rotated from "Neutral" position. Tighten locknut (5) to secure adjustment nut (6). Fill gearcase with approximately 170 mL (5.7 ozs.) of SAE 90 hypoid outboard gear oil.

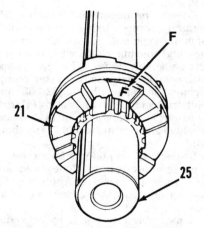

Fig. SZ6-34—Install clutch (21) on propeller shaft (25) with mark (F) facing forward gear.

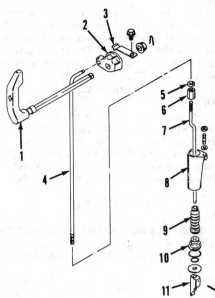

Fig. SZ6-35—Exploded view of shift control linkage components.

1. Shift lever
2. Lever
3. Detent spring
4. Upper shift rod
5. Locknut
6. Adjustment nut
7. Lower shift rod
8. Collar
9. Boot
10. Guide
11. Cam

SUZUKI DT8C, DT8C SAIL, DT9.9C and DT9.9C SAIL

CONDENSED SERVICE DATA

NOTE: Metric fasteners are used throughout outboard motor.

TUNE-UP

Hp/rpm	8/4700-5700
	(6.0 kW)
	9.9/5300-5700
	(7.4 kW)
Bore	54.0 mm
	(2.13 in.)
Stroke	46.0 mm
	(1.81 in.)
Number of Cylinders	2
Displacement	211 cc
	(12.9 cu. in.)
Spark Plug	NGK B6HS-10
Electrode Gap	0.9-1.0 mm
	(0.035-0.039 in.)
Ignition Type	CDI
Ignition Timing	11° ATDC at 600 rpm (1)
Maximum Timing Advance	28° BTDC at 2000 rpm
Carburetor Make	Mikuni B24
Compression Ratio	7.2:1
Idle Speed (in gear)	600-650 rpm
Fuel:Oil Ratio	See Text

(1)—On 1988 DT9.9C models, ignition timing is 12 degrees ATDC at 600 rpm.

SIZES-CLEARANCES

Piston Ring End Gap	0.15-0.30 mm
	(0.006-0.012 in.)
Wear Limit	0.8 mm
	(0.030 in.)
Piston-to-Cylinder Clearance	0.052-0.067 mm
	(0.0020-0.0026 in.)

SIZES—CLEARANCES CONT.

Wear Limit	0.147 mm
	(0.0058 in.)
Piston Pin Diameter	11.995-12.000 mm
	(0.4722-0.4724 in.)
Wear Limit	11.980 mm
	(0.4716 in.)
Cylinder Bore Diameter	54.000-54.015 mm
	(2.1260-2.1266 in.)
Piston Diameter	53.940-53.955 mm
	(2.1236-2.1242 in.)
Allowable Crankshaft Runout	0.05 mm
	(0.002 in.)
Allowable Connecting Rod Small End Side Shake	4.0 mm
	(0.157 in.)

TIGHTENING TORQUES

Crankcase Screws	20-26 N·m
	(15-19 ft.-lbs.)
Cylinder Head Screws	21-25 N·m
	(15-18 ft.-lbs.)
Flywheel Nut	80-90 N·m
	(59-66 ft.-lbs.)
Standard Screws:	
5 mm	2-4 N·m
	(18-35 in.-lbs.)
6 mm	4-7 N·m
	(35-62 in.-lbs.)
8 mm	10-16 N·m
	(7-12 ft.-lbs.)
10 mm	22-35 N·m
	(16-26 ft.-lbs.)

LUBRICATION

The power head is lubricated by oil mixed with the fuel. All models are equipped with automatic oil injection. The recommended oil is Suzuki Outboard Motor Oil or a good quality NMMA certified TC-W oil. Recommended fuel is unleaded gasoline with a minimum octane rating of 85.

On a new or rebuilt engine, the first tank of fuel should be mixed with a recommended oil at a 50:1 ratio and used in addition with the oil injection system to ensure sufficient lubrication during engine break-in. Gasoline and oil should be thoroughly mixed in a separate container. After first tank of fuel is depleted, switch to straight gasoline in fuel tank.

Recommended lower unit lubricant is Suzuki Outboard Motor Gear Oil or a good quality SAE 90 hypoid gear oil. Gearcase capacity is 175 mL (5.9 oz.). Gearcase oil should be changed after initial 10 hours of operation and after every 100 hours of operation thereafter. Reinstall drain and vent plugs securely, using new gaskets if necessary to ensure a watertight seal.

FUEL SYSTEM

CARBURETOR. A Mikuni B24-15 carburetor is used on 8 hp models and a Mikuni B24-18 carburetor is used on 9.9 hp models. Refer to Fig. SZ7-1 for exploded view of carburetor assembly. Initial adjustment of pilot screw (2) from a lightly seated position is 1-1/2 to 2 turns out on Model DT8C and 1-3/4 to 2-1/4 turns out on Model DT9.9C. Final adjustment should be made with engine at normal operating temperature and running in forward gear. Adjust idle speed to 600-650 rpm in forward gear.

Main fuel metering is controlled by fixed main jet (15). Standard main jet size for normal operation is #105 on Model DT8C and #137.5 on Model DT9.9C. Standard pilot jet (5) size for normal operation is #85 on Model DT8C and #65 on Model DT9.9C.

To check float level, remove float bowl (10) and invert carburetor. Measure float level from carburetor body-to-float bowl mating surface to top of float at a point 180 degrees from inlet valve as shown in Fig. SZ7-2. Float level should be 23-

25 mm (0.9-1.0 in.). Adjust float level by bending float tang.

FUEL PUMP. The fuel pump is an integral part of carburetor. Fuel pump assembly can be overhauled without carburetor removal. Refer to Fig SZ7-1 to disassemble pump. Note position of cover (21) and check valve assembly (18) for reference during reassembly. Inspect all components for damage or excessive wear and renew if necessary. Clean all passages with a suitable solvent and blow dry with compressed air.

REED VALVES. The reed valves are located between intake manifold and crankcase. The reed petals should seat very lightly against reed plate throughout entire length of reed petal with the least possible tension. Tip of reed petal must not stand open more than 0.2 mm (0.008 in.) from contact surface. Renew reed petal if not to specification. Reed stop opening should be 7.8 mm (0.310 in.).

Renew reeds if petals are broken, cracked, warped, rusted or bent. Never attempt to bend reed petal or to straighten a damaged reed. Never install bent or damaged reed. Seating surface of reed plate should be smooth and flat. When installing reeds or reed stop, make sure that petals are centered over inlet holes in reed plate, and that reed stops are centered over reed petals. Apply Suzuki Thread Lock 1342 or a suitable equivalent thread locking compound to reed petal mounting screws.

SPEED CONTROL LINKAGE. Throttle opening and timing advance must be synchronized to occur simultaneously. Check and adjust, if necessary, the ignition timing as outlined in the IGNITION section prior to speed control linkage adjustment.

To adjust speed control linkage, rotate throttle to wide open position. With throttle full open, front tab on stator stopper (2—Fig. SZ7-3) should touch boss (3) on engine block. If not, adjust carburetor link rod (9—Fig. SZ7-4) so tab contacts boss. Note that rod (9) should be approximately 37.5 mm (1.5 in.) long measured where shown in Fig. SZ7-4. Loosen nuts (3—Fig. SZ7-5) and adjust throttle cables (2) so zero clearance exists between lever (6) and stop (7), and zero clearance exists between throttle lever (10—Fig. SZ7-4) and stop on carburetor. Rotate throttle grip to fully close throttle. With throttle closed, the rear tab on stator stopper (2—Fig. SZ7-3) should touch boss (3) on engine block. If not, adjust stator link rod (4—Fig. SZ7-5) so rear tab contacts boss.

Make sure throttle lever and stator begin movement simultaneously as throttle grip is rotated. If not, repeat adjustment procedure. Ignition timing should be rechecked after adjustments are completed.

OIL INJECTION

All models are equipped a Mikuni oil pump, driven by drive gear on crankshaft. Oil pump output is proportional to engine speed and is not adjustable. Refer to Fig. SZ7-6 for oil injection system schematic and Fig. SZ7-7 for exploded view of oil pump assembly.

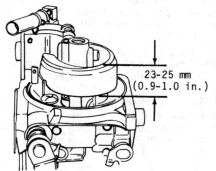

Fig. SZ7-1—Exploded view of carburetor and integral fuel pump assembly.

1. Body
2. Pilot screw
3. Throttle stop screw
4. Spring
5. Pilot jet
6. Gasket
7. Inlet needle
8. Pin
9. Float
10. Float bowl
11. Gasket
12. Screw
13. Drain screw
14. Main nozzle
15. Main jet
16. Gasket
17. Diaphragm
18. Check valve assy.
19. Diaphragm
20. Gasket
21. Cover

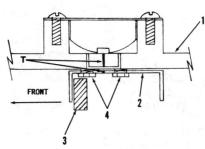

Fig. SZ7-3—Refer to text for speed control and ignition timing adjustment procedures.

1. Stator
2. Stator stopper
3. Boss
4. Screws
T. Timing marks

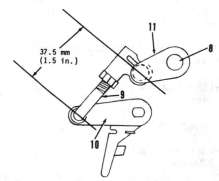

Fig. SZ7-4—View of carburetor linkage on port side of engine. Refer to text for adjustment procedures.

8. Throttle shaft
9. Carburetor link rod
10. Throttle lever
11. Throttle shaft lever

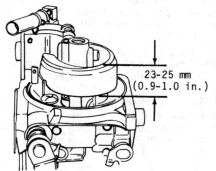

Fig. SZ7-2—Float level should be 23-25 mm (0.9-1.0 in.) measured 180 degrees from inlet valve as shown.

Fig. SZ7-5—View of speed control linkage on starboard side of engine. Refer to text for adjustment procedure.

1. Idle speed control knob
2. Cable assy's.
3. Nuts
4. Stator link rod
5. Cable drum
6. Throttle lever
7. Throttle stop

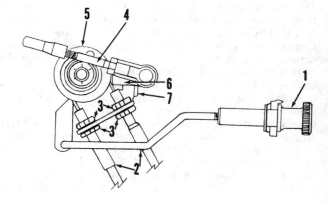

Illustrations Courtesy Suzuki America Corp.

BLEED OIL INJECTION SYSTEM.

Air must be purged from injection system if oil pump, oil lines or tank have been removed or renewed, or if unit has been in long term storage.

Fill fuel tank with a 50:1 mixture of gasoline and a recommended oil to ensure proper lubrication during bleeding

procedure. Fill oil tank with a recommended oil. Loosen bleed screw (S—Fig. SZ7-7) two or three turns. Start engine and allow to idle (600-650 rpm) until air free oil is discharged from bleed screw (S). Be sure to securely retighten bleed screw.

CHECKING OIL PUMP OUTPUT.

Start engine and allow to warm-up to normal operating temperature. Remove oil tank and connect Suzuki oil measuring gage 09900-21602 to oil line. Fill oil measuring gage with a recommended oil and bleed system as previously described. Refill oil measuring gage to an upper reference mark. Start engine and maintain speed at 1500 rpm for five minutes. Pump output should be 1.2-1.8 mL (0.04-0.06 oz.) in five minutes at

1500 rpm. Renew oil pump if not to specification.

When installing oil pump, lubricate pump driven gear (3—Fig. SZ7-7) with a recommended oil and be certain driven gear shaft properly engages oil pump.

IGNITION

All models are equipped with breakerless capacitor discharge ignition. Refer to Fig. SZ7-8 for wiring diagram on models with electric start.

IGNITION TIMING. To check ignition timing, make sure timing marks (T—Fig. SZ7-3) on stator (1) and stator stopper (2) are aligned as shown. Loosen screws (4) and move stopper (2) to adjust. Im-

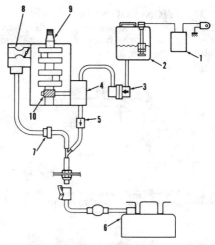

Fig. SZ7-6—Diagram of automatic oil injection system.

1. CDI unit
2. Oil tank
3. Oil filter
4. Oil pump
5. Check valve
6. Fuel tank
7. Fuel filter
8. Carburetor
9. Crankshaft
10. Oil pump driven gear

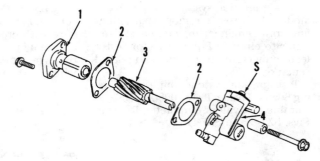

Fig. SZ7-7—Exploded view of automatic oil pump assembly.

1. Retainer
2. Gasket
3. Driven gear
4. Pump assy.
S. Bleed screw

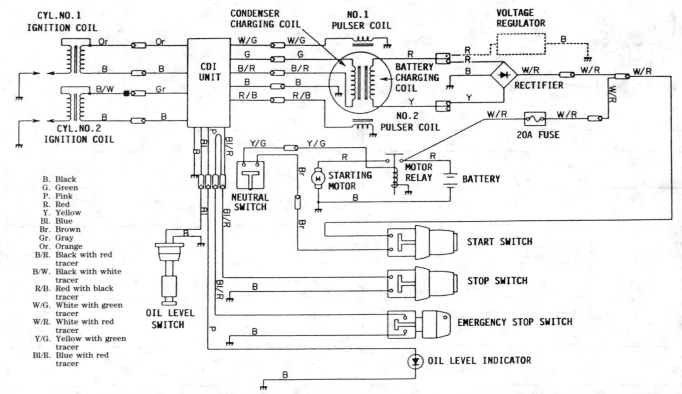

B. Black
G. Green
P. Pink
R. Red
Y. Yellow
Bl. Blue
Br. Brown
Gr. Gray
Or. Orange
B/R. Black with red tracer
B/W. Black with white tracer
R/B. Red with black tracer
W/G. White with green tracer
W/R. White with red tracer
Y/G. Yellow with green tracer
Bl/R. Blue with red tracer

Fig. SZ7-8—Wiring diagram typical of all models. Diagram shown is on models equipped with electric start and optional voltage regulator. Manual start models are similar.

merse lower unit in water, connect a suitable power timing light, start engine and warm-up to normal operating temperature. Refer to Fig. SZ7-9 for view of timing marks and pointer. Ignition timing at 600 rpm should be 9-13 degrees ATDC on Model DT8C and 10-14 degrees ATDC on Model DT9.9C. Total timing advance at 2000 rpm or over should be 16-20 degrees BTDC on Model DT8C and 26-30 degrees BTDC on Model DT9.9C.

TROUBLE-SHOOTING. If ignition malfunction occurs, use only approved procedures to prevent damage to ignition components. Check spark plugs, wiring and wiring connections. Use Stevens Model CD-77 peak voltage tester or Suzuki Pocket Tester 09900-25002 to test ignition components and circuits. A suitable ohmmeter may be substituted for Suzuki Pocket Tester 09900-25002.

To test ignition system using Stevens Model CD-77 tester, remove spark plugs and crank engine using manual starter. Refer to chart in Fig. SZ7-10 for tester lead connections, test values and related remarks.

Test ignition system components using Suzuki Pocket Tester 09900-25002 or suitable equivalent ohmmeter. Refer to Figs. SZ7-8 and SZ7-11.

NOTE: The following ignition system resistance specifications are based on an ambient temperature of 20° C (68° F).

CONDENSER CHARGING COIL. Disconnect condenser charging coil and connect tester between condenser charging coil leads. Resistance should be 230-240 ohms. Renew coil if resistance is not to specification.

BATTERY CHARGING COIL. Disconnect battery charging coil. On manual start models, connect tester between red and yellow wires. Resistance should be 0.1-0.4 ohms. On electric start models, connect tester between yellow with red tracer wire and yellow wire, then between red and yellow wires. Resistance should be 0.1-0.4 ohms on each test. Renew coil if resistance is not to specification.

PULSER COILS. Disconnect pulser coils and connect tester between white wire with green tracer and black wire on number 1 pulser coil and between red wire with black tracer and black wire on number 2 pulser coil. Resistance

should be 170-250 ohms on each coil. Renew pulser coil(s) if resistance is not to specification. Note that number 1 and number 2 pulser coils have different color wires and must not be interchanged. Refer to Fig. SZ7-11. The firing order will be altered and engine will not start if pulser coils are interchanged. Air gap between pulser coils and flywheel magnets should be 0.75 mm (0.030 in.). Refer to Fig. SZ7-12.

IGNITION COILS. Disconnect ignition coils. Check primary windings by connecting tester between orange and black wires on number 1 coil and be-

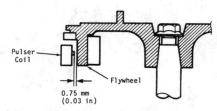

Fig. SZ7-12—Air gap between pulser coils and flywheel magnets should be 0.75 mm (0.030 in.) as shown.

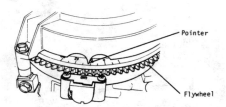

Fig. SZ7-9—View of timing pointer and flywheel timing marks.

Fig. SZ7-11—Pulser coils must be installed on stator in location shown for proper ignition system operation. Pulser coils are identified by wire color code.
R/B. Red with black trace
W/G. White with green tracer

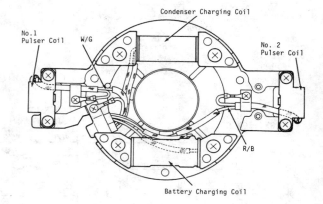

ITEM		DATA	METER LEAD CONNECTION	REMARKS
Condenser charging coil		80V or over (Meter setting: POS500)	Red: Green Black: Black/Red	Connect CDI unit
Pulser coil		3.0V or over (Meter setting: SEN50)	Red: White/Green (No. 1), Red/Black (No. 2) Black: Black	Connect CDI unit
Battery charging coil	Manual Start Models	1.3V or over (Meter setting: POS50)	Red: Red Black: Yellow	Disconnect rectifier
		1.6V or over (Meter setting: POS50)	Red: Red/Yellow Black: Yellow	
	Electric Start Models	1.6V or over (Meter setting: POS50)	Red: Red Black: Yellow	
CDI to coil		85V or over (Meter setting: POS500)	Red: Orange (No. 1), Gray (No. 2) Black: Black	Connect ignition coil

Fig. SZ7-10—Use chart shown when trouble-shooting ignition system using Stevens Model CD-77 peak voltage tester. Remove spark plugs and crank engine with manual rewind starter when performing tests.

POWER HEAD

tween black wire with white tracer and black wire on number 2 coil. Primary resistance should be 0.1-0.4 ohms on both coils. Renew coil(s) if not to specification.

To check secondary windings, connect tester between orange wire and end of spark plug lead on number 1 coil and black wire with white tracer and end of spark plug lead on number 2 coil. Secondary resistance should be 2700-4100 ohms on both coils. Renew coil(s) if resistance is not to specification.

RECTIFIER. Disconnect rectifier and connect tester leads according to chart in Fig. SZ7-13. Renew rectifier if resistance values are not as shown.

COOLING SYSTEM

WATER PUMP. A rubber impeller type water pump is mounted between drive shaft housing and gearcase. Impeller key (4—Fig. SZ7-14) engages impeller (3) and drive shaft causing impeller to rotate with drive shaft. If cooling system malfunction is noted, inspect water intake for plugging or partial restriction. If water intake is not restricted, check thermostat for proper operation. Refer to THERMOSTAT section. If thermostat operation is accept-

able, remove gearcase as outlined in the appropriate section and check condition of water pump, water tube, water passages and seals. Inspect impeller (3) and impeller plate (2) for excessive wear or other damage.

Install seal (6) into housing (5) with lip facing away from impeller. Apply a suitable water-resistant grease to seal lip. When installing housing over impeller, rotate drive shaft in clockwise direction in order to seat impeller vanes in the proper direction. Avoid turning drive shaft in opposite direction after water pump is reassembled. Lubricate seals (8 and 10) with a suitable water resistant grease when installing water tube.

THERMOSTAT. Cooling system is equipped with a thermostat (4—Fig. SZ7-15) to regulate operating temperature. Thermostat can be removed from cylinder block after removing cover (6). If thermostat malfunction is suspected, check for foreign material in thermostat valve seat. Test thermostat by suspending thermostat in water with a suitable thermometer. As water is heated, thermostat should start to open at 48°-52°C (118°-126°F). Thermostat should be renewed if opening temperature is not within specified range.

REMOVE AND REINSTALL. The following removal and reinstallation procedures are based on Model DT9.9C equipped with electric start. All other models are similar.

Remove engine cover and manual starter. Disconnect wires, wiring harnesses and cables that interfere with power head removal. Remove idle speed control knob, throttle cables and throttle control lever. Remove oil tank, carburetor air intake cover and carburetor. Note that plug located adjacent to choke knob in lower engine cover can be removed to gain access to lower carburetor mounting screw. Remove two nuts and four screws securing power head to drive shaft housing and lift off power head.

Before reinstalling power head, make sure drive shaft splines are clean. Coat drive shaft splines with a suitable water-resistant grease. Rotate propeller while lowering power head in place to align drive shaft and crankshaft splines. Apply a suitable silicone sealant to power head securing screws and studs and tighten to 18-28 N·m (13-20 ft.-lbs.). The remainder of installation is the reverse order of removal. Refer to SPEED CONTROL LINKAGE to synchronize throttle opening and ignition advance.

DISASSEMBLY. Power head disassembly may be accomplished in the following manner. Remove exhaust tube, CDI unit, rectifier, ignition coils, starter relay and starter motor. Remove throttle cable bracket and neutral switch. Remove spark plugs, oil pump, throttle control lever and clutch shaft.

		(+) LEAD OF TESTER		
		Black	White/Red	Yellow	Red
LEAD OF TESTER (-)	Black		5,500–8,500Ω	2,200–3,200Ω	2,200–3,200Ω
	White/Red	∞		∞	∞
	Yellow	∞	2,200–3,200Ω		∞
	Red	∞	1,700–2,700Ω	∞	

Fig. SZ7-13—To test rectifier, connect tester leads to rectifier wires as shown in chart.

Fig. SZ7-15—Exploded view of crankcase and cylinder block assembly.

1. Crankcase
2. Cylinder block
3. Gasket
4. Thermostat
5. Gasket
6. Thermostat cover
7. Cylinder head
8. Gasket
9. Exhaust plate
10. Gasket
11. Exhaust cover

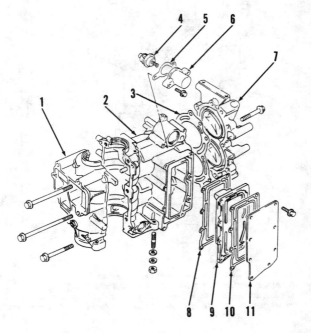

Fig. SZ7-14—Exploded view of water pump assembly.

1. Gasket
2. Plate
3. Impeller
4. Key
5. Housing
6. Seal
7. Stud
8. Seal
9. Water tube
10. Seal

Using a suitable flywheel holding tool, remove flywheel nut and remove flywheel using a suitable flywheel puller. Remove stator assembly and retainers and spacer under stator. Remove cylinder head, exhaust cover, thermostat cover and thermostat. Remove six screws securing crankcase to cylinder block and remove one seal housing screw (Fig. SZ7-16). Separate crankcase from cylinder block and lift crankshaft assembly out of crankcase.

Engine components are now accessible for overhaul as outlined in the appropriate following sections.

REASSEMBLY. Reassemble engine in reverse order of disassembly referring to specific service sections. Make sure all seal and gasket surfaces are clean and free from nicks and burrs. Make sure all carbon, salt, dirt and sand are cleaned from the combustion chambers, exhaust ports and water passages. Renew all gaskets and seals.

All friction surfaces should be coated with an approved two-stroke oil during reassembly. Apply Suzuki Bond 1207B or a suitable equivalent sealer to crankcase and cylinder block mating surfaces. Tighten crankcase screws to specified torque in sequence shown in Fig. SZ7-16. After crankcase is reassembled, rotate crankshaft to check for binding or abnormal noise.

CYLINDER HEAD AND BLOCK. Check cylinder head and block mating surfaces for distortion using a suitable straightedge and feeler gage. Maximum allowable warpage is 0.03 mm (0.0012 in.) for block and head. Cylinder head and block mating surfaces may be lapped if warpage exceeds specified amount. Do not remove more material than necessary. Tighten cylinder head screws to 21-25 N·m (16-18 ft.-lbs.) in sequence shown in Fig. SZ7-17.

PISTONS, PINS, RINGS AND CYLINDERS. Piston-to-cylinder bore clearance should be 0.052-0.067 mm (0.0020-0.0026 in.) with a wear limit of 0.147 mm (0.0058 in.). Measure piston diameter at 90 degrees to piston pin, 19 mm (0.75 in.) up from bottom of skirt. Measure cylinder bore diameter 25 mm (0.98 in.) down from top of bore. Maximum allowable cylinder bore taper and/or out-of-round is 0.10 mm (0.004 in.). Pistons and rings are available in oversizes of 0.25 mm (0.010 in.) and 0.50 mm (0.020 in.).

Standard piston pin diameter is 11.995-12.000 mm (0.4722-0.4724 in.) with a wear limit of 11.980 mm (0.4716 in.). Standard piston pin bore diameter is 11.998-12.010 mm (0.4724-0.4728 in.) with a wear limit of 12.030 mm (0.4736 in.). Oversize piston pin is not available. Renew piston and pin as a unit.

Piston ring end gap should be 0.15-0.30 mm (0.006-0.012 in.). Maximum allowable ring end gap is 0.8 mm (0.031 in.). Pistons are equipped with locating pins to prevent ring rotation. Install rings with marked side facing up. Install pistons on connecting rods with arrow on piston crown facing exhaust port. Always renew piston pin retainers when installing pistons.

CONNECTING RODS, BEARINGS AND CRANKSHAFT. Connecting rods, bearings and crankshaft are a pressed together unit. Crankshaft should be disassembled ONLY by experienced service personnel using the proper service equipment.

Caged roller bearings are used at both large and small ends of connecting rods. Determine connecting rod big end bearing wear by measuring rod small end side-to-side play as shown in Fig. SZ7-19. Renew connecting rod (8—Fig. SZ7-18), bearing (9) and crankpin (6) if small end play exceeds 4.0 mm (0.157 in.). Maximum allowable crankshaft runout is 0.05 mm (0.002 in.). During reassembly, apply Suzuki Super Grease "A" or equivalent to lip of seals (10 and 22). Apply a suitable water-resistant grease to seals (24 and 26).

MANUAL STARTER

Refer to Fig. SZ7-20 for exploded view of manual starter assembly. Starter may be removed from power head as an assembly by loosening nut (N), disconnecting neutral start cable (1) and removing three screws securing housing (6) to power head.

To disassemble starter, remove cotter pin (2), washer (3), lever (4), spring (5) and cable (1). Invert starter assembly, lift out a length of starter rope and place rope into notch in pulley (9). While holding rope, carefully allow rope pulley (9) to rotate clockwise, releasing tension on rewind spring (8). Remove screw (14), plate (12), pawl (11), spring (10) and pulley (9). Remove pulley stopper (7). Using suitable hand and eye protection, carefully remove rewind spring (8). Use caution when removing spring (8) as rapidly uncoiling spring may cause personal injury.

Reassemble in the reverse order of disassembly noting the following. Apply a suitable water-resistant grease to rewind spring. Wind rewind spring into housing in a counterclockwise direction, starting with outer coil. Use caution when installing rewind spring into housing to prevent spring from uncoiling. Apply a suitable water-resistant grease to rope pulley and both sides of plate (12).

Wind rope on pulley (9) 2-1/2 turns in counterclockwise direction (viewed from flywheel side of starter) and place rope into notch of pulley. Holding rope in notch, rotate pulley four turns counterclockwise to preload rewind spring.

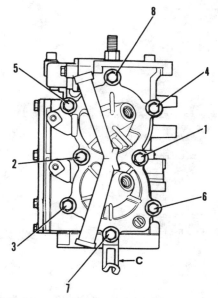

Oil Seal Housing Screw

Fig. SZ7-16—To separate crankcase from cylinder block, remove six crankcase screws and one oil seal housing screw. When reassembling, tighten crankcase screws in sequence shown to 20-26 N·m (15-19 ft.-lbs.).

Fig. SZ7-17—Tighten cylinder head bolts in sequence shown to 21-25 N·m (16-18 ft.-lbs.). Note location of clamp (C).

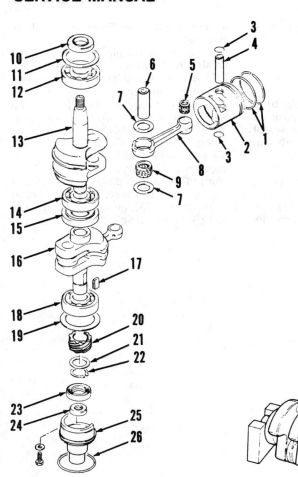

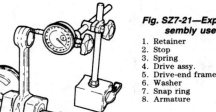

Fig. SZ7-18—Exploded view of crankshaft, connecting rod and piston assembly.

1. Piston rings
2. Piston
3. Retainer
4. Piston pin
5. Needle bearing
6. Crankpin
7. Washer
8. Connecting rod
9. Needle bearing
10. Seal
11. Thrust washer
12. Bearing
13. Upper crankshaft assy.
14. Bearing
15. Seal
16. Lower crankshaft assy.
17. Key
18. Bearing
19. Thrust washer
20. Oil pump drive gear
21. Washer
22. Snap ring
23. Seal
24. Seal
25. Seal housing
26. Seal

Fig. SZ7-21—Exploded view of electric starter assembly used on models so equipped.

1. Retainer	9. Washer
2. Stop	10. Frame assy.
3. Spring	11. Brush springs
4. Drive assy.	12. Commutator-end
5. Drive-end frame	frame
6. Washer	13. Through-bolt
7. Snap ring	14. Brushes
8. Armature	

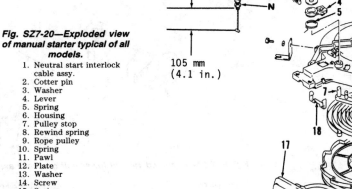

Fig. SZ7-19—Measure connecting rod small end side-to-side play as shown to determine condition of rod, rod bearing and crankpin. Maximum allowable play is 4.0 mm (0.157 in.).

LOWER UNIT

PROPELLER AND RUBBER DAMP-ER. Spline drive propeller with rubber

Install starter assembly on power head. With clutch lever in neutral position, adjust nut (N) so neutral start inner cable length is 105 mm (4.1 in.) as shown and reconnect cable to power head.

ELECTRIC STARTER

Some models are equipped with the electric starter shown in Fig. SZ7-21. Disassembly is evident after referral to exploded view and inspection of unit. Standard commutator outside diameter is 20 mm (0.79 in.). Minimum allowable commutator diameter is 19 mm (0.75 in.). Resurface commutator if taper exceeds 0.05 mm (0.002 in.). Renew armature if commutator taper exceeds 0.4 mm (0.016 in.). Undercut mica between commutator segments to 1.8 mm (0.07 in.) deep. Do not exceed 2.0 mm (0.08 in.) deep. Minimum brush length is 4.0 mm (0.16 in.).

Lubricate starter bushings and inside diameter of drive with Suzuki Super Grease "A" or a suitable equivalent. Tighten starter through-bolts to 15-20 N·m (11-15 ft.-lbs.). Bench test starter prior to installing on power head.

Fig. SZ7-20—Exploded view of manual starter typical of all models.

1. Neutral start interlock cable assy.
2. Cotter pin
3. Washer
4. Lever
5. Spring
6. Housing
7. Pulley stop
8. Rewind spring
9. Rope pulley
10. Spring
11. Pawl
12. Plate
13. Washer
14. Screw
15. Spring
16. Rope
17. Rope guide
18. Retainer
N. Nut

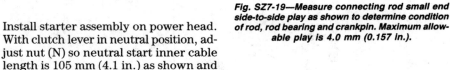

105 mm
(4.1 in.)

hub is used to provide shock protection for lower unit gears and shafts. Three-blade propellers are used. Renew propeller if blades are chipped, broken or worn excessively thin. Standard propeller for Sail models has a diameter of 254 mm (10 in.) and 165.1 mm (6.5 in.) pitch. Propeller for all other models is available in the following sizes: 235 mm (9-1/4 in.) diameter with 177.8 mm (7 in.) pitch; 228.6 mm (9 in.) diameter with 209.5 mm (8-1/4 in.) pitch; 235 mm (9-1/4 in.) diameter with 228.6 mm (9 in.) pitch. Propeller should be selected to provide full throttle operation within the specified range of 4700-5700 rpm on

8 hp models and 5300-5700 rpm on 9.9 hp models.

R&R AND OVERHAUL. Refer to Fig. SZ7-22 for exploded view of lower unit gearcase assembly. During disassembly, note location and thickness of all shims and washers for aid in reassembly.

Remove drain plug (2), vent plug (3) and drain gearcase lubricant. Loosen jam nut (56) and turn adjuster (55) to separate lower shift rod (54) from upper shift rod. Remove four screws and

separate gearcase from drive shaft housing.

Remove cotter pin (30), nut (29), washer (28), spacer (27) and propeller (25). Remove bearing carrier (22) retaining screws and attach a suitable slide hammer to propeller shaft (16). Using slide hammer, carefully withdraw propeller shaft assembly and bearing carrier (22) from gearcase. Refer to Fig. SZ7-14 and WATER PUMP section and remove water pump assembly. Lift drive shaft (47—Fig. SZ7-22) and bearing housing (39) from gearcase. Remove forward gear (9), shim (8), pinion gear (31), shift rod (54) and collar (42).

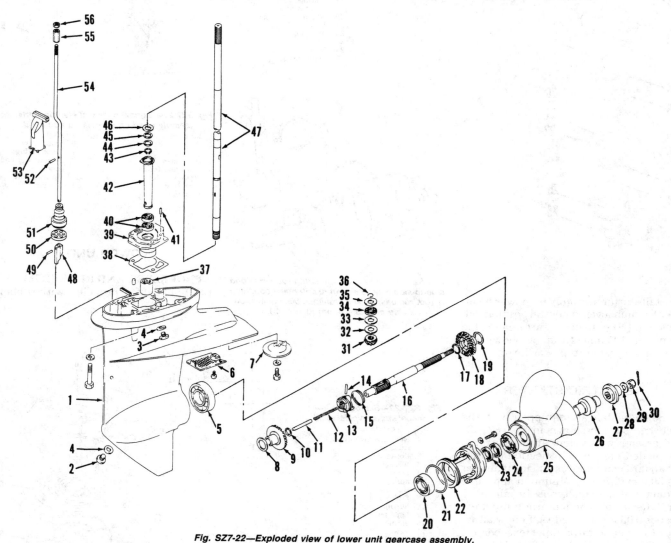

Fig. SZ7-22—Exploded view of lower unit gearcase assembly.

1. Gearcase
2. Drain plug
3. Vent plug
4. Gasket
5. Bearing
6. Water filter
7. Anode
8. Shim
9. Forward gear
10. Washer (1.0 mm [0.039 in.])
11. Rod
12. Spring
13. Dog clutch
14. Pin
15. Retainer
16. Propeller shaft
17. Thrust washer
18. Reverse gear
19. Shim
20. Bearing
21. "O" ring
22. Bearing carrier
23. Seal
24. Spacer
25. Propeller
26. Bushing
27. Spacer
28. Washer
29. Nut
30. Cotter pin
31. Pinion gear
32. Shim
33. Thrust washer (2.75 mm [0.108 in.])
34. Thrust bearing
35. Thrust washer (2.75 mm [0.108 in.])
36. Snap ring
37. Bearing
38. Gasket
39. Bearing housing
40. Seal
41. Pin
42. Collar
43. Snap ring
44. Washer (1.0 mm [0.039 in.])
45. Washer (0.5 mm [0.020 in.])
46. Washer (1.0 mm [0.039 in.])
47. Drive shaft
48. Shift cam
49. Pin
50. Guide
51. Boot
52. Pin
53. Shift rod stop
54. Lower shift rod
55. Adjuster
56. Jam nut

Illustrations Courtesy Suzuki America Corp.

Pull rod (11) and spring (12) from shaft (16). Remove retainer (15) from dog clutch (13), push out pin (14) and slide dog clutch (13) off shaft (16). Remove pinion bearing (37) by driving down into propeller shaft cavity.

Inspect all components for excessive wear or other damage and renew as necessary. Renew all seals, "O" rings and gaskets. Coat all friction surfaces and bearings with an approved gear lubricant during reassembly. Apply a suitable water-resistant grease to sealing surfaces and seal lips.

Reassemble lower unit gearcase in reverse order of disassembly while noting the following: Renew all gaskets and seals. Apply a suitable water-resistant grease to lip area of all seals. Place pinion bearing (37—SZ7-22) into gearcase with stamped mark (S—Fig. SZ7-23) facing up. Using Suzuki special tools or suitable equivalent arranged as shown in Fig. SZ7-23, pull bearing into gearcase until top of pinion bearing is 162 mm (6.4 in.) from top surface of gearcase as shown in Fig. SZ7-23.

To determine the correct pinion gear shim (32—Fig. SZ7-22) thickness, assemble shim (32) thrust washers (33 and 35) and thrust bearing (34) as shown in Fig. SZ7-24.

NOTE: Inside diameter of upper thrust washer (35) is 18 mm. Inside diameter of lower thrust washer (33) is 17 mm. Make sure thrust washers are installed in the correct location.

Measure thickness (T) of shim and thrust bearing assembly (32, 33, 34 and 35). If thickness (T) is within 9.95-10.05 mm (0.392-0.396 in.), shim (32) thickness is acceptable and may be reinstalled. Add or subtract from shim (32) thickness to obtain specified thickness (T). Pinion gear shim (32) is available in thicknesses of 0.5 mm (0.020 in.) through 1.0 mm (0.39 in.), in 0.1 mm (0.004 in.) increments. Select shim(s) (32) so as not to allow more than two shims stacked together to obtain correct thickness (T).

Drive shaft (47—Fig. SZ7-22) end play should be 0.10-0.30 mm (0.004-0.012 in.). Adjust thickness of forward gear shim (8) to obtain proper end play. Note final end play reading (after adjustment) for reference during reverse gear adjustment.

Install dog clutch (13) on propeller shaft (16) with side stamped "F" facing forward gear (9). Refer to Fig. SZ7-25. Propeller shaft end play should be 0.2-0.4 mm (0.008-0.016 in.). Adjust thickness of reverse gear thrust washer (17) to obtain proper end play.

At this time, recheck drive shaft end play. If drive shaft end play is the same as end play previously noted, proceed with reassembly. If not, adjust thickness of reverse gear shim (19) so end play is equal to forward gear end play setting.

After reassembly, connect Suzuki leak tester 09950-69511 and pump assembly 09821-00004 or a suitable equivalent pressure tester to oil drain plug hole. Pressurize drive unit to 100 kPa (14.5 psi). If pressure falls off, locate leak and repair as necessary.

Apply a suitable water-resistant grease to propeller shaft splines prior to installing propeller. Tighten propeller nut to 15-20 N·m (11-15 ft.-lbs.). Apply a suitable silicone sealant to gearcase-to-drive shaft housing mating surface and threads of gearcase screws. Tighten screws to 15-20 N·m (11-15 ft.-lbs.). Fill gearcase with approximately 175 mL (5.9 oz.) of Suzuki Outboard Motor Gear Oil or equivalent. Gearcase oil should be rechecked and added to if necessary after two or three minutes of operation.

Adjust shift rod adjustment nut (55) so proper engagement of forward, neutral and reverse gears is obtained. The shift lever should have an equal angle of travel for both forward and reverse when lever is rotated from neutral position. Tighten jam nut (56) to secure adjustment nut (55).

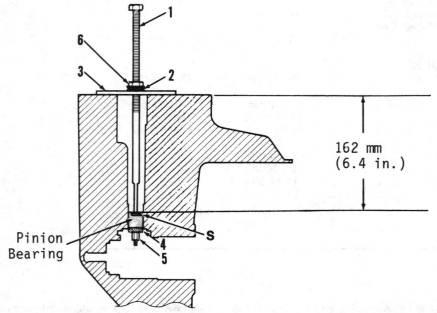

Fig. SZ7-23—Install pinion bearing using Suzuki special tools shown or suitable equivalent. Place bearing into gearcase with stamped marking (S) facing up. Turning nut (6), draw bearing into gearcase until top of bearing is 162 mm (6.4 in.) from top surface of gearcase as shown.

1. Installer shaft
   09951-49910
2. Thrust bearing
   09951-69910
3. Plate 09951-39913
4. Washer 09951-19210
5. Nut 09951-29910
6. Nut

Fig. SZ7-24—Refer to text for pinion gear shimming procedure. Note that inside diameter of upper thrust washer (35) is 18 mm and lower thrust washer (33) is 17 mm. Make certain upper and lower thrust washers are located in the proper position.

32. Shim(s)
33. Thrust washer
34. Thrust bearing
35. Thrust washer

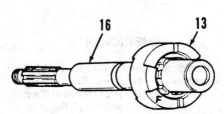

Fig. SZ7-25—Install dog clutch (13) on propeller shaft (16) with side stamped "F" facing forward gear (9—Fig. SZ7-22).

SUZUKI DT9.9 AND DT16
(PRIOR TO 1983)

CONDENSED SERVICE DATA

NOTE: Metric fasteners are used throughout outboard motor.

TUNE-UP	DT9.9	DT16
Horsepower	9.9	16
Bore	56 mm	59 mm
Stroke	52 mm	52 mm
Displacement	256 cc	284 cc
Spark Plug:		
NGK	B6HS	B7HS
Electrode gap	0.6-0.7 mm	0.6-0.7 mm
Magneto:		
Breaker point gap	Breakerless	Breakerless
Carburetor:		
Make	Mikuni	Mikuni
Model	BV24-16	BV24-19
Fuel:Oil Ratio	50:1	50:1
SIZES—CLEARANCES		
Piston Ring End Gap	0.15-0.35 mm	0.15-0.35 mm
Piston Pin Diameter	13.995-14.000 mm	13.995-14.000 mm
Piston to Cylinder Wall		
Clearance	0.042-0.058 mm	0.042-0.058 mm
Max. Crankshaft Runout at		
Main Bearing Journal	0.05 mm	0.05 mm
Max. Connecting Rod Small End		
Side Shake	4.0 mm	4.0 mm
TIGHTENING TORQUES		
Cylinder Head	18-28 N·m	18-28 N·m
Crankcase:		
6 mm	8-12 N·m	8-12 N·m
8 mm	18-28 N·m	18-28 N·m
Flywheel Nut	80-90 N·m	80-90 N·m
Standard Screws:		
5 mm	2-4 N·m	2-4 N·m
6 mm	4-7 N·m	4-7 N·m
8 mm	10-16 N·m	10-16 N·m
10 mm	22-35 N·m	22-35 N·m

LUBRICATION

The power head is lubricated by oil mixed with the fuel. Fuel:oil ratios should be 30:1 during break-in of a new or rebuilt engine and 50:1 for normal service when using a NMMA certified two-stroke engine oil or Suzuki "CCI" oil. When using any other type of two-stroke engine oil, fuel:oil ratios should be 20:1 during break-in and 30:1 for normal service. Manufacturer recommends regular or no-lead automotive gasoline having an 85-95 octane rating. Gasoline and oil should be thoroughly mixed.

The lower unit gears and bearings are lubricated by oil contained in the gear-case. SAE 90 hypoid outboard gear oil is recommended. Oil capacity of gear-case with integral exhaust outlet in the lower housing is approximately 220 mL. Oil capacity of gearcase with through-the-propeller exhaust is approximately 200 mL. Reinstall vent and fill plugs securely using a new gasket, if necessary, to ensure a water tight seal.

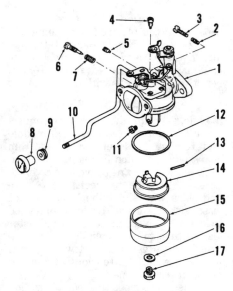

Fig. SZ5-1 — Exploded view of Mikuni BV24 type carburetor.

1. Body	10. Choke actuating rod
2. Spring	11. Main jet
3. Throttle stop screw	12. Gasket
4. Pilot jet	13. Float shaft
5. Air jet	14. Float
6. Pilot air screw	15. Float bowl
7. Spring	16. Gasket
8. Choke knob	17. Bowl retaining screw
9. Bushing	

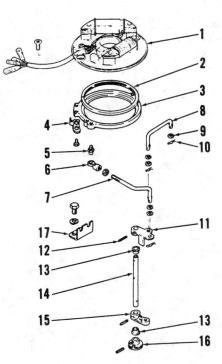

Fig. SZ5-2 — Exploded view of speed control linkage.

1. Stator assembly	10. Clip
2. Bushing	11. Linkage connector
3. Speed control ring	12. Roll pin
4. Control ring stop	13. Bushing
5. Ball stud	14. Shaft
6. Ball socket	15. Lever
7. Stator link rod	16. Throttle drum
8. Carburetor link rod	17. Cable mounting plate
9. Washer	

Fig. SZ5-3 — Exploded view of inlet manifold and reed valve assembly.

1. Inlet manifold	4. Reed petals
2. Gasket	5. Reed stop
3. Reed plate	6. Gasket

Fig. SZ5-4 — Exploded view of diaphragm type fuel pump.

I. Inlet hose	5. Pump valves
O. Outlet hose	6. Lower body
1. Cover	7. Diaphragm set
2. Gasket	8. Pump base
3. Filter	9. Gasket
4. Upper body	10. Insulator block

FUEL SYSTEM

CARBURETOR. A Mikuni BV24 type carburetor is used on all models. Refer to Fig. SZ5-1 for exploded view of carburetor. Initial setting of pilot air screw (6) should be 1 to 1-1/2 turns from a lightly seated position on DT9.9 models and 1-3/4 to 2-1/4 turns on DT16 models. Final carburetor adjustment should be made with engine at normal operating temperature and running in forward gear. Adjust throttle stop screw (3) so engine idles at approximately 600-650 rpm. Adjust pilot air screw so engine idles smoothly and will accelerate cleanly without hesitation. If necessary, readjust throttle stop screw to obtain 600-650 rpm idle speed.

Main fuel metering is controlled by main jet (11). Standard main jet size for normal operation is #92.5 on DT9.9 models and #117.5 on DT16 models.

To check float level, remove float bowl and invert carburetor. Float surface nearest main jet should be 18.5-20.5 mm away from gasket surface of carburetor. Adjust float level by bending float tang.

SPEED CONTROL LINKAGE. The speed control grip is attached to the magneto stator plate and moving the speed control will advance or retard the ignition timing. Throttle linkage, which is fixed and not adjustable, is synchronized to open the carburetor throttle as magneto timing is advanced.

To synchronize linkage, first check ignition timing to be sure it is set correctly as outlined in IGNITION section. Disconnect ball socket (6 – Fig. SZ5-2) from speed control ring (3). Set speed control grip at slow speed position. Rotate stator clockwise until lower tab of stop (4) contacts boss on cylinder block. Adjust length of stator link rod (7) as required so linkage may be attached without moving stator. Turn speed control grip to maximum speed position. Upper tab of stop (4) should contact boss on magneto cover. If full slow speed or high speed positions are unobtainable, check speed control cable adjustment and for bent or worn speed control linkage.

REED VALVES. The inlet reed valves are located on a reed plate between inlet manifold and crankcase. The reed petals should seat very lightly against the reed plate throughout their entire length, with the least possible tension. Tip of reed petal must not stand open more than 0.2 mm from contact surface. Reed stop opening should be 8.3 mm.

Renew reeds if petals are broken, cracked, warped, rusted or bent. Never attempt to bend a reed petal or to straighten a damaged reed. Never install a bent or damaged reed. Seating surface of reed plate should be smooth and flat. When installing reeds or reed stop, make sure that petals are centered over the inlet holes in reed plate, and that the reed stops are centered over reed petals.

FUEL PUMP. A diaphragm type fuel pump is mounted on the side of power head cylinder block and is actuated by pressure and vacuum pulsations from the engine crankcase.

When servicing pump, scribe reference marks across pump body to aid in reassembly. Defective or questionable parts should be renewed. Diaphragm should be renewed if air leaks or cracks are found, or if deterioration is evident.

IGNITION

All models are equipped with a breakerless, capacitor discharge ignition system. Refer to Fig. SZ5-5 for wiring diagram.

Full throttle and full advance should occur simultaneously. Ignition timing is

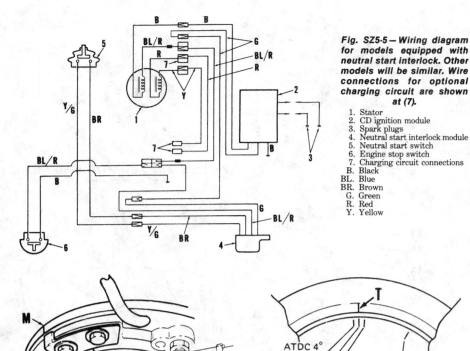

Fig. SZ5-5 — Wiring diagram for models equipped with neutral start interlock. Other models will be similar. Wire connections for optional charging circuit are shown at (7).

1. Stator
2. CD ignition module
3. Spark plugs
4. Neutral start interlock module
5. Neutral start switch
6. Engine stop switch
7. Charging circuit connections
B. Black
BL. Blue
BR. Brown
G. Green
R. Red
Y. Yellow

Check condition of charge coil by separating the blue/red wire connector and black wire connector at stator and attach a tester lead to each wire. Charge coil may be considered satisfactory if resistance reading is within the limits of 135-165 ohms.

To check condition of CD ignition module, separate the black wire connector and green wire connector at module and remove high tension wires from spark plugs. Attach tester positive lead to green wire and negative lead to black wire. Resistance between green wire and black wire should be 100k ohms or less. With tester positive lead connected to green wire, connect negative tester lead in turn to each cylinder's high tension wire. Resistance between green wire and each high tension wire should be above 100k ohms.

Connect tester positive lead to ignition module black wire and negative tester lead to green wire. Attaching negative lead to green wire should cause tester needle to show deflection then return toward infinite resistance. With tester positive lead connected to black wire, connect negative tester lead in turn to each cylinder's high tension wires. Resistance betwen black wire and each high tension wire should be above 100k ohms.

Connect positive tester lead to upper cylinder high tension wire and negative tester lead to green ignition module wire. Resistance should be above 100k ohms. Then connect tester negative lead to black ignition module wire and note reading. Resistance should be above 100k ohms. With tester positive lead connected to upper cylinder high tension

Fig. SZ5-6 — Adjust ignition timing statically by aligning stop (4) with mark (M). Refer to text.

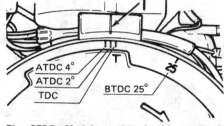

Fig. SZ5-7 — Models equipped with overhead type starter have timing marks shown in top view while models with gear type starter have timing marks shown in bottom view.

limited by control ring stop (4—Fig. SZ5-6) contacting bosses on cylinder block and magneto cover. Ignition timing should be 2 degrees ATDC when lower tab on stop contacts boss on cylinder block (idle speed ignition timing) and 25 degrees BTDC when upper tab contacts boss on magneto cover (full throttle ignition timing).

Static adjustment of ignition timing is correct if lower tab end surface (L) on control ring stop (4) is aligned with scribed mark (M) on magneto base plate. Loosen control ring stop retaining cap screws and reposition stop to adjust timing.

Ignition timing may also be checked and adjusted using a suitable power timing light. Immerse outboard in water and connect timing light to upper spark plug. Set engine throttle at full retard position and start engine. Timing marks should be aligned as shown in Fig. SZ5-7. To check advance ignition timing, run engine at wide open throttle and note timing marks which should indicate 25 degrees BTDC. Reposition control ring stop to adjust ignition timing.

If ignition malfunction occurs, check condition of spark plugs, all wires and connections before trouble-shooting ignition circuit. Using Suzuki pocket tester number 09900-25002 or a suitable ohmmeter, refer to the following test specifications and procedures to aid trouble-shooting.

Fig. SZ5-8 — Exploded view of water pump assembly. Inset shows water pump used on models with exhaust exiting through gearcase outlet.

4. "O" ring
5. Drive shaft tube
6. Water tube
7. Water tube guide
8. "O" ring
9. Pump housing
10. Impeller drive key
11. Impeller
12. Back plate
13. Gasket

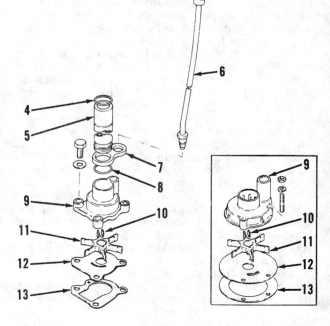

Illustrations Courtesy Suzuki America Corp.

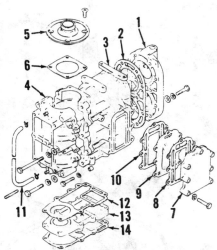

Fig. SZ5-9 — Exploded view of cylinder block assembly.

1.	Cylinder head	8.	Gasket
2.	Gasket	9.	Plate
3.	Cylinder block	10.	Gasket
4.	Crankcase half	11.	Lubrication hose
5.	Upper seal housing	12.	Gasket
6.	Gasket	13.	Lower seal housing
7.	Exhaust cover	14.	Gasket

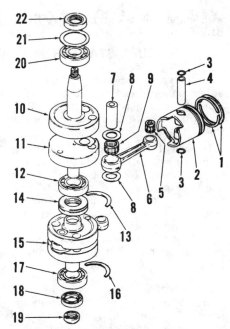

Fig. SZ5-10 — Exploded view of piston and crankshaft assembly.

1.	Piston rings	12.	Roller bearing
2.	Piston	13.	Thrust ring
3.	Retainer	14.	Seal
4.	Piston pin	15.	Lower crank assembly
5.	Roller bearing	16.	Thrust ring
6.	Connecting rod	17.	Ball bearing
7.	Crank pin	18.	Crankshaft seal
8.	Crank pin washer	19.	Drive shaft seal
9.	Roller bearing	20.	Ball bearing
10.	Crank half	21.	Shim
11.	Crank half	22.	Crankshaft seal

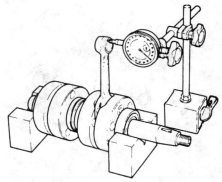

Fig. SZ5-11 — Move small connecting rod end side to side as shown to determine rod, bearing and crank pin wear. See text.

wire, connect negative tester lead to bottom cylinder high tension wire. Resistance between upper and bottom high tension wires should be 2200-2900 ohms. Connect tester positive lead to bottom cylinder high tension wire and repeat test procedure in this paragraph. Resistance readings should be the same as the upper cylinder readings.

COOLING SYSTEM

WATER PUMP. A rubber impeller type water pump is mounted between the drive shaft housing and gearcase. A key in the drive shaft is used to turn the pump impeller. If cooling system problems are encountered, check water intake for plugging or partial stoppage, then if not corrected, remove gearcase as outlined in the appropriate section and check condition of the water pump, water passages and sealing surfaces.

When water pump is disassembled, check condition of impeller (11 – Fig. SZ5-8) and plate (12) for excessive wear. Turn drive shaft clockwise (viewed from top) while placing pump housing over impeller. Avoid turning drive shaft in opposite direction when water pump is assembled.

POWER HEAD

REMOVE AND REINSTALL. To remove the power head, first remove upper cover and disconnect linkage, fuel lines and wires which interfere with power head removal. Remove carburetor, fuel pump, CD ignition coil module, recoil starter, upper magneto housing,

flywheel, stator assembly, lower magneto housing and disconnect neutral interlock rod before detaching power head from drive shaft housing. Remove screws which secure power head assembly to drive shaft housing and lift off power head.

Before reinstalling power head, make certain drive shaft splines are clean then coat them with a light coating of water-resistant grease. Apply a coat of silicone sealer to mating surfaces of power head and drive shaft housing and install a new gasket. Install power head on drive shaft housing and tighten retaining cap screws to 6-10 N·m. The remainder of installation is the reverse of removal procedure.

DISASSEMBLY. Disassembly and inspection may be accomplished in the following manner. Remove cylinder head and clean carbon from combustion chamber and any foreign material accumulation in water passages. Remove exhaust cover, intake manifold, reed valves and upper and lower oil seal housings. Separate crankcase half (4 – Fig. SZ5-9) from cylinder block (3) after removal of crankcase retaining cap screws. Crankshaft and piston assembly may now be removed.

Engine components are now ready for overhaul as outlined in the appropriate following paragraphs. Refer to the following section for assembly procedure.

ASSEMBLY. Refer to specific service sections when assembling the crankshaft, connecting rod, piston and reed valves. Make sure all joint and gasket surfaces are clean, free from nicks and burrs and hardened cement or carbon.

Whenever the power head is disassembled, it is recommended that all gasket surfaces and mating surfaces without gaskets be carefully checked for nicks, burrs and warped surfaces which might interfere with a tight seal. Cylinder head, head end of cylinder block and some mating surfaces of manifold and crankcase should be checked on a surface plate and lapped if necessary to provide a smooth surface. Do not remove any more metal than is necessary.

When assembling power head, first lubricate all friction surfaces and bearings with engine oil. Place thrust rings (13 and 16 – Fig. SZ5-10) in cylinder block, then install crankshaft assembly. Apply a coat of Suzuki Bond No. 4 or a suitable sealer to mating surfaces of cylinder half and cylinder block and position crankcase half on cylinder block. Using a crossing pattern, tighten the 6 mm crankcase screws to 8-12 N·m and 8 mm crankcase screws to 18-28 N·m. Cylinder head gasket should be installed without the application of a gasket sealer. Position cylinder head and gasket on cylinder block and tighten head screws in a crossing pattern to 18-28 N·m.

Install crankshaft seal (22 – Fig. SZ5-10) into upper seal housing with open side towards bearing (20). Install drive shaft seal (19) followed by crankshaft seal (18) into lower seal housing with open sides toward each other. Apply a suitable high temperature grease

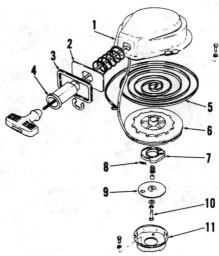

Fig. SZ5-12 — Exploded view of overhead type manual starter.

1. Housing	7. Pawl
2. Plate	8. Pawl spring
3. Grommet	9. Plate
4. Rope guide	10. Cap screw
5. Recoil spring	11. Starter cup
6. Rope pulley	

to lip portion of seals, then install upper and lower seal housings to cylinder block assembly.

RINGS, PISTONS AND CYLINDERS. The piston is fitted with two piston rings. Rings are interchangeable in grooves but must be installed with manufacturers marking toward closed end of piston. Piston ring end gap should be 0.15-0.35 mm with a maximum allowable ring end gap of 0.70 mm. Piston rings are retained in position by locating pins. Piston to cylinder wall clearance should be 0.042-0.058 mm. Pistons and rings are available in standard size as well as 0.25 mm and 0.50 mm oversizes. Cylinder should be bored to an oversize if cylinder is out of round or taper exceeds 0.10 mm. Install piston on connecting rod so arrow on piston crown will point towards exhaust port when piston is in cylinder.

CONNECTING ROD, BEARINGS AND CRANKSHAFT. Connecting rod, bearings and crankshaft are a press together unit. Crankshaft should be disassembled ONLY by experienced service personnel and with suitable service equipment.

Caged roller bearings are used at both large and small ends of the connecting rod. Determine rod bearing wear from side to side as shown in Fig. SZ5-11. Normal side to side movement is 4.0 mm or less. Maximum limit of crankshaft runout is 0.05 mm measured at bearing surfaces with crankshaft ends supported.

When installing crankshaft, lubricate pistons, rings, cylinders and bearings

with engine oil as outlined in ASSEMBLY section.

MANUAL STARTER

The power head may be equipped with either an overhead type starter (Fig. SZ5-12) or a gear type starter (Fig. SZ5-13). Refer to following service sections.

Overhead Type Starter. On models equipped with an overhead type starter, starter may be disassembled for overhaul or renewal of individual components as follows: Remove engine top cowl and three cap screws securing starter assembly to power head. If starter spring remains under tension, pull starter rope and hold rope pulley (6 – Fig. SZ5-12) with notch in pulley adjacent to rope outlet. Pull rope back through outlet so that it engages notch in pulley and allow pulley to slowly unwind. Remove cap screw (10) and disassemble unit. Be careful when removing rewind spring (5); a rapidly uncoiling starter spring could cause serious injury.

Rewind spring is wound in counterclockwise direction in starter housing. Rope is wound on rope pulley in counterclockwise direction as viewed with pulley in housing. Reassemble starter assembly by reversing disassembly procedure. To place tension on rewind spring, pass rope through rope outlet in housing and install rope handle. Pull rope out and hold rope pulley so notch on pulley is adjacent to rope outlet. Pull rope back through outlet between notch in pulley and housing. Turn rope pulley counterclockwise six complete revolutions to place tension on spring. Do not place more tension on rewind spring than is necessary to draw rope handle up against housing.

Gear Type Starter. On models with gear type starter, starter may be removed and disassembled for overhaul or renewal of individual components as follows: Remove engine top cowl, then remove rope handle and allow rope to wind onto rope pulley. Remove the nut and three cap screws securing starter assembly to power head and withdraw assembly. Loosen jam nut (2 – Fig. SZ5-13) and unscrew bolt (1), then using a suitable punch, drive out pin (12). Slide starter pinion (3) with spring clip (5) from starter reel (13). Remove snap ring (6) and washer (7), then carefully withdraw reel (13) from housing (9) so rewind spring (11) will not uncoil from housing; a rapidly uncoiling rewind spring could cause serious injury. Broken rewind spring or rope may be renewed at this point.

Rewind spring is wound in a clockwise

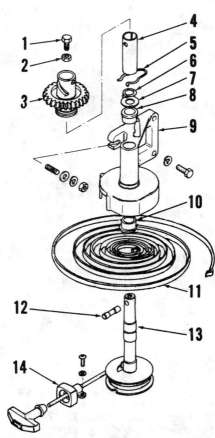

Fig. SZ5-13 — Exploded view of gear type manual starter used on some models.

1. Screw	8. Bushing
2. Nut	9. Housing
3. Starter pinion	10. Bushing
4. Bushing	11. Rewind spring
5. Spring clip	12. Pin
6. Snap ring	13. Starter reel
7. Washer	14. Rope guide

direction into housing as viewed from bottom. Wind rope onto pulley in a clockwise direction as viewed from bottom. Insert reel (13) into housing, engaging eye in end of spring with notch at reel base. Install washer (7) and snap ring (6), then place starter pinion (3) with spring clip (5) on shaft. Make certain spring clip is centered over lug on housing. Install pin (12) and secure in position with bolt (1) and nut (2). Thread rope through starter housing and attach rope handle. Hold pulley so notch on pulley is adjacent to rope outlet. Pull a loop of rope back through outlet between notch in pulley and housing. While grasping rope, turn rope pulley one complete revolution clockwise as viewed from bottom to place tension on spring. Do not place more tension on rewind spring than is necessary to draw rope handle up against housing.

LOWER UNIT

Early Models

PROPELLER AND RUBBER DAMPER. A rubber damper (41 – Fig.

Fig. SZ5-14 — Exploded view of early model lower unit assembly. Note that exhaust exits through an outlet in lower housing.

1. Seal
2. Snap ring
3. Snap ring
4. Bearing
5. Snap ring
6. Washer
7. Drive shaft
8. Needle bearing
9. Lower housing
10. Vent plug
11. Plate
12. Water filter
13. Bearing race
14. "O" ring
15. Bushing
16. Fill plug
17. Gearcase
18. Thrust washer
19. Thrust bearing
20. Thrust washer
21. Shims
22. Pinion gear
23. Bearing
24. Push rod
25. Push pin
26. Spring
27. Shim
28. Forward gear
29. Thrust washer
30. Clutch
31. Shift pin
32. Propeller shaft
33. Thrust washer
34. Reverse gear
35. Shim
36. "O" ring
37. Bearing
38. Seal
39. End cap
40. Stopper
41. Propeller hub
42. Propeller
43. Propeller nut
44. Cotter key

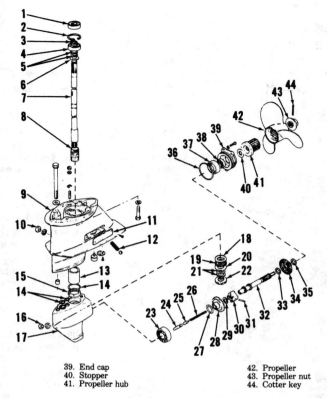

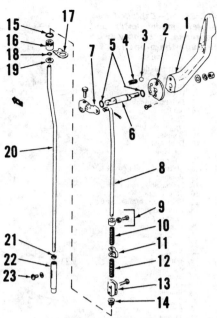

Fig. SZ5-15 — Exploded view of shift control linkage used on early models.

1. Shift handle
2. Detent plate
3. Detent ball
4. Spring
5. "O" ring
6. Shaft
7. Shift lever
8. Upper shift rod
9. Stopper
10. Spring
11. Reverse lock holder
12. Spring
13. Coupler
14. Bushing
15. "O" ring
16. Shift rod guide
17. Guide retainer
18. "O" ring
19. Washer
20. Lower shift rod
21. Nut
22. Shift cam
23. Shift cam retainer screw

SZ5-14) is used to provide shock protection for lower unit gears and shafts. Three-bladed propellers are used. Standard propeller for DT9.9 models has a 205 mm pitch and a 225 mm diameter while standard propeller for DT16 models has a 230 mm pitch and 225 mm diameter. Optional propellers for all models are available from the manufacturer and should be selected to provide full throttle operation within the recommended limits of 4500-5500 rpm on DT9.9 models and 5200-5800 rpm on DT16 models.

R&R AND OVERHAUL. Refer to Fig. SZ5-14 for exploded view of lower unit gearcase assembly used on early models which are identified by a lower housing exhaust outlet. During disassembly, note the location of all shims and thrust washers to aid in reassembly. To remove gearcase, first unscrew drain plug (16) and drain gear lubricant. Remove propeller, then disconnect shift linkage at coupler located externally between lower unit and power head. Remove the four cap screws securing lower unit to drive shaft housing and separate the lower unit assembly from drive shaft housing. Remove water pump assembly (Fig. SZ5-8) and gearcase end cap (39 – Fig. SZ5-14). Extract propeller shaft and reverse gear assembly. Remove shift cam retaining screw (23 – Fig. SZ5-15) located in gear-

case side and the two cap screws securing gearcase (17 – Fig. SZ5-14) to lower housing (9). Detach the gearcase while simultaneously removing pinion gear (22), shims (21) and thrust bearing assembly (18, 19 and 20). Extract forward gear (28) with shim (27). Remove drive shaft seal (1) and snap rings (2 and 3). Withdraw drive shaft (7) through gearcase side of lower housing.

Inspect shafts for wear on seal lip contact areas and on splines. Inspect clutch and gears for wear on engagement areas of dog teeth. Inspect gears for wear and damage. Inspect shift cam for excessive wear on ramp. All seals and "O" rings should be renewed when unit is reassembled.

To check gear mesh pattern and gear backlash, make a trial assembly using original shims and thrust washers. Assemble forward gear and pinion gear into gearcase, then attach gearcase to lower housing. Check mesh pattern of pinion gear and forward gear. Mesh pattern is adjusted by varying thickness of shims (21). Gear backlash should be 0.05-0.15 mm and is adjusted by varying thickness of forward gear shim (27) and reverse gear shim (35). Propeller shaft end play should be 0.05-0.50 mm and is adjusted by increasing or decreasing the thickness of thrust washers (29) and (33) in equal increments.

Reassemble lower unit by reversing disassembly procedure while noting the

following: Apply water-resistant grease to all "O" rings. Apply a coat of liquid gasket to mating surfaces of lower housing and gearcase and to mating surfaces of gearcase and gearcase end cap.

With lower unit installed, adjust shift linkage by first ensuring lower unit is in neutral. Set shift control handle exactly between "F" and "R" positions, then tighten screws securing shift rod coupler (13 – Fig. SZ5-15). Fill gearcase with approximately 220 mL of SAE 90 hypoid outboard gear oil.

Late Models

PROPELLER AND DRIVE CLUTCH. Late Model DT9.9 and DT16 models have a through-the-propeller exhaust system. Protection for the motor is built into a special cushioning clutch in the propeller hub. No adjustment is possible on the propeller or clutch. Three-bladed propellers are used. Standard propeller for DT9.9 models has a 203 mm pitch and a 235 mm diameter while standard propeller for DT16 models has a 230 mm pitch and 235 mm diameter. Optional propellers for all models are available from the manufacturer and should be selected to provide full throttle operation within the

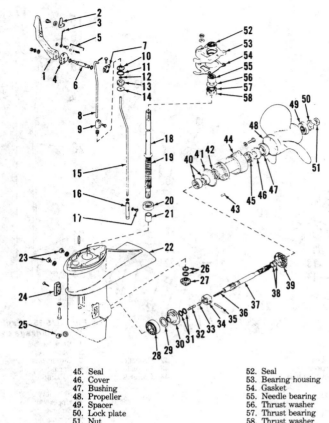

1. Shift handle
2. Interlock plate
3. Interlock rod
4. Detent plate
5. Detent ball assembly
6. Shaft
7. Shift lever
8. Upper shift rod
9. Coupler
10. Dust seal
11. "O" ring
12. "O" ring
13. Shift rod guide
14. Washer
15. Lower shift rod
16. Shift cam
17. Shift cam retainer screw
18. Drive shaft
19. Spring
20. Bearing
21. Bearing race
22. Gearcase
23. Vent plugs
24. Water filter
25. Fill plug
26. Shim
27. Pinion gear
28. Bearing
29. Shim
30. Forward gear
31. Thrust washer
32. Push rod
33. Push pin
34. Clutch
35. Shift pin
36. Spring
37. Propeller shaft
38. Thrust washer
39. Reverse gear
40. Needle bearing
41. "O" ring
42. Shim
43. Pin
44. Bearing housing

45. Seal
46. Cover
47. Bushing
48. Propeller
49. Spacer
50. Lock plate
51. Nut

52. Seal
53. Bearing housing
54. Gasket
55. Needle bearing
56. Thrust washer
57. Thrust bearing
58. Thrust washer

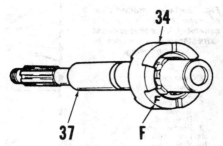

Fig. SZ5-17—Install clutch (34) so (F) mark is towards forward gear.

recommended limits of 4500-5500 rpm on DT9.9 models and 5200-5800 rpm on DT16 models.

R&R AND OVERHAUL. Refer to Fig. SZ5-16 for exploded view of lower unit gearcase assembly used on late models with through-the-propeller exhaust system. During disassembly note the location of all shims and thrust washers to aid in reassembly. To remove gearcase, first unscrew drain plug (25) and drain gear lubricant. Remove propeller, then disconnect shift linkage at coupler (9) located externally between lower unit and power head. Remove the cap screws securing lower unit to drive shaft housing and separate the lower unit assembly from drive shaft housing. Unscrew bearing housing (44) and using a suitable puller, extract propeller shaft and reverse gear assembly. Remove water pump assembly (Fig. SZ5-8) and drive shaft bearing housing (53—Fig. SZ5-16). Withdraw drive shaft while simultaneously removing pinion gear (27). Extract forward gear (30) with shim (29). Remove shift cam retaining screw (17) and withdraw lower shift rod (15).

Inspect shafts for wear on seal lip contact areas and on splines. Inspect clutch and gears for wear on engagement areas of dog teeth. Inspect gears for wear and damage. Inspect shift cam for excessive wear on ramp. All seals, "O"

rings and gaskets should be renewed when unit is reassembled.

To check gear mesh pattern and gear backlash, make a trial assembly using original shims and thrust washers. Assemble forward gear and pinion gear into gearcase, then insert drive shaft. Check mesh pattern of pinion gear and forward gear. Mesh pattern is adjusted by varying thickness of shims (26). Gear backlash should be 0.05-0.50 mm and is adjusted by varying thickness of forward gear shim (29) and reverse gear shim (42). Propeller shaft end play should be 0.05-0.50 mm and is adjusted by increasing or decreasing the thickness of thrust washers (31) and (38) in equal increments.

Reassemble lower unit by reversing disassembly procedure while noting the following: Install clutch (34) on propeller shaft (37) so "F" marked side (see Fig. SZ5-17) is towards forward gear (30—Fig. SZ5-16). Install seal (45) so seal lip is towards propeller. Apply water-resistant grease to all "O" rings and to lip portion of seals. Apply silicone sealer to lower unit and drive shaft housing mating surfaces.

With lower unit installed, adjust shift linkage by first ensuring lower unit is in neutral. Set shift control handle exactly between "F" and "R" positions, then tighten screws securing shift rod connector (9). Fill gearcase with approximately 200 mL of SAE 90 hypoid outboard gear oil.

SUZUKI DT20 and DT25
(PRIOR TO 1983)

CONDENSED SERVICE DATA

NOTE: Metric fasteners are used throughout outboard motor.

TUNE-UP	DT20	DT25
Hp	19.8	25
Bore	64 mm	68 mm
Stroke	61.5 mm	61.5 mm
Displacement	396 cc	447 cc
Spark Plug:		
NGK	B7HS	B7HS
Electrode Gap	0.6-0.7 mm	0.6-0.7 mm
Magneto:		
Breaker Point Gap	Breakerless	Breakerless
Carburetor:		
Make	Mikuni	Mikuni
Model	BV28-22	BV32-28
Fuel:Oil Ratio	50:1	50:1
SIZES—CLEARANCES		
Piston Ring End Gap	0.15-0.35 mm	0.15-0.35 mm
Piston Pin Diameter	15.995-16.000 mm	15.995-16.000 mm
Piston to Cylinder Wall Clearance	0.060-0.090 mm	0.060-0.090 mm
Max. Crankshaft Runout at Main		
Bearing Journal	0.05 mm	0.05 mm
Max. Con. Rod Small End Side		
Shake	5.0 mm	5.0 mm
TIGHTENING TORQUES		
Cylinder Head	18-28 N·m	18-28 N·m
Crankcase	18-28 N·m	18-28 N·m
Exhaust Cover	8-12 N·m	8-12 N·m
Flywheel Nut	100-110 N·m	100-110 N·m
Standard Screws:		
5 mm	2-4 N·m	2-4 N·m
6 mm	4-7 N·m	4-7 N·m
8 mm	10-16 N·m	10-16 N·m
10 mm	22-35 N·m	22-35 N·m

LUBRICATION

The power head is lubricated by oil mixed with the fuel. Fuel:oil ratios should be 30:1 during break-in of a new or rebuilt engine and 50:1 for normal service when using a BIA certified two-stroke engine oil or Suzuki "CCI" oil. When using any other type of two-stroke engine oil, fuel:oil ratios should be 20:1 during break-in and 30:1 for normal service. Manufacturer recommends regular or no-lead automotive gasoline having an 85-95 octane rating. Gasoline and oil should be thoroughly mixed.

The lower unit gears and bearings are lubricated by oil contained in the gearcase. SAE 90 hypoid outboard gear oil should be used. Gearcases with exhaust outlet in gearcase require 380 mL of gear oil while through-the-propeller exhaust models require 300 mL of gear oil. Reinstall vent and fill plugs securely using a new gasket, if necessary, to ensure a water tight seal.

FUEL SYSTEM

CARBURETOR. A Mikuni carburetor is used on all models. Refer to Fig. SZ8-1 for exploded view. Initial setting of pilot air screw (5) from a lightly seated position should be 1½-2 turns on DT20 models and 1¼-1¾ turns on DT25 models. Final carburetor adjustment should be made with engine at normal operating temperature and running in forward gear. Adjust throttle stop

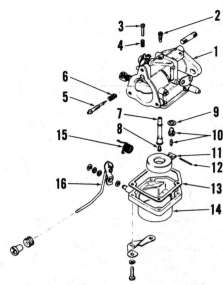

Fig. SZ8-1 — Exploded view of Mikuni carburetor typical of all models.

1. Throttle body	9. Gasket
2. Pilot jet	10. Inlet valve
3. Throttle stop screw	11. Float
4. Spring	12. Float pin
5. Pilot air screw	13. Gasket
6. Spring	14. Float bowl
7. Main nozzle	15. Spring
8. Main jet	16. Choke linkage

screw (3) so engine idles at approximately 600-650 rpm. Adjust pilot air screw so engine idles smoothly and will accelerate cleanly without hesitation. If necessary, readjust throttle stop screw to obtain 600-650 rpm idle speed.

Main fuel metering is controlled by main jet (8). Standard main jet size for normal operation is #130 on DT20 models and #160 on DT25 models.

To check float level, remove float bowl and invert carburetor. Distance (A – Fig. SZ8-2) between main jet and bottom of float should be 10.4-12.4 mm. Adjust float level by bending float tang.

REED VALVES. The inlet reed valves are located on a reed plate between inlet manifold and crankcase. The reed petals should seat very lightly against the reed plate throughout their entire length with the least possible tension. Tip of reed petal must not stand open more than 0.2 mm from contact surface. Reed stop opening should be 11.0 mm.

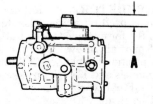

Fig. SZ8-2 — Float level (A) should be 10.4-12.4 mm.

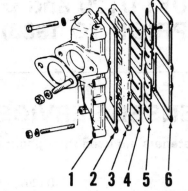

Fig. SZ8-3 — Exploded view of intake manifold and reed valve assembly.

1. Manifold	4. Reed petals
2. Gasket	5. Reed stop
3. Reed plate	6. Gasket

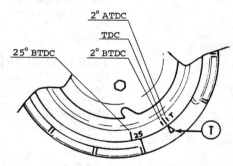

Fig. SZ8-4 — Exploded view of diaphragm type fuel pump assembly.

1. Cover	6. Gasket
2. Diaphragm	7. Body
3. Valve	8. "O" ring
4. Body	9. Insulator block
5. Fuel outlet	

Renew reeds if petals are broken, cracked, warped, rusted or bent. Never attempt to bend a reed petal or to straighten a damaged reed. Never install a bent or damaged reed. Seating surface of reed plate should be smooth and flat. When installing reeds or reed stop, make sure that petals are centered over the inlet holes in reed plate, and that the reed stops are centered over reed petals.

FUEL PUMP. A diaphragm fuel pump is mounted on the side of power head cylinder block and is actuated by pressure and vacuum pulsations from the engine crankcases.

When servicing pump, scribe reference marks across pump body to aid in reassembly. Defective or questionable parts should be renewed. Diaphragm should be renewed if air leaks or cracks are found, or if deterioration is evident.

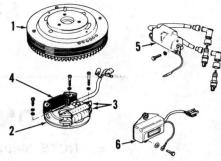

Fig. SZ8-6 — Exploded view of pointless electronic ignition components.

1. Flywheel	4. Lighting coil
2. Stator plate	5. Ignition coil
3. Ignition charge coils	6. CD ignition module

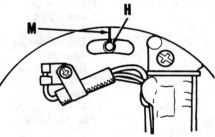

Fig. SZ8-7 — Set ignition timing statically by centering mark (M) on stator plate over screw hole (H).

Fig. SZ8-8 — View of ignition timing pointer (T) and flywheel timing marks.

IGNITION

All models are equipped with a pointless electronic ignition system. Refer to Fig. SZ8-8A for wiring diagram

Two capacitor charge coils (3 – Fig. SZ8-6) automatically advance ignition timing electronically as engine speed increases. Stator plate position is fixed.

Ignition timing should be 0° (TDC) at 1000 rpm and 25° BTDC at 5000 rpm. Initial setting of ignition timing may be accomplished by centering mark (M – Fig. SZ8-7) on stator plate over stator plate retaining screw hole (H). Final ignition timing check can be made

Illustrations Courtesy Suzuki America Corp.

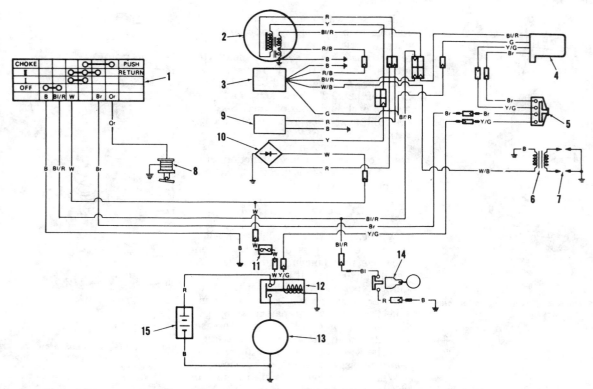

Fig. SZ8-8A—Wiring diagram for models equipped with electric starter, optional charging system, electric choke and emergency stop switch. Other models are similar.

1. Ignition switch	5. Neutral switch	13. Starter motor	R. Red	9. Regulator	W. White
2. Stator	6. Ignition coil	14. Emergency stop	Y. Yellow	10. Rectifier	BR. Brown
3. CD module	7. Spark plugs	switch	B. Black	11. 20 amp fuse	BL. Blue
4. NSI module	8. Choke solenoid	15. Battery	G. Green	12. Starter solenoid	OR. Orange

using a suitable power timing light. Immerse outboard in water and connect timing light to upper spark plug. Set engine throttle at full retard position and start engine. Timing marks should be aligned as shown in Fig. SZ8-8. To check advance ignition timing, run engine at wide open throttle and note timing marks. Reposition stator plate to adjust ignition timing.

If ignition malfunction occurs, check and make sure malfunction is not due to spark plug, wiring or wiring connection failure. If spark is absent at both cylinders, first check neutral start interlock (NSI) operation. Check neutral switch adjustment, switch should depress at least 1 mm when shift linkage is in neutral position. Check condition of neutral switch (5–Fig. SZ8-8A) using Suzuki pocket tester number 09900-25002 or a suitable ohmmeter. Separate the wire connectors between switch (5) and NSI module (4) and attach a tester lead to each wire connected to switch. With shift linkage in neutral position, tester should read zero resistance. Moving shift linkage to "F"

or "R" positions, should cause tester to read infinite resistance. Renew neutral switch if required.

To check condition of NSI module, use tester or ohmmeter in conjunction with test chart shown in Fig. SZ8-9. Renew NSI module if required.

Troubleshoot ignition circuit using Suzuki pocket tester number 09900-25002 or ohmmeter as follows: Check condition of low speed charge coil by separating the blue/red wire connector and red/black wire connector at stator and attach a tester lead to each wire. Low speed charge coil may be con-

	— Tester's minus terminal			
+ Tester's plus terminal		Blue/Red	Green	Brown	Yellow/Green
	Blue/Red		A	B	C
	Green	B		B	C
	Brown	A	A		C
	Yellow/Green	C	C	B	

Fig. SZ8-9 — Use chart shown above and values listed below to test condition of NSI module.

A. 200 ohms or less
B. 200 ohms or more
C. Tester needle should show deflection then return toward infinite resistance

Fig. SZ8-10 — Use chart shown above and values listed below to test condition of CD ignition module.

A. 200 ohms or less
B. 200 ohms or more
C. Tester needle should show deflection then return toward infinite resistance

	— Tester's minus terminal				
+ Tester's plus terminal		Green	Blue/Red	Red/Black	Black	White/Black
	Green		B	B	B	B
	Blue/Red	C		B	A	A
	Red/Black	C	B		A	A
	Black	C	B	B		A
	White/Black	C	B	B	C	

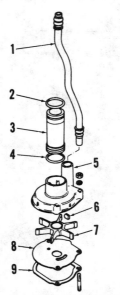

Fig. SZ8-11 — Exploded view of water pump assembly.

1. Water tube
2. "O" ring
3. Seal tube
4. "O" ring
5. Pump housing
6. Key
7. Impeller
8. Plate
9. Gasket

sidered satisfactory if resistance reading is within the limits of 122-149 ohms. Check condition of high speed charge coil by separating the black wire connector and red/black wire connector at stator and attach a tester lead to each wire. High speed charge coil may be considered satisfactory if resistance reading is within the limits of 1.62-1.98 ohms.

To check condition of ignition coil, separate the black wire connector and white/black wire connector at coil and remove high tension wires from spark plugs. Attach tester positive lead to black wire and negative lead to white/black wire. Primary coil resistance reading should be within the limits of 0.28-0.38 ohms. Attach a tester lead to each high tension wire. Secondary coil resistance reading should be within the limits of 2975-4025 ohms.

To check condition of CD module, use tester or ohmmeter in conjunction with test chart shown in Fig. SZ8-10. Renew CD module if required.

COOLING SYSTEM

WATER PUMP. A rubber impeller type water pump is mounted between the drive shaft housing and gearcase. A key in the drive shaft is used to turn the pump impeller. If cooling system problems are encountered, check water intake for plugging or partial stoppage, then if not corrected, remove gearcase as outlined in the appropriate section and check condition of the water pump, water passages and sealing surfaces.

When water pump is disassembled, check condition of impeller (7 – Fig. SZ8-11) and plate (8) for excessive wear. Turn drive shaft clockwise (viewed from top) while placing pump housing over impeller. Avoid turning drive shaft in opposite direction when water pump is assembled.

THERMOSTAT. A thermostat is used to regulate operating temperature. The thermostat is calibrated to control temperature within the range of 61°-64°C. Thermostat can be removed

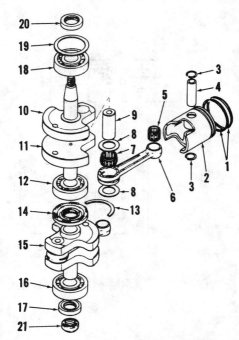

Fig. SZ8-13 — Exploded view of crankshaft assembly typical of all models.

1. Piston rings
2. Piston
3. Piston pin clip
4. Piston pin
5. Roller bearing
6. Connecting rod
7. Roller bearing
8. Thrust washer
9. Crank pin
10. Top crank half
11. Crank half
12. Ball bearing
13. Thrust ring
14. Labyrinth seal
15. Lower crankshaft assembly
16. Ball bearing
17. Crankshaft seal
18. Ball bearing
19. Shim
20. Crankshaft seal
21. Drive shaft seal

for inspection or renewal by removing thermostat housing cover located at top of cylinder head. Refer to Fig. SZ8-12 for exploded view of cylinder block assembly showing thermostat (16) and associated parts.

POWER HEAD

REMOVE AND REINSTALL. To remove the power head, first remove upper cover and disconnect linkage, fuel lines and wires which interfere with power head removal. Remove carburetor, fuel pump, CD module, rectifier, ignition coil, neutral safety interlock switch, interlock rod, recoil or electric starter, magneto housing, flywheel and stator assembly before detaching power head from lower unit. Remove screws securing power head assembly to lower unit and lift off the power head.

Before reinstalling power head, make certain drive shaft splines are clean then coat them with a light coating of water resistant grease. Apply a suitable sealer to mating surfaces of power head and lower unit and install a new gasket. The remainder of installation is the reverse of removal procedure.

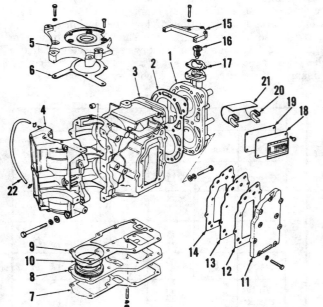

Fig. SZ8-12 — Exploded view of crankcase assembly typical of all models.

1. Cylinder head
2. Head gasket
3. Cylinder block
4. Crankcase half
5. Upper seal housing
6. Gasket
7. Gasket
8. Lower seal housing
9. Gasket
10. "O" ring
11. Exhaust cover
12. Gasket
13. Plate
14. Gasket
15. Cover
16. Thermostat
17. Cover
18. Cover
19. Gasket
20. Grommet
21. Wire connection box
22. Lubrication hose

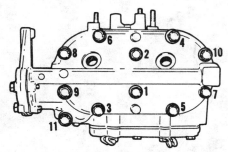

Fig. SZ8-14—Cylinder head cap screws should be tightened in the sequence shown above.

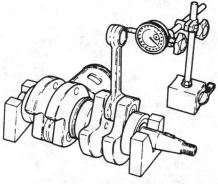

Fig. SZ8-15—Maximum side to side shake at small end of connecting rod should be 5.0 mm or less.

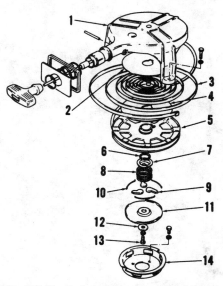

Fig. SZ8-17—Exploded view of overhead starter assembly used on some models.

1. Starter housing	8. Spring
2. Retainer	9. Pawl
3. Rewind spring	10. Clip
4. Retainer	11. Drive plate
5. Rope pulley	12. Washer
6. Washer	13. Cap screw
7. Spring guide	14. Starter cup

DISASSEMBLY. Disassembly and inspection may be accomplished in the following manner. Remove exhaust tube from lower oil seal housing (8–Fig. SZ8-12) then remove lower oil seal housing. Remove upper oil seal housing, exhaust cover, intake manifold and reed valves. Remove cylinder head and clean carbon from combustion chamber and any foreign material accumulation in water passages. Crankcase half (4) may be separated from cylinder block (3) and crankshaft and piston assembly removed after removal of crankcase retaining cap screws.

Engine components are now ready for overhaul as outlined in the appropriate following paragraphs. Refer to the following section for assembly procedure.

ASSEMBLY. Refer to specific service sections when assembling the crankshaft, connecting rod, piston and reed valves. Make sure all joints and gasket surfaces are clean, free from nicks and burrs and hardened cement or carbon. Whenever the power head is disassembled, it is recommended that all gasket surfaces and mating surfaces without gaskets be carefully checked for nicks, burrs and warped surfaces which might interfere with a tight seal. Cylinder head, head end of cylinder block and some mating surfaces of manifold and crankcase should be checked on a surface plate and lapped if necessary to provide a smooth surface. Do not remove any more metal than is necessary.

When assembling power head, first lubricate all friction surfaces and bearings with engine oil. Place thrust ring (13–Fig. SZ8-13) in cylinder block, then install crankshaft assembly. Apply a coat of Suzuki Bond No. 4 or a suitable sealer to mating surfaces of cylinder half and cylinder block and position crankcase half on cylinder block. Using a crossing pattern, tighten the crankcase screws to 18-28 N·m. Cylinder head gasket should be installed without the

application of a gasket sealer. Position cylinder head and gasket on cylinder block and tighten head screws in sequence shown in Fig. SZ8-14 to 18-28 N·m.

Install crankshaft seal (20–Fig. SZ8-13) into upper seal housing with open side towards bearing (18). Install drive shaft seal (21) followed by crankshaft seal (17) into lower seal housing with open sides toward each other. Apply a suitable high temperature grease to lip portion of seals, then install upper and lower seal housings to cylinder block assembly.

RINGS, PISTONS AND CYLINDERS. The piston is fitted with two piston rings. Rings are interchangeable in grooves but must be installed with manufacturers marking toward closed end of piston. DT20 models should have a piston ring end gap of 0.15-0.35 mm with a maximum allowable ring end gap of 0.070 mm. DT25 models should have a piston ring end gap of 0.20-0.40 mm with a maximum allowable ring end gap of 0.80 mm. On all models, piston to cylinder wall clearance should be 0.060-0.090 mm. Pistons and rings are available in standard size as well as 0.25 mm and 0.50 mm oversizes. Cylinder should be bored to an oversize if cylinder is out-of-round or taper exceeds 0.10 mm. Install piston on connecting rod so arrow on piston crown will point towards exhaust port when piston is in cylinder.

CONNECTING ROD, BEARINGS AND CRANKSHAFT. Connecting rod, bearings and crankshaft are a pressed-together unit. Crankshaft should be disassembled ONLY by experienced service personnel and with suitable service equipment.

Caged roller bearings are used at both large and small ends of the connecting rod. Determine rod bearing wear by

measuring connecting rod small end side-to-side movement as shown in Fig. SZ8-15. Normal side-to-side movement is 5.0 mm or less. Standard limit of crankshaft runout is 0.05 mm measured at bearing surfaces with crankshaft ends supported.

When installing crankshaft, lubricate pistons, rings, cylinders and bearings with engine oil as outlined in ASSEMBLY section.

STARTERS

MANUAL STARTER. Refer to Fig. SZ8-17 for exploded view of overhead type manual starter assembly and to Fig. SZ8-18 for exploded view of gear type manual starter.

Overhead Type Starter. On models equipped with an overhead type starter, starter may be disassembled for overhaul or renewal of individual components as follows: Remove engine top cowl and three cap screws securing starter assembly to power head. If starter spring remains under tension, pull starter rope and hold rope pulley (5–Fig. SZ8-17) with notch in pulley adjacent to rope outlet. Pull rope back through outlet so that it engages notch in pulley and allow pulley to slowly unwind. Remove cap screw (13) and disassemble unit. Be careful when removing rewind spring (3); a rapidly uncoiling starter spring could cause serious injury.

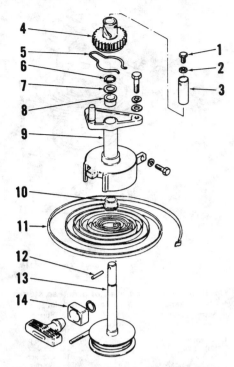

Fig. SZ8-18 — Exploded view of gear type starter assembly used on some models.

1. Bolt	8. Bushing
2. Nut	9. Housing
3. Pinion bushing	10. Bushing
4. Pinion	11. Rewind spring
5. Spring clip	12. Pin
6. Snap ring	13. Reel
7. Washer	14. Rope guide

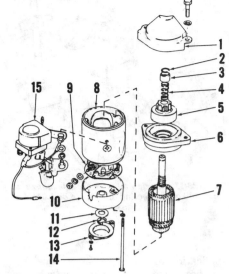

Fig. SZ8-19 — Exploded view of electric starter motor.

1. Drive cover	
2. "C" ring	9. Brush assembly
3. Stop	10. Brush cover
4. Spring	11. Thrust washer
5. Drive	12. "E" clip
6. Frame head	13. End cap
7. Armature	14. Through bolt
8. Frame	15. Starter solenoid

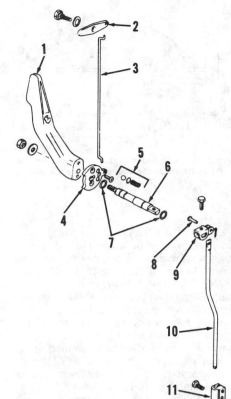

Fig. SZ8-20 — Exploded view of upper shift linkage assembly used on all models.

1. Shift handle	
2. Interlock plate	7. "O" rings
3. Interlock rod	8. Pin
4. Detent plate	9. Shift arm
5. Detent assembly	10. Upper shift rod
6. Shaft	11. Connector

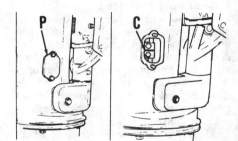

Fig. SZ8-21 — View of drive shaft housing showing location of shift linkage cover plate (P) and shift linkage connector (C).

Rewind spring is wound in a counterclockwise direction in starter housing. Rope is wound on rope pulley in a counterclockwise direction as viewed with pulley in housing. Reassemble starter assembly by reversing disassembly procedure. To place tension on rewind spring, pass rope through rope outlet in housing and install rope handle. Pull rope out and hold rope pulley so notch on pulley is adjacent to rope outlet. Pull rope back through outlet between notch in pulley and housing. Turn rope pulley counterclockwise four complete revolutions to place tension on spring. Do not place more tension on rewind spring than is necessary to draw rope handle up against housing.

Gear Type Starter. On models equipped with gear type starter, starter may be removed and disassembled for overhaul or renewal of individual components as follows: Remove engine top cowl, then remove rope handle and allow rope to wind onto rope pulley. Remove the cap screws securing starter assembly to power head and withdraw assembly. Loosen jam nut (2–Fig. SZ8-18) and unscrew bolt (1), then using a suitable punch, drive out pin (12). Slide starter pinion (4) with spring clip (5)

from starter reel (13). Remove snap ring (6) and washer (7), then carefully withdraw reel (13) from housing (9) so rewind spring (11) will not uncoil from housing; a rapidly uncoiling rewind spring could cause serious injury. Broken rewind spring or rope may be renewed at this point.

Rewind spring is wound in a clockwise direction into housing as viewed from bottom. Wind rope onto pulley in a clockwise direction as viewed from bottom. Insert reel (13) into housing, engaging eye in end of spring with notch at reel base. Install washer (7) and snap ring (6), then place starter pinion (4) with spring clip (5) on shaft. Make certain spring clip is centered over lug on housing. Install pin (12) and secure in position with bolt (1) and nut (2). Thread rope through starter housing and attach rope handle. Hold pulley so notch on pulley is adjacent to rope outlet. Pull a loop of rope back through outlet between notch in pulley and housing. While grasping rope, turn rope pulley clockwise, as viewed from bottom, one complete revolution to place tension on spring. Do not place more tension on rewind spring than is necessary to draw rope handle up against housing.

ELECTRIC STARTER. Some models are equipped with electric starter shown in Fig. SZ8-19. Disassembly is evident after inspection of unit and reference to exploded view.

Starter brushes have a standard length of 14.0 mm and should be renewed if worn to 9.5 mm or less. After reassembly, bench test starter before installing on power head.

LOWER UNIT

DT20 Models

PROPELLER AND RUBBER DAMPER. A rubber damper (58 – Fig. SZ8-22) is used to provide shock protection for lower unit gears and shafts. Three-bladed propellers are used. Standard propeller has a 255 mm pitch and a 225 mm diameter. Optional propellers are available from the manufacturer and should be selected to provide full throttle operation within the recommended limits of 5200-5700 rpm.

DT25 Models

PROPELLER AND DRIVE CLUTCH. DT25 models have a through-the-propeller exhaust system. Protection for the motor is built into a special cushioning clutch in the propeller hub. No adjustment is possible on the propeller or clutch. Three-bladed propellers are used. Standard propeller has a 230 mm pitch and a 235 mm diameter. Optional propellers are available from the manufacturer and should be selected to provide full throttle operation within the recommended limits of 5200-5700 rpm.

All Models

R&R AND OVERHAUL. Refer to Fig. SZ8-22 for exploded view of lower unit gearcase assembly used on DT20 models and to Fig. SZ8-23 for exploded view of lower unit gearcase assembly used on DT25 models. The following service procedures will apply to both models except where noted. During disassembly, note the location of all shims and thrust washers to aid in reassembly. To remove gearcase, first unscrew drain plug (18) and drain gear lubricant. Remove cover plate (P–Fig. SZ8-21) located on drive shaft housing and disconnect shift linkage at connector (C). Remove the cap screws securing gearcase to drive shaft housing and separate gearcase assembly from drive shaft housing. Remove water pump assembly (Fig. SZ8-11) and shift yoke pilot screw (32–Fig. SZ8-22 or Fig. SZ8-23) from lower gearcase cover (19). Remove propeller and unscrew the six cap screws securing lower gearcase cover (19) and detach cover. Propeller shaft (43), complete with gears and bearings, may now be removed. Remove snap ring (35) and pinion gear (34) from drive shaft (6). Drive shaft (6) and related components may be withdrawn from upper gearcase after removal of retaining ring (1) on all models and snap ring (3–Fig. SZ8-23) on DT25 models.

On all models, inspect gears for wear on teeth and in engagement dogs. Inspect clutch (42–Fig. SZ8-22 or SZ8-23) for wear on engagement surfaces. Inspect shafts for wear on splines and on friction surfaces of gears and oil seals. Check shift yoke (31) and shift cradle (30) for excessive wear. All seals and "O" rings should be renewed when unit is reassembled.

Backlash between pinion gear (34) and drive gears (40 and 46) should be

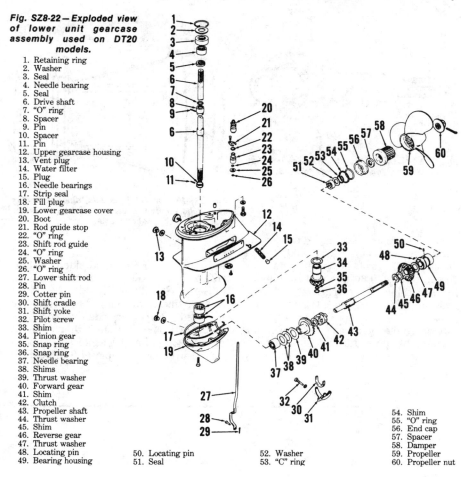

Fig. SZ8-22 – Exploded view of lower unit gearcase assembly used on DT20 models.

1. Retaining ring
2. Washer
3. Seal
4. Needle bearing
5. Seal
6. Drive shaft
7. "O" ring
8. Spacer
9. Pin
10. Spacer
11. Pin
12. Upper gearcase housing
13. Vent plug
14. Water filter
15. Plug
16. Needle bearings
17. Strip seal
18. Fill plug
19. Lower gearcase cover
20. Boot
21. Rod guide stop
22. "O" ring
23. Shift rod guide
24. "O" ring
25. Washer
26. "O" ring
27. Lower shift rod
28. Pin
29. Cotter pin
30. Shift cradle
31. Shift yoke
32. Pilot screw
33. Shim
34. Pinion gear
35. Snap ring
36. Snap ring
37. Needle bearing
38. Shims
39. Thrust washer
40. Forward gear
41. Shim
42. Clutch
43. Propeller shaft
44. Thrust washer
45. Shim
46. Reverse gear
47. Thrust washer
48. Locating pin
49. Bearing housing

50. Locating pin
51. Seal

52. Washer
53. "C" ring

54. Shim
55. "O" ring
56. End cap
57. Spacer
58. Damper
59. Propeller
60. Propeller nut

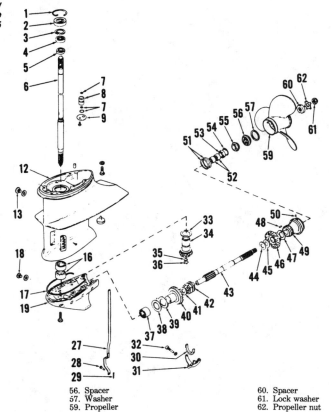

Fig. SZ8-23 – Exploded view of lower unit gearcase assembly used on DT25 models.

1. Retaining ring
2. Seal
3. Snap ring
4. Bearing
5. Seal
6. Drive shaft
7. "O" ring
8. Shift rod guide
9. Rod guide stop
12. Upper gearcase housing
13. Vent plug
16. Needle bearings
17. Strip seal
18. Fill plug
19. Lower gearcase cover
27. Lower shift rod
28. Pin
29. Cotter pin
30. Shift cradle
31. Shift yoke
32. Pilot screw
33. Shim
34. Pinion gear
35. Snap ring
36. Snap ring
37. Needle bearing
38. Shim
39. Thrust washer
40. Forward gear
41. Shim
42. Dog clutch
43. Propeller shaft
44. Thrust washer
45. Shim
46. Reverse gear
47. Thrust washer
48. Locating pin
49. Bearing housing
50. Locating pin
51. "O" rings
52. Needle bearings
53. Seal
54. Snap ring
55. End cap

56. Spacer
57. Washer
59. Propeller

60. Spacer
61. Lock washer
62. Propeller nut

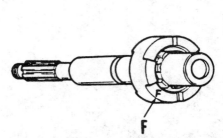

Fig. SZ8-24—Install clutch on propeller shaft with "F" marked side towards forward gear.

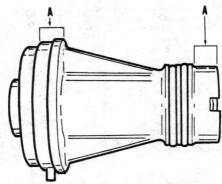

Fig. SZ8-25—On DT25 models, silicone sealer should be applied to bearing housing in areas shown at A.

0.05-0.30 mm and is adjusted by varying thickness of shims (38) and thrust washer (47). Propeller shaft end play should be 0.05-0.30 mm and is adjusted by increasing or decreasing the thickness of thrust washer (41) and shims (45).

Reassemble gearcase by reversing disassembly procedure while noting the following: Install clutch (42) on propeller shaft (43) so "F" marked side (see Fig. SZ8-24) is towards forward gear (40 – Fig. SZ8-22 or Fig. SZ8-23). Make certain thrust washers (39 and 47) are installed with copper side towards drive gears (40 and 46) and that hole in reverse gear thrust washer (47) is positioned over locating pin (48) in bearing housing (49). On DT20 models (Fig. SZ8-22), apply a 5 mm wide bead of silicone sealer to each side of "O" ring groove on bearing housing (49). On DT25 models (Fig. SZ8-23), silicone sealer should be applied to bearing housing (49) in areas shown at (A – Fig. SZ8-25). When installing propeller shaft assembly on all models, tab of thrust washer (39 – Fig. SZ8-22 or Fig. SZ8-23) must engage locating notch in upper gearcase while hole in bearing housing (49) must engage locating pin (50) in upper gearcase. Apply water-resistant grease to all "O" rings and to lip portion of seals. Apply silicone sealer to upper and lower gearcase mating surfaces and to mating surfaces of drive shaft housing and gearcase assembly.

With gearcase assembly installed, adjust shift linkage by first ensuring gearcase is in neutral. Set shift control handle exactly between "F" and "R" positions, then tighten shift rod connector (C – Fig. SZ8-21). Fill gearcase with outboard gear oil as outlined in LUBRICATION section.

SUZUKI DT20 (1986-1988) AND DT25 (1985-1988)

CONDENSED SERVICE DATA

NOTE: Metric fasteners are used throughout outboard motor.

TUNE-UP

Hp/rpm 20/4800-5500
                                          25/4800-5500

Bore:
  DT20 . . . . .67 mm
                                          (2.64 in.)
  DT25 . . . . .71 mm
                                          (2.80 in.)
Stroke . . . . .63 mm
                                          (2.48 in.)
Number of Cylinders 2
Displacement:
  DT20 . . . . .444 cc
                                          (27.10 cu. in.)
  DT25 . . . . .499 cc
                                          (30.45 cu. in.)
Spark Plug:
  NGK BR7HS
Electrode Gap . . . . .0.8-0.9 mm
                                          (0.031-0.035 in.)
Ignition Type . . . . .CDI
Carburetor Make . . . . .Mikuni
Idle Speed (in gear) . . . . .650-700 rpm
Fuel:Oil Ratio . . . . .See Text

SIZES—CLEARANCES

Piston Ring End Gap . . . . .0.2-0.4 mm
                                          (0.008-0.016 in.)
Piston-to-Cylinder Clearance:
  Prior to 1987 . . . . .0.067-0.082 mm
                                          (0.0026-0.0032 in.)
  After 1986 .0.087-0.102 mm
                                          (0.0034-0.0040 in.)
Piston Pin Diameter . . . . .17.995-18.000 mm
                                          (0.7085-0.7087 in.)
Max. Crankshaft Runout at Main
  Bearing Journal . . . . .0.05 mm
                                          (0.002 in.)
Max. Connecting Rod Small End
  Side Shake . . . . .5.0 mm
                                          (0.20 in.)

TIGHTENING TORQUES

Power Head Mounting Screws . . . . .15-20 N·m
                                          (11-14 ft.-lbs.)

TIGHTENING TORQUES CONT.

Crankcase:
  6 mm . . . . .8-12 N·m
                                          (6-8 ft.-lbs.)
  8 mm . . . . .20-26 N·m
                                          (14-19 ft.-lbs.)
Flywheel Nut . . . . .130-150 N·m
                                          (94-108 ft.-lbs.)
Cylinder Head Screws:
  6 mm . . . . .8-12 N·m
                                          (6-8 ft.-lbs.)
  8 mm . . . . .20-26 N·m
                                          (14-19 ft.-lbs.)
Gearcase Pinion Nut . . . . .18-22 N·m
                                          (13-16 ft.-lbs.)
Propeller Shaft Nut . . . . .27-30 N·m
                                          (19-21 ft.-lbs.)
Standard Screws:
  Unmarked or Marked "4"
    5 mm . . . . .2-4 N·m
                                          (2-3 ft.-lbs.)
    6 mm . . . . .4-7 N·m
                                          (3-5 ft.-lbs.)
    8 mm . . . . .10-16 N·m
                                          (7-12 ft.-lbs.)
    10 mm . . . . .22-35 N·m
                                          (16-26 ft.-lbs.)
  Stainless Steel
    5 mm . . . . .2-4 N·m
                                          (2-3 ft.-lbs.)
    6 mm . . . . .6-10 N·m
                                          (5-7 ft.-lbs.)
    8 mm . . . . .15-20 N·m
                                          (11-15 ft.-lbs.)
    10 mm . . . . .34-41 N·m
                                          (25-30 ft.-lbs.)
  Marked "7" or SAE Grade 5
    5 mm . . . . .3-6 N·m
                                          (2-5 ft.-lbs.)
    6 mm . . . . .8-12 N·m
                                          (6-9 in.-lbs.)
    8 mm . . . . .18-28 N·m
                                          (13-20 ft.-lbs.)
    10 mm . . . . .40-60 N·m
                                          (29-44 ft.-lbs.)

LUBRICATION

The power head is lubricated by oil mixed with the fuel. During break-in of a new or rebuilt engine, fuel:oil ratio should be 30:1 on 1985 DT25 models and 25:1 on 1986 and later DT25 and all DT20 models. Fuel:oil ratio for normal service should be 50:1 on 1985 DT25 models and 100:1 on 1986 and later DT25 and all DT20 models. Recommended oil is Suzuki Outboard Motor Oil or a good quality NMMA certified TC-W engine oil. Recommended fuel is regular or unleaded gasoline having an 85 minimum octane rating. Manufacturer does not recommended using gasoline containing alcohol additives. However, unleaded gasoline containing ethanol (grain alcohol) may be used providing ethanol content does not exceed five percent and minimum octane rating is 85.

NOTE: Manufacturer recommends NOT using any gasoline containing methanol (wood alcohol).

The lower unit gears and bearings are lubricated with approximately 230 mL (7.8 ozs.) of SAE 90 hypoid gear oil. After checking or refilling lower unit, reinstall vent and fill plugs securely using new gaskets to ensure a water tight seal.

FUEL SYSTEM

CARBURETOR. A Mikuni B32-24 carburetor is used on all DT25 models and 1986 DT20 models. On 1987 and 1988 DT20 models, a Mikuni B28-22 carburetor is used. Refer to Fig. SZ9-1 for exploded view of carburetor typical of all models.

Initial setting of pilot air screw (6) from a lightly seated position is 3/4 to 1-1/4 turns on all models prior to 1987, 1-3/4 to 2-1/4 turns on 1987 and later DT20 models and 1-1/4 to 1-3/4 turns on 1987 and later DT25 models. Final adjustment should be made with engine at normal operating temperature and running in forward gear. Adjust idle speed screw (2) so engine idles at approximately 650-700 rpm. Adjust pilot air screw (6) so engine idles smoothly and will accelerate cleanly without hesitation. Readjust idle speed to 650-700 rpm if necessary.

Standard pilot jet is #67.5 on 1986 Model DT20, #90 on 1987 and later DT20 models and #90 on all DT25 models.

Main fuel metering is controlled by main jet (10). Standard main jet for normal operation is #142.5 on 1986 DT20 models and all DT25 models. Standard main jet for normal operation on 1987 and later DT20 models is #120.

To check float level, remove float bowl (14) and invert carburetor body (1). Distance (D—Fig. SZ9-2) between main jet and bottom of float should be 10-12 mm (0.390-0.470 in.) on all models prior to 1987, 11.5-13.5 mm (0.450-0.530 in.) on 1987 and later DT20 models and 11-12 mm (0.430-0.470 in.) on 1987 and later DT25 models. Bend float tang to adjust float level.

FUEL FILTER. A fuel filter assembly is used to filter the fuel prior to entering the fuel pump assembly. Periodically unscrew cup (5—Fig. SZ9-3) from base (1) and withdraw filter element (4). Clean cup (5) and filter element (4) in a suitable solvent and blow dry with clean compressed air. Inspect filter element (4). If excessive blockage or damage is noted, then the element must be renewed.

Reassembly is reverse order of disassembly. Renew "O" ring (3) and, if needed, seal (2) during reassembly.

FUEL PUMP. A diaphragm fuel pump (Fig. SZ9-4) is mounted on the side of power head cylinder block and is actuated by pressure and vacuum pulsations from the engine crankcase.

When servicing pump, scribe reference marks across pump body to aid reassembly. Defective or questionable parts should be renewed. Diaphragm should be renewed if air leaks or cracks are found, or if deterioration is evident.

REED VALVES. The reed valves are located on a reed plate located behind the intake manifold. The intake manifold must be removed in order to remove reed plate and service reed valves.

Renew reed valves (2—Fig. SZ9-5) if petals are broken, cracked, warped,

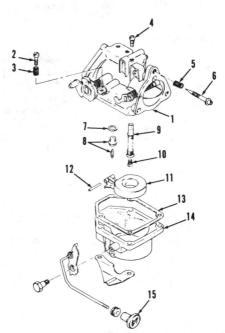

Fig. SZ9-1—Exploded view of Mikuni B32-24 carburetor.

1. Body
2. Idle speed screw
3. Spring
4. Pilot jet
5. Spring
6. Pilot air screw
7. Gasket
8. Needle & seat
9. Main nozzle
10. Main jet
11. Float
12. Pin
13. Gasket
14. Float bowl
15. Choke knob

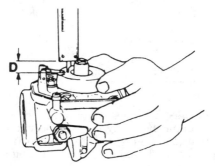

Fig. SZ9-2—Measure float level from bottom of main jet to bottom of float as shown. Measurement should be taken at a point 180 degrees from inlet needle valve. Refer to text for float level specifications.

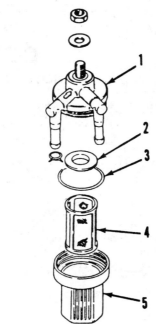

Fig. SZ9-3—Exploded view of fuel filter assembly.

1. Base
2. Seal
3. "O" ring
4. Element
5. Cup

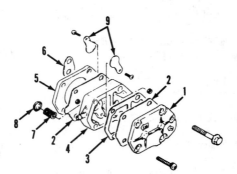

Fig. SZ9-4—Exploded view of diaphragm type fuel pump.

1. Cover
2. Diaphragm
3. Gasket
4. Valve body
5. Plate
6. Gasket
7. Spring
8. Spring seat
9. Check valve

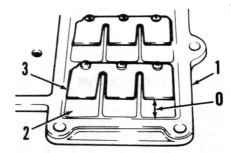

Fig. SZ9-5—View indentifying reed plate (1), reed valves (2) and reed stops (3). Reed stop opening (O) should be 6.0-6.4 mm (0.24-0.25 in.).

rusted or bent. Tip of reed petal must not stand open more than 0.2 mm (0.008 in.) from contact surface. Reed stop opening (O) should be 6.0-6.4 mm (0.24-0.25 in.).

SPEED CONTROL LINKAGE. Place twist grip in the full closed position. Stator plate stopper (P—Fig. SZ9-8) should be in contact with cylinder block boss (D). Adjust rod (A—Fig. SZ9-6) length until mark (M) on throttle cam (C) is centered with roller (R). Rotate twist grip to the full throttle position. Stator plate stopper should be in contact with cylinder block boss. Adjust rod (B) length until throttle limiter (L) contacts stopper (S) on bottom engine cover.

IGNITION

A breakerless, capacitor discharge ignition system is used. Refer to Fig. SZ9-7 for wiring diagram.

Full throttle and full ignition advance should occur simultaneously. The ignition timing is mechanically advanced and must be synchronized with throttle opening.

To check ignition timing, first immerse lower unit of outboard motor in water. Connect a suitable tachometer to the engine. Connect a power timing light to upper spark plug. Start the engine and warm up to normal operating temperature. Shift into "Forward" gear and note ignition timing. Timing pointer (T—Fig. SZ9-8) should be aligned with 2 degrees ATDC mark (A) on flywheel. If necessary, loosen locknut and rotate screws (S) until recommended idle speed timing is obtained. Maximum advance timing should be 25 degrees BTDC (M) at 5000 rpm. Stop engine and loosen cap

screws (C) and slide stator plate stopper (P) in slots to adjust maximum advance timing. Retighten cap screws (C) after recommended maximum advance timing is obtained. Reset idle speed timing as previously recommended.

If ignition malfunction occurs, check condition of spark plugs, all wires and connections before trouble-shooting ignition circuit. Using Suzuki pocket tester 09900-25002 or a suitable ohmmeter, refer to the following test specifications and procedures to aid troubleshooting.

To check secondary coil resistance of CDI unit, detach spark plug wires at spark plugs. Connect a tester lead to terminal end of each spark plug wire. Secondary coil resistance should be 2136-3204 ohms at 20° C (68° F) on early models (prior to 1987) and 2100-3200 ohms on 1987 and later models.

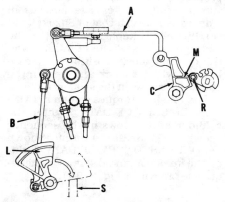

Fig. SZ9-6 — View of speed control linkage. Adjust components as outlined in text.

A. Rod
B. Rod
C. Throttle cam
L. Throttle limiter
M. Mark
R. Roller
S. Stopper

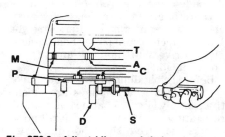

Fig. SZ9-8 — Adjust idle speed timing and maximum advance timing as outlined in text.

A. 2° ATDC mark
C. Cap screws
D. Cylinder block boss
M. 25° BTDC mark
P. Stator plate stopper
S. Idle speed timing adjustment screw
T. Timing pointer

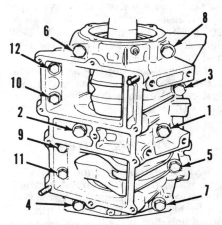

Fig. SZ9-9 — Tighten crankcase screws in the sequence shown. Refer to CONDENSED SERVICE DATA for screw torques.

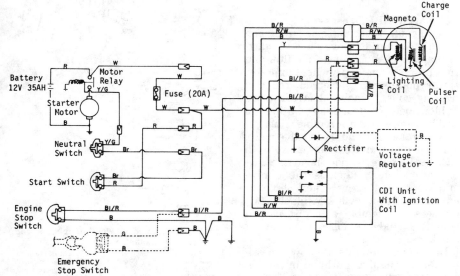

Fig. SZ9-7—Wiring diagram of electrical system on models with electric starter.

B. Black
G. Green
R. Red
W. White
Y. Yellow
Bl. Blue
Br. Brown
B/R. Black with red tracer
Bl/R. Blue with red tracer
R/W. Red with white tracer
Y/G. Yellow with green tracer

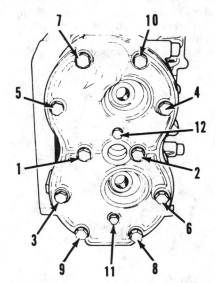

Fig. SZ9-10 — Tighten cylinder head screws in sequence shown. Refer to CONDENSED SERVICE DATA for screw torques.

Remove top cover of electrical parts holder for access to wire connectors. Remove top three-wire connector and separate. To check charge coil (Fig. SZ9-7), connect a tester lead to black wire with red tracer and black wire of three-wire connector leading to stator plate. Charge coil is acceptable if resistance is 102-154 ohms at 20° C (68° F) on models prior to 1987 and 100-160 ohms at 20° C (68° F) on 1987 and later models.

To check pulser coil, connect a tester lead to red wire with white tracer and black wire of three-wire connector leading to stator plate. Pulser coil is acceptable if resistance is 27.9-47.9 ohms at 20° C (68° F) on models prior to 1987 and 40-60 ohms at 20° C (68° F) on 1987 and later models.

Check condition of battery charging coil by separating connectors of yellow wire and red wire. Connect a tester lead to terminal end of wires leading to stator plate. Battery charging coil is acceptable if resistance is 0.24-0.36 ohms at 20° C (68° F) on models prior to 1987 and 0.2-0.6 ohm at 20° C (68° F) on 1987 and later models.

If all ignition components are found acceptable in previous tests and ignition system malfunction is still evident, renew CDI unit.

COOLING SYSTEM

WATER PUMP. A rubber impeller type water pump is mounted between the drive shaft housing and gearcase. A key in the drive shaft is used to turn the pump impeller. If cooling system problems are encountered, check water intakes for plugging or partial stoppage. If water intakes are clear, remove gearcase as outlined under LOWER UNIT and check condition of the water pump, water passages and sealing surfaces.

When water pump is disassembled, check condition of impeller (8—Fig. SZ9-

19) and plate (9) for excessive wear. Turn drive shaft clockwise (viewed from top) while placing pump housing over impeller. Avoid turning drive shaft in opposite direction when water pump is assembled.

THERMOSTAT. A thermostat (7—Fig. SZ9-14) is used to regulate operating temperature. The thermostat should start to open within the temperature range of 48.5°-51.5° C (119°-125° F). Thermostat can be removed for inspection or renewal by removing cylinder head cover (6).

POWER HEAD

REMOVE AND REINSTALL. To remove power head, first remove engine top cover. Disconnect throttle cables, throttle limiting rod, fuel inlet hose at lower engine cover connector, choke knob and wires which will interfere with power head removal. Label wires, if needed, for later reference. Remove carburetor air intake cover, motor relay and electric starter motor. Remove eight screws which secure power head assembly to drive shaft housing and lift off power head.

Before reinstalling power head, make certain drive shaft splines are clean, then apply light coating of water-resistant grease to splines. Install power head on drive shaft housing. Coat threads of retaining cap screws with silicone sealer and tighten screws to 15-20 N·m (11-14 ft.-lbs.). The remainder of installation is the reverse of removal procedure. Refer to SPEED CONTROL LINKAGE for synchronizing throttle opening with ignition advance.

DISASSEMBLY. Disassembly and inspection may be accomplished in the following manner. Remove electric starter bracket, exhaust tube, fuel filter and fuel pump. Remove flywheel and key, stator plate with pulser, charge and lighting coils. Remove electrical parts holder, speed control linkage, upper oil seal housing and stator retainer ring. Remove intake manifold, reed valve plate, exhaust cover and exhaust plate with gaskets. Remove cylinder head and cover with gaskets. Remove the twelve crankcase cap screws, then separate crankcase from cylinder block. Lift crankshaft assembly with pistons and connecting rod assemblies from cylinder block.

Engine components are now accessible for overhaul as outlined in the appropriate following paragraphs. Clean carbon from cylinder head and combustion chambers and remove any foreign material accumulation in water pas-

sages. Inspect components for damage and renew if needed. Refer to the following section for assembly procedure.

ASSEMBLY. Refer to specific service sections when assembling the crankshaft, connecting rods, pistons and reed valves. Make sure all joint and gasket surfaces are clean and free from nicks and burrs. Make sure all carbon, salt, dirt and sand are cleaned from the combustion chambers, exhaust ports and water passages.

Lubricate crankpin bearings and cylinder walls of cylinder block with Suzuki Outboard Motor Oil or a suitable NMMA certified TC-W engine oil. Install crankshaft assembly in crankcase. Make sure flange of lower oil seal (7—Fig. SZ9-12) and middle labyrinth seal (5) fits properly in crankcase grooves. Make sure bearing pins engage notches in crankcase. Spread a coat of Suzuki Bond No. 1215 or a suitable equivalent on the mating surfaces of the crankcase and the cylinder block. Position crankcase half on cylinder block and tighten the crankcase screws in the sequence shown in Fig. SZ9-9 to torques shown in CONDENSED SERVICE DATA. Tighten the cylinder head screws in the sequence shown in Fig. SZ9-10 to torques shown in CONDENSED SERVICE DATA. Tighten the intake manifold screws in the sequence shown in Fig. SZ9-11.

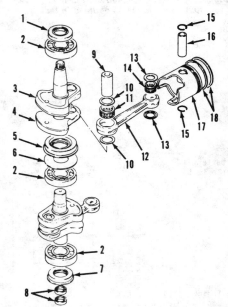

Fig. SZ9-12—Exploded view of piston and crankshaft assembly.

1. Seal	10. Thrust washers
2. Ball bearings	11. Roller bearing
3. Crank half	12. Connecting rod
4. Crank half	13. Thrust washers
5. Labyrinth seal	14. Roller bearing
6. Washer	15. Circlips
7. Seal	16. Piston pin
8. Seals	17. Piston
9. Crank pin	18. Piston rings

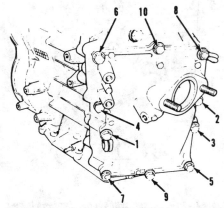

Fig. SZ9-11—Securely tighten intake manifold screws in sequence shown.

PISTONS, PINS, RINGS AND CYLINDERS. Each piston is fitted with two piston rings. Piston ring end gap should be 0.2-0.4 mm (0.008-0.016 in.) with maximum allowable ring end gap of 0.8 mm (0.031 in.). Piston rings are retained in position by locating pins. Install marked side of piston ring toward top of piston. Piston-to-cylinder clearance should be 0.067-0.082 mm (0.0026-0.0032 in.) on models prior to 1987 and 0.087-0.102 mm (0.0034-0.0040 in.) on 1987 and later models. Pistons and rings are available in standard size as well as 0.25 mm (0.010 in.) and 0.50 mm (0.020 in.) oversizes. Cylinders should be bored to next oversize if either cylinder is out-of-round or tapered in excess of 0.10 mm (0.004 in.). Standard piston pin diameter is 17.995-18.000 mm (0.7085-0.7087 in.). Install pistons on connecting rods so arrow on piston crown faces exhaust port side of cylinder.

CONNECTING RODS, BEARINGS AND CRANKSHAFT. Connecting rods, bearings and crankshaft are a press to-gether unit. Crankshaft should be disassembled ONLY by experienced service personnel and with suitable service equipment.

Caged roller bearings are used at both large and small ends of the connecting rods. Determine rod bearing wear from side to side as shown in Fig. SZ9-13. Normal side to side movement is 5.0 mm (0.20 in.) or less. Maximum limit of crankshaft runout is 0.05 mm (0.002 in.) measured at bearing surfaces with crankshaft ends supported.

Apply Suzuki Super Grease "A" or a suitable high temperature grease to lip portion of lower crankshaft seal prior to installation.

MANUAL STARTER

Refer to Fig. SZ9-15 for an exploded view of manual starter assembly. Starter may be removed as a complete unit by detaching the neutral start cable and removing the three cap screws securing starter assembly to power head. To disassemble starter, proceed as follows: Remove starter handle (16 – Fig. SZ9-15) and allow starter rope (14) to slowly wind onto pulley (4). Detach neutral start components. Invert starter housing (1) and remove cap screw (17). Withdraw plate (10) and spring (9).

Remove drive pawl (6) and return spring (5). Remove snap ring (8). Lift pulley (4) with starter rope (14) from starter housing. Use suitable hand and eye protection, and withdraw rewind spring (2) from starter housing (1). Be careful when removing rewind spring (2); a rapidly uncoiling starter spring could cause serious injury.

To reassemble, coat rewind spring area of starter housing (1) with a suitable water resistant grease. Install rewind spring (2) in starter housing. Rewind spring (2) must wind in a counterclockwise direction from the outer end. Wrap starter rope (14) in a clockwise direction 2½ turns onto pulley (4) when viewed from the flywheel side. Reassemble starter assembly by reversing disassembly procedure making certain rewind spring's hook properly engages groove in pulley (4). Apply water resistant grease to friction side of drive plate (10). Make sure slot (S – Fig. SZ9-16) in drive plate properly engages tab (T) on starter housing boss and spring (9) fits into groove (G) in pulley (4).

To place tension on rewind spring (2 – Fig. SZ9-15), pass starter rope (14) through rope outlet in housing (1),

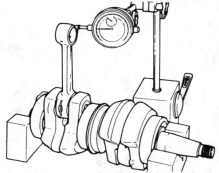

Fig. SZ9-13 – Move connecting rod small end side to side to determine connecting rod, bearing and crank pin wear. Refer to text.

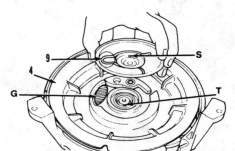

Fig. SZ9-15 – Exploded view of manual starter assembly.

1. Housing	10. Plate
2. Rewind spring	11. Spring
3. Bushing	12. Rope guide
4. Pulley	13. Rubber plate
5. Return spring	14. Starter rope
6. Drive pawl	15. Clip
7. Spacer	16. Handle
8. Snap ring	17. Cap screw
9. Spring	

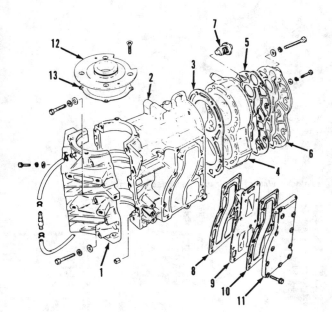

Fig. SZ9-14 – Exploded view of cylinder block and crankcase assembly.

1. Crankcase
2. Cylinder block
3. Gasket
4. Cylinder head
5. Gasket
6. Cylinder head cover
7. Thermostat
8. Gasket
9. Exhaust plate
10. Gasket
11. Exhaust cover
12. Upper oil seal housing
13. Gasket

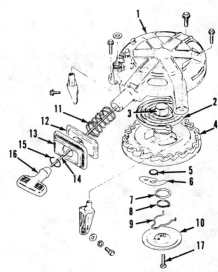

Fig. SZ9-16 – During reassembly, slot (S) in drive plate must properly engage tab (T) on starter housing boss and spring (9) must fit into groove (G) in pulley (4).

spring (11), rope guide (12), rubber plate (13) and install rope handle (16). With rope starter (14) inserted in slot of pulley (4), rotate pulley 4 turns counterclockwise when viewed from the flywheel side. Secure pulley, then release starter rope (14) from slot in pulley and allow starter rope to slowly wind onto pulley. Do not place any more tension on rewind spring (2) than is necessary to draw rope handle up against housing.

Remount manual starter assembly and reassemble neutral start cable and associated components. With the gear shift lever in the "Forward" or "Reverse" position, mark (M–Fig. SZ9-17) in lever (L) must be between marks (X and Y) on starter housing (1). Adjust the length of the neutral start cable to obtain the correct adjustment.

ELECTRIC STARTER

Some models are equipped with electric starter shown in Fig. SZ9-18. Disassembly is evident after inspection of unit and reference to exploded view. Standard commutator outside diameter is 30 mm (1.18 in.) and should be renewed if worn to a diameter of 29 mm

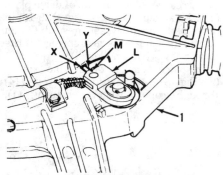

Fig. SZ9-17—For proper neutral start cable adjustment, mark (M) in lever (L) must be between marks (X and Y) on starter housing (1) when gear shift lever is in "Forward" or "Reverse" position.

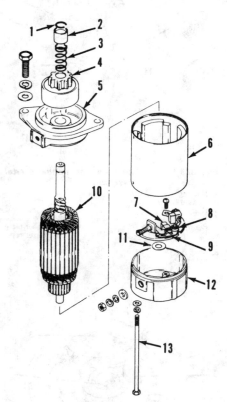

Fig. SZ9-18—Exploded view of electric starter motor.

1. Retainer
2. Stop
3. Spring
4. Drive
5. Frame head
6. Frame
7. Brush
8. Spring
9. Brush holder
10. Armature
11. Thrust washer
12. Frame end
13. Through-bolt

Fig. SZ9-19—Exploded view of lower unit gearcase assembly.

1. Grommet	28. Rod	42. Reverse gear
2. Water tube	29. Shim	43. Shim
3. Grommet	30. Forward gear	44. "O" ring
4. Seal tube	15. Drive shaft	31. Shim	45. Bearing
5. Grommet	16. Washer	32. Spring guide	46. Bearing carrier
6. Water pump housing	17. Spring	33. Pin	47. Bearing
7. Key	18. Thrust washer	34. Dog clutch	48. Seals
8. Impeller	19. Washer	35. Retainer	49. Spacer
9. Plate	20. Collar	36. Spring	50. Ratchet hub
10. Gasket	21. Snap ring	37. Propeller shaft	51. Propeller
11. Upper bearing housing	22. Bearing	38. Shim	52. Spacer
12. Seal	23. Level plug	39. Pinion gear	53. Washer
13. Bearing	24. Gasket	40. Nut	54. Nut
14. "O" ring	25. Drain plug	41. Shim	55. Cotter pin
	26. Housing		
	27. Bearing		

(1.14 in.) or less. Starter brushes have a standard length of 12.5 mm (0.492 in.) and should be renewed if worn to 9 mm (0.354 in.) or less. During reassembly, make sure upper and lower alignment marks on frame (6—Fig. SZ9-18) align with notches in frame head (5) and frame end (12). After reassembly, bench test starter before installing on power head.

LOWER UNIT

PROPELLER AND RUBBER DAMPER. A ratchet hub (50—Fig. SZ9-19) is used to provide shock protection for lower unit gears and shafts. Three-bladed propellers are used. Standard propeller has a 260.3 mm (10¼ in.) diameter and a 304.8 mm (12 in.) pitch on short shaft models and 279.4 mm (11 in.) pitch on long shaft models. Optional propellers are available from the manufacturer and should be selected to provide full throttle operation within the recommended limits of 4800-5500 rpm.

R&R AND OVERHAUL. Refer to Fig. SZ9-19 for exploded view of lower unit gearcase assembly. During disassembly, note the location of all shims and washers to aid in reassembly. To remove gearcase, first remove drain plug (25) and level (vent) plug (23) and drain gear lubricant. Loosen shift rod locknut (9—Fig. SZ9-22) and turn adjustment nut (8) until upper and lower shift rods are separated. Remove cotter pin (55—Fig. SZ9-19), nut (54), washer (53), spacer (52) and withdraw propeller (51) with ratchet hub (50). Withdraw spacer (49). Remove six lower cap screws. Withdraw lower unit assembly from drive shaft housing.

Remove bearing carrier (46) retaining screws. Being careful, use a suitable slide hammer and extract bearing carrier with propeller shaft assembly. Disassemble water pump assembly. Remove pinion nut (40) and withdraw pinion gear (39) and shim (38). Remove cap screws securing upper bearing housing, then use two 6 mm cap screws positioned as shown in Fig. SZ9-20 and tighten screws in equal increments to withdraw upper bearing housing with drive shaft components. Remove forward gear (30—Fig. SZ9-19), shim (29) and bearing (27). Remove screw from

side of gearcase securing guide holder (13—Fig. SZ9-22) and withdraw lower shift linkage components.

Inspect all components for excessive wear and damage. Apply a water resistant grease to lip portion of all seals. All seals and "O" rings should be renewed when unit is reassembled.

Reassemble lower unit by reversing disassembly procedure while noting the following: Install dog clutch 34—Fig. SZ9-21) on propeller shaft (37) so "F" marked side is toward forward gear. Tighten pinion nut (40—Fig. SZ9-19) to 18-22 N·m (13-16 ft.-lbs.). Tighten water pump housing (6) cap screws to 6-10 N·m (4-7 ft.-lbs.). Tighten bearing carrier (46) cap screws to 6-10 N·m (4-7 ft.-lbs.). Tighten propeller retaining nut to 27-30

N·m (19-21 ft.-lbs.). Assembled backlash between pinion gear (39) and forward gear (30) should be 0.1-0.2 mm (0.004-0.008 in.). Adjust thickness of shim (38) or shim (29) until recommended backlash is obtained. Recheck mesh pattern between pinion gear and forward gear to determine if correct tooth contact is being made. Adjust pinion gear shim (38) or forward gear shim (29), if needed, to obtain correct mesh pattern. Assembled propeller shaft end play should be 0.2-0.4 mm (0.008-0.016 in.). Adjust thickness of shim (41) until recommended end play is obtained. Apply silicone sealer to lower unit and drive shaft housing mating surfaces. Tighten lower unit cap screws to 15-20 N·m (11-15 ft.-lbs.).

Adjust shift rod adjustment nut (8—Fig. SZ9-22) until the proper engagement of "Forward," Neutral" and "Reverse" is obtained. Tighten locknut (9) to secure adjustment nut (8) position. Fill gearcase with approximately 230 mL (7.77 ozs.) of SAE 90 hypoid outboard gear oil.

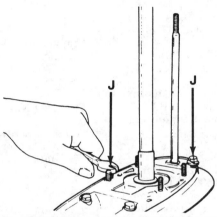

Fig. SZ9-20—Use two 6 mm jackscrews positioned as shown to withdraw upper bearing housing with drive shaft components.

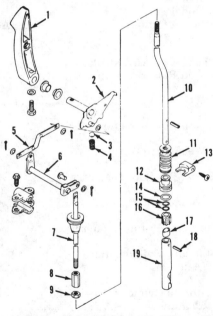

Fig. SZ9-22—Exploded view of shift control linkage components.

1. Shift lever	11. Dust seal
2. Cam	12. Rod guide
3. Detent ball	13. Guide holder
4. Detent spring	14. "O" ring
5. Rod	15. "O" rings
6. Shaft	16. Guide
7. Upper shift rod	17. Spacer
8. Adjustment nut	18. Pin
9. Locknut	19. Shift cam
10. Lower shift rod	

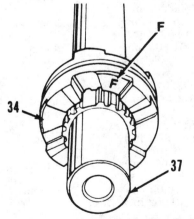

Fig. SZ9-21—Install dog clutch (34) on propeller shaft (37) so "F" mark (F) is toward forward gear.

SUZUKI DT25C

CONDENSED SERVICE DATA

NOTE: Metric fasteners are used throughout outboard motor.

TUNE-UP

Hp/rpm . . . . .25/5000-5600 rpm
(18.6 kW)
Number of Cylinders 3
Bore . . . . .62 mm
(2.44 in.)
Stroke . . . . .60 mm
(2.36 in.)
Displacement . . . . .543 cc
(33.1 cu. in.)
Spark Plug . . . . .NGK B7HS-10
Electrode Gap . . . . .0.9-1.0 mm
(0.035-0.039 in.)
Ignition . . . . .CDI
Carburetor:
Make . . . . .Mikuni
Model B26-20
Fuel:Oil Ratio . . . . .Automatic Metering

SIZES-CLEARANCES

Piston Ring End Gap . . . . .0.15-0.35 mm
(0.006-0.014 in.)
Wear Limit . . . . .0.8 mm
(0.030 in.)
Piston Pin Diameter . . . . .15.995-16.000 mm
(0.6297-0.6299 in.)
Wear Limit . . . . .15.980 mm
(0.6291 in.)
Piston Pin Bore Diameter . . . . .16.002-16.010 mm
(0.6300-0.6303 in.)
Wear Limit . . . . .16.030 mm
(0.6311 in.)
Standard Piston Diameter . . . . .61.920-61.935 mm
(2.4378-2.4384 in.)
Standard Cylinder Bore
Diameter . . . . .62.000-62.015 mm
(2.4409-2.4415 in.)
Piston-to-Cylinder
Clearance . . . . .0.072-0.087 mm
(0.0028-0.0034 in.)
Wear Limit . . . . .0.167 mm
(0.0066 in.)
Max. Crankshaft Runout
at Main Journal . . . . .0.05 mm
(0.002 in.)

SIZES—CLEARANCES CONT.

Max. Connecting Rod Small
End Side Shake . . . . .5.0 mm
(0.20 in.)

TIGHTENING TORQUES
Cylinder Head:
6 mm . . . . .8-12 N·m
(6-9 ft.-lbs.)
8 mm . . . . .21-25 N·m
(15-18 ft.-lbs.)
Crankcase:
6 mm . . . . .8-12 N·m
(6-9 ft.-lbs.)
8 mm . . . . .20-26 N·m
(15-19 ft.-lbs.)
Flywheel Nut . . . . .130-150 N·m
(96-111 ft.-lbs.)
Standard Screws—
Unmarked or Marked "4":
5 mm . . . . .2-4 N·m
(18-35 in.-lbs.)
6 mm . . . . .4-7 N·m
(35-62 in.-lbs.)
8 mm . . . . .10-16 N·m
(7-12 ft.-lbs.)
10 mm . . . . .22-35 N·m
(16-26 ft.-lbs.)
Stainless Steel:
5 mm . . . . .2-4 N·m
(18-35 in.-lbs.)
6 mm . . . . .6-10 N·m
(53-88 in.-lbs.)
8 mm . . . . .15-20 N·m
(11-15 ft.-lbs.)
10 mm . . . . .34-41 N·m
(25-30 ft.-lbs.)
Marked "7":
5 mm . . . . .3-6 N·m
(27-53 in.-lbs.)
6 mm . . . . .8-12 N·m
(6-9 ft.-lbs.)
8 mm . . . . .18-28 N·m
(13-21 ft.-lbs.)
10 mm . . . . .40-60 N·m
(29-44 ft.-lbs.)

LUBRICATION

The power head is lubricated by oil mixed with the fuel. Model DT25C is equipped with automatic oil injection. Recommended oil is Suzuki Outboard Motor Oil or a good quality NMMA cer-tified TC-W engine oil. Recommended fuel is regular or unleaded gasoline hav-ing an 85 minimum octane rating. Man-ufacturer does not recommended using gasoline containing alcohol additives. However, unleaded gasoline containing ethanol (grain alcohol) may be used providing ethanol content does not ex-ceed five percent and minimum octane rating is 85.

NOTE: Manufacturer recommends NOT using any gasoline containing methanol (wood alcohol).

During break-in (first 10 hours of operation) of a new or rebuilt engine, mix a recommended oil with the fuel at a 50:1 ratio in combination with the oil injection system to ensure adequate lubrication during break-in process. Be certain oil and fuel is thoroughly mixed in fuel tank. After initial 10 hours of operation, switch to straight gasoline in the fuel tank.

The lower unit gears and bearings are lubricated with oil contained in the gearcase. Recommended gearcase oil is Suzuki Outboard Motor Gear Oil or a suitable equivalent SAE 90 hypoid gear oil. Gearcase capacity is approximately 230 mL (7.8 ozs.). Lower unit oil should be changed after the first 10 hours of operation and after every 100 hours or seasonally thereafter. Reinstall drain and vent plugs securely, using a new gasket if necessary, to ensure water tight seal.

FUEL SYSTEM

CARBURETOR. Three Mikuni B26-20 carburetors are used. Refer to Fig. SZ10-1 for exploded view. Initial setting of pilot air screw (12) is 1-1/2 to 2 turns out from a lightly seated position. Final adjustment should be made with engine at normal operating temperature and running in forward gear. Adjust idle speed with idle speed switch located on outside of lower cover so engine idles at approximately 650-700 rpm. Adjust pilot air screw so engine idles smoothly and will accelerate cleanly without hesitation. Readjust idle speed to 650-700 rpm if necessary.

Main fuel metering is controlled by main jet (5). Standard main jet for normal operation is #125. Standard pilot jet (11) for normal operation is #70.

To check float level, remove float bowl (7) and invert carburetor body (1). Measure float level from float bowl mating surface to bottom of float at 180 degrees from needle valve as shown in Fig. SZ10-2. Float level should be 16.5-18.5 mm (0.65-0.73 in.). Bend tang on float to adjust float level.

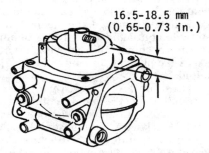

Fig. SZ10-2—Measure float level from float bowl mating surface to bottom of float 180 degrees from needle valve as shown. Bend tang on float to adjust float level.

FUEL FILTER. A fuel filter assembly is used to filter the fuel prior to entering the fuel pump. Periodically unscrew bowl (5—Fig. SZ10-3) and withdraw filter element (4). Clean bowl and filter element in a suitable solvent and blow dry with clean compressed air. Inspect filter element for excessive blockage or other damage and renew if necessary. Reassemble in reverse order of disassembly. Renew "O" ring (3) and seal (2) upon reassembly.

FUEL PUMP. A diaphragm-type fuel pump is used. Refer to Fig. SZ10-4 for exploded view. Fuel pump is mounted on the side of power head cylinder block and is actuated by crankcase pulsations.

When servicing pump, scribe reference marks on pump body to aid alignment during reassembly. Defective or questionable components should be renewed. Diaphragm should be renewed if air leaks or cracks are noted, or if deterioration is evident.

REED VALVES. The reed valves are located behind the intake manifold. The intake manifold must be removed to access reed block and valves assembly.

Renew reed valves (2—Fig. SZ10-5) if petals are broken, cracked, warped, rusted or bent, or if tip of petal stands open in excess of 0.2 mm (0.008 in.) from seat area. Do not attempt to bend or straighten a damaged reed petal. Reed stop opening (O) should be 3.8 mm (0.15 in.). When reassembling reed valve assembly, apply Suzuki Thread Lock 1342 or a suitable equivalent thread locking compound to threads of screws (4).

SPEED CONTROL LINKAGE. To adjust speed control linkage, loosen throttle lever adjusting screws (1—Fig. SZ10-6) on top and bottom carburetors and rotate throttle levers (2) counterclock-

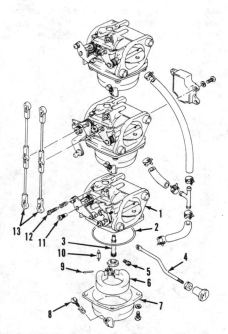

Fig. SZ10-1—Exploded view of Mikuni B26-20 carburetors used.

1. Body	
2. Gasket	8. Drain screw
3. High speed nozzle	9. Float pin
4. Choke rod	10. Needle valve
5. Main jet	11. Pilot jet
6. Float	12. Pilot screw
7. Float bowl	13. Throttle control rods

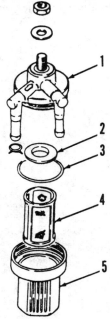

Fig. SZ10-3—Exploded view of fuel filter assembly.

1. Base
2. Seal
3. "O" ring
4. Filter
5. Bowl

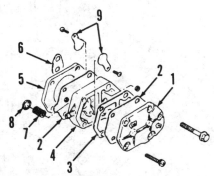

Fig. SZ10-4—Exploded view of fuel pump assembly.

1. Cover	
2. Diaphragm	
3. Gasket	6. Gasket
4. Valve body	7. Spring
5. Plate	8. Spring seat
	9. Check valve

wise to full closed position. Hold levers (2) closed and retighten screws (1). Adjust throttle link (4) so throttle arm (3) is against stopper (5) and clearance (C) is 0.5-1.5 mm (0.020-0.060 in.) with throttle in fully closed position. Make sure throttle plates are synchronized at full closed and full open positions.

If throttle cables require adjustment, loosen cable adjustment nuts and adjust cables so core wires are tight with no free movement in drum (6). Make sure arm (3) contacts stopper (5) when throttle is fully closed. Oil injection pump control linkage should be checked and/or adjusted after speed control linkage adjustment. Refer to OIL INJECTION section.

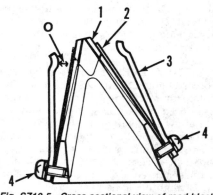

Fig. SZ10-5—Cross-sectional view of reed block and valves assembly.

1. Reed block
2. Reed petal
3. Reed stop
4. Screw
O. Reed stop opening

OIL INJECTION

CONTROL LINKAGE ADJUSTMENT. Make sure speed control linkage is properly adjusted. Initial length of pump control rod (5—Fig. SZ10-7) should be 77.5 mm (3.05 in.) as shown. With throttle in fully closed position, clearance (C) between lever stopper (6) and boss (7) on pump housing should be 1 mm (0.040 in.) or less, but stopper (6) should not contact boss (7). To adjust, loosen nuts (4) and adjust length of rod (5) as necessary. Make sure nuts (4) are securely tightened after adjustment. After adjusting pump control linkage, recheck speed control linkage and readjust if necessary. Refer to SPEED CONTROL LINKAGE section.

OIL FLOW SENSOR. Inline filter contained in oil flow sensor should be periodically removed and cleaned in a suitable nonflammable solvent. Manufacturer recommends renewing filter if excessive plugging or contamination is noted.

To test oil flow sensor, remove sensor and connect a suitable ohmmeter between sensor red wire with blue tracer and black wire. Plug sensor inlet and connect a vacuum source to sensor outlet. With vacuum applied, ohmmeter should show continuity. Remove vacuum source and sensor should show infinity.

BLEEDING PUMP. To bleed trapped air from oil supply lines or pump, proceed as follows: Fill fuel tank with a 50:1 mixture of recommended gasoline and oil. Fill oil tank with a recommended oil. Loosen bleed screw (B—Fig. SZ10-7 or SZ10-8) two or three turns. Start engine and allow to idle at 650-700 rpm until no air bubbles are noted at bleed screw (B).

CHECKING OIL PUMP OUTPUT. Start engine and allow to warm-up for approximately five minutes. Stop engine, disconnect oil pump control rod from carburetor and remove oil tank. Connect oil gage 09900-20205 or a suitable equivalent to oil pump supply hose. Fill oil gage with a recommended oil until oil is even with an upper reference mark. Bleed system as previously described. With oil pump control rod in fully closed position, start engine and allow to run at 1500 rpm for five minutes. Oil consumption should be 1.0-1.9 mL (0.035-0.065 oz.) in five minutes at 1500 rpm. Move oil pump control rod to fully open position, restart engine and allow to run at 1500 rpm for two minutes. Oil consumption should be 1.2-1.7 mL (0.04-0.06 oz.) in two minutes at 1500 rpm. Renew oil pump assembly (2—Fig. SZ10-8) if pump output is not as specified. After reinstalling oil tank, bleed air from oil injection system as previously described.

NOTE: Results of oil pump output test may vary according to weather conditions, testing error or other conditions. The manufacturer recommends repeating output test procedure two or three times to ensure the proper test results are obtained.

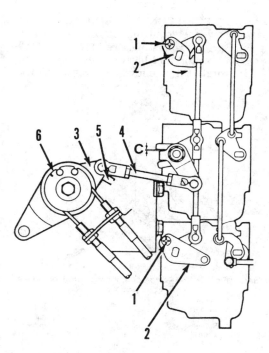

Fig. SZ10-6—View of speed control linkage. Adjust linkage as described in text.

1. Screw
2. Throttle lever
3. Throttle arm
4. Link rod
5. Stopper
6. Cable drum

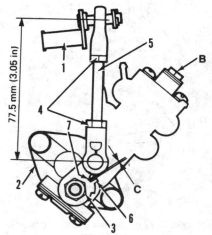

Fig. SZ10-7—View of oil injection pump and control linkage. Refer to text for control linkage adjustment.

1. Throttle lever
2. Pump assy.
3. Pump lever
4. Adjustment nuts
5. Control rod
6. Stopper
7. Boss
B. Bleed screw

COOLING SYSTEM

WATER PUMP. A rubber impeller-type water pump is mounted between the drive shaft housing and gearcase. Key (7—Fig. SZ10-9) in the drive shaft is used to turn the impeller (6). If cooling system malfunction is encountered, check water intakes for plugging or partial restriction. If water intakes are clear, remove gearcase as outlined in LOWER UNIT section and check condition of water pump, water passages and sealing surfaces.

When water pump is disassembled, inspect impeller (6) and plate (8) for excessive wear or other damage. Turn drive shaft clockwise (viewed from top) while placing pump housing (5) over impeller. Avoid turning drive shaft in opposite direction after water pump is reassembled.

THERMOSTAT. A thermostat is used to regulate operating temperature. Test thermostat by submersing in heated water with a suitable thermometer. Thermostat should start to open at 48°-52° C (118°-126° F). Thermostat can be removed for inspection or renewal after removing thermostat cover located in cylinder head.

ENGINE TEMPERATURE SENSOR. Engine temperature sensor is located at lower side of engine block. Sensor is normally open and changes to closed circuit when engine temperature reaches 36°-44° C (97°-111° F). When sensor is open, ignition timing is automatically advanced which increases idle speed and allows engine to warm-up quicker. When sensor closes, ignition timing and idle speed return to normal idle setting.

WATER FLOW SENSOR. Water flow sensor is located in cylinder head cover. Water flow sensor is designed to warn operator should cooling water flow to engine become insufficient. To test sensor, remove sensor from cylinder head cover and make sure sensor float moves freely. If not, remove pin securing float and carefully clean float and pin with water. Note that one side of pin hole in sensor is smaller than other side. Drive pin out toward larger hole. Connect a suitable ohmmeter between sensor wires and move float up and down. Ohmmeter reading should be zero ohm with float in down position and infinity with float in up position.

IGNITION

A breakerless, integrated circuit, capacitor discharge ignition system is used. Refer to Fig. SZ10-10 for wiring diagram. An integral ignition control module monitors throttle valve position (throttle valve sensor) and flywheel position (counter coil) and calculates and automatically adjusts ignition timing for optimum performance at all speeds above idle. Refer to Fig. SZ10-11. With throttle valves fully closed (idle speed), timing and idle speed are controlled by idle speed switch. Refer to IDLE SPEED SWITCH section.

TROUBLE-SHOOTING. If ignition malfunction occurs, check condition of spark plugs, all wires and connections before trouble-shooting ignition system. Use only approved procedures to prevent damage to the components. The fuel system should be checked first to make certain that faulty operation is not the result of incorrect fuel mixture or contaminated fuel. Use Suzuki Pocket Tester 09900-25002 or a suitable ohmmeter to test ignition components and circuits. Refer to Figs. SZ10-10 and SZ10-12 when trouble-shooting ignition system.

CONDENSER CHARGING COIL. Flywheel must be removed for access to condenser charging coil. Make sure a suitable puller is used to remove flywheel. Disconnect condenser charging coil (5—Fig. SZ10-12) and connect tester between black wire with red tracer and green wire. Resistance should be 170-250 ohms. Renew condenser charging coil if resistance is not as specified.

PULSER COIL. Three pulser coils (2, 4 and 6—Fig. SZ10-12) are used, and if removed, must be reinstalled in original position on stator or engine will not start. Note color of pulser coil wires or mark coils for reference. Pulser coils-to-flywheel air gap should be 0.5 mm (0.020 in.) as shown in Fig. SZ10-13.

To test pulser coils, separate connectors leading from pulser coils. Attach one tester lead to a good engine ground and remaining tester lead to red wire with black tracer on number 1 coil, white wire with black tracer on number 2 coil and red wire with white tracer on number 3 coil. Renew pulser coil(s) if resistance is not within 170-250 ohms.

COUNTER COIL. Separate connector leading from counter coil (7—Fig. SZ10-12). Connect tester leads to orange wire with green tracer and black wire with green tracer. Counter coil can be considered acceptable if resistance is within 160-240 ohms. Air gap between counter coil and flywheel ring gear teeth should be 0.5 mm (0.020 in.).

NOTE: Air gap between counter coil and flywheel ring gear teeth must be set to exactly 0.5 mm (0.020 in.) for proper operation of outboard motor. Make sure air gap is properly adjusted.

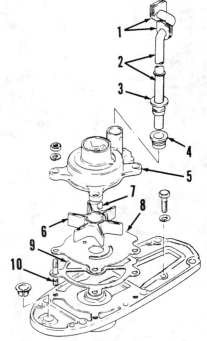

Fig. SZ10-9—Exploded view of water pump assembly.

1. Grommet	6. Impeller
2. Water tube	7. Key
3. Grommet	8. Plate
4. Grommet	9. Gasket
5. Housing	10. Stud

Fig. SZ10-8—Exploded view of oil injection pump assembly.

1. Gasket
2. Pump assy.
3. Pump lever
4. Adjusting nut
5. Control rod
6. Retainer
7. Driven gear

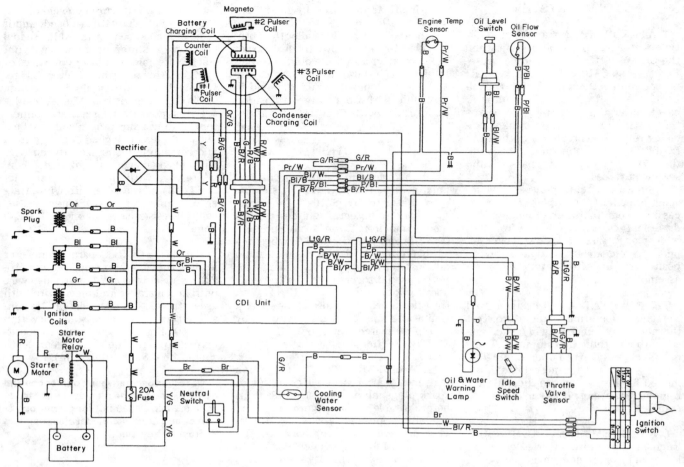

Fig. SZ10-10—Wiring diagram of electrical system on models equipped with electric starter.

B. Black	B/W. Black with white tracer	W/B. White with black tracer	Bl/R. Blue with red tracer
G. Green	G/R. Green with red tracer	W/R. White with red tracer	Bl/W. Blue with white tracer
P. Pink	R/B. Red with black tracer	Y/B. Yellow with black tracer	Or/G. Orange with green tracer
R. Red			
Y. Yellow	R/G. Red with green tracer	Y/G. Yellow with green tracer	P/Bl. Pink with blue tracer
W. White	R/W. Red with white tracer	Bl/B. Blue with black tracer	Pr/W. Purple with white tracer
Bl. Blue			
Br. Brown	R/Y. Red with yellow tracer	Bl/P. Blue with pink tracer	Lt G/R. Light green with red tracer
Gr. Gray			
Or. Orange			
Pr. Purple			
B/G. Black with green tracer			
B/R. Black with red tracer			

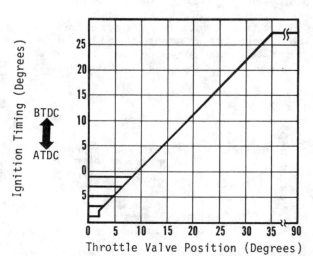

Fig. SZ10-11—Chart showing ignition timing in relation to throttle valve position.

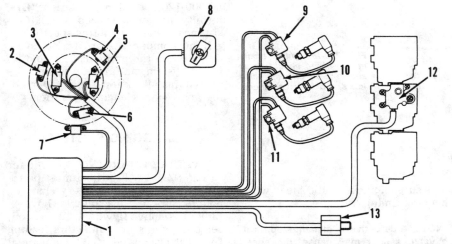

Fig. SZ10-12—Diagram of ignition system components.

1. CDI module
2. Number 2 pulser coil
3. Battery charging coil
4. Number 3 pulser coil
5. Condenser charging coil
6. Number 1 pulser coil
7. Counter coil
8. Idle speed switch
9. Number 1 ignition coil
10. Number 2 ignition coil
11. Number 3 ignition coil
12. Throttle valve sensor
13. Engine temperature sensor

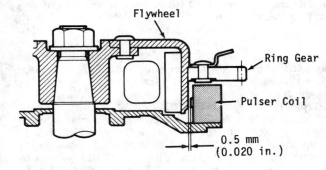

Fig. SZ10-13—Air gap between pulser coils and flywheel should be 0.5 mm (0.020 in.) as shown.

IGNITION COILS. Three ignition coils are used. Refer to Fig. SZ10-12. Separate wires at connectors leading from ignition coils and disconnect spark plug wires from coils. To test primary windings, connect tester between the following wires: Number 1 coil—orange wire and black wire; number 2 coil—blue wire and black wire; number 3 coil—gray wire and black wire. Primary winding resistance on all coils should be 0.1-0.4 ohm. Renew coil(s) if primary resistance is not as specified.

To test secondary windings, attach one tester lead to each spark plug wire terminal and remaining tester lead to orange wire on number 1 coil, blue wire on number 2 coil and gray wire on number 3 coil. Renew coil(s) if resistance is not within 1900-2700 ohms.

THROTTLE VALVE SENSOR. To test throttle valve sensor (5—Fig. SZ10-14), remove alignment pin attached to black cover over throttle valve sensor and insert alignment pin (1) into hole in sensor and sensor cam (3). Align slot in cam (3) with throttle shaft. Disconnect throttle valve sensor connector (4). Connect test harness 09930-89530 or suitable jumper wires to a battery as shown in Fig. SZ10-14. Battery voltage must be

six volts or more. Connect positive (+) lead of a suitable digital voltmeter to test harness light green wire with red tracer and voltmeter negative (–) lead to battery negative (–) terminal as shown. With throttle fully closed, voltmeter reading should be 0.45-0.55 volt. If not, remove rubber cap (2) and turn adjustment screw (under cap) as necessary to obtain the correct voltage reading. Note that turning adjustment screw clockwise will increase voltage and counterclockwise will decrease voltage.

NOTE: The manufacturer recommends using only a nonmetallic screwdriver to turn sensor adjusting screw or sensor voltmeter reading may not be valid. If metal screw-

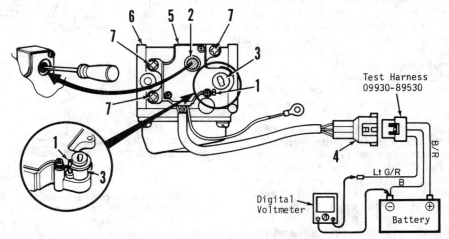

Fig. SZ10-14—Refer to text for throttle valve sensor testing and installation procedure.

1. Alignment pin
2. Cap (adjustment screw)
3. Sensor cam
4. Connector
5. Throttle valve sensor assy.
6. Carburetor
7. Mounting screw
B. Black
B/R. Black with red tracer
Lt G/R. Light green with red tracer

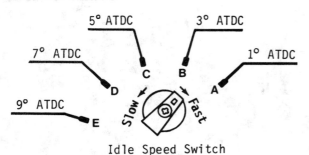

Fig. SZ10-15—Ignition timing at idle speed should be as shown at the corresponding idle speed switch positions.

driver must be used, remove screwdriver from area of throttle valve sensor after adjustment to prevent erroneous voltmeter reading.

If sensor output voltage at closed throttle is below 0.45 volt, idle speed ignition timing will be fixed at 5 degrees BTDC and idle speed switch will be inoperative. If sensor output voltage at closed throttle is above 0.55 volt, ignition timing at idle speed will not be correct. Refer to IDLE SPEED SWITCH section.

Once the specified voltage reading is obtained at closed throttle, remove alignment pin and open carburetor to wide-open throttle. Voltmeter reading should now be 2.7 volts or more. Do not attempt to adjust wide-open throttle sensor voltage. If wide-open throttle sensor voltage is not 2.7 volts or higher, renew sensor.

If throttle valve sensor is removed or renewed, install as follows: Insert alignment pin (1) as shown to align cam and sensor shaft. Align slot in sensor cam with carburetor throttle shaft and install sensor on carburetor. Lightly tighten mounting screws (7) to allow for adjustment of sensor position on carburetor. Connect test harness and digital voltmeter as shown in Fig. SZ10-14. Make sure battery voltage is 6 volts or more. Sensor output voltage at closed throttle should be 0.45-0.55 volt. If not, move position of sensor on carburetor to obtain specified voltage and securely tighten screws (7). Recheck voltage after tightening screws (7) and if necessary, remove cap (2) and turn adjustment screw to obtain 0.45-0.55 volt. Be sure to reinstall cap (2). After obtaining the correct voltage at closed throttle, remove alignment pin and check sensor output voltage at wide-open throttle. Voltage should be 2.7 volts or higher. Do not attempt to adjust wide-open throttle voltage.

IDLE SPEED SWITCH. Idle speed switch (8—Fig. SZ10-12) malfunction can be quickly verified by checking ignition timing and engine rpm while switching position of idle speed switch.

Make sure engine is at idle speed when checking timing.

NOTE: A defective or maladjusted throttle valve sensor may cause idle speed switch to be inoperative or ignition timing at idle speed to be incorrect. Prior to testing idle speed switch, make sure throttle valve sensor is operating properly and correctly adjusted. Refer to THROTTLE VALVE SENSOR section.

Ignition timing at idle speed should be as shown in Fig. SZ10-15. Note that each position of switch should change engine idle speed approximately 50 rpm. If timing and engine rpm do not change with each switch position, idle speed switch is defective and must be renewed.

To test idle speed switch with Suzuki Pocket Tester 09900-25002 or a suitable ohmmeter, disconnect idle switch and connect tester between black wires with white tracer (Fig. SZ10-10). Switch resistance should be as follows: Position (A—Fig. SZ10-15)—zero ohm; position (B)—9,000-13,000 ohms; position (C)—26,500-39,500 ohms; position (D)—

80,000-120,000 ohms; position (E)—infinity. Renew idle speed switch if resistance values are not as specified.

If no components are found to be defective in the previous tests and ignition system malfunction is still suspected, install a known good CDI module and recheck engine operation.

CHARGING SYSTEM

BATTERY CHARGING COIL. Refer to Fig. SZ10-10. Flywheel must be removed for access to battery charging coil. Be sure to use a suitable flywheel puller to remove flywheel. To test coil, separate wires at connectors leading from battery charging coil. On manual start models, connect one lead of Suzuki Pocket Tester 09900-25002 to terminal of yellow wire with red tracer and remaining tester lead to terminal of yellow wire. On models equipped with electric start, connect one tester lead to red wire and remaining tester lead to yellow wire. Battery charging coil can be considered acceptable if resistance is within 0.2-0.6 ohm.

RECTIFIER. Use Suzuki Pocket Tester 09900-25002 or equivalent ohmmeter to test rectifier. Refer to Fig. SZ10-16 for view of rectifier assembly and to chart in Fig. SZ10-17 for rectifier test data. Renew rectifier if test results are not as shown in chart.

POWER HEAD

REMOVE AND REINSTALL. To remove power head, remove engine cover, disconnect neutral start interlock cable from lever and remove rewind starter assembly. Remove electric parts holder cover and rectifier cover. Disconnect battery cables, disconnect CDI module wires, and remove CDI module and electric parts holder. Remove oil tank and disconnect throttle valve sensor, choke solenoid, warning lamp, idle speed switch and fuel hose. Disconnect ignition coil wires, remove silencer cover and disconnect choke lever. Remove eight cap screws and separate power head from drive shaft housing.

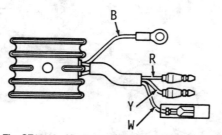

Fig. SZ10-16—View of rectifier assembly. Refer to chart in Fig. SZ10-17 to test rectifier.

Fig. SZ10-17—Refer to Fig. SZ10-16 and use chart shown to test rectifier assembly.

		(+)LEAD OF TESTER			
		Black	White	Yellow	Red
(−)LEAD OF TESTER	Black		5,500-8,500Ω	2,200-3,200Ω	2,200-3,200Ω
	White	∞		∞	∞
	Yellow	∞	2,200-3,200Ω		∞
	Red	∞	1,700-2,700Ω	∞	

Illustrations Courtesy Suzuki America Corp.

Before reinstalling power head, make certain drive shaft splines are clean, then apply a light coat of water-resistant grease to shaft splines. Install power head on drive shaft housing while rotating propeller shaft to assist alignment of drive shaft and crankshaft splines. Apply a suitable silicone sealant to threads of retaining screws, then tighten screws to 15-20 N·m (11-15 ft.-lbs.). Remainder of installation is the reverse of removal procedure. Refer to SPEED CONTROL LINKAGE for adjustment procedure.

DISASSEMBLY. Disassemble power head as follows: Remove exhaust tube, carburetors, throttle control lever, rectifier, starter relay and starter motor. Remove fuel filter, fuel pump, oil pump, oil hoses, choke solenoid and intake manifold screws. Carefully pry off intake manifold using a screwdriver or suitable tool. Use caution not to damage mating surfaces. Remove rewind starter mounting brackets, ignition coils, engine temperature sensor, counter coil and starter pulley. Use a suitable puller and remove flywheel. Remove stator assembly, cylinder head, exhaust cover, thermostat cover and thermostat. Remove 14 crankcase screws and carefully separate crankcase from cylinder block. Crankshaft assembly can now be removed from crankcase.

REASSEMBLY. Refer to specific service sections when reassembling the crankshaft, connecting rods, pistons and reed valves. Make sure all joint and gasket surfaces are clean and free from nicks and burrs. Cylinder head and block mating surfaces should not be warped in excess of 0.30 mm (0.012 in.). Cylinder head and block mating surfaces may be lapped using #400 or finer emery paper. Use caution when lapping to not remove any more material than necessary to true mating surfaces. Make sure all carbon, salt, dirt and sand are cleaned from the combustion chambers, exhaust ports and water passages. Lubricate crankpin bearings and cylinder walls with Suzuki Outboard Motor Oil or a suitable NMMA certified TC-W engine oil. Coat crankcase-to-cylinder block mating surface with Suzuki Bond 1207B or suitable equivalent sealant. Tighten crankcase screws in sequence shown in Fig. SZ10-18. Tighten 6mm screws to 8-12 N·m (6-9 ft.-lbs.) and 8 mm screws to 20-26 N·m (15-19 ft.-lbs.). Make sure two long clamps (L) are mounted on crankcase where shown. Rotate crankshaft after reassembling crankcase to check for locking or abnormal noise. If locking or abnormal noise is noted, crankcase must be disassem-

bled to determine cause and repaired. Tighten cylinder head screws in sequence shown in Fig. SZ10-19. Tighten 6 mm screws to 8-12 N·m (6-9 ft.-lbs.) and 8 mm screws to 21-25 N·m (15-18 ft.-lbs.). Install clamps (C) where shown. Make sure mating surface of flywheel is clean prior to installation. Tighten flywheel nut to 130-150 N·m (96-111 ft.-lbs.) using appropriate tools. Refer to CONDENSED SERVICE DATA for other fastener tightening values.

PISTONS, PINS, RINGS AND CYLINDERS. Refer to CONDENSED SERVICE DATA for pistons, pins, rings and cylinder service specifications. Each piston is fitted with two piston

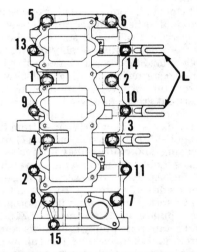

Fig. SZ10-18—Tighten crankcase screws in sequence shown. Tighten 6 mm screws to 8-12 N·m (6-9 ft.-lbs.) and 8 mm screws to 20-26 N·m (15-19 ft.-lbs.). Make sure long clamps (L) are positioned as shown.

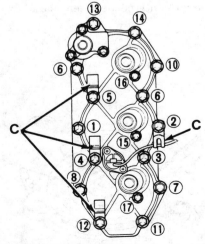

Fig. SZ10-19—Tighten cylinder head screws in sequence shown. Tighten 6 mm screws to 8-12 N·m (6-9 ft.-lbs.) and 8 mm screws to 21-25 N·m (15-18 ft.-lbs.). Note location of clamps (C).

rings. Pistons are equipped with locating pins in ring grooves to prevent piston ring rotation. Measure piston diameter 23 mm (0.9 in.) up from bottom of skirt at a right angle to piston pin bore. Pistons and rings are available in standard size and 0.25 mm (0.010 in.) and 0.50 mm (0.020 in.) oversize. Install pistons on connecting rods so arrow on piston crown will face exhaust ports upon reassembly. All cylinders should be bored to next oversize if any cylinder is out-of-round or tapered in excess of 0.10 mm (0.004 in.).

CRANKSHAFT, CONNECTING RODS AND BEARINGS. Connecting rods, bearings and crankshaft are a press together unit. Crankshaft should be disassembled ONLY by experienced service personnel using appropriate service equipment.

Determine connecting rod bearing wear from side-to-side movement as shown in Fig. SZ10-21. Normal side-to-side movement is 5.0 mm (0.197 in.) or less. If movement exceeds 5.0 mm (0.197 in.), connecting rod, crankpin and crankpin needle bearing should be renewed. Maximum allowable crankshaft runout is 0.05 mm (0.002 in.) measured at bearing surfaces with ends of crankshaft supported in V-blocks.

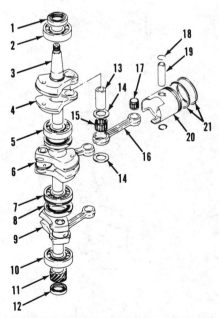

Fig. SZ10-20—Exploded view of piston and crankshaft assembly.

1. Seal
2. Main bearing
3. Crank half
4. Crank half
5. Main bearing
6. Center crankshaft assy.
7. Main bearing
8. Seal
9. Lower crankshaft assy.
10. Main bearing
11. Oil pump drive gear
12. Seal
13. Crank pin
14. Thrust washer
15. Needle bearing
16. Connecting rod
17. Needle bearing
18. Retainer
19. Piston pin
20. Piston
21. Piston rings

Apply Suzuki Super Grease "A" or a suitable equivalent to seal lips. When installing crankshaft assembly into cylinder block, make sure seals properly engage grooves in block. Make sure bearing pins properly engage notches in cylinder block.

MANUAL STARTER

Refer to Fig. SZ10-22 for exploded view of manual rewind starter assem-

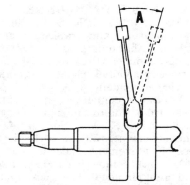

Fig. SZ10-21—Move connecting rod small end side-to-side to determine connecting rod, bearing and crankpin wear. Maximum allowable small end play is 5.0 mm (0.197 in.).

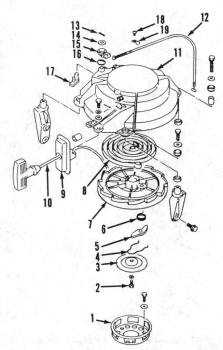

Fig. SZ10-22—Exploded view of manual starter assembly.

1. Cup
2. Screw
3. Plate
4. Friction spring
5. Pawl
6. Spring
7. Rope pulley
8. Rewind spring
9. Rope guide
10. Rope
11. Housing
12. Neutral start cable
13. Cotter pin
14. Washer
15. Arm
16. Spring
17. Lever
18. Screw
19. Clamp

bly. To remove starter assembly, remove screw (18) and clamp (19), detach neutral start cable (12) and remove three screws securing starter assembly to power head. To disassemble starter, remove cotter pin (13), washer (14), arm (15), spring (16) and lever (17). To relieve rewind spring tension, invert starter housing and grasp a section of rope, place rope into notch (N—Fig. SZ10-23) provided in rope pulley (7). Holding rope as shown, allow pulley (7) to rotate clockwise relieving rewind spring tension. Remove screw (2—Fig. SZ10-22), plate (3) and friction spring (4). Remove pawl (5) and spring (6), then carefully lift out rope pulley (7) making sure rewind spring (8) remains in housing (11). Using suitable hand and eye protection, carefully remove rewind spring (8) from housing (11).

Inspect all components for excessive wear or other damage and renew as necessary. Reassemble starter in the reverse order of disassembly noting the following: Starting with inner coil, wind rewind spring into housing in clockwise direction. Apply a suitable water-resistant grease to rewind spring. Wind rope onto pulley (7) 2-1/2 turns in counterclockwise direction (viewed from flywheel side) and install pulley (7) into housing. Make sure pulley properly engages hook on inner coil of rewind spring. Apply water-resistant grease to both sides of plate (3). To preload rewind spring, place rope into notch of rope pulley as shown in Fig. SZ10-23 and rotate rope pulley four turns counterclockwise. Release rope and allow remaining rope to wind onto pulley. Install starter assembly on power head and connect neutral start cable. With clutch lever in neutral position, slot (S—Fig. SZ10-24) should align with mark (N) on housing (11). With clutch lever in forward or reverse gear, slot (S) should centered between marks (M).

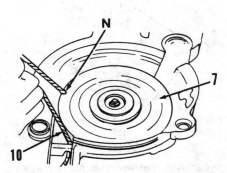

Fig. SZ10-23—To relieve rewind spring tension, grasp rope (10) as shown, place rope into notch (N) and allow pulley (7) to rotate clockwise.

Loosen screw (18) and move cable (12) to adjust. Make sure starter will operate only in neutral position.

ELECTRIC STARTER

Refer to Fig. SZ10-25 for exploded view of electric starter assembly used on models so equipped. Disassembly is evident after inspection of unit and referral to exploded view. Standard commutator outside diameter is 30 mm (1.18 in.). Renew armature (6) if commutator is worn to less than 29 mm (1.14 in.). Standard undercut between commutator segments is 0.5-0.8 mm (0.020-0.031 in.) with a minimum allowable undercut of 0.2 mm (0.008 in.). Renew brushes (8) if worn to 9 mm (0.354 in.) or less. During reassembly, make sure upper and lower alignment marks on frame (7) align with notches in end frames (5 and 10). Tighten through-bolts (11) to 15-20 N·m (11-15 ft.-lbs.). Bench test starter prior to installing on power head.

LOWER UNIT

PROPELLER AND DRIVE CLUTCH. Protection for the motor is built into a special cushioning clutch in the propeller hub. No adjustment is possible on the propeller or clutch. Three-blade propellers are used. Propellers are available from the manufacturer in various diameters and pitches and should be selected to provide optimum performance at full throttle within the recommended limits of 5000-5600 rpm.

R&R AND OVERHAUL. Refer to Fig. SZ10-26 for exploded view of lower unit gearcase assembly. During disassembly, note the location of all shims and washers to aid in reassembly.

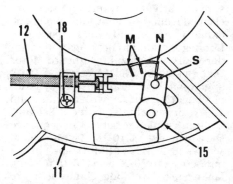

Fig. SZ10-24—With clutch lever in neutral position, slot (S) in arm (15) should align with mark (N) on housing (11). With clutch lever in forward or reverse gear, slot (S) should be in center of marks (M). Loosen screw (18) and move cable (12) to adjust.

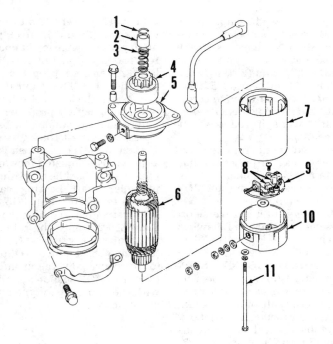

Fig. SZ10-25—Exploded view of electric starter assembly.

1. Retainer
2. Stop
3. Spring
4. Drive assy.
5. End frame
6. Armature
7. Frame
8. Brushes
9. Brush holder
10. End frame
11. Through-bolt

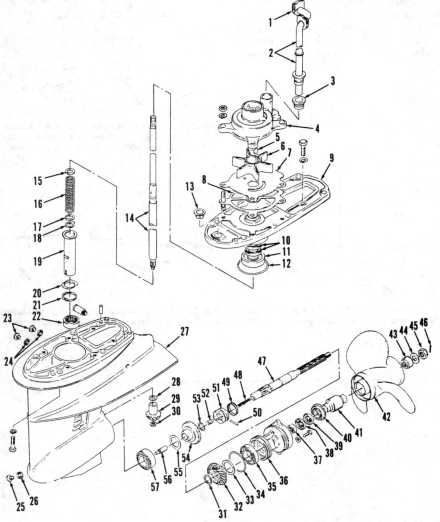

1. Grommet
2. Water tube
3. Grommet
4. Water pump housing
5. Key
6. Impeller
7. Plate
8. Gasket
9. Bearing housing
10. Seal
11. Bearing
12. "O" ring
13. Bushing
14. Drive shaft
15. Washer
16. Spring
17. Thrust washer
18. Washer
19. Collar
20. Barrier
21. Snap ring
22. Bearing
23. Level plug
24. Gasket
25. Drain plug
26. Gasket
27. Gearcase
28. Shim
29. Pinion gear
30. Nut
31. Shim
32. Reverse gear
33. Shim
34. "O" ring
35. Bearing
36. Bearing carrier
37. Bearing
38. Seal
39. Seal
40. Spacer
41. Bushing
42. Propeller
43. Spacer
44. Washer
45. Nut
46. Cotter pin
47. Propeller shaft
48. Spring
49. Retainer
50. Pin
51. Dog clutch
52. Pin
53. Thrust washer
54. Forward gear
55. Shim
56. Push rod
57. Bearing

Fig. SZ10-26—Exploded view of lower unit gearcase assembly.

To remove gearcase, first remove drain plug (25) and level plugs (23) and drain gearcase lubricant. Loosen shift rod locknut (6—Fig. SZ10-27) and turn adjustment nut (5) until upper and lower shift rods are separated. Remove six screws and separate gearcase assembly from drive shaft housing. Remove propeller and two screws securing bearing carrier (36—Fig. SZ10-26) to gearcase (27). Using a suitable slide hammer type puller, carefully extract bearing carrier and propeller shaft assembly. Remove water pump housing (4), impeller (6), key (5), plate (7) and gasket (8). Install drive shaft holder 09921-29610 or equivalent on upper spline of drive shaft (14), then remove pinion gear nut (30) by turning drive shaft. Remove two remaining screws securing bearing housing (9) to gearcase. Use two 6 mm screws positioned as shown in Fig. SZ10-

28 and tighten screws in equal increments to withdraw upper bearing housing and drive shaft components. Reach into gearcase and remove pinion gear (29—Fig. SZ10-26), shim (28), forward gear (54), shim (55) and bearing (57). Refer to Fig. SZ10-29 and remove screw securing shift rod guide holder (10—Fig. SZ10-27). Lift lower shift rod assembly out top of gearcase.

Inspect all components for excessive wear or other damage. Apply a suitable water-resistant grease to lip area of all seals. Renew all seals, gaskets and "O" rings upon reassembly.

Reassemble lower unit in reverse order of disassembly noting the following: Install dog clutch (51—Fig. SZ10-30) on propeller shaft (47) so side marked "F" is toward forward gear (54—Fig. SZ10-26). If removed, install pinion bearing (22) into gearcase using a suitable driver. Be sure lettered side of bearing (22) faces up. Apply Suzuki Thread Lock 1342 or a suitable equivalent to threads of pinion nut (30) and tighten nut to 27-30 N·m (20-22 ft.-lbs.). Forward gear-to-pinion gear backlash should be 0.1-0.2 mm (0.004-0.008 in.). Adjust thickness of shims (28 and 55) to obtain specified backlash. After obtaining the proper backlash, check pinion gear-to-forward

gear mesh pattern. Add and subtract from shims (28 and 55) to obtain correct mesh pattern while maintaining the correct forward gear-to-pinion gear backlash. Assembled propeller shaft end play should be 0.2-0.4 mm (0.008-0.016 in.). Adjust thickness of shim (31) to obtain the specified propeller shaft end play. Recheck pinion gear backlash. If necessary, adjust thickness of reverse gear shim (33) so backlash is the same as previously adjusted forward gear-to-pinion gear backlash setting. Tighten propeller shaft bearing carrier (36) screws to 15-20 N·m (11-15 ft.-lbs.).

Adjust shift rod adjustment nut (5—Fig. SZ10-27) until the proper engagement of "Forward," "Neutral" and "Reverse" is obtained. Tighten locknut (6) to secure adjustment nut. Refer to LUBRICATION section and fill gearcase with the appropriate type and amount of lubricant.

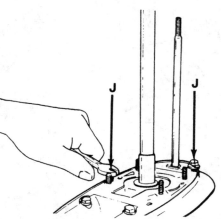

Fig. SZ10-27—Exploded view of shift control linkage components.

1. Shift lever	10. Guide holder
2. Lever	11. Guide
3. Boot	12. "O" ring
4. Upper shift rod	13. "O" ring
5. Adjustment nut	14. Spacer
6. Locknut	15. Magnet
7. Lower shift rod	16. Shift cam
8. Pin	17. Pin
9. Boot	

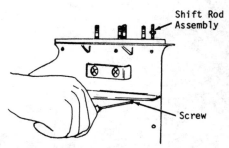

Fig. SZ10-29—To remove lower shift rod assembly, remove screw shown securing shift rod guide holder and pull shift rod out top of gearcase.

Fig. SZ10-28—Use two 6 mm jackscrews (J) to withdraw upper bearing housing with drive shaft components.

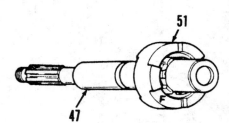

Fig. SZ10-30—Install dog clutch (51) on propeller shaft (47) so side marked "F" is toward forward gear.

TANAKA

TANAKA KOGYO U.S.A.
7509 S. 228th St.
Kent, Washington 98031

TOB-120, TOB-175 AND TOB-300

CONDENSED SERVICE DATA

NOTE: Metric fasteners are used throughout outboard motor.

TUNE-UP	TOB-120	TOB-175	TOB-300
Hp/rpm	1.2/8000	1.75/7500	3/7500
Bore	30 mm	36 mm	41 mm
	(1.19 in.)	(1.42 in.)	(1.61 in.)
Stroke	30 mm	30 mm	38 mm
	(1.19 in.)	(1.19 in.)	(1.50 in.)
Number of Cylinders	1	1	1
Displacement	22 cc	30.5 cc	50 cc
	(1.39 cu. in.)	(1.86 cu. in.)	(3.05 cu. in.)
Breaker Point Gap	0.35 mm*	0.35 mm*	0.35 mm*
	(0.013 in.)	(0.013 in.)	(0.013 in.)
Ignition Timing	28° BTDC	25° BTDC	25°BTDC
Spark Plug:			
Champion	RCJ-8	RCJ-8	RCJ-8
Electrode Gap	0.63 mm	0.63 mm	0.63 mm
	(0.025 in.)	(0.025 in.)	(0.025 in.)
Armature Air Gap	0.35 mm	0.35 mm	0.35 mm
	(0.013 in.)	(0.013 in.)	(0.013 in.)
Fuel:Oil Ratio	50:1	50:1	50:1

*TOB-120 models with serial number C-119047 and after, TOB-175 models with serial number C-190852 and after and TOB-300 models with serial number C-183863 and after are equipped with a breakerless ignition system.

SIZES—CLEARANCES	TOB-120	TOB-175	TOB-300
Piston Skirt Clearance	0.04-0.08 mm	0.105-0.160 mm	0.04-0.08 mm
	(0.0016-0.0031 in.)	(0.0041-0.0062 in.)	(0.0016-0.0031 in.)
Piston Ring Side Clearance	0.045-0.080 mm	0.055-0.090 mm	0.045-0.080 mm
	(0.0018-0.0031 in.)	(0.0022-0.0035 in.)	(0.0018-0.0031 in.)
Piston Ring End Gap	0.05-0.25 mm	0.10-0.35 mm	0.10-0.35 mm
	(0.0020-0.0098 in.)	(0.0039-0.0138 in.)	(0.0039-0.0138 in.)
Piston Pin Diameter	8.991-9.000 mm	9.990-10.000 mm	9.990-10.000 mm
	(0.352-0.354 in.)	(0.393-0.394 in.)	(0.393-0.394 in.)
Crankshaft End Play	0.05-0.25 mm	0.05-0.25 mm	0.05-0.25 mm
	(0.002-0.010 in.)	(0.002-0.010 in.)	(0.002-0.010 in.)
Lower Unit Gear Backlash	0.05-0.15 mm	0.05-0.15 mm	0.05-0.15 mm
	(0.0020-0.0059 in.)	(0.0020-0.0059 in.)	(0.0020-0.0059 in.)

TIGHTENING TORQUES

Flywheel and Drive Clutch Flange:
M7 . . . . .19.6-22.6 N·m
    (14-16 ft.-lbs.)
M8 . . . . .19.6-24.6 N·m
    (14-18 ft.-lbs.)
M10 . . . . .34.4-39.3 N·m
    (25-29 ft.-lbs.)

Standard Screws:
M4 . . . . .2-3 N·m
    (1-2 ft.-lbs.)
M5 . . . . .3.9-4.9 N·m
    (3-4 ft.-lbs.)
M6 . . . . .5.9-6.9 N·m
    (4-5 ft.-lbs.)
M8 . . . . .14.7-19.7 N·m
    (11-14 ft.-lbs.)

Fig. TK1-1 — View showing location of gearcase lubricant fill screw. A hex-head screw is used on TOB-175 and TOB-300 models. Drain lubricant by removing gear housing cover.

LUBRICATION

The power head is lubricated by oil mixed with the fuel. Recommended fuel:oil ratio is 50:1. Oil should be BIA certified TC-W.

Lower unit is lubricated by oil contained in gearcase. To fill grease, remove fill screw (F – Fig. TK1-1) and fill gearcase with unit upright until lubricant flows out of fill screw hole. Use a SAE 90 outboard gear lubricant.

FUEL SYSTEM

CARBURETOR. Refer to Fig. TK1-2, TK1-3 or TK1-4 for an exploded view of float type carburetor used. Air flow through carburetor is controlled by throttle slide (8). Jet needle (7) position in throttle slide is determined by clip (6). Recommended clip (6) position is third notch from the top on TOB-120 and TOB-175 models and second notch from the top on TOB-300 models. Jet needle (7) passes through main jet (11) or needle jet (24) and alters fuel flow through main jet according to throttle slide movement. As the throttle slide is raised to admit more air through the carburetor, jet needle (7) will be withdrawn from the main jet or needle jet allowing more fuel to flow into carburetor bore. Relocating jet needle clip (6) on jet needle (7) will change fuel delivery. Moving the clip to a higher groove in the jet needle will lean the air:fuel mixture; placing the clip in a lower groove will richen the mixture. Full throttle mixture is controlled by size of main jet (11). Recommended main jet (11) is number 50 on TOB-120 models, number 68 on TOB-175 models and number 74 on TOB-300 models.

An idle speed adjustment screw (22) is provided on TOB-175 and TOB-300 models. Adjust as follows: Start engine

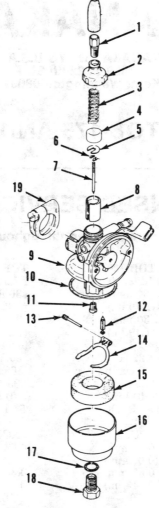

Fig. TK1-2 — Exploded view of carburetor used on TOB-120 models.

1. Cable guide	
2. Cap	
3. Spring	11. Main jet
4. Throttle stop	12. Needle valve
5. Clip retainer	13. Float pin
6. Clip	14. Float arm
7. Jet needle	15. Float
8. Throttle slide	16. Float bowl
9. Body	17. Gasket
10. Gasket	18. Drain plug
	19. Clamp

and allow to warm-up to normal operating temperature. Completely close throttle, then turn screw (22) clockwise to increase engine speed or counterclockwise to decrease engine speed. Do not reduce engine idle speed below smooth engine operation.

IGNITION

Air gap between ignition coil legs and flywheel must be adjusted for optimum ignition output. Loosen coil mounting screws and install tool 020-29351-150 on TOB-120 models, 020-29333-280 on TOB-175 models and 020-29355-000 on TOB-300 models in flywheel housing as shown in Fig. TK1-5. Position ignition coil so legs contact tool and tighten igni-

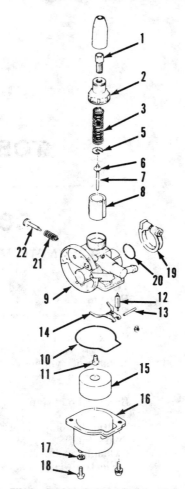

Fig. TK1-3 — Exploded view of carburetor used on TOB-175 models. Refer to Fig. TK1-2 for parts identification except for: 20. "O" ring, 21. Spring and 22. Idle speed adjustment screw.

tion coil mounting screws. If special tool is not available adjust armature air gap to 0.35 mm (0.013 in.).

On models so equipped, breaker point gap should be 0.35 mm (0.013 in.). The outside surface of the flywheel is marked with a "T", for TDC, and a "M", for correct ignition timing. The breaker points must start to open when the "M" mark is aligned with the match mark on the crankcase. Reposition magneto base plate to adjust ignition timing.

COOLING SYSTEM

The power head is air-cooled by a fan built into the flywheel. The fan shroud must be in place and power head cooling fins must be clean and unbroken or engine may overheat.

POWER HEAD

DISASSEMBLY. To disassemble power head, remove cover, fuel tank, re-

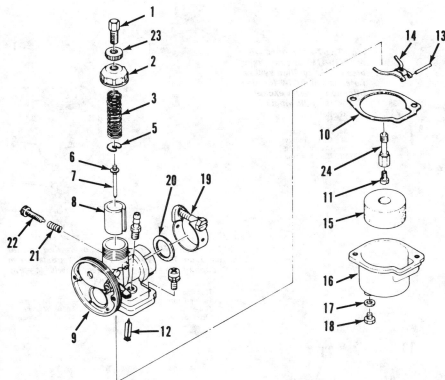

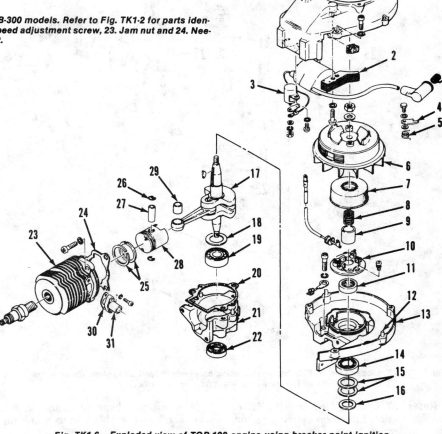

REASSEMBLY. To reassemble power head, reverse disassembly procedure. Crankcase and cylinder mating surfaces should be flat and free of nicks and gouges. Be sure piston rings are correctly positioned around piston ring locating pins in piston ring grooves when installing cylinder.

PISTON, PIN, RINGS AND CYLINDER. All models are equipped with a closed end cylinder. Oversize pistons and rings are not available.

Piston rings are pinned in piston ring grooves. Piston rings on TOB-120 models are interchangeable. On TOB-175 and TOB-300 models, install cast iron ring in lower ring groove and chrome ring in upper ring groove.

Install piston on connecting rod with arrow on top of piston facing toward exhaust port side of cylinder. Install new piston pin retaining clips.

Fig. TK1-4 — Exploded view of carburetor used on TOB-300 models. Refer to Fig. TK1-2 for parts identification except for: 20. Gasket, 21. Spring, 22. Idle speed adjustment screw, 23. Jam nut and 24. Needle jet.

wind starter, flywheel, muffler, carburetor and any other component that will interfere with power head removal. Unscrew power head from adapter plate or clutch case and separate power head from lower unit.

Remove breaker point plate (models so equipped) and cooling shroud. On TOB-175 and TOB-300 models, disassemble clutch unit. Remove cylinder base nuts or screws and separate cylinder from crankcase. Remove piston pin clips, drive out piston pin and remove piston. On TOB-175 models, remove intake manifold assembly. Unscrew crankcase screws and separate crankcase halves. Remove crankshaft and rod assembly from crankcase half.

Fig. TK1-5 — View showing use of tool (T) to set armature air gap. Refer to text.

Fig. TK1-6 — Exploded view of TOB-120 engine using breaker point ignition.

1. Shroud	10. Breaker point plate assy.	17. Crankshaft & rod assy.	24. Gasket
2. Ignition coil	11. Seal	18. Thrust washer	25. Piston rings
3. Condenser	12. Dowel pin	19. Ball bearing	26. Clip
4. Starter pawl	13. Upper crankcase half	20. Gasket	27. Piston pin
5. Pawl spring	14. Ball bearing	21. Lower crankcase half	28. Piston
6. Flywheel	15. Shims	22. Seal	29. Bushing
7. Cover	16. Thrust washer	23. Cylinder	30. Gasket
8. Spring			31. Intake manifold
9. Breaker point cam			

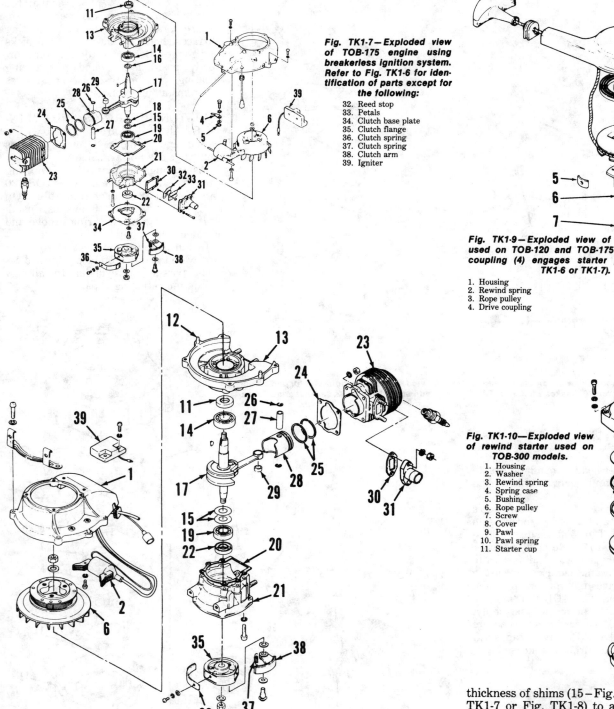

Fig. TK1-7 — Exploded view of TOB-175 engine using breakerless ignition system. Refer to Fig. TK1-6 for identification of parts except for the following:

32. Reed stop
33. Petals
34. Clutch base plate
35. Clutch flange
36. Clutch spring
37. Clutch spring
38. Clutch arm
39. Igniter

Fig. TK1-8 — Exploded view of TOB-300 engine using breakerless ignition system. Refer to Fig. TK1-6 or Fig. TK1-7 for identification of parts.

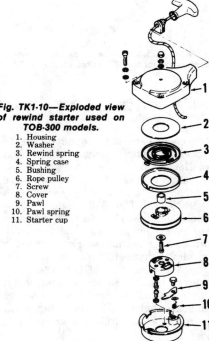

Fig. TK1-9 — Exploded view of rewind starter used on TOB-120 and TOB-175 models. Drive coupling (4) engages starter pawls (4 — Fig. TK1-6 or TK1-7).

1. Housing
2. Rewind spring
3. Rope pulley
4. Drive coupling
5. Rope guide
6. Washer
7. Pulley shaft

Fig. TK1-10 — Exploded view of rewind starter used on TOB-300 models.

1. Housing
2. Washer
3. Rewind spring
4. Spring case
5. Bushing
6. Rope pulley
7. Screw
8. Cover
9. Pawl
10. Pawl spring
11. Starter cup

Refer to CONDENSED SERVICE DATA section for recommended piston skirt clearance.

CONNECTING ROD AND CRANKSHAFT. Connecting rod is one-piece which rides on bearing rollers around crankpin. Crankshaft halves are pressed on crankpin to retain connecting rod.

Connecting rod, bearing, crankpin and crankshaft can be obtained as a unit only.

The crankshaft is supported at both ends by ball bearings. Bearing should be renewed if damaged or excessively worn.

Crankshaft end play should be 0.05-0.25 mm (0.002-0.010 in.). Vary thickness of shims (15 — Fig. TK1-6, Fig. TK1-7 or Fig. TK1-8) to adjust crankshaft end play.

MANUAL STARTER

All models are equipped with a pawl type rewind starter. Refer to Fig. TK1-9 or Fig. TK1-10 for an exploded view of starter. Overhaul of starter is evident after inspection of unit and referral to exploded view. Rewind spring on TOB-120 and TOB-175 models must be wound in counterclockwise direction from outer end in starter housing (1)

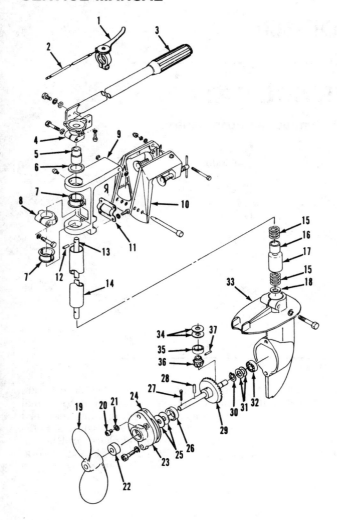

Fig. TK1-11—Exploded view of mounting brackets, steering components, throttle components and lower unit used on TOB-120 models.

1. Throttle lever
2. Throttle cable
3. Steering handle
4. Adapter plate
5. Coupling
6. Thrust washer
7. Bushings
8. Stop cam
9. Tilt bracket
10. Transom bracket
11. Tilt pin holder
12. Pin
13. Drive shaft
14. Drive shaft tube
15. Springs
16. Bushing
17. Bushing holder
18. Gasket
19. Propeller
20. Fill screw
21. Gasket
22. Seal
23. Cover
24. Gasket
25. Shims
26. Bushing
27. Cotter pin
28. Shear pin
29. Gear & shaft assy.
30. Snap ring
31. Shims
32. Bearing
33. Gearcase housing
34. Shims
35. Bushing
36. Pinion gear
37. Pin

while rewind spring on TOB-300 models must be wound in clockwise direction in spring case (4–Fig. TK1-10). Rope is wrapped around pulley in counterclockwise direction as viewed from drive side on TOB-120 and TOB-175 models and clockwise direction on TOB-300 models.

LOWER UNIT

Standard propeller on TOB-120 models is two bladed with a diameter of 150 mm (5-29/32 in.) and a pitch of 72 mm (2-13/16 in.). Standard propeller on TOB-175 models is three bladed with a diameter of 171 mm (6-47/64 in.) and a pitch of 104.4 mm (4-7/64 in.). Standard propeller on TOB-300 models is three bladed with a diameter of 182 mm (7-11/64 in.) and a pitch of 130 mm (5⅛ in.).

Refer to Fig. TK1-11 or TK1-12 for an exploded view of lower unit. Overhaul is evident after inspection of unit and referral to exploded view. Be careful not to lose or damage shims during disassembly. Inspect components and renew any which are damaged or excessively worn.

Assembled backlash between pinion (36–Fig. TK1-11 or TK1-12) and gear (29–Fig. TK1-11) on TOB-120 models or (50–Fig. TK1-12) on TOB-175 and TOB-300 models should be 0.05-0.15 mm (0.002-0.006 in.). Vary thickness of shims (25 and 31–Fig. TK1-11 or TK1-12) until backlash is within the recommended limits.

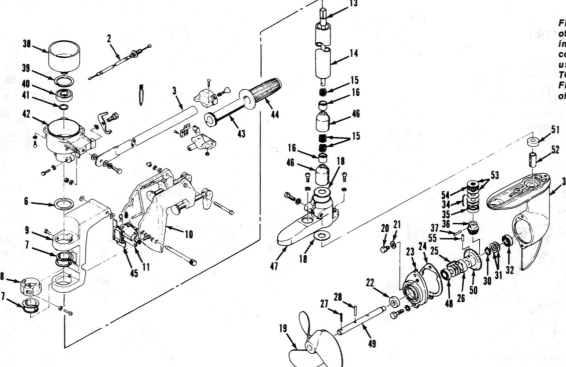

Fig. TK1-12 — Exploded view of mounting brackets, steering components, throttle components and lower unit used on TOB-175 and TOB-300 models. Refer to Fig. TK1-11 for identification of components except for the following:

38. Clutch shaft
39. Snap ring
40. Bearing
41. Snap ring
42. Clutch case
43. Twist grip
44. Rubber cover
45. Guide bracket
46. Bushing holders
47. Drive shaft housing
48. Bearing
49. Propeller shaft
50. Drive gear
51. Seal
52. Bushing
53. Thrust washers
54. Thrust bearing
55. Pin

TANAKA TOB-550

CONDENSED SERVICE DATA

NOTE: Metric fasteners are used throughout outboard motor.

TUNE-UP	TOB-550
Hp/rpm	5.5/6000
Bore	54 mm
	(2.13 in.)
Stroke	48 mm
	(1.89 in.)
Number of Cylinders	1
Displacement	110 cc
	(6.7 cu. in.)
Ignition Type	CDI
Spark Plug:	
NGK	BPR-7HS
Electrode Gap	0.65 mm
	(0.025 in.)
Fuel:Oil Ratio	50:1

LUBRICATION

The power head is lubricated by oil mixed with the fuel. Recommended fuel:oil ratio is 50:1. Oil should be BIA certified TC-W.

Lower unit is lubricated by oil contained in gearcase. To fill gearcase, remove fill screw (F–Fig. TK2-1) and level screw (L). Add SAE 90 outboard gear lubricant through fill screw hole until lubricant is at base of level screw hole. Reinstall screws with new gaskets.

FUEL SYSTEM

CARBURETOR. Refer to Fig. TK2-2 for an exploded view of float type carburetor used. A fuel pump, integral with the carburetor is used. The fuel pump is operated by crankcase pressure changes from the up and down movement of the piston. MAKE SURE the hose connect-

ing the crankcase fitting to the fuel pump fitting is in good condition and fits tight on fittings.

NOTE: Fuel pump and engine malfunction will result if the fuel pump and all connections are not airtight.

To adjust engine idle speed, start engine and allow to warm-up to normal operating temperature. Shift outboard motor directional lever into "FORWARD" position and place throttle control in "SLOW" position. Propeller rotation should stop. If not, adjust engine

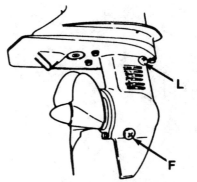

Fig. TK2-1—View showing lower unit gearcase drain and fill screw (F) and oil level (vent) screw (L).

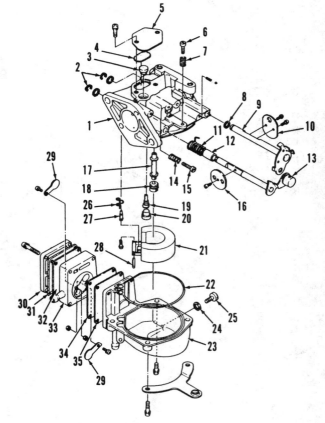

Fig. TK2-2—Exploded view of carburetor and fuel pump used.

1. Body
2. Clips
3. Plug
4. Gasket
5. Plate
6. Idle speed screw
7. Spring
8. "O" ring
9. Choke shaft
10. Choke plate
11. Spring
12. Sleeve
13. Throttle shaft
14. Spring
15. Air screw
16. Throttle plate
17. Main nozzle
18. Main jet
19. Slow jet
20. Plug
21. Float
22. Gasket
23. Float bowl
24. Gasket
25. Drain plug
26. Clip
27. Needle valve assy.
28. Pin
29. Check valves
30. Cover
31. Gasket
32. Diaphragm
33. Pump body
34. Diaphragm
35. Gasket

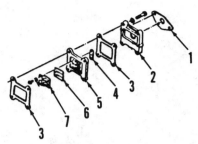

Fig. TK2-3—Exploded view of intake manifold and reed valve assembly.

1. Gasket
2. Intake manifold
3. Gasket
4. Plate
5. Reed plate
6. Reed petals
7. Reed stop

idle speed screw (6) until propeller rotation stops.

REED VALVE. The inlet reed valve assembly is located between carburetor and crankcase, and should be checked whenever the carburetor is removed for service.

Reed petals (6–Fig. TK2-3) should seat very lightly against reed plate (5) throughout their entire length, with the least possible tension. Inspect reed petals for cracks or signs of distortion. Do not attempt to straighten bent reed petals or reed stops.

IGNITION

The standard spark plug is NGK BPR-7HS with an electrode gap of 0.65 mm (0.025 in.).

A capacitor discharge ignition (CDI) system is used. If engine malfunction is noted and the ignition system is suspected, make sure the spark plug and all electrical wiring are in good condition before servicing CDI components.

COOLING SYSTEM

The power head is air-cooled by a fan mounted on top of the flywheel. The fan shroud and cylinder shroud must be in place and power head cooling fins must be clean and unbroken or engine may overheat.

A water tube (14–Fig. TK2-9) in the drive shaft housing directs water through the drive shaft housing (10) to cool exiting exhaust gases. The water tube should be kept clean of any blockage.

POWER HEAD

R&R AND OVERHAUL. To remove power head, remove rewind starter, cover, engine shrouds, muffler, carburetor/fuel pump and any other component that will interfere with power head removal. Unscrew power head from clutch case and separate power head from lower unit.

Refer to Fig. TK2-6 for an exploded view of power head components. Disassembly of power head is evident after inspection of unit and referral to exploded view.

Note that connecting rod is one-piece which rides on bearing rollers around crankpin. Crankshaft halves are pressed on crankpin to retain connecting rod. Connecting rod, bearing, crankpin and crankshaft can be obtained as a unit only. Oversize pistons and rings are not available.

To reassemble power head, reverse disassembly procedure. Crankcase and cylinder mating surfaces should be flat and free of nicks and gouges.

MANUAL STARTER

A pawl type rewind starter is used. Refer to Fig. TK2-7 for an exploded view of starter. Overhaul of starter is evident after inspection of unit and referral to exploded view. Rewind spring (2) must be wound in clockwise direction from outer end in starter housing (1). Starter rope (12) is wrapped around pulley (3) in a clockwise direction as viewed from flywheel side.

LOWER UNIT

Standard propeller is three bladed with a diameter of 197 mm (7¾ in.) and a pitch of 254 mm (10 in.).

Refer to Fig. TK2-9 for an exploded view of lower unit. Overhaul is evident after inspection of unit and referral to exploded view. Inspect components and renew any which are damaged or excessively worn.

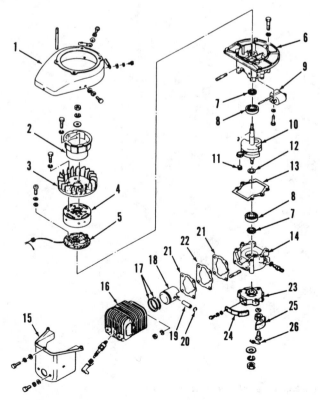

Fig. TK2-6—Exploded view of engine assembly.

1. Top shroud
2. Starter cup
3. Fan
4. Flywheel
5. Stator plate & primary coil
6. Crankcase half
7. Seals
8. Ball bearings
9. Ignition coil
10. Crankshaft & rod assy.
11. Needle bearing
12. Shim
13. Gasket
14. Crankcase half
15. Cylinder shroud
16. Cylinder
17. Piston rings
18. Piston
19. Piston pin
20. Clips
21. Gaskets
22. Spacer
23. Clutch flange
24. Clutch spring
25. Clutch arm
26. Clutch spring

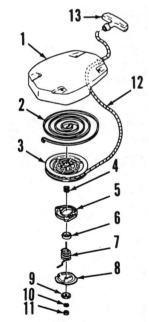

Fig. TK2-7—Exploded view of rewind starter.

1. Starter housing
2. Rewind spring
3. Pulley
4. Friction spring
5. Ratchet
6. Case
7. Return spring
8. Friction plate
9. Thrust washer
10. Washer
11. Nut
12. Starter rope
13. Handle

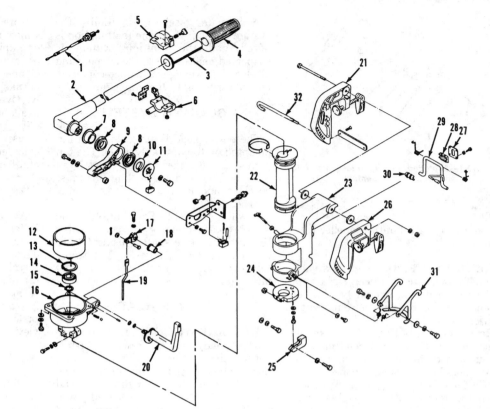

Fig. TK2-8—Exploded view of mounting brackets, steering components and throttle components.

1. Throttle cable
2. Steering handle
3. Twist grip
4. Rubber cover
5. Upper holder
6. Lower holder
7. Bushing
8. Cushions
9. Bracket
10. Grommet
11. Stop
12. Clutch shaft
13. Snap ring
14. Bearing
15. Snap ring
16. Clutch case
17. Shift link
18. Bushing
19. Shift rod
20. Shift handle
21. Transom bracket
22. Thrust bracket
23. Tilt bracket
24. Thrust bracket plate
25. Return cam
26. Transom bracket
27. Plate
28. Holder half
29. Shallow water & trailer lever
30. Holder half
31. Tilt pin holder
32. Tilt pin

1. Gasket
2. Gasket
3. Muffler inner pipe
4. Flange
5. Muffler outer pipe
6. Drive shaft tube
7. Drive shaft
8. Gasket
9. Shift rod guide
10. Drive shaft housing
11. Shift rod
12. Seal
13. Hose fitting & bracket
14. Water hose
15. Water pickup
16. Spring clamp
17. Boot
18. Drive shaft guide
19. Gasket
20. Seals
21. Pin
22. Shift cam
23. Bushing
24. Spinner
25. Cotter pin
26. Propeller & hub
27. Shear pin
28. Cover
29. "O" ring
30. Seals
31. Bearing
32. Reverse gear
33. Shim
34. Propeller shaft
35. Retainer
36. Dog clutch
37. Pin
38. Spring
39. Shift pin
40. Forward gear
41. Bearing
42. Clip
43. Pinion gear
44. Washer
45. Clip
46. Bushing
47. Gearcase housing
48. Gasket
49. Level screw
50. Fill screw

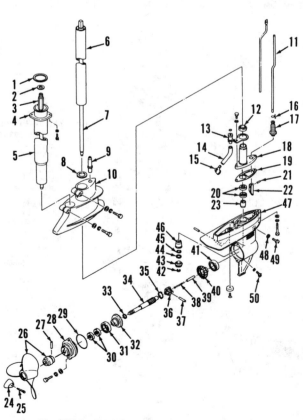

Fig. TK2-9—Exploded view of lower unit assembly.

TOHATSU

TOHATSU U.S.A.
1211 Avenue of the Americas
New York, NY 10036

TOHATSU 2.5 AND 3.5 HP

CONDENSED SERVICE DATA

NOTE: Metric fasteners are used throughout outboard motor.

TUNE-UP

Hp/rpm 2.5/4500
. . . . .3.5/4750
Bore . . . . .47 mm
. . . .(1.85 in.)
Stroke . . . . .43 mm
. . . .(1.69 in.)
Displacement . . . . .74.6 cc
. . . .(4.5 cu.in.)
Number of Cylinders 1
Spark Plug:
 2.5 HP
  Champion RL87YC
  Electrode Gap . . . . .1 mm
. . . .(0.040 in.)
 3.5 HP
  NGK B7HS
  Champion L81Y
  Electrode Gap . . . . .0.6-0.7 mm
. . . .(0.024-0.028 in.)
Breaker Point Gap . . . . .0.3-0.4 mm
. . . .(0.012-0.016 in.)
Ignition Timing . . . . .Fixed

TUNE-UP CONT.
Carburetor Make . . . . .TK
Idle Speed:
 2.5 HP . . . . .900-1000 rpm
 3.5 HP . . . . .1100-1300 rpm
Fuel:Oil Ratio 50:1
Gearcase Oil Capacity . . . . .90 mL
. . . .(3 oz.)

SIZES—CLEARANCES
Piston Ring End Gap .0.18-0.33 mm
. . . .(0.006-0.012 in.)
Piston Ring Side Clearance . . . . .0.01-0.05 mm
. . . .(0.0003-0.0010 in.)
Piston Clearance . . . . .0.06-0.15 mm
. . . .(0.002-0.005 in.)
Max. Connecting Rod Side Clearance . . . . .0.5 mm
. . . .(0.020 in.)
Max. Crankshaft Runout at Main
 Bearing Journal . . . . .0.5 mm
. . . .(0.001 in.)
Connecting Rod Small End Side Shake . . . . .0.6-1.5 mm
. . . .(0.022-0.056 in.)

LUBRICATION

The power head is lubricated by oil mixed with the fuel. Recommended oil is Tohatsu outboard motor oil mixed at a fuel:oil ratio of 50:1. During engine break-in the fuel:oil ratio should be 20:1 for a period of 10 operating hours.

Lower unit gears and bearings are lubricated by oil contained in the gearcase. Recommended oil is SAE 80 gear oil. Oil should be changed after initial 10 hours of operation and after every 200 hours of operation.

FUEL SYSTEM

CARBURETOR. The TK type carburetor shown in Fig. T1-1 is used on both 2.5 and 3.5 hp models. Standard main jet (19) size for normal operation is number 94 for 2.5 hp models and number 88 for 3.5 hp models. Normal position of clip (7) is second groove from the top on 2.5 hp models and in one of the middle grooves on 3.5 hp models of jet needle (8). Inserting clip in a higher groove will lean midrange mixture while insertion in a lower groove will richen midrange mixture.

To check fuel level adjustment with carburetor mounted on power head, connect a drain hose to drain plug hole in fuel bowl and hold hose up alongside carburetor. Open fuel valve and note level of fuel in hose. Fuel level should be 20-22

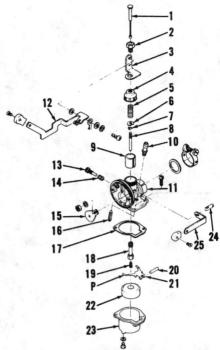

Fig. T1-1—Exploded view of TK type carburetor used on both 2.5 and 3.5 hp models.

1. Throttle wire
2. Guide screw
3. Bracket
4. Cap
5. Spring
6. Retainer
7. Clip
8. Jet needle
9. Throttle slide
10. Fuel inlet
11. Body
12. Throttle lever
13. Idle speed screw
14. Spring
15. Choke plate
16. Fuel inlet valve
17. Gasket
18. Needle jet
19. Main jet
20. Float arm pin
21. Float arm
22. Float
23. Float bowl
24. Shaft
25. Choke lever

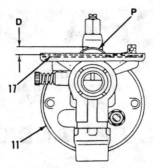

Fig. T1-2—Float level is measured by inverting carburetor body (11) and measuring distance (D) from top of carburetor bowl gasket (17) to base of float arm pad (P). Bend float arms evenly to adjust.

mm (0.787-0.866 in.) below center of carburetor throttle bore. Fuel level may be adjusted by bending pads (P) of float arm (21).

To determine the float level with carburetor removed, invert carburetor body (11–Fig. T1-2) and measure distance (D) from top of carburetor bowl gasket (17) to base of float arm pad (P). Distance should be 2.3 mm (0.090 in.) and is adjusted by bending float arm pads (P) evenly until the correct distance is obtained.

Adjust idle speed screw (13–Fig. T1-1) so engine idles at 900-1000 rpm on 2.5 hp models and 1100-1300 rpm on 3.5 hp models with engine at normal operating temperature.

REED VALVE. The reed valve is located on inside of crankcase. Inspect reed valve (4–Fig. T1-3) and renew if cracked, bent or otherwise damaged. Do not attempt to straighten reed valve. Reed valve stop height (H–Fig. T1-4) should be 6.0-6.2 mm (0.236-0.244 in.).

SPEED CONTROL LINKAGE. Engine speed is regulated by position of throttle lever (12–Fig. T1-1). As throttle lever (12) is raised or lowered, car-

buretor throttle slide (9) is operated via throttle wire (1).

IGNITION

Breaker point gap should be 0.3-0.4 mm (0.012-0.016 in.) and is adjustable through opening in flywheel. The flywheel must be removed for breaker point renewal. Tighten flywheel nut to 41 N·m (30 ft.-lbs.). Ignition timing is fixed but can be adjusted by changing breaker point gap within recommended breaker point gap setting.

Recommended spark plug on 2.5 hp models is Champion RL87YC with an electrode gap of 1 mm (0.040 in.). Recommended spark plug on 3.5 hp models is Champion L81Y or NGK B7HS with an electrode gap of 0.6-0.7 mm (0.024-0.028 in.).

COOLING SYSTEM

WATER PUMP. A rubber impeller type water pump is located in the gearcase and mounted on and driven by the propeller shaft.

When cooling system problems are encountered, first check the water inlet for plugging or partial stoppage, then if not

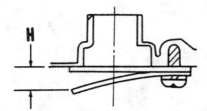

Fig. T1-4—Reed valve stop height (H) should be 6.0-6.2 mm (0.236-0.244 in.).

corrected, remove propeller and gearcase cap for access to pump impeller. Refer to Fig. T1-7 for an exploded view of water pump.

POWER HEAD

REMOVE AND REINSTALL. To remove power head, remove motor covers, fuel tank and manual starter. Remove starter cup, unscrew flywheel nut and remove flywheel using a suitable puller. Disconnect ignition wires and remove ignition assembly. Remove carburetor. Unscrew the six screws securing power head and separate power head from drive shaft housing.

Reverse removal procedure when installing power head. Apply water resistant grease to ends of crankshaft and upper drive shaft. Install a new gasket between power head and drive shaft housing.

DISASSEMBLY. To disassemble power head, detach cylinder head (26–Fig. T1-3) and head plate (3). Unscrew six screws securing crankcase (2) to cylinder block (24) and separate crankcase from cylinder block. Crankshaft assembly is now accessible and can be removed from cylinder block (24). Refer to specific service sections for overhaul.

ASSEMBLY. All friction surfaces and bearings must be lubricated with

Fig. T1-3—Exploded view of engine.

1. Plug
2. Crankcase
3. Head plate
4. Reed valve
5. Reed valve stop
6. Seal
7. Locating ring
8. Ball bearing
9. Key
10. Upper crankshaft half
11. Connecting rod
12. Roller bearing
13. Crankpin
14. Lower crankshaft half
15. Ball bearing
16. Locating ring
17. Seal
18. Roller bearing
19. Circlip
20. Piston ring
21. Piston
22. Piston pin
23. Dowel
24. Cylinder block
25. Head gasket
26. Cylinder head

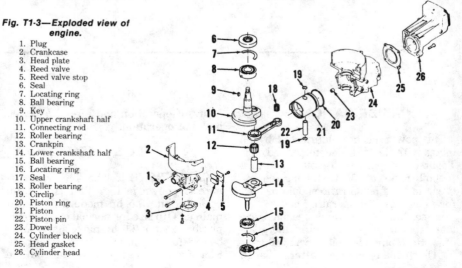

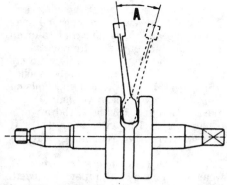

Fig. T1-5—Measure connecting rod small end shake (A) by moving small end side to side. Maximum allowable rod small end shake is 1.5 mm (0.056 in.).

Fig. T1-7—Exploded view of gearcase.

1. Lower drive shaft
2. Seal
3. Snap ring
4. Ball bearing
5. Sleeve
6. Ball bearing
7. Gearcase
8. Pinion gear
9. Ball bearing
10. Thrust washer
11. Gear
12. Propeller shaft
13. Impeller drive pin
14. Shear pin
15. Ball bearing
16. Seal
17. "O" ring
18. Water pump housing
19. Impeller
20. Cap

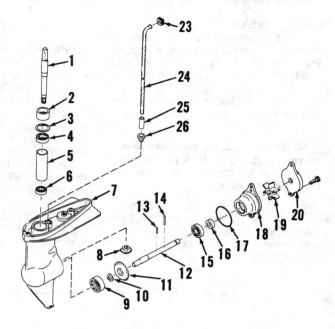

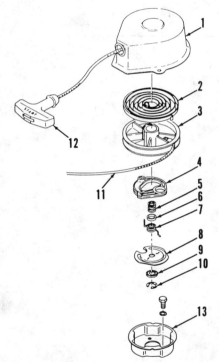

Fig. T1-6—Exploded view of manual starter assembly.

1. Housing
2. Rewind spring
3. Pulley
4. Ratchet
5. Spring
6. Sleeve
7. Return spring
8. Friction plate
9. Thrust washer
10. Clip
11. Starter rope
12. Handle
13. Starter cup

engine oil during reassembly. Install piston on connecting rod so arrow on piston crown points towards flywheel end of crankshaft on 2.5 hp models and towards exhaust port on 3.5 hp models. Insert piston in cylinder block while being sure piston ring properly engages locating pin in piston ring groove. Install crankshaft assembly in cylinder block with locating rings (7 and 16–Fig. T1-3) properly positioned in grooves of cylinder block (24). Check frequently as power head is being assembled for binding of working parts. If binding or lock-

ing is encountered, correct cause before proceeding with assembly.

Apply a nonhardening gasket sealer to sealing surface of cylinder block (24). Make sure entire surface is coated, but avoid an excess application. Install crankcase half (2) on cylinder block while being sure locating pins in bearings (8 and 15) correctly engage notches in cylinder block (24). Install head plate (3).

PISTON, PIN, RING AND CYLINDER. The standard cylinder bore is 47 mm (1.850 in.) with a maximum wear limit of 47.05 mm (1.852 in.). Bore cylinder to 0.5 mm (0.020 in.) oversize if maximum wear limit is exceeded or cylinder bore is tapered or out-of-round more than 0.06 mm (0.002 in.). Piston and piston ring are available in standard size and 0.5 mm (0.020 in.) oversize.

The piston pin is retained by clips (19–Fig. T1-3) which should be renewed if removed. The piston pin rides in a roller bearing in rod small end. Install piston on connecting rod so arrow on piston crown points towards flywheel end of crankshaft on 2.5 hp models and towards exhaust port on 3.5 hp models. Recommended piston ring end gap is 0.18-0.33 mm (0.006-0.012 in.). Recommended piston ring side clearance is 0.01-0.05 mm (0.0003-0.0010 in.).

CRANKSHAFT AND CONNECTING ROD. Crankshaft, connecting rod, crankpin and bearing are assembled as a pressed-together unit. Renew crankshaft assembly as a complete unit.

Determine connecting rod deflection (A–Fig. T1-5) by moving small rod end from side-to-side. Normal side-to-side movement is 0.6-1.5 mm (0.022-0.056

in.). Renew crankshaft assembly if side movement exceeds 1.5 mm (0.056 in.).

MANUAL STARTER

To overhaul the manual starter, proceed as follows: Remove the screws retaining the engine's port and starboard side covers, then withdraw covers. Remove the screws retaining the manual starter assembly to the power head and withdraw.

To disassemble, untie starter rope (11–Fig. T1-6) at handle (12) and allow rope to wind into the starter. Invert the unit and remove clip (10), then withdraw thrust washer (9), friction plate (8), return spring (7), sleeve (6), spring (5) and ratchet (4). Remove pulley (3) while being careful not to dislodge rewind spring (2). Remove starter rope (11) from pulley (3) if renewal is required. If rewind spring (2) must be removed, care must be used to prevent spring from uncoiling dangerously.

Reassembly is the reverse order of disassembly. Apply a water resistant grease to rewind spring area of starter housing (1). Install rewind spring (2) with coils wrapped in a counterclockwise direction from outer spring end. Wrap starter rope (11) around pulley (3) in a counterclockwise direction when viewed from the bottom side. Install pulley (3) in starter housing (1) making sure pulley properly engages rewind spring (2). Thread rope end through starter housing (1) and secure on handle (12).

NOTE: Lubricate all friction surfaces with a suitable water resistant grease during reassembly.

Install ratchet (4) so ratchet tooth points counterclockwise when viewed from the bottom side. Assemble remaining components. Apply tension to rewind spring (2) by engaging starter rope (11) in pulley (3) notch and turning pulley counterclockwise, then release starter rope (11) from pulley notch.

NOTE: Do not apply any more tension on rewind spring (2) than is required to draw starter handle (12) back into the proper released position.

Check starter action, then remount manual starter assembly and engine's side covers to complete reassembly.

LOWER UNIT

PROPELLER AND SHEAR PIN. Lower unit protection is provided by a shear pin (14 – Fig. T1-7). Be sure correct shear pin is installed for maximum protection to lower unit.

On 2.5 hp models, standard propeller is three-bladed with a diameter of 188 mm (7.4 in.) and a pitch of 114 mm (4.5 in.). On 3.5 hp models, standard propeller is two-bladed with a diameter of 180 mm (7-5/64 in.) and a pitch of 166 mm (6-17/32 in.). Propeller rotation is clockwise.

R&R AND OVERHAUL. To remove gearcase, unscrew two screws securing gearcase to drive shaft housing and separate. Unscrew drain plug and level (vent) plug and allow lubricant to drain into a suitable container. Remove cotter pin and withdraw propeller. Remove cap (20 – Fig. T1-7), water pump impeller (19), pin (13) and water pump housing (18). Withdraw lower drive shaft (1). Remove pinion gear (8) and withdraw propeller shaft (12) with gear (11). If necessary, remove remaining bearings from gearcase.

Inspect all components for excessive wear and damage and renew if needed. Reassembly is reverse order of disassembly. Fill gearcase with lubricant until lubricant begins to overflow from level (vent) plug port.

TOHATSU 5 HP
(Prior to 1985)

CONDENSED SERVICE DATA

NOTE: Metric fasteners are used throughout outboard motor.

TUNE-UP

Hp/rpm..5/5000
Bore...52 mm
Stroke ....43 mm
Displacement ....91 cc
Number of cylinders.........................2
Spark Plug:
  NGK....................................B7HS
  Champion...............................L81Y
  Electrode Gap ....0.6-0.7 mm
Breaker Point Gap ....0.3-0.4 mm
Ignition Timing (BTDC) ....2.9-3.7 mm
                             27-31 degrees

Carburetor:
  Make ....TK
  Model R14F-2A
  Idle Speed ....1100-1200 rpm
  Fuel:Oil Ratio 50:1

SIZES—CLEARANCES

Piston Ring End Gap ....0.15-0.35 mm
Piston Ring Side Clearance ....0.03-0.07 mm
Piston Clearance ....0.07-0.10 mm
Piston Pin Clearance in Piston .....0.007-0.010 mm
Connecting Rod Side Clearance:
  Standard ....0.16-0.32 mm
  Limit ....0.5 mm
Connecting Rod Small End Shake:
  Standard ....0.8 mm
  Limit ....1.6 mm

LUBRICATION

The power head is lubricated by oil mixed with the fuel. Recommended oil is Tohatsu outboard motor oil mixed at a fuel:oil ratio of 50:1. During engine break-in the fuel:oil ratio should be 20:1 for a period of 10 operating hours.

Lower unit gears and bearings are lubricated by oil contained in the gearcase. Recommended oil is SAE 80 gear oil. Oil should be changed after initial 10 hours of operation.

FUEL SYSTEM

CARBURETOR. The TK Model R14F-2A carburetor shown in Fig. T2-1 is used. Standard main jet (22) size for normal operation is #90. Normal position of clip (4) is in the middle groove of jet needle (5). Inserting clip in a higher groove will lean mid-range mixture while insertion in a lower groove will richen mid-range mixture. Throttle valve (6) cutaway is 0.5 mm. Needle jet (21) diameter is 2.095 mm.

To check fuel level adjustment, connect a drain hose to drain plug hole in fuel bowl and hold hose up alongside carburetor. Open fuel valve and note level of fuel in hose. Fuel level should be 17.5 mm below center of carburetor throttle bore. Fuel level may be adjusted by bending pads (P) of float arm (20).

Adjust idle speed screw (8) so engine idles at 1100-1200 rpm with forward gear engaged.

REED VALVE. The reed valve is attached to reed valve plate (4 – Fig. T2-2) which is mounted on inside of intake manifold (2). Inspect reed valve (6) and renew if cracked, bent or otherwise damaged. Do not attempt to straighten reed valve. Reed valve seating surface of reed plate (4) should be flat. Reed valve stop height (H – Fig. T2-3) should be 5.0-5.2 mm.

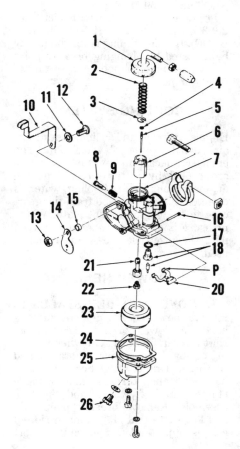

Fig. T2-1 – Exploded view of TK Model R14F-2A carburetor.

1. Cap
2. Spring
3. Retainer
4. Clip
5. Jet Needle
6. Throttle slide
7. Body
8. Idle speed screw
9. Spring
10. Choke lever
11. Washer
12. Special screw
13. Locknut
14. Choke plate
15. Sleeve
16. Float pin
17. Gasket
18. Fuel inlet valve
20. Float arm
21. Needle jet
22. Main jet
23. Float
24. Gasket
25. Float bowl
26. Drain screw

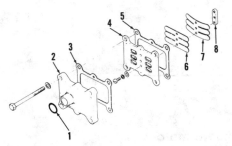

Fig. T2-2 — Exploded view of reed valve assembly.

1. "O" ring
2. Intake manifold
3. Gasket
4. Plate
5. Gasket
6. Reed valve
7. Reed valve stop
8. Retainer

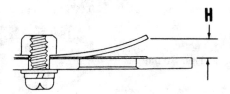

Fig. T2-3 — Reed valve stop height (H) should be 5.0-5.2 mm.

IGNITION

Breaker point gap should be 0.3-0.4 mm and is adjustable through opening in flywheel. The flywheel must be removed for breaker point renewal. Tighten flywheel nut to 59-78 N·m.

Ignition should occur with piston at 2.9-3.7 mm BTDC (27-31 degrees BTDC). Ignition timing is fixed but may be adjusted by changing breaker point gap within breaker point gap setting of 0.3-0.4 mm.

COOLING SYSTEM

Engine cylinder and cylinder head are air cooled by the flywheel fan. The engine crankcase and exhaust port areas are cooled by water directed at the engine mount plate. Cooling water is directed by a water tube from the gearcase to the engine mount plate. Water pressure is attained from water forced past the propeller; no water pump is used.

POWER HEAD

REMOVE AND REINSTALL. To remove power head, detach carrying handle and lower power head cover (hold shift lever in forward gear when removing cover). Remove manual starter and fuel tank. Unscrew flywheel nut which has left-hand threads and remove starter cup, flywheel and ignition assembly. Remove breaker point cam and key (note that "R" stamped side of cam is up). Remove fuel tank support

Fig. T2-4 — View of ignition system components.

1. Starter cup
2. Flywheel
3. Breaker point cam
4. Ignition switch
5. Spark plug
6. Breaker points
7. Condenser
8. Ignition coil
9. Lighting coil
10. Stator plate

and carburetor. Unscrew engine mounting screws and lift off engine.

To install power head, reverse removal procedure. Install breaker point cam with "R" stamped side up. Note that flywheel retaining nut has left-hand threads. Apply water resistant grease to ends of crankshaft and drive shaft.

DISASSEMBLY. To disassemble power head, remove lower cap (35 – Fig. T2-5) and engine mount plate

Fig. T2-5 — Exploded view of engine.

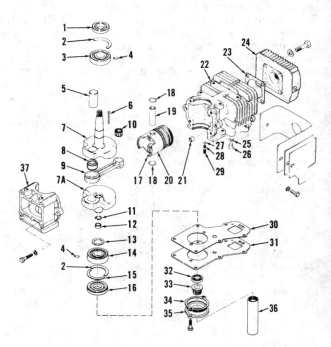

1. Seal
2. Retainer
3. Ball bearing
4. Pin
5. Crankpin
6. Key
7. Upper crankshaft half
7A. Lower crankshaft half
8. Roller bearing
9. Connecting rod
10. Roller bearing
11. Snap ring
12. Plug
13. Shim
14. Ball bearing
15. Retainer
16. Seal
17. Piston
18. Circlip
19. Piston pin
20. Piston rings
21. Dowel pin
22. Cylinder
23. Head gasket
24. Cylinder head
25. Gasket
26. Plug
27. Check valve ball
28. Spring
29. Plug
30. Gasket
31. Base plate
32. Seal
33. Bushing
34. Gasket
35. Cap
36. Tube
37. Crankcase

(31). Remove intake manifold and reed valve assembly. Remove cylinder head. Remove crankcase screws and separate crankcase from cylinder. Crankshaft assembly is now accessible and may be removed from cylinder. Refer to specific service sections for overhaul.

ASSEMBLY. Before reassembling engine, be sure all joints and gasket surfaces are clean, free from nicks and burrs and hardened cement or carbon. Mating surfaces may be lapped to remove high spots or nicks, however, only a minimum amount of metal should be removed.

All friction surfaces and bearings should be thoroughly lubricated with engine oil during reassembly. Coat mating surfaces with a non-hardening gasket sealer.

When assembling engine, be sure piston ring ends properly mate with locating pin in piston groove. Bearing retainers (2 and 15 – Fig. T2-5) must fit in crankcase and cylinder grooves. Be sure bearing locating pins (4) properly engage notches in crankcase. Rotate crankshaft after tightening crankcase screws and check for binding.

PISTON, PIN, RINGS AND CYLINDER. The cylinder is equipped with an iron liner which may be bored to accept oversize pistons. Piston and piston rings are available in standard size and 0.5 and 1.0 mm oversize.

The piston pin is retained by circlips (18 – Fig. T2-5) which should be renewed if removed. The piston pin rides in a roller bearing in rod small end. Install

504

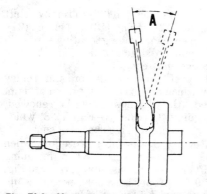

Fig. T2-6— *Measure connecting rod small end shake (A) by moving small end side to side. Maximum allowable rod small end shake is 1.6 mm.*

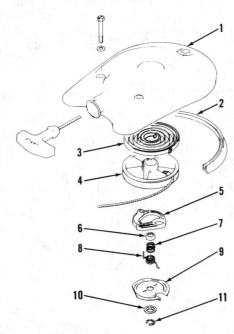

Fig. T2-7 — *Exploded view of manual starter.*

1. Starter housing
2. Grommet
3. Rewind spring
4. Rope pulley
5. Ratchet
6. Sleeve
7. Spring
8. Return spring
9. Friction plate
10. Thrust washer
11. "E" ring

piston on connecting rod so arrow in piston crown points towards exhaust port.

CRANKSHAFT AND CONNECTING ROD. Crankshaft, connecting rod, crankpin and bearing are assembled as a pressed together unit. Disassembly and assembly of crankshaft should be performed by a shop experienced in repair of this type crankshaft. Individual crankshaft components are available.

Determine rod bearing wear by moving small rod end from side to side as shown in Fig. T2-6. Normal side to side movement is 0.8 mm; renew worn com-

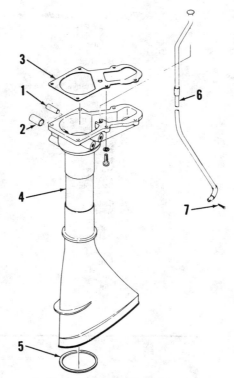

Fig. T2-8 — Exploded view of drive shaft housing.

1. Shift lever stop pin
2. Shift shaft bushing
3. Gasket
4. Drive shaft housing
5. "O" ring
6. Water tube
7. Cotter pin

ponents if side movement exceeds 1.6 mm.

Bearing numbers are 6204E2C3 for upper main bearing (3 – Fig. T2-5) and 6204ZE2C3 for lower main bearing (14). Install oil seals (1 and 16) with open side towards bearing.

MANUAL STARTER

Refer to Fig. T2-7 for an exploded view of manual starter. To disassemble starter, first remove starter from fuel tank then remove rope handle and allow rope to wind into starter. Detach "E" clip (11) and remove thrust washer (10), friction plate (9), return spring (8), sleeve (6), spring (7) and ratchet (5). Remove rope pulley (4) while being careful not to dislodge rewind spring (3). If rewind spring must be removed, care must be used not to allow spring to uncoil uncontrolled.

Install rewind spring with coils wrapped in a counterclockwise direction from outer spring end. Wrap rope around pulley in a counterclockwise direction as viewed with pulley in starter housing. Install ratchet so tooth points counterclockwise. Assemble remaining components. Apply tension to rewind spring by engaging rope in rope pulley notch and turning pulley counterclock-

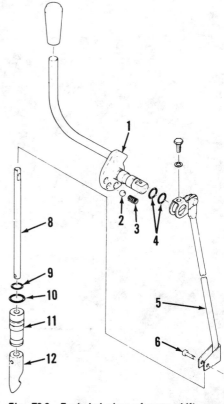

Fig. T2-9 — Exploded view of gear shift components.

1. Shift lever
2. Detent ball
3. Spring
4. "O" rings
5. Upper shift rod
6. Pin
8. Lower shift rod
9. "O" ring
10. "O" ring
11. Bushing
12. Shift cam

wise. Check starter action and install on power head.

LOWER UNIT

PROPELLER AND SHEAR PIN. Lower unit protection is provided by a shear pin (19 – Fig. T2-10). Be sure correct shear pin is installed for maximum protection to lower unit.

Standard propeller is three-bladed with 188 mm diameter and 157 mm pitch. Propeller rotation is clockwise.

R&R AND OVERHAUL. To remove gearcase it is first necessary to remove power head as previously outlined. Detach upper shift rod (5 – Fig. T2-9) from shift lever (1). Drive out water tube retaining pin (5 – Fig. T2-10). Unscrew five screws securing gearcase to drive shaft housing and separate gearcase from drive shaft housing. Drain gearcase oil and remove propeller and shear pin. Remove cap (29) retaining screws and withdraw propeller shaft assembly. Detach oil seal retainer plate (2), withdraw drive shaft (1) and remove pinion gear (10) and forward gear (16).

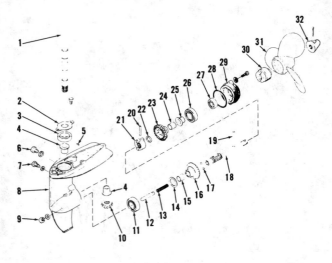

Fig. T2-10 — Exploded view of gearcase.

1. Drive shaft
2. Retainer
3. Seal
4. Bushing
5. Water tube pin
6. Vent plug
7. Shift bushing locating screw
8. Gearcase
9. Fill plug
10. Pinion gear
11. Ball bearing
12. Shift plunger
13. Spring
14. Shim
15. Bushing
16. Forward gear
17. Washer
18. Propeller shaft
19. Shear pin
20. Clutch pin
21. Clutch
23. Washer
24. Bushing
25. Collar
26. Ball bearing
27. Seal
28. "O" ring
29. Cap
30. Propeller hub
31. Propeller
32. Nut

Drive out clutch pin (20) to remove shift plunger (12), spring (13) and clutch (21). Unscrew cam bushing locating screw (7) and pull up shift rod (8 – Fig. T2-9) to remove shift cam.

Inspect components for and renew any which are excessively worn or damaged. All "O" rings should be renewed, including "O" ring (5 – Fig. T2-8) which may remain in drive shaft housing.

Reverse disassembly procedure when assembling gearcase. When installing shift cam and rod assembly, refer to Fig. T2-9 for proper assembly; note that upper shift rod (5) is aft of lower shift rod (8). Backlash between pinion gear (10 – Fig. T2-10) and forward gear (16) should be 0.05-0.10 mm and is adjusted using shims (14). Clutch spring (13) pressure should be 19.6 newtons at 40.5 mm length.

TOHATSU 5 HP
(1985 and After)

CONDENSED SERVICE DATA

NOTE: Metric fasteners are used throughout outboard motor.

TUNE-UP

Hp/rpm 5/5000
Bore . . . . 55 mm
                     (2.16 in.)
Stroke . . . . 43 mm
                     (1.69 in.)
Number of Cylinders 1
Displacement . . . . 102 cc
                  (6.22 cu. in.)
Spark Plug:
  NGK BP7HS10
  Champion L82YC
    Electrode Gap . . . . 1.0 mm
                   (0.040 in.)
Ignition Type . . . . Breakerless CD
Carburetor:
  Make . . . . Keihin Seiki
  Model . . . . BCK 21-15
Idle Speed (in gear) . . . . 850 rpm
Fuel:Oil Ratio 50:1

SIZES—CLEARANCES

Piston Ring End Gap . . . . 0.2-0.4 mm
                (0.008-0.016 in.)
Piston Ring Side Clearance:
  Top Ring . . . . 0.03-0.07 mm
                (0.001-0.003 in.)
  Bottom Ring . . . . 0.02-0.06 mm
                (0.001-0.002 in.)
Piston Clearance . . . . 0.03-0.06 mm
                (0.001-0.002 in.)

SIZES—CLEARANCES CONT.

Piston Pin Clearance in Piston . . . . Interference to
             0.008 mm Loose
            (Interference to
            0.0003 in. Loose)
Connecting Rod Side Clearance:
  Standard . . . . 0.13-0.37 mm
                (0.005-0.015 in.)
  Limit . . . . 0.5 mm
                (0.020 in.)
Crankshaft Runout . . . . 0.05 mm
                (0.002 in.).

TIGHTENING TORQUES

Cylinder Head . . . . 23.5-25.5 N·m
             (208-226 in.-lbs.)
Crankcase . . . . 9.8-10.7 N·m
             (87-95 in.-lbs.)
Flywheel . . . . 49-58.9 N·m
             (36-43 ft.-lbs.)
Spark Plug . . . . 24.5-29.4 N·m
             (217-260 in.-lbs.)
Standard Screws:
  No. 4 . . . . 1.2-1.8 N·m
             (11-16 in.-lbs.)
  No. 5 . . . . 2.6-3.5 N·m
             (23-31 in.-lbs.)
  No. 6 . . . . 4.6-6.2 N·m
             (41-55 in.-lbs.)
  No. 8 . . . . 11.2-15.1 N·m
             (99-134 in.-lbs.)

LUBRICATION

The power head is lubricated by oil mixed with the fuel. Recommended oil is Tohatsu outboard motor oil mixed at a fuel:oil ratio of 50:1. During engine break-in the fuel:oil ratio should be 20:1 for a period of 10 operating hours.

Lower unit gears and bearings are lubricated by oil contained in the gearcase. Recommended oil is Tohatsu gear oil or SAE 80 gear oil. Approximate capacity of gearcase is 195 mL (6.59 ozs). Oil should be changed after initial 20 hours of operation and after every 200 hours of operation.

FUEL SYSTEM

CARBURETOR. The Keihin Seiki Model BCK 21-15 carburetor with integral fuel pump shown in Fig. T3-1 is used. Standard main jet (11) size for normal service is #78 on early models, and #80 on later models (after serial number 31100). Standard slow jet (8) size is #55.

Initial setting for fuel mixture screw (3) is 1¾ to 2¼ turns open from lightly seated position. Recommended idle speed is 850 rpm in gear with engine at normal operating temperature. Adjust fuel mixture screw (3) until optimum idle speed is obtained, then readjust idle speed screw (5).

To determine the float level, invert carburetor body (1) and measure distance from carburetor body to base of float (14). Distance should be 12-16 mm (0.47-0.63 in.) and is adjusted by bending tang on float arm.

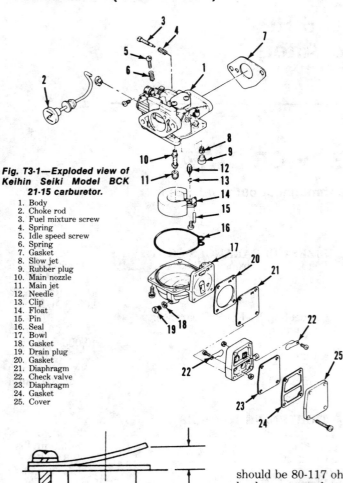

Fig. T3-1—Exploded view of Keihin Seiki Model BCK 21-15 carburetor.

1. Body
2. Choke rod
3. Fuel mixture screw
4. Spring
5. Idle speed screw
6. Spring
7. Gasket
8. Slow jet
9. Rubber plug
10. Main nozzle
11. Main jet
12. Needle
13. Clip
14. Float
15. Pin
16. Seal
17. Bowl
18. Gasket
19. Drain plug
20. Gasket
21. Diaphragm
22. Check valve
23. Diaphragm
24. Gasket
25. Cover

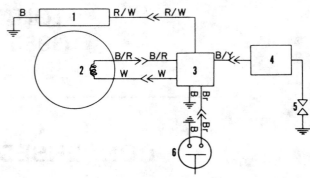

Fig. T3-3—Wiring diagram of CD ignition system.

1. Pulser coil
2. Exciter coil
3. CDI module
4. Ignition coil
5. Spark plug
6. Stop switch

B. Black
W. White
Br. Brown

B/R. Black with red tracer
B/Y. Black with yellow tracer
R/W. Red with white tracer

Fig. T3-2—Reed valve stop height (H) should be 6.0-6.2 mm (0.23-0.24 in.).

REED VALVE. The reed valve is attached on inside of crankcase. Inspect reed valve (2–Fig. T3-6) and renew if cracked, bent or otherwise damaged. Do not attempt to straighten reed valve. Reed valve stop height (H–Fig. T3-2) should be 6.0-6.2 mm (0.23-0.24 in.).

IGNITION

All models are equipped with a breakerless capacitor discharge ignition system. The ignition exciter and pulser coils as well as the lighting coil are located under the flywheel. Flywheel nut has left-hand threads. Tighten flywheel nut to 49-58.9 N·m (434-521 in.-lbs.).

The following checks using an ohmmeter can be used to locate faulty ignition system components. Refer to Fig. T3-3. Disconnect wire connectors between stator plate and CD ignition module, then connect on ohmmeter lead to stator plate. Connect remaining ohmmeter lead to red/white stator lead to check pulser coil. Ohmmeter reading

should be 80-117 ohms. With ohmmeter leads connected to black/red lead and white lead to check exciter coil, ohmmeter reading should be 93-140 ohms. To check the CD ignition module, disconnect module leads and refer to chart in Fig. T3-4 for desired ohmmeter readings.

IGNITION TIMING. Ignition timing is electrically advanced as engine speed is increased. An idle speed (5 degrees BTDC) timing mark (I—Fig. T3-5) and a full throttle (30 degrees BTDC) timing mark (F) are stamped on the side of the

flywheel. The timing marks should align with the mating surfaces (S) of the crankcase when engine is operated at respective speed.

COOLING SYSTEM

A rubber impeller type water pump is mounted between the drive shaft housing and gearcase. The impeller is driven by a key in the drive shaft.

Whenever cooling system problems are encountered, check water inlet for plugging or partial stoppage. Then if not corrected, remove gearcase and check condition of the water pump, water passages and sealing surfaces.

When water pump is disassembled, check condition of impeller (5–Fig. T3-11), liner (4) and plate (7). Turn drive shaft clockwise (viewed from top) while placing pump housing over impeller. Avoid turning drive shaft in opposite direction when water pump is assembled.

POWER HEAD

REMOVE AND REINSTALL. To remove power head, first remove engine cover. Remove CDI module, manual

		TESTER (−) TERMINAL				
		Red/White	White	Black/Red	Black	Black/Yellow	Brown
TESTER (+) TERMINAL	Red/White			A	B	B	A
	White	B		C	B	B	C
	Black/Red	B	D		B	B	B
	Black	B	F	E		B	E
	Black/Yellow	C	C	C	C		C
	Brown	B	D	B	B	B	

Fig. T3-4—Use the above chart and a suitable ohmmeter to test CD ignition module.

A. Infinity
B. Zero
C. Tester needle should show deflection then return toward infinite resistance.
D. Tester needle should show deflection then return to approximately 18k ohms.
E. Tester needle should show deflection then return to approximately 1000k ohms.
F. Tester needle should show deflection then return to approximately 10k ohms.

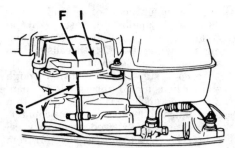

Fig. T3-5—View identifying idle speed (5 degrees BTDC) timing mark (I), full throttle (30 degrees BTDC) timing mark (F) and crankcase mating surfaces (S). Refer to text.

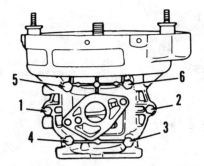

Fig. T3-7 — Tighten crankcase screws to 9.8-10.7 N·m (87-95 in.-lbs.) following sequence shown above.

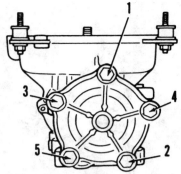

Fig. T3-8—Tighten cylinder head screws to 23.5-25.5 N·m (208-226 in.-lbs.) following sequence shown above.

starter lockout rod, throttle cable and choke rod. Remove fuel cock rod, fuel tank hose and fuel tank. Unscrew engine mounting screws and lift off engine.

To install power head, reverse removal procedure.

DISASSEMBLY. Remove lower seal housing (15 – Fig. T3-6). Remove ignition coil, spark plug and manual starter. Remove flywheel, then remove exciter coil and pulser coil. Remove carburetor assembly. Remove cylinder head. Remove crankcase screws and separate crankcase from cylinder block. Crankshaft assembly is now accessible and can be removed from cylinder block. Refer to specific service sections for overhaul.

ASSEMBLY. Before reassembling engine, be sure all joints and gasket surfaces are clean, free from nicks and burrs and hardened cement or carbon. Mating surfaces can be lapped to remove high spots or nicks, however,

only a minimum amount of metal should be removed.

All friction surfaces and bearings should be thoroughly lubricated with engine oil during reassembly. Coat mating surfaces of crankcase and cylinder block with Three Bond 1104 packing agent or a suitable equivalent.

Before assembling power head, install bearing retainers (5 – Fig. T3-6) in cylinder block grooves. Install crankshaft assembly in cylinder block while being sure piston rings properly mate with locating pin in piston ring grooves and bearing locating pins mate with notches in cylinder block. Tighten crankcase screws to 9.8-10.7 N·m (87-95 in.-lbs.) following sequence shown in Fig. T3-7. Tighten cylinder head screws to 23.5-25.5 N·m (208-226 in.-lbs.) following sequence shown in Fig. T3-8.

PISTON, PIN, RINGS AND CYLINDER. The cylinder is equipped with an iron liner which can be bored to accept

an oversize piston. Piston and piston rings are available in standard size and 0.5 mm (0.020 in.) oversize.

The piston pin (19—Fig. T3-6) is retained in piston by retaining rings (18) which should be renewed if removed. The piston pin rides in a roller bearing in connecting rod small end. Install piston on connecting rod so "UP" marking on piston crown faces toward flywheel end of crankshaft.

CRANKSHAFT AND CONNECTING ROD. Crankshaft, connecting rod, crankpin and bearing are assembled as a pressed-together unit. Disassembly and assembly of crankshaft should be performed by a shop experienced in repair of this type crankshaft. Individual crankshaft components are available.

Connecting rod side clearance should be 0.13-0.37 mm (0.005-0.015 in.) with a maximum limit of 0.5 (0.020 in.). Crankshaft runout should not exceed 0.05 mm (0.002 in.).

Upper and lower main bearings are interchangeable. Install oil seals (4 – Fig. T3-6) with open side towards bearing.

MANUAL STARTER

Refer to Fig. T3-9 for an exploded view of manual starter. To overhaul the manual starter, proceed as follows: Remove engine cover. Remove screws retaining manual starter to engine. Remove starter lockout rod (16) from rod keeper (15). Withdraw the starter assembly.

Check pawl (27) for freedom of movement and excessive wear or damage of engagement area. Renew or lubricate pawl (27) with a suitable water-resistant grease if needed.

To disassemble, remove clip (28) and withdraw pawl (27) and pawl springs (25 and 26). Untie starter rope (3) at anchor (1) and allow the rope to wind into the starter. Remove bolt (24), washer (23) and spindle (22). Carefully lift pulley (30) with starter rope (3) from housing (5). BE CAREFUL not to dislodge rewind

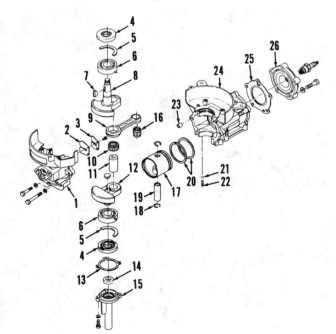

Fig. T3-6—Exploded view of engine assembly. On models after serial number 31350, bearing retainers (5) are full-circle design.

1. Crankcase
2. Reed valve
3. Reed stop
4. Seal
5. Bearing retainer
6. Bearing
7. Key
8. Upper crank half
9. Connecting rod
10. Roller bearing
11. Crankpin
12. Lower crank half
13. Gasket
14. Seal
15. Lower seal housing
16. Roller bearing
17. Piston
18. Retaining ring
19. Piston pin
20. Piston rings
21. Check ball
22. Spring
23. Dowel pin
24. Cylinder block
25. Gasket
26. Cylinder head

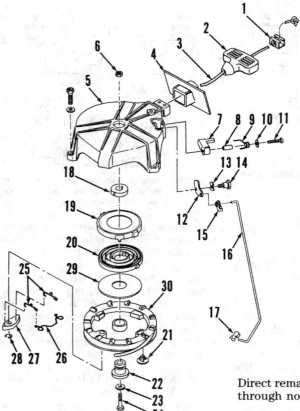

Fig. T3-9—Exploded view of manual starter.

1. Anchor
2. Handle
3. Starter rope
4. Rope guide
5. Starter housing
6. Nut
7. Starter lock
8. Sleeve
9. Spring
10. Washer
11. Screw
12. Cam
13. Wave washer
14. Shoulder screw
15. Rod keeper
16. Rod
17. Rod keeper
18. Spring guide
19. Spring case
20. Rewind spring
21. Spring case stop
22. Spindle
23. Washer
24. Bolt
25. Spring
26. Spring
27. Pawl
28. Clip
29. Washer
30. Pulley

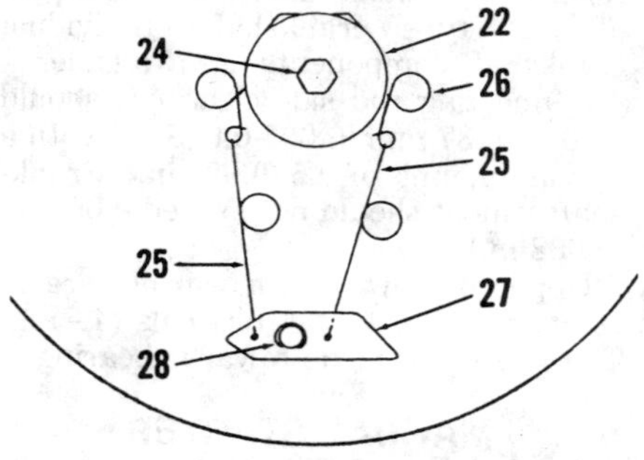

Fig. T3-10—Drawing showing proper installation of starter pawl (27) and springs (25 and 26). Refer to Fig. T3-9 for complete identification of parts.

spring (20) when removing pulley (30). Remove starter rope (3) from pulley (30) if renewal is required. If renewal of rewind spring (20) is required, use extreme caution when removing rewind spring (20) from spring case (19).

Inspect all components for damage and excessive wear and renew if needed.

To reassemble, first apply a coating of a suitable water-resistant grease to rewind spring area of spring case (19). Install rewind spring (20) in spring case (19) so spring coils wind in a counterclockwise direction from the outer end. Make sure the spring's outer hook is properly secured. Wind starter rope (3) onto pulley (30) 2-3 turns counterclockwise when viewed from flywheel side.

Direct remaining starter rope (3) length through notch in pulley (30).

NOTE: Lubricate all friction surfaces with a suitable water resistant grease during reassembly.

Assemble pulley (30) to starter housing making sure that pulley hub properly

Fig. T3-11—Exploded view of lower unit assembly.

1. Water pump housing
2. Pickup tube
3. Grommets
4. Liner
5. Impeller
6. Gasket
7. Plate
8. Gasket
9. Water pump base
10. Seal
11. Shim
12. Gasket
13. Retainer
14. Drive shaft
15. Key
16. Bearing
17. Bearing
18. Gearcase
19. Gasket
20. Fill plug
21. Drain plug
22. Bearing
23. Shim
24. Drive gear
25. Shift plunger
26. Spring holder
27. Dog clutch
28. Pin
29. Pinion gear
30. Spring
31. Propeller shaft
32. Thrust washer
33. Drive gear
34. Bearing
35. Seal
36. "O" ring
37. Bearing carrier
38. Spacer
39. Propeller
40. Washer
41. Nut
42. Cotter pin

engages inner hook of rewind spring (20). Install spindle (22), washer (23) and bolt (24). Apply a suitable thread fastening solution on bolt (24) threads and install nut (6) and securely tighten.

Thread starter rope (3) through starter housing (5), rope guide (4), handle (2) and anchor (1) and secure with a knot. Turn pulley (30) 2-3 turns counterclockwise when viewed from flywheel side, then release starter rope (3) from pulley notch and allow rope to slowly wind onto pulley.

NOTE: Do not apply any more tension on rewind spring (20) than is required to draw starter handle (2) back into the proper released position.

Install springs (25 and 26), pawl (27) and clip (28) as shown in Fig. T3-10. Remount manual starter assembly. Reconnect starter lockout rod (16—Fig. T3-5) to rod keeper (15) and check for proper operation of starter lockout assembly.

Complete reassembly.

LOWER UNIT

PROPELLER. Standard propeller has three blades with a diameter of 200 mm (7-7/8 in.) and a pitch of 200 mm

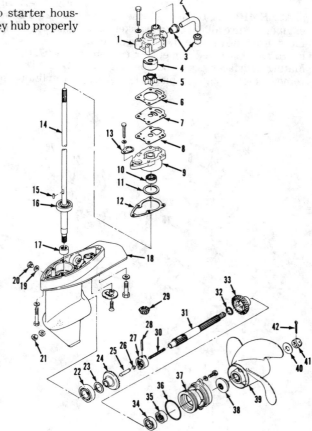

(7-7/8 in.). Optional propellers are available from the manufacturer and should be selected to provide full-throttle operation within the recommended limits of 4500-5500 rpm.

R&R AND OVERHAUL. To remove gearcase, first place shift lever in reverse position. Disconnect lower shift rod by removing plug in side of drive shaft housing and loosening cap screw (9 – Fig. T3-12). Remove screws securing gearcase to drive shaft housing and separate gearcase from drive shaft housing. Drain lubricant from gearcase. Remove cotter pin (42 – Fig. T3-11), nut (41), washer (40) and withdraw propeller (39) and spacer (38). Remove bearing carrier (37) retaining screws and withdraw propeller shaft assembly. Remove pinion gear (29). Remove water pump assembly and retainer (13) screw. Remove water pump base (9), drive shaft (14) and lower shift rod assembly. Withdraw drive gear (24).

Inspect components and renew any which are excessively worn or damaged. All gaskets and "O" rings should be renewed. Clearance between bushing in drive gear (24) and propeller shaft should be 0.030-0.058 mm (0.0012-0.0023 in.). Clearance between bushing in drive gear (33) and propeller shaft should be 0.040-0.070 mm (0.0016-0.0028 in.).

Reverse disassembly procedure when assembling gearcase. Recommended backlash between drive gear (24) and pinion gear (29) is 0.05-0.15 mm (0.002-0.006 in.). Shims (11 and 23) are available in a service packet with shims ranging from 0.1 mm through 0.15 mm.

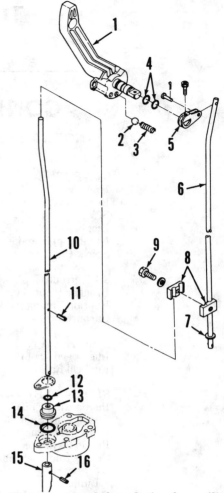

Fig. T3-12—Exploded view of shift control components.

1. Shift lever
2. Detent ball
3. Spring
4. "O" rings
5. Lever
6. Upper shift rod
7. Washer
8. Clamp assy.
9. Cap screw
10. Lower shift rod
11. Pin
12. "O" ring
13. Bushing
14. "O" ring
15. Shift cam
16. Pin

Place shift lever in reverse position and verify shift cam (15 – Fig. T3-12) is in reverse position, then tighten cap screw (9) to secure shift rods in clamp (8). Refer to LUBRICATION section and refill gearcase.

TOHATSU 8 AND 9.8 HP
(Prior to 1987)

CONDENSED SERVICE DATA

NOTE: Metric fasteners are used throughout outboard motor.

TUNE-UP	8 Hp	9.8 Hp
Hp/rpm	8/6000	9.8/5000
Bore	45 mm	52 mm
Stroke	43 mm	43 mm
Displacement	137 cc	183 cc
Number of cylinders	2	2
Spark Plug:		
NGK	B7HS	B7HS
Electrode Gap	0.6-0.7 mm	0.6-0.7 mm
Breaker Point Gap	0.3-0.4 mm	0.3-0.4 mm
Ignition Timing (BTDC)	23½-26½ degrees	23½-26½ degrees
Carburetor:		
Make	TK	TK
Model	PA17C-4	PA17C-4
Idle Speed – rpm	1100-1200	1100-1200
Fuel:Oil Ratio	50:1	50:1
SIZES – CLEARANCES		
Piston Ring End Gap	0.18-0.33 mm	0.15-0.35 mm
Piston Ring Side Clearance	0.01-0.05 mm	0.03-0.07 mm
Piston Clearance	0.06-0.12 mm	0.06-0.12 mm
Piston Clearance in Piston	0.007-0.010 mm	0.007-0.010 mm
Connecting Rod Side Clearance:		
Standard	0.16-0.42 mm	0.16-0.42 mm
Limit	0.6 mm	0.6 mm
Connecting Rod Small End Shake:		
Standard	0.9 mm	0.9 mm
Limit	1.7 mm	1.7 mm
Gearcase Capacity	185 cc	185 cc
TIGHTENING TORQUES		
(All values in newton meters)		
Crankcase	19.6-26.5	19.6-26.5
Cylinder Head	19.6-26.5	19.6-26.5
Flywheel	64-73	64-73
Spark Plug	24.5-29.4	24.5-29.4

LUBRICATION

The power head is lubricated by oil mixed with the fuel. Recommended oil is Tohatsu outboard motor oil mixed at a fuel:oil ratio of 50:1. During engine break-in the fuel:oil ratio should be 20:1 for a period of 10 operating hours.

Lower unit gears and bearings are lubricated by oil contained in the gearcase. Recommended oil is SAE 80 gear oil. Oil should be changed after initial 20 hours of operation and after every 200 hours of operation.

FUEL SYSTEM

CARBURETOR. Refer to Fig. T4-1 for an exploded view of TK Model PA17C-4 carburetor used on both models. Standard main jet (26) size for normal operation is #92. Normal position of clip (6) is in the middle groove of jet needle (7). Inserting clip in a higher groove will lean mid-range mixture while insertion in a lower groove will richen mid-range mixture. Throttle valve (8) cutaway is 2.0 mm. Needle jet (25) diameter is 2.580 mm.

Float height is measured with carburetor inverted as shown in Fig. T4-2. Float height (H) with gasket removed should be 15 mm.

Adjust idle speed screw (9 – Fig. T4-1) so engine idles at 1100-1200 rpm with forward gear engaged.

REED VALVE. The reed valve is attached to reed valve plate (4 – Fig. T4-3) which is mounted on inside of intake manifold (2). Inspect reed valve (5) and renew if cracked, bent or otherwise damaged. Do not attempt to straighten

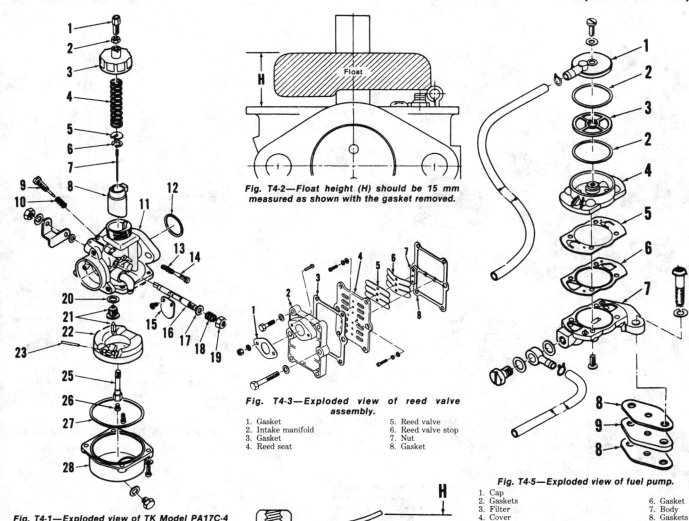

Fig. T4-1—Exploded view of TK Model PA17C-4 carburetor.

1. Cable adjuster	15. Choke plate
2. Nut	16. Choke shaft
3. Cap	17. Washer
4. Spring	18. Spring
5. Retainer	19. Nut
6. Clip	20. Gasket
7. Jet needle	21. Fuel inlet valve
8. Throttle slide	22. Float
9. Idle speed screw	23. Float pin
10. Spring	25. Needle jet
11. Body	26. Main jet
12. Gasket	27. Gasket
13. Spring	28. Fuel bowl
14. Idle mixture screw	

Fig. T4-2—Float height (H) should be 15 mm measured as shown with the gasket removed.

Fig. T4-3—Exploded view of reed valve assembly.

1. Gasket	5. Reed valve
2. Intake manifold	6. Reed valve stop
3. Gasket	7. Nut
4. Reed seat	8. Gasket

Fig T4-4—Reed valve stop height (H) should be 5.5 mm.

Fig. T4-5—Exploded view of fuel pump.

1. Cap		6. Gasket
2. Gaskets		7. Body
3. Filter		8. Gaskets
4. Cover		9. Insulator
5. Diaphragm		

reed valve. Reed valve seating surface of reed plate (4) should be flat. Reed valve stop height (H – Fig. T4-4) should be 5.5 mm.

FUEL PUMP. A diaphragm type fuel pump is mounted on starboard side of upper cylinder. The fuel pump is operated by crankcase pulsations. Refer to Fig. T4-5 for an exploded view of fuel pump. Individual components are available.

IGNITION

Breaker point gap should be 0.3-0.4 mm and is adjustable through opening in

flywheel. The flywheel must be removed for breaker point renewal. Flywheel nut has left-hand threads. Tighten flywheel nut to 59 N·m.

Ignition timing may be checked and adjusted as follows: Remove manual starter and starter flange attached to flywheel. Connect a point checker or ohmmeter to blue wire leading from magneto (top cylinder primary lead). Rotate flywheel clockwise. Top cylinder breaker points should open when top cylinder ignition mark (U – Fig. T4-7) is aligned with ignition mark (I) on magneto base. Adjust top cylinder ignition timing by removing flywheel (flywheel nut has left-hand threads), loosening stator plate retaining screws and rotating stator plate. Reinstall flywheel. After top cylinder ignition timing is checked and adjusted, check bottom

cylinder ignition timing by connecting point checker to black wire leading from magneto (bottom cylinder primary lead). Rotate flywheel clockwise. Bottom cylinder breaker points should open when bottom cylinder ignition mark (L) is aligned with ignition mark (I). Adjust bottom cylinder ignition timing by adjusting point gap of bottom cylinder breaker points within breaker point gap setting of 0.3-0.4 mm.

COOLING SYSTEM

THERMOSTAT. A thermostat (40 – Fig. T4-8) is located in the cylinder head. Thermostat should begin opening at 50°-54°C (122°-130°F) with a maximum opening of 3 mm at 65°C (149°F).

WATER PUMP. A rubber impeller type water pump is mounted between the drive shaft housing and gearcase. The impeller is driven by a Woodruff key in the drive shaft.

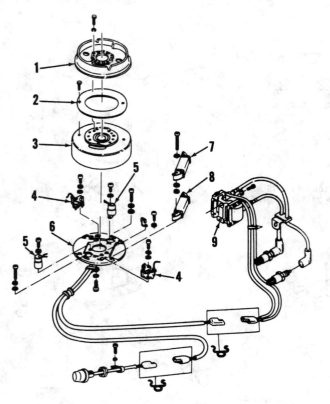

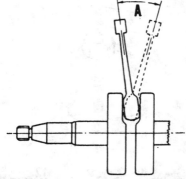

Fig. T4-6—Exploded view of ignition system components.
1. Starter cup
2. Plate
3. Flywheel
4. Breaker points
5. Condenser
6. Stator plate
7. Upper primary coil
8. Lower primary coil
9. Secondary ignition coils

Fig. T4-9—Measure connecting rod small end shake (A) by moving small end side to side. Maximum allowable rod small end shake is 1.7 mm.

POWER HEAD

REMOVE AND REINSTALL. To remove power head, remove upper motor cover and disconnect throttle cable, ignition switch wire and fuel line. Detach choke linkage. Unscrew fasteners and remove power head.

To install power head, reverse removal procedure. Apply water resistant grease to ends of crankshaft and drive shaft.

DISASSEMBLY. To disassemble power head, remove carburetor, fuel

Whenever cooling problems are encountered, check water inlet for plugging or partial stoppage and thermostat for proper operation, then if not corrected, remove gearcase and check condition of the water pump, water passages and sealing surfaces.

When water pump is disassembled, check condition of impeller (5–Fig. T4-13), liner (4) and plate (6). Turn drive shaft clockwise (viewed from top) while placing pump housing over impeller.

Avoid turning drive shaft in opposite direction when water pump is assembled.

Fig. T4-8—Exploded view of engine. Plate (30) and gasket (31) are only used on 9.8 hp models.

1. Magneto base
2. Oil seal
3. Seal retainer
4. "O" ring
5. Ball bearing
6. Piston rings
7. Circlip
8. Piston pin
9. Piston
10. Bushing
11. Key
12. Crankpin
13. Crank half
14. Roller bearing
15. Connecting rod
16. Crank half
17. Seal
18. Seal locating screw
19. Retainer
20. Crank half
21. Snap ring
22. Plug
23. Crank half
24. Shim
25. Seal
26. Seal
27. Gasket
28. Seal plate
29. Gasket
30. Plate
31. Gasket
32. Crankcase
33. Dowel pin
34. Check ball
35. Spring
36. Plug
37. Cylinder block
38. Head gasket
39. Cylinder head
40. Thermostat
41. Gasket
42. Cover
43. Gaskets
44. Inner exhaust cover
45. Outer exhaust cover

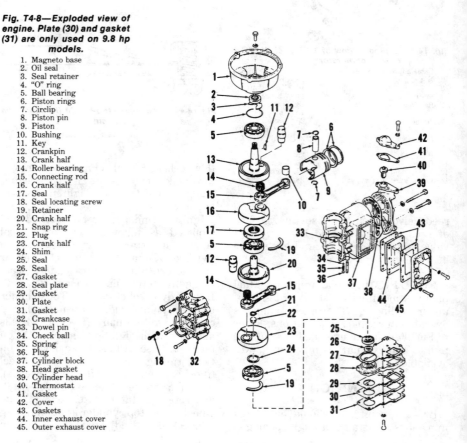

Fig. T4-7—Drawing showing location of timing marks on flywheel and magneto base.

I. Ignition mark
L. Lower cylinder mark
T. TDC mark
U. Upper cylinder mark

Illustrations Courtesy Tohatsu

pump and manual starter. Remove flywheel (flywheel nut has left-hand threads). Punch match marks in stator plate and magneto base for future reference and remove ignition components. Remove magneto base (1 – Fig. T4-8), intake manifold (2 – Fig. T4-3) and reed valve. Detach cylinder head, exhaust cover (45 – Fig. T4-8), exhaust plate (44) and seal plate (27). Unscrew seal locating screw (18). Remove crankcase screws and separate crankcase from cylinder. Crankshaft assembly is now accessible and may be removed from cylinder. Refer to specific service sections for overhaul.

ASSEMBLY. Before reassembling engine, be sure all joints and gasket surfaces are clean, free from nicks and burrs and hardened cement or carbon. Mating surfaces may be lapped to remove high spots or nicks, however, only a minimum amount of metal should be removed.

All friction surfaces and bearings should be thoroughly lubricated with engine oil during reassembly. Coat mating surfaces with a nonhardening gasket sealer.

Before assembling engine, install bearing retainers (19) in cylinder block grooves. Install crankshaft assembly in cylinder block while being sure piston rings properly mate with locating pin in piston ring groove and bearing locating pins mate with notches in cylinder block. Hole in labyrinth seal circumference must point towards hole in crankcase for locating screw. Before tightening crankcase screws, install seal locating screw (18) and seal washer. Tighten crankcase screws to 19.6-26 N·m. Rotate crankshaft after tightening screws and check for binding.

PISTON, PIN, RINGS AND CYLINDER. The cylinders are equipped with iron liners which may be bored to accept oversize pistons. Pistons and rings are available in standard size and 0.5 and 1.0 mm oversize.

The piston pin is retained by circlips (7 – Fig. T4-8) which should be renewed if removed. The piston pin rides in a renewable plain bushing in rod small

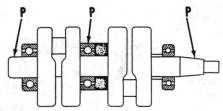

Fig. T4-10—With outer bearings supported in vee blocks, maximum runout measured at points (P) must not exceed 0.05 mm.

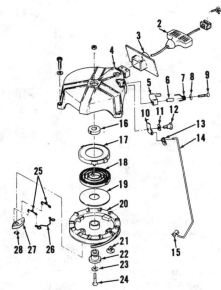

Fig. T4-11—Exploded view of manual starter.

2. Handle	16. Spring guide
3. Guide	17. Spring case
4. Starter housing	18. Rewind spring
5. Starter lock	19. Washer
6. Sleeve	20. Rope pulley
7. Spring	21. Spring case stop
8. Washer	22. Spindle
9. Screw	23. Washer
10. Cam	24. Bolt
11. Wave washer	25. Spring
12. Shoulder screw	26. Spring
13. Rod keeper	27. Pawl
14. Rod	28. "E" ring
15. Rod keeper	

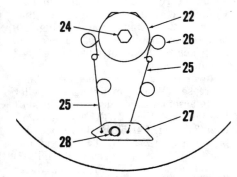

Fig. T4-12 — Drawing showing proper installation of starter pawl and springs. Refer to Fig. T4-11 for parts installation.

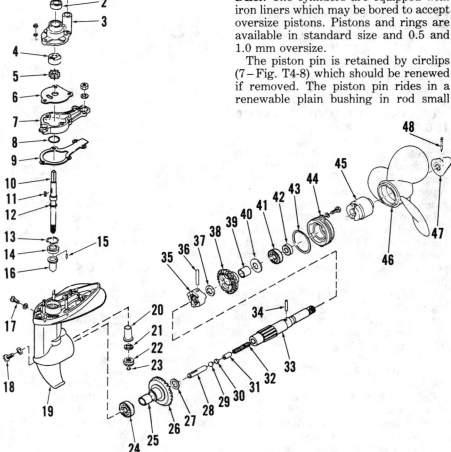

Fig. T4-13—Exploded view of gearcase. Note that water pump shown is used on early models and can be identified by aluminum housing (3) and base (7). Water pump used on later models is similar and can be identified by plastic housing (3) and base (7).

1. Grommet	13. Retainer	25. Bushing	37. Thrust washer
2. Seal	14. Seal	26. Forward gear	38. Reverse gear
3. Water pump housing	15. Pin	27. Thrust washer	39. Bushing
4. Liner	16. Bushing	28. Shift plunger	40. Washer
5. Impeller	17. Vent plug	29. Ball	41. Ball bearing #6203
6. Plate	18. Fill plug	30. Thrust piece	42. Seal
7. Water pump base	19. Gearcase	31. Push rod	43. "O" ring
8. "O" ring	20. Bushing	32. Spring	44. Bearing housing
9. Gasket	21. Thrust washer	33. Propeller shaft	45. Propeller hub
10. Drive shaft	22. Pinion gear	34. Shear pin	46. Propeller
11. Key	23. Snap ring	35. Clutch pin	47. Nut
12. Thrust washer	24. Ball bearing #6005	36. Clutch	48. Cotter pin

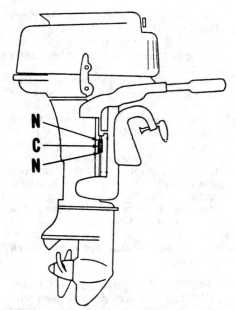

Fig. T4-14—Locknut (N) and connector (C) must be unscrewed to separate upper and lower shift rods. Note that upper locknut has left-hand threads.

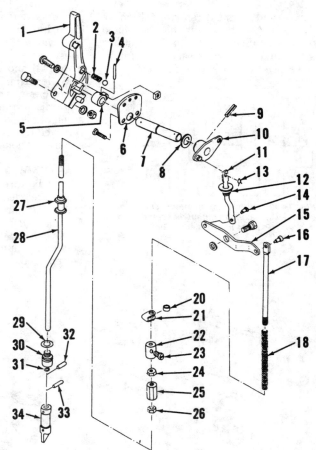

Fig. T4-15—Exploded view of shift mechanism components.

1. Shift lever
2. Spring
3. Detent ball
4. Pin
5. Collar
6. Detent plate
7. Shaft
8. Shim
9. Roll pin
10. Arm
11. Shift rod
12. Grommet
13. Clip
14. Pin
15. Lever
16. Pin
17. Shift rod
18. Spring
19. Spacer
21. Clamp
22. Stop
23. Screw
24. Nut (L.H.)
25. Connector
26. Nut
27. Grommet
28. Shift rod
29. "O" ring
30. Bushing
31. "O" ring
32. Pin
33. Pin
34. Shift cam

end. Install piston on connecting rod so arrow in piston crown points towards exhaust port.

CRANKSHAFT AND CONNECTING ROD.

Crankshaft, connecting rods, crankpins and bearings are assembled as a pressed-together unit. Disassembly and assembly of crankshaft should be performed by a shop experienced in repair of this type crankshaft. Individual crankshaft components are available.

Determine rod bearing wear by moving small rod end from side to side as shown in Fig. T4-9. Normal side to side movement is 0.9 mm; renew worn components if side movement exceeds 1.7 mm.

Check crankshaft runout by supporting outer main bearings in vee blocks. Maximum allowable crankshaft runout measured at points (P–Fig. T4-10) is 0.05 mm.

MANUAL STARTER

Refer to Fig. T4-11 for an exploded view of manual starter. To disassemble starter, remove starter then remove rope handle and allow rope to wind into starter. unscrew pulley retaining bolt (24) and remove rope pulley (20). If necessary, detach rewind case (17) with spring from rope pulley. If rewind spring must be removed, care must be used not to allow spring to uncoil uncontrolled.

Reverse disassembly procedure when assembling starter. Rewind spring should be wound in a clockwise direction from outer end when installed in spring case (17). Wind rope around pulley in a counterclockwise direction as viewed with pulley installed in starter housing. Convex side of spring guide (16) must be adjacent to starter housing surface. Refer to Fig. T4-12 for a typical view of correct installation of pawl (27) and springs (25 and 26).

LOWER UNIT

PROPELLER AND SHEAR PIN.

Lower unit protection is provided by shear pin (34–Fig. T4-13). Be sure correct shear pin is installed for maximum protection to lower unit.

Standard propeller has three blades on all models. Propeller on standard 8 hp models has 220 mm diameter and 197 mm pitch while long-shaft 8 hp models has 230 mm diameter and 152 mm pitch. Propeller on 9.8 hp models has 230 mm diameter and 220 mm pitch. Propeller rotation is clockwise.

R&R AND OVERHAUL.

To remove gearcase, first disconnect shift rod by unscrewing coupler (C–Fig. T4-14). Remove screws securing gearcase to drive shaft housing and separate gearcase from drive shaft housing. Drain lubricant from gearcase and remove propeller and shear pin. Remove bearing housing (44–Fig. T4-13) retaining screws and withdraw propeller shaft assembly. Detach snap ring (23) and remove pinion gear (22). Unscrew water pump retaining screws and remove water pump and lower drive shaft. Separate water pump from drive shaft. Forward gear (26) and bearing (24) may now be removed from gearcase; it may be necessary to heat gearcase in boiling water when removing bearing. Drive out clutch pin (35) and slide clutch (36) off propeller shaft. Withdraw shift rod and cam (34–Fig. T4-15) assembly.

Inspect components and renew any which are excessively worn or damaged. All seals and "O" rings should be renewed. Clutch spring (32–Fig. T4-13) free length should be 78.0-78.5 mm and should be renewed if 76.5 mm or less. Clearance between forward gear bushing (25), pinion gear bushing (20) and shafts should be 0.035-0.065 mm. Propeller shaft runout must not exceed 0.5 mm.

Reverse disassembly when assembling gearcase. When installing propeller shaft assembly, be sure notch in shift plunger (28–Fig. T4-13) engages shift cam (34–Fig. T4-15). Backlash between pinion gear (22–Fig. T4-13) and forward and reverse gears (26 and 38) should be 0.12-0.15 mm. Install water pump impeller so vanes are pointing in correct direction (drive shaft rotation is clockwise when viewed at top).

TOHATSU 8 HP
(1987 and After)

CONDENSED SERVICE DATA

NOTE: Metric fasteners are used throughout outboard motor.

TUNE-UP

Hp/rpm 8/5000
(6.0 kW)
Bore .... 50 mm
(1.97 in.)
Stroke .... 43 mm
(1.69 in.)
Displacement .... 169 cc
(10.3 cu. in.)
Number of Cylinders 2
Spark Plug:
NGK BP7HS-10
Champion L82YC
Electrode Gap .... 0.9-1.0 mm
(0.035-0.039 in.)
Ignition Type .... Breakerless
Ignition Timing .... See Text
Carburetor:
Make .... Keihin Seiki
Model .... BCK 21-15
Idle Speed (In Forward
Gear) .... 700-800 rpm
Fuel:Oil Ratio 50:1

SIZES—CLEARANCES

Piston Ring End Gap .... 0.18-0.33 mm
(0.007-0.013 in.)
Wear Limit .... 0.8 mm
(0.031 in.)
Piston Ring Side Clearance ... 0.01-0.05 mm
(0.0004-0.0020 in.)
Wear Limit .... 0.08 mm
(0.0031 in.)

SIZES—CLEARANCES CONT.

Piston Clearance .... 0.02-0.05 mm
(0.0008-0.0020 in.)
Wear Limit .... 0.15 mm
(0.006 in.)
Connecting Rod Side
Clearance .... 0.2-0.4 mm
(0.008-0.016 in.)
Wear Limit .... 0.6 mm
(0.024 in.)
Maximum Crankshaft
Runout .... 0.05 mm
(0.002 in.)

TIGHTENING TORQUES

Crankcase .... 11.8-13.7 N·m
(9-10 ft.-lbs.)
Cylinder Head .... 7.9-9.8 N·m
(6-7 ft.-lbs.)
Exhaust Cover .... 7.9-9.8 N·m
(6-7 ft.-lbs.)
Flywheel .... 49.0-58.9 N·m
(36-43 ft.-lbs.)
Intake Manifold .... 11.8-13.7 N·m
(9-10 ft.-lbs.)
Spark Plug .... 24.5-29.4 N·m
(18-22 ft.-lbs.)
Standard Screws:
4 mm .... 1.5-2.0 N·m
(13-18 in.-lbs.)
5 mm .... 2.4-3.4 N·m
(21-30 in.-lbs.)
6 mm .... 4.9-6.4 N·m
(43-57 in.-lbs.)

LUBRICATION

The power head is lubricated by oil mixed with the fuel. Recommended oil is Tohatsu outboard motor oil mixed at a 50:1 ratio. During engine break-in (first 10 hours of operation) of a new or rebuilt engine, fuel:oil ratio should be 20:1.

Lower unit gears and bearings are lubricated by oil contained in the gearcase. Recommended oil is Genuine Tohatsu gear oil or a suitable equivalent SAE 80 gear oil. Gearcase oil should be changed after initial 10 hours of opera-tion and after every 200 hours of oper-ation or once per boating season thereafter.

FUEL SYSTEM

CARBURETOR. Refer to Fig. T4-25 for exploded view of Keihin Seiki BCK 21-15 carburetor equipped with integral fuel pump. Standard main jet (11) size for normal operation is #98. Standard slow jet (8) size for normal operation is #48. To check float level, invert carbu-retor and measure from float bowl mat-ing surface to bottom of float as shown in Fig. T4-26. Float level should be 12-16 mm (0.47-0.63 in.). Bend float tang to adjust. Fuel pump is mounted to side of carburetor and is actuated by crank-case pulsations. Renew diaphragms (21 and 23) if air leaks, cracks or deterio-ration is noted. Make sure check valves (22) are seating properly.

Initial setting of pilot screw (3) is 2-1/8 to 2-5/8 turns out from a lightly seated position. Adjust idle speed screw (5) to 700-800 rpm with lower unit in forward gear. Adjust pilot screw (3) to obtain highest engine speed, then readjust idle speed screw to 700-800 rpm (in forward gear).

REED VALVE. Reed valves are mounted on reed plate located between intake manifold and crankcase. Renew reed valves if petals are broken, cracked, warped, rusted or bent. Tip of reed petals must not stand open more than 0.2 mm (0.008 in.) from seat. Reed stop opening (O—Fig. T4-27) should be 5.0-5.2 mm (0.197-0.205 in.). When reassembling reed valves, make sure notch on corner of reed valves and reed stops are aligned. Screws (1) are treat-ed with thread locking compound and should be renewed if removed. Tighten screws (1) to 0.7-0.9 N·m (6-8 in.-lbs.).

SPEED CONTROL LINKAGE. Throttle opening and ignition timing advance must be synchronized to occur simultaneously. Adjust stator link rod so stator rotates counterclockwise and contacts stop when throttle is rotated fully closed, and stator rotates fully clockwise against stop when throttle is fully opened.

IGNITION

A breakerless, capacitor discharge ignition system is used. Refer to Fig. T4-28 for diagram of electrical system. Recommended spark plug is NGK BP7HS-10 or Champion L82YC. Electrode gap should be 0.9-1.0 mm (0.035-0.039 in.). Spark plug should be removed and inspected after every 50 hours of operation. Renew spark plug as necessary.

Exciter coil and battery charging coil (on models so equipped) are located under the flywheel. Tighten flywheel nut to 49.0-58.9 N·m (36-43 ft.-lbs.). Flywheel nut has right-hand threads.

To test exciter coil, disconnect black and green exciter coil wires between CDI module and stator plate. Refer to Fig. T4-28. Connect a suitable ohmmeter between black and green wires. Exciter coil can be considered acceptable if resistance is within 224-336 ohms.

To test CDI module, disconnect module leads and refer to chart and wiring diagram in Fig. T4-29. Renew CDI module if test results are not as specified.

NOTE: To prevent damage to CDI module, do not short circuit or disconnect exciter coil or CDI module wires while engine is running. Do not disconnect spark plug wires while engine is running. When testing module, use only an ohmmeter with internal battery rated at three volts or less.

Ignition coil is integrated in the CDI module. To test ignition coil, disconnect spark plug wires at spark plugs and connect a suitable ohmmeter between plug wires. Ignition coil secondary resistance should be 2080-3120 ohms. No provision for testing coil primary resistance is available. Renew ignition coil if secondary resistance is not as specified.

Ignition timing should be 4 degrees ATDC at 700 rpm and 24 degrees BTDC at 5000 rpm. Check alignment of timing marks on port side of stator plate with mating surfaces of crankcase and cylinder block to check timing. Adjust length of stator plate link rod to adjust timing.

COOLING SYSTEM

THERMOSTAT. A thermostat is located in the cylinder block under the cylinder head. Test by submersing thermostat in heated water with a suitable thermometer. Thermostat should begin to open at 50.5°-53.5° C (123°-128° F) and be fully open at 65° C (149° F).

WATER PUMP. A rubber impeller type water pump is mounted between the drive shaft housing and lower unit

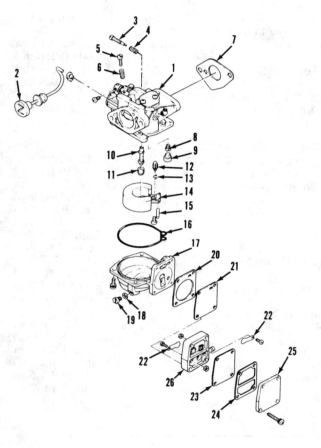

Fig. T4-25—Exploded view of Keihin Seiki Model BCK 21-15 carburetor with integral fuel pump.

1. Body
2. Choke rod
3. Pilot screw
4. Spring
5. Idle speed screw
6. Spring
7. Gasket
8. Slow jet
9. Rubber plug
10. Main nozzle
11. Main jet
12. Inlet needle
13. Clip
14. Float
15. Pin
16. Seal
17. Float bowl
18. Gasket
19. Drain plug
20. Gasket
21. Diaphragm
22. Check valve
23. Diaphragm
24. Gasket
25. Cover

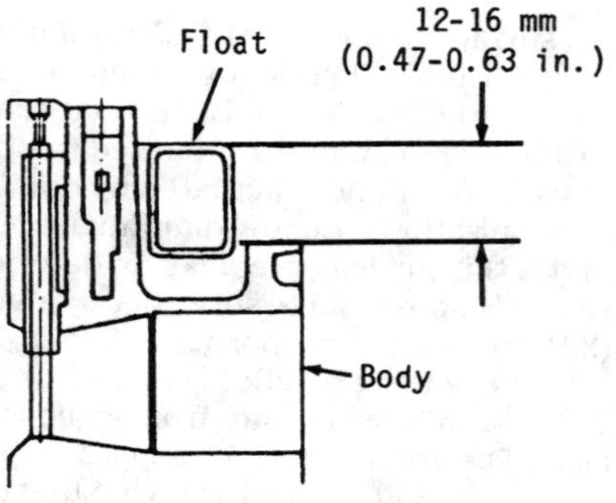

Fig. T4-26—To check float level, invert carburetor and measure from float bowl mating surface to bottom of float as shown.

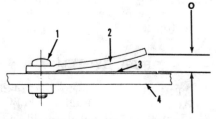

Fig. T4-27—Side view of reed valve assembly. Reed stop opening (O) should be 5.0-5.2 mm (0.197-0.205 in.) measured as shown.

1. Screw
2. Reed stop
3. Reed petal
4. Seat

gearcase. The impeller (3—Fig. T4-30) is driven by key (4) in the drive shaft.

If cooling system malfunction is noted, inspect water inlet for plugging or partial restriction and thermostat for proper operation. Separate lower unit from drive shaft housing to inspect water pump, water passages and sealing surfaces.

Inspect condition of impeller (3), liner (2) and plate (6). Note location of pin in top of liner (2) when installing liner in housing (1). Install seal (10) into base (9) with seal lip facing upward. Rotate drive shaft clockwise (viewed from top) while placing pump housing over im-

peller. Avoid turning drive shaft in opposite direction after water pump is reassembled.

POWER HEAD

REMOVE AND REINSTALL. To remove power head, remove upper cover and disconnect ignition wires, neutral start lock rod, throttle cable, choke rod and fuel hose. Remove six drive shaft housing screws and separate power head from drive shaft housing.

Reinstall power head in reverse order of removal. Make sure crankshaft and drive shaft splines are clean and apply

a suitable water resistant grease to splines. Tighten drive shaft housing-to-power head screws to 7.8-9.8 N·m (6-7 ft.-lbs.).

DISASSEMBLY. Disassemble power head as follows: Remove two screws securing bearing carrier (12—Fig. T4-31) and separate carrier assembly and gasket (8) from crankcase and cylinder block assembly. Remove manual starter assembly and starter pulley. Remove CDI module and carburetor. Using a suitable flywheel puller, remove flywheel and stator plate. Refer to Fig. T4-32 and loosen cylinder head screws in reverse order of tightening sequence. Remove cylinder head and thermostat. Remove inner and outer exhaust covers. Remove ten crankcase screws, separate intake manifold and reed valve assembly from crankcase and carefully pry crankcase from cylinder block using a screwdriver or other suitable tool. Use caution not to damage mating surfaces. A boss is provided on crankcase and cylinder block for prying. Lift crankshaft assembly with pistons and connecting rod assemblies from cylinder block.

ASSEMBLY. Refer to specific service sections when assembling the crankshaft, connecting rods, pistons and reed valves. Make sure all joints and gasket surfaces are clean, free from nicks,

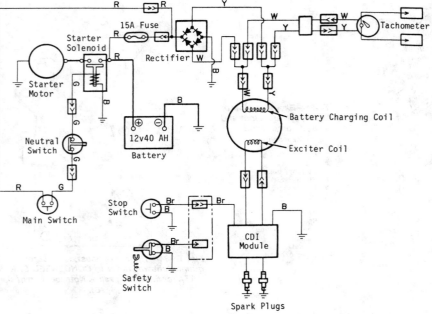

Fig. T4-28—Electrical system diagram on models equipped with electric starter.

B. Black
G. Green
R. Red
W. White
Y. Yellow
Br. Brown

Tester Terminal And Lead Wire Identification		Tester (+) Lead			
		Green	Brown	Black-1	Black-2
Tester (–) Lead	Green		Continuity	Pointer swings once, then infinity	Pointer swings once then infinity
	Brown	Infinity		Infinity	Infinity
	Black-1	Continuity	Continuity		Zero
	Black-2	Continuity	Continuity	Zero	

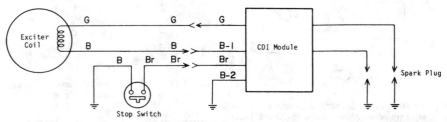

Fig. T4-29—Refer to wiring diagram and chart when testing CDI module. Use an ohmmeter with three-volt or less battery.

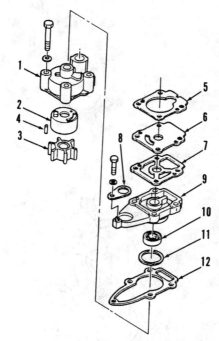

Fig. T4-30—Exploded view of water pump.

1. Housing
2. Liner
3. Impeller
4. Key
5. Gasket
6. Plate
7. Gasket
8. Retainer
9. Base
10. Seal
11. Shim
12. Gasket

burrs, hardened gasket sealant or carbon. Mating surfaces may be lapped to remove high spots or nicks, however, only a minimum amount of metal should be removed.

All friction surfaces and bearings should be thoroughly lubricated with a recommended engine oil during reassembly. Coat crankcase-to-cylinder block mating surfaces with Three Bond 1104-1 or a suitable equivalent gasket sealing compound. Refer to Figs. T4-33 and T4-34 for crankcase and exhaust cover fastener tightening sequences. Refer to CONDENSED SERVICE DATA for torque value. Rotate crankshaft af-

ter tightening crankcase screws and check for binding or unusual noise. If binding or noise is noted, engine must be disassembled and inspected to determine cause and repaired.

PISTONS, PINS, RINGS AND CYLINDER. Refer to CONDENSED SERVICE DATA for service specifications. Pistons and rings are available in 0.5 mm (0.020 in.) oversize. Measure piston diameter at right angle to piston pin 10 cm (3.9 in.) up from bottom of skirt. Cylinder should be bored to 50.50-50.51 mm (1.9881-1.9885 in.) if oversize piston and rings are used.

Piston pins (7—Fig. T4-35) are retained in position by retainers (6). Retainers should be renewed if removed. Install pistons on connecting rods so ''UP'' mark on piston crown is toward flywheel side of engine. Pistons are equipped with locating pins to prevent ring rotation.

CRANKSHAFT AND CONNECTING RODS. Crankshaft, connecting rods, crankpins and crankpin bearings are assembled as a pressed-together unit. The manufacturer recommends that crankshaft should not be disassembled and should be renewed as a unit assembly. Refer to CONDENSED SERVICE DATA for service specifications. Check crank-

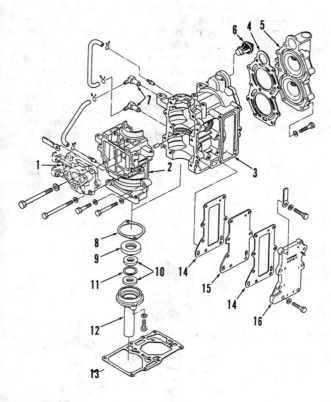

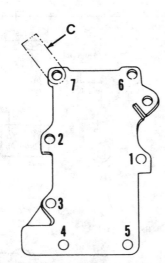

Fig. T4-31—Exploded view of crankcase, cylinder block and related components.

1. Intake manifold
2. Crankcase
3. Cylinder block
4. Gasket
5. Cylinder head
6. Thermostat
7. Check valve
8. Gasket
9. Seal
10. Seal
11. Spacer
12. Bearing housing
13. Gasket
14. Gasket
15. Inner exhaust cover
16. Outer exhaust cover

Fig. T4-34—Tighten exhaust cover screws in sequence shown. Refer to CONDENSED SERVICE DATA for tightening value. Note location of clamp (C).

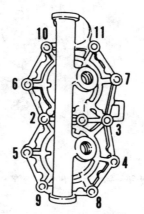

Fig. T4-32—Tighten cylinder head screws in sequence shown.

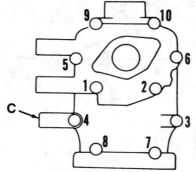

Fig. T4-33—Tighten crankcase-to-cylinder block screws in sequence shown. Refer to CONDENSED SERVICE DATA for torque value. Note location of clamp (C).

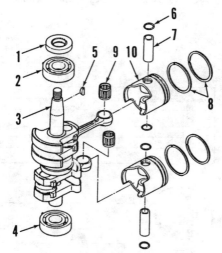

Fig. T4-35—Exploded view of crankshaft assembly, pistons, pins and rings.

1. Seal
2. Main bearing
3. Crankshaft assy.
4. Main bearing
5. Woodruff key
6. Retainer
7. Piston pin
8. Piston rings
9. Needle bearing
10. Piston

shaft runout by supporting outer main bearings in V-blocks. Maximum allowable crankshaft runout measured at points (P—Fig. T4-36) is 0.05 mm (0.002 in.). Connecting rod big end side play should be 0.2-0.4 mm (0.008-0.016 in.). Make sure locating pins on main bearings are properly engaged in notches in cylinder block when installing crankshaft assembly.

MANUAL STARTER

Refer to Fig. T4-37 for exploded view of manual starter assembly. To disassemble starter, remove screws securing housing (12—Fig. T4-37) to power head and lift off starter assembly. Remove rope handle and carefully allow rope pulley (19) to unwind, relieving tension on rewind spring (18). Remove screw (24), friction plate (23), pawls (22), springs (21) and spring (20). Carefully remove rope pulley (19) allowing rewind spring (18) to remain in housing (12).

Inspect all components for excessive wear or other damage and renew as necessary. Reassemble starter in the reverse order of disassembly noting the following: Apply a suitable water-resistant grease to rewind spring, friction plate (23) and shank of screw (24). To preload rewind spring, rotate pulley (19) in counterclockwise direction (viewed from flywheel side). With rope extended completely, rope pulley should still be able to rotate 1/4 to 1-1/4 turns. Apply a suitable thread locking compound to threads of screw (24) and tighten screw to 3.4-3.9 N·m (2-3 ft.-lbs.). If power head is equipped with neutral start interlock device, make sure manual starter is inoperable when lower unit is in gear.

ELECTRIC STARTER

Some models are equipped with an electric starter motor. Models equipped with electric start are also equipped with a battery charging system and neutral start interlock. Refer to Fig. T4-28

for wiring diagram for models equipped with electric start. Minimum allowable brush length is 4 mm (5/32 in.).

LOWER UNIT

PROPELLER AND RUBBER HUB. Lower unit protection is provided by a splined rubber cushion hub in the propeller. Propeller hub is not serviceable. Standard propeller for short shaft models is three-blade with 6.5 inch (165.1 mm) diameter and 8.5 inch (215.9 mm) pitch. Standard propeller for long shaft models is three-blade with 6.5 inch (165.1 mm) diameter and 7.5 inch (190.5 mm) pitch. Various propellers are available from the manufacturer to obtain optimum performance depending on outboard usage. Select propeller to allow a properly tuned and adjusted engine to operate within the recommended limit of 4500-5000 rpm at wide open throttle.

R&R AND OVERHAUL. To remove lower unit, drive out lower roll pin (3—Fig. T4-39) from upper and lower shift rod coupler (1) as shown in Fig. T4-40. Drain gearcase lubricant, remove four

gearcase-to-drive shaft housing screws and separate gearcase assembly from drive shaft housing. Remove propeller (28—Fig. T4-38) and spacer (27). Remove two screws securing bearing carrier (25) and pull propeller shaft assembly from gearcase. To disassemble propeller shaft, lightly press in push rod (37) and drive out pin (34), then remove dog clutch (35), push rod (37), spring seat (36) and spring (33). Remove water pump housing (1), impeller (3), key (14) and plate (5). Remove screw securing retainer (8) and lift off water pump base (7), drive shaft (12) and lower shift rod (12—Fig. T4-39) as an assembly. Remove pinion gear (20—Fig. T4-38), forward gear (38) and shim (39) from gearcase.

Inspect all components for excessive wear or other damage and renew as necessary. Renew all seals, "O" rings and gaskets. Clearance between inside diameter of forward gear (38) and propeller shaft (32) should be 0.03-0.058 mm (0.0012-0.0023 in.). Renew forward gear (38) if clearance exceeds 0.1 mm (0.004 in.). Make sure forward gear bearing surface of propeller shaft (32) is not excessively worn. Clearance between propeller shaft (32) and inside di-

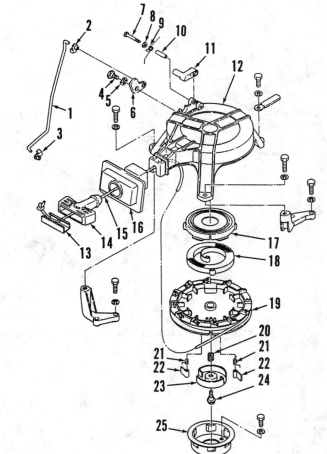

Fig. T4-37—Exploded view of manual rewind starter.

1. Neutral start interlock rod
2. Retainer
3. Retainer
4. Screw
5. Wave washer
6. Cam
7. Screw
8. Washer
9. Spring
10. Spring
11. Lock lever
12. Housing
13. Rope anchor
14. Handle
15. Rope
16. Rope guide
17. Cover
18. Rewind spring
19. Rope pulley
20. Friction spring
21. Spring
22. Pawl
23. Friction plate
24. Screw
25. Cup

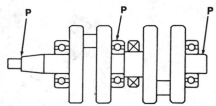

Fig. T4-36—With outer bearings supported in V-blocks, measure crankshaft runout at points (P). Renew crankshaft assembly if runout exceeds 0.05 mm (0.002 in.).

ameter of bearing carrier (25) bushing should be 0.06-0.09 mm (0.0024-0.0035 in.). Renew bearing carrier (25) if clearance exceeds 0.15 mm (0.006 in.).

Reassemble gearcase in the reverse order of disassembly noting the following: Renew roll pin (34) when installing dog clutch (35) on propeller shaft (32), making sure roll pin (34) does not extend past sides of dog clutch. Apply a suitable water resistant grease to "O"

rings (9 and 11—Fig. T4-39) when reconnecting shift rod (12) to shift cam (6). Renew roll pin (5) and make certain roll pin does not extend beyond sides of cam (6). Use Tohatsu tool 332-72256-0 or equivalent to properly drive needle bearing (16—Fig. T4-38) into gearcase. Backlash between forward gear (38) and pinion gear (20) should be 0.05-0.15 mm (0.002-0.006 in.) with maximum allowable backlash of 0.3 mm (0.012 in.). Adjust backlash by varying thickness of shim (10).

After reassembly, fill gearcase with approximately 320 mL (11 oz.) of the

recommended gear oil. Refer to LUBRICATION section. To adjust shift lever linkage, loosen screw securing detent spring (18—Fig. T4-39) and move shift lever (22) into the reverse position. Retighten screw and make sure lower unit gear engagement is synchronized with the detents on detent lever (16).

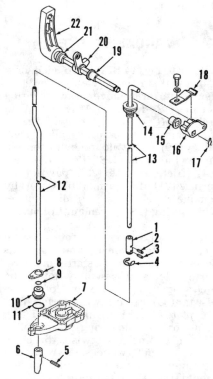

Fig. T4-39—Exploded view of shift control components.

1. Coupler	13. Upper shift rod
2. Roll pin	14. Boot
3. Roll pin	15. Bushing
4. "E" ring	16. Detent lever
5. Roll pin	17. Clip
6. Shift cam	18. Detent spring
7. Water pump base	19. Bushing
8. Retainer	20. Neutral start
9. "O" ring	interlock lever
10. Bushing	21. Seal
11. "O" ring	22. Shift lever
12. Lower shift rod	

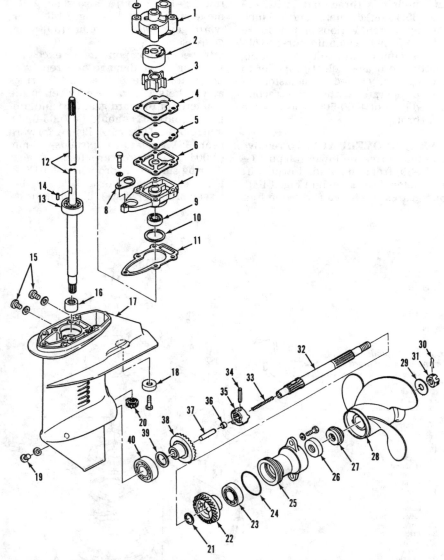

Fig. T4-38—Exploded view of water pump and lower unit gearcase assembly.

1. Housing	15. Plug	28. Propeller
2. Liner	16. Needle bearing	29. Washer
3. Impeller	17. Gearcase	30. Cotter pin
4. Gasket	18. Anode	31. Nut
5. Plate	19. Plug	32. Propeller shaft
6. Gasket	20. Pinion gear	33. Spring
7. Base	21. Thrust washer	34. Pin
8. Retainer	22. Reverse gear	35. Dog clutch
9. Seal	23. Bearing	36. Spring seat
10. Shim	24. "O" ring	37. Push rod
11. Gasket	25. Bearing carrier	38. Forward gear
12. Drive shaft	26. Seal	39. Shim
13. Bearing	27. Spacer	40. Bearing
14. Key		

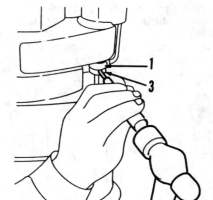

Fig. T4-40—Drive out lower roll pin (3) from shift coupler (1) to disconnect upper and lower shift rods. Refer to Fig. T4-39.

TOHATSU 9.9, 12, 15 AND 18 HP

CONDENSED SERVICE DATA

NOTE: Metric fasteners are used throughout outboard motor.

TUNE-UP

Hp/rpm	9.9/4800
	12/5000
	15/5500
	18/5500
Bore:	
9.9, 12 & 15 HP	55 mm
	(2.16 in.)
18 HP	60 mm
	(2.36 in.)
Stroke	52 mm
	(2.05 in.)
Number of Cylinders	2
Displacement:	
9.9, 12 & 15 HP	247 cc
	(15.07 cu. in.)
18 HP	294 cc
	(17.94 cu. in.)
Spark Plug	See Text
Ignition Type	Breakerless CD
Carburetor Make	TK
Idle Speed (in gear)	800-850 rpm
Fuel:Oil Ratio	50:1

SIZES—CLEARANCES

Piston Ring End Gap	0.20-0.40 mm
	(0.008-0.016 in.)
Piston Ring Side Clearance:	
Top	0.03-0.07 mm
	(0.0012-0.0028 in.)
Bottom	0.02-0.06 mm
	(0.0008-0.0024 in.)
Piston Clearance	0.05-0.09 mm
	(0.0020-0.0035 in.)
Piston Pin Clearance in Piston	0.013-0.030 mm
	(0.0005-0.0012 in.)

SIZES—CLEARANCES CONT.

Connecting Rod Side Clearance:	
Standard	0.2-0.4 mm
	(0.008-0.016 in.)
Limit	0.6 mm
	(0.024 in.)
Crankshaft Runout	0.05 mm
	(0.002 in.)

TIGHTENING TORQUES

Crankcase	23.5-25.4 N·m
	(208-225 in.-lbs.)
Cylinder Head	23.5-25.4 N·m
	(208-225 in.-lbs.)
Exhaust Cover	7.8-9.8 N·m
	(69-87 in.-lbs.)
Flywheel Nut	67-88 N·m
	(49-65 ft.-lbs.)
Gearcase	17.6-19.6 N·m
	(156-173 in.-lbs.)
Intake Manifold	7.8-9.8 N·m
	(69-87 in.-lbs.)
Pinion Gear Nut	23.5-25.4 N·m
	(208-225 in.-lbs.)
Standard Screws:	
No. 4	1.2-1.8 N·m
	(11-16 in.-lbs.)
No. 5	2.6-3.5 N·m
	(23-31 in.-lbs.)
No. 6	4.6-6.2 N·m
	(41-55 in.-lbs.)
No. 8	11.2-15.1 N·m
	(99-134 in.-lbs.)
No. 10	22.6-30.9 N·m
	(200-273 in.-lbs.)

LUBRICATION

The power head is lubricated by oil mixed with the fuel. Recommended oil is Tohatsu outboard motor oil mixed at a fuel:oil ratio of 50:1. During engine break-in the fuel:oil ratio should be 20:1 for a period of 10 operating hours.

Lower unit gears and bearings are lubricated by oil contained in the gearcase. Recommended oil is Tohatsu gear oil or a SAE 80 gear oil. Gearcase oil capacity on M12B, M15A and M18A models is 440 mL (14.9 oz.), and on M9.9B, M12C, M15B and M18C models is 300 mL (10.1 oz.). Oil should be changed after initial 10 hours of operation and every 200 hours of operation thereafter.

FUEL SYSTEM

CARBURETOR. Refer to Fig. T5-1 for exploded view of TK carburetor used. Note that on late models, float (19) and float arm (17) are a one-piece unit. Standard main jet (23) size for normal operation is #86 on Model M12B, #110 on Model M15A and #108 on Model M18A. Standard main jet (23) size on Models M9.9B, M12C and M15B is #108 or #120. Standard main jet (23) size on Model M18C is #120. Initial setting of idle mixture screw (11) is 1-1/2 turns open on Model M18C and 1-1/8 to 1-5/8 turns open on all other models. Final mixture adjustment should be performed with engine running at normal operating temperature. Adjust idle speed screw (12) so engine idle speed is 800-850 rpm with lower unit in forward gear. Adjust mixture screw (11) to obtain highest engine speed, then reset idle speed to 800-850 rpm (in gear).

To check float level, remove float bowl and invert carburetor. On models with separate float and float arm, measure from float bowl mating surface to float arm pads (P—Fig. T5-1) as shown in Fig. T5-2. Height (H) of each pad should be 2 mm (0.080 in.). On models with a one-peice float and arm, set float parallel with float bowl mating surface. Bend float arm on all models to adjust.

FUEL PUMP. A diaphragm type fuel pump is mounted on side of carburetor as shown in Fig. T5-1. The fuel pump is operated by crankcase pulsations through an external line (1—Fig. T5-3). Individual pump components are available.

REED VALVE. The inlet reed valves are located on reed plate between inlet manifold and crankcase. The reed petals should seat very lightly against the reed plate throughout their entire length, with the least possible tension. Check seating visually. Reed stop set-

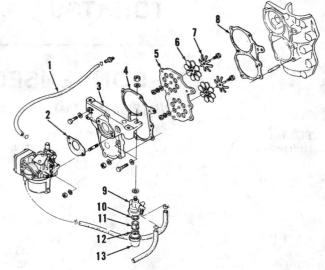

Fig. T5-3—Exploded view of fuel filter, intake manifold and reed valve assemblies. Reed plate (5), reed valve (6) and reed stop (7) shown are used on M12B, M15A and M18A models. Refer to Fig. T5-4 for components used on M9.9B, M12C, M15B and M18C models.

1. Fuel pump pulse hose
2. Gasket
3. Intake manifold
4. Gasket
5. Reed plate
6. Reed valve
7. Reed stop
8. Gasket
9. Fuel filter
10. Gasket
11. Filter element
12. Gasket
13. Bowl

ting should be 3.9-4.1 mm (0.15-0.16 in.) on M12B, M15A and M18A models, and 6-6.2 mm (0.23-0.24 in.) on M9.9B, M12C, M15B and M18C models when measured as shown in Fig. T5-5.

Renew reeds if petals are broken, cracked, warped, rusted or bent. Never attempt to bend a reed petal or to straighten a damaged reed. Seating surface of reed plate should be smooth and flat. When installing reeds or reed stop, make sure that petals are centered over the inlet holes in reed plate, and that the reed stops are centered over reed petals.

SPEED CONTROL LINKAGE. Check to see if full throttle and idle markings on speed control grip are synchronized with bellcrank (9—Fig. T5-6) when it touches ignition stop screws (8 and 10). Adjust length of link (11) to synchronize throttle grip and bellcrank. Shift gearcase to reverse and turn speed control grip toward full throttle. Speed control should not rotate any farther when

throttle roller (5) centerline is aligned with first mark (M) on throttle cam. Adjust reverse throttle stop screw (2) to align roller centerline with mark.

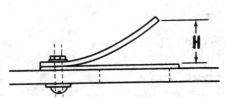

Fig. T5-5—Height (H) of reed stops should be 3.9-4.1 mm (0.15-0.16 in.) on M12B, M15A and M18A models, and 6-6.2 mm (0.23-0.24 in.) on M9.9B, M12C, M15B and M18C models.

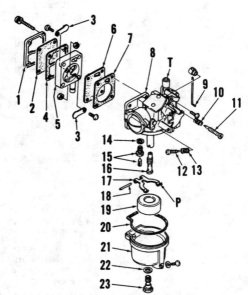

Fig. T5-1—Exploded view of TK carburetor used. Note that on late models, float (19) and float arm (17) are a unit assembly.

1. Fuel pump cover
2. Diaphragm
3. Check valve
4. Gasket
5. Pump body
6. Diaphragm
7. Gasket
8. Carburetor body
9. Rod
10. Spring
11. Idle mixture screw
12. Idle speed screw
13. Spring
14. Gasket
15. Fuel inlet valve
16. Main nozzle
17. Float arm
18. Float pin
19. Float
20. Gasket
21. Fuel bowl
22. Gasket
23. Main jet

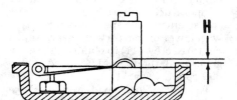

Fig. T5-2—With carburetor body inverted on models with separate float and float arm, height (H) of float arm pads above body rim should be 2 mm (0.079 in.). Bend float arm pads to adjust height.

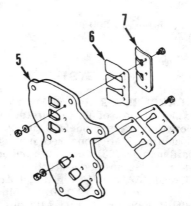

Fig. T5-4—Exploded view of reed plate (5), reed valve (6) and reed stop (7) used on M9.9B, M12C, M15B and M18C models.

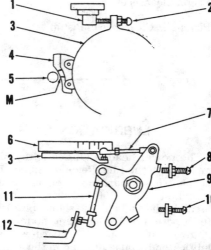

Fig. T5-6—Drawings of speed control linkage. Refer to text for adjustment.

1. Reverse speed stop
2. Reverse speed stop screw
3. Speed control ring
4. Throttle cam
5. Throttle roller
6. Stator plate
7. Link
8. Full advance stop screw
9. Bellcrank
10. Idle speed ignition stop screw
11. Link
12. Speed control shaft

IGNITION

All models are equipped with a breakerless capacitor discharge ignition system. The ignition exciter, trigger and lighting coils are located under the flywheel. Flywheel nut has left-hand threads. Tighten flywheel nut to 69-88 N·m (51-65 ft.-lbs.).

Standard spark plug on M12B, M15A and M18A models is NGK B7HS with an electrode gap of 0.6-0.7 mm (0.024-0.028 in.). Standard spark plug on M9.9B, M12C, M15B and M18C models is NGK B7HS-10 with an electrode gap of 0.9-1.0 mm (0.035-0.040 in.).

Early models are equipped with ignition system manufactured by Lida Electric Company. On Model M12B after serial number 32490, Model M15A after serial number 51975 and Model M18A after serial number 12405, ignition system manufactured by Kokusan Denki Company is used. A later design ignition system manufactured by Kokusan is used on Model M9.9B after serial number 96045, Model M12C after serial number 51685, Model M15B after serial number 72540 and Model M18C after serial number 34730. On early design Kokusan ignition system, CDI module and ignition coil are a unit assembly. On late design Kokusan ignition system, ignition coil is separate from CDI module.

Disconnect three-wire connector between stator plate and CDI module and check ignition components with a suitable ohmmeter.

NOTE: When testing CDI module, the manufacturer recommends using an ohmmeter with internal battery rated at three volts maximum to prevent damage to CDI module.

On early models, connect one tester lead to stator plate. Connect remaining tester lead to red stator lead to test exciter coil. Exciter coil resistance should be 290 ohms for Lida Electric exciter coil and 275 ohms on early Kokusan exciter coil. To test trigger coil, connect tester leads between stator plate and blue stator lead. Trigger coil resistance should be 20 ohms on Lida Electric trigger coil and 30 ohms on early Kokusan trigger coil. To test lighting coil, connect tester leads between yellow stator leads. Lighting coil resistance should be 0.34 ohm for Lida Electric and early Kokusan lighting coils.

On late model Kokusan ignition system (separate CDI module and ignition coil), disconnect three-wire connector between stator plate and CDI module. To test Exciter coil, connect tester between red and black stator leads. Exciter coil resistance should be 280 ohms. To test trigger coil, connect tester between blue and black stator leads. Trigger coil resistance should be 58 ohms. To test lighting coil, connect tester between yellow and white stator leads. Lighting coil resistance should be 0.33 ohm. Test ignition coil primary winding resistance by connecting tester between black coil lead with yellow tracer and coil ground. Primary winding resistance should be 0.29 ohm. Connect tester leads between coil high tension leads to check coil secondary resistance. Ignition coil secondary winding resistance should be 5000 ohms.

To check the CDI module, disconnect module leads and refer to charts in Figs. T5-10, T5-11 and T5-12 for correct tester connections and desired test results.

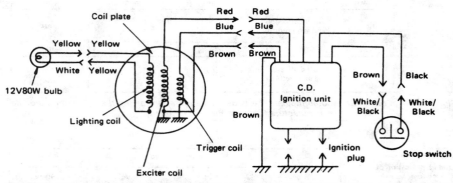

Fig. T5-8—Wiring schematic typical of early models. Refer to Fig. T5-9 for later models ignition circuit. Refer to Fig. T5-23 for wiring diagram on models equipped with electric starter.

Fig. T5-7—Exploded view of ignition components typical of all early models. Later models are similar except ignition coil is separate from CD module (7).

1. Flywheel
2. Trigger coil
3. Exciter coil
4. Lighting coil
5. Stator plate
6. Throttle cam
7. CD module
8. Ignition switch

Fig. T5-9—Wiring schematic typical of models equipped with late design Kokusan ignition system. Early Kokusan ignition system is similar except CDI module and ignition coil are a unit assembly.

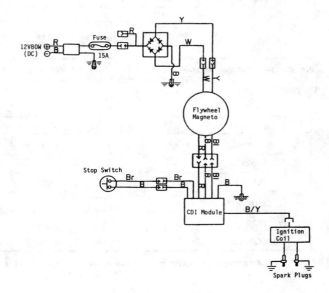

IGNITION TIMING. To adjust ignition timing, disconnect lower link (11—Fig. T5-6). Measure length of upper link (7) from back of locknut to center of bent end as shown in Fig. T5-13. Length should be 47 mm (1.85 in.) and is adjusted by turning link end. Rotate bellcrank (9—Fig. T5-6) so it contacts maximum advance screw (8) and note which timing mark on stator plate (6) is aligned with crankcase and cylinder block mating surface. Maximum advance ignition timing should be as follows:

HP	Serial Number	BTDC
9.9	Prior to 96046	16.5°-19.5°
	After 96045	20.5°-23.5°
12	Prior to 51686	16.5°-19.5°
	After 51685	20.5°-23.5°
15	60001-61250	20.5°-23.5°
	61251-62540	16.5°-19.5°
	After 72540	20.5°-23.5°
18	Prior to 21301	23.5°-26.5°
	After 21300	20.5°-23.5°

Turn maximum advance screw (8) to adjust timing. Rotate bellcrank (9) so it contacts idle speed ignition timing screw (10). Idle speed ignition timing should be 0-2 degrees ATDC on models prior to 1988 and 4-5 degrees ATDC on 1988 and later models. Turn idle speed ignition timing screw (10) to adjust timing.

COOLING SYSTEM

THERMOSTAT. A thermostat (32—Fig. T5-14) is located in the cylinder head. Thermostat should begin opening at 50.5°-53.5° C (123°-128° F) and should be fully open at 65° C (149° F).

WATER PUMP. A rubber impeller type water pump is mounted between the drive shaft housing and gearcase. The impeller is driven by a Woodruff key in the drive shaft.

Whenever cooling problems are encountered, check water inlet for plugging or partial restriction and thermostat for proper operation, then if not corrected, remove gearcase and check condition of water pump, water passages and sealing surfaces.

When water pump is disassembled, check condition of impeller (7—Fig. T5-25), liner (6) and plate (8). Note locating pin in top of liner (6) when installing liner in pump housing. Turn drive shaft clockwise (viewed from top) while placing pump housing over impeller. Avoid turning drive shaft in opposite direction when water pump is assembled.

POWER HEAD

REMOVE AND REINSTALL. To remove power head, remove upper motor cover and disconnect ignition wires. Detach throttle safety stop link and disconnect fuel feed line from filter. Detach lower speed control link (11—Fig. T5-6) from speed control lever (12). Unscrew cap screws securing power head to drive shaft housing. Lift power head off drive shaft housing while also disengaging choke control knob and lever.

To install power head, reverse removal procedure. Apply water resistant grease to ends of crankshaft and drive shaft.

DISASSEMBLY. To disassemble power head, detach safety start link and remove rewind starter. Remove electric starter on models so equipped. Remove flywheel (flywheel nut has left-hand threads) and detach upper speed control link (7—Fig. T5-15). Disconnect wires and remove ignition stator plate assembly, retainer plate (P) and speed control ring (R). Remove carburetor and CDI module. Remove the cylinder head while noting cylinder head screws are marked "T." Remove exhaust cover assembly. Remove intake manifold and reed valve assembly. Unscrew center crankshaft seal locating screw (20—Fig. T5-16). Unscrew ten crankcase screws and separate crankcase from cylinder block. Note that there are prying slots provided between crankcase and cylinder block. Remove oil seal housing (1—

Connection of tester leads and identification of CD module leads		Tester (+) lead			
		Brown	Red	Blue	Black
Tester (−) lead	Brown		infinity	infinity	infinity
	Red	Small deflection and soon returns			zero
	Blue	300Ω ~ 1000Ω	infinity		infinity
	Black	Small deflection and soon returns	zero	infinity	

Fig. T5-10—An ohmmeter should indicate the above readings when testing the CD ignition module manufactured by Lida Electric Company.

Connection of tester leads and identification of CD module leads		Tester (+) lead			
		Brown	Red	Blue	Black
Tester (−) lead	Brown		zero	infinity	zero
	Red	Small deflection and soon returns to 220kΩ		infinity	zero
	Blue	zero	zero		zero
	Black	Small deflection and soon returns	Small deflection and soon returns	infinity	

Fig. T5-11—An ohmmeter should indicate the above readings when testing early model Kokusan Denki CD ignition module with integral ignition coil.

NEGATIVE (−) TESTER LEAD	POSITIVE (+) TESTER LEAD				
		BROWN	BLACK	BLUE	RED	BLACK/YELLOW
BROWN		Infinity	Infinity	Infinity	Infinity
BLACK	90Ω		4Ω	50Ω	Infinity
BLUE	150Ω	3Ω		Continuity	Infinity
RED	3Ω	100Ω	100Ω		Infinity
BLACK/YELLOW	Infinity	Infinity	Infinity	Infinity	

Fig. T5-12—An ohmmeter should indicate the above readings when testing CDI module with separate ignition coil.

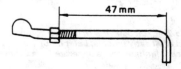

Fig. T5-13—Length of speed control link (7—Fig. T5-6) should be 47 mm (1.85 in.) when measured as shown. Adjust link end as required.

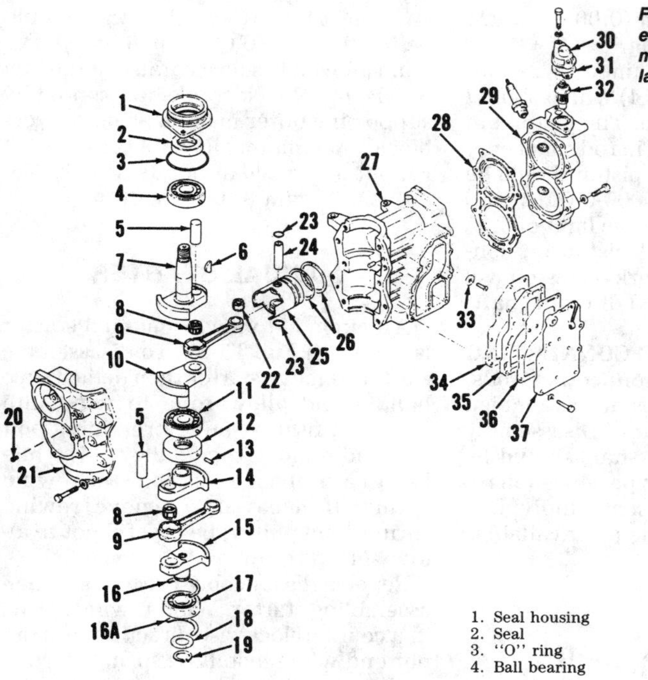

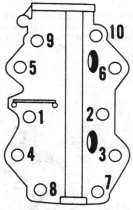

Fig. T5-14—Exploded view of engine assembly typical of all models. Retainer (16A) on later models is a full circle design.

5. Crankpin
6. Key
7. Crank half
8. Roller bearing
9. Connecting rod
10. Crank half
11. Ball bearing
12. Labyrinth seal
13. Dowel pin
14. Crank half
15. Crank half
16. Retainer
16A. Retainer
17. Ball bearing
18. Spacer
19. Snap ring
20. Seal locating screw
21. Crankcase
22. Roller bearing
23. Retaining ring
24. Piston pin
25. Piston
26. Piston rings
27. Cylinder block
28. Head gasket
29. Cylinder head
30. Thermostat housing
31. Gasket
32. Thermostat
33. Anode
34. Gasket
35. Inner exhaust cover
36. Gasket
37. Outer exhaust cover

1. Seal housing
2. Seal
3. "O" ring
4. Ball bearing

PISTONS, PINS, RINGS AND CYLINDERS.

The cylinders are equipped with iron liners which can be bored to accept oversize pistons. Pistons and rings are available in standard size and 0.5 mm (0.020 in.) oversize. Piston to cylinder wall clearance, measured at a point perpendicular to piston pin and 12 mm (0.47 in.) from bottom of piston skirt, should be 0.05-0.09 mm (0.0020-0.0035 in.) with a wear limit of 0.20 mm (0.008 in.). Piston ring end gap should

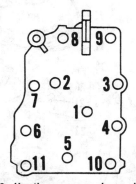

Fig. T5-17—Use the sequence shown above and tighten cylinder head screws to 23.5-25.4 N·m (17-19 ft.-lbs.).

Fig. T5-14) and lift crankshaft assembly out of cylinder block. Individual components may now be serviced as outlined in following service sections.

ASSEMBLY. Before reassembling engine, be sure all joints and gasket surfaces are clean, free from nicks and burrs and hardened cement or carbon. Mating surfaces may be lapped to remove high spots or nicks, however, only a minimum amount of metal should be removed.

All friction surfaces and bearings should be thoroughly lubricated with engine oil during reassembly. Coat mating surfaces with a non-hardening gasket sealer.

Install seal (2—Fig. T5-14) in seal housing (1) so seal lip is toward engine. Install lower bearing retainer (16A) in groove in cylinder block. Install crankshaft assembly in cylinder block while being sure rings properly mate with locating pin in piston ring groove and bearing locating pins mate with notches in cylinder block. Install inner bearing retainer (16) in cylinder block groove. Hole in crankshaft labyrinth seal circumference must point toward hole in crankcase for locating screw. Install seal housing (1) and align mounting hole. Install crankcase but do not tighten crankcase screws. Apply sealer to labyrinth seal locating screw (20) and install in crankcase. Tighten crankcase screws to 23.5-25.4 N·m (17-19 ft.-lbs.). Rotate crankshaft after tightening crankcase screws and check for binding. Complete remainder of assembly by

reversing disassembly procedure. Note tightening sequences in Figs. T5-17 and T5-18 for cylinder head and exhaust cover fasteners. Note in Fig. T5-19 the position of long and short screws securing the intake manifold. Refer to CONDENSED SERVICE DATA for recommended tightening torque values.

Fig. T5-15—View of top of engine with stator plate removed.

Fig. T5-16—View showing location of labyrinth seal locating screw (20).

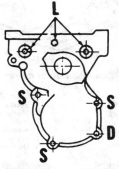

Fig. T5-18—Use the sequence shown above and tighten exhaust cover screws to 7.8-9.8 N·m (69-87 in.-lbs.).

Fig. T5-19—View showing location of long (L) and short (S) screws retaining the intake manifold. A stud (D) is located as shown.

be 0.20-0.40 mm (0.008-0.016 in.). Piston ring side clearance should be 0.03-0.07 mm (0.0012-0.0028 in.) for the top

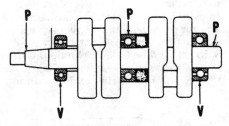

Fig. T5-20—With outer bearings supported in vee blocks (V), maximum runout of crankshaft measured at points (P) must not exceed 0.05 mm (0.002 in.).

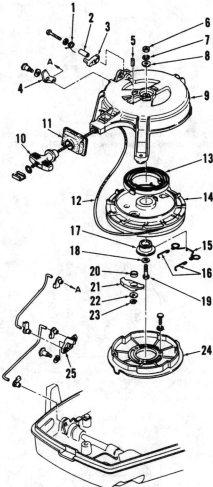

Fig. T5-21—Exploded view of manual starter assembly.

1. Spring
2. Spacer
3. Starter lock
4. Cam
5. Spring pin
6. Nut
7. Lockwasher
8. Washer
9. Starter housing
10. Rope handle
11. Rope guide
12. Rope
13. Rewind spring
14. Rope pulley
15. Spring
16. Links
17. Hub
18. Washer
19. Screw
20. Bushing
21. Pawl
22. Washer
23. "E" ring
24. Starter drive flange
25. Reverse throttle stop

ring and 0.02-0.06 mm (0.0008-0.0024 in.) for the bottom ring.

The piston pin is retained by retaining rings (23—Fig. T5-14) which should be renewed if removed. The piston pin rides in a roller bearing in rod small end. Piston pin clearance in piston should be 0.013-0.030 mm (0.0005-0.0012 in.) with a maximum allowable limit of 0.05 mm (0.002 in.). Install piston on connecting rod so "UP" mark on piston will be toward flywheel end of crankshaft.

CRANKSHAFT AND CONNECTING RODS. Crankshaft, connecting rods, crankpins and bearings are assembled as a pressed together unit. Disassembly and assembly of crankshaft should be performed by a shop experienced in repair of this type crankshaft. Individual crankshaft components are available.

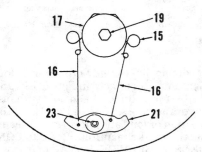

Fig. T5-22—Drawing showing proper installation of starter pawl, links and spring. Refer to Fig. T5-21 for parts identification.

Connecting rod side clearance should be 0.2-0.4 mm (0.008-0.016 in.). Maximum allowable side clearance is 0.6 mm (0.024 in.). Check crankshaft runout by supporting outer main bearings in vee-blocks. Maximum allowable crankshaft runout measured at points (P—Fig. T5-20) is 0.05 mm (0.002 in.).

MANUAL STARTER

An exploded view of manual starter is shown in Fig. T5-21. To disassemble starter, remove starter then detach rope handle and allow rope to wind into starter. Unscrew pulley retaining bolt (19) and remove rope pulley (14) while being careful not to dislodge the rewind spring. If necessary, remove rewind spring from pulley; be careful not to allow spring to unwind uncontrolled.

Reverse disassembly procedure when assembling starter. Wind rewind spring in a counterclockwise direction from inner end when installing spring on rope pulley. Wind rope around pulley in a counterclockwise direction as viewed with pulley installed in starter housing. Refer to Fig. T5-22 for drawing showing correct installation of pawl (21), spring (15) and links (16). Spring (15) must engage the groove in hub (17). Preload the rewind spring by turning the rope pulley three revolutions counterclockwise before passing rope end through rope outlet.

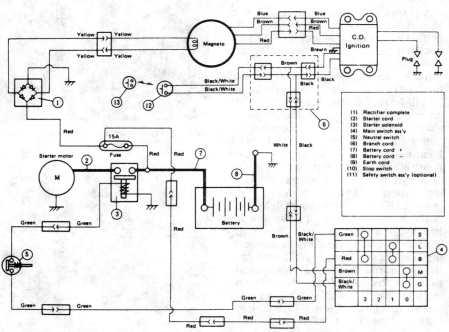

(1) Rectifier complete
(2) Starter cord
(3) Starter solenoid
(4) Main switch ass'y
(5) Neutral switch
(6) Branch cord
(7) Battery cord +
(8) Battery cord −
(9) Earth cord
(10) Stop switch
(11) Safety switch ass'y (optional)

	Green		S
Red			L
			B
Brown			M
Black/White			G
	3 2 1 0		

Fig. T5-23—Wiring schematic on models equipped with electric starter. Note that on late models, CD ignition module and ignition coil are separate components.

ELECTRIC STARTER

Some models are equipped with an electric starter motor. Models equipped with an electric starter are also equipped with a battery charging system and a neutral safety start switch. Refer to Fig. T5-23 for a wiring schematic of electric starter equipped models.

Minimum starter brush length is 4 mm (0.157 in.) and minimum commutator diameter is 19.7 mm (0.775 in.).

LOWER UNIT

PROPELLER AND SHEAR PIN.
Lower unit protection is provided by shear pin (34–Fig. T5-25) on M12B, M15A and M18A models. Be sure correct shear pin is installed for maximum protection to lower unit. Lower unit protection is provided by a clutch in propeller (63–Fig. T5-26) on M9.9B, M12C, M15B and M18C models.

Standard propeller has three blades and is designed for clockwise rotation. Various propellers are available to obtain best performance depending on outboard usage. Desired operating range at maximum engine speed is 4500-5300 rpm for 9.9 and 12 hp models and 4750-5500 rpm for 15 and 18 hp models.

R&R AND OVERHAUL.
To remove gearcase, first disconnect shift rod by driving out upper spring pin (P–Fig. T5-24) in the shift rod connector. Remove four nuts securing gearcase to drive shaft housing and separate gearcase from drive shaft housing. Drain lubricant from gearcase and remove propeller. On Models M12B, M15A and M18A, remove shear pin. Unscrew retaining screws and remove water pump housing (5–Fig. T5-25), impeller (7) and key (15). Remove pump base plate (9); do not lose shims (12) which may adhere to bottom of plate. Unscrew cap (42) or carrier (60–Fig. T5-26) retaining screws and withdraw propeller shaft assembly from gearcase. Remove pinion gear nut

(25–Fig. T5-25) then pull drive shaft (14) out of gearcase; it may be necessary to tap on gearcase with a soft-faced mallet when pulling out drive shaft. Remove pinion gear (24) and forward

gear (28). If necessary, use a suitable puller and remove roller bearing (16) by pulling towards top of gearcase. A suitable puller may be used to remove ball bearing (26). Remove retainer (56) and

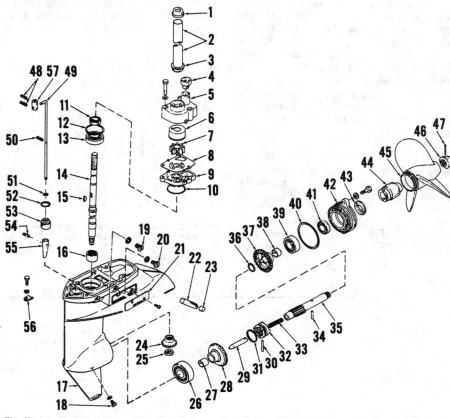

Fig. T5-25—Exploded view of lower unit assembly used on M12B, M15A and M18A models. Lower unit assembly used on Models M9.9B, M12C, M15B and M18C is similar except for components noted in Fig. T5-26.

1. Grommet	15. Key	29. Shift plunger	43. Washer
2. Drive shaft tube	16. Roller bearing	30. Pin	44. Prop hub
3. Grommet	17. Gearcase	31. Retainer spring	45. Propeller
4. Water tube grommet	18. Fill plug	32. Clutch	46. Nut
5. Water pump housing	19. Vent plug	33. Spring	47. Cotter pin
6. Liner	20. Water plug	34. Shear pin	48. Spring pins
7. Impeller	21. Water intake cover	35. Propeller shaft	49. Lower shift rod
8. Plate	22. Strainer	36. Thrust washer	50. Spring pin
9. Water pump base	23. Plug	37. Reverse gear	51. "O" ring
10. "O" ring	24. Pinion gear	38. Bushing	52. "O" ring
11. Seal	25. Nut	39. Ball bearing	53. Bushing
12. Shims	26. Ball bearing	40. "O" ring	54. Spring pin
13. Ball bearing	27. Bushing	41. Seal	55. Shift cam
14. Drive shaft	28. Forward gear	42. Cap	56. Retainer
			57. Coupler

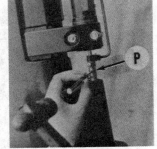

Fig. T5-24—Drive out upper spring pin (P) from coupler to disconnect upper and lower shift rods.

Fig. T5-26—Exploded view of propeller shaft components used on Models M9.9B, M12C, M15B and M18C. Refer to Fig. T5-25 for identification of components except for the following:

58. Spring holder
59. Bearing
60. Carrier
61. Seal
62. Thrust holder
63. Propeller
64. Washer
65. Nut
66. Cotter pin

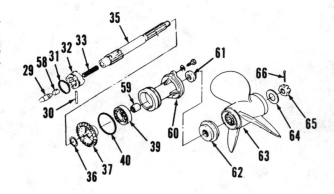

pull lower shift rod and cam assembly out of gearcase.

To remove dog clutch (32) from propeller shaft, remove retaining spring (31) and push out pin (30) while pushing in shift plunger (29).

Inspect components and renew any which are damaged or excessively worn. Clearance between propeller shaft and gear bushings should be 0.018-0.092 mm (0.0007-0.0036 in.) with a maximum allowable clearance of 0.15 mm (0.0059 in.). Bushings (27 and 38) are only available with their respective gears.

To reassemble gearcase, reverse disassembly procedure while noting the following points: Cam side of shift cam (55) and bent end of shift rod (49) must be on opposite sides of shift rod. Pin (54) must not extend past sides of shift cam (55). Apply a suitable grease to shift rod and bushing (53) during assembly. Tohatsu tool part number 362-72246-0 may be used to properly install roller bearing (16). Install dog clutch (32) so groove (G – Fig. T5-27) is towards shift plunger (29 – Fig. T5-25). Backlash be-

tween pinion gear (24) and forward gear (28) or reverse gear (37) should be 0.08-0.13 mm (0.003-0.005 in.) not to exceed 0.35 mm (0.014 in.). Adjust backlash using shims (12). Tighten pinion gear nut (25) to 23.5-25.4 N·m (208-225 in.-lbs.).

After gearcase has been attached to drive shaft housing, synchronize gear engagement in gearcase with detents on

shift plate (6 – Fig. T5-28). Loosen screw (5) and rotate shift plate (6) so correct detent notch is engaged then retighten screw (5).

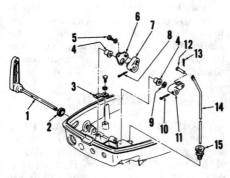

Fig. T5-28—Exploded view of shift control components.

1. Shift control lever	9. Wave washer
2. Seal	10. Cotter pin
3. Detent spring	11. Lever
4. Bushing	12. Pin
5. Screw	13. Cotter pin
6. Detent plate	14. Upper shift rod
7. Lever	15. Grommet
8. Cotter pin	

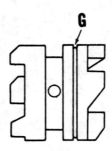

Fig. T5-27 — Install clutch so end with groove (G) is towards shift plunger (29 – Fig. T5-25 or Fig. T5-26).

TOHATSU 25 HP
(Prior to 1985)

CONDENSED SERVICE DATA

NOTE: Metric fasteners are used throughout outboard motor.

TUNE-UP

Hp/rpm	25/5000
Bore	66 mm
Stroke	58 mm
Displacement	397 cc
Number of cylinders	2
Spark plug –	
NGK	B7HS
Electrode gap	0.6-0.7 mm
Breaker point gap	Breakerless CD
Ignition timing (BTDC)	25 degrees
Carburetor –	
Make	Keihin
Model	1000-286-00
Idle speed – rpm	1000-1100 rpm
Fuel:oil ratio	50:1

SIZES – CLEARANCES

Piston ring end gap	0.20-0.35 mm

SIZES – CLEARANCES CONT.

Piston ring side clearance	0.02-0.06 mm
Piston clearance	0.10-0.15 mm
Piston pin clearance in piston	0.001-0.018 mm
Connecting rod side clearance	0.25-0.80 mm
Connecting rod small end shake –	
Standard	1.0 mm
Limit	2.0 mm
Gearcase capacity	260 cc

TIGHTENING TORQUES
(All values in newton meters.)

Crankcase	23.5-25.4
Cylinder head	49-53
Flywheel	79-98
Spark plug	24.5-29.4

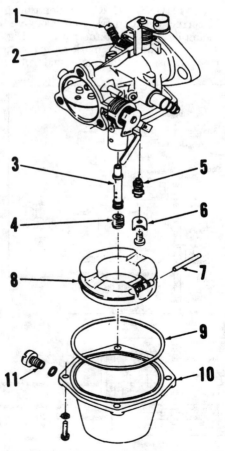

Fig. T6-1—Exploded view of Keihin carburetor used on 25 hp models.

1. Idle mixture screw	7. Float pin
2. Idle speed screw	8. Float
3. Nozzle	9. Gasket
4. Main jet	10. Fuel bowl
5. Fuel inlet valve	11. Drain screw
6. Inlet valve retainer	

LUBRICATION

The power head is lubricated by oil mixed with the fuel. Recommended oil is Tohatsu outboard motor oil mixed at a fuel:oil ratio of 50:1. During engine break-in the fuel:oil ratio should be 20:1 for a period of 10 operating hours.

Lower unit gears and bearings are lubricated by oil contained in the gearcase. Recommended oil is SAE 80 gear oil. Oil should be changed after initial 10 hours of operation and after every 200 hours of operation thereafter.

FUEL SYSTEM

CARBURETOR. An exploded view of the Keihin carburetor used is shown in Fig. T6-1. Standard main jet (4) size is #155 for normal operation. Initial setting of idle mixture screw (1) is 1⅛ turns open. Adjust idle speed screw (2) so engine idles at 1000-1100 rpm with lower unit engaged in forward gear.

Float height is determined by removing fuel bowl and inverting carburetor. Measure from carburetor body rim to bottom of float as shown in Fig. T6-2.

Float height (H) should be 18 mm and may be adjusted by bending tang of float arm.

FUEL PUMP. A diaphragm type fuel pump is mounted on the starboard side of the cylinder block. The pump is operated by crankcase pulsations. Refer to Fig. T6-3 for an exploded view of fuel pump.

REED VALVES. Two pyramid type reed valve assemblies (one for each cylinder) are located between the intake manifold and crankcase. Remove intake manifold for access to reed valve assembly (5 – Fig. T6-4).

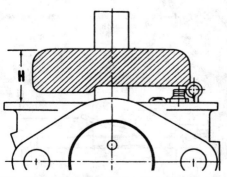

Fig. T6-2—Float height (H) with carburetor inverted should be 18 mm.

Renew reeds if petals are broken, cracked, warped or bent. Do not attempt to bend or straighten reeds. Reed seating surface on reed block (5) should be smooth and flat. Reed stop setting should be 9.0 mm when measured as shown in Fig. T6-5.

IGNITION

All models are equipped with a breakerless, capacitor discharge ignition system. The ignition exciter and trigger coils as well as the lighting or battery charging coil are located under the flywheel. Flywheel nut has left-hand threads. Tighten flywheel nut to 79-98 N·m.

The following checks using an ohmmeter may be made to locate faulty ignition system components. Disconnect three-wire connector between stator plate and CD ignition module, then connect one ohmmeter lead to stator plate. Connect remaining ohmmeter lead to white/red stator lead to check exciter coil. Ohmmeter reading should be 216-324 ohms or exciter coil is faulty. With ohmmeter leads connected to white/red and blue stator leads ohmmeter should read 16-24 ohms or trigger coil is faulty. If the CD ignition module is believed faulty, install a new or good module and check ignition operation.

IGNITION TIMING. Ignition timing is correct when mark near elongated mounting hole on stator plate (8 – Fig. T6-6) is aligned with mark on magneto base. Loosen stator plate and rotate

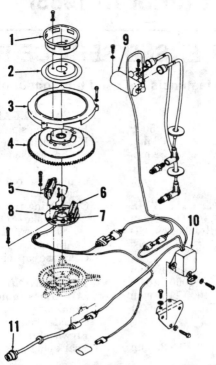

Fig. T6-6—Exploded view of ignition system. Flywheel (4), coils (6 and 7) and stator plate (8) are available only as a unit assembly.

1. Starter cup
2. Cover
3. Gear cover
4. Flywheel
5. Lighting coil
6. Trigger coil
7. Charge coil
8. Stator plate
9. Ignition coil
10. Ignition module
11. Ignition switch

Fig. T6-3—Exploded view of fuel pump.

1. Cover
2. Spring
3. Spring seat
4. Diaphragm
5. Gasket
6. Retainer
7. Check valve
8. Gasket
9. Pump body
10. Gasket
11. Spring
12. Gasket
13. Plate

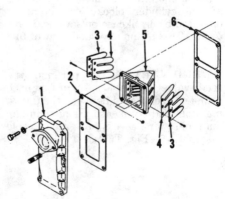

Fig. T6-4—Exploded view of reed valve assembly.

1. Intake manifold
2. Gasket
3. Reed stop
4. Reed valve
5. Reed block
6. Gasket

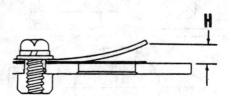

Fig. T6-5—Reed valve stop height (H) should be 9.0 mm.

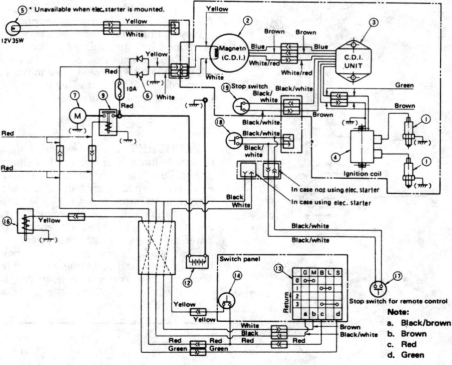

Fig. T6-8—Wiring schematic of electrical system. Components outside ignition system box are only used on electric start models.

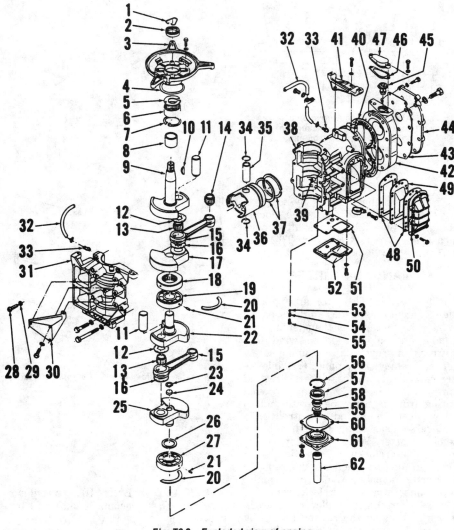

Fig. T6-9—Exploded view of engine.

1. Retainer	17. Crank half	47. Thermostat housing
2. Seal	18. Labyrinth seal	48. Gasket
3. Magneto base	19. Ball bearing	49. Inner exhaust cover
4. "O" ring	20. Retainer	50. Outer exhaust cover
5. Shield	21. Pin	51. Gasket
6. Roller bearing	22. Crank half	52. Exhaust pipe
7. Snap ring	23. Snap ring	53. Check ball
8. Inner race	24. Plug	54. Spring
9. Crank half	25. Crank half	55. Plug
10. Key	26. Shim	56. Snap ring
11. Crankpin	27. Ball bearing	57. Seal
12. Thrust washer	28. Labyrinth seal screw	58. Seal
13. Roller bearing	29. Seal washer	59. Bushing
14. Roller bearing	30. Starter bracket	60. Gasket
15. Connecting rod	31. Crankcase	61. Seal housing
16. Thrust washer		62. Drive shaft tube
	32. Bleeder hose	
	33. Fitting	
	34. Circlip	
	35. Piston pin	
	36. Piston	
	37. Piston rings	
	38. Cylinder block	
	39. Dowel	
	40. Cyl. head gasket	
	41. Ign. coil bracket	
	42. Cylinder head	
	43. Gasket	
	44. Cyl. head cover	
	45. Thermostat	
	46. Gasket	

stator plate to align marks. Ignition timing should be 25° BTDC at 5500 rpm.

COOLING SYSTEM

THERMOSTAT. A thermostat (45 – Fig. T6-9) is located in the cylinder head. Thermostat should begin opening at 50°-54°C (122°-129°F) and be fully open at 65°C (149°F). Thermostat opening at maximum opening should be 3.0 mm.

WATER PUMP. A rubber impeller type water pump is mounted between the drive shaft housing and gearcase. The impeller is driven by a Woodruff key in the drive shaft.

Whenever cooling problems are encountered, check water inlet for plugging or partial stoppage and thermostat for proper operation, then if not corrected, remove gearcase and check condition of the water pump, water passages and sealing surfaces.

When water pump is disassembled, check condition of impeller (6 – Fig. T6-13), liner (5) and plate (7). Turn drive shaft clockwise (viewed from top) while placing pump housing over impeller.

Avoid turning drive shaft in opposite direction when water pump is assembled.

POWER HEAD

REMOVE AND REINSTALL. To remove power head, remove upper motor cover and disconnect ignition wires. Detach throttle wire and disconnect fuel line. Disengage choke control. Unscrew power head retaining nuts and lift power head off drive shaft housing.

To install power head, reverse removal procedure. Apply water resistant grease to ends of crankshaft and drive shaft.

DISASSEMBLY. To disassemble power head, disconnect fuel lines and remove carburetor, fuel filter and fuel pump. Remove electric starter, if so equipped. Remove manual starter, disconnect ignition wires and remove ignition module and ignition coil. Remove flywheel ring gear cover, starter cup and flywheel (flywheel nut has left-hand threads). Remove stator plate. Remove cylinder head and exhaust cover assemblies. Remove intake manifold and reed valve assembly. Remove magneto base (3 – Fig. T6-9) and seal housing (61). Disconnect crankcase bleeder hose. Unscrew labyrinth seal retaining screw (28) located inside crankcase intake passage. Unscrew crankcase screws and separate crankcase from cylinder block. Lift crankshaft assembly out of cylinder block. Individual components may now be serviced as outlined in following service sections.

ASSEMBLY. Before reassembling engine, be sure all joints and gasket surfaces are clean, free from nicks and burrs and hardened cement or carbon. Mating surfaces may be lapped to remove high spots or nicks, however, only a minimum amount of metal should be removed.

All friction surfaces and bearings should be thoroughly lubricated with engine oil during reassembly. Coat mating surfaces with a non-hardening gasket sealer.

The upper main bearing (6 – Fig. T6-9) is located in magneto base (3). Install shield (5) and snap ring (7) so the end gaps are aligned with notch in magneto base bore. Install crankshaft assembly in cylinder block while being sure piston rings properly mate with locating pins in piston ring grooves and labyrinth seal locating pin is inserted in hole in cylinder block. Install bearing retainers (20) then mate crankcase with cylinder block, but do not tighten crankcase screws. Be sure bearing inner race (8) is installed on crankshaft, then install magneto base (3)

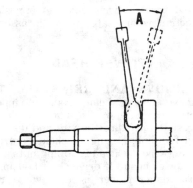

Fig. T6-10—Measure connecting rod small end shake (A) by moving small end side to side. Maximum allowable rod small end shake is 2.0 mm.

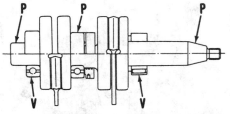

Fig. T6-11—With outer bearing supported in vee blocks (V), maximum runout measured at points (P) must not exceed 0.05 mm.

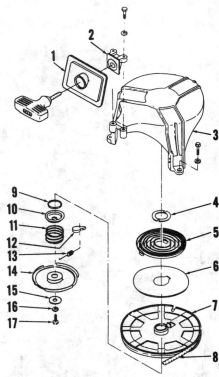

Fig. T6-12—Exploded view of manual starter.

1. Grommet	
2. Rope guide	
3. Starter housing	10. Spring set
4. Washer	11. Spring
5. Rewind spring	12. Pawl
6. Washer	13. Spring
7. Rope pulley	14. Friction plate
8. Rope	15. Washer
9. Washer	16. Lockwasher
	17. Screw

and seal housing (61) with oil groove in seal housing aligned with oil hole in cylinder block; do not tighten magneto base or seal housing screws. Tighten crankcase screws to 23.5-25.4 N·m and install labyrinth locating screw (28) with a seal washer. Tighten magneto base and seal housing screws. Complete remainder of assembly by reversing disassembly procedure. Install intake manifold so carburetor will be directed towards top cylinder.

PISTON, PIN, RINGS AND CYLINDER. The cylinders are equipped with iron liners which may be bored to accept oversize pistons. Pistons and piston rings are available in standard size and 0.5 and 1.0 mm oversizes. Piston to cylinder wall clearance measured perpendicular to piston pin should be 0.10-0.15 mm with a wear limit of 0.20 mm. Piston ring end gap should be 0.20-0.35 mm while piston ring side clearance should be 0.02-0.06 mm.

The piston pin is retained by circlips (34 – Fig. T6-9) which should be renewed if removed. The piston pin rides in a roller bearing in rod small end. Piston pin clearance in piston should be 0.001-0.018 mm. Install piston on connecting rod so arrow on piston crown will point towards exhaust port.

CRANKSHAFT AND CONNECTING ROD. Crankshaft, connecting rods, crankpins and bearings are assembled as a pressed together unit. Disassembly and assembly of crankshaft should be performed by a shop experienced in repair of this type crankshaft. Individual crankshaft components are available.

Determine rod bearing wear by moving small rod end from side to side as shown in Fig. T6-10. Normal side to side movement is 1.0 mm while maximum allowable limit is 2.0 mm. Connecting rod side clearance should be 0.25-0.80 mm.

Check crankshaft runout by supporting outer main bearings in vee blocks. Maximum allowable crankshaft runout measured at points (P – Fig. T6-11) is 0.05 mm.

MANUAL STARTER

Refer to Fig. T6-12 for an exploded view of manual starter. To disassemble starter, remove starter then detach rope handle and allow rope to wind into starter. Unscrew pulley retaining screw (17) and remove rope pulley (7) while being careful not to dislodge the rewind spring. If necessary, remove rewind spring from housing; be careful not to allow spring to unwind uncontrolled.

Reverse disassembly procedure to assemble starter. Wind rewind spring (5) in a counterclockwise direction from outer spring end when installing spring in starter housing. Wind rope around rope pulley in a counterclockwise direction as viewed with pulley installed in housing. Preload the rewind spring by turning the rope pulley 2½ revolutions counterclockwise before passing rope end through rope outlet.

ELECTRIC STARTER

Some models are equipped with an electric starter. Models equipped with an electric starter are also equipped with a battery charging system.

Minimum starter brush length is 12 mm and minimum commutator diameter is 31.5 mm.

LOWER UNIT

PROPELLER AND SHEAR PIN. Lower unit protection is provided by a shear pin (44 – Fig. T6-13). Be sure correct shear pin is installed for maximum protection to lower unit.

Standard propeller has three blades and is designed for clockwise rotation. Various propellers are available to obtain best performance depending on outboard usage. Desired operating range at maximum engine speed is 4800-5500 rpm.

R&R AND OVERHAUL. To remove gearcase, first disconnect shift rod by unscrewing coupler (C – Fig. T6-14). Unscrew nuts securing gearcase to drive shaft housing and separate gearcase from drive shaft housing. Remove propeller and shear pin then drain lubricant. Unscrew cap (52 – Fig. T6-13) retaining screws and withdraw propeller shaft assembly from gearcase. Unscrew water pump retaining screws and withdraw drive shaft assembly from gearcase. To separate upper and lower gearcases unscrew two retaining screws; note that lower screw (31) is located inside lower gearcase. Refer to Fig. T6-13 and disassemble drive shaft and propeller shaft assemblies as required. Remove forward gear (34) and bearing (32); bearing removal will be easier after heating gearcase in 90°C temperature water. Remove retainer (28) and pull lower shift rod and cam assembly out of gearcase.

Inspect components for excessive wear and damage. Drive shaft runout should not exceed 0.5 mm. Inner diameter of bushings (33 and 47) should be 17.03-17.05 mm with a wear limit of 17.08 mm. Bushings (33 and 47) are available only as an assembled unit with

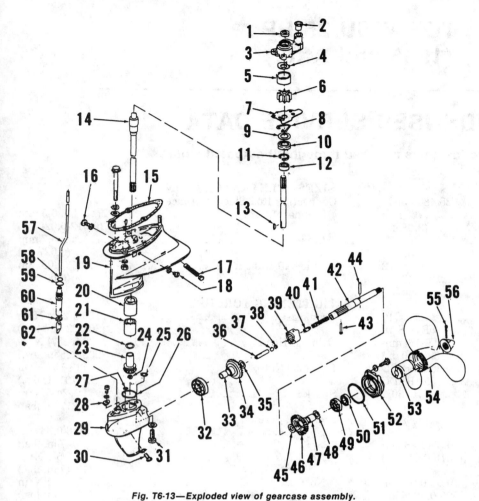

Fig. T6-13—Exploded view of gearcase assembly.

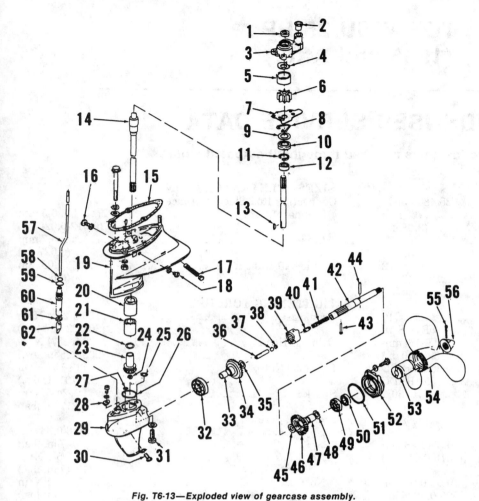

Fig. T6-14—Drawing showing location of shift rod coupler (C) and locknuts (N).

gear. Clearance between gear bushings (33 and 47) and propeller shaft should be 0.035-0.065 mm. Spring (41) free length should be 78.0-78.5 mm with a minimum length of 76.5. Spring pressure should be 71.0 newtons at 64 mm.

To reassemble gearcases, reverse disassembly procedure while noting the following points: Install shift rod assembly so sloping side of shift cam (62) will be towards propeller shaft. Backlash between pinion gear (23) and forward gear (34) or reverse gear (46) should be 0.12-0.15 mm with a maximum of 0.4 mm. Adjust backlash using shims (22).

After attaching gearcase to drive shaft housing, adjust shift rod coupler (C – Fig. T6-14) so gear engagement is synchronized with shift control lever position.

1. Seal	17. Screen	32. Ball bearing
2. Water tube grommet	18. Flushing plug	33. Bushing
3. Water pump housing	19. Upper gear case	34. Forward gear
4. Plate	20. Outer race	35. Thrust washer
5. Liner	21. Bearing	36. Shift plunger
6. Impeller	22. Shim	37. Ball
7. Plate	23. Pinion gear & bearing	38. Thrust piece
8. Retainer	assy.	39. Clutch
9. Shield	24. Snap ring	40. Push rod
10. Seal	25. "O" ring	41. Spring
11. Snap ring	26. "O" ring	42. Propeller shaft
12. Bushing	27. "O" ring	43. Pin
13. Key	28. Retainer	44. Shear pin
14. Drive shaft	29. Lower gearcase	45. Thrust washer
15. Gasket	30. Fill plug	46. Reverse gear
16. Vent plug	31. Screw	47. Bushing

48. Washer	55. Nut
49. Ball bearing	56. Nut
50. Seal	57. Lower shift rod
51. "O" ring	58. "O" ring
52. Cap	59. "O" ring
53. Hub	60. Bushing
54. Propeller	61. Nut
55. Cotter pin	62. Shift cam

TOHATSU 25 HP
(1985 and After)

CONDENSED SERVICE DATA

NOTE: Metric fasteners are used throughout outboard motor.

TUNE-UP

Hp/rpm	25/4800-5500
Bore	68 mm
	(2.68 in.)
Stroke	59 mm
	(2.32 in.)
Number of Cylinders	2
Displacement	430 cc
	(26.2 cu. in.)
Spark Plug:	
Champion	L82C10
NGK	B7HS-10
Electrode Gap	0.9-1.0 mm
	(0.035-0.040 in.)
Ignition Type	Breakerless CD
Ignition Timing	25° BTDC
Fuel:Oil Ratio	50:1

SIZES—CLEARANCES

Piston Ring End Gap	0.33-0.48 mm
	(0.013-0.019 in.)
Piston Ring Side Clearance:	
Top	0.05-0.09 mm
	(0.0020-0.0035 in.)
Bottom	0.02-0.06 mm
	(0.0008-0.0024 in.)
Piston Clearance	0.06-0.10 mm
	(0.0024-0.0040 in.)
Piston Pin Clearance in Piston	0.001-0.013 mm
	(0.00004-0.00051 in.)

SIZES—CLEARANCES CONT.

Connecting Rod Side Clearance:	
Standard	0.3-0.5 mm
	(0.012-0.020 in.)
Limit	0.7 mm
	(0.027 in.)
Crankshaft Runout	0.05 mm
	(0.002 in.)

TIGHTENING TORQUES

Crankcase	23.5-25.4 N·m
	(208-225 in.-lbs.)
Cylinder Head	23.5-25.4 N·m
	(208-225 in.-lbs.)
Flywheel Nut	118-137 N·m
	(87-101 ft.-lbs.)
Spark Plug	24.5 N·m
	(217 in.-lbs.)
Standard Screws:	
No. 3	0.6-0.8 N·m
	(5-7 in.-lbs.)
No. 4	1.5-2 N·m
	(13-17 in.-lbs.)
No. 5	2.4-3.4 N·m
	(22-30 in.-lbs.)
No. 6	4.9-6.4 N·m
	(43-56 in.-lbs.)
No. 8	11.3-15.2 N·m
	(100-135 in.-lbs.)
No. 10	22.6-30.9 N·m
	(200-273 in.-lbs.)

LUBRICATION

The power head is lubricated by oil mixed with the fuel. Recommended oil is Tohatsu outboard motor oil mixed at a fuel:oil ratio of 50:1. During engine break-in the fuel:oil ratio should be 20:1 for a period of 10 operating hours.

Lower unit gears and bearings are lubricated by oil contained in the gearcase. Recommended oil is Tohatsu gear oil or a SAE 80 gear oil. Gearcase oil capacity is 430 mL (14.5 oz.). Oil should be changed after initial 10 hours of operation and after every 200 hours of operation thereafter.

FUEL SYSTEM

CARBURETOR. Refer to Fig. T7-1 for an exploded view of carburetor. Stan-dard main jet (9) size for normal opera-tion is #175 on Models M25A and M25B, #165 on Model M25C prior to serial number 27906 and #155 on Model M25C after serial number 27905. Standard slow jet (10) size for normal service is #75 on Models M25A and M25B, and #88 on Model M25C. Initial setting of idle mixture screw (3) is 5/8 to 1-1/8 turns open on Model M25B and 1-1/4 to 1-1/2 turns open on Model M25C. Adjust idle mixture and idle speed after motor tem-perature has normalized. Idle speed screw (1) should be adjusted so engine idles at 900-950 rpm on Models M25A and M25B, and 850-900 rpm on Model M25C with gearcase engaged in forward gear.

Adjust float level so float is parallel to gasket surface with carburetor inverted and fuel bowl removed. Note clip (14) which secures inlet valve to float.

SPEED CONTROL LINKAGE. Car-buretor throttle opening and ignition timing are synchronized by the speed control linkage so the carburetor throt-tle valve is opened as the ignition timing is advanced.

To adjust speed control linkage, disconnect lower link (7—Fig. T7-2) and rotate bellcrank so "S" mark on throttle cam (4) is aligned with center of throttle lever roller (7—Fig. T7-1). Rotate speed control grip to "START" position. Ad-just length of lower link (7—Fig. T7-2) by turning link ends so link can be at-tached to bellcrank and speed control rod (8) without disturbing position of bellcrank or speed control rod. Recheck adjustment and refer to IGNITION TIMING section and check ignition tim-ing.

All models are equipped with a re-verse speed limiting rod (24—Fig. T7-13)

Tohatsu 25 HP (1985 & After)

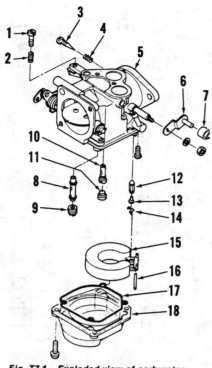

Fig. T7-1 — Exploded view of carburetor.

1. Idle speed screw
2. Spring
3. Idle mixture screw
4. Spring
5. Body
6. Lever
7. Roller
8. Main fuel nozzle
9. Main jet
10. Slow jet
11. Rubber cap
12. Fuel inlet valve
13. Pin
14. Clip
15. Float
16. Float pin
17. "O" ring
18. Fuel bowl

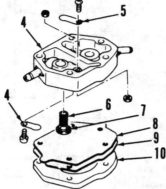

Fig. T7-3 — Exploded view of fuel pump.

1. Cover
2. Diaphragm
3. Gasket
4. Check valve
5. Body
6. Spring
7. Spring seat
8. Diaphragm
9. Gasket
10. Base

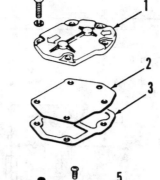

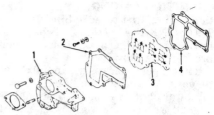

Fig. T7-4 — View of reed valve assembly.

1. Intake manifold
2. Gasket
3. Reed valve assy.
4. Gasket

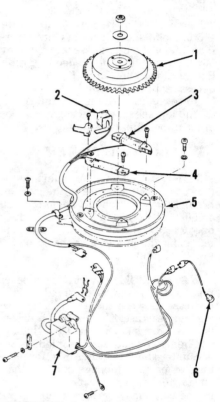

Fig. T7-5 — Exploded view of ignition system.

1. Flywheel
2. Trigger coil
3. Lighting coil
4. Exciter coil
5. Stator plate
6. Ignition switch
7. Ignition module

and lever (21) which prevents excessive engine speed when motor is in reverse gear. With motor in reverse gear, adjust length of rod (24) by turning rod ends (15) so mark "R" on throttle cam (4— Fig. T7-2) is aligned with center of throttle roller.

FUEL PUMP. A diaphragm type fuel pump is mounted on the starboard side of the cylinder block. The pump is operated by crankcase pulsations. Refer to Fig. T7-3 for an exploded view of fuel pump.

REED VALVES. The reed valves are attached to a plate which is located between the intake manifold and the crankcase as shown in Fig. T7-4. Inspect reed valves and renew if cracked, bent or otherwise damaged. Do not attempt to straighten a reed valve petal. Reed valve seating surface of reed plate should be flat. Reed valve is available only as an assembly consisting of reed plate, reed petals and reed stops.

IGNITION

All models are equipped with a breakerless, capacitor discharge ignition system. The ignition exciter and trigger coils as well as the lighting coil are located under the flywheel. The flywheel nut has left-hand threads. Tighten flywheel nut to 118-137 N·m (87-101 ft.-lbs.).

The following checks using an ohmmeter can be made to locate faulty ignition system components. Disconnect three-wire connector between stator plate and CD ignition module, then connect one ohmmeter lead to stator plate. Connect remaining ohmmeter lead to red stator lead to check exciter coil. Ohmmeter reading should be 290 ohms. With ohmmeter leads connected to stator plate and blue stator lead to check trigger coil, ohmmeter reading should be 20 ohms. To check the CD ignition module, disconnect module leads and refer to chart in Fig. T7-6 for desired ohmmeter readings.

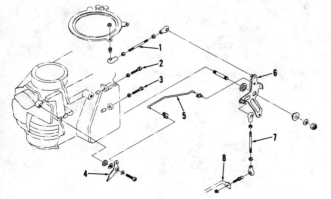

Fig. T7-2 — View of speed control linkage.

1. Stator control link
2. Maximum timing screw
3. Idle timing screw
4. Throttle cam
5. Link
6. Bellcrank
7. Lower link
8. Control rod

Illustrations Courtesy Tohatsu

IGNITION TIMING. To adjust ignition timing, first refer to SPEED CONTROL LINKAGE section and check adjustment of speed control linkage, then proceed as follows:

Rotate speed control grip to full throttle position. The 25 degree BTDC mark on stator plate (5—Fig. T7-5) should be aligned with the mating surface line of the crankcase and cylinder block. If not, turn maximum ignition timing adjustment screw (2—Fig. T7-2). Rotate speed control grip to fully closed position. The 2 degree ATDC mark on the stator plate should be aligned with the mating surface line of the crankcase and cylinder block. If not, turn idle speed ignition timing adjustment screw (3). It may be necessary to adjust length of upper link (1) to set ignition timing for full throttle and idle speed. Recheck ignition timing if upper link (1) is detached.

COOLING SYSTEM

THERMOSTAT. A thermostat (25–Fig. T7-8) is locate in the cylinder head. Thermostat should begin opening at 50°-54°C (122°-129°F) and be fully open at 65°C (149°F). Thermostat opening at maximum opening should be 3.0 mm (0.118 in.).

WATER PUMP. A rubber impeller type water pump is mounted on the gearcase between the drive shaft housing and gearcase. The impeller is driven by a Woodruff key in the drive shaft.

Whenever cooling problems are encountered, check water inlet for plugging or partial stoppage and the thermostat for proper operation, then if not corrected, remove gearcase and check condition of the water pump, water passages and sealing surfaces.

When water pump is disassembled, check condition of impeller (4–Fig. T7-14), liner (3) and plate (5). Turn drive shaft clockwise (viewed from top) while placing pump housing over impeller. Avoid turning drive shaft in opposite direction when water pump is assembled. Tighten pump housing screws in a crossing pattern.

POWER HEAD

REMOVE AND REINSTALL. To remove power head, remove upper

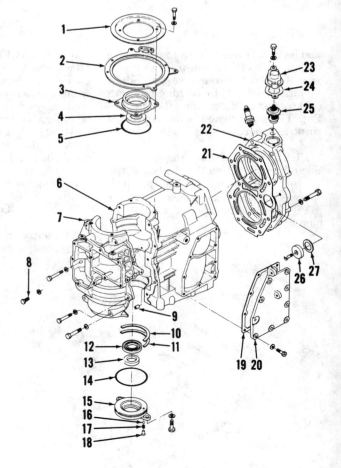

Fig. T7-7—Wiring diagram typical of electric start models. Other models are similar.

1. Stator plate
2. Ignition module
3. Starter safety switch
4. Rectifier
5. Fuse
6. Electric starter motor
7. Solenoid
8. Neutral switch
9. Choke solenoid
10. Choke solenoid switch

B. Black
G. Green
R. Red
W. White
Y. Yellow
Bl. Blue
Br. Brown
B/W. Black with white tracer

Fig. T7-8—Exploded view of crankcase and cylinder block assembly.

1. Retainer
2. Magneto ring
3. Seal housing
4. Seal
5. "O" ring
6. Cylinder block
7. Crankcase
8. Labyrinth seal locating screw
9. Dowel
10. Inner bearing retainer
11. Lower bearing retainer
12. Seal
13. Seal
14. "O" ring
15. Seal housing
16. Check ball
17. Spring
18. Plug
19. Gasket
20. Exhaust cover
21. Gasket
22. Cylinder head
23. Thermostat cover
24. Gasket
25. Thermostat
26. Anode
27. Gasket

Connection of Tester Leads and Ident. of CD Module Leads		Tester (+) Lead			
		BROWN	RED	BLUE	BLACK
Tester (-) Lead	BROWN		Infinity	Infinity	Infinity
	RED	Small deflection and soon returns			Zero
	BLUE	300Ω - 1000Ω	Infinity		Infinity
	BLACK	Small deflection and soon returns	Zero	Infinity	

Fig. T6-6—An ohmmeter should indicate the above readings when testing the CD ignition module.

Illustrations Courtesy Tohatsu

motor cover and disconnect ignition wires. Detach speed control lower link (7 – Fig. T7-2). Detach starter lockout rod from shift shaft, disconnect fuel hoses and disengage choke control. Unscrew power head retaining screws and lift power head off drive shaft housing.

To install power head, reverse removal procedure. Apply water resistant grease to ends of crankshaft and drive shaft.

DISASSEMBLY. To disassemble power head, disconnect fuel lines and remove carburetor, fuel filter and fuel pump. Remove electric starter, if so equipped. Remove manual starter, disconnect ignition wires and remove ignition module. Detach speed control linkage. Remove flywheel, stator plate assembly, retainer (1 – Fig. T7-8) and magneto ring (2). Remove exhaust cover (20) and cylinder head (22). Remove intake manifold and reed valve. Remove upper and lower seal housings (3 and 15). Unscrew labyrinth seal locating screw (8) and crankcase retaining screws. Separate crankcase from cylinder block and lift crankshaft assembly out of cylinder block. Individual components may now be serv-

iced as outlined in following service sections.

ASSEMBLY. Before reassembling engine, be sure all joints and gasket surfaces are clean, free from nicks and burrs and hardened cement or carbon. Mating surfaces may be lapped to remove high spots or nicks, however, only a minimum amount of metal should be removed.

All friction surfaces and bearings should be thoroughly lubricated with engine oil during reassembly. Coat mating surfaces with a nonhardening gasket sealer.

Note the following points when assembling power head: Position lower bearing retainer (11 – Fig. T7-8) in cylinder block groove before installing crankshaft; position inner bearing retainer (10) in cylinder block groove after crankshaft has been installed. Be sure piston rings properly mate with piston ring groove pins, and locating pins in bearings and labyrinth seal engage holes or notches in cylinder block when installing crankshaft assembly in cylinder block. Tighten crankcase screws in steps to 23.5-25.4 N·m (208-225 in.-lbs.) using a crossing pattern; tighten the center screws first. Install seals (4 and 12) in seal housings so lips are toward engine. Install seal (13) in seal housing (15) so lip is away from engine. Tighten cylinder head retaining screws to 23.5-25.4 N·m (208-225 in.-lbs.) using the tightening sequence shown in Fig. T7-10.

PISTONS, PINS, RINGS AND CYLINDERS. The cylinders are equipped with an iron liner which may be bored to accept oversize pistons. Pistons and piston rings are available in standard size and 0.5 mm (0.020 in.) oversize. Each piston ring is located in the piston ring groove by a pin in each ring groove.

The piston pin is retained by retaining rings (37—Fig. T7-9) which should be renewed if removed. The piston pin rides in a roller bearing in rod small end. Install piston on connecting rod so arrow on piston crown will point toward exhaust port.

CRANKSHAFT AND CONNECTING RODS. Crankshaft, connecting rods, crankpins and bearings are assembled as a pressed-together unit. Disassembly and assembly of crankshaft should be performed by a shop experienced in repair of this type crankshaft. Individual crankshaft components are available. Refer to Fig. T7-11 for correct installation of crankshaft bearings and labyrinth seal so locating pins are on correct side.

MANUAL STARTER

Refer to Fig. T7-12 for an exploded view of manual starter. The starter may be disassembled after removing motor

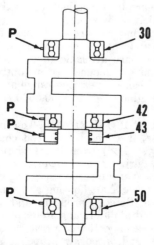

Fig. T7-9—Exploded view of crankshaft, connecting rod and piston assembly.

30. Bearing	42. Bearing
31. Crankshaft half	43. Labyrinth seal
32. Key	44. Pin
33. Crankpin	45. Crankpin
34. Roller bearing	46. Crankshaft half
35. Connecting rod	47. Roller bearing
36. Roller bearing	48. Connecting rod
37. Retaining ring	49. Crankshaft half
38. Piston pin	50. Bearing
39. Piston	51. Shim
40. Piston rings	52. Spacer
41. Crankshaft half	53. Snap ring

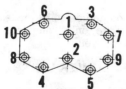

Fig. T7-10 — Tighten cylinder head screws in sequence shown above.

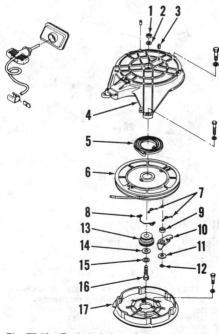

Fig. T7-12 — Exploded view of manual starter.

1. Nut		
2. Washer		
3. Pin	10. Pawl	
4. Starter housing	11. Washer	
5. Rewind spring	12. "E" ring	
6. Rope pulley	13. Shaft	
7. Spring links	14. Washer	
8. Spring	15. Lockwasher	
9. Bushing	16. Screw	
	17. Starter cup	

Fig. T7-11 — When reassembling crankshaft install bearings (30, 42 and 50) and labyrinth seal (43) so locating pins (P) are positioned as shown.

cover, detaching starter lock-out linkage and removing starter from power head. Remove rope handle and allow rope to wind into starter. Remove screw (16) and shaft (13), then carefully lift pulley (6) out of housing while being careful not to disturb rewind spring (5). If rewind spring must be removed care should be used not to allow spring to uncoil uncontrolled. Inspect pawl (10) for wear and freedom of movement. Renew and grease pawl if required.

When assembling starter, wind rewind spring in housing in a counterclockwise direction from outer end. Wind rope around rope pulley in a counterclockwise direction as viewed with pulley in housing. Pawl spring (8) must engage groove in shaft (13). Rotate pulley three turns counterclockwise before passing rope through rope outlet to preload rewind spring.

A starter lock-out mechanism (Fig. T7-13) is used to prevent starter usage when motor is in forward or reverse gear. Adjust length of lock-out rod (13) by turning rod end so starter will operate with motor in neutral gear but not in forward or reverse gear.

ELECTRIC STARTER

Some models are equipped with an electric starter. Models equipped with an electric starter are also equipped with a battery charging system. Refer to Fig. T7-7 for a wiring diagram. Starter

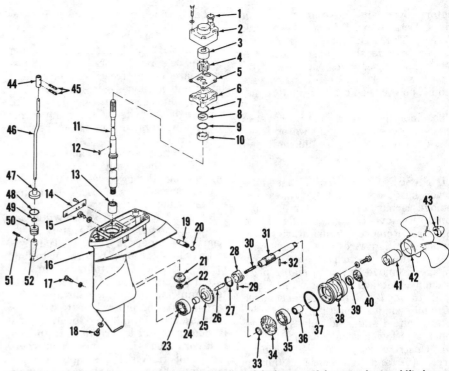

Fig. T7-14 — Exploded view of gearcase typical of all models. Later models use a shorter shift plunger (26) and spring (30) guide. Lower end of drive shaft (11) is fitted with a collar and spring.

1. Bushing	12. Key	21. Pinion gear	31. Propeller shaft	42. Propeller
2. Water pump housing	13. Bearing	22. Nut	32. Shear pin	43. Nut
3. Liner	14. Water inlet cover	23. Bearing	33. Thrust washer	44. Coupler
4. Impeller	15. Vent plug	24. Bushing	34. Reverse gear	45. Pin
5. Plate	16. Gearcase	25. Forward gear	35. Bearing	46. Lower shift rod
6. Pump base	17. Shift bushing	26. Shift plunger	36. Bearing	47. Guide
7. "O" ring	retaining screw	27. Wire retainer	37. "O" ring	48. "O" ring
8. Seal	18. Fill plug	28. Clutch	38. Bearing housing	49. "O" ring
9. Shim	19. Screen	29. Pin	39. Seal	50. Bushing
10. Bearing	20. Plug	30. Spring	40. Spacer	51. Pin
11. Drive shaft			41. Hub	52. Shift cam

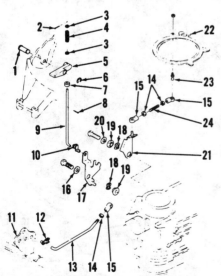

Fig. T7-13 — Exploded view of starter lock-out and reverse speed limiting mechanism.

1. Pin	13. Rod
2. Cotter pin	14. Locknut
3. Washer	15. Rod end
4. Spring	16. Washer
5. Pawl	17. Lever
6. "E" ring	18. Wave washer
7. Collar	19. Bushing
8. Cotter pin	20. Washer
9. Rod	21. Pivot arm
10. Rod end	22. Magneto ring
11. Shift shaft detent	23. Pivot stud
plate	24. Reverse speed
12. Rod end	limiting rod

drive pinion and on some models, brush assembly, are only components serviceable on starter.

LOWER UNIT

PROPELLER AND SHEAR PIN. Lower unit protection is provided by a shear pin (32 – Fig. T7-14). Be sure correct shear pin is installed for maximum protection to lower unit.

The standard propeller has three blades and rotates clockwise. Various propellers are available to obtain best performance depending on outboard usage. Desired operating range at maximum engine speed is 4800-5500 rpm.

R&R AND OVERHAUL. To remove gearcase, disconnect shift rod coupler (44 – Fig. T7-14) from lower shift rod (46) by driving out lower pin (45). Unscrew five cap screws securing gearcase to drive shaft housing and remove gearcase. Remove propeller and shear pin then drain lubricant. Remove water pump assembly. Remove bearing housing (38) and withdraw propeller shaft assembly. Drive out pin (29) to separate clutch (28) and spring (30 from propeller

Fig. T7-15 — Install clutch so end with groove (G) is towards forward gear end of propeller shaft.

shaft. Unscrew pinion gear nut (22) and pull drive shaft (11) from gearcase. Pinion gear (21) and forward gear (25) with bearing may now be removed. Use a suitable puller and remove roller bearing (13) by pulling towards gearcase top. Unscrew shift bushing retaining screw (17) and remove shift components (46 through 52) from gearcase.

Inspect components for excessive wear and damage. To reassemble gearcase, reverse disassembly procedure while noting the following points: Lubricate all "O" rings and seals prior to assembly. Backlash between pinion gear and forward or reverse gear should be 0.08-0.13 mm (0.003-0.005 in.) and is adjusted by varying thickness of shim (9). Apply Loctite during final assembly and tighten pinion gear nut (22) to 23.5-25.4 N·m (208-225 in.-lbs.). Install clutch (28) on propeller shaft so grooved end is towards forward gear (25); see Fig. T7-15. When attaching gearcase to drive shaft housing, tighten fore and aft screws before tightening side screws.

YAMAHA

YAMAHA MOTOR CORPORATION U.S.A., Marine Division
6555 Katella Avenue
Cypress, CA 90630

YAMAHA 2 HP

CONDENSED SERVICE DATA

NOTE: Metric fasteners are used throughout outboard motor.

TUNE-UP

Hp/rpm	2/4000-5000
Bore	39 mm
	(1.54 in.)
Stroke	36 mm
	(1.42 in.)
Displacement	43 cc
	(2.6 cu. in.)
Number of Cylinders	1
Spark Plug – NGK	B5HS
Electrode Gap	0.5-0.6 mm
	(0.020-0.024 in.)
Breaker Point Gap	0.35 mm
	(0.014 in.)
Ignition Timing	See Text
Idle Speed	1150-1250 rpm
Fuel:Oil Ratio	100:1
Gearcase Oil Capacity	45 mL
	(1.5 oz.)

SIZES—CLEARANCES

Piston Ring End Gap	0.1-0.3 mm
	(0.004-0.012 in.)
Piston Ring Side Clearance	0.03-0.07 mm
	(0.0012-0.0028 in.)
Standard Cylinder Bore Diameter	39.0-39.02 mm
	(1.535-1.536 in.)
Max. Allowable Taper	0.08 mm
	(0.003 in.)
Max. Allowable Out-of-Round	0.05 mm
	(0.002 in.)

SIZES—CLEARANCES CONT.

Piston Skirt Clearance	0.03-0.04 mm
	(0.0012-0.0016 in.)
Connecting Rod Big End Side Clearance	0.30-0.60 mm
	(0.012-0.024 in.)
Max. Allowable Crankshaft Runout	0.02 mm
	(0.0008 in.)
Lower Unit Gear Backlash	0.08-0.30 mm
	(0.003-0.012 in.)

TIGHTENING TORQUES

Crankcase	10 N·m
	(7 ft.-lbs.)
Cylinder Head	10 N·m
	(7 ft.-lbs.)
Flywheel	44 N·m
	(32 ft.-lbs.)
Standard Screws:	
5 mm	5 N·m
	(4 ft.-lbs.)
6 mm	8 N·m
	(6 ft.-lbs.)
8 mm	18 N·m
	(13 ft.-lbs.)
10 mm	36 N·m
	(25 ft.-lbs.)
12 mm	43 N·m
	(31 ft.-lbs.)

LUBRICATION

The power head is lubricated by oil mixed with the fuel. Fuel should be regular leaded, low lead or unleaded gasoline with a minimum pump octane rating of 84. Recommended oil is YAMALUBE 100/1 Two-Cycle Lubricant. Normal fuel:oil ratio is 100:1. Mix fuel and oil at a ratio of 25:1 for the first 10 hours of operation.

Lower unit gears and bearings are lubricated by oil contained in the gearcase. Recommended oil is YAMALUBE Gearcase Lube. Lubricant is drained by removing vent and drain plugs in gearcase. Refill through drain plug hole until oil has reached level of top (vent) plug hole.

FUEL SYSTEM

CARBURETOR. Exploded view of carburetor is shown in Fig. Y1-1. Standard main jet (27) size is #96 for normal operation. Jet clip (12) should be in third from top groove on jet needle (13). Inserting clip (12) into a higher groove will lean midrange mixture while insertion into a lower groove will enrich midrange mixture. Throttle valve (14) cutaway is 0.75 mm (0.030 in.). Main nozzle (26) inside diameter is 2.085 mm (0.0821 in.).

To determine float level, invert carburetor body (25–Fig. Y1-2) and measure distance (D) from gasket surface of body to float pads (P) of float arm. Distance (D) should be 3.5-4.5 mm (0.14-0.18 in.).

When installing carburetor on spigot of intake manifold (1–Fig. Y1-4), place "O" ring inside carburetor bore then install carburetor on spigot. Lightly push carburetor towards intake manifold so spigot end is seated against "O" ring and tighten carburetor retaining clamp. Be sure carburetor is in a vertical position. Adjust idle speed screw (20–Fig. Y1-1) so engine idles at 1150-1250 rpm with engine at normal operating temperature.

SPEED CONTROL LINKAGE. The engine speed is regulated by the position of the throttle lever. As the throttle lever is raised or lowered, the carburetor's throttle valve (14–Fig. Y1-1) is operated via throttle rod (1).

REED VALVE. The inlet reed valve unit is mounted on the crankcase side of the intake manifold. The reed valve assembly should be checked whenever the carburetor is removed. Reed petal (2–Fig. Y1-4) should seat very lightly against intake manifold (1) surface throughout entire length. Renew petal if broken, cracked, warped, rusted or bent. Seating surface on intake manifold (1) must be smooth and flat. Reed stop (3) opening should be 6 mm (0.24 in.).

IGNITION

Breaker point gap should be 0.35 mm (0.014 in.) and is adjustable through opening in the flywheel. The flywheel must be removed for breaker point renewal. Tighten flywheel nut to 44 N·m (32 ft.-lbs.).

To obtain the correct ignition timing, proceed as follows: Install a suitable dial indicator in the spark plug hole and place piston at TDC. Properly synchronize indicator face with piston position. Disconnect the white wire leading to the stop switch at the connector located below the magneto base plate. Using a suitable continuity tester, connect one tester lead to the white wire leading to the breaker point assembly and the other tester lead to an engine ground. Rotate the flywheel counterclockwise until the continuity tester indicates the breaker points just close, then note the dial indicator. The dial indicator should read between 0.99 and 1.23 mm (0.039 and 0.049 in.). If not, adjust the breaker point gap. If indicator reads less than 0.99 mm (0.039 in.), in-

crease breaker point gap. If indicator reads more than 1.23 mm (0.049 in.), decrease breaker point gap.

Check ignition coil primary winding resistance by connecting a suitable ohmmeter between coil primary wire (white) and coil body. Primary resistance should be 0.95-1.17 ohms at 20° C (68° F). To check ignition coil secondary winding resistance, connect ohmmeter between coil high tension lead terminal and coil body. Secondary resistance should be 5445-6655 ohms at 20° C (68° F).

COOLING SYSTEM

WATER PUMP. A rubber impeller type water pump is located in the gearcase and mounted on and driven by the lower unit drive shaft.

When cooling system problems are encountered, first check the water inlet for plugging or partial stoppage; then if not corrected, remove the gearcase and overhaul pump. Refer to Fig. Y1-6 for an exploded view of water pump assembly. When reassembling, apply water-resistant grease to water tube seals (1 and 3) and oil seal (7). Note that on 1989 models, double-lip seal (7) has been replaced by two single-lip seals.

POWER HEAD

REMOVE AND REINSTALL. To remove power head, remove power head cover, unscrew six screws securing power head to drive shaft housing and

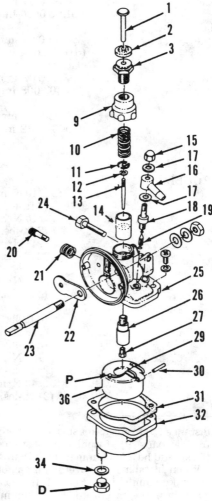

Fig. Y1-1 — Exploded view of carburetor.

D. Drain plug	19. Fuel inlet valve
P. Float pad	20. Idle speed screw
1. Throttle rod	21. Spring
2. Cover	22. Choke valve
3. Nut	23. Choke shaft
9. Cap nut	24. Cap screw
10. Spring	25. Body
11. Retainer	26. Main nozzle
12. Clip	27. Main jet
13. Jet needle	29. Float arm
14. Throttle valve	30. Float pin
15. Nut	31. Gasket
16. Fuel inlet	32. Float bowl
17. Washers	34. Gasket
18. Fuel inlet seat	36. Float

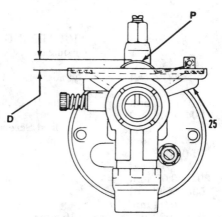

Fig. Y1-2 — With carburetor body (25) inverted as shown, distance (D) from the body's gasket surface to float pads (P) should be 3.5-4.5 mm (0.14-0.18 in.).

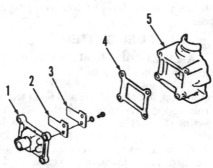

Fig. Y1-4 — Exploded view of intake manifold and reed valve assembly.

1. Intake manifold	
2. Reed petal	4. Gasket
3. Reed stop	5. Crankcase half

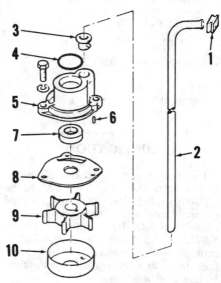

Fig. Y1-6—Exploded view of water pump. Note that on 1989 models, double-lip seal (7) is replaced with two single-lip seals.

1. Seal	6. Dowel pin
2. Water tube	7. Oil seal
3. Seal	8. Plate
4. "O" ring	9. Impeller
5. Pump housing	10. Liner

separate power head from drive shaft housing. Before reinstalling power head, apply water-resistant grease to ends of crankshaft and upper drive shaft. Install new gaskets between power head, exhaust plate and drive shaft housing.

DISASSEMBLY. Disconnect fuel line and remove fuel tank. Disconnect stop switch leads and remove control panel assembly. Remove carburetor, flywheel and magneto components. Remove intake manifold (1–Fig. Y1-4), then remove cylinder head (26–Fig. Y1-8). Unscrew two crankcase screws, separate crankcase half (5) from cylinder block and remove crankshaft assembly from cylinder block. Disassemble crankshaft assembly as required for service.

Refer to the following section for assembly procedure.

ASSEMBLY. Refer to specific service sections when assembling the crankshaft, connecting rod and piston. Install crankshaft assembly into cylinder block being sure pins in outer races of main bearings properly seat in slots of cylinder block. Apply Yamaha Bond No. 4 or a suitable equivalent to cylinder block and crankcase half mating surfaces and position crankcase half on cylinder block. Install two crankcase

screws and tighten in equal increments until a final torque of 10 N·m (7 ft.-lbs.). Install intake manifold with gasket and tighten screws in a criss-cross pattern in equal increments until a final torque of 10 N·m (7 ft.-lbs.). Install cylinder head gasket and cylinder head. Tighten cylinder head screws in a criss-cross pattern to a torque of 5 N·m (4 ft.-lbs.), then to a torque of 10 N·m (7 ft.-lbs.). Reverse disassembly procedure for remainder of assembly.

PISTONS, PIN, RINGS AND CYLINDER. The piston is fitted with two piston rings which should have a ring end gap of 0.1-0.3 mm (0.004-0.012 in.). The piston pin is fully floating and secured by clips (18–Fig. Y1-8). Piston clearance should be 0.03-0.04 mm (0.0012-0.0016 in.). Measure piston diameter at right angle to piston pin approximately 10 mm (0.4 in.) from bottom of piston skirt. Install piston on connecting rod with the side of the piston crown stamped "UP" facing toward flywheel side of crankshaft.

CONNECTING ROD, CRANKSHAFT AND CRANKCASE. The connecting rod rides on a roller bearing around the crankpin. Crankshaft, crankpin, bearing and connecting rod are available only as a unit assembly. Maximum al-

lowable side clearance between rod and crankshaft is 0.5 mm (0.020 in.). Determine rod bearing wear by moving small rod end from side-to-side as shown in Fig. Y1-10. Renew crankshaft assembly if side movement exceeds 2.0 (0.08 in.).

Use a suitable press to remove and install main bearings (7 and 14–Fig. Y1-8). Install bearings on crankshaft with identifying markings facing away from crankshaft. Grease lips of seals (6 and 16) and install with open side towards bearing.

MANUAL STARTER

The manual starter must be disassembled to renew starter rope (2–Fig. Y1-12) or any other internal starter component.

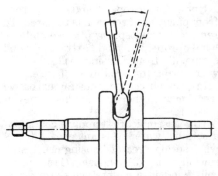

Fig. Y1-10—Move small end of connecting rod side-to-side as shown to determine rod, bearing and crankpin wear. Renew crankshaft assembly if side movement exceeds 2.0 mm (0.080 in.).

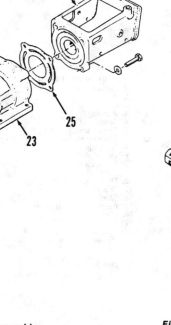

Fig. Y1-8—Exploded view of power head assembly.

Fig. Y1-12—Exploded view of manual rewind starter.

5. Crankcase half	11. Roller bearing	16. Seal
6. Seal	12. Connecting rod	17. Needle bearings
7. Bearing	13. Crankshaft half	18. Clips
8. Crankshaft half	14. Bearing	19. Piston pin
9. Key	15. Spacer	20. Piston
10. Crankpin		

21. Piston rings	
22. Dowel pins	
23. Cylinder block	
24. Plug	
25. Gasket	
26. Cylinder head	

1. Starter housing	6. Spring clip
2. Starter rope	7. Plate
3. Rewind spring	8. Cap screw
4. Pulley	9. Return spring
5. Drive pawl	10. Handle

To overhaul the manual starter, proceed as follows: Remove the engine's bottom and side covers. Remove the screws securing the manual starter to the power head and withdraw.

To disassemble, untie starter rope (2) at handle (10) and allow the rope to wind into the starter. Invert the manual starter and remove cap screw (8), then withdraw plate (7), spring clip (6), drive pawl spring (9) and drive pawl (5). Lift pulley (4) with starter rope (2) from starter housing (1). BE CAREFUL when removing pulley (4) as rewind spring (3) may be dislodged.

NOTE: Should pulley (4) not lift free from rewind spring (3), insert a suitable screwdriver blade through hole in pulley (4) to hold rewind spring (3) securely in housing (1).

Untie starter rope (2) and remove rope from pulley (4) if renewal is required. To remove rewind spring (3), use suitable hand protection and extract rewind spring (3) from housing (1). Allow rewind spring to uncoil in a safe area.

Inspect all components for excessive wear or any other damage and renew if needed.

To reassemble, first apply a coating of a suitable water-resistant grease to rewind spring area of housing (1). Install rewind spring (3) in housing (1) so spring coils wind in a counterclockwise direction from the outer end. Make sure the spring's outer hook is properly secured in starter housing. Wind starter rope (2) onto pulley (4) approximately 3 turns counterclockwise when viewed from the flywheel side. Direct remaining starter rope (2) length through notch in pulley (4).

NOTE: Lubricate all friction surfaces with suitable water-resistant grease during reassembly.

Assemble pulley (4) to starter housing making sure that slot in pulley's drum properly engages hook end in rewind spring (3). Thread starter rope (2) through housing (1) and handle (10) and secure. Install drive pawl (5), return spring (9), spring clip (6) and plate (7). Apply a suitable thread fastening solution on cap screw (8) threads and securely tighten. Turn pulley (4) 2-3 turns counterclockwise when viewed from the flywheel side, then release starter rope (2) from pulley (4) notch and allow rope to slowly wind onto pulley.

NOTE: Do not apply any more tension on rewind spring (3) than is required to draw starter handle (10) back into the proper released position.

LOWER UNIT

PROPELLER AND SHEAR PIN. Lower unit protection is provided by shear pin (16 – Fig. Y1-15). Be sure correct shear pin is installed for maximum protection to lower unit.

Standard propeller size is 184 mm (7¼ in.) diameter with a 114 mm (4½ in.) pitch with clockwise rotation. An optional propeller is offered with 184 mm (7¼ in.) diameter and a pitch of 127 mm (5 in.) or 140 mm (5½ in.).

R&R AND OVERHAUL. To remove gearcase, first remove vent and drain plugs and allow lubricant to drain into a suitable container. Unscrew two screws securing gearcase to drive shaft housing and separate gearcase from drive shaft housing. Remove cotter pin (21 – Fig. Y1-15) and remove propeller. Remove water pump. Unscrew and remove shaft carrier (18), then detach "E" ring (8). Withdraw drive shaft (1) while simultaneously removing pinion gear (7), thrust washer (6) and shims (5). Remove propeller shaft (15) and shims (14). If necessary, use a suitable puller and remove bearing (13) and bushings (4).

Inspect all components for excessive wear and damage. If removed, install three bushings (4) and bearing (13). To check mesh position and gear backlash, make a trial assembly with components (1, 5, 6, 7, 8, 14 and 15). Mesh position is adjusted using shims (5) while shims (14) are used to adjust gear backlash. Gear backlash should be 0.08-0.3 mm (0.003-0.012 in.). Make final assembly by reversing disassembly procedure.

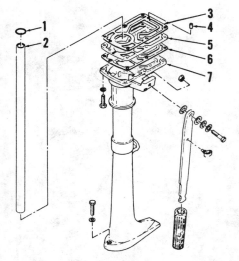

Fig. Y1-14 — Exploded view of drive shaft housing.

1. "O" ring	
2. Drive shaft tube	5. Exhaust plate
3. Gasket	6. Gasket
4. Dowel pin	7. Drive shaft housing

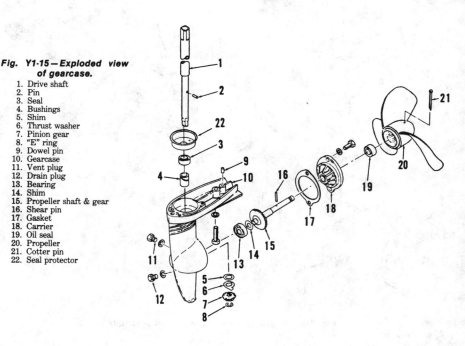

Fig. Y1-15 — Exploded view of gearcase.

1. Drive shaft
2. Pin
3. Seal
4. Bushings
5. Shim
6. Thrust washer
7. Pinion gear
8. "E" ring
9. Dowel pin
10. Gearcase
11. Vent plug
12. Drain plug
13. Bearing
14. Shim
15. Propeller shaft & gear
16. Shear pin
17. Gasket
18. Carrier
19. Oil seal
20. Propeller
21. Cotter pin
22. Seal protector

YAMAHA 3 HP

CONDENSED SERVICE DATA

NOTE: Metric fasteners are used throughout outboard motor.

TUNE-UP
Hp/rpm 3/5000
  (2.2 kW)
Bore.................................46 mm
  (1.81 in.)
Stroke ....42 mm
  (1.65 in.)
Displacement ....70 cc
  (4.3 cu. in.)
Number of Cylinders.............................1
Spark Plug—NGK B6HS-10
  Electrode Gap ....0.9-1.0 mm
  (0.035-0.039 in.)
Ignition Type ....CDI
Idle Speed (in gear) ....1000-1100 rpm
Fuel:Oil Ratio.......................100:1
Gearcase Oil Capacity....................75 mL
  (2.5 oz.)

SIZES—CLEARANCES
Piston Ring End Gap ....0.1-0.3 mm
  (0.004-0.012 in.)
Piston Ring Side
  Clearance:
    Top Ring ....0.02-0.06 mm
      (0.0008-0.0024 in.)
    Second Ring ....0.03-0.07 mm
      (0.0012-0.0028 in.)
Standard Cylinder Bore
  Diameter.....................46.00-46.02 mm
    (1.811-1.812 in.)
Max. Allowable Taper....................0.08 mm
  (0.003 in.)
Max. Allowable Out-of-Round ....0.05 mm
  (0.002 in.)

SIZES—CLEARANCES CONT.
Piston-to-Cylinder Clearance.........0.030-0.035 mm
  (0.0012-0.0014 in.)
Max. Allowable Crankshaft
  Runout ....0.03 mm
    (0.0012 in.)
Max. Connecting Rod Small
  End Shake ....2.0 mm
    (0.079 in.)
Connecting Rod Side Clearance ....0.30-0.95 mm
  (0.012-0.037 in.)

TIGHTENING TORQUES
Crankcase ....6.0-9.5 N·m
  (53-84 in.-lbs.)
Cylinder Head ....6.0-9.5 N·m
  (53-84 in.-lbs.)
Flywheel Nut ....40-50 N·m
  (29-37 ft.-lbs.)
Spark Plug ....25 N·m
  (18 ft.-lbs.)
Standard Screws:
  5 mm ....5 N·m
    (44 in.-lbs.)
  6 mm ....8 N·m
    (71 in.-lbs.)
  8 mm ....18 N·m
    (13 ft.-lbs.)
  10 mm ....36 N·m
    (26 ft.-lbs.)
  12 mm ....43 N·m
    (32 ft.-lbs.)

LUBRICATION

The power head is lubricated by oil mixed with the fuel. Fuel should be regular leaded, low leaded or unleaded gasoline with a minimum pump octane rating of 84. Recommended oil is YAMALUBE 100/1 Two-Cycle Outboard Oil. The recommended fuel:oil ratio for normal operation is 100:1. During the initial 10 hours of operation (break-in), the fuel:oil ratio should be 25:1.

Lower unit gears and bearings are lubricated by oil contained in the gearcase. Recommended oil is YAMALUBE Gearcase Lubricant or a suitable equivalent SAE 90 hypoid gear lube. Lubricant is drained by removing vent and drain plugs in gearcase. Refill through drain plug hole until oil reaches level of top (vent) plug hole.

FUEL SYSTEM

CARBURETOR. Refer to Fig. Y1-25 for exploded view of carburetor and fuel pump assembly. Standard main jet (8) size is #65 on carburetor with stamped mark 6L500 and #68 on carburetor stamped 6L501. Standard pilot jet (9) size is #40 on all carburetors. Initial setting of idle mixture screw (5) is 1 to 1-1/2 turns out from a lightly seated position. Recommended idle speed is 1000-1100 rpm with lower unit in gear and engine at normal operating temperature.

To determine float level, remove float bowl (17) and invert carburetor. Measure distance from carburetor body gasket surface to top of float as shown in Fig. Y1-26. Distance should be 12-16 mm (0.47-0.63 in.). If float level is not as specified, renew inlet needle (11—Fig. Y1-25).

FUEL PUMP. A diaphragm type fuel pump is mounted on the side of carburetor. The fuel pump is operated by crankcase pulsations transferred through passageways in the crankcase, reed valve plate and carburetor body. Passageways must be clear of obstructions for proper fuel pump operation. Renew diaphragms (19 and 22—Fig. Y1-25) if cracking, stretching or other damage is noted. Inspect check valves (21) for cracking, bending or other damage and renew as necessary.

SPEED CONTROL LINKAGE. Ignition timing spark advance is controlled electronically. No adjustment is provided or necessary to synchronize throttle opening and timing advance.

To adjust throttle cable, loosen screw (3—Fig. Y1-27) and reposition core wire (1) in throttle lever (2) as necessary to obtain wide open throttle with twist grip in the "FAST" position.

REED VALVE. Reed valves are attached to intake manifold located between carburetor and crankcase. Reed petals should seat squarely and smooth-

ly along their entire length and should be free of cracks, nicks, tears and burrs. Renew reed petals if petals are bent or warped in excess of 1.5 mm (0.060 in.). Do not attempt to straighten or repair bent or damaged reeds. Reed stop opening should be 3.8-4.2 mm (0.15-0.16 in.) measured as shown in Fig. Y1-28. Carefully bend reed stop to adjust opening. Tighten intake manifold-to-crankcase screws to 6.0-9.5 N·m (53-84 in.-lbs.).

IGNITION

The standard spark plug is NGK B6HS-10 with recommended electrode gap of 0.9-1.0 mm (0.035-0.039 in.). Tighten spark plug to 25 N·m (18 ft.-lbs.).

A capacitor discharge ignition (CDI) system is used. If engine malfunction is noted and ignition system is suspected, make sure spark plug and electrical wiring are in good condition and all electrical connections are clean and tight before proceeding to trouble-shooting CDI system. Be sure to eliminate any obvious problems such as a defective engine stop switch.

Use Yamaha Digital Multimeter YU-33263 or a suitable equivalent ohmmeter to test CDI system. Refer to Figs. Y1-29 and Y1-30 and test CDI system as follows: Separate wiring connectors between magneto base (6—Fig. Y1-29) and CDI module (10).

To test low-speed pulser coil (7), connect tester red lead to green wire with white tracer (G/W—Fig. Y1-30) and black tester lead to black (B) wire. Resistance should be approximately 279-341 ohms.

NOTE: Low-speed pulser coil only affects CDI operation at cranking speed to 1500 rpm. High-speed pulser coil becomes operational at speeds above 1700 rpm. If engine will not start, test low-speed pulser. If engine starts but runs poorly at speeds over 1500 rpm, test high-speed pulser.

To test high-speed pulser coil (5—Fig. Y1-29), connect red tester lead to red wire with white tracer (R/W—Fig. Y1-30) and black tester lead to black (B) wire. Resistance should be approximately 30-36 ohms.

Test charge coil (4—Fig. Y1-29) by connecting red tester lead to brown wire (Br—Fig. Y1-30) and black tester lead to black (B) wire. Charge coil resistance should be approximately 248-302 ohms.

To test ignition coil (11—Fig. Y1-29), disconnect high tension lead at spark plug and coil primary leads. Test coil primary winding resistance by connecting red tester lead to orange (Or—Fig. Y1-30) wire and black tester lead to black (B) wire. Primary resistance should be approximately 0.08-0.12 ohm. Connect red tester lead to spark plug end of high tension lead and black tester lead to black (B) wire to test condition

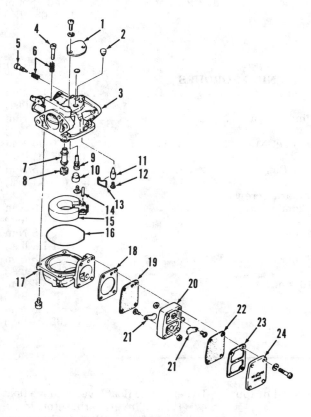

Fig. Y1-25—Exploded view of carburetor with integral fuel pump.

1. Cover
2. Plug
3. Body
4. Idle speed screw
5. Idle mixture screw
6. Spring
7. Main nozzle
8. Main jet
9. Pilot jet
10. Plug
11. Inlet needle
12. Pin
13. Spring clip
14. Float pin
15. Float
16. Seal
17. Float bowl
18. Gasket
19. Diaphragm
20. Pump body
21. Check valve
22. Diaphragm
23. Gasket
24. Cover

Fig. Y1-26—Float level should be 12-16 mm (0.47-0.63 in.) measured as shown. Refer to text.

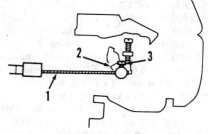

Fig. Y1-27—Adjust throttle cable by loosening screw (3) on lever (2) and repositioning core wire (1). Refer to text.

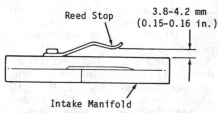

Fig. Y1-28—Reed stop opening should be 3.8-4.2 mm (0.15-0.16 in.) measured as shown. Bend reed stop to adjust opening.

of coil secondary windings. Secondary resistance should be approximately 2080-3120 ohms.

NOTE: Ignition system resistance data is based on ambient temperature of 20° C (68° F). Individual resistance readings at different temperatures using different testers may vary, however, if readings vary greatly from specified limits, component being tested is most likely defective.

To test CDI module, disconnect all module wires and remove CDI module from outboard motor. Use a suitable ohmmeter and refer to chart in Fig. Y1-31. With reference to chart, perform CDI module resistance tests.

Renew any components that are not within manufacturer's recommended limits.

Fig. Y1-31—Use chart and values listed below to test condition of CDI module.
A. Zero
B. Infinity
C. 25,000 ohms
D. 23,000 ohms
E. 120,000 ohms
F. 12,000 ohms
G. 9,000 ohms
H. 4,000 ohms
I. Tester needle swings once, then returns to infinity
B. Black
W. White
Br. Brown
Or. Orange
G/W. Green with white tracer
R/W. Red with white tracer

CDI Module Leads

Pos. Tester Lead / Neg. Tester Lead	W	Br	G/W	R/W	B	Or
W		A	B	B	B	I
Br	A		B	B	B	I
G/W	D	D		C	G	B
R/W	E	E	B		F	B
B	H	H		F		I
Or	B	B	B	B	B	

(Left side label: CDI Module Leads)

Ignition timing is not adjustable but may be checked to confirm proper op-

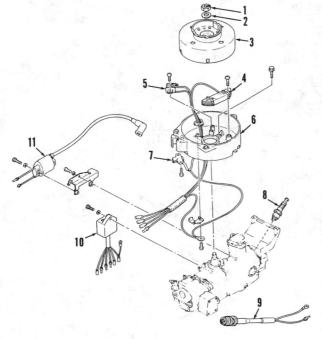

Fig. Y1-29—View identifying CDI system components.
1. Nut
2. Washer
3. Flywheel rotor
4. Charge coil
5. High-speed pulser coil
6. Magneto base
7. Low-speed pulser coil
8. Spark plug
9. Stop switch
10. CDI module
11. Ignition coil

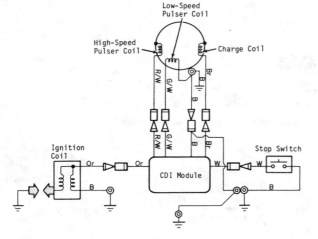

Fig. Y1-30—Wiring schematic of CDI system.
B. Black
W. White
Br. Brown
Or. Orange
G/W. Green with white tracer
R/W. Red with white tracer

eration of the electronic, automatic timing advance system. Connect a suitable tachometer and timing light to engine. Two timing windows are located in bottom of magneto base. Refer to Fig. Y1-32. Timing mark should be visible in slow-speed window at engine speed up to 1500 rpm and visible in high-speed window at speeds above 4500 rpm. If timing mark is not visible in either window, check flywheel rotor for proper mounting or sheared key. If flywheel rotor and key are in acceptable condition and properly mounted, check pulser coils and CDI module.

COOLING SYSTEM

THERMOSTAT. A thermostat is located under thermostat cover in top side of cylinder block adjacent to cylinder head. Refer to Fig. Y1-35. Thermostat should be closed at temperatures below 48° C (118° F) and open at 62° C (144° F). Minimum thermostat valve lift (L—Fig. Y1-33) is 3 mm (0.12 in.).

WATER PUMP. A rubber impeller type water pump is mounted between the drive shaft housing and gearcase. The impeller is driven by pin (7—Fig. Y1-34) in drive shaft.

If cooling system malfunction is noted, check water inlet for plugging or partial restriction and thermostat for proper operation. If cooling system malfunction is still evident, remove gearcase as outlined under LOWER UNIT section and check condition of the water pump, water passages and sealing surfaces.

When water pump is disassembled, check condition of impeller (5), lining (4) and plate (6). When installing housing (1) over impeller (5), rotate drive shaft in a clockwise direction (viewed from top). Avoid turning drive shaft in opposite direction after water pump is reassembled.

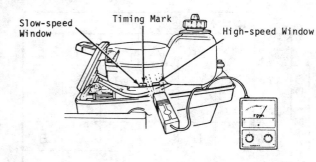

Fig. Y1-32—Timing mark should be visible in slow-speed window (left side of magneto base) at idle speed to 1500 rpm and visible in high-speed window (right side) at above 4500 rpm. Refer to text.

POWER HEAD

REMOVE AND REINSTALL. Remove manual starter. Using a suitable puller, remove flywheel. Refer to Fig. Y1-29 and disconnect magneto wiring and remove magneto base along with ignition components. Disconnect fuel line, throttle cable and remove fuel tank. Remove power head mounting screws and lift off power head assembly.

Prior to reinstalling power head, apply a suitable water-resistant grease to drive shaft splines. Install new gasket (33—Fig. Y1-35). Tighten power head screws to 6-9.5 N·m (53-84 in.-lbs.).

DISASSEMBLY. Remove cylinder head (12—Fig. Y1-35) and exhaust tube (32). Remove carburetor (1) and intake manifold (3). Remove six crankcase screws and separate crankcase (5) from cylinder block (7). Lift out crankshaft and piston assembly from cylinder block. Do not remove bearings (17 and 27) from crankshaft unless bearing renewal is required.

REASSEMBLY. Refer to specific service sections when reassembling the crankshaft, connecting rod and piston. When reassembling power head, make sure all joints and gasket surfaces are clean and free from nicks and burrs. All friction surfaces and bearings must be

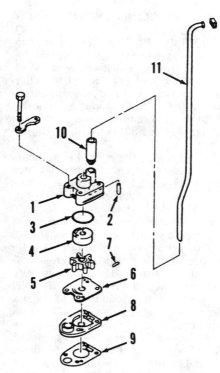

Fig. Y1-33—Minimum thermostat valve lift (L) is 3 mm (0.12 in.).

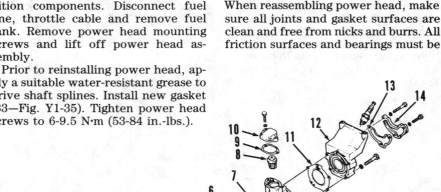

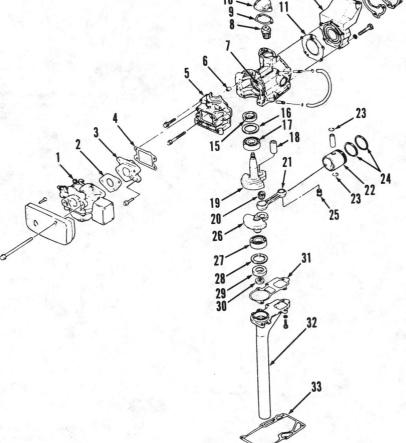

Fig. Y1-35—Exploded view of power head assembly.

Fig. Y1-34—Exploded view of water pump.

1. Housing
2. Dowel pin
3. "O" ring
4. Liner
5. Impeller
6. Plate
7. Impeller drive pin
8. Base
9. Gasket
10. Seal
11. Water tube

1. Carburetor
2. Gasket
3. Intake manifold & reed valve assy.
4. Gasket
5. Crankcase
6. Dowel pin
7. Cylinder block
8. Thermostat
9. Gasket
10. Cover
11. Gasket
12. Cylinder head
13. Gasket
14. Cover
15. Seal
16. Washer
17. Bearing
18. Crankpin
19. Crankshaft half
20. Needle bearing
21. Connecting rod
22. Piston
23. Retainer
24. Piston rings
25. Needle bearing
26. Crankshaft half
27. Bearing
28. Washer
29. Seal
30. Seal
31. Gasket
32. Exhaust tube
33. Gasket

lubricated with engine oil during reassembly. Make sure locating pins on crankshaft ball bearings fit into the slots in cylinder block. Check frequently as power head is being assembled for binding of working parts. If binding or unusual noise is noted, correct cause before proceeding with reassembly.

Crankcase-to-cylinder block sealing surfaces should be lightly and evenly coated with a suitable nonhardening gasket compound. Make sure entire surface is coated, but avoid excess application as compound may be squeezed into crankcase, bearings or passages.

Tighten crankcase, cylinder head, intake manifold and exhaust tube screws in two steps, first to 3.0 N·m (27 in.-lbs.), then to 6.0-9.5 N·m (53-84 in.-lbs.). Tighten crankcase screws following sequence shown in Fig. Y1-36 and cylinder head screws following sequence shown in Fig. Y1-37.

CYLINDER HEAD, CYLINDER, PISTON AND RINGS. Maximum allowable cylinder head warpage is 0.1 mm (0.004 in.). Cylinder head may be lapped if warpage exceeds specified amount. Do not remove more metal than required to true head mating surface.

Bore cylinder to next oversize if cylinder bore is tapered in excess of 0.08 mm (0.003 in.) or out-of-round in excess of 0.05 mm (0.002 in.). Piston-to-cylinder clearance should be 0.030-0.035 mm (0.0012-0.0014 in.). Measure piston diameter at a right angle to piston pin bore, 10 mm (0.4 in.) from bottom of skirt. Oversize piston is available in diameters of 46.25 mm (1.821 in.) and 46.50 mm (1.831 in.).

Top piston ring is semi-keystone shape. Refer to CONDENSED SERVICE DATA for ring service specifications.

Install piston rings with markings facing upward. Make sure ring end gaps are properly positioned around locating pins in ring grooves. Install piston on connecting rod with "UP" mark on piston crown facing flywheel end of engine. Piston pin retainer clips (23—Fig. Y1-35) should be renewed if removed from piston.

CRANKSHAFT, BEARINGS AND CONNECTING ROD. The connecting rod rides on a roller needle bearing around crankpin. Crankshaft, crankpin, bearing and connecting rod are available only as a unit assembly. Maximum allowable side clearance between connecting rod big end and crankshaft is 0.30-0.95 mm (0.012-0.037 in.). Maximum allowable crankshaft runout is 0.03 mm (0.0012 in.). Support ends of crankshaft in V-blocks and measure runout at crankshaft bearings to determine runout. Determine rod, rod bearing and crankpin wear by moving rod small end side-to-side as shown in Fig. Y1-38. Renew crankshaft assembly if side play exceeds 2.0 mm (0.079 in.). Make sure crankshaft bearing locating pins are properly positioned in notches in cylinder block upon reassembly.

MANUAL STARTER

Refer to Fig. Y1-39 for exploded view of manual starter assembly. To disassemble starter proceed as follows: Remove starter assembly from power head. Invert starter, grasp rope and place into notch located in outer periphery of pulley (7). While holding rope in notch, carefully allow rewind spring to unwind, relieving tension on rewind spring (6). Remove screw (12), plate (11), springs (10 and 9) and pawl (8). Lift pulley (7) from housing (5). BE CAREFUL when removing pulley (7) as rewind spring may dislodge from housing. To remove rewind spring (6) from housing (5), place housing upright on a flat surface and tap top of housing until spring falls free and uncoils.

Inspect all components for excessive wear or damage and renew as necessary. New starter rope length should be 165 cm (65 in.).

Prior to reassembly, apply a suitable water-resistant grease to rewind spring, spring area of housing (5) and friction plate (11). Wind rewind spring (6) into housing (5) in counterclockwise direction starting with outer coil. Make sure hook on outer coil of rewind spring is

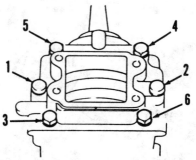

Fig. Y1-36—Tighten crankcase screws in two steps, in sequence shown to final value of 6.0-9.5 N·m (53-84 in.-lbs.).

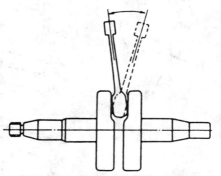

Fig. Y1-38—Renew crankshaft assembly if connecting rod small end side-to-side play exceeds 2.0 mm (0.079 in.).

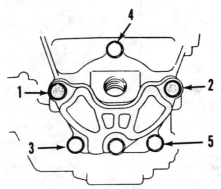

Fig. Y1-37—Tighten cylinder head screws in two steps, in sequence shown to final value of 6.0-9.5 N·m (53-84 in.-lbs.).

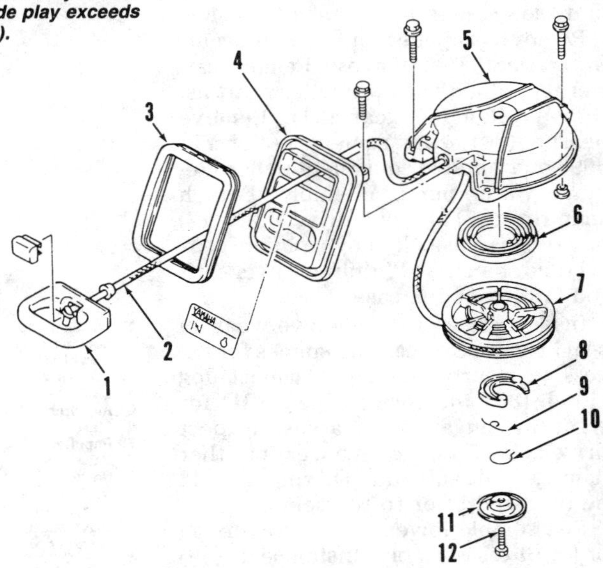

Fig. Y1-39—Exploded view of manual rewind starter.
1. Handle
2. Rope
3. Seal
4. Rope guide
5. Housing
6. Rewind spring
7. Pulley
8. Pawl
9. Spring
10. Friction spring
11. Friction plate
12. Screw

properly engaged in housing. Wind rope 1-1/2 turns counterclockwise (viewed from flywheel side) onto pulley (7), place rope into notch in outer periphery of pulley and install pulley into housing. Make sure inner hook of rewind spring properly engages pulley. Install pawl (8), spring (9), spring (10), plate (11) and securely tighten screw (12). Holding rope in notch of pulley (7), rotate pulley six revolutions counterclockwise and pass rope through rope guide (4) and seal (3). Fasten rope to handle (1), then allow rope to slowly wind into starter.

NOTE: Do not apply more tension on rewind spring than necessary to draw handle snug against housing.

Reinstall starter assembly on power head and tighten securely.

LOWER UNIT

PROPELLER AND DRIVE HUB. Lower unit protection is provided by a cushion type hub in the propeller. Various propellers are available from the manufacturer. Select a propeller that will allow a properly tuned and adjusted engine to operate in the 4500-5500 rpm range at full throttle.

R&R AND OVERHAUL. Note location of all shims for reference during reassembly. Secure outboard motor in a suitable stand, remove vent and drain plugs and drain gearcase lubricant. Remove cover on starboard side of drive shaft housing and loosen shift linkage clamp screw (16—Fig. Y1-40) enough to allow lower shift rod (18) to separate from upper shift rod (15). Do not remove screw (16) completely. Remove four screws securing gearcase and separate gearcase from drive shaft housing.

Remove propeller and screws securing carrier (38) to gearcase. Remove carrier (38) along with propeller shaft assembly. Remove gear (31). Remove bearing (30) using Yamaha puller YB-6096 or a suitable equivalent puller. Remove water pump assembly. Detach snap ring (28) and pull drive shaft (12) out of gearcase. Remove pinion gear (27) and shim (26). Withdraw lower shift rod (18) from gearcase.

Inspect shafts for excessive wear on seal lip contact areas and splines for excessive wear or damage. Inspect dog clutch (33) and forward gear (31) for wear on engagement areas. Inspect drive gears for excessive wear or other damage. All seals and "O" rings should be renewed prior to reassembly.

Reassemble lower unit by reversing order of disassembly. Install seals (39)

into carrier (38) with lips facing propeller. Install original shims (26 and 29). Pinion gear-to-forward gear backlash should be 0.15-1.2 mm (0.006-0.047 in.). Vary thickness of shim (26) to adjust backlash. Shim (26) is available in thicknesses of 2.0 mm (0.079 in.) through 2.3 mm (0.090 in.) in 0.1 mm (0.004 in.) increments. If the proper backlash cannot be obtained by adjusting shim (26),

add or subtract thickness of shim (29). Note that shim (29) is available in original thickness only. Tighten propeller nut to 8-12 N·m (6-9 ft.-lbs.).

Apply a suitable water-resistant grease to drive shaft spines and water tube prior to installing lower unit on drive shaft housing. Tighten lower unit mounting screws to 6.0-9.5 N·m (53-84 in.-lbs.).

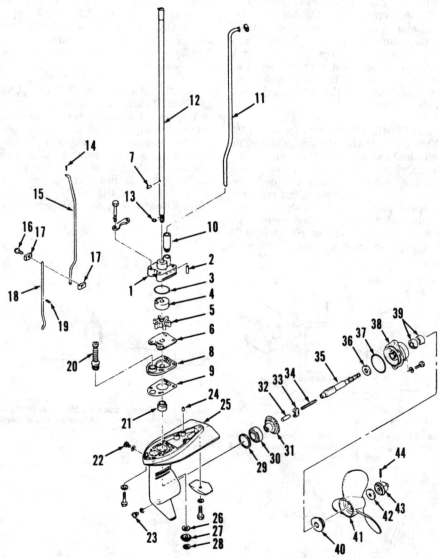

Fig. Y1-40—Exploded view of lower unit gearcase assembly.

1. Water pump housing	15. Upper shift rod	30. Bearing
2. Dowel pin	16. Screw	31. Forward gear
3. "O" ring	17. Clamp	32. Pin
4. Liner	18. Lower shift rod	33. Dog clutch
5. Impeller	19. Pin	34. Spring
6. Plate	20. Boot	35. Propeller shaft
7. Impeller drive pin	21. Bushing	36. Spacer
8. Base	22. Vent plug	37. "O" ring
9. Gasket	23. Drain plug	38. Bearing carrier
10. Seal	24. Dowel pin	39. Seals
11. Water tube	25. Gearcase	40. Spacer
12. Drive shaft	26. Shim	41. Propeller
13. Retainer	27. Pinion gear	42. Spacer
14. Clip	28. Snap ring	43. Nut
	29. Shim	44. Cotter pin

YAMAHA 4 AND 5 HP

CONDENSED SERVICE MANUAL

NOTE: Metric fasteners are used throughout outboard motor.

TUNE-UP
Hp/rpm 4/4500-5500
5/4500-5500
Bore:
4 HP . . . . .50 mm
(1.97 in.)
5 HP . . . . .54 mm
(2.13 in.)
Stroke:
4 HP . . . . .42 mm
(1.65 in.)
5 HP . . . . .45 mm
(1.77 in.)
Number of Cylinders 1
Displacement:
4 HP . . . . .83 cc
(5 cu. in.)
5 HP . . . . .103 cc
(6.3 cu. in.)
Spark Plug – NGK B7HS
Electrode Gap .0.5-0.6 mm
(0.020-0.024 in.)
Ignition Type . . . . .CDI
Idle Speed (in gear) . . . . .950-1050 rpm
Fuel:Oil Ratio 100:1
Gearcase Oil Capacity .105 mL
(3.5 oz.)

SIZES—CLEARANCES
Piston Ring End Gap . . . . .0.15-0.35 mm
(0.006-0.014 in.)
Piston Ring Side
Clearance . . . . .0.03-0.07 mm
(0.002-0.003 in.)

SIZES—CLEARANCES CONT.
Piston Skirt Clearance . . . . .0.030-0.035 mm
(0.0012-0.0014 in.)
Crankshaft Runout—Max . . . . .0.03 mm
(0.0012 in.)
Connecting Rod Small End
Shake—Max . . . . .2.0 mm
(0.079 in.)
Connecting Rod Side
Clearance . . . . .0.2-0.7 mm
(0.008-0.028 in.)

TIGHTENING TORQUES
Crankcase . . . . .12 N·m
(106 in.-lbs.)
Cylinder Head Cover . . . . .8 N·m
(71 in.-lbs.)
Exhaust Cover . . . . .8 N·m
(71 in.-lbs.)
Flywheel . . . . .45 N·m
(33 ft.-lbs.)
Spark Plug . . . . .25 N·m
(18 ft.-lbs.)
Standard Screws:
5 mm . . . . .5 N·m
(44 in.-lbs.)
6 mm . . . . .8 N·m
(71 in.-lbs.)
8 mm . . . . .18 N·m
(13 ft.-lbs.)
10 mm . . . . .36 N·m
(25 ft.-lbs.)
12 mm . . . . .43 N·m
(31 ft.-lbs.)

LUBRICATION

The power head is lubricated by oil mixed with the fuel. Fuel should be regular leaded, low leaded or unleaded gasoline with a minimum pump octane rating of 84. Recommended oil is YAMALUBE 100/1 Two-Cycle Lubricant. The recommended fuel:oil ratio for normal operation is 100:1. During the first 10 hours of operation, the fuel:oil ratio should be increased to 25:1.

Lower unit gears and bearings are lubricated by oil contained in the gearcase. Recommended oil is YAMALUBE Gearcase Lube. Lubricant is drained by removing vent and drain plugs in gearcase. Refill through drain plug hole until oil has reached level of top (vent) plug hole.

FUEL SYSTEM

CARBURETOR. The fuel pump and carburetor are a complete unit. The standard recommended main jet (12—Fig. Y2-1) size is #80 on 4 hp models and #82 on 5 hp models. The standard recommended pilot jet (9) size is #46 on both 4 and 5 hp models. Initial adjustment of idle mixture screw (5) is 1-5/8 to 2-1/8 turns out from a lightly seated position on 4 hp models and 1-3/8 to 1-7/8 turns out from a lightly seated position on 5 hp models. Recommended idle speed is 950-1050 rpm in gear with the engine at normal operation temperature.

To determine the float level, invert carburetor body (3 – Fig. Y2-2) with needle valve (10 – Fig. Y2-1) and float lever (13 – Fig. Y2-2) installed. Measure distance (D) from carburetor body sealing surface to top of float lever hump. Distance should be 1.0-3.0 mm (0.040-0.118 in.) and is adjusted by bending the arms of float lever (13).

FUEL PUMP. A diaphragm type fuel pump is mounted on the side of the carburetor. The fuel pump is operated by crankcase pulsations transferred through passageways in the crankcase, reed valve plate and carburetor body. Passageways must be clear of obstructions or fuel pump will not operate properly. Refer to Fig. Y2-1 for an exploded view of fuel pump.

SPEED CONTROL LINKAGE. The engine speed is regulated by the position

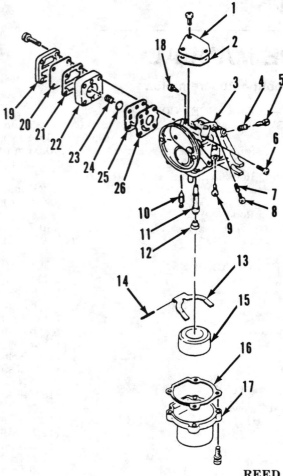

white tracer (B/W) at connector and spark plug boot from spark plug. Remove ignition coil from mounting bracket. Use a suitable ohmmeter and connect red tester lead to black wire with white tracer (B/W) and black tester lead to black wire (B). The primary winding resistance reading should be 0.2-0.3 ohms. Leave black tester lead connected to black wire (B). Connect red tester lead to terminal end in spark plug boot. The secondary winding resistance reading should be 2000-3000 ohms. Use Yamaha tester YU-33261 or a suitable equivalent to perform a power test. Connect tester leads as outlined in tester's handbook. On Yamaha tester YU-33261, a steady spark should jump a 8 mm (0.31 in.) gap with voltage selector switch in "CDI" position. A surface insulation test can be performed using tester YU-33261 or a suitable equivalent and following tester's handbook.

To check source (charge) coil, disconnect black wire (B), brown wire (Br), white wire with red tracer (W/R) and white wire with green tracer (W/G) at connectors leading from magneto base plate. Use a suitable ohmmeter and connect red tester lead to brown wire (Br) and black tester lead to black wire (B). The ohmmeter should read 250-300 ohms.

To check low speed pulser (trigger) coil, disconnect wires as outlined under source (charge) coil. Use a suitable ohmmeter and connect red tester lead to

REED VALVE. A reed valve plate is mounted between the carburetor and crankcase. Reed petals should seat squarely and smoothly along their entire length and should be free of cracks, nicks, tears and burrs. Do not attempt to straighten or repair bent or damaged reeds. If reed stop (S–Fig. Y2-4) is removed, install new retaining screws and apply a thread fastening solution on screw threads. Reed stop height (H) should be 7.0 mm (0.28 in.). Bend reed stop (S) to adjust height (H).

IGNITION

The standard spark plug on both the 4 and 5 hp models is NGK B7HS with an electrode gap of 0.5-0.6 mm (0.020-0.024 in.).

Both the 4 and 5 hp models are equipped with a capacitor discharge ignition (CDI) system. If engine malfunction is noted and the ignition system is suspected, make sure the spark plug and all electrical wiring are in good condition and all electrical connections are tight before proceeding to trouble-shooting the CD ignition system.

Proceed as follows to test CDI system components: Refer to Fig. Y2-5. To test ignition coil, disconnect black wire with

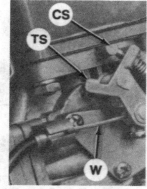

Fig. Y2-3 — View depicting control cable inner wire (W), carburetor stop (CS) and throttle arm stop (TS). Refer to text.

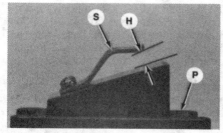

Fig. Y2-4 — View showing reed plate assembly (P). Reed stop height (H) should be 7.0 mm (0.28 in.). Bend reed stop (S) to adjust height (H).

Fig. Y2-2 — With carburetor body (3) inverted, check float level by measuring distance (D) from carburetor body sealing surface to top of float lever (13) hump. Distance should be 1.5-2.5 mm (0.06-0.10 in.) and is adjusted by bending the arms of float lever (13).

of the carburetor's throttle plate. The throttle plate is controlled by the twist grip via a control cable. When the twist grip is placed in the "FAST" position, stopper (TS–Fig. Y2-3) on the carburetor's throttle arm should contact carburetor stop (CS). If not, reposition the control cable inner wire (W) length until the correct positioning is obtained.

white wire with green tracer (W/G) and black tester lead to black wire (B). The ohmmeter should read 189-231 ohms.

To check high speed pulser (trigger) coil, disconnect wires as outlined under source (charge) coil. Use a suitable ohmmeter and connect red tester lead to white wire with red tracer (W/R) and black tester lead to black wire (B). The ohmmeter should read 30-36 ohms.

To test CDI module, first disconnect all wires at connectors and remove CDI module from outboard motor. Use a suitable ohmmeter and refer to Fig. Y2-6. With reference to chart, perform CDI module resistance tests.

Renew any components that are not within the manufacturer's recommended limits.

COOLING SYSTEM

WATER PUMP. A rubber impeller type water pump is mounted between the drive shaft housing and gearcase. The impeller is driven by a dowel pin in the drive shaft.

Whenever cooling problems are encountered, check water inlet for plugging or partial stoppage and thermostat behind exhaust cover for proper operation. If cooling problems persist, remove gearcase as outlined under LOWER UNIT section and check condition of the water pump, water passages and sealing surfaces.

When water pump is disassembled, check condition of impeller (5 – Fig. Y2-7), lining (3) and plate (6). Turn drive shaft clockwise (viewed from top) while placing pump housing over impeller. Avoid turning drive shaft in opposite direction when water pump is assembled.

POWER HEAD

REMOVE AND REINSTALL. Clamp outboard motor to a suitable stand and remove engine top cowl. Remove integral fuel tank (4 hp models), spark plug, manual rewind starter and carburetor/fuel pump assembly. Remove starter cup and flywheel as a complete

unit. Withdraw flywheel key from crankshaft slot. Remove two magneto base mounting screws, detach wires at connectors and lift magneto base from power head.

NOTE: Magneto base contains upper crankshaft seal and "O" ring. Renewal is required prior to magneto base installation.

Disconnect starter lockout rod from cable's actuating lever located on engine's starboard side. Remove seven cap screws retaining power head to drive shaft housing and lift off power head.

Installation is the reverse order of removal. Install a new gasket between power head and drive shaft housing. Securely tighten power head retaining screws. Tighten flywheel nut to 45 N·m (33 ft.-lbs.) and spark plug to 25 N·m (18 ft.-lbs.).

DISASSEMBLY. Remove the two reed plate retaining screws and

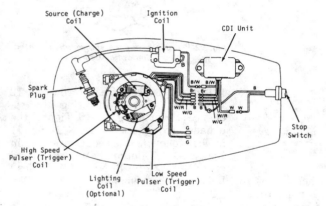

Fig. Y2-5 — View identifying CDI system components.

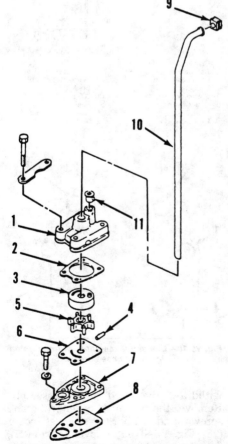

Fig. Y2-7—Exploded view of water pump.

1. Body	7. Base
2. Gasket	8. Gasket
3. Lining	9. Seal
4. Dowel pin	10. Water tube
5. Impeller	11. Seal
6. Plate	

		CDI UNIT LEADS					
Red Ohmmeter Lead	Black Ohmmeter Lead	Stop	Charge	Pulser High Speed	Pulser Low Speed	Earth (Ground)	Ignition
		W	Br	W/R	W/G	B	B/W
Stop	W		A	B	B	B	H
Charge	Br	A		B	B	B	H
Pulser High Speed	W/R	C	C		B	E	H
Pulser Low Speed	W/G	C	C	D		F	H
Earth (Ground)	B	G	G	E	B		H
Ignition	B/W	H	H	H	B	H	

Fig. Y2-6—Use chart and values listed below to test condition of CD ignition module. Before making test (H), connect CDI module black wire and black wire with white tracer together, then disconnect wires and perform desired test.

A. Zero
B. Infinity
C. 12,000-28,000 ohms
D. 16,000-36,000 ohms

E. 7,500-17,500 ohms
F. 4,500-14,500 ohms
G. 2,200-6,200 ohms

H. Tester needle should deflect to 200,000-500,000 ohms, then return to infinity

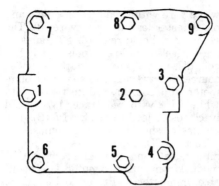

Fig. Y2-11 — Use sequence shown when tightening exhaust cover screws. All screws are the same length except for the following: Screw (9) is 35 mm (1.38 in.) long and screw (3) is 16 mm (0.63 in.) long.

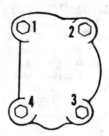

Fig. Y2-12 — Use sequence shown when tightening cylinder head screws.

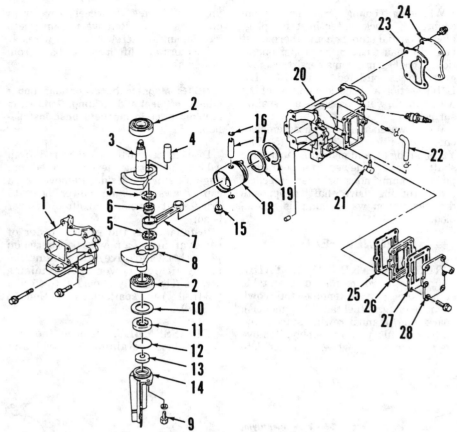

Fig. Y2-8 — Exploded view of power head assembly.

1. Crankcase housing
2. Ball bearing
3. Crankshaft half
4. Crankpin
5. Thrust washer
6. Roller bearing
7. Connecting rod
8. Crankshaft half
9. Cap screw
10. Washer
11. Seal
12. "O" ring
13. Seal
14. Lower crankshaft seal housing
15. Needle bearing
16. Piston pin clips
17. Piston pin
18. Piston
19. Piston rings
20. Cylinder block
21. Check valve
22. Recirculation hose
23. Gasket
24. Cylinder head cover
25. Gasket
26. Inner cover
27. Gasket
28. Exhaust cover

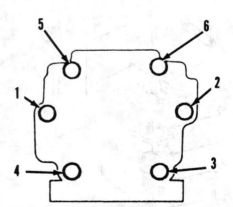

Fig. Y2-10 — Use sequence shown when tightening crankcase screws.

withdraw the reed plate assembly. Remove the exhaust cover retaining screws and withdraw exhaust cover (28 – Fig. Y2-8), outer cover gasket (27), inner cover (26) and inner cover gasket (25). Remove cap screw (9), then tap lower crankshaft seal housing (14) with a rubber mallet to remove. Remove recirculation hose (22). Remove six cap

screws securing crankcase housing (1) to cylinder block (20). While being careful, pry crankcase housing from cylinder block. Lift crankshaft and piston assembly from cylinder block. Remove the four cylinder head cover retaining screws and withdraw cylinder head cover and gasket.

ASSEMBLY. When reassembling, make sure all joints and gasket surfaces are clean and free from nicks and burrs. All friction surfaces and bearings must be lubricated with engine oil during reassembly. Make sure locating pins on crankshaft ball bearings fit into the slots in cylinder block. Check frequently as power head is being assembled for binding of working parts. If binding or locking is encountered, correct cause before proceeding with assembly.

Gasket and sealing surfaces should be lightly and evenly coated with Yamaha Bond No. 4 or an equivalent nonhardening gasket cement. Make sure entire surface is coated, but avoid an excess application as cement may be squeezed into crankcase, bearings or passages.

Tighten the crankcase screws to 12 N·m (106 in.-lbs.) following the sequence shown in Fig. Y2-10. Tighten the exhaust cover screws to 8 N·m (71 in.-lbs.) following the sequence shown in Fig. Y2-11. Tighten the cylinder head cover screws to 8 N·m (71 in.-lbs.) following the sequence shown in Fig. Y2-12.

Complete remainder of reassembly in the reverse order of disassembly.

CYLINDER, RINGS AND PISTON. Cylinder bore should be measured in several locations to determine if an out-of-round or tapered condition exists. Maximum allowable out-of-round is 0.05 mm (0.002 in.). Maximum allowable taper is 0.08 mm (0.003 in.).

NOTE: Cylinder sleeve and cylinder head are cast into the cylinder block. If cylinder is out-of-round or tapered, or if excessive scoring is noted, the cylinder block must be renewed.

Recommended piston skirt-to-cylinder clearance is 0.030-0.035 mm (0.0012-0.0014 in.). Measure piston diameter at a right angle to piston pin bore, 10 mm (0.4 in.) from bottom of skirt. Recommended piston ring end gap is 0.15-0.35 mm (0.006-0.014 in.) for both rings. Piston ring side clearance should be 0.03-0.07 mm (0.001-0.003

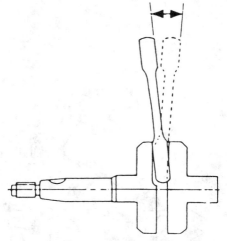

Fig. Y2-13 — Move connecting rod small end side to side as shown to determine rod, rod bearing and crankpin wear. Refer to text.

Fig. Y2-14 — Exploded view of manual rewind starter.
1. Nut
2. Starter housing
3. Rewind spring
4. Pulley
5. Spring
6. Drive pawl
7. Clip
8. Bolt
9. Shaft
10. Starter rope
11. Rope guide
12. Seal
13. Handle
14. Washer

in.) for both rings. Note that top ring is semi-keystone shaped. Measure top ring side clearance on bottom side of ring. Make sure piston rings properly align with location pins in ring grooves.

Piston pin should not have any noticeable play in rod small end bearing or piston pin bore in piston. When reassembling, install new piston pin retaining clips (16—Fig. Y2-8). Install piston on connecting rod so "UP" mark on piston crown is toward flywheel side of engine. Coat bearings, piston, rings and cylinder bore with a recommended engine oil during reassembly.

CRANKSHAFT, BEARINGS AND ROD. The connecting rod rides on a roller bearing around the crankpin. Crankshaft, crankpin, bearing and connecting rod are available only as a unit assembly. Maximum allowable side clearance between rod and crankshaft is 0.7 mm (0.028 in.). Maximum runout of crankshaft is 0.03 mm (0.0012 in.) with crankshaft ends supported. Determine rod, rod bearing and crankpin wear by moving small rod end from side to side as shown in Fig. Y2-13. Renew crankshaft assembly if side movement exceeds 2.0 mm (0.0787 in.).

Protect crankshaft end and use a suitable press to remove and install main ball bearings (2—Fig. Y2-8).

MANUAL STARTER

A starter lockout assembly is used to prevent starter engagement when the gear shift lever is in the forward or reverse position.

The manual starter must be disassembled to renew starter rope (10—Fig. Y2-14) and rewind spring (3).

To overhaul the manual starter, proceed as follows: Remove the engine's top cowl. Remove the screws retaining the manual starter to the engine. Remove the starter lockout cable at the starter housing. Note plunger and spring located at cable end, care should be used not to lose components should they fall free. Withdraw the starter assembly.

Check pawl (6) for freedom of movement, excessive wear of engagement area and any other damage. Renew or lubricate pawl (6) with a suitable water resistant grease and return starter to service if no other damage is noted.

To disassemble, remove clip (7) and withdraw pawl (6) and pawl spring (5). Untie starter rope (10) at handle (13) and allow the rope to wind into the starter. Remove bolt (8), washer (14) and shaft (9), then place a suitable screwdriver blade through hole (H—Fig. Y2-15) to hold rewind spring (3—Fig. Y2-14) securely in housing (2). Carefully lift pulley (4) with starter rope (10) from housing (2). BE CAREFUL when removing pulley (4) as the rewind spring may be dislodged. Untie starter rope (10) and remove rope from pulley (4) if renewal is required. To remove rewind spring (3) from housing (2), invert housing so it sits upright on a flat surface, then tap the housing top until rewind spring (3) falls free and uncoils.

Inspect all components for damage and excessive wear and renew if needed.

To reassemble, first apply a coating of a suitable water-resistant grease to rewind spring area of housing (2). Install rewind spring (3) in housing (2) so spring coils wind in a counterclockwise direction from the outer end. Make sure the spring's outer hook is properly secured over starter housing (2) pin. Wind starter rope (10) onto pulley (4) approximately 2½ turns counterclockwise when viewed from the flywheel side. Direct remaining starter rope (10) length through notch in pulley (4).

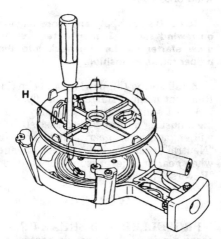

Fig. Y2-15 — Pulley hole (H) is used during pulley withdrawal. Refer to text.

NOTE: Lubricate all friction surfaces with a suitable water-resistant grease during reassembly.

Assemble pulley (4) to starter housing making sure that pulley's pin engages hook end in rewind spring (3). Install shaft (9), washer (14) and bolt (8). Apply a thread fastening solution on bolt (8) threads and install nut (1) and securely tighten.

Thread starter rope (10) through starter housing (2), rope guide (11) and handle (13) and secure with a knot. Turn pulley (4) two turns counterclockwise when viewed from the flywheel side, then release starter rope (10) from

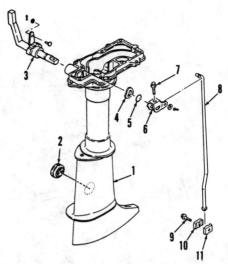

Fig. Y2-17 — View of drive shaft housing and gear shift linkage.

1. Drive shaft housing	
2. Cover	7. Cap screw
3. Shift handle	8. Upper shift rod
4. Wave washer	9. Screw
5. "O" ring	10. Clamp half
6. Shift lever	11. Clamp half

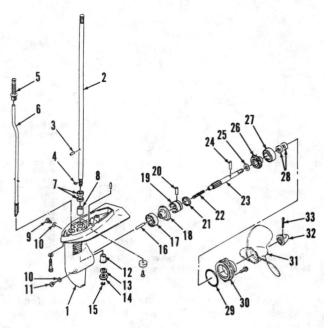

Fig. Y2-18 — Exploded view of lower unit gearcase assembly.

1. Gearcase housing
2. Drive shaft
3. Dowel pin
4. Clip
5. Boot
6. Shift rod
7. Seals
8. Bushing
9. Vent plug
10. Gasket
11. Drain plug
12. Bushing
13. Thrust washer
14. Pinion
15. Snap ring
16. Shift plunger
17. Ball bearing
18. Forward gear
19. Dog clutch
20. Pin
21. Clip
22. Spring
23. Propeller shaft
24. Shear pin
25. Thrust washer
26. Reverse gear
27. Ball bearing
28. Seals
29. "O" ring
30. Gearcase housing cover
31. Propeller
32. Spinner
33. Cotter pin

pulley notch and allow rope to slowly wind onto pulley.

NOTE: Do not apply any more tension on rewind spring (3) than is required to draw starter handle (13) back into the proper released position.

Install spring (5), pawl (6) and clip (7). Remount manual starter assembly.

Adjust starter lockout assembly turning adjusting nuts at cable end so starter will engage when gear shift lever is in "Neutral" position, but will not engage when gear shift lever is in "Forward" or "Reverse" position.

LOWER UNIT

PROPELLER AND SHEAR PIN. A shear pin is used to provide protection for the propeller and lower unit. Select a propeller that will allow the engine at full throttle to reach maximum operating rpm range (4500-5500).

R&R AND OVERHAUL. Clamp outboard motor to an appropriate stand and remove gearcase drain plug and vent plug. Allow gearcase lubricant to drain into a suitable container. Remove cover (2 – Fig. Y2-17) and LOOSEN shift link-

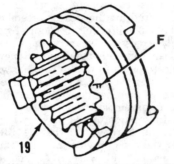

Fig. Y2-19 — Install dog clutch (19) so "F" mark (F) is toward forward gear.

age clamp screw (9). Remove the two cap screws retaining gearcase housing to drive shaft housing and withdraw gearcase housing.

Disassemble gearcase as follows: Remove cotter pin (33 – Fig. Y2-18), spinner (32), propeller (31) and shear pin (24). Remove water pump assembly (Fig. Y2-7). Withdraw shift rod (6 – Fig. Y2-18). Remove two cap screws retaining gearcase housing cover (30). Extract cover (30) with components (16 and 19 through 29). Pry snap ring (15) from end of drive shaft and withdraw drive shaft from gearcase. Remove pinion (14) and thrust washer (13). Withdraw forward gear

(18) from gearcase housing. Detach retainer clip (21) and drive out pin (20) to remove shift plunger (16), dog clutch (19) and spring (22).

Inspect shafts for wear on seal lip contact areas and on splines. Inspect dog clutch and gears for wear on engagement areas of dog teeth. Inspect gears for excessive wear and damage. Inspect shift cam for excessive wear on ramp. All seals and "O" ring should be renewed when unit is reassembled.

NOTE: No adjustment of gear mesh pattern and gear backlash is provided. The parts were machined at very close tolerances and require no shimming when in good condition and are properly assembled.

Reverse disassembly for reassembly while noting the following: Install dog clutch (19) with "F" marked side (Fig. Y2-19) toward forward gear (18 – Fig. Y2-18). Apply a water resistant grease to the lip surfaces of all seals.

Adjust shift linkage by depressing shift rod (6) downward to bottom stop. Make sure lower unit is in reverse gear. Move shift handle (3 – Fig. Y2-17) to "Reverse" and tighten clamp screw (9).

YAMAHA 6 AND 8 HP

CONDENSED SERVICE DATA

NOTE: Metric fasteners are used throughout outboard motor.

TUNE-UP

Hp/rpm	6/5000
	8/5500
Bore	50 mm
	(1.97 in.)
Stroke	42 mm
	(1.65 in.)
Number of Cylinders	2
Displacement	165 cc
	(10.1 cu. in.)
Spark Plug	
NGK	B7HS-10
Electrode Gap	0.9-1.0 mm
	(0.035-0.039 in.)
Ignition Type	CDI
Idle Speed (in gear)	750-850 rpm
Fuel:Oil Ratio	100:1
Gearcase Oil Capacity	160 mL
	(5.4 oz.)

SIZES—CLEARANCES

Piston Ring End Gap	0.15-0.35 mm
	(0.006-0.014 in.)
Piston Ring Side Clearance:	
Top Ring	0.02-0.06 mm
	(0.0008-0.0024 in.)
Second Ring	0.03-0.07 mm
	(0.0012-0.0028 in.)
Standard Cylinder Bore	
Diameter	50.0 mm
	(1.968 in.)
Max. Allowable Taper	0.08 mm
	(0.003 in.)
Max. Allowable Out-of-Round	0.05 mm
	(0.002 in.)

SIZES—CLEARANCES CONT.

Piston Skirt Clearance	0.040-0.045 mm
	(0.0016-0.0018 in.)
Crankshaft Runout—Max	0.03 mm
	(0.0012 in.)
Connecting Rod Small End	
Shake—Max	2.0 mm
	(0.079 in.)
Connecting Rod Side Clearance	0.2-0.7 mm
	(0.008-0.028 in.)

TIGHTENING TORQUES

Crankcase/Intake Manifold	12 N·m
	(106 in.-lbs.)
Cylinder Head Cover	10 N·m
	(89 in.-lbs.)
Exhaust Cover	10 N·m
	(89 in.-lbs.)
Flywheel	45 N·m
	(32 ft.-lbs.)
Spark Plug	28 N·m
	(20 ft.-lbs.)
Standard Screws:	
5 mm	4 N·m
	(36 in.-lbs.)
6 mm	8 N·m
	(70 in.-lbs.)
8 mm	18 N·m
	(13 ft.-lbs.)
10 mm	36 N·m
	(26 ft.-lbs.)
12 mm	42 N·m
	(31 ft.-lbs.)

LUBRICATION

The power head is lubricated by oil mixed with the fuel. Fuel should be regular leaded, low lead or unleaded gasoline with a minimum pump octane rating of 84. Recommended oil is YAMALUBE 100/1 Two-Cycle Lubricant. The recommended fuel:oil ratio for normal operation is 100:1. During the first 10 hours of operation, the fuel:oil ratio should be increased to 25:1.

Lower unit gears and bearings are lubricated by oil contained in the gearcase. Recommended oil is YAMALUBE Gearcase Lube. Lubricant is drained by removing vent and drain plugs in gearcase. Refill through drain plug hole until oil has reached level of top (vent) plug hole.

FUEL SYSTEM

CARBURETOR. The fuel pump and carburetor are a complete unit. Standard main jet (11–Fig. Y4-1) size is #98. Standard pilot jet (10) size #45. Initial adjustment of idle mixture screw (7) is 7/8-1 3/8 turns out from a lightly seated position. Recommended idle speed is 750-850 rpm in gear with the engine at normal operating temperature. Rotate screw (5) to adjust idle speed.

To determine the float level, invert carburetor body (1) with float bowl (19) and seal (18) removed. Measure float height as shown in Fig. Y4-2. Distance from carburetor body sealing surface to top of float should be 14 mm (9/16 in.). Bend tang on float arm to adjust.

FUEL PUMP. The fuel pump is an integral part of the carburetor. Refer to Fig. Y4-1 for an exploded view of fuel pump assembly. Note that fuel pump assembly can be overhauled without carburetor removal.

SPEED CONTROL LINKAGE. To synchronize ignition timing and throttle opening, proceed as follows: Remove both spark plugs and install a dial indicator in the number 1 (top) cylinder. Use the dial indicator to verify when piston is at TDC. With piston at TDC, timing pointer (P–Fig. Y4-3) must align with TDC mark on flywheel (F).

Disconnect magneto base plate control rod (R–Fig. Y4-4) from magneto base plate control lever (L). Rotate flywheel to align 35° BTDC mark (M–Fig. Y4-3)

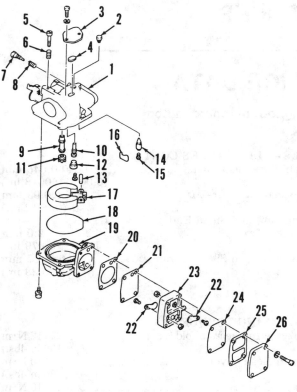

Fig. Y4-1—Exploded view of carburetor/fuel pump assembly.

1. Body
2. Plug
3. Cover
4. Packing
5. Idle speed screw
6. Spring
7. Idle mixture screw
8. Spring
9. Main nozzle
10. Pilot jet
11. Main jet
12. Plug
13. Pin
14. Needle valve
15. Pin
16. Clip
17. Float
18. Seal
19. Float bowl
20. Gasket
21. Diaphragm
22. Check valve
23. Pump body
24. Diaphragm
25. Gasket
26. Pump outer cover

(R) to slide over ball joint on magneto base plate control lever (L).

REED VALVE. A reed valve plate is mounted between the intake manifold and crankcase. Reed petals should seat squarely and smoothly along their entire length and should be free of cracks, nicks, tears and burrs. Do not attempt to straighten or repair bent or damaged reeds. If reed stop (S–Fig. Y4-7) is removed, install new retaining screws and apply a thread fastening solution on screw threads. Reed stop height should be 4.3-4.7 mm (0.169-0.185 in.). To check reed stop height, a drill bit (B) within recommended tolerance can be inserted between reed petals and reed stop as shown in Fig. Y4-7 or use a suitable measuring tool. Bend reed stop (S) to adjust reed stop height. If reed stop height is 0.1 mm (0.004 in.) above or below recommended tolerance, manufacturer recommends renewing reed stop (S).

IGNITION

The standard spark plug is NGK B7HS-10. Electrode gap should be 0.9-1.0 mm (0.035-0.039 in.).

Models are equipped with a capacitor discharge ignition (CDI) system. If engine malfunction is noted and the ignition system is suspected, make sure the

on flywheel with timing pointer (P). Loosen cap screw (S–Fig. Y4-5) and rotate magneto base plate until timing pointer (T) on magneto base plate is aligned with mark stamped on base of flywheel (F). Move stop bracket (B) until light contact is made with stop tab on timing pointer (T). Tighten cap screw (S).

Rotate twist grip to wide-open throttle (WOT), then adjust maximum throttle cable (A–Fig. Y4-6) until carburetor throttle lever (C–Fig. Y4-4) is in contact with WOT stop (W). Adjust idle throttle cable (I–Fig. Y4-6) to remove cable slack. With timing at maximum advance position as previously outlined and carburetor throttle lever (C–Fig. Y4-4) against WOT stop (W), adjust ball socket at end of magneto base plate control rod

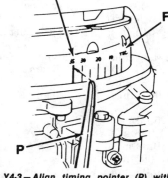

Fig. Y4-3—Align timing pointer (P) with 35° BTDC mark (M) on flywheel (F) during adjustment of speed control linkage. Refer to text.

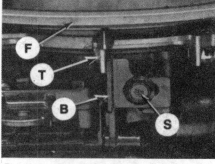

Fig. Y4-5—Cap screw (S) retains stop bracket (B). Timing pointer (T) should align with mark stamped on base of flywheel (F) when timing is at maximum advance position.

Fig. Y4-2—View showing procedure for checking float level. Refer to text.

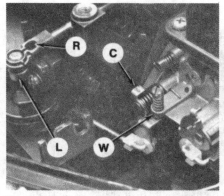

Fig. Y4-4—View identifying carburetor throttle lever (C), magneto base plate control lever (L), magneto base plate control rod (R) and WOT stop (W).

Fig. Y4-6—Loosen jam nuts (N) to adjust maximum advance throttle cable (A) and idle throttle cable (I).

spark plugs and all electrical wiring are in good condition and all electrical con-

Fig. Y4-7—View showing reed valve plate assembly. A drill bit (B) within recommended tolerance can be inserted between reed petals and reed stop (S) to check reed stop height. Refer to text.

nections are tight before proceeding to trouble-shooting the CD ignition system.

Proceed as follows to test CDI system components: Refer to Fig. Y4-8. To test ignition coil, disconnect black wire (B) and orange wire (Or) at connectors and spark plug boots from spark plugs. Use a suitable ohmmeter and connect black tester lead to black wire (B) and red tester lead to orange wire (Or). The resistance reading should be 0.36-0.44 ohms. Connect one tester lead to terminal end in one of the spark plug boots and the other tester lead to the terminal end in the other spark plug boot. The resistance reading should be 3150-3850 ohms. Use Yamaha tester YU-33261 or a suitable equivalent to perform a power test. Connect tester leads as outlined in tester's handbook. On Yamaha tester YU-33261, a steady spark should jump a

8 mm (0.31 in.) gap with voltage selector switch in "CDI" position. A surface insulation test can be performed using tester YU-33261 or a suitable equivalent and following tester's handbook.

To check source (charge) coil, disconnect black wire (B) and brown wire (Br) at connectors leading from magneto base plate. Use a suitable ohmmeter and connect red tester lead to brown wire (Br) and black tester lead to black wire (B). The ohmmeter should read 81-99 ohms.

To check trigger coil, disconnect black wire (B) and white wire with red tracer (W/R) at connectors leading from magneto base plate. Use a suitable ohmmeter and connect red tester lead to white wire with red tracer (W/R) and black tester lead to black wire (B). The ohmmeter should read 92-112 ohms.

To test CDI module, first disconnect all wires at connectors and remove CDI module from outboard motor. Use a suitable ohmmeter and refer to Fig. Y4-9. With reference to chart, perform CDI module resistance tests.

Renew any components that are not within the manufacturer's recommended limits.

COOLING SYSTEM

WATER PUMP. A rubber impeller type water pump is mounted between the drive shaft housing and gearcase. The impeller is driven by a Woodruff key in the drive shaft.

Whenever cooling problems are encountered, check water inlets for plugging or partial stoppage and thermostat behind cylinder head cover for proper operation. If cooling problems persist, remove gearcase as outlined under LOWER UNIT section and check condition of the water pump, water passages and sealing surfaces.

When water pump is disassembled, check condition of impeller (5 – Fig. Y4-10), lining (4) and plate (7). Turn drive shaft clockwise (viewed from top) while placing pump housing over impeller. Avoid turning drive shaft in opposite direction when water pump is assembled. Securely tighten water pump housing retaining screws.

POWER HEAD

REMOVE AND REINSTALL. Clamp outboard motor to a suitable stand and remove engine top cowl. Remove manual rewind starter, flywheel, tool kit and bracket and carburetor/fuel pump assembly. Withdraw flywheel key from crankshaft slot. Disconnect speed control linkage. Remove CDI module and ignition coil.

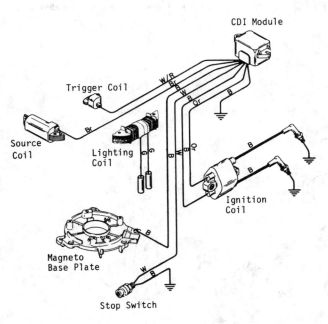

Fig. Y4-8 – View identifying CDI system components. Wires are identified as follows.

B. Black
G. Green
W. White
Br. Brown
Or. Orange
W/R. White wire with red tracer

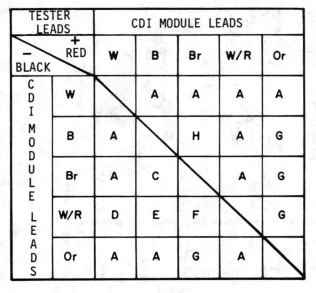

TESTER LEADS − BLACK / + RED	CDI MODULE LEADS				
	W	B	Br	W/R	Or
C D I M O D U L E L E A D S — W		A	A	A	A
B	A		H	A	G
Br	A	C		A	G
W/R	D	E	F		G
Or	A	A	A	A	

Fig. Y4-9—Use chart and values listed below to test condition of CD ignition module. Wires are identified in Fig. Y4-8. Before making test (G), connect CDI module's black wire and orange wire together. Then disconnect wires and perform desired test.

A. Infinity
C. 63,000-95,000 ohms
D. 8,000-14,000 ohms
E. 14,000-22,000 ohms
F. 30,000-46,000 ohms
G. Tester needle swings once then returns to infinity
H. 7,000-12,000 ohms

Remove three magneto base plate mounting screws, detach wires at connectors and lift magneto base plate from power head. Remove six cap screws retaining power head to drive shaft housing and lift off power head.

Installation is reverse order of removal. Install a new gasket between power head and drive shaft housing. Tighten power head retaining screws to 8 N·m (70 in.-lbs.). Tighten flywheel nut to 45 N·m (32 ft.-lbs.).

DISASSEMBLY. Remove lower oil seal housing (20 – Fig. Y4-11), exhaust manifold (22) and gasket (21). Remove three friction plate (8) cap screws and withdraw friction plate (8), nylon ring (7) and retaining ring (9). Remove six intake manifold cap screws and withdraw intake manifold and reed valve plate assembly. Remove upper oil seal housing (10). Remove cylinder head cover (6) and withdraw nylon spacer (4) and thermostat (3). Remove seven exhaust cover cap screws and separate outer exhaust cover (16) from inner exhaust cover (14). Remove four remaining crankcase cover cap screws and separate crankcase cover (2) from cylinder block (1) while being careful not to damage mating surfaces.

Engine components are now accessible for removal and overhaul as outlined in the appropriate service paragraphs.

ASSEMBLY. When reassembling, make sure all joints and gasket surfaces are clean and free from nicks and burrs. All friction surfaces and bearings must be lubricated with engine oil during reassembly. Make sure locating pins on

crankshaft ball bearings and labyrinth seal fit into the slots in cylinder block. Check frequently as power head is being assembled for binding of working parts. If binding or locking is encountered, correct cause before proceeding with assembly.

Apply Yamaha Bond No. 4 to sealing surface of crankcase cover (2—Fig. Y4-11) and crankcase sealing surface of cylinder block (1). Make sure entire surface is coated, but avoid an excess application as sealant may be squeezed into crankcase, bearings or passages. Install crankcase cover (2) and tighten screws in a counterclockwise sequence starting with top, starboard screw to 12 N·m (106 in.-lbs.). Tighten the intake manifold screws to 12 N·m (106 in.-lbs.) following the sequence shown in Fig. Y4-12. Tighten the exhaust cover screws to 10 N·m (89 in.-lbs.) following the sequence shown in Fig. Y4-13. Tighten

the cylinder head cover screws to 10 N·m (89 in.-lbs.) following the sequence shown in Fig. Y4-14, then complete reassembly.

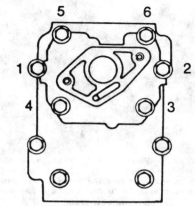

Fig. Y4-12 — Tighten intake manifold screws to 12 N·m (106 in.-lbs.) in sequence shown.

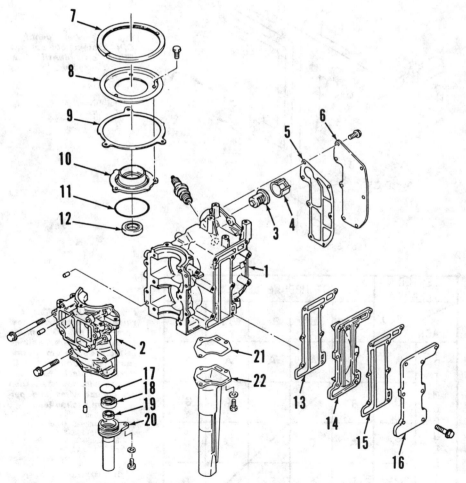

Fig. Y4-11 — Exploded view of crankcase and cylinder block assembly.

1. Cylinder block	7. Nylon ring	12. Seal
2. Crankcase cover	8. Friction plate	13. Gasket
3. Thermostat	9. Retaining ring	14. Inner exhaust cover
4. Nylon spacer	10. Upper oil seal housing	15. Gasket
5. Gasket	11. "O" ring	16. Outer exhaust cover
6. Cylinder head cover		

17. "O" ring	
18. Seal	
19. Seal	
20. Lower oil seal housing	
21. Gasket	
22. Exhaust manifold	

Fig. Y4-10 — Exploded view of water pump assembly.

1. Seal
2. Plate (2)
3. Housing
4. Liner
5. Impeller
6. Gasket
7. Plate

CYLINDERS, RINGS AND PISTONS. Cylinder bores should be measured in several different locations to determine if an out-of-round or tapered condition exits. Inspect cylinder walls for scoring. If cylinder bore is out-of-round more than 0.05 mm (0.002 in.), tapered more than 0.08 mm (0.003 in.) or excessive scoring is noted, cylinder block (1—Fig. Y4-11) and crankcase cover (2) must be renewed.

NOTE: To deglaze cylinder walls, lightly hone following hone manufacturer's recommendations.

Recommended piston skirt-to-cylinder clearance is 0.040-0.045 mm (0.0016-0.0018 in.). Measure piston diameter at a right angle to piston pin bore, 10 mm (0.39 in.) from bottom of skirt. Recommended piston ring end gap is 0.15-0.35 mm (0.006-0.014 in.) for both rings. The top (semi-keystone) piston ring should have a side clearance of 0.02-0.06 mm (0.0008-0.0024 in.) and bottom (square) piston ring should have a side clearance of 0.03-0.07 mm (0.0012-0.0028 in.). Make sure piston rings properly align with locating pins in ring grooves and identifying letter faces up.

When reassembling, install new pistons pin retaining clips (11—Fig. Y4-15) and make sure that pistons are installed with "UP" mark facing toward flywheel side of engine. Coat bearings, pistons, rings and cylinder bores with a suitable engine oil during assembly.

CRANKSHAFT, BEARINGS AND CONNECTING RODS. The connecting rods ride on roller bearings around the crankpins. Crankshaft, crankpins, bearings and connecting rods are available as a unit assembly only. Maximum allowable side clearance between connecting rod and crankshaft is 0.2-0.7 mm (0.008-0.028 in.). Maximum runout of crankshaft is 0.03 mm (0.0012 in.) with crankshaft ends supported. Determine rod, rod bearing and crankpin wear by moving rod small end side-to-side as shown in Fig. Y4-16. Renew crankshaft assembly if side-to-side movement exceeds 2.0 mm (0.079 in.).

Protect crankshaft end and use a suitable press to remove and install main ball bearings (1—Fig. Y4-15).

MANUAL STARTER

A starter lockout assembly is used to prevent starter engagement when the gear shift lever is in the forward or reverse position.

The manual starter must be disassembled to renew starter rope (11—Fig. Y4-17) and rewind spring.

To remove the manual starter, proceed as follows: Remove the engine top cover. Remove the screws retaining the starter assembly to the engine. Remove the starter lockout cable at the starter housing. Note plunger and spring located at cable end, care must be used not to lose components should they fall free. Withdraw the starter assembly.

Check pawl (7) for freedom of movement, excessive wear of engagement area and any other damage and renew if necessary. Lubricate pawl (7) with a suitable water-resistant grease and return starter to service if no other damage is noted.

To disassemble, remove clip (8) and withdraw pawl (7) and pawl spring assembly (6). Remove cover (15) and untie starter rope (11) at handle (14) and allow the rope to wind into the starter. Remove bolt (10), washer (9) and shaft (5), then place a suitable screwdriver blade through hole (H—Fig. Y4-18) to hold rewind spring (3—Fig. Y4-17) securely in housing (2). Carefully lift pulley (4) with starter rope (11) from housing (2). BE CAREFUL when removing (4) as the rewind spring may be dislodged. Untie starter rope (11) and remove rope from pulley (4) if renewal is required. To remove rewind spring (3) from housing (2), invert housing so it sits upright on a flat surface, then tap the housing top until rewind spring (3) fall free and uncoils.

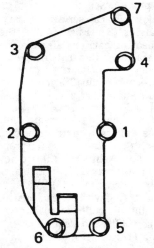

Fig. Y4-13 — Tighten exhaust cover screws to 10 N·m (89 in.-lbs.) in sequence shown.

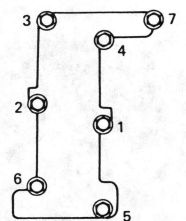

Fig. Y4-14 — Tighten cylinder head cover screws to 10 N·m (89 in.-lbs.) in sequence shown.

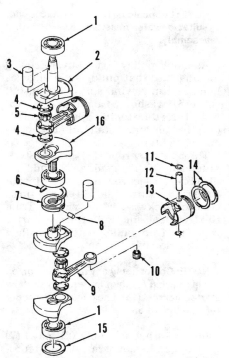

Fig. Y4-15 — Exploded view of crankshaft assembly.

1. Ball bearings	9. Connecting rod
2. Crank half	10. Roller bearing
3. Crankpin	11. Retaining clip
4. Thrust washers	12. Piston pin
5. Roller bearing	13. Piston
6. Snap ring	14. Piston rings
7. Labyrinth seal	15. Washer
8. Pin	16. Crank half

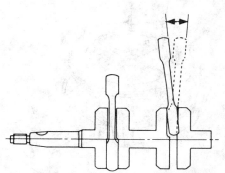

Fig. Y4-16—Move connecting rod small end side-to-side as shown to determine rod, rod bearing and crankpin wear. Refer to text.

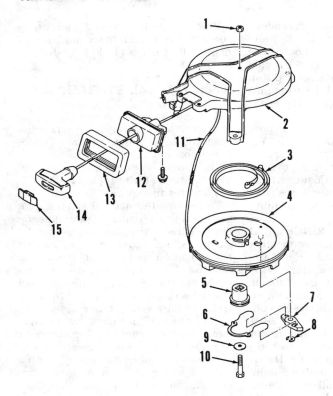

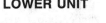

Fig. Y4-17 — Exploded view of manual rewind starter.

1. Nut
2. Housing
3. Rewind spring
4. Pulley
5. Shaft
6. Pawl spring assy.
7. Pawl
8. Clip
9. Washer
10. Bolt
11. Starter rope
12. Rope guide
13. Seal
14. Handle
15. Cover

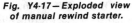

LOWER UNIT

PROPELLER AND DRIVE HUB. Lower unit protection is provided by a cushion type hub in the propeller. Various propellers are available from the manufacturer. Select a propeller that will allow a properly tuned and adjusted engine to operate at full throttle in the specified range of 4000-5000 rpm on 6 hp models and 4500-5500 rpm on 8 hp models.

R&R AND OVERHAUL. Most lower unit service can be performed after removing lower unit gearcase from the drive shaft housing. Remove gearcase as follows: Clamp outboard motor to a suitable stand, remove propeller and drain lubricant. Place shift lever in "Reverse" and tilt outboard motor to full up position. Loosen cap screw (S – Fig. Y4-19) so lower shift rod slides freely in clamp (C). Remove four cap screws retaining gearcase to drive shaft housing. Withdraw gearcase assembly. Remove water pump assembly.

Remove two cap screws securing bearing carrier (36 – Fig. Y4-20), then extract bearing carrier (36) with propeller shaft assembly. Separate propeller shaft assembly from bearing carrier (36). Remove spring clip (28) and push out pin (27) to remove dog clutch (26). Lift out shim (30), reverse gear (31) and shim (32) from bearing carrier (36). Use suitable pullers to extract bearing (33) and seals (37). Remove water pump base (9) and lower shift rod (2). Remove clip (6), pinion gear (20) and shim (19). Withdraw drive shaft (4). Withdraw forward gear (23) with cone of bearing (22). Use a suitable puller to withdraw cup of bearing (22) and shim (21). Drive bushing (18) down into gear cavity for removal.

Inspect shafts for wear on seal lip contact areas and on splines. Inspect dog clutch and gears for wear and damage

Inspect all components for damage and excessive wear and renew if needed.

To reassemble, first apply a coating of a suitable water-resistant grease to rewind spring area of housing (2). Install rewind spring (3) into housing (2) so spring coils wind in counterclockwise direction from the outer end. Make sure the outer hook of rewind spring is properly secured over starter housing (2) pin. Wind starter rope (11) onto pulley (4) approximately 1-1/2 turns counterclockwise when viewed from the fly-

wheel side. Direct remaining starter rope (11) through notch in pulley (4).

NOTE: Lubricate all friction surfaces with a suitable water-resistant grease during reassembly.

Assemble pulley (4) to starter housing making sure that pulley's pin engages hook end in rewind spring (3). Install shaft (5), washer (9) and bolt (10). Apply a thread fastening solution on bolt (10) threads and install nut (1) and securely tighten.

Thread starter rope (11) through starter housing (2), rope guide (12) and handle (14) and secure with a knot. Install cover (15). Turn pulley (4) three turns counterclockwise when viewed from the flywheel side, then release starter rope (11) from pulley notch and allow rope to slowly wind onto pulley.

NOTE: Do not apply any more tension on rewind spring (3) than is required to draw starter handle (14) back into the proper released position.

Install spring assembly (6), pawl (7) and clip (8). Remount manual starter assembly.

Adjust starter lockout assembly by turning adjusting nuts at cable end so starter will engage when gear shift lever is in "Neutral" position, but will not engage when gear shift lever is in "Forward" or "Reverse" position.

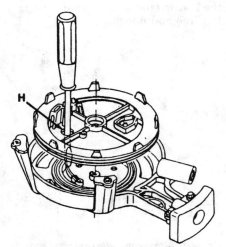

Fig. Y4-18—Pulley hole (H) is used during pulley withdrawal. Refer to text.

Fig. Y4-19—Loosen cap screw (S) so lower shift rod slides freely in clamp (C) before removing gearcase.

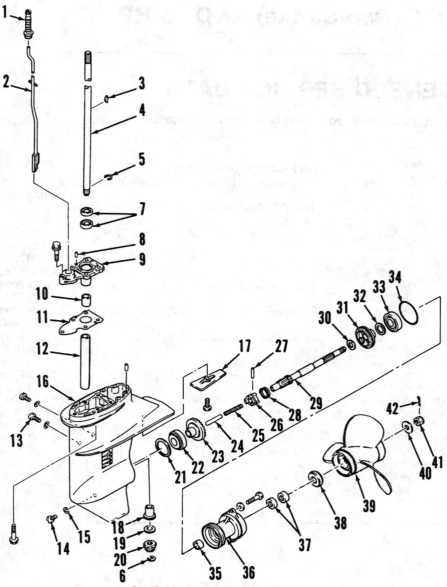

Fig. Y4-20 — Exploded view of gearcase.

on engagement areas. Inspect shift cam for excessive wear on ramp. All seals and "O" rings should be renewed when unit is assembled.

Gear backlash and mesh position should be checked on reassembly. Install forward gear (23) with original shim (21) in gearcase. Position pinion gear (20) with original shim (19) in gearcase then install drive shaft (4). Secure pinion gear to drive shaft with clip (6). Forward gear (23) and pinion gear (20) should mesh evenly when drive shaft (4) is pulled up and rotated. Adjust mesh position by varying thickness of shim (19). Forward and reverse gear backlash should be 0.25-0.75 mm (0.01-0.03 in.) and is adjusted by shims (21 and 32).

Reassemble gearcase by reversing disassembly procedure while noting the following: Install seals (7) into water pump base (9) so seal lips are facing top of housing. Install seals (37) into bearing carrier (36) so seal lips are facing propeller. Install dog clutch (26) on propeller shaft (29) so side marked "F" (Fig. Y4-21) is facing toward forward gear (23—Fig. Y4-20). Apply a light coat of water-resistant grease to drive shaft upper splines. Tighten gearcase-to-drive shaft housing screws to 8 N·m (70 in.-lbs.).

With gearcase assembled and installed, synchronize gear engagement with shift lever. Tighten cap screw (S—Fig. Y4-19) to secure shift rods in clamp (C).

1. Boot	12. Sleeve	22. Bearing	32. Shim
2. Lower shift rod	13. Level plug	23. Forward gear	33. Bearing
3. Key	14. Drain plug	24. Shift pin	34. "O" ring
4. Drive shaft	15. Gasket	25. Spring	35. Bushing
5. Clip	16. Housing	26. Dog clutch	36. Bearing carrier
6. Clip	17. Anode	27. Pin	37. Seals
7. Seals	18. Bushing	28. Spring clip	38. Thrust hub
8. Dowel pin	19. Shim	29. Propeller shaft	39. Propeller
9. Water pump base	20. Pinion gear	30. Thrust washer	40. Washer
10. Bushing	21. Shim	31. Reverse gear	41. Nut
11. Gasket			42. Cotter pin

Fig. Y4-21 — Install dog clutch so "F" mark (F) is toward forward gear.

YAMAHA 9.9 (Two-Stroke) AND 15 HP

CONDENSED SERVICE DATA

NOTE: Metric fasteners are used throughout outboard motor.

TUNE-UP

Hp/rpm 9.9/5000
                                    15/5500
Bore ....56 mm
                                    (2.205 in.)
Stroke ....50 mm
                                    (1.968 in.)
Number of Cylinders 2
Displacement ....246 cc
                                    (15 cu. in.)
Spark Plug – NGK B7HS-10
  Electrode Gap ....0.9-1.0 mm
                                    (0.036-0.040 in.)
Ignition Type ....CDI
Idle Speed (in gear) ....670-770 rpm
Fuel:Oil Ratio 100:1

SIZES—CLEARANCES

Piston Ring End Gap ....0.15-0.35 mm
                                    (0.006-0.014 in.)
Piston Ring Side Clearance ....0.04-0.08 mm
                                    (0.0016-0.0032 in.)
Piston Skirt Clearance ....0.035-0.040 mm
                                    (0.0014-0.0016 in.)
Crankshaft Runout – Max. ....0.03 mm
                                    (0.0012 in.)

SIZES—CLEARANCES CONT.

Connecting Rod Small End Shake – Max. ....2.0 mm
                                    (0.078 in.)

TIGHTENING TORQUES
Crankcase:
  M6 ....12 N·m
                                    (9 ft.-lbs.)
  M8 ....30 N·m
                                    (22 ft.-lbs.)
Cylinder Head ....17 N·m
                                    (12 ft.-lbs.)
Flywheel ....100 N·m
                                    (74 ft.-lbs.)
Spark Plug ....28 N·m
                                    (20 ft.-lbs.)
Standard Screws:
  5 mm ....4 N·m
                                    (3 ft.-lbs.)
  6 mm ....8 N·m
                                    (6 ft.-lbs.)
  8 mm ....18 N·m
                                    (13 ft.-lbs.)
  10 mm ....36 N·m
                                    (26 ft.-lbs.)
  12 mm ....42 N·m
                                    (30 ft.-lbs.)

LUBRICATION

The power head is lubricated by oil mixed with the fuel. Fuel should be regular leaded, low lead or unleaded gasoline with a minimum pump octane rating of 84. Recommended oil is YAMALUBE 100/1 Two-Cycle Lubricant. The recommended fuel:oil ratio for normal operation is 100:1. During the first 10 hours of operation, the fuel:oil ratio should be increased to 25:1.

Lower unit gears and bearings are lubricated by oil contained in the gearcase. Recommended oil is YAMALUBE Gearcase Lube. Lubricant is drained by removing vent and drain plugs in gearcase. Refill through drain plug hole until oil has reached level of top (vent) plug hole.

FUEL SYSTEM

CARBURETOR. Refer to Fig. Y6-1 for exploded view of carburetor. Normal main jet (21) size is #104 on 9.9 hp

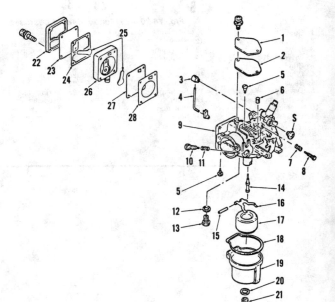

Fig. Y6-1 – Exploded view of carburetor and fuel pump.

1. Cover
2. Gasket
3. Rod end
4. Throttle rod
5. Screw
6. Pilot jet
7. Spring
8. Idle mixture screw
9. Carburetor body
10. Idle speed screw
11. Spring
12. Gasket
13. Fuel inlet valve
14. Main nozzle
15. Pin
16. Float lever
17. Float
18. Gasket
19. Float bowl
20. Gasket
21. Main jet
22. Fuel pump cover
23. Diaphragm
24. Gasket
25. Check valves
26. Pump body
27. Diaphragm
28. Gasket

models and #135 on 15 hp models. Normal pilot jet (6) size is #52 on 9.9 hp models and #56 on 15 hp models. Initial setting of idle mixture screw (8) from a lightly seated position is 1-1/4 to 1-3/4 turns out on 9.9 hp models and 1-1/8 to 1-5/8 turns out on 15 hp models. Adjust idle speed to 670-770 rpm with outboard motor in forward gear and at normal operating temperature.

To set float level, invert carburetor and measure from carburetor body to bottom of float lever as shown in Fig. Y6-2. Height (H) of float lever should be 1.5-2.5 mm (0.06-0.10 in.) and is adjusted by bending float arms evenly.

SPEED CONTROL LINKAGE. Before synchronizing throttle control and ignition, ignition timing should be checked and adjusted if required. Disconnect adjustable link (L—Fig. Y6-4) between magneto control lever (M) and magneto base plate. Turn twist grip to "FAST" position. Rotate magneto base plate to full advanced position then install adjustable link (L) between magneto base plate and magneto control lever (M). Adjust length of link as required so link fits easily over mounting points. With twist grip still in full throttle po-

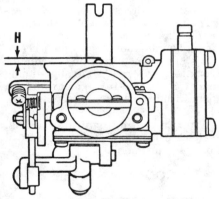

Fig. Y6-2—For correct float level, height (H) of float lever should be 1.5-2.5 mm (0.06-0.10 in.). Refer to text.

Fig. Y6-4—View identifying speed control components. Refer to text.

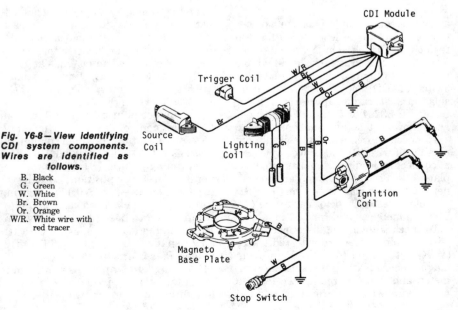

Fig. Y6-6—View of reed valve assembly. Height (H) of reed valve stops (T) should be 1.3 mm (0.05 in.) on 9.9 hp models and 4 mm (0.16 in.) on 15 hp models.

sition, carburetor throttle plate should be in wide-open position. Loosen screw (S—Fig. Y6-1) and adjust throttle rod (4) in rod end (3) to obtain wide-open throttle, then retighten screw (S).

Place outboard motor in "Neutral" position. Loosen locknut (N—Fig. Y6-4) and screw (R), then start engine. Allow engine to warm up to normal operating temperature. Rotate twist grip until engine speed is between 1000 and 1600 rpm, then adjust screw (R) until end of screw (R) contacts stopper (P). Stop engine and tighten locknut (N).

REED VALVE. A pyramid type reed valve is mounted between the carburetor and crankcase. Reed petals should seat squarely and smoothly along their entire length and should be free of cracks, nicks, tears and burrs. Do not attempt to straighten or repair bent or damaged reeds. Reed petal ends should not stand open more than 0.2 mm (0.008 in.). Reed stop height (H–Fig. Y6-6) should be 1.3 mm (0.05 in.) on 9.9 hp

models and 4 mm (0.16 in.) on 15 hp models.

FUEL PUMP. A diaphragm type fuel pump is mounted on the side of the carburetor. The fuel pump is operated by crankcase pulsations transferred through passageways in the crankcase, reed valve plate and carburetor body. Passageways must be clear of obstructions or fuel pump will not operate properly. Refer to Fig. Y6-1 for an exploded view of fuel pump.

IGNITION

The standard spark plug is NGK B7HS-10 with an electrode gap of 0.9-1.0 mm (0.036-0.040 in.).

Models are equippped with a capacitor discharge ignition (CDI) system. If engine malfunction is noted and the ignition system is suspected, make sure the spark plugs and all electrical wiring are in good condition and all electrical connections are tight before proceeding to trouble-shooting the CD ignition system.

Proceed as follows to test CDI system components: Refer to Fig. Y6-8. To test ignition coil, disconnect black wire (B) and orange wire (Or) at connectors and spark plug boots from spark plugs. Use a suitable ohmmeter and connect black tester lead to black wire (B) and red tester lead to orange wire (Or). The resistance reading should be 0.12-0.18 ohms. Connect one tester lead to terminal end in one of the spark plug boots and the other tester lead to the terminal end in the other spark plug boot. The resistance reading should be 2800-4200 ohms. Use Yamaha tester YU-33261 or

Fig. Y6-8—View identifying CDI system components. Wires are identified as follows.

B. Black
G. Green
W. White
Br. Brown
Or. Orange
W/R. White wire with red tracer

TESTER LEADS	CDI MODULE LEADS				
+ RED / **− BLACK**	**W**	**B**	**Br**	**W/R**	**Or**
W		A	A	A	A
B	A		H	A	G
Br	A	C		A	G
W/R	D	E	F		G
Or	A	A	G	A	

Fig. Y6-9—Use chart and values listed below to test condition of CD ignition module. Wires are identified in Fig. Y6-8. Before making test (G), connect CDI module's black wire and orange wire together. Then disconnect wires and perform desired test.

A. Infinity
C. 63,000-95,000 ohms
D. 8,000-14,000 ohms
E. 14,000-22,000 ohms
F. 30,000-46,000 ohms
G. Tester needle swings once then returns to infinity
H. 7,000-12,000 ohms

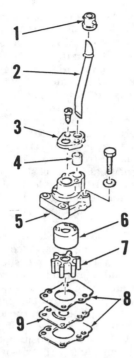

Fig. Y6-13—Exploded view of water pump.
1. Seal
2. Water tube
3. Cover
4. Seal
5. Water pump body
6. Lining
7. Impeller
8. Gaskets
9. Plate

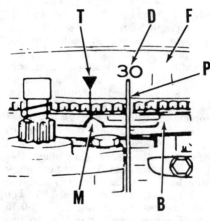

Fig. Y6-10 — Refer to text for setting ignition timing.

B. Magneto base plate
D. 30° BTDC mark
F. Flywheel
M. Magneto base plate timing mark
P. Timing pointer
T. Triangle shaped timing mark

Fig. Y6-11 — Refer to text for setting ignition timing.

C. Throttle cam
D. Idle ignition timing adjustment screw
S. Screws

a suitable equivalent to perform a power test. Connect tester leads as outlined in tester's handbook. On Yamaha tester YU-33261, a steady spark should jump 8 mm (0.31 in.) gap with voltage selector switch in "CDI" position. A surface insulation test can be performed using tester YU-33261 or a suitable equivalent and following tester's handbook.

To check source (charge) coil, disconnect black wire (B) and brown wire (Br) at connectors leading from magneto base plate. Use a suitable ohmmeter and connect red tester lead to brown wire (Br) and black tester lead to black wire (B). The ohmmeter should read 81-99 ohms.

To check trigger coil, disconnect black wire (B) and white wire with red tracer (W/R) at connectors leading from magneto base plate. Use a suitable ohmmeter and connect red tester lead to white wire with red tracer (W/R) and

black tester lead to black wire (B). The ohmmeter should read 92-112 ohms.

To test CDI module, first disconnect all wires at connectors and remove CDI module from outboard motor. Use a suitable ohmmeter and refer to Fig. Y6-9. With reference to chart, perform CDI module resistance tests.

Renew any components that are not within the manufacturer's recommended limits.

Ignition timing can be checked and adjusted as follows: Remove both spark plugs and install a dial indicator in the number 1 (top) cylinder. Use the dial indicator to verify when piston is at TDC. With piston at TDC, timing pointer (P – Fig. Y6-10) must align with TDC mark on flywheel (F).

Disconnect adjustable link between magneto control lever and magneto base plate. Rotate flywheel to align 30 degrees BTDC mark (D) on flywheel with timing pointer (P). Place shift lever in "Forward" position. Loosen two cap screws (S—Fig. Y6-11) securing throttle cam to magneto base plate. Position magneto base plate (B—Fig. Y6-10) so timing mark (M) aligns with triangle shaped timing mark (T) on flywheel. Place throttle cam (C—Fig. Y6-11) so magneto stop on base of cam is in contact with stop on cylinder block. Retighten two cap screws (S).

Rotate flywheel to align 5 degrees BTDC mark on flywheel with timing pointer. Rotate magneto base plate until idle ignition timing adjustment screw (D) is in contact with stop on cylinder block. Adjust screw (D) to align timing mark (M—Fig. Y6-10) on magneto base plate with triangle shaped timing mark (T) on flywheel.

After adjusting ignition timing, recheck carburetor and speed control linkage adjustments.

COOLING SYSTEM

WATER PUMP. A rubber impeller type water pump is mounted between the drive shaft housing and gearcase. The impeller is driven by a Woodruff key in the drive shaft.

Whenever cooling problems are encountered, check water inlet for plugging or partial stoppage and thermostat in cylinder head for proper operation. If cooling problem persists, remove gearcase and check condition of the water pump, water passages and sealing surfaces.

When water pump is disassembled, check condition of impeller (7—Fig. Y6-13), lining (6) and plate (9). Turn drive shaft clockwise (viewed from top) while placing pump housing over impeller. Avoid turning drive shaft in opposite direction when water pump is assembled.

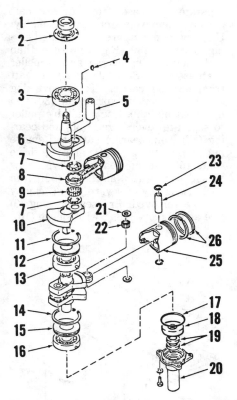

Fig. Y6-15 — Exploded view of crankshaft assembly.

1. Seal	14. Snap ring
2. Plate	15. Seal
3. Ball bearing	16. Ball bearing
4. Key	17. "O" ring
5. Crankpin	18. Seal
6. Crankshaft	19. Seals
7. Thrust washer	20. Seal housing
8. Connecting rod	21. Thrust washers
9. Roller bearing	22. Needle bearings (25)
10. Crankshaft	23. Piston pin clips
11. Snap ring	24. Piston pin
12. Seal	25. Piston
13. Ball bearing	26. Piston rings

POWER HEAD

R&R AND OVERHAUL. The power head can be removed for disassembly and overhaul as follows: Clamp outboard motor to a suitable stand and remove engine top cowl. Remove manual starter and, if so equipped, electric starter. Remove fuel system components, flywheel, magneto base plate and ignition coil, then disconnect speed control linkage. Remove any other component that will interfere with power head removal. Remove six screws securing power head to drive shaft housing and lift off power head. Disconnect crankcase recirculation hose. Remove cylinder head, lower oil seal housing (20—Fig. Y6-15) and exhaust cover. Carefully remove crankcase half while being careful not to damage mating surfaces.

Engine components are now accessible for removal and overhaul as outlined in the appropriate following paragraphs. Assemble as outlined in the ASSEMBLY paragraphs.

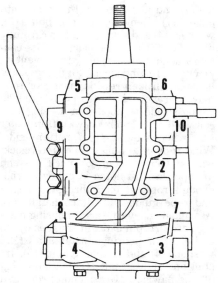

Fig. Y6-16 — Tighten crankcase screws in sequence shown above.

ASSEMBLY. When reassembling, make sure all joints and gasket surfaces are clean, free from nicks and burrs and hardened cement or carbon. The crankcase and inlet manifold must be completely sealed against water leakage and pressure. Mating surfaces of water intake and exhaust areas between power head and drive shaft housing must form a tight seal.

Whenever the power head is disassembled, it is recommended that all gasket surfaces and mating surfaces without gaskets be carefully checked for nicks, burrs and warped surfaces which might interfere with a tight seal. Cylinder head, cylinder block and crankcase should be checked on a surface plate and lapped if necessary to provide a smooth surface. Do not remove any more metal than is necessary.

All friction surfaces and needle bearings should be lubricated with engine oil during reassembly. Seals should be filled with Yamaha Grease A or an equivalent water-resistant grease. Check frequently as power head is being assembled for binding of working parts. If binding or locking is encountered, correct cause before proceeding with assembly.

Mating surfaces of crankcase should be lightly and evenly coated with Yamaha Bond No. 4 or a suitable equivalent. Make sure entire surface is coated, but avoid an excess application as sealant may be squeezed into crankcase, bearings or passages. Tighten M6 crankcase screws to 12 N·m (9 ft.-lbs.) and M8 crankcase screws to 30 N·m (22 ft.-lbs.) following tightening sequence shown in Fig. Y6-16. Tighten cylinder head screws to 17 N·m (12 ft.-lbs.) following tightening sequence shown in Fig. Y6-17.

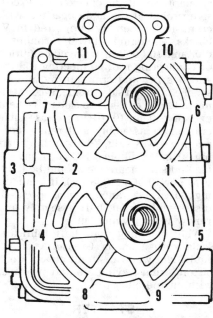

Fig. Y6-17 — Tighten cylinder head screws in sequence shown above.

Before attaching power head to drive shaft housing, make certain drive shaft splines are clean then coat splines with a light coating of Yamaha Grease A or an equivalent water-resistant grease. Tighten power head retaining screws to 18 N·m (13 ft.-lbs.).

CYLINDERS, RINGS AND PISTONS. Cylinder bores should be measured in several different locations to determine if an out-of-round or tapered condition exists. Bore and hone cylinder to fit an oversize piston and ring set if cylinder is 0.05 mm (0.002 in.) out-of-round or if cylinder is tapered in excess of 0.08 mm (0.003 in.). Be sure to chamfer edges of ports in cylinder after boring to prevent rings from hanging up on sharp edges.

Recommended piston skirt-to-cylinder clearance is 0.035-0.040 mm (0.0014-0.0016 in.). Recommended piston ring end gap is 0.15-0.35 mm (0.006-0.014 in.) for both rings. Piston ring side clearance should be 0.04-0.08 mm (0.0016-0.0031 in.) for both rings. Top piston ring is semi-keystone shaped. Install piston rings with manufacturer's markings toward top of piston.

When reassembling, install new piston pin retaining clips (23—Fig. Y6-15) and make sure that piston is positioned on connecting rod so "UP" mark on piston crown is toward flywheel end of engine. Coat bearings, pistons, rings and cylinder bores with a suitable engine oil during reassembly.

CRANKSHAFT, BEARINGS AND CONNECTING RODS. The crankshaft assembly should be checked for excessive runout at the main bearings with crankshaft assembly supported in V-blocks. Maximum allowable runout is 0.03 mm (0.0012 in.). Check condition of connecting rod, connecting rod big end bearing and crankpin by moving small end of rod side-to-side. If connecting rod small end side-to-side movement exceeds 2.0 mm (0.079 in.), disassemble crankshaft assembly and renew connecting rod (8—Fig. Y6-15), roller bearing (9) and crankpin (5). Connecting rod big end side clearance should be 0.20-0.70 mm (0.008-0.028 in.). If connecting rod side clearance is not as specified, disassemble crankshaft assembly and renew worn components.

When installing crankshaft, lubricate seals with Yamaha Grease A or an equivalent water-resistant grease. Coat pistons, rings, cylinders and bearings with engine oil.

STARTER

MANUAL STARTER. Starter may be disassembled for overhaul or renewal of individual components as follows: Remove engine top cowl and three screws securing starter assembly to power head. Check pawl (10—Fig. Y6-19) for wear on engagement area and freedom of movement. Renew or grease as necessary. Remove rope handle (4) and allow rope (5) to wind onto pulley (7). Remove nut (1), bolt (15), washer (14) and shaft (13), then carefully lift pulley (7) out of housing (2). Use caution when removing pulley to prevent injury from rewind spring (6) flying out of housing. Broken rewind spring or rope may be renewed at this point. Rewind spring should be hooked in housing with coil winding counterclockwise from outer end when viewed from bottom side. Wind rope onto pulley (7) counterclockwise as viewed from bottom. Hook end of rope through notch in pulley leaving enough rope to feed through housing and rope guide and attach handle (4). Assemble pulley to starter housing making sure that pin in drum engages eye in end of rewind spring. Install shaft (13), washer (14) and retaining bolt (15). Install and tighten nut (1). Install spring (9) and pawl (10). Grasp end of rope and turn pulley three or four turns counterclockwise.

NOTE: Do not apply any more tension on rewind spring (6) than is required to draw starter handle (4) back into the proper released position.

Thread rope through starter housing and rope guide and attach rope handle (4). All friction surfaces should be greased with Yamaha Grease A or a suitable water-resistant grease.

Adjust starter safety cable by turning adjusting nuts at cable end so starter will operate when outboard motor is in neutral position, but will not engage when outboard motor is in forward or reverse gear.

ELECTRIC STARTER. Some models are equipped with the 12-volt electric starter shown in Fig. Y6-21. Commutator undercut should be 0.5-0.8 mm (0.02-0.03 in.). Minimum brush wear limit is 4.5 mm (0.18 in.).

LOWER UNIT

PROPELLER AND DRIVE HUB. Lower unit protection is provided by a cushion type hub in the propeller. Select a propeller that will allow the engine to reach maximum engine speed of 4500-5500 rpm.

R&R AND OVERHAUL. Most lower unit service can be performed after removing lower unit gearcase from the drive shaft housing. Remove gearcase as follows: Clamp motor to a suitable stand, remove propeller and drain lubricant. Loosen shift rod locknut (N—Fig. Y6-23) and unscrew coupler (C) to disconnect upper shift rod from lower shift rod (3). Unscrew four screws and

separate gearcase from drive shaft housing. Remove water pump assembly. Unscrew two cap screws securing bearing carrier (39—Fig. Y6-24), then withdraw bearing carrier and propeller shaft assembly. Separate propeller shaft from bearing carrier. To remove dog clutch (28), remove spring clip (30) and drive out pin (29). Use a suitable puller to separate reverse gear (35) and bearing (37) from bearing carrier. Remove nut (22), pinion gear (21) and pull drive shaft (5) out of gearcase. Withdraw thrust bearing (23) and shim (20) from gearcase cavity. Forward gear (27) may now be removed. Pry seal housing (9) free and remove along with sleeve (10).

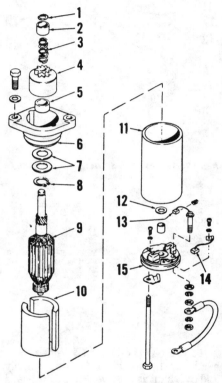

Fig. Y6-21—Exploded view of electric starter motor used on some models.

1. Snap ring		9. Armature	
2. Collar		10. Magnets	
3. Spring		11. Housing	
4. Starter drive		12. Washer	
5. Bushing		13. Positive brush	
6. End frame		14. Negative brush	
7. Washers		15. End cap	
8. Snap ring			

Fig. Y6-19—Exploded view of manual starter.

1. Nut			
2. Housing		9. Spring	
3. Rope guide		10. Pawl	
4. Handle		11. "E" clip	
5. Rope		12. Bushing	
6. Rewind spring		13. Shaft	
7. Pulley		14. Washer	
8. Pin		15. Bolt	

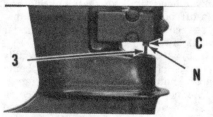

Fig. Y6-23—Loosen locknut (N) and unscrew coupler (C) from lower shift rod (3) before removing gearcase.

Drive needle bearings (19) down into gear cavity for removal. Unscrew retainer (1) and withdraw shift rod and cam (3).

Inspect shafts for wear on seal lip contact areas and on splines. Inspect clutch and gears for wear on engagement areas of dog teeth. Inspect gears for wear and damage. Inspect shift cam for excessive wear on ramp. All seals and "O" rings should be renewed when unit is assembled.

Gear backlash and mesh position should be checked on reassembly. Install forward gear (27) and bearing (25) with original shim (26) in gearcase. Position pinion gear (21) and thrust bearing (23) with original shim (20) in gearcase, then install drive shaft (5). Secure pinion gear to drive shaft with nut (22).

Tighten nut (22) to 25 N·m (18 ft.-lbs.). Invert gearcase housing. Forward gear (27) and pinion gear (21) should mesh evenly when drive shaft (5) is rotated. Adjust mesh position by varying thickness of shim (20). Forward gear backlash should be 0.23-0.69 mm (0.009-0.027 in.) and is adjusted by varying thickness of shim (26). Reverse gear backlash should be 0.80-1.15 mm (0.031-0.045 in.) and is adjusted by varying thickness of shim (36).

Reassemble gearcase by reversing disassembly procedure while noting the following: Install seals (6) in seal housing (9) so lips are toward top of housing. Install seals (41) in bearing carrier (39) so lips are toward propeller. Install dog clutch (28) so "F" marked side (Fig. Y6-25) is toward forward gear. Apply a light coat of Yamaha Grease A or a suitable water-resistant grease to drive shaft splines.

With gearcase assembled and installed, synchronize gear engagement with gear selector handle by turning shift rod coupler (C—Fig. Y6-23), then tighten locknut (N) against coupler.

Fig. Y6-24—Exploded view of gearcase assembly. Note that on late models, set of two needle bearings (19) are replaced with a single needle bearing. If renewing bearings (19) on early models equipped with two bearing set, be sure to install single bearing design.

10. Sleeve
11. Gasket
12. Seal
13. Retainer
14. Dowel pin
15. Dowel pin
16. Vent plug
17. Gearcase
18. Drain plug
19. Needle bearings
20. Shim
21. Pinion gear
22. Nut
23. Thrust bearing
24. Trim tab
25. Ball bearing
26. Shim
27. Forward gear
28. Dog clutch
29. Pin
30. Spring clip
31. Shift pin
32. Spring
33. Propeller shaft
34. Thrust washer
35. Reverse gear
36. Shim
37. Ball bearing
38. "O" ring
39. Bearing carrier
41. Seals
42. Thrust hub
44. Seal
45. Water tube
46. Retainer
47. Seal

1. Retainer
2. Boot
3. Shift rod & cam
4. Key
5. Drive shaft
6. Seals
7. Bushing
8. Dowel pin
9. Seal housing

Fig. Y6-25 — Install dog clutch (28 — Fig. Y6-24) so "F" mark (F) is towards forward gear.

YAMAHA 25 HP
(Prior to 1988)

CONDENSED SERVICE DATA

NOTE: Metric fasteners are used throughout outboard motor.

TUNE-UP
Hp/rpm	25/4500-5500
Bore	73 mm
	(2.87 in.)
Stroke	61 mm
	(2.40 in.)
Number of Cylinders	2
Displacement	496 cc
	(30.3 cu. in.)
Spark Plug–NGK	B7HS
Electrode Gap	0.5-0.6 mm
	(0.020-0.024 in.)
Ignition	CDI
Idle Speed (in gear)	750-850 rpm
Fuel:Oil Ratio	100:1

SIZES–CLEARANCES
Piston Ring End Gap	0.2-0.4 mm
	(0.008-0.016 in.)
Lower Piston Ring Side Clearance	0.04-0.08 mm
	(0.0016-0.0032 in.)
Piston Skirt Clearance	0.060-0.065 mm
	(0.0024-0.0026 in.)
Crankshaft Runout–Max	0.03 mm
	(0.0012 in.)

SIZES—CLEARANCES CONT.
Connecting Rod Small End Shake:	
Standard	0.8 mm
	(0.030 in.)
Limit	2.0 mm
	(0.080 in.)
Connecting Rod Big End Side Clearance	0.38-0.48 mm
	(0.015-0.019 in.)

TIGHTENING TORQUES
Crankcase	27 N·m
	(19 ft.-lbs.)
Cylinder Head	27 N·m
	(19 ft.-lbs.)
Flywheel	160 N·m
	(118 ft.-lbs.)
Standard Screws:	
5 mm	5 N·m
	(44 in.-lbs.)
6 mm	8 N·m
	(71 in.-lbs.)
8 mm	18 N·m
	(13 ft.-lbs.)
10 mm	36 N·m
	(25 ft.-lbs.)
12 mm	43 N·m
	(31 ft.-lbs.)

LUBRICATION

The power head is lubricated by oil mixed with the fuel. Fuel should be regular leaded, low lead or unleaded gasoline with a minimum pump octane rating of 84. Recommended oil is YAMALUBE 100/1 Two-Cycle Lubricant. Normal fuel:oil ratio is 100:1. During the first 10 hours of operation, the fuel:oil ratio should be increased to 25:1.

Lower unit gears and bearings are lubricated by oil contained in the gearcase. Recommended oil is YAMALUBE Gearcase Lube. Lubricant is drained by removing vent and drain plugs in the gearcase. Refill through drain plug hole until oil has reached level of top (vent) plug hole.

FUEL SYSTEM

CARBURETOR. Refer to Fig. Y8-1 for an exploded view of carburetor. Recommended standard main jet (15–Fig. Y8-1) size is #133 and recommended standard pilot jet (6) size is #60. Main jet (15) size should be reduced from standard recommendation by one size

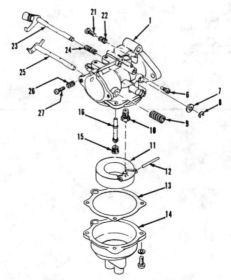

Fig. Y8-1—Exploded view of carburetor.

1. Body		15. Main jet	
6. Pilot jet		16. Main nozzle	
7. Washer		21. Idle mixture screw	
8. Clip		22. Spring	
9. Spring		23. Throttle shaft	
10. Fuel inlet valve		24. Spring	
11. Float		25. Choke shaft	
12. Pin		26. Spring	
13. Gasket		27. Idle speed screw	
14. Float bowl			

for altitudes of 2500 to 5000 feet (750 to 1500 m), two sizes for altitudes of 5000 to 7500 feet (1500 to 2250 m) and three sizes for altitudes of 7500 feet (2250 m) and up. Initial adjustment of idle mixture screw (21) is 1⅛ to 1⅝ turns out from a lightly seated position. Recommended idle speed is 750-850 rpm (in gear) with the engine at normal operating temperature.

To check float level, remove float bowl (14) and invert carburetor. While holding carburetor at approximately a 60 degree angle as shown in Fig. Y8-2, measure from gasket surface of carburetor body (1) to top of float (11). Measurement should be 17.5-18.5 mm (0.69-0.73 in.). Bend float tang (T) to adjust.

FUEL FILTER. A fuel filter assembly (1–Fig. Y8-3) is connected between fuel supply line (2) and fuel pump inlet line (3). With the engine stopped, periodically unscrew fuel filter cup (7) from filter base (4) and withdraw filter element (6), "O" ring (5) and gasket (8). Clean cup (7) and filter element (6) in a suitable solvent and blow dry with clean compressed air. Inspect filter element (6). If excessive blockage or damage is noted, renew element.

Reassembly is reverse order of disassembly. Renew "O" ring (5) and gasket (8) during reassembly.

FUEL PUMP. The diaphragm type fuel pump is located on the port side of the engine. Refer to Fig. Y8-4 for an exploded view of fuel pump. Alternating pressure and vacuum pulsations in the crankcase actuates the diaphragm and check valves in the pump. Fuel pump assembly uses reed valve type check valves.

Make certain that all gaskets, diaphragms and check valves are in

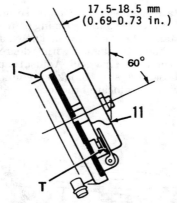

17.5-18.5 mm (0.69-0.73 in.)

60°

Fig. Y8-2—Measure float level between gasket surface of carburetor body (1) and top of float (11) with carburetor at a 60 degree angle as shown. Bend float tang (T) to adjust.

good condition when reassembling unit. Coat fuel pump mounting gasket with a nonhardening type gasket sealer making certain that passage in center is not blocked with gasket sealer.

REED VALVE. The reed valve assembly is located between the intake manifold and crankcase. Refer to Fig. Y8-6 for a view of reed valve assembly.

Cracked, warped, chipped or bent reed petals will impair operation and should be renewed. Do not attempt to straighten or repair bent or damaged reed petals. Reed petals should seat smoothly against reed plate along their entire length. Make sure reed petals are centered over reed plate passages. Height of reed stop should be 4.7-5.3 mm (0.19-0.21 in.). Renew reed stop if height adjustment is 0.2 mm (0.008 in.) more or less than specified, or damage is noted.

SPEED CONTROL LINKAGE. To synchronize ignition and throttle control linkage, first make sure the ignition timing is properly adjusted. Detach magneto base plate control rod (4—Fig. Y8-9) from magneto control lever (8). Place magneto base plate in full advanced position. Shift outboard motor to forward gear position, then rotate twist grip to full throttle position. Adjust length of magneto base plate control rod (4) until rod end slides onto magneto lever ball socket without disturbing position of magneto lever. Rec-

ommended length of control rod (4) is 78.5-79.5 mm (3.09-3.13 in.).

Detach throttle cam control rod (1) from throttle control lever (9). Rotate carburetor throttle shaft to wide-open throttle stop, then rotate throttle cam (2) until cam contacts throttle shaft roller (3). Rotate twist grip to full throttle position and adjust length of throttle cam control rod (1) until rod end slides onto throttle control lever ball socket without disturbing position of throttle control lever. Recommended length of rod (1) is 170.5 mm (6.71 in.).

With twist grip held in the full throttle position, blockout lever (11) should contact bottom cowling stopper (12). If not, readjust blockout lever control rod (10). Recommended length of rod (10) is 93.5-94.5 mm (3.68-3.72 in.).

Loosen nuts (13) on throttle cable pull side (6) and adjust nuts (13) until all slack is removed from cable (6). Loosen nuts (13) on throttle cable loose side (7) and adjust nuts (13) to provide 1-2 mm (0.040-0.080 in.) slack in cable (7). Be sure nuts (13) are securely retightened.

IGNITION

The standard spark plug is NGK B7HS with an electrode gap of 0.5-0.6 mm (0.020-0.024 in.).

All models are equipped with a capacitor discharge ignition (CDI) system. If engine malfunction is noted and the ignition system is suspected,

Fig. Y8-4—Exploded view of fuel pump assembly.
1. Base
2. Gasket
3. Diaphragm
4. Check valves
5. Spring plate
6. Spring
7. Body
8. Gasket
9. Diaphragm
10. Cover

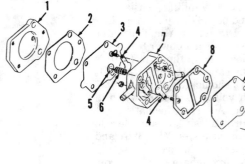

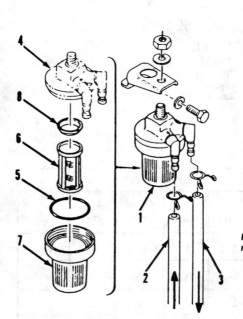

Fig. Y8-3—Exploded view of fuel filter assembly, fuel hoses and mounting brackets.

1. Fuel filter assy.	5. "O" ring
2. Fuel supply line	6. Filter element
3. Fuel pump inlet line	7. Cup
4. Filter base	8. Gasket

Fig. Y8-6—Exploded view of reed valve and intake manifold assembly.
1. Crankcase half
2. Gasket
3. Reed valve assy.
4. Gasket
5. Intake manifold

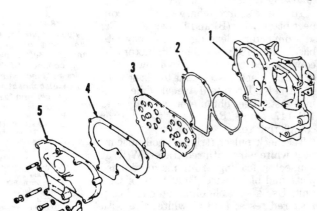

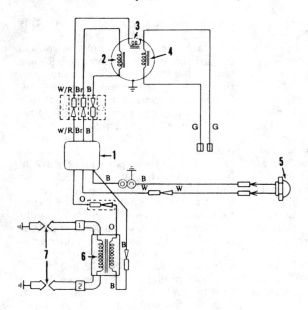

Fig. Y8-9—View of speed control linkage. Refer to text for adjustment procedure.

1. Throttle cam control rod
2. Throttle cam
3. Throttle shaft roller
4. Magneto control rod
5. Cable adjust nuts
6. Throttle cable (pull side)
7. Throttle cable (loose side)
8. Magneto control lever
9. Throttle control lever
10. Blockout lever control rod
11. Blockout lever
12. Stopper
13. Locknuts
14. Magneto base plate

To test CDI module, first disconnect all wires at connectors and remove CDI module from outboard motor. Use a suitable ohmmeter and refer to Fig. Y8-12. With reference to chart, perform CDI module resistance tests.

Renew any components that are not within the manufacturer's recommended limits.

To check ignition timing, rotate flywheel clockwise so timing pointer (TP—Fig. Y8-13) is aligned with 25 degrees BTDC mark on flywheel.

NOTE: Rotate engine in normal direction of rotation (clockwise) only. Water pump impeller may be damaged if engine rotation is reversed.

Rotate magneto base plate so stop bracket tab (T) contacts timing pointer. The stamped mark on the magneto base plate should be aligned with 0 degrees (TDC) mark on flywheel. Adjust timing by loosening stop bracket retaining screws and relocate bracket.

make sure the spark plugs and all electrical connections are tight before proceeding to trouble-shooting the CD ignition system.

Proceed as follows to test CDI system components: Refer to Fig. Y8-11. To test ignition coil, disconnect black wire (B) and orange wire (O) at connectors and spark plug boots from spark plugs. Use a suitable ohmmeter and connect red tester lead to orange wire (O) and black tester lead to black wire (B). The primary winding resistance reading should be 0.08-0.10 ohms. Connect red tester lead to terminal end in one spark plug boot and black tester lead to terminal end in remaining spark plug boot. The secondary winding resistance reading should be 2,975-4,025 ohms. Use a suitable coil tester or Yamaha tester YU-33261 to perform a power test. Connect tester leads as outlined in tester's handbook. On Yamaha tester YU-33261, a steady spark should jump a 8 mm (0.31 in.) gap with voltage selector switch in "CDI" position. A surface insulation test can be performed using a suitable coil tester or Yamaha tester YU-33261 and following tester's handbook.

To check source (charge) coil, disconnect black wire (B) and brown wire (Br) at connectors leading from magneto base plate. Use a suitable ohmmeter and connect red tester lead to brown wire (Br) and black tester lead to black wire (B). DO NOT rotate flywheel while making test. The ohmmeter should read 121-147 ohms. Reconnect wires after completing test.

To check pulser (trigger) coil, disconnect white wire with red tracer (W/R) at connector leading from magneto base plate and black wire (B) at back of CDI unit. Use a suitable ohmmeter and connect red tester lead to white wire with red tracer (W/R) and black tester lead to

black wire (B). DO NOT rotate flywheel while making test. The ohmmeter should read 12.6-15.4 ohms.

Fig. Y8-11 — View identifying CDI system components.

1. CDI module
2. Charge coil
3. Pulser coil
4. Lighting coil
5. Stop switch
6. Ignition coil
7. Spark plugs

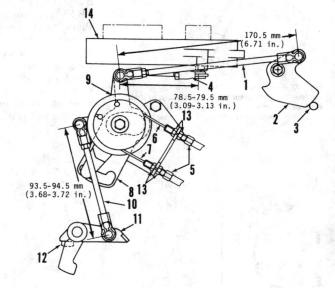

Fig. Y8-12—Use chart and values listed below to test condition of CD ignition module. Before making test (J), connect CDI's orange wire and black wire together. Then disconnect wires and perform test.

A. Zero
B. Infinity
C. 9,000-19,000 ohms
D. 2,000-6,000 ohms
E. 80,000-160,000 ohms
F. 70,000-150,000 ohms
G. 33,000-63,000 ohms
H. 7,000-17,000 ohms
I. 15,000-35,000 ohms
J. Tester needle should show deflection then return toward infinite resistance

Red Test Lead \ Black Test Lead	CDI UNIT LEADS				
	White	Black	Brown	White w/Red	Orange
White	A	B	B	B	B
Black	C	A	D	B	J
Brown	E	F	A	B	J
White w/Red	G	H	I	A	J
Orange	B	B	B	B	A

COOLING SYSTEM

WATER PUMP. A rubber impeller type water pump is mounted between the drive shaft housing and gearcase. Water pump impeller (6–Fig. Y8-15) is driven by a key in the drive shaft.

When cooling system problems are encountered, first check water inlet for plugging or partial stoppage. Be sure thermostat located in cylinder head operates properly. If the water pump is suspected defective, separate gearcase from drive shaft housing and inspect pump. Make sure all seals and mating surfaces are in good condition and water passages are unobstructed. Check impeller (6) and plate (7) for excessive wear. When reassembling, coat gasket surfaces with a thin coating of YAMAHA Bond No. 4.

POWER HEAD

R&R AND OVERHAUL. The power head can be removed for disassembly and overhaul as follows: Clamp outboard

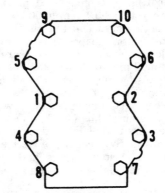

Fig. Y8-17—Tighten crankcase screws in sequence shown above.

motor to a suitable stand and remove engine cowl and starter assembly. Disconnect speed control cables, fuel line and any wiring that will interfere with power head removal. Remove or disconnect any component that will interfere with power head removal. Remove six screws securing power head to drive shaft housing and lift power head free. Remove flywheel, ignition components, carburetor, intake manifold and reed valve assembly. Remove screws retaining exhaust cover (18–Fig. Y8-20) and withdraw. Crankcase halves can be separated after removal of ten screws securing crankcase half (1) to cylinder block.

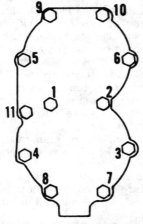

Fig. Y8-18—Tighten cylinder head screws in sequence shown above.

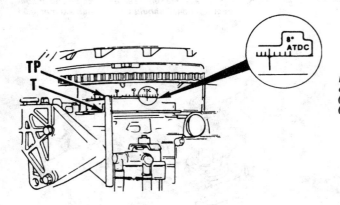

Fig. Y8-13—Full advance occurs when stop bracket tab (T) contacts timing pointer (TP). Refer to text for ignition timing adjustment.

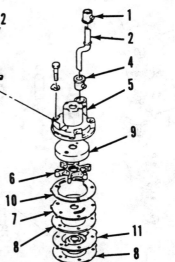
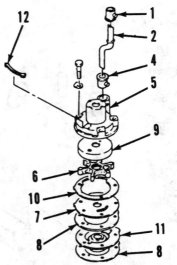

Fig. Y8-15—Exploded view of water pump assembly.

1. Seal
2. Water tube
4. Seal
5. Pump housing
6. Impeller
7. Plate
8. Gasket
9. Liner
10. Gasket
11. Base
12. Spacer

Fig. Y8-20—Exploded view of cylinder block assembly.

1. Crankcase
2. Cylinder block
3. Oil seal housing
4. Gasket
5. Oil seal
6. Check valve
7. Dowel pin
8. Gasket
9. Cylinder head
10. Thermostat cover
11. Gasket
12. Spacer
13. Thermostat
14. Anode
15. Gasket
16. Inner exhaust plate
17. Gasket
18. Exhaust cover

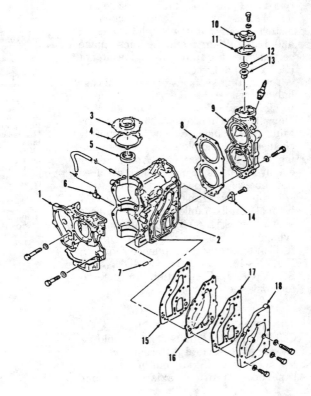

Crankshaft and pistons are now accessible for removal and overhaul as outlined in the appropriate following paragraphs.

ASSEMBLY. Two-stroke engine design dictates that intake manifold and crankcase are completely sealed against both vacuum and pressure. Exhaust manifold and cylinder head must be sealed against water leakage and pressure. Mating surfaces of water intake and exhaust areas between power head and drive shaft housing must form a tight seal.

Whenever the power head is disassembled, it is recommended that all gasket surfaces of crankcase halves be carefully checked for nicks, burrs or warped surfaces which might interfere with a tight seal. The cylinder head, head end of cylinder block, and the mating surfaces of manifolds and crankcase should be checked and lapped, if necessary, to provide a smooth surface. Do not remove any more metal than is necessary to obtain a smooth finish. Thoroughly clean the parts with new oil on a soft shop towel, then wash with soap and water.

Mating surface of crankcase halves may be checked on the lapping block, and high spots or nicks removed, but surfaces must not be lowered. If extreme care is used, a slightly damaged crankcase can be salvaged in this manner. In case of doubt, renew the crankcase assembly.

The crankcase halves are positively located during assembly by the use of two dowel pins. Check to make sure that dowel pins are not bent, nicked or distorted and that dowel holes are clean and true. When installing pins, make certain they are fully seated, but do not use excessive force.

The mating surfaces of the crankcase halves must be sealed during reassembly using Yamaha Bond No. 4 or nonhardening type of gasket sealer. Make certain that surfaces are thoroughly cleaned of oil and old sealer before making a fresh application. Apply sealer evenly and use sparingly, so excess does not squeeze into crankcase cavity.

Tighten the crankcase screws to 27 N·m (19 ft.-lbs.) following the sequence shown in Fig. Y8-17. Tighten the cylinder head screws to 27 N·m (19 ft.-lbs.) following the sequence shown in Fig. Y8-18. Refer to CONDENSED SERVICE DATA section for general torquing specifications.

PISTONS, PINS, RINGS AND CYLINDERS. Cylinder bore should be measured in several different locations to determine if an out-of-round or tapered condition exists. Inspect

cylinder wall for scoring. If minor scoring is noted, cylinders should be honed to smooth out cylinder wall.

Recommended piston skirt to cylinder clearance is 0.060-0.065 mm (0.0024-0.0026 in.). Recommended piston ring end gap is 0.2-0.4 mm (0.008-0.016 in.) for both rings. The top piston ring is semi-keystone shaped. The recommended lower piston ring side clearance is 0.04-0.08 mm (0.0016-0.0032 in.). Make sure piston rings properly align with locating pins in ring grooves.

When reassembling, install new piston pin retaining clips (4 – Fig. Y8-22) and make sure that "UP" on dome of piston is towards flywheel end of engine. Coat bearings, pistons, rings and cylinder bores with engine oil during assembly.

CONNECTING RODS, CRANKSHAFT AND BEARINGS. The crankshaft assembly should only be disassembled if the necessary tools and experience are available to service this type of crankshaft.

Maximum crankshaft runout measured at bearing outer races with crankshaft ends supported in lathe centers is 0.03 mm (0.0012 in.). Maximum connecting rod big end side clearance should be 0.38-0.48 mm (0.015-0.019 in.). Side-to-side shake of connecting rod small end measured as shown in Fig. Y8-23 should be a maximum of 2.0 mm (0.08 in.).

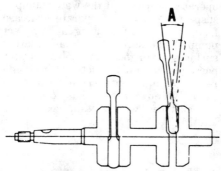

Fig. Y8-23 — Maximum shake at small end of connecting rod (A) should be less than 2.0 mm (0.08 in.).

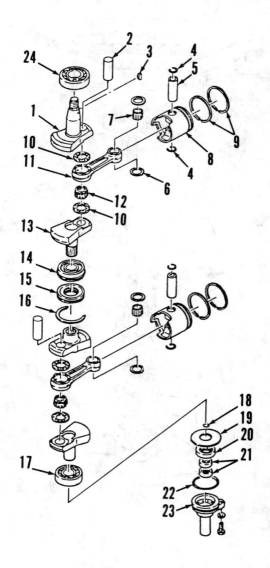

Fig. Y8-22—Exploded view of crankshaft assembly.

1. Crank half
2. Crankpin
3. Key
4. Clip
5. Piston pin
6. Washer
7. Needle bearings
8. Piston
9. Piston rings
10. Thrust washer
11. Connecting rod
12. Roller bearing
13. Crank half
14. Bearing & snap ring
15. Labyrinth seal
16. Snap ring
17. Bearing
18. "O" ring
19. Washer
20. Oil seal
21. Oil seals
22. "O" ring
23. Lower oil seal housing
24. Bearing

Crankcase, connecting rods and center section components are available only as a unit assembly. Outer main bearings (17 and 24 – Fig. Y8-22) are available individually.

Thirty-four needle bearings (7) are used in each connecting rod small end. Rollers can be held in place with petroleum jelly while installing piston.

Lubricate bearings, pistons, rings and cylinders with engine oil prior to installation. Tighten crankcase and cylinder head screws as outlined in ASSEMBLY section.

STARTER

MANUAL STARTER. When starter rope (5 – Fig. Y8-25) is pulled, pulley (7) will rotate. As pulley (7) rotates, drive pawl (10) moves to engage with the flywheel thus cranking the engine.

When starter rope (5) is released, pulley (7) is rotated in the reverse direction by force from rewind spring (6). As pulley (7) rotates, the starter rope is rewound and drive pawl (10) is disengaged from the flywheel.

Safety plunger (20) engages lugs on pulley (7) to prevent starter engagement when the gear shift lever is in the forward or reverse position.

To overhaul the manual starter, proceed as follows: Remove the engine top cover. Remove the screws retaining the manual starter to the engine. Remove starter lockout cable (18) at starter housing (2). Note plunger (20) and spring (19) located at cable end; care should be used not to lose components should they fall free. Withdraw the starter assembly.

Check pawl (10) for freedom of movement and excessive wear of engagement area or any other damage. Renew or lubricate pawl (10) with a suitable water-resistant grease and return starter to service if no other damage is noted.

To disassemble, remove clip (11) and withdraw pawl (10) and pawl spring (9). Untie starter rope (5) at handle (4) and allow the rope to wind into the starter. Remove bolt (15), washer (14) and shaft (13), then place a suitable screwdriver blade through hole (H – Fig. Y8-26) to hold rewind spring (6 – Fig. Y8-25) securely in housing (2). Carefully lift pulley (7) with starter rope (5) from housing (2). BE CAREFUL when removing pulley (7) to prevent possible injury from rewind spring. Untie starter rope (5) and remove rope from pulley (7) if renewal is required. To remove rewind spring (6) from housing (2), invert hous-

ing so it sits upright on a flat surface, then tap the housing top until rewind spring (6) falls free and uncoils.

Inspect all components for damage and excessive wear and renew if needed.

To reassemble, first apply a coating of Yamaha Grease A or a suitable water-resistant grease to rewind spring area of housing (2). Install rewind spring (6) in housing (2) so spring coils wind in a counterclockwise direction from the outer end. Make sure the spring outer hook is properly secured around starter housing pin (8). Wind starter rope (5) onto pulley (7) approximately 2½ turns

Fig. Y8-26—View showing proper installation of pawl spring (9), pawl (10) and clip (11). Pulley hole (H) is used during pulley withdrawal. Refer to text.

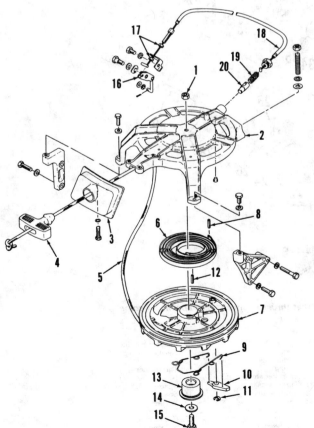

Fig. Y8-25—Exploded view of manual starter assembly.

1. Nut
2. Housing
3. Rope guide
4. Handle
5. Starter rope
6. Rewind spring
7. Pulley
8. Pin
9. Pawl spring
10. Pawl
11. Clip
12. Pin
13. Shaft
14. Washer
15. Bolt
16. Lever & link
17. Adjusting nuts
18. Starter lockout cable
19. Spring
20. Plunger

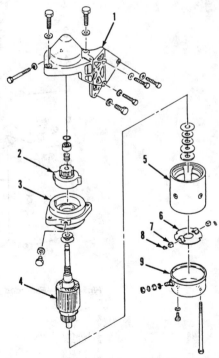

Fig. Y8-28—Exploded view of electric starter.

1. End frame
2. Drive assy.
3. Frame cover
4. Armature
5. Frame
6. Brush plate
7. Brush
8. Brush spring
9. End cover

counterclockwise when viewed from the flywheel side. Direct remaining starter rope (5) length through notch in pulley (7).

NOTE: Lubricate all friction surfaces with Yamaha Grease A or a suitable water-resistant grease during reassembly.

Assembly pulley (7) to starter housing making sure that pin (12) engages hook end in rewind spring (6). Install shaft (13), washer (14) and bolt (15). Apply a thread fastening solution on bolt (15)

threads, then install nut (1) and securely tighten.

Thread starter rope (5) through starter housing (2), rope guide (3) and handle (4) and secure with a knot. Turn pulley (7) 2 to 3 turns counterclockwise when viewed from the flywheel side, then release starter rope (5) from pulley notch and allow rope to slowly wind onto pulley.

NOTE: Do not apply any more tension on rewind spring (6) than is required to draw starter handle (4) back into the proper released position.

Install spring (9), pawl (10) and clip (11) as shown in Fig. Y8-26. Remount manual starter assembly.

Adjust starter lockout assembly by turning adjusting nuts (17 – Fig. Y8-25) at cable (18) end so starter will engage when gear shift lever is in neutral position, but will not engage when gear shift lever is in forward or reverse position. Plunger (20) end should recess in starter housing (2) 1 mm (0.04 in.) when gear shift lever is in neutral position.

ELECTRIC STARTER. Some models are equipped with an electric

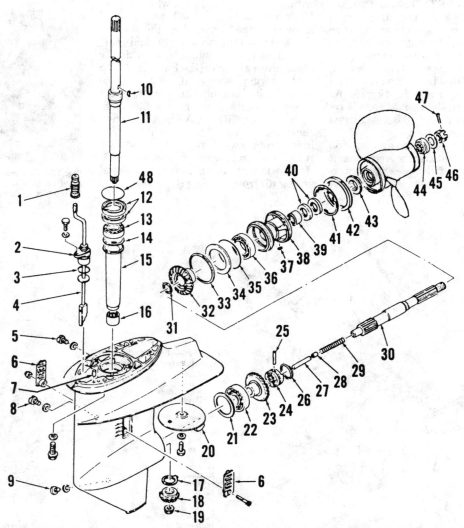

Fig. Y8-30—Exploded view of gearcase assembly. Note that thrust washer (17) is absent on some models.

1. Boot	14. Shim	25. Pin	37. Key
2. Retainer	15. Drive shaft tube	26. Spring clip	38. Bearing housing
3. "O" ring	16. Needle bearing	27. Spring plunger	39. Needle bearing
4. Lower shift rod	17. Thrust washer	28. Spring guide	40. Oil seals
5. Vent plug	18. Pinion gear	29. Spring	41. Tab washer
6. Water inlet cover	19. Nut	30. Propeller shaft	42. Nut
7. Dowel	20. Trim tab	31. Thrust washer	43. Spacer
8. Oil level plug	21. Shim	32. Reverse gear	44. Spacer
9. Drain plug	22. Tapered roller	33. Shim	45. Washer
10. Key	bearing	34. Thrust washer	46. Nut
11. Drive shaft	23. Forward gear	35. "O" ring	47. Cotter pin
12. Oil seals	24. Dog clutch	36. Ball bearing	48. "O" ring
13. Bearing			

starter motor. Refer to Fig. Y8-28 for an exploded view of the starter motor. Commutator undercut should be 0.5-0.8 mm (0.02-0.03 in.) with a minimum limit of 0.2 mm (0.008 in.). Minimum brush length is 10 mm (0.394 in.).

During reassembly, adjust shims so armature end play is 1.5-2.0 mm (0.06-0.08 in.).

LOWER UNIT

PROPELLER AND DRIVE HUB. Lower unit protection is provided by a cushion type hub in the propeller. Standard propeller rotates clockwise. Select a propeller that will allow the engine at full throttle to reach maximum operating range of 4500-5500 rpm.

R&R AND OVERHAUL. Most service on lower unit can be performed after detaching gearcase from drive shaft housing. To remove gearcase, attach outboard motor to a suitable stand and remove vent and drain plugs in gearcase to allow lubricant to drain. Loosen locknut (21 – Fig. Y8-31) and remove coupler nut (20). Remove four bolts securing gearcase to drive shaft housing and carefully separate gearcase from drive shaft housing. Remove water pump being careful not to lose impeller key (10 – Fig. Y8-30). Remove propeller.

Disassemble gearcase by bending back locking tab of lockwasher (41), then remove nut (42) and lockwasher (41). Using a suitable puller attached to propeller shaft, extract components (24 through 40) from gearcase. Disassemble propeller shaft assembly as required being careful not to lose shims (33). Detach spring clip (26) and pin (25) to remove dog clutch (24), spring guide (28) and spring (29). Use a suitable puller to separate ball bearing (36) from reverse gear (32).

To remove drive shaft, unscrew pinion gear nut (19) and withdraw drive shaft (11). Forward gear (23) and bearing (22)

cone may now be removed. Use a suitable puller to extract bearing cup; do not lose shims (21). Pull oil seals (12) and bearing (13) out of gearcase being careful not to lose shims (14). Remove drive shaft tube (15) then drive bearing (16) down into gear cavity. Lower shift

rod (4) may be removed after unscrewing retainer (2).

Inspect gears for wear on teeth and in engagement dogs. Inspect dog clutch (24) for wear on engagement surfaces. Inspect shafts for wear on splines and on friction surfaces of gears and oil seals. Check shift cam for excessive wear on shift ramps. All seals and "O" rings should be renewed during reassembly.

Assemble gearcase by reversing disassembly procedure. Install oil seals (12) with lips away from bearing (13). Install thrust washer (17) with grooved side facing pinion gear (18). Tighten pinion gear nut (19) to 34-38 N·m (25-28 ft.-lbs.). Forward gear backlash should be 0.2-0.5 mm (0.008-0.020 in.) and reverse gear backlash should be 0.7-1.0 mm (0.028-0.039 in.).

Install dog clutch (24) so "F" marked side (see Fig. Y8-32) is towards forward gear (23 – Fig. Y8-30). Shift plunger (27) is installed with round end towards cam on lower shift rod (4). Apply Yamaha Grease A or a water resistant grease to drive shaft upper splines.

With gearcase assembled and installed, synchronize gear engagement with gear selector handle by turning shift rod adjusting coupler nut (20 – Fig. Y8-31), then tighten locknut (21).

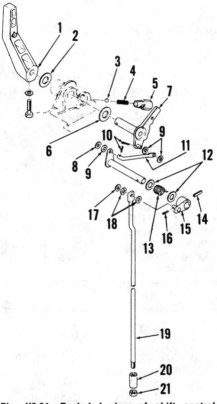

Fig. Y8-31—Exploded view of shift control linkage.

1. Shift control handle	
2. Washer	
3. Detent ball	12. Washers
4. Spring	13. Spring
5. Guide	14. Pin
6. Washer	15. Arm
7. Cam	16. Cotter pin
8. Washer	17. Washer
9. Washer	18. Washers
10. Pins	19. Upper shift rod
11. Link	20. Coupler nut
	21. Locknut

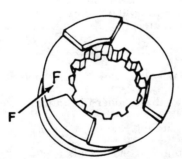

Fig. Y8-32—Install dog clutch so "F" mark (F) is towards forward gear.

YAMAHA 25 HP
(1988 and After)

CONDENSED SERVICE DATA

NOTE: Metric fasteners are used throughout outboard motor.

TUNE-UP

Hp/rpm	25/5500
	(18.6 kW)
Bore	67 mm
	(2.64 in.)
Stroke	56 mm
	(2.20 in.)
Displacement	395 cc
	(24.1 cu. in.)
Number of Cylinders	2
Ignition Type	CDI
Spark Plug	B7HS-10
Electrode Gap	0.9-1.0 mm
	(0.035-0.039 in.)
Idle Speed (in gear)	600-700 rpm
Speed Range at Full Throttle	5000-6000 rpm
Fuel:Oil Ratio	Automatic Metering
Gearcase Oil Capacity	375 mL
	(12.7 oz.)

SIZES—CLEARANCES

Standard Cylinder Bore	
Diameter	67.00-67.02 mm
	(2.6378-2.6386 in.)
Max. Allowable Taper	0.08 mm
	(0.003 in.)
Max. Allowable Out-of-Round	0.05 mm
	(0.002 in.)
Piston-to-Cylinder Clearance	0.040-0.045 mm
	(0.0016-0.0018 in.)
Piston Ring End Gap	0.40-0.60 mm
	(0.016-0.024 in.)
Piston Ring Side Clearance:	
Top Ring	0.02-0.06 mm
	(0.0008-0.0024 in.)
Second Ring	0.03-0.07 mm
	(0.0012-0.0028 in.)
Max. Allowable Crankshaft	
Runout	0.03 mm
	(0.0012 in.)

SIZES—CLEARANCES CONT.

Connecting Rod Side Clearance	1.90-2.10 mm
	(0.075-0.083 in.)
Max. Connecting Rod Small End	
Side Play	2.0 mm
	(0.079 in.)

TIGHTENING TORQUES

Crankcase:	
6 mm	11 N·m
	(8 ft.-lbs.)
8 mm	28 N·m
	(21 ft.-lbs.)
Cylinder Head:	
6 mm	11 N·m
	(8 ft.-lbs.)
8 mm	28 N·m
	(21 ft.-lbs.)
Exhaust Cover	8 N·m
	(71 in.-lbs.)
Flywheel Nut	100 N·m
	(74 ft.-lbs.)
Intake Manifold	8 N·m
	(71 in.-lbs.)
Power Head-to-Drive Shaft	
Housing	21 N·m
	(15 ft.-lbs.)
Spark Plug	25 N·m
	(18 ft.-lbs.)
Standard Screws:	
5 mm	5.0 N·m
	(44 in.-lbs.)
6 mm	8.0 N·m
	(71 in.-lbs.)
8 mm	18 N·m
	(13 ft.-lbs.)
10 mm	36 N·m
	(26 ft.-lbs.)
12 mm	43 N·m
	(32 ft.-lbs.)

LUBRICATION

Models are equipped with automatic oil injection. Recommended oil is YAMALUBE Two-Cycle Outboard Oil or a suitable equivalent NMMA certified TC-W II engine oil. Recommended fuel is regular leaded, low lead or unleaded gasoline with a minimum pump octane rating of 84.

Engines require additional lubrication during the first 10 hours of operation (break-in period) of a new or rebuilt engine. Fill fuel tank with recommended fuel and oil mixed at a 100:1 ratio and use in combination with normal oil injection system. Make sure fuel and oil is thoroughly mixed in a separate container prior to pouring into fuel tank.

Lower unit gears and bearings are lubricated by oil contained in the gearcase. Recommended oil is YAMALUBE Gearcase Lubricant or a suitable equivalent SAE 90 gearlube. Lubricant is drained by removing vent and drain plugs in the gearcase. Refill through drain plug hole until oil reaches level of vent plug hole. Gearcase oil capacity is 375 mL (12.7 ozs.). Lower unit lubricant should be changed after every 100 hours of operation.

FUEL SYSTEM

CARBURETOR. Refer to Fig. Y9-1 for exploded view of carburetor with in-

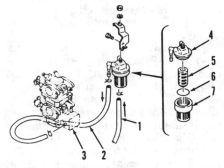

Fig. Y9-3—Exploded view of fuel filter assembly.

1. Fuel inlet hose
2. Fuel outlet hose
3. Fuel pump
4. Base
5. Filter element
6. "O" ring
7. Cup

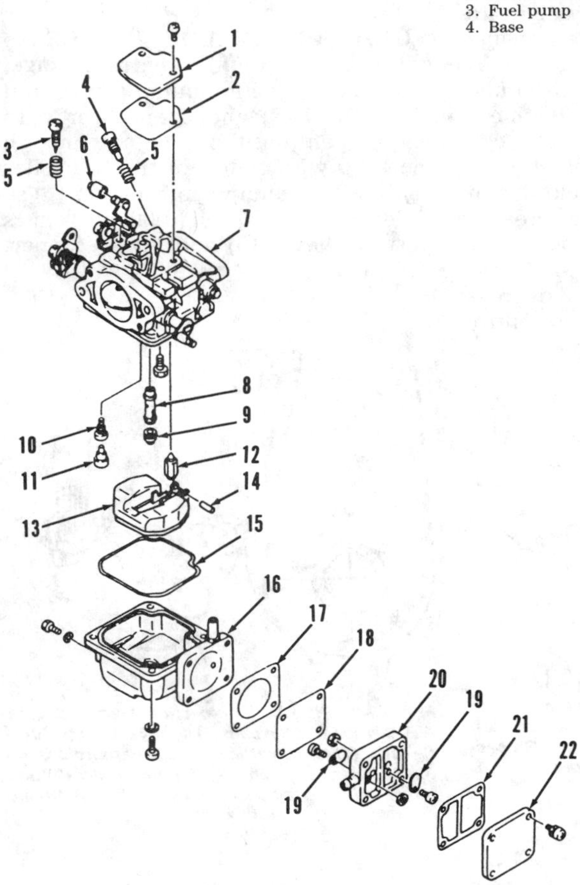

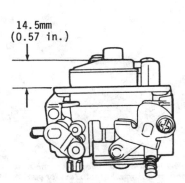

Fig. Y9-1—Exploded view of lower carburetor with integral fuel pump. Upper carburetor is the same except fuel pump is absent.

1. Cover
2. Gasket
3. Idle speed screw
4. Idle mixture screw
5. Spring
6. Roller
7. Body
8. Main nozzle
9. Main jet
10. Pilot jet
11. Plug
12. Inlet needle
13. Float
14. Pin
15. Seal
16. Float bowl
17. Gasket
18. Diaphragm
19. Check valve
20. Pump body
21. Gasket
22. Cover

tegral fuel pump. Standard main jet (9) size is #125. Standard pilot jet (10) size is #60. Initial adjustment of idle mixture screw (4) is 2-1/4 to 2-3/4 turns out from a lightly seated position. Idle speed should be 600-700 rpm with lower unit in forward gear and engine running at normal operating temperature.

To determine float level, remove float bowl (16), invert carburetor and measure as shown in Fig. Y9-2. Float level should be 14.5 mm (0.57 in.). If float level is not as specified, inspect needle valve seat in body (7—Fig. Y9-1) for wear or damage and renew inlet needle (12).

FUEL FILTER. An inline type fuel filter is used. After every 50 hours of operation, unscrew cup (7—Fig. Y9-3) and withdraw filter element (5). Thoroughly clean cup (7) and element (5) in a suitable solvent and dry with compressed air. Renew element if damage or excessive blockage is noted.

FUEL PUMP. Refer to Fig. Y9-1 for exploded view of fuel pump. Pump is activated by crankcase pulsations. Make certain that all gaskets, diaphragms and check valves are in acceptable condition when reassembling unit. Inspect check valves (19) for cracks or bending and renew as necessary. Renew diaphragm (18) if cracking, stretching or other damage is noted.

REED VALVE. Reed valve assemblies (1—Fig. Y9-4) are located between crankcase and intake manifold (3). Reed petals (2—Fig. Y9-5) should seat squarely and smoothly along entire length and should be free of cracks, nicks, tears and burrs. Renew reed valve assembly if reed petals stand open from seat (B) more than 1.5 mm (0.059 in.). Do not attempt to straighten or repair bent or damaged reed petals. Reed stop height (H) should be 5.8-6.2 mm (0.23-0.24 in.).

14.5mm (0.57 in.)

Fig. Y9-2—To determine float level, invert carburetor and measure from float bowl mating surface to bottom of float as shown. If float level is not 14.5 mm (0.57 in.), renew inlet needle (12—Fig. Y9-1).

Fig. Y9-4—Exploded view of reed valve assemblies and related components.

1. Reed valve assy.
2. Gasket
3. Intake manifold
4. Gaskets
5. Carburetors
S. Screws

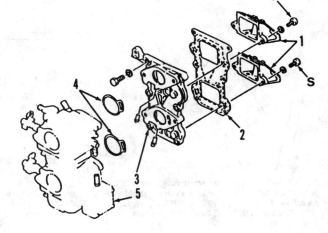

Bend reed stop (1) to adjust. Reed valves are available as a unit assembly only. Apply a suitable thread locking compound to threads of screws (S—Fig. Y9-4) during reassembly.

SPEED CONTROL LINKAGE. The carburetor throttle valves must be synchronized to open as the ignition is advanced to obtain optimum performance. To adjust speed control linkage, proceed as follows: Remove spark plugs and install Yamaha Dial Gage YU-3097 or a suitable equivalent dial indicator into the number 1 spark plug hole. While observing dial indicator, rotate flywheel in a clockwise direction until piston is a TDC.

NOTE: Water pump impeller may be damaged if engine is turned in opposite direction of normal rotation. Rotate flywheel in a CLOCKWISE direction only.

Rotate flywheel in clockwise direction to position number 1 piston at 3.34 mm (0.131 in.) BTDC. Refer to Fig. Y9-6 and loosen timing pointer screw and align

pointer with 25 degrees BTDC mark on flywheel. Be sure to retighten screw securely.

Next, position magneto control lever (5—Fig. Y9-7) in the fully advanced position. Loosen locknut (4) and adjust length of rod (2) so marks (M) on flywheel (1) and magneto base (3) are aligned. Rotate flywheel clockwise and align timing pointer with 7 degrees ATDC mark on flywheel, then loosen locknut (Fig. Y9-8) and adjust fully retarded adjustment screw so marks (M) on flywheel and magneto base are realigned.

Connect a suitable timing light to number 1 spark plug lead, start engine and warm to normal operating temperature. Check timing with engine at idle speed and fully retarded adjustment screw (Fig. Y9-8) contacting stop on cylinder block. Timing should be 4-6 degrees ATDC. If not, loosen locknut and turn fully retarded adjustment screw as necessary. Note that turning screw clockwise will advance timing. Fully advanced timing should be 24-26 degrees BTDC. Adjust length of magneto control

rod (2—Fig. Y9-7) to adjust full advance timing.

To adjust timing pick-up point, open throttle slowly until throttle cam (3—Fig. Y9-9) lightly contacts throttle roller (1). Pick-up timing should be 2-4 degrees ATDC when throttle cam (3) just contacts roller (1) and throttle valves in carburetors begin to open. Loosen screw (2) and move roller (1) to adjust. Note that screw (2) has left-hand threads.

OIL INJECTION

OIL PUMP CONTROL LINKAGE. To adjust injection pump control linkage, disconnect injection pump control rod (4—Fig. Y9-10) and open throttle to wide open position, aligning match mark (2) with center of throttle roller (1). Position pump control lever (5) so a clearance of 0.5 mm (0.020 in.) exists between lever (5) and lever stopper.

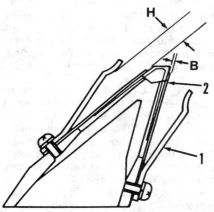

Fig. Y9-5—Reed valve stopper (1) height (H) should be 5.8-6.2 mm (0.23-0.24 in.). Bend stopper (1) to adjust. Renew reed valve assembly if reed petal (2) warpage (B) exceeds 1.5 mm (0.059 in.).

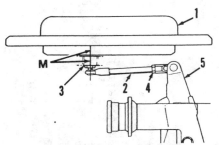

Fig. Y9-7—View showing alignment of timing marks (M) on flywheel (1) and magneto base (3). Refer to text in SPEED CONTROL LINKAGE section for adjustment procedure.

1. Flywheel
2. Magneto control rod
3. Magneto base
4. Locknut
5. Magneto control lever
M. Marks

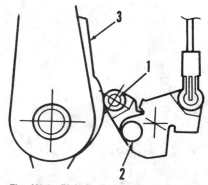

Fig. Y9-9—Pick-up timing should be 1 degree ATDC when throttle cam (3) lightly contacts throttle roller (1) and throttle valves in carburetors begin to open. Loosen adjustment screw (2) and move roller to adjust. Screw (2) has left-hand threads.

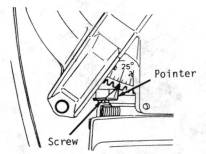

Fig. Y9-6—Timing pointer should align with 25 degree mark on flywheel with number 1 piston located at 3.34 mm (0.131 in.) BTDC. Refer to SPEED CONTROL LINKAGE section.

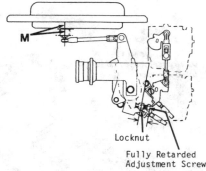

Fig. Y9-8—Refer to text under SPEED CONTROL LINKAGE section for proper adjustment of fully retarded adjustment screw.

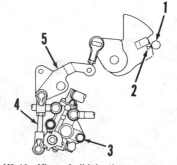

Fig. Y9-10—View of oil injection pump assembly and control linkage. Refer to text for control linkage adjustment procedure.

1. Throttle roller
2. Match mark
3. Injection pump assy.
4. Control rod
5. Lever

With lever (5) in this position, adjust rod (4) so rod will connect to lever (5) without disturbing position of lever (5). Make sure carburetor throttle valves will open fully after adjustment.

BLEEDING PUMP. Oil injection system is self-bleeding. Oil from tank (1—Fig. Y9-11) flows through delivery hose (2) to pump (4) and then back to tank through return hose (6). Check valve (7) prevents oil from reversing flow.

To bleed air from system, fill oil tank with a recommended oil. To ensure proper lubrication, use a 100:1 fuel:oil mixture in fuel tank during bleeding process. Start engine and run at idle speed until all air is purged from system and oil flows from discharge hoses (5).

CHECKING OIL PUMP OUTPUT. Fill fuel tank with a 100:1 ratio mixture of recommended gasoline and engine oil. Fill oil tank with recommended engine oil.

NOTE: The manufacturer recommends using only genuine Yamaha Two-Cycle Outboard Motor Oil when checking oil pump output. Oil of different make or viscosity will produce inaccurate output results.

Start engine and allow to warm to normal operating temperature. Make sure all air is bled from system. Adjust idle speed to 1500 rpm with idle speed screw. Remove oil pump control rod and fix pump lever to the full throttle position. Measure oil pump output from each discharge hose for three minutes using an accurate graduated container. Oil pump output should be 1.4-3.0 mL (0.047-0.101 oz.) at 1500 rpm in three minutes. Renew oil pump assembly if output is not as specified.

IGNITION

Capacitor discharge ignition (CDI) is used. Standard spark plug is NGK B7HS-10. Electrode gap should be 0.9-1.0 mm (0.035-0.039 in.).

If engine malfunction is noted and the ignition system is suspected, make sure the spark plugs are in acceptable condition, all electrical connections are clean and tight and fuel system is operating properly before trouble-shooting ignition system.

Pulser coils, charge coil and lighting coil are located under the flywheel. Use a suitable flywheel puller when removing flywheel. Tilt flywheel away from timing pointer when lifting flywheel off crankshaft to avoid damaging pointer. Refer to Fig. Y9-12 when testing ignition system components. Disconnect six wires leading from magneto base to test magneto components.

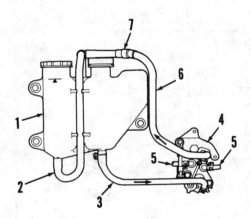

Fig. Y9-11—View of oil tank, injection pump and hoses.

1. Tank
2. Drain hose
3. Delivery hose
4. Injection pump assy.
5. Discharge hoses
6. Return hose
7. Check valve

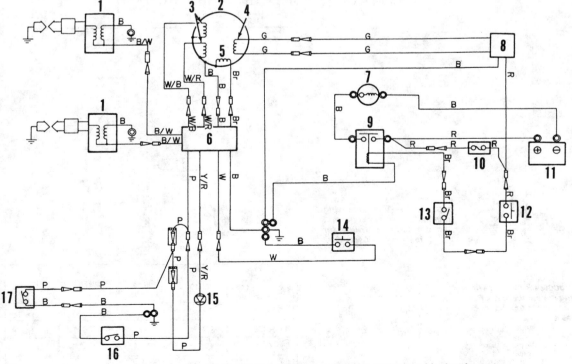

1. Ignition coil
2. Magneto
3. Pulser coils
4. Lighting coil
5. Charge coil
6. CDI module
7. Starter motor
8. Rectifier
9. Relay
10. Fuse (10 amp)
11. Battery
12. Starter switch
13. Neutral switch
14. Stop switch
15. Warning lamp
16. Oil level sensor
17. Temperature switch
B. Black
G. Green
P. Pink
R. Red
W. White
Br. Brown
B/W. Black with white tracer
W/B. White with black tracer
W/R. White with red tracer
Y/R. Yellow with red tracer

Fig. Y9-12—Wiring schematic on models equipped with electric starter.

NOTE: The following resistance values are based on ambient temperature of 20° C (68° F). Resistance will vary approximately 10 ohms per 0.56° C (1° F) change in ambient temperature. In addition, resistance readings may vary somewhat between testers of different manufacture. If readings vary greatly from the following values, component is most likely defective and should be renewed. Test entire ignition system before failing a component whose resistance is only slightly out of specification.

To test pulser (trigger) coils, connect a suitable ohmmeter between (B) and (W/B) wires, then (B) and (W/R) wires. Resistance for both tests should be 218-432 ohms.

Test charge coil by connecting ohmmeter between wires (B) and (Br). Charge coil resistance should be 560-840 ohms.

To test lighting coil, connect ohmmeter between two wires (G). Lighting coil resistance should be 560-840 ohms.

Check ignition coils primary winding resistance by connecting ohmmeter between wires (B) and (B/W). Primary resistance should be 0.10-0.14 ohm.

To check ignition coil secondary resistance, connect ohmmeter between wire (B) and high tension lead. Secondary resistance should be 1680-2520 ohms. If available, perform ignition coil power test and surface insulation test using Yamaha coil tester YU-33261 or a suitable equivalent coil tester. Follow tester manufacturer's instructions regarding tester connections and test procedure.

To test CDI module, disconnect module wires at connectors and remove module from outboard motor. Use a suitable ohmmeter to test module. With reference to Fig. Y9-13 and chart in Fig. Y9-14, perform CDI module resistance tests.

To check ignition timing, refer to SPEED CONTROL LINKAGE section. Timing should be 4-6 degrees ATDC at full retarded (idle speed) and 24-26 degrees BTDC at maximum advance (wide open throttle).

To test lighting system rectifier, refer to Fig. Y9-15 and test rectifier using a suitable ohmmeter.

COOLING SYSTEM

THERMOSTAT. Engines are equipped with a thermostat to control engine operating temperature. Thermostat is located under cover in top side of cylinder head. Test thermostat by heating in water. Thermostat should be fully closed at temperatures 48° C (118° F)

Fig. Y9-14—Use chart and values listed to test condition of CDI module. Refer to Fig. Y9-13 for view of CDI module and wiring color code identification.

- A. 1,120-1,680 ohms
- B. 3,120-4,680 ohms
- C. 3,200-4,800 ohms
- D. 4,000-6,000 ohms
- E. 4,800-7,200 ohms
- F. 7,200-10,800 ohms
- G. 8,000-12,000 ohms
- H. 8,960-13,440 ohms
- I. 15,200-22,800 ohms
- J. 16,000-24,000 ohms
- K. 17,600-26,400 ohms
- L. 32,000-48,000 ohms
- M. 41,600-62,400 ohms
- N. 51,200-76,800 ohms
- O. 54,400-81,600 ohms
- P. 65,600-98,400 ohms
- Q. 80,000-120,000 ohms
- R. 112,000-168,000 ohms
- S. 120,000-180,000 ohms
- T. Tester needle deflects toward zero ohm, then returns to 80,000-120,000 ohms
- U. Tester needle deflects toward zero ohm, then returns to infinity
- V. Infinity

Pos. Tester Lead / Neg. Tester Lead	STOP W	GROUND B	CHARGE Br	PULSER W/R	PULSER W/B	IGNITION B/W1	IGNITION B/W2	THERMO SWITCH P	OVER-HEAT Y/R
W		F	I	V	V	J	J	M	H
B	L		B	V	V	C	C	J	A
Br	J	G		U	U	I	I	K	G
W/R	S	N	P		V	T	Q	R	O
W/B	S	N	P	V		Q	T	R	O
B/W1	V	V	V	V	V		V	V	V
B/W2	V	V	V	V	V	V		V	V
P	V	V	V	V	V	V	V		V
Y/R	L	A	D	V	V	E	E	K	

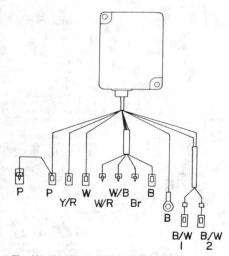

Fig. Y9-13—View of CDI module identifying wiring color code for performing resistance tests. Refer to chart in Fig. Y9-14 for proper test connections and results.

- B. Black
- P. Pink
- W. White
- Br. Brown
- B/W. Black with white tracer
- W/B. White with black tracer
- W/R. White with red tracer
- Y/R. Yellow with red tracer

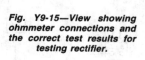

Fig. Y9-15—View showing ohmmeter connections and the correct test results for testing rectifier.

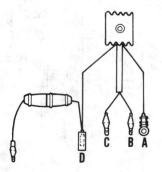

Positive(+) Tester Lead / Negative(-) Tester Lead	(A) BLACK	(B) GREEN	(C) GREEN	(D) RED
(A) BLACK		Continuity	Continuity	Continuity
(B) GREEN	∞		Continuity	Continuity
(C) GREEN	∞	∞		Continuity
(D) RED	∞	∞	∞	

and below. At 60° C (172° F), thermostat valve should open a minimum of 3.0 mm (0.12 in.).

WATER PUMP. A rubber impeller type water pump is mounted between the drive shaft housing and gearcase. Water pump impeller (6—Fig. Y9-16) is driven by a key in the drive shaft.

If cooling system malfunction is noted, check water inlet for plugging or partial restriction. Be sure thermostat is operating properly.

To service water pump, separate lower unit gearcase from drive shaft housing. Make sure all seals and mating surfaces are in good condition and water passages are unobstructed. Check impeller (6), liner (5) and plate (7) for excessive wear or other damage. Apply a suitable water-resistant grease to impeller during reassembly. Rotate drive shaft clockwise when installing housing (3) over impeller to set impeller vanes in the proper direction. Avoid turning drive shaft in opposite direction after installing housing. Apply a suitable thread locking compound to screws (1) during reassembly.

POWER HEAD

REMOVE AND REINSTALL. The power head can be removed for disassembly and overhaul as follows: Clamp outboard motor to a suitable stand and remove engine cowl and starter assembly. Disconnect speed control cables, fuel line and any wiring that will interfere with power head removal. Remove or disconnect any component that will interfere with power head removal. Remove six screws securing power head to drive shaft housing and lift power head free.

Reinstall power head by reversing order of removal. Install a new gasket between power head and drive shaft housing. Make sure crankshaft and drive shaft splines are clean and apply a suitable water-resistant grease to splines. Tighten drive shaft housing-to-power head screws to 18 N·m (13 ft.-lbs.).

DISASSEMBLY. Refer to Fig. Y9-17. Remove cylinder head cover (14) and cylinder head (9). Remove intake manifold, reed valve assembly, outer and inner exhaust covers (5 and 7) and oil seal housing (11—Fig. Y9-18). Remove 10 crankcase screws and carefully separate crankcase from cylinder block. Crankshaft and pistons are now accessible for removal and overhaul as outlined in the appropriate following service sections.

REASSEMBLY. Refer to specific service sections when reassembling power head. Renew all seals and gaskets. Make sure all joints and gasket surfaces are clean, free from nicks and burrs, hardened carbon or gasket compound. The crankcase, cylinder block and intake manifold mating surfaces must be completely sealed against water leakage and pressure.

Whenever power head is disassembled, it is recommended that all gasket surfaces and mating surfaces without gaskets be carefully checked for nicks, burrs and warped surfaces which might interfere with a tight seal. Cylinder head, cylinder block and crankcase should be checked on a surface plate and lapped if necessary to provide a smooth surface. Do not remove any more metal that necessary to true mating surface.

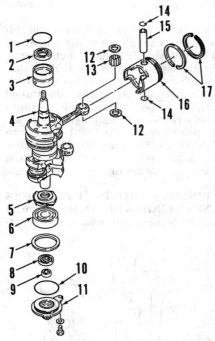

Fig. Y9-18—Exploded view of crankshaft, connecting rods and pistons assembly.

1. "O" ring	10. "O" ring
2. Seal	11. Seal housing
3. Bearing	12. Washer
4. Crankshaft assy.	13. Needle bearing
5. Oil pump drive gear	rollers
6. Bearing	14. Retainer
7. Washer	15. Piston pin
8. Seal	16. Piston
9. Seal	17. Piston rings

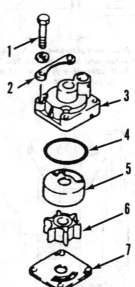
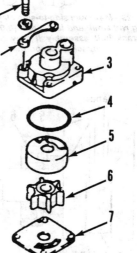

Fig. Y9-16—Exploded view of water pump assembly.

1. Screw	5. Liner
2. Plate	6. Impeller
3. Housing	7. Plate
4. "O" ring	

Fig. Y9-17—Exploded view of cylinder block assembly.

1. Crankcase
2. Dowel pin
3. Cylinder block
4. Gasket
5. Inner exhaust cover
6. Gasket
7. Outer exhaust cover
8. Gasket
9. Cylinder head
10. Thermostat
11. Gasket
12. Cover
13. Gasket
14. Cylinder head cover

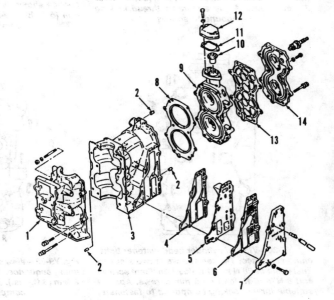

All friction surfaces and bearings should be lubricated with engine oil during reassembly. Apply a suitable water-resistant grease to lip area of all seals. As power head is reassembled, frequently check rotation of crankshaft for binding or unusual noise. If binding or noise is noted, the cause must be corrected before proceeding with reassembly.

Mating surfaces of crankcase and cylinder block should be lightly and evenly coated with Yamaha GasketMaker or a suitable equivalent sealant. Make sure entire surface is coated, but avoid excess application. Apply a suitable thread locking compound to threads of crankcase screws and tighten screws in sequence shown in Fig. Y9-19. Refer to Figs. Y9-20, Y9-21 and Y9-22 for cylinder head, exhaust cover and intake manifold fastener tightening sequences.

PISTONS, RINGS, CYLINDERS AND CYLINDER HEAD. Make sure all carbon deposits are removed from cyl-inder head and combustion chamber. If cylinder head mating surface is warped in excess of 0.1 mm (0.004 in.), resurface head on a suitable lapping block using 400-600 grit sandpaper. Do not remove any more material than necessary to true head mating surface.

Measure piston diameter 10 mm (0.39 in.) up from bottom of skirt at a right angle to piston pin bore. Refer to CONDENSED SERVICE DATA for piston, rings and cylinder bore service specifications. Pistons and rings are available in 0.25 mm and 0.50 mm oversizes. Bore cylinders to next oversize if excessive out-of-round, taper or scoring is evident in cylinder bore.

Upper piston ring is semi-keystone design. Second ring should be installed on piston with manufacturer's marking facing up. Make sure piston ring end gaps are properly located around ring locating pins in ring groove. Install pistons on connecting rods with "UP" mark on piston crown facing flywheel end of engine. Piston pin retainers (14—Fig. Y9-18) should be renewed during reassemby.

CRANKSHAFT, CONNECTING RODS AND BEARINGS. Crankshaft and connecting rods are available as a unit assembly only. Do not remove bearing (6—Fig. Y9-18) unless bearing renewal is required. Connecting rods are equipped with 31 needle rollers (13) per rod. Use a suitable needle bearing assembly grease to hold needle rollers in place during reassembly.

Measure crankshaft runout at main bearings with crankshaft supported in V-blocks. Maximum allowable runout is 0.03 mm (0.0012 in.). Measure connecting rod small end side-to-side play as shown in Fig. Y9-23. Renew crankshaft assembly if side-to-side play exceeds 2.0 mm (0.080 in.). Connecting rod big end side clearance should be 1.90-2.10 mm (0.075-0.083 in.). Renew crankshaft assembly if not as specified. Install seals (8 and 9—Fig. Y9-18) with lips facing down.

STARTER

MANUAL STARTER. To disassemble starter, disconnect neutral start inter-

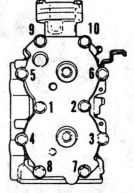

Fig. Y9-19—Tighten crankcase-to-cylinder block screws in sequence shown. Screws should be tightened in two steps to final value of 28 N·m (21 ft.-lbs.) for 8 mm screws and 11 N·m (8 ft.-lbs.) for 6 mm screws. Apply a suitable thread locking compound to screws.

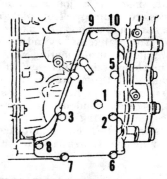

Fig. Y9-21—Tighten exhaust cover screws in sequence shown, in two steps, to final value of 8 N·m (6 ft.-lbs.). Apply a suitable thread locking compound to screws.

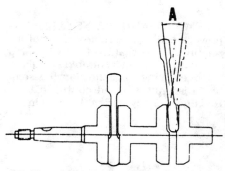

Fig. Y9-23—Maximum side-to-side play (A) at connecting rod small end is 2.0 mm (0.080 in.). Renew crankshaft assembly if play (A) exceeds specified amount.

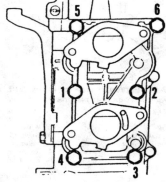

Fig. Y9-20—View of cylinder head fastener tightening sequence. Tighten screws in two steps to final value of 28 N·m (21 ft.-lbs.) on 8 mm screws and 8 N·m (6 ft.-lbs.) on 6 mm screws. Apply a suitable thread locking compound to fasteners.

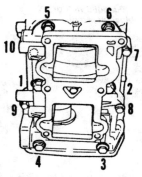

Fig. Y9-22—View of intake manifold fastener tightening sequence. Tighten screws in two steps to 8 N·m (6 ft.-lbs.). Apply a suitable thread locking compound to fasteners.

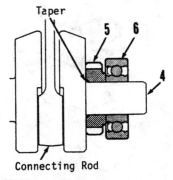

Fig. Y9-24—Install oil pump drive gear (5) on crankshaft (4) with taper on inside diameter of gear facing connecting rod as shown.

4. Crankshaft assy.
5. Drive gear
6. Bearing

lock cable (24—Fig. Y9-25) from starter housing (7) and remove screws (5) securing starter to power head. Lift off starter and lay down in inverted position. Lift a length of rope and place rope into notch (N—Fig. Y9-26) in pulley. Insert a suitable screwdriver (Fig. Y9-26) through neutral start plunger hole to secure pulley from unwinding. Uncoil rope from pulley, remove screwdriver and carefully allow pulley to unwind, relieving rewind spring tension. Remove screw (16—Fig. Y9-25) and lift off pulley being careful not to dislodge rewind spring. If rewind spring requires removal, wear suitable hand and eye protection to prevent personal injury

due to rewind spring flying out of housing. If necessary, remove "E" ring (15), pawl (14), pawl spring (13) and shaft (12).

Inspect all components for excessive wear or other damage and renew as necessary. New starter rope (3) should be 195 cm (77 in.) long. To install rewind spring, apply Yamaha grease C or equivalent to rewind spring area of housing. Secure hook in outer coil of rewind spring to post in housing. Starting with outer coil, wind spring into housing in counterclockwise direction. Insert rope through seal (3), rope guide (4) and secure to pulley with a suitable knot. Wind rope three turns onto pulley in

counterclockwise direction and place rope into notch (N—Fig. Y9-26). Install pulley into housing making sure hook on inner coil of rewind spring properly engages pulley. Apply a suitable water-resistant grease to shaft (12—Fig. Y9-25) and insert shaft into pulley. Apply a suitable thread locking compound to nut (6), install screw (16) and secure with nut (6). With rope positioned in notch in pulley, preload rewind spring two turns in counterclockwise direction and allow rope to wind onto pulley. Apply water-resistant grease to hole in pawl (14) and secure pawl with "E" ring (15). If drum (18) is removed, apply thread locking compound to screws (17), install drum (18) on flywheel and tighten screws securely. Install starter on power head and apply thread locking compound to screws (5).

To adjust neutral start interlock cable, shift gearcase into neutral gear, loosen jam nuts and turn adjusting nut (Fig. Y9-27) as necessary to align edge of plunger with hole in housing as shown.

ELECTRIC STARTER. Some models are equipped with an electric starter. Refer to Fig. Y9-28 for exploded view of starter motor.

Renew brush plate (15) and brushes (13) if brush length is 4.5 mm (0.18 in.) or less. Standard commutator diameter is 20 mm (0.79 in.) with minimum allowable diameter of 19.7 mm (0.77 in.). Maximum allowable armature runout is 0.05 mm (0.002 in.). Commutator should be undercut 0.5-0.8 mm (0.020-0.031 in.) with minimum limit of 0.2 mm (0.008 in.).

LOWER UNIT

PROPELLER AND DRIVE HUB. Lower unit protection is provided by a cushion type hub in the propeller. Various propellers are available from the manufacturer. Select a propeller that will allow a properly tuned and adjusted engine to operate at full throttle in the 5000-6000 rpm range.

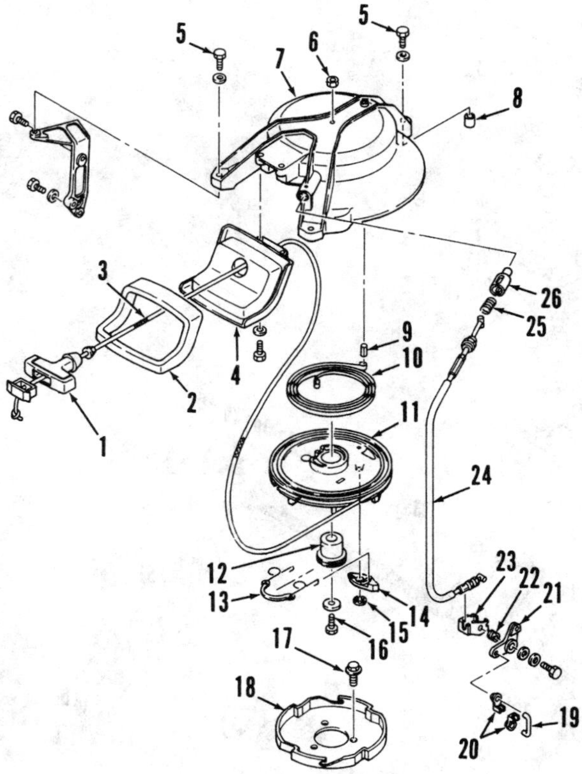

Fig. Y9-25—Exploded view of manual rewind starter assembly.

1. Handle
2. Seal
3. Rope
4. Rope guide
5. Screw
6. Nut
7. Housing
8. Spacer
9. Pin
10. Rewind spring
11. Rope pulley
12. Shaft
13. Pawl spring
14. Pawl
15. "E" ring
16. Screw
17. Screw
18. Drum
19. Link
20. Connector
21. Arm
22. Collar
23. Cable anchor
24. Cable assy.
25. Spring
26. Plunger

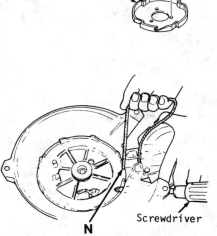

Fig. Y9-26—Insert a suitable screwdriver through neutral start plunger hole in housing as shown to hold rope pulley from turning. Refer to text.

Fig. Y9-27—To adjust neutral start interlock cable, shift gearcase to neutral, loosen jam nuts and turn adjusting nut so edge of plunger is even with hole in housing.

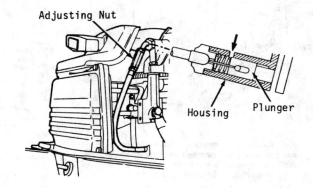

R&R AND OVERHAUL. Place outboard motor in a suitable stand, remove vent and drain plugs and allow gearcase oil to drain. Disengage reverse interlock hook (1—Fig. Y9-29) from shift rod, loosen nut (2) and turn adjustment nut (3) to separate upper and lower shift rods. Remove four screws securing gearcase to drive shaft housing, remove gearcase and secure in a suitable holding fixture.

Note location of all shims and washers for reference during reassembly. Remove water pump housing (3—Fig. Y9-30), impeller (6), impeller key (15) and plate (7). Remove four screws and lift off seal housing (12), lower shift rod (17) and boot (9). Remove screws (46) and using two screwdrivers or similar tools (Fig. Y9-31), pry carrier (42—Fig. Y9-30) out of gearcase along with components (32 through 40). To remove pinion gear nut (23), reach into gear cavity and hold nut (23) secure using Yamaha special tool YB-6078 or equivalent wrench. Use Yamaha drive shaft socket YB-6368 or other suitable tool to turn drive shaft (14) until nut (23) falls free. Pull drive

shaft out top of gearcase, then reach into gear cavity and extract nut (23), pinion gear (24), bearing (26) and shims (25 and 27). Use a suitable slide hammer type puller to remove forward gear bearing (31) from gearcase. Remove drive shaft sleeve (18). To remove bearing (19), insert a suitable driver into drive shaft bore and drive bearing (19) down into gear cavity. Remove bearing (11) and seals (8) from seal housing (12). Remove seals (44) and bearing (43) from carrier (42). Remove retainer spring (33) from dog clutch (34), push out pin (35) and slide dog clutch (34) off propeller shaft (36) to complete disassembly.

Inspect all components for excessive wear, corrosion or other damage and renew as necessary. Renew all seals, "O" rings and gaskets during reassembly.

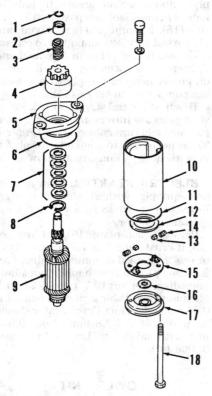

Fig. Y9-28—Exploded view of electric starter motor.

1. Snap ring	10. Frame assy.
2. Collar	11. "O" ring
3. Spring	12. Washer
4. Drive gear	13. Brush
5. Front frame	14. Spring
6. "O" ring	15. Brush plate
7. Washers	16. Washer
8. Snap ring	17. End frame
9. Armature	18. Through-bolt

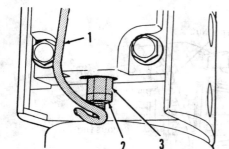

Fig. Y9-29—To separate upper and lower shift rods, disengage reverse interlock hook (1) from shift rod, loosen jam nut (2) and turn adjustment nut (3) until shift rods separate.

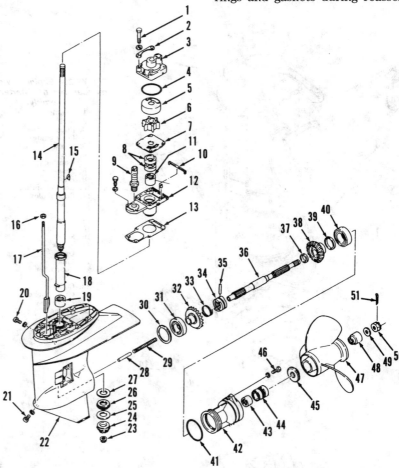

Fig. Y9-30—Exploded view of lower unit gearcase assembly.

1. Screw	18. Sleeve	35. Pin
2. Plate	19. Needle bearing	36. Propeller shaft
3. Water pump	20. Vent plug	37. Thrust washer
housing	21. Drain plug	38. Reverse gear
4. "O" ring	22. Gearcase	39. Shim
5. Liner	23. Nut	40. Bearing
6. Impeller	24. Pinion gear	41. "O" ring
7. Plate	25. Shim	42. Bearing carrier
8. Seals	26. Thrust bearing	43. Bearing
9. Shift rod boot	27. Thrust washer	44. Seals
10. Seal	28. Shift plunger	45. Spacer
11. Needle bearing	29. Spring	46. Screw
12. Seal housing	30. Shim	47. Propeller
13. Gasket	31. Bearing	48. Spacer
14. Drive shaft	32. Forward gear	49. Washer
15. Impeller key	33. Retainer spring	50. Nut
16. Nut	34. Dog clutch	51. Cotter pin
17. Lower shift rod		

Apply a suitable water-resistant grease to lip area of all seals. Make sure all bearings and gears are thoroughly lubricated with a recommended gearcase oil during reassembly. Refer to LUBRICATION section.

If renewing gearcase housing only, while installing the original internal components, proceed as follows: Remove trim tab and note numbers following "F," "R" and "P" letters cast into bottom side of antiventilation plate. Compare numbers on new gearcase with numbers on old gearcase and adjust original shims accordingly.

NOTE: Numbers following prefix letters "F," "R" and "P" must be divided by 100 to obtain the correct shim adjustment amount.

If necessary, determine correct thickness of pinion gear shim (25) as follows:
1. Remove trim tab and note number following "P." Divide number following "P" by 100 and add the sum to 49.00.
2. Place thrust bearing (26) and washer (27) together and measure thickness using a suitable micrometer. Subtract thickness from sum obtained in step 1.
3. Subtract remainder obtained in step 2 from 42.5 mm.
4. If remainder obtained in step 3 is less than 1.60 mm, use a 1.50 mm thick pinion shim (25). If more than 1.61 mm, use a 1.60 mm thick pinion shim (25).

Install bearing (19) into gearcase using a suitable driver. Install drive shaft sleeve (18). Place original shims (30) into position and install bearing (31). Install drive shaft (14), pinion gear (24), shim (25), thrust bearing (26) and washer (27). Tighten pinion nut (23) to 50 N·m (37 ft.-lbs.). Install shift rod (17) and boot (9). Reassemble propeller shaft components (28, 29, 33, 34, 35 and 36). Place original shim (39) on reverse gear (38) and insert gear and shim assembly into bearing (40). Coat "O" ring (41) with Yamaha GasketMaker or equivalent sealing compound and install carrier assembly into gearcase.

To check forward gear backlash, forward gear must be fixed in place to prevent turning. Install a suitable puller as shown in Fig. Y9-32 and apply pressure to propeller shaft, forcing shaft into forward gear. Forward gear backlash

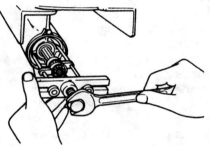

Fig. Y9-32—When checking forward gear backlash, lock forward gear in place by applying pressure to propeller shaft with a puller assembly as shown.

should be 0.15-0.25 mm (0.006-0.010 in.). Vary thickness of shim (30) to adjust backlash.

Reverse gear must be secured from turning to properly check backlash. Install propeller on propeller shaft backwards without spacer (45). Install nut (50) and tighten until reverse gear will not turn. Reverse gear backlash should be 0.40-0.55 mm (0.016-0.022 in.). Vary thickness of shim (39) to adjust backlash.

NOTE: If forward and reverse gear backlash is out of specification, adjust thickness of pinion shim (25), forward gear shim (30) and reverse gear shim (39) as necessary to obtain the correct backlash. If forward gear only, or reverse gear only backlash is out of specification, adjust thickness of respective shim to obtain the correct backlash.

Complete remainder of reassembly by reversing disassembly. Tighten propeller nut to 35 N·m (26 ft.-lbs.). Apply a suitable water-resistant grease to drive shaft spines and end of water tube. Install lower unit to drive shaft housing and tighten lower unit mounting screws to 40 N·m (29 ft.-lbs.).

Shift lower unit to reverse gear and connect upper and lower shift rods. Adjust nuts to 3.5-5.0 mm (0.14-0.20 in.) above housing as shown in Fig. Y9-33. Reconnect reverse interlock rod as shown in Fig. Y9-33. Fill gearcase with an approved gearcase oil as recommended in LUBRICATION section.

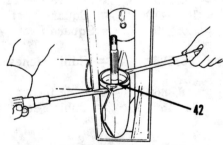

Fig. Y9-31—Carefully pry bearing carrier (42) from gearcase as shown.

Fig. Y9-33—To adjust shift linkage, shift lower unit into reverse gear and set nuts 3.5-5.0 mm (0.14-0.20 in.) above housing as shown. Reverse interlock rod should be hooked around shift rod as shown.

METRIC CONVERSION

Cubic meters	= .02832	x Cubic Feet
Cubic meters	x 1.308	= Cubic Yards
Cubic meters	= .765	x Cubic Yards
Liters	x 61.023	= Cubic Inches
Liters	= .01639	x Cubic Inches
Liters	x .26418	= U.S. Gallons
Liters	= 3.7854	x U.S. Gallons
Grams	x 15.4324	= Grains
Grams	= .0648	x Grains
Grams	x .03527	= Ounces, avoirdupois
Grams	= 28.3495	x Ounces, avoirdupois
Kilograms	x 2.2046	= Pounds
Kilograms	= .4536	x Pounds
Kilograms per square centimeter	x 14.2231	= Pounds per square Inch
Kilograms per square centimeter	= .0703	x Pounds per square Inch
Kilograms per cubic meter	x .06243	= Pounds per cubic Foot
Kilograms per cubic meter	= 16.01890	x Pounds per cubic Foot

Metric tons (1,000 kilograms)	x 1.1023	= Tons (2,000 Pounds)
Metric tons (1,000 kilograms)	= .9072	x Tons (2,000 Pounds)
Kilowatts	= 1.3405	x Horsepower
Kilowatts	x .746	= Horsepower
Millimeters	x .03937	= Inches
Millimeters	= 25.400	x Inches
Meters	x 3.2809	= Feet
Meters	= .3048	x Feet
Kilometers	x .621377	= Miles
Kilometers	= 1.6093	x Miles
Square centimeters	x .15500	= Square Inches
Square centimeters	= 6.4515	x Square Inches
Square meters	x 10.76410	= Square Feet
Square meters	= .09290	x Square Feet
Cubic centimeters	x .061025	= Cubic Inches
Cubic centimeters	= 16.3866	x Cubic Inches
Cubic meters	x 35.3156	= Cubic Feet

Millimeters to Inches — Decimal and Fractional Equivalents

MM	INCHES		MM	INCHES		MM	INCHES		MM	INCHES		MM	INCHES		MM	INCHES	
1	0.0394	1/32 +	51	2.0079	2.0 +	101	3.9764	3 31/32 +	151	5.9449	5 15/16 +	201	7.9134	7 29/32 +	251	9.8819	9 7/8 +
2	0.0787	5/64 +	52	2.0472	2 1/16 −	102	4.0157	4 1/64 +	152	5.9842	5 31/32 +	202	7.9527	7 15/16 +	252	9.9212	9 59/64 +
3	0.1181	1/8 −	53	2.0866	2 3/32 −	103	4.0551	4 1/16 −	153	6.0236	6 1/32 −	203	7.9921	8.0 −	253	9.9606	9 61/64 −
4	0.1575	5/32 +	54	2.1260	2 1/8 +	104	4.0945	4 3/32 +	154	6.0630	6 1/16 +	204	8.0315	8 1/32 +	254	10.0000	10.0
5	0.1969	3/16 +	55	2.1654	2 5/32 +	105	4.1339	4 1/8 +	155	6.1024	6 3/32 +	205	8.0709	8 1/16 +	255	10.0393	10 1/32 +
6	0.2362	1/4 −	56	2.2047	2 7/32 −	106	4.1732	4 11/64 +	156	6.1417	6 9/64 +	206	8.1102	8 1/8 −	256	10.0787	10 5/64 +
7	0.2756	9/32 −	57	2.2441	2 1/4 −	107	4.2126	4 7/32 −	157	6.1811	6 3/16 −	207	8.1496	8 5/32 −	257	10.1181	10 1/8 −
8	0.3150	5/16 +	58	2.2835	2 9/32 +	108	4.2520	4 1/4 +	158	6.2205	6 7/32 +	208	8.1890	8 3/16 +	258	10.1575	10 5/32 +
9	0.3543	11/32 +	59	2.3228	2 5/16 +	109	4.2913	4 9/32 +	159	6.2598	6 1/4 +	209	8.2283	8 7/32 +	259	10.1968	10 3/16 +
10	0.3937	13/32 −	60	2.3622	2 3/8 −	110	4.3307	4 21/64 +	160	6.2992	6 19/64 +	210	8.2677	8 9/32 −	260	10.2362	10 1/4 −
11	0.4331	7/16 −	61	2.4016	2 13/32 −	111	4.3701	4 3/8 −	161	6.3386	6 11/32 −	211	8.3071	8 5/16 −	261	10.2756	10 9/32 −
12	0.4724	15/32 +	62	2.4409	2 7/16 +	112	4.4094	4 13/32 +	162	6.3779	6 3/8 +	212	8.3464	8 11/32 +	262	10.3149	10 5/16 +
13	0.5118	1/2 +	63	2.4803	2 15/32 +	113	4.4488	4 7/16 +	163	6.4173	6 13/32 +	213	8.3858	8 3/8 +	263	10.3543	10 11/32 +
14	0.5512	9/16 −	64	2.5197	2 17/32 −	114	4.4882	4 1/2 −	164	6.4567	6 15/32 −	214	8.4252	8 7/16 −	264	10.3937	10 13/32 −
15	0.5906	19/32 −	65	2.5591	2 9/16 −	115	4.5276	4 17/32 −	165	6.4961	6 1/2 −	215	8.4646	8 15/32 −	265	10.4330	10 7/16 −
16	0.6299	5/8 +	66	2.5984	2 19/32 +	116	4.5669	4 9/16 +	166	6.5354	6 17/32 +	216	8.5039	8 1/2 +	266	10.4724	10 15/32 +
17	0.6693	21/32 +	67	2.6378	2 5/8 +	117	4.6063	4 39/64 −	167	6.5748	6 9/16 +	217	8.5433	8 17/32 +	267	10.5118	10 1/2 +
18	0.7087	23/32 −	68	2.6772	2 11/16 −	118	4.6457	4 41/64 +	168	6.6142	6 5/8 −	218	8.5827	8 19/32 −	268	10.5512	10 9/16 −
19	0.7480	3/4 −	69	2.7165	2 23/32 −	119	4.6850	4 11/16 −	169	6.6535	6 21/32 −	219	8.6220	8 5/8 −	269	10.5905	10 19/32 −
20	0.7874	25/32 +	70	2.7559	2 3/4 +	120	4.7244	4 23/32 +	170	6.6929	6 11/16 +	220	8.6614	8 21/32 +	270	10.6299	10 5/8 +
21	0.8268	13/16 +	71	2.7953	2 25/32 +	121	4.7638	4 49/64 −	171	6.7323	6 23/32 +	221	8.7008	8 11/16 +	271	10.6693	10 21/32 +
22	0.8661	7/8 −	72	2.8346	2 27/32 −	122	4.8031	4 51/64 +	172	6.7716	6 25/32 −	222	8.7401	8 3/4 −	272	10.7086	10 23/32 −
23	0.9055	29/32 −	73	2.8740	2 7/8 −	123	4.8425	4 27/32 −	173	6.8110	6 13/16 −	223	8.7795	8 25/32 −	273	10.7480	10 3/4 −
24	0.9449	15/16 +	74	2.9134	2 29/32 +	124	4.8819	4 7/8 +	174	6.8504	6 27/32 +	224	8.8189	8 13/16 +	274	10.7874	10 25/32 +
25	0.9843	31/32 +	75	2.9528	2 15/16 +	125	4.9213	4 59/64 −	175	6.8898	6 7/8 +	225	8.8583	8 27/32 +	275	10.8268	10 13/16 +
26	1.0236	1 1/32 −	76	2.9921	3.0 −	126	4.9606	4 61/64 +	176	6.9291	6 15/16 −	226	8.8976	8 29/32 −	276	10.8661	10 7/8 −
27	1.0630	1 1/16 +	77	3.0315	3 1/32 +	127	5.0000	5.0	177	6.9685	6 31/32 −	227	8.9370	8 15/16 −	277	10.9055	10 29/32 −
28	1.1024	1 3/32 +	78	3.0709	3 1/16 +	128	5.0394	5 1/32 +	178	7.0079	7.0 +	228	8.9764	8 31/32 +	278	10.9449	10 15/16 +
29	1.1417	1 9/64 +	79	3.1102	3 1/8 −	129	5.0787	5 5/64 +	179	7.0472	7 1/16 −	229	9.0157	9 1/64 +	279	10.9842	10 31/32 +
30	1.1811	1 3/16 −	80	3.1496	3 5/32 −	130	5.1181	5 1/8 −	180	7.0866	7 3/32 −	230	9.0551	9 1/16 −	280	11.0236	11 1/32 −
31	1.2205	1 7/32 +	81	3.1890	3 3/16 +	131	5.1575	5 5/32 +	181	7.1260	7 1/8 +	231	9.0945	9 3/32 +	281	11.0630	11 1/16 +
32	1.2598	1 1/4 +	82	3.2283	3 7/32 +	132	5.1968	5 3/16 +	182	7.1653	7 5/32 +	232	9.1338	9 1/8 +	282	11.1023	11 3/32 +
33	1.2992	1 19/64 +	83	3.2677	3 9/32 −	133	5.2362	5 1/4 −	183	7.2047	7 7/32 −	233	9.1732	9 11/64 +	283	11.1417	11 9/64 +
34	1.3386	1 11/32 −	84	3.3071	3 5/16 −	134	5.2756	5 9/32 −	184	7.2441	7 1/4 −	234	9.2126	9 7/32 −	284	11.1811	11 3/16 −
35	1.3780	1 3/8 +	85	3.3465	3 11/32 +	135	5.3150	5 5/16 +	185	7.2835	7 9/32 +	235	9.2520	9 1/4 +	285	11.2204	11 7/32 +
36	1.4173	1 13/32 +	86	3.3858	3 3/8 +	136	5.3543	5 11/32 +	186	7.3228	7 5/16 +	236	9.2913	9 9/32 +	286	11.2598	11 1/4 +
37	1.4567	1 15/32 −	87	3.4252	3 7/16 −	137	5.3937	5 13/32 −	187	7.3622	7 3/8 −	237	9.3307	9 21/64 +	287	11.2992	11 19/64 +
38	1.4961	1 1/2 −	88	3.4646	3 15/32 −	138	5.4331	5 7/16 −	188	7.4016	7 13/32 −	238	9.3701	9 3/8 −	288	11.3386	11 11/32 −
39	1.5354	1 17/32 +	89	3.5039	3 1/2 +	139	5.4724	5 15/32 +	189	7.4409	7 7/16 +	239	9.4094	9 13/32 +	289	11.3779	11 3/8 +
40	1.5748	1 9/16 +	90	3.5433	3 17/32 +	140	5.5118	5 1/2 +	190	7.4803	7 15/32 +	240	9.4488	9 7/16 +	290	11.4173	11 13/32 +
41	1.6142	1 5/8 −	91	3.5827	3 19/32 −	141	5.5512	5 9/16 −	191	7.5197	7 17/32 −	241	9.4882	9 1/2 −	291	11.4567	11 15/32 −
42	1.6535	1 21/32 −	92	3.6220	3 5/8 −	142	5.5905	5 19/32 −	192	7.5590	7 9/16 −	242	9.5275	9 17/32 −	292	11.4960	11 1/2 −
43	1.6929	1 11/16 +	93	3.6614	3 21/32 +	143	5.6299	5 5/8 +	193	7.5984	7 19/32 +	243	9.5669	9 9/16 +	293	11.5354	11 17/32 +
44	1.7323	1 23/32 +	94	3.7008	3 11/16 +	144	5.6693	5 21/32 +	194	7.6378	7 5/8 +	244	9.6063	9 39/64 −	294	11.5748	11 9/16 +
45	1.7717	1 25/32 −	95	3.7402	3 3/4 −	145	5.7087	5 23/32 −	195	7.6772	7 11/16 −	245	9.6457	9 41/64 +	295	11.6142	11 5/8 −
46	1.8110	1 13/16 −	96	3.7795	3 25/32 −	146	5.7480	5 3/4 −	196	7.7165	7 23/32 −	246	9.6850	9 11/16 −	296	11.6535	11 21/32 −
47	1.8504	1 27/32 +	97	3.8189	3 13/16 +	147	5.7874	5 25/32 +	197	7.7559	7 3/4 +	247	9.7244	9 23/32 +	297	11.6929	11 11/16 +
48	1.8898	1 7/8 +	98	3.8583	3 27/32 +	148	5.8268	5 13/16 +	198	7.7953	7 25/32 +	248	9.7638	9 49/64 −	298	11.7323	11 23/32 +
49	1.9291	1 15/16 −	99	3.8976	3 29/32 −	149	5.8661	5 7/8 −	199	7.8346	7 27/32 −	249	9.8031	9 51/64 +	299	11.7716	11 25/32 −
50	1.9685	1 31/32 −	100	3.9370	3 15/16 −	150	5.9055	5 29/32 −	200	7.8740	7 7/8 −	250	9.8425	9 27/32 −	300	11.8110	11 13/16 −

NOTE. The + or − sign indicates that the decimal equivalent is larger or smaller than the fractional equivalent.

MAINTENANCE LOG

MAINTENANCE LOG

NOTES

NOTES

NOTES

NOTES